Introduction

The *Time Out Eating & Drinking Guide* is the most authoritative and comprehensive guide to good restaurants, gastropubs and cafés in the capital. This is not just because we have a great passion for food, and for finding the best places to eat and drink in London. What you have in your hands is the only London guide for which anonymous critics pay for their meal and drinks just like a regular customer (Time Out then reimburses their expenses). We do not tell the restaurants we are coming, nor do we reveal who we are after the meal. Restaurants can exert no pressure on us as to the content of their reviews, and do not pay to be included in the guide. Our editors select all the establishments featured on merit and interest alone.

We want our readers to know just what the experience of eating at each restaurant might be like for them, and take pains to ensure that our reviewers remain totally objective on your behalf. Our insistence on undercover reporting means that our experience is much more likely to reflect your experience. This can't be said of well-known newspaper restaurant columnists: they often receive preferential treatment from restaurant kitchens who have their photographs pinned up to ensure the critics do not go unrecognised (and those critics are inclined to feel insulted or ill-treated if they are not recognised, adding further bias to their reviews).

Many of our reviewers have extraordinary expertise in specialist areas. Several are trained cooks or former chefs, others are well-established food and/or wine authors, and some are simply dedicated enthusiasts who have lived abroad and learned much about a particular region's cuisine. Our contributors include chefs who have worked in the grand hotels of India and in kaiseki restaurants of Japan, expert bakers and baristas, award-winning wine writers, and food lovers hailing from Iran, Russia and Malaysia.

For the weekly *Time Out London* magazine alone, our reviewers visit around 200 new places every year. Their better discoveries are then included in this guide. Reviewers also check other new openings as well as revisiting places included in previous editions. We also take in feedback and recommendations from users of the Time Out website (www.timeout.com/restaurants). Then we eliminate the also-rans to create the list of London's best eateries that this guide represents. We hope you find it useful, and that it helps you get more enjoyment from eating out in the capital.

Contents

timeout.com/restaurants

Features

Restaurants

Cheap Eats

Drinking

Maps & Indexes

Published by

Time Out Guides Limited
Universal House
251 Tottenham Court Road
London W1T 7AB
Tel +44 (0)20 7813 3000
Fax +44 (0)20 7813 6001
email guides@timeout.com
www.timeout.com

Sections in this guide were written by

African & Caribbean Lauren Bravo, Haben Habelatsie, Nana Ocran, Yolanda Zappaterra; **The Americas (North American)** Jenni Muir, Nora Ryan **(Latin American)** Sally Peck, Patrick Welch; **Brasseries** Claire Fogg, Jenni Muir; **British** Sarah Guy, Celia Plender, Caroline Stacey; **Chinese** Tania Ballantine, Phil Harriss, Florentyna Leow, Jeffrey Ng, Sally Peck, Willa Zehn; **East European** Simon Coppock, Katrina Kollegaeva; **Fish** Claire Fogg, Jenni Muir, Emma Perry; **French** Emily Boyce, Sarah Guy, Jenni Muir, Natasha Polyviou; **Gastropubs** Alexi Duggins, Lewis Esson, Sarah Guy, Jenni Muir, Nick Rider, Nora Ryan; **Global** Jessica Cargill Thompson, Phil Harriss; **Greek** Alexi Duggins; **Hotels & Haute Cuisine** Silvija Davidson, Richard Ehrlich, Euan Ferguson, Roopa Gulati, Ruth Jarvis, Jenni Muir, Jeffrey Ng; **Indian** Euan Ferguson, Roopa Gulati, Phil Harriss, Jenni Muir, Eleanor Smallwood; **Italian** Emily Boyce, Silvija Davidson, Richard Ehrlich, Lewis Esson, Yolanda Zappaterra; **Japanese** Kei Kikuchi, Charmaine Mok, Celia Plender; **Jewish** Judy Jackson; **Korean** Celia Plender, Charmaine Mok, Yolanda Zappaterra; **Malaysian, Indonesian & Singaporean** Jeffrey Ng; **Middle Eastern** William Crow, Jenni Muir, Cyrus Shahrad, Janet Zmroczek; **Modern European** Simon Coppock, Claire Fogg, Sarah Guy, Jenni Muir, Cath Phillips, Nick Rider, Ros Sales; **North African** Caroline Hire, Caroline Stacey, Jamie Warburton; **Pan-Asian & Fusion** Tania Ballantine, Lauren Bravo, Jenni Muir, Jeffrey Ng; Caroline Hire, Chris Moss, Nick Rider, Nora Ryan, Elizabeth Winding; **Steakhouses** Simon Coppock, Alexi Duggins, Chris Moss; **Thai** Lewis Esson, Caroline Hire, Charmaine Mok; **Turkish** Euan Ferguson, Neil McQuillian, Caroline Anna Norman, Natasha Polyviou; **Vietnamese** Euan Ferguson; **Budget** Tania Ballantine, Lauren Bravo, William Crow, Anne Faber, Charlotte Morgan, Celia Plender, Jamie Warburton; **Cafés** Zena Alkayat, Jessica Cargill Thompson, Caroline Hire, Jael Marschner, Neil McQuillian, Emma Perry; **Coffee Bars** Zena Alkayat, Euan Ferguson, Jenni Muir; **Fish & Chips** Alexi Duggins, Anne Faber, Euan Ferguson, Jenni Muir, Peter Watts; **Ice-cream Parlours** Zena Alkayat, Lisa Harris, Jenni Muir, Celia Plender; **Pizza & Pasta** Emily Boyce, Anne Faber, Peter Watts; **Bars** Euan Ferguson, *Time Out London's Best Bars*; **Eating & Entertainment** William Crow, Jamie Warburton; **Wine Bars** Ruth Jarvis.

Additional reviews by Zena Alkayat, Ramona Andrews, Tania Ballantine, Emily Boyce, Lauren Bravo, Jessica Cargill Thompson, Simon Coppock, Silvija Davidson, Guy Dimond, Alexi Duggins, Richard Ehrlich, Lewis Esson, Anne Faber, Euan Ferguson, Jan Fuscoe, Sarah Guy, Roopa Gulati, Lisa Harris, Caroline Hire, Ruth Jarvis, Emily Kerrigan, Katrina Kollegaeva, Susan Low, Jael Marschner, Neil McQuillian, Charmaine Mok, Chris Moss, Jenni Muir, Jeffrey Ng, Amanda Nicolas, Anna Norman, Emma Perry, Cath Phillips, Celia Plender, Natasha Polyviou, Nick Rider, Nora Ryan, Ros Sales, Cyrus Shahrad, Shalinee Singh, Caroline Stacey, Eleanor Smallwood, Peter Watts, Elizabeth Winding, Yolanda Zappaterra, Janet Zmroczek.

The Editor would like to thank Edoardo Albert, Tania Ballantine, Jessica Cargill Thompson, Simon Coppock, William Crow, Guy Dimond, Alexi Duggins, Euan Ferguson, Susan Low, Emma Perry, John Watson. Thanks to our sponsor, MasterCard.

Maps JS Graphics (john@jsgraphics.co.uk). Maps 1-18 and 24 are based on material supplied by Alan Collinson and Julie Snook through Copyright Exchange. London Underground map supplied by Transport for London.

Photography by pages 10 (left), 61, 79 (centre), 83, 97, 134, 135, 156 (right), 169 (top), 227 (right), 232, 234 (centre), 237, 260, 287, 299, 304 (left) Tricia de Courcy Ling; pages 10 (centre), 11 (top), 14 (left), 20, 21, 25 (left), 32, 37, 41, 44, 50, 51, 60, 63, 64, 69 (bottom and centre left), 73, 75, 79, 80, 81, 84, 86, 108, 115 (bottom left), 117, 118, 137, 139, 144, 154, 156 (centre), 157, 170 (centre), 171, 180, 182 (right), 183, 190, 193, 202, 218, 227 (left), 231, 246 (centre), 252, 253, 259 (centre), 263, 266, 298, 303 Ming Tang-Evans; pages 10 (right), 12 (right), 48 (left), 78, 119, 133, 138, 145, 211, 236, 246, 268 (centre) Michael Franke; pages 11 (middle and bottom), 24, 37 (right), 42, 43, 123, 125, 156 (left), 165, 167, 185, 186, 210, 212, 219, 247 (top), 282, 314, 317, 319, 324 (right), 327 (top) Britta Jaschinski; pages 12 (left), 26, 36, 38, 48, 49, 52, 56, 60 (centre), 65, 72, 77, 84 (right), 85, 90, 101, 103, 104, 151, 168, 169 (bottom), 170 (right), 173, 176, 191, 194, 196, 227 (centre), 228, 234 (left), 235, 239, 241, 259, 261, 268 (right), 269, 271, 277, 280, 283, 286, 289, 294, 295, 297, 304, 308, 309, 324, 328 Rob Greig; pages 12 (middle), 25 (right), 74 (centre), 170 (left), 179, 185 (right), 189, 274 (right), 278, 308 (right), 310, 311 Michelle Grant; pages 14 (top), 20 (right), 115 (top), 148, 172, 265, 320 (right) Alys Tomlinson; pages 25 (centre), 53, 96, 194 (right), 201, 232 (bottom right), 281 Ed Marshall; page 28 David Loftus; page 39 Richard Lewisham; pages 46, 57, 247 (bottom), 307, 327 (bottom) Scott Wishart; page 47 (right) Mark Whitfield; pages 63 (centre left), 265 (centre) Thomas Skovsende; pages 69 (top and centre right) 182 (centre) Heloise Bergman; page 69 (bottom right) Katy Peters; pages 74, 122, 178, 182 (left), 320 Jonathan Perugia; page 112 Andre Ainsworth; page 115 (bottom right) Ben Rowe; pages 116 Gus Gregory; page 118 (left) North Road; page 121 David Tett; page 127 (left), 128 (centre) Mandarin Oriental; page 127, 128 Ashley-Palmer Watts; page 128 (top right) Eddie Judd; pages 130, 131 Neil Setchfield; pages 177, 225 Martin Daly; pages 202 (centre), 274 (centre), 276 (centre) Jitka Hynkova; page 204 Steve Wallington; pages 222, 234 (right), 240, 292 Celia Topping; page 224 (centre) Olivia Rutherford; pages 268 (left), 272 Christina Theisen; pages 274 (left), 276 (centre) Oliver Knight; page 274 Karen Thomas Photography.com; page 314 (center) Experimental Cocktail Club; page 315 (left) Andreas von Einsiedel; page 315 (right) Jefferson Smith; page 321 Heloise Bergman.

The following images were provided by the featured establishments: pages 14 (right), 31, 47 (left), 111, 162, 187, 195, 203, 318.

Printed by Wyndeham Group.
Time Out Group uses paper products that are environmentally friendly, from well-managed forests and mills that used certified (PEFC) Chain of Custody pulp in their production.

ISBN 978-1-9050-4263-0
ISSN 1750-4643
Distribution by Comag Specialists (01895 433 800). For further distribution details, see timeout.com.

About the guide

LISTED BY AREA
The restaurants in this guide are listed by cuisine type: British, Chinese, Indian, Middle Eastern etc. Then, within each chapter, they are listed by geographical area: ten main areas (in this example, South West), then by neighbourhood (Wandsworth). If you are not sure where to look for a restaurant, there are two indexes at the back of the guide to help: an A-Z Index (starting on p371) listing restaurants by name, and an Area Index (starting on p354), where you can see all the places we list in a specific neighbourhood.

STARS
A red star ★ means that a venue is, of its type, very good indeed. A green star ★ identifies budget-conscious eateries – expect to pay £20 per head for a three-course meal, or its equivalent (not including drinks and service).

NEW
The NEW symbol means new to this edition of the *Eating & Drinking Guide*. In most cases, these are brand-new venues.

TIME OUT HOT 50
The HOT 50 symbol means the venue is among what we consider to be London's top 50 iconic eating and drinking experiences. For details of the complete 50, *see p8*.

AWARD NOMINEES
Winners and runners-up in Time Out's Eating & Drinking Awards 2011. For more information on the awards, *see p10*.

OPENING HOURS
Times given are for last orders rather than closing times (except in cafés and bars).

PRICES
We have listed the cheapest and most expensive main courses available in each restaurant. In the case of many oriental restaurants, prices may seem lower – but remember that you often need to order several such dishes to have a full meal.

COVER CHARGE
An old-fashioned fixed charge may be imposed by the restaurateur to cover the cost of rolls and butter, crudités, cleaning table linen and similar extras.

MAP REFERENCE
All restaurants that appear on our street maps (starting on p330) are given a reference to the map and grid square where they can be found.

SERVICES
These are listed below the review.

Babies and children We've tried to reflect the degree of welcome extended to babies and children in restaurants. If you find no mention of either, take it that the restaurant is unsuitable.

Disabled: toilet means the restaurant has a specially adapted toilet, which implies that customers with walking disabilities or wheelchairs can get into the restaurant. However, we recommend phoning to double-check.

Vegetarian menu Most restaurants claim to have a vegetarian dish on the menu. We've highlighted those that have made a more concerted effort to attract and cater for vegetarian (and vegan) diners.

South West
Wandsworth

★ ★ **Bite Trash** HOT 50
2011 RUNNER-UP BEST NEW CHEAP EATS
1 Wandsworth Bridge, SW18 6JM (9876 4321).
Wandsworth Town rail. **Open/meals served** 8am-round midnight daily. **Main courses** £2.50-£7.50. **Cover** £1.
Credit AmEx, MC, V.
This converted Winnebago by Wandsworth Bridge roundabout brings the taste of Lower East Side drugstores to Old York Road. Settle back in one of the peeling red-vinyl bench seats for intimate communal dining, or eat alfresco on the red, white and blue striped Lay-Z-Boys, with their sensational views of Homebase and SW18's landmark advertising signage. While the *8 Mile* soundtrack plays on loop, gung-ho staff in Calvin Klein underpants, baseball caps and rollerskates bring complimentary bags of Cheetos to tear open at table. The menu majors on sharing plates of classic recipes, such as honey mustard pretzels, and fat-free Irish cheddar popcorn, with credible suppliers (Kraft, Kellogg's, Sara Lee) listed. A special of peanut butter and pepperoni pizzette, the only hot dish available, came topped with aerosol cheese and jalapeño peppers. The short, focused drinks list (Budweiser, Pepsi, iced tea) won't frighten nearby McDonalds, though the mash-up-style sundae of grape jelly, Pop-tart, frozen cookie dough and marshmallow fluff proves the multinational stands well back from the cutting edge when it comes to this high-energy cuisine.
Available for hire: vacation lets. Babies and children welcome: travel cot; skateboards. Disabled: ramps; john. Tables outdoors (6, sidewalk). Takeout and delivery service.
Map 21 A4.

Anonymous, unbiased reviews
The reviews in the *Eating & Drinking Guide* are based on the experiences of Time Out restaurant reviewers. Venues are always visited anonymously, and Time Out pays the bill. No payment or PR invitation of any kind has secured or influenced a review. The editors select which places are listed in this guide, and are not influenced in any way by the wishes of the restaurants themselves. Restaurants cannot volunteer or pay to be listed; we list only those we consider to be worthy of inclusion. Advertising and sponsorship has no effect whatsoever on the editorial content of the *Eating & Drinking Guide*. An advertiser may receive a bad review, or no review at all.

Busaba Eathai
Londoner's favourite Thai restaurant
busaba.com

Time Out's Hot 50

We have picked 50 places, entirely subjectively, that we believe offer some of London's most interesting eating experiences. We're not saying these venues have the best food and drink in the capital, but we believe each adds something life-enhancing to our city. Here they are, in alphabetical order. Each review is marked with a HOT 50 symbol in the relevant chapter of the guide.

Amaya
Indian p139.
Sparkling and sophisticated modern Indian grill.

Baltic
East European p77.
Classic East European dishes are given a contemporary spin at this still-glamorous restaurant and jazz bar.

Barrafina
Spanish p239.
A pint-sized space attracting mile-long queues for its stylish, authentic tapas and fine selection of sherries and Spanish wines.

Barshu
Chinese p67.
The fiery flavours of Sichuanese cooking, served in style.

Bentley's Oyster Bar & Grill
Fish p80.
Take a seat at the art nouveau bar for freshly shucked oysters and London's best fish pie.

Bistrot Bruno Loubet
French p86.
The Zetter hotel is a colourful setting for Bruno Loubet's modern French cooking.

Bistrotheque
French p95.
Bistro food, modish bar and camp cabaret make for an original combination at this east London hotspot.

Buen Ayre
The Americas p36.
Argentinian parrillada (steak grill) with everything from ribeyes to sweetbreads.

Busaba Eathai
Thai p253.
Great value Thai cooking in an exquisite canteen setting.

Le Café Anglais
Modern European p211.
Rowley Leigh's buzzy Bayswater brasserie.

Cah Chi
Korean p188.
Head to Raynes Park or Earlsfield for a taste of home-style Korean cooking.

Caravan
Brasseries p37.
A restaurant, bar and coffee roastery where beans are ethically sourced and expertly blended to suit the season.

Czechoslovak Restaurant
East European p78.
The city's only Czech restaurant and bar is a piece of living history.

Eyre Brothers
Global p121.
Mozambique meets the Mediterranean at David and Rob Eyre's sleek Shoreditch restaurant and tapas bar.

La Fromagerie
Cafés p282.
Dine among the deli ingredients at this charming fine food store.

Gelupo
Ice-cream Parlours p305.
Seaside hues of white and blue make this a sunny spot to enjoy superb Sicilian-style gelati and granita.

Hakkasan
Chinese p61.
Alan Yau may have sold up, but this remains a hot destination for Chinese cooking and cocktails.

Harwood Arms
Gastropubs p107.
British country produce stars at this Fulham pub dining room.

Hawksmoor
Steakhouses p249.
Will Beckett and Huw Gott's very British steakhouse and cocktail bar with fabulous interior of reclaimed materials.

Hix Soho
British p53, Bars p317.
Mark Hix's fun British restaurant with characterful downstairs bar.

The Ledbury
Hotels & Haute Cuisine p136.
Always a fine restaurant, now officially legend as brave staff made headlines around the world.

Locanda Locatelli
Italian p159.
A sexy, lounge-like dining room serving fine Italian cuisine and impressive wines.

Lola Rojo
Spanish p240.
Bringing a slice of Spain's nueva cocina to Battersea.

Mandalay
Global p118.
Sample first-rate Burmese fare at this otherwise basic caff.

Masa
Global p122.
The Middle East meets the Indian subcontinent in an unsung corner of Harrow.

Momo
North African p225.
A great Maghrebi soundtrack, cool Marrakech decor and some of the best Moroccan food in London.

Moro
Spanish p235.
Enduringly popular Exmouth Market restaurant with a menu that stretches from Spain right along the Mediterranean.

Nahm
Thai p252.
Royal Thai cuisine served with style and grace in a glittering dining room.

Ottolenghi
Brasseries p47.
Glamorous café by day, exquisite fusion restaurant by night.

Petersham Nurseries Café
Modern European p223.
The surrounding gardens inspire Skye Gyngell's inventive, flavour-packed cooking style.

Poppies
Fish & Chips p301.
Retro Spitalfields chippie with top-notch frying and more than a hint of happy days.

Princess Victoria
Gastropubs p105.
Brilliant conversion of a Victorian gin palace to pub and restaurant.

The Providores & Tapa Room
Pan-Asian & Fusion p229.
World-beating fusion fare served all day, from banana and pecan french toast to grilled scallops with crab and quinoa dumplings.

Rasa Samudra
Indian p139.
A rare opportunity to sample the authentic and surprisingly fiery fish cookery of Kerala.

The River Café
Italian p163.
The wood-fired oven takes centre stage in this world-famous, yet relaxed, Hammersmith classic.

Roka
Japanese p171.
Spectacularly designed restaurant based around a central grill, and great for Fitzrovia people-watching.

St John
British p50.
Fergus Henderson's uncompromising approach to food, and especially meat, has inspired a new generation of chefs both here and abroad.

Sakonis
Indian p155.
The original Indian vegetarian chat (snack) house, serving South Indian and Gujarati dishes.

Sketch: Lecture Room & Library
Hotels & Haute Cuisine p134.
Pierre Gagnaire's astonishing food isn't the only talking point at this stylish celebration of art and luxury.

Song Que
Vietnamese p269.
Authentic Vietnamese dishes at affordable prices.

Spuntino
The Americas p27.
A slice of New York's Lower East Side in the heart of London's Soho.

Sweetings
Fish p79.
Old-world bonhomie and classic British fish dishes since 1889.

Terroirs
Wine Bars p327.
Natural wines and small plates pioneer that's inspired a vat of imitators.

Towpath
Cafés p290.
Quirky waterside café in N1.

Les Trois Garçons
French p96.
Home to hippo heads, stuffed bulldogs and a collection of vintage handbags, as well as some terrific French food.

Viajante
Hotels & Haute Cuisine p136.
Nuno Mendes' Bethnal Green outpost of cutting-edge cuisine.

Vinoteca
Wine Bars p325.
A model wine bar with well-priced, well-rendered cooking, and all wines available to take home at retail price.

Wapping Food
Modern European p221.
Victorian pumping station museum/art-gallery serving inventive modern cooking and an Australian wine list.

The Wolseley
Brasseries p40.
A decade on, and this former car showroom still feels like one of London's most exciting destinations, day or night.

Yashin
Japanese p178.
An artistic antidote to the sushi lunchbox chains.

Time Out's 22nd annual
Eating & Drinking
Awards 2011

Manchurian Legends

Malina

Pollen Street Social

Time Out has an unrivalled reputation for promoting the best of London's eating and drinking places – something of which we are very proud. It is not just those with the grandest credentials that we champion, either, but the little places that are, in their own field, worthy of note. This is the ethos behind our broad coverage of London's gastronomic delights – from weekly reviews in *Time Out* magazine to our numerous guides. And this is why our annual Eating & Drinking Awards take in not only London's restaurant elite, but also representatives from neighbourhood restaurants, gastropubs and cafés, as independently selected by a panel of Time Out judges.

The award categories, which vary each year, reflect the diverse needs and tastes of London's diners and drinkers; this year's award for Best New Fine Dining shows that haute cuisine restaurants are thriving, despite the recession, while Best Sushi Bar reflects Londoners' enduring love for Japanese food. With new reviews appearing each week in *Time Out* magazine (and on our website, www.timeout.com/restaurants), the list of potential candidates can seem dauntingly long. The judges revisit every shortlisted venue as normal paying punters (we never accept PR invitations or freebies), so that a final decision can be reached.

And the winners are...

BEST NEW BAR

WINNER
Worship Street Whistling Shop *See p319.*

RUNNERS-UP
Booking Office *See p315.*
Experimental Cocktail Club *See p314.*
Zetter Townhouse *See p314.*

BEST NEW CHEAP EATS

WINNER
Manchurian Legends *See p61.*

RUNNERS-UP
Ariana II *See p122.*
KaoSarn *See p257.*
Meza *See p197.*

BEST NEW DESIGN

WINNER
Massimo (Italian) *See p162.*

RUNNERS-UP
NOPI (Pan-Asian & Fusion) *See p229.*
Riding House Café (Brasseries) *See p39.*
Spuntino (The Americas) *See p27.*

BEST NEW FINE DINING

WINNER
Pollen Street Social (Hotels & Haute Cuisine)
See p134.

RUNNERS-UP
Dinner by Heston Blumenthal (Hotels & Haute
Cuisine) *See p129.*
Hedone (Hotels & Haute Cuisine) *See p135.*
Medlar (Modern European) *See p215.*

BEST NEW LOCAL RESTAURANT

WINNER
Malina (East European) *See p75.*

RUNNERS-UP
Brawn (Modern European) *See p220.*
Corner Room (Modern European) *See p219.*
Kateh (Middle Eastern) *See p197.*

BEST NEW RESTAURANT

WINNER
Hawksmoor Seven Dials (Steakhouses) *See p249.*

RUNNERS-UP
Kopapa (Brasseries) *See p38.*
Morito (Spanish & Portuguese) *See p234.*
Spuntino (The Americas) *See p27.*

BEST PARK CAFÉ

WINNER
Lido Café (Brockwell Lido) *See p293.*

RUNNERS-UP
Fulham Palace Café *See p292.*
Lido Café (Serpentine) *See p291.*
Pavilion Café (Highgate) *See p293.*

BEST SUSHI BAR

WINNER
Yashin *See p178.*

RUNNERS-UP
Atari-ya *See p178.*
Dinings *See p172.*
Sushi of Shiori *See p171.*

Yashin

Worship Street Whistling Shop

Hawksmoor Seven Dials

AWARDS 2011

This year's judges:
Jessica Cargill Thompson, Simon Coppock, Alexi Duggins, Euan Ferguson, Susan Low, Charmaine Mok, Jenni Muir, Emma Perry

Where to...

Got the hunger, the people, the occasion, but not the venue? These suggestions will help you find the perfect spot to eat, drink and be merry.

GO FOR BREAKFAST
Breakfast is offered every day unless stated otherwise. *See also* **Brasseries** and **Cafés**.

Albion British p59
Bentley's Oyster Bar & Grill Fish p80
Bistrot Bruno Loubet French p86
Botanist Modern European p202
Canteen British p59
Cecconi's Italian p159
Chiswell Street Dining Rooms Modern
 European p202
Cinnamon Club (Mon-Fri) Indian p145
The Diner The Americas p28
Dishoom Indian p137
Dorchester Grill Room British p51
Fifteen (Trattoria) Italian p167
Fifth Floor (Café, Mon-Sat)
 Modern European p207
Garufa The Americas p36
Goring Hotel British p55
Grazing Goat Gastropubs p102
Lutyens French p85
The Luxe Modern European p220
The Modern Pantry (Mon-Fri)
 Pan-Asian & Fusion p227
NOPI Pan-Asian & Fusion p229
Orange Public House & Hotel
 Gastropubs p102
The Providores & Tapa Room
 Pan-Asian & Fusion p229
Queen Adelaide Gastropubs p105
Roast (Mon-Sat) British p58
St John (Leicester Square branch) British p50
Sakonis (Sat, Sun) Indian p155
Simpson's-in-the-Strand (Mon-Fri) British p55

Smiths of Smithfield Modern European p205
Sotheby's Café (Mon-Fri)
 Modern European p207
York & Albany Modern European p221

EAT/DRINK BY THE WATERSIDE
See also the Southbank Centre branches of **Giraffe** and **Wagamama**.

Blueprint Café Modern European p218
Dock Kitchen Modern European p213
Lido Café (Brockwell Lido) Cafés p293
Lido Café (Serpentine) Cafés p291
Camino (Docklands branch) Spanish p237
Gaucho (Tower Bridge and Richmond branches)
 The Americas p30
Narrow Gastropubs p111

Le Pont de la Tour Modern European p218
Royal China (Docklands branch) Chinese p69
Serpentine Bar & Kitchen Cafés p291
Skylon Modern European p217

ENJOY THE VIEW
Blueprint Café Modern European p218
Le Coq d'Argent French p84
Galvin at Windows Hotels & Haute
 Cuisine p132
Oxo Tower Restaurant, Bar & Brasserie
 Modern European p217
Inn The Park British p52
Min Jiang Chinese p71
Paramount Modern European p203
Plateau Modern European p220
Roast British p58

Rhodes Twenty Four British p49
Skylon Modern European p217
Tate Modern Café Brasseries p45
Smiths of Smithfield (Top Floor)
 Modern European p205

SHARE DISHES
Angels & Gypsies Spanish p241
Barrica Spanish p235
Bocca di Lupo Italian p161
Caravan Brasseries p37
Club Gascon French p87
Dinings Japanese p172
Ibérica Food & Culture Spanish p236
Lalibela African & Caribbean p22
Norfolk Arms Gastropubs p100
Ottolenghi Brasseries p47
La Petite Maison French p91
Tayyabs Indian p153
Terroirs Wine Bars p327
Tom's Kitchen Brasseries p43
Vine Gastropubs p115

TAKE AFTERNOON TEA
See also **Cafés** and **Hotels & Haute Cuisine**.

Bob Bob Ricard Brasseries p40
Botanist Modern European p202
Chiswell Street Dining Rooms
 Modern European p202
Les Deux Salons French p87
National Dining Rooms (Bakery)
 British p55
Northall British p55
Quince Turkish p259

THE
BLUES
KITCHEN

BLUES BAR &
SOUL FOOD DINER

WHERE TO...

Where to... get in first

DUE TO OPEN SEPT 2011
Bread Street Kitchen
One New Change, 10 Bread Street, EC4M 9AB (7592 1616, www.gordon ramsay.com/breadstreetkitchen/).
Gordon Ramsay Holdings is soon to open a casual all-day diner within the City's New Change shopping development. Expect a wood-burning oven and grill, own-made charcuterie, a Manhattan-style deli and an open kitchen.

DUE TO OPEN OCT 2011
Fornata
15 Kingly Street, W1B 5PS (www.fornata.com).
From the team behind Babbo comes this new all-day Italian establishment in Soho. It will have an open kitchen serving Italian coffee and pastries at breakfast, southern Italian oven-baked dishes at lunch, and aperitivos and antipasti come nightfall.

Cuisine de Bar by Poilâne
39 Cadogan Gardens, SW3 2TB (www.poilane.fr).
All-day dining in Chelsea from acclaimed Parisian bakery Poilâne. Breads, pastries, salads and light suppers will be served in the airy dining space, by the fireside lounge, or up at the eating bar, where savoury tartines are made to order.

Hawksmoor Guildhall
10-12 Basinghall Street, EC2V 5BQ (www.thehawksmoor.co.uk).
The third branch of popular steakhouse Hawksmoor, this time located in the City. In addition to the usual high-end steaks and burgers, this site will offer a bar, walk-in wine tasting room and the first Enomatic in London dedicated to port.

Soif
27 Battersea Rise, SW11 1HG
Another triplet arrives – from the same stable as Terroirs and Brawn. Like its siblings, natural wines will be teamed with rustic small plates of Gallic-leaning cooking, with occasional influences from Britain and the Med.

Union Jack's
Central St Giles, 1 St Giles High Street, WC2H 8AG.
Celebrity chef Jamie Oliver turns his hand to his native cuisine with the launch of this accessible Brit restaurant concept (expect more to follow), in Covent Garden's new Central St Giles development.

Aurelia
13-14 Cork Street, W1S 3NS (www.aureliamayfair.com).
The team behind La Petite Maison and Roka is due to launch a venture on the site once home to Mulligan's of Mayfair. The chefs may be ex-Roka, but the menu will lean more towards the Med than Japan.

DUE TO OPEN NOV 2011
Cabana
Central St Giles, 1 St Giles High Street, WC2H 8AG.
Having sold his stake in Hush, Villandry and Sake no Hana, Jamie Barber is set to launch a Brazilian barbecue restaurant in the new Central St Giles development.

34
34 Grosvenor Square, W1K 2HD (www.34-restaurant.co.uk).
Pitched at carnivores, this latest addition to the Caprice Holdings group will offer rare-breed meats and seasonal game cooked over a bespoke charcoal grill, within an art deco-inspired dining room.

Mishkin's
25 Catherine Street, WC2B 5JS.
Prolific restaurant duo Russell Norman and Richard Beatty (who gave us Spuntino and Polpo and its offshoots) are planning, for their fifth eaterie, to create a witty twist on a traditional East End Jewish deli.

Bill Granger
175 Westbourne Grove, W11 2SB.
Having moved to west London a couple of years ago, popular Aussie chef Bill Granger is finally gearing up to open his first restaurant in the area. The exact name is yet to be confirmed, but it will serve a casual, all-day menu that leans heavily on his Asian-inspired dishes.

LONDON HAS NOWHERE QUITE AS HALLUCINATORY AS THE WAPPING PROJECT

WAPPING FOOD
THE WAPPING PROJECT
WAPPING HYDRAULIC POWER STATION
WAPPING WALL
E1W 3SG
020 7680 2080

Photo Credit: Lianna Fowler photographed by thomas zanon-larcher, directed by Jules Wright (2010)

Restaurants

African & Caribbean

Many of London's African eateries are at the promulgation phase of their lives, with restaurateurs and chefs keen to explain the intricacies of their cuisine to other Londoners – as well as catering to expats hungry for the cooking of their homeland. Eritrea is particularly well represented, with **Mosob**, **Asmara** and **Adulis** all offering the spicy stews and spongy injera flatbread that typify the cuisine. A similar cooking style is offered by Ethiopian specialists **Lalibela** and **Queen of Sheba**. You can also try Somali cooking at the **Village**, and uncompromisingly authentic west African cooking at **805 Bar Restaurant**.

Meanwhile, the capital's Caribbean restaurants have come of age in the past decade, offering much more than the colourful decorations, rum cocktails and home-style soul food that had almost become a cliché. There's now a broader choice of eating establishments: from upbeat cafés (**Jerk City**, **Savannah Jerk**) to restaurants that offer updated, classy versions of classic dishes (**Mango Room**), along with venues that are ripe for a celebratory meal (**Caribbean Scene**).

AFRICAN

West

Hammersmith

★ The Village
95 Fulham Palace Road, W6 8JA (8741 7453). Hammersmith tube. **Meals served** 11.30am-11.30pm daily. **Main courses** £7-£8. **Set lunch** £6. **Unlicensed** no alcohol allowed. **Credit** AmEx, MC, V. Somali
Located in a vast Hammersmith basement, the Village is a relaxed space where, on our visit, the informality was underscored by most customers appearing to be Somali friends of the employees. Service was quite slow, despite few people dining, and although our waiter was geniality itself, this didn't compensate for him mixing up our orders (they were eventually corrected). From the all-halal menu we enjoyed a perfectly cooked sea bass, subtly seasoned and accompanied by salad dressed with lemon and olive oil. The drawback was the soggy Somali bread (wholemeal bread soaked in a coriander sauce). Likewise, tiramisu sponge for pudding was scrumptious, but spoiled by an abundance of very sweet cream on top. The decor keeps things simple, with tables and chairs of dark wood and the odd piece of traditional Somali striped cloth or panels of patterned bamboo on the walls. Somali folk music plays in the background. To drink, try something from the tempting range of fruit shakes (no alcohol is served), such as avocado, banana and mango. *Available for hire. Babies and children admitted. Takeaway service.* **Map 20 C5**.

Westbourne Park

★ Mosob
339 Harrow Road, W9 3RB (7266 2012, www.mosob.co.uk). Westbourne Park tube. **Meals served** 6-11pm Mon-Thur; 6-11.30pm Fri; 3-11.30pm Sat; 3-11pm Sun. **Main courses** £7.50-£10. **Set meal** £14.50-£19.95 per person (minimum 2). **Credit** MC, V. Eritrean
A mosob is a hand-woven table traditionally used in Eritrea at mealtimes. It is large enough for a family to sit around, giving comfortable access to the same plate. Mosob, the restaurant, has recreated this community spirit by providing extremely friendly service in its modern yet atmospheric dining room. The walls are adorned with Eritrean artefacts and covered in wallpaper patterned with tiny mosobs. Customers are of mixed age and background. The menu offers the staple Eritrean dishes of tsebhi (spicy tomato-based stews) and alicha ahmelti (spiced carrots, cabbage, split peas and onions), as well as less well-known dishes such as bamia (okra stewed in spices, onions and tomatoes). Stews are eaten with rice or injera. Disappointingly, our bamia was dominated by a potent combination of red onion and berbere spice mix. Nevertheless, the meal began and ended well. Mosob's samosas, stuffed with spiced potatoes, lentils and carrots, made an appetising starter; and we finished with a sweet, pleasant torta macao: chocolate cream on crushed biscuit. *Babies and children welcome: high chairs. Booking advisable. Separate room for parties, seats 22. Takeaway service.* **Map 1 A4**.

South

Brixton

★ Asmara
386 Coldharbour Lane, SW9 8LF (7737 4144). Brixton tube/rail. **Dinner served** 5.30pm-midnight daily. **Main courses** £7.20-£10. **Set meal** £30 (2 people) vegetarian, £32 (2 people) meat. **Credit** MC, V. Eritrean
Asmara, named after Eritrea's capital, makes its inspiration clear to customers with a gold-plated map of the homeland above a central bar. The ground floor was half full on our visit, but tables were served by just one waiter (with another staff member working behind the bar). In spite of this, service was speedy and very welcoming. We ordered the silver pollack kilwa (an Eritrean word meaning 'frying', in this case with green chillies and spices) and alicha (a stew of potatoes, cabbage and carrots), which was a little overcooked. Dishes are served on injera and portions are large. To finish, spiced tea with cinnamon and cloves was soothing to our full stomachs. Asmara has an intimate atmosphere, with low ceilings, a small interior and amiable staff who are happy to describe the dishes in detail. Windows are draped with pieces of

netzela (a cotton cloth often used by Eritrean women as a shawl). Paintings of Eritrean landscapes and simple country life provide an absorbing backdrop to the palatable food. *Babies and children welcome: high chairs. Booking advisable. Separate room for parties, seats 35. Takeaway service. Vegan dishes. Vegetarian menu.* **Map 22 E2**.

Kennington

Adulis

44-46 Brixton Road, SW9 6BT (7587 0055, www.adulis.co.uk). Oval tube. **Meals served** 4pm-midnight Mon-Wed; noon-midnight Thur-Sun. **Main courses** £10.95-£13.95. **Credit** MC, V. Eritrean

Named after the ancient port city by the Red Sea, Adulis endeavours to keep the tastes and ambience of Eritrean cuisine alive in London. There are immaculately patterned bamboo throws draped over chairs, and paintings of pastoral Eritrean scenes lining the walls. We enjoyed the set combination of vegetarian dishes, which included spicy lentil stew, a flavoursome but fiery experience. Each stew was infused with the organic herbs and spices (chilli powder, paprika and coriander, among others) that the restaurant imports from Eritrea. Portions are large, and most main courses are served with freshly made injera bread. For desserts, expect the likes of cheesecake and banoffi pie – perhaps it's best to finish with the coffee ceremony, performed by a cheerful woman wearing a traditional dress of white cotton with brightly coloured embroidery. The coffee was served in a jebena, a patterned clay pot that holds enough for around six very small cups. Other traditional drinks include mies, a wine made from fermented honey. Service on our Saturday night visit was very friendly, but the speed declined after 9pm as the restaurant filled. Nevertheless, Adulis has character and authenticity aplenty. *Babies and children welcome: high chairs. Booking advisable weekends. Separate room for parties, seats 100. Takeaway service.* **Map 16 M13**.

South East

Peckham

805 Bar Restaurant

805 Old Kent Road, SE15 1NX (7639 0808, www.805restaurant.com). Elephant & Castle tube/rail then 53 bus. **Meals served** 2pm-midnight daily. **Main courses** £11-£16. **Set meal** £9-£15. **Credit** MC, V. Nigerian

Popular with Nigerians to whom it offers a taste of home, 805 Bar Restaurant is a lively eatery with a bright, white interior decorated with colourful African art. There's a choice of two dining areas: the smarter executive suite (which can also be hired for events) and the main dining room, which is less pristine but equally popular. Fans come here to wolf down large Nigerian-style portions of cowfoot, spiced chicken gizzards, fish pepper soup, jollof rice and some excellent whole-baked fish. Our dishes were a little hit-and-miss. Tilapia with fried plantain and jollof rice was beautifully cooked, but chicken thighs in tomato sauce was disappointingly dry. Salad garnish dressed in salad cream was a little unexpected too. Although welcoming, service was slow due to some problems in the kitchen, but a free

Mango Room. See p24.

drink was offered without any prompting. Prices are on the high side, though in recompense, portions are generous. Fans of Nigerian and West African cuisine should head here, but although there are plenty of 'safe' options, much of the food might be challenging for the uninitiated.
Babies and children welcome: high chairs. Disabled: toilet. Separate room for parties, seats 55. Tables outdoors (6, pavement). Takeaway service.

North
Kentish Town

★ Queen of Sheba
12 Fortress Road, NW5 2EU (7284 3947, www.thequeenofsheba.co.uk). Kentish Town tube/rail. **Meals served** 5.30-11pm daily. **Main courses** £5-£10.50. **Set meal** £30 (2-3 people). **Credit** MC, V. Ethiopian
One of the biggest joys of an Ethiopian meal is the element of ceremony, and despite low-key surroundings, the Queen of Sheba happily obliges in this. Its simple, café-style set-up might not be as cosy or atmospheric as some, with the bustle of Kentish Town inescapable through the windows, but all the right aromas, trinkets and other cultural touches are present. More crucially, the flavours are here too. The menu offers a well-described range of we'ts and t'ibs (spicy stews), with ample choice for vegetarians and plenty of milder dishes for the spice-shy. The Sheba special kifto – traditional spiced steak tartare served with a cheese and spinach mixture – was delicious, as was the chef's

special of bozena shiro, a creamy chickpea and fried meat stew. A fiery side dish of stuffed chillies defeated us, but the sympathetic serving team were on hand with some milk. Platefuls of perfectly sour injera come as standard with each main course, and the stews are presented and spooned on to the flatbread for you, in cheerful ritual by the relaxed yet attentive staff. The only disappointment is a lack of decent desserts; the headily spiced coffee just about compensates.
Available for hire. Babies and children welcome: high chairs. Booking advisable Fri, Sat. Takeaway service. Vegan dishes. Vegetarian menu. **Map 26 B4**.

Tufnell Park

Lalibela
137 Fortress Road, NW5 2HR (7284 0600). Tufnell Park tube or 134 bus. **Dinner served** 6pm-midnight Mon-Sat. **Main courses** £11-£12.95. **Credit** MC, V. Ethiopian
If you're hankering after a dining experience that feels as far from Tufnell Park as possible, Lalibela won't disappoint. Atmospheric to the limit, its two floors are fitted out with carved wood, knick-knacks, pictures, lamps and, in one corner, a full-sized mannequin. Devoted locals and curious foodies flock here, as much for the rituals as for the food. Starters of salads and kebabs are mostly unremarkable; the magic is in the mains. Stews simmering gently over tea lights are mopped up with handfuls of spongy, sour injera. Lamb and pumpkin wot with tropical spices was rich and fragrant, while a range of spinach-based t'ibs (spicy stews) were far tastier than their menu description

suggests. Vegetarians are well catered for. Desserts seemed surplus to requirements after the immense main courses, but we enjoyed a slab of syrupy baklava. Afterwards came the unmissable finale, where roasting coffee beans are brought to fragrance the table before potent coffee is served in traditional dainty glasses. Service was cheerful if slow; this is a restaurant that encourages lingering. Prices have shot up in recent years, but the belt-straining portions and overall charm keep Lalibela's disciples spreading the word.
Babies and children welcome: high chairs. Booking advisable. Takeaway service. Vegetarian menu. **Map 26 B3**.

CARIBBEAN
Central
Clerkenwell & Farringdon

Cottons
70 Exmouth Market, EC1R 4QP (7833 3332, www.cottons-restaurant.co.uk). Farringdon tube/rail or bus 19, 38, 341. **Lunch served** noon-4pm, **dinner served** 5-11pm daily. **Main courses** £12.50-£14.50. **Credit** MC, V.
Authenticity cuts two ways. At Cottons, it runs to the less appealing aspects of some restaurants in the Caribbean: shambolic service, schizophrenic decor that combines rum shack with yacht club, and soul food with misplaced airs of pretension. It's a shame, as the initial vibe is a nice one. A brightly

AFRICAN & CARIBBEAN

coloured dining room dotted with boxing and travel posters looks on to a sweet little bar stuffed with an amazing rum selection and various cocktails on one side, and Exmouth Market on the other. The menu is also appealing, with a broad selection of hearty traditional dishes, including papaya and mango salad, grilled jerk chicken caesar salad, curry goat and a mixed jerk meat or fish grill. The latter promised parrotfish, tilapia, snapper and tiger prawns, but turned out to be two unidentifiable steaks and a chewy fillet topped with one burnt king prawn. The meat version was little better; pork ribs and belly pork had been replaced by ham because, said our waitress unapologetically, the pork hadn't been delivered. Punchy jerk sauce and perfect plantain made some amends, but our disappointment remained – standards have slipped at this once very good restaurant.
Available for hire. Babies and children welcome: high chairs. Disabled: toilet. Entertainment: DJs 9.30pm-2am Fri, Sat. Separate room for parties, seats 65. Tables outdoors (5, patio). Takeaway service. **Map 5 N4.**
For branch see index.

Soho

★ Jerk City
189 Wardour Street, W1F 8ZD (7287 2878). Tottenham Court Road tube. **Meals served** 11am-9pm Mon-Wed; 11am-10pm Thur-Sat; noon-8pm Sun. **Main courses** £6-£8.50. **Credit** MC, V.
Caribbean food is not widely available in central London, so this Soho gem is worth discovering. From the outside, Jerk City resembles a red-fronted caff. Dishes are chalked on a big board behind the front counter, and cooked in a subterranean kitchen by a chef-cum-waitress. If you're eating in, try to come in the late afternoon when a lull after the lunchtime rush means you're likely to have a choice of seating at the smattering of brown wooden tables. Jerk City's repertoire of Caribbean staples includes curried, stewed or jerk chicken (marinated in hot peppers and herbs before being chargrilled), vegetable roti, braised oxtail with butter beans, peppered steak in rich gravy, and curried prawns with diced potatoes. Portions are generous, so a medium-sized ackee and saltfish at £7.75 was good value: large chunks of salted cod were blended with ackee, onions and sweet peppers, served with a sizeable helping of coconut-flavoured rice and peas, plus a side salad of fresh tomato, lettuce and cucumber. Accompany this with a smooth, sweet Guinness punch for a laid-back treat.
Babies and children welcome: high chairs; nappy-changing facilities. Takeaway service. **Map 17 B3.**

Savannah Jerk
187 Wardour Street, W1F 8ZB (7437 7770, www.savannahjerk.com). Tottenham Court Road tube. **Meals served** 11am-11pm Mon-Fri; 2-11pm Sat. **Credit** AmEx, MC, V.
Any Caribbean cooking worth its salt(fish) should have the effect of transporting you to a desert island, and Savannah Jerk manages the feat with ease. If you're looking for a huge plate of spicy comfort food containing ingredients such as green banana, boiled yam, dumpling and sweet potato, and dishes such as macaroni pie, rich flavoursome mutton curry served with rice and peas, or stewed chicken turned a dark, chocolatey brown from

caramelised sugar, this is the place to head. The short menu covers all the classics of everyday Caribbean cuisine: jerk chicken, oxtail, ackee and saltfish, stewed chicken, and Trinidad roti (a choice of meat, chicken and prawn curries with diced potatoes wrapped in soft flatbread). Drinks are authentic too; Guinness punch, Ting (fizzy grapefruit juice), ginger beer (great with jerk chicken) and the ubiquitous Red Stripe all feature alongside a long list of rums. Despite the restaurant's spacious, smart dining room, this isn't fancy stuff, just Caribbean cooking that flavours hearty ingredients with hints of scotch bonnet, ginger and allspice, bringing a big smile to your face and a 'mmmm' to your heart.
Takeaway service. **Map 17 B3.**

South East
Crystal Palace

★ Keno's at Island Fusion
57B Westow Hill, SE19 1TS (8239 8517). Crystal Palace or Gypsy Hill rail. **Meals served** 1pm-midnight Mon-Sat; 3-10pm Sun. **Main courses** £6-£8. **No credit cards.**
For years, this place was simply known as Island Fusion, but in June 2011, new management added the moniker Keno's, a shortened name for the St Vincentian Kennedy family who now run things. We willed the restaurant to be as comforting as before, with an equally enticing Caribbean menu. However, previously added twists, such as sweet potato mash, popadoms and seafood platters, have been replaced by a more standard menu featuring many of the dishes you'd expect from the Caribbean islands. That's not to fault the food, though. An order of oxtail and another of brown stew fish came with generous portions of rice and peas, and plain rice respectively. Both dishes were well proportioned and, at £6 each, a bargain – but both needed a little more sauce to raise them from good to very good meals. Other main courses include curried or stewed chicken or mutton, ackee and saltfish, and a special Keno's sweet sticky chicken that promises savoury flavours and the chef's secret sauce. Service was friendly if slightly hesitant. Weekly activities feature dominoes, chess, film screenings, musicians and rum nights.
Available for hire. Babies and children welcome (until 7pm): high chairs. Takeaway service; delivery service (over £10 within 3-mile radius).

East
Stratford

Caribbean Scene
1 Gerry Raffles Square, E15 1BG (8522 8660, www.caribbeanscene.co.uk). Stratford tube/rail/DLR. **Breakfast served** 8-11am, **meals served** noon-10pm daily. **Main courses** £7.50-£9.50. **Credit** AmEx, MC, V.
The folk at Caribbean Scene know what their largely Afro-Caribbean customers want: decent, cheap food in a lively environment, with efficient, friendly service. Yes, there are the inevitable brightly coloured wall murals, but when these celebrate the likes of Gary Sobers and Usain Bolt you can't help but smile; likewise at the plasma screens sheltered by little thatched roofs, showing cute images of school kids on days out to the

Menu

Menu

CARIBBEAN

Ackee: a red-skinned fruit with yellow flesh that looks like scrambled eggs when cooked; traditionally served in a Jamaican dish of salt cod, onion and peppers.

Bammy or **bammie:** pancake-shaped, deep-fried cassava (qv) bread, often served with fried fish.

Breadfruit: this football-sized fruit has sweet creamy flesh that's a cross between sweet potato and chestnut. Eaten as a vegetable.

Bush tea: herbal tea made from cerese (a Jamaican vine plant), mint or fennel.

Callaloo: the spinach-like leaves of either taro or malanga, often used as a base for a thick soup flavoured with pork or crab meat.

Coo-coo: a polenta-like cake of cornmeal and okra.

Cow foot: a stew made from the hoof of the cow, boiled with vegetables. The cartilage gives the stew a gummy or gelatinous texture.

Curried goat: usually lamb in London; the meat is marinated and slow-cooked until tender.

Dasheen: a root vegetable with a texture similar to yam (qv).

Escoveitched (or **escovitch**) fish: fish fried or grilled, then pickled in a tangy sauce with onions, sweet peppers and vinegar; similar to escabèche.

Festival: deep-fried, slightly sweet dumpling often served with fried fish.

Foo-foo: a Barbadian dish of pounded plantains, seasoned, rolled into balls and served hot.

Jerk: chicken or pork marinated in chilli spices, slowly roasted or barbecued.

Patty or **pattie:** a savoury pastry snack, made with turmeric-coloured shortcrust pastry, usually filled with beef, saltfish or vegetables.

Peas or **beans:** black-eyed beans, black beans, green peas and red kidney beans.

Pepperpot: traditionally a stew of meat and casssereep, a juice obtained from cassava (qv).

Phoulorie: a Trinidadian snack of fried doughballs often eaten with a sweet tamarind sauce.

Plantain or **plantin:** a savoury variety of banana that is cooked like potato.

Rice and peas: rice cooked with kidney or gungo beans, pepper seasoning and coconut milk.

Saltfish: salt cod, classically mixed with ackee (qv) or callaloo (qv).

Sorrel: not the herb, but a type of hibiscus with a sour-sweet flavour.

Soursop: a dark green, slightly spiny fruit; the pulp, blended with milk and sugar, is a refreshing drink.

Yam: a large tuber, with a yellow or white flesh and slightly nutty flavour.

Olympic Park. The menu gets it right too, with the obvious Jamaican dishes – jerk chicken, ackee and saltfish, curry goat – joined by representatives from Cuba, Nevis, Guyana and Trinidad. Hence, you'll also find oxtail stew, brown stew chicken, roti, and curry chicken, the latter two showing the influence of Indian cookery on the islands. Flavouring and spices in all of these were spot on, the scotch bonnet peppers giving a true taste of the cuisine without the fierce heat that sometimes accompanies it. Even the music went beyond the predictable reggae, giving us upbeat, fun soca, which the kids eating with their families around us obviously loved – and took us straight back to carnival.

Babies and children welcome: children's menu; high chairs. Disabled: toilet. Takeaway service.
For branch see index.

North

Camden Town & Chalk Farm

★ Mango Room

10-12 Kentish Town Road, NW1 8NH (7482 5065, www.mangoroom.co.uk). Camden Town tube. **Meals served** noon-11pm daily. **Main courses** £10-£14. **Credit** AmEx, MC, V.

Classy dining at the dodgier end of Kentish Town Road might sound incongruous, but the Mango Room sits comfortably in its locality. The atmosphere is created by the cheerful diners rather than any arresting decor. Instead of trying to whisk you to a distant clime, the furnishings encourage you to enjoy the view of Camden streetlife, while sipping a tropical cocktail and appreciating the muted reggae soundtrack. Service is efficient, if not effusive. The menu consists of a soulful collection of Caribbean favourites – jerk chicken, rice and peas, and curried goat, all elegantly presented – alongside more unusual dishes such as barracuda and salmon carpaccio. Main courses are served in delicate portions, but there are plenty of starchy side dishes to bulk them out. Salt cod fritters were delicious, flavourful and dense in their crispy batter shell; and a sunny plateful of bream with coconut and pepper sauce arrived perfectly cooked, to be mopped up with good roti bread. Nicely caramelised plantain and wonderfully tender roast honey and ginger duck completed a fine meal. Desserts (such as mango and banana crème brûlée) hold their own, but aren't as exciting. After lingering as long as possible, we left with a post-holiday glow.

Babies and children welcome: high chairs. Booking advisable weekends. Separate room for parties, seats 20. Takeaway service. Vegan dishes. **Map 27 D2.**

Lalibela. See p22.

The Americas

NORTH AMERICAN

This year's openings should put to rest any idea that North American cuisine is restricted to burger joints and diners. Jamie Oliver partnered with US meat and barbecuing expert Adam Perry Lang to launch glitzy **Barbecoa** in St Paul's One New Change (a shopping mall, how appropriate). It may not have had Oliver's usual Midas touch, despite being preceded by his US television series and hit American cookbook, but it's a welcome move upmarket for fans of pulled pork, barbecued ribs and butt ends. Hot on its hooves came the **Pitt Cue Co** food truck – not a restaurant, but certainly a hipster eaterie attracting connoisseurs with its 'pickle back and skin' (bourbon chased by a shot of pickle brine, with pork crackling on the side). For a different slice of the American pie, head to **Spuntino** in Soho, a London evocation of the Italian-American bars of New York's Lower East Side. Old favourites performed well this year too, including Covent Garden swisherie **Christopher's**, plus Tom Conran's bijou diner **Lucky 7** and **Dollar Grills & Martinis**, a good choice for burgers, of course.

Central

City

Barbecoa NEW

20 New Change Passage, EC4M 9AG (3005 8555, www.barbecoa.com). St Paul's tube. **Meals served** 11.45am-11pm Mon-Sat; noon-10pm Sun. **Main courses** £16-£65. **Credit** AmEx, MC, V.
Slated by critics when it first opened, Jamie Oliver's joint venture with American barbecue expert Adam Perry Lang has, in fact, much to recommend it. The sensational view of St Paul's makes it worth a visit alone, and the Tom Dixon-designed interior is smartly sexy. A quadrangle of dining rooms is built around the kitchen. The space is huge, but makes a good choice for party groups looking to splash out. Service is more formal than at other JO establishments, yet retains the signature affability. The menu is a strange but probably astute mix of steaks, Texas 'cue classics, and the pukka Italianate dishes with which Oliver has charmed the world. Sweet, succulent, smoky pulled pork shoulder is as close as meat gets to producing the endorphin rush of chocolate, and here is much better than the short rib with worcestershire glaze. Creamed spinach was straight out of America's classic steakhouses. Add duck-fat chips or pit-smoked beans with burnt ends, and there's your obesity epidemic explained. Return another time for desserts of vin santo rose cake with candied vanilla lemons, and baked cheesecake with chocolate gingersnap crust and lime meringue. Pity there are so few American bottles on the wine list.
Babies and children welcome: high chairs; nappy-changing facilities. Booking advisable. Disabled: lift; toilet. Separate room for parties, seats 50. Tables outdoors (4, terrace). **Map 11 P6**.

Clerkenwell & Farringdon

Dollar Grills & Martinis

2 Exmouth Market, EC1R 4PX (7278 0077, www.dollargrillsandmartinis.com). Farringdon tube/rail or bus 19, 38, 341.
Bar **Open/food served** 5pm-1am Tue, Wed; 5pm-1.30am Thur; 5pm-3am Fri, Sat. **Main courses** £5.
Restaurant **Lunch served** noon-5pm daily. **Dinner served** 5-11pm Mon-Thur; 5-11.30pm Fri, Sat; 5-10pm Sun. **Main courses** £8-£24.
Both **Credit** AmEx, MC, V.
Glossy black tiling, glowing chandeliers and gleaming cutlery – the luxe interior of Dollar Grills & Martinis is primped and polished like a well-manicured Manhattanite: no underdressed tables or straggly stray chairs here. This pedigree extends to the menu, which features a list of grain-fed USDA-certified steaks, from a 9oz rump to an 18oz chateaubriand (for two). We plumped for the wagyu beefburger, a more affordable way to enjoy this prime breed, and it didn't disappoint. It was served in a rich brioche bun, with jack cheese and sweet-cure bacon topping off the medium-rare patty perfectly. We were less excited about the burgers named after Las Vegas casinos, the peanut satay, relish and avocado topping of the MGM Grand being a rather ill-advised combination. Taking a gamble on the baby back ribs paid in full – the almost too-generous portion was meltingly tender. Cocktails are part of the appeal here, the downstairs bar featuring a dedicated team of mixologists at the weekend, shaking up rhubarb negronis and fig sours. Knowledgeable American staff make the service every bit as smooth as the atmosphere, and the £6 weekday lunch menu (burger, steak, spaghetti and meatballs, among other options) is a real deal compared to the evening prices.
Babies and children admitted. Booking advisable weekends. Entertainment: DJs 9pm Thur-Sat. Tables outdoors (10, pavement). Takeaway service. **Map 5 N4**.

Covent Garden

Christopher's

18 Wellington Street, WC2E 7DD (7240 4222, www.christophersgrill.com). Covent Garden tube.
Bar **Open/food served** noon-midnight Mon-Fri; 11.30am-1am Sat; 11.30am-10.30pm Sun.
Restaurant **Lunch served** noon-3pm Mon-Fri.

Spuntino

Brunch served 11.30am-3.30pm Sat, Sun.
Dinner served 5-11.30pm Mon-Sat; 5-10.30pm Sun.
Both **Main courses** £14-£34. **Set meal**
(5-7pm, 10-11pm Mon-Sat) £16.95 2 courses,
£21.50 3 courses. **Credit** AmEx, MC, V.
Scarlett O'Hara would approve of the sweeping
staircase that guarantees a grand entrance into
Christopher's sumptuous dining room, housed on
the first floor of a striking mid 19th-century
building in Covent Garden. The menu, described as
neo-American, lists USDA prime steaks, maryland
crab cakes and new york cheesecake next to
Modern European and pan-Asian dishes. A starter
of lobster bisque came with a trio of floating
Chinese-style dumplings packed with lobster meat.
Clever presentation extended to a roast of missouri-
rubbed roast rump of lamb served with pumpkin
confit and an avocado-filled tamale wrapped in a
corn husk. Located a whisker away from the
Lyceum Theatre, home of *The Lion King*,
Christopher's offers a competitively priced pre- and
post-theatre menu. Smoked salmon fish cakes and
charcoal-grilled leg of lamb with chickpea mash
and horseradish crème fraîche were both executed
to a high standard, if not better than those dishes
we ordered from the carte. American wines are
represented well, but diners can also sip one of the
many imaginative martinis produced by the busy
cocktail bar downstairs. Efficient service saw
dropped cutlery and used glasses replaced without
hesitation, adding to the overall impression that
Christopher's is a class act.
Available for hire. Babies and children welcome:
children's menu; high chairs. Booking advisable.
Separate room for parties, seats 40. **Map 18 F4**.

Joe Allen

13 Exeter Street, WC2E 7DT (7836 0651,
www.joeallen.co.uk). Covent Garden tube.
Breakfast served 8-11.30am Mon-Fri. **Meals
served** noon-12.30am Mon-Fri; 11.30am-
12.30am Sat; 11.30am-11.30pm Sun. **Brunch
served** 11.30am-4pm Sat, Sun. **Main courses**
£9.50-£22.50. **Set brunch** £19.50 2 courses,
£21.50 3 courses incl drink. **Set meal** (noon-
3pm Mon-Fri, 5-6.45pm Mon-Sat) £16 2 courses,
£18 3 courses. **Credit** AmEx, MC, V.
'Off Broadway or just off the Strand?' we asked
ourselves, descending the stairs to Joe Allen's
basement restaurant, set among the backstreets
and stage doors of Covent Garden. There's more
than a touch of New York to this dimly lit dining
room, filled floor to ceiling with posters and signed
photographs that serve as a love letter to London's
theatreland. Brunch is a big deal in the Big Apple
and so it seemed appropriate to order the perfectly
spiced bloody mary, available on our special Sunday
menu. Macaroni in cheese sauce elicited strings of
gooey goodness with every forkful, and a starter of
butternut squash soup was pleasingly smooth.
With half a dozen ways to order eggs here, it's no
surprise that the smoked salmon and dill omelette
got points for presentation and taste. Slow-cooked
pork belly, however, saw the crackling burnt rather
than bubbling. Finally, a dessert of vanilla tart and
raspberry coulis acted as an encore to a good-value
set meal. Ask waiting staff about the Joe Allen
burger, not listed on the menu. It gets top billing
from theatre staff regulars, thankful for a kitchen
that closes well after curtain call.
Babies and children welcome: booster seats;
high chairs. Booking advisable. Entertainment:
pianist 9pm-1am Mon-Sat. Tables outdoors
(2, pavement). Takeaway service. **Map 18 E4**.

Soho

★ **Spuntino** `NEW` `HOT 50`
2011 RUNNER-UP BEST NEW RESTAURANT
2011 RUNNER-UP BEST NEW DESIGN
61 Rupert Street, W1D 7PW (no phone,
www.spuntino.co.uk). Piccadilly Circus tube.
Meals served 11am-midnight Mon-Sat;
noon-11pm Sun. **Main courses** £5.50-£10.
Credit AmEx, MC, V.
You can spot this speakeasy-like eaterie by the
queue snaking out the door – the signage certainly
isn't clear. The narrow, dimly lit space is artfully
contrived to look semi-derelict. A U-shaped, pewter-
topped bar is surrounded by heavy-duty industrial
stools; the ceiling of distressed, ornate tin tiles – a
fantastic architectural salvage find – suggests
faded grandeur, while the floor's hefty wooden
planks say spit 'n' sawdust. The loud retro-rock
soundtrack is reminiscent of Stateside college radio
stations, yet the overall effect is very pleasant. The
menu, sometimes described as Italian-American,
isn't so in a mounds-of-pasta way. Food is served as
small plates; some are based on typical Italian
ingredients, and some – such as a dark, salty mix
of calamari with chickpeas and squid ink – would
be right at home in the Old Country. Sliders, the
mini burgers that are de rigueur in New York bars,
are offered too. Our lamb and pickled cucumber

version hit the taste buds in the right places, as did
a salad of duck ham (made from the cured breast),
pecorino and mint. Pizzette are properly thin-
crusted, with imaginative toppings such as
courgette, chilli and mint. Spuntino is very of-the-
minute, and is reasonably good value. But be
prepared to arrive early (before 7pm) or you'll have
to join the queue.
Babies and children admitted. Bookings not
accepted. **Map 17 B4**.

West
Westbourne Park

Lucky 7
127 Westbourne Park Road, W2 5QL
(7727 6771, www.lucky7london.co.uk). Royal
Oak or Westbourne Park tube. **Meals served**
noon-10.30pm Mon; 10am-10.30pm Tue-Thur;
9am-11pm Fri, Sat; 9am-10.30pm Sun. **Main
courses** £6.95-£12.95. **Credit** MC, V.
The diner-style interior of Lucky 7 comes straight
out of central casting, with Cadillac-sized booths,
kitsch adverts and vintage neon signs all competing
for attention in this boutique-sized slice of
Americana. Only the bottle of West Indian pepper
sauce on each table is a clue to the Westbourne Park
location. The open kitchen specialises in breakfasts,

Budget bites

America (both North and South) has always
excelled at fast food. We don't mean dodgy
burger chains, but homely stalls and New
York-style food trucks, where you can grab
a tasty, cheap snack made fresh in front
of you. Fortunately, such ventures are an
increasingly common sight on London's
streets – try these specialists for size.

Big Apple Hot Dogs
Outside 239 Old Street, EC1V 9EY
(07989 387441 mobile, www.bigapple
hotdogs.com). Old Street tube/rail.
Open noon-6pm Mon-Fri. **Main courses**
£2.50-£4. **No credit cards**.
For a classy version of that much-maligned
American snack-food favourite, look out
for this mobile cart appearing weekdays
on Old Street. Choose your size and meat
combination (pork, beef, pork and beef),
then top with your preferred condiments.
The specially commissioned sausages are
made from free-range pork, while the buns
are baked by Anderson's bakery of Hoxton.
Even non-hot dog fans will be converted
by the taste: coarsely meaty, flavoursome
and evocative of baseball games, world
fairs and competitive eating.
Map 6 Q4.

Daddy Donkey
Leather Lane Market, EC1N 7TE
(7267 6042, www.daddydonkey.co.uk).
Chancery Lane tube or Farringdon tube/
rail. **Open** 7.30am-4pm Mon-Fri. **Main
courses** £5.25-£5.95. **No credit cards**.
As well as cheap handbags and
homewares, Leather Lane Market is the

place to buy first-rate Mexican fast food,
thanks to this consistently good daytime-
only stall. The Daddy D burrito includes
black beans, rice, lettuce and cheese
or sour cream in a flour tortilla, with a
choice of six fillings – such as tomatillo
beef (shredded beef cooked with green
tomatillos and lime salsa) and picadillo
(ground beef cooked with garlic, onion,
paprika, cumin, oregano, chipotle and
tomato). A 'naked burrito' ditches the
tortilla in favour of salad. Add a side
of chipotle coleslaw or freshly made
guacamole. Expect to queue.
Map 5 N5.

Pitt Cue Co
Under Hungerford Bridge, Belvedere
Road, SE1 8XX (no phone, www.pittcue.
co.uk). Waterloo tube/rail. **Open** *May-Sept*
noon-8.30pm daily. **Main courses** £5-£8.
No credit cards.
This summertime food truck, set beneath
Hungerford Bridge on the South Bank, is
the place for good ol' American barbecue.
It's a meat fest, with pork, chicken, pork
ribs and beef brisket all available, served in
a cardboard box with either marvellous root
beer beans (red kidney beans slow-cooked
with tomatoes and the namesake soda), or
crunchy red cabbage and parsley coleslaw.
You also get pickles, chargrilled bread
(useful for mopping up the meat juices) and
optional scotch bonnet hot sauce. To drink,
there's a short menu of cocktails, plus ale
from the nearby Kernel Brewery. Check the
website for the latest opening times.
Map 10 M8.

burgers and shakes with a West Coast influence by way of Mexico. Our 'Kalfornian' burger was piled high with monterey jack cheese, guacamole and sour cream, and would probably be made illegal on health grounds in the state that shares its name. A huge stack of onion rings had been beer-battered to perfection – the best we've eaten outside the US. 'Exterminator chilli' was pleasingly, eye-wateringly hot, the vegetarian version being an alternative to the mainly meat-focused menu. The no-bookings policy became clear when the shared booths filled up with after-school kids slurping on peanut butter shakes, and groups of local hipsters looking for a bacon cheeseburger hit. Fans of American beer will appreciate the Samuel Adams and Blue Moon brews. Ice-cream sundaes and pies (apple, pecan) complete the authentic diner experience.

Babies and children welcome: children's menu. Bookings not accepted. Takeaway service. **Map 7 A5**.

South
Clapham

Bodean's
169 Clapham High Street, SW4 7SS (7622 4248, www.bodeansbbq.com). Clapham Common tube. **Lunch served** noon-3pm, **dinner served** 5.30-11pm Mon-Fri. **Meals served** noon-11pm Sat; noon-10.30pm Sun. **Main courses** £7-£21. **Credit** AmEx, MC, V.

Walking into Bodean's is an invitation to have a good time. Decked out with Americana – from beer trays and antler lamps on the walls, to flatscreen TVs showing baseball or the NFL – the Clapham branch of this mini-chain has gone the whole hog on its rib-shack theme, with country and western music and chummy staff to boot. Much of the restaurant consists of leather booths, encouraging a relaxed, family-style approach to dining. Sadly, the quality of cooking has slipped since the place first opened, but any lack of finesse is made up for in portion sizes. Buffalo chicken wings are large and meaty, and while some baby back ribs were rather tough, even a half rack (served with hand-cut chips) should satisfy a hungry carnivore. Surprisingly, given the focus on meat, it was a rich, creamy slice of 'Eli's' baked cheesecake that stole the show. US beers include Sierra Nevada Pale Ale (bottled) and Blue Moon (draught). In spite of the kitchen's shortcomings, and an irksome no-bookings policy (except for groups), it's a popular spot with twentysomethings midweek and families at weekends – a fun place to visit for a slice of American pie.

Available for hire. Babies and children welcome: children's menu; high chairs; nappy-changing facilities. Bookings not accepted for fewer than 8 people. Tables outdoors (3, pavement). Takeaway service. **Map 22 B2**.
For branches see index.

North
Camden Town & Chalk Farm

★ The Diner
2 Jamestown Road, NW1 7BY (7485 5223, www.goodlifediner.com). Camden Town tube. **Meals served** 10am-11pm Mon-Thur; 10am-midnight Fri; 9am-midnight Sat; 9am-11pm Sun. **Main courses** £5.20-£9. **Credit** AmEx, MC, V.

There's a fanboy's attention to detail in the decor here (white piping on the red leather booths, buffalo horns protruding from feature brickwork, 'Love in an Elevator' blaring from the speakers), so the genuine warmth of the welcome at Camden's Diner stands out as pleasingly inauthentic. The menu celebrates the good, bad and ugly of cuisine Americana, from eggs benedict to bacon chilli cheese dogs and strawberry peanut butter milkshakes. Results are variable, though the yankee doodle dandy breakfasts (served all day) are a Saturday ritual for local families, as well as teens and tourists preparing to hit the market. Our lumberjack-themed plate of fluffy pancakes with crisp bacon, maple syrup and eggs cooked to a lacy brown finish on the hotplate was highly pleasurable and big enough to set us up for a day's tree-felling. The sunny staff are well drilled; filter coffee refills aren't just promised but offered, and who are we to question the wisdom of pushing a blueberry, amaretto and vanilla hard shake at 11.30am? This is Camden, after all. Something's certainly working well: the Diner's five branches now stretch from Kensal Rise to Shoreditch.

Babies and children welcome: high chairs; nappy-changing facilities. Booking advisable weekends. Disabled: toilet. Tables outdoors (13, terrace; 8, pavement). Takeaway service. **Map 27 C2**.
For branches see index.

Barbecoa. See p25.

LATIN AMERICAN

Recent years have seen Londoners enjoying a greater choice of Mexican eateries – there has been a spate of new openings and the burrito is now a well-established lunchtime favourite, though the capital is lacking specialists in any regional Mexican cuisine. Despite their lack of sophistication, there are good meals to be had at **Mestizo** and **Taqueira**, which remain our top picks in this sector. Argentinian restaurants are thriving too: in this edition we welcome **Casa Malevo** and **Moo!**, both from the hand of Alberto Abbate (of well-regarded Battersea steakhouse Santa Maria del Sur). They are very different establishments however: Casa Malevo is swanky, Moo! cheap and casual. Hackney's **Buen Ayre** and the **Gaucho** chain, also both Argentinian, remain very popular, but when it comes to the cooking of other Latin American countries, London is not faring so well. For a sampler of what we're missing, head to Islington's pan-Latin American spot **Sabor**.

THE AMERICAS

Central
Covent Garden

Cantina Laredo
10 Upper St Martin's Lane, WC2H 9FB (7420 0630, www.cantinalaredo.com). Covent Garden or Leicester Square tube. **Meals served** noon-11.30pm Mon-Thur; noon-midnight Fri, Sat; noon-10.30pm Sun. **Main courses** £14.95-£29.95. **Credit** AmEx, MC, V. Mexican
Walking into Cantina Laredo, with its bright decor, thumping soundtrack and friendly greeters, you could be in any US mall. Complimentary tortilla chips arrive at the table virtually as you do, along with two complex and tasty salsas – one warm, and filled with low notes, another chilled and spicy. Sadly, flavours diminish from here. Oaxaca quesadillas con hongos, a 'signature dish' of toasted flour tortillas filled with melted cheese and mushrooms, were bland. Another 'special' of pork tamales topped with a chipotle-wine sauce, and served with sides of rice and 'sautéed vegetables' (sweetcorn, courgette and carrot with cumin), continued the dull, heavy theme. The chain claims to specialise in seafood, but prawn fajitas, served with flour tortillas, guacamole, sour cream, a ton of fried onion and six measly prawns, seemed outrageously priced at nearly £18. Cocktails are a highlight; a virgin apple mojito made a refreshing, light accompaniment to the heavy food. If Starbucks-style predictability appeals, Laredo might be your kind of Mexican: the chillies aren't too hot, the flavours aren't too challenging, and the service is attentive and efficient. If, however, you like a bit of tang in your taco, you'll leave this US chain disappointed.
Available for hire. Babies and children welcome: children's menu; high chairs; nappy-changing facilities. Disabled: toilet. Separate room for parties, seats 20. Tables outdoors (9, pavement). Takeaway service. Vegetarian menu. **Map 18 D4.**

Wahaca
66 Chandos Place, WC2N 4HG (7240 1883, www.wahaca.co.uk). Covent Garden or Leicester Square tube. **Meals served** noon-11pm Mon-Sat; noon-10.30pm Sun. **Main courses** £6-£10. **Credit** AmEx, MC, V. Mexican
With an increasing variety of good, moderately priced restaurants in and around Covent Garden, this large basement branch of *MasterChef* winner Thomasina Miers' Mexican 'street food' chain is nowadays healthily rather than unpleasantly busy. As at the other branches, decor is deliberately, cheerfully, market-stall bright. It matches well with the tapas-style sharing ethos that makes Wahaca popular with families. At night, the buzzy atmosphere, decent tequilas and Mexican beer (served also in chelada or michelada beer-cocktails) appeal to local workers and tourists. Although fairly enjoyable, a meal here seems like Mexican ever so slightly out of focus: 'British steak, the Mexican way' (slivers of steak with green rice, spring onions and house salsas); a quesadilla of new potatoes, broad beans, peas, feta and mint; a chicken taquito with tomato and lancashire cheese; 'baja cheese' made from farmhouse cheddar and mozzarella. Still, service is swift and bustling yet warm, and the menu is very approachable. Choose between 'platos fuertes' (main dishes such as burritos or a succulent pork pibil) or 'street food' (small plates to share). Puddings include the welcome but unsurprising churros, a passionfruit cheesecake and dulce de leche ice-cream.
Babies and children welcome: high chairs; nappy-changing facilities. Bookings not accepted. Disabled: toilet. Vegetarian menu. **Map 18 D5.** **For branches see index.**

Fitzrovia

Gaucho Charlotte Street
60A Charlotte Street, W1T 2NU (7580 6252, www.gauchorestaurants.co.uk). Goodge Street or Tottenham Court Road tube. **Meals served** noon-11pm Mon-Sat; noon-10.30pm Sun. **Main courses** £15.95-£52.50. **Credit** AmEx, MC, V. Argentinian
The foyer is rather sterile, but the basement dining room of this branch of the burgeoning Argentinian steakhouse chain has the familiar monochromatic, slightly bling look of the other outlets. Yet there's no doubting the cowskin booths, leather furniture and shiny surfaces work; you have to give Gaucho credit for creating the smooth, sophisticated urban grill idea. Empanada and baby scallop starters were tasty and, importantly, not filling – the former could have been juicier but the seasoning was spot-on, while the scallops' maize cancha (toasted corn kernels), mango and roasted yellow pepper adornments worked nicely. As the typically Peruvian/Ecuadorean cancha indicates, Gaucho is increasingly an ambassador for Latin American food, as well as for prime beef steaks: a savvy idea, as Peru is a rising star on the international gastronomic scene. As always, the ribeye and rump steaks were magnificent, and the sides of chips and green salad were simple and effective. The house chimichurri lacks punch, but you don't really need dressing on meat of this quality. An ever-evolving wine list boasts the best range of Argentinian reds in the world (probably), and the group wine tasting sessions held here are ideal for work parties.
Babies and children welcome: high chairs. Booking advisable. Disabled: lift; toilet. Dress: smart casual. Separate room for parties, seats 10. **Map 3 J5.** **For branches see index.**

Mestizo
103 Hampstead Road, NW1 3EL (7387 4064, www.mestizomx.com). Warren Street tube or Euston tube/rail. **Meals served** noon-11pm Mon-Sat. **Lunch served** noon-4pm, **dinner served** 5-10pm Sun. **Main courses** £9.80-£24. **Credit** AmEx, MC, V. Mexican
With its deep red walls, cream leather seating and backlit bar proudly showcasing tequilas, Mestizo has the air of a smart nightspot. Evenings see plenty of émigrés from the hotels around Euston Road join New Yorkers in knocking back the best margaritas they've discovered in London. Turn up for Sunday brunch, however, and you'll find a relaxed family-friendly vibe with numerous expat Mexicans enjoying the all-you-can-eat buffet. Staff bring complimentary jugs of hibiscus-flavoured agua fresca (think Mexican Ribena) and the sweet, milky, rice-based horchata to quell any fires started by the searing menudo (braised belly pork with guajillo chilli and tomato sauce). Quesadillas (tinga, pastor, chorizo and potato, and more) are cooked to order on a hotplate, while other authentic dishes such as pozole (a spicy pork stew) are available to serve yourself from metal buffet trays. Enchilada papa suiza (potato and cheese) smothered with tomatillo salsa is blissfully squidgy, cheesy and tangy, and the choice of stuffed peppers delightful. A small table at the end houses the day's desserts – a creamy tart topped with strawberry sauce, maybe. Staff are friendly and hardworking, though it can be difficult to catch their attention when so much is going on.
Available for hire. Babies and children welcome: high chairs. Booking advisable weekends. Disabled: toilet. Separate room for parties, seats 60. Takeaway service. **Map 3 J3.**

Marble Arch

★ Casa Malevo NEW
23 Connaught Street, W2 2AY (7402 1988, www.casamalevo.com). Marble Arch tube. **Lunch served** noon-2.30pm, **dinner served** 6-10.30pm Mon-Fri. **Brunch served** noon-4pm Sat, Sun. **Main courses** £12-£24. **Credit** AmEx, DC, MC, V. Argentinian
Having sold Argentinian steaks in Hackney, Arsenal and Queenstown Road, Alberto Abbate has joined forces with chef Diego Jacquet (whose pedigree includes the Zetter hotel and stints at New

Casa Malevo

Wahaca. See p30.

York's Aquavit and El Bulli in Spain), to create a high-end restaurant suited to this swanky part of town. On the downside, this translates to a small dining room with surroundings so discreet and classy they border on dull, and portions that are either haute or stingy, according to your point of view. Having said that, there's no faulting the flavour of the food. The basic parrilla (Argentinian grill) fare of fine steaks, chorizo sausage and blood sausage is what Jacquet's kitchen cooks up, and is of the same quality as at Abbate's Santa Maria del Sur restaurant. The key extras are subtle and buttery mollejas (sweetbreads), and superior empanadas filled with cuts of tender beef rather than the usual minced beef. We tried two of the smaller (225g) steaks and found the ribeye superior to the sirloin for taste, tenderness and girth. The wine list features hefty Argentinian malbecs and is squarely pitched at affluent locals, with most bottles costing £25-plus, though there are 375ml carafes for smaller wallets.

Available for hire. Babies and children welcome: high chairs. Booking advisable. Separate room for parties, seats 12. Tables outdoors (3, pavement). Map 8 F6.

Soho

Floridita

100 Wardour Street, W1F 0TN (7314 4000, www.floriditalondon.com). Tottenham Court Road tube.
Bar **Open** 5.30pm-2am Tue, Wed; 5.30pm-3am Thur-Sat.
Restaurant **Dinner served** 5.30pm-11am Tue-Sat. **Main courses** £12.50-£30.
Admission (after 8pm Fri, Sat) £10.
Both **Credit** AmEx, MC, V. Cuban
Previous visits to this Soho mega restaurant have been disappointing and our last was no different: screeching metal chair legs, fussy service, tacky decor and – God, please no! – toilet attendants. Despite this large nightclubby bar-restaurant having a branch in Havana, and a salsa band that plays from 7.30pm, the menu is mostly pan-Latin American rather than Cuban: think Mexican quesadillas, ceviche, Argentinian empanadas, Brazilian steaks, Cuban lobster – and burgers. The fish in our grouper and prawn ceviche was chunky, flavourful and citrusy, but the dish had just one prawn.Rump steak kebab had none of that typical juicy, salty picanha flavour and its chipotle and guacamole sauces could have been from a supermarket tub. Barbecued organic chicken with lemon, garlic and pico de gallo salsa and flatbread was better, but for £17.50 not nearly good enough. Sides of mangetout with shallots, and basmati rice, were passable, but again expensive. Yes, the cocktails are good, but you could spend £100 in the restaurant on a very mediocre meal for two.
Booking advisable. Disabled: toilet. Dress: smart casual. Entertainment: musicians, DJ 7.30pm Tue-Thur, 8pm Fri, Sat. Separate rooms for parties, seating 52-72. Map 17 B3.

Strand

★ Lupita NEW
13-15 Villiers Street, WC2N 6ND (7930 5355, www.lupita.co.uk). Embankment tube or Charing Cross tube/rail. **Meals served** noon-11pm Mon-Thur; noon-11.30pm Fri, Sat; noon-9pm Sun. **Main courses** £5.95-£9.95. **Credit** AmEx, MC, V. Mexican

Brazilian bonanza

The capital has a few rodizio specialists: Brazilian all-you-can-eat venues, where waiters serve food straight on to your plate at the table, and continue serving until you say stop. Rodizio refers to the style of service, not the cuisine – though, in London, such places tend to be churrascarias (grill houses) that major in meat. Remember that the cheaper meat and cuts tend to be delivered first, so don't fill up on chicken, ham, sausages and bread before the more expensive sirloin, fillet steak and rump arrive.

Rodizio is occasionally served at Sabor Brasileiro, but it focuses on traditional Brazilian dishes, priced by weight.

Amber Grill Rodizio
47 Station Road, NW10 4UP (8963 1588, www.ambergrill.co.uk). Willesden Junction tube/rail. **Lunch served** noon-6pm, **dinner served** 6-11pm daily. **Main courses** £6-£19. **Set lunch** £6-£12. **Set dinner** £19.50 buffet. **Credit** MC, V. Brazilian
The service is so warm and enthusiastic at Amber Grill Rodizio, it's a shame to report its attempt at a classic Brazilian dining experience falls flat. Things looked promising enough as skewers heavy with various cuts of pork, chicken, lamb and beef were ferried from the grill to our plates, but the chicken hearts were rubbery, the beef shank tough, and the spiced sausages tiny and crisp. Only the sublimely tender picanha (rump steak) impressed, and, generously, appeared at the table more than once. Even the all-you-can-eat hot and cold buffet was a mixed beast, with some tired salads among the bland feijão (black beans) and tepid rice. Still, live music on Saturdays (along with excellent caipirinhas) could completely lift a meal here.
Available for hire. Babies and children welcome: high chairs. Booking advisable. Entertainment: musicians 7.30pm Sat. Tables outdoors (2, pavement).

Rodizio Preto
72 Wilton Road, SW1V 1DE (7233 8668, www.rodiziopreto.co.uk). Victoria tube/rail. **Meals served** noon-midnight Mon-Sat; noon-10pm Sun. **Buffet** £19.95 (£14.95 vegetarian). **Credit** AmEx, MC, V. Brazilian
The vibe is relaxed at this all-you-can-eat Brazilian place, despite the surprisingly formal dining room, the centrepiece of which is the buffet bar. Load up on salads, olives and feijão, but don't overdo it, because if you've opted for the rodizio menu – as you should – you'll be brought plate after plate of meat fresh from the grill: rump, sirloin, chilli-flavoured chicken, chicken heart… There are 15 selections in all, and staff give you as much time as you need to get through the lot. The chicken, in its various forms, was best;

the steak was a tad dry, although the fillet wrapped in bacon was deliciously tender and dripping with flavour. Desserts are palate-cleansers, and the wine and beer list suitably uncomplicated.
Babies and children welcome: high chairs. Booking advisable weekends. Tables outdoors (6, pavement). Vegetarian menu. **Map 15 J10.**

Rodizio Rico
111 Westbourne Grove, W2 4UW (7792 4035, www.rodiziorico.com). Bayswater tube. **Dinner served** 6pm-midnight Mon-Fri. **Meals served** noon-midnight Sat, Sun. **Buffet** £23.50 (£19.50 vegetarian). **Credit** MC, V. Brazilian
The all-you-can-eat meat deal only makes economic sense if you intend to really pig out. Refreshingly, instead of the cheaper grills (chicken hearts and legs, sausage), waiters first offered us skewers of rump, topside, pork and lamb. But once the novelty of the experience wears off – 'Wow! Someone keeps bringing us swords of meat!' – there's time to assess the quality, and we weren't overly impressed. Many of the carnivorous offerings were nautically salty; the beef was tragically overcooked. Sides, from the buffet, ranged from perky salads to service-station standard garlic bread and croquettes.
Babies and children welcome: high chairs. Booking advisable; essential weekends. Separate room for parties, seats 55. Tables outdoors (6, pavement). Takeaway service. Vegetarian menu. **Map 7 B6.**
For branches see index.

Sabor Brasileiro
639 Harrow Road, NW10 5NU (8969 1149, www.saborbrasileiro.info). Kensal Green tube/rail. **Meals served** noon-7pm Mon-Sat; noon-5pm Sun. **Main courses** £10/kg. **Buffet** £9.80. **No credit cards.** Brazilian
This might just be how the girl from Ipanema kept her figure – paying by weight for your lunch can make you a little cautious. Sabor Brasileiro is a *comida por kilo* restaurant, with electronic scales alongside the metal trays of traditional Brazilian fare. On offer was beef stew with cassava, roasted cuts of pork, chicken and beef on the bone, beans, garlicky pumpkin, and farofa to sprinkle, though sadly no collard greens. You'll get a decent plateful for around £6; alternatively, the all-you-can-eat deal costs £9.80. Juices of acai, acerola, cupuaçu and more familiar fruits were sweet enough to serve as dessert. Panelled in light wood, with just a thin strip of tinted window, the space has a sauna-like feel. Rodizio is sometimes offered at weekends.
Available for hire evenings. Babies and children welcome: high chairs. Booking advisable. Takeaway service.

The owners of Lupita showed some savvy when choosing Villiers Street – the narrow, crowded hill that runs between Embankment tube and Charing Cross station – as the place to set up shop. By day, this good-looking, capable Mexican restaurant gets passing trade from tourists and office workers; by night, it's descended on by commuters and revellers, many of whom are tipsy and hungry. Choose carefully, and you can construct an interesting meal here. Choose drunkenly, and you can have large helpings of well-made stodge to sustain you on the journey home. Many dishes qualify in both categories, such as the quesadillas nopales: two folded flour pancakes, stuffed with cheese and Mexican cactus. Elsewhere, results are more mixed; had it not been for the addition of some of the excellent salsas, our carnitas – shredded barbecued pork, served on an open corn taco – would have been a tad plain. Likewise, though fresh and satisfying, 'guacamole artesanal' could have done with an extra squeeze of lime (and wasn't made at the table, as promised by the menu). The mostly Mexican staff were calm under pressure, despite the occasionally boisterous customers they have to deal with.
Babies and children welcome: high chairs. Disabled: toilet. Tables outdoors (5, pavement). Takeaway service. **Map 10 L7.**

West
Westbourne Grove

★★ Taqueria
139-143 Westbourne Grove, W11 2RS (7229 4734, www.taqueria.co.uk). Notting Hill Gate tube. **Meals served** noon-11pm Mon-Thur; noon-11.30pm Fri, Sat; noon-10.30pm Sun. **Main courses** £3.90-£8.75. **Set lunch** (noon-4.30pm Mon-Fri) £6.50 1 course. **Credit** MC, V. Mexican
Great Mexican food, whether haute cuisine or cowboy grub, relies on good, smoky chillies, authentic herbs and top-quality fresh ingredients. As Taqueria is owned by the Cool Chile Company, Britain's premier importer of Mexican ingredients, it has a head start on the competition. The deal is sealed by a cheerful dining room – bright from floor-to-ceiling windows, and decorated with old Mexican film posters – and the ethical arsenal of free-range eggs and meat, and organic dairy products, making this an excellent little spot. Among the selection of traditional street snacks, sope is outstanding: a fried nest of ground maize topped with refried beans, crumbled cheese and own-made chorizo. Tacos carnitas featured wonderfully tender slow-cooked pork, green salsa, pickled jalapeño and sharp onion. Tacos with garlicky grilled prawns and smooth guacamole gained great depth from a smoky chilli chipotle garnish. As you might guess from the low prices, dishes are modest in size, which should leave room for the delicious desserts. Fried plantain with ice-cream and cajeta (goat's milk toffee) is the best take on a banana split we've seen. Drinks include aguas frescas, tequilas, Mexican bottled beers, assorted margaritas and other cocktails, and own-made Mexican hot chocolate (with cinnamon and almonds). There are special menus at lunchtimes and for children.
Available for hire. Babies and children welcome: high chairs. Bookings not accepted Fri-Sun. **Map 7 A6.**

South
Battersea

Santa Maria del Sur
129 Queenstown Road, SW8 3RH (7622 2088, www.santamariadelsur.co.uk). Queenstown Road rail. **Lunch served** noon-3pm Sat, Sun. **Dinner served** 6-10pm daily. **Main courses** £19-£25. **Credit** MC, V. Argentinian
Battersea's friendly Argentinian grill is all about carefully selected cuts of beef, perfectly seasoned and lovingly cooked. The rump steak comes thick and bloody, the sirloin tender and smooth to slice. There are, however, plenty of other Hispanic treats to savour – empanadas, serrano ham, chorizo, marinated ox tongue and, for pudding, flan (crème caramel) – not to mention great fat chips (seasoned before frying for a tasty crispy coating). Trouble is, the steaks don't leave room for much else. Yes, there are a couple of token vegetarian dishes, and some fish (tuna), but you don't come to a restaurant with an open parrilla grill conspicuous through the window, and pictures of beef cattle hung around the walls, if you aren't partial to the red stuff. The extensive wine list showcases the best of South America's vineyards, including some high-end (high-priced) numbers, but there are also several imported beers such as Quilmes from Argentina and Cusqueña from Peru. Although open for lunch at weekends, Santa Maria del Sur is more of an evening venue, its crepuscular corners conducive to candlelit dinners or group nights out. Swing by on Monday nights for live Argentinian music and top tango artistes from Buenos Aires.
Babies and children welcome: high chairs. Booking advisable weekends. Entertainment: musicians, tango 8.30pm Mon. Tables outdoors (5, pavement).

South East
Bermondsey

Constancia
52 Tanner Street, SE1 3PH (7234 0676, www.constancia.co.uk). Bermondsey tube or London Bridge tube/rail. **Dinner served** 6-10.30pm Mon-Sat. **Meals served** 1.30-9.30pm Sun. **Main courses** £17.60-£25. **Credit** AmEx, MC, V. Argentinian
It's always a good sign when a restaurant is busy on a Monday night. And on our last visit to Constancia, a few minutes' walk from the river down Tower Bridge Road, we could see why this good-looking Argentinian steakhouse is a hit. It's a simple but effective set-up: relaxed but efficient staff serving large portions of grass-fed Argentinian beef accompanied by simple sides and good, reasonably priced Argentinian wine. Starters range from empanadas (spinach, cheese and onion, or meat) to black pudding or Tuscan prosciutto. Go easy, though – main courses are huge. We opted for a mixed parrillada, which produced a barbecue of cooked morcilla sausage (made by the owner's aunt), portobello mushrooms with pesto, provolone cheese and two steaks: an 11oz ribeye and a 10oz sirloin. All were enjoyable, but the ribeye came out on top for being prodigiously tender and juicy (the sirloin was a little too crispy and tough on the outside). If you can still manage more, finish with the cheesecake of the day, ice-cream, crème

caramel, or brownie pimped with dulce de leche, melted chocolate and vanilla ice-cream.
Babies and children admitted. Booking advisable dinner Fri, Sat. **Map 12 R9.**

Blackheath

Buenos Aires Café
17 Royal Parade, SE3 0TL (8318 5333, www.buenosairesltd.com). Blackheath rail. **Lunch served** noon-3pm Mon-Fri; noon-4pm Sat, Sun. **Dinner served** 6-10.30pm daily. **Main courses** £9-£22. **Credit** MC, V. Argentinian
Unlike its Greenwich outpost, the Blackheath Village branch of Buenos Aires is more restaurant than café, with large windows offering spectacular views across the heath. There are tables outside, on the ground floor or in the more intimate first-floor dining room (a suntrap when we arrived at sunset). Stripped floors and whitewashed walls covered in framed photos and prints add to the warmth. Argentina's large Italian immigrant population has shaped the country's cuisine, which is reflected in the menu here. Pizza and pasta are given nearly as much space as beef. There's plenty of choice for vegetarians, although we found the wild mushroom ravioli to be light on mushroom flavour and the pasta itself a little too thick. As for the meat, a pallid beef, pork, bacon and white wine sausage seemed poached rather than grilled, and made an unremarkable starter. In contrast, the ribeye (from grass-fed, free-range Argentinian cattle) that followed was perfectly cooked and as flavourful as the menu promised. Pair it with one of the fine malbecs from the predominantly Argentinian wine list. Service was generally attentive, if occasionally forgetful. No matter: the restaurant's charm, coupled with the high-quality food, is enough to warrant repeat visits.
Available for hire. Babies and children welcome: booster seats. Booking essential. Tables outdoors (4, pavement).
For branch see index.

East
Spitalfields

Boho Mexica
151-153 Commercial Street, E1 6BJ (7377 8418, www.bohomexica.co.uk). Liverpool Street tube/rail. **Lunch served** noon-2.30pm Mon-Fri. **Dinner served** 5.30-10pm Mon, Tue; 5.30-11pm Wed-Fri. **Meals served** 2-11pm Sat; 1-10pm Sun. **Main courses** £8.95-£12.50. **Set lunch** £9.95 2 courses. **Credit** AmEx, MC, V. Mexican
Although this cute little place presents itself as a classier sort of Mexican restaurant, it's not above recognising that many Londoners still come looking for happy hours and margaritas. But Boho Mexica is far from being a Chiquito-style Tex-Mex: it's an inviting space, decorated with cool retro Latino posters and regularly bubbling over with the lively chatter of off-duty Spitalfields workers. All dishes, we are told, 'arrive when ready'. (Better than arriving before they're ready.) This seems to be a pre-emptive excuse for a slackness of service that saw one of our mains being served a good five minutes before the other. The menu makes for an interesting read; the chef is clearly keen to encourage diners away from the ubiquitous folded wraps and towards the varied cuisine of Mexico. So dishes such as caldo tlapeño (a smoky chicken

broth with avocado and chipotle) appear, as does sautéed prawns in ancho chilli sauce. Dishes don't always impress: a recent visit found some flavours unremarkable, and textures indistinct. A tamale tasted of not much; corn bread with rajas poblanos was too mushy. A fun place to drink, then, but the kitchen needs a bit more zing in its step.
Babies and children admitted. Booking advisable. Disabled: toilet. Separate room for parties, seats 20. **Map 6 R5.**

Whitechapel

Moo!
4 Cobb Street, E1 7LB (7377 9929, www.moogrill.co.uk). Aldgate or Aldgate East tube or Liverpool Street tube/rail. **Breakfast served** 8-11am Mon-Fri. **Dinner served** 6-11pm Mon-Fri; 6-10pm Sat. **Meals served** noon-5pm Sun. **Main courses** £5-£16. **Credit** AmEx, MC, V. Argentinian
'Hola, amigos!' Cheerful host José Luis greets customers like old friends as they enter his cosy, wood-panelled Argentinian steak and wine bar. He only stops smiling when recommending how each cut should be cooked; José is a man who takes his meat seriously. Busy at lunchtime with Liverpool Street suits hungry for a hefty steak sandwich, Moo! also buzzes with early-evening drinkers matching their ribeye or sirloin and chips with a predominantly Argentinian wine list. Meat is sourced from Argentina via Smithfield Market, and the quality certainly shows. Ribeye was tender, with an even distribution of fat through the meat fibres, and rich with the taste of the grill. For a good snack, try the empanadas: little pastry pockets of melting cheese with ham, beef or sweetcorn. A choripan sandwich featured chorizo split lengthways and laden with onion, peppers and chimichurri sauce. There are also lomito sandwiches, overflowing with beef, chicken or aubergine, with optional extras of ham, cheese and a fried egg. The crème caramel (made by José Luis's mum) was light and decadently sweet, served with a splodge of rich dulce de leche. Milkshakes were

too expensive at £3, but the fresh orange and apple juices were definitely worth paying for.
Booking advisable. Separate room for parties, seats 20. Takeaway service; delivery service (over £15 within 1-mile radius). **Map 12 R6.**

North East
Hackney

Buen Ayre   `HOT 50`
50 Broadway Market, E8 4QJ (7275 9900, www.buenayre.co.uk). London Fields rail or bus 26, 48, 55. **Lunch served** noon-3pm Fri; noon-3.30pm Sat, Sun. **Dinner served** 6-10.30pm daily. **Main courses** £13-£25. **Credit** MC, V. Argentinian
While some of London's Argentinian restaurants might put on airs and graces, Buen Ayre has that scruffy, laid-back charm that its near-namesake capital does so well. Tattooed staff wear denim shorts and T-shirts, while shabby Boca Juniors flags and random bovine-themed art adorn the walls. The main event, unsurprisingly, is beef, which crackles on the huge charcoal grill (there are vegetarian dishes too, but be warned: this much cow may well horrify some). Go easy on the starters; a dish of serrano ham, palm hearts and thousand island dressing was a mere distraction from the giant steaks that followed: a sirloin that was soft and juicy on the inside and smoky and charred on the outside, and a ribeye that, although lacking in flavour, was rescued by its accompanying chimichurri sauce, butter bean and roast pepper garnish, and a side order of rocket and garlic salad. Groups might want to investigate the parrilladas (mixed grills). We savoured a thick Bodegas Norton malbec from the all-Argentinian wine list. We don't reckon these are the best steaks in London, but for casual Buenos Aires bonhomie and good value, Buen Ayre is top of the pile.
Babies and children welcome: high chairs. Booking advisable. Disabled: toilet. Tables outdoors (5, garden).

North
Highbury

Garufa
104 Highbury Park, N5 2XE (7226 0070, www.garufa.co.uk). Arsenal tube. **Meals served** 10am-10.30pm daily. **Main courses** £12-£26. **Set lunch** £9.80-£12.50 1 course incl drink. **Credit** MC, V. Argentinian
A likeable neighbourhood spot with traditional wood decor, Garufa is unusual in keeping brasserie hours. Hence you can rock up for breakfast, pop in late afternoon for a drink and complimentary small bites (here called 'Argie Aperitif Time'), or bring a date to share a mixed grill supper. Cottage cheese and chive omelette, toasted sandwiches, and a choice of revueltos (scrambled egg dishes) are among the breakfast options, but most people come for the hearty full Argentine, featuring 150g rump steak, chimichurri, cheese-topped mushrooms and scrambled eggs, plus a piquant (if slightly gristly) sausage. It's also worth making room for Garufa's sensationally crisp empanadas: classic beef, or sweet and salty ham and cheese. Orange juice, straight from the extractor, was a sumptuous foam of citrus that could almost garnish a haute cuisine dish. Less pleasing was the bloody mary, which contained plenty of vodka but lacked the requisite seasonings. Service too was a little thin, though still well meaning and kind. The Monday tango nights are for the authentic music aficionado.
Available for hire. Babies and children welcome: children's menu (until 5pm); high chairs; nappy-changing facilities. Booking advisable dinner. Entertainment: tango 8pm Mon. Takeaway service.

Islington

Sabor
108 Essex Road, N1 8LX (7226 5551, www.sabor.co.uk). Angel tube or Essex Road rail or bus 38, 73. **Dinner served** 6-10pm Tue, Wed; 6-11pm Thur, Fri. **Meals served** noon-11pm Sat, Sun. **Main courses** £12-£19. **Set lunch** £16 2 courses, £17.50 3 courses. **Credit** MC, V. Pan-Latin American
Here is that rarest of creatures: a Latin American restaurant that doesn't fall into clichés of ponchos and maracas for decor. Instead, Sabor opts for light, bright furnishings that befit its pan-Latin American cuisine. The menu rounds up Argentinian empanadas, Cuban ropa vieja beef brisket and Brazilian moqueca fish stew, but on our last visit it was the fish starters that outshone the rest. Tuna tiradito (Peruvian-style sashimi) was delicate and not overpowered by its salsa, while cod ceviche was chunky, tangy and nicely complemented by crunchy toasted corn kernels. We later wished the ceviches had been main courses, as our 8oz ribeye steak with plantain was disappointing, arriving well done rather than medium-rare, as requested. Grilled lamb with sweet fruit salsa and white and brown quinoa was perfectly tender and delicious, but not as good as the preceding raw fish. Service was relaxed yet competent: tap water was replenished without us having to ask, food arrived promptly and we weren't ushered out until after we'd finished nattering and polished off our bottle of Argentinian tempranillo.
Available for hire. Babies and children welcome: high chairs. Booking advisable. Vegetarian menu. **Map 5 P1.**

Lupita. See p33.

Brasseries

With a stonking 11 new arrivals joining the Brasseries chapter for this edition, it's clear restaurateurs and their customers are seeing the benefits of all-day opening and flexible dining. These user-friendly eateries range from the designer glamour of **Galoupet** in Knightsbridge, to the faux-boheme of **Elliot's** in Borough Market and the **Riding House Café** in Fitzrovia, and the 'hey, let's open a restaurant' vibe of Hackney's **Railroad** and **A Little of What You Fancy**. Far more than a spot for breakfast or drinks-plus-nibbles, Peter Gordon's **Kopapa** was so good it made the finals of our Best New Restaurant award. Some old favourites have fallen in the fashion stakes, with service and cooking standards declining too, but we still love the **Wolseley**, **Tom's Kitchen** and **Ottolenghi**, while recent newcomers **Caravan** and **Hackney Pearl** continue in fine form. There's a place here to suit every mood, every appetite and, mostly importantly, any time, but, as we've said before, the real winners amid all this competition are Londoners.

Central

Belgravia

Chelsea Brasserie

7-12 Sloane Square, SW1W 8EG (7881 5999, www.chelsea-brasserie.co.uk). Sloane Square tube. **Lunch served** noon-3pm Mon-Sat. **Brunch served** 11.15am-3.30pm Sun. **Dinner served** 6-10.30pm Mon-Sat. **Main courses** £16-£22.50. **Set dinner** (6-7.30pm) £19.75 2 courses, £24.50 3 courses. **Credit** MC, V.

Time seemingly stands still: this could be the 1980s, or the 1990s, given the red walls, exposed brickwork and cacophonous mix of big, bold paintings (some with aggressive-looking abstract swishes). The Chelsea Brasserie is bigger than you'd imagine, stretching into an extensive L-shape beyond the modest entrance on Sloane Square. The top-notch location brings bustle, especially pre- and post-theatre (the Royal Court is just across the square), but not noteworthy dining. Head chef Simon Henbery's menu of European stalwarts is perfectly adequate, albeit with occasional pretensions to something more: terrine de foie gras is served with Poilâne bread, for instance, and a dessert wine is from a region 'close to Sauternes'. A glistening chickpea and chorizo starter was light and well balanced; poached hake fillet moist, if burdened with a still-cold doubloon of parsley and lemon butter. A flavourful grilled pork chop with cider jus worked well with the tangy celeriac and apple remoulade. Service seemed a little smug,

which was a shame, as this is a serviceable stop-off, if not a destination in its own right.
Babies and children welcome: children's menu; high chairs. Booking essential. Disabled: lift; toilet. Dress: smart casual. Separate room for parties, seats 14. Tables outdoors (4, pavement). **Map 15 G10**.

City

Café Below

St Mary-le-Bow, Cheapside, EC2V 6AU (7329 0789, www.cafebelow.co.uk). St Paul's tube or Bank tube/DLR. **Breakfast served** 7.30-11am, **lunch served** 11.30am-3pm, **snacks served** 2.30-5.30pm, **dinner served** 5.30-9pm Mon-Fri. **Main courses** £7.50-£15. **Credit** MC, V.

This budget-priced haven in the undercroft below St Mary-le-Bow Church started life in 1989 as homely vegetarian cafeteria The Place Below, but smartened up slightly a few years ago – and added meat. It's still a busy takeaway and eat-in lunch spot for City workers (arrive by 12.30pm to bag a table), but now opens from breakfast, via afternoon tea and early evening nibbles, to dinner. The daily changing seasonal menu features soup, salads, hearty sandwiches and hot dishes, and suppliers are name-checked (Tudge's sausages and bacon, Brindisa chorizo, River Farm smoked salmon). There are vegetarian specials aplenty, such as a comforting spinach and mung bean casserole with a coriander and pepper salsa, alongside the likes of noodles with slow-braised pork slivers, pak choi and a light ginger-chilli dressing. Drinks include

Meantime beer, Dunkertons cider, and wine. Stone walls and wooden tables mean this is a noisy venue when packed; it's calmer come the evening when the menu is less café, more restaurant. Pan-fried sea bream, creamed leeks and crushed new potatoes, and rump steak with red wine sauce, are typical dinner dishes – but prices remain very reasonable. A welcome addition is the waiter-service outdoor eating area in Bow Churchyard.
Available for hire. Babies and children welcome: high chairs. Booking advisable dinner. Tables outdoors (20, churchyard). Takeaway service. Vegan dishes. **Map 11 P6**.

Clerkenwell & Farringdon

★ Caravan [HOT 50]

11-13 Exmouth Market, EC1R 4QD (7833 8115, www.caravanonexmouth.co.uk). Farringdon tube/rail or bus 19, 38, 341. **Meals served** 8am-10.30pm Mon-Fri; 10am-10.30pm Sat; 10am-4pm Sun. **Main courses** £4.50-£16. **Credit** AmEx, MC, V.

An immediate success when it opened in early 2010, this restaurant-bar continues to thrive. The easygoing atmosphere, likeable staff, quietly modish interior and intriguing but user-friendly menu all play their part. The menu consists of small plates of interesting food (plus some larger dishes, such as veal schnitzel). We always order the savoury-but-sweet treat of spicy pork-filled, honey-glazed gypsy bun. Other dishes come and go, but you might find smoked eel, new potato and baby gem with curry powder mayonnaise and a quail's egg, or seared

Kopapa

onglet with miso, green beans and peanut dressing. Snacks and side dishes include cornbread with chipotle butter (delightfully rich) and gypsy potatoes (a little gloopy). Puddings run from affogato to spiced roast pineapple with cacao sauce and coconut sorbet. Breakfasts and brunches offer the same heady mix of the familiar and the new; try baked eggs with tomato and pepper ragout, greek yoghurt and chorizo. The wine list has plenty by the glass, and the bar ensures there's a good choice of cocktails. Coffee is taken seriously – in the basement is a roastery. Our only gripe: if the music in the bar gets turned up (and it increasingly does), it's hard to chat.

Available for hire. Babies and children welcome: high chairs; nappy-changing facilities. Booking advisable dinner. Tables outdoors (7, pavement). Takeaway service. **Map 5 N4**.

Covent Garden

Bill's NEW

13 Slingsby Place, St Martin's Courtyard, WC2E 9AB (7240 8183, www.billsproducestore. co.uk). Covent Garden tube. **Meals served** 8am-11pm Mon-Fri; 9am-11pm Sat; 9am-10.30pm Sun. **Main courses** £8.95-£15.95. **Credit** AmEx, MC, V.

The original branch of Bill's opened in Lewes, East Sussex in 2001, with a simple plan to be an old-fashioned grocer, mid-market deli, and informal café. Judging by the mini-chain's success (there's a phenomenally busy branch in Brighton and others in Cambridge and Reading), Bill's is getting it right. This is its first foray into London, helped along by investment from restaurateur Richard Caring (who owns the Ivy, among many other eateries). Apart from a lone box of complimentary clementines, fresh produce is notably absent: instead, there are tables over two floors, with bunches of dangling chillies, and deli shelves stretching to the ceiling. Wooden tables look pre-loved and there are recipes writ large on the walls, while staff are chummy and efficient. We tried a beetroot salad (both golden and fuchsia, with lentils and parsley), a chorizo brioche sandwich with houmous, yoghurt and some brilliant skin-on chips, and a simple but fragrant dish of grilled chicken with lemon, rosemary and garlic. Housed in a plum spot in the new St Martin's Courtyard development, Bill's very helpfully suits a range of purposes: early breakfast, quick lunch, afternoon coffee or a substantial dinner.

Babies and children welcome: children's menu; high chairs; nappy-changing facilities. Bookings not accepted lunch. Disabled: toilet. Tables outdoors (6, courtyard). **Map 18 D4**.

Kopapa NEW

2011 RUNNER-UP BEST NEW RESTAURANT
32-34 Monmouth Street, WC2H 9HA (7240 6076, www.kopapa.co.uk). Covent Garden or Leicester Square tube. **Breakfast served** 8.30-11am Mon-Fri. **Brunch served** 10am-3pm Sat, Sun. **Meals served** noon-10.45pm Mon-Fri; 3.30-10.45pm Sat; 3.30-9.30pm Sun. **Main courses** £10.50-£20. **Credit** AmEx, DC, MC, V.

At Kopapa, chef and co-owner Peter Gordon brings his particular style of global pick 'n' mix cooking to Covent Garden. As at sister restaurant the Providores, it's a mash-up of Asian, Middle Eastern, European and American ingredients – to which the all-day menu, served in fashionably tapas-sized portions, is particularly well suited. Some ingredients will test the mettle of even dedicated food nerds, but the combinations generally work, as in pepper- and chilli-salted squid with smoked aioli, in which the fiery elements were cooled by the soothing dip. A generous piece of pork belly, nicely cooked and not too fatty, was spiced up with hot and sour chilli-pickled plums. In some dishes there can be just a flavour too many; for example, duck leg spring roll with sichuan pepper and guindilla chillies, served with tamarind aioli for dipping, just didn't need feta too. With its closely spaced tables and hard surfaces, the

acoustics can get a bit loud, and costs soon spiral if you get caught up in the excitement of ordering. Service is as laid-back and friendly as you'd expect, and there are some lovely wines on the list, including an appealing Kiwi selection.
Babies and children welcome: high chairs; nappy-changing facilities. Booking advisable. Disabled: toilet. Tables outdoors (3, pavement). **Map 18 D3**.

Fitzrovia

Riding House Café NEW
2011 RUNNER-UP BEST NEW DESIGN
43 Great Titchfield Street, W1W 7PQ (7927 0840, www.ridinghousecafe.co.uk). Oxford Circus tube. **Breakfast served** 8am-noon, **dinner served** 6-10pm Mon-Sat. **Lunch served** noon-3pm Mon-Fri. **Main courses** £9.50-£25. **Credit** AmEx, MC, V.
Salvage is a current decor trend, but few take it to such lengths as the Riding House Café. Every piece of furniture, every fixture, every fitting is either reclaimed or bespoke. The stout legs of the dining room tables are hewn from snooker tables; ex-theatre seats have been shipped from California; and the private dining room is actually an old English stable, demolished, transported and rebuilt, tying in with the loose equestrian theme that comes from the location (next to Riding House Street). Add stuffed squirrels as wall lights, and the steady stream of customers is never short of something to talk about. The day starts with breakfast: a couple of smoothies with chocolate and peanut butter temper healthful options such as carrot juice, bircher muesli and a fruit plate with yoghurt. Eggs come all the expected ways, or there's chorizo hash browns, or cured sea trout with crème fraîche and toast. Lunch and dinner menus reveal gastropub sensibilities (the same team run the Garrison in Bermondsey), with everything from fish and chips to rack of pork with lentils, smoked sausage and horseradish. Alternatively, the choice of small plates (cleverly listed at £3, £4 or £5 each) is very appealing. The wine list offers a 20-strong 'house selection' by glass, carafe or bottle, and plenty more besides. It's all very smartly conceived; staff are keen too.
Babies and children welcome: children's menu; high chairs; nappy-changing facilities. Booking advisable. Disabled: toilet. Separate room for parties, seats 16. **Map 9 J5**.

King's Cross

St Pancras Grand
Upper Concourse, St Pancras International, Euston Road, N1C 4QL (7870 9900, www.searcys.co.uk/stpancrasgrand). King's Cross tube/rail. **Meals served** 7am-10.30pm Mon-Sat; 8am-10.30pm Sun. **Main courses** £9.75-£23.50. **Set meal** £20 2 courses, £25 3 courses. **Credit** AmEx, MC, V.
We can only assume that the prices charged at the St Pancras Grand are for the fabulous art deco-style interior (courtesy of Martin Brudnizki) and great views of the glass and steel roof of the train station – sadly, the food (courtesy of Searcys) doesn't match up to the surroundings. Perhaps, on our Sunday visit, we should have opted for the roast, as many of our fellow diners did. Instead, we chose cheese and onion soufflé – perfectly cooked, brown and crispy outside, creamy and fluffy within. We should have stopped there. Barbecued plaice was

so small that it only provided a few meagre morsels of fish, and the accompanying vegetables, though fresh, lacked flavour. A dessert of apparently own-made sherbets was awful: the three scoops of pink, purple and pale yellow ice were almost entirely flavourless, though the pink one tasted vaguely (and oddly) of orange. There is a reasonable-value set meal, but ordering à la carte came in at £40 a head (including a glass of very nice pinot) – far too much for a disappointing lunch.
Available for hire. Babies and children welcome: children's menu; high chair. Booking advisable dinner and weekends. Disabled: toilet. Entertainment: jazz 1-4pm Sun. Separate rooms for parties, seating 14 and 15. **Map 4 L3**.

Knightsbridge

Galoupet NEW
13 Beauchamp Place, SW3 1NQ (7036 3600, www.galoupet.co.uk). Knightsbridge tube. **Meals served** 8am-11pm Mon-Thur; 8am-11.30pm Fri, Sat; 9am-11pm Sun. **Main courses** £8-£12. **Set breakfast** (8am-noon Mon-Sat; 9am-3pm Sun) £10. **Set lunch** (noon-3pm daily) £15 2 courses. **Set dinner** (6-11pm Mon-Thur, Sun; 6-11.30pm Fri, Sat) £55 tasting menu. **Credit** AmEx, MC, V.
Glitzy Galoupet is run by the owners of a vineyard in Provence, and the choice of bottles is fabulous, if a tad pricey. A wall of wine dispensers is the first thing you notice on entering the light-filled, entry-level bistro; downstairs is a more formal dining room, though the same menu is served in both areas. And what a menu it is, ranging from breakfasts of free-range eggs baked in the Josper grill with white pudding, back bacon and apple, or porridge with coconut, palm sugar and dates, to an elegant five-course seasonal tasting carte. Many ingredients are drawn from the Mediterranean, but this is not a Provençal restaurant: dishes are intriguing fusion affairs, often featuring superb British and Irish produce (Scottish girolles, Norfolk White free-range chicken, O'Shea's sausages) alongside flavourings such as miso, sumac and chilli jam. Some are more successful than others: we liked lamb with chilli, pickled fennel and pistachio, but onglet steak with mandarin, peanut brittle and papaya was too westernised and therefore lacked the harmony that would have come from fish sauce and spices. However, it's worth noting that feedback from our web users has been extremely positive. If you're

looking for a smart spot to rest those Manolos during a shopping spree, Galoupet fits the bill.
Available for hire. Babies and children welcome: children's menu; high chairs. Booking advisable. Disabled: toilet. **Map 14 F9**.

Mayfair

Sketch: The Parlour
9 Conduit Street, W1S 2XG (7659 4500, www.sketch.uk.com). Oxford Circus tube. **Meals served** 10am-9pm, **tea served** 1-6.30pm Mon-Sat. **Main courses** £4-£8.50. **Set tea** £10.50-£27; £38 incl glass of champagne. **Credit** AmEx, MC, V.
'Comfort food', cocktails and afternoon tea are the mainstays of Sketch's most egalitarian dining area. You can walk into Parlour without a booking, and it's open early until late (although it's members only after 9pm), making a great introduction to the always-surprising world of this expensively refurbed Georgian townhouse. When Sketch opened almost ten years ago, it was the decor that grabbed the headlines – maximalist, opulent, over the top, playful, arty and original. There's still constantly something new to attract the eye: a saucily embroidered sofa, a mid-century tea set, a hopscotch court painted in the entrance hall. And the toilets are the most extraordinary in London. It's all brilliant fun. That our evaluation of the cooking comes so late in this review might tell you that food isn't the most important part of the operation. Although the afternoon tea is classy, lunch – familiar dishes such as macaroni cheese, beef tartare, smoked salmon bagel – is merely decent and doesn't begin to justify the hefty prices. Superstar chef Pierre Gagnaire's creative touch is more evident in dishes such as the 'club sandwich', with thai mayonnaise and 'sweet and sour coriander onions'. Occasionally forgetful service comes from a series of stunners, who can be haughty.
Babies and children welcome: high chairs. Separate room for parties, seats 45-200. Takeaway service. **Map 9 J6**.

Truc Vert
42 North Audley Street, W1K 6ZR (7491 9988, www.trucvert.co.uk). Bond Street tube. **Meals served** 7.30am-10pm Mon-Fri; 9am-10pm Sat; 9am-4pm Sun. **Main courses** £14.95-£19. **Credit** AmEx, MC, V.

Riding House Café

Even though it's in the centre of town, deli-restaurant Truc Vert has the warm welcome, user-friendly menu and happy chatter of an ideal neighbourhood brasserie. It's just that the prices are higher. Customers are a mix of well-heeled locals, business people and tourists. The interior is country-kitchen functional by day, softened at night by tablecloths and dimmed lighting. Staff are cheery and aren't trying to turn tables. In the evening, therefore, diners can linger over, say, chicken and vegetable broth followed by nicely baked hake fillet with ragout of leek, samphire, carrot, broad bean and roast cherry tomato, with lamb's lettuce salad and olive salsa. There's always a steak too: an excellent bavette came with sautéed savoy cabbage, roast onion, and a stack of (unexpectedly cold) butternut squash. The day starts with big breakfasts, buttermilk pancakes or croissants; lunch sees quiche and salad combos, cheese and charcuterie plates as well as sizeable mains. In the afternoon there's a tapas menu of dishes such as grilled thai-marinated tiger prawns, meatball with spiced tomato sauce, and fried squid rings with lime mayonnaise. An equally accommodating wine list runs alongside various teas, coffees, organic bottled juices, lagers and a Devon cider.

Available for hire. Babies and children welcome: high chairs; nappy-changing facilities. Booking advisable. Entertainment: jazz 7-10pm Fri, Sat. Tables outdoors (12, pavement). Takeaway service. **Map 9 G6.**

Piccadilly

★ The Wolseley `HOT 50`
160 Piccadilly, W1J 9EB (7499 6996, www.thewolseley.com). Green Park tube. **Breakfast served** 7-11.30am Mon-Fri; 8-11.30am Sat, Sun. **Lunch served** noon-3pm Mon-Fri; noon-3.30pm Sat, Sun. **Tea served** 3-6.30pm Mon-Fri; 3.30-5.30pm Sat; 3.30-6.30pm Sun. **Dinner served** 5.30pm-midnight Mon-Sat; 5.30-11pm Sun. **All-day menu served** 11.30am-midnight daily. **Main courses** £6.75-£28.75. **Set tea** £9.75-£21; £29 incl glass of champagne. **Cover** £2. **Credit** AmEx, DC, MC, V.
This opulent brasserie is something of an enigma. With its loyal following and dedicated book, *Breakfast at The Wolseley* by AA Gill, it has the hallmarks of a grand café that has witnessed decades come and go, yet it has been open less than a decade. In fact, the marble pillars, stately staircases and noble arches that lend it such a Venetian flavour are the stamp, not of a European café, but of a former bank and car showroom. Not that it matters much, for famed restaurateurs Chris Corbin and Jeremy King have created a venue that feels every inch the sine qua non of London's chic café culture. Breakfast-goers are spoilt for choice: pastry baskets are accompanied by the finest

MasterCard Priceless Tip

Les Deux Salons (see p87) is a new, quintessentially French brasserie in the heart of Covent Garden from the award-winning team behind hit restaurants Arbutus and Wild Honey. Service is superb and the food a cut above.

condiments, and French baguettes arrive with a soothing bowl of hot chocolate. Savouries such as kedgeree topped with a poached egg carry through to lunch and dinner, and are bolstered by a well-considered carte, which flexes from a simple hamburger to lobster and caviar. Beloved of tourists, business folk, A-listers and many others, this Johnny-come-lately is having a ball. And with a reported 1,000 covers a day, booking ahead is definitely advised.

Babies and children welcome: high chairs; nappy-changing facilities. Booking advisable. Disabled: toilet. Separate room for parties, seats 12. **Map 9 J7.**

Soho

Bob Bob Ricard
1 Upper James Street, W1F 9DF (3145 1000, www.bobbobricard.com). Piccadilly Circus tube. **Meals served** noon-11pm Tue-Sat. **Main courses** £12-£40. **Set meal** (noon-6pm) £19.50 2 courses; £24.50 3 courses. **Credit** AmEx, MC, V.
Bob Bob Ricard sounds fun, but, most importantly, it is fun. It has turquoise booth seating, art nouveau styling, sub-Arctic vodka shots, very proper English afternoon tea, and a whole host of other eccentricities that shouldn't work together, but, one way or another, definitely, defiantly, do. Self-professed 'luxury' brands often verge on the starchy, but not so here. If anything, it's high-end trashy – as attested by the presence of a champagne button by each table: a temptingly decadent way to place an order. Top-notch wines and fizz are encouragingly priced (somewhat bizarrely, the drinks menu price-matches against notable London restaurants), food somewhat less so, primarily because the portions are fairly modest. Yet the menu is lengthy and strikingly charcterful, encompassing chicken kiev and that lesser-spotted Russian speciality, jellied ox tongue, as well as legions of tamer choices, such as roast leg of lamb with caramelised onions and 'old Bay' crispy fried chicken, spiced and served with coleslaw. This singularly eclectic mix of Russian and English dishes is served from lunch through to closing without pause, making it a surprising – and surprisingly useful – find in the heart of Soho.
Booking advisable. Disabled: toilet. Separate room for parties, seats 10. **Map 17 A4.**

Kettner's
29 Romilly Street, W1D 5HP (7734 6112, www.kettners.com). Leicester Square or Piccadilly Circus tube. **Meals served** noon-11pm Mon-Wed; noon-11.30pm Thur-Sat; noon-9.30pm Sun. **Main courses** £11.50-£27.50. **Set meal** (noon-6.30pm) £14.50 2 courses, £18.50 3 courses. **Credit** AmEx, MC, V.
Smack bang in the centre of Soho, Kettner's has been a stalwart of West End dining since 1867; more recently it served as a branch of Pizza Express. After a 2009 refurb and subsequent renaissance, the venue seems finally to have found a classic French-inspired menu worthy of its grand townhouse surroundings. Diners were wall-to-wall on our visit. Bayonne ham and celeriac remoulade came laced with a nose-tingling dose of dijon mustard; and crottin goat's cheese saw artistry in an accompanying arrangement of roasted red and yellow beetroot slivers. Expertly constructed dishes kept arriving. Duck confit sat on a cake of sarladaise potatoes. Rump steak was cooked rare, exactly as ordered, served with stilton sauce and a

superb portion of chips. Reproduction French furniture, candelabras and rococo-inspired flourishes make the interior very easy on the eye ideal for impressing a date, the in-laws, or hosting a special birthday, all of which seemed to be happening around us on an evening punctuated by champagne corks popping. Kettner's has long been famous for serving the fizzy stuff (there's a champagne bar alongside the restaurant) – and we certainly toast the improved menu and service.
Babies and children welcome: children's menu; high chairs. Booking advisable Fri, Sat. Disabled: toilet. Entertainment: pianist 6.30-9.30pm Mon-Thur, 7.30-10.30pm Fri, Sat, 6.30-8.30pm Sun. Separate rooms for parties, seating 12-85. **Map 17 C4.**

Princi
135 Wardour Street, W1F 0UT (7478 8888, www.princi.co.uk). Leicester Square or Tottenham Court Road tube. **Meals served** 7am-midnight Mon-Sat; 8.30am-10pm Sun. **Main courses** £5-£12. **Credit** AmEx, MC, V.
It's hard to think of many international jet-setting experiences that can be had for less than a tenner in grimy Soho, but Princi comes close. Everything about this Milanese-font bakery is glamorous, from the staff's smart uniforms (Armani, natch) to the sandstone and black marble interior, designed by Claudio Silvestrin. But it's the food that is the most alluring aspect of this upmarket take on the traditional Italian panetteria. Displayed in gorgeous glass counters and huge plate-glass windows are fresh-baked pizza, lasagne, breads sumptuous-looking salads and all manner of cakes and traditional Italian pâtisserie, including the best sfogliate (slivered layers of crisp pastry wrapped around Italian custard to form a shell) this side of Naples. Some things grate: service is at the counter, making it difficult then to grab a seat at the often-packed tables; and on our last visit, little breakfast cakes that had been inadvertently decorated with sea salt rather than sugar were fussed over and apologies made, but mysteriously no compensation or reimbursement was forthcoming. Still, these are minor quibbles; stand at one of the marble plinths sipping Princi's excellent caffè latte and you really feel like you're in the beating heart of a stylish Italian city.
Babies and children admitted. Bookings not accepted. Disabled: toilet. Takeaway service; delivery service (over £100 within 3-mile radius). **Map 17 B4.**

West
Chiswick

High Road Brasserie
162-166 Chiswick High Road, W4 1PR (8742 7474, www.highroadhouse.co.uk). Turnham Green tube. **Breakfast served** 7am-noon Mon-Fri; 8am-noon Sat, Sun. **Brunch served** noon-5pm Sat, Sun. **Dinner served** 5-10.30pm Sat; 5-10pm Sun. **Meals served** noon-11pm Mon-Thur; noon-midnight Fri. **Main courses** £10-£22. **Set lunch** (noon-5pm Mon-Fri) £12.50 2 courses, £15.50 3 courses. **Credit** AmEx, MC, V.
Part of Soho House, this stylish establishment lies under the group's High Road House hotel and members' club. The wide pavement permits a large outdoor seating area, while the interior resembles

a Parisian brasserie, with touches such as patterned Victorian floor tiles and green banquettes along the walls. It's a proper brasserie in terms of opening hours: breakfast is served, and there are brunch, lunch and a diverse all-day/dinner menus. You can also have just a drink or snack any time, as well as afternoon tea. When it opened in 2006, it buzzed with locals, tourists and shoppers of all ages. Nowadays, however, it's often all too easy to get a table. Instead of excitement, we've noticed a rather lackadaisical vibe, not helped by staff who can be offhand and a core clientele betraying the self-important insensitivity that cause many to give Chiswick a wide berth. The menu that once delighted – with its mix of Brit nursery/school/pub food and US brunch mainstays – now seems passé and rather twee, while portions have shrunk and prices seem to have risen in equal measure.
Babies and children welcome: crayons; high chairs; nappy-changing facilities. Booking advisable dinner and weekends. Disabled: toilet. Tables outdoors (8, pavement).

Sam's Brasserie & Bar

11 Barley Mow Passage, W4 4PH (8987 0555, www.samsbrasserie.co.uk). Chiswick Park or Turnham Green tube. **Open** 9am-midnight Mon-Wed, Sun; 9am-12.30am Thur-Sat. **Meals served** 9am-10.30pm daily. **Main courses** £9.50-£18.50. **Set lunch** (noon-3pm Mon-Fri) £13.50 2 courses, £16.50 3 courses. **Credit** AmEx, MC, V.

Sam Harrison's well-regarded establishment makes more effort than most to attract custom, with regular jazz and soul nights, wine tastings, BYO Mondays, and an accommodating menu that runs from breakfast via weekend brunch to full-blown dining; there's a children's menu too. The ex-industrial space is equally appealing, with a separate bar (remodelled in autumn 2011) and a large dining area in white and grey, with oversized lampshades and thoughtfully planned seating. It's smart enough for a special occasion, informal enough for a family lunch. Well-made cocktails and a discerning and affordable wine list are other bonuses, and staff provide helpful, well-drilled service. A shame, then, that our food lacked sparkle. A starter salad of octopus, spring onion, pepper and chilli contained no hint of chilli and needed a tangier dressing; saffron risotto (a main) with peas, red pepper and manchego cheese was dull; french fries were tepid. Best dishes were a thick, flavourful gazpacho, and cardamom-tinged rice pudding with a caramel crust that managed to be both soothing and luxurious. Seafood (Colchester rock oysters, whole prawns with tarragon mayo, South Coast mussels in a white wine broth) is a strong point, but elsewhere the kitchen needs a bit more pzazz.
Babies and children welcome: children's menu; high chairs; toys. Booking advisable Thur-Sat. Disabled: toilet. Separate room for parties, seats 26.
For branch (Harrison's) see index.

Ladbroke Grove

Electric Brasserie

191 Portobello Road, W11 2ED (7908 9696, www.the-electric.co.uk). Ladbroke Grove tube. **Meals served** 8am-11pm Mon-Fri; 8am-5pm, 6-11pm Sat; 8am-5pm, 6-10pm Sun. **Main courses** £10-£28. **Set lunch** (noon-5pm Mon-Fri) £13.50 2 courses, £16.50 3 courses. **Credit** AmEx, MC, V.

Bill's. See p38.

Railroad. See p46.

The Electric Brasserie's populist menu keeps this Portobello Road institution constantly buzzing – we were lucky to get a seat among the tightly packed tables on our Wednesday night walk-in. Much entertainment is to be had watching the highly charged open kitchen turn out a succession of steaks, seafood and salads at an eye-watering pace. A scotch egg with caper mayonnaise was outstanding, the highlight of our small plate selection, though almost bettered by mashed broad beans served with parmesan-crusted flatbreads. Calamares and garlicky aïoli was our nod to the Electric's emphasis on fish (from oyster platters to lobster and whole baked sea bream). It was the thrill of the grill that appealed for our main courses, however. The house cheeseburger's brioche bun matched the glossy leather banquettes of the art deco-inspired dining room; and the succulent, smoky 'roast' chicken came perfectly paired with a rich pesto. A well-stocked bar-café out front acts as an all-day meeting place for plugged-in locals (many visiting the cinema next door), while an ever-changing cocktail list ensures the operation remains current and never loses its spark.
Available for hire. Babies and children welcome: booster seats; children's menu; crayons; high chairs; nappy-changing facilities. Booking advisable Thur-Sun. Disabled: toilet. Tables outdoors (6, terrace).
Map 19 B3.

Westbourne Grove

Daylesford Organic
208-212 Westbourne Grove, W11 2RH (7313 8050, www.daylesfordorganic.com). Ladbroke Grove or Notting Hill Gate tube. **Meals served** *8.30am-7pm Mon-Sat; 10am-4pm Sun.* **Main courses** £9.95-£13.95. **Credit** *AmEx, MC, V.*
Daylesford's London outlets are in carefully chosen sites: here, on an upmarket shopping street, another in a villagey part of Pimlico, and one in Selfridges. All ideal locations for chichi café-delis serving (mostly) organic brasserie fare: smoked salmon with herb leaf salad and melba toast; welsh rarebit with chutney and mixed leaves; rare roast beef with horseradish and mustard dressing; and a selection of salads (bulgar wheat with broad beans, red onion, parsley and mint; beetroot with red onion, red pepper, spinach and spiced almonds). At the Westbourne Grove branch, there's seating at communal tables and on bar stools. There's always a queue at weekends, and on our visit there weren't enough waiting staff to keep pace with the brunching masses. We plumped for soup of the day (chilled tomato, cucumber and fennel), caesar salad, beef burger, and (best of all) yoghurt panna cotta with raspberries. All were good, but unmemorable, and all seemed slightly more expensive than justified; the modestly sized burger, for example, cost £12.95. The prices are partly a result of careful sourcing (much of the produce comes from Daylesford's organic estate; bread and dairy products are also made there), and it's unlikely that their core customers are counting the pennies – but this isn't the place for a quick, inexpensive lunch.
Babies and children welcome: crayons; high chairs; nappy-changing facilities. Bookings not accepted. Disabled: toilet. Tables outdoors (6, pavement). Takeaway service. Vegan dishes.
Map 7 A6.
For branch see index.

South West

Barnes

The Depot

Tideway Yard, 125 Mortlake High Street, SW14 8SN (8878 9462, www.depotbrasserie. co.uk). Barnes Bridge or Mortlake rail, or bus 209. **Lunch served** noon-3pm Mon-Fri; noon-3.30pm Sat; noon-5pm Sun. **Brunch served** 9.30-11.30am Sat. **Dinner served** 6-11pm Mon-Sat; 6-10pm Sun. **Main courses** £10.95-£19.50. **Set lunch** (Mon-Fri) £12.95 2 courses, £15.95 3 courses. **Credit** AmEx, DC, MC, V.

A full house on a Wednesday evening is proof of the continuing popularity of this Thameside stalwart, in business since 1984. Bag a window seat, if you can, for optimal sunset viewing, though the rest of the interior is pleasant too – with polished wooden floor and tables, bare brick walls and some comfortable striped banquettes. There's also a separate bar area with deep armchairs, and outdoor tables in the front courtyard. The seasonal menu is divided by category ('Veggies & salads', 'Fish & shellfish', 'Meats & grills') with, helpfully, many dishes available in starter and main course sizes. Puddings, usually a highlight, were a slight disappointment this time; walnut frangipane tart came with figs (dried-out chunks) inside the tart rather than on the side, as the menu description suggested. But the rest of the meal worked a treat: perfectly cooked slow-roast shoulder of lamb with good-quality golden polenta; and brazen hake atop creamy mash and spinach, with a soothing parsley sauce dotted with mussels. Helpings are hearty, the cheery young staff on the ball, and the wine list long and varied enough in price and content to please all-comers.
Available for hire. Babies and children welcome: children's menu; crayons; high chairs; nappy-changing facilities. Booking advisable. Tables outdoors (11, courtyard).

Chelsea

Gallery Mess

Saatchi Gallery, Duke of York's HQ, King's Road, SW3 4LY (7730 8135, www.saatchi-gallery.co.uk). Sloane Square tube. **Breakfast served** 10-11.30am Sat, Sun. **Meals served** 11.30am-9.30pm Mon-Sat; 11.30am-6.30pm Sun. **Main courses** £11-£18.50. **Set tea** (2.30-6pm) £9.50. **Credit** AmEx, MC, V.

What to expect from the brasserie at the gallery of Charles Saatchi, arguably the most powerful man in contemporary art? Instances of the super-collector's taste are evident, as you'd hope (artworks are selected from web showcase Saatchi Online). A giant sculpted shoe clings to the back wall, and a gaping-mouthed neon nude kneels resplendent on all fours high above the tables, but there the outrageousness ends and the professionalism begins. Gallery Mess – with its enviable Chelsea location, listed interior with vaulted ceiling, and terrace overlooking Duke of York Square – is a grown-up operation, every bit as slick and assured as Saatchi's meteoric career. Clientele are a fairly mixed group, from out-there art appreciators to the conservative gentlefolk of SW3. Thankfully, staff are courteous regardless. The seasonal menu offers light, well-balanced dishes, seeing the day through from breakfast to late supper. Chicken breast with

quinoa and pomegranate salad was fresh and sparky; south-coast fish in a bag came with a bird's nest of potato strips and a tangle of potato fries, served on a newspaper-print square of paper. Such dishes are artfully presented (of course), but there's substance to this style: a new 'sensation', perhaps.
Babies and children welcome: high chairs; nappy-changing facilities. Booking advisable lunch and dinner. Disabled: toilet. Separate room for parties, seats 30. Tables outdoors until 5.30pm Nov-Apr; until 9.30pm May-Oct (30, terrace). Map 14 F11.

★ Tom's Kitchen

27 Cale Street, SW3 3QP (7349 0202, www.tomskitchen.co.uk). Sloane Square or South Kensington tube. **Breakfast served** 8-11am, **lunch served** noon-3pm Mon-Fri. **Brunch served** 10am-4pm Sat, Sun. **Dinner served** 6-11pm daily. **Main courses** £14.50-£29.50. **Credit** AmEx, MC, V.

Although Tom Aikens first made his mark in haute cuisine, this brasserie is his stab at a more egalitarian style of cooking and service. It offers 'food for everyone and anyone' – as long as they can afford it. This is primarily a local for Chelsea Green residents; wear Thomas Pink or Joseph and you'll fit right in. Still, the place is highly likeable. It's the comfort food that gets the attention – macaroni cheese, fish pie, beef burger, calf's liver with mash – but the menu is lengthy and extends to the likes of pan-fried foie gras with duck egg and Ventreche bacon. We've had complaints of poor service, and suspect that on very busy nights the tables would feel unpleasantly cramped. However, with an upbeat crowd and a bit of room for manoeuvre, the vibe is jolly good fun. Even better is a quiet breakfast time, when you can linger over superb pancakes and well-made coffee. The decor – white brick tiles, marble counters, sleekly chunky wood furniture – was ahead of its time and still looks the business. The branch at Somerset House doesn't have quite the same verve, but the location is a draw nevertheless.
Babies and children welcome: high chairs; nappy-changing facilities. Booking advisable dinner and weekends. Disabled: toilet. Separate rooms for parties, seating 22 and 40.
Map 14 E11.
For branch see index.

A Little of What You Fancy. See p46.

Homa. See p46.

South

Waterloo

★ Giraffe

Riverside Level 1, Royal Festival Hall, Belvedere Road, SE1 8XX (7928 2004, www.giraffe.net). Embankment tube or Waterloo tube/rail. **Meals served** 8am-10.45pm Mon-Fri; 9am-10.45pm Sat; 9am-10.30pm Sun. **Main courses** £8-£16. **Credit** AmEx, MC, V.

If you don't love Giraffe, you probably don't have children. It's not that giving birth suddenly creates a taste for burritos or pesto oil, but new parents have a heightened appreciation of such elements as well-spaced tables, buggy parking, unflappable staff and ground floor toilets. Giraffe's crayons, sheet of games and spot-on kid's menu have given many a couple the simple luxury of a breather on a hectic day out – and the food's not bad. The menu shuffles a pack of ideas gleaned from hippy travel guides (world music plays in the background) and swooshes them with contemporary dish styling, such as wooden boards and dinky pots. Best dishes tend to be classics: a generous torpedo roll of minute steak; the house bacon and cheese burger; chilli beef enchiladas; and breakfast pancakes. Lunch deals, an early-bird menu and Bar Buddies (50% off selected drinks 5-7pm Mon-Fri) are deal sweeteners, and the Italian house white wine is very acceptable. Skip desserts in favour of extra chips, a fruit smoothie, Union coffee or a cocktail (we like the 'mellow yellow' mojito with mint, lime and passionfruit).
Babies and children welcome: children's menu; crayons; high chairs; nappy-changing facilities. Disabled: toilet. Tables outdoors (40, terrace). Takeaway service. **Map 10 M8.**
For branches see index.

South East

Bankside

Elliot's NEW

12 Stoney Street, SE1 9AD (8980 0030, www.elliotscafe.com). London Bridge tube/rail. **Breakfast served** 7.30-11am, **lunch served** 12.30-2.30pm, **dinner served** 5.30-10pm Mon-Sat. **Main courses** £4-£19. **Credit** AmEx, MC, V.

Elliot's stands out as one of the most enjoyable of London's new-wave tapas-style eateries. Owners Brett Redman and Rob Green (of the Pavilion Café in Victoria Park) aim to take inspiration from their Brorough Market location and work with the traders to produce a menu that reflects what is available on the stalls each day. This is wittily reflected in the menu design – Courier type on paper that looks like someone's been doodling on it. They are baking their own breads (and, for breakfast, pretty brioche striped with chocolate), using traditional methods and organic flours stoneground in Dorset. The kitchen isn't open literally all day – there's a gap between before lunch, and a bar snack menu only between 2.30pm and 5.30pm, but you can always pop in for a drink. In season, expect the likes of squirrel rillettes, and partridge with corn, leeks and bacon, but the food isn't entirely British: there's the likes of squid with romesco sauce, prosciutto with pickled peaches, and a main of caponata on toast. Finish with farmhouse cheese, or ices – maybe damson ripple, or vanilla ice-cream with bottled wild cherry plums. We love the drinks list, which embraces New Forest cider, London microbrewed ales, and en vogue natural wines.

Bookings not accepted. Tables outdoors (4, pavement). Vegetarian menu. **Map 11 P8**.

The Table

83 Southwark Street, SE1 0HX (7401 2760, www.thetablecafe.com). Southwark tube or London Bridge tube/rail. **Meals served** 7.30am-4.30pm Mon-Fri. **Brunch served** 8.30am-4pm Sat, Sun. **Dinner served** 6-10.30pm Tue-Sat. **Main courses** £14-£25. **Credit** AmEx, MC, V.
Dining at the Table is a bit like eating in a design showroom – the steel fittings, new wooden tables and clean lines create a minimalist space that's brought to life by the open kitchen. A potentially soulless vibe is avoided thanks the relaxed busyness of the engaged chefs. The sound of gentle conversation pervades the space, which is as suited to business breakfasts and sole diners as it is to couples and small groups. Dedication to top-drawer ingredients is evident in the displays of wines, condiments and (Chegworth Valley) juices. The modern approach extends to the menu, whose contemporary British dishes – very much in the 'local is best' camp – are infused with Mediterranean flavours. A starter of smoked haddock was made light and fresh with mint and coriander. Sea bass stuffed with dill was perfectly complemented by chargrilled fennel and tomato, while ham hock 'tartine' with chickpea and rose harissa salad and poached duck egg was tasty and attractively presented. Quality produce makes up for the fact that portions are on the small side. Weekend brunches, when the huge windows provide a lovely light, are a treat here.
Babies and children welcome: high chairs. Disabled: toilet. Tables outdoors (8, terrace). Takeaway service. **Map 11 O8**.

Tate Modern Café: Level 2

2nd floor, Tate Modern, Sumner Street, SE1 9TG (7401 5014, www.tate.org.uk). Southwark tube or London Bridge tube/rail. **Meals served** 10am-5.30pm Mon-Thur, Sun; 10am-9.30pm Fri; 10am-6.30pm Sat. **Main courses** £8.95-£11.15. **Credit** AmEx, DC, MC, V.
Tate Modern's big, bustling entrance-level café has something for everyone: light snacks (meat platters, bloomer sandwiches); main courses that aim higher than they need to (pork cutlet with a salad of pak choi and shiitake) plus a proper wine list; posh breakfasts (duck egg!); afternoon tea; floor-to-ceiling views out to the Thames; and award-winning industrial chic design. It's suitably patriotic too, promoting Cornish mackerel, crisp-battered fish and chips, St Jude's ice-cream, and some particularly interesting English cheeses. An exciting beer menu has been lovingly sourced from smaller UK breweries – our Kernel Black IPA coming from mere streets away. Children are enthusiastically catered for, with a free children's meal for every adult main course at lunch – though portions are small and the dishes nursery staples: over-eights might find themselves hungry, and more sophisticated youngsters may prefer a smaller portion of an adult meal. Although it was clear from all our dishes that ingredients are fresh and good quality, we'd have preferred the burger a lot rarer (or, at least, to have been asked how we wanted it cooked). It's usually very busy; try to get a window table for a more relaxed, less institutional experience.

Babies and children welcome: children's menu; high chairs; nappy-changing facilities. Disabled: toilet. **Map 11 O7**.

Blackheath

Chapters All Day Dining

43-45 Montpelier Vale, SE3 0TJ (8333 2666, www.chaptersrestaurants.com). Blackheath rail. **Breakfast served** 8-11.30am Mon-Fri; 8am-noon Sat; 9am-noon Sun. **Lunch served** noon-3pm Mon-Sat; 11am-4pm Sun. **Tea served** 3-6pm Mon-Sat; 4-6pm Sun. **Dinner served** 6-11pm Mon-Sat; 6-9pm Sun. **Main courses** £9.45-£30.50. **Credit** AmEx, MC, V.
The aptly named 'All Day Dining' branch of Chapters is a buzzy, bright place to visit for a coffee and catch-up with friends at the pavement tables, a hearty brunch or a dinner with the parents. The spacious dining room is all modern furniture and exposed brickwork, and you can perch on stylish aluminium bar chairs for a bloody mary or two. Unlike formal, Michelin-starred sister restaurant Chapter One (based in Bromley), here you'll find classy cooking in a casual setting. Various menus cover every mealtime. Brunch dishes can be quite heavy, such as slow-roast pork belly with an assortment of trimmings. A fish special of expertly pan-fried lemon sole accompanied by an unctuous pearl barley risotto was lighter. Spatchcock chicken had been imbued with a delicate smokiness from the charcoal embers of the Josper oven and arrived dripping with flavoursome juices. Desserts are quite small; a raspberry tart was inhaled in seconds. On previous visits, service was the epitome of continental efficiency, though on this occasion our entertaining waiter was more engaged in flirting with a neighbouring table than listening to our order – but it's just such variation from the norm that gives Chapters its edge.
Babies and children welcome: children's menu; high chairs; nappy-changing facilities. Booking essential dinner and weekends. Disabled: toilet. Separate room for parties, seats 50. Tables outdoors (4, pavement).

Crystal Palace

Joanna's

56 Westow Hill, SE19 1RX (8670 4052, www.joannas.uk.com). Crystal Palace or Gipsy Hill rail. **Breakfast served** 10am-noon daily. **Meals served** noon-11pm Mon-Sat; noon-10.30pm Sun. **Main courses** £11.75-£32.50. **Set meal** (lunch Mon-Sat) £10 2 courses, £13.95 3 courses. **Credit** AmEx, MC, V.
It's not the most conspicuous of restaurants (the bottle-blue frontage is easily overlooked amid Westow Hill's clutter of pubs and plumbing shops), but Joanna's has been bringing a slice of the high life to one of London's highest points since it opened as an American-style grill and piano bar in 1978 (a framed photo of Frank Sinatra hints at its raucous past). And there remains a dash of Americana in the deco-style interior – walls replete with modern art of the Vettriano variety, long bar gleaming and ceiling fans whirring, wooden floor set with champagne buckets and patrolled by smart, black-shirted staff – but the laid-back vibe and brasserie menu is resolutely European. Our starter of beetroot carpaccio with goat's cheese fritters was excellent, its earthiness contrasting wonderfully with the sweetness of a raisin, orange

and pine nut dressing. Also superb was a main of spiced duck confit in a sweet citrus sauce with wilted chard and mash – the duck skin perfectly crisp, the meat melting off the bone. An Aberdeen Angus burger with cheese and bacon was juicy and generous, and suggests that the founders' affection for Stateside cuisine hasn't entirely been forgotten.
Babies and children welcome until 6pm: booster seats; children's menu; high chairs. Booking advisable; essential weekends. Tables outdoors (3, pavement).

East
Shoreditch

Water House

10 Orsman Road, N1 5QJ (7033 0123, www.waterhouserestaurant.co.uk). Haggerston rail or bus 67, 242. **Lunch served** noon-4pm Mon-Fri, Sun. **Dinner served** 6-10pm Tue-Sat. **Main courses** £10.50-£17. **Credit** MC, V.
Described as a social enterprise and 'training restaurant' owned by the Shoreditch Trust, Water House – whose USP is its location bang on the Regent's Canal just north of Shoreditch – has all the accoutrements of a professional operation, with a modish interior, sparkling glassware and an Italian-slanted Modern European menu. Its slightly tucked-away location means it's generally quiet at the weekend – which can have its advantages: good weather meant we could eat on the canalside terrace. A starter of smoked mackerel niçoise was a good mix of fresh ingredients in a zesty dressing. Other starters are more specifically Italian: the likes of panzanella salad, or buffalo mozzarella with speck, figs and balsamic. Carbonara with black squid ink pasta was a generous portion, warmly comforting and subtly flavoured. Roasted lemon and thyme risotto was less successful: flavours had gone awry – it was oversalted and too much lemon lent a harsh taste. But we had asked the kitchen to leave out the butter, so perhaps this sent things askew. Still, sunny service, sunny weather and an enjoyable bottle of Backsberg chenin blanc, for a very reasonable £17.80, made for an all-round enjoyable experience.
Babies and children welcome: high chairs. Booking advisable. Disabled: toilet. Tables outdoors (8, towpath). Takeaway service. **Map 6 R2**.

Spitalfields

Breakfast Club NEW

12-16 Artillery Lane, E1 7LS (7078 9633, www.thebreakfastclubcafes.com). Liverpool Street tube/rail or Shoreditch High Street rail. **Meals served** 7.30am-10.30pm Mon-Wed; 7.30am-11.30pm Thur, Fri; 9am-11.30pm Sat; 9am-10pm Sun. **Main courses** £3.50-£10.20. **Credit** AmEx, MC, V.
Breakfast Club's Spitalfields branch resembles a cool version of an American burger bar: faux tin ceiling, 'booths' created from a row of reclaimed locker-room seats, zinc bar stools around original brick columns, and walls covered in eclectic memorabilia and signage, including a neon 'Sex and Drugs and Bacon Rolls'. There's a real sense of fun here – even the loos have My Little Pony wallpaper – and, on the night of our visit, the mainly suited crowd clearly enjoyed the buzzy atmosphere.

Hackney Pearl

Evening opening sees the menu extend beyond breakfast and brunch to a huge range of burgers, wings, nachos and salads, along with the (genius, this) 'late, late breakfast' – an enormous fry-up of sausages, bacon, black pudding, eggs and, for the health-conscious, the option of brown toast. Food is good if not outstanding: a halloumi starter was better than the feta and (jarred, pitted) olives, and a lovely cheeseburger was let down by watery coleslaw and disappointing chips. Genial service is a real plus, happy hour takes £4 off a £20 bottle of wine and, if you keep 'em peeled (at the giant Smeg fridge and the Janitor's Cupboard), your evening could get a whole lot better.
Available for hire. Babies and children welcome: high chairs; nappy-changing facilities. Bookings not accepted before 5pm weekends. Disabled: toilet. Takeaway service. **Map 12 R5.**
For branches see index.

North East
Dalston

A Little of What You Fancy NEW
464 Kingsland Road, E8 4AE (7275 0060, www.alittleofwhatyoufancy.info). Dalston Junction rail or bus 67, 242. **Breakfast served** 9am-noon Tue-Fri. **Lunch served** noon-4pm Tue-Fri; 10am-4pm Sat; noon-5pm Sun. **Dinner served** 7-9.45pm Tue, Wed; 7-10pm Thur-Sat. **Main courses** £12-£19. **Credit** MC, V.
Despite its subdued frontage, ALOWYF stands out against Kingsland Road's Turkish and Vietnamese cafés as a beacon of trad Brit cooking. As you might guess from the name, it's as twee as a Pastels pin badge. The narrow, cosy, candlelit space is run by two friends, with school-salvaged furniture (complete with compass-etched graffiti), wooden boxes of oranges and lemons, and a cabinet showcasing someone's homemade jam. Dishes are comfortably British in style, with a few adopted French influences, and have a reassuringly own-made manner. We started with two scoops of chicken liver pâté with toast and gherkins; and an

earthy salad of roast beetroot, strathdon blue cheese and pickled walnuts. Both were generous in size and assembled with care. Mains followed suit: a saucer-sized smoked haddock fish cake came with tartare sauce and caperberries, while plentiful chunks of meat snuggled into the rich gravy of a beef bourguignon. A compact drinks list offers a couple of beers from the Kernel microbrewery in Southwark, and a few wines by the glass, carafe or bottle. The selection of small plates is handy for accompanying a drink.
Available for hire. Babies and children welcome until 7pm: high chairs. Booking advisable Thur-Sat. Disabled: toilet. Takeaway service.

Hackney

Railroad NEW
120-122 Morning Lane, E9 6LH (8985 2858, www.railroadhackney.co.uk). Hackney Central rail. **Lunch served** 10am-5pm Mon, Tue, Sun; 10am-4pm Wed-Sat. **Dinner served** 7.30-10pm Wed-Sat. **Main courses** £10-£14. **Credit** MC, V.
A lo-fi, low-key, DIY operation, Railroad has been created by knocking together a former barber's and a Nigerian wine bar, giving them a lick of paint and embellishing with nothing more than a spot of foliage, a vast mirror and team shots of George Best and Bobby Charlton. There's some salvaged furniture and a tiny wedge of a kitchen, which contains a top-of-the-range espresso machine and delivers food of a standard that belies the humble interior. On our visit, we had a short wait before ordering because dinner was still in the oven. From the daily-changing menu, we trid starters of breaded quail with fish sauce, and deep-fried spiced chickpeas; for mains, we sampled spinach and potato curry, shot through with nigella, mustard seeds and curry leaves, and also chorizo, lentil and tomato stew, served with chunks of own-made bread. Dessert – also oven-fresh – was a simple slice of almond and pear tart. Such places could be celebrated as an example of what can be done with a bit of ambition and imagination. The downstairs space hosts poetry readings and open-mic nights.
Available for hire. Babies and children admitted. Booking advisable Fri, Sat. Takeaway service.

Hackney Wick

★ Hackney Pearl
11 Prince Edward Road, E9 5LX (8510 3605, www.thehackneypearl.com). Hackney Wick rail. **Open** 8am-11pm Tue-Fri; 10am-11pm Sat, Sun. **Lunch served** noon-4pm, **dinner served** 6-10pm Tue-Sun. **Brunch served** 10am-4pm Tue-Fri; 10am-1pm Sat, Sun. **Main courses** £10-£14. **Credit** MC, V.
The Hackney Pearl really is a pearl of the east – Hackney's post-industrial far east, that is. In the incongruous surroundings of Hackney Wick, it's a laid-back combination of neighbourhood hangout and restaurant, with a friendly, unpretentious atmosphere and brilliant, generous food that punches well above its weight. The spacious, light interior has a retro-meets-boho vibe, with Formica tables and old copies of *National Geographic* set on shelves. Staff lean towards the bohemian too, but they're professional with it. Food comes in big flavours with some lively matches; witness a starter of salt beef brisket, plums, watercress and walnuts, or the more traditional (and lovely) potted prawns with rocket and toast. A broad bean and pea bruschetta with shaved pecorino was a vivid, coarsely mashed heap bursting with freshness and flavour. From a choice of four mains, only one, a huge, creamy, flavourful roast tomato and thyme risotto, was meatless. Lamb chop came supersized, tender and simply grilled, with herby baba ganoush, chilli and garlic greens. Our waiter warned us the 'strawberry eton mess' was without strawberries, but it was still an indulgent, luxurious mess – this time with cherries.
Available for hire. Babies and children welcome: high-chairs; nappy-changing facilities. Booking advisable. Disabled: toilet. Tables outdoors (7, terrace). Takeaway service.

Stoke Newington

Homa NEW
71-73 Stoke Newington Church Street, N16 0AS (7254 2072, www.homalondon.co.uk). Stoke Newington rail or bus 73, 393, 476. **Open** 9am-11.30pm Tue-Sat; 10am-11.30pm Sun. **Lunch served** noon-3pm Tue-Fri; noon-4pm Sat; noon-5pm Sun. **Brunch served** 10am-3pm Tue-Fri; 10am-4pm Sat, Sun. **Dinner served** 6-10.30pm Tue-Sat; 6-10pm Sun. **Main courses** £6.50-£18. **Credit** MC, V.
This continental-style brasserie has all the right ingredients to attract a loyal following, and shortly after opening was already pulling in laid-back groups and date-night couples. There's a front terrace, funky black and white-tiled bar area, and a restaurant decked out in cool, modern grey. Service is friendly and informal. The concise menu crosses southern Mediterranean borders: crisp, thin-based pizzas alternate with tapas and main courses such as confit duck. Silky pappardelle with fragrant Scottish girolles was a simple pleasure. The wine list geographically matches the food on offer, and is fairly priced, from £13.50 at £18 a bottle. For a £7.50 corkage fee, a more extensive and expensive selection can be ordered from the deli upstairs. At breakfast or between meals, it's best to head to the brightly lit, raised ground floor, open from 9am until dinner. A marble breakfast bar is given over to pastries and coffee, and fry-ups have a continental flavour, using Italian sausages and hams. A longer marble slab is laid with scenic

platters of salads, grilled vegetables and grains for a more pick 'n' mix approach to lunch, while a large central table and long wooden bars provide communal seating. *Babies and children welcome: high chairs; nappy-changing facilities. Booking advisable. Disabled: toilet. Separate room for parties, seats 40. Tables outdoors (14, terrace). Takeaway service.* **Map 25 B1.**

North
Camden Town & Chalk Farm

Made in Camden NEW
Roundhouse, Chalk Farm Road, NW1 8EH (7424 8495, www.madeincamden.com). Chalk Farm tube. **Lunch served** noon-2.30pm Mon-Fri. **Brunch served** 10.30am-3pm Sat, Sun. **Dinner served** 6-10.30pm daily. **Main courses** £4.40-£16. **Set lunch** £10 2 courses. **Credit** AmEx, MC, V.

We've had mixed experiences at this revamped café-bar and restaurant in the Roundhouse. Gig-goers will be pleasantly surprised by the quality of food, service and decor compared to other concert venues, but to work as a destination in its own right (which it undoubtedly seeks to do), more consistency is required from the kitchen and waitstaff. On the plus side: astute recipes stylishly presented, Caravan coffee and a terrific choice of draught and bottled beers. From the brunch menu, we liked onglet open sandwich with red onions and horseradish cream, and an Iranian-style omelette of leeks, walnuts and raisins; from the dinner menu, crab and sweetcorn fritters, and lamb köfte with pearl barley tabouleh. Desserts (glamorous takes on trifle and rice pudding) were gorgeous in both looks and taste. However, brunch pancakes were flabby and greasy, and the service, although friendly, was aggravating, thanks to long waits for food and distracted staff. Coffees, when they finally arrived, were lukewarm. Made in Camden's challenge is to smooth out the peaks and troughs of concert custom; when the audience descends on the bar, diners are left to stew. At least, the confident blend of sleek contemporary design and old-rocker images hits the right note. *Babies and children welcome: high chairs; nappy-changing facilities. Booking advisable. Disabled: toilet.* **Map 27 B1.**

Islington

★ Ottolenghi HOT 50
287 Upper Street, N1 2TZ (7288 1454, www.ottolenghi.co.uk). Angel tube or Highbury & Islington tube/rail. **Meals served** 8am-10pm Mon-Wed; 8am-10.30pm Thur-Sat; 9am-7pm Sun. **Main courses** £5.50-£12. **Credit** AmEx, MC, V.

Conversation at Ottolenghi almost inevitably turns to the desirability, or viability, of cooking this way at home. The cookbooks have been a worldwide hit, and even the savoury dishes, which exude healthful vitality, provide eye-candy – but in practice the list of ingredients deters all but the keenest cooks. It's dizzying enough reading the menu, which features combinations such as faro, arborio and wild rice with feta, courgette flower, dried Iranian lime and herbs. Lunchtime typically sees around ten salads offered alongside six main courses, though we soon clocked why the bright, friendly staff kept asking

whether we'd come for 'a late lunch or coffee and cake' – only two of the mains were still available. No matter, a selection of four salads works as a main course too; have three if you're not so hungry. Chargrilled salmon with spicy aubergine choka (similar to baba ganoush, though less creamy) was surprisingly fridge-cold, but refreshing and delicious. Best of the salads was butternut squash with sweetcorn, feta, pumpkin seeds and chilli. Dinner (this is the only branch that offers it) sees the perennially busy kitchen crank up several notches, turning out elegantly plated fusion combinations that add Caribbean, Japanese and Thai ingredients to the core larder of British and Mediterranean produce. *Babies and children welcome: high chairs. Booking advisable dinner; not accepted lunch. Takeaway service.* **Map 5 O1.** **For branches see index.**

Kentish Town

Kentish Canteen NEW
300 Kentish Town Road, NW5 2TG (7485 7331, www.kentishcanteen.co.uk). Kentish Town tube. **Meals served** 9am-10.30pm daily. **Main courses** £11-£12. **Credit** AmEx, MC, V.

This bright, brash addition to the eateries clustered around Kentish Town station is proving popular with locals looking for quality weekend breakfasts, and office workers wanting to trade up from the nearby sandwich bars. The menu is a mix of deli-café, gastropub and Mediterranean favourites. We love the rock-star luxury of being able to order french toast with bacon and maple syrup at 3pm, and the option to choose two salads (summer green slaw, caponata, mohgrabieh, tomato and feta) as a main course. The cooking can be very good indeed, although the long wait for our main courses was frustrating. We have fond memories of chargrilled chicken with punchy anchoïade dressing, sauté potatoes and broccolini, and were impressed by the freshness of the crab in a plate of lemony, chilli-flecked linguine, a dish that determinedly put quality before quantity. Desserts can be restaurant (chocolate and amaretti torte with candied orange and mascarpone – as good as you'll find anywhere) or cakey (walnut brownie, Joyce's double lemon slice). The acoustics aren't great – every drop of

cutlery set our teeth on edge – and the view of traffic, with a tiny strip of Hampstead Heath, isn't the best, but this place has plenty going for it. *Available for hire. Babies and children welcome: children's menu; high chairs; nappy-changing facilities. Booking advisable Sat, Sun. Disabled: toilet. Separate room for parties, seats 45. Tables outdoors (9, terrace). Takeaway service.* **Map 26 B4.**

North West
Queen's Park

Hugo's
21-25 Lonsdale Road, NW6 6RA (7372 1232). Queen's Park tube/rail. **Meals served** 9.30am-5.30pm Mon; 9.30am-11pm Tue-Sat. **Main courses** £7.50-£15.80. **Credit** MC, V.

Popular with all ages, this spacious café is sited on a gentrified backstreet, flanked by local businesses and workshops. Decor has been freshened up since our last visit, with pale grey walls softening the old deep maroon shades. Velvet drapes, glinting fairy lights and sturdy church-like furniture remain unchanged, adding to the quirky appeal. The broad menu covers regular café staples – burgers, pastas, risottos and sandwiches, but also the likes of duck confit and quinoa salads – and is perhaps trying too hard to tick all the boxes. A tapas platter didn't deliver: houmous paired with focaccia was an odd marriage, while an orange-coloured chicken pâté was bland and offputting. Mains were average too. Fish stew had a pleasing tomato and garlic flavour, but was soupy in consistency and marred by an abundance of overcooked salmon. The downward spiral continued: tough and gristly ribeye, topped with squishy onions, was redeemed only by crisp fries on the side. Hugo's isn't cheap, and service although well meaning, is slow. Drop by for a traditional breakfast or brunch for a more rewarding experience. *Available for hire. Babies and children welcome: crayons; high chairs; nappy-changing facilities. Booking advisable weekends. Entertainment: musicians 6.30pm Tue, 8pm Sun. Tables outdoors (7, pavement). Takeaway service.* **Map 1 A1.**

Made in Camden

British

Ask anyone who can remember World War II what they think of British restaurants, and you might be told of the communal kitchens set up by the wartime government to feed coupon-less diners during rationing. The term 'British restaurant' was preferred by Churchill to the original name, 'Community Feeding Centres'. We've come a long way since – or have we? The renaissance in British cuisine has always looked to our culinary past, as well as keeping an eye on contemporary competition. Hence at two of London's most lustrous stars in this section – **St John** and **Hix** – you might find the likes of braised ox kidney with bacon and mash (St John), or lamb's tongue with braised lettuce hearts and green sauce (Hix): offal dishes that had largely disappeared from menus by the prosperous final decades of the 20th century. Such has been the skill and verve brought by Fergus Henderson (St John), Gary Rhodes (**Rhodes 24**) and Mark Hix, among others, to reinvigorating our native cuisine, that even old-timers such as the **Dorchester Grill Room** and **Simpson's-in-the-Strand** have a new-found confidence in providing singularly British food.

Newcomers have followed suit too. Heck, you can even get mince and potatoes at the glamorous **Dean Street Townhouse**. Heston Blumenthal and Marcus Wareing have got in on the act, opening **Dinner** (*see p129*) and **Gilbert Scott**, at the Mandarin Oriental and refurbished St Pancras hotels respectively. Indeed, British hotel dining rooms seem to be undergoing a rebirth with the reopening of the **Savoy Grill** and, just down the road, newcomer **Northall** at the Corinthia. So not only is Britain revelling in a passion for its own cuisine, it's singing about it to visitors as well – now that is confidence.

Central
City

Paternoster Chop House
Warwick Court, Paternoster Square, EC4M 7DX (7029 9400, www.paternosterchophouse.co.uk). St Paul's tube. **Lunch served** noon-3.30pm Mon-Fri; noon-4pm Sun. **Dinner served** 5.30-10.30pm Mon-Fri. **Main courses** £15-£25. **Set meal** (Mon-Fri) £22 2 courses, £26.50 3 courses. **Set lunch** (Sun) £22 2 courses incl tea or coffee, £27 3 courses incl tea or coffee. **Credit** AmEx, MC, V.
A stone's throw from St Paul's Cathedral, Paternoster Chop House is spacious and modern. On a summer evening visit, tipsy City workers were crammed beneath the outside awning; inside saw a similar crowd, along with the odd tourist. Despite the half empty dining room, we were squeezed on to a small table between a pillar and another couple, making the meal less relaxing than it might have been. The simple menu didn't disappoint, though, with well-sourced, skilfully cooked meat, sustainable fish and a few classic British puds. The

'beast of the day', roast Galloway beef, was perfectly tender and flavour-filled, if a little overpowered by a nose-tinglingly hot beetroot and horseradish purée. Huntsham Court Farm Middle White pork hit the spot with creamy fat, crunchy crackling and a well-balanced apple sauce. Sticky toffee pudding also made the grade. The globetrotting wine list holds a few English bottles. Our waiter was prompt and polite, but just a little indifferent. For a meat-heavy meal with clients, or after-work drinks and nibbles from the bar menu, Paternoster fits the bill, but it's possibly not the place for a special occasion.
Available for hire. Babies and children welcome: crayons (Sun); high chairs; toys (Sun). Booking advisable. Disabled: toilet. Separate room for parties, seats 13. Tables outdoors (20, courtyard). **Map 11 O6**.
For branch (Butlers Wharf Chop House) see index.

Restaurant at St Paul's
St Paul's Cathedral, St Paul's Churchyard, EC4M 8AD (7248 2469, www.restaurantat stpauls.co.uk). St Paul's tube. Café **Open/meals served** 9am-5pm Mon-Sat; 10am-4pm Sun. *Restaurant* **Lunch served** noon-3pm, **tea served** 3-4.30pm daily. **Set lunch** £21.50 2 courses, £25.95 3 courses. **Set tea** £9.95-£21.25. *Both* **Credit** MC, V.
If you're expecting a florid interior, the simplicity of the formal restaurant in the crypt of St Paul's Cathedral could prove a little disappointing. Vaulted ceilings and a bit of tapestry are the only elements suggesting church or history: otherwise, it's reminiscent of the sort of brasserie restaurants found in market towns – contemporary chairs and black placemats alongside heritage-green hues and a country dresser-style waiters' station. However, that suits a menu that does its best to showcase the garden (or, rather, allotment) of England. Yes, there is a smattering of parmesan, olives and truffle, but the overall impression is of Suffolk bacon, heritage vegetables, farmhouse cheddar and cider. Best of our dishes was a small tart of artichoke and watercress – a surprising combination that didn't resort to quiche-y custard to unify the differing textures of the veg. Grey mullet with apple, fennel and purple potato salad was a good tasting combination let down by undercooked potatoes. Desserts suited the season: daintily presented fruit and cream concoctions, rather than rib-sticking

puds. Service looked the part, but was less efficient than it could have been, and although the room was by no means full (a mix of quiet City workers and tourists), the wait for dishes was over-long. *Babies and children welcome: high chairs. Booking advisable. Disabled: lift; toilet.* **Map 11 O6**.

★ Rhodes Twenty Four

24th floor, Tower 42, Old Broad Street, EC2N 1HQ (7877 7703, www.rhodes24.co.uk). Bank tube/DLR or Liverpool Street tube/rail. **Lunch served** noon-2.15pm, **dinner served** 6-8.30pm Mon-Fri. **Main courses** £16.50-£31. **Credit** AmEx, DC, MC, V.

The view from the 24th floor is awe-inspiring day or night, though we have a slight preference for the twinkling evening cityscape. Also, at dinner the usual business clientele is leavened by dating couples and family groups. Bargain hunters should check for the regular lunch deals; the special summer set lunch on our visit was a steal for this quality. Decor is pale and low-key, focusing attention on the floor-to-ceiling windows. Well-drilled staff ensure everything runs smoothly, while the kitchen produces hit after hit. The real showstopper was a plate of pork: pork belly on a chunky apple ring, roast loin on carrots, and braised cheek on mash – a sublime dish. Beside this, pan-fried haddock with baby leeks and smoked bacon and cockle chowder was almost unassuming. Starters were excellent too. An earthy, deep green watercress soup came with little ticklemore goat's cheese fritters, while a good portion of wood pigeon was served with beetroot tartlet and sour cream dressing. High standards were maintained by the signature dessert plate, which held Gary Rhodes' version of a jaffa cake, an almost liquid bread and butter pudding, and an addictive warm date pudding with toffee sauce. Of the extras, a white tomato soup amuse-bouche scored top marks, and the bread rolls were also good. Petits fours were generous but misguided: mini muffins are just too heavy after a three-course meal. Have an aperitif (there's a short cocktail list) first, or a coffee in the bar later, to make the most of those amazing views. *Available for hire. Babies and children welcome: high chair. Booking essential, 2-4 wks in advance. Disabled: lift; toilet. Dress: smart casual.* **Map 12 Q6**. **For branch (Rhodes W1) see index**.

Clerkenwell & Farringdon

Medcalf

38-40 Exmouth Market, EC1R 4QE (7833 3533, www.medcalfbar.co.uk). Farringdon tube/rail or 19, 38, 341 bus. **Lunch served** noon-3pm Mon-Sat; noon-3.30pm Sun. **Dinner served** 6-10pm Mon-Thur, Sat; 6-10.30pm Fri. **Main courses** £12.50-£22. **Credit** MC, V.

Bold food with understated execution helps Medcalf to embody the best of British dining. The look reflects the 'reclaimed furniture' chic of Exmouth Market; the only hint of the building's former life as a butcher's is an eccentric wooden carving table and a vintage sign above the door. However, the kitchen's dedication to quality produce would make any butcher proud. Both oversized Great Garnett Farm pork chop, and an exuberant pan-fried whole plaice in anchovy butter, elicited gasps of excitement – and yet each dish highlighted just three simple ingredients. This is grown-up food with no pretensions, where great produce does all the work.

Gilbert Scott. See p51.

Service was precise but relaxed, perfectly pitched for the mature, creative types wandering in from Clerkenwell's cobbled streets. Waitresses made astute pairing recommendations, including a particularly cheeky cider whisky aperitif. The drinks list also contains a fantastic independent beer selection. Medcalf's design is as tasteful as the menu: a slightly ramshackle streetside terrace; refined dining inside, mostly for couples; and cool leather booths at the back, from where groups of friends spill on to the green courtyard. Even the toilets have a minimalist, farmhouse feel. The subtle combination of classy seasonal food with high-end retro style is a winner.
Babies and children welcome: high chairs. Booking advisable dinner. Disabled: toilet. Separate room for parties, seats 18. Tables outdoors (7, pavement; 5, garden). **Map 5 N4.**

★ St John `HOT 50`
26 St John Street, EC1M 4AY (3301 8069, www.stjohnrestaurant.com). Barbican tube or Farringdon tube/rail. **Lunch served** noon-3pm Mon-Fri; 1-3pm Sun. **Dinner served** 6-11pm Mon-Sat. **Main courses** £13.50-£23.80. **Credit** AmEx, DC, MC, V.
With dazzling white walls, painted floorboards (that could do with a new coat), and Shaker pegs around the walls, the dining room at Fergus Henderson's renowned restaurant is a bright, unfussy space. The airier bar (with baker's oven in one corner – loaves can be taken away) is great for rustic snacks, including a proper doorstep cheese and chutney sandwich, or the more sophisticated likes of the celebrated bone marrow with parsley salad. It tends to attract younger, less formal customers, but even the restaurant is not somewhere to dress up for; a lone, scruffy, elderly diner asked for offal, knowing his request would be satisfied with ox heart or chitterling on our summer visit, the menu kicked off with peas in their pod: delightful to eat, and a simple, nostalgic treat. A knubbly, liver-boosted terrine, and a robustly dressed salad of salsify, leeks and watercress with tiny capers, followed by gamey mains of rabbit and pigeon, were wonderfully subtle, seasonal dishes that spoke of a damp, green, agrarian country – not the Technicolor Mediterranean version of summer we've become used to. Courgettes cooked to a flavourful mush, and a carrot also slow-cooked to acquire the flavour of the roast rabbit it accompanied, may not suit all tastes. But desserts such as treacle tart or buttermilk pudding with raspberries (a welcome variation on panna cotta), or breathtakingly buttery eccles cakes are unmissable delights. Wines are almost all French and not overpriced. Knowledgeable, proficient and affable staff are another strength. World fame hasn't gone to St John's head; it has kept its integrity. A national treasure.
Babies and children welcome: high chairs. Booking advisable dinner and weekends. Disabled: toilet (bar). Separate room for parties, seats 18. **Map 5 O5.**
For branch (St John Hotel) see index.

Covent Garden

Rules
35 Maiden Lane, WC2E 7LB (7836 5314, www.rules.co.uk). Covent Garden tube. **Meals served** noon-11.30pm Mon-Sat; noon-10.30pm Sun. **Main courses** £18.95-£28.95. **Credit** AmEx, MC, V.

From Charles Dickens to Edward VII, Rules has played host to an impressive list of diners in the 200 or so years since it opened. These days, you're more likely to rub shoulders with business people, families and tourists than royalty, but that doesn't detract from the atmosphere. The dark dining room is kitted out with velvet booths and immaculately set tables. The walls are covered in yellowing pictures. The restaurant prides itself on pies, puddings and Rhone Valley wines. Game is also a major feature, much of which comes from Rules' own Lartington Estate in Scotland. Sadly, it wasn't in season on our visit, so a generous, potato-topped game pie was filled with farmed venison instead. Subtle pan-fried cod (served with a fried egg and mustard sauce) had been smoked on the premises. Bright green mussel and parsley soup was served at table from a silver tureen. The cooking is reasonable, but unlikely to knock your socks off. For a taste of the past or a family celebration, Rules makes a charming choice – the friendly waiters will even sing 'happy birthday' on your big day.
Babies and children welcome: high chairs. Booking advisable. Dress: smart casual. Separate rooms for parties, seating 8-18. **Map 18 E5.**

Gloucester Road

★ Launceston Place
1A Launceston Place, W8 5RL (7937 6912, www.danddlondon.com). Gloucester Road tube. **Lunch served** noon-2.30pm Tue-Sat; noon-3pm Sun. **Dinner served** 6-10.30pm Mon-Sat; 6.30-9.30pm Sun. **Set lunch** £22 3 courses; (Sun) £22 3 courses. **Set dinner** £45 3 courses, £60 tasting menu. **Credit** AmEx, MC, V.
We're not the only ones to proclaim chef Tristan Welch's cleverness, but his restaurant remains surprisingly off-radar for many food lovers, despite his TV appearances. Perhaps it's the location – tucked away in a residential quarter of Kensington; perhaps being part of the huge D&D London restaurant group dilutes the message. But

Launceston Place offers characterful cooking of great style and originality. British fare is served with such elegance; the ribbon tying together an appetiser of warm potato crisps was the only twee note in our modishly presented tasting menu. Although Welch is a fine-dining exponent at heart, you'll find ingredients such as oats (used as a bed for smoked partridge, whisky and heather) and duck hearts (served on toast with wild garlic and morels). There's invariably an adroit combination or two; witness our venison tartare with quails' eggs, English mustard and walnut dressing. Other elements are disarmingly simple, such as pickled herring served instead of olives; Sunday roast of Longhorn beef with horseradish; and the excellent bread. Wine buffs will adore exploring the acclaimed wine list – the chatty sommelier can help those with less knowledge, but rest assured it's worth spending a few pounds extra. Sumptuous decor includes soft banquettes and shimmery, 1930s-inspired fabrics to sit on, and walls decked with contemporary landscape paintings, witty wallpaper and bitter chocolate paint.
Available for hire. Babies and children welcome: high chairs. Booking advisable. Disabled: toilet. Separate room for parties, seats 10. **Map 7 C9.**

Holborn

Great Queen Street
32 Great Queen Street, WC2B 5AA (7242 0622). Covent Garden or Holborn tube. Bar **Open** 5-11.30pm Tue-Sat. *Restaurant* **Lunch served** noon-2.30pm Mon-Sat; noon-3pm Sun. **Dinner served** 6-10.30pm Mon-Sat. **Main courses** £10.80-£22. *Both* **Credit** MC, V.
In an area strangely devoid of many top-notch eating options, Great Queen Street shines out as a central London beacon of civilised dining. The long, low-lit space filled with rough-hewn tables is suited as much to drawn-out lunches as it is to post-work meals. Relaxed staff confidently attend to a varied

Great Queen Street

range of customers, from food-lovers drawn by the Anchor & Hope connection (the owners' gastropub in Waterloo), to tourists who found the place simply by wandering past. As at the sister venue, food is stripped-back British, with a strong emphasis on seasonal produce. Prosecco and strawberry fizz made a fine aperitif, despite its unhurried arrival, complemented by a rustic pair of flavourful starters: borlotti beans with peppers from Kent; and cockles, peas and bacon. Next came mains of fried breaded pig's cheek and broad bean purée, and hake with lentils and green sauce (aka salsa verde); the hake, in particular, was both hearty yet full of summery vibrancy, while the pig's cheek was like an old-school school lunch, but somehow in a good way. Wine available in a range of measures (from 125ml) is another plus, and desserts of chocolate tart and brioche summer pudding left us perfectly contented, with a resolution to return.
Babies and children admitted. Booking advisable. Disabled: toilet. Tables outdoors (4, pavement). Map 18 E3.

King's Cross

Gilbert Scott NEW
St Pancras Renaissance London Hotel, Euston Road, NW1 2AR (7278 3888, www.thegilbertscott.co.uk). King's Cross tube/rail. **Lunch served** noon-3pm, **dinner served** 5.30-11pm daily. **Main courses** £16-£25. **Set dinner** (5.30-6.30pm) £19 2 courses, £24 3 courses. **Credit** AmEx, MC, V.
A huge restaurant and destination bar within the refurbished Grade-I listed St Pancras hotel, this Marcus Wareing outfit, named after the building's architect, Sir George Gilbert Scott, offers modern interpretations of historic British dishes – the en-vogue solution for elite chefs confounded that any decent pub can produce a good roast dinner and sticky toffee pudding. The disconcertingly long menu namechecks the likes of Mrs Beeton and Queen Anne, plus (more reassuringly) quality ingredients such as Dorset snails, harbourne blue cheese, Colchester oysters and Morecambe Bay shrimps. Wareing has correctly identified that haslet (a traditional product of Lincolnshire pork butchers, here served with greengages) is worthy of a wider audience, but anyone reluctant to experiment will find safe ports such as smoked salmon and soda bread, fish and chips, and eton mess. A £2 cover charge brings a choice of excellent breads. We didn't like the reservation confirmation hoo-haa or the two-hour dining slot, but that was early days – perhaps the lukewarm reviews will have knocked off some of the arrogance. Frankly, it's the building that's the destination, and to enjoy the fabulous setting we'd rather take drinks in the Booking Office bar next door.
Babies and children admitted: high chairs. Booking advisable. Disabled: lift; toilet. Dress: smart casual. Separate room for parties, seats 12. Map 24 B2.

Mayfair

Corrigan's Mayfair
28 Upper Grosvenor Street, W1K 7EH (7499 9943, www.corrigansmayfair.com). Marble Arch tube. **Lunch served** noon-2.30pm Mon-Fri; noon-3.45pm Sun. **Dinner served** 6-10.30pm Mon-Sat; 6-9.15pm Sun. **Main courses** £21-£38. **Set lunch** (Mon-Fri) £27 3 courses incl carafe of wine. **Set meal** (Sun) £27 3 courses. **Cover** £2. **Credit** AmEx, MC, V.
Much though we've enjoyed midweek dinners at Corrigan's, there's no denying the lure of the Sunday lunch deal. If you can resist the extras, such as canapés at £4 a pop (and we couldn't – but the spicy cheese sables were worth it) or the glorious-looking aged rib of beef with yorkshire pudding (£10 supplement), then £27 buys three immaculate courses. Even the £2 a head cover charge is hard to begrudge when bread and petits fours (madeleines warm from the oven) are this good. Punchy starters of heritage beetroot with goat's cheese gnocchi, and shellfish ravioli with sauce americaine whetted the appetite for satisfying mains of English duck with savoy cabbage and girolles, and a large fish pie made with haddock, sea bass and john dory. English strawberry pudding, with buttermilk ice-cream and honeycomb, had a fabulous jelly at the bottom, as did pear and lime panna cotta with yoghurt sorbet. Staff are professional but not without humour. The well-stocked wine list is unstuffy, with an emphasis on biodynamic and organic wines. All this occurs in a calm, pleasant room given interest by the low-key hunting, shooting and fishing motifs: we loved the beautiful feathered lampshades and a handsome silver coffee pot topped by a perky game bird.
Babies and children welcome: high chairs. Booking advisable. Disabled: toilet. Separate rooms for parties, seating 4-30. Map 9 G7.

Dorchester Grill Room
The Dorchester, 53 Park Lane, W1K 1QA (7629 8888, www.thedorchester.com). Hyde Park Corner tube. **Breakfast served** 7-10.30am Mon-Fri; 8-11am Sat, Sun. **Lunch served** noon-2.30pm Mon-Fri; 12.30-3pm Sat; 12.30-3.30pm Sun. **Dinner served** 6.30-10.30pm Mon-Fri; 6.30-11pm Sat; 7-10.30pm Sun. **Main courses** £19-£46. **Set lunch** (Mon-Sat) £23 2 courses, £27 3 courses. **Set dinner** (6.30-7.30pm) £29 2 courses, £33 3 courses. **Set meal** £70 tasting menu (£90 incl wine). **Credit** AmEx, DC, MC, V.
You can't help but be cheered by the gloriously extrovert decor of the Grill Room – all tartans, red high-backed settles, and murals of capering clan chieftains. Such furnishings dispel any notions of posh hotel stuffiness, and also unite a disparate clientele of wealthy travellers, soft-business diners, ladies who lunch, and people enjoying an internet deal. The rise of British food has allowed the Grill to meet the demand for conservative hotel classics – game, decent roasts, simply cooked fish – within a fashionable context. Chef Brian Hughson slides top-drawer ingredients such as smoked salmon and mackerel, scallops, grouse, wood pigeon, veal sweetbread and pig's head (and that's just the starters) on to the plate with well-judged accompaniments (the sweetbreads, for example, come with a shellfish cream). Cooking and presentation are detailed, precise and beautifully judged (a little over-foaming aside). We don't know of anywhere else that would dare charge £19.50 for a main course of anna potatoes with summer vegetables – though it was both good-looking (with its microdot purées) and exquisite-tasting (each component custom-cooked). The Angus beef, carved at table, was a full-flavoured marbled joint. A meal here is a boat-pushing prospect, with all the fine-dining accessories you'd expect, including a powerhouse wine list – with a helpful cut-down 'sommelier's choice' for people not wanting to browse the world's great cellars.
Babies and children welcome (Sat, Sun): high chairs. Booking advisable; essential weekends. Disabled: toilet. Dress: smart casual. Map 9 G7.

Hix at the Albemarle
Brown's Hotel, 33-34 Albemarle Street, W1S 4BP (7493 6020, www.thealbemarlerestaurant. com). Green Park tube. **Lunch served** noon-3pm Mon-Sat; 12.30-4pm Sun. **Dinner served** 5.30-11pm Mon-Sat; 7-10.30pm Sun. **Main courses** £14.50-£32.50. **Set lunch** (Sun) £31.50 2 courses, £37.50 3 courses. **Set meal** £27.50 2 courses, £32.50 3 courses. **Credit** AmEx, DC, MC, V.

Hix

Mark Hix is director of food at this stylish hotel dining room (Marcus Verberne is executive chef), and his influence can be seen in the modern British menu and also in the modern British art. The wood-panelled room is a relaxing and attractive place in which to eat, and staff are attentive (quick to proffer spare reading glasses, for example) without being obsequious. Compared to previous meals here, a midweek dinner lacked a certain something: deep-fried Cornish lamb's sweetbreads with whipped peas, smoked bacon and a poached Burford Brown egg was excellent, but mixed beets with ragstone goat's cheese and wild herbs, although pretty, lacked oomph; heritage tomato and lovage salad was similarly timid. Mains had more character: fish and chips brought a lightly battered chunk of coley, plus superb chips and light pea purée; a sizeable chargrilled Halesworth pork chop with marrow, capers and anchovies also pleased. Only Newlyn monkfish curry disappointed – the bland fish not helped by a one-dimensional curry. To finish: ginger parkin was more sticky toffee pud than a parkin, but nonetheless good; lemon jelly with lemon curd sorbet was a big hit; gooseberry fool with shortbread was average. Better than all of them were the chocolate truffle petits fours. But even with this slightly uneven experience, we still had a great evening in one of London's more enjoyable hotel restaurants.
Babies and children welcome: children's menu; crayons; high chairs. Booking advisable. Disabled: toilet (hotel). Separate rooms for parties, seating 2-70. Vegetarian menu.
Map 9 J7.

St James's

Inn The Park
St James's Park, SW1A 2BJ (7451 9999, www.innthepark.com). St James's Park tube.
Breakfast served 8-11am Mon-Fri; 9-11am Sat, Sun. **Lunch served** noon-3pm Mon-Fri; noon-4pm Sat, Sun. **Tea served** 3-5pm Mon-Fri; 4-5pm Sat, Sun. **Dinner served** 6-8.30pm daily. **Main courses** £10.50-£18.50. **Credit** MC, V.
On a rare balmy English summer evening, with its floor-to-ceiling windows rolled back, Inn The Park has one of the most enviable positions in town – in the heart of St James's Park. The restaurant's airy contemporary interior is sympathetic to the outside space, right down to the bumblebee motif on the glasses. Attention to detail was reflected in a menu that offered seasonality in spades, from pea and lovage salad with honey and own-made ricotta, to globe artichoke with cobnut vinaigrette. Sadly, the menu promised more than it delivered, the lobster, squid and crayfish salad being a rather mean smattering of seafood amid an overgrown plate of frisée, making the £16.50 price tag questionable. Shetland smoked salmon and haddock fish cakes too seemed like a starter portion. That left room for the cheeseboard, which reads as a showcase of British cheeses: blue horizon, keltic gold and an intriguing Cornish miss muffet. A mistake in the kitchen meant we received two cheeses rather than three, but this was soon rectified along with a requested extra portion of the top-notch wheaten bread, which only then managed to sate our grumbling stomachs. Could, and should, do better.
Babies and children welcome: children's menu; high chairs. Booking advisable. Disabled: toilet. Tables outdoors (23, terrace). Takeaway service.
Map 10 K8.

Wiltons

55 Jermyn Street, SW1Y 6LX (7629 9955, www.wiltons.co.uk). Green Park or Piccadilly Circus tube. **Lunch served** noon-2.30pm, **dinner served** 5.30-10.30pm Mon-Fri. **Main courses** £22-£60. **Set lunch** £45 2 courses. **Set dinner** (5.30-6.30pm) £35 2 courses, £45 3 courses; (5.30-10.30pm) £80 tasting menu (£150 incl wine). **Credit** AmEx, DC, MC, V.

Five minutes from Piccadilly, Wiltons offers a retreat from the modern world – along with plush furnishings, formally dressed waiters (and patrons) and a handful of private rooms. This bastion of a bygone era has been serving traditional British food since 1742 (when it opened as a shellfish stand on Haymarket). Popular choices include potted shrimps, lunchtime carvery meats, British cheeses, and game when in season. No meal here is cheap, but if you're looking to save a few pennies, try the pre-theatre menu (£35 for two courses, £45 for three); pay an extra fiver for a glass of French wine (Sancerre, Bourgogne pinot noir and the like). A decent-sized pork chop was tender and juicy within its crunchy breadcrumb coating. Sauced at the table from a silver gravy boat, it was complemented by buttery caramelised apples, creamy mash and perfectly al dente runner beans. Sherry trifle, piped with sweet, dense vanilla cream, had just the right amount of booze as well as plump strawberries, though the sponge was a little too soggy. A selection of rich chocolate truffles rounded off the meal perfectly; one of them was even emblazoned with Wiltons' logo, a champagne-swilling lobster.
Babies and children welcome: high chairs. Booking advisable. Disabled: lift; toilet. Dress: smart; jacket required. Separate room for parties, seats 20. **Map 17 B5**.

Soho

Dean Street Townhouse

69-71 Dean Street, W1D 4QJ (7434 1775, www.deanstreettownhouse.com). Piccadilly Circus or Tottenham Court Road tube. **Breakfast served** 7-11.30am, **tea served** 3-5pm daily. **Meals served** 11.30am-11.30pm Mon-Sat; 11.30am-10.30pm Sun. **Main courses** £15-£24. **Set dinner** (5-7.30pm) £17 2 courses, £21 3 courses. **Credit** AmEx, MC, V.

Opened to rave reviews in 2010, this all-day hotel restaurant in magnificent Georgian buildings has effortlessly established itself as one of the places to drink, eat and be in Soho. Many customers (a starry, but not flashy throng) seem to be regulars – they are greeted as such by friendly, professional staff. A long wooden bar sets the tone: nuts replenished, icy tap water in a jug, any drink from draught beer to a soho mule with a refreshing gingery kick. Country house wallpaper, which on closer inspection has a rather rude motif, sums it up – the best of traditional, but also contemporary, classy, clever. The outstanding art collection of mostly black and white pictures features work by, among others, Tracey Emin, Mat Collishaw and Peter Blake. The Townhouse is properly British too, with some provocatively retro dishes – it takes chutzpah to put mince and potatoes on a menu, and skill to reinvent a resistible relic as a plate of appetisingly browned, savoury, juicy beef. Summer salad was a riot of garden produce: perfectly seasoned and subtly dressed baby carrots, lightly cooked, thin slices of radish, watercress, beetroot, peas and spring onions. More heart-threatening

classics include soft, fluffy smoked haddock soufflé with buttery sauce; fish (juicy inside crisp batter) with chips and marrowfat peas; a glorious trifle of plums and sherry-soaked sponge. But with everything from roast chicken with sage and onion stuffing, to cod with braised lettuce and brown shrimps, this is somewhere you can imagine becoming a habit. If only such knowing simplicity were a little less expensive.
Babies and children welcome: high chairs; nappy-changing facilities. Booking essential. Disabled: toilet. Separate room for parties, seats 12. Tables outdoors (7, terrace). **Map 17 B3**.

★ Hix `HOT 50`

66-70 Brewer Street, W1F 9UP (7292 3518, www.hixsoho.co.uk). Piccadilly Circus tube. **Meals served** noon-midnight daily. **Main courses** £14.75-£35.50. **Set meal** (4.30-6.30pm, 10.30-11.30pm Mon-Sat; noon-10.30pm Sun) £17.50 2 courses, £22.50 3 courses. **Credit** AmEx, DC, MC, V.

When Mark Hix's second London restaurant opened in late 2009, he had the city's gourmets eating out of his hand. As a former chef-director of Caprice Holdings, writer for the *Independent* and general man about town, his social status was always going to help, but what impresses is that Hix Soho remains one of the most convivial spots in town whether you're A-list or no-list. The place seems to sum up everything that's great about dining in London's most libertine precinct: permanently buzzing, clubby, informal, arty. It's the sort of venue where you could sit with friends, eat some great food and get merrily pissed without feeling out of place. Hix's signature cooking, which celebrates seasonal British produce in an unshowy yet precise fashion, is generally spot-on. Starters might include Herefordshire snail and mushroom tart, or chilled cucumber soup with scallop and samphire; a real treat is the roast free-range chicken with garlic sauce to share. Meat and fish certainly dominate the menu. The basement Mark's Bar is worthy of mention too. Dimly lit, lively and a former contender for Time Out's Best Bar award, it features historical British cocktails and Hix's own-brand ales from Dorset.

Available for hire. Babies and children welcome: high chairs; nappy-changing facilities. Booking advisable. Disabled: toilet. Separate room for parties, seats 10. **Map 17 A4**.
For branches see index.

Quo Vadis

26-29 Dean Street, W1D 3LL (7437 9585, www.quovadissoho.co.uk). Leicester Square, Piccadilly Circus or Tottenham Court Road tube. **Lunch served** noon-2.30pm, **dinner served** 5.30-10.30pm Mon-Sat. **Main courses** £17-£24. **Set meal** (noon-2.30pm, 5.30-6.30pm) £17.50 2 courses, £19.50 3 courses. **Cover** £2. **Credit** AmEx, MC, V.

A stalwart of the Soho scene (with a long history as an Italian restaurant), Quo Vadis is now a showcase for high-class contemporary British cooking and restauration. Stained-glass windows cast a pretty light into the train carriage-like row of rooms, divided by partitions and vast vases, with foxed mirrors and plump, butterscotch-leather banquettes. It's as smooth, rich and reassuring as salted caramel, of course, as the on-trend flavour. The pleasingly seasonal menu ranges from scotch egg to less yeoman-like dishes based on well-sourced prime ingredients – such as beef, hung for a lengthy 56 days. These steaks (not extortionately priced) are served with notable triple-cooked chips. Although the kitchen knows how to keep expense-account diners happy, it's brave enough to offer calf's brains, and to use humble, undervalued runner beans in a starter salad with (skinned) tomatoes and teeny-weeny diced cucumber and peas; shame the dressing was a little vinegary. Another starter – of two large, perfectly grilled sardines – was exemplary, and resembled a Braque still-life with its muslin-wrapped half-lemon. Crisp, golden, salty grilled skin was also a feature of both gurnard (a sustainable species), and juicy duck with perfectly caramelised carrots and a very sweet jus. The cauliflower purée with the fish was rather too creamy. Prices aren't unreasonable for the finesse of the cooking, though tablecloths on the pub-like wooden tables would be more apt. The good wine list sweeps across Europe's refreshing best. Upstairs, you'll find a grand bar, a members' club and private dining.

Savoy Grill. *See p55.*

Babies and children admitted. Booking advisable. Separate rooms for parties, seating 12 and 24. Tables outdoors (6, terrace). **Map 17 B3.**

Strand

Savoy Grill

100 Strand, WC2R 0EW (7592 1600, www.gordonramsay.com). Embankment tube or Charing Cross tube/rail. **Lunch served** noon-3pm, **dinner served** 5.30-10.45pm daily. **Main courses** £24-£38. **Credit** AmEx, DC, MC, V.
The glamour of the Savoy Grill has only been enhanced by its recent three-year renovation. A deep springy carpet cushions the noise, while grand pillars and heavy, expensive silverware add to the sense of opulence. One of the better restaurants from the troubled Gordon Ramsay Holdings stable, the menu here nods to tradition, with seafood, grills and imaginative British dishes. A starter of potted salt beef was slow-cooked and tender, the accompanying buckwheat crispbreads good for scooping up the buttery, salty strands of meat. A 'mutton pie' was a clever play on shepherd's pie, with a potato garnish piped on top of a neat cylinder of dark, intensely flavoured, slow-cooked meat. Not everything went as smoothly as you'd hope: eggs en cocotte were overcooked, and our waitress inexplicably disappeared for around 25 minutes, leaving us with no wines to go with our main courses. But we forgave these shortcomings with the arrival of a baked alaska, with Grand Marnier flambéed at the table and a pretty, warm meringue, and an arctic centre of mandarin sorbet. The Savoy Grill can be expensive – particularly if you're fond of wine – but it's not overpriced. Tables can be hard to come by, so book well ahead.
Available for hire. Babies and children welcome: high chairs; nappy-changing facilities. Booking essential. Disabled: toilet. Dress: smart casual. Separate room for parties, seats 40. **Map 18 E5.**

Simpson's-in-the-Strand

100 Strand, WC2R 0EW (7836 9112, www.simpsonsinthestrand.co.uk). Embankment tube or Charing Cross tube/rail. **Breakfast served** 7.15-10.30am Mon-Fri. **Lunch served** 12.15-2.45pm Mon-Sat; 12.15-3pm Sun. **Dinner served** 5.45-10.45pm Mon-Sat; (Grand Divan) 6-9pm Sun. **Main courses** £16-£33.50. **Set dinner** (5.45-7pm) £25.75 2 courses, £31 3 courses. **Credit** AmEx, DC, MC, V.
What could be more British than roast beef and yorkshire pudding? Order Simpson's signature dish and you'll be treated to a dedicated carver at your table, resplendent in chef's whites and serving 28-day-aged Scottish rib from a trolley with a dome the size of St Paul's Cathedral. If this feels like a throwback to another era, you won't be surprised to hear Simpson's hasn't changed its trolley-service fare since it switched from being a gentleman's chess club to an all-British restaurant in the mid 1800s. We lapped up the tradition along with the various sauces that were served by a succession of waiters brandishing silver tureens. Lobster sauce over sea trout and crayfish tails, red wine sauce over stuffed loin of pork and creamed potatoes and, finally, madagascan vanilla custard poured over a distinctly British steamed treacle sponge. The imposing wood-panelled dining room, tailcoat-attired staff and resident pianist all add to the sense of Britain's history. With strong literary links that

include mentions in EM Forster's *Howards End*, the Sherlock Holmes stories, and custom from Charles Dickens and George Bernard Shaw, Simpson's-in-the-Strand is firmly written into the fabric of London's restaurant scene. Long may it continue.
Babies and children welcome: high chairs. Booking advisable. Disabled: toilet. Dress: smart; no trainers, T-shirts or sportswear. Separate rooms for parties, seating 25 and 150. **Map 18 E5.**

Trafalgar Square

National Dining Rooms

Sainsbury Wing, National Gallery, WC2N 5DN (7747 2525, www.thenationaldiningrooms.co.uk). Charing Cross tube/rail.
Bakery **Meals served** 10am-5.30pm Mon-Thur, Sat, Sun; 10am-8.30pm Fri. **Main courses** £8-£12.
Restaurant **Lunch served** noon-3.15pm daily. **Dinner served** 5-7pm Fri. **Main courses** £18. **Set meal** £24 2 courses, £27 3 courses.
Both **Credit** AmEx, MC, V.
Here you'll find art-lovers and fans of the Peyton & Byrne bakeries. Both sets of enthusiasts are glad that the adjoining restaurant is committed to using the best seasonal British produce, which the kitchen handles with confidence. The lofty space is part-gentlemen's club (green leather chairs, studded banquettes), part-gallery (a huge Paula Rego mural dominates). Service on our visit was friendly, if a little too relaxed (staff assumed we wanted a 'bakery' rather than restaurant lunch, and we had a long wait before plates were cleared), but there was no denying the quality of the food. Baby courgettes in a fairy-light tempura batter, with their flowers stuffed with creamy blue cheese, made a great starter. Mains were just as impressive: a substantial Cornish plaice was served with fresh samphire and peas; and toothsome Bickfield beef came with heritage tomatoes, broccoli and courgettes in a moreish meaty gravy. Traditionalists love the desserts of fruit crumble, treacle tart and strawberry parfait, and the drinks list offers several wines by the glass. On one of the hottest days of summer, the only conceivable drink was a deliciously cool and delicately flowery glass of Provençal rosé.
Babies and children welcome: children's menu; high chairs. Booking advisable. Disabled: toilet. **Map 17 C5.**

Victoria

Goring Hotel

Beeston Place, Grosvenor Gardens, SW1W 0JW (7396 9000, www.goringhotel.co.uk). Victoria tube/rail. **Breakfast served** 7-10am Mon-Fri; 7-10.30am Sat; 7.30-10.30am Sun. **Lunch served** 12.30-2.30pm Mon-Fri, Sun. **Dinner served** 6-10pm daily. **Set lunch** (Mon-Fri) £35 3 courses; (Sun) £40 3 courses. **Set dinner** (6-6.30pm) £32 2 courses; £48.50 3 courses. **Credit** AmEx, DC, MC, V.
London's only family-run five-star hotel combines the old-style traditions of beef wellington, wooden panelling and a statue of the Queen Mum, with modern touches such as the 'not quite a trifle', striking Swarovski chandeliers and, on our visit, a pop-up beach bar in the garden. The Goring hit the headlines in 2011 when it hosted the Middleton family before the royal wedding; you can enjoy pre-dinner cocktails in the drawing room where Kate

had 'that dress' sewn on to her, or stand at the buzzing bar before slipping into the serene dining room. Astute attention to detail characterises the place as grandiose yet funky: strips of beetroot jelly in one starter mimicked the coloured stripes running down the waiter's waistcoat, for example, and imperial columns jut up to the ceiling to match miniature crystal obelisks on each table. Mushroom and truffle flavours permeated a main of roast Suffolk chicken. First-rate mashed potato, whipped into a satisfyingly sticky purée, had a faint aroma of leeks and butter. Roasted skate wing with black butter and miniature capers was a fine rendition too. We'd also recommend succumbing to the British cheese trolley.
Babies and children welcome: high chairs. Booking essential. Disabled: toilet (hotel). Dress: smart casual. Separate rooms for parties, seating 6-40. Tables outdoors (9, terrace). **Map 15 H9.**

Westminster

Northall **NEW**

Corinthia Hotel London, 10 Northumberland Avenue, WC2N 5AE (7930 8181, www.the northall.co.uk). Embankment tube. **Breakfast served** 6-10.30am, **lunch served** noon-3pm, **tea served** 5.30-7pm, **dinner served** 5.30-11pm daily. **Main courses** £24-£39. **Set meal** £18.50 2 courses, £22.50 3 courses. **Credit** AmEx, MC, V.
Like the other dining rooms in this luxury hotel, Northall is a showstopper: grand and luxuriously appointed with select modern flourishes, it overlooks Embankment station through huge curved glass windows. Seafood and shellfish dominate a menu that takes provenance porn to new depths, with every dish listing a producer's name. Our delicious salad of ox tongue (from Lake District Farm) and warm hen's egg came with diced pickle and soft herbs, while scallops with fermented lemon dressing were equally impressive: the molluscs springy, the dressing tingly. Mains hit the same heights. A Cumbrian beef burger was one of the best we've had in London, tasting of not much more than first-class steak – and all the better for it. Perfectly roasted fillet of pollack was scattered with deep-fried pieces of squid and apostrophised with smears of sticky ink sauce – the only let-down was the soggy 'triple-cooked chips'. But desserts picked things up again: a vivid apple chiboust (a sort of thick custard) was presented on a spicy gingerbread base and sharpened by apple sorbet. Service was slick, if a little restrained, but the biggest detractor is the bill, which given the setting, is unsurprisingly steep. The 'daily market menu', at £22.50 for three courses, is a more affordable, if less exciting, option.
Babies and children welcome: high chairs. Booking advisable. Disabled: toilet. **Map 10 L8.**

West

Bayswater

Hereford Road

3 Hereford Road, W2 4AB (7727 1144, www.herefordroad.org). Bayswater tube. **Lunch served** noon-3pm Mon-Fri; noon-3.30pm Sat; noon-4pm Sun. **Dinner served** 6-10.30pm Mon-Sat; 6-10pm Sun. **Main courses** £9.50-£14.50. **Set lunch** (Mon-Fri) £13 2 courses, £15.50 3 courses. **Credit** AmEx, MC, V.

BRITISH

Tom Pemberton (who was previously head chef at St John Bread & Wine) took over this former butcher's shop in 2007 and has made it into a destination restaurant focusing on modern British cooking. Inside, the dining room can feel a little on the austere side, though the tables by the bar are quite romantic, and noise levels can be deafening when the rear room fills up. But Hereford Road serves some of the best British food around, cooked with intelligence, care and a degree of edginess. Pemberton dares to serve parts of animals that many restaurants choose to chuck away. So soft, squidgy calf's brain is pan-fried with black butter, and the faggots should not be missed. The menu changes daily; on our latest visit, we were delighted with a roast suckling pig served with fresh watercress, which added a peppery hint, and accompanied by apple sauce. Desserts may appear conventional, but they go beyond the home kitchen. We enjoyed every mouthful of a buttermilk pudding counterbalanced by the tartness of gooseberries. To drink, the Old World wine list has ample choice by the glass. Food prices continue to be keen, especially at lunchtimes, and service is willing and helpful.

Babies and children welcome: high chairs. Booking advisable. Disabled: toilet. Tables outdoors (3, pavement). **Map 7 B6.**

South West
Parsons Green

Manson
676 Fulham Road, SW6 5SA (7384 9559, www.mansonrestaurant.co.uk). Parsons Green tube. **Lunch served** noon-3pm Mon-Fri. **Brunch served** noon-4pm Sat. **Dinner served** 6-10.30pm Mon-Sat. **Meals served** noon-6pm Sun. **Main courses** £10-£20. **Set meal** (noon-3pm, 6-7pm Mon-Fri) £13.50 2 courses, £17.50 3 courses. **Credit** AmEx, MC, V.

Following the arrival of head chef Alan Stewart (ex-Chez Bruce and Launceston Place) in spring 2011, Manson has changed its menu from Modern European to British. The buzzwords 'seasonal' and 'local' actually mean something here, with summer berries, Kentish tomatoes, samphire and sea aster all making an appearance on our July visit, and the restaurant baking (very tasty) bread twice-daily, churning butter and doing its own butchering. Produce comes from around the British Isles, as well as SW6 allotments. Simple but judicious flavour combinations are the result. A roundel of Devon Brown crabmeat topped with pickled cucumber, in a gazpacho-like chilled soup, made a fresh, light starter. Scottish girolles, mini potato dumplings and a rich but delicate smoked butter sauce matched well with wild black bream (crispy skin, moist flesh); top marks too for perfectly cooked Herdwick lamb with aubergine and courgettes. A dessert of blackberries, frozen yoghurt and lemon curd was too plain, however. The room has a companionable, rustic feel, thanks to chunky wooden tables, industrial lamps and dark brown leather seating (including some cosy window booths). Young women in butcher's aprons provided cheery, helpful service. There's a good-value set lunch, plus Saturday brunch and Sunday roasts.

Babies and children admitted. Booking advisable. Tables outdoors (4, pavement).

Wandsworth

Steam
55-57 East Hill, SW18 2QE (8704 4680, www.steamwinebar.com). Clapham Junction or Wandsworth Town rail or bus 37, 87, 170, 337. **Lunch served** 11am-3.30pm Sat; 11am-4pm Sun. **Dinner served** 6-10.30pm Tue-Sat. **Main courses** £10-£18.50. **Set dinner** £15 2 courses, £18.50 3 courses. **Credit** AmEx, MC, V.

Steam is a thriving local wine bar with a decent restaurant. The wine list is of moderate length and

Northall. See p55.

ambition (by-the-glass drinkers would appreciate whites that go beyond pinot grigio, chardonnay and sauvignon blanc, for example). The dark-hued dining area at the back features a short, quite conservative menu, heavy on steak and chips – there were no fewer than three varieties on our visit – along with a short list of pasta and fish dishes. A starter of pan-fried scallops with romano peppers, pak choi and fennel salad featured bivalves that were properly seared outside and tender within, thanks to spot-on timing. A generously proportioned main course of fresh egg linguine with lobster, tomato and chilli overdid it on the chilli, overwhelming the delicate seafood. Desserts are old-fashioned faves such as sticky toffee pudding (ours was served scaldingly hot), cheesecakes and the like. The set-price dinner menu is decent value (£15 for two courses, £18.50 for three) and the Sunday lunch menu features more than simple roasts. One to bear in mind if you're in the neighbourhood.
Available for hire. Babies and children welcome: children's menu; high chairs; nappy-changing facilities. Disabled: toilet. Separate room for parties, seats 20. Tables outdoors (2, pavement).

Old Brewery

South East
East Dulwich

Franklins
157 Lordship Lane, SE22 8HX (8299 9598, www.franklinsrestaurant.com). East Dulwich rail.
Meals served 11am-10.30pm Mon-Fri; 10am-10.30pm Sat; noon-10pm Sun. **Main courses** £11-£18. **Set lunch** (noon-5pm Mon-Fri Jan-Nov) £13.95 2 courses, £16.95 3 courses.
Credit MC, V.
Offering largely UK-sourced produce, much from nearby Kent, Franklins gets full marks for provenance. But the feel-good factor doesn't end there, as the restaurant offers a small but well-put-together, seasonal menu with plenty of appeal for lovers of Modern European food. On this occasion, crisp and delicate salt beef fritters were paired with a zingy radish and caper salad. To follow, chicken, bacon and leek pie, with short, crumbly pastry, showed a remarkably light touch. Even raspberry ripple ice-cream made a point of showcasing its seasonality, bursting with plump whole fruit. Staff went out of their way to make our visit enjoyable. There are three eating areas: a table near the bar offers a laid-back bistro feel; the restaurant at the rear is great for leisurely dining and allows you to peer into the kitchen; for private parties or a cosy tête-à-tête, ask for a table downstairs. Decor is modern: simple dark wood floor and furnishings, huge restored mirrors and exposed brick walls hung with colourful art (for sale). Franklins is popular with locals as somewhere to go for a smart night out, a relaxed Saturday brunch, or simply good food in stylish surroundings.
Available for hire. Babies and children welcome: high chairs; nappy-changing facilities. Booking advisable. Disabled: toilet. Separate room for parties, seats 34. Tables outdoors (4, pavement).
Map 23 C4.

Greenwich

Old Brewery
Pepys Building, Old Royal Naval College, SE10 9LW (3327 1280, www.oldbrewerygreenwich. com). Cutty Sark DLR.

Café **Meals served** 10am-5pm daily.
Main courses £6-£16.50.
Bar **Open** 11am-11pm daily. **Lunch served** noon-5pm, **dinner served** 6-10.30pm daily.
Main courses £6-£16.50.
Restaurant **Dinner served** 6-10.30pm daily. **Main courses** £10.50-£17.50.
All **Credit** MC, V.
Tucked away in a corner of the magnificent Old Royal Naval College, this cavernous restaurant-cum-café occupies a former 18th-century brewhouse. It's probably best to avoid the packed-out, cosy bar on sunny afternoons; instead, sup from the choice of more than 50 ales (including those brewed by owners Meantime) in the popular walled courtyard. Impressive floor-to-ceiling copper brewing tuns stand at one end of the restaurant but even these are overshadowed by the centrepiece: an undulating wave of suspended Meantime beer bottles. A painted potted history of

British brewing adorns the maroon walls. Despite low lighting and comfortable booths, the echoing, high-ceilinged room feels intimate only when all tables are full. The menu, which is heavy on meat and fish, changes seasonally. A generous portion of whitebait was perfectly spiced and well paired with the recommended Meantime Helles lager, but limp chips let down a fresh, flavoursome battered haddock. Thai basil transformed a traditional eton mess, yet lukewarm poached apricots were one-dimensional and came with a bitter brandy-snap basket: all in all, a meal of highs and lows. Service was welcoming, but the quality of both food and service has veered from jaw-droppingly good to yawningly average on previous visits. This is a good local restaurant, nonetheless.
Babies and children welcome: high chairs; nappy-changing facilities. Booking advisable. Disabled: toilet. Tables outdoors (20, garden). Takeaway service.

Rivington Grill

178 Greenwich High Road, SE10 8NN (8293 9270, www.rivingtongrill.co.uk). Greenwich rail/DLR. **Breakfast served** 10am-noon, **lunch served** noon-5pm Thur-Sun. **Dinner served** 5-11pm Tue-Sat; 5-10pm Sun. **Main courses** £11.50-£32.50. **Set lunch** (Sun) £19.75 3 courses. **Credit** AmEx, MC, V.

Sister to the edgier Shoreditch original, this Greenwich branch of Rivington Grill has an appropriately maritime feel, with brass railings and mirror-lined mezzanine. Both restaurants carry a meat- and fish-focused menu, though with far more vegetarian choices here. Even at sunset on a summer's evening, both the main dining room and the mezzanine were gloomy and devoid of atmosphere, but our eyes lit up on perusing the menu. The likes of 'smoked mackerel, samphire and cucumber pickle, potato salad' sounded simple and delicious. There's a good range of wines by the glass too, but that's where our fun ended. Listless service and expensive, below-average food made us feel as gloomy as the interior. After wrestling the tough outer skin from the bone-in smoked mackerel, the ice-cold fish turned out to be flavourful, even though overshadowed by a pleasingly salty pickle. To follow, the buttery, crumbly pastry of a half-filled pie was better than the few mouthfuls of chicken, ham and leek it contained, and a side salad of heirloom tomatoes and lovage outshone a tough, overcooked lamb chop. A £7.75 cheese plate with three tiny nuggets of fridge-cold cheese compounded our misery. We left disappointed, and £60 a head poorer.

Available for hire. Babies and children welcome: high chairs; nappy-changing facilities. Booking advisable. Disabled: toilet. Separate room for parties, seats 40. Tables outdoors (8, terrace). **For branch (Rivington Grill) see index.**

London Bridge & Borough

Roast

The Floral Hall, Borough Market, Stoney Street, SE1 1TL (7940 1300, www.roast-restaurant.com). London Bridge tube/rail. **Breakfast served** 7-11am Mon-Fri; 8-11.30am Sat. **Lunch served** noon-2.45pm Mon, Tue; noon-3.45pm Wed-Sat; 11.30am-3pm Sun. **Dinner served** 5.30-11pm Mon-Fri; 6-11pm Sat; 4-9.45pm Sun. **Main courses** £16.50-£35. **Set meal** (Sun) £28 2 courses, £32 3 courses. **Credit** AmEx, MC, V.

If the name 'roast' conjures up images of boring, old-fashioned British food, think again. Roast may serve British food, but boring it ain't. Set smack in the middle of Borough Market (with superb views of market stalls from the upstairs dining room), the restaurant is ideally sited to pick the best of British bread, cheese, fish, fowl – and meat, for which the kitchen is renowned. It's a buzzing place, from breakfast (with hangover-healing platefuls of eggs benedict or Orkney kippers) all the way until dinner. There's a lively bar too. The same, bracingly pricey but extensive carte is served at lunch and dinner; set-price menus aren't much of a bargain either. Portions, though, are hearty. Sautéed duck livers served with girolles and crisp shards of bacon were rather overcooked, but the earthy flavours were spot-on. Meat ranges from handsome beef rib roasts to rare-breed suckling pig, but non-carnivores can eat well too. Simply grilled Cornish pilchards, enjoyed with a cool glass of Chapel Down rosé, were a proper treat. We also relished the buttermilk panna cotta with strawberries and mint: a chic updated classic. Tourists eager to try real British food should beat a path here, with Londoners in tow.

Available for hire. Babies and children welcome: children's menu; high chairs. Booking advisable. Disabled: lift; toilet. Dress: smart casual. **Map 11 P8**.

East

Docklands

Boisdale Canary Wharf

Cabot Place, E14 4QT (7715 5818, www. boisdale-cw.co.uk). Canary Wharf tube/DLR. **Lunch served** noon-2.30pm Mon-Fri. **Dinner served** 6-11pm Mon-Sat. **Main courses** £14.50-£47.50. **Set lunch** £22.50 2 courses. **Set meal** £19.75 2 courses. **Credit** AmEx, MC, V.

Much like its siblings in Bishopsgate and Belgravia, this latest branch of Boisdale combines Caledonia and Americana, the tartan and hunting trophies cheek by jowl with portraits of iconic US musicians (a nod to the regular blues nights). The food is only sort-of Scottish – it makes use of good Scottish ingredients, which isn't the same thing. The steak is Aberdeenshire beef, plus there's Loch Duart smoked salmon, haggis and West Coast langoustines. A two-course menu offers decent value at £19.75, but everything else is expensive.

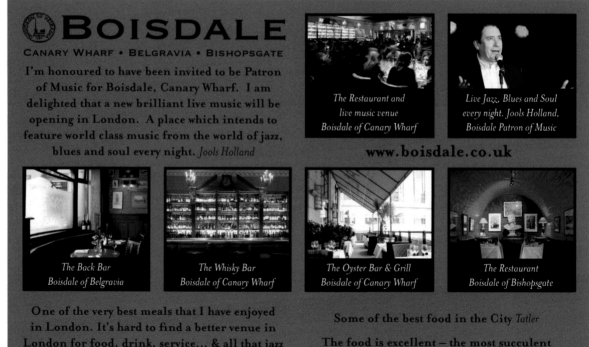

Our scallop starter (£16.75) was overpowered by the accompanying fried shallots, while prawn cocktail had too much shredded onion in the marie rose sauce. Mains were better: roast chicken and rumbledethumps (a traditional Scottish dish of mashed potato, onion and cabbage) was reliable, but nothing that would set the heather on fire. What makes Boisdale worth a visit is the remarkable whisky menu. Just about every expression from every Scottish distillery, silent and active, in the last century seems to be represented here. (Strangely, there are no Scottish tasters at all.) Well-off Wharfers, who won't be deterred by the prices, will find Boisdale a lively place to entertain. The rest of us are better off in the bar.

Available for hire. Babies and children admitted. Booking advisable Wed-Sat. Disabled: lift; toilet. Dress: smart casual; no shorts. Separate rooms for parties, seating 12-40. Tables outdoors (15, terrace). **Map 24 B2.**
For branches see index.

Shoreditch

Albion
2-4 Boundary Street, E2 7DD (7729 1051, www.albioncaff.co.uk). Shoreditch High Street rail. **Meals served** 8am-11pm daily. **Main courses** £8-£12. **Credit** AmEx, MC, V.
To get a table in Terence Conran's trendy British café in Shoreditch, Banksy country, enter through the gift shop. Well, the deli, which sells fine British produce, as well as the breads, pastries and cakes – the victoria sandwich a WI-worthy triumph – baked for the café. The shop is a good showcase of what the UK does best, as is the café menu, with its pleasing selection of breakfast, gentlemen's and country club dishes. So there is kedgeree; excellent, piquant and perfectly cooked devilled kidneys; omelette; and Welsh rabbit. A cliff of golden puff pastry overhung a creamy, slightly runny chicken and ham pie; fish pie was full of flavour and variety thanks to smoked haddock, squid, mussel and egg. Cold roast beef and potato salad or cold poached salmon are genteel dishes – the fat, golden, dripping-fried chips are a prolier joy. Albion doesn't take bookings except for groups and, as we waited, we spotted a design flaw. According to the severe east European maîtresse d', the stools next to the stainless steel kitchen counter laden with freshly baked goodies aren't to be used for 'health and safety' reasons, because they're too close to the food. At weekends, when there's a queue for brunch, this could be even more annoying. Once we were installed at the refectory tables, each equipped with ketchup and HP sauce bottles and family-style messy butter, all was forgiven.
Babies and children welcome: high chairs; nappy-changing facilities. Bookings not accepted for fewer than 7 people. Disabled: toilet. Tables outdoors (10, pavement). Takeaway service. **Map 6 R4.**

Rochelle Canteen
Rochelle School, Arnold Circus, E2 7ES (7729 5677, www.arnoldandhenderson.com). Shoreditch High Street rail. **Breakfast served** 9-11am, **lunch served** noon-3pm Mon-Fri. **Main courses** £8.50-£15. **Unlicensed. Corkage** £5. **Credit** MC, V.
Rochelle Canteen actually merits the description 'hidden gem', lying as it does behind a high brick wall in what was once a Victorian school playground. Everything is kept simple and

uncluttered, from plain chairs and tables to dish descriptions – it's left to diners, many of them artists or creatives of some sort, to provide visual interest. The compact menu evolves from day to day; there's always a vegetarian main: girolles, black cabbage and polenta, for example, or aubergine and olive stew. The only problem with a delicious summer lunch of ham, bobby beans and soft boiled egg (a tasty, well-balanced starter, with pea shoots for added flavour), followed by roast chicken, lemon potatoes and aïoli (seasonal comfort food) was that portions were super-sized – meaning we couldn't manage either of the two desserts on offer (apple and calvados trifle or chocolate tart with crème fraîche). On the downside, another starter, purple sprouting broccoli and anchovy, was nice enough but had very little fish flavour, and a macchiato was grainy. The restaurant (and a catering business) is run by Melanie Arnold and Margot Henderson. The latter is married to Fergus Henderson of St John fame, and the restaurants share a similar vision.
Available for hire. Babies and children welcome: high chairs; nappy-changing facilities. Booking advisable Thur, Fri. Tables outdoors (12, courtyard). **Map 6 S4.**

Spitalfields

Canteen
2 Crispin Place, off Brushfield Street, E1 6DW (0845 686 1122, www.canteen.co.uk). Liverpool Street tube/rail. **Meals served** 8am-11pm Mon-Fri; 9am-11pm Sat; 9am-10pm Sun. **Main courses** £8-£14.50. **Credit** AmEx, MC, V.
For a time, Canteen was one of the more talked-about restaurants in the back-to-basics British mould. It may have faded from the spotlight, but the kitchen's honest, simple cooking and emphasis on seasonality and provenance is still admirable. The venue is more of a spot for a business meeting (arts-based, probably) or an easy catch-up rather than a special-occasion meal: it's called Canteen for a reason. The space is nonetheless smart and stylish, albeit in a no-frills way, the only decorative touch being a large wall map of the British Isles. Long modern benches make up most of the interior seating – be sure to book a booth table if you're after more comfort – while the exterior is popular on warm evenings with those who don't mind an echoing atmosphere. The menu is unapologetically nostalgic, featuring classic British dishes, revived in contemporary fashion (so, without the stodge). Daily specials always feature a roast and simply cooked fish, and this pattern is replicated on a wider scale on the à la carte. Aside from the fish and roasts, highlights are the pies, all-day breakfasts and puddings – all made using top-quality ingredients. We'll certainly return for seconds of the baked cheesecake topped with caramel and roasted nuts.
Babies and children welcome: high chairs. Bookings not accepted lunch Sat, Sun. Disabled: toilet. Tables outdoors (10, plaza). Takeaway service. **Map 12 R5.**
For branches see index.

St John Bread & Wine
94-96 Commercial Street, E1 6LZ (7251 0848, www.stjohnbreadandwine.com). Liverpool Street tube/rail. **Breakfast served** 9-11am Mon, Sat, Sun; 8am-11pm Tue-Fri. **Lunch served** noon-6pm Mon-Fri; noon-4pm Sat, Sun. **Dinner served** 6-10.30pm Mon-Sat; 6-9pm Sun. **Main courses** £2.50-£15. **Credit** AmEx, MC, V.

The clean, spare lines of a former bank make a good canvas for the St John look: painted white, with wooden chairs and tables, and little decoration. Here, there's an open kitchen and a bakery hatch to draw the eye, plus big blackboards listing food and drink. Opened in 2003, this was the second of Fergus Henderson and Trevor Gulliver's St John 'chain', and its lineage is clear from the daily-changing menu. Breakfast on an Old Spot bacon sandwich; take elevenses of seed cake and a glass of Madeira; then move through lunch and dinner with dishes such as smoked sprats and horseradish, cold Middle White and celeriac remoulade, or quail and blackcurrant jelly. The venue is more brasserie-like than the original Smithfield site – diners tend to share dishes over a glass of wine (from a resolutely French list) – though there are also hearty mains, such as rabbit with lentils and trotter, or plaice with brown butter and samphire. Finish with bread pudding with butterscotch sauce, or (our favourite) apple sorbet and Polish vodka. Wines and baked goods (fabulous sourdough bread, mighty eccles cakes) can also be taken away. Staff are on the ball, and the enjoyable buzz encourages repeat visits.
Available for hire. Babies and children welcome: high chairs. Booking advisable. Takeaway service. **Map 12 S5.**
For branch (St John Hotel) see index.

North

Camden Town & Chalk Farm

★ Market
43 Parkway, NW1 7PN (7267 9700, www.marketrestaurant.co.uk). Camden Town tube. **Lunch served** noon-2.30pm, **dinner served** 6-10.30pm Mon-Sat. **Meals served** 1-3.30pm Sun. **Main courses** £13-£16. **Set lunch** (Mon-Fri) £10 2 courses. **Credit** AmEx, DC, MC, V.
Offering pretty much everything you want in a local restaurant, Market is difficult to find fault with, and, given its easy-going charm, you'd feel churlish to try. Service is friendly, efficient and wonderfully unobtrusive, hitting just the right note for a not-too-smart, not-too-casual destination that is both a treat and a bargain. Decor is simple: banquettes where possible, a big vase of flowers, exposed brickwork and a small hatch into the rear kitchen. The chairs are a tad uncomfortable, but you'll still want to linger over the likes of pork belly with roast quince, and seared scallops with cauliflower purée and hazelnuts. The daily-changing menu mixes classics of the modern British canon with proper traditional dishes (fish and chips, bacon collar, a Sunday roast). The pies have a deserved reputation, but we're particularly fond of the precision-grilled onglet and chips. Offal has proved a good choice too, with sautéed kidneys on toast being a highlight of our last visit. Sticky toffee pudding is the hard-to-refuse dessert, but there's also own-made ice-creams, grilled figs in season, and cheese. Wrapping up this attractive package is a pleasingly unpretentious wine list featuring 20 or so each of red and white.
Babies and children welcome: high chairs. Booking advisable. Separate room for parties, seats 12. Tables outdoors (2, pavement). **Map 3 H1.**

Chinese

Gradually, Londoners are starting to discover the full glories of Chinese cuisine. We've rapidly moved on from the Bamboo Curtain days when 'real' Chinese food – as opposed to chop suey takeaway fodder, or luxury-ingredient stir-fries (beloved of money-grabbing posh venues in the south-western suburbs) – was the preserve of the capital's Chinese community. Dim sum was the first bastion to be breached. These afternoon snacks and dumplings, at their best exquisitely delicate, are now popular choices at fashionable establishments such as **Hakkasan**, as well as at longer-established experts such as **Royal China**. Regional cuisine was next to be explored, so in addition to top-class Cantonese food (more common because of the UK's links with Hong Kong), you can now sample Sichuan cooking at the likes of **Barshu**, **Ba Shan** and **Seventeen**. The process is far from complete, however. Of the four great cuisines of China, Shanghainese food is still a rarity in our city, limited to a few specials at venues such as **Shanghai Dalston**. The same was true for northern Chinese cuisine, though London now has the new **Manchurian Legends** (specialising in food from the north-east of the country) joining the well-established **North China** (where the northern repertoire seems to have shrunk of late).

Central

Belgravia

Hunan
51 Pimlico Road, SW1W 8NE (7730 5712, www.hunanlondon.com). Sloane Square tube. **Lunch served** 12.30-2pm, **dinner served** 6.30-11pm Mon-Sat. **Set lunch** £28.80 per person (minimum 2). **Set dinner** £42.80 per person (minimum 2). **Credit** AmEx, DC, MC, V.
The dining areas of this family-run restaurant are comfortably snug, and apart from the collection of Chinese artefacts over the door, the space is neutral in tone. In contrast, the cooking is far from mainstream. The 'leave it to us' menu of a dozen or more small tasting dishes is the USP, and this should satisfy the most daring of diners. Textures and offal took centre stage on our visit, starting with spicy cold octopus and mustard greens with light soy sauce, followed by pig's tongue wrapped inside the ear of the piggy. Then a short respite with steamed pork and chicken soup served in a bamboo cup, before the arrival of claret-coloured, deep-fried pig's intestine, served with hoi sin sauce, as well as moreish beef tripe with a dash of rice vinegar. Although too many of the dishes we ordered were accompanied by shredded white cabbage, we enjoyed Hunan's interesting take on Chinese regional cooking. Service is attentive, though staff spent a lot of their time shuffling and announcing dishes between tables. There's a well-crafted wine list as well.
Babies and children admitted. Booking essential. Vegetarian menu. **Map 15 G11**.

Chinatown

Imperial China
White Bear Yard, 25A Lisle Street, WC2H 7BA (7734 3388, www.imperial-china.co.uk). Leicester Square or Piccadilly Circus tube. **Meals served** noon-11.30pm Mon-Sat; 11.30am-10.30pm Sun. **Dim sum served** noon-5pm daily. **Main courses** £5.90-£26.50. **Dim sum** £2.30-£3.60. **Set meal** £19-£35 per person (minimum 2). **Minimum** £10. **Credit** AmEx, MC, V.
A little courtyard, including a bridge over a carp pool (watch the whoppers blowing bubbles), gives Imperial China a sense of space and tranquillity unique in Chinatown. In summer, open french windows accentuate the vibe, as does the roomy wood-panelled interior and the serene staff, smart in their dinky tunics. Dim sum has long been the speciality here; the list is long and varied, and we can vouch for the deep-fried stuffed pastry with pork (juicy filling, delectable pastry), the unusual steamed glutinous rice with meat wrapped in yam (dense but satisfying logs) and the enticingly fruity 'steamed beef with pineapple dumplings in butterfly shape'. Other choices were passable but lacked delicacy: the fried taro paste croquette missing its melting layer, the prawn cheung fun a little floury. Most annoying was the delivery of dishes. Gai lan (perfectly crunchy chinese broccoli) had gone cold when the next dish arrived. The wine list could do with more than three choices by the glass too. Next time we'll sample the full menu, especially the alluring list headed 'typical Chinese dishes, may not be suitable for Europeans' taste': baked lobster coated with salted duck egg; salted fish cubes with aubergine in hotpot…
Babies and children admitted. Booking advisable. Disabled: toilet. Separate rooms for parties, seating 10-70. Tables outdoors (5, courtyard). **Map 17 C4**.

Joy King Lau
3 Leicester Street, WC2H 7BL (7437 1132, www.joykinglau.com). Leicester Square or Piccadilly Circus tube. **Meals served** noon-11.30pm Mon-Sat; 11.30am-10.30pm Sun. **Dim sum served** noon-5pm Mon-Sat; 11am-5pm Sun. **Main courses** £7.50-£18. **Dim sum** £2.40-£4.50. **Set meal** £11.50-£35 per person (minimum 2). **Credit** AmEx, MC, V.
The joy of Joy King Lau is its steadfast refusal to deviate from the old Chinatown line. While others promote regional cuisine, smarten their premises and slicken their service, here you get a voluminous roll-call of Cantonese classics, a utilitarian three-storey eating den, and hurtling staff who veer between sweetly swift and abrasively brusque. We were barged out of the slightly gloomy ground floor

and squeezed into an antediluvian lift up to the surprisingly airy, light second floor. It's best to come during the day and order dim sum; the full menu of myriad stir-fries is prosaic in comparison. Portions are large; nearby, four diners were tucking into heaped meal-in-one platefuls of noodles with messy gusto. The dim sum seems to have improved of late. All our snacks were served piping hot and full of flavour. Best was the grilled dried shrimp cheung fun, still radiating heat from its crisp exterior; best bargain was the 'assorted meat glutinous rice', a hefty helping full of ham, pork, chicken and sausages for £3.80. Fried snacks are brought first, so our deep-fried custard buns had to be consumed early. Yes, some snacks lack finesse, but we left satisfied and replete.

Babies and children welcome: high chairs. Booking advisable weekends. Takeaway service. **Map 17 C5**.

★ Manchurian Legends NEW

2011 WINNER BEST NEW CHEAP EATS
12 Macclesfield Street, W1D 5BP (7437 8785). Leicester Square or Piccadilly Circus tube.
Meals served noon-11pm daily. **Main courses** £7.50-£12.80. **Set lunch** £5.50-£11 2 courses. **Set dinner** £18.80-£23.80 2 courses. **Credit** MC, V.
When it comes to restaurants, London hasn't had many Manchurian candidates to date. A few dishes from the region, now known as Dongbei, pop up on Chinese menus, but this offshoot of the Leong's Legends chain (a pioneer in bigging up Taiwanese cuisine) is the first to specialise in Dongbei cooking. The region has long winters, so expect rich, warming, slow-cooked dishes, and plenty of pork belly. Vegetarians, be warned: of the 13 offerings in the menu's 'vegetable and tofu dishes', six contained pork. Some recipes are a major departure from standard Chinatown fare, such as the sweet, sticky sauce covering a crispy, fatty lamb skewer sprinkled with cumin seeds and dried chilli. More generic Chinese dishes impressed too, such as the meltingly soft deep-fried squid scattered with garlic and chilli. It's all served in what they describe as a '1910s classy ambience', which translates to a functional black and white tiled interior broken up by a collection of retro objets d'arts: a rotating dial phone sits atop the bar, and a vintage gramophone perches on a bookcase (curiously lined with DVDs). Service is friendly, attentive and geared up for those unfamiliar with the cuisine, with cutlery offered instead of chopsticks, and doggy bags proffered for those who over-order.
Babies and children admitted. Booking advisable. Disabled: toilet. **Map 17 C4**.

Fitzrovia

Hakkasan HOT 50

8 Hanway Place, W1T 1HD (7927 7000, www.hakkasan.com). Tottenham Court Road tube.
Bar **Open** noon-12.30am Mon-Wed; noon-1.30am Thur-Sat; noon-midnight Sun.
Restaurant **Lunch/dim sum served** noon-3pm Mon-Fri; noon-4pm Sat, Sun. **Dinner served** 6-11pm Mon-Wed, Sun; 6pm-midnight Thur-Sat. **Main courses** £9.50-£58. **Dim sum** £3-£20. *Both* **Credit** AmEx, MC, V.
Once the hottest ticket in town, the Hanway Place branch of Hakkasan is in danger of being eclipsed by its shiny new Mayfair sibling, where staff are notably friendlier. For now, the original continues

Manchurian Legends

first class authentic Chinese cuisine

5 - 9 Glentworth Street, London, NW1 5PG
Tel: 0207 486 3515 Fax: 0207 486 3401

A breathtaking Oriental gem near Baker Street Station
Welcome to the newly refurbished Phoenix Palace Chinese Restaurant

- Vibrant oriental setting
- Dim-sum served daily
- Private party function rooms
- Disabled facilites
- Receptions & canapes catered for

to play to packed houses – primarily City slickers, cosmocrats and special-occasion dates – drawn to the high-end modern Cantonese cooking and the sexy subterranean setting. The kitchen still comes up with flashes of brilliance, but overall standards have slipped. High points include the smouldering sweetness of jasmine tea-smoked pork ribs; a signature dish of roasted silver cod, the moist flakes of fish offset by a silky, delicately honeyed champagne sauce; and the simple, clean flavours of a blood-orange sorbet. Yet our basket of steamed dim sum was woefully inadequate, with poorly balanced luxury ingredients and pastry that was both too thick to showcase its expensive contents and too brittle to remain intact when handled. The other disappointment on our most recent visit was the service. Good-looking they may be, but the door girl was frosty, the reception team aloof, and our waiter well meaning but witless. Excellent people-watching opportunities and exotic cocktails help compensate, but only if your pockets are extremely deep.

Available for hire. Babies and children admitted. Booking essential, 6 weeks in advance. Disabled: lift; toilet. Entertainment: DJs 9pm daily. **Map 17 C2**.

Knightsbridge

Mr Chow

151 Knightsbridge, SW1X 7PA (7589 7347, www.mrchow.com). Knightsbridge tube. **Lunch served** 12.30-3pm Tue-Sun. **Dinner served** 7pm-midnight daily. **Main courses** £12.50-£32. **Set lunch** £24. **Set dinner** £39-£46. **Cover** £2. **Credit** AmEx, DC, MC, V.

This pioneer of fashionable Chinese restaurants opened its doors in 1968, and its appeal among Knightsbridge's opulent diners has endured through the decades. On our visit, the venue was so busy that there was a logjam at reception. The buzz and clamour is certainly impressive, but this is no place for strapped wallets: a bowl of rice costs £5.50, and the service charge is 13% on top of a cover charge. We found ourselves squeezed into a swish, dark room furnished with rosewood chairs and filled with original modern art. The silver sculpture of three Cantonese roast ducks, hanging from the ceiling, is a neat touch. The food is more akin to a Hollywood pastiche of the cuisine than authentic Chinese, but the kitchen showed ample skill with a whole stone crab, its soft flesh sautéed with egg white. Squid ink rice noodles – a clever, almost Mediterranean take on ho fun – was delicious, and crispy beef was also right on the money, but we felt cheated by bland gai lan (chinese broccoli), which had been par-boiled rather than stir-fried with oyster sauce. Staff, despite being rushed off their feet, were charming.

Babies and children admitted. Booking advisable; essential dinner. Separate rooms for parties, seating 20-75. **Map 8 F9**.

Marylebone

Phoenix Palace

5 Glentworth Street, NW1 5PG (7486 3515, www.phoenixpalace.co.uk). Baker Street tube. **Meals served** noon-11.30pm Mon-Sat; 11am-10.30pm Sun. **Dim sum served** noon-5pm Mon-Sat; 11am-5pm Sun. **Main courses** £6.50-£25. **Dim sum** £2.80-£4.70. **Set meal** £20-£48 per person (minimum 2). **Credit** AmEx, MC, V.

Hakkasan (Mayfair). See p61.

Royal China Club

Phoenix Palace is a grande dame among London's Chinese restaurants: a little gaudy and slightly overdressed, but perfectly well mannered. Thankfully, the chintzy decor doesn't detract from the food, so the authentic Cantonese cooking here is unlikely to disappoint. With the likes of abalone, crab and lobster up for grabs, shellfish is king of the Palace, but the choice of exotic meats is almost as regal. Ostrich, kangaroo and venison offer a rare twist to the usual repertoire. Our 'Chinese tapas' of pigs' trotters in rice wine made an unctuous beginning to the meal. We can also vouch for the beef with pickled ginger and pineapple – a quirky cousin of the Cantonese classic sweet and sour, with a fine balance of flavours (including a pleasant bite from the ginger). Cantonese pipa beancurd, made of fried mashed beancurd served atop broccoli and braised mushrooms, pleased both vegetarians and meat-eaters. The French-based wine list includes stupendous vintages at more than £200 a bottle (handy if you're entertaining a head of state), but

also a varied choice of Chinese spirits. With excellent service to boot, this is an ideal spot for a feed – whether you're holding court or simply sharing a midweek meal.
Babies and children welcome: high chairs. Booking advisable. Separate rooms for parties, seating 12-30. Takeaway service; delivery service (over £10 within 1-mile radius). **Map 2 F4**.

★ Royal China Club

40-42 Baker Street, W1U 7AJ (7486 3898, www.royalchinagroup.co.uk). Baker Street or Marble Arch tube. **Meals served** noon-11pm daily. **Dim sum served** noon-4.45pm daily. **Main courses** £9.50-£120. **Dim sum** £3.80-£7. **Credit** AmEx, MC, V.
Dim sum doesn't get any classier – or better – than this in London. The sleek brown dining room, lined with gold leaf embellishments, is as serene and stately as the giant lobsters that promenade in the central fish tank. Friendly waiting staff glide by

the elegant tables. The kitchen produces perfectly executed versions of classic Cantonese cuisine. In particular, this is a wonderful place to splash out on seafood, as the ingredients are top-notch. The delicacy of xiao long bao (soup dumplings made of balls of pork or crab, encased in a wrapper that holds the soup inside) typifies the lightness of touch; attempts at this eastern Chinese speciality elsewhere in the capital tend to be leaden. Cheung fun – of the unorthodox duck variety, or the more typical prawn – are similarly delicate and just as delectable. The à la carte menu features seafood not often found in London (sea cucumber, shark's fin), as well as the occasional instance of creative flair (lobster balls in mixed fruit juice with puffed rice). A dim sum meal here is the ideal Sunday afternoon treat – but it's probably best to book ahead; the queues can be extensive.
Babies and children admitted. Booking advisable Sat, Sun. Separate room for parties, seats 24. Takeaway service. **Map 9 G5**.

Mayfair

★ China Tang

*The Dorchester, 53 Park Lane, W1K 1QA
(7629 9988, www.thedorchester.com). Hyde
Park Corner tube.* **Meals/dim sum served**
noon-midnight daily. **Main courses** £12-£48.
Dim sum £5-£8. **Set lunch** £15. **Credit**
AmEx, DC, MC, V.

The Dorchester's luxurious Cantonese restaurant
offers a fabulous mix of art deco design and David
Tang's gutsy modern take on Chinese cookery. The
opulent underground dining rooms counterbalance
shiny dark wood with bold patterns to fine effect.
Cocktails, food – and prices – all match the decor
in decadence; the international clientele struggles
to compete with such beautiful surroundings. To
impress fellow diners, splash out on Japanese
abalone or an entire suckling pig (£150).
Alternatively, you might stick to humble Cantonese
dishes, which are executed to an admirable
standard. Light prawn and pork won tons come in
a skilfully contrasted rich broth. First-rate tofu
served with diced chicken, ginger and salted fish
in a clay pot is a model of southern Chinese
restraint: subtle flavours combining to create the
ultimate comfort dish. The barbecued meats are
among London's best – don't miss the tender char
siu barbecued pork doused in Shaoxing wine, or
the expertly roasted duck, with rich meat, paper-
thin crisp skin, and not a hint of white fat. And to
top off a treat here, visit the toilets; thanks to
polished design and a bizarre reading of the
Arabian Nights over the tannoy, they're surely a
candidate for the best in town.
*Babies and children welcome: high chairs.
Booking advisable. Disabled: lift; toilet. Separate
rooms for parties, seating 18-50.* **Map 9 G7.**

★ Princess Garden

*8-10 North Audley Street, W1K 6ZD (7493
3223, www.princessgardenofmayfair.com). Bond
Street tube.* **Lunch served** noon-4pm Mon-Fri;
noon-4.30pm Sat, Sun. **Dinner served** 6.30-
11pm Mon-Sat; 6.30-10.30pm Sun. **Dim sum
served** noon-4pm daily. **Main courses** £7.50-
£12. **Dim sum** £2.30-£3.80. **Set lunch** £12 per
person (minimum 2). **Set dinner** £30-£85 per
person (minimum 2). **Credit** AmEx, DC, MC, V.
Stepping through Princess Garden's large glass
doors, you are transported at once from Mayfair to
Hong Kong. The restaurant is stylishly decorated
in muted tones, with Chinese art and elegant
antiques adding visual interest. An international
clientele increases the cosmopolitan feel. Dim sum
is served at lunchtime, with a limited assortment
available as starters in the evening. On the full
menu, familiar classics such as crispy seaweed,
lemon chicken and stir-fried beef are listed
alongside northern dishes, Cantonese classics and
modern inventions. Peking duck is a popular choice,
as is beggar's chicken (with advance notice): a
whole chicken roasted in a clay shell. Luxury
ingredients figure prominently too: abalone, lobster,
sea bass, dover sole and veal. We liked the drunken
chicken, a cold appetiser steeped in fragrant
Shaoxing wine. To follow, veal stir-fried in a honey
barbecue sauce was flavourful and tender, while
prawns and scallops with asparagus stir-fried in
XO sauce seemed surprisingly bland despite the
strong seasoning. The highlight was steamed sole
in egg whites; cooked to perfection, the delicate fish
blended seamlessly with the silky, savoury custard.

China Tang

Complementing the smart menu is a thoughtful, mostly French wine list. Polite, attentive service adds to the calm atmosphere.
Babies and children welcome: high chairs. Booking advisable. Separate rooms for parties, seating 6-50. Takeaway service. **Map 9 G6**.

Paddington

Pearl Liang
8 Sheldon Square, W2 6EZ (7289 7000, www.pearlliang.co.uk). Paddington tube/rail. **Dim sum served** noon-11pm daily. **Meals served** noon-4.45pm daily. **Main courses** £8.80-£60. **Dim sum** £2.70-£4.50. **Set meal** £25 per person 3 courses (minimum 2); £38 per person 5 courses (minimum 4). **Credit** AmEx, MC, V.
If you find yourself stuck at Paddington station with a hunger for the Orient, head west to this modern hideaway shielded by tall glass buildings. A giant abacus and small goldfish pond greet you at reception, then you enter a stylish room decked out in glossy pink, with wooden lattice screens and modish low chairs clad in mauve. The place was already heaving when we arrived, and we found ourselves having to eat in the bar. Pearl Liang's menu is rooted in Cantonese cookery, although chicken satay and Thai green curry make an appearance. Dim sum (served daytime only) is a strong suit. The meal started with silky dumplings filled with crabmeat and topped with egg white and salmon roe. We also sampled a supple fried octopus cake with chives that had us fighting over the last piece. The kitchen can falter, however; consommé served with sheets of beancurd and bamboo pith had little flavour, and prawn won tun in a spicy broth was marred by too much vinegar. Aloof service can let the side down too, but keen prices and the chic interior made us forget the few shortcomings.
Babies and children welcome: high chairs. Booking advisable. Disabled: toilet. Separate room for parties, seats 40. Takeaway service. Vegetarian menu. **Map 8 D5**.

Soho

Ba Shan
24 Romilly Street, W1D 5AH (7287 3266). Leicester Square tube. **Meals served** noon-11pm Mon-Thur, Sun; noon-11.30pm Fri, Sat. **Main courses** £7.90-£16.50. **Credit** AmEx, MC, V.
At the entrance of Ba Shan – the newer sibling to fellow spice merchant Barshu – you'll find a dare from Chairman Mao to all who enter: 'If you don't eat chillies, you won't be a revolutionary.' Diners are able to take up the challenge wholeheartedly thanks to the restaurant's wide choice of fiery Hunanese and Sichuanese dishes. The menu, once defined by its choice of xiao chi or small eats, is now more conventionally organised into a range of meat, seafood and vegetarian dishes. Our palates were aroused by the bamboo chicken, with its dried chillies, Sichuan pepper-tinged bites of chicken breast and earthy mushrooms. Flavourful too was a generous portion of crunchy stir-fried potato slivers with a strong, vinegary bite. We also sampled spicy bean-thread noodles with cabbage, which showed the kitchen's ability to harmonise the contrasting textures of slippery and crisp. The furnishings here add to the revolutionary fervour; traditional folk art and Cultural Revolution posters decorating the walls celebrate Hunan province, the homeland of Chairman Mao. However, while the food and atmosphere are inspiring, the service on our visit was disappointingly slow and inattentive.
Babies and children admitted: high chairs. Booking advisable. Disabled: toilet. Separate room for parties, seats 12. **Map 17 C4**.

Barshu   HOT 50
28 Frith Street, W1D 5LF (7287 6688, www.bar-shu.co.uk). Leicester Square or Tottenham Court Road tube. **Meals served** noon-11pm Mon-Thur, Sun; noon-11.30pm Fri, Sat. **Main courses** £8.90-£28.90. **Credit** AmEx, MC, V.
In 2006, Barshu exploded on to the London scene and, along with sister restaurants Baozi Inn and Ba Shan, has become the capital's flag bearer for Sichuan cooking. The dining rooms on three floors are reminiscent of a Beijing teahouse, furnished with heavy-duty dark wood, decorated with woodcarvings, and softened by red lanterns. Our lunch began with a skilful assembly of slices of tender pork adorned with soft silk gourd. Offal also makes an appearance, with fast-fried ducks' tongues, and beef tripe with chilli. The menu entices diners towards the fiery stuff, almost daring you to take on the dishes marked 'very hot'. So it was hardly surprising when we received a blistering smack in the face from some beautifully cooked, spicy dry-fried lamb ribs, the meat almost falling off the bone, served with crunchy preserved mustard greens. Gong bau prawns with celery and cashew nuts also ensured an immediate endorphin high. So, Barshu is still a scorcher, although we felt like shaking the glum staff, who insist on moving around with the handbrake on.
Available for hire. Babies and children welcome: high chairs. Booking advisable. Disabled: toilet. Separate room for parties, seats 24. **Map 17 C4**.

★ Yauatcha
15 Broadwick Street, W1F 0DL (7494 8888, www.yauatcha.com). Leicester Square, Piccadilly Circus or Tottenham Court Road tube. **Dim sum served** noon-11.45pm Mon-Sat; noon-10.30pm Sun. **Dim sum** £4-£15. **Set meal** (3-6pm Mon-Fri) £14.44 per person (maximum 2). **Credit** AmEx, MC, V.
Alan Yau's stylish café still has an impressive buzz and energy eight years after opening. In the bright ground-floor dining room – and its sexy cavernous counterpart below – traditional Chinese design and materials are juxtaposed with bursts of modernist colour. And as with the decor, so with the food. The extensive, regionally organised tea and wine lists perfectly complement a sophisticated menu that's imbued with Cantonese classics. A la carte choices are extensive (from fresh sea bass with osmanthus sauce to braised Somerset lamb with black bean sauce), but Yauatcha is justly renowned for the quality and creativity of its dim sum. Char siu buns feature wonderfully savoury and sweet diced pork and onion inside steamed buns so light and airy they make the versions in nearby Chinatown seem like sugary bricks. Typical of the exemplary preparation is the magical prawn and tofu cheung fun; flavourful plump prawns are wrapped in deep-fried crunchy tofu skin and placed within soft light rice-flour pasta, creating an expertly judged interplay of textures. Many diners come here primarily to see and be seen, but they're also treated to one of the best meals Soho has to offer.
Babies and children admitted. Booking advisable. Disabled: lift; toilet. **Map 17 B3**.

Dim sum

Dim sum menus are roughly divided into steamed dumplings, deep-fried dumplings, sweet dishes and so on. Try to order a selection of different types of food, with plenty of light steamed dumplings to counterbalance the heavier deep-fried snacks. If you are eating with a large group, make sure you order multiples of everything, as most portions consist of about three items. Tea is the traditional accompaniment. Musty bo lay (pu'er in Mandarin), grassy Dragon Well (long jing) or fragrant Iron Buddha (tie guan yin) are alternatives to the jasmine blossom that is usually served by default to non-Chinese guests. Waiters should leave the teapots filled throughout the meal; leave the teapot lid tilted at an angle or upside down to signal that you want a top-up.

Char siu bao: steamed bun stuffed with barbecued pork in a sweet-savoury sauce.
Char siu puff pastry or **roast pork puff:** triangular puff-pastry snack, filled with barbecued pork, scattered with sesame seeds and oven-baked.
Cheung fun: sheets of steamed rice pasta wrapped around fresh prawns, barbecued pork, deep-fried dough sticks, or other fillings, with a sweet soy-based sauce.
Chiu chow fun gwor: soft steamed dumpling with a wheat-starch wrapper, filled with pork, vegetables and peanuts.
Chive dumpling: steamed prawn meat and chinese chives in a translucent wrapper.
Har gau: steamed minced prawn dumpling with a translucent wheat-starch wrapper.
Nor mai gai or **steamed glutinous rice in lotus leaf:** lotus-leaf parcel enclosing moist sticky rice with chicken, mushrooms, salty duck-egg yolks and other bits and pieces, infused with the herby fragrance of the leaf.
Paper-wrapped prawns: tissue-thin rice paper enclosing prawn meat, sometimes scattered with sesame seeds, deep-fried.
Sago cream with yam: cool, sweet soup of coconut milk with sago pearls and taro.
Scallop dumpling: delicate steamed dumpling filled with scallop (sometimes prawn) and vegetables.
Shark's fin dumpling: small steamed dumpling with a wheaten wrapper pinched into a frilly cockscomb shape on top, stuffed with a mix of pork, prawn and slippery strands of shark's fin.
Siu loon bao or **xiao long bao:** Shanghai-style round dumpling with a whirled pattern on top and a minced pork and soup filling.
Siu mai: little dumpling with an open top, a wheat-flour wrapper and a minced pork filling. Traditionally topped with crab coral, although minced carrot and other substitutes are common.
Taro croquette or **yam croquette:** egg-shaped, deep-fried dumpling with a frizzy, melt-in-your-mouth outer layer of mashed taro, and a savoury minced pork filling.
Turnip paste: a heavy slab of creamy paste made from glutinous rice flour and white oriental radishes, studded with wind-dried pork, sausage and dried shrimps and fried.

CHINESE

West

Acton

North China

305 Uxbridge Road, W3 9QU (8992 9183, www.northchina.co.uk). Acton Town tube or 207 bus. **Lunch served** noon-2.30pm daily. **Dinner served** 6-11pm Mon-Fri, Sun; 6-11.30pm Fri, Sat. **Main courses** £5.50-£12.80. **Set meal** £14.50-£22.50 per person (minimum 2). **Credit** AmEx, MC, V.

Don't get too excited: although its name suggests you'll find a Beijing influence to the food at this long-established local, most of North China's menu features classic Cantonese takeaway dishes. We unearthed the few northern Chinese offerings, hoping to sample some of the hearty cuisine of the Chinese capital. The most famous northern Chinese dish, peking duck, is a popular option (its anglicised cousin, crispy aromatic duck, also features prominently). However, we preferred the simpler northern fare. Handmade, grilled dumplings – thick, chewy skins filled with juicy pork – came in a mighty portion (eight dumplings to share). Lamb casserole, with savoury brown sauce, was mouth-meltingly tender and richly satisfying. But there were inconsistencies to the meal; own-made stir-fried noodles with chicken was uninspired, lacking any depth of flavour; and a large plate of garlic-flecked french beans was equally bland, and greasy. Yet though the food was of variable quality, service was pleasantly attentive throughout and our teacups were always kept full. Although not a destination restaurant, North China is an agreeable spot for a meal, with bay windows, ochre walls and attractive black and white photos of Chinese life.

Babies and children welcome: high chairs. Booking advisable; essential dinner Fri, Sat. Separate room for parties, seats 36. Takeaway service; delivery service (over £20 within 2-mile radius). Vegetarian menu.

Bayswater

Gold Mine

102 Queensway, W2 3RR (7792 8331). Bayswater tube. **Meals served** noon-11pm daily. **Main courses** £7-£30. **Set meal** £15.50-£20.50 per person 3 courses (minimum 2). **Credit** MC, V.

With glistening ducks in the window and a tiny Queensway shopfront, Gold Mine is something of a Tardis. Step inside, and what you thought was a Chinese café is a mid-range proper restaurant, tricked out in typical style with bright lighting and mirrors, plumply upholstered chairs and carpet underfoot. Waitresses in waistcoats and dickie bows squeeze between the tightly packed tables to dish up Cantonese-leaning takeaway favourites (sesame prawns on toast, spare ribs) plus more exotic options (frogs' legs with bitter melon, or sichuan kung po eel), but results are mixed. The signature duck was full-flavoured yet dry, and a dish of cold crunchy lettuce leaves with a warm filling of diced chicken, water-chestnuts and mushrooms could have won fans with its interplay of temperature and texture, were it not for the overpowering tang of undercooked garlic. Likewise, tender strips of beef in black bean sauce were smothered by ribbons of white onion. Only a near-perfect dish of crispy noodles topped with succulent king prawns, squid and scallops saved the day. Service can be brusque, but large portions and low prices have nonetheless made this a favourite with the younger section of the local Chinese community.

Available for hire. Babies and children welcome: high chairs. Booking advisable. Takeaway service. **Map 7 C6.**

Magic Wok

100 Queensway, W2 3RR (7792 9767). Bayswater or Queensway tube. **Meals served** noon-11pm daily. **Main courses** £6.50-£18. **Set meal** £14-£29 per person (minimum 2). **Credit** AmEx, MC, V.

Friendly, proficient staff, fair prices and a massive choice of Cantonese food – including some dishes rarely found on an English-language menu in London – are major draws to this Queensway old-stager. The decor is not, unless you're partial to worn brown carpets, yellowing ceiling tiles and a general paucity of space. Try to get a table in the more roomy back area, which is cheered up by traditional Chinese paintings of flowers and peacocks, or perhaps the smaller but brighter first-floor room. We were crammed in by the front counter, with our elbows tucked in. The menu soon distracted us from such minor discomforts: we were wowed by salted fish with chicken and aubergine (one of several enticing hotpots); stewed trotter; and stir-fried goose webs with dried lip mew and sea cucumber. Beef brisket and noodle soup was a splendid bowlful of tender meat, greenery and plentiful noodles in a cockle-warming stock – a meal in itself for £6.50. We also sampled a more

CHINESE

mundane dish of mixed seafood (plump prawns, curly squid, limp sliced scallops) with gai lan (chinese broccoli) in a gingery sauce. Tourists mix with multifarious regulars (some Chinese, some not, some young, others not) to produce a happy throng. *Babies and children admitted. Booking advisable dinner. Separate room for parties, seats 30. Takeaway service. Vegetarian menu.* **Map 7 C6**.

Mandarin Kitchen

14-16 Queensway, W2 3RX (7727 9012). Bayswater or Queensway tube. **Meals served** noon-11.30pm daily. **Main courses** £5.90-£28. **Set meal** £10.90 per person (minimum 2); £20 per person (minimum 4). **Credit** MC, V.

Even on a Monday night in summer, queues were forming at Mandarin Kitchen's entrance. Most were tourists with out-of-date guidebooks. Why out-of-date? We reckon this place is living on its reputation. In the past, advocates were willing to overlook the hustling service and the gloomy, cave-like interior (with yellowing arched ceilings and torn banquettes) for some of Chinese London's best seafood. The service has improved somewhat (though on arriving for a 7.30pm booking we were asked 'can you come back in an hour?'), and Chinese business-people still hold banquets at the large round tables (feasting on lobster, braised whole abalone, or stuffed boneless chicken with prawn paste), but much of our food seemed perfunctorily prepared and arrived lukewarm. The best dish was a cold starter: a refreshing assembly of jellyfish, smoked chicken and arctic clam spiced with XO sauce. But peking dumplings were claggy and near cold. MK's most famous dish, lobster with noodles, featured nicely resilient crustacean flesh, but overcooked, insipid noodles. Deep-fried oysters had stodgy batter. Only a dish of steamed belly pork was faultless. So, standards seem to have dropped, but while those tourists keep queuing, the management doesn't appear to care. *Babies and children welcome: booster seats. Booking advisable dinner. Takeaway service.* **Map 7 C7**.

Royal China

13 Queensway, W2 4QJ (7221 2535, www2.royalchinagroup.biz). Bayswater or Queensway tube. **Meals served** noon-11pm Mon-Thur; noon-11.30pm Fri, Sat; 11am-10pm Sun. **Dim sum served** noon-4.45pm Mon-Sat; 11am-4.45pm Sun. **Main courses** £7.50-£50. **Dim sum** £2.30-£5. **Set meal** £30-£38 per person (minimum 2). **Credit** AmEx, MC, V.

One of the early standard-bearers for upmarket oriental cooking, the original Royal China on Queensway has been doing a roaring trade for over a decade and a half now. During this time it has spawned a clutch of equally popular offspring in all corners of the capital. Service here can be a tad offhand, but orders are rarely wrong, and though the signature interiors of black lacquer and gold are looking somewhat tired, none of this puts off legions of fans from squeezing into the bustling, brightly lit dining room. The kitchen's strong suit is seafood, with highlights including soft-shell crab crusted with salt and slivers of chilli; and sweet, velvety scallops in oyster sauce with crunchy asparagus – a textbook Cantonese interplay of texture and delicate flavour. Meat eaters should try the slippery minced pork dumplings in a soy and garlic broth, or a knockout dish of tender veal in sweet, sticky black bean sauce studded with red peppers and onions. While dinner doesn't come

Gold Mine

Chinatown on the cheap

CHINESE

With its garish red lanterns and hotchpotch of low-priced restaurants playing cheesy Mandopop, Chinatown has long been a favourite haunt of local students, wandering tourists and cash-strapped diners. Broadly Cantonese menus are the norm among the budget establishments. Many of these lists contain Anglo-Canto takeaway fodder, and are further diluted by generic South-east Asian dishes, but there's good eating to be found if you know where to look.

Decor, ambience and service often leave much to be desired. Efforts at interior design are usually non-existent, while service is more about utility than smiles – at best brusque and efficient, at worst rude and sullen. And don't be surprised if you end up sharing tables with strangers. In general, you'll get better treatment if you eat at off-peak times, when staff will be less eager to slam your bill on the table and kick you out. It also pays to try a 'xie xie' or 'mm goi sai' – that's 'thank you' in Mandarin and Cantonese, respectively – after ordering. Even if you completely mangle the pronunciation, the attempt will usually be appreciated.

Receipts are often not itemised, and some places (HK Diner being one) have a minimum order per head – a fine-print condition that leaves unsuspecting diners irate. Check the menu beforehand, and ask for a receipt breakdown; very often it will have included the service charge.

At some restaurants, Mandarin or Cantonese speakers will receive Chinese-language menus that often contain a slightly different set of dishes. Savvier diners keen on more authenticity could ask for the Chinese menu, and hope that staff will provide a few translations. Alternatively, point at whatever your neighbouring Chinese diners are eating.

Baozi Inn

25 Newport Court, WC2H 7JS (7287 6877). *Leicester Square tube.* **Meals served** noon-10.30pm Mon-Thur, Sun; noon-11pm Fri, Sat. **Main courses** £6.50-£6.90. **No credit cards.**
At Baozi Inn, kitsch Communist Revolution decor meets northern Chinese street food tidied up for London. True to Sichuanese form, red is present in most dishes – if not as a slick of potent chilli oil, then in lashings of sliced or whole chillies. Beware of the generously portioned spicy beef noodles: the soup is topped with a layer of tongue-numbing chilli oil. Dan dan noodles, cucumber salad and crescent dumplings are all good choices, especially when accompanied by fresh, unsweetened hot soy milk. The kitchen occasionally gets things wrong, but when it's on song – which is often – the food is spicy, delicious and cheap.
Babies and children admitted. Bookings not accepted. Takeaway service.
Map 17 C4.

Café de Hong Kong

47-49 Charing Cross Road, WC2H 0AN (7534 9898). *Leicester Square tube.* **Meals served** 11.30am-11pm Mon-Sat; 11am-10.30pm Sun. **Main courses** £5-£6. **Credit** (over £10) MC, V.
Not a French-style HK café, misleadingly enough, but a fun, buzzing diner just a few steps from Leicester Square tube station. This Chinese-student favourite serves Anglo-Canto fare with the odd British dish thrown in – noodle dishes, roast meats (decent, though nothing special), plus assorted snacks such as chicken wings, sesame prawn toasts and duck's tongues. Bubble teas, juices and grass jelly combos provide the liquid accompaniment. Food can be hit and miss, and occasionally a bit too greasy, but the café is certainly a worthwhile pitstop.
Babies and children admitted. Takeaway service. **Map 17 C4.**

Café TPT

21 Wardour Street, W1D 6PN (7734 7980). *Leicester Square or Piccadilly Circus tube.* Meals served noon-1am daily. **Main courses** £6.50-£22. **Set meal** £10-£19.50 per person (minimum 2). **Credit** AmEx, MC, V.
Given TPT's fast service and massive menu, with portions to match, you can forgive its slightly cramped seating (there's also an upstairs dining area) and occasional culinary misses. This is one of the friendlier, more relaxed Chinatown joints. Avoid the sloppy baked pork chop rice, and the posh pseudo-laksa, and order cold chicken strips with crunchy-tender jellyfish, sizzling stuffed beancurd, or beef ho fun fresh from the wok. The bubble teas and the sweet, silky beancurd dessert (chilled tau foo fah) are sublime, and pots of hot tea (plus refills) cost just 50p a head.
Available for hire. Babies and children welcome: high chairs. Takeaway service. Vegetarian menu. **Map 17 B5.**

Canton

11 Newport Place, WC2H 7JR (7437 6220). *Leicester Square tube.* **Meals served** noon-11.30pm Mon-Thur, Sun; noon-12.30am Fri, Sat. **Main courses** £5-£10. **Set meal** £10-£16. **Credit** AmEx, MC, V.
Yet another Chinatown stalwart intent on snappy, high-volume turnover, Canton is nevertheless still an excellent spot, especially for solitary dining. Food can be by turns heavily salted or remarkably bland (and, unforgivably, the roast meats are sometimes served stone cold). Skip the thick-skinned pork dumplings, and avoid drinking too much of the tongue-numbing broths (which taste like they contain much MSG). But when the tea is hot and a vast heap of tasty beef fried rice costs just £5, hungry, bleary-eyed travellers leave satisfied. Expect change from a tenner.

Babies and children admitted. Separate room for parties, seats 22. Takeaway service. **Map 17 C4.**

Cha Cha Moon

15-21 Ganton Street, W1F 9BN (7297 9800, www.chachamoon.com). *Oxford Circus tube.* **Meals served** 11.30am-11pm Mon-Thur; 11.30am-11.30pm Fri, Sat; noon-10.30pm Sun. **Main courses** £7-£8. **Credit** AmEx, MC, V.
It aspires to Wagamama's success, with more pretensions to authenticity, but we reckon Cha Cha Moon was better in the days when Alan Yau was still directly overseeing the operation. Recently, we've experienced charmless service, even for Chinatown, with orders mixed up and food arriving at arbitrary times. We've also endured depressingly tasteless noodle dishes, and cardboard-like pancakes dotted with spring onion. Prices are about £6 for a main, for what can be quite sub-standard food. We can recommend the pretty and rather delicious Shibuya cocktail, but better Chinese eating is to be had nearby for the same price.
Babies and children admitted. Bookings not accepted. Disabled: toilet. Tables outdoors (8, courtyard). Takeaway service. **Map 17 A4.**

Four Seasons

12 Gerrard Street, W1D 5PR (7494 0870, www.fs-restaurants.co.uk). *Leicester Square or Piccadilly Circus tube.* **Meals served** noon-midnight Mon-Sat; 11am-midnight Sun. **Main courses** £7.50-£24. **Set meal** £14.50-£34. **Credit** AmEx, MC, V.
The famed Soho purveyor of the golden trio of roasted meats: duck, char siu (barbecued pork) and siew yoke (crispy belly pork). Any of them – or all three – on a plate with rice is reason enough to return for more of the same, but it's also worth trying other dishes on the extensive menu. Soya chicken is usually recommended, as are the stir-fried green beans with pork. Staff are particularly offhand during busy hours, and the meal-end plate of oranges is a not-so-subtle hint that there are other customers waiting.
Available for hire. Babies and children welcome: high chairs. Booking advisable. Takeaway service. Vegetarian menu. **Map 17 C4.** **For branches see index.**

HK Diner

22 Wardour Street, W1D 6QQ (7434 9544). *Leicester Square or Piccadilly Circus tube.* **Meals served** 11am-4am daily. **Main courses** £5-£25. **Set meal** £10-£30 per person (minimum 2). **Minimum** £6. **Credit** MC, V.
Open until 4am every day, HK Diner is a favourite with students, the post-clubbing crowd and chef Jun Tanaka. It's charming,

in a cheerful greasy-spoon kind of way. The café-style food is consistently decent, and some waiters aren't immune to smiles and a little banter. But the real stars are the impeccably shaken bubble teas; for just £3.30 a pop, the HK original, black sesame or Japanese grape will send you straight to tapioca heaven. Have back-up choices in mind, though, as certain flavours are apt to run out. And watch out for the minimum £6 a head charge.
Babies and children welcome: high chairs. Takeaway service. Vegetarian menu. **Map 17 C4.**

Leong's Legends
4 Macclesfield Street, W1D 6AX (7287 0288). Leicester Square or Piccadilly Circus tube. **Meals served** noon-11pm Mon-Thur, Sun; noon-11.30pm Fri, Sat. **Dim sum served** noon-5pm daily. **Main courses** £4.50-£18.50. **Dim sum** £1.90-£6. **Credit** (over £12) MC, V.
Arrive in the afternoon when this dark-panelled, teahouse-style Taiwanese specialist is half-empty, or risk queues and hurried dining. Select any of the following: xiao long bao (crab or the original pork); luscious, soup-filled baozi (an absolute steal at eight for £6.50); meltingly tender belly pork and rice (a fantastic cheap lunch for £5.20); aubergine with mashed garlic and tao pan sauce; or the super-garlicky, salty-spicy chilli garlic crab, already cracked for convenient eating. We don't, however, recommend the congee. Dishes sometimes arrive at staggered intervals. Try to ignore the purist next to you moaning about how it's not all that Taiwanese food, and then leave only marginally poorer.
Babies and children admitted. Bookings not accepted. Takeaway service. **Map 17 C4. For branches see index.**

Wong Kei
41-43 Wardour Street, W1D 6PY (7437 8408). Leicester Square or Piccadilly Circus tube. **Meals served** noon-11.30pm Mon-Sat; noon-10.30pm Sun. **Main courses** £4.40-£8. **Set meal** £8.50-£13.50 per person (minimum 2). **No credit cards**.
A faithful coterie of customers still visits the vast old restaurant known affectionately as 'Wonkies', in the nostalgic hope of being verbally abused by the waiters. Sadly, the rudeness was apparently (mostly) an act for the tourists; these days, the service is simply blunt and efficient – which is no bad thing in a multistorey restaurant with seating for scores of diners. The menu remains almost biblical in length, with dozens of stir-fries covering everything from pork to seafood. The rice can often be overcooked and the roast meats cold, but you do get free tea and huge portions for low prices.
Babies and children admitted. Disabled: toilet. Takeaway service. Vegetarian menu. **Map 17 B4.**

cheap, the outstanding selection of skilfully made dim sum is remarkably good value for the quality. Small wonder that the epic queues during weekend lunchtimes frequently spill on to the street.
Babies and children admitted. Booking advisable (not accepted lunch Sat, Sun). Separate rooms for parties, seating 20-40. Takeaway service. Vegetarian menu. **Map 7 C7. For branches see index.**

Kensington

Min Jiang
10th floor, Royal Garden Hotel, 2-4 Kensington High Street, W8 4PT (7361 1988, www.minjiang.co.uk). High Street Kensington tube. **Lunch/dim sum served** noon-3pm, **dinner served** 6-10.30pm daily. **Main courses** £10-£48. **Dim sum** £3.60-£5.20. **Set lunch** (Mon-Fri) £20.50. **Set dinner** £50-£70 per person (minimum 2). **Credit** AmEx, MC, V.
The best time to visit Min Jiang is for lunch, when you can enjoy a panoramic view of London from the tenth floor of the Royal Garden Hotel (which includes a glimpse of Kensington Palace). At night, you only get to see your own reflection. Dining takes place in a calm and modern room that's smartly adorned with reproduction Ming vases. Despite the visual attractions, the food doesn't take a back seat. Beijing duck is a speciality, but we chose from the dim sum menu, which we've found to be consistently good. Cheung fun, the supple steamed rice-noodle roll, arrived packed with shiitake mushrooms and was excellent. Steamed shanghai dumplings came with a delicious spicy dip. From the main menu, braised belly of pork, rich and sticky, was served with small rice buns. Flavours can be a little muted, though; our Sichuan-inspired stir-fried string beans with minced chicken could have done with more firepower. Service is pleasant, but can get stretched when the room fills up.
Babies and children welcome: high chairs; nappy-changing facilities. Booking advisable: essential Thur-Sun. Disabled: lift; toilet. Separate room for parties, seats 20. **Map 7 B8.**

Notting Hill

Seventeen **NEW**
17 Notting Hill Gate, W11 3JQ (7985 0006, www.seventeen-london.com). Notting Hill Gate tube. **Meals served** noon-11.30pm daily. **Main courses** £7-£24.80. **Set meal** £24.80-£35.80 per person 4 courses (minimum 2). **Credit** AmEx, MC, V.
Covering two floors, the interior of this modern Chinese restaurant seems more suited to the trendy Xintiandi area of Shanghai than to an anonymous part of Notting Hill. Moody colours and chic furnishings predominate. The broad menu covers Cantonese, Shanghainese and Sichuan cuisines, and includes a selection of offal dishes such as pork lung slices and pig's tripe. We started with a credible xiao long bun from the very short dim sum menu, followed by an overcooked razor clam served with a slapdash combo of spring onions and Shaoxing wine. 'Sea and land' pot, in which plump prawns and scallops complemented the meaty flavour of thinly sliced beef fillet, was let down by a bland Sichuan vinegar chilli sauce. We would have traded everything for another plate of the soft Japanese-style tofu, which had marvellous flavour and texture. It arrived with mixed vegetables, including carrots carved in the shape of small

ducks, and a sauce sexed up with abalone. The manager apart, staff were glum and seemed to verge on the narcoleptic; we really wished for a brighter atmosphere at lunch.
Babies and children welcome: nappy-changing facilities. Booking advisable weekends. Disabled: toilet. Separate room for parties, seats 10-16. Takeaway service; delivery service (over £20 within 3-mile radius). Vegetarian menu. **Map 7 B7.**

South East
Elephant & Castle

Dragon Castle
100 Walworth Road, SE17 1JL (7277 3388, http://dragoncastle.eu). Elephant & Castle tube/ rail. **Meals served** noon-11.30pm Mon-Sat; 11.30am-10.30pm Sun. **Dim sum served** noon-4.30pm daily. **Main courses** £5.50-£25. **Dim sum** £2.20-£3.90. **Set meals** £15.80-£34.80 per person (minimum 2). **Credit** AmEx, MC, V.
For south Londoners looking for a credible alternative to Chinatown, Dragon Castle is just the ticket. Styled in the manner of a banqueting restaurant – complete with stone dragons guarding the entrance, koi carp pond in the foyer and traditional lanterns in the tall windows – it offers an extensive selection of Cantonese-inspired high-street favourites (sweet and sour pork, egg fried rice, prawns with garlic and ginger) alongside lesser-seen delicacies such as cold sliced abalone. The real draw, however, is the excellent-value dim sum. Highlights include properly prepared prawn and chive fun gwor, with fragrant innards shining through the wafer-thin steamed parcels (the pastry neither too sticky nor too weak: a mark of the kitchen's skill), and slippery char siu cheung fun, the classic rice-noodle roll stuffed in this case with smoky, honeyed pork morsels and served in a puddle of sweet soy-based sauce. The experience is not without its downsides, though; our yam fritters were tough and greasy, the siu mai (steamed pork dumplings) a touch overcooked, and service varied from brisk and efficient one moment to absent-minded and indifferent the next – though with prices averaging £2.70 a plate, no one's complaining.
Babies and children welcome: high chairs. Booking advisable Fri, Sat. Disabled: toilet. Separate room for parties, seats 60. Takeaway service. Vegetarian menu.

East
Docklands

Yi-Ban
London Regatta Centre, Dockside Road, E16 2QT (7473 6699, www.yi-ban.co.uk). Royal Albert DLR. **Meals served** noon-11pm Mon-Sat; 11am-10.30pm Sun. **Dim sum served** noon-5pm daily. **Main courses** £4-£30. **Dim sum** £2.20-£4. **Set meal** £22-£38 per person (minimum 2). **Credit** AmEx, MC, V.
On the first floor of a concrete building that is the London Regatta Centre, Yi-Ban boasts sweeping views of London City Airport; the sight and sound of the planes should keep young children fascinated. The dining room, furnished in pale wood and cream leather, exudes serenity. This is a popular spot for weddings at the weekends, and is also frequented

Seventeen. See p71.

by the local Vietnamese community. Service is fleet-footed and friendly. The menu is packed with Cantonese dishes, and hotpots feature strongly. We ordered prawn cheung fun from the dim sum selection, which was a fair rendition, although the rice noodle was a touch gooey. For the main dishes, we went off-piste and were rewarded with sweet and tender frogs' legs: the amphibians coated in batter, then deep-fried and imbued with garlic and spicy salt. Bitter melon stuffed with minced pork and served with a black bean sauce was tasty, but the melon could have done with more cooking. While we deliberated between desserts of mango pudding and coconut mousse, complimentary fresh oranges made an entrance and we were sorted.

Babies and children welcome: booster seats; high chairs. Booking advisable. Disabled: toilet. Entertainment: jazz 8pm Fri, Sat. Takeaway service. Vegetarian menu.

North East
Dalston

★ Shanghai Dalston
41 Kingsland High Street, E8 2JS (7254 2878, www.shanghaidalston.co.uk). Dalston Kingsland rail or 38, 67, 76, 149 bus. **Meals served** noon-11pm, **dim sum served** noon-5pm daily. **Main courses** £5.50-£7.80. **Dim sum** £2.10-£4.50. **Set meal** £15.80-£19 per person (minimum 2). **Credit** MC, V.

Operating in a former pie and mash shop, Shanghai Dalston is a testament to London's multi-culturalism. Grab a seat in one of the wooden booths in the front half of the restaurant and admire the Edwardian furnishings – tiled walls, a marble bar, and mirrors aplenty. Karaoke rooms can be hired too, adding another dimension to this remarkable venue. The kitchen produces a range of regional dishes from across China, including interpretations of fiery Sichuanese and mild Shanghainese flavours. But its strength is the Cantonese selection, of which dim sum is the star. Vegetarian yam croquettes were perfectly fried, producing a crisp, flaky outer coating; ha gau crystal prawn dumplings were generously filled with plump and sweet prawns; and the pan-fried turnip paste with meat in XO sauce was moreish. We also enjoyed the roast meats: roast duck was tender, and although the crispy pork slices were slightly over-salted, the crackling was irresistibly crunchy. Takeaway is also available, but the helpful, attentive staff make dining-in a pleasure.

Babies and children welcome: high chairs. Booking advisable. Disabled: toilet. Separate rooms for parties, both seating 45. Takeaway service. **Map 25 B5.**

North
Camden Town & Chalk Farm

★ Yum Cha Silks & Spice
27-28 Chalk Farm Road, NW1 8AG (7482 2228, www.yumchasilksandspice.co.uk). Chalk Farm tube. **Meals/dim sum served** noon-11pm Mon-Thur; noon-midnight Fri, Sat; noon-10.30pm Sun. **Main courses** £7.25-£8.50. **Dim sum** £3.50-£5.20. **Credit** AmEx, MC, V.

Just across from the melee of Camden's Stables Market, Yum Cha ('drink tea') is named after the Hong Kong institution also known as dim sum. It's decorated with red silks and crafts from across Asia, including a large gold reclining Buddha. An impressively diverse choice of dim sum is offered day and night (with prices higher in the evening), plus dozens of main-course dishes from South-east Asia and China. A half-price dim sum deal from Monday to Wednesday, along with karaoke rooms for hire, makes this a lively and inexpensive party venue. Nevertheless, we reckon the kitchen, a culinary jack-of-all-trades, does nothing particularly well. True, we enjoyed the Japanese whole baby octopus, nicely balanced by the sharpness of worcestershire sauce, but beef mee goreng (spicy fried noodles) lacked character and was short on beef. Siew long bao (steamed pork soup dumplings) was disappointing too; the delicate skins burst, spilling out the prized soup before we got a taste. Sichuan pork dumpling topped with spicy oil and crushed peanuts proved to be bland. Service was ill-informed. Though dishes such as Sichuan spicy duck tongues, and morning glory with balanchan shrimp paste bode well, Yum Cha failed to dazzle.
Babies and children welcome: high chairs. Booking advisable weekends. Disabled: toilet. Separate rooms for parties, seating 10-60. Tables outdoors (10, pavement). Takeaway service; delivery service (over £15 within 3-mile radius). **Map 27 C1**.

Outer London
Ilford, Essex

Mandarin Palace
559-561 Cranbrook Road, Ilford, Essex, IG2 6JZ (8550 7661). Gants Hill tube. **Lunch served** noon-4pm Mon-Sat. **Dinner served** 6.30-11.30pm Mon-Thur; 6.30pm-midnight Fri, Sat. **Meals served** noon-11.30pm Sun. **Dim sum served** noon-4pm Mon-Sat; noon-5pm Sun. **Main courses** £8.50-£30. **Dim sum** £2.50-£4.50. **Set meal** £24 per person (minimum 2); £29 per person (minimum 4). **Credit** AmEx, MC, V.
Enter Mandarin Palace and it can seem as if the owner has had a field day shopping in a Shanghai emporium, what with the assorted Chinese vases, lanterns and screens. The menu offers several set options from £24, with dishes such as shredded veal with coriander in a bird's nest providing a little diversion. We tucked into some praiseworthy dim sum, starting with comforting grilled pork dumplings with a rice vinegar dip, followed by a delightful fried turnip paste with spiky XO sauce. The kitchen fluffed its lines, however, with dreadfully chewy spare ribs and black bean sauce. In contrast, we enjoyed the sweet and spongy water-chestnut paste so much that a scuffle with chopsticks broke out for the last remaining piece. Over lunch, keep your eyes peeled and you might spot a few diners sporting the sort of fake tans inspired by *The Only Way is Essex*. During our stay, service was curt, and Gants Hill roundabout is hardly a beauty spot – but the appetising food quickly made us forget the downsides.
Babies and children welcome: high chairs. Separate room for parties, seats 50. Takeaway service; delivery service (over £20 within 2-mile radius).
For branch see index.

Dragon Castle. See p71.

East European

To anyone analysing the culture of expat communities in a great metropolis, London's eastern European restaurant scene offers plenty of scope for research. In this section we group together venues offering food from the Czech Republic and eastwards as far as Russia. Each tells a tale of 20th- and 21st-century migration. Glorious survivors of an earlier age are the **Czechoslovak Restaurant** and the **Gay Hussar**, which once provided a rendezvous for refugees from the Soviet Bloc. New arrival **Malina**, winner of our Best New Local Restaurant award 2011, also has echoes of the old days; it is owned by the Polish couple who for years ran the venerable Daquise (before it was taken over by a Polish company to become **Gessler Daquise**). Other establishments such as the Russian **Trojka** or Georgian **Tbilisi** aim to be a showcase for the cuisine of their homeland. But although Poland entered the EU in 2004, it took several years before many Polish restaurants catering for recent émigrés began trading. As the community has become established, however, budget venues have started appearing – **Oasis** being one of the most recent.

Central
Soho

★ Gay Hussar
2 Greek Street, W1D 4NB (7437 0973, www.gayhussar.co.uk). Tottenham Court Road tube. **Lunch served** 12.15-2.30pm, **dinner served** 5.30-10.45pm Mon-Sat. **Main courses** £12.25-£17.50. **Set lunch** £19 2 courses, £22 3 courses. **Credit** AmEx, DC, MC, V. Hungarian
This Soho landmark, in business for over half a century, doesn't so much rest on its laurels as luxuriate among them. From the famously entertaining collection of politician caricatures, displayed above tables arranged railway-carriage style along each wall of a narrow dining room, to the unsmiling service, the Gay Hussar remains exactly how you remember, or imagine, it. As for the classic Hungarian food, the menu description of the paprika potatoes tells you much: 'contains meat'. Gusto is required to do justice to the likes of very smoky sliced goose breast on a richly flavoured cassoulet, served with lattice crisps and sauerkraut and a dollop of redcurrant sauce, or the veal goulash with galuska (the meat tender, the amorphous little white dumplings dense and bouncy). Although starters are unnecessary for anyone with less than Ken Clarke's appetite, the chilled wild cherry soup is worth a slurp – sweet and creamy, it's almost like a yoghurt, rather than the savoury appetiser you might expect. The mid-priced Hungarian wines are better than the house

selection. It was all very enjoyable, with the exception of an unimpressive cold fish terrine. Despite, or more likely because of, the retro feel, Soho trendies are starting to dine here between the Hungarian émigrés and wielders of walking sticks.
Babies and children welcome: high chairs. Booking essential dinner. Separate rooms for parties, seating 12 and 24. **Map 17 C3.**

South Kensington

Gessler Daquise
20 Thurloe Street, SW7 2LT (7589 6117, http://gesslerlondon.com). South Kensington tube. **Meals served** noon-11pm daily. **Main courses** £6-£14.50. **Set lunch** (noon-4pm Mon-Fri) £9 2 courses. **Credit** MC, V. Polish
When Daquise changed hands in 2008, after more than 60 years of serving South Kensington locals and Polish émigrés, many regulars bemoaned the loss of generous portions and warm service. On our recent return, £8 for a few spears of asparagus with breadcrumbs seemed excessive, and the old-fashioned silver service performed by the chefs themselves was baffling – although a twinkle in our waiter's eye made the process almost fun. The luminous interior, with stripped wooden floors, soft linen napkins and 'old-money' furnishings, is both elegant and relaxing, attracting families and lone diners. A changing seasonal menu combines Polish classics with several Jewish influences – goose meat, liver, not so much pork – and refined French-style consommés and reduced sauces. Sorrel soup with boiled egg was deliciously tangy, while a

delicately light bouillon with beef tripe had a slightly spicy flavour. To follow, simply boiled chicken with own-made klezki (translated as noodles, but more like gnocchi) was properly cockle-warming, if rather bland. Turn down the overblown service and add some good old Polish rye bread, and Daquise could stay a South Ken favourite for another century.
Babies and children admitted. Booking advisable. **Map 14 D10.**

West
Hammersmith

Knaypa
268 King Street, W6 0SP (8563 2887, www.theknaypa.co.uk). Hammersmith tube. **Dinner served** 6-10.30pm Mon-Fri. **Meals served** noon-10.30pm Sat; noon-9.30pm Sun. **Main courses** £10-£15. **Credit** AmEx, MC, V. Polish
An interior of sombre rococo-esque decor, curved ceilings and formal tableware certainly gives Knaypa a distinctive look. On our last visit, however, we spotted a more playful side to this Polish venue, shown by the art on its walls (a studenty mismatch of witticisms and sexy innuendos) and a few fun, if not always successful, additions to the menu. We loved the zurek, a classic aromatic soup of greens and chopped egg, which arrived in a bread pot with a shaped lid. Less appetising, though, were the chunks of breaded

camembert, bitter from over-frying, and a gigantic platter of traditional Polish goodies (large enough as a main course for three) that had the peculiar addition of grilled processed smoked cheese. The menu is substantial, full of the usual repertoire: from hearty stews of meat and sauerkraut, to loaded dumplings and obligatory soups. Families and parties are warmly welcomed, drawn to the elaborate buffet menu, the whole roasted pig stuffed with buckwheat, and the locally made cakes. Knaypa is situated in one of the heartlands of London's Polish community, and rightfully attracts those looking for comforting food, smiling service and good value.

Available for hire. Babies and children welcome: high chairs; nappy-changing facilities. Booking advisable weekends. Separate room for parties, seats 38. Tables outdoors (2, pavement). Vegetarian menu. **Map 20 A4**.

Malina NEW

2011 WINNER BEST NEW
LOCAL RESTAURANT
166 Shepherd's Bush Road, W6 7PB (7603 8881, www.malinarestaurant.com). Goldhawk Road or Hammersmith tube. **Lunch served** noon-3pm, **dinner served** 5.30-11pm Mon-Fri. **Meals served** noon-11pm Sat, Sun. **Main courses** £9.90-£14.90. **Set lunch** (Sun) £12.50 3 courses. **Credit** AmEx, MC, V. Polish
If you regard 'home cooking' as a synonym for unrefined, this Polish newcomer will sweep your prejudice aside: the barszcz z uszkami (beetroot soup with mushroom tortellini) here combines intense colour and jewel-like clarity with deep flavour, the pasta maintaining perfect consistency. Other dishes were nearly as good: saczewicz (lentil dumplings) had great length of flavour, and were prettily presented with a fine dice of onion on top; blini with gravadlax and caviar was also attractive, and served in a generous but not overwhelming portion. Only the bigos (meat, sausage and dried mushroom stew) looked a little rough-handed – a slap of somewhat dry stew and a slosh of mash and sauerkraut – but it still packed the requisite flavour punch. If you expect somewhere focusing on fine home cooking to excel on hospitality, you're bang on: from the free appetiser of bacon pâté with dark rye bread to the own-made raspberry liqueur that saluted our departure (malina means 'raspberry') and a very friendly waitress, Malina is incredibly obliging. Quiet on our visit, this is a dining secret we hope more people discover.
Available for hire. Babies and children welcome: high chairs. Booking advisable Fri, Sat. Separate room for parties, seats 10. **Map 20 C3**.

Kensington

Mimino

197C Kensington High Street, W8 6BA (7937 1551, www.mimino.co.uk). Kensington High Street tube. **Dinner served** 7-11pm Mon-Thur; 6pm-midnight Fri, Sat. **Main courses** £10-£15. **Credit** MC, V. Georgian
To get the best out of Mimino, come on a cooler day with a merry group of friends, as the dark basement dining room, with no natural light, is hardly enticing even with its atmospheric paintings and plush furniture. On a recent visit, several large parties in a room with poor acoustics made for a taut experience. The usual bounteous portions were lacking too, though the distinctive Georgian spicing

was still evident. Dishes containing walnuts (a proud mainstay of the cuisine) scored highest, such as the delicious steamed pkhali of leek and walnuts, and succulent rolls of aubergine with walnut sauce, sprinkled with pomegranate seeds. Unfortunately, the normally popular lobio, a starter of red kidney beans with herbs, lacked flavour. Also underwhelming was the lamb shashlik (kebab) – generally a prized part of every Georgian male's culinary repertoire – though the dish was saved by tangy plum sauce and lovely crunchy pickled cabbage. The wisest option is to choose simple food (say, khachapuri bread made with freshly rolled dough and melting cheese) and accompany it with nectar-like Georgian red wine.
Available for hire. Babies and children welcome: high chairs. Booking advisable weekends. Takeaway service. **Map 7 A9**.

Shepherd's Bush

Tatra

24 Goldhawk Road, W12 8DH (8749 8193, www.tatrarestaurant.co.uk). Goldhawk Road tube. **Lunch served** noon-4pm, **dinner served** 6-11pm Mon-Fri. **Meals served** noon-11pm Sat; noon-10pm Sun. **Main courses** £10-£16. **Credit** AmEx, MC, V. Polish
If you believe buckwheat is for health freaks, Tatra will force a rethink. In this striking, if rather 1980s-styled eaterie (plenty of painted black wood, bare brick and faux leather seating), the buckwheat 'risotto', and golabki of cabbage leaves, buckwheat and mushrooms are objects of desire. No butter is spared either on plump dumplings with sauerkraut and cottage cheese. The young chef plays with the

Malina

modern Polish and eastern European repertoires, producing occasionally risky pairings and unexpected results. Thus savoury black pudding with apples came with a sweet dressing of herbs and overly reduced balsamic vinegar. We preferred the smoked Polish sausag with a tangy mix of Polish and American mustards. In general, the classics worked better: bigos, a delectable stew of sauerkraut, beef, pork sausage and potatoes; and stuffed cabbage parcels with creamy mushroom sauce. Portion sizes seemed a little smaller in relation to price than previously – and near-burnt ingredients marred an otherwise lovely cottage cheese and rum pancake for pudding. The own-flavoured vodkas were as delicious as ever; Tatra has a dozen varieties ranging from puréed fruit to freshly grated horseradish, served from frozen.
Available for hire. Babies and children welcome: high chairs. Booking advisable weekends. Disabled: toilet. **Map 20 B2**₁

South

Waterloo

★ Baltic   `HOT 50`
74 Blackfriars Road, SE1 8HA (7928 1111, www.balticrestaurant.co.uk). Southwark tube.
Lunch served noon-3pm, **dinner served** 5.30-11.15pm Mon-Sat. **Meals served** noon-10.30pm Sun. **Main courses** £10.50-£17. **Set meal** £14.50 2 courses, £17.50 3 courses. **Credit** AmEx, MC, V. East European
Following the closure of Wódka in July 2011, handsome Baltic – with its amber-shard chandelier and Hanseatic-style red brickwork against a cool Scandinavian white backdrop – is now the flag bearer for owner Jan Woroniecki's modern take on classic central and eastern European cuisine. Our meal began with a telling-off from the waiter (for taking two pieces of the lovely rye bread instead of one), but, friendly, though occasionally elusive, service soon resumed. It's hard to resist the stupendous vodka list; home-infused treats such as caraway vodka sit alongside many top-quality clear varieties. A starter of subtly smoky black pudding, with sweetly caramelised onion and apple on a crisp potato pancake, was a dream combination with spiky horseradish vodka. A main course of meltingly tender shin of beef in a robustly herbed broth with just-cooked vegetables, delicate potato dumplings and nutty kasza seemed a rash order on a hot evening – but we had no regrets. The cooling air-con did double service as an antidote to the occasionally intrusive bass thud from the bar and loud party chatter next door. A rather miserly pudding of soft cheese and sultana pancake was forgiven thanks to two must-try dessert vodkas: warmly spiced orange, and fragrant pear.
Babies and children admitted: high chairs. Disabled: toilet. Separate room for parties, seats 30. Tables outdoors (4, terrace). **Map 11 N8**.

South East

Elephant & Castle

★ Mamuska!
1st floor, Elephant & Castle Shopping Centre, SE1 6TE (07986 352810 mobile, www. mamuska.net). Elephant & Castle tube/rail.
Meals served 7am-midnight Mon-Wed; 7am-12.30am Thur-Sat; 9am-midnight Sun. **Main courses** £5. **No credit cards.** Polish
Since opening in 2009, Mamuska! has found favour with students and comfortably off couples who enjoy its contemporary take on a Polish milk bar and relish the hearty, interesting food. Truth be told, local competition is limited in the culinary wasteland of Elephant & Castle, but valiant attempts are made here to counteract the grotty, shopping centre location with rotating exhibitions of modern art, quirkily mismatched furniture and a monochrome colour scheme on breeze-block walls. Most customers are eastern European, as evidenced by the weekly Polish music nights and counter service that's as likely to see you greeted in Polish as English. Punters come to while away weekend afternoons with big bottles of Zywiec beer, or to wolf down gigantic portions of stodgy, homely cuisine at bargain basement prices. Cooking tends towards the basic, but the all-day breakfast option of the 'Big Daddy' – rich, oaty Polish black pudding, parsley-scattered pan-fried potatoes, eggs, gherkin, tomato and thick bacon – is perennially reliable. Belt-bustingly satisfying too are the hefty helpings of pierogi (filled with minced pork, or cheese and potato, or cheese and fruit) and the towering stacks of fluffy potato pancakes swimming in rich goulash.
Available for hire. Babies and children welcome: children's menu; high chairs. Booking advisable. Takeaway service; delivery service (over £20 within 3-mile radius).

North

Camden Town & Chalk Farm

Trojka
101 Regents Park Road, NW1 8UR (7483 3765, www.troykarestaurant.co.uk). Chalk Farm tube.
Meals served 8am-10pm Mon-Fri; 9am-10.30pm Sat, Sun. **Main courses** £8-£13.95. **Set lunch** (Mon-Fri) £5.95 1 course, £7.95 2 courses. **Credit** MC, V. Russian
Custom was so sparse on one visit to Trojka that we wondered if this Primrose Hill stalwart had finally fallen out of favour. So, it was a pleasure on our latest excursion to find the place bustling with locals, families, yoga bunnies and distinguished émigrés. Staff were efficient rather than friendly, but the room is cosseting; with rich red walls, gold trimmings, colourful Russian dolls and glinting mirrors, it feels like an old velvet musical box. Landscape paintings, stained glass and traditional dark wood furniture add a sense of history. The menu offers café standards (cooked breakfasts, average cappuccino, hamburgers) alongside Russian and East European classics (caviar and blinis, pierogi, bigos, zakuski). There's a specials board too, promoting the likes of veal and chicken shepherd's pie with stroganoff sauce, and risotto. Salt beef sandwich featured caraway-flavoured rye bread with a crisp, thin crust and puffy tender crumb, though the beef needed its accompanying dollop of mustard and tangy dill pickle. The crunchy coleslaw on the side was perfect: nothing fancy, but well balanced. We love the cream cheese and sultana pancakes for dessert, but look in the cake counter to see if anything takes your fancy.

Oasis

Georgian
27 Balham Hill, SW12 9DX (8675 4975). Clapham South tube. **Open** 7am-6pm Mon; 7am-11pm Tue-Sun. **Main courses** £12.50-£15. **Unlicensed**. **Corkage** no charge. **No credit cards.** Georgian
You can have breakfast (scrambled eggs, toast with Marmite) at this pleasant café with cream walls and open brickwork, but it's the Georgian dishes that are the draw. Khachapuri was the highlight, the pastry soft and flaky and the cheese within soft, warm and oozing. Pelmenis – ravioli-like dumplings filled with minced pork and beef and served with a minted yoghurt sauce – are ideal for cold winter days, and work well with a side order of ajika, a spicy relish. And don't forget the cakes: the counter has an impressive display of appetising confections made from fruit, cream and sugar, most of them baked.
Available for hire. Babies and children welcome: high chairs. Tables outdoors (3, pavement). Takeaway service. Vegetarian menu.

Oasis
236 Neasden Lane, NW10 0AA (8450 5178). Neasden tube. **Meals served** 10am-10pm Mon-Thur, Sun; 10am-11pm Fri, Sat. **Main courses** £3-£9. **No credit cards.** Polish
A cheerful, orange-hued restaurant brightening up its locality by Neasden roundabout, Oasis provides a refuge for Poles of hearty appetite. Its menu is packed with enough eastern European ballast to see off the harshest of Gdansk winters – at paltry prices. Start with gloriously tangy barszcz harbouring delicate mushroom dumplings, or maybe a vast bowlful of beef stroganoff, before embarking on fried trout with rosemary, or bigos (an immense helping of sauerkraut hiding chunks of chicken and wonderfully smoky bacon nuggets). Nalesniki (filled pancakes) will finish you off, though the choice of Polish beers might cause a revival.
Babies and children welcome: children's menu; high chairs. Booking advisable. Separate room for parties, seats 40. Takeaway service. Vegetarian menu.

Menu

EAST EUROPEAN

Dishes followed by (Cz) indicate a Czech dish; (G) Georgian; (H) Hungarian; (P) Polish; (R) Russian. Others have no particular affiliation.

Bigos (P): classic hunter's stew made with sauerkraut, various meats and sausage, mushrooms and juniper.
Borscht: beetroot soup. There are many varieties: Ukrainian borscht is thick with vegetables; the Polish version (**barszcz**) is clear. There are also white and green types. Often garnished with sour cream, boiled egg or mini dumplings.
Caviar: fish roe. Most highly prized is that of the sturgeon (beluga, oscietra and sevruga, in descending order of expense), though keta or salmon caviar is underrated.
Chlodnik (P): cold beetroot soup, bright pink in colour, served with sour cream.
Galabki, golabki or golubtsy: cabbage parcels, usually stuffed with rice or kasha (qv) and sometimes meat.
Golonka (P): pork knuckle, often cooked in beer.
Goulash or gulasz (H): rich beef soup.
Kasha or kasza: buckwheat, delicious roasted: fluffy, with a nutty flavour.
Kaszanka (P): type of blood sausage that's made with buckwheat.
Khachapuri (G): flatbread; sometimes called Georgian pizza.
Kielbasa (P): sausage. Poland has dozens of widely differing styles.
Knedliky (Cz): bread dumplings.
Kolduny (P): small meat-filled dumplings (scaled-down pierogi, qv) often served in beetroot soup.
Koulebiaka, kulebiak or cou_lebiac (R): type of pie made with layered salmon or sturgeon, with eggs, dill, rice and mushrooms.
Krupnik (P): barley soup, and the name of a honey vodka (because of the golden colour of barley).
Latke: grated potato pancakes, fried.
Makowiec or makietki (P): poppy seed cake.
Mizeria (P): cucumber salad; very thinly sliced and dressed with sour cream.
Nalesniki (P): cream cheese pancakes.
Paczki (P): doughnuts, often filled with plum jam.
Pierogi (P): ravioli-style dumplings. Typical fillings are sauerkraut and mushroom, curd cheese or fruit (cherries, apples).
Pirogi (large) or **pirozhki** (small) **(R):** filled pies made with yeasty dough.
Placki (P): potato pancakes.
Shashlik: Caucasian spit-roasted meat.
Uszka or ushka: small ear-shaped dumplings served in soup.
Zakuski (R) or zakaski (P): starters, traditionally covering a whole table. The many dishes can include pickles, marinated vegetables and fish, herring, smoked eel, aspic, mushrooms, radishes with butter, salads and caviar.
Zrazy (P): beef rolls stuffed with bacon, pickled cucumber and mustard.
Zurek (P): sour rye soup.

Babies and children welcome: high chairs. Booking advisable dinner Fri, Sat. Entertainment: Russian folk music 8-10.30pm Fri, Sat. Tables outdoors (4, pavement). Takeaway service. **Map 27 A1.**

Highbury

★ Tbilisi

91 Holloway Road, N7 8LT (7607 2536). Highbury & Islington tube/rail. **Dinner served** 6.30-11pm daily. **Main courses** £8-£11. **Credit** AmEx, MC, V. Georgian
'Honest food, prepared with care' is now an annoying cliché, but the words summarise perfectly the efforts of this well-established Georgian eaterie. From its modestly priced menu of almost exclusively Georgian dishes, to the warm, unobtrusive service, the simply furnished room of reds and blacks, and the vintage cutlery, Tbilisi is a retreat from frenzied Holloway Road. The kitchen has made some welcome changes since our last visit: cornflour is mostly out; fresh spicing is in. Cleverly, the majority of starters – comprising deliciously flaky khachapuri cheese bread and mainly vegetable-based mezes – can be served as a trio for two to share. A tangy purée of spinach with pomegranate seeds stood out, being both cool and warming from intricate spicing. A main course of aubergine in walnut sauce came with a little (undressed) salad, while a spicy stew of tender beef sprinkled with pickled cucumbers reminded us of good old Hungarian goulash. The wine list is Georgian too, which in even the simplest saperavi house red rewarding with its complex structure. Tbilisi may be a little twee, but is nevertheless great for a quiet, comforting midweek supper.
Available for hire. Babies and children welcome: high chairs. Booking advisable Fri, Sat. Separate room for parties, seats 40. Takeaway service.

North West
St John's Wood

★ Tamada

122 Boundary Road, NW8 0RH (7372 2882, www.tamada.co.uk). Kilburn Park or St John's Wood tube, or Kilburn High Road rail. **Lunch served** 1-4pm Sat, Sun. **Dinner served** 6-11pm Tue-Sun. **Main courses** £9-£18. **Credit** AmEx, MC, V. Georgian
When this chic Georgian restaurant opened in 2009, we recommended it with a caveat: a saintly supply of patience was needed to deal with the slow service. The kitchen appears to have speeded up, but the floor service still seems overstretched. Our waitress was charming yet unable to stop to answer questions about the menu, which those unfamiliar with the cuisine may find enticing but mysterious. Georgian food is made to fill you up, though it's much more besides, and Tamada is perhaps London's best place to sample its complexities. It has the air of a small art gallery – modern paintings by Georgian artists, a few artfully placed Caucasian ornaments – with bare tables laid with thick napkins, heavy cutlery and featherlight glassware. Starters include deeply flavoured citeli lobio (mashed red beans with walnuts and spices, garnished with pomegranate seeds), and hearty salad olivie (vegetables with hard-boiled eggs, dill and mayonnaise). We loved the layers of ingredients in chaqapuli: lamb casserole with red wine, tarragon and wild plum sauce. Jarkoe (layered

---

and baked veal with onions, potatoes and herbs) was tempting, but took 45 minutes to cook. You could put that time to good use working through the delightful all-Georgian wine list, which showcases some excellent bottles from this undervalued viticultura area. Several are available by the glass.
Babies and children welcome: high chair. Booking advisable Fri, Sat. Tables outdoors (4, pavement). Takeaway service. **Map 1 C1.**

West Hampstead

★ Czechoslovak Restaurant `HOT 50`

74 West End Lane, NW6 2LX (7372 1193, www.czechoslovak-restaurant.co.uk). West Hampstead tube. **Dinner served** 5-10pm Tue-Fri. **Meals served** noon-10pm Sat, Sun. **Main courses** £4-£12. **Credit** MC, V. Czech
Eating here is an experience. Set in what was once a suburban house (look for the old-fashioned model of a chef in the front garden) and featuring a map of Czechoslovakia as a socialist republic, this long-running social club for Czechs and Slovaks seems adrift from the normal run of time. Food is eaten in the rear bar (to a background of Czech sport on the TV) or a barely more formal dining room (under photos of a cardinal, a fighter ace and the dear departed Queen Mum), and it's simple in the unrefined sense. Order a Czech sausage from the beer bites and that's what you get: fried or steamed sausage, rye bread and a splodge each of tomato sauce, mustard and horseradish. The menu is meat-focused (including an underpowered segedinský pork goulash), but there are also fish options (a good trout schnitzel) and sides (the cucumber salad comes, Czech style, in a big bowl of sweetened water). Be sure to go off-piste with the drinks. Moravian wine and the Budvar Dark are very fine, but the guest bottles are a treat; the brilliantly lugubrious young barman supplied an excellent Kozel Černý beer on our last visit.
Babies and children welcome: high chairs. Booking advisable weekends. Disabled: toilet. Separate room for parties, seats 25. Vegetarian menu. **Map 28 A3.**

Mamuska! See p77.

Fish

At last, London's fish restaurants are starting to become aware of the 21st-century peril of our seas – the danger that some of Britain's favourite species will become extinct unless we pursue a more sustainable course. At high-profile restaurants such as **J Sheekey**, you'll now find the likes of devilled mackerel and pan-fried pollack on the menu, while its equally illustrious stablemate, **Scott's**, might serve ray wing or Cornish gurnard. Rediscovering ingredients from Britain's culinary heritage is currently much in vogue, so recipes using long-forgotten fish sit well with the fashion. Also on-trend is foraging, with the UK's salt marshes, estuaries and coastline providing rich pickings, not least ingredient-of-the-moment sea aster. Traditional oyster bars are also experiencing a renaissance. The rejuvenation of **Bentley's** started the craze; newcomers include a Soho branch of **Wright Brothers** (some of whose oysters come from its own farm in Cornwall), the **Bennett Oyster Bar & Brasserie** in Battersea (which takes care to source all its seafood from around the British coast), and the Corinthia Hotel's Italian-inspired **Massimo** (*see p162*). To discover which types of fish and seafood are certified as sustainable, visit the Marine Stewardship Council's website, www.msc.org. For London's best chippies, see the Fish & Chips chapter, starting on page 298.

Central
Belgravia

Olivomare
10 Lower Belgrave Street, SW1W 0LJ (7730 9022, http://olivorestaurants.com). Victoria tube/rail. **Lunch served** noon-2.30pm Mon-Fri; noon-3pm Sat, Sun. **Dinner served** 7-11pm Mon-Sat; 7-10.30pm Sun. **Main courses** £19.50-£22. **Credit** AmEx, MC, V.

Gleaming white and uncompromisingly stark, save for a pop of colour from fresh flowers at the bar, Olivomare is intriguing. Lurking beneath its slick façade is a traditional Sardinian seafood restaurant – one of a clutch of Belgravia dining establishments from Italian owner Mauro Sanno, each with a strong reputation. The upmarket prices are indicative of the address and the provenance of ingredients, rather than the complexity of the well-considered menu. Authentic seafood, fish and pasta dishes are fuss-free, employing fresh, high-quality produce, true to the motherland's rustic roots. The likes of salty spaghetti bottarga (cured grey mullet roe), paper-thin carasau bread and the sherry-like Vernaccia di Oristano house aperitif fly the Sardinian flag. Red mullet ravioli was subtly sweetened with roasted peppers, but the pasta itself was over-resistant to the bite. Chargrilled cuttlefish, a single slab in black ink dressing, lingering and powerful, was heavier-going than anticipated. At times, the staff's coolness verged on the haughty, which marred the experience, as did the squeezed-in tables within ready eavesdropping distance of each other. Olivomare is a small restaurant with ambition, let down by its slightly brittle atmosphere. *Babies and children admitted. Booking advisable. Disabled: toilet. Tables outdoors (4, terrace).* **Map 15 H10**.

City

★ Sweetings [HOT 50]
39 Queen Victoria Street, EC4N 4SA (7248 3062). Mansion House tube. **Lunch served** 11.30am-3pm Mon-Fri. **Main courses** £15-£33. **Credit** AmEx, MC, V.

Operating on the same site since 1889, Sweetings has scarcely changed over the years and is all the better for it. Bookings aren't taken, so arrive early – we prefer the back area (past the linen-covered side counters), where you'll be seated at monogrammed chairs at long tables, possibly beside the dumb waiter and elbow to elbow with a striped shirt (diners are predominantly City gents). The short menu has a few nods to modernity, but in the main sticks to tradition: expect oysters, potted shrimps and prawn and crab cocktails to start, followed by excellent but simply cooked fish (poached or fried). Portions are substantial: skate wing with black butter sauce scarcely fitted on the plate, and swordfish with freshly made tomato salsa featured two big juicy steaks. Vegetables are simple (peas and mash, chips or potatoes) and puddings, unsurprisingly, are a public schoolboy's dream: crumble, spotted dick, bread and butter pud, and, on our summer visit, strawberries and cream. Pricing is reasonable, fish sustainable and service friendly and solicitous – in short, Sweetings is an absolute old-fashioned treat. *Available for hire (dinner only). Babies and children admitted. Bookings not accepted. Takeaway service.* **Map 11 P6**.

Leicester Square

J Sheekey
28-32 St Martin's Court, WC2N 4AL (7240 2565, www.j-sheekey.co.uk). Leicester Square tube. **Lunch served** noon-3pm Mon-Sat; noon-3.30pm Sun. **Dinner served** 5.30pm-midnight Mon-Sat; 6-11pm Sun. **Main courses** £13.50-£39.50. **Set lunch** (Sat, Sun) £26.50 3 courses. **Credit** AmEx, DC, MC, V.

This grande dame of Theatreland has no need to show off: its reputation as an iconic seafood restaurant precedes it. Passers-by can't see in from the street, which lends low-key mystery to the warren of tables, mostly tucked-up booths squeezed under lowish ceilings. Black and white portraits of stars of the stage and screen line the walls, but decor is modest, and seemingly untouched by the passage of time. Waiting staff are smartly suited, professional and courteous. Dining is more casual than you might imagine from a Caprice Holdings venue: trad, not stuffy, and increasingly touristy. Importantly, head chef Richard Kirkwood's menu is so delightfully varied – fruits de mer, potted shrimps, pickled herrings, pan-fried ray wing, even fried cod tongues – that you never feel in the slightest bit limited. Baked smoked haddock tart had the touch of a fine pastry chef, while a special of slip soles benefited from buttery, lemon-spiced shrimps. Dishes aren't cheap (mains hover around £20, and sevruga or beluga caviar cost serious cash), but the freshness is phenomenal. According to the menu, meat dishes are also available, but really, why bother? Note that the grand, horseshoe-shaped Oyster Bar next door (a 2008 addition) keeps conveniently long hours, and booking is not required.

Babies and children welcome: colouring books; high chairs. Booking essential. Disabled: toilet. Vegan dishes. Vegetarian menu. **Map 18 D5**.

Mayfair

Scott's

20 Mount Street, W1K 2HE (7495 7309, www.scotts-restaurant.com). Bond Street or Green Park tube. **Meals served** noon-10.30pm Mon-Sat; noon-10pm Sun. **Main courses** £15-£42. **Cover** £2. **Credit** AmEx, MC, V.
Celebrity hangout du jour, Scott's is currently eclipsing the Ivy as London's pre-eminent see-and-be-seen spot. Occupying a distinguished building in the heart of Mayfair, this bustling seafood favourite is convenient for guests at the Connaught or Dorchester, and indeed oozes something of those hotels' upmarket exclusivity. It's polished and pristine, with a handsome mosaic floor, but above all, discreet – mobiles are politely ushered away and staff are attentive. The high-ceilinged dining room is centred around a marble-topped oyster bar, and noise levels can rise, mainly because the restaurant is so popular (you'll find it busy late into a Monday night). Like at others in the well-bred Caprice group, you have a good idea of what to expect: innovation takes a backseat to reliability. The menu is shorter than at sister restaurant J Sheekey, but when the seasonality is this good, there's much to appreciate. With head chef Dave McCarthy at the helm, you can be assured of sublime roasted shellfish platters to share and cleverly judged mains, such as the cod fillet confidently paired with padrón peppers and chorizo. Portions are a good size, with sides reasonably priced, although our tender-stem broccoli verged on undercooked. Ties aren't required, but clientele look the part nonetheless.

Babies and children welcome: high chairs. Booking essential. Disabled: toilet. Separate room for parties, seats 40. Tables outdoors (7, pavement). Vegetarian menu. **Map 9 G7**.

Piccadilly

★ Bentley's Oyster Bar & Grill HOT 50

11-15 Swallow Street, W1B 4DG (7734 4756, www.bentleysoysterbarandgrill.co.uk). Piccadilly Circus tube.
Oyster Bar **Breakfast served** 7.30-10.30am Mon-Fri. **Meals served** noon-11pm Mon-Sat; noon-9.30pm Sun. **Main courses** £8.75-£36.
Restaurant **Lunch served** noon-2.30pm Mon-Fri. **Dinner served** 5.30-10.30pm Mon-Sat. **Main courses** £18.95-£38.
Both **Credit** AmEx, MC, V.
A grand old spot refurbished with love, Bentley's marries British traditions with chef-patron Richard Corrigan's fine-dining sensibilities. Staff are formally dressed and fastidious in their work, yet ready for a chat when time allows. We prefer the convivial ground-floor oyster bar to the stiffer upstairs restaurant. Glasses and cutlery sparkle against the wood panelling; chairs feature velvet stripes and studded red leather; walls are hung with angling trophies, zoological drawings and staff photos from the old days. Outside are umbrella-shaded pavement tables with garden chairs. A blackboard advertises daily specials from across the globe: Vietnamese-style sea bass, say, scallops with white peach and jalapeño pepper, or roast brill with girolles, leeks and young capers. But it's always tempting to opt for the benchmark fish pie and a bottle of green Tabasco. A good choice for business lunches and pre- or post-theatre sustenance, Bentley's is now open for breakfast too: it's wonderful to watch London unfold while eating thick-cut cold-smoked salmon with scrambled eggs, toast and a handful of sprightly watercress, or the Irish breakfast including black pudding and a baked oyster. Artisan suppliers are name-checked in typical Corrigan style; our only query regarded the use of teabags.

Booking advisable. Disabled: toilet. Dress: smart casual; no shorts. Separate rooms for parties, seating 14 and 60. **Map 17 A5**.

Bennett Oyster Bar & Brasserie

FISH

FishWorks

*79 Swallow Street, W1B 4DE (7734 5813,
www.fishworks.co.uk). Piccadilly Circus tube.*
Meals served 10am-10.30pm Mon-Sat;
10am-10pm Sun. **Main courses** £14.50-£60.
Set meal (noon-7pm) £15 2 courses. **Credit**
AmEx, MC, V.

There's an old industry cliché that the best place to
open a restaurant is next to a highly successful one,
so perhaps FishWorks decision to go head-to-head
with Bentley's on Swallow Street is not as impudent
or as reckless as it seems. The new owners of the
once-burgeoning chain have given their flagship
site a classier, more understated look than you may
remember from the brand's previous incarnation
(now it's all North Sea grey and dark wood), though
the up-front-and-personal fish retail counters
remain, as do the cookery courses. The waistcoated
staff are very knowledgeable, but, on our visit, were
a little too relaxed, forgetting to bring the wine.
Check the board for daily specials – perhaps ray
and king scallops, or a choice of whole roast turbot
or monkfish to share. The 'ocean platter' of hot and
cold seafood is the best way to sample a range of
species: 12 are served, with pots of calorie- and
allium-laden sauces. Ours was terrific all round, but
the incredibly sweet, mild and fresh-tasting brown
crabmeat warrants special mention. For the kids,
there's fish fingers and spaghetti with tomato sauce.
Finish with crowd-pleasing desserts such as crème
brûlée, chocolate pudding or eton mess. FishWorks
offers its own-label wine at £24 a bottle, but the
South African chenin blanc is a good choice if
you're looking for something cheaper.

*Available for hire. Babies and children welcome:
children's menu; high chairs; nappy-changing
facilities. Booking advisable. Disabled: toilet.*
Map 17 A5.
For branches see index.

Soho

Wright Brothers Soho

*12-13 Kingly Street, W1B 5PW (7434 3611,
www.thewrightbrothers.co.uk). Oxford Circus
or Piccadilly Circus tube.* **Meals served**
noon-10.45pm Mon-Sat; noon-6pm Sun.
Main courses £12-£18.50. **No credit cards**.
Wright Bros may have started in a cramped corner
of Borough Market, but this new branch sprawls
over three floors, from Kingly Street to the heart of
the Kingly Court retail development off Carnaby
Street. You'll find several outdoor benches
punctuated with Wrights' trademark beer barrels;
inside, there's diner-style bar seating, and more
traditional restaurant tables both upstairs (quieter)
and down (lively), by the gleaming open kitchen.
On our first visit, the brown shrimps, scallops, and
sardines on toast were the best catches. Ox cheek,
ale and oyster pie, served in a cast-iron dish with
two oysters on the side for diners to plop into the
pie and cook last-minute, featured superb pastry
and full-flavoured sauce – but was excessively
priced at £16.50. Indeed, given the need for side veg
(green beans £4), and wines starting at £20 a bottle
(try the beers instead), it all seems a bit steep. Roast
pollack with morcilla and potatoes (a blackboard
special on another visit) could have been more
generous. Better was the friendly waitress's
recommendation of juicy deep-fried oysters served
with lush tarragon mayonnaise, and the elegant
understatement of caramel cream with pistachio
biscotti (though the portion was tiny). Still, it's
pitched right for the post-work crowd, and end-of-
week evenings get very busy.
*Available for hire. Babies and children welcome;
high chairs; nappy-changing facilities. Booking
advisable. Disabled: toilet. Tables outdoors
(3, courtyard).* **Map 17 A4**.
**For branch (Wright Brothers Oyster
& Porter House) see index**.

West
Notting Hill

Geales

*2 Farmer Street, W8 7SN (7727 7528,
www.geales.com). Notting Hill Gate tube.* **Lunch
served** noon-3pm Tue-Fri. **Dinner served**
6-10.30pm Mon-Fri. **Meals served** noon-
10.30pm Sat; noon-9.30pm Sun. **Main courses**
£8-£29.50. **Set lunch** (noon-3pm Tue-Fri)
£11.95 2 courses. **Credit** AmEx, MC, V.
In business since 1939, Geales is the ultimate posh
chippy and well positioned for its well-heeled
clintele. Comfortingly old-fashioned fare is cooked
with respect for quality ingredients, and served in
unusually cosseting yet family-friendly surrounds.
Plates of precision-fried scampi and whitebait will
transport diners straight to seaside holidays on the
Isle of Wight; prices are on the high side compared
to local takeaway joints, but still cheaper than the
Solent ferry. The 'seaside pick'n'mix' is a nice light
alternative to starters if you want to fully enjoy the
tangy, crunchy, beer-battered fish (pollack, cod,
haddock, sole) and tartare sauce – chips, rather

meanly, are charged extra at £3.45 a bowl, but
they're good. Moules marinière tasted wonderfully
fresh with a creamy lemon- and parsley-accented
broth. We were most impressed with the hazelnut
brownie too, served with a scoop of blood orange
sorbet. Wine prices start at £15.75 a bottle and
escalate sharply, but rest assured the cheapest
viognier is a sound choice. A replica Chelsea Green
branch opened in 2010, where we've enjoyed crisp-
shelled fish cakes of smoked haddock and salmon.
Geales describes itself as no-frills, but the interior
is all flouncy double tablecloths of black and white
check, crystal wall sconces, and feel-the-depth
high-backed chairs, so it's probably best to take
that with a pinch of (flaky sea) salt.
*Babies and children welcome: children's menu;
high chairs. Booking advisable Fri, Sat. Separate
room for parties, seats 12. Tables outdoors
(6, pavement).* **Map 7 A7**.
For branch see index.

South
Battersea

Bennett Oyster Bar
& Brasserie NEW

*7-9 Battersea Square, SW11 3RA (7223 5545,
www.bennettsbrasserie.com). Clapham Junction
rail or bus 19.* **Meals served** 11am-11pm Mon-
Wed; 11am-midnight Fri; 9am-midnight Sat;
9am-6pm Sun. **Main courses** £12-£25.
Credit AmEx, MC, V.
Unperturbed by the absence of passing trade in this
notoriously out-of-the-way spot, Bennett has gone
to town on its interiors, using enough marble and
brass in its dining room, fine-wine shop and oyster
bar to trick out a palace. It has a timeless, Anglo-
Continental brasserie feel, with bronze-tinted
mirrors and British racing green paintwork, while
the food is largely well executed. A sensational
starter of razor clams saw succulent pieces of flesh
mixed with chunks of unctuous boar meat and
grainy-textured butter beans, while steamed steak
and oyster pudding featured tender, good-quality
meat, and a crust that gave off the appealing aroma
of piping-hot suet. There are meat dishes too: roast
duck breast, though well sourced, was slightly
overcooked, and the numerous chunks of orange,
fennel and beetroot on the plate might have been
overdoing it. Likewise, our baked alaska, correctly
frozen in the centre yet warm on the outside, had
too much going on. Bennett is a lovely place, with
gracious staff and a cracking wine list of 150 or so
bins. But its main appeal is as a neighbourhood
brasserie useful for a drink, breakfast or lunch bite,
rather than as a destination restaurant.
*Available for hire. Babies and children welcome:
high chairs. Booking advisable weekends.
Disabled: toilet. Separate room for parties, seats
22. Tables outdoors (6, patio).* **Map 21 B2**.

South East
London Bridge
& Borough

Applebee's Café

*5 Stoney Street, SE1 9AA (7407 5777,
www.applebeesfish.com). London Bridge tube/
rail.* **Lunch served** noon-3.30pm Tue-Thur;

11.30am-4pm Fri; 11.30am-4.30pm Sat. **Dinner served** 6-10pm Tue-Thur, Sat; 6-10.30pm Fri. **Main courses** £11.50-£23. **Set lunch** £14.50-£17.50 2 courses. **Credit** MC, V.

Applebee's is generally busiest on market days, when Borough's food stalls bring Londoners and tourists flocking for high-quality comestibles. Once their hessian bags are bulging with top-notch produce, many of these shoppers head here in search of first-rate fish. Even when the market isn't in full swing, lunchtimes are lively, with a hotplate out front selling seafood wraps, and a full menu of fish dishes inside; vegetarian and meat options are non-existent. With a mouthful of horseradish- and apple-crusted cod fillet, it's impossible not to pause conversation just to appreciate the culinary magic taking place on your tongue. Lobster and scallop ravioli in saffron sauce was equally diverting. It's a darkish, intimate space, with muddy-orange banquettes on one side facing the open kitchen on the other. Waiting staff were relaxed to the point of inattentiveness, although they were friendly enough when they remembered to come over. More often, we had to wave to attract their attention. Puddings were almost as good as the mains – a chocolate fondant oozed expertly, and raspberry and saffron crème brûlée delighted – so we trotted off happy and replete.

Available for hire. Babies and children admitted. Booking advisable. Disabled: toilet. Tables outdoors (4, pavement). Takeaway service.
Map 11 P8.

North East
South Woodford

Ark Fish Restaurant
142 Hermon Hill, E18 1QH (8989 5345, www.arkfishrestaurant.com). South Woodford tube. **Lunch served** noon-2.15pm Tue-Sat. **Dinner served** 5.30-9.45pm Tue-Thur; 5.30-10.15pm Fri, Sat. **Meals served** noon-8.45pm Sun. **Main courses** £9.95-£19.95. **Credit** MC, V.

Big bay windows, blue seats and an extensive fish menu make you feel as if you're relaxing at the seaside, rather than looking out on to the A113 through South Woodford. Ark is a family-run institution – an outpost of the old, now long-gone, East End with the freshest fish from Billingsgate and a loyal local following. Appetisers include fresh peeled prawns, cockles, winkles and whelks, while starters encompass crab, smoked salmon and oysters. Baked crab came with a light cheese crust, perfectly judged to let the delicate flavour of the crustacean win through. Seared scallops in garlic butter were plump, silky and plentiful. For mains, your chosen fish (cod, haddock, lemon sole, dover sole, salmon and so forth) can be deep-fried, grilled or poached, but it pays to first check the specials board, which is usually full of enticing options. A huge portion of juicy grilled haddock with samphire and beurre blanc would have had Michel Roux weeping with gratitude; sea bass with lightly curried vegetables was no slouch either. Afterwards, we shared a sticky toffee pudding that was a perfect dome of featherlight sponge in a moat of cream. Ark offers top-class ingredients cooked with precision and without any fine-dining pretensions – how refreshing.

Babies and children welcome: children's menu; high chairs. Bookings not accepted.

North
Finsbury Park

Chez Liline
101 Stroud Green Road, N4 3PX (7263 6550, www.chezliline.co.uk). Finsbury Park tube/rail. **Lunch served** noon-3pm, **dinner served** 6.30-11pm Tue-Sun. **Main courses** £12.75-£22.75. **Set lunch** £10 2 courses. **Set dinner** £12.50 2 courses. **Credit** AmEx, MC, V.

The fish shop next door offers some clue as to how seriously Chez Liline takes its fish – the same family owns both. The restaurant decor may be plain, with blue tablecloths, wooden chairs and white walls, yet the cooking is anything but. Chez Liline specialises in Mauritian seafood dishes, which combine French, Indian, African and Chinese influences. The wine list has some interesting French bottles too. To start, tender squid sautéed with garlic and herbs (basil, tarragon and thyme) was more than the sum of its simple parts; and a warm salad of chargrilled seafood and fresh leaves tossed in vinaigrette was also well executed. Main courses continued the high standard. The distinct flavours of fennel and asparagus were skilfully balanced with sublimely delicate sea bass. Cuttlefish curry with rice and pickled vegetables (Mauritian dish of the day) provided perfectly cooked cuttlefish in a a rich sauce that complementing rather than overpowered. Attentive but unhurried service makes this a great venue for a convivial evening with friends, although a woman eating on her own seemed frustrated by the pace. Stroud Green Road may not be the most glamorous destination, but Chez Liline is worth a visit. Do check it's open before you set out, though: we've been disappointed by locked doors, especially at lunchtime.

Available for hire. Babies and children welcome: high chairs. Booking advisable. Tables outdoors (2, pavement).

Outer London
Croydon, Surrey

Fish & Grill
48-50 South End, Croydon, Surrey, CR0 1DP (8774 4060, www.fishandgrill.co.uk). South Croydon rail or bus 119, 466. **Lunch served** noon-3pm, **dinner served** 5-11pm Mon-Thur. **Meals served** noon-11pm Fri; 10am-11pm Sat; 10am-10.30pm Sun. **Main courses** £10.95-£44. **Set lunch** £14.95 2 courses, £17.95 3 courses. **Credit** AmEx, MC, V.

The Fish & Grill is Malcolm John's second Croydon eaterie. It's a large, handsome space, with polished dark wood, high-backed seats and banquettes, and modern prints on the walls, designed to attract business lunchers and special-occasion diners. Whether due to size, layout or understaffing, service can be slow and muddled; we had to leave our seats and seek out staff. The menu and its execution, however, were not compromised. Seared scallops were pearlescent perfection, with accompanying green beans nicely snappy and hazelnut butter the right shade of brown; 28-day aged Aberdeen Angus beef fillet was beautifully pink and tender (and a generous size); chips were triple-cooked; a special of sautéed ceps and crayfish showed great attention to the quality of the seasonal mushrooms. Flavours tend towards the robust, whether in a powerfully dressed rocket salad, lobster fettuccine sauced with roast shell-scented bisque, or briny buttered sea vegetables. As perfect a crème brûlée as you could hope to find, with aromatic Keralan vanilla much in evidence, was worth the wait. The approachably priced wine list, helpfully structured according to flavour profile, completes the winning formula.

Available for hire. Babies and children welcome: children's menu; high chairs. Booking advisable Fri, Sat. Disabled: toilet. Tables outdoors (3, pavement).
For branch see index.

Geales. See p81.

FISH

French

London's relationship with French restaurants is curious. Time was when no self-respecting luxury hotel here could operate without a French chef, but during the renaissance of British cuisine in the 1990s, Gallic cooking was seen almost as a culinary colonial overlord. Young British chefs of the time, though needing to show knowledge of the classic French repertoire, sought to subvert it – like fledgling nations demonstrating their independence. Now, there's confidence aplenty in modern British food, and as a consequence, French restaurants, placed on a less exalted plane, tend to have jettisoned much of their former stuffiness. Take new arrival **Cigalon**, prouder of its regional (southern) roots than of any Gallic stereotypes; or **Les Deux Salons**, where, in handsome belle époque surroundings, chef Anthony Demetre creates simple yet expertly rendered dishes with a complete lack of pretension. More-established top performers emphasise the tie-loosening exuberance of today's French restaurants: **La Petite Maison**, with its Niçois specialities; **Bar Boulud**, the informal yet classy bistro of American super-chef Daniel Boulud; and the exhilaratingly creative **Trinity** and **Bistrot Bruno Loubet**. But there's also space for the polished stars of classical French cuisine – the likes of **Morgan M** or the luxe operators to be found in our Hotels & Haute Cuisine chapter (*see p127*).

Central
Belgravia

Le Cercle
1 Wilbraham Place, SW1X 9AE (7901 9999, www.lecercle.co.uk). Sloane Square tube.
Bar **Open/snacks served** noon-midnight Tue-Sat.
Restaurant **Lunch served** noon-2pm Tue-Sat.
Dinner served 5.30-10.45pm Tue-Sat.
Both **Main courses** £9-£29. **Set lunch** £15 3 courses, £19.50 4 courses. **Set dinner** (5-7pm, 10-11pm) £17.50 3 courses, £21 4 courses.
Tapas £6-£16. **Credit** AmEx, MC, V.
Through the automatic doors into the foyer, past the concierge, and down the staircase – each step towards your table at Le Cercle draws you nearer to the gentle burble emanating from the elegant, high-ceilinged dining space. The design is reminiscent of Frank Lloyd Wright, with clean, modern lines juxtaposed with natural textures of stone and wood. Diners are bathed in softly diffused light and soothing film music. This Club Gascon offshoot whispers moneyed taste, from the wine collection along one wall to the discreetly sheathed booths behind billowy muslin drapes. The menu has recently become more flexible, and features a carefully calibrated mixture of culinary classicism and strident modernity. Miniature ravioli of comté

cheese and basil set the tone for our meal, with dainty pasta pillows floating in buttery foam. Foam and decorative plating are key themes – the second course of firm but flaky haddock also arrived in its own bubbly herb bath, while a dish of intensely flavoured pork belly rested on a raft of puy lentils. The small but satisfying cheeseboard completed a refreshing French fine-dining experience, though we've found that the formal service can be patchy. *Available for hire. Babies and children admitted. Booking advisable dinner and Sat, Sun. Disabled: lift; toilet. Dress: smart casual. Separate room for parties, seats 12. Vegan dishes.* **Map 15 G10**.

Roussillon
16 St Barnabas Street, SW1W 8PE (7730 5550, www.roussillon.co.uk). Sloane Square tube.
Lunch served noon-2.30pm Mon-Fri. **Dinner served** 6.30-10.30pm Mon-Sat. **Set lunch** £35 3 courses incl half bottle of wine. **Set dinner** £65 3 courses. **Set meal** £65-£75 tasting menu.
Credit AmEx, MC, V.
You might spot a red-coated Chelsea pensioner on your way to this calm, sober restaurant not far from Sloane Square, and you'll likely encounter an older clientele inside too. The lunch deal is excellent value, including half a bottle of very good wine from a choice of ten, and several interesting little bites in addition to the three courses. It's a shame this is only available during the week; dinner prices are eye-watering. Roussillon is renowned for

revering seasonal vegetables. It has a vegetarian tasting menu, and even the decor plays homage to veg in colourful contemporary artwork on the walls. Sometimes this enthusiasm for produce leads to over-abundance in a dish; cod came with artichokes, samphire and sorrel, but we weren't convinced the delicate flavour of each ingredient gained much in combination. Raspberry louis was described as a light mousse, which indeed it was, albeit covered in chocolate with a layer of jelly and praline: a dessert for the very sweet-toothed. Service is attentive if sometimes, like the food, fussy; a splatter on the tablecloth was immediately covered with a napkin as if too shameful to behold. *Booking essential lunch Mon-Fri; dinner Mon-Sat. Separate room for parties, seats 28. Vegetarian menu.* **Map 15 G11**.

City

Le Coq d'Argent
No.1 Poultry, EC2R 8EJ (7395 5000, www.coqdargent.co.uk). Bank tube/DLR.
Brasserie **Lunch served** 11.30am-3pm Mon-Fri. **Main courses** £12-£18.50.
Restaurant **Breakfast served** 7.30-10am Mon-Fri. **Lunch served** 11.30am-3pm Mon-Fri; noon-3pm Sun. **Dinner served** 6-10pm Mon-Fri; 6.30-10pm Sat. **Main courses** £17.50-£24. **Set lunch** £28 2 courses, £32 3 courses.
Both **Credit** AmEx, DC, MC, V.

High-fliers will feel at home at this rooftop establishment, part of the D&D London stable. They can admire the expanding City skyline from the outdoor terraces or dramatic lawned garden while splashing some cash on the French-slanted food. You have the choice of brassiere and restaurant, both with covered outdoor seating and sharing the smart interior of linen-draped tables, grey leather club chairs and wood partitions (the furnishings don't seem to have changed much since this was a Conran restaurant). Oysters, foie gras, lemon sole and rump steak are typical offerings in the restaurant, for which an expense account would be handy – most mains hover around the £25 mark. We ate lunch in the brasserie (on the viewless terrace encircling the lift shaft, which is used for drinkers come the evening). Lemon-grilled salmon, served with horseradishy new potatoes, came crisp-skinned but the fish was underdone; a salad of goat's cheese, palm hearts and leaves lacked zing. Fat chips, served in a dinky silver bowl, were tasty but cost £4.50 (ouch). Dessert made amends: upside-down blackcurrant cake, dramatically presented in a little glass bowl, with a scoop of almond milk ice-cream perched on a silver spoon. Despite the plethora of black-garbed staff whisking busily about, service was amateurish, with the waiter asking how the food was before we'd tasted a morsel.
Available for hire. Babies and children welcome: high chairs. Booking advisable. Disabled: lift; toilet. Entertainment (jazz 12.30-4pm Sun). Tables outdoors (34, terrace). **Map 11 P6**.

Lutyens

85 Fleet Street, EC4Y 1AE (7583 8385, www.lutyens-restaurant.co.uk). City Thameslink or Blackfriars rail, or bus 4, 11, 15, 23, 26.
Bar **Open** noon-midnight, **breakfast served** 7.30-10.30am, **meals served** noon-9pm Mon-Fri. **Main courses** £12.50-£18.
Restaurant **Lunch served** noon-3.30pm, **dinner served** 5.30-10pm Mon-Fri. **Main courses** £12.50-£33. **Set meal** (5.30-10pm) £39.50 3 courses incl half bottle of wine.
Both **Credit** AmEx, MC, V.
Lutyens is classic Conran: not just a 130-seat restaurant, but a handsome bar, a members' club, four private dining rooms, and menus with seafood to the fore. What's more, it's in a historic building, designed by Sir Edwin Lutyens and the former home of Reuters – look at the gorgeous Lutyens-designed postbox-clock at the entrance. In the bar, a slimmed down menu lists the likes of crab salad and (excellent) steak tartare with chips and salad, or tapas, cheese or charcuterie boards to share. The roomy, light restaurant beyond gently references the 1930s, and is a pleasant space in which to knock back half a dozen rock oysters (spéciale de claire) and deliciously rich if slightly sinewy roast wood pigeon with seared foie gras. It's all quite pricey, which makes the menu compris a bargain: £39.50 buys a half bottle of wine, three courses plus coffee and petits fours. Of this, only the biscuity petits fours and bitter coffee disappointed; otherwise, soufflé suisse (twice-baked cheese), ribeye steak with bone marrow sauce, and summer fruits with lemon verbena and basil ice-cream were all impeccable. Best, however, was raspberry mojito granita, from the main menu – a chilly, fruity eye-opener of a dessert.
Babies and children welcome: high chairs. Booking essential. Disabled: lift; toilet. Separate rooms for parties, seating 6-20. **Map 11 N6**.

Les Deux Salons. See p87.

Chabrot Bistrot d'Amis. See p88.

See p88.

FRENCH

Sauterelle

Royal Exchange, EC3V 3LR (7618 2483, www.sauterelle-restaurant.co.uk). Bank tube/ DLR. **Lunch served** noon-2.30pm, **dinner served** 6-9.30pm Mon-Fri. **Main courses** £10-£35. **Set meal** £20 2 courses, £25 3 courses. **Credit** AmEx, MC, V.

The imposing Royal Exchange building houses three branches of the upmarket D&D restaurant group. City slickers can discuss the day's events over oysters in the Grand Café downstairs, a cocktail in the Mezzanine Lounge, or a smart meal at Sauterelle, also at mezzanine level. If the view down over the bustling courtyard and glittering designer boutiques isn't enough to entertain you, peer over the pass to watch the chefs preparing their fresh, modern take on French food. The set menu is great value, and no less inventive than the carte, with cheaper cuts such as ox cheek slow-cooked and paired with vibrant herby bulgar wheat. Care is taken in presentation, and a green and yellow courgette salad sang of Mediterranean sunshine. Less convincingly, confit salmon was served asymmetrically on the edge of a plate, threatening to tip into our laps. Service is swift and smiling, though the sommelier's attempt to push the more expensive wines by the glass wasn't so charming. And the trek down to toilets shared with the rest of the building slightly takes the sheen off the glamorous setting.

Available for hire, seats 26. Babies and children welcome: high chairs; nappy-changing facilities. Booking advisable. Disabled: lift; toilet. Dress: smart casual. Separate room for parties. **Map 12 Q6**.

Clerkenwell & Farringdon

★ Bistrot Bruno Loubet `HOT 50`

St John's Square, 86-88 Clerkenwell Road, EC1M 5RJ (7324 4455, www.bistrot brunoloubet.com). Farringdon tube/rail. **Breakfast served** 7-10.30am Mon-Fri; 7.30-11am Sat, Sun. **Lunch served** noon-2.30pm Mon-Fri. **Brunch served** noon-3pm Sat, Sun. **Dinner served** 6-10.30pm Mon-Sat; 6-10pm Sun. **Main courses** £13.50-£21.50. **Credit** AmEx, MC, V.

Although Bistrot Bruno Loubet is the restaurant at the Zetter hotel, it doesn't feel like a hotel dining room. The big windows looking on to St John's Square help, as does the slightly quirky decor, but most of all it's the sheer joie de vivre of Bruno Loubet's menu. From starters such as beetroot ravioli, rocket salad, fried breadcrumbs and parmesan (fast becoming a classic), or own-made duck pastrami, coleslaw and piccalilli, to mains such as pan-fried sea bream with cauliflower and parsley purée and squid ink stew, or rabbit 'tournedos' with artichoke barigoule and lovage pesto – there's an inventiveness at work that makes every dish seem like a must-try. And we defy anyone to resist chocolate fondant with a salted liquid fudge centre, or not be intrigued by the green peppercorn ice-cream accompanying English strawberries and lemon marshmallow. Prices aren't greedy, either on the menu or on the wine list, the latter having lots of choice by the glass and carafe. The adjacent bar ensures a fine set of cocktails too. Not a classic French restaurant, then – and all the better for it.

Babies and children welcome: high chairs. Booking essential. Disabled: toilet. Separate rooms for parties, seating 40-50. Tables outdoors (9, terrace). **Map 5 O4**.

Club Gascon

57 West Smithfield, EC1A 9DS (7796 0600, www.clubgascon.com). Barbican tube or Farringdon tube/rail. **Lunch served** noon-2pm Mon-Fri. **Dinner served** 7-10pm Mon-Thur; 7-10.30pm Fri, Sat. **Dishes** £12-£26. **Set lunch** £22 2 courses. **Set meal** £55 5 courses (£85 incl wine). **Credit** AmEx, MC, V.
Diners need a sense of adventure at Club Gascon, as well as deep pockets (it's unsettling to hear a £23 dish described as a 'taster-size plate'). Still, it's a pleasure to sit back and enjoy the ride. Ignore some of the odder bits of crockery and decoration in the low-lit room and focus on the south-west France menu. This is divided into sections ('La route du sel', 'L'océane' and so on). From 'Le potager', watercress quinoa risotto with pine sauce and baby cress was sublime, as was pressed duck foie gras piperade with roast crab (from 'Les foies gras'), though the crab seemed a bit of a spare part. Meat dishes were a little disappointing. Barbecued rack of lamb (which arrived still cooking) was good, but accompanying violet mustard fritters (odd-tasting, unappealing cubes) and tempura caperberries weren't; French rabbit ballotine with octopus and fennel salad and braised chorizo lost points thanks to a bland bunny. An exquisite pudding (gariguette strawberries with izarra parfait and java pepper sorbet) and a charming cheese course (ossau-iraty, a ewe's milk cheese, beautifully laid out among grapes made crunchy with muesli and verjus) restored our faith in chef Pascal Aussignac's alchemy. The extras – bread, amuse-bouche – are also praiseworthy; we particularly loved the chocolate petits fours, served on a lacy web of chocolate. If you're straying beyond the selection of wines by the glass, consult the sommelier.
Available for hire. Booking essential.
Map 11 O5.

Le Comptoir Gascon

61-63 Charterhouse Street, EC1M 6HJ (7608 0851, www.comptoirgascon.com). Farringdon tube/rail. **Lunch served** noon-2.15pm Tue-Fri. **Brunch served** 9am-3pm Sat. **Dinner served** 7-9.45pm Tue, Wed, Sat; 7-10.45pm Thur, Fri. **Main courses** £10-£15. **Credit** AmEx, MC, V.
The persistent popularity of this buzzy brasserie is due to an uncomplicated but welcome formula: great food of distinctive character, simply but pleasingly presented, sensibly priced and served by well-informed yet unobtrusive staff in appealing surroundings. That the venue doubles as a deli adds to its charm and sense of place (in this case southwest France), even if the tables are closely packed and the wait for food can be long at busy times. In contrast, wine from an interesting and wallet-friendly list is served swiftly, and generous carafes help conversation flow. Among the deeply savoury dishes are a number of unmissables: duck rillettes served warm in a mini Staub casserole; 'piggy treats', a rich platter of largely own-made charcuterie, ranging from black and white puddings to tender slivers of pig's ear; anything with foie gras (not least the 'Winner burger' in a brioche bun); and the goose-fat fried chips sprinkled with 'crazy salt' (espelette pepper and sea salt). Due respect is paid to the 'vegetal', and refreshing ways with greenery (sparky leaves dressed with lemon confit) temper the overall richness. Desserts plunge you back into hefty Gascon territory of Agen prunes and rich pâtisserie, though a chocolate and armagnac cake proved dark and elegant.

Babies and children welcome: high chairs. Booking advisable. Tables outdoors (4, pavement). **Map 11 O5.**

Covent Garden

Clos Maggiore

33 King Street, WC2E 8JD (7379 9696, www.closmaggiore.com). Covent Garden or Leicester Square tube. **Lunch served** noon-2.15pm daily. **Dinner served** 5-11pm Mon-Sat; 5-10pm Sun. **Main courses** £15.50-£21.50. **Set lunch** (Mon-Fri) £19.50 2 courses incl half bottle of wine or 3 courses; (Sat, Sun) £22.50 3 courses, £27.50 2 courses incl half bottle of wine. **Set dinner** (Fri, Sat) £22.50 2 courses; (Sun) £22.50 2 courses incl half bottle of wine or 3 courses. **Set meal** £59 tasting menu. **Credit** AmEx, MC, V.
The idiosyncratic conservatory at Clos Maggiore, with its shrub-covered walls and canopy of fake flowers, comes across as enchanting or kitsch, depending on your sensibilities. A sliding glass roof lets in fresh air on sunny days, and adds to the atmosphere at night. The piped muzak and old-fashioned, rustic Gallic decorations (a plaster cockerel, for instance) seem to suit the more mature, buttoned-up clientele of business diners and ladies-who-lunch. The Covent Garden location also makes the place an ideal pre-theatre venue, particularly given the keenly priced set menus. A typically generous portion of foie gras parfait with brioche set the scene for a rich meal that also took in translucent, overly oily pollack with a solid slab of squid ink and spinach lasagne. Unusually for a trad French restaurant, the vegetarian choices are more than token gestures; we enjoyed a vol-au-vent with earthy girolles, trompettes and broad beans. Some Italian accents are also evident. Caponata, burrata and tagliatelle have infiltrated recent menus, and on our visit an exceptional parmesan focaccia was disappearing quickly from the breadbasket. Dessert was a high spot: lavender-infused crème brûlée and fluffy, not-too-sweet pistachio madeleines. A drinks list that runs to a staggering 2,000 wines and around a dozen teas earns further bonus points.
Babies and children welcome: high chairs. Booking advisable; essential weekends, 1 mth in advance for conservatory. Separate room for parties, seats 23. Vegetarian menu.
Map 18 D4.

★ Les Deux Salons

42-44 William IV Street, WC2N 4DD (7420 2050, www.lesdeuxsalons.co.uk). Charing Cross tube/rail. **Lunch served** noon-3pm, **tea served** 3-5pm daily. **Dinner served** 5-11pm Mon-Thur; 5-11.30pm Fri, Sat; 5-10.30pm Sun. **Main courses** £15.95-£23.95. **Set lunch** (Mon-Sat) £15.50 3 courses. **Set dinner** (5-6.30pm Mon-Sat) £15.95 3 courses. **Credit** AmEx, MC, V.
The decor is cliché on a grand scale – brass rails, tiled floor, red booths, ball-shaped lights, linen curtains and tablecloths – and the location, a former Pitcher & Piano, is geared to tourists and theatre-goers, but if you were expecting standard French brasserie fare from the kitchen, you'll be pleasantly surprised. Oh, there are reassuring dishes such as salade niçoise and crème brûlée (good, though not brilliant), but Patrick Demetre and Will Smith, the team behind hit Modern European restaurants Arbutus and Wild Honey, aim higher. Ox cheek with watercress, bone marrow and a deceptively rich salsify salsa, served

in a black Staub cast-iron plate, was inventive yet unfussy, and one of the best dishes we've eaten all year. Pale juicy pork belly pepped up with a slice of saucisson, crunchy spring greens, carrots and lentils was another classily hearty winner. A Josper oven cooks everything from andouillette and calf's liver to burgers. Look to the page of specials on the table for seasonal bargains. Carafes of 250ml make it easy to have a different wine with each course. A huge cheeseboard tempts, but it would be a shame to miss out on the pretty paris-brest plump with praline cream and sprinkled with toasted almonds. Service is superb.
Babies and children welcome: high chairs. Booking advisable. Disabled: toilet. Separate rooms for parties, seating 10 & 25. **Map 18 D5.**

Mon Plaisir

21 Monmouth Street, WC2H 9DD (7836 7243, www.monplaisir.co.uk). Covent Garden tube. **Meals served** noon-11.15pm Mon-Fri. **Lunch served** noon-3pm, **dinner served** 5.45-11.15pm Sat. **Main courses** £16.95-£23.95. **Set lunch** £10.95 2 courses, £14.95 3 courses. **Set meal** (5.45-7pm Mon-Sat; after 10pm Mon-Thur) £12.95 2 courses, £14.95 3 courses incl glass of wine & coffee. **Credit** AmEx, MC, V.
The self-proclaimed oldest French restaurant in the capital is part of central London's disappearing old guard. Perennially busy on weekday lunchtimes, Mon Plaisir draws in tourists and loyal regulars in equal numbers. The appeal is the sociable atmosphere, and sense of history and tradition. While the food is of a high quality, and skilfully prepared, it can't be described as cutting-edge. Classic dishes make up the bulk of the menu, with clichés creeping in (although that's partly the aim). So, coq au vin takes its place beside confit of lamb and steak tartare – vegetarians may struggle here. Diners on a budget might flinch at the prices on the evening à la carte, but will be pleasantly surprised by the good-value lunch deals, which normally feature one fish dish (a very tasty whiting with hazelnut crust on the day we visited) and one meat choice (lamb shoulder casserole, perhaps). The pre- and post-theatre menus are also a steal. Desserts – the likes of plum clafoutis – transport you to holidays in the French countryside.
Babies and children admitted: high chairs. Booking advisable. Separate room for parties, seats 25. **Map 18 D3.**

Fitzrovia

Elena's L'Étoile

30 Charlotte Street, W1T 2NG (7636 7189, www.elenasletoile.co.uk). Goodge Street or Tottenham Court Road tube. **Lunch served** noon-2.30pm Mon-Fri. **Dinner served** 6-10.30pm Mon-Sat. **Main courses** £15.75-£20.25. **Credit** AmEx, DC, MC, V.
A feature of Charlotte Street for over a century, Elena's L'Etoile – partly named after renowned London maître d' Elena Salvoni (it was simply called L'Etoile, 'the star', until it changed hands in the 1990s) – is resolutely old-school in both its ambience and its rather tired but reliable menu. When you're seated on a red-velvet chair, one of the medley of waiters will insist on tucking a blanched linen napkin into your shirt. The sunflower-yellow walls plastered with celeb-signed photographs from yesteryear (from Sir Cliff to Mavis from Corrie via, er, Eamonn Holmes) remain

intact. Where once this was a haven for Fleet Street editors and advertising executives, now you're more likely to be sat beside a party of Japanese tourists, but it's a fun place to visit if you're after a slice of nostalgia. Chicken liver parfait with red onion marmalade and toasted brioche, and chilled melon soup with peppermint tea sorbet give an idea of the type of starters on offer, while salmon and leek fish cakes, and a trio of slow-cooked pork are firm fixtures when it comes to mains. Desserts – such as the pave of Valrhona chocolate, and lemon tart with clotted cream and marinated berries – are suitably calorific.

Babies and children admitted. Booking advisable; essential lunch. Separate rooms for parties, seating 10, 16 and 32. Map 17 B1.

Villandry

170 Great Portland Street, W1W 5QB (7631 3131, www.villandry.com). Great Portland Street tube.
Bar Open 8am-11pm Mon-Fri; 9am-11pm Sat. **Breakfast served** 8-11.30am, **meals served** noon-10pm Mon-Sat. **Main courses** £11.50-£22.50.
Restaurant **Lunch served** noon-3pm Mon-Fri; 11am-4pm Sun. **Brunch served** 11am-6pm Sat. **Dinner served** 6-10.30pm Mon-Sat. **Main courses** £13-£19.80.
Both **Credit** AmEx, MC, V.
Villandry was bought by Le Pain Quotidien founder Philippe Le Roux in mid 2011, but there were no significant changes to the formula by autumn. The charcuterie area is still packing them in at lunchtimes, with a menu that includes salads and sandwiches as well as meat, cheese and vegetarian platters. The menus in the bar area and airy restaurant at the back have changed little, and feature fine ingredients from the British Isles such as Loch Duart salmon and 28-day dry-aged Galloway beef, along with classic European favourites such as moules frites. We tried a summer special of seared salmon with new potatoes, asparagus and peas in herb mayonnaise, while sitting at a linen-cloth covered table in the restaurant. The fish and asparagus were cooked to perfection, but some of the potatoes tasted like they'd been reheated. A strawberry tart to follow was excellent, and chocolate truffle petits fours substantial enough to have been pudding in their own right. At the front, the foodstore continues its decline, with everything breathtakingly expensive; however, items from the on-site bakery are very reasonable, with pain au chocolat at £1.60 and chocolate torte at £2.10. The incongruous baby shop has gone, but the takeaway area is still going strong, selling stir-fries and falafal wraps to order (a bit dry on our last try). Service throughout this Great Portland Street monolith remains personal and friendly even when busy, so in all, there's no sign of it crumbling yet.

Available for hire. Babies and children welcome: children's menu; high chairs. Booking advisable. Tables outdoors (13, pavement). Takeaway service. Map 3 H5.
For branches (French Kitchen) see index.

Holborn

Cigalon NEW

115 Chancery Lane, WC2A 1PP (7242 8373, www.cigalon.co.uk). Chancery Lane or Temple tube. **Lunch served** noon-2.45pm, **dinner**

served 6-9.45pm Mon-Fri. **Main courses** £12.50-£21. **Set meal** £19.50 2 courses, £24 3 courses. **Credit** AmEx, MC, V.
Cigalon's background music of cheerfully chirping crickets brings an aural sense of Provençal to the shadowy law courts of Chancery Lane. Here you'll find elegant, well-conceived French food with an excellent, well-priced set menu. Executive chef Pascal Aussignac closely manages his restaurants – including prestigious Club Gascon and Le Cercle – he even designed Cigalon's interiors himself. The decor is as evocative of Provençal as the menu; reeds hide a mirrored wall, which creates a sense of sitting on an open terrace; soft lavender-coloured booths scoop out secluded tables; and olive trees, dried fruit and forest shadows imprinted on the wall are rustic – yet the food is distinctly refined. King prawn ceviche was served with upbeat basil granite and chilled melon soup that evoked a cool summer evening. Classic beef onglet certainly had the wow factor: hefty steak slices mixed through a crisp, vibrant green salad, served on a heavy platter. A meringue with delicate raspberry notes was served with apricots two ways – roasted, and turned into a slightly sharper lemon verbena and apricot sorbet. Selected wines come by the glass or carafe; the wine list is divided into Provence and Corsican wines, then 'the Rest of France' is given brief page space too.
Available for hire. Babies and children welcome: high chairs. Booking advisable lunch Mon-Fri. Separate room for parties, seats 8.
Map 11 N6.

Knightsbridge

★ Bar Boulud

Mandarin Oriental Hyde Park, 66 Knightsbridge, SW1X 7LA (7201 3899, www.barboulud.com). Knightsbridge tube.
Lunch served noon-2.30pm, **tea served** 3.30-5pm, **dinner served** 5.30-10.30pm daily. **Main courses** £12-£28. **Set meal** (lunch, 5.30-7pm) £22 3 courses. **Credit** AmEx, MC, V.
This London bistro of American super-chef Daniel Boulud may be situated inside one of London's grand hotels, but the dining here is refreshingly informal, and adults with children are welcomed with sincerity. The open-plan kitchen lies at the centre of a big dining area decorated in oak and claret leather; the room bristles with happy customers. Food is French but comes with New York style, so expect to find piggie burger next to the fruits de mer. There's stellar charcuterie from Gilles Verot, and when we visited on a Sunday, a £22 lunch menu including coffee. The cooking doesn't push any boundaries, but food is delivered with aplomb, and prices are reasonable for Knightsbridge. Symmetrical goat's cheese terrine with a mosaic of vegetables came with a tomato-basil pesto and sweet vine-ripened tomatoes. And in a dish of croustilles de porc, we loved the crisp texture of the pig's ear (served with gribiche sauce), and the highly audible crunchiness of the pork scratchings. Next, pappardelle with duck confit and oyster mushrooms was comforting, and to finish, raspberry came up trumps (in the form of fruit, coulis, sorbet) in a mascarpone-filled pavlova. Order camomile infusion and it comes with the real flowers – classy.
Babies and children welcome: high chairs. Booking advisable. Disabled: toilet. Dress: smart casual. Separate rooms for parties, seating 16.
Map 8 F9.

Chabrot Bistrot d'Amis NEW

9 Knightsbridge Green, SW1X 7QL (7225 2238, www.chabrot.co.uk). Knightsbridge tube. **Lunch served** noon-3pm, **dinner served** 6.30-11pm daily. **Set meal** (noon-3pm, 6.30-7.30pm) £12.50 1 course, £15.50 1 course incl glass of wine, £17.50 2 courses incl glass of wine. **Credit** AmEx, MC, V.
Clearly a labour of love from a top-pedigree team of 'amis' (with experience ranging from Le Gavroche to Nobu), this intimate new bistro is unrestrainedly Gallic. Close tables are covered with tea-towel tablecloths and sparkling cutlery; aged brandies adorn shelves around the room; smart and cordial waiters ferry plates of snails, oysters and bone marrow to the Francophone diners. The menu isn't ground-breaking, covering bistro classics with a lean towards south-west France, but the attention to detail and small touches elevate it. Bread was exceptional. A plate of charcuterie included rillettes, jesus du pays basque, garlicky saucisson and earthy andouille (thinly sliced sausage made mostly from pig's intestines). From a list of specials we chose monkfish 'cassoulet', a deconstructed and fancified version with a slice of fish topped with chorizo perched on a scoop of white beans and tomato sauce. But for a handful of prestige French bottles, everything on the one-page wine list is sensibly priced and there's a good choice by the glass and carafe too. Best of all, there's a terrific-value set meal: £15.50 gets you the plat du jour plus a glass of house red or white; add £2 and you'll get a coffee and small dessert.
Available for hire. Babies and children admitted. Booking advisable. Separate room for parties, seats 20. Map 8 F9.

Racine

239 Brompton Road, SW3 2EP (7584 4477, www.racine-restaurant.com). Knightsbridge or South Kensington tube. **Lunch served** noon-3pm Mon-Fri; noon-3.30pm Sat, Sun. **Dinner served** 6-10.30pm Mon-Sat; 6-10pm Sun. **Main courses** £12.50-£20.75. **Set meal** (lunch, 6-7.30pm Mon-Sat) £15.50 2 courses, £17.75 3 courses; (lunch, 6-7.30pm Sun) £18 2 courses, £20 3 courses. **Credit** AmEx, MC, V.
Racine is clearly doing something right; since opening in 2002, the place has continued to hum with a throng of locals and visitors. Furnishings provide little to write home about. The predominantly brown colour scheme is cheered up slightly with mirrors, but such sobriety serves to focus attention on the resolutely French cooking of chef-patron Henry Harris. There are invariably some Lyonnais classics on the menu, and most recently, we were thrilled by the pan-fried calf's brains with black butter, which came with a few capers for that extra pinch of sharpness. Another winning dish was grilled rabbit, which arrived with a velvety dijon mustard sauce finished with tasty pieces of smoked bacon. Beef comes from Cork, via Knightsbridge butcher Jack O'Shea, and the côte de boeuf (for two, served with béarnaise sauce, £77) is hung for 44 days. Cooking here is classic and comforting, pretty much delivering what's on the tin. Dessert of petit pots of chocolate is another crowd-pleaser. The lunch and early dinner prix-fixe represent good value in this exclusive part of town. Additional draws include the assiduous service and a mostly French wine list containing 20 options by the glass.
Available for hire. Babies and children welcome: high chairs. Booking essential. Separate room for parties, seats 22. Map 14 E10.

Marylebone

FRENCH

Galvin Bistrot de Luxe

*66 Baker Street, W1U 7DJ (7935 4007,
www.galvinrestaurants.com). Baker Street tube.*
Lunch served noon-2.30pm Mon-Sat; noon-
3pm Sun. **Dinner served** 6-10.30pm Mon-
Wed; 6-10.45pm Thur-Sat; 6-9.30pm Sun.
Main courses £16-£21.50. **Set lunch** £17.50
3 courses. **Set dinner** (6-7pm) £19.50 3 courses.
Credit AmEx, MC, V.
With its elegant dark-wood panelling, crisp linen
and precise combination of class and conviviality,
this is one of London's best renderings of a classic
Parisian bistro – equally well primed for a business
lunch, a treat for two or a get-together with friends.
Exceptional service, charming and responsive,
adds to the experience, and the wine list offers an
impressive, predominantly French selection at quite
hefty prices. At its best, the cooking is both refined
and deliciously enjoyable. In a terrine of chicken
confit, foie gras and globe artichokes, flavours and
textures were finely intertwined. To follow, saddle

of rabbit was ideally matched with an exquisitely
subtle curry sauce. Our gripe is with the oddly
uninformative menu. Ordering a 'gazpacho
andalou', we expected – as you would – a refreshing
summer soup, but what came was unusually acrid
and had a fierce, entirely un-gazpacho back-taste
of hot spice. Cod with mussels and a courgette and
saffron ragout sounded like an original stew, but
was only a pretty conventional piece of fish with a
non-ragout-like light sauce and (unannounced)
peas. Creative variations on classic dishes, fine, but
if you don't tell diners what they're ordering it's no
surprise if some complain.
*Babies and children welcome: high chairs.
Booking advisable. Disabled: toilet. Separate
room for parties, seats 22. Tables outdoors
(3, pavement).* **Map 9 G5**.
**For branch (Galvin at Windows)
see index.**

The Wallace

*Wallace Collection, Hertford House, Manchester
Square, W1U 3BN (7563 9505, www.thewallace
restaurant.co.uk). Bond Street tube.*

Café **Meals served** 10am-4.30pm daily.
Main courses £6.50-£12.50.
Restaurant **Lunch served** noon-3pm Mon-
Fri; noon-3.30pm Sat, Sun. **Dinner served**
5-9.30pm Fri, Sat. **Main courses** £14.50-£21.50.
Set lunch £22 2 courses, £26 3 courses.
Both **Credit** MC, V.
Peyton & Byrne's operation at the Wallace is well
known for its elegant afternoon teas, served in the
museum's attractive glass-roofed courtyard. Less
commonly known is the fact you can also eat here
on a Friday and Saturday night; on our visit, only
a handful of tables were filled. Unfortunately, the
restaurant's charms by day appear to be its
downfall by night. Being ushered in through closed-
up galleries felt a little creepy, and the garden-
furniture seating was uncomfortable by the end of
the evening. The menu reads well, including a
selection of fruits de mer and rustic terrines, but
everything we tried was disappointing. Sea bass
had been drowned in a pungent marinade; when we
asked what was in it, the waitress disappeared to
ask the chef and never came back. Bayonne ham
was served tooth-tinglingly cold, and an oddly

Bistro du Vin

flavourless steak came with flaccid chips. Our wine was kept out of reach, leaving us empty-glassed for long stretches. If the Wallace could attract a few more punters, the atmosphere would be much improved, but at present there's little to tempt folk. Available for hire. Babies and children welcome: children's menu; high chairs. Booking advisable restaurant. Disabled: lift; toilet. **Map 9 G5**.

Mayfair

★ La Petite Maison

54 Brooks Mews, W1K 4EG (7495 4774, www.lpmlondon.co.uk). Bond Street tube. **Lunch served** noon-2.30pm Mon-Fri; 12.30-2.45pm Sat; 12.30-3.30pm Sun. **Dinner served** 6-10.30pm Mon-Sat; 6.30-9pm Sun. **Main courses** £13.50-£35. **Credit** AmEx, MC, V.
The London offshoot of one of Nice's most feted and famous restaurants, La Petite Maison has breezy, white-painted walls, waiters in striped aprons, and trademark table centrepieces of fresh lemons and tomatoes. It certainly looks the part – as do the customers, with their open-necked shirts, prosperous tans, and conversations revolving around yachts and golf. (The smaller tables along the banquette are a tight squeeze, so expect to leave with a working knowledge of your neighbour's handicap.) The kitchen offers polished takes on time-honoured Niçois classics, such as pissaladière – artfully reinvented as dainty little rectangles, topped with lusciously buttery onion, a dot of black olive and symmetrical slivers of anchovy. Crab and lobster salad evinced a similar finesse, and served on ice was almost too pretty to eat. Mains were simpler, but no less delicious – though salt-baked sea bass couldn't compete with our honey-marinated chargrilled lamb cutlets paired with silky, smoky aubergine purée. The downside, alas, is the eye-watering prices (over £30 for many of the mains), with myriad little extras on top: £5.50 for a simple side dish, say, and a 13.5% service charge. Add a seriously expensive wine list, and, rather soberingly, you'll pay the best part of a train fare to Nice for the meal.
Babies and children admitted: high chairs. Booking advisable. Tables outdoors (10, terrace). **Map 9 H6**.

Soho

Bistro du Vin NEW

36 Dean Street, W1D 4PS (7432 4800, www.bistroduvinandbar.com). Tottenham Court Road tube. **Lunch served** noon-2.30pm Mon-Fri; noon-3pm Sat, Sun. **Dinner served** 5-10.30pm Mon-Sat; 5-10pm Sun. **Main courses** £11.95-£32. **Set meal** (lunch, 5-7.30pm daily) £18.50 2 courses, £24.50 3 courses. **Credit** AmEx, MC, V.
The Hotel du Vin chain is a collection of tasteful boutique hotels in prime UK locations, where comfortable rooms come with the guarantee of decent cooking and a great wine list. The second London-based Bistro du Vin to open in as many months, this Soho site, like its Clerkenwell predecessor, is a restaurant-only spin-off for the brand. It's nonetheless recognisably HdV: a British aesthetic with an Anglo-French menu that's good but not too challenging. The knowingly placed grocer's scales and butcher's blocks may smack of rustic kitsch, but slick, unpretentious staff make the experience memorable. Likewise, while the meat- and fish-focused menu mostly plays it safe

(steak, moules frites), this branch does take a few more risks than its provincial counterparts, offering the likes of sweetbreads and roast bone marrow. Our saucisson à la Lyonnaise with mustardy ratte potatoes was proficiently cooked, with well-sourced ingredients. Charcuterie and cheese also feature strongly, and are showcased in a glass-walled fridge, with a 'cheese aficionado' on hand to give tours and help with selections. What's more, both London branches boast a by-the-glass dispenser, allowing you to sample interesting wines from a list masterminded by Ronan Sayburn, one of the country's top sommeliers.
Available for hire. Babies and children admitted. Booking advisable. Disabled: toilet. Separate room for parties, seats 20. Tables outdoors (2, pavement). **Map 17 B3**.
For branch see index.

Gauthier Soho

21 Romilly Street, W1D 5AF (7494 3111, www.gauthiersoho.co.uk). Leicester Square or Piccadilly Circus tube. **Lunch served** noon-2.30pm Mon-Fri. **Dinner served** 5.30-10.30pm daily. **Set lunch** £18 2 courses, £25 3 courses. **Set dinner** (5.30-7pm, 9.30-10.30pm) £18 2 courses (£26 incl half bottle of wine), £25 3 courses (£33 incl half bottle of wine); (7-9.30pm) £35 3 courses, £45 4 courses, £55 5 courses. **Set meal** £68 tasting menu (£124 incl wine). **Credit** AmEx, MC, V.
This refined townhouse restaurant, set across several floors, is very much at the 'haute' end of French cuisine, with almost as many waiters as diners, exquisite amuse-bouches and a seriously reverential atmosphere. While there are several multi-course menus (including a vegetarian choice), there's also a good-value set lunch/pre-theatre option (rising to excellent value if you take up the addition of half a bottle of wine). From the latter, starters were more impressive than mains: a lovely langoustine and basil velouté had a tiny scallop-flavoured tortellino infused with a waft of lemon; a powerful beetroot risotto came with a pretty parmesan crisp. To follow, however, a charming arrangement of summer baby vegetables (stuffed with herbs and truffle, with a basil reduction) was insipid. Ginger-marinated organic salmon, with sprouting broccoli and red pepper and a fish reduction, was also a bit so-what. One quirk on the menu is the introduction of calorie counts: who knew that the plate of unpasteurised French cheeses with garnish and biscuits racked up fewer calories (376) than strawberry vacherin (strawberries, meringue and vanilla ice-cream, 487) or golden louis XV (dark chocolate and praline, 480)? The charming sommelier will help you tackle the long wine list.
Available for hire. Babies and children admitted. Booking advisable. Separate rooms for parties, seating 4-16. **Map 17 C4**.

South Kensington

Cassis Bistro NEW

232 Brompton Road, SW3 2BB (7581 1101, www.cassisbistro.co.uk). South Kensington tube. **Meals served** 11.30am-11pm Mon-Fri; 11am-11pm Sat, Sun. **Main courses** £11-£34. **Set lunch** (noon-3pm Mon-Fri) £17 2 courses, £20 3 courses. **Credit** AmEx, MC, V.
Owned by wealthy restaurateur Marlon Abela (who boasts a collection that includes the Greenhouse and Umu), Cassis, on first glance, is a French

restaurant so tasteful it borders on dull. It has the expensive cutlery, the well-chosen art on the walls, the gracious serving staff and the 'right' location. As for the food, it's pretty damn good, fairly expensive, and with few surprises. However, there's a sense of playfulness about the menu that we liked. The 'petites bouchées' gave a knowing wink to 1970s dinner parties. Pastis-flambéed snails, puff pastry and garlic butter were… vol-au-vents. And eggs mimosa (hard-boiled eggs with the yolks mixed and restuffed), came beautifully impregnated with crab mayonnaise. Some aspects of the meal stood out – the breads were a highlight – while others struggled to make an impact. The pâtés were perfectly correct but a touch prosaic, while pan-fried red mullet with fregola (Sardinian couscous) would have been bland but for the addition of little brown shrimps. The wine list is stacked full of fantastic bottles (France, Italy, Spain) at prices that aren't rapacious, though a sommelier is on hand should you wish to up your game to some of the 700 options from the longer list.
Available for hire. Babies and children welcome: high chairs; nappy-changing facilities. Booking advisable. Disabled: toilet. Tables outdoors (5, terrace). **Map 14 E10**.

West

Bayswater

Angelus

4 Bathurst Street, W2 2SD (7402 0083, www.angelusrestaurant.co.uk). Lancaster Gate tube. **Meals served** 11am-11pm Mon-Sat; 11am-10pm Sun. **Main courses** £18-£33. **Set lunch** £32 3 courses (£40 incl half bottle of wine). **Credit** AmEx, MC, V.
Owner Thierry Tomasin has created an intimate restaurant out of what was once an elegant pub: lots of dark wood with art nouveau curves, and plenty of mirrors and natural light. Staff are charming, but not above pushing the menu's pricier end – we had to ask for the cheaper all-day list, and the astounding price of a very average bloody mary (£13) was only revealed when we got the bill. There are few bargains on the French-leaning wine list either. From the all-day menu, a steak baguette with french fries was satisfying, far more substantial and much tastier than our tiny portion of rubbery goujons de poisson for £9. However, it took a 'tasting plate' to reveal the kitchen's true capabilities: a ramekin of delectable gazpacho; chicken and ham terrine with grain-mustard dressing; bayonne ham with pea and mint mousse and broad beans; a zingy salad of crayfish and mango with avocado purée; and a sinfully good foie gras crème brûlée with toasted nut and fruit bread – a snip at £13. An assiette of desserts was also a joy, from the baby pineapple soufflé to the chocolate and cherry cake. Do eat here, but keep a sharp eye on the prices when you do so.
Babies and children admitted. Booking advisable. Disabled: lift; toilet. Separate room for parties, seats 22. Tables outdoors (5, terrace). **Map 8 D6**.

Chiswick

La Trompette

5-7 Devonshire Road, W4 2EU (8747 1836, www.latrompette.co.uk). Turnham Green tube. **Lunch served** noon-2.30pm Mon-Sat;

12.30-3pm Sun. **Dinner served** 6.30-10.30pm Mon-Sat; 6.30-9.30pm Sun. **Set lunch** (Mon-Fri) £26 3 courses; (Sat) £27.50 3 courses; (Sun) £32.50 3 courses. **Set dinner** £39.50 3 courses, £49.50 4 courses. **Credit** AmEx, MC, V.
An established destination, with links to the Ledbury, Chez Bruce and the Glasshouse, La Trompette has earned an enthusiastic following of business types, mature diners and romancing couples. The dining room is furnished in shades of brown and beige, punctuated by crisp white napery: a fitting setting for high-quality cooking that's mostly classic French, but makes occasional forays to the Mediterranean. Creamy fennel soup, notable for its delicate aniseed-like flavour, was an outstanding example of simple elegance. Less impressive, duck confit tortellini, served with sweet creamed cabbage and mustard and bacon foam, had ambition yet lacked punch. Mains, however, were splendid. A juicy, golden-hued chicken breast, surrounded by plump, smoky-tasting morels, broad beans, peas and macaroni, was full of garden-fresh flavour. Equally enjoyable, crisp-skinned bream fillet, accompanied by crushed potatoes, paired well with tangy clam vinaigrette flecked with chives and diced tomatoes. Puddings are exceptional; strawberry sorbet and meringue fingers made a light, fresh-flavoured finale to a satisfying meal. The wine list is extensive, and service professional and unobtrusive, if at times slow between courses. In summer, the glass frontage opens on to a neatly appointed outdoor dining area.
Available for hire. Babies and children welcome: high chairs. Booking essential. Disabled: toilet. Tables outdoors (7, terrace).

Le Vacherin
76-77 South Parade, W4 5LF (8742 2121, www.levacherin.co.uk). Chiswick Park tube/rail. **Lunch served** noon-3pm Tue-Sun. **Dinner served** 6-10.30pm Mon-Thur; 6-11pm Fri, Sat; 6-10pm Sun. **Set lunch** £25 3 courses. **Set dinner** (Mon-Thur) £14.95 2 courses; £19.95-£35 3 courses; (Fri-Sun) £35 3 courses. **Credit** AmEx, MC, V.
This pair of dining rooms recreates a classic bistro look for its clientele of well-heeled locals. Parisian prints, white tablecloths, mirrors and draped curtains set the scene for some traditional French cooking. Evenings are well populated, but on our Saturday daytime visit, the restaurant was almost empty – and yet the vibe remained relaxed and the French service team friendly and low-key. Dishes varied in quality. Smoked duck breast, although tender and well matched with apple and celeriac remoulade, was let down by a shortfall of shredded apple. Cream of pea soup was too heavy in texture for a first course. Things picked up with mains. Succulent steak, accompanied by a plump, wine- and stock-braised shallot, and crisp chips, was outstanding for its sticky reduction of thyme-infused jus. Almost as impressive, fried sea bream fillet topped with buttery brown shrimps was tastefully contrasted with the salty bite of samphire. Desserts are star performers. Our favourite: dinky profiteroles filled with custardy cream, served with full-flavoured coffee ice-cream and warm caramel sauce. Despite occasional hiccups, this neighbourhood gem is great value.
Babies and children welcome: high chairs. Booking advisable. Separate room for parties, seats 30.
For branches (Brasserie Vacherin, Le Cassoulet) see index.

Holland Park
The Belvedere
Holland House, off Abbotsbury Road, in Holland Park, W8 6LU (7602 1238, www.belvedererestaurant.co.uk). Holland Park tube. **Lunch served** noon-2.15pm Mon-Sat; noon-2pm, 2.30-4.30pm Sun. **Dinner served** 6-10.30pm Mon-Sat. **Main courses** £12-£22. **Set meal** (lunch, 6-7pm Mon-Fri) £15.95 2 courses, £19.95 3 courses; (lunch Sat, Sun) £27.50 3 courses. **Credit** AmEx, MC, V.
With its swish setting inside Holland Park, the Belvedere is the kind of restaurant you want to dress up for, whether or not you're off to the opera afterwards. It's easy to imagine yourself in an art deco hotel lounge, with gilt mirrors, oriental-patterned wallpapers and the piano tinkling away as you enter the room; all that's missing is Hercule Poirot. There are playful touches, with bright artwork like Warhol's Marilyn Monroe to dilute the sense that you're in a period piece. Likewise, the menu features some slightly incongruous items, with fish and chips sitting alongside the Franco-Italian classics. There's also a selection of Sunday roasts – with jus, not gravy. Back on track, the wine list places formidable French vintages to the fore. Staying more or less across the Channel, a chicory salad combined two colours of the bitter leaf, with the right balance of roquefort, pears and walnuts. Calf's liver was nicely charred, and paired with an intense sauce diable, but tuna steak with aubergine caviar had a slightly mushy texture and was under-seasoned. Oddly, the waiters offer a grinding of black pepper over every dish, Pizza Express-style, but they serve their white-haired and well-to-do clientele with smooth efficiency.
Available for hire. Babies and children welcome: high chairs. Booking essential. Separate room for parties, seats 20. Tables outdoors (8, terrace).
Map 7 A8.

South West
Fulham
★ My Dining Room
18 Farm Lane, SW6 1PP (7381 3331, www.mydiningroom.net). Fulham Broadway tube or bus 11, 14, 211.
Bar **Open** 11am-midnight Mon-Sat; 11am-11.30pm Sun. **Meals served** noon-11pm Mon-Sat; 11am-10.30pm Sun.
Restaurant **Meals served** noon-10.30pm daily.
Both **Main courses** £9.95-£20. **Set lunch** (noon-4pm Mon-Fri) £9.95 2 courses, £13.50 3 courses. **Set meal** (6-10.30pm daily) £15 2 courses, £19.50 3 courses. **Credit** AmEx, MC, V.
You can't judge a restaurant by its name. 'My Dining Room' sounds like a contrived attempt at the personal touch (how long before we get iDining?), yet this expansive bar-restaurant is a genuinely charming enterprise. French venues aren't known for their warmth, but you'll find an easy-going Gallic flair here. Even cynics might have softened had they been welcomed, like us, with a disarming smile and: 'Good evening, or is it afternoon? Good evenoon'. Loungey sofas, bar snacks and books set the tone near the entrance; towards the back is the 'dining room', fittingly appointed with deep-hued wallpaper, sturdy old-

school dressers and an avenue of overhead lights. The à la carte, billed as 'honest French cooking', changes monthly, while the prix fixe offers interesting dishes at an appealing price. Leg of rabbit was delicately braised and remarkably tender, while a robust cassoulet incorporated quality toulouse sausage and succulent pork belly. Desserts, such as almond baba or apple tarte tatin with cider sorbet (cooked to order), are a cut above. The kitchen even creates vegetarian dishes, such as the tempting aubergine millefeuille. In all, this is a relaxed, uncomplicated spot that's deserving of a place in your list of go-to restaurants.
Babies and children welcome: high chairs. Booking advisable. Disabled: toilet. Tables outdoors (5, pavement; 4, terrace). **Map 13 A13**.

Wandsworth
★ Chez Bruce
2 Bellevue Road, SW17 7EG (8672 0114, www.chezbruce.co.uk). Wandsworth Common rail. **Lunch served** noon-2pm Mon-Fri; noon-3pm Sat, Sun. **Dinner served** 6.30-10pm Mon-Thur; 6.30-10.30pm Fri, Sat; 7-9pm Sun. **Set lunch** (Mon-Fri) £27.50 3 courses; (Sat, Sun) £35 3 courses. **Set dinner** £45 3 courses. **Credit** AmEx, DC, MC, V.
Lauded by nearly every guide, critic, website and diner, chef Bruce Poole's restaurant offers a wine list and cooking that is among London's very best. Pitched firmly at the City bonus and special anniversary crowd, the atmosphere is hushed, the prices high. But once you get past the shock of finding a Mayfair restaurant overlooking Wandsworth Common, the sybaritic pleasures reel you in. The bright colours of some dishes evoke the Mediterranean, such as a starter of yellow tagliatelle with broad beans and amber girolles. With others it's the flavours that have most impact, such as a dun-hued courgette soup with the sharp, oxalic tang of sorrel, topped with the crunch of fresh croutons. Both fish and meat cookery show mastery of timing, with a firm fillet of plaice near-translucent, and roast rump of lamb pink and very tender. Little details and add-ons consistently impress; the neatly carved lamb came with a faultless caponata, perfectly crisp, Greek-style boureki glazed with thyme honey, and a tiny lamb meatball in a sweet jus. There's no carte, just set menus, which makes it hard to resist the desserts; one of the lighter options might be a simple strawberry jelly, set in a glass with a black pepper tuile and yoghurt sorbet. Some unusually imaginative wines are available by the glass; try a violet-scented zweigelt red from Austria, or a white Terlaner from the Italian Tyrol, with its tropical fruit nose. Of course, there's also a huge fine wines list, at prices that would cover the annual insurance of one of the Audis or BMWs parked nearby.
Babies and children welcome (lunch): high chairs. Booking essential. Disabled: toilet. Separate room for parties, seats 16.
For branch (The Glasshouse) see index.

South
Battersea
Entrée NEW
2 Battersea Rise, SW11 1ED (7223 5147, www.entreebattersea.co.uk). Clapham Junction rail. **Lunch served** noon-3.30pm Sat, Sun.

The smart way of giving

Treat the foodie in your life to the ultimate culinary adventure

Browse the full range of gift boxes from Time Out
timeout.com/smartbox

Dinner served 6-10.30pm daily. **Main courses** £13.50-£19.50. **Set lunch** £18 2 courses, £21 3 courses. **Set meal** (6-7.30pm) £20 2 courses, £24 3 courses. **Credit** AmEx, MC, V.

This little bistro, at the Clapham Common end of Battersea Rise, opened in spring 2010 but looks like an unreconstructed 1970s wine bar – peeling tables, low lighting, French ephemera used as wallpaper, and a piano by the entrance. In reality, a kitchen of considerable ambition and ability is hiding under the ooh-la-la. A starter of sweetbreads was perfectly tender in its delicately flavoured chicken jus, served with an onion purée sautéed in duck fat. Stone bass (a sustainable fish appearing more often on menus under this name, as the fisherman's version – Atlantic wreckfish – doesn't attract so many orders) proved to be a firmly textured, slightly sweet white fillet, pan-seared and served with roasted fennel, soy beans and a bouillabaisse sauce. The menu strays towards the Far East with a few ingredients (green papaya, say, or edamame), but mostly the dishes hail from within a day's march of Gaul, such as the ravioli of feta and courgette topped with tempura-fried courgette flowers. We were impressed by the obvious care and attention to detail in the cooking, which exceeded expectations that had been lowered by the rather dated surroundings and modest pricing. Service, from young and enthusiastic staff, was smiling and solicitous.
Available for hire. Babies and children admitted (weekends). Booking essential Sat, Sun. Dress: smart casual. Separate room for parties, seats 20. **Map 21 C4.**

Clapham

★ Trinity
4 The Polygon, SW4 0JG (7622 1199, www.trinityrestaurant.co.uk). Clapham Common tube. **Lunch served** 12.30-2.30pm Tue-Fri; noon-2pm Sat; noon-4pm Sun. **Dinner served** 6.30-10.30pm Mon-Sat. **Main courses** £17-£28. **Set lunch** (Tue-Sat) £20 3 courses. **Set meal** (Tue-Sat) £40 tasting menu (£70 incl wine). **Cover** £1.50 lunch, £2 dinner. **Credit** AmEx, MC, V.

Chef-proprietor Adam Byatt opened Trinity in 2006 to a string of hugely positive reviews; now the restaurant is even better. On our last two visits, we were wowed by the cheery atmosphere, charming service and stunning food. A starter with the terse description 'chicken dumplings, sweetcorn, tarragon' didn't do justice to the delicate quenelles of chicken mousse, one rolled in very fine black soot to render it charcoal black. The dabs and squiggles of tarragon pesto on the dark Vera Wang plates also gave a very striking effect. Main courses showed further creativity: just-cooked cod, the skin seared crisp, on a very buttery potato fondant with a moat of white gazpacho and fresh, hand-shelled almonds. To underline the Spanish inspiration of this dish, migas (Spanish-style fried breadcrumbs) garnished the side. A seam of butter ran through the menu, as Trinity makes its own – and very good it is too. Béarnaise sauce was served with some nicely carved bavette and a huge chunk of bone marrow, encased in thighbone the size of a pepper mill. The wine list is also more than up to scratch, and the setting is unassuming yet classy (white walls and table linen creating a look of simple elegance). Absolutely everyone on our dinner visit was having a ball – not always the case in some

high-minded restaurants – and Sunday lunch was fabulous too. If you've not yet been here, make sure that Trinity's on your wish list.
Babies and children welcome: high chairs. Booking essential. Disabled: toilet. **Map 22 A1.**

Tooting

★ French Café
16-18 Ritherdone Road, SW17 8QD (8767 2660, www.the-french-cafe.co.uk). Tooting Bec tube or Balham tube/rail or bus 155. **Open** 11am-10pm Mon-Fri; 9am-10pm Sat; 9am-9pm Sun. **Main courses** £6.50-£14.95. **Set meal** £9.95 2 courses. **Credit** AmEx, MC, V.

A little bit of the Continent has come to Tooting Bec. The de rigueur trappings of a proper bistro – all-day opening, decent breakfasts as well as lunch and dinner, outdoor tables in good weather – make French Café a welcome addition to this leafy neighbourhood. It's a popular spot for locals to sit and read the papers while idling over a coffee and croissants, or more substantial brunch dishes (weekends only) such as croque monsieur or eggs benedict. In the evening, the kitchen switches gear and serves up easy-going French classics such as steak frites, or rabbit cooked with mustard, and there are rillettes and pâtés galore. We've found that it's pretty hard to go wrong with the slow-cooked dishes, such as beef bourguignon, rich with red wine and lardons, or crisp-skinned confit of duck with puy lentils. Wines too are mostly French and well-priced. The prix-fixe menu can be good value, but choose carefully: poor-quality baguettes and a reliance on what appears to be bagged lettuce leaves in several dishes can let the side down. Those grumbles aside, this is a notable neighbourhood restaurant with a friendly vibe.
Available for hire. Babies and children welcome: high chairs; nappy-changing facilities. Booking advisable weekends. Disabled: toilet. Tables outdoors (6, terrace).

Waterloo

RSJ
33 Coin Street, SE1 9NR (7928 4554, www.rsj.uk.com). Waterloo tube/rail. **Lunch served** noon-2.30pm Mon-Fri. **Dinner served** 5.30-11pm Mon-Sat. **Main courses** £12-£19. **Set meal** £16.95 2 courses, £18.95 3 courses. **Credit** AmEx, DC, MC, V.

When it opened more than three decades ago, RSJ was a pioneer of the Modern French-British restaurant movement. The current ethos would seem to be, 'if it ain't broke, don't fix it'. The smart, Scandi-esque design of the upstairs dining room, offset by butter-yellow walls and plain wooden floors, is a little sober but none the worse for it. RSJ has long been a haunt for wine lovers, with quite possibly the best selection of wines from France's Loire Valley in the UK. By-the-glass options make a good starting point if you're unfamiliar with these well-priced, underrated (and food-friendly) wines. The short, frequently changing menu roams around France and the Med, frequently giving an unexpected twist here and there, as in linguine served with crab meat and chilli, spiked with ginger. The fixed-price menu is a bargain; star dishes were a pea and mint soup and a thick tranche of cod cooked just-so and served on crushed potatoes with avocado and mango salsa. In all, a reliable, unassuming spot that should figure prominently on the radar for South Bank diners.

Babies and children admitted. Booking advisable. Separate rooms for parties, seating 25-40. **Map 11 N8.**

East
Bethnal Green

Bistrotheque   `HOT 50`
23-27 Wadeson Street, E2 9DR (8983 7900, www.bistrotheque.com). Bethnal Green tube/rail or Cambridge Heath rail, or bus 55.
Bar **Open** 6pm-midnight Tue-Sat; 6-11pm Sun.
Restaurant **Brunch served** 11am-4pm Sat, Sun. **Dinner served** 6.30-10.30pm Mon-Thur, Sun; 6.30-11pm Fri, Sat. **Main courses** £12-£22. **Set dinner** (6.30-7.30pm Mon-Thur) £17.50 3 courses; (6.30-7.15pm Fri, Sat) £30 3 courses.
Both **Credit** AmEx, MC, V.

Hidden in an unlikely location down a gritty Hackney side street, Bistrotheque has become a key player on the east London after-dark scene. This is largely because of the cabaret shows that take place side by side with the restaurant; the three-in-one venue also has a bar downstairs, and dinner and show packages are popular. The airy first-floor restaurant sports an industrial-chic look, with whitewashed brick walls, bell jar-like light fixtures and steel beams that hint at its former incarnation as a warehouse. The menu draws elements from France and Britain – typical dishes include trout with samphire and Jersey royals; rock oysters; steak tartare; and ribeye with stilton. A smoked trout salad was lifted with refreshing fennel and a chipotle-spiked dressing, though both a cauliflower soup starter and a rabbit confit main were perfectly fine but unremarkable in their simplicity. Desserts, on the other hand, benefited from a lack of fussiness – roast peaches with thyme-scented mascarpone were ambrosial, while brownie-like chocolate cake didn't disappoint in its decadence, the richness cut with tart raspberries. Service from the trendily coiffed staff was perfunctory and disengaged; perhaps there's a warmer atmosphere during weekend brunches, which are accompanied by a pianist and singing.
Babies and children admitted: high chairs. Booking advisable. Disabled: toilet. Entertainment: cabaret (check website or phone for details); pianist noon-4pm Sun. Separate rooms for parties, seating 50-80.

Shoreditch

Boundary
2-4 Boundary Street, entrance at 9 Redchurch Street, E2 7DD (7729 1051, www.theboundary.co.uk). Shoreditch High Street rail. **Lunch served** noon-5pm Sat, Sun. **Dinner served** 6-11.30pm Mon-Sat. **Main courses** £17.50-£32. **Set lunch** £19.50 2 courses, £24.50 3 courses. **Credit** AmEx, MC, V.

Boundary is one of three eateries in a Conran complex on ultra-fashionable Redchurch Street: the more casual Albion café and the summer Rooftop bar make up the trio and there's also a hotel, as evidenced by the glossy international crowd in this snazzy basement restaurant. The interior decoration is a talking point. From the galley window on to the kitchen and the cartographic ceiling artwork twinkling with inlaid lights, to the art deco-style silverware and the skylight-illuminated booths upholstered in warm jewel tones, there's a lot going on here, but it's realised with impeccable taste. Staff tend to stand on ceremony (en route to our table we were greeted by every waiter and the sommelier), but aren't so starched as to be unwelcoming. Classic selling points include extravagant seafood platters, rotisserie meats and charcuterie assembled with dramatic flourishes from tableside trolleys. A Sunday lunch of rôti chicken was presented unadorned, letting the high-quality main event speak for itself; the accompanying jug of tarragon sauce did little to enhance it. Pea and mint soup, with its concentrated, vibrant flavours, presented summer in a bowl. Oenophiles will enjoy exploring the extensive wine list, which runs to 620 bins with several available by the glass. Peter Weeden (ex-Coq d'Argent) was appointed head chef as we went to press; tweaks are to be expected, though Boundary's gastronomic raison d'être is expected to remain constant.

Available for hire. Babies and children welcome: high chairs; nappy-changing facilities. Booking advisable dinner. Disabled: lift; toilet. **Map 6 R4**.

Les Trois Garçons [HOT 50]

1 Club Row, E1 6JX (7613 1924, www.les troisgarcons.com). Shoreditch High Street rail. **Lunch served** noon-2.30pm Mon-Fri. **Dinner served** 6-9.30pm Mon-Thur; 6-10.30pm Fri, Sat. **Set lunch** £17.50 2 courses, £22 3 courses. **Set dinner** £40.50 2 courses, £47 3 courses, £60 tasting menu (£99 incl wine). **Credit** AmEx, DC, MC, V.

Housed in an attractive Victorian pub, Les Trois Garçons has a look that's more blinged-up curiosity shop than East End boozer. Chandeliers and vintage handbags hang from the ceiling. Heavy curtains swathe the windows, and bejewelled, stuffed animals are everywhere you turn. For over a decade, well-heeled diners have been flocking from all over the place to try the modern French food. Pissaladière d'descargots de Dorset came with plump and juicy snails tinged with chilli and garlic, but they were slightly overpowered by sweet caramelised onions and the puff pastry case. A trio of pork included deliciously smoky pea and pork croquettes, tender braised shoulder and strips of

roasted belly – all balanced by savoury sea aster. Disappointingly, the fish of the day (crisp-skinned john dory with pearl barley risotto) came to the table lukewarm and had to be sent back. This was dealt with efficiently, if not apologetically. Though the standard of cooking varied, we couldn't fault the smooth Bourgueil we chose from the French-skewed wine list; a pudding of citrusy lavender sorbet was also notable. If you're after a posh meal in a quirky setting, Les Trois Garçons fits the bill – but the experience doesn't come cheap.

Available for hire. Booking advisable. Children admitted over 12yrs. Separate room for parties, seats 10. **Map 6 S4**. .

Spitalfields

Galvin La Chapelle

St Boltoph's Hall, 35 Spital Square, E1 6DY (7299 0400, www.galvinrestaurants.com). Liverpool Street tube/rail or Shoreditch High Street rail. **Lunch served** 11.50am-2.30pm daily. **Dinner served** 5.50-10.30pm Mon-Sat; 5.50-9.30pm Sun. **Main courses** £10-£30. **Set lunch** £25.50 3 courses. **Set dinner** £29.50 3 courses. **Credit** AmEx, DC, MC, V.

Brother Jeff's patch of the Galvin empire, La Chapelle is no mere branch of Baker Street's Bistrot de Luxe, but an altogether more elegant destination for modern French cuisine. Look at the 100ft-high vaulted ceiling for an inkling of the building's former life as a parish hall – it's now Grade II listed. Deeply padded brown leather chairs and crisp linens add to the sense of airy opulence. Service is as smooth and lush as béarnaise, with staff persuasively suggesting champagne aperitifs, offering another delve into the excellent bread basket, and pointing out the menu's signature dishes – lasagne of Dorset crab sounded too good to refuse. Classic assiette of lamb (including a nutty fried sweetbread, stuffed courgette flower and shallot purée) worked better than the intriguing combination of roast salmon with white peach, mussels and verjus beurre blanc. Sunny fruit flavours were put to more effective use in a starter of foie gras ballotine with cherries and spiced brioche, and banana and passionfruit soufflé with white chocolate sauce. The restaurant claims to

have the world's largest collection of Hermitage La Chapelle, with bottles dating from 1952. Without a City bonus, wine prices may seem unkind, but the cheapest red (a Portuguese Ribatejo, £22) is a big, smooth wowser. We like the more casual next-door Café a Vin very much too.

Babies and children welcome: high chairs. Booking advisable. Disabled: toilet. Separate room for parties, seats 16. Tables outdoors (60, terrace). **Map 12 R5**. **For branch (Galvin Café a Vin) see index**.

North

Camden Town & Chalk Farm

L'Absinthe

40 Chalcot Road, NW1 8LS (7483 4848, http://labsinthe.co.uk). Chalk Farm tube. **Lunch served** noon-2.30pm Mon-Fri; noon-4pm Sat, Sun. **Dinner served** 6-10.30pm Tue-Sat; 6-9.30pm Sun. **Main courses** £9.50-£15.75. **Set lunch** (Tue-Fri) £9.95 2 courses, £12.50 3 courses; (Sun) £14.95 2 courses, £18.50 3 courses. **Credit** AmEx, MC, V.

This jolly spot dispenses bonhomie and joie de vivre by the bucketload, and wines by the glass, pot and bottle – with a very friendly policy of only charging shop price plus corkage on the latter. Good on them, for this was once considered an unlikely site (we remember eating Italian, Indian), but L'Absinthe has proved such a hit it's expanded into the building next door, from where it now offers a traiteur, deli-café and takeaway foodstuffs. The secret of success may lie in its lack of pretension – despite the Primrose Hill location, cooking is unfussy, the presentation homely and prices correspondingly keen. Opt for the set lunch menu, with its choice of two dishes per course, and dining is even cheaper. From the carte, beef bourguignon with mash was precisely that – no galette of celeriac or parmesan tuile to garnish. Marinated herring came with radicchio, shallot dressing and a disc of potato salad, but was otherwise another typically straightforward dish.

Galvin La Chapelle

We wish the béarnaise served with the steak frites hadn't been left to stand so long before serving, but chocolate and coffee mousse was a paragon. Consideration is given to quality British suppliers, with Chalk Farm smoked salmon and Marshfield organic ice-cream from the West Country among the discerning choices.

Babies and children welcome: high chairs. Booking advisable. Tables outdoors (5, pavement). **Map 27 B2.**

Highgate

Côte

2 Highgate High Street, N6 5JL (8348 9107, www.cote-restaurants.co.uk). Archway tube.
Meals served 8am-11pm Mon-Fri; 9am-11pm Sat; 9am-10.30pm Sun. **Main courses** £8.95-£17.95. **Set meal** (noon-7pm Mon-Fri) £9.95 2 courses, £11.95 3 courses. **Credit** AmEx, MC, V.
Côte's premise is to offer simple French bistro cooking at fair prices, but there are so many menus (carte, set, specials, children's, lunch rapide) that it all seems rather complicated. At least everybody is bound to find something to enjoy. Unlike many French restaurants, vegetarians have a decent choice, and that's not the only advantage of dining at a chain such as this: staff are well drilled, groups accommodated, and the elderly and young families made comfortable. Cooking ranges from not bad to very good. The crème caramel compares favourably to those of more esteemed kitchens, and fresh vegetables sang in a dish of buckwheat galettes stuffed with spinach and mushrooms then bathed in cream. Steak frites is reliably good, so too nibbles of fougasse bread with reblochon cheese, and the saucisson sec, but we found our fresh tuna niçoise a bit flat. Similarly, the most affordable wines are serviceable rather than special. This Highgate Village branch has particularly good premises, including a huge decked terrace for semi-alfresco eating, and leafy views from the capacious front dining room. Worth a bit of a journey, then, though with 14 branches in London, it shouldn't be difficult to find a Côte near you.
Babies and children welcome: children's menu; high chairs' nappy-changing facilities. Booking advisable. Disabled: toilet. Tables outdoors (15, terrace).
For branches see index.

Islington

Almeida

30 Almeida Street, N1 1AD (7354 4777, www.almeida-restaurant.co.uk). Angel tube or Highbury & Islington tube/rail. **Lunch served** noon-2.30pm Tue-Sat. **Dinner served** 5.30-10.30pm Mon-Sat. **Meals served** noon-3.30pm Sun. **Main courses** £9.50-£15.50. **Set dinner** £28.50 2 courses, £33.50 3 courses. **Set meal** (5.30-6.30pm daily; 9.30-10.30pm Mon-Sat) £15.95 2 courses, £18.95 3 courses. **Credit** AmEx, MC, V.
Cheerful tubs of red geraniums, and pavement tables sporting umbrellas are persuasive calls to lunch at this outpost of the D&D group. At Sunday lunch there's a pleasing level of bonhomie inside too, with diners chatting between tables – though you never lose the sense that best manners are expected. It's a shame to miss one of the trolleys (charcuterie, cheese) as they add to the sense of occasion, and the contents are damn good. Specify foie gras and chicken liver parfait, rillettes (pork,

Cassis Bistro. See p91.

STREET**SMART**
HELPING THE HOMELESS

"All it takes is one well-fed quid next time you're dining at any of the damned fine establishments taking part in this glorious campaign, and that tiny extra sum will go straight to an excellently worthwhile cause. Go on, it'll make you feel good about that expanding waistband."
Ian Rankin, author

STREETSMART
HELPING THE HOMELESS

Download our free
iPhone® app now

Available on the
App Store

iPhone is a registered trademark of Apple Inc.

For a list of participating restaurants and details of how to take part, visit **www.streetsmart.org.uk**

duck), and a little bayonne ham if you like, or simply ask for a bit of everything, which would see three different saucissons added, plus cornichons, superb piccalilli and the chutney du saison. Crab tian, our other starter, had much to compete with. Next, we could have had roast beef, lamb, or suckling pig, but opted for fried sea bass with pan-crusted herb gnocchi, cucumber and shellfish foam, and 'local day boat' fish gratin – a French take on fish pie featuring big chunks of fish and crustaceans, and a chive-flecked cream sauce. The cheapest wine (£19), a French sauvignon blanc, suited both perfectly. Service was bright, friendly and keen, if rather distracted; staff handled an error with our bill gracefully.

Babies and children welcome: children's menu; high chairs; nappy-changing facilities. Booking advisable. Disabled: toilet. Separate rooms for parties, seating 10 and 20. Tables outdoors (8, pavement). **Map 5 O1.**

★ Morgan M

489 Liverpool Road, N7 8NS (7609 3560, www.morganm.com). Highbury & Islington tube/ rail. **Lunch served** noon-1.30pm Wed-Fri, Sun. **Dinner served** 7-8.30pm Tue-Sat. **Set lunch** (Wed-Fri) £24.50 2 courses, £28.50 3 courses, £43-£48 tasting menu. **Set dinner** £43 3 courses, £48-£52 tasting menu. **Credit** MC, V.
Morgan Meunier's pub conversion, located on an unassuming suburban street, could well be London's gastronomic Shangri-La for French food. This is haute cuisine at its most elevated, characterised by winning pairings of seasonal ingredients prepared in a classical French style with unreserved labour-intensive skill. Service front of house is faultless, the intimate dining room stylish, and the tables double-clothed. The lunchtime sitting offers two or three courses from the à la carte, while dinner increases to three courses or a six-course tasting menu with optional, predominantly French, wine matches. All menus come with own-made breads, amuse-bouches, sorbet entremets and mignardises of salted caramels and macarons, so it's worth setting aside a few hours for the experience. Plump seared scallops on asparagus-flecked fregola pasta with a velvety champagne velouté knocked our socks off, as did the cardamom-braised duck with polenta in a red wine and liquorice jus. The cheese trolley is a tour de force; you'll smell it before you see it, and its lip-smacking specimens provide a mouthful of France's terroir at its best. A new branch is planned for Smithfield.
Babies and children admitted (lunch, Sun). Booking essential weekends. Dress: smart casual. Separate room for parties, seats 12. Vegetarian menu.

North West
Queen's Park

Penk's
79 Salusbury Road, NW6 6NH (7604 4484, www.penks.com). Queen's Park tube/rail. **Lunch served** noon-3pm Mon-Fri. **Dinner served** 6-10.30pm Mon-Thur; 6-11pm Fri. **Meals served** 10am-11pm Sat; 10am-10pm Sun. **Main courses** £12-£18.50. **Set meal** (noon-3pm, 6-7.30pm) £16.50 2 courses. **Credit** MC, V.
A classic, oft-changing and well-executed bistro menu keeps Queen's Park diners coming back to this neighbourhood stalwart. There certainly

wasn't much to grumble about when the Burgundy-style roast chicken breast arrived, or indeed the grilled fillet of bream on warm salad – but, then again, there wasn't much to rave about either. It seems the kitchen likes to play things safe, with tried and tested standards: a disappointing trait considering the prices (around £13 for a main dish, £7 for starters), and one that left us craving a little more imagination and daring. Still, high-quality produce is used and there's an exciting wine list to explore. Penk's homely vibe well suits the food too, and quiz nights and meal deals add to the community feel. Service is casual rather than slick, with dressed-down, sociable staff who are eager to please. The simple decor is similarly comfortable. A well-worn sofa faces fold-back windows at the front (a nice spot to share a Spanish charcuterie board), while candle-topped tables for two dominate the space further back. In all, a cosy, if not thrilling, set-up.
Available for hire. Babies and children welcome until 8pm Mon-Fri; lunch weekends: high chairs. Booking advisable. Separate room for parties, seats 14. Tables outdoors (2, pavement).

St John's Wood

L'Aventure
3 Blenheim Terrace, NW8 0EH (7624 6232, www.laventure.co.uk). St John's Wood tube or bus 139, 189. **Lunch served** 12.30-2.30pm Mon-Fri. **Dinner served** 7-11pm Mon-Sat. **Set lunch** £18.50 2 courses, £21.50 3 courses. **Set dinner** £31 2 courses, £39.50 3 courses. **Credit** AmEx, MC, V.
Just off Abbey Road but about as un-rock 'n' roll as it gets, L'Aventure is in the upmarket, verging on fussy mould of the neighbourhood French restaurant circa 1985. Tables are rather crammed in, with long white tablecloths threatening to trip you as you squeeze to a seat. Service during our meal was very attentive at the start; it needed to be to help decipher the menu, handwritten and in French only. As the room filled, so the waiters became less visible, returning eventually to present a miscalculated bill. Still, the meal (of a minimum two courses) was enjoyable, with sauces a highlight. Duck in a cassis sauce had fresh blackcurrants for sweet-sharp flavour, while a creamy sauce dugléré (tomatoes, herbs and cream) was delicate enough for a fillet of brill. It's a shame the accompaniments – boiled new potatoes and vegetables – were quite dull. For pudding, we savoured every drop of a vanilla sauce with poached peaches, but the fruit was a little hard. A duo of crème brûlées had us playing spot-the-difference; the cherry in one of them was certainly subtle. An unalloyed pleasure, however, was the well-chilled half-bottle of Muscadet from the French-only list.
Babies and children admitted. Booking advisable dinner. Tables outdoors (6, terrace). **Map 1 C2.**

Outer London
Richmond, Surrey

Chez Lindsay
11 Hill Rise, Richmond, Surrey, TW10 6UQ (8948 7473, www.chezlindsay.co.uk). Richmond tube/rail.
Crêperie Meals served 11am-10.45pm Mon-Sat; noon-10pm Sun. **Main courses** £3.95-£11.50.

Restaurant Meals served noon-10.45pm Mon-Sat; noon-10pm Sun. **Main courses** £10.75-£25. **Set lunch** (noon-7pm Mon-Fri) £10.75 2 courses, £13.75 3 courses. **Set meal** (7-10.45pm Mon-Fri; all day Sat, Sun) £21.75 2 courses, £25.75 3 courses.
Both **Credit** MC, V.
Ditch the wine glasses in favour of bolées à cidre at this laid-back, sunny bistro specialising in Breton cuisine. A half-litre pichet of the house cider, an off-dry organic number from Normandy, was a good match for a big bowl of mussels (a popular choice, judging by the metal lids piling up around us). There are meat and fish mains, several cooked with cider, but most fun is to be had with the buckwheat galettes. The edges of these savoury pancakes are tucked under to enclose a filling below as well as on top, such as creamy leeks with scallops, or melted cheese and ratatouille. The latter was offered on the weekend set menu, which, at over £20 for two courses, can work out steeper than the combined carte prices. In contrast, the weekday prix-fixe lunch is a steal. Perhaps it was the effect of a double-pancake meal, but our crêpe, too light on chocolate sauce, fell flat. The fruit sorbets might have been a better bet. Staff are cheerful and enthusiastic, some almost too much so; there are only so many times you can smile and nod when asked 'Ça va? C'est bon?'
Babies and children welcome: high chairs. Booking advisable. Separate room for parties, seats 36.

Twickenham, Middlesex

Brula
43 Crown Road, Twickenham, Middx, TW1 3EJ (8892 0602, www.brula.co.uk). St Margaret's rail. **Lunch served** noon-3pm daily. **Dinner served** 6-10.30pm Mon-Sat. **Main courses** £14-£20. **Set lunch** £14 2 courses, £18 3 courses. **Set dinner** £19 2 courses, £25 3 courses. **Credit** AmEx, MC, V.
A heart-warming mix of birthday celebrations and dates keeps Brula humming on Saturday nights – deservedly so, as this professionally run local is streets ahead of most neighbourhood restaurants. The interior is comfortable and undemanding rather than fashionable, with any excitement being contained in the modern French menu. Sauté of king scallops with chilled pea panna cotta, radish, black pudding, chilli and mint dressing was almost too pretty to eat, while three glorious curried mussels, part of a starter of Cornish crab, cauliflower remoulade, pickled apple and coriander, made the dish the evening's star turn. Mains – roast lamb provençal with tapenade dressing, sautéed spinach and cherry tomatoes with peppers and anchovies; and asparagus and broad bean tart with truffle oil, red pepper coulis, courgette ribbons and hazelnuts – were good without being memorable. Similarly, desserts (chouquettes with almond ice-cream and chocolate sauce, and crème brûlée) looked a treat, but needed something to lift them above OK-for-the-price. The drinks list has a great selection of house wines (by the glass, carafe and bottle), which includes some organic and 'natural' bottles. Service is charming and on the ball. We'd happily become regulars: Brula is a rare restaurant that understands the meaning of hospitality.
Babies and children admitted. Booking advisable. Separate rooms for parties, seating 8, 10 and 24. Vegetarian menu.

Gastropubs

Reports of the gastropub's demise have been overstated, but perhaps that reflects our love-hate relationship with the genus. Fans of the boozer often despair when a local gets 'gastroed', and yet it's a commitment to cooking quality food on the premises (instead of microwaving catering companies' ready-prepared dishes) that has saved many a pub from demise. This time, we're including six of the best and most useful new food-minded hostelries (there have been many more) and, as ever, they are a broad church, ranging from refurbished pubs serving great pizzas (**New Cross House**), to chef-led establishments that exude a formal restaurant vibe (Claude Bosi's **Fox & Grapes** in Wimbledon). But it's the places that cater to all-comers that we tend to prefer, such as the capacious **Vine** in Kentish Town, where you can settle in the bar, head to the restaurant, or drink and dine on a smart garden terrace, and West Dulwich's yet-again-relaunched **Rosendale**, which offers much of the same, plus a play area for kids. These places aren't just foodie, but friendly to drinkers too – we all say cheers to that.

Central

Bloomsbury

Norfolk Arms
28 Leigh Street, WC1H 9EP (7388 3937, www.norfolkarms.co.uk). Euston tube/rail.
Open 11am-11pm Mon-Sat; noon-10.30pm Sun.
Lunch served noon-3pm Mon-Fri; noon-4pm Sat. **Dinner served** 6-10.15pm Mon-Sat.
Meals served noon-10.15pm Sun. **Tapas served** noon-10.15pm daily. **Main courses** £9.50-£13. **Tapas** £2-£12. **Credit** AmEx, MC, V.
This remodelled Victorian pub wears its gastro credentials out front for all to see. Legs of jamón hang in the windows; bunches of dried chillies line the bare plaster walls; and onions hang from the orange, retro light fittings. Such culinary decorations add to an interior decor consisting of dark green marble pillars, and high ceilings panelled with plaster frescoes of cherubic faces. It's worth booking for weekday evenings, when an after-work crowd clutter the outdoor tables, and groups of thirtysomething diners soon fill the interior. Things are quieter at weekends, but at busy periods the jovial staff become rushed and it can take numerous attempts to attract their attention. The menu revolves around sharing, with a tapas-heavy selection including some Greek and English dishes. Quality is variable. A smoked eel and soft-boiled egg salad was delicately flavoured, and a vegetable meze mix saw garlicky, unctuous carrots sitting alongside fluffy Greek-style pitta.

However, fried paprika pork belly was tough and chewy, and a scotch egg didn't noticeably differ from one you'd find in a service station. Still, a range of Iberian drinks such as sangria, Sagres beer and a small selection of sherries nicely peps up the long wine list.
Babies and children admitted: high chairs. Booking advisable. Separate rooms for parties, seating 10 and 20. Tables outdoors (9, pavement). **Map 4 L3.**

City

★ White Swan Pub & Dining Room
108 Fetter Lane, EC4A 1ES (7242 9696, www.thewhiteswanlondon.com). Chancery Lane tube. **Open** 11am-11pm Mon; 11am-midnight Tue-Thur; 11am-1am Fri. **Lunch served** noon-3pm, **dinner served** 6-10pm Mon-Fri. **Main courses** £14.50-£20. **Set lunch** (noon-1pm) £14.50 2 courses; (noon-3pm) £26 2 courses, £29.75 3 courses. **Credit** AmEx, MC, V.
Between the City and the lawyers' haunts around Holborn, this branch of the ETM Group – also responsible for the Gun, the Cadogan Arms and several other London gastropubs – caters well for its smart customers. The wood-lined ground-floor bar has an ample beer selection and superior pub food; the comfortable dining room upstairs is very much a proper restaurant, with a sophisticated, inventive Modern European menu. Even barristers and commodity-checkers appreciate a bargain, though, and the express lunch menu (you must

finish by 1pm) is a snip: two courses for £14.50, with three choices for both. Ingredients were especially impressive: a lovely, refreshing salad featured broad and borlotti beans and sugar snaps, all beautifully fresh, and berkswell cheese, an English sheep's cheese to rival any older European variety. To follow, pan-fried skirt steak with braised cheek, artichoke and bone marrow was a great, rich, generous mix, especially the punchy-flavoured cheek braised in red wine. Stay on after 1pm and you can also choose from an extensive additional range that's still fine value; in the evening, there's a slightly shorter carte. As well as beers and cocktails, drinks include a serious wine list, with much available by the glass.
Available for hire. Babies and children admitted. Booking advisable. Separate room for parties, seats 52. **Map 11 N6.**
For branch (Well) see index.

Clerkenwell & Farringdon

Coach & Horses
26-28 Ray Street, EC1R 3DJ (7278 8990, www.thecoachandhorses.com). Farringdon tube/rail. **Open** noon-11pm Mon-Fri; 6-11pm Sat; 12.30-5pm Sun. **Lunch served** noon-3pm Mon-Fri; 1-4pm Sun. **Dinner served** 6-10pm Mon-Sat. **Main courses** £12.50-£15. **Credit** AmEx, MC, V.
Tucked away off Clerkenwell Road, this Victorian boozer, with its wood-panelled interior and etched-glass windows, is endearingly shabby. It's also a proper pub, with outdoor tables at the front and as

many drinkers as diners. Three real ales and assorted continental lagers are offered alongside a better-than-average wine list. Standards seem to have slipped on the food front, however. The menu features several unusual dishes – some more appealing than others. We enjoyed the starter plate of rich, smoky sprats with horseradish and dill potato salad, but the idea of beetroot and hazelnut risotto didn't appeal. Heritage tomato salad (a starter) produced cold, largely flavourless chunks of tomato and an excess of rocket, while a main course sea trout steak was raw in the centre and the accompanying cold pearl barley too oily and studded with an absurd number of pickled garlic cloves (at least a dozen). Portions are massive; Desperate Dan would have approved of the size of the steak bavette and chips (at least, both components were decently cooked). Best was a warm, soft chocolate tart with clotted cream. In all, however, fair pricing, a relaxed vibe and friendly, attentive service don't compensate for the slapdash approach of the kitchen.

Available for hire. Babies and children welcome: high chairs. Booking advisable. Separate room for parties, seats 30. Tables outdoors (5, garden). **Map 5 N4**.

★ Eagle

159 Farringdon Road, EC1R 3AL (7837 1353). Farringdon tube/rail. **Open** noon-11pm Mon-Sat; noon-5pm Sun. **Lunch served** 12.30-3pm Mon-Fri; 12.30-3.30pm Sat, Sun. **Dinner served** 6.30-10.30pm Mon-Sat. **Main courses** £5-£15. **Credit** MC, V.

Despite the slide of many gastropubs into aping fancy restaurants, the Eagle – one of the originals – remains pleasingly unreconstructed. Scuffed cream walls and bare wood dominate the dining area; diners share tables; ordering is done at the bar (behind which the kitchen is crammed); instead of menus, dishes are scrawled on blackboards; and food options tend far more towards hearty mains than three-course dining. On our trip, desserts were limited to a custard tart, and smaller dishes seemed more akin to side helpings than starters, including a basket of doorstep-thick bread slices and a portion of oily boquerones cut through with a refreshing vinegar tang. Next, chicken tagine came with a sloppy, rich sauce spiked with ras el hanout and topped with plump almonds toasted to crunchy, smoky perfection, while a pork belly and lentil salad featuring orange segments and big slices of beef tomato was all zingy lightness of flavour. This isn't an ideal destination for a summer's day, though. The few outdoor tables soon fill up, and despite a window-lined dining area, the kitchen's location renders approaching the bar an uncomfortably hot experience. Cool off after the meal with a pint of Eagle IPA.

Babies and children admitted. Bookings not accepted. Tables outdoors (4, pavement). **Map 5 N4**.

Peasant

240 St John Street, EC1V 4PH (7336 7726, www.thepeasant.co.uk). Angel tube or Farringdon tube/rail. *Bar* **Open** noon-11pm Mon-Sat; noon-10.30pm Sun. **Meals served** noon-10.45pm Mon-Sat; noon-9.30pm Sun. **Main courses** £8.50-£14. *Restaurant* **Brunch served** noon-3pm Sun. **Dinner served** 6-11pm Tue-Sat. **Main courses** £9.50-£16. *Both* **Credit** AmEx, MC, V.

Princess of Shoreditch. See p112.

We arrived at the Peasant to a 1980s soundtrack, and suspect the decor hasn't changed much since those days. The first-floor restaurant was hosting a wine tasting, so we opted for the bar menu and discovered that the once-great cooking of one of London's first gastropubs seems to have dipped spectacularly. A 'broad beans, beetroot and baby turnip' starter arrived without beans, went back and was presented again with a few tough beans added, plus a single halved turnip so hard that it flew off the plate during our attempt to spear it. 'Trout rillettes' on toast was better, but not rillettes – more 'trout mixed in horseradish'. The best dish was the well-done ('medium rare' was ordered) house burger: a generous, well-seasoned patty on a bun with bacon and cheese, served with tasty hand-cut chips. The crowd-pleasing drinks list includes speciality beers and wines from around the world. Our friendly, lone barman did his best, but failed to offer new glasses when we switched from white to red wine. During a quiet night here, both the food and service were disappointing.

Babies and children welcome until 9pm: high chairs. Booking advisable. Tables outdoors (5, garden terrace; 5, pavement). **Map 5 O4.**

Marylebone

Duke of Wellington

94A Crawford Street, W1H 2HQ (7723 2790, www.thedukew1.co.uk). Baker Street tube or Marylebone tube/rail. **Open** noon-11pm Mon-Sat; noon-10.30pm Sun. **Lunch served** noon-3pm Mon-Fri; noon-4pm Sat; 12.30-4.30pm Sun. **Dinner served** 6.30-10pm Mon-Fri; 7-10pm Sat; 7-9pm Sun. **Main courses** £13-£38. **Set lunch** (noon-1.30pm Mon-Thur) £14.95 2 courses. **Credit** AmEx, MC, V.

Very much a local Marylebone spot – with the requisite polo shirts and pearls on show – the Duke of Wellington is a good bet for a weekday evening catch-up over decent grub, with the upstairs dining room available for formal occasions. That this isn't a 'destination' place might explain the lack of cohesion in terms of mood: the loudish music, upmarket gastropub decor (gilt mirrors, vintage furniture) and random wall pictures – from Pop art-style prints to a framed copy of the *Sun* ('British Warship Sunk by Argies', a Duke of Wellington connection?) – don't especially gel, but the vibe is friendly and cheerful nonetheless. Warm sourdough got the meal off to a good start, while starters of Cornish crab, and pork and pistachio terrine – both on toast – were tasty and generous. Mains, while nothing out of the ordinary, elicited no complaints, with perfectly cooked plaice with black butter and capers just winning out ahead of spatchcock quails with peas cooked the French way (with onions and butter). Buttermilk pudding with berries, for dessert, resembled an inferior panna cotta. The wine list is so hefty that it has a contents page attached. Staff can get flustered when the place is busy.

Babies and children admitted: high chairs. Separate room for parties, seats 25. Tables outdoors (6, pavement). **Map 2 F5.**

Grazing Goat NEW

6 New Quebec Street, W1H 7RQ (7724 7243, www.thegrazinggoat.co.uk). Marble Arch tube. *Bar* **Open** 7.30am-11.30pm Mon-Sat; 7.30am-10.30pm Sun. **Breakfast served** 7.30-11.30am, **meals served** noon-9.30pm daily. *Restaurant* **Lunch served** noon-3.30pm, **dinner served** 6-9.30pm daily. *Both* **Main courses** £10.50-£21.50. **Set lunch** (Mon-Fri) £11.50-£14.50 1 course incl glass of wine or pint of beer. **Credit** AmEx, MC, V.

Another proficient operation from the Cubitt House group – the people who brought us elegant spots such as the Thomas Cubitt and Pantechnicon Rooms in Belgravia, and the Orange Public House in Pimlico. Marble Arch may seem a bit north for them, but this is Portman Village, where their contemporary country house look goes down as smoothly as a glass of champers. Certainly, this ex-pub is a destination for real ale enthusiasts (Deuchars IPA the only tap beer on our visit); the wine list is well chosen, but the prices are West End-high, with £18 the starting point for bottles of pinot grigio and merlot. There's also a choice of ten cocktails, as well as fresh juices including watermelon, and an apple, lemon and lime combo. Food is mostly British, with plenty of French and Mediterranean influences, though, refreshingly, this is a chorizo-free zone. You'll find a ploughman's, roasts (with suppliers name-checked), and a lamb and rosemary pie, but also the likes of seared scallops with cauliflower, fennel and saffron dressing, and stuffed courgette flower with goat's cheese and tomato and basil. Breakfast sounds a treat, with own-made muffins and granola, blueberry pancakes and the expected full english (including black pudding) and eggs benedict.

Available for hire. Babies and children welcome: high chairs; nappy-changing facilities. Booking advisable. Disabled: toilet. Separate room for parties, seats 70. Tables outdoors (10, pavement). **Map 8 F6.**

Honey Pot NEW

20 Homer Street, W1H 4NA (7724 9685, www.thehoneypot-pub.co.uk). Edgware Road tube or Marylebone tube/rail. **Open** noon-11.30pm Mon-Sat. **Meals served** noon-10.30pm daily. **Main courses** £4.50-£24.90. **Set meal** £14.95 2 courses, £19.95 3 courses. **Credit** AmEx, MC, V.

There's much to admire at this tapas tavern: terrific small plates, courteous and attentive service, and a wealth of wine. A former Victorian boozer, it's brightened by enormous windows and a rear conservatory, while the main bar area is partitioned from a small crowd of dining tables using sherry barrels, all surrounded by dangling jamón, wine decanters and cans of olive oil. Confidently cooked tapas dishes steal the show: you can kick off with classic tortilla (or a more unusual version, made with morcilla – Spanish black pudding – and butternut squash); a heap of deep-fried whitebait; or snails with chorizo and a fried egg. Meat-lovers will be pleased to find a handful of well-cooked steaks, as well as the traditional charcuterie selection. Finish with simple but effective puds, from honey-baked figs served with nutty praline ice-cream, to a plate of Spanish cheeses with quince jam and bread. For liquid refreshment, there's a

solid choice of Meantime beers on tap, plus the pub's Honey Pot lager, brewed at London Bridge. The wine list, numbering some 130 bins, offers 32 choices by the tumbler.

Available for hire. Babies and children admitted. Booking advisable dinner Thur & Fri. Disabled: toilet. Separate room for parties, seats 45. Tables outdoors (5, pavement). **Map 2 F5.**

Queen's Head & Artichoke

30-32 Albany Street, NW1 4EA (7916 6206, www.theartichoke.net). Great Portland Street or Regent's Park tube. **Open** 11am-11pm Mon-Sat; noon-10.30pm Sun. **Lunch served** noon-3pm Mon-Fri; 12.30-4pm Sat. **Dinner served** 6-10.30pm Mon-Sat. **Meals served** 12.30-10.15pm Sun. **Tapas served** noon-10.30pm Mon-Sat; 12.30-10.15pm Sun. **Main courses** £9.50-£16. **Tapas** £1.50-£12.50. **Credit** AmEx, MC, V.

This refined and friendly gastropub on the edge of Regent's Park serves outstanding Spanish tapas in a very English setting. The Spanish chef has, unusually, succeeded in making his mark on classic tapas without compromising the dishes' essential qualities. Ham croquettes, for example, were slightly oversized, but the béchamel filling was almost mousse-like, and aromatic nutmeg left a warm aftertaste among the fine crumb coating. Manchego cheese spring roll was a risky fusion – a gooey, crispy risk that certainly paid off. Main courses didn't live up to the tapas; marrow stuffed with marinated artichoke hearts, caramelised onion and feta was a good flavour combination, but the varying textures did not cohere. Dessert pulled it back, however: a bowl of fresh raspberry sorbet, creamy salted caramel and intense dark chocolate ice-cream hit all the right notes. You can eat downstairs in the bar or upstairs in the Regency-style dining room, complete with fireplace and ornate clocks. It's all rather grand, with extensive windows and dark wood panelling, but the atmosphere is jovial. The enclosed courtyard is a colourful, cushioned hideaway for open-air dining during the summer months.

Babies and children welcome: high chairs. Separate room for parties, seats 50. Tables outdoors (6, garden; 8, pavement). **Map 3 H4.**

Pimlico

★ Orange Public House & Hotel

37 Pimlico Road, SW1W 8NE (7881 9844, www.theorange.co.uk). Sloane Square tube. **Open** 8am-11.30pm Mon-Thur; 8am-midnight Fri, Sat; 8am-10.30pm Sun. **Breakfast served** 8am-11.30am, **meals served** noon-9.30pm daily. **Main courses** £12.50-£16.50. **Credit** AmEx, MC, V.

Pimlico has clearly taken to the new-style Orange. The revamped pub has a bar, some outdoor tables and a dining room (plus a few B&B rooms), all tastefully and unfussily done out, and packed on a Saturday night. The menu is a happy blend of new and familiar, and apart from tiny quibbles – too much red onion in an otherwise finger-licking roast chicken and green bean salad with tarragon and garlic dressing; a so-so baked cheesecake with roast peach and basil anglaise – it works beautifully. A zingy starter of fried squid, prawns, artichoke and lemon was lifted by the tempura lemon; a generous portion of tuna carpaccio with violet artichokes and fried capers had carefully nuanced layers of flavour.

Next, slow-cooked veal shin, soft polenta and radicchio was comfort food heaven, while crab, chilli and lime mascarpone pizza sounded like it shouldn't have worked, but did. Puddings are pricey (mostly £7), but in the case of a superb coffee brûlée with peanut biscuits and caramel ice-cream, totally justified. A short global wine list and a few real ales (Harveys Sussex Best, Adnams) is supplemented by a short cocktail list – we were taken with the Basil Fawlty (Belvedere vodka, apple juice, passionfruit and own-made basil syrup). Intelligent staff keep the whole operation zipping along nicely. *Babies and children welcome: high chairs; nappy-changing facilities. Booking advisable. Disabled: toilet. Separate rooms for parties, seating up to 75. Tables outdoors (5, pavement).*
Map 15 G11.
For branches (Pantechnicon Rooms, Thomas Cubitt) see index.

West
Chiswick

Devonshire Arms NEW
126 Devonshire Road, W4 2JJ (8742 2302, www.devonshirearmspub.com). Turnham Green tube. **Open** noon-11pm daily. **Lunch served** noon-3.30pm, **dinner served** 6-10.30pm daily. **Main courses** £10.50-£22. **Credit** MC, V.
The Devonshire Arms is not substantially different in layout from the days when it was part of Gordon Ramsay Holdings; if anything, it seems less pretentious, with charming vintage lights and spriggy wallpaper adding an appealing hint of granny's sitting room to the dark green painted bar. The new owners have form – running Islington's Drapers Arms – and this spot is something of a mirror image, with its residential surrounds and appealing garden. Three real ales are offered, with Harveys Sussex Best the lynchpin and two on rotation (on our visit, Sambrook's Wandle and Woodforde's Wherry). Wines start at a neighbourly £3.90 per glass and 14 or so are offered by the 500ml carafe; we liked the informed-insider tone of the tasting notes (other pubs would do well to study). Bar food typically includes scotch quail eggs, haggis and pork sausage roll, and rillettes with rhubarb chutney. Next door, in the main dining area, the British natural larder forms the basis of dishes – wood pigeon and grouse in season, Scottish girolles, Devon crab, Cornish skate, samphire. We enjoyed perfectly grilled steak and chips, and john dory with a summery borlotti bean broth, though starters underwhelmed. Desserts are pub classics, with subtle diversions such as orange panna cotta with Grand Marnier sauce.
Available for hire. Babies and children welcome: children's menu (Sat, Sun); high chairs; nappy-changing facilities. Tables outdoors (3, pavement; 10, garden).
For branch (Drapers Arms) see index.

Duke of Sussex
75 South Parade, W4 5LF (8742 8801, www.thedukeofsussex.co.uk). Chiswick Park tube. **Open** noon-11pm Mon-Thur, Sun; noon-midnight Fri, Sat. **Meals served** noon-10.30pm Mon-Sat; noon-9.30pm Sun. **Main courses** £11-£17.50. **Credit** MC, V.
The dining room of this impressive Victorian pub opposite Acton Green Common has been sympathetically restored: hung with art deco-style

chandeliers (cleverly gilded and coloured), and adorned with carved cherubs around a magnificent vast skylight. Tables are well spaced, and there are sizeable banquettes to suit large groups. The room leads to a spacious beer garden via splendid french windows – take your glass of Rioja or pint of Sagres out here in summer. The atmosphere is buzzy and jolly, like the staff, and the bar can become positively clamorous with young, well-heeled punters, partly due to the acoustics created by the high ceiling. The menu is an appetising blend of traditional British food (roast beef with all the trimmings, fish and chips) and tempting Spanish dishes, such as delicious tapas, black rice with grilled cod and aïoli, and seafood paella in large portions. A highlight is the bread, made daily on the premises in white and brown versions. Desserts are a bit hit and miss; the meringues seemed shop-bought, but the fruit filling them was fresh and tasty. Prices are fair: yet another reason for the Duke's popularity.
Babies and children welcome: high chairs. Booking advisable dinner. Disabled: toilet. Tables outdoors (37, back garden; 3, front garden).

★ Roebuck
122 Chiswick High Road, W4 1PU (8995 4392, www.theroebuckchiswick.co.uk). Turnham Green tube. **Open** 11am-11pm Mon-Sat; noon-10.30pm Sun. **Lunch served** noon-4pm Mon-Fri; noon-5pm Sat, Sun. **Dinner served** 6-10pm Mon-Thur, Sun; 6-10.30pm Fri, Sat. **Main courses** £9.50-£18.50. **Set lunch** (Mon-Fri) £5 1 course. **Set dinner** (Mon, Sun) £12.50 2 courses. **Credit** AmEx, MC, V.
If Carlsberg did gastropubs, they'd be just like the Roebuck. The bar is spacious, the seating comfy; alfresco tables populate the wide Chiswick pavement in summer, and there's a beautiful garden at the back. The cool dining room has widely spaced tables from where you can watch your food being cooked. Cheerful and helpful staff bring a regularly refreshed, succinct menu that seems to have something for everyone – including some of the best hand-cut triple-cooked chips in the known universe. Prices are very reasonable for this part of town, with a chargrilled sirloin steak accompanied by those cosmic chips and peppercorn sauce for only £16, and melt-in-the-mouth, slow-cooked pork

Honey Pot

GASTROPUBS

Fox & Grapes. See p107.

belly with parsley mash, savoy cabbage and glazed beetroot at £14.50. 'Seasonal' and 'fresh' seem to be the watchwords, even for the amazing-value £5 lunches on weekdays (a great draw for locals), and the two-course dinner on Sunday and Monday evenings (a mere £12.50). The drinks menu is impressive and the wine list cleverly arranged by type; you'll almost certainly like it if you usually go for sauvignons, pinot grigios, chardonnays or merlots. Probably the best gastropub to be found in this part of the world.
Available for hire. Babies and children welcome until 7pm: children's menu; high chairs. Disabled: toilet. Tables outdoors (20, garden; 3, pavement).

Ealing

Ealing Park Tavern
222 South Ealing Road, W5 4RL (8758 1879, www.ealingparktavern.com). South Ealing tube.
Open noon-11pm Mon-Thur, Sun; noon-midnight Fri, Sat. **Lunch served** noon-4pm, **dinner served** 6-10pm daily. **Main courses** £10-£15. **Credit** AmEx, MC, V.
We're long-time fans of this pub and dining room so were disappointed to find it wasn't up to its usual high standards on a recent visit. A procession of staff we encountered were tetchy and humourless, whereas the norm in our experience has always been easy-going friendliness and confident hospitality. They voiced concern over the number of groups taking lunch that Sunday, yet the dining room was no more or less busy than we've found it before. Indeed, they should be used to plenty of custom, for this has been easily the best restaurant in the area for some years, as well suited to date night as family gatherings, or beer and tapas after work. Food from the showpiece open kitchen was generally fine, but also lacklustre. Chilli salt squid tasted good with its mango, onion and coriander salad, but the coating was soft and gluey, not crisp or crunchy. The yorkshires that came with the roasts were stone cold, and coffee crème brûlée with double chocolate chip cookie was over-rich. However there was much enthusiasm for our plates of Loch Duart salmon with vine tomatoes, green beans and hollandaise, and roast saddle of lamb with pistachio stuffing and pea purée. Fortunately, the wine list and beer range still provide great fun for discerning drinkers.
Available for hire. Babies and children welcome (until 6.30pm): children's menu (Sat, Sun); high chairs. Tables outdoors (20, garden).

Shepherd's Bush

Anglesea Arms
35 Wingate Road, W6 0UR (8749 1291). Goldhawk Road or Ravenscourt Park tube.
Open 11am-11pm Mon-Sat; noon-10.30pm Sun. **Lunch served** 12.30-2.45pm Mon-Fri; 12.30-3pm Sat; 12.30-3.30pm Sun. **Dinner served** 7-10pm Mon; 7-10.30pm Tue-Sat; 6.30-9.30pm Sun. **Main courses** £13-£17. **Credit** MC, V.
At the end of a pretty little street off Goldhawk Road, you'll find this welcoming gastropub. On summer evenings, the front terrace soon fills with drinkers. Inside, the bar is traditional pub-cosy: a wood-panelled boozer with Union Jack cushions, the customary battered chesterfield, church pews, well-scratched tables and a mounted hog's head. Perhaps the latter is a nod to the piggy bar snacks

GASTROPUBS

chalked on the wall, along with pints of prawns, oysters, Neal's Yard cheeses and pasties. All the gastropub boxes are ticked here: real ales (from Otter, plus regularly changing guest ales); fancy cocktails; and a dining room of exposed brickwork and an open kitchen. Any French bistro would be proud of the food: 'à la franglaise' as one item on the menu boasts. It's easy to see why affluent locals keep the pub busy. Terrines, whole globe artichokes, soups and seasonal salads are typical starters. For mains, a grilled pork chop with a delightful fennel gratin showed the kitchen at its best. We were also keen on the mackerel with its summery sweetcorn and tomato salad. To finish, a vanilla-speckled buttermilk panna cotta was slick and well executed – as is the Anglesea in general. *Babies and children admitted. Tables outdoors (9, pavement).* Map 20 A3.

★ Princess Victoria HOT 50
217 Uxbridge Road, W12 9DH (8749 5886, www.princessvictoria.co.uk). Shepherd's Bush tube. **Open** 11.30am-11pm Mon-Thur, Sun; 11.30am-midnight Sat. **Lunch served** noon-3pm Mon-Sat; noon-4.30pm Sun. **Dinner served** 6.30-10.30pm Mon-Sat; 6.30-9.30pm Sun. **Main courses** £10.50-£16.50. **Set lunch** (Mon-Fri) £12.50 2 courses, £15 3 courses. **Credit** MC, V.
It's a delight to see how this former 'dram shop' and gin palace has been transformed from a dark and unwelcoming drinking den to a bright, beautiful pub pouring energy into all areas of operation: bar, kitchen and community. Emblematic of this change was the discovery of three gorgeous, delicately decorated lightwells dating from the early 20th century, which had been boarded up. They now illuminate the uncommonly large dining room (with an attractive central table seating 15, party organisers, note) and equally commodious bar, both agreeably styled as weathered Edwardian dining meets Farrow & Ball. The menu runs from snack to feast, with a penchant for the rustic, porcine, piscine and Mediterranean. Gentle own-made black pudding featured on a fine pork board (along with crispy pig cheeks) and also in a Tamworth pork, pearl barley and bacon main dish that showed an aptitude for handling big textures and flavours. This was also true of an excellent chargrilled squid and chorizo salad with romesco sauce. Bizarrely, lamb and sweetbread fricassée contained unadvertised potatoes, and the accompanying boulangère potatoes unadvertised lamb. A chocolate and espresso sundae was a bit throwaway, but, in general, quality and value were high. And you've got to love a menu that stipulates a ten-minute wait for cooked-to-order scotch eggs. Lots of smarts and little pretension have gone into a very strong wine list, with plenty by the glass and carafe. The harp-shaped bar also dispenses cask ales, and own-made ginger ale and lemonade. *Babies and children welcome: high chairs. Booking advisable. Separate room for parties, seats 60. Tables outdoors (10, garden).* Map 20 A2.

Queen Adelaide
412 Uxbridge Road, W12 0NR (8746 2573, www.thequeenadelaidew12.co.uk). Shepherd's Bush Market tube. **Open** noon-midnight Mon-Thur; noon-12.30am Fri; 10am-12.30am Sat; 10am-11pm Sun. **Breakfast served** 10am-noon Sat, Sun. **Lunch served** noon-4pm Mon-Fri;

noon-5pm Sat. **Dinner served** 6-10.30pm Mon-Sat. **Meals served** noon-9.30pm Sun. **Main courses** £10.50-£17.50. **Set lunch** (Mon-Fri) £10 2 courses. **Credit** AmEx, MC, V.
A characteristic feature of any self-respecting gastropub is the chalkboard menu. The Queen Adelaide houses a board at least ten feet tall, which is an indication of the sheer size of this sympathetically restored boozer in Shepherd's Bush. Spoilt for choice over seating, we headed for the dedicated wood-panelled dining area in preference to the centre bar and sun-trapped tables out front. An imaginative breakfast menu (served at the weekend) allows stacks of pancakes to be washed down with 'hair of the dog'; eggs benedict came cloaked in an excellent hollandaise, though the yolks were overcooked. Lunch and dinner deviate from standard British pub fare of beer-battered cod and sausages and mash to dishes showing Mediterranean and American influences. A starter ramekin of chilli-flecked crab was infused with garlic butter and served with a generous side of toasted soldiers. Barbecue ribs were meltingly tender, with the correct ratio of sauce to meat. Desserts take you back firmly into the British camp, with sticky toffee pudding and Pimm's jelly flying the flag. Eton mess stood out as a triumph of own-made meringue packed into a sundae glass; an extra-long spoon was provided and we scraped out every last morsel.
Available for hire. Babies and children welcome: children's menu; high chairs; nappy-changing facilities. Booking advisable. Disabled: toilet. Tables outdoors (12, terrace). Takeaway service; delivery service. Map 20 A1.

Westbourne Park

Cow
89 Westbourne Park Road, W2 5QH (7221 0021, www.thecowlondon.co.uk). Royal Oak or Westbourne Park tube. **Open** noon-11pm Mon-Sat; noon-10.30pm Sun. **Lunch served** noon-3.30pm daily. **Dinner served** 6-10.30pm Mon-Sat; 6-10pm Sun. **Main courses** £10-£15. **Set lunch** (Sun) £24 2 courses, £26 3 courses. **Credit** MC, V.
Tom Conran's Cow is a rural Irish pub as imagined by Disney – all cutesy cottage-style net curtains, Guinness advertising and glossy 1950s Technicolor paintwork. The bar menu is dedicated to the classic pairing of stout and seafood. Lucky Notting Hill regulars can soak up any excess of the black stuff with platters of oysters, dressed crab or pints of prawns and mayonnaise. We ate in the more formal first-floor dining room, and, once seated, were presented with a basket of pillowy focaccia, olives and vivid-pink radishes. Together, these took more than just the edge off our hunger and made ordering a starter impossible. There's nothing on the Cow's menu to scare the horses; comforting classics are the order of the day. Tables of tourists were happily feasting on portions of fish and chips or lamb shanks with mountainous servings of mashed potatoes. A massive pork chop came with a pot of English mustard ready to slather over the accompanying caramelised apples and black pudding. Everything was very competently prepared, but we left feeling the real craic was to be had sitting at the bar with a black velvet and a dozen of Ireland's finest oysters.
Available for hire. Babies and children admitted (restaurant only). Tables outdoors (2, pavement). Map 7 A5.

Barnes

★ Brown Dog
28 Cross Street, SW13 0AP (8392 2200, www.thebrowndog.co.uk). Barnes Bridge rail. **Open** noon-11pm daily. **Lunch served** noon-3pm Mon-Fri; noon-4pm Sat, Sun. **Dinner served** 7-10pm Mon-Sat; 6-9pm Sun. **Main courses** £13.95-£16.95. **Credit** AmEx, MC, V.
Dogs of any colour are welcome at this backstreet gastropub, as are drinkers, who might want to sample the lengthy wine list or one of the London-brewed real ales (Sambrook's Wandle and Twickenham Original). But the focus is on food, with the small main room packed with wooden tables and chairs. Prints and old metal signs clutter the walls. It's a charming spot, especially in the evening when the polished red ceiling, candles and handsome copper globe lights above the bar create a twinkling setting for some appealing food. Although many starters are simple (half-pint of prawns with mayo, salty padrón peppers, whole globe artichoke), ingredients are top-quality and attention is paid to the details; plump Maldon rock oysters came with a shallot vinegar infused with coriander seeds. Full marks for the Scottish côte de boeuf (cooked rare, as requested), served with proper hand-cut fries and roasted tomatoes. Flavours don't always shine through, however: a summery broad bean, pea and mint risotto was ultra-creamy, but lacked zing; and poached nectarines with amaretto biscuits and cream tasted more of the poaching wine than the fruit. Approachable, enthusiastic service and a contented hum from other diners made amends.
Available for hire. Babies and children welcome: high chairs. Booking advisable. Tables outdoors (12, garden). Vegetarian menu.

Chelsea

Cadogan Arms
298 King's Road, SW3 5UG (7352 6500, www.thecadoganarmschelsea.com). Sloane Square tube then bus 19, 22 or 319. **Open** 11am-11pm Mon-Sat; 11am-10.30pm Sun. **Lunch served** noon-3.30pm, **dinner served** 6-10.30pm Mon-Fri. **Meals served** noon-10.30pm Sat; noon-9pm Sun. **Main courses** £11-£22. **Credit** AmEx, MC, V.
Chelsea's shooting set probably feels quite at home among the trophy antlers and stuffed birds adorning the walls of the small dining area at the back of the Cadogan Arms. A majestic buffalo head peered down as we tucked into a pleasurable starter of scallops and sweetcorn purée, topped with shards of crisp bacon. Waiting staff told us they had served over 100 covers since noon by the time we arrived on a Sunday evening. The high demand on the kitchen might explain a lacklustre main course of pork belly. Chewy and seemingly not slow-roasted as advertised, this was accompanied by an overcooked yorkshire pudding of prawn cracker-like consistency. All was forgiven, however, when our pan-fried monkfish arrived, bathing in a mussel-dotted broth with flashes of green broad beans and braised gem lettuce. To drink, order something from the well-ordered wine list, or a pint of Adnams or London Pride. Unlike the taxidermy ducks surrounding us,

GASTROPUBS

The OWL & PUSSYCAT

....

34 Redchurch Street
Shoreditch London E2 7DP
020 3487 0088
owlandpussycatshoreditch.com

Pub - Restaurant - Garden

The FELLOW
Pub & Dining Room

....

24 York Way London N1 9AA
Reservations: 020 7833 4395
thefellow.co.uk

service was decidedly unstuffy; a bottle of chilled tap water is brought to table as a matter of course. We'll definitely return, if only to appease the food envy we experienced from the aroma of truffle-scented pasta wafting past our table.
Available for hire. Babies and children welcome: children's menu; high chairs. Booking advisable. Separate room for parties, seats 50.
Map 14 E12.

Lots Road Pub & Dining Room

114 Lots Road, SW10 0RJ (7352 6645, www.lotsroadpub.com). Fulham Broadway tube or Imperial Wharf rail. **Open** 11am-11pm Mon-Sat; noon-10.30pm. **Lunch served** noon-3pm Mon; noon-4pm Tue-Sat; noon-5pm Sun. **Dinner served** 6-10.30pm Mon-Sat; 6-9.30pm Sun. **Main courses** £10-£17. **Set meal** (Mon, dinner Sun) £10 2 courses. **Credit** AmEx, MC, V.
As this popular corner pub is located on a road better known for its high-end design shops and auction house, with plush Chelsea Harbour opposite, you might expect the place to be more expensive and pretentious than it is. The menu focuses on British pub classics done well, if not exceptionally so. Sausage and mash comes in a generous portion, with rich onion gravy, but perhaps not the world's most flavoursome bangers. Starters are also pretty large; size-wise, there wasn't much difference between a smoked mackerel starter (a plump fillet piled on fennel, potatoes and leaves) and our chicken salad main. There's also a roast on Sundays and a £10 set menu on Mondays, with a few more restaurant-style dishes available each day. Desserts are simple but well selected – salted caramel ice-cream was sublime. Tables are laid out in a U-shape around the bar; it can get very noisy towards the back. Customers come to drink as much as eat here, with the likes of Doom Bar bitter and Aspall cider on tap. The wine list provides recommendations, Amazon website-style, for those who like pinot grigio or cabernet sauvignon, encouraging drinkers to branch out from their favourites.
Available for hire. Babies and children welcome: children's menu; high chairs. Booking advisable lunch Sun. Disabled: toilet. **Map 21 A1**.

Pig's Ear

35 Old Church Street, SW3 5BS (7352 2908, www.thepigsear.info). Sloane Square tube then bus 19, 22 or 319.
Pub **Open** noon-11pm Mon-Sat; noon-10.30pm Sun. **Lunch served** 12.30-3pm, **dinner served** 7-10pm Mon-Fri. **Meals served** noon-11pm Sat; noon-10.30pm Sun. **Main courses** £12-£15.
Restaurant **Dinner served** 7-10.30pm Tue-Sat. **Meals served** noon-9pm Sun. **Main courses** £12-£20.
Both **Credit** AmEx, MC, V.
It might be situated on a genteel backstreet two minutes' walk from the chi-chi King's Road, but the bar of this lovingly scuffed gastropub is as keen to populate itself with punk merchandise as it is with the polo-shirt brigade who frequent it. A promo cartoon for the Sex Pistols' 'Holidays in the Sun' above the bar advertises a 'cheap holiday in other people's misery', while a Clash 'Sandinista!' poster claims to be 'written with love, sealed with a kick'. Beers come from Battersea's Sambrook's Brewery. The tiny dining area at the back opts for more self-consciously kitsch pub trappings. There's the kind of battered dark wooden furniture

you'd expect to find in Hogwarts' dining hall, posters of dogs playing pool, a stuffed stag's head and cases of pin-mounted butterflies adorning the faded aquamarine wood panelling. Food tends towards the hearty and meaty, although nothing impressed on our Sunday afternoon visit. A '32-day aged' beef sirloin arrived doused in a sticky, salty gravy, and the pleasantly runny yolk of an own-made scotch egg was let down by its watery meat casing. Service can verge on the distracted, even when not busy. Sad, as the Pig's Ear has wowed us in the past.
Available for hire. Babies and children welcome: high chairs. Booking advisable (dining room).
Map 14 E12.

Fulham

★ Harwood Arms   HOT 50

Corner of Walham Grove & Farm Lane, SW6 1QP (7386 1847, www.harwoodarms.com). Fulham Broadway tube. **Open** 5.30-11pm Mon; noon-11pm Tue-Fri; noon-midnight Sat; noon-10pm Sun. **Dinner served** 5.30-10pm Mon. **Meals served** noon-10pm Tue-Sat; noon-9pm Sun. **Main courses** £16.50-£18. **Credit** AmEx, MC, V.
The Harwood Arms is a smart restaurant with the conceit that it's a gastropub. While you can pop in for a pint – and a few local toffs do – dinner reservations are so sought after that you'll have to book days, or even weeks, in advance. If you manage to bag a table, you're in for a treat that reminds you just how good simple, classic British cooking can be. Scotch eggs are a signature dish: served piping hot, with the interior molten, and the venison shell pliable and thrillingly flavourful. Game is always a strong hand: on our visit, a shoulder of venison for two people, served on a wooden slab with horn-handled carving tools, looked like something from a Tudor banquet. The deer meat was unusually tender, the slow-braised fibres of meat moist, the accompanying buttery mash as rich as custard; and it came with a celeriac salad to refresh the palate. A starter of country terrine was also exemplary, the texture delicate and even, the bosky flavours complex. Puddings are all as proper and correct as Mary Poppins – trifles, fools, possets – and true Brit, without any dodgy Dick Van Dyke accents. Drinks haven't been forgotten: the regularly changing real ales usually feature Battersea's Sambrook's and three guests, while the wine list is a corker, with over 30 wines available by the glass. It's an attractive spot too, with cream and grey paintwork, and plenty of natural light thanks to the big windows.
Available for hire. Babies and children welcome: children's menu; high chairs. Booking advisable dinner. **Map 13 A12**.

Putney

Spencer

237 Lower Richmond Road, SW15 1HJ (8788 0640, www.thespencerpub.com). Putney Bridge tube or Putney rail or bus 22, 265, 485. **Open** 11am-midnight Mon-Sat; 11am-11pm Sun. **Lunch served** noon-3pm, **dinner served** 6-10pm Mon-Sat. **Meals served** noon-9pm Sun. **Main courses** £8.95-£24.50. **Credit** AmEx, MC, V.
The Spencer may have dropped the 'Arms' from its name, but they are still proudly painted on the grey-green walls of this large corner pub. Mismatched

wooden tables complete the predictable shabby-chic look. In summer, you can sit out on Putney Common: not London's most impressive green space, but a calm enough spot in which to enjoy a pint of London Pride or Landlord, or, more likely, a glass of something from the extensive wine list. When ordering food, our advice would be to stick with the main courses – there are plenty to choose from, whether you're after a quality burger or something more sophisticated – as starters and desserts seem a bit uninspiring. A grilled half-chicken (free-range, of course) with lemon and garlic was lip-smackingly juicy, and came with a mountain of skinny chips. Monkfish and chorizo brochette on a hillock of not-very-herby tabouleh looked quite sad in comparison. Despite a focus on the grill, vegetarians are well catered for, with a halloumi burger/meat-free roast on Sundays and several pastas and salads. Friendly Aussie waiting staff add to the lively, down-to-earth vibe that characterises this neighbourhood hangout.
Babies and children welcome until 9pm: high chairs; nappy-changing facilities. Disabled: toilet. Tables outdoors (12, pavement).

Wimbledon

Earl Spencer

260-262 Merton Road, SW18 5JL (8870 9244, www.theearlspencer.co.uk). Southfields tube. **Open** 11am-11pm Mon-Thur; 11am-midnight Fri, Sat; noon-10.30pm Sun. **Lunch served** 12.30-2.30pm Mon-Sat; 12.30-3pm Sun. **Dinner served** 7-10pm Mon-Sat; 7-9.30pm Sun. **Main courses** £8.50-£14. **Set lunch** (Mon-Fri) £7.50 1 course. **Credit** AmEx, MC, V.
A cavernous Edwardian pub that's more deserving of the 'gastronomic' epithet than most. The Earl Spencer was refurbished and reopened back in 2003, yet has never felt like a calculated exercise in filling a gap in the market. It serves inviting food, less formulaic than most, and gives the impression the menu has followed a steady evolution. Chef Justin Aubrey's starters veer from simple tomato soup to inspired devilled lambs' kidneys and bacon on toast, with Cox apple and shallot salad – both dishes, slightly perplexingly, priced identically. Rugged potato and spinach croquettes, a little under-seasoned, came with an overly runny taleggio dip. Better was the main of red bream on a plate laden with a rainbow of veg: sautéed potatoes, black cabbage, carrots, and roast pepper and olive relish. Service is friendly, though far from polished. A side of corn on the cob was missing from our piri piri chicken, never to materialise despite our enquiries. However, you can sit where you like, order and pay at the bar, choose cask-conditioned ales, and get a complimentary basket of own-made bread. For the refreshing lack of conceit alone, this pub is quite a find.
Babies and children welcome: high chairs. Bookings not accepted lunch Sun. Separate room for parties, seats 70. Tables outdoors (10, patio).

Fox & Grapes   NEW

9 Camp Road, SW19 4UN (8619 1300, www.foxandgrapeswimbledon.co.uk). Wimbledon tube/rail then bus 93. **Open** noon-11pm Mon-Thur; 11am-midnight Fri, Sat; noon-10.30pm Sun. **Lunch served** noon-3pm Mon-Sat; noon-4pm Sun. **Dinner served** 6-9.30pm Mon-Sat; 6-9pm Sun. **Main courses** £13.50-£31.50. **Set lunch** (Mon-Sat) £17.50 2 courses, £19.50 3 courses. **Credit** MC, V.

Earl Spencer. See p107.

In spite of its bucolic, quasi-rural location, the old Fox & Grapes was a bit of an under-achiever. But now that Claude Bosi (of Mayfair's fine-dining restaurant Hibiscus) and his team have taken it over and given it a huge refurb, it has morphed into a smart restaurant-posing-as-gastropub. A menu based around British pub favourites has been deconstructed, refined and put back together. Highlights of our visit included a chunk of crisp-skinned roast pork belly teamed with rich, dark black pudding and a translucent, golden cider sauce. Another dish that impressed was a fillet of pollack, once again perfectly judged, with a heap of puy lentils in a mustardy sauce. A starter of pork pie was properly made using hot water crust pastry, while the jelly inside was delicately flavoured with apple. Only the puddings let the side down: a medieval dessert of junket ('set' milk) was just a little too watery. The Fox & Grapes has a nice vibe; Bosi's brother Cedrid is managing the place, and although bookings in the first weeks were muddled, it was full of appreciative diners who had travelled by taxi or 4x4 (it's a bit out of the way, in the middle of Wimbledon Common). Book well ahead if you want to get a prime dinner slot.

Available for hire. Babies and children welcome: children's menu; high chairs; nappy-changing facilities. Booking advisable Thur-Sun.

South

Balham

Avalon

16 Balham Hill, SW12 9EB (8675 8613, www.theavalonlondon.com). Clapham South tube. **Open** noon-11pm Mon-Wed; noon-midnight Thur; noon-1am Fri, Sat; noon-10.30pm Sun. **Lunch served** noon-3.30pm Mon-Fri; noon-4pm Sat. **Dinner served** 6-10.30pm Mon-Sat. **Meals served** noon-9pm Sun. **Main courses** £9.50-£21. **Credit** AmEx, MC, V.

Setting a standard for gentrified good looks, the Avalon is a grown-up pub and dining room that has become a firm local favourite. The restaurant's walls are lined with milky-white tiles and vintage sepia prints for a classic period look, while the more informal main boozer boasts a huge Greco-Roman-style mural, comfy vintage sofas and a sweeping wooden bar. Best of all for summer, there's a peaceful decked rear garden – complete with mature trees and a four-tiered fountain. The cooking, sadly, doesn't quite live up to the rarefied setting. Gastropub favourites are generously portioned, yet ours lacked finesse, with risotto primavera on the starchy side and a well-cooked steak let down by its watery béarnaise sauce. Better to play safe with a simple burger or the pie of the day, and a drink from the bar (there's Landlord on tap, plus a great range of spirits). Service, likewise, is a little amateurish, with condiments forgotten and empty glasses unnoticed. Not that such shortcomings make one jot of difference – the Avalon has been playing to packed houses since opening, with Balham and Clapham's middle classes flocking here, particularly on Sundays when a traditional roast is the draw.

Babies and children welcome: children's menu; crayons; high chairs; nappy-changing facilities. Booking advisable weekends. Disabled: toilet. Separate room for parties, seats 20. Tables outdoors (22, garden; 10, pavement; 10 courtyard)..

Battersea

Draft House

*94 Northcote Road, SW11 6QW (7924 1814,
www.drafthouse.co.uk). Clapham Junction rail.*
Open noon-11pm Mon-Fri; 10am-11pm Sat;
10am-10.30pm Sun. **Meals served** noon-
10pm Mon-Sat; 10am-9pm Sun. **Main courses**
£5.75-£16.50. **Credit** AmEx, MC, V.
One of a three-strong chain, this buzzing boozer
on a modest corner plot throbs with a good-time
vibe. The dedicated dining area at the back fills up
steadily over an evening, seemingly as carousers
from the front bar decide that solid sustenance may
be necessary given their advancing state of
marination. True to its name, the Draft House puts
beer centre stage, taking provenance, cellaring and
pouring seriously. The brews are indeed
impressive, and the option of one-third pint
measures reinforces the spirit of discovery. If only
the same care were taken with the food. Staples
include haddock and chips, salmon and crab cakes,
and an 8oz burger (the menu recommends beer
matches). Yet in the instances where ambition crept
in, we found the results disappointing. A starter of
squid, chorizo and caper berries was eye-
wateringly hot, and a little sweet, while ham hock
and cheddar croquettes came with an unpleasant
glutinous mustard-based dip. Both dishes were
served at nuclear temperatures. Food felt
perfunctory, service was misjudged, and at times
the commercialism was transparent: a £16.50
ribeye was served with only a garnish – a portion
of chips or fries cost extra. Ouch!
*Babies and children welcome: high chairs;
nappy-changing facilities. Booking advisable
dinner Thur-Sat; lunch Sun. Disabled: toilet.
Tables outdoors (8, pavement).* **Map 21 C5.**
For branches see index.

Streatham

Manor Arms NEW

*13 Mitcham Lane, SW16 6LQ (3195 6888,
www.themanorarms.com). Streatham rail or bus
249.* **Open** 11am-11pm Mon-Fri; 10am-midnight
Sat; noon-midnight Sun. **Lunch served** noon-
3pm Mon-Fri; 11am-4pm Sat. **Dinner served**
6-10pm Mon-Sat. **Meals served** noon-9pm Sun.
Main courses £9-£15. **Set lunch** (Mon-Fri)
£10 2 courses, £11.50 3 courses. **Set dinner**
(Mon-Fri) £11.50 2 courses, £15.50 3 courses.
Credit AmEx, MC, V.
A sweeping, pewter-clad bar dominates the ground
floor of this light and refreshingly modern art deco
space. It's still a proper pub, though, with original
1930s oak panelling lining the walls and hand-
pulled pints including Purity Pure Gold (a golden
ale from Warwickshire), Sambrook's Wandle from
Battersea, and Adnams Broadside from Suffolk.
But most people are here to dine. A salad of mixed
beets, soft goat's cheese and pickled walnuts was
a good start. Rib steak was a cut above, and as
you'd expect for £21, correctly rare, moist and
flavourful. Chips were of the skinny, french fry
variety. Less impressive were the fish goujons,
which resembled leftover scraps. Potted shrimps
came warm and molten (rather than chilly and set),
while a panna cotta was also melting: a product of
the too-hot open kitchen, where delayed dishes
were disintegrating before delivery. Not that we
cared, because the grub was still good. A good
wine list and Wayne Collins cocktail list offer

diversion, but it's the congenial atmosphere and
friendly service that are the most potent draws.
*Available for hire. Babies and children welcome:
children's menu; high chairs; nappy-changing
facilities. Booking advisable Sun. Disabled: toilet.
Tables outdoors (20, garden).*

Tooting

★ Antelope

*76 Mitcham Road, SW17 9NG (8672 3888,
www.theantelopepub.com). Tooting Broadway
tube.* **Open** 4pm-midnight Mon-Thur; 4pm-
1am Fri; noon-1am Sat; noon-11pm Sun.
Dinner served 6-10.30 Mon-Fri; 6-10.30pm Sat.
Lunch served noon-4pm Sat; noon-5pm Sun.
Main courses £8.50-£15. **Credit** MC, V.
With beaten-down sofas and mismatched chairs
and tables, 'shabby chic' is a term that was made
for the Antelope. Hunting trophies mounted on the
walls, heavy wood panelling, period fireplaces and
heritage paints all combine to create the feel of a
stately home, yet there's nothing dusty about this
place. With ambient tunes and a laid-back clientele,
it's retro cool with a modern twist. The pub is huge,
with three large, high-ceilinged rooms and a beer
garden. There's a big screen for watching sports, a
pool table, stacks of board games, and high chairs
too, suiting the full range of customers. The menu
is far from shabby; changing daily, it's a roll-call of
well-thought-out, well-crafted dishes. Pan-fried
squid with pangritata was cooked to perfection,
whipped off the heat the second it was done. A beef
burger (not the typical pub staple) excelled, arriving
with sweet confit onions and a fresh tomato relish.
To finish: a warm brownie and fior di latte ice-
cream. In short, the Antelope is a must for lovers
of great grub in an informal setting.
*Available for hire. Babies and children welcome:
high chairs. Booking advisable. Disabled: toilet.
Separate room for parties, seats 150. Tables
outdoors (20, garden).*

Waterloo

★ Anchor & Hope

*36 The Cut, SE1 8LP (7928 9898). Southwark
tube or Waterloo tube/rail.* **Open** 5-11pm
Mon; 11am-11pm Tue-Sat; 12.30-5pm Sun.
Lunch served noon-2.30pm Tue-Sat; 2pm
sitting Sun. **Dinner served** 6-10.30pm Mon-
Sat. **Main courses** £12-£20. **Credit** MC, V.
The menu is British at the A&H, and so is the
seating policy, with no reservations from Monday
to Saturday, meaning that diners wanting to
sample the robust seasonal cooking must often
queue until a table becomes free. Fortunately,
draught Young's and Bombardier are on hand. On
busy weekday evenings, things can get noisy, and
some diners are seated on communal tables, so this
isn't an ideal spot for an intimate dinner. But
despite the manager's advance warning of a wait
of up to an hour ('Whatever you do, don't turn up
starving'), a Saturday afternoon visit saw us shown
straight to a table in the relaxed rear dining room.
Here, burgundy walls are hung with for-sale
contemporary art, and heavily weathered wooden
tables are surrounded by mismatched chairs.
Chatter fills the place. The nose-to-tail menu
features dishes such as calf's brains and brown
butter on toast, and a roughly minced Middle
White faggot that was so creamily rich it could
have contained foie gras. Vegetarian dishes are
limited, but a softball-sized, sweet globe artichoke

came with velvety dijon vinaigrette. Make sure you
leave room for dessert; a precision-baked custard
tart encased with light, springy shortcrust pastry
was a highlight of our most recent visit.
*Babies and children welcome: high chairs.
Bookings not accepted Mon-Sat; advisable Sun.
Tables outdoors (5, pavement).* **Map 11 N8.**

South East

Dulwich

★ Rosendale NEW

*65 Rosendale Road, SE21 8EZ (8761 9008,
www.therosendale.co.uk). West Dulwich rail.*
Bar Open noon-11pm Mon-Thur, Sun; noon-
1am Fri, Sat. **Lunch served** noon-3.30pm,
dinner served 6-10.30pm daily. **Main
courses** £9.50-£16.
Restaurant **Lunch served** noon-3.30pm
Mon-Fri; noon-4pm Sat. **Dinner served**
6-10.30pm Mon-Sat. **Meals served** noon-9pm
Sun. **Main courses** £9-£16.
Both Credit AmEx, MC, V.
Recently taken over by Renaissance Pubs (which
also owns the Avalon in Balham and other south
London gastropubs), the Rosendale has been given
a stylish makeover, and the new menu is one to be
savoured. If it's an old-school pub you're after, stick
by the bar to enjoy a pint of real ale, catch the big
game and tuck into the predominantly British-
themed bar menu, including welsh rarebit, scotch
egg and beer-battered fish and chips. The
restaurant is all pressed napkins and polished
cutlery, but still charmingly laid-back. Old theatre
posters and antique prints line the walls, with sepia-
photo wallpaper and huge steel chandeliers adding
interest. As well as pub favourites such as burgers,
you'll also find more ambitious fare. Traditional
niçoise was given a modern makeover in a jasmine
tea-smoked sea trout salad with duck egg, roasted
tomatoes, olives and beans. For families, it's an
absolute find: parents can enjoy a grown-up lunch
alfresco, while kids roam in the play area. The
children's menu is equally appealing and includes
a cupcake to decorate for dessert. Also worth
knowing: there are two rooms available for private
parties and a huge beer garden for sunny days.
*Babies and children welcome: high chairs; nappy-
changing facilities; play area. Disabled: toilet.
Separate rooms for parties, seating 25-100.
Tables outdoors (40, garden).*

East Dulwich

Herne Tavern

*2 Forest Hill Road, SE22 0RR (8299 9521,
www.theherne.net). East Dulwich or Peckham
rail or bus 12, 197.* **Open** noon-1am Mon-Thur,
Sun; noon-2am Fri, Sat. **Lunch served** noon-
2.30pm Mon-Fri; noon-4pm Sat, Sun. **Dinner
served** 5.30-9.30pm Mon-Sat; 6-9pm Sun.
Main courses £8.50-£15. **Set meal** (Mon-Fri)
£11.50 2 courses, £15 3 courses. **Credit** MC, V.
The Herne has one of the largest, loveliest and
most child-friendly beer gardens in south London,
and consequently any mildly clement day will see
it packed with local families. Inside, the bar ticks
all the 'fantasy pub' boxes: real ale, decent wine
list, posh crisps, wood panelling, leather sofas, real
fire, discreet TV (big events get shown in the
garden barn), loyal regulars, a pub quiz… But the
food seems to have been sidelined. With the

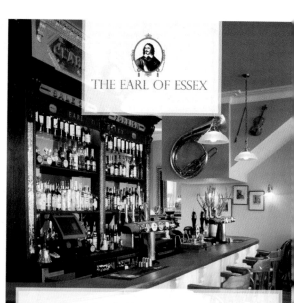

exception of the hugely popular Sunday roasts, the menu is dull and the cooking average. Steak and chips, fish and chips, tuna niçoise, chocolate brownie, English cheeses, blah, blah... often served with indifference. It's as if the food is there just to soak up your pint – which is what most visitors seem to use it for. Staff, a crucial interface between diner and chef, don't appear to have been coached in what they're serving. When we asked one fresh-faced barmaid about the guest ales – in a pub that runs an annual beer festival – she just shrugged and looked blank. Food lovers may prefer to decamp to sister restaurant, the Palmerston; pub-lovers may never want to go home.
Babies and children welcome: children's menu; high chairs; nappy-changing facilities. Separate room for parties, seats 60. Tables outdoors (25, garden).

Palmerston

91 Lordship Lane, SE22 8EP (8693 1629, www.thepalmerston.net). East Dulwich rail or bus 185, 176, P13. **Open** noon-11pm Mon-Thur; noon-midnight Fri, Sat; noon-10.30pm Sun. **Lunch served** noon-2.30pm Mon-Fri; noon-3pm Sat, Sun. **Dinner served** 7-10pm Mon-Sat; 7-9.30pm Sun. **Main courses** £11-£16. **Set lunch** (Mon-Fri) £12.50 2 courses, £16 3 courses. **Credit** MC, V.

From a table at the Palmerston, you can watch the whole of East Dulwich go by if you sit there long enough – and that wouldn't be unpleasant in these relaxed wood-panelled surrounds. Twinned with the Herne pub, the Palmerston is where the owners concentrate their gastronomic efforts. The thick, bloody, 28-day Galloway ribeye is the biggest draw, but we've found more creative dishes to be hit and miss. A chilled spiced apple soup offered an unexpectedly complex combination of flavours, but 'rare roast beef' was disappointingly dry and towards the brown end of the spectrum, though the accompanying salad of pickled girolles and minted peas exhibited freshness and zing. Desserts – well-executed gastropub staples – are worth ordering; the vanilla custard with raspberries and shortbread was so light that two portions wouldn't have been a challenge. Opening in 2004 to critical acclaim, and catching East Dulwich just at the tipping point of its gentrification, the Palmerston has of late been resting on its laurels. Now that the local food scene has upped the ante considerably (no one is ever short of an artisanal loaf or free-range sausage in SE22), the pub may have to raise its game to remain a contender.
Babies and children welcome: high chairs; nappy-changing facilities. Booking advisable dinner and weekends. Tables outdoors (8, pavement). **Map 23 C4.**

New Cross

New Cross House NEW

316 New Cross Road, SE14 6AF (8691 8875, www.thenewcrosshouse.com). New Cross or New Cross Gate rail. **Open** noon-midnight Mon-Thur, Sun; noon-1am Fri, Sat. **Meals served** noon-10pm Mon-Sat; noon-9.30pm Sun. **Main courses** £7-£10.50. **Credit** MC, V.

New owner Capital Pubs does a great trade in revamping old, tired boozers and giving them a fresh lease of life. New Cross House is no different, pitched at local denizens craving a friendly, comforting pub with good food and drink, rather than a destination gastro-temple. The newly expanded ground-floor space is light and airy, with bentwood chairs and cosy leather booths. There are good brews and cider from Sharp's, as well as the company's own Bonobo or Weasel beers. Taking centre stage among the food offerings is a large wood-fired pizza oven, with thin-crusted choices including one combining pork, mozzarella, tomato and garlic mushrooms, though a well-intended chorizo, fennel salami, mozzarella and pecorino version was far too salty. Better are the small snacks, such as breaded halloumi with a parmesan and cauliflower dip, or a light salad of smoked chicken with poached egg. There are roasts too, though you'll get brisket instead of rose-pink slabs of beef. The local area may have cheaper options, but the service here is chummy, the food and drink decent, and there's even a piano out front for some old-fashioned pub sing-songs.
Available for hire. Babies and children welcome: high chairs; nappy-changing facilities. Booking advisable Fri-Sun. Disabled: toilet. Tables outdoors (30, garden).

East

Docklands

Gun

27 Coldharbour, E14 9NS (7515 5222, www.thegundocklands.com). Canary Wharf tube or Blackwall DLR. **Open** 11am-midnight Mon-Sat; 11am-11pm Sun. **Lunch served** noon-3pm Mon-Fri; noon-4pm Sat, Sun. **Dinner served** 6-10.30pm Mon-Sat; 6.30-9.30pm Sun. **Main courses** £13-£22. **Set lunch** (Mon-Thur) £15-£18 3 courses. **Credit** AmEx, MC, V.

This riverside pub has much to recommend it: fabulous Thames views from the terrace, great history (Emma Hamilton and Nelson may have trysted here), a convivial vibe, decent beer (including ale from Dark Star and Adnams) and imaginative cooking. Even so, our latest visit was disappointing: service was friendly but inattentive (we were offered only the dinner menu, though the cheaper pub menu included an extremely popular burger); specials weren't pointed out, despite the board offering the likes of grouse (shot on the Glorious 12th); and, despite waiting almost 40 minutes for a smoked trout, the fish arrived fridge-cold and meagre. A small fillet was presented atop lettuce and Jersey royals, with a couple of green beans and half a quail's egg. To follow, a much-anticipated 35-day-aged Angus ribeye was too fatty and, though accurately cooked, offered few choice mouthfuls. This came with good twice-fried chips, over-buttery and under-vinegared béarnaise and a pile of undressed watercress; it cost £27. We've eaten better here, and feel sure our experience was an aberration as the terrace and dining room were both busy on a Sunday night. On form, the Gun is a pub we'd love to have as our local.
Available for hire. Babies and children welcome: high chairs. Booking advisable. Disabled: toilet. Separate rooms for parties, seating 16 and 22. Tables outdoors (26, terrace). **Map 24 C2.**

Limehouse

Narrow

44 Narrow Street, E14 8DP (7592 7950, www.gordonramsay.com/thenarrow). Limehouse DLR. **Open** 11.30am-11pm Mon-Fri; noon-11.30pm Sat; noon-10.30pm Sun. **Lunch served** 11.30am-3pm Mon-Fri; noon-4pm Sat, Sun. **Dinner served** 6-10.30pm Mon-Fri; 5.30-10.30pm Sat, Sun. **Main courses** £10-£17. **Set meal** (6-9pm Mon-Thur; 6-7pm Fri-Sun) £18 2 courses, £22 3 courses. **Credit** AmEx, MC, V.

Very much a pub that trades on its location. On a sunny day, the riverside setting sees the Narrow full of an after-work crowd taking in the sweeping views of the Thames from the outdoor terrace (where summer barbecues are offered at weekends), or from the tall, river-facing windows of the conservatory-like dining area. Inside, there's a contemporary rustic feel, with the clean white wooden decor jazzed up by armchairs striped like a public schoolboy's blazer, and a collection of objets d'art that includes a vintage radio, old metal tankards, a watering can and artfully arranged piles of weathered hardbacks. As you'd expect from a Gordon Ramsay establishment, the bar

Rosendale. See p109.

menu throws bloodthirsty offerings such as devilled duck hearts into a list of sandwiches, burgers and fish and chips. The restaurant menu leans more towards fine dining, though we reckon that results are generally underwhelming these days. Pork shoulder sat on polenta as bland as wallpaper paste; a black pudding and pig's cheek croquette came with a flavourless ginger jelly; and knickerbocker glory was a curiously grainy mélange. The Narrow's tasteful selection of real ales and bottled beers, and a decent wine list, make it a far better option for a drink.
Babies and children welcome: high chairs. Booking essential. Disabled: toilet. Separate room for parties, seats 18. Tables outdoors (36, riverside terrace).

Shoreditch

Princess of Shoreditch

76-78 Paul Street, EC2A 4NE (7729 9270, www.theprincessofshoreditch.com). Old Street tube/rail. **Open** noon-11pm Mon-Sat; noon-10pm Sun. **Lunch served** noon-3pm Mon-Fri; noon-4pm Sat. **Dinner served** 6.30-10pm Mon-Sat. **Meals served** noon-8pm Sun. **Main courses** £11.50-£19. **Set lunch** (Tue-Fri) £14 2 courses, £18 3 courses. **Credit** AmEx, MC, V.

The attractive dining room at the Princess is accessed via a slightly challenging wrought-iron spiral staircase. It's a decorous spot, a world away from the booze-fuelled din of the altogether-more-basic ground floor. An ambitious, seasonal menu contains no bargains: for these prices we'd have liked more comfort (the tables are too close together, with legs that get in the way). Most dishes, however, justified their prices: crispy blacksticks blue cheese, candied walnut and pear salad; razor clams in tomato and chilli sauce with garden herb crust; and ham hock, spring bean and pea salad with shaved parmesan and mint and lemon dressing – all made pleasing summer starters. Grilled sea bass with orange and tomato gazpacho was one of several spritely fish mains, but pink roasted rack of Blackface lamb with summer beans, potatoes and crispy pancetta was more like medium raw than medium rare, making it rather heavy-going. Puddings ended the meal positively: a lava-like warm chocolate fondant with vanilla ice-cream, and an almost too-sweet (but good) sticky toffee pudding. Drinks run from pints (try Sambrook's Wandle Ale, from Battersea) to regularly changing wines. Service is low-key yet attentive. It's a popular venue – book or take your chances in the bar.
Available for hire. Booking advisable. Children admitted until 6pm: high chairs. Tables outdoors (3, pavement). **Map 6 Q4.**

North East

Hackney

Prince Arthur

95 Forest Road, E8 3BH (7249 9996, www.theprincearthurlondonfields.com). Dalston Kingsland or London Fields rail or bus 38, 242, 277. **Open** 4-11pm Mon-Thur; 3-11pm Fri; 11am-11pm Sat, Sun. **Lunch served** noon-4.30pm Sat. **Dinner served** 6-10pm Mon-Sat. **Meals served** noon-9pm Sun. **Main courses** £11-£23. **Set meal** (6-10pm Mon-Wed) £15 2 courses. **Credit** MC, V.

Manor Arms. See p109.

A traditional pub atmosphere prevails at the Prince Arthur, thanks to the no-nonsense furnishings of heavy wooden tables and dark green leather stools; many punters ignore the 'gastro' leanings and treat it purely as a place for a pint. The food disappointed on our visit – which is puzzling, as that's not in keeping with other Martin Brothers venues such as the Gun and the Cadogan Arms. Fish pie is topped with garish yellow cheese and tasted offputtingly close to a ready meal, while stilton and onion tart suffered from greasiness and heavy, slightly burnt pastry. Both came with the same dreary frisée lettuce salad. The rest of the menu consists of standards including fish and chips, burgers and steaks. We had to ask for the prix fixe promoted online as we weren't offered it – bad form in any case, but worse since the carte prices are a tad steep for the quality of ingredients and the lack of finesse displayed by the kitchen. Other niggles included a half-hour wait to pay the bill, despite asking for it twice – the pub wasn't overly busy but the waiters were harried and inattentive. A lacklustre experience, but hopefully an atypical one. *Babies and children welcome: children's menu; high chairs; nappy-changing facilities. Disabled: toilet. Tables outdoors (4, pavement).*

North

Archway

St John's

91 Junction Road, N19 5QU (7272 1587, www.stjohnstavern.com). Archway tube.
Bar Open/meals served 5-11pm Mon-Thur; noon-11pm Fri, Sat; noon-10.30pm Sun.
Main courses £2.75-£7.
Restaurant **Lunch served** noon-3.30pm Fri; noon-4pm Sat, Sun. **Dinner served** 6.30-11pm Mon-Sat; 6.30-9.30pm Sun. **Main courses** £11.25-£18.50.
Both **Credit** AmEx, MC, V.
The team at this attractive Victorian pub have worked with English Heritage to restore its original architectural details with great success. The airy front bar (where you can also eat) benefits from huge windows letting in plenty of cheering natural light, while the huge, gold-ceilinged dining hall next door features an intriguing gallery of pictures, a semi-open kitchen and its own bar for easy drinks service. Welcoming, intelligent staff promptly brought crayons and paper to amuse the child in our group, while we perused the paper menu and blackboard highlighting a discerning range of credible ingredient suppliers. It's worth forking out £2.50 for the fabulous own-made sourdough with Cornish salted butter, but you'll probably want to save room for desserts such as lavender crème brûlée and steamed cherry sponge. Pork with sauerkraut, apple and mash was a pale assembly, but tasty and succulent. Hake came with an inspired chorizo and samphire dressing, but was too salty (not for the first time, in our experience). There were other quibbles too. The room wasn't full – we dined alongside a modest stag do, groups of couples, and families – yet such was the long wait between courses that we spent 90 minutes on a two-course lunch. And the prices of wines by the glass looked very reasonable until we clocked their 125ml size; bottles cost upwards of £15, but a few 375ml carafes are offered. *Babies and children welcome: high chairs. Booking essential weekends. Tables outdoors (10, patio). Map 26 B1.*

Crouch End

Queens Pub & Dining Room

26 Broadway Parade, N8 9DE (8340 2031, www.thequeenscrouchend.co.uk). Finsbury Park tube/rail then bus W7, or Crouch Hill rail. **Open** noon-11pm Mon-Thur, Sun; noon-midnight Fri, Sat. **Meals served** noon-10pm Mon-Sat; noon-9pm Sun. **Main courses** £9-£16. **Set meal** (noon-3pm Mon-Fri; noon-6pm Sat) £5 1 course. **Credit** AmEx, MC, V.
There was a time when the then-Hornsey Council, dominated by Methodists, strove to keep pubs and the demon drink out of its newly built borough. Local builder JC Hill fought many battles with the council and in 1899 built the Queens on an unprecedentedly lavish scale, to convince the councillors it was a grand amenity and not some dingy drinking den (though even then they refused him a licence for two years). Finely preserved and restored, with its baroque plasterwork, stained glass, floral iron grilles and mahogany partitions, the Queens remains a wonderful monument to late Victorian extravagance. Since becoming gastrofied a few years ago, the dining room has provided a distinctive backdrop to the enjoyment of fresh modern-pub food. Beer-battered haddock and chips, a menu standard, is everything you could ask for; the steaks and a variety of more intricate dishes are nicely done too. On Sundays, there are generous roasts, and weekday £5 lunch specials also help maintain custom. The Queens is big enough to have entirely separate and similarly imposing bar areas, and a garden as well. The suits-all drinks range includes quality ales and a concise but varied and good-value wine list. *Babies and children admitted. Disabled: toilet. Separate room for parties, seats 50. Tables outdoors (12, garden).*

Villiers Terrace

120 Park Road, N8 8JP (8245 6827, www.villiersterracelondon.com). Finsbury Park tube/rail then bus W7, or Hornsey rail. **Open** noon-11pm Mon, Tue; noon-midnight Wed; noon-1am Thur-Sat; noon-11pm Sun. **Meals served** noon-10.30pm daily. **Main courses** £11-£16.50. **Set menu** (noon-3pm, 6-7pm Mon-Fri) £10.50 2 courses, £14 3 courses. **Credit** MC, V.
Aesthetically, Villiers Terrace is the fussiest gastropub in Crouch End, with its 'wooden log store' bar area, statement wallpaper and bold colour combinations. It's usually quiet in the daytime and packed in the evening, when quizzes, cocktail nights or DJs create a party atmosphere. Service seems to run from nonchalant to churlish, and you can feel almost forgotten in the walled garden – but the food is a sheer pleasure. On our latest visit, citrus cured salmon with kohlrabi, horseradish crème fraîche and ginger made a wonderful start. Next, roast chicken breast with chorizo and pea paella was lifted into sublime territory with a sweet smoked paprika finish, while miso-marinated cod fillet with mashed potato and pak choi in a soy and sherry sauce was heavenly. OK, so the texture of the vanilla panna cotta was more like a mousse than a set cream, but the flavours again were superb. If the management could just sort out the staff's attitude (we got short shrift when asking for bread with our starter, and half a pint of lager took over 20 minutes to arrive), this place would become a firm favourite.

Babies and children welcome: children's menu; high chairs; nappy-changing facilities. Booking advisable dinner Wed-Sun. Entertainment: DJs 10pm Fri, Sat. Separate room for parties, seats 50. Tables outdoors (20, garden; 10, terrace).

East Finchley

Bald-Faced Stag

69 High Road, N2 8AB (8442 1201, www.thebaldfacedstagn2.co.uk). East Finchley tube. **Open** noon-11pm Mon-Wed, Sun; noon-11.30pm Thur; noon-midnight Fri; 10am-midnight Sat. **Breakfast served** 10am-2.30pm Sat. **Lunch served** noon-3.30pm Mon-Fri; noon-4.30pm Sat. **Dinner served** 6-10.30pm Mon-Sat. **Meals served** noon-9.30pm Sun. **Main courses** £11.50-£18. **Set lunch** (Mon-Fri) £9.90 2 courses, £12.90 3 courses. **Credit** MC, V.
Weekend breakfasts are a clever new addition to the line-up at this likeable neighbourhood gastropub. The Bald-Faced Stag is large enough to suit many occasions. Its pleasant garden, featuring a huge sycamore tree, welcomes diners, drinkers and smokers (the latter doing little to diminish the atmosphere, given the traffic on the A1000). Effort is put into the draught beer selection, with Cornish Trelawny and Sambrook's Wandle on tap during our visit. Many customers, though, come for the interesting choice of 16 wines by the glass. The capacious, purpose-built dining room apes classic gastropub decor; the bar is more cheerful. Curiously, the set lunch menu showed better cooking and greater generosity than our à la carte options, which unanimously disappointed. Nicely cooked, fresh-tasting pollack was let down by gritty spinach and an over-mild sweetcorn velouté. Much better was the crisp-topped slab of pork belly with ham-hock potato cake and red cabbage, preceded by tender chicken livers on balsamic-flavoured toast. Sticky toffee pudding was a good rendition, whereas a slice of blueberry cheesecake (meagre, ugly, broken) was outclassed by its accompanying raspberry ripple ice-cream (not a good flavour match either). Service needed a giddy-up to show its friendly efficiency. *Babies and children admitted (until 7pm). Disabled: toilet. Separate room for parties, capacity 25. Tables outdoors (10, garden; 10, patio).*

Finsbury Park

Old Dairy

1-3 Crouch Hill, N4 4AP (7263 3337, www.theolddairyn4.co.uk). Crouch Hill rail. **Open** noon-11pm Mon-Thur; noon-1am Fri, Sat; noon-10.30pm Sun. **Lunch served** noon-3.30pm Tue-Fri. **Dinner served** 6-10pm Mon-Fri. **Meals served** noon-10pm Sat; noon-9pm Sun. **Main courses** £11-£18. **Credit** AmEx, MC, V.
This outpost of the Realpubs empire is a neighbourhood favourite, thanks to its friendly staff and efforts to create a community spirit. There are BYO nights on Mondays, quiz nights on Tuesdays, and regular daytime parent and toddler music sessions. Staff are extremely helpful, and the building (yes, an old dairy), though cavernous, manages to be welcoming due to the evidence of its past life (the intricate relief panels on the exterior are works of art) and some judicious carving-up of interior space into bar and restaurant areas. The new banquette seating near the open kitchen is highly popular. The menu (the same in bar and

restaurant) gives only cursory nods towards provenance ('Suffolk farm chicken' tells us little), but the choice of food is tempting: from spaghetti with chilli, clams and mussels, to lamb rump with broad bean and mint salad. A starter of ham hock salad, puy lentils and crispy poached egg was excellent, and puddings (lemon and orange posset, chocolate brownie) were also very good. Main courses let the meal down, though, with an overcooked grilled sole, and limp vegetables accompanying the roast beef – but you forgive a lot when service is so good.
Available for hire. Babies and children welcome: children's menu; high chairs; nappy-changing facilities. Booking essential Sun. Disabled: toilet.

Islington

Charles Lamb
16 Elia Street, N1 8DE (7837 5040, www.the charleslambpub.com). Angel tube. **Open** 4-11pm Mon, Tue; noon-11pm Wed-Sat; noon-10.30pm Sun. **Lunch served** noon-3pm Wed-Fri; noon-4pm Sun; noon-6pm Sun. **Dinner served** 6-9.30pm Mon-Sat. **Main courses** £9-£13.50. **Credit** AmEx, MC, V.
A charming pub with a lovely atmosphere, but in many ways, it's coasting. The set-up is appealing, the two small cream-painted rooms hung with interesting pictures and maps (notably Stephen Walter's depiction of London as an island), and packed with wooden tables, chairs and benches. The blackboard menu is tempting (cider-baked pork chop, fish pie, apple crumble and cream) and nicely priced (£4.50-£12), but on recent visits we've found the execution lacking: pork rillettes with toast and cornichons had liquefied; apple, beetroot and goat's cheese salad was missing the beetroot; and ratatouille on bruschetta with mozzarella and salad would be deemed average in a student caff. There's an attractive range of drinks (real ales, Breton cider, a decent wine list), but ours were served in an amateur fashion, the most serious offence being a half of Dark Star's Hophead poured straight into a boiling hot glass. In short, all so different from the professionalism on show at nearby sister bar 69 Colebrooke Row. Pity, as the Charles Lamb has been a real favourite in the past.
Babies and children admitted. Bookings not accepted. Tables outdoors (4, pavement). **Map 5 O2.**

Compass
58 Penton Street, N1 9PZ (7837 3891, www.thecompassn1.co.uk). Angel tube. **Open** 5-11pm Mon-Thur; 5pm-midnight Fri; noon-midnight Sat; noon-10.30pm Sun. **Lunch served** noon-3pm Sat. **Dinner served** 5-10pm Mon-Sat. **Meals served** noon-8pm Sun. **Main courses** £9-£15. **Credit** MC, V.
A proper boozer-like gastropub at the end of Chapel Market, the Compass is a laid-back and low-key hangout, with diners sitting alongside drinkers in the relaxed, dark-painted bar. Food is pretty typical of the genre – rump of lamb, risotto, confit duck – with the odd more adventurous dish thrown in, such as our starter of ox heart: a big success. Thin, tender curls of ox heart had a distinct, but not over-strong, flavour: a good foil for the tartness of the accompanying pickled beetroot and horseradish. Grilled sardines with herbs and chilli was a generous portion of fresh, plump, perfectly grilled herby fish, although the chilli was not much in evidence. A confit duck main was again a large helping, with

mushy butter beans: robust, homely and full of flavour. We also sampled a fall-off-the-bone tender whole grilled plaice, served with salty strands of samphire and clams. A Capito pinot grigio made a fine, fresh accompaniment, and a shared pudding of lemon tart ended the meal well. Staff are professional, the pace is leisurely, there are three real ales (plus a real cider) on tap, and our food was great. Just what a gastropub experience should be.
Babies and children welcome: high chairs. Booking advisable. Disabled: toilet. Separate room for parties, seats 40. Tables outdoors (8, pavement). **Map 5 N2.**

Duke of Cambridge
30 St Peter's Street, N1 8JT (7359 3066, www.dukeorganic.co.uk). Angel tube. **Open** noon-11pm Mon-Sat; noon-10.30pm Sun. **Lunch served** 12.30-3pm Mon-Sat; 12.30-3.30pm Sun. **Dinner served** 6.30-10.30pm Mon-Sat; 6.30-10pm Sun. **Main courses** £13-£21. **Credit** MC, V.
A pioneer of all things green and ethical, the Duke of Cambridge is the UK's only gastropub to be certified by the Soil Association. From its beers and bitters to its pies and puddings, everything is organic – and the owners have the (recycled) paperwork to prove it. For such a serious-minded place it's surprisingly relaxed, thanks in part to the calm residential location and its open-door policy to children and dogs. Draught ales from Freedom, Pitfield and St Peter's breweries attract beer connoisseurs from far and wide, while locals come for the food. Pass through the big airy bar to find an intimate restaurant, furnished with recycled tables and chairs. A short blackboard menu showcases Home Counties-sourced produce such as Tamworth pork, Sussex-bred beef and MSC-certified fish, including line-caught coley and grey mullet. On our last visit, we were impressed by a smoked sprat starter with redcurrant compote, and a hearty pork belly stew with lightly spiced kidney beans. With organic and ethically sourced food commanding top dollar, the bar snacks are playing an increasingly important role; warm chorizo, olives with herbs and own-made houmous serve to soak up the beer as well as enticing drinkers to sample more of what's available.
Available for hire. Babies and children welcome: high chairs; nappy-changing facilities. Booking advisable. Tables outdoors 4, pavement. **Map 5 O2.**

Marquess Tavern
32 Canonbury Street, N1 2TB (7354 2975, www.themarquesstavern.co.uk). Highbury & Islington tube/rail or Essex Road rail. **Open** 5-11pm Mon-Thur; 4pm-midnight Fri; noon-midnight Sat; noon-10.30pm Sun. **Lunch served** noon-5pm Sat, Sun. **Dinner served** 6-10pm Mon-Sat; 6-8.30pm Sun. **Main courses** £10-£17. **Credit** AmEx, MC, V.
The Marquess has the feeling of a gastropub slowly morphing back into a boozer. The main bar in the handsome, high-ceilinged tavern was always kept as a place for drinking, but these days it's the focus of attention, with a short wine list, several beers on tap and a selection of bottled options (including Kelpie's Seaweed Ale from Scotland and Jever Pilsener from Germany). The lovely dining room has off-white walls and nicely spaced wooden tables, and is much quieter, though the bar's disco music can still be heard. The biggest change lies in the menu: gastro fare is served only on Friday and

Saturday, and roasts on Sunday; from Monday to Saturday, thin-crust pizzas are available. A two-for-one special offer bought a capricciosa (mushrooms, artichokes, black olives, cherry tomatoes, garlic cloves, prosciutto, salami) and a quattro formaggi (gorgonzola, ricotta, parmesan, buffalo mozzarella); both acceptable at £10 for two, but not worth £10 each. Far better was a well-flavoured globe artichoke with pine nut crumble and garlic mayonnaise, followed by ribeye with grilled cherry tomatoes, salad and parsley butter cooked just-so. A side of honey- and thyme-glazed parsnips looked limp but tasted fine; chips were average. An eagerly anticipated fresh fruit salad with Mount Gay rum and apricot ripple ice-cream was a disappointment, with no alcohol apparent and gloopy fruit. Service was charming, but then again, staff didn't have many diners to take care of. In short, no longer a destination gastropub, but a nice spot for a drink.
Available for hire. Babies and children welcome until 7pm: high chairs. Tables outdoors (6, patio).

Kentish Town

★ Bull & Last
168 Highgate Road, NW5 1QS (7267 3641, www.thebullandlast.co.uk). Kentish Town tube/rail then bus 214, C2, or Gospel Oak rail then bus C11. **Open** noon-11pm Mon-Thur; noon-midnight Fri, Sat; noon-10.30pm Sun. **Lunch served** noon-3pm Mon-Fri; 12.30-3.30pm Sat, Sun. **Dinner served** 6.30-10pm Mon-Sat; 7-9pm Sun. **Main courses** £12-£25. **Credit** MC, V.
Unlike some gastropubs with gourmet pretensions, the Bull & Last proudly sells real ales. Doom Bar is a mainstay, but you may find Truman's Runner, or Sambrook's Wandle, both London beers. There are certainly good wines available by glass and bottle too, but ordering them doesn't feel right in this near-perfect neighbourhood boozer. Tucker is first-rate: even the bread basket's a wowser – three varieties on our latest visit, including a wonderfully cake-like brown loaf. Brown crab macaroni showed the kitchen's high-end aspirations with its premium ingredients and elegant presentation. A salad of English peas, rocket and jersey royals was a little more rustic, but still secreted a swirl of cow's curd and sumptuously fresh and creamy pea fritters. Properly chewy-tender, maroon-centred onglet came with garlic butter and fat wedges of crusty triple-cooked chips. Squeeze in some own-made ice-cream for dessert: there are flavours aplenty. Unfortunately, the superb food is not matched by the service. Staff are friendly, keen, intelligent, kind – and it's nice not to be rushed – but the waits to place orders and then to receive dishes are protracted, making even a great meal feel almost an hour too long. Frustrating.
Babies and children welcome: high chairs; nappy-changing facilities. Booking advisable. Separate room for parties, seats 70. Tables outdoors (5, pavement). **Map 26 A3.**
For branch (Prince of Wales) see index.

★ Junction Tavern
101 Fortess Road, NW5 1AG (7485 9400, www.junctiontavern.co.uk). Tufnell Park tube or Kentish Town tube/rail. **Open** noon-11pm Mon-Fri; 11.30am-11pm Sat; noon-10.30pm Sun. **Lunch served** noon-3pm Mon-Fri; 11.30am-4pm Sat. **Dinner served** 6-10.30pm Mon-Fri; 6.30-10.30pm Sat. **Meals served** noon-9.30pm Sun. **Main courses** £12.30-£17.50. **Set lunch** (Sun) £16 2 courses. **Credit** MC, V.

Bull & Last

sauce featured excellent freshly cooked seafood, first-rate greens and an original blend of flavours. To follow, warm salmon salad with asparagus and decoratively cut strips of cucumber was also very nicely done. Another main, chicken leg stuffed with pork and pistachio and wrapped in bacon, with parmesan mash, spinach and a Madeira jus, sounded like it might all be too much, but was deliciously subtle, the contrasting ingredients handled with skill. A weekday lunch menu also offers varied sandwiches and salads, and there's another extensive menu with roasts for Sunday lunch. The main dining area artfully combines comfy booths and contemporary colours with the original features of this Victorian pub; the long bar still has a proper-pub feel, with a regularly changing ale selection as well as a varied wine list. Largely different menus are served at other outlets of the Realpubs group, but all have an enterprising approach. The Oxford also hosts jazz on Mondays, and comedy on Thursdays.

Available for hire. Babies and children admitted until 8pm. Booking advisable dinner. Disabled: toilet. Entertainment: musicians 8.30pm Mon; quiz 7.30pm Tue; comedy 7pm Thur, Sat. Separate room for parties, seats 50. Tables outdoors (7, pavement). **Map 26 B5**.

Vine NEW

86 Highgate Road, NW5 1PB (7209 0038, www.thevinelondon.co.uk). Tufnell Park tube or Kentish Town tube/rail. **Open** noon-11pm Mon-Wed; noon-midnight Thur-Sat; noon-10.30pm Sun. **Meals served** noon-10.30pm Mon-Sat; noon-9.30pm Sun. **Main courses** £10.50-£18. **Credit** AmEx, MC, V.

Yet another grape in the Realpubs bunch, but this one is intriguingly different – as it should be, given the company also runs the Oxford about ten minutes' walk away. Their fashionable solution is to offer around 25 cicchetti (Venetian tapas) all day, as well as a selection of starters and mains comprising classy Italian dishes and classic gastropub fare. As a result the menu is much larger than many food-minded pubs would deem sensible, but cooking from the shiny new open kitchen installed at the rear (the refurbishment works have been extensive, though decor is unfussy) is more than competent. Highlights over a couple of visits have been the full-flavoured cicchetti of squid, tomato, chilli and garlic, and arancini (risotto fritters) filled with basil, plus a large plate of soft herb polenta served with sautéed wild mushrooms. There's a choice of around ten afters, though we suspect the ices are the pick of them. True to Realpubs style, the beers are interesting and well kept (local Camden Town Brewery pale ale is among the options) and the wine list holds some real treats. Perhaps best of all is the opportunity to sit under the elegant umbrellas of the pub's front terrace: without the red buses, you might think you were by the Mediterranean.

Babies and children welcome: high chairs. Booking advisable. Disabled: toilet. Separate rooms for parties, seating 35. Tables outdoors (20, garden; 20, terrace). **Map 26 A4**.

Muswell Hill

Clissold Arms

105 Fortis Green, N2 9HR (8444 4224, www.clissoldarms.co.uk). East Finchley tube. **Open** noon-11pm Mon-Thur; noon-midnight Fri, Sat; noon-11pm Sun. **Lunch served**

Today, the stalwart Junction seems a typical quality gastropub, so it's easy to forget that on opening it was something of a trailblazer, showing dining pubs who'd strayed too far into restaurant territory the way back to quality ales. Staff are very friendly and enthuse about the beers (do browse the sizeable list of guest ales); we settled on two London options: Sambrook's Junction Ale and Tottenham's Redemption pale ale. You can eat throughout the pub; maybe the modestly proportioned dining room with its claret-coloured walls, glass chandeliers and huge clear windows looking on to Fortess Road is a hair's breadth more elegant than the warm, wood-panelled bar. There's also a cheerful, if noisy, conservatory and attractive garden tables. The appealing Saturday brunch menu changes weekly, but typically proffers a choice of pancakes, eggs benedict and its variations, a cheeseburger, and a clever, satisfying twist on smoked haddock kedgeree with fried egg and mustard cream. Roasts are served all day on Sundays, though you can also dine à la carte at certain hours – in which case you'll find a can't-go-wrong mix of British and other European dishes. Having booked over the phone just an hour in advance, we were impressed to see a high chair ready and waiting at the table for the baby. A big bottle of tap water arrived promptly too: proper hospitality.

Babies and children admitted until 7pm: high chair; booster seats. Booking advisable weekends. Tables outdoors (20, garden). **Map 26 B4**.

Oxford

256 Kentish Town Road, NW5 2AA (7485 3521, www.theoxfordnw5.co.uk). Kentish Town tube/rail. **Open** noon-11.30pm Mon, Tue; noon-midnight Wed-Sat; noon-10.30pm Sun. **Lunch served** noon-3.30pm Mon-Fri; noon-4.30pm Sat. **Dinner served** 6-10pm Mon-Wed; 6-10.30pm Thur-Sat. **Meals served** noon-10pm Sun. **Main courses** £11-£15. **Credit** AmEx, MC, V.

The gastropub concept has its established repertoire (sausage and mash, beer-battered fish and chips), so it's a pleasure to find more adventurous cooking here. At the Oxford, a salad of fried squid and spring onion with sweet chilli

Adam & Eve

noon-3pm Mon-Fri; noon-4pm Sat. **Dinner served** 6-10pm Mon-Fri; 6.30-10.30pm Sat. **Meals served** noon-9pm Sun. **Main courses** £10.25-£22.95. **Credit** AmEx, MC, V.

With Kinks memorabilia neatly displayed in the front room (the band's first gig was here) and tightly packed tables full of middle-aged Muswell Hill-types in carefully pressed linen matching the crisp white tablecloths, the Clissold Arms is more restaurant than pub these days – with matching prices. A large party room twinkling with fairy lights, a buzzing open kitchen and smart outdoor terrace create a glam, contemporary vibe. Smooth, friendly service on our visit was slightly rushed, but staff helped us navigate the impressive wine list. The menu seems less complicated of late, but lacks seasonality (containing plentiful slow-cooked meat in midsummer), though fat chips cooked in dripping are irresistible whatever the weather. A meagre salt and pepper squid starter with roasted red peppers and balsamic dressing was bland. Tempting hunks of bread never came our way; they cost extra. So we welcomed the generous portion of grilled cod in light tomatoey broth, flecked with smoky paprika and served with spinach and new potatoes. Seafood linguine in a robust tomato and basil sauce was stingy on the clams; a rich, gooey brownie with ice-cream and chocolate sauce showed more generosity. Locals love it (it's often fully booked at weekends).

Available for hire. Babies and children welcome: children's menu; high chairs; nappy-changing facilities. Booking advisable dinner Thur-Sat; lunch Sun. Disabled: toilet. Tables outdoors (25, garden; 15, terrace).

North West
Hampstead

★ Horseshoe
28 Heath Street, NW3 6TE (7431 7206). Hampstead tube. **Open** 10am-11pm Mon-Thur; 10am-midnight Fri, Sat; 10am-10.30pm Sun. **Lunch served** noon-3.30pm Mon-Sat; noon-4.30pm Sun. **Dinner served** 6-10pm Mon-Thur; 6.30-11pm Fri, Sat; 6.30-9.30pm Sun. **Main courses** £8-£15. **Set lunch** £8 1 course incl glass of wine. **Credit** AmEx, MC, V.

Camden Town Brewery, currently gushing like a spilt pint through London's food scene, began life in the cellar of this appealing pub. Beneath the Pentameters theatre, the former Three Horseshoes has been thoroughly gastroed, with grey-green exterior, white walls, blond wood bar and huge plate-glass windows that are often open to make the airy spot feel even brighter. Staff on our visit were decidedly unwelcoming, but became friendlier as the

meal progressed. All life is here: businessmen having informal lunch meetings, couples escaping their workplaces, tourists with backpacks, ladies clutching designer handbags and toy dogs. The daily lunch specials are terrific – Saxmundham sausage sandwich with onions, say, plus a glass of wine or juice for £8. Extras such as bread (Flour Station's tortano ring) underline the serious sourcing. We chose from a well-judged lunch menu. Deep-fried cod cheeks were wonderfully fresh and crisp, served with a verdant swoop of silky pea purée. Salad of black figs with grilled goat's cheese and walnuts was a nice idea that suffered from overpowering chèvre. The wine list is good value, but it's a shame to miss the fabulous Camden Town beers – sparkling pale ale was perfect refreshment on a hot day.

Available for hire. Babies and children welcome: high chairs; nappy-changing facilities. Booking advisable. Tables outdoors (2, pavement). **Map 28 B2**.

Wells
30 Well Walk, NW3 1BX (7794 3785, www.thewellshampstead.co.uk). Hampstead tube. **Open** noon-11pm Mon-Sat; noon-10.30pm Sun. **Lunch served** noon-3pm Mon-Fri; noon-4pm Sat, Sun. **Dinner served** 6-10pm Mon-Fri; 7-10pm Sat, Sun. **Main courses** £9.95-£18.95. **Credit** AmEx, MC, V.

As locals go, the Wells is Hampstead-classy, a genteel Georgian building that's more bar and restaurant than foodie boozer. Weekday lunchtimes are best, when the place isn't packed (unlike at weekends), and ground-floor diners are a happy mix of business people in neatly pressed shirts, boho-leaning celebrities, and glossy-haired mums with designer specs and nappy bags. There's London Pride and Grolsch on tap, though wine tends to be the drink of choice and the intelligently organised list sells it well. Food is Modern European in style with plenty drawn from the Mediterranean, but there's pubby fare too: cumberland sausage and mash, hamburger with cheese or bacon, sticky toffee pud. The 28-day-aged ribeye with shallot and tarragon butter is a favourite, but this time we chose confit duck (a spot-on mix of crisp skin and flaky, tender meat), and juicy, pink-centred rump of lamb served with pomme purée, minted peas and hispi cabbage. Vegetarians might order a seasonal plate of gnocchi or vegetable bake combining pumpkin, courgette and aubergine. Kids' dishes are available though unadvertised, yet the menu promotes bowls of dog food – that's Hampstead. Upstairs are three elegant dining rooms to book for special occasions. *Babies and children welcome: children's menu; colouring books; high chairs. Disabled: toilet. Separate room for parties, seats 12. Tables outdoors (8, patio).* **Map 28 C2**.

Kilburn

Salusbury

50-52 Salusbury Road, NW6 6NN (7328 3286). Queens Park tube/rail. **Open** 5-11pm Mon; noon-11pm Tue, Wed; noon-midnight Thur-Sat; noon-10.30pm Sun. **Lunch served** 12.30-2.30pm Tue-Fri; 12.30-3.30pm Sat, Sun. **Dinner served** 7-10.15pm Mon-Sat; 7-10pm Sun. **Main courses** £11.80-£16.40. **Credit** MC, V.
The Salusbury is a modern affair, with several concerns taking place under one roof. There's a food store, where you can buy delicatessen staples or sit and eat pizza, a separate wine shop, and the pub and dining room. The bar – with its traditional decor and groups of punters drinking Breton cider, Asahi beer or Italian wine – contrasts markedly with the plush dining room, walled off around the side. Here, leather banquettes and smart upholstered chairs attract wealthy customers. Service was attentive and helpful on our trip, but the food, despite a promising menu, was disappointing. Minestrone had all the flavour of boiled vegetables in their cooking water; beans, pasta and garlic weren't in evidence, and the vegetables were chopped as fine as bricks. Beef carpaccio had a silky-smooth texture, yet lacked seasoning. Main courses varied in quality too. Pappardelle pasta with duck ragù was our only wholly successful dish; the own-made pasta had bite and flavour, and the ragù was rich and meaty. Another main, Elwy Valley lamb chops, was unappealingly greasy, served with decent mash but watery spinach. The Salusbury may look the part, but something seems to be awry in the kitchen.
Available for hire. Babies and children welcome until 7pm; high chairs. Tables outdoors (6, pavement).

Mill Hill

Adam & Eve **NEW**

The Ridgeway, NW7 1RL (8959 1553, www.adamandevemillhill.co.uk). Mill Hill East tube then bus 240. **Open** noon-11pm Mon-Thur; noon-midnight Fri, Sat; noon-10.30pm Sun. **Lunch served** noon-3pm Mon-Fri; noon-5pm Sat, Sun. **Dinner served** 6-10pm daily. **Main courses** £10.95-£20. **Set lunch** (Mon-Fri) £12 2 courses, £14 3 courses; (Sun) £14 1 course, £18 2 courses, £22 3 courses. **Credit** MC, V.
The Adam & Eve is an elegant, airy Edwardian inn with well-chosen wallpapers offsetting the Farrow & Ball heritage paint that softens the extensive wood panelling. Tom Dixon copper pendants seem to be as essential in today's gastropubs as mismatched old furniture and a blackboard menu – and they're here, along with a set of antlers and framed prints depicting the biblical Fall. This place may not push the envelope, but it has put the clichés together very well. What a boon for Mill Hill Village – even with a kitchen of serious intent, locals can pop in for a quick pint, and families are given a warm welcome (there are also lovely private rooms upstairs for parties). The menu changes daily and is a crowd-pleasing mix of British pub fare and Mediterranean touches. Start, maybe, with watermelon and feta salad, or St James Smokehouse salmon with grated egg, capers and horseradish cream. Continue with a burger or steak from the grill, or slow-roast leg of Elwy Valley lamb with roast butternut squash, pearl barley and baby spinach. Desserts don't ruffle any feathers either (lemon posset, crème brûlée), and are all the better for it. Beer fans will be satisfied by the great choice of real ales (Flying Scotsman, Deuchars IPA and Directors were among those offered on our visit), and around 20 wines are available in two sizes of glass, with the house options coming from Italy. *Available for hire. Babies and children welcome: children's menu; high chairs; nappy-changing facilities. Booking advisable lunch Sat, Sun; dinner. Disabled: toilet. Separate room for parties, seats 70. Tables outdoors (12, garden).*

Spencer. See p107.

Global

Diners who revel in London's joyous ethnic diversity will find much to explore in this chapter – it's the place where we put many restaurants that simply don't fit comfortably anywhere else in the guide. And really, it's one of the most exciting collections to explore, with many lovely restaurants and perennial favourites that could easily be overlooked by people searching for better-known cuisines: we think particularly of little Burmese eaterie **Mandalay**, and the glamorous swagger of Iberia-by-way-of-Mozambique **Eyre Brothers**. There are several new options here too, including **North Road** for contemporary Scandinavian cooking, **Bistro Délicat** for traditional Austrian specialities, and **Samarqand**, an upmarket, Russian-owned party spot serving the melting-pot cuisine of Uzbekistan. So go on – try a meal less ordinary.

Central

Clerkenwell & Farringdon

North Road NEW
69-73 St John Street, EC1M 4AN (3217 0033, www.northroadrestaurant.co.uk). Farringdon tube/rail. **Lunch served** noon-2.30pm Mon-Fri. **Dinner served** 6-10.30pm Mon-Thur; 6-11pm Fri, Sat. **Main courses** £17-£28. **Set lunch** £20 3 courses. **Set dinner** (6-7pm Mon-Fri) £22 3 courses incl glass of wine. **Credit** AmEx, MC, V. Scandinavian

When this Scandinavian restaurant opened, it was inevitably compared to 'World's Best Restaurant' Noma, but while there is much to admire about chef-patron Christoffer Hruskova's efforts – combining local ingredients with Nordic sentiments – they don't always hit the mark. Certainly, there were flashes of brilliance: a terrific trio of amuse-bouches showcased the classic Scandinavian flavours of smoke and salt (only sharp was absent) ahead of a delicate rose veal tartare with quail's yolk, beautifully offset by the bite of horseradish in a thin cream, and golden shards of crispy, briny chicken skin. Equally impressive was roe deer wrapped in paper-thin parcels of burnt hay – a signature dish – seeing the ruby-red morsels of game imbued with a smoky essence against a backdrop of sweet beetroot and bone marrow. However, Herdwick lamb belly with sweetbreads was not only crying out for something astringent to cut through the soft, fatty meat, but came wincingly over-seasoned. Likewise, a pudding of caramel sauce teamed with a feeble 'carrot' sorbet and limp 'elderflower' cream, tasted as beige as it looked. Given the high-end pricing, you

expect better. Happily, the restrained space oozes Scandinavian serenity and style, while staff are gracious and effortlessly professional.
Available for hire. Babies and children admitted. Booking advisable. Disabled: toilet. Separate rooms for parties, seating 10-20. **Map 5 O5.**

Edgware Road

★ ★ Mandalay HOT 50
444 Edgware Road, W2 1EG (7258 3696, www.mandalayway.com). Edgware Road tube. **Lunch served** noon-2.30pm, **dinner served** 6-10.30pm Mon-Sat. **Main courses** £4.40-£7.90. **Set lunch** £3.90 1 course, £5.90 3 courses. **Credit** AmEx, DC, MC, V. Burmese

The Ally family's modest dining establishment on a rundown stretch of Edgware Road has drawn much acclaim over the past 18 years – and not only because it is London's only Burmese restaurant. Behind the plate-glass frontage, Mandalay is a cosy little spot, fiercely loved by its many regulars (student types, locals and some Burmese exiles). Hearth-like tiled flooring, plastic tablecloths and space for just 28 diners add to the homely setting, as does friendly, informative service. The cuisine is a mix of Indian, Chinese and Thai styles, along with several nationally distinctive dishes. Hence, the menu is full of excitement, with much that's rarely found in London – and almost everything is superb. Highlights of a recent meal were the assorted fritters (shrimps, chicken and vegetables in a tempura-like batter, served with three dipping sauces), a Thai-style green papaya and cucumber salad (an excellent foil for the fritters), and the laksa-like coconut and chicken noodles. We can also vouch for the vegetarian pairing of lentil rice

with the burmese omelette curry (the thick omelette floating in a copious spicy tomato sauce). Only the rough and ready toilets detract from this top performer.
Available for hire weekdays. Babies and children welcome: high chairs. Booking essential dinner. Takeaway service. **Map 2 D4.**

Marylebone

Samarqand NEW
18 Thayer Street, W1U 3JY (7935 9393, http://samarqand-restaurant.com). Bond Street tube. **Meals served** noon-11pm Mon-Thur; noon-11.30pm Fri, Sat; noon-10.30pm Sun. **Main courses** £12-£16. **Set lunch** £13.95 2 courses, £15.95 3 courses. **Credit** AmEx, MC, V. Uzbek

Samarqand is a city forever at a crossroads, where dishes echo those of Turkey, China and more recently, Russia. Celebrating the food of contemporary Uzbekistan, this is a smart operation, furnished in a five-star-hotel style of expensive dark wood and mood lighting, with charming service throughout. Starters include soups or samosas scattered with rocket leaves, while plov (a close relative of pilau) is prepared the Uzbek way, correctly glistening with so much fat it resembled stir-fried rice rather than the delicate rice dishes of Iran or India. Likewise, the lagman noodles were exemplary: freshly made and served in a simple beef and vegetable broth. Meat-filled wheat pasta dumplings is another dish that crops up from Korea to Poland, but this version, manty – minced lamb dumplings, served with yoghurt dips – is distinctively Central Asian. Our fellow diners were mostly monied Russians (Samarqand is part of a Russian restaurant group), enjoying the extensive list of vodkas and high-priced wines. Sadly, many of the rear alcoves have been turned into private dining areas (some with karaoke facilities) pitched at expat Russian speakers in party mood. Be prepared if you visit on a Friday or Saturday night. *Available for hire. Babies and children welcome: high chairs. Separate rooms for parties, seating 8-14.* **Map 9 G5**.

South Kensington

Madsen

20 Old Brompton Road, SW7 3DL (7225 2772, www.madsenrestaurant.com). South Kensington tube. **Open** noon-11pm Mon-Thur; noon-midnight Fri, Sat; noon-5pm Sun. **Lunch served** noon-4pm daily. **Dinner served** 5-10pm Mon-Thur; 6-10.45pm Fri, Sat. **Main courses** £11.50-£17.50. **Set lunch** £9.50 smushi; £14.95 vegetarian; £14.50 2 courses, £18.95 3 courses. **Set dinner** £24.95 2 courses, £29.50 3 courses. **Credit** MC, V. Danish
For a restaurant just around the corner from the South Ken museums, Madsen isn't nearly as packed as you'd expect. Instead, it's a cool, calm corner of Scandinavia: all elegant wooden ply furniture and classic Louis Poulsen lights, with dishes as simple, fresh and elegantly presented as the decor. Interesting lunch deals include 'smushi' mini open sandwiches (smørrebrød) on rye, with traditional toppings such as thinly sliced pork with red cabbage (flæskesteg), Greenland prawns, or roast beef with pickled cucumber. The set lunch delivered some big fat pork meatballs (frikadeller) and a summery apple and elderflower trifle. Both dishes were pleasant, rather than thrilling. What turned out to be the star is something you might dismiss as a cliché: the pickled herrings. These are marinated on site, in onion, creamy dill, and tomato versions, combining freshness, sweetness, sourness and meatiness all on the same plate. Considering Denmark's brewing prowess, it's a shame there were only two beers on our visit – though who could resist the amusingly named Swedish bestseller 'God Lager'? Blankets (IKEA, of course) provided for alfresco diners are a nice touch – a northern European custom we'd do well to adopt here. *Available for hire. Babies and children welcome: children's menu; crayons; high chairs; nappy-changing facilities. Booking advisable evenings. Separate room for parties, seats 14. Tables outdoors (4, terrace). Takeaway service.* **Map 14 D10**.

South West
Colliers Wood

Chakalaka

Horse & Groom, 145 Haydons Road, SW19 1AN (8544 2693, www.chakalakarestaurant. com). South Wimbledon tube or Haydons Road rail. **Meals served** noon-11.30pm Mon-Fri; noon-11pm Sat, Sun. **Main courses** £11.95-£19.95. **No credit cards**. South African
Chakalaka had three branches in spring 2010, but is now reduced to this outlet inside a Colliers Wood pub. A pragmatic response to the recession it may be – this part of south-west London is a bolt-hole for South Africans – but our recent visit saw no expatriates dining. The pub has been halved by a small partition, with Chakalaka on one side (zebra print, grass matting and picture of an elephant)

Bistro Délicat. See p121.

GLOBAL

galoupet

At Galoupet, we believe that enjoying food and wine with family and friends is one of the greatest **pleasures** in life. We follow the pattern of the **seasons**, our wine list always features 36 wines available by the glass and every dish on our menu is carefully matched with a wine that complements the flavours of the dish. We're open breakfast, lunch and dinner from 8am.

Wine Tasting • Merchant • Restaurant

13 Beauchamp Place, Knightsbridge, London SW3 1NQ
Tel 0207 036 3600   eat@galoupet.co.uk   galoupet.co.uk

bravely trying to keep things vaguely formal, as the crowd on the bar side gears up for a night's drinking. The 'combo platters' (spicy wings, mini samosas, wedges) are aimed at party groups; the more South African dishes are mainly meaty and variable in quality. Boerewors with spicy tomato salsa and mealie pap was rustic and full-flavoured; other starters include kudu carpaccio, and marinated ostrich salad. Mains continue the carnivorous theme, with peri-peri ribs and a macho steak selection, but springbok bourguignon gained nothing from the substitution of beef, while the accompanying mash was unappetisingly claggy. And a zigzag of balsamic reduction over every dish is not sophisticated, even in the outer boroughs. The all-SA wine list is commendable, though on our visit there were no native beers.
Available for hire. Babies and children admitted.

South
Balham

★ Fat Delicatessen
7 Chestnut Grove, SW12 8JA (8675 6174, www.fatdelicatessen.co.uk). Balham tube/rail. **Meals served** 8am-8pm Mon-Wed; 8am-10pm Thur, Fri; 9am-10pm Sat; 11am-6pm Sun. **Main courses** £4-£8. **Credit** MC, V. Mediterranean
With its shabby tiled floor and plain wooden tables, this corridor of a café may not look like much, but someone out back really knows how to cook. You'll find gutsy, Med-leaning dishes on the compact menu, as well as a daily changing specials board. Baked sardines with a salad of tomatoes and red onions spoke of summer sunshine, and the full-flavoured lamb, chorizo and chickpea stew is deservedly popular (team it with a basket of breads for a good-value meal big enough for two). Alternatively, stroll up to the deli counter to pick out charcuterie, artisan cheeses, wholesome salads or the tart of the day – leek and goat's cheese, say. Just save room for something sweet; the chewy brownies or moist lemon and polenta cake are both worth sampling. Almost everything at the Fat Deli is available to take away, from bakes in the chill counter for home cooking, to the gourmet store-cupboard goods lining the shelves – all of which encourage a steady stream of customers throughout the day. The relaxed, neighbourhood vibe is occasionally too laid-back, with the well-meaning staff sometimes slow and absent-minded. Head elsewhere if you're in a hurry.
Available for hire. Babies and children welcome: high chairs. Booking advisable dinner Thur-Sat. Disabled: toilet. Takeaway service.

Battersea

Bistro Délicat [NEW]
124 Northcote Road, SW11 6QU (7924 3566, www.bistrodelicat.com). Clapham Junction rail. **Lunch served** 11.30am-4pm Mon-Fri; 10.30am-4pm Sat, Sun. **Dinner served** 6-10.30pm daily. **Main courses** £11-£18. **Set lunch** £12.50 2 courses, £15.50 3 courses. **Credit** AmEx, MC, V. Austrian
Don't come to this Austrian brasserie expecting dark wood, steins of beer and pork knuckles: with its chummy service and casual, camp vibe, it's styled more like the fashionable cafés of modern-day Vienna. The menu borrows from France (tuna tartare niçoise, croque monsieur, bouillabaisse) and

northern Europe (perfectly cooked grilled scallops with pork belly), but what makes Délicat worth a special journey are the Austrian specialities. The wiener schnitzel is as good a version as you'll find in London: the veal beaten thin, hand-breaded and crisply fried, and finished with nice details such as a muslin-wrapped half lemon. Schlutzkrapfen, a kind of ravioli from the borders of Italy, filled with curd cheese, spinach and sage butter, was robust but well made. Some other dishes weren't quite as convincing. Beef consommé came cloudy, not clear, and the accompanying thin pancake slivers had sunk into the soup (though it tasted fine). Cakes were conspicuously absent, so we finished with apricot knödel: sweet dumplings served with cooked apricot and ice-cream. The wine list, though brief, has one of the capital's best selections of Austrian bottles. On sunny days, the pavement tables are an additional draw.
Available for hire. Babies and children welcome: children's menu; high chairs. Booking advisable Thur-Sat. Tables outdoors (5, pavement). **Map 21 C5.**

South East
Crystal Palace

Mediterranea
21 Westow Street, SE19 3RY (8771 7327). Crystal Palace or Gipsy Hill rail. **Lunch served** noon-2.30pm Mon-Thur; noon-3.30pm Fri, Sat. **Dinner served** 6-10pm Tue-Thur; 6-11pm Fri, Sat. **Meals served** noon-10pm Sun. **Main courses** £9.50-£15.90. **Credit** AmEx, MC, V. Mediterranean
Located on the Crystal Palace triangle, Mediterranea has plenty of competition from other restaurants, but entering this little Sardinian-run establishment is a breath of fresh air. All bright aqua blues, colourful paintings and starched white tablecloths, the place feels clean and sun-kissed even on a rainy Friday lunchtime. The menu, which is amended seasonally, offers a small but well-chosen selection of food. It has a Sardinian slant, but also Greek, Italian and Spanish influences. The emphasis is on dishes made from scratch, and the own-made asparagus ravioli and creamy, smooth panna cotta with raspberries were both expertly and beautifully executed. There's a pizza menu too and, at weekends, the restaurant offers child-sized portions – which no doubt contributes to its popularity with families. The simple formula also appeals to a spectrum of other diners, with couples, small groups of friends and a smattering of businessmen in evidence during the week. Staff are highly professional, considerate and keen to talk through dishes. Prices are fair too, which along with the well-presented, unfussy food and the laid-back surroundings make Mediterranea a place that locals visit time and again.
Available for hire. Babies and children welcome: high chairs. Booking advisable weekends.

East
Shoreditch

★ Eyre Brothers [HOT 50]
70 Leonard Street, EC2A 4QX (7613 5346, www.eyrebrothers.co.uk). Old Street tube/rail. **Lunch served** noon-2.45pm Mon-Fri. **Dinner**

Samarqand. See p118.

served 6.30-10.45pm Mon-Fri; 7-11pm Sat. **Main courses** £15-£27.50. **Credit** AmEx, DC, MC, V. Mediterranean

David and Robert Eyre's restaurant celebrates the entire Iberian peninsula, revelling in such dishes as feijoada de bacalhau (meaty salt cod and haricot beans), rustic pork casserole, peri-peri prawns (a favourite of Mozambique, where the brothers grew up), Basque cheeses and Ibérico hams. Signature dish is the marinated acorn-fed Ibérico pig, grilled over charcoal and served medium rare to spotlight the lean, succulent qualities of the fillet – this is not pork as you know it. Throughout, flavours are strong and ballsy: not fancy, but packing a punch derived from confident seasoning, marinating and grilling; the aromas hit you as soon as the dishes arrive. Typical tapas and petiscos are available at the bar (or some as a starter). The wine list is almost exclusively Iberian, with sherries, ports, Madeiras and cavas well represented. Attentive, informed service (staff also know when to leave you be), a relaxed environment and comfortable banquettes meant that nearly three and a half hours passed without us noticing. Good food, even rustic good food, comes at a price, but Eyre Brothers is a consistently great performer. Consequently, booking (there's a handy online service) is advisable.
Available for hire. Babies and children admitted. Booking advisable Thur-Sat. Disabled: toilet. **Map 6 Q4**.

North
Stoke Newington

El Olivo
24 Stoke Newington Church Street, N16 0LU (7254 7897). Stoke Newington rail or bus 38. **Meals served** 8am-midnight daily.

Ariana II

Main courses £7.95-£14.95. **Set lunch** (noon-5pm) £5.95-£9.95 2 courses; £7.95 3 courses. **Credit** MC, V. Mediterranean

Just across from Stoke Newington's farmers' market, this small restaurant plays to the masses, with a pick'n'mix approach to tapas that takes in classic Spanish small plates (patatas bravas, gazpacho) as well as Turkish meze (houmous, köfte). Catch-all menus like this can often flounder, yet the food is fresh, robust and, for the most part, flavoursome. Fried calamari rings were light and not rubbery, while peppers stuffed with minced lamb and herbs also hit the right notes. Better yet was the paella, served sizzling fiercely in a pan and studded with chunks of lamb, chorizo and chicken (a steal at £8.25 per person), and accompanied by a simple salad of ripe avocado. Desserts, neither Spanish nor Turkish, were the only real disappointment: crème brûlée was thin and watery, while tiramisu not only lacked alcohol but came full of cloying cream. Happily, the wine list has plenty of choice from Spain and the New World, and little passing the £20 mark. Likewise, the dark wood and lively chatter makes for a welcoming ambience: it may not be worth crossing town for, but for locals seeking a relaxed hangout, El Olivo fits the bill.
Available for hire. Babies and children welcome: high chairs. Tables outdoors (2, pavement). Takeaway service. **Map 25 C1**.

North West
Kilburn

Ariana II `NEW`
2011 RUNNER-UP BEST NEW CHEAP EATS
241 Kilburn High Road, NW6 7JN (3490 6709). Kilburn tube or Brondesbury rail. **Meals served** noon-11pm daily. **Main courses**

£6-£12. **Set meal** £12.50 per person (minimum 2) 3 courses. **Unlicensed. Corkage** no charge. **Credit** MC, V. Afghan

Unable to find the right centrally located site Mohammad Wali (the man behind restaurant Ariana I, in Manhattan, who also has family in London) chose to set up shop in the less-than-salubrious environs of Kilburn High Road. Simply decorated, this BYO restaurant combines a broad-ranging list of perfectly prepared Afghan dishes with low prices. Dishes unique to Afghanistan include aushak: delicately translucent ravioli filled with a julienne of leeks, then topped with a spicy meat sauce and a drizzle of yoghurt, and served with a disc of tandoor-cooked Afghan flatbread. Mantu is another dumpling dish, this time filled with lamb. Marinated and grilled kebabs are more familiar, but we skipped over these in favour of the house speciality of Kabuli palow (pilau). A heap of long-grained brown basmati rice concealed pieces of lamb shank so tender they had long since escaped the bone. This luxe version featured raisins, almonds and pistachios, and was delicately flavoured with cinnamon, cumin and mint. Some vegetable side dishes resembled North Indian classics (such as the okra, well spiced and oozing red oil), while others are more subtle and Turkish-leaning, such as the baudinjan buranee: fried and mashed aubergine.
Available for hire. Babies and children welcome: high chairs. Booking advisable Thur-Sun. Separate room for parties, seats 40. Takeaway service; delivery service (over £12 within 3-mile radius).

Outer London
Harrow, Middlesex

Masa `HOT 50`
24-26 Headstone Drive, Harrow, Middx, HA3 5QH (8861 6213). Harrow & Wealdstone tube/rail. **Meals served** 12.30-11pm daily. **Main courses** £5.95-£13. **Set meal** £23.95 (2 people); £33 (2-3 people); £55 (4-5 people). **Unlicensed. Corkage** no charge. **Credit** MC, V. Afghan

The drab shopping parade location is soon forgotten as you enter this hugely enjoyable restaurant. A spectacular chandelier, heavy wooden furniture, and maroon and white walls displaying colourful still-lifes produce a lavish air that's only partially dissipated by the droning TV and a glass display counter. Afghani food is a blend of Middle Eastern and North Indian cuisines, and at Masa you can expect sublime rice and naans, tangy meze-like dips, juicy kebabs and rich curries. A selection of four dips is the best bet for a shared starter, perhaps including grilled aubergine with garlic, walnut and yoghurt. Ordering chicken corn soup – a cornfloury version of the Chinese standard – was a mistake. Kingfish and quail are barbecued options to follow, along with the usual chicken and lamb kebabs, but you'll also find a few uniquely Afghan dishes. Try the mantoo: nicely chewy pasta parcels overflowing with tangy minced lamb and yoghurt. Rich, tender kidney bean curry made a fitting sidekick, as did a glass of yoghurty dogh (there's no licence). Good-natured staff and a laid-back Anglo-Afghan crowd (some in traditional garb, some not) add to the exotic vibe.
Babies and children welcome: high chairs. Disabled: toilet. Takeaway service; delivery service (over £12 within 3-mile radius).

Greek

This may be one of the guide's shortest chapters, yet it contains some of the capital's most enduring and popular restaurants. London's Hellenic dining scene has been as steady as a yacht on the Aegean for some years now. You'll find tavernas, usually Greek-Cypriot, in the areas where members of the community tended to settle: Camden remains a stronghold. Then there are the establishments that double as fish and chip shops, most notably **George's** in South Woodford, and **Vrisaki** in Wood Green. For a relaxing holiday island buzz, try Primrose Hill's **Lemonia**, or the roof terrace at **Daphne**. Food of the mainland is the speciality at Notting Hill's **Greek Affair**, but there hasn't been a truly upmarket Greek restaurant in the capital since the original **Real Greek** in Hoxton was sold and subsequently turned into a souvlaki chain. In June 2011 the Real Greek was sold once again, to businessmen who helped run it while it was part of Clapham House Group. It's always been profitable, they've been quoted as saying, and they have plans for expansion – appropriately the first scheduled opening is next to the Olympic Park.

West
Bayswater

Aphrodite Taverna
15 Hereford Road, W2 4AB (7229 2206, www.aphroditerestaurant.co.uk). Bayswater, Notting Hill Gate or Queensway tube. **Meals served** noon-midnight Mon-Sat. **Main courses** £9.50-£23.50. **Set mezédes** £19 vegetarian, £22 meat, £31 fish per person (minimum 2). **Cover** £1. **Credit** AmEx, MC, V.
Aphrodite's quiet, leafy backstreet location makes its scattering of outdoor tables a relaxed summer spot for watching promenading middle-aged couples and well-heeled urban trendies. Inside, cosy taverna chintz dominates. Mini bouzoukis, gourds, plaster Parthenons and Greek pottery frescoes clutter a dining area overlooked by big paintings of Greek-Cypriots in traditional costume. Tables of regulars on first-name terms with the staff and conversing in Greek add to the charming atmosphere. The food is hearty and appetising, yet slips aren't unknown. A slab of halloumi was cut thickly enough to allow a smoky chargrilled crust, while staying meltingly soft in the middle; rich afélia arrived generously studded with coriander seeds; and huge roast potatoes were cooked the typically Greek way (pleasingly soft, oily and crust-free). However, a very oniony sausage-shaped portion of keftédes came with a disappointingly thin, watery tomato sauce, and while the lamb soúvla featured a caveman-like portion of meat hunks, it lacked the

dish's signature smoky punch. Enthusiastic service sees the chef occasionally emerge to greet diners, and a matron who makes a point of checking the cooking's up to scratch, but at quiet times, waiters can hover too attentively.
Available for hire. Babies and children welcome: high chairs. Booking advisable dinner. Tables outdoors (12, terrace). Takeaway service. Vegetarian menu. **Map 7 B6.**

Notting Hill

Greek Affair
1 Hillgate Street, W8 7SP (7792 5226, www.greekaffair.co.uk). Notting Hill Gate tube. **Lunch served** noon-3pm Tue-Sun. **Dinner served** 6-11pm daily. **Main courses** £8.50-£10.50. **Credit** AmEx, MC, V.
This contemporarily styled Notting Hill stalwart isn't afraid to buck the trends of London's Hellenic culinary scene. OK, in chi-chi west London, there's nothing too surprising about an interior that takes traditional trappings such as framed recipes for avgolemono soup, spanakorizo and keftédes, and cosily mixes them up with sleek grey walls, big scuffed tables and fairy lights. Yet in contrast to the capital's Greek-Cypriot norm, Greek Affair bases its menu on the food of the Greek mainland and islands. What's more, it bucks the unwritten rule of 'feed 'em till they burst' by promising 'nothing in excess'. Even the 'grand meze' selection is easily devoured without needing to loosen the belt. But with taramosaláta free from pink food colouring, a meltingly tender kléftiko perfectly balanced by a

fragrant lemon sauce, and flavour-packed, batter-free calamares, there's enough quality to make up for the diminished quantity. The beans in our fasólia gigantes were undercooked and chewy, and some might be disappointed by the substitution of sesame seed-coated crusty bread for the customary basket of pitta, but if the table of City boys happily singing 1970s pop hits is any indicator, most punters leave pretty pleased.
Babies and children welcome: high chairs. Booking advisable. Tables outdoors (10, roof garden). Takeaway service. Vegetarian menu. **Map 19 C5.**

South West
Earl's Court

As Greek As It Gets
233 Earl's Court Road, SW5 9AH (7244 7777, www.asgreekasitgets.co.uk). Earl's Court tube. **Lunch served** noon-3pm, **dinner served** 5-11pm Mon-Fri. **Meals served** noon-11pm Sat, Sun. **Main courses** £10-£15. **Credit** MC, V.
Despite the name, the interior of this place is intriguingly un-Hellenic, except for a map of the Greek islands that dominates the entrance. The distracting TV screens have vanished; instead, gold-edged mirrors and black and white portraits adorn the dark walls, and a glitzy glass chandelier hangs over the dining room. The lengthy menu consists mainly of Greek classics, some of which come with a modern twist. A starter of feta

wrapped in crisp filo pastry got an aniseed kick from ouzo liquor. Fava bean croquettes surprised with their golf ball size: four was a very generous portion, though the addition of capers to an already highly seasoned batter made them too salty. Mains cover traditional moussaká, chicken or pork gyros, and meat skewers. Kléftiko wasn't served on the bone, as is usual; instead, a few dry chunks of meat had been cooked in parchment paper, and came with a small side salad. Pork gyros in a pitta wrap was also on the dry side, but a generous slap of creamy tzatziki made up for it. Our friendly Cypriot waitress helped with the Greek wine selection, some of which is available in a 375ml carafe.

Available for hire. Babies and children welcome: high chairs. Booking advisable weekends. Tables outdoors (2, pavement). Takeaway service. **Map 13 B11**.

South East
Bankside

The Real Greek
Riverside House, 2A Southwark Bridge Road, SE1 9HA (7620 0162, www.therealgreek.com). London Bridge tube/rail. **Meals served** noon-11pm daily. **Tapas** £4-£7. **Set meal** £25.95-£29.95. **Credit** AmEx, MC, V.

There's no doubt that this chain lacks the homely charms that most London Greek restaurants trade upon. Customer turnover is quick, and – particularly given this branch's tourist-friendly, riverside location – service can be impersonal, if not downright inattentive. But the Real Greek also lacks the amateurish qualities that can characterise the cooking in some of the capital's Hellenic eateries. Food rarely sparkles, but order one of the souvláki wraps and you're in for a reliable, hearty feed. The focus is on Greek rather than Greek-Cypriot dishes, with the various sharing menus named after the nation's provinces. Rather than typical Cypriot pitta bread, you're offered the far superior fluffy flatbread of the mother country. On a sunny day, the outdoor tables are a pleasant place to take in the Thames views. Inside, decor is smart and tasteful (all dark wood furnishings and twinkly lighting), but the restaurant's large size means that it tends to feel either jarringly empty or swamped by the procession of tourists who frequent the place. Also, despite claims that a Mediterranean diet is 'healthy', the inclusion of calorific values on the Real Greek's menu is thought-provoking.

Available for hire. Babies and children welcome: high chairs. Disabled: toilet. Tables outdoors (23, terrace). Takeaway service. **Map 11 P7**. **For branches see index**.

North East
South Woodford

George's Fish & Souvlaki Bar
164 George Lane, E18 1AY (8989 3970, www.georgesfishbar.co.uk). South Woodford tube. **Lunch served** noon-2.30pm Mon-Thur; noon-3pm Fri, Sat. **Dinner served** 5-10.30pm Mon-Sat. **Meals served** 1-9pm Sun. **Main courses** £11-£13.50. **Set lunch** £7.95-£10.95 2 courses. **Set mezédes** £22.50. **Credit** MC, V.

A small outdoor seating area and a big blue canopy belie the fact that there's an impressively versatile fish and chip shop at the heart of this local restaurant. To reach the little pink chandeliers and the tealight-garnished tables of the rear dining area, you'll need to step past deep-fat fryers, takeaway priceboards and as many chippy industry awards as you can shake a saveloy at (including something entitled 'Keith Chegwin's Perfect Portion' award). The menu offers pickled onions, mushy peas and a range of sustainably sourced seafood (available battered, fried in matzo meal or grilled), along with classic Greek-Cypriot dishes served with huge helpings of chunky chips. It's the Hellenic food that's the highlight. A portion of keftédes had a delicate cinnamon fragrance, and a cold meze mix featured intensely tangy tahini plus a refreshing tzatziki run through with finely grated cucumber. On Sundays, there's an offer of two courses for £10.95, but be warned: on our end-of-week visit, several dishes had run out.

Available for hire. Babies and children welcome: children's menu; high chairs. Booking advisable Thur-Sun. Tables outdoors (8, patio). Takeaway service.

North
Camden Town & Chalk Farm

Daphne
83 Bayham Street, NW1 0AG (7267 7322). Camden Town or Mornington Crescent tube.

GREEK

Lunch served noon-2.30pm, **dinner served** 6-11.30pm Mon-Sat. **Main courses** £9-£14.50. **Set lunch** £7.75 2 courses, £9.25 3 courses. **Set mezédes** £16.50 meat or vegetarian, £20.50 fish per person (minimum 2). **Credit** MC, V.

The Greekness of this three-floor family-run restaurant doesn't stop at its menu. The patron checks diners are ready to order with 'Endaxi?' ('OK?'), and the jovial matron trades jokes about the veracity of the Greek legend of Daphne. Service is super-attentive, and a dropped napkin was whisked from the floor and replaced before we could even react. The small roof terrace lined with baskets of flowers makes a lovely venue for a summer's meal, while the interior varies from the ground floor's floral patterned booths and monochrome photos of Cypriot village women, to the more earthily Mediterranean feel of the wine rack-lined first-floor dining room. A blackboard list of specials offers an extensive choice of seafood, but on previous visits the fish has paled against the more typically Hellenic fare. A portion of moussaká came in a full-to-the-brim soup bowl, topped by a rich crust of cheese; the filling in our spanakópitta was tart and satisfyingly creamy; and two skewers of lamb souvláki were grilled to charcoaly, succulent perfection. Unfortunately, many main courses require the additional purchase of side dishes, but diners are treated to a complimentary portion of loukoúmi on paying.

Available for hire. Babies and children welcome: high chairs. Booking advisable. Tables outdoors (7, roof terrace; 2, veranda). Takeaway service. Vegetarian menu. **Map 27 D2**.

★ Lemonia

89 Regent's Park Road, NW1 8UY (7586 7454). Chalk Farm tube. **Lunch served** noon-3pm Mon-Fri; noon-3.30pm Sun. **Dinner served** 6-11.30pm Mon-Sat. **Main courses** £10.50-£15. **Set lunch** (Mon-Fri) £9.75 2 courses, £11.50 3 courses. **Set mezédes** £19.50 per person (minimum 2). **Credit** MC, V.

A row of hanging flower baskets and large-paned windows folding out on to Primrose Hill's main shopping street herald London's classiest Greek restaurant. Inside, it's a sunny place, filled with carefree locals who treat it as something akin to the neighbourhood chippie, and groups of friends who have made the journey for a fun evening out. Booking is prudent at all times: even on a weeknight in the depths of the recession, people were patiently waiting for tables – though, rest assured, there is a large number of covers, and service is brisk without being pushy. The menu is extensive; add a sheet of specials and the set menu and deciding what to eat is a challenge. We eventually settled on the clichés: deliciously smoky grills of tender calamari and lamb shashlik, with spanakópitta and succulent cheesy courgette fritters to start. Come dessert, a crisp, nut-filled tunnel of syrup-soaked kataïfi outclassed the galaktopoúreko, whose bland custard filling was slightly too thick with starch. The only real disappointment, however, was the wine list: we noticed high mark-ups on bottles available cheaply in Majestic. Still, Lemonia's delicious food and happy vibe easily compensate.

Babies and children admitted. Booking essential. Separate room for parties, seats 40. Tables outdoors (6, pavement). **Map 27 A1**.

Carob Tree. See p126.

GREEK

Menu

Dishes followed by (G) indicate a specifically Greek dish; those marked (GC) indicate a Greek-Cypriot speciality; those without an initial have no particular regional affiliation. Spellings on menus often vary.

Afélia (GC): pork cubes stewed in wine, coriander and other herbs.

Avgolémono (G): a sauce made of lemon, egg yolks and chicken stock. Also a soup made with rice, chicken stock, lemon and whole eggs.

Dolmádes (G) or **koupépia (GC):** young vine leaves stuffed with rice, spices and (usually) minced meat.

Fasólia plakí or **pilaki:** white beans in a tomato, oregano, bay, parsley and garlic sauce.

Garídes: prawns (usually king prawns in the UK), fried or grilled.

Gígantes or **gígandes:** white butter beans baked in tomato sauce; pronounced 'yígandes'.

Halloumi (GC) or **hallúmi:** a cheese that is traditionally made from sheep or goat's milk, but increasingly from cow's milk. Best served fried or grilled.

Horiátiki: Greek 'peasant' salad made from tomato, cucumber, onion, feta and sometimes green pepper, dressed with ladolémono (a mixture of oil and lemon).

Hórta: salad of cooked wild greens.

Houmous, hoúmmous or **húmmus (GC):** a dip of puréed chickpeas, sesame seed paste, lemon juice and garlic, garnished with paprika. Originally an Arabic dish.

Htipití or **khtipití:** tangy purée of matured cheeses, flavoured with red peppers.

Kalamári, kalamarákia or **calamares:** small squid, usually sliced into rings, with the pieces battered and fried.

Kataífi or **katayfi:** syrup-soaked 'shredded-wheat' rolls.

Keftédes or **keftedákia (G):** herby meatballs made with minced pork or lamb (rarely beef), egg, breadcrumbs and possibly grated potato.

Kléftiko (GC): slow-roasted lamb (often shoulder), served on the bone and flavoured with oregano and other herbs.

Kopanistí (G): a cheese dip with a tanginess traditionally coming from natural fermentation, but often boosted with chilli.

Koukiá: broad beans.

Loukánika or **lukánika:** spicy coarse-ground sausages, usually pork and heavily herbed.

Loukoumédes: tiny, spongy dough fritters, dipped in honey.

Loukoúmi or **lukúmi:** 'turkish delight' made using syrup, rosewater and pectin, and often studded with nuts.

Loúntza (GC): smoked pork loin.

Marídes: picarel, often mistranslated as (or substituted by) 'whitebait' – small fish best coated in flour and flash-fried.

Melitzanosaláta: grilled aubergine purée.

Meze (the plural is **mezédes**, pronounced 'mezédhes'): a selection of either hot or cold appetisers and main dishes.

Moussaká(s) (G): a baked dish of mince (usually lamb), aubergine and potato slices, topped with béchamel sauce.

Papoutsáki: aubergine 'shoes', slices stuffed with mince, topped with sauce, usually béchamel-like.

Pourgoúri or **bourgoúri (GC):** a pilaf of cracked wheat, often prepared with stock, onions, crumbled vermicelli and spices.

Saganáki (G): fried cheese, usually kefalotyri; also refers to anything (mussels, spinach) served in a cheese-based red sauce.

Sheftaliá (GC): little pig-gut skins stuffed with minced pork and lamb, onion, parsley, breadcrumbs and spices, then grilled.

Soutzoukákia or **soutzoúki (G):** baked meat rissoles, which are often topped with a tomato-based sauce.

Soúvla: large cuts of lamb or pork, slow-roasted on a rotary spit.

Souvláki: chunks of meat quick-grilled on a skewer (known in London takeaways as kebab or shish kebab).

Spanakópitta: small turnovers stuffed with spinach, dill and often feta or some other crumbly tart cheese.

Stifádo: a rich meat stew (often made using beef or rabbit) with onions, red wine, tomatoes, cinnamon and bay.

Taboúlleh: generic Middle Eastern starter of pourgoúri (qv), chopped parsley, cucumber chunks, tomatoes and spring onions.

Taramá, properly **taramosaláta:** fish roe pâté, originally made of dried, salted grey mullet roe, but now more often smoked cod roe, plus olive oil, lemon juice and breadcrumbs.

Tavás (GC): lamb, onion, tomato and cumin, cooked in earthenware casseroles.

Tsakistés (GC): split green olives marinated in lemon, garlic, coriander seeds and other optional flavourings.

Tyrópitta (G): similar to spanakópitta (qv) but usually without spinach and with more feta.

Tzatzíki, dzadzíki (G) or **talatoúra (GC):** a dip of shredded cucumber, yoghurt, garlic, lemon juice and mint.

Kentish Town

★ Carob Tree

15 Highgate Road, NW5 1QX (7267 9880). Gospel Oak rail or bus C2, C11, 214. **Lunch served** noon-3pm, **dinner served** 6-10.30pm Tue-Fri. **Meals served** noon-10.30pm Sat; noon-9pm Sun. **Main courses** £3.20-£20. **Credit** MC, V.

Packed as soon as it opened a couple of years ago, Carob Tree is now less of a hotspot, despite its enviable position opposite Hampstead Heath and a smart modern decor that avoids taverna clichés. Could it be the welcome? We, and another party, arrived to an empty restaurant towards the end of lunchtime, to the staff's clear dismay; only when the waitress accepted we were staying did her mood switch to friendly and helpful. The specials board set above the open-plan kitchen proffered Cornish brill for two, French sea bass, grilled jumbo prawns and beef moussaká. Cypriot dips and sauces, says to the menu, are made in a prep kitchen to Carob Tree's recipes – the rich, almost caramelised flavour of the aubergine dip was far superior to anything from a factory, and served with a generous basket of hot pitta. A squeeze of lemon shot the spicy chargrilled pastourma into the realms of the heavenly; potato salad arrived chilled, but wasn't the worse for it. Combined with a bottle of chardonnay (the cheapest white), it was a delightful meal. With more cash to flash, we might have had chargrilled veal chop or lamb cutlets, but part of this restaurant's appeal is that you can have enjoyable food whatever your budget.
Available for hire. Babies and children welcome: high chairs. Booking advisable. Disabled: toilet. Tables outdoors (10, garden). Vegetarian menu.

Wood Green

Vrisaki

73 Myddleton Road, N22 8LZ (8889 8760). Bounds Green or Wood Green tube. **Meals served** noon-11.30pm Mon-Sat; noon-9pm Sun. **Main courses** £10-£18. **Set mezédes** £19 per person (minimum 2). **Credit** AmEx, MC, V.

Among the photos of budget celeb patrons lining Vrisaki's chip-shop interior (Antony Costa, George Graham, Jodie Marsh), there's one that sums the place up perfectly. 'She has survived' proclaims a *Daily Mirror* article on Gloria Gaynor, accompanied by a note from the singer thanking the restaurant for 'a wonderful dining experience', thus allaying fears that she might have been unable to withstand the gargantuan quantity of food that is the forte here. The first course of the mixed meze selection features no less than 18 dishes, with the charmingly frank waiters acting almost like personal trainers as they encourage you to eat enough of the dips, salads and seafood medleys to clear space for more dishes. Food quality (generally underwhelming on our previous visit) seems to have improved a notch. Huge asparagus spears were topped with bushy dill sprigs; and a selection of chargrilled sheftaliá (Cypriot sausage enveloped in caul fat), pork souvláki and quail had plenty of charcoaly tang. The seafood disappointed, though. A caper-strewn trout was doused in mouth-puckering quantities of lemon, and the cold meze's seafood medleys were watery and gritty.
Available for hire. Babies and children welcome: high chairs. Booking advisable: essential weekends. Takeaway service.

Hotels & Haute Cuisine

Look at this year's clutch of new haute cuisine establishments and you may wonder what happened to the recession. It's true: while other parts of the restaurant trade have been suffering, fine dining is on a bit of a high. Perhaps it's a sign that, although people may be eating out less, when they do splash out, they want a guaranteed memorable experience – and, thanks to hit TV programmes such as *MasterChef* and *Saturday Kitchen*, they're more aware of what that experience might be and where to find it. Or maybe it simply proves that gastronomes are more concerned with food quality and artistry than prices. Certainly, none of these places is cheap, but, for the most part, celebrities and the super-rich do their conspicuous consumption elsewhere. Jason Atherton's well-funded **Pollen Street Social** is our favourite of the new haute hotspots – and winner of our 2011 Best New Fine Dining award – but we're also fond of **Hedone**, bravely opening in out-of-centre Chiswick. You might expect most of the places in this chapter to receive top marks from our critics, and many do, so we'll take this opportunity to point you in the direction of some that deserve greater recognition: **Texture**, the **Greenhouse**, **Viajante** and **Hélène Darroze at the Connaught** performed particularly well this year.

Central
Belgravia

Pétrus
1 Kinnerton Street, SW1X 8EA (7592 1609, www.gordonramsay.com). Knightsbridge tube. **Lunch served** noon-2.15pm, **dinner served** 6.30-10pm Mon-Sat. **Set lunch** £30 3 courses. **Set dinner** £60 3 courses. **Set meal** £70 tasting menu. **Credit** AmEx, MC, V.
There's a sense of calm as you enter this deluxe dining room. A modern, smart set-up, accentuated by beige tones and an eye-catching cylindrical wine vault, Pétrus is also a convivial spot, less buttoned-up than its peers. The welcome is sociable and gracious. Food consists of the Gordon Ramsay take on modern French cuisine (as interpreted by executive chef Mark Askew), so expect tried and tested dishes such as fillet of lemon sole with clams and champagne velouté. The lunch menu is good value, and the set pieces – such as watercress mousse with tiny cubes of potatoes and salmon tartare, or a pre-dessert of passionfruit ice-cream served in a chocolate cornetto – are so eminently likeable that we wished there were seconds. To start, we were impressed by the clear flavours of silky ravioli bursting with quail meat and wild mushrooms (served with salad and a splash of cep sauce). The kitchen then produced a juicy braised neck of Devon lamb teamed with spring vegetables and a thyme jus. The accompanying carrots of differing colours (including burgundy) were equally alluring. Cheeses, especially a ripe, runny saint-félicien, are worth the £12 supplement. Although the cooking generally plays it safe and might not quicken the pulse, the food is reliably excellent. Orange and vanilla baked alaska with a Grand Marnier sauce was beautiful to behold, and tickled our palate right to the end. The wine list, befitting this restaurant's name, is crammed with class too. *Available for hire. Babies and children welcome: high chairs. Booking advisable. Disabled: toilet. Dress: smart casual. Vegetarian menu.* **Map 9 G9**.

City

Bonds
Threadneedles, 5 Threadneedle Street, EC2R 8AY (7657 8088, www.theetoncollection.com). Bank tube/DLR. **Breakfast served** 6.30-10.30am Mon-Fri; 7.30-11am Sat, Sun. **Lunch served** noon-2.30pm, **dinner served** 6-10pm Mon-Fri. **Main courses** £12.95-£26.95. **Set meal** (noon-2.30pm, 6-8pm) £19.95 3 courses incl glass of wine. **Credit** AmEx, DC, MC, V.
Looking for a wise investment? Consider this hotel restaurant set in a former Victorian bank. Look left as you walk through the bar to see the original main hall with its stunning glass-painted dome. The restaurant is a calm, discreet modern space with walnut-panelled walls, brown banquettes and large pendant lamps. Statement flowers and red accents (chair seats, water glasses) provide a splash of colour, while black-waistcoated staff provide graceful, professional service. A hushed, but not stuffy atmosphere prevailed at lunch – perhaps because most diners (unusually for a City venue) were women. Look out for the regularly changing special deals: our August visit coincided with a set lunch/early evening menu of three courses including a glass for wine for £19.95 – a cracking bargain, considering you'd pay the same for one of the cheaper mains on the carte. Carefully sourced, seasonal ingredients, precision-cooking and immaculate presentation are the hallmarks of head chef Barry Tonks. Our dishes sang: Scottish beef

Dinner by Heston Blumenthal

tartare was nicely tangy and well textured; Scottish salmon a la plancha (crisp skin, firm flesh) came with creamy tomato and saffron risotto; eton mess fitted its description of 'a classic tuck-shop treat'. Best was a main of slow-cooked, rare-breed pork belly with potato fondant, crushed peas, tomatoes and black pudding with apple purée, the plate as carefully composed as a Cubist painting. The wine list is aimed at expense-accounters, though there are bottles under £20.

Available for hire. Babies and children admitted. Booking advisable. Disabled: lift; toilet. Separate rooms for parties, seating 8, 14 and 16. **Map 12 Q6.**

Fitzrovia

Pied à Terre

34 Charlotte Street, W1T 2NH (7636 1178, www.pied-a-terre.co.uk). Goodge Street or Tottenham Court Road tube. **Lunch served** noon-2.30pm Mon-Fri. **Dinner served** 6-10.45pm Mon-Sat. **Set lunch** £23.50 2 courses, £29.50 5 courses. **Set dinner** £75 3 courses. **Set meal** £95 tasting menu. **Credit** AmEx, MC, V.
A change at the helm after a decade at this highly rated restaurant: Shane Osborn cedes the apron to Marcus Eaves, Osborn's protégé and former chef at sister restaurant, L'Autre Pied. The kitchen continues to perform, but some other things could do with a tweak. The muted decor in an already awkward space is beginning to feel tired, and the service is capable but lacks a certain sparkle. On the plate (pretty, textured plates, that is), the house style is creative and complex, employing multiple ingredients, techniques and flavours to generally delightful effect. Bread, including savoury brioche, light cheese rolls and Guinness loaf, is a highlight. On our last visit, for the good-value set lunch, slow-cooked lamb with smoked garlic, roast shallot and an air-dried herb powder was technical and implausibly flavoursome; plaice with a pistou of white beans, brown shrimps and basil cream sauce had been beautifully plated but was detrimentally over-salted. We didn't see as much as we'd hoped of Eaves' inspired and delicate presentation, but there were hints of it in the plaice and the hors d'oeuvres (exceptional, notably the sesame tuiles), so it presumably features on the more complex à la carte (sample dish: slow-cooked veal cheek with sweetbreads, grelot onions, morteau sausage and kaffir lime jus). The wine list is interesting at the lower end and knowledgeable at the upper; the enthusiastic sommelier doesn't discriminate.
Babies and children admitted. Booking advisable; essential weekends. Dress: smart casual. Separate room for parties, seats 13. Vegetarian menu. **Map 17 B1.**

Roux at the Landau

The Landau, 1C Portland Place, W1B 1JA (7965 0165, www.thelandau.com). Oxford Circus tube. **Breakfast served** 7-10.30am Mon-Fri; 7am-noon Sat, Sun. **Lunch served** 12.30-2.30pm Mon-Fri. **Dinner served** 5.30-10.30pm Mon-Sat. **Main courses** £19-£42. **Set meal** (12.30-2.30pm, 5.30-7pm) £47.50 3 courses incl half bottle of wine, mineral water, coffee, £80 tasting menu (£140 incl wine). **Credit** AmEx, DC, MC, V.
The kitchen at this sumptuous venue is overseen by Albert and Michel Roux Jr, and run by head chef Chris King. It couldn't feel less like a hotel restaurant, with its impressive high ceiling,

extensive wood panelling, pastel-coloured palette, and expansive curved bay window. Cooking, although based on classic French techniques, also celebrates Mediterranean and Middle Eastern flavours with flair. Creamy salt cod brandade made a tasty partner for squid rings fried in inky-hued tempura batter. Equally memorable, courgette strips, anointed with olive oil and scattered with toasted pine nuts and raisins, were given an aromatic flourish with chickpea fritters seasoned with Middle Eastern spices. Mains were just as creative. Our favourite: plump lamb cutlets, juicy and meltingly tender, partnered by slow-simmered cracked wheat, finished with shredded green olives and marjoram. Simple, yet so tasty, was chorizo-filled rabbit leg served with auburn-hued saffron rice, which shone with an unashamedly bold Spanish character. Desserts were impeccable. Especially notable: a warm, fragrant apricot soufflé, flecked with diced fruit and served with pistachio ice-cream. Service, like the cooking, is hard to fault. Expect big-budget expenditure for choices from the carte; set menus provide more affordable options matched with moderately priced wines.
Babies and children welcome: high chairs. Booking advisable; essential weekends. Disabled: toilet. Dress: smart casual. Separate room for parties, seats 16. **Map 9 H5.**

Holborn

Pearl Bar & Restaurant

Chancery Court Hotel, 252 High Holborn, WC1V 7EN (7829 7000, www.pearl-restaurant.com). Holborn tube.
Bar **Open** 11am-11pm Mon-Fri; 6-11pm Sat.
Restaurant **Lunch served** noon-2.30pm Mon-Fri. **Dinner served** 6-10pm Mon-Sat. **Set lunch** £22 1 course, £26.50 2 courses, £29.50 3 courses. **Set dinner** £38 1 course, £50 2 courses, £60 3 courses. **Set meal** £70 tasting menu (£120 incl wine).
Both **Credit** AmEx, DC, MC, V.
Exec chef Jun Tanaka worked with a roll-call of stellar names, from the Roux family to Marco Pierre White, before alighting at what has become his signature restaurant, in the luxury Chancery Court hotel. After seven years, his Asian-accented modern French dishes remain as fresh and artful as ever, pleasing both the eye and the palate with a balance of delicacy and intensity, and a broad spectrum of flavour. Lobster in gazpacho was outstanding for its sculptural presentation, all pretty in pink; an artichoke raviolo was delicate in every respect. If we were really fussy, we'd say the beef bone marrow didn't truly lend itself to the herb-powder gussying-up, and the monkfish with seaweed, cucumber, squid and seashore vegetables, though teasingly complex, seemed a tad wet and ungenerous. Prices are high; we might have said too much, but they pay for the all-round wow factor as well as the food. The interior is spectacular, conjuring grandeur, intimacy and style out of an early 20th-century building that weaves in lovely strand-of-pearl lighting as a nod to its past as the head office of Pearl Assurance. A meal is punctuated by intricate hors d'oeuvres, palate teasers and pre-desserts. Staff spoil you but don't fuss; seating is comfortable and well spaced; and the atmosphere hushed but humming. The wine list, though, is ill conceived. It includes some stellar bottles, but is overlong and poorly categorised and explained, with too little by the glass or under £40. That said, the bar staff know an unfeasible amount about cachaça.

Babies and children welcome: high chairs. Booking advisable. Disabled: toilet. Dress: smart casual. Entertainment: pianist 7.30pm Wed-Sat. Separate room for parties, seats 12. **Map 18 F2.**

Knightsbridge

The Capital

The Capital, 22-24 Basil Street, SW3 1AT (7591 1202, www.capitalhotel.co.uk). Knightsbridge tube. **Breakfast served** 7.30-10.30am, **lunch served** noon-2.30pm, **dinner served** 6.30-10.30pm daily. **Main courses** £24-£40. **Set lunch** £24.50 2 courses, £39.50 3 courses. **Set meal** £55 tasting menu (£98 incl wine). **Credit** AmEx, DC, MC, V.
An oasis of calm among hectic nearby department stores, this discreet old-school hotel restaurant offers indulgence – at a price. It's an intimate dining room favoured by tourists and mature regulars, the corporate vibe softened by splashes of bold pink upholstery. Jérôme Ponchelle oversees kitchen affairs, giving top billing to new-wave dishes as well as French classics. On our lunchtime visit, we ordered from the extremely well-priced set menu. Prawn ravioli, its filling deliciously chunky, made a marvellous match with an Asian-inspired broth of lemony coconut milk infused with ginger and mild chillies. Roast, boned quail served with lentils wasn't as notable – especially as we couldn't detect any of the promised bacon aromas in its foamy garnish. We loved the sea-fresh creativity of roast cod fillet, however, which came glistening with juicy mussels and surrounded by buttery seaweed sauce. Sadly, the meal was let down by a simple staple of roast lamb; tough and unyielding, it was an unequal partner to an outstanding meaty jus. Desserts didn't hit the mark either: an excellent vanilla ice-cream was overshadowed by dry, powdery brownies and grainy chocolate sauce. In compensation, service was seamless and the wine list, although pricey, has a decent selection by the glass.
Available for hire. Babies and children welcome: high chairs. Booking advisable. Disabled: toilet. Dress: smart casual. Separate rooms for parties, seating 10, 14 and 24. **Map 8 F9.**

Dinner by Heston Blumenthal NEW
2011 RUNNER-UP BEST NEW FINE DINING
Mandarin Oriental Hyde Park, 66 Knightsbridge, SW1X 7LA (7201 3833, www.dinnerbyheston.com). Knightsbridge tube. **Lunch served** noon-2.30pm, **dinner served** 6.30-10.30pm daily. **Main courses** £26.50-£72. **Set lunch** (Mon-Fri) £28 3 courses. **Credit** AmEx, DC, MC, V.
With Heston Blumenthal now a fully-fledged celebrity, complete with advertising campaigns and media coverage of his personal life, it was inevitable his London debut would cause a stir. The clamour for tables isn't quite as bad as it was in the early stages, but this warm, relaxing room is still a hotspot attracting high-profile clientele. Worth noting, though, that dinner is not actually by Blumenthal, but under the command of Ashley Palmer-Watts, executive head chef of the Fat Duck group and still involved with Blumenthal's Bray establishments. The pair developed the menu of historically-inspired British dishes together. Dating each recipe on the menu labours the point rather irritatingly, especially since what appears on the plate looks perfectly modern, and flavour combinations and cooking techniques are no more outlandish or thought-provoking than at any other

good fine-dining establishment. We especially liked the salamagundy (essentially a salad) of chicken oysters, bone marrow and horseradish cream, and the cucumber ketchup that accompanied perfectly cooked seared scallops. 'Powdered duck' (two legs rubbed with spices and roast) was overly rich, but the accompanying potato purée was heaven. After our fatty duck, lemon suet pudding with lemon caramel was a little heavy-going, but nevertheless delicious and nicely cooked. A freebie of earl grey ganache delighted too. Service (almost of the Jamie Oliver school) was charming in its lack of posturing, but a little disorganised.
Babies and children welcome: high chairs; nappy-changing facilities (hotel). Booking essential. Disabled: toilet (hotel). Dress: smart casual. Separate rooms for parties, seating 6 and 10. Tables outdoors (15, terrace). **Map 8 F9**.

Koffmann's

The Berkeley, Wilton Place, SW1X 7RL (7107 8844, www.the-berkeley.co.uk). Hyde Park Corner or Knightsbridge tube. **Lunch served** noon-2.30pm Mon-Fri; noon-3pm Sat, Sun. **Dinner served** 6-10.30pm daily. **Main courses** £19-£34. **Set lunch** (Mon-Sat) £21.50 2 courses, £25.50 3 courses; (Sun) £22.50 2 courses, £26.50 3 courses. **Credit** AmEx, MC, V.

The return of Pierre Koffmann, one of the best chefs of his generation, guaranteed a procession of chefs and gourmets through the doors when this restaurant – a brasserie dedicated to the cooking of Koffmann's native Gascony – opened in 2010. Things have since settled into a smooth groove, with front of house managed by the charming Eric Garnier and Clare Harrison (Koffmann's partner), whose warm personality always wins us over. The Berkeley's basement dining room feels more formal than a brasserie, with textured wallpaper and shades of cream and olive green. Many diners come here to experience the creations first made famous at Koffmann's old restaurant, La Tante Claire – and the pig's trotter stuffed with chicken mousse and morels will not disappoint. An extensive regional French wine list provides back-up. We decided on the good-value lunch menu. First up, a beautifully rich and smooth liver parfait with toasted Poilâne bread. The French know how to cook a roast chicken, and Koffmann's version, with the leg paired with gratin potatoes and girolles, is terrific. It's also heartening not to be charged extra for vegetables served with the main courses. The humble spud, especially, is treated with respect, with a different variety arriving each day; the chips are irresistible. We deviated into the carte at the end for pistachio soufflé, which ensured we left fully content.
Available for hire. Babies and children welcome: high chairs; nappy-changing facilities. Booking advisable. Disabled: toilet (hotel). Dress: smart casual. Separate room for parties, seats 16. **Map 9 G9**.

Marcus Wareing at the Berkeley

The Berkeley, Wilton Place, SW1X 7RL (7235 1200, www.the-berkeley.co.uk). Hyde Park Corner or Knightsbridge tube. **Lunch served** noon-2.30pm Mon-Fri. **Dinner served** 6-10.30pm Mon-Fri; 6.30-10.30pm Sat. **Set lunch** £30 2 courses, £38 3 courses (£50 incl 2 glasses of wine). **Set meal** £80 3 courses, £98 tasting menu, £110 seasonal menu (incl wine). **Credit** AmEx, DC, MC, V.

Despite Marcus Wareing's recent opening of British restaurant Gilbert Scott, no one has taken an eye off the ball at this flagship destination; cooking remains superbly executed. The Berkeley is a powerbroker's stomping ground, and the claret colour scheme and plush fittings reflect the somewhat formal tone. Even so, this is a popular haunt. On our weekday visit, the dining area was filled with the appreciative buzz of conversation from occupied tables. Dishes are often complex in nature, but always well crafted. A soft scoop of creamy burrata cheese complemented the intense fruitiness of sliced heritage tomatoes and minted melon balls: a marvellous set of contrasts. The summery theme continued with a splendidly tender chicken breast, crowned with glistening skin, surrounded by a moat of creamy elderflower sauce. Desserts delivered the

goods too. Wareing's signature custard tart was delectable, the filling silky-smooth and wobbly, its pastry, crisp and buttery. Fitting finales include old-fashioned trolleys offering cheese selections and mounds of truffles; it's all rather grand. Prices are pitched at the sharp end, but it's worth sampling the set lunch menu and accompanying wines for a more affordable meal. Service is smoothly assured and utterly professional.
Babies and children welcome: high chairs. Booking essential. Dress: smart; jacket preferred. Separate rooms for parties, seating 8 and 16. Vegetarian menu. **Map 9 G9**.

One-O-One

101 Knightsbridge, SW1X 7RN (7290 7101, www.oneoonerestaurant.com). Knightsbridge tube.

Roganic

Lunch served noon-2.30pm Mon-Fri; 12.30-2.30pm Sat, Sun. **Dinner served** 6.30-10pm daily. **Main courses** £28-£39. **Set lunch** £17 2 dishes-£37 6 dishes. **Set dinner** £45 6 courses, £55 tasting menu. **Credit** AmEx, DC, MC, V.

Breton chef Pascal Proyart is serious about seafood. It's a shame that the decor at the hotel restaurant in which he presides lacks character, warmth and intimacy. On our Sunday lunch visit, the spacious dining area was sparsely occupied by a few mature diners and a solitary young family: a pity, as the cooking, which draws upon a roll-call of global influences, is exemplary. Although à la carte options are seriously expensive, the set lunches are exceptionally good value. Farmed tilapia (from Yorkshire), filleted and steamed to juicy sweetness

– surrounded by a gingery coconut broth with crunchy, flash-fried water chestnuts and sesame-crusted mussels – made a marvellously light start to a series of taster plates. We also loved the more robustly flavoured mackerel bruschetta, steeped in red pepper juiciness and scented with saffron. The carte contains a few meat dishes, but One-O-One is unashamedly a fish and seafood destination. Desserts are as indulgent as they are tasty; warm brownies, accompanied by coffee mousse and salted caramel ice-cream, and sabayon-coated berries with sorbet, are two excellent choices that rounded off a fabulous meal.

Available for hire. Babies and children welcome: high chairs. Booking advisable Thur-Sun. Disabled: toilet. Dress: smart casual. Separate room for parties, seats 10. **Map 8 F9**.

Marylebone

Roganic NEW
19 Blandford Street, W1U 3DH (7486 0380, www.roganic.co.uk). Baker Street or Bond Street tube. **Lunch served** noon-2pm, **dinner served** 6-9pm Tue-Sat. **Set lunch** (Tue-Fri) £29 3 courses. **Set meal** £55 6 courses, £80 10 courses. **Credit** AmEx, MC, V.

Chef-proprietor Simon Rogan's occasionally wacky but always cutting-edge cooking at L'Enclume in Cumbria is well regarded. This, his first London venture, is run by head chef Ben Spalding (previously at L'Autre Pied and Rhodes W1), but overseen by Rogan. Adventurous, beautifully presented dishes showcase offbeat home-grown and foraged produce: expect such curiosities as heritage potatoes anointed with onion ash, lovage and leafy wood sorrel. Friendly waiters know the menu inside out, but our meal was hit and miss. Highlights were the less fussy dishes – most notably sweet glazed Kentish mackerel fillets drizzled with fragrant elderflower honey, though we also loved meaty, tender Cumbrian hogget (one- to two-year-old lamb) with its musky partner of artichoke purée, and a nostalgic dessert of fruity cherry soda coupled with a tingly strawberry-sherbet marshmallow. On the downside, some dishes seemed over-crafted: an excessively salty finger of brill, coated in reduced chicken stock mixed with crunchy salt, and an under-seasoned beetroot jelly matched with floppy curd, both missed the mark. Housed in a modestly sized place, Roganic is on a short two-year lease, which might explain the sparse furnishings – low-hanging steel lamps, splashes of modern art and 1970s-style fixtures.

Available for hire. Babies and children admitted. Booking advisable. Dress: smart casual. Separate room for parties, seats 10. Vegetarian menu. **Map 9 G5**.

★ Texture
34 Portman Street, W1H 7BY (7224 0028, www.texture-restaurant.co.uk). Marble Arch tube. **Bar Open** noon-midnight Tue-Sat. *Restaurant* **Lunch served** noon-2.30pm, **dinner served** 6.30-11pm Tue-Sat. **Main courses** £27.50-£31.50. **Set lunch** £19.90 2 courses, £24 3 courses. **Set meal** £76 tasting menu (£58 vegetarian). *Both* **Credit** AmEx, MC, V.

The recent rise of modern Scandinavian cooking has had gastronomes drooling, and while Icelandic chef Agnar Sverrisson's kitchen doesn't display its northern influences as brazenly as some, the dishes here include many nods to his homeland. The ethos is evident in the cooking, which overlooks the butter and cream traditional to French cuisine in favour of light, pure flavours. From the minute the amuse arrives – new-season peas with hazelnuts and mint 'snow', say – it's clear you're embarking on a special culinary experience. A starter of Atlantic prawns came with pea mousse and delicate shards of rye bread; Icelandic lamb and cod also feature regularly across the menu. The star of a delightful meal was a square of English pork belly, plated with a puffy crisp of crackling, gooseberries, samphire, pak choi and peach purée. Desserts are similarly thrilling; we relished a 'soup' of passionfruit, lemongrass and ginger with basil sorbet and pineapple. The inventiveness is amped up in two tasting menus. Clockwork service is pleasantly informal, and the luminous, airy room is suitably Nordic too: the

Roganic

ornately corniced Georgian townhouse displaying sculptural branches and mossy plants. One of the most exciting places to eat in London.

Available for hire. Babies and children admitted. Booking advisable. Disabled: toilet. Separate room for parties, seats 16. Vegetarian menu. Map 9 G6.

Mayfair

Alain Ducasse at the Dorchester

The Dorchester, 53 Park Lane, W1K 1QA (7629 8866, www.alainducasse-dorchester.com). Hyde Park Corner tube. **Lunch served** noon-1.30pm Tue-Fri. **Dinner served** 6.30-9.30pm Tue-Sat. **Set lunch** £50 3 courses incl 2 glasses of wine, mineral water, coffee. **Set dinner** £78 3 courses, £95 4 courses. **Set meal** £115 tasting menu (£210 incl wine), £180 seasonal menu. **Credit** AmEx, DC, MC, V.

Alain Ducasse's top-end restaurants have earned him world acclaim, and this is his only UK establishment, currently holder of three Michelin stars. At the helm, executive head chef Jocelyn Herland creates contemporary French dishes using seasonal British and French produce. There's no denying their quality, but a lack of wow-factor combined with stratospheric pricing can leave some guests feeling disappointed. Designer Patrick Jouin is behind the taupe-toned interior and its centrepiece, a table curtained by thousands of shimmering fibre optics. As you'd expect, the restaurant holds an extravagant collection of wines, mainly French, which are on show in one corner. Among the signature dishes are a lobster and truffled chicken starter with pasta, and a rum baba with chantilly cream, doused in your choice of rum. Haute cuisine dining is usually a leisurely affair, but a three-course express lunch has recently been added. From this regularly changing choice, we tried a starter of vegetables in spicy tomato sauce, slow-cooked and served in an Alain Ducasse-branded casserole. It had simple yet beautifully balanced flavours, as did a main of roast john dory with a sticky black olive jus. But it's the desserts that are the stars; a rhubarb, strawberry and vanilla millefeuille sang out our meal on a high note.

Booking essential, 2 mths in advance. Children admitted (over 10 years old). Disabled: toilet (hotel). Dress: smart. Separate rooms for parties, seating 8-24. Map 9 G7.

Galvin at Windows

28th floor, London Hilton, Park Lane, W1K 1BE (7208 4021, www.galvinatwindows.com). Green Park or Hyde Park Corner tube. **Lunch served** noon-2.30pm Mon-Fri; 11.45am-3pm Sun. **Dinner served** 6-10.30pm Mon-Wed; 6-11pm Thur-Sat. **Set lunch** £25 2 courses, £29 3 courses (£45 incl half bottle of wine, mineral water and coffee). **Set dinner** £39-£65 3 courses. **Set meal** £85 tasting menu (£125 incl wine). **Credit** AmEx, DC, MC, V.

It might sound like a hair salon, but this is one serious destination restaurant. The stunning panoramic views from the Hilton's 28th floor provide a theatrical backdrop that combines with a beautifully uniformed battery of staff and a glammed-up international clientele to create a real sense of occasion. You can partake in this whether you order from the relatively moderate £39 (£29 at lunch) chef's menu or the £65 prestige menu (both three courses, the latter with more luxurious ingredients). The food is French-influenced, with British and Italian notes;

haute, but not esoterically so, and attractive rather than artsy. Starters of intense gazpacho and poached breast of wood pigeon evidenced good ingredients and technique. Mains showed an affinity for the meaty, such as duck breast with blackcurrant jus teamed with a sausage roll – delicious, but unbalanced. Ratatouille-stuffed courgette (the only vegetarian option) was more allotment overspill than fine dining. The whole was prefaced by good bread and amuse-bouche, accompanied by relaxed but impeccable silver service, and ended with a bill presented with cute marshmallows. The wine list is as high-end and wide-ranging as you'd expect, but refreshed by a 'natural' wines section and good options by the glass; and the digestif trolley positively rattled with vintage armagnacs. Seating is comfortable and well spaced, decor low-key luxurious, and acoustics allow both privacy and buzz; and if prices are perhaps a bit high, then so is the location. You can request a particular aspect when you book: we'd suggest the north side for a romantic sunset behind the Wembley arch.

Available for hire. Babies and children welcome: high chairs. Booking advisable. Disabled: lift; toilet (hotel). Dress: smart casual. Separate room for parties, seats 30. Map 9 G8.

★ Le Gavroche

43 Upper Brook Street, W1K 7QR (7408 0881, www.le-gavroche.co.uk). Marble Arch tube. **Lunch served** noon-2pm Mon-Fri. **Dinner served** 6.30-11pm Mon-Sat. **Main courses** £25-£65. **Set lunch** £51 3 courses incl half bottle of wine, mineral water, coffee. **Set dinner** £100 tasting menu (£158 incl wine). **Credit** AmEx, DC, MC, V.

Le Gavroche's set lunch is famously good value – the £51 charge includes a half bottle of wine, coffee and petits fours – and you'll need to book well ahead to snag a table. Come for dinner, however, and you can expect to pay around £230 for two, much more if you don't keep an eye on the drinks and opt for dishes of luxury ingredients (the fillet of beef is £42.40, and a strawberry tasting dessert is more expensive than some mains). Still, it's not just the prices that add a sense of grandeur. The basement dining room with its green fabric walls, original Picasso's, flashing cloches and air of exclusivity is a great choice for special occasions, and not entirely populated by royalty or the super-rich. Uniformed staff work in hierarchy, but can still be chatty, particularly the knowledgeable sommelier (Gavroche buys all its wines direct from producers), who confidently offered several different recommendations of wine for our disparate choice of dishes. We opted, in the end, for a slightly sparkling white from Corsica. Light, creamy gratin of langoustines and snails made a heavenly start, while salad of roast bone marrow with air-dried ham, croutons and piccalilli dressing proved the kitchen has a grasp of current food trends. Equally modern, yet original, was a pleasing main of john dory with chorizo, wild rice and pickled red pepper. To finish, we returned to the old school for a heady dessert of omelette rothschild with apricot and cointreau compote. In all, a great pleasure, if and when you can afford it.

Available for hire. Babies and children admitted. Booking essential. Dress: jacket; smart jeans accepted; no trainers. Map 9 G7.

★ Greenhouse

27A Hay's Mews, W1J 5NY (7499 3331, www.greenhouserestaurant.co.uk). Green Park tube. **Lunch served** noon-2.30pm Mon-Fri.

Dinner served 6.30-11pm Mon-Sat. **Set lunch** £25 2 courses, £29 3 courses. **Set meal** £65 2 courses, £75 3 courses, £90 tasting menu (£75 vegetarian). **Credit** AmEx, MC, V.

The Greenhouse manages that elusive trick of wearing its Michelin star lightly, while maintaining an unwavering commitment to the standards expected at this level of dining. The restrained and discreet room allows the food to take centre stage. Cooking is French in principle, but Lyon-born chef Antonin Bonnet is unafraid to employ global influences. His playful dishes might see scallops with lime and honey, or Brittany chicken given an almost Thai twist with purple basil, grapefruit and shallots. The kitchen has confidence enough in its ability and sourcing to send out the likes of an artichoke and broad bean salad garnished only with a light vinaigrette, smoked quails' eggs and peppery leaves. Besuited and perfectly mannered staff are adept at reading a table and customising service accordingly; oenophiles will get to know the sommelier well as they get to grips with the spectacular and award-winning 93-page wine list. Differently priced menus make for a real mix of diners: sober-suited Mayfair businessmen won't expect much change from £100 with the à la carte, but the set lunch, at £29 for three courses plus pre- and post- freebies, makes an excellent introduction to the consistently faultless Greenhouse experience.

Available for hire. Babies and children admitted. Booking essential. Disabled: toilet. Dress: smart casual. Separate room for parties, seats 10. Vegetarian menu. Map 9 H7.

★ Hélène Darroze at the Connaught

The Connaught, Carlos Place, W1K 2AL (3147 7200, www.the-connaught.co.uk). Bond Street tube. **Lunch served** noon-2.30pm Tue-Fri. **Dinner served** 6.30-10.15pm Tue-Sat. **Brunch served** 11am-3pm Sat. **Set lunch/brunch** £35 3 courses (£42 incl 2 glasses of wine). **Set meal** £80 3 courses, £85 5 courses, £115 tasting menu. **Credit** AmEx, DC, MC, V.

There's a certain defiance evident in Hélène Darroze's evolving menu. Asian flavours are overt, from tandoori spices, via sarawak and lampong pepper, to gomasio and miso; Scottish salmon is presented as homage to the Japanese architect Tadao Ando. Ingredients and concepts are sourced from Spain and Italy, as well as Britain and Darroze's home ground of south-west France. Design on the plate is intricate, feminine, at times impossibly pretty. Yet it all works as a nicely balanced, entirely enjoyable eating experience – exciting but never needlessly challenging. As such, it matches the Connaught's furnishings beautifully: dark wood softened with olive tones and gold swirls, deeply comfortable chairs and banquettes, elegant tableware. Staff are efficient, as expected, but display a marked absence of froideur, happy to engage in conversation if diners are so inclined. Which all makes for remarkably relaxing high-end dining. The set lunch (notably the wine-inclusive deal, which includes two small glassfuls, to match each savoury course) remains an absolute pleasure. That said, while some dishes appeared seamlessly seasoned and virtually flawless – from a wild mushroom velouté of perfect texture, temperature and woodsiness, via a deceptively simple dish of plump, moreish aubergine ravioli, to a visually stunning revelation of 'blue fish' ceviche (could mackerel conceivably prove so startlingly fresh?) – all was not quite perfect. The fiercely reduced sauce

Pollen Street Social. See p134.

accompanying stuffed tomato seemed out of kilter until diluted by tomato juices, which then rendered the whole thing rather watery. Hashed lamb (and duck and foie gras) filling was a clever take on tradition, but not endlessly exciting. However, the brilliantly textured and nuanced chocolate dessert remains one of the best expressions of chocolate we've encountered. So, a treat, all told.
Available for hire. Babies and children welcome: high chairs. Booking advisable; essential weekends. Disabled: toilet (hotel). Dress: smart; no jeans or trainers. Separate room for parties, seats 20.
Map 9 H7.

Hibiscus
29 Maddox Street, W1S 2PA (7629 2999, www.hibiscusrestaurant.co.uk). Oxford Circus tube.
Lunch served noon-2.30pm Mon-Sat. **Dinner served** 6.30-10pm Mon-Thur; 6-10pm Fri, Sat.
Set lunch £33.50 3 courses, £90 6 courses.
Set dinner £80 3 courses, £100 tasting menu.
Credit AmEx, MC, V.
When Hibiscus first opened, it was stunning, but our recent meal disappointed on many levels. Perhaps this could be put down to the summer holiday season. Undercooked, chewy quail, and veal kidneys with a spaghetti junction of nerves and veins suggested insufficient hands on deck; then again, our Scottish girolles were among the cleanest wild mushrooms we've encountered. Equally dismaying, however, was the sheer failure of Claude Bosi's famously daring combinations of ingredients and concepts to please the palate: toasted rice and fresh and candied almonds provided no crunch or flavour contrast to a bland, creamy 'royale' of supposedly aged parmesan; crushed, minty peas and pistachio lent colour contrast but curiously jarring texture and flavour to a tartare of salmon with coconut velouté; crisped shrimp shells and salty potato wafers proved an umami overload on duck-fat sautéed kidney; and a single, screamingly acidic apricot half drowned out the delicate girolles. On the plus side, we loved the moist granary bread and the faultless desserts. Perfectly poached peach with a frangipane 'stone' was beautifully offset by a delicate almond milk ice; a rich yet flaky bakewell tart with flavour-packed cherry gel indicated an angelic pâtissier. The atmosphere in the olive-toned dining room struck a nice balance between the overtly formal and almost relaxed. Yet a gentle buzz of excitement from a motley crowd, stimulated by successive arrays of startlingly designed crockery, couldn't quite dissipate our sense of sampling food fashioned for the terminally bored. We hope this is a blip as we've enjoyed many meals here in the past.
Babies and children welcome: high chairs. Booking essential. Disabled: toilet. Separate room for parties, seats 18. Vegetarian menu.
Map 9 J6.

Maze
10-13 Grosvenor Square, W1K 6JP (7107 0000, www.gordonramsay.com). Bond Street tube. **Lunch served** noon-2.30pm, **dinner served** 6-10.30pm daily. **Main courses** £10-£30. **Set meal** (lunch daily; 6-7pm, 10-11pm Mon-Thur, Sun) £25 3 dishes (£45 incl wine), £36 4 dishes (£56 incl wine). **Set meal** £70 tasting menu (£125 incl wine). **Credit** AmEx, MC, V.
A quick lunch suggested that this Gordon Ramsay satellite could use a bit of sprucing up. The room remains the same long, low-slung, split-level space,

with decoration unchanged since opening, and the bar still features imaginative (and hugely expensive) cocktails. But the food, though good, just lacked sparkle. There are several options for ordering, of which the most affordable by far is a fixed-price menu of small dishes served at lunch and early evening. That's what we ate, with mixed results. Chilled pea soup with shreds of ham hock and a pea salad was perfectly pleasant, yet not exceptional. An ingenious assembly of marinated beetroot, goat's curd and pine nuts was very tasty but a little too fiddly. The star of the show was salmon served with leek fondue and delectable brown shrimps, dressed with a vinaigrette and horseradish foam – perfectly roasted salmon, well-judged accompaniments. The dish showed that there's talent in the kitchen. Maze was packed on our visit, and always is, according to our waiter. Service is careful and exceptionally friendly. Standard quibble: a pricey wine list, with very little under £40. If and when this pioneering restaurant regains its ability to dazzle and astonish, the wine prices will seem more acceptable. Amusement for geeks: the wine list is presented on an iPad.
Available for hire. Babies and children welcome: high chairs. Booking essential. Disabled: toilet. Dress: smart casual; no trainers. Separate rooms for parties, seating 8, 10 and 40. **Map 9 G6**.

★ Pollen Street Social NEW
2011 WINNER BEST NEW FINE DINING
8 Pollen Street, W1S 1NQ (7290 7600, www.pollenstreetsocial.com). Oxford Circus tube.
Bar Open/tapas served noon-midnight Mon-Sat. **Tapas** £3.50-£16.
Restaurant **Lunch served** noon-2.45pm, **dinner served** 6-10.45pm Mon-Sat. **Main courses** £21-£24.50. **Set lunch** £20 2 courses, £23.50 3 courses.
Both **Credit** AmEx, MC, V.
Jason Atherton, formerly of Maze, has certainly put Pollen Street on the map. The huge Mayfair site comprises large lounge bar and restaurant areas, a dessert bar, a private dining-cum-sommelier's room, showcase kitchen, glass-walled wine cellar and meat-ageing room (apologies if we've forgotten something). The social aspect is best exemplified in the no-bookings bar, where you can order simple, classy tapas, choose from the carte, or just have dessert. Surprisingly, the puddings disappointed on our lunchtime visit. Presentation of the wild strawberry and vanilla cheesecake and lemon meringue with cream cheese and lime sorbet was overwrought, and couldn't hide that the basic recipes simply weren't special enough. But we were bowled over by a stunning black and white starter of cauliflower and squid, which looked almost like risotto, and exquisitely fresh hake with smoked mussels. A generous plate of roast Dingley Dell pork belly and loin with apple, curly kale, mulled brambles and cobnut paste brought intrigue to a classic flavour combination. Service – welcoming, smiling, disarming – was sensational; smooth too. Wines begin at £6.50 a glass or £22 a bottle and there aren't many bottles for under £30, but the cocktails, including some deliciously fruity virgin options, are good. Vegetarians have a dedicated menu featuring dishes such as penne with salsify cream, girolles and summer truffle. PSS is highly welcoming, then, and a must-visit for fans of fine dining, though we've yet to decide whether the gift each customer is given to take home is charming or smarmy.

Hedone

Available for hire. Babies and children welcome (restaurant): high chairs. Booking advisable. Disabled: toilet. Separate room for parties, seats 14. Vegetarian menu. **Map 9 J6**.

Sketch: Lecture Room & Library HOT 50
9 Conduit Street, W1S 2XJ (7659 4500, www.sketch.uk.com). Oxford Circus tube.
Lunch served noon-2.30pm Tue-Fri. **Dinner served** 7-10.30pm Tue-Sat. **Main courses** £35-£55. **Set lunch** £30 2 courses, £35 3 courses, £48 3 courses incl half bottle of wine, mineral water. **Set meal** £95 tasting menu.
Credit AmEx, MC, V.
Of the three main restaurants in the universally expensive Sketch, the Lecture Room & Library offers the best value. The 'gourmet rapide' lunch, at £30 for two courses including coffee, costs less than it did when the place opened in 2002. That's not to say anything here is remotely cheap – à la carte starters average £35, mains £40. But every dish is a fantastically complex yet unified assembly of ingredients, all presented with chef-patron Pierre Gagnaire's trademark attention to detail and subtlety. A starter on the set lunch might include four separate plates: strawberry and tomato soup; grilled sardine with Thai spices and raspberry and sorrel purée; soft-boiled eggs à la bordelaise with grilled leeks; and foie gras with pickled cherries and chocolate. Mains are equally elaborate and just as perfectly executed: 'pig' comes as cocotte of chop with sage; black pudding with aged rum; chard gratin with Ibérico ham; crunchy ear with kimchi and black radish. Service is immaculately mannered, and the room itself still has the power to wow. The handsomely proportioned Georgian space has been sexed up and given a colourful

Maghrebi twist, creating something far removed from the usual beige blah of high-end restaurants. *Available for hire. Babies and children welcome: high chairs. Booking advisable. Dress: smart casual. Separate rooms for parties, seating 24 and 50.* **Map 9 J6.**

The Square
6-10 Bruton Street, W1J 6PU (7495 7100, www.squarerestaurant.com). Bond Street or Green Park tube. **Lunch served** noon-2.15pm Mon-Fri. **Dinner served** 6.30-10pm Mon-Fri; 6.30-10.30pm Sat; 6.30-9.30pm Sun. **Set lunch** £30 2 courses, £35 3 courses. **Set dinner** £65 2 courses, £80 3 courses. **Set meal** £105 tasting menu (£170 incl wine). **Credit** AmEx, MC, V.
A few tables were already occupied when we arrived for a noon booking at Philip Howard's acclaimed Mayfair restaurant. By the time we left,

the place was packed – and this is normal lunchtime trade. Small wonder: even ordering the set lunch, we were bowled over. This may be fancy cooking, but it isn't prissy. Flavours are big and complex, and saucing is exquisite. A plump ravioli of king crab and red mullet sat in a sublime bouillabaisse-flavoured vinaigrette. The savoury velouté under a dazzling assembly of roast rabbit was good enough to drink in a cup. Garnishes are equally well judged. Plaice fillet came with cloud-like mashed potatoes and nuggets of razor clam; beef tartare and carpaccio with beautifully roasted beetroot and exquisite salad leaves. Raspberry crumble tarte with poached white peach and raspberry ripple ice-cream was heavenly. Complaint: the wine list is magnificent and international in scope, but you won't find much under £40. Complaint: a very slight clumsiness from some waiters; one kept saying 'you're

welcome' even when we hadn't said 'thank you'. The room is large, but has just 65 covers, which means plenty of space between tables. Some will find the decor impersonal, but you'll probably be focusing on the food – and you won't find it wanting. *Available for hire. Babies and children admitted. Booking advisable. Disabled: toilet. Dress: smart; smart jeans accepted; no trainers. Separate room for parties, seats 18.* **Map 9 H7.**

Piccadilly

The Ritz
150 Piccadilly, W1J 9BR (7493 8181, www.theritzhotel.co.uk). Green Park tube. *Bar* **Open** 11.30am-midnight Mon-Sat; noon-10.30pm Sun. *Restaurant* **Breakfast served** 7-10am Mon-Sat; 8-10am Sun. **Lunch served** 12.30-2.30pm daily. **Tea served** (reserved sittings) 11.30am, 1.30pm, 3.30pm, 5.30pm, 7.30pm daily. **Dinner served** 5.30-10.30pm Mon-Sat; 7-10pm Sun. **Main courses** £37-£49. **Set lunch** £39 3 courses. **Set tea** £40. **Set dinner** £48 3 courses, £65 4 courses; (Fri, Sat) £95 4 courses. *Both* **Credit** AmEx, MC, V.
Tell someone you're going to the Ritz and the reaction will probably be an admiring gasp – the famous hotel still carries an enviable reputation. Its public dining room is perhaps the most spectacularly gilded in London. This, along with the courteous, formal service and the sense of theatre (the cloched plates, the silverware, the coat-tailed waiters) must be what keeps the place so popular with foreign businessmen, celebrating families and elderly lunchers – because it's not the food. A few modern touches enliven the proficient and rich classical French dishes, although Londoners used to fine-dining restaurants will find the cooking unremarkable and anachronistic (along with the dress policy: 'gentlemen' must arrive jacketed and tied and remain so for the duration). On our recent visit, both a starter of scallops with pea purée and a main of braised halibut with spring veg were victims of over-enthusiastic salting. The cost too is offputting: £39 at lunch for three courses (although this includes service); the wine list has no glasses below £10 and no bottles below £50. The Ritz without doubt still has a place in London, but sensible diners will find far better places to part with their cash.
Babies and children welcome: children's menu; high chairs. Booking advisable restaurant; essential afternoon tea. Dress: jacket and tie; no jeans or trainers. Entertainment: dinner dance Fri, Sat (restaurant); pianist daily. Separate rooms for parties, seating 16-60. Tables outdoors (8, terrace). **Map 9 J7.**

West
Chiswick

Hedone [NEW]
2011 RUNNER-UP BEST NEW FINE DINING
301-303 Chiswick High Road, W4 4HH (8747 0377, www.hedonerestaurant.com). Chiswick Park tube. **Lunch served** 12.30-2.15pm Fri, Sat. **Dinner served** 6.30-10pm Tue-Sat. **Set lunch** £30 3 courses, £40 4 courses, £50 5 courses. **Set dinner** £50 4 courses, £60 5 courses, £70 6 courses. **Credit** AmEx, MC, V.

Rarely does a fine restaurant appear with such clarity of vision. Mikael Jonsson's Hedone, although undeniably a haute cuisine establishment, is on par with Fergus Henderson's St John and Nico Ladenis's first Queenstown Road restaurant, Chez Nico, both for its culinary single-mindedness and bold choice of location. The almost-Gunnersbury site is mostly delightful (the lack of loos will be sorted with downstairs refurbishment, they told us) with an atelier-style open kitchen, soft touch-me banquettes, and a sophisticated Nordic-leaning decor of blonde wood, red tiles and open brickwork; the illustrated ceiling is charming. The limited-choice menu increases in price according to the number of courses you order. Things began well with exceptionally good sourdough. Tart of ceps, thyme and coffee jelly was breathtaking, as was the john dory, exquisitely fresh and cooked just-so. We also liked the aged beef with braised endive and a dessert of chilli-marmalade chocolate bar, but the too-plain blueberry tart was something a *BBC Good Food* reader could knock out confidently. And, for a chef reportedly obsessed with ingredient quality, our cheeseboard was blah and meanly portioned. We have mixed feelings about the wine list too – it's all good, but hardly kind – and, on our most recent visit, the sommelier was a little cavalier, which resulted in him bringing the wrong bottle. A terrific debut then, but not without faults.
Available for hire. Babies and children welcome: high chairs; nappy-changing facilities. Booking advisable. Disabled: toilet. Dress: smart casual.

Westbourne Grove

★ The Ledbury `HOT 50`
127 Ledbury Road, W11 2AQ (7792 9090, www.theledbury.com). Westbourne Park tube. **Lunch served** noon-2.30pm Tue-Sat; noon-3pm Sun. **Dinner served** 6.30-10.30pm Mon-Sat; 7-10pm Sun. **Set lunch** (Tue-Sat) £27.50 2 courses, £33.50 3 courses; (Sun) £40 3 courses. **Set dinner** £75 3 courses, £95 tasting menu. **Credit** AmEx, MC, V.
There are few chefs that produce a set menu of dishes that you want to try as much as their à la carte, but the Ledbury's Brett Graham – an Australian in the quiet achiever mould – does so as a matter of routine. This makes securing a table at lunchtime as difficult as snaring one for dinner, despite the edge-of-Notting Hill location. Dishes change seasonally and according to availability of ingredients – we were delighted by a special of scallop ceviche with shaved fennel, seaweed-flavoured oil and a fluffy pile of frozen horseradish – though there are signature components that appear regularly, such as celeriac baked in ash. Our meal contained many thrills: grilled mackerel with avocado, mustard and shiso was relatively simple, but the combination of flavours was astonishingly good. Crisp-skinned cod came with a hint of buckwheat, nasturtium and umami-packed smoked eel brandade. By the time (superb) lovage ice-cream appeared with pavé of milk chocolate, we were prepared to hail Graham as London's cleverest chef. Service was friendly, though occasionally absent-minded (we had to nag for more bread and our petits fours) and the wait between courses was so long the kitchen sent out an extra dish to ease the pain. The beer list is a treat, but don't expect any bargains on Australian wine – few bottles cost under £30.
Available for hire. Babies and children admitted. Booking essential. Disabled: toilet. Tables outdoors (9, terrace). **Map 19 C3**.

South West
Chelsea

★ Gordon Ramsay
68 Royal Hospital Road, SW3 4HP (7352 4441, www.gordonramsay.com). Sloane Square tube. **Lunch served** noon-2.15pm, **dinner served** 6.30-10.15pm Mon-Fri. **Set lunch** £45 3 courses. **Set meal** £90 3 courses, £120 tasting menu. **Credit** AmEx, DC, MC, V.
'It's supposed to be fun.' The words came from a senior waiter when we praised the service that makes eating here such a profound pleasure. The staff treated us royally, even though we were clearly the lowest-spending customers in the place. The carte is replete with luxuries, but the set lunch menu creates splendour from relatively humble ingredients. Ravioli of smoked potato and a poached egg, served on crushed peas and broad beans, was startling and sublime. Shin of beef was braised to melting tenderness, shredded, and served inside a cylinder of paper-thin pastry with layers of confit potatoes and a topping of creamed mushrooms. Slow-cooked belly of pork came with heavenly garnishes including choucroute and a wedge of the best black pudding on earth. A dessert juxtaposing banana parfait with peanut butter mousse, bitter chocolate and caramelised bananas created perfect harmony from contrasting flavours and textures. In a league of its own: a starter combining Sichuan pork, prawns and tiny morsels of assorted vegetables – each ingredient had thrillingly intense flavour. The atmosphere in the small, quietly elegant room was jolly, not hushed or reverential. Staff chatted with customers; customers chatted across the tables. The complaint, as ever, is the wine list: hardly anything under £40. Apart from that, we found nothing to fault. This is a great restaurant, and it's fun.
Available for hire. Booking essential. Children admitted. Dress: smart; jacket preferred.
Map 14 F12.
For branch see index.

East
Bethnal Green

★ Viajante `HOT 50`
Town Hall Hotel, Patriot Square, E2 9NF (7871 0461, www.viajante.co.uk). Bethnal Green tube or Cambridge Heath rail. **Lunch served** noon-2pm Wed-Sun. **Dinner served** 6-9.30pm daily. **Set lunch** £28 3 courses (£46 with wine), £50 6 courses (£90 with wine), £70 9 courses (£130 with wine). **Set dinner** £65 6 courses (£115 with wine), £90 12 courses (£170 with wine). **Credit** AmEx, MC, V.
The hottest table in town a year or so ago, Bethnal Green's Viajante remains a fun destination for style-conscious gastronauts. Nuno Mendes's cooking is creative and forward-looking, yet firmly rooted in tradition and peasant foodways (he worked on the family's farm in Portugal). His native cuisine plays a part, but Japanese, Thai and South American flavours are just as likely to appear, as do molecular gastronomy ideas. Opt for three, six or nine courses at lunch, six or 12 at dinner – it's generally worth splashing out on the wine pairings, which add an extra £18 to £80 to the meal depending on how many dishes you're having. Seafood typically appears in many forms, and is a strong suit. Raw mackerel is not to everyone's taste, but here was sensationally matched with sour cherries and lettuce. Yuzu-flavoured crab came wrapped like cannelloni in a sheet of spiced milk, and garnished with tobiko (flying fish roe) and basil purée – thrilling. Eyebrows raised with the slightly sticky texture of cod tripe, but topped with onion and filaments of crispy potato, the dish took on a wonderfully comforting quality that continued, though in a different vein, with acorn-fed Iberian pork loin served (by Mendes himself) with cereal grains and almond cream. Treats of frozen marzipan with celery and lime (it worked), and foam-topped strawberries with stracciatella and pine finished the colourful procession. Not every dish here is delicious (a canapé of potatoes with yeast and black olives was, to our palates, hideous), but it's unfailingly interesting.
Booking advisable. Children admitted over 11yrs. Disabled: toilet. Separate room for parties, seats 22.

Outer London
Richmond, Surrey

The Bingham
61-63 Petersham Road, Richmond, Surrey, TW10 6UT (8940 0902, www.thebingham.co.uk). Richmond tube/rail. **Breakfast served** 7-10am Mon-Fri; 8-10am Sat, Sun. **Lunch served** noon-2.15pm Mon-Sat; 12.30-4pm Sun. **Dinner served** 7-10pm Mon-Thur; 6.30-10.30pm Fri, Sat. **Set lunch** £22.50 2 courses, £26 3 courses. **Set meal** £55 3 courses, £75 tasting menu (£125 incl wine). **Credit** AmEx, DC, MC, V.
This boutique hotel makes the most of its geographical serendipity – the views over the Thames from its terrace are sublime. Dining takes place in a chic room with twinkling chandeliers and flourishes of caramel leather and gold velour. Service is young and a little green; the staff's relaxed manner does much to lighten the formality. Head chef Shay Cooper has devised several menus, ranging from a two-course set lunch to a seven-course tasting menu; there's even a children's menu. The setting could easily overshadow the food, but we found much to enjoy from the kitchen. Own-made breads followed by an agreeable foie gras parfait with apple and elderflower foam was a fine start. We also relished the flavours and textures of roast quail with soft cep custard, crunchy artichoke and morsels of luscious black garlic. Less thrilling were the indifferent ingredients used in a dish of hake fillet with chickpea gnocchi, squid, samphire, and red pepper reduction. Portions are modest, but the dishes arrive attractively presented without being too dressy. Vanilla panna cotta came with poached rhubarb, rhubarb sorbet and a little vacherin: a winning combination that was superbly rounded off by a ravishing rhubarb and ginger consommé. The diverse wine list contains the odd affordable bottle and a good selection by the glass. We left with our spirits lifted; the Bingham is a tonic for the stresses of daily life.
Babies and children welcome: children's menu; high chairs; nappy-changing facilities. Booking advisable Thur-Sun. Disabled: toilet. Dress: smart casual. Separate room for parties, seats 90. Tables outdoors (8, balcony).

Indian

We call this section 'Indian', but it includes restaurants specialising in most of the cuisines of the subcontinent: Pakistani, Sri Lankan, the diaspora cooking of Indians in East Africa and, of course, the regions that make up the modern state of India. No matter what your taste – smoky grilled meats, fruity vegetarian curries, Keralan seafood, regal birianis or contemporary creative cooking – London will have an estimable exponent, and the capital's best places hold their own against any in the world, including those on the subcontinent itself.

Fine dining establishments have dominated the city's Indian restaurant scene over the past few years, but this is one cuisine where price bears little relationship to quality. If delicious authenticity is your aim, you can eat very well very cheaply indeed. Places such as **Apollo Banana Leaf**, **Lahore Kebab House** and **Ram's** beat several of their glossier counterparts when it came to rating meals this year. Furthermore, thanks to **Masala Zone**, **Dishoom** and Islington's new **Delhi Grill**, India's street-food snacks and café culture have moved from traditional community areas such as Southall, Wembley and Tooting to the mainstream – a trend that we hope continues. If you're looking for a smarter spot for business or a special occasion, you'll be pleased to hear that our favourite restaurants this year also include stalwart performers **Rasa Samudra**, **Moti Mahal** and the **Cinnamon Club**, which are all centrally located.

Central
Covent Garden

Dishoom
12 Upper St Martin's Lane, WC2H 9FB *(7420 9320, www.dishoom.com). Covent Garden or Leicester Square tube.* **Meals served** 8am-11pm Mon-Fri; 10am-11pm Sat; 10am-10pm Sun. **Main courses** £1.70-£10.50. **Credit** AmEx, MC, V. Pan-Indian
Dishoom ticks many design characteristics of the Victorian Irani cafés of Bombay, but occupies a new, purpose-built development near Covent Garden, so lacks any ageing charm. The feel is clever and corporate rather than soulful or stylish, but it's clean, well run and handy. More good news: the kitchen generally lives up to the promise of the tempting menu, which runs from breakfast via lunchtime roti wraps to small plates to share over pre-theatre cocktails, and wind-down beers and ruby murray. Connoisseurs of Irani cafés will relish the keema pau (spiced minced lamb on a Portuguese-style bread roll), chilli cheese toast, house black dal and Indian soft drinks, but Dishoom's Anglo innovations are welcome too. Bacon and sausages seasoned with sweetly fiery chilli jam and fresh coriander appear in naan breakfast rolls, and alongside the piquant Bombay omelette. Fruit roomali (crêpe-like roti bread stuffed with fresh fruits, mascarpone and honey) was more reminiscent of international health spa cuisine than anything we've ordered in India, but the masala chai is strong and satisfying enough to convert an espresso fiend – and you can buy it to take away. There's usually no need to book and, come evening, they won't take reservations for fewer than six. *Babies and children welcome: high chairs. Bookings not accepted for fewer than 6 after 5pm. Disabled: toilet. Tables outdoors (7, pavement). Takeaway service.* **Map 18 D4**.

★ Moti Mahal
45 Great Queen Street, WC2B 5AA (7240 9329, www.motimahal-uk.com). Covent Garden or Holborn tube. **Lunch served** noon-3pm Mon-Fri. **Dinner served** 5.30-11pm Mon-Sat. **Main courses** £9-£28. **Set lunch** £15-£20. **Set dinner** £25-£56. **Credit** AmEx, MC, V. Modern Indian
Since 2005, chef Anirudh Arora's elegant restaurant has flown the Tiranga for top-class Indian food. Initial impressions are of innocuous, classic fine dining – cream banquettes, heavy napery, a legion of slick staff – but the dining room isn't so formal as to deter tourists roaming Covent Garden with backpacks and comfy shoes. The staff's tendency to upsell a bit too enthusiastically is our only criticism, along with the fact that it's easy to part with a load of cash here. Appealing lunch and dinner deals represent value for money – although the heavily marked-up wine list should be approached with caution. However the most important aspect, the food, is almost beyond reproach: sophisticated and complex, with a respect for the immense variations of cuisines that come under the heading 'Indian'. Familiar curries such as rogan josh and murgh makhani are reimagined with new subtleties; the 'Grand Trunk Road' à la carte offers imaginative versions of regional dishes such as katli (stuffed aubergine with pear chutney, from the Punjab), or Lucknow keema kaleji (chicken liver and lamb with black cardamom and ginger). A meal here, from beginning to end, is hard to fault. *Available for hire. Babies and children welcome: high chairs. Booking advisable dinner. Dress: smart casual. Tables outdoors (5, pavement). Vegetarian menu.* **Map 18 E3**.

Sitaaray
167 Drury Lane, WC2B 5PG (7269 6422, www.sitaaray.com). Covent Garden or Holborn tube. **Lunch served** noon-3pm, **dinner served** 5.30-11pm Mon-Sat. **Set lunch** £14.50 2 courses. **Set dinner** (5.30-7pm) £14.50-£16.50 2 courses, £22.95 buffet. **Credit** MC, V. Pan-Indian

INDIAN

Dishoom. See p137.

INDIAN

'Bollywood or bust' might be a more apt title for this extraordinary little duplex dedicated to Indian film. Enter Sitaaray's ground floor or mezzanine and you're assailed by dance music and movie clips from plentiful flatscreen TVs. Take a seat in the boudoir-like interior and prepare to be assailed by food. Though there are à la carte options, the buffet deal is the draw. Warning bells should sound: belt-busting feeds in theme joints rarely cause gastronomic joy – but they do here. Sitaaray's feast includes eight portions of kebabs and snacks, served à point by ultra-competent staff. Best are the amritsari fish (exquisitely fresh in its crisp batter), the pâté-like disc of peppered lamb kebab, and the expertly seared dill chicken tikka. Then comes the main course: thali-sized pots of creamy makhani dal, delicious mixed veg in a fenugreek-based masala, and… chicken tikka masala (why?). More is offered should you stagger to a completion. We had no complaint about any dish, though the meal was unbalanced (too much chicken, not enough vegetables): come with friends and make sure some order the vegetarian version of the feast. Desserts are an impossibility, but try to find space for a movie-themed cocktail.

Babies and children admitted. Booking advisable dinner. Disabled: toilet. Takeaway service. **Map 18 E3**.

Fitzrovia

★ Rasa Samudra HOT 50
5 Charlotte Street, W1T 1RE (7637 0222, www.rasarestaurants.com). Goodge Street tube. **Lunch served** noon-3pm Mon-Sat. **Dinner served** 6-10.30pm Mon-Wed, Sun; 6-10.45pm Thur-Sat. **Main courses** £6.50-£12.95. **Set meal** £22.50 vegetarian, £30 seafood. **Credit** AmEx, MC, V. South Indian
The eight London restaurants in the Rasa chain peerlessly recreate the intricacies and colour of South Indian food, but this remains the flagship. In service and style, it's the smartest of the group (as befits its position on the business-lunch hotspot of Charlotte Street), with a vibrant pink colour scheme adorned by statues, paintings and ornaments from the subcontinent. As well as the vegetarian cooking

of the south-western state of Kerala that Rasa does so well, Samudra specialises in seafood. It's hard not to order too much: just about everything on the menu reads delightfully. Begin with snacks such as pappadavadai (popadoms fried with cumin and sesame seeds), then move on to starters proper, such as Mysore bonda (fried potato balls with chilli, ginger and cashew nuts) or crab thoran. The main-course fish dishes are superb – try fiery varutharacha meen curry (tilapia fillet in roasted coconut, tamarind and red chilli gravy) – or mop up a yoghurty beet cheera pachadi (beetroot and spinach) with one of the spiced breads. The indecisive, or the more impecunious, should go for the vegetarian or seafood 'feasts'. Round the back, on Rathbone Street, is Rasa Express W1, where a superb vegetarian meal box to eat in or take away costs an astounding £3.50.
Babies and children welcome: high chairs. Booking advisable. Separate rooms for parties, seating 12-25. Takeaway service. Vegan dishes. Vegetarian menu. **Map 17 B1**.
For branches (Rasa, Rasa Express, Rasa Maricham, Rasa Mudra, Rasa Travancore, Rasa W1) see index.

Knightsbridge

Amaya HOT 50
Halkin Arcade, Motcomb Street, SW1X 8JT (7823 1166, www.amaya.biz). Knightsbridge tube. **Lunch served** 12.30-2.15pm Mon-Sat; 12.45-2.45pm Sun. **Dinner served** 6.30-11.30pm Mon-Sat; 6.30-10.30pm Sun. **Main courses** £19-£24. **Set lunch** £19.50-£32. **Set dinner** £42-£70 tasting menu. **Credit** AmEx, DC, MC, V. Modern Indian
There's no doubt that Amaya has style. It's a seductively romantic venue, the shiny black granite floor, rosewood furnishings and muted lighting lending an upmarket vibe to proceedings, enhanced by views of chefs in action at the grill, tandoor and griddle. Part of the same group as Chutney Mary, Veeraswamy and the Masala Zone chain, the restaurant has gained acclaim for its splendid grazing menu: the fresh, light flavours of the salads and relishes, and the array of bite-sized delicacies.

Signature dishes include shredded mango and green papaya piled into lettuce cups; crunchy, lightly smoked and seared broccoli florets partnered by sweet yoghurt; and dori kebab (velvety textured pounded lamb on a skewer, spiced with ginger and cardamom, and grilled over coals). We love the chicken morsels, steeped in fragrant paprika before being seared in a clay oven. Sadly, on our last two trips here, we noticed a drop in quality both in cooking and service. Watercress and spinach griddle cakes stuffed with chopped figs, although tasty, were served cold, and our much-anticipated biriani wasn't quite as aromatic with sweet spices as on earlier visits. Staff can be harried too. Amaya is a world-class restaurant – let's hope top-class service is resumed soon.
Booking advisable. Children admitted until 8pm. Disabled: toilet. Dress: smart casual. Separate room for parties, seats 14. **Map 9 G9**.

Haandi
7 Cheval Place, SW7 1EW (7823 7373, www.haandi-restaurants.com). Knightsbridge tube. **Lunch served** noon-3pm daily. **Dinner served** 5.30-11pm Mon-Thur, Sun; 5.30-11.30pm Fri, Sat. **Main courses** £6-£16. **Set lunch** £11.95. **Credit** AmEx, MC, V. East African Indian
Haandi is well established across East Africa, and now has a brace of branches in London. There are two separate entrances to the Knightsbridge restaurant (the one on Cheval Place is a better bet for parking if you're coming by car). The dimly lit and rather old-fashioned dining room is decked out with potted plants and cane chairs; the centrepiece is the glass-fronted kitchen where you can enjoy watching the chefs hard at work. Prices for the homely Punjabi cooking are fair, especially for such a smart neighbourhood, and the set lunch is good value at £11.95. We can never resist the tandoori lamb chops; the juiciness of the meat and the smoky flavour had us fighting over the last remaining piece. Vegetarian dishes are generally a safe bet; whole baby aubergines cooked in onion masala was tasty, although chewy ladies fingers let down a bhindi masala. Succulent prawns lababdar arrived with tomatoes and onions; the dish was

Moti Mahal. See p137.

INDIAN

lifted by coriander. Nans and popadoms were less thrilling. Pistachio kulfi is a good way to end a meal here. Service was spotty, and has a way to go. *Available for hire. Babies and children admitted. Booking advisable. Separate room for parties, seats 30. Takeaway service; delivery service (over £10 within 2-mile radius).* **Map 14 E9**. **For branch see index**.

Marylebone

★ Roti Chai NEW

3-4 Portman Mews South, W1H 6HS (7408 0101, www.rotichai.com). Marble Arch tube. **Meals served** noon-10.30pm Mon-Sat. **Main courses** £4.50-£8.50. **Credit** AmEx, MC, V. Pan-Indian

Spacious new brasserie Roti Chai takes its name from those most humble of fuel foods – 'bread' and 'tea' – and aims to transform the everyday into a style statement. The pared-back decor, a quirky mix of industrial chic and cleverly presented Indian groceries, will appeal to both hipsters and nostalgic Indians. The youthful staff are friendly, and know their stuff. Street snacks are to the fore. Bhel puri – puffed rice, tossed with diced onions and coriander, cloaked in a sweet-sour tamarind sauce spiked with cumin – was crunchy and delicious. Lightly textured dokhla (a Gujarati savoury sponge made from ground chickpea flour spiced with mustard seeds) arrived warm from the steamer, and paired well with coconut chutney. Chickpea curry, a Punjabi classic, was outstanding for its smoky character – a marvellous complement to the base of golden-hued onions fried with astringent ginger and garam masala. Not everything worked: minced chicken, simmered with livers, veered towards blandness. Steamy masala chai (served in chunky glass tumblers) was authentically milky, with lovely cinnamon and ginger notes. There's also a small array of decent wines by the glass, and a basement bar is promised soon. *Available for hire. Babies and children welcome: high chairs; nappy-changing facilities. Bookings. Disabled: toilet. Vegan dishes. Vegetarian menu.* **Map 9 G6**.

★ Trishna London

15-17 Blandford Street, W1U 3DG (7935 5624, www.trishnalondon.com). Bond Street tube. **Lunch served** noon-2.45pm Mon-Sat; 12.30-3.15pm Sun. **Dinner served** 6-10.45pm Mon-Sat; 6.30-9.45pm Sun. **Main courses** £8-£20. **Set lunch** £15 2 courses, £18 3 courses, £21 4 courses. **Set dinner** (6-6.30pm Mon-Sat; 6.30-7pm Sun) £20 4 courses. **Credit** AmEx, MC, V. South Indian

Urbane, multinational staff and customers, double-fronted premises decked out with oak flooring and taupe or whitewashed brick walls, and a menu of inventive, exquisitely presented south-west Indian coastal dishes place Trishna in the top bracket of subcontinental dining in the capital. It's a branch of a Mumbai restaurant, but influences owe more to Mod Euro sources. Though prices are high, the £20 four-course early-evening meal is a belter: full of good ideas and good food. After popadoms and decent chutneys, we were treated to a playful pastiche of fish and chips (matchstick potatoes, breadcrumbed ultra-fresh pollock and crushed peas topped with mustard seeds and curry leaf); guinea fowl tikka well-teamed with nutty green lentils boosted by fennel seeds and star anise; a main course of sea bass in a sublime coconutty sauce,

Pan-Indian menu

Spellings of Indian dishes vary widely; dishes such as gosht may appear in several versions on different menus as the word is transliterated from (in this case) Hindi. There are umpteen languages and several scripts in the Indian subcontinent, the most commonly seen on London menus being Punjabi, Hindi, Bengali and Gujarati. For the sake of consistency, however, we have tried to adhere to uniform spellings. The following are common throughout the subcontinent.

Aloo: potato.
Ayre: a white fish much used in Bengali cuisine.
Baingan: aubergine.
Bateira, batera or **bater**: quail.
Bengali: Bengal, before Partition in 1947, was a large province covering Calcutta (now in India's West Bengal) and modern-day Bangladesh. 'Bengali' and 'Bangladeshi' cooking is quite different, and the term 'Bengali' is often misused in London's Indian restaurants.
Bhajee: vegetables cooked with spices, usually 'dry' rather than sauced.
Bhajia or **bhaji**: vegetables dipped in chickpea-flour batter and deep-fried; also called pakoras.
Bhatura: deep-fried doughy discs.
Bhindi: okra.
Brinjal: aubergine.
Bulchao or **balchao**: a Goan vinegary pickle made with small dried prawns (with shells) and lots of garlic.
Chana or **channa**: chickpeas.
Chapati: a flat wholewheat griddle bread.
Chat or **chaat**: various savoury snacks featuring combinations of pooris (qv), diced onion and potato, chickpeas, crumbled samosas and pakoras, chutneys and spices.
Dahi: yoghurt.
Dahl or **dal**: a lentil curry similar to thick lentil soup. Countless regional variations exist.
Dhansak: a Parsi (qv) casserole of meat, lentils and vegetables, with a mix of hot and tangy flavours.
Dhaniya: coriander.
Ghee: clarified butter used for frying.
Gobi: cauliflower.
Gosht, josh or **ghosh**: meat, usually lamb.
Gram flour: chickpea flour.
Kachori: crisp pastry rounds with spiced mung dal or pea filling.
Lassi: a yoghurt drink, ordered with salt or sugar, sometimes with fruit. Ideal to quench a fiery palate.
Machi or **machli**: fish.
Masala or **masaladar**: mixed spices.
Methi: fenugreek, either dried (seeds) or fresh (green leaves).
Murgh or **murg**: chicken.
Mutter, muter or **mattar**: peas.

Nan or **naan**: teardrop-shaped flatbread cooked in a tandoor.
Palak or **paalak**: spinach; also called saag.
Paan or **pan**: betel leaf stuffed with chopped 'betel nuts', coconut and spices such as fennel seeds, and folded into a triangle. Available sweet or salty, and eaten at the end of a meal as a digestive.
Paneer or **panir**: Indian cheese, a bit like tofu in texture and taste.
Paratha: a large griddle-fried bread that is sometimes stuffed (with spicy mashed potato or minced lamb, for instance).
Parsi or **Parsee**: a religious minority based in Mumbai, but originally from Persia, renowned for its cooking.
Pilau, pillau or **pullao**: flavoured rice cooked with meat or vegetables. In most British Indian restaurants, pilau rice is simply rice flavoured and coloured with turmeric or (rarely) saffron.
Poori or **puri**: a disc of deep-fried wholewheat bread; the frying makes it puff up like an air-filled cushion.
Popadom, poppadom, papadum or **papad**: large thin wafers made with lentil paste, and flavoured with pepper, garlic or chilli. Eaten in the UK with pickles and relishes as a starter while waiting for the meal to arrive.
Raita: a yoghurt mix, usually with cucumber.
Roti: a round, sometimes unleavened, bread, thicker than a chapati and cooked in a tandoor or griddle. Roomali roti is a very thin, soft disc of roti.
Saag or **sag**: spinach; also called palak.
Tamarind: the pods of this East African tree, grown in India, are made into a paste that imparts a sour, fruity taste – popular in some regional cuisines, including Gujarati and South Indian.
Thali: literally 'metal plate'. A large plate with rice, bread, metal containers of dal and vegetable curries, pickles and yoghurt.
Vadai or **wada**: a spicy vegetable or lentil fritter; **dahi wada** are lentil fritters soaked in yoghurt, topped with tamarind and date chutneys.
Vindaloo: originally, a hot and spicy pork curry from Goa that should authentically be soured with vinegar and cooked with garlic. In London restaurants, the term is usually misused to signify simply very hot dishes.
Xacuti: a Goan dish made with lamb or chicken pieces, coconut and a complex mix of roasted then ground spices.

THREE OF THE VERY BEST
INDIAN RESTAURANTS

AMAYA

This award winning, Michelin starred, restaurant presents an unmistakable experience for lunch and dinner in Belgravia.

Halkin Arcade, Motcomb Street
Knightsbridge, London SW1

Telephone: 020 7823 1166

CHUTNEY MARY

The rich setting, interesting art and romantic candle lighting are secondary details in London's temple of great Indian food.

535 Kings Road
Chelsea, London SW10

Telephone: 020 7351 3113

VEERASWAMY

Divine dishes, lovingly prepared and beautifully served in sumptuous surroundings overlooking Regent Street.

Mezzanine Floor, Victory House
99 Regent Street, London W1

Telephone: 020 7734 1401

For outside catering, please contact our Head Office on 020 7724 2525
www.realindianfood.com

plus side dishes of dal, and spinach dotted with sweetcorn; then a dessert of carrot halva matched with lychee sorbet. Wine is taken seriously, with flights suggested for each set meal and a formidable Old World-centric list. Perhaps the sea bass was a mite overcooked, but we're pushed to think of any other complaints. Small wonder the place buzzed like a hive on a rainy Monday evening.

Available for hire. Babies and children welcome: high chairs. Booking advisable evenings. Separate room for parties, seats 12. Tables outdoors (3, patio). Vegetarian menu. **Map 9 G5.**

Mayfair

Benares

12A Berkeley Square House, Berkeley Square, W1J 6BS (7629 8886, www.benaresrestaurant. com). Green Park tube. **Lunch served** noon-2.30pm Mon-Sat; noon-3pm Sun. **Dinner served** 5.30-10.30pm Mon-Sat; 6-10pm Sun. **Main courses** £24-£54. **Set meal** (lunch, 5.30-6.30pm) £20 2 courses, £25 3 courses. **Credit** AmEx, DC, MC, V. Modern Indian

The Berkeley Square location, between a luxury car showroom and a bank, tells you much you need to know about Atul Kochhar's Benares. Even the most out-of-touch super-rich customer wouldn't mistake it for a curry house, such is the effort put into making this a fine dining experience, but somewhere here they seem to have forgotten the importance of hospitality. A swarm of uniformed waiters working to a pretentious hierarchy was irritating and inefficient; the host at a neighbouring table ticked one off for being rude. We felt pressured to order more drinks than we wanted, and an unrequested bottle of water was opened and placed at the centre of our table. The cooking, at least, was very good, with the superb quality of ingredients shining through, despite tidgy portion sizes. We have fond memories of the elegant rogan josh, though most of the menus (there are five or so) offer more contemporary creations, such as steamed chutney sole with 'textures of coconut', and tandoori pigeon with vanilla beetroot and beet purée. We'd gladly return to the lively cocktail bar, which hummed with happy customers, for delicious concoctions such as the Mumbai martini flavoured with ginger and curry leaves.

Available for hire. Babies and children welcome: high chairs. Booking advisable. Disabled: toilet. Dress: smart casual. Separate rooms for parties, seating 14, 22 and 30. Takeaway service. **Map 9 H7.**

Tamarind

20-22 Queen Street, W1J 5PR (7629 3561, www.tamarindrestaurant.com). Green Park tube. **Lunch served** noon-2.45pm Mon-Fri, Sun. **Dinner served** 5.30-11pm Mon-Sat; 6-10.45pm Sun. **Main courses** £17.95-£24. **Set lunch** (Mon-Fri) £17.50 2 courses, £19.50 3 courses, £28 tasting menu. **Set dinner** (5.30-6.45pm, 10.30-11pm) £27.50 3 courses. **Credit** AmEx, DC, MC, V. Pan-Indian

Popular with business groups and wealthy tourists, this smart, spacious basement venue is furnished in subdued, earthy colours, offset by crisp white napery and speckled mirrors. Cooking is traditional rather than flamboyant, with a focus on North Indian spice blends, tandoori kebabs and grilled meats. A first course of shaped, skewered lamb mince, grilled over coals, was memorable for its toasted cumin and ginger spicing, and hits of chilli

and crunchy red onion. We were also impressed with the chaat: crunchy pastry discs, topped with sweet yoghurt, tamarind chutney, chickpeas, blueberries and mint relish. Main courses, however, were merely average. Chicken chunks in a tomato and red pepper sauce lacked the hoped-for astringency of pounded coriander seeds and cracked peppercorns, while the yellow dal was extremely bland – more suited to invalid food than fine dining. Things picked up with a vegetarian main course of soft paneer cubes and peppers tossed in a creamy tomato sauce, but we couldn't detect any nuttiness from the promised melon-seed spicing. Service is spot-on and professional, which helps compensate for the uneven cooking. We've had better meals in the past at this long-established and acclaimed restaurant.

Babies and children welcome: children's menu; high chairs. Booking essential. Takeaway service. Vegan dishes. Vegetarian menu. **Map 9 H7.**

Veeraswamy

Mezzanine Floor, Victory House, 99-101 Regent Street, entrance on Swallow Street, W1B 4RS (7734 1401, www.veeraswamy.com). Piccadilly Circus tube. **Lunch served** noon-2.30pm Mon-Fri; 12.30-2.45pm Sat, Sun. **Dinner served** 5.30-10.45pm Mon-Sat; 6-10.15pm Sun. **Main courses** £15-£32. **Set meal** (lunch, 5.30-6.30pm Mon-Sat) £17.75 2 courses; (lunch Sun) £24 3 courses. **Set dinner** £45 tasting menu. **Credit** AmEx, DC, MC, V. Pan-Indian

Billed as London's oldest surviving Indian restaurant, Veeraswamy remains a destination for tourists and corporate types on elastic expense accounts. A lift (accessed by a narrow entrance) whisks diners to an expansive, airy first floor overlooking Regent Street. Decor is a mix of colourful hanging lamps, ornate chandeliers and memorabilia from a bygone era. Even on our weekday supper, most tables were full and the restaurant buzzed with conversation. Yet all is not rosy here: the food is expensive and we're not convinced the current quality of cooking meets expectations. Lamb rogan josh was fine (miniature shanks of lamb on the bone, simmered in an aromatic masala featuring mild kashmiri chillies), making a great match with the hot breads – our only complaint, the stingy portions of naan and parathas. Chicken dopiaza was more disappointing; although the chicken pieces were succulent, the addition of pickled slivers of harsh-tasting lemon preserve overshadowed any delicate spicing. Puddings were also a let-down. Tandoori nectarine wedges, dunked in a jam-like berry sauce, were underwhelming and overpriced. In addition, service, although well meaning, simply wasn't up to scratch. Established in 1926, and owned by the Masala World group, Veeraswamy seems to be trading on past glories.

Booking advisable weekends. Children admitted until 8pm. Disabled: lift; toilet. Dress: smart casual. Separate room for parties, seats 24. **Map 17 A5.**

Soho

★ Imli

167-169 Wardour Street, W1F 8WR (7287 4243, www.imli.co.uk). Oxford Circus or Tottenham Court Road tube. **Meals served** noon-11pm Mon-Sat; noon-10pm Sun. **Tapas** £3.95-£7.95. **Set lunch** £8.50-£9.95. **Credit** AmEx, MC, V. Pan-Indian

North Indian menu

Under the blanket term 'North Indian', we have included dishes originating in the Punjab (the region separating India and Pakistan), Kashmir and all points down to Hyderabad. Southall has some of London's best Punjabi restaurants, where breads cooked in the tandoor oven are often preferred to rice, marinated meat kebabs are popular, and dals are thick and buttery.

Bhuna gosht: a dry, spicy dish of lamb.
Biriani or **biryani:** a royal Moghul (qv) version of pilau rice, in which meat or vegetables are cooked together with basmati rice, spices and saffron. It's difficult to find an authentic biriani in London restaurants.
Dopiaza or **do pyaza:** cooked with onions.
Dum: a Kashmiri cooking technique where food is simmered in a casserole (typically a clay pot sealed with dough), allowing spices to permeate.
Gurda: kidneys.
Haandi: an earthenware or metal cooking pot, with handles on either side and a lid.
Jalfrezi: chicken or vegetable dishes cooked with fresh green chillies – a popular cooking style in Mumbai.
Jhingri, jhinga or **chingri:** prawns.
Karahi or **karai:** a small iron or metal wok-like cooking dish. Similar to the 'balti' dish made famous in Birmingham.
Kheema or **keema:** minced lamb, as in kheema nan (stuffed nan).
Kofta: meatballs or vegetable dumplings.
Korma: braised in yoghurt and/or cream and nuts. Often mild, but rich.
Makhani: cooked with butter (makhan) and sometimes tomatoes, as in **murgh makhani.**
Massalam: marinated, then casseroled chicken dish, originating in Muslim areas.
Moghul, Mogul or **Moglai:** from the Moghul period of Indian history, used in the culinary sense to describe typical North Indian Muslim dishes.
Pasanda: thin fillets of lamb cut from the leg and flattened with a mallet. In Britain, the term usually applies to a creamy sauce virtually identical to a korma (qv).
Punjabi: Since Partition, the Punjab has been two adjoining states, one in India, one in Pakistan. Lahore is the main town on the Pakistani side, which is predominantly Muslim; Amritsar on the Indian side is the Sikh capital. Punjabi dishes tend to be thick stews or cooked in a tandoor (qv).
Roghan gosht or **rogan josh:** lamb cooked in spicy sauce, a Kashmiri speciality.
Seekh kebab: ground lamb, skewered and grilled.
Tandoor: clay oven originating in north-west India in which food is cooked without oil.
Tarka: spices and flavourings are cooked separately, then added to dal at a final stage.
Tikka: meat, fish or paneer cut into cubes, then marinated in spicy yoghurt and baked in a tandoor (qv).

INDIAN

Bangalore

affordable innovative modern Indian brasserie cooking

Bangalore CITY & Bbar

Corbet Court, Gracechurch Street, EC3V OAT
Opposite Leadenhall Market

Continuous service 11 to 11 Monday to Saturday
Reservations 020 7220 9195
or online **www.bangaloreexpress.co.uk**

Bangalore WATERLOO

Waterloo Road SE1 8UL

Continuous service 11 to 11, 7 days a week
Reservations 020 7021 0886
or online **www.bangaloreexpress.co.uk**

Bangalore TAILOR-MADE

**Event catering for every occasion however large
or small in a venue of your choice**

FREE Private Party Venue Hire available
Call us on 020 7265 1785
or visit **www.bangaloretailormade.co.uk**

(an approved caterer to Royal Borough of Kensington and Chelsea)

Rasa Samudra. See p139.

A more egalitarian offshoot of the upmarket Tamarind in Mayfair, Imli feels tailor-made for busy Soho lunchers. It's slick and modern without being overbearing; the food largely consists of small-plate Indian 'tapas', ideal for sharing; and only unprepared diners visit here and pay full price for a meal – there are usually discounts aplenty available from the website. Even without the special offers, Imli is good value. The lunchtime sharing platters bring a selection of small dishes: mainly vegetarian curries and Indian snacks such as papdi chaat (crisp fried wafers with tamarind sauce, yoghurt and chickpeas), aloo tikka (fried potato cake) or tarka dal. The à la carte menu offers a bit more variation, including pan-Indian street food and larger mains, sometimes with a welcome twist (see the samosa chaat, smothered in chickpeas, yoghurt and two vibrant chutneys). We've had complaints ourselves about service in the past, noting indifferent staff not always prepared to engage with customers over menu queries, but are pleased to report that on our last visit all concerned were smiling, helpful and efficient.
Babies and children welcome: children's menu; high chairs. Booking advisable Thur-Sat. Disabled: toilet. Separate room for parties, seats 45. Takeaway service; delivery service (over £20 within half-mile radius). **Map 17 B3**.

★ Masala Zone
9 Marshall Street, W1F 7ER (7287 9966, www.masalazone.com). Oxford Circus tube. **Meals served** noon-11pm Mon-Sat; 12.30-10.30pm Sun. **Main courses** £7.75-£13. **Set meal** £5.50 1 course, £8.50-£9.20 2 courses, £10.75-£11.45 3 courses. **Credit** AmEx, DC, MC, V. Pan-Indian
Even though the fast-ish food concept of the Masala Zone chain is clearly designed to reach a wider public, it is reassuring to see plenty of Indian customers still enjoying lunch here. There are certainly cheaper places they could go, and others more highfaluting (a notable few run by the Zone's owners – Camellia and Namita Panjabi and Ranjit Mathrani), but this place offers a persuasive mix of good cooking, keen prices, stylish surroundings and friendly service. Thalis (grand and regular) form the crux of the menu, but you'll also find around 15 curries, birianis served with dal, grills and street snacks. Bubbly crisp-shelled chicken and pea samosas had a juicy filling that didn't stint on chilli powder; we quelled the fire with thick vanilla lassi and a refreshing apple and mint juice combo. Rarely seen Sindhi dishes include chana dabalroti, the rich vegetarian version featuring chickpeas, lotus root (apparently) and chunks of bread in a tomatoey masala. It was a lip-smacking mixed grill that scored highest on our last visit, though: fat, juicy prawns, tender smoky mutton chops and generous hunks of chicken tikka – great value at £10.75, served with naan, salad and zingy mint raita.
Available for hire. Babies and children welcome: children's menu; high chairs. Booking advisable. Takeaway service; delivery service (over £15 within 1.5-mile radius). **Map 17 A3**.
For branches see index.

Red Fort
77 Dean Street, W1D 3SH (7437 2115, www.redfort.co.uk). Leicester Square or Tottenham Court Road tube. Bar **Open** 5pm-1am Tue-Sat. *Restaurant* **Lunch served** noon-2.30pm

Mon-Fri. **Dinner served** 5.30-11.30pm daily.
Main courses £15-£18. **Set lunch** £12
2 courses. **Set meal** (5.30-7pm) £16
2 courses incl tea or coffee.
Both **Credit** AmEx, MC, V. North Indian
The Red Fort remains a landmark among London's
North Indian restaurants, maintaining high
standards despite changes of chef, interior and
menu over two decades. With the high standards
go high prices – though on our visit, packs of
guffawing office workers filled the sleekly furnished
dining room, drawn by an online half-price food
offer. This proved to be an excellent deal, with no
diminution of culinary standards. A simple starter
of seekh kebab was a princely version, the lamb
finely minced to a paste-like consistency, then
sensitively flavoured with a garam masala of
freshly ground spices: quite sublime. Although
every curry house makes similar claims, the Red
Fort's menu really does contain original recipes
from the courtly cooking of the Moghuls. That
curry house staple, bhuna gosht, showed regal
lineage, with chunks of lamb in a warming, ginger-
flecked curry. Even the simplest of our dishes, from
the dals to the breads, was perfectly evocative of
the real India, both past and present. The seafood
dishes tend towards the contemporary, the
samundari ratan seafood stew containing scallops,
an ingredient not seen in the kitchens of the Raj. A
perfect venue for smart occasions, where the whiff
of fenugreek won't offend.
*Babies and children admitted. Booking advisable.
Dress: smart casual. Vegan dishes. Vegetarian
menu.* **Map 17 B3**.

Westminster

★ Cinnamon Club
*Old Westminster Library, 30-32 Great
Smith Street, SW1P 3BU (7222 2555,
www.cinnamonclub.com). St James's Park or
Westminster tube.* **Breakfast served** 7.30-
9.30am Mon-Fri. **Lunch served** noon-2.45pm,
dinner served 6-10.45pm Mon-Sat. **Main
courses** £14-£32. **Set meal** £19 2 courses,
£22 3 courses. **Credit** AmEx, DC, MC, V.
Modern Indian
Housed in a former Victorian library, Cinnamon
Club has become a magnet for power-brokers and
politicians. Expect a colonial-style atmosphere,
with high ceilings, a gallery of books and leather
seating adding to the clubby vibe. Service is as
smooth as Indian silk, friendly and focused.
Executive chef Vivek Singh's accomplished take
on Modern Indian cuisine is based on robust
flavours from across the subcontinent. Starters of
crisp-fried courgette flowers, filled with tender
marrow flecked with fiery red chillies, made a
marvellous match with tangy tamarind sauce. A
dressed-up Mumbai beach staple, pau bhaji, was
equally satisfying – crushed potatoes, folded into
softened tomatoes, red onions, peas, ginger and tart
pomegranate, and served with a buttery roll. Mains
too were top-drawer; a fillet of fried sea bass,
cooked to perfection, combined memorably with
fruity green mango and coconut chutney. Only the
murgh methi (a juicy sautéed chicken breast) was
let down by its plain appearance, and needed a
sauce to enliven the mustardy accompaniment of
fenugreek leaves. Puds, especially the molten
chocolate mousse, hit the sweet spot. Such quality
doesn't come cheap, and the wine list, although
expansive, is expensive too. A special-occasion
establishment to savour.

Namaaste Kitchen. See p153.

South Indian menu

Much South Indian food consists of rice, lentil- and semolina-based dishes. Fish features strongly in non-vegetarian restaurants, and coconut, mustard seeds, curry leaves and red chillies are widely used. If you want to try South Indian snacks such as dosas, idlis or uppama, go at lunchtime, which is when these dishes are traditionally eaten, and they're more likely to be cooked fresh to order. In the evening, try the thalis and rice- and curry-based meals, including vegetable stir-fries like thorans and pachadis.

Adai: fermented rice and lentil pancakes, with a nuttier flavour than dosais (qv).
Avial: a mixed vegetable curry from Kerala with a coconut and yoghurt sauce.
Bonda: spiced mashed potatoes, dipped in chickpea-flour batter and deep-fried.
Dosai or **dosa**: thin, shallow-fried pancake, often sculpted into interesting shapes; the very thin ones are called **paper dosai**. Most dosais are made with fermented rice and lentil batter, but variants include **rava dosai**, made with 'cream of wheat' semolina. **Masala dosais** come with a spicy potato filling. All variations are traditionally served with sambar (qv) and coconut chutney.
Gobi 65: cauliflower marinated in spices, then dipped in chickpea-flour batter and deep-fried. It is usually lurid pink due to the addition of food colouring.
Idli: steamed sponges of ground rice and lentil batter. Eaten with sambar (qv) and coconut chutney.
Kadala: black chickpea curry.
Kancheepuram idli: idli (qv) flavoured with whole black peppercorns and other spices.
Kappa: cassava root traditionally served with kadala (qv).
Kootu: mild vegetable curry in a creamy coconut and yoghurt sauce.
Pachadi: spicy vegetable side dish cooked with yoghurt.
Rasam: consommé made with lentils; it tastes both peppery-hot and tamarind-sour, but there are many regional variations.
Sambar or **sambhar**: a variation on dal made with a specific hot blend of spices, plus coconut, tamarind and vegetables – particularly drumsticks (a pod-like vegetable, like a longer, woodier version of okra; you strip out the edible interior with your teeth).
Thoran: stir-fried with mustard seeds, curry leaves, chillies and fresh grated coconut.
Uppama: a popular breakfast dish in which onions, spices and, occasionally, vegetables are cooked with semolina using a risotto-like technique.
Uthappam: a spicy, crisp pancake/pizza made with lentil- and rice-flour batter, often topped with tomato, onions and chillies.
Vellappam: a bowl-shaped, crumpet-like rice pancake (same as appam or hoppers, qv, Sri Lankan menu).

Babies and children welcome: high chairs. Booking advisable. Disabled: lift; toilet. Dress: smart casual. Separate rooms for parties, seating 30-60. **Map 16 K9**.
For branch (Cinnamon Kitchen) see index.

West
Hammersmith

Sagar
157 King Street, W6 9JT (8741 8563, www.sagarveg.co.uk). Hammersmith tube. **Lunch served** noon-3pm Mon-Fri. **Dinner served** 5.30-10.45pm Mon-Thur. **Meals served** noon-11.30pm Fri, Sat; noon-10.45pm Sun. **Main courses** £4.25-£13. **Thalis** £12.25-£14.95. **Credit** AmEx, MC, V.
South Indian vegetarian
Popular with students and aficionados of South Indian vegetarian cuisine, Sagar has gained renown for its keenly priced homely cooking – so much so that the owners now have four outposts across London. Unlike many cafés on King Street, this, the original branch, is an attractive, upmarket-looking place, furnished with blond wood fittings and a restrained display of Indian artefacts. As for the food, the good news first: the dosas are wonderful – golden and crisp on the outside and lightly spongy underneath – making an ideal foil for the filling of crushed potato masala seasoned with nutty-tasting mustard seeds. However, we've recently noticed a drop in standards at this branch. It's the accompaniments that are the problem. The sambar has lacked many of the soft and flavoursome vegetables (aubergines, onions and tomatoes) that make this lentil and tamarind gravy appealing. Equally dispiriting, the coconut and coriander chutney was without the much-loved peppery addition of curry leaves and popped mustard seeds. We hope that success isn't making the management complacent; Sagar has been one of the best places to sample vegetarian South Indian cooking – and we miss its exacting culinary standards.
Babies and children welcome: high chair. Booking advisable. Takeaway service. Vegan dishes. Vegetarian menu. **Map 20 B4**.
For branches see index.

Kensington

Zaika
1 Kensington High Street, W8 5NP (7795 6533, www.zaika-restaurant.co.uk). High Street Kensington tube. **Lunch served** noon-2.45pm Tue-Sun. **Dinner served** 6-10.45pm Mon-Sat; 6-9.45pm Sun. **Main courses** £17-£29. **Set lunch** £21 2 courses incl tea or coffee, £25 3 courses incl tea or coffee. **Set meal** £45-£60 tasting menu. **Credit** AmEx, DC, MC, V.
Modern Indian
A sweet waft of incense hits you upon entering Zaika. The interior has a confused mishmash of styles – including some magnificent carved stone from the bank that once occupied the building, now draped with lounge-bar purple and crimson velvet – with gold swirled glass and a few Indian handicrafts thrown in for good measure. This provides the setting for a menu of refined Anglo-Indian food that comes with as many flourishes as the decor. Our dinner started with an amuse-bouche of intense coconutty broth laced with truffle oil.

Baby lamb samosas came with mango chutney and a squiggle of tamarind, neither of which had the necessary tartness to cut through the rather heavy meat and pastry. Tandoori chicken (with a matching squiggle, this time in green) was much better, tender with a vibrant herb marinade. A vegetarian biriani (cooked under a flaky, fennel seed-flecked crust) was very attractive to behold, though the overcooked rice inside lacked a little flair. Cardamom and rose crème brûlée was, however, divine. So, hits and misses delivered by (on our visit) rather surly waiting staff.
Available for hire. Babies and children welcome: high chair. Booking advisable; essential weekends. Vegetarian menu. **Map 7 C8**.

South West
East Sheen

Mango & Silk
199 Upper Richmond Road West, SW14 8QT (8876 6220, www.mangoandsilk.co.uk). Mortlake rail or bus 33, 337, 493. **Lunch served** noon-3pm Sun (group reservation only Sat). **Dinner served** 6-10pm Tue-Thur, Sun; 6-10.30pm Fri, Sat. **Main courses** £7.95-£10.50. **Set buffet** (Sun) £12.95. **Credit** AmEx, MC, V. Pan-Indian
From the moment you step into this little gem of a suburban 'Indian', you know you've found something special. Owner Radhika Verma greets guests on arrival and continues to be unobtrusively solicitous throughout. The decor is simple and understated, in pale neutrals and pastels, with gleaming white tablecloths and subdued lighting – although tables for two are quite small for multi-dished meals. But it's the food that makes Mango & Silk such a find. Verma has managed to persuade award-winning chef (ex-Bombay Brasserie) Udit Sarkhel to return to the kitchen. Each dish of our meal seemed better than the last: lamb samosas with spiced yoghurt, and murgh malai kebabs (creamy chicken with cashew nuts), set the scene for main courses of delicious, if modestly portioned, macher malai (Bengali fish curry with mustard and coconut) and a perfect jardaloo ma gosht (lamb masala with apricots). The accompanying peshwari naan was among the best Indian breads we've tasted. On Sunday lunchtimes there's a regional Indian buffet with special deals for children, and every evening (apart from Fridays and Saturdays) staff serve thali platters with a starter and a dessert – usually fresh, silky mango, of course.
Babies and children welcome: booster seats; crayons; nappy-changing facilities. Booking advisable. Disabled: toilet. Tables outdoors (2, decking). Takeaway service.

Chelsea

Chutney Mary
535 King's Road, SW10 0SZ (7351 3113, www.chutneymary.com). Fulham Broadway tube or bus 11, 22. **Lunch served** 12.30-2.45pm Sat, Sun. **Dinner served** 6.30-11.15pm Mon-Sat; 6.30-10.15pm Sun. **Main courses** £16.50-£29.50. **Set lunch** £22 3 courses. **Set dinner** £45 tasting menu. **Credit** AmEx, DC, MC, V. Pan-Indian
With a formula that has been working for over 20 years, Chutney Mary continues to produce upmarket Indian food for a clientele of equally upmarket Chelsea diners. Descending to the lower-

INDIAN

Delhi Grill. See p153.

ground level, you enter the large yet intimate dining room where flickering candlelight is reflected by mirrored walls. There's also a verdant conservatory, perfect for lunch or a summer's evening. The menu focuses on banquet-style cooking from different Indian regions. You can try a selection with the tasting menu, or a thoughtfully balanced thali in which each dish is bright with colours from natural ingredients. From the kitchen of the Nawab of Ranpur comes lamb, slow-cooked in onion gravy heady with mace and Himalayan screwpine. Travel west for Bengali prawns or south to Goa for chicken cloaked in a buttery green chilli and coconut masala. Vegetarians are well catered for too, and the enjoyable Anglo-Indian puddings plus the great wine list are further incentives to visit. Dishes are rich with complex spicing; these curries leave you full, unlike the lighter cooking found at some more modern Indian restaurants. But although Chutney Mary may not be as cutting edge as it was in the 1990s, the kitchen still produces reliably good food. *Babies and children welcome under 10yrs until 8pm; high chairs. Booking advisable; essential Thur-Sat. Dress: smart casual. Separate room for parties, seats 28.* **Map 13 C13**.

Painted Heron
112 Cheyne Walk, SW10 0DJ (7351 5232, www.thepaintedheron.com). Sloane Square tube or 11, 19, 22, 319 bus. **Dinner served** 6-11pm Mon-Fri. **Meals served** 11am-11pm Sat, Sun. **Main courses** £13.50-£22. **Set meal** £45 6 courses (minimum 2). **Set brunch** (11am-5pm Sat, Sun) £20. **Credit** AmEx, MC, V.
Modern Indian
A recent refurb has softened the interior of this classy establishment. The restrained grey carpet, wooden tables and modern art produce an elegant, subtle effect, well suited to business diners. In contrast, the cooking is flamboyant, showcasing European ingredients alongside regional Indian traditions. The results aren't always consistent, though. Seared chicken tikka morsels, steeped in lemony yoghurt and fried in spicy gram-flour batter, were splendid – especially when matched with zesty kumquat and cranberry chutney. On the other hand, masala scrambled eggs made a bland starter; we wished for more green chillies and fried onions to revive it. Star main course was mutton chops, simmered in a smooth masala and spiked with naga chillies; sharp and piquant, rather than searingly hot, this garlicky home-style curry went well with hot chapatis. Our other choice, lamb nihari, was a rich and deliciously smoky curry, seasoned with cardamom and black cumin; however, it could have been cooked longer to render the meat meltingly tender. Although the standard menu is priced at the sharp end, the weekend brunch (until 5pm) is fantastic value – it's surprising there weren't more takers for this inexpensive taste of Modern Indian flavours. *Available for hire. Babies and children welcome: high chairs. Booking advisable weekends.* **Map 14 D13**.

South
Tooting

★ Apollo Banana Leaf
190 Tooting High Street, SW17 0SF (8696 1423, www.apollobananaleaf.co.uk). Tooting Broadway tube. **Lunch served** noon-3pm,

Gujarati menu

Most Gujarati restaurants are located in north-west London, mainly in Wembley, Sudbury, Kingsbury, Kenton, Harrow, Rayners Lane and Hendon, and they tend to be no-frills, family-run eateries.

Unlike North Indian food, Gujarati dishes are not normally cooked in a base sauce of onions, garlic, tomatoes and spices. Instead they're tempered; whole spices such as cumin, red chillies, mustard seeds, ajwain (carom) seeds, asafoetida powder and curry leaves are sizzled in hot oil for a few seconds. The tempering is added at the start or the end of cooking, depending on the dish.

Commonplace items like grains, beans and flours – transformed into various shapes by boiling, steaming and frying – are the basis of many dishes. Coriander, coconut, yoghurt, jaggery (cane sugar), tamarind, sesame seeds, chickpea flour and cocum (a sun-dried, sour, plum-like fruit) are also widely used.

Each region has its own cooking style. Kathiyawad, a humid area in western Gujarat, and Kutch, a desert in the north-west, have spawned styles that are less reliant on fresh produce. Kathiyawadi food is rich with dairy products and grains such as dark millet, and is pepped up with chilli powder. Kutchis make liberal use of chickpea flour (as do Kathiyawadis) and their staple diet is based on khichadi. In central Gujarat towns such as Baroda and Ahmedabad, grains are widely used; they appear in snacks that are the backbone of menus in London's Gujarati restaurants.

The gourmet heartland, however, is Surat – one of the few regions with heavy rainfall and lush vegetation. Surat boasts an abundance of green vegetables like papadi (a type of broad bean) and ponk (fresh green millet). A must-try Surti speciality is undhiyu. Surti food uses 'green masala' (fresh coriander, coconut, green chillies and ginger), as opposed to the 'red masala' (red chilli powder, crushed coriander, cumin and turmeric) more commonly used in western and central regions.

The best time to visit Gujarati restaurants is for Sunday lunch, which is when you'll find little-seen regional specialities on the menu – but you will almost certainly need to book ahead.

Bhakarvadi: pastry spirals stuffed with whole spices and, occasionally, potatoes.
Bhel poori: a snack originating from street stalls in Mumbai, which contains crisp, deep-fried pooris, puffed rice, sev (qv), chopped onion, tomato, potato and more, plus chutneys (chilli, mint and tamarind).
Dhokla: a steamed savoury gram-flour cake.
Farsan: Gujarati snacks.
Ganthia: Gujarati name for crisply fried savoury confections made from chickpea flour; they come in all shapes.
Ghughara: sweet or savoury pasties.
Kadhi: yoghurt and chickpea flour curry, often cooked with dumplings or vegetables.
Khandvi: tight rolls of 'pasta' sheets (made from gram flour and curds) tempered with sesame and mustard seeds.
Khichadi or **khichdi**: rice and lentils mixed with ghee and spices.
Mithi roti: round griddle-cooked bread stuffed with a cardamom-and-saffron-flavoured lentil paste. Also called puran poli.
Mogo: deep-fried cassava, often served as chips together with a sweet and sour tamarind chutney. An East African Asian dish.
Pani poori: bite-sized pooris that are filled with sprouted beans, chickpeas, potato, onion, chutneys, sev (qv) and a thin, spiced watery sauce.
Patra: a savoury snack made of the arvi leaf (colocasia) stuffed with spiced chickpea-flour batter, steamed, then cut into slices in the style of a swiss roll. The slices are then shallow-fried with sesame and mustard seeds.
Pau bhajee: a robustly spiced dish of mashed potatoes and vegetables, served with a shallow-fried white bread roll.
Puran poli: see mithi roti.
Ragda pattice or **ragada patties**: mashed potato patties covered with a chickpea or dried-pea sauce, topped with onions, sev (qv) and spicy chutney.
Sev: deep-fried chickpea-flour vermicelli.
Thepla: savoury flatbread.

dinner served 6-10.30pm Mon-Thur. **Meals served** noon-10.30pm Fri-Sun. **Main courses** £3.50-£6.75. **Unlicensed. Corkage** no charge. **Credit** MC, V. Sri Lankan

With its lurid, tightly packed interiors and filmic soundtrack, you might mistake Apollo Banana Leaf for just another curry house, but looks can be deceptive. True, the laminated menu contains mainstream interlopers such as chicken tikka, but that's not where the kitchen's heart – or skill – lies. The Sri Lankan crew showcase the best of their native cuisine, with a focus on seafood, vegetables and the odd bit of mutton. Kick off with traditional 'short eats' (street snacks) such as breaded cutlets (fish cakes) spiked with green chilli and curry leaves, or moreish deep-fried mutton rolls (giant croquettes) combining tender, full-flavoured meat and soft potato. Disappointingly, the edges of our plain dosa were soggy, rather than wafer-thin and crisp, but the stuffed masala version won plaudits for its filling of mustard seed-studded crushed potatoes. Other highlights include a shell-on crab curry – hugely messy but worth doing battle with, both for the sweet morsels of meat and the rich, creamy sauce – and a terrific dish of whole spiced ladies' fingers (okra). Sweet-natured service, ludicrously cheap prices and a no-corkage BYO policy all increase the appeal.

Babies and children welcome: high chairs.
Booking advisable weekends. Takeaway service.

South East
East Dulwich

Indian Mischief NEW
71 Lordship Lane, SE22 8EP (8693 1627).
East Dulwich rail. **Dinner served** 6-11pm Mon-Thur, Sun; 6pm-midnight Fri. **No credit cards.** Gujarati vegetarian

Opened in autumn 2010, this venture from two of Lordship Lane's longest-running and most respected food retailers (the Cheese Block and wholefood grocer SMBS) offers East Dulwich locals something different to the usual high-street curry house. The cooking is South Indian and Gujarati vegetarian, with lots of spicy potatoes and pulses, and aims to educate as well as satisfy. Carefully presented starters include traditional snack foods such as dhokla (savoury sponge cakes), mehdu vada (crispy lentil doughnuts) and bhel poori, while the popular dosas are a head-turning curl of crisp pancake accompanied by fresh sambars and chutneys. Alongside the main menu are daily specials, such as smoky baingan bharta (roasted aubergine curry) – perfect for warming up a drab Sunday evening. The emphasis throughout is on freshness, flavour and careful spicing, rather than powerful chilli kicks. Beers include Taj Mahal and Jaipur IPA, and you can finish with Indian-style cardamom coffee or spiced masala tea. A playful note in the window encourages diners to try eating with their hands.
Map 23 C4.

East
Whitechapel

Café Spice Namaste
16 Prescot Street, E1 8AZ (7488 9242,
www.cafespice.co.uk). Aldgate East or Tower Hill
tube or Tower Gateway DLR. **Lunch served**

noon-3pm Mon-Fri. **Dinner served** 6.15-10.30pm Mon-Fri; 6.30-10.30pm Sat. **Main courses** £12.50-£18.55. **Set meal** £30 4 courses, £40 5 courses, £65 tasting menu. **Credit** AmEx, DC, MC, V. Pan-Indian

Near Tower Hill, this airy recycled 19th-century courthouse makes an unusual venue, but is well suited to Namaste's position as one of the UK's most innovative and award-winning Indian restaurants. The high-ceilinged interior is enlivened by sumptuous drapery and stained glass in saturated hues. The menu ('Indian cuisine with specialities and influences from all over Asia, often with a European twist') reflects the inspired eclecticism of celebrated chef-patron, author and sustainability champion Cyrus Todiwala OBE. Provenance details abound, and the seasonal 'speciality menu' offered both Soay and Rhug Estate salt marsh lamb. However, the Soay in a curry sauce was distinctly chewy and arrived in a vol-au-vent that could have graced a church hall buffet. House speciality guizzado de chorize javali – spiced wild boar chipolatas cooked in a rich vindaloo masala – was served with a bog-standard bread roll rather than the menu's usual toasted pitta. In a version of fish and chips, the coley had a pleasant spiced batter and the gently aromatic version of tartare sauce was a delight, but the fish, though nicely cooked, was riddled with pin bones. In summary, the twist was doing all the shouting, but the execution was far from capital.

Babies and children welcome: high chairs.
Disabled: toilet. Tables outdoors (8, garden).
Takeaway service; delivery service (within 2-mile radius). **Map 12 S7.**

★ Lahore Kebab House
2 Umberston Street, E1 1PY (7488 2551,
www.lahore-kebabhouse.com). Aldgate East
or Whitechapel tube. **Meals served** noon-

midnight daily. **Main courses** £5.50-£9.50. **Unlicensed. Corkage** no charge. **Credit** MC, V. Pakistani

Along with nearby Tayyabs – opened by an uncle of Lahore's founder – and Needoo, this Pakistani grill forms the sacred trinity of Whitechapel curry houses. Those who have woken up to the uniform blandness of Brick Lane's restaurants flock here to discover the typically fiery and exuberant dishes of the Punjab that it has been cooking for more than 40 years. You'll usually have to queue; diners pack into tables over two floors, as industrious waiters ferry huge trays of karahi serving dishes. Music is loud, TV screens are permanently on, the crowd is often in party mood: it's not subtle, but it's very cheap and the food is cracking. We've found dishes to be much spicier than elsewhere in the area. Starters, such as barbecued chicken leg, moist seekh kebabs or deep-fried cassava chips, are great to share; tandoori bread is perfectly puffy and buttery. The adventurous can avoid the more common curries and work their way through the uncompromising specials: nihari, with slow-cooked lamb shanks; chicken curry served on the bone; or paya – spiced sheep's trotters. We imagine we'll still be praising LKH in another 40 years' time.

Babies and children welcome: high chairs.
Disabled: toilet. Takeaway service; delivery service (by taxi).
For branches see index.

★ Needoo Grill
87 New Road, E1 1HH (7247 0648,
www.needoogrill.co.uk). Whitechapel tube.
Meals served 11.30am-11.30pm daily. **Main courses** £6-£6.50. **Credit** MC, V. Pakistani

It's impossible to write about Needoo Grill without mentioning Tayyabs, just around the corner. Needoo was opened in late 2009 by a former Tayyabs manager, and in both looks (slick and

Indian Mischief

Sri Lankan menu

Sri Lanka has three main groups: Sinhalese, Tamil and Muslim. The cuisine has evolved by absorbing South Indian, Portuguese, Dutch, Malaysian, Arabic and Chinese flavours over the years. Cinnamon, cloves, curry leaves, nutmeg and fresh coriander are combined with South-east Asian ingredients such as lemongrass, pandan leaves, sesame oil, dried fish and rice noodles. Fresh coconut, onions, green chillies and limes are used liberally, and there are about two dozen types of rice.

Curries come in three main varieties: white (cooked in coconut milk), yellow (with turmeric and mild curry powder) and black (with roasted curry powder, normally used with meat). Hoppers (saucer-shaped pancakes) are generally eaten for breakfast with kithul palm syrup and buffalo-milk yoghurt, while string hoppers (steamed, rice-flour noodles formed into flat discs) usually accompany fiery curries.

Ambul thiyal: sour fish curry cooked dry with spices.

Badun: black. 'Black' curries are fried; they're dry and usually very hot.

Devilled: meat, seafood or vegetable dishes fried with onions in a sweetish sauce; usually served as starters.

Godamba roti: flaky, thin Sri Lankan bread, sometimes wrapped around egg or potato.

Hoppers: confusingly, hoppers come in two forms, either as saucer-shaped, rice-flour pancakes (try the sweet and delectable milk hopper) or as string hoppers (qv). Hoppers are also known as **appam**.

Katta sambol: onion, lemon and chilli relish; fearsomely hot.

Kiri: white. 'White' curries are based on coconut milk and are usually mild.

Kiri hodi: coconut milk curry with onions and turmeric; a soothing gravy.

Kuttu roti, kottu or **kothu roti**: strips of thin bread (resembling pasta), mixed with mutton, chicken, prawns or veg to form a 'bread biriani'; very filling.

Lamprais or **lumprice**: a biriani-style dish where meat and rice are cooked together, often by baking in banana leaves.

Lunnu miris: a relish of ground onion, chilli and maldives fish (qv).

Maldives fish: small, dried fish with a very intense flavour; an ingredient used in sambols (qv).

Pittu: rice flour and coconut steamed in bamboo to make a 'log'; an alternative to rice.

Pol sambol: a mix of coconut, chilli, onions, maldives fish (qv) and lemon juice.

Sambols: strongly flavoured relishes, often served hot; they are usually chilli-hot too.

Seeni sambol: sweet and spicy, caramelised onion relish.

String hoppers: fine rice flour noodles formed into flat discs. Usually served steamed. Also called **idiappa**.

Vellappam: appam (qv) served with vegetable curry.

sparkly) and food (Punjabi curries and grills) it is clearly inspired by the Whitechapel stalwart. However, prices are generally slightly lower, and the cooking slightly less exalted, though still very good. The lamb chops might lack the punch of Tayyabs's legendary rendition, yet nearly everything else – sizzling tikka starters, fried samosas and bhajias, unstrained meat and veg curries (such as karahi lamb with spinach, or dark, slow-cooked makhani dal) – is almost on a par. We'd love to see the restaurant use its less-established status to branch out and serve a few more unusual Punjabi dishes; as it is, the place feels like a Tayyabs overspill, which is how many people use it (takeaway is easier, and the queues, though frequent, are nowhere near as intimidating). That said, if Needoo were located anywhere else in London it could be seen with an objective eye; this remains a reliable venue to eat no-nonsense, decently cooked Pakistani and northern Indian food.
Available for hire. Babies and children welcome: high chairs. Tables outdoors (8, pavement). Takeaway service. Vegetarian menu.

★ Tayyabs
83 Fieldgate Street, E1 1JU (7247 9543, www.tayyabs.co.uk). Aldgate East or Whitechapel tube. **Meals served** noon-11.30pm daily. **Main courses** £6.50-£28.50. **Unlicensed. Corkage** no charge. **Credit** AmEx, MC, V. Pakistani
Since Mohammed Tayyab first opened his Punjabi grill in 1972, it has grown from a small, low-key café for locals in a Whitechapel backstreet, to one of the busiest restaurants in London: two floors of packed-in tables, flashy decor, an army of waiters and endless streams of diners who flow in from across the city. This popularity is no mystery: food is consistently superb, and even if portion sizes appear to have shrunk in recent years, the no-corkage BYO and general cheapness make Tayyabs irresistible. The lamb chops, bashed thin, marinated in lime, chilli, ginger and a masala of other spices, are transcendentally good; also sublime are the powerfully flavoured curries (best on the menu is the unappetising-sounding 'dry meat' – slow-cooked lamb), juicy shish kebabs, equally appealing vegetable dishes (lentils with baby aubergine is a favourite), and the hot, buttery breads. For the full experience, try one of the daily specials (quail curry on Tuesdays, say). A trip here is an essential London experience, but note: Tayyabs is a hectic place, staff can be curt and there are half-hour queues most nights. Go midweek for a more pleasant time, and always book.
Babies and children welcome: high chairs. Booking advisable. Separate room for parties, seats 35. Takeaway service.

North
Camden Town & Chalk Farm

Namaaste Kitchen
64 Parkway, NW1 7AH (7485 5977, www.namaastekitchen.co.uk). Camden Town tube. **Lunch served** noon-2.30pm, **dinner served** 5.30-11.30pm Mon-Thur. **Meals served** noon-11.30pm Fri, Sat; noon-11pm Sun. **Main courses** £7.50-£18.95. **Set lunch** £8.95 2 courses, £11.50 3 courses. **Credit** AmEx, MC, V. Modern Indian

Namaaste Kitchen showcases South Asia's culinary heritage (seafood dishes from the Malabar coast, Moghul-inspired classics, Pakistani street food) and aims to be creative while respecting tradition. Nevertheless, there is a sense of trying too hard. Starters encouraged us to expect an artily inventive meal, then mains turned out to be earthy and rustic – this kitchen (a pity the tossing and skewering action has been relegated to the back of the restaurant) should decide whether it's producing modern or traditional cooking. Still, apart from some disappointing breads, and service that needed tightening, we enjoyed the meal. Smokily succulent tandoori lamb cutlets were impressive, so too chicken livers fried with onion and green chilli masala, served over a tart apple disc with stood-up pieces of white toast. Tender rabbit, a classic from Rajasthan, worked well with a cooked-down tomato masala spiced with nigella, fennel and toasted fenugreek seeds. Mixed vegetable curry was memorable too. The design tries to overcome the confines of a long narrow space with a mix of open brickwork, contemporary furnishings and obligatory bar with flatscreen TV.
Available for hire. Babies and children welcome: high chairs. Booking advisable. Separate room for parties, seats 20. Takeaway service; delivery service (over £15 within 3-mile radius). Vegan dishes. Vegetarian menu. **Map 27 C3.**

Islington

★ Delhi Grill NEW
21 Chapel Market, N1 9EZ (7278 8100, www.delhigrill.com). Angel tube. **Lunch served** noon-2.45pm, **dinner served** 6-10.30pm Tue-Sun. **Main courses** £3.95-£8.95. **Credit** AmEx, MC, V. Punjabi
On the former site of Rooburoo, Delhi Grill is a family concern started by brothers Aman and Preet Grewal. They've selected their relatives' best recipes for a short, focused menu in homage to India's dhaba (roadside canteens). Dishes are split equally between items from the tandoor and those from the pot, but look to the specials board before ordering – August proffered dhal gosht, aloo puri and vegetable pakora; if available, the on-the-bone goat curry is a must, as is rajmah, a Punjabi dish of kidney beans. We've generally found most satisfaction from the slow-cooked sauce dishes, but a 'Delhi Grill' for two at just £7.50 will see off any cravings for meat – it includes lamb chops, chicken tikkas and punchy seekh kebabs. The own-made, silky-smooth beetroot chutney has become something of a signature. On our most recent visit, service was sweet but slow and as the room filled up, we became more and more frustrated: it takes more than enthusiasm and a good idea to move from daytime roti stall to proper restaurant, no matter how casual. But we like this spot. The cooking is great and the decor – in which old Indian newspapers serve as wallpaper alongside cheerful blue paint – is fun.
Available for hire. Babies and children admitted. Booking advisable Thur-Sat. Disabled: toilet. Takeaway service. Vegan dishes. **Map 5 N2.**

North West
Neasden

★ Shayona NEW
54-62 Meadow Garth, NW10 8HD (8965 3365, www.shayonarestaurants.com). Harlesden or

Shayona. See p153.

Neasden tube. **Meals served** 11.30am-10pm Mon-Fri; 11am-9.30pm Sat, Sun. **Main courses** £4.95-£6.25. **Set lunch** £6.99 buffet. **Set meal** £13.50 4 courses, £16.50 6 courses. **Unlicensed** no alcohol allowed. **Credit** MC, V. Pan-Indian vegetarian

Shayona is run on behalf of Neasden's spectacular Swaminarayan Temple by a well-established catering firm. However, the restaurant inhabits a structure in the car park that resembles a cash-and-carry establishment. But if you head inside, past the sweet and snack counters, you'll find a restaurant that is notably smarter than the average temple canteen in India. The coffee and cream tones of the large dining room are offset by vibrant wall paintings, artificial foliage and graceful chandeliers, while the local Hindu community pack out the tables, even midweek. The draw is a menu that, while vegetarian and *sattvic* (a diet based on 'pure' food that excludes pungent-smelling ingredients), also includes dishes from across the subcontinent. Sample a selection with the good-value Shayona platter served with four chutneys – we relished the crisp samosa, the uncommonly light bateta wada (a ball of spiced mashed potato in deep-fried batter) and the spongy methi gota (fenugreek dumpling). To follow, there's a choice of South Indian 'light meals', including dosas and idlis, and a list of curries that again roams happily through the subcontinent; the dal makhani was luxuriously buttery. Drink fresh juices or lassi – there's no alcohol – to complete an uplifting, if not religious, experience.
Available for hire. Babies and children welcome: high chairs. Booking advisable. Disabled: toilet. Takeaway service. Vegetarian menu.

Swiss Cottage

Eriki

4-6 Northways Parade, Finchley Road, NW3 5EN (7722 0606, www.eriki.co.uk). Swiss Cottage tube. **Lunch served** noon-2.30pm Mon-Fri, Sun. **Dinner served** 6-10.30pm daily. **Main courses** £10-£12. **Set lunch** £12.95 2 courses. **Credit** MC, V. Pan-Indian
On a road that seems blighted with empty shops and 'to let' signs, Eriki stands out as a quality outfit. High-backed chairs of wood and metal, a zebrano-style floor, and elegantly framed tapestries on maroon walls transport diners to the luxurious serenity of a swish spa. The pan-Indian menu, which stretches from Kerala to the Punjab, is just right for the location, though the uniforms of the courteous staff are perhaps a tad too formal for the establishment. Salmon, calamares, scallops and prawns all feature among the starters; vegetarians will be happy with their lot too. Birianis come in copper handis, most everything else is served in asymmetrical bowls. Dahi baigan (aubergine in spiced yoghurt) was sumptuously textured, but the spicing, despite the presence of onion seeds and a touch of fresh coriander, was more reminiscent of Anglo curry powder than the promised panch poran. Much better was the coupe glass of ras malai with mango sauce. Wines by the glass are limited, but the Australian house chardonnay is a treat. For a decadent finish, try a post-prandial cocktail, such as the Smoky Fig made with scotch, fig liqueur and lime.
Available for hire. Babies and children admitted. Booking advisable. Takeaway service; delivery service (6-9.45pm, over £20 within 4-mile radius). Vegetarian menu. **Map 28 B4**.

Outer London

Harrow, Middlesex

★ Ram's

203 Kenton Road, Harrow, Middx, HA3 0HD (8907 2022, http://ramsrestaurant.co.uk). Kenton tube/rail. **Lunch served** noon-3pm, **dinner served** 6-11pm daily. **Main courses** £4-£5. **Set meal** £22 (unlimited food & soft drinks). **Thalis** £4.99-£8.99. **Credit** MC, V.
Gujarati vegetarian

Ram's may be a large, very simply decorated café with functional furniture and wipe-clean surfaces, but it's held in high regard and booking is prudent even on weeknights. The main draw is the vegetarian Surti cuisine (from Surat, a district of Gujarat), though the lengthy menu includes dishes from the Punjab right down to Kerala, plus a couple of Indochinese options such as hakka noodles. As in Surat, the choice of wheat breads is a point of pride, and Ram's speciality, puran puri, is easily the best we've found in London. The delectable dahi puri (crisp-shelled Mumbai street snacks doused in tangy yoghurt) challenge all rivals too. Another highlight: kachori, deep-fried globes of sweet peas and spices, served with smooth fresh chutneys. Of the main courses, Surti choices of spinach and fenugreek bhajia, and dal dhokri (strips of lentil pancake cooked in dal) easily outclassed the claggy vegetable biriani. Had we any room after the creamy saffron and almond lassi with nut flakes bouncing around the glass, we might have ordered the own-made kulfi, falooda or shrikhand. Staff couldn't have been nicer, though a couple of large parties meant that our food took some time to arrive.
Available for hire. Babies and children welcome: high chairs. Booking advisable weekends. Takeaway service; delivery service (over £25 within 2-mile radius).

Southall, Middlesex

★ Brilliant

72-76 Western Road, Southall, Middx, UB2 5DZ (8574 1928, www.brilliantrestaurant.com). Southall rail. **Lunch served** noon-3pm Tue-Fri. **Dinner served** 6-11.30pm Tue-Sun. **Main courses** £4.50-£14. **Credit** AmEx, MC, V.
East African Indian

About a mile from central Southall, on a Tuesday night, Brilliant still attracts a full house to its glam ground-floor dining room. Multinational business diners, couples and friends create a lively hubbub in the attractive space, where three flatscreen TVs, burnished copper highlights and African sculptures provide yet more entertainment. Yes, you'll find some old-school curry house trappings – plate heaters, hot flannels, chocolate mints with the bill – but the food (Punjabi by way of Kenya) easily transcends the genre. Savour the robust spicing in the methi chicken, or the buttery tang of the tarka dal. Staff remain solicitous and prompt even at full throttle. Faultless too is the light spicy batter in the sublimely fresh fish pakora starter; try it with the superb own-made pickles (six big bowlfuls, provided gratis; the lemon pickle and the mint relish go well with the fish). Established in the 1970s by the Kenyan Asian Anand family, Brilliant is great for group dining: share a butter chicken to start, followed by a 'full bowl' (feeding five) of palak lamb. Upstairs is a banqueting hall, part of the Anands' extensive catering operation.

Babies and children welcome: high chairs. Booking advisable weekends. Separate room for parties, seats 120. Takeaway service. Vegetarian menu.

★ ★ New Asian Tandoori Centre (Roxy)

114-118 The Green, Southall, Middx, UB2 4BQ (8574 2597). Southall rail. **Meals served** 8am-11pm Mon-Thur; 8am-midnight Fri-Sun. **Main courses** £4.50-£7.50. **Credit** MC, V. Punjabi

Busy, good value and no frills, the Roxy – as locals still know it – is the perfect venue for the assertive flavours of Punjabi cooking. The hectic takeaway section opens into an energetic dining room with little adornment. It's almost always packed with Southall families and groups, as well as curry fans from further afield, drawn by some of London's most authentic North Indian food. Eating here is a thrilling experience; the menu offers little help to the uninitiated, and lurid pictures of dishes above the takeaway counter do little to encourage orders either. But almost everything is brilliant, especially the Punjabi specialities. 'Boneless chicken curry' sounds basic, but provides a fine introduction to the lively masalas from this northern region. Dal makhani (served weekends only) is a deep, rich dish of slow-cooked black lentils with the typically Punjabi addition of cream and butter. And kadhi, originally a Gujarati dish but popular here too, is gently spiced yoghurt and balls of fried gram flour. We've found the grills more restrained in flavour than in some of the Whitechapel Punjabi venues, but that's a minor complaint. This is an all-round winner.
Babies and children welcome: high chairs. Disabled: toilet. Separate room for parties, seats 60. Takeaway service. Vegetarian menu.

Wembley, Middlesex

★ Sakonis `HOT 50`

129 Ealing Road, Wembley, Middlesex, HA0 4BP (8903 9601, www.sakonis.co.uk). Alperton tube. **Breakfast served** 9-11am Sat, Sun. **Meals served** noon-10pm daily. **Main courses** £2-£4.99. **Set buffet** (breakfast) £4.50; (noon-4pm Mon-Fri, noon-5pm Sat, Sun) £8.99; (6-9.30pm) £11.99. **Credit** MC, V.
Gujarati/South Indian vegetarian

A landmark on Ealing Road, Sakonis attracts a cross-section of the local Indian vegetarian population. It's a huge, café-style operation; behind the pavement tables you'll find a snack-and-sweet takeaway counter, then a pan bar (where the betel-leaf digestifs are made to order), followed by the capacious white dining area (resembling a windowless canteen), the buffet counter and, finally, the kitchen. Sit at an easy-wipe table and choose between the lengthy menu and the buffet. Either way you'll be well looked after by the plentiful staff. Gujarati and South Indian dishes abound in both options, and such is the throughput of customers, most buffet choices remain fresh and (where appropriate) crisp. Some 30 dishes plus various chutneys and salads feature along the stainless-steel counter. Start with pooris and other crisp snacks before moving on to a masala dosa (cooked to order, ours was a little dry), an Indo-Chinese dish (crisp chilli paneer was better than the rather lank hakka noodles) or one of many curries. We particularly relished the upma (nutty with mustard seeds), the khadi, and the enthusiastic Sunday lunchers.
Babies and children welcome: high chairs. Takeaway service. Vegetarian menu.
For branch see index.

Sweets menu

Even though there isn't a tradition of serving puddings at everyday meals in South Asia, there is much ceremony associated with distributing sweetmeats at auspicious events, especially weddings and religious festivals. Desserts served at many Indian restaurants in London include the likes of gulab jamun, cardamom-scented rice pudding, creamy kulfi, and soft, syrup-drenched cheese dumplings. In the home, family meals don't often include a dessert; you're more likely to be treated to a platter of seasonal fruit. Winter warmers also have their place, including comforting, fudge-like carrot halwa, a Punjabi favourite and popular street snack. Winter is also the season for weddings, where other halwas, made with wholewheat flour, semolina, lentils and pumpkin, might be served.

Barfi: sweetmeat usually made with reduced milk, and flavoured with nuts, fruit, sweet spices or coconut.
Bibenca or **bibinca:** soft, layered cake from Goa made with eggs, coconut milk and jaggery.
Falooda or **faluda:** thick milky drink (originally from the Middle East), resembling a cross between a milkshake and a sundae. It's flavoured with either rose syrup or saffron, and also contains agar-agar, vermicelli, nuts and ice-cream. Very popular with Gujarati families, faloodas make perfect partners to deep-fried snacks.
Gajar halwa: grated carrots, cooked in sweetened cardamom milk until soft, then fried in ghee until almost caramelised; usually served warm.
Gulab jamun: brown dumplings (made from dried milk and flour), deep-fried and drenched in rose-flavoured sugar syrup, best served warm. A traditional Bengali sweet, now ubiquitous in Indian restaurants.
Halwa: a fudge-like sweet, made with semolina, wholewheat flour or ground pulses cooked with syrup or reduced milk, and flavoured with nuts, saffron or sweet spices.
Jalebis: spirals of batter, deep-fried and dipped in syrup, best eaten warm.
Kheer: milky rice pudding, flavoured with cardamom and nuts. Popular throughout India (there are many regional variations).
Kulfi: ice-cream made from reduced milk, flavoured with nuts, saffron or fruit.
Payasam: a South Indian pudding made of reduced coconut or cow's milk with sago, nuts and cardamom. **Semiya payasam** is made with added vermicelli.
Rasgullas: soft paneer cheese balls, simmered and dipped in rose-scented syrup, served cold.
Ras malai: soft paneer cheese patties in sweet and thickened milk, served cold.
Shrikhand: hung (concentrated) sweet yoghurt with saffron, nuts and cardamom, sometimes with fruit added. A traditional Gujarati favourite, eaten with pooris.

Italian

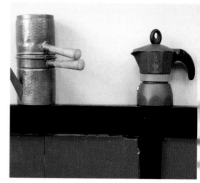

London didn't need another high-priced Italian restaurant, let alone one in a hotel, but when it came to our award for Best New Design 2011, **Massimo** restaurant and oyster bar in Westminster's new Corinthia Hotel won in grand style. It is the antithesis of the trend of the past few years, which has seen approachable neighbourhood spots such as Archway's **500 Restaurant**, and the bacaros of Russell Norman and Richard Beatty (**Polpo** and its siblings) attracting queues. However, this year has also seen the rebirth of the Italian deli-café, with notable players such as Sardo and importer-restaurateur Machiavelli bringing first-rate ingredients to the takeaway lunch market. Still, it's not all about fashion: regular readers will note our favourite Italian restaurants are hardy perennials: **Assaggi** in Bayswater, wine specialist **Enoteca Turi** in Putney, **Locanda Locatelli** in Marylebone and **Theo Randall at the Intercontinental** in Mayfair. And only two of them are in hotels.

Central
Belgravia

Olivo
21 Eccleston Street, SW1W 9LX (7730 2505, www.olivorestaurants.com). Sloane Square tube or Victoria tube/rail. **Lunch served** noon-2.30pm Mon-Fri. **Dinner served** 6-10.30pm Mon-Sat; 6.30-10.30pm Sun. **Main courses** £13-£23. **Set lunch** £23 2 courses, £27.50 3 courses. **Credit** AmEx, MC, V.
You could easily miss Olivo's understated exterior if it weren't for the telltale olive trees. Inside, the distinctive Mediterranean palette of blue and yellow is in need of a lick of paint, and some might think the white paper tablecloths don't befit the prices charged. The menu is a mix of Sardinian specialities and Italian standards. Stuffed calamari had a good chargrilled flavour, but the portion was meagre. Malloreddus (small, curled pasta shells from Sardinia) came in a bland sauce, though the own-made sausage pieces – when we found them – were punchy. We enjoyed a seafood brochette with Sardinian couscous: fresh and summery on the plate and on the palate. To finish, our dessert of panna cotta looked a flop, but was redeemed by a sharp raspberry coulis. The impressive Italian wine list contains several bottles from Sardinia. Staff are friendly and helpful; a mix-up with the wine was cheerfully rectified, and some pyjama-clad kids playing with iPads were indulged in the Italian way. The owners run a mini-chain of Italian establishments in Belgravia, including Olivomare fish restaurant and a deli. However, crowds were thin at Olivo; perhaps rival Sardo has tempted lovers of Sardinian cuisine north of Oxford Street. *Babies and children admitted. Booking advisable.* **Map 15 H10**.
For branch (Oliveto) see index.

City

L'Anima
1 Snowden Street, EC2A 2DQ (7422 7000, www.lanima.co.uk). Liverpool Street tube/rail. *Bar* **Open/meals served** 9am-midnight Mon-Fri; 5.30-11pm Sat. **Main courses** £15-£33. *Restaurant* **Lunch served** 11.45am-3pm Mon-Fri. **Dinner served** 5.30-11pm Mon-Fri; 5.30-11.30pm Sat. **Main courses** £15-£33. **Set lunch** £24.50 2 courses, £28.50 3 courses. *Both* **Credit** AmEx, DC, MC, V.
This vast, ultra-minimalist room in the soulless precincts of the City uses a glass wall to divide dining room and 'lounge area'. The dining room has more comfortable seating, and tablecloths. We lunched in the lounge, and while unforgiving acoustics sometimes made conversation difficult, the extraordinary food seemed to make everything else irrelevant. Two of us shared three starters and came away full. Linguini with crab, lemon and chilli was sauced impeccably, the chilli lending a warm glow rather than scorching fire to the delicate flavour of the crab. Stoccafisso (reconstituted dried fish) with scallops and anchovy sauce consisted of two plump bivalves, each on a mound of the fish, with elegant daubs of the sauce inviting a finishing swipe of the excellent own-made bread. A huge fritto misto – fish and shellfish with delectable shreds of courgette and enoki mushrooms – was a wonder of precise deep-frying that left us gasping for superlatives. The wine list caters generously for the bonus boys, but has good bottles under £25. Service was flawless. A full meal à la carte is expensive, but with one glass of wine and a bottle of water, our bill came to a shade over £60. *Babies and children welcome: high chairs. Booking advisable. Disabled: toilet. Dress: smart casual. Separate rooms for parties, seating 6-14.* **Map 6 R5**.

Carluccio's Caffè
12 West Smithfield, EC1A 9JR (7329 5904, www.carluccios.com). Barbican tube or Farringdon tube/rail. **Meals served** 8am-11pm Mon-Fri; 9am-11pm Sat; 9am-10.30pm Sun. **Main courses** £7.95-£30. **Set meal** £9.95 2 courses. **Credit** AmEx, DC, MC, V.
Quality varies between branches, of course, but in the main Carluccio's makes a decent job of being everyone's favourite Italian chain restaurant. The Smithfield site is handy for Barts Hospital as well as nearby offices; at weekends, it's more of a hangout for local residents. Specials supplement a menu of tried and tested dishes. You'll find antipasti sharing plates, hearty salads, pastas (penne alla luganica, with an Italian sausage sauce, is spicy comfort food), a daily-changing risotto and mains that encompass pollo alla cacciatora (roast chicken breast with tomato and herb sauce and potatoes) and fritto misto (crispy calamari, whitebait, prawns and sea bass fillet, floured, fried and served with garlic mayonnaise). Puddings feature vanilla and rum panna cotta, tiramisu and a selection of ices. There's a breakfast menu too. Service is generally good, and staff are great with youngsters (what's

more, the children's menu is excellent value). This branch has a small shop at the front, a big deli counter along one side, and a restaurant in a big airy room at the rear, done out in the company's trademark blue and white colour scheme.
Babies and children welcome: children's menu; high chairs; nappy-changing facilities. Disabled: toilet. Tables outdoors (5, pavement). Takeaway service. Vegetarian menu. **Map 11 O5.**
For branches see index.

Covent Garden

Jamie's Italian Covent Garden

11 Upper St Martin's Lane, WC2H 9FB (3326 6390, www.jamieoliver.com/italian). Covent Garden or Leicester Square tube. **Meals served** noon-11.30pm Mon-Sat; noon-10.30pm Sun. **Main courses** £9.85-£15.95. **Credit** AmEx, DC, MC, V.

Jamie Oliver has got everything right at his chain of mid-priced restaurants designed to compete with the likes of Carluccio's, Giraffe and Strada. It certainly leaves those last two in the shade. At our latest visit to the Covent Garden branch, someone knocked a nearly full bottle of red wine off a neighbour's table and the staff couldn't have been nicer about it. They supplied colouring sheets, crayons and retro View-Masters (with picture menus) to the kids, and didn't get flustered when we changed our order three times. What's really a very large space is divided artfully by a central bar, bread station, welcome point and meat bar (featuring cured meats hanging from the ceiling). There's also a second basement floor and an unusually large number of alfresco tables front and back. We chose small portions of pasta so that we could try the enticing antipasti too, but you can also order pasta dishes in main-course sizes; in addition, there's a choice of fish or meat dishes, such as steaks, fish stew and whole roasted sea bass. Prawn linguine and a spring vegetable pasta dish were both full of flavour. Crispy polenta chips sprinkled with rosemary, sea salt and parmesan, and a courgette flower stuffed with four cheeses offered interesting tastes and textures. The children wolfed down their burger and spaghetti bolognese too. No wonder the place is packed.
Babies and children welcome: children's menu; high chairs; nappy-changing facilities. Bookings not accepted for fewer than 6 people. Disabled: toilet. Tables outdoors (15, courtyard; 4, pavement). **Map 18 D4.**
For branches see index.

Fitzrovia

Mennula

10 Charlotte Street, W1T 2LT (7636 2833, www.mennula.com). Goodge Street or Tottenham Court Road tube. **Lunch served** noon-3pm Mon-Fri; 12.30-3pm Sun. **Dinner served** 6-11pm Mon-Sat; 6-9.30pm Sun. **Main courses** £9.50-£29. **Set meal** £45-£55 4 courses, £59 tasting menu. **Credit** AmEx, MC, V.

The last time we reviewed this unusually smart Sicilian restaurant, we were excited by the food – nicely balanced between rustic and sophisticated, Sicilian and pan-Italian. However, the early promise was only partly realised on our follow-up visit. Yes, the room remains an attractive white L-shape with comfortable booths, but the service was still distracted (and distracting), and food quantity and quality fell slightly short of the level that the prices demand. For £12.50, a tuna salad starter needed to be special, but a quail's egg on top wasn't enough to flavour the unexciting fish. Octopus salad, with cherry tomatoes and potato purée, was appealing, but similarly short on zing. Monkfish osso buco (an odd description, there being no bone nor deep flavours involved) was less thrilling than it sounded, and the accompanying risotto over-buttered. And warm calf's liver salad was merely some tasty but not-so-tender liver set next to a green salad. Attractive presentation and good bookends – small squares of bread, arancini, olives, almonds (after which Mennula is named) and cannoli – plus an all-Italian wine list with a well-chosen selection from Sicily's resurgent producers, swings the overall verdict to a thumbs-up: but it walks the line.
Available for hire. Booking advisable dinner. Children admitted. Dress: smart casual. Separate room for parties, seats 14. Tables outdoors (2, pavement). **Map 17 B1.**

Sardo

45 Grafton Way, W1T 5DQ (7387 2521, www.sardo-restaurant.com). Warren Street tube. **Lunch served** noon-3pm Mon-Fri. **Dinner served** 6-11pm Mon-Sat. **Main courses** £12-£19.90. **Credit** AmEx, MC, V.

Fashions in the restaurant world come and go, but Sardo's popularity remains undiminished: the place was packed on a Tuesday night with a smart West End crowd including dating couples and a birthday celebration. The long narrow room – white paintwork, pale grey wood panelling, soft wall lighting, white tablecloths and rush-seat chairs – provides a muted backdrop for some classy food. There's a monthly changing menu and daily specials, but it's the Sardinian dishes that most customers turn to. Rightly so: from the basket of breads (including pane carasau flatbread) to pasta and meat, all our dishes were excellent. Bottarga (dried mullet roe, a signature Sardinian ingredient) provided a delicate yet intense flavouring for perfectly cooked spaghetti. Simplicity and quality were key also to linguine al granchio, with its sauce of white crab meat, parsley, chilli and olive oil. Salsiccia sarda – a slightly spicy, fennel-tinged spiral sausage – came with sautéed potatoes, green beans and carrots. Desserts include tiramisu and Sardinian cheeses. Service from black-clad staff was deft, informed and friendly; take advantage of their expertise to explore the predominantly Sardinian wine list, which has plenty of choice by the glass. We can recommend the ruby-red, rich, smooth Mandrolisai Superiore.
Available for hire. Babies and children admitted. Booking advisable. Separate room for parties, seats 36. Tables outdoors (3, patio). **Map 3 J4.**
For branch see index.

Knightsbridge

Zafferano

15 Lowndes Street, SW1X 9EY (7235 5800, www.zafferanorestaurant.com). Knightsbridge tube. **Lunch served** noon-2.30pm Mon-Fri;

Tinello. See p161.

Donna Margherita, nominated by Time Out as London's best Pizza 2010 (best in the south)

"This out-of-the-way trattoria is a local gem, with attentive service and a gently buzzing atmosphere... two days later we forsook our usual takeaway for another taste of Donna Margherita's Italy."
- Time Out Online 2008

"... it was the best thing I have eaten in ages"
- Metro Life 2006

"Perhaps the most authentic Neapolitan restaurant in London"
- Harden's Restaurant Guide 2010

"Donna Margherita is one of London's best"
- Evening Standard 2009

Battersea, 183 Lavender Hill, SW11 5TE | 020 7228 2660 | www.donna-margherita.com

12.30-3pm Sat, Sun. **Dinner served** 7-11pm Mon-Sat; 7-10.30pm Sun. **Main courses** (lunch Mon-Fri) £18-£25. **Set meal** (lunch Sat, Sun; dinner daily) £34.50 2 courses, £44.50 3 courses, £49.50 4 courses. **Credit** AmEx, DC, MC, V.

As Zafferano is located in one of the swankiest parts of town, it's encouraging that the welcome from staff comes with no hint of snootiness. Inside, the dining area – filled with the scent of fresh flowers and furnished with brightly striped seat covers – projects a relaxing rather than a ritzy image. Giorgio Locatelli helped propel this restaurant to its peak, before opening his own place, but British chef Andy Needham hasn't let standards slip since taking over. The mantra here is all about sourcing the best ingredients; much is flown from Italy on the day of serving. Take our simple octopus salad paired with potatoes and a few taggiasche olives: so fresh you could almost taste the sun. The pasta dishes are always hard to resist, and pappardelle with pig's cheek and a hint of saffron was top drawer. The kitchen resists temptation to complicate things, so a juicy pan-fried veal cutlet arrived with just artichokes and potato purée. Desserts such as vanilla panna cotta with strawberries and basil sugar are lovely treats too. The only downside is that prices have crept steadily upwards (though the set menu is good value); unnecessarily high wine premiums can take the shine off dining here.
Babies and children welcome: high chairs. Booking essential. Disabled: toilet. Dress: smart casual. Separate room for parties, seats 20. **Map 15 G9.**

Marylebone

Il Baretto
43 Blandford Street, W1U 7HF (7486 7340, www.ilbaretto.co.uk). Baker Street or Bond Street tube. **Lunch served** noon-3pm Mon-Fri; 12.30-4pm Sat, Sun. **Dinner served** 6-10.30pm Mon-Fri; 6.30-10pm Sat, Sun. **Main courses** £14.50-£31.50. **Credit** AmEx, MC, V.

Basement spaces can be a difficult proposition for a restaurant designer. A tricksy, awkward room layout, echoing acoustics and austere black and smoked glass fittings all conspire to create a rather gloomy sense of oppression at Il Baretto. Service too is off-kilter, veering from obsequious to matey, with a constant undertow of upselling: buy bottled water, buy bread, buy wine, buy another starter… On the other hand, we were perfectly happy with our shared starter, a dazzlingly pretty broad bean and rocket salad topped with razor-thin slices of tart, feisty pecorino cheese. And we wanted to leave space for our primo – beautifully al dente paccheri smothered in a dense 'nduja sauce and grated smoked ricotta, its rustic smokiness setting off to perfection the spiciness of the soft Calabrian sausage and tomato sauce. Grilled lamb chops, piled high and deliciously moist, worked well as a follow-up, particularly when they were teamed with foot-long matchsticks of deep-fried courgettes coated in barely-there batter, and a bowl of delicate, glistening green beans. Yes, the food is great, but it seems overpriced, and the service and decor are wide of the mark. Il Baretto feels like it's in danger of becoming an irrelevant haunt for the local ladies who lunch.
Babies and children welcome: high chairs. Booking essential. Tables outdoors (2, pavement). **Map 9 G5.**

★ Locanda Locatelli   HOT 50
8 Seymour Street, W1H 7JZ (7935 9088, www.locandalocatelli.com). Marble Arch tube. **Lunch served** noon-3pm Mon-Sat; noon-3.30pm Sun. **Dinner served** 6.45-11pm Mon-Thur; 6.45-11.30pm Fri, Sat; 6.45-10.15pm Sun. **Main courses** £12.50-£31.50. **Credit** AmEx, MC, V.

The decor, with its frosted glass curtains and mirrors, may strike some as more Miami Beach than West End, but at night Giorgio Locatelli's dining room is cosy and warm, and a fitting setting for some of London's best Italian food. Our meal this year was flawless from beginning (a groaning bread basket and deeply pungent extra virgin olive oil) to end (exquisite petits fours). Starters: sardines 'en saor' (with sultanas and pine nuts), and creamy salt cod with gorgeous cherry tomatoes and paper-thin polenta crisps. Mains: own-made strozzapreti (rolled pasta) with a rich tomato sauce featuring spicy 'nduja sausage, olives and heavenly ricotta; and chargrilled lamb with minted peas and crushed potato. Mind you, at nearly £30, the lamb could have been more generously portioned. For dessert, a diminutive pair of lovely cannoli was served with strawberries and pistachio ice-cream. The wine list is an encyclopaedia of classic Italy and lesser-known treasures, and includes some bottles under or around £30. The downer was in the service: assertive refilling of wine glasses even after we had asked to do the pouring ourselves, and a long wait for a requested VAT receipt. However, those are minor quibbles. Locatelli maintains high standards year after year.
Available for hire. Babies and children welcome: high chairs. Booking advisable. Disabled: toilet. Dress: smart casual. Separate room for parties, seats 50. **Map 9 G6.**

Mayfair

Alloro
19-20 Dover Street, W1S 4LU (7495 4768, www.alloro-restaurant.co.uk). Green Park tube. *Bar* **Open** noon-10pm Mon-Fri; 7-10pm Sat. **Lunch served** noon-2.30pm Mon-Fri. **Dinner served** 7-10.30pm Mon-Sat. **Main courses** £16-£20.
Restaurant **Lunch served** noon-2.30pm Mon-Fri. **Dinner served** 7-10.30pm Mon-Sat. **Main courses** £16-£20. **Set lunch** £29.50 2 courses, £35 3 courses. **Set dinner** £34 2 courses, £39 3 courses, £43 4 courses. *Both* **Credit** AmEx, DC, MC, V.

If the term 'fine dining', often associated with Italian food, has become devalued, Alloro rehabilitates it. The veteran operation continues to ooze class – from the intuitive, plentiful staff to the comfortable shades-of-taupe aesthetic and precise on-plate presentation. Prices are high, but neither ingredient quality nor portion sizes are scrimped on, and dining costs haven't risen in two years. The menu is a fixed price for two or three courses (or four at dinner), with some fairly steep supplements. Italian dishes are most prominent in the antipasti and primi; the main courses are pan-European modern classics. We started with strozzapreti with a beef ragù, whose slight dryness we forgave instantly for its depth of flavour and affinity for the house-made pasta. Mains read simply – meat or fish with salad or vegetables – but taste and texture are expertly elicited. Plaice with tempura vegetables had a light batter that complemented the delicate, creamy fish with crackle and seasoning. The

thoughtful wine list represents Italy's regions and grape types knowledgeably, and within a wide span of prices. Our only cavil was that a lone luncher was served a large bottle of mineral water; such peccadilloes would doubtless have gone unnoticed by the relaxed Mayfair business crowd.
Available for hire. Babies and children admitted. Booking advisable. Dress: smart casual. **Map 9 J7.**

Cecconi's
5A Burlington Gardens, W1S 3EP (7434 1500, www.cecconis.co.uk). Green Park or Piccadilly tube. **Breakfast served** 7am-noon Mon-Fri; 8am-noon Sat, Sun. **Brunch served** noon-5pm Sat, Sun. **Meals served** noon-11.30pm Mon-Sat. **Main courses** £14-£26. **Credit** AmEx, MC, V.

Achingly fashionable in the noughties, this all-day Italian brasserie has mellowed into a sleekly self-assured Mayfair stalwart – and remains hugely popular. On a Monday evening, our squeezed-in two-hour slot wasn't mere maître d' posturing: come 8pm, every table in the place was occupied. Designed by Ilse Crawford, the dining room's monochrome marble floor, apple-green upholstery and velvet banquettes have stood the test of time; perhaps the best perches in the house are along the low-lit central bar, with its elegant art deco lamps and suave, white-suited barmen. The menu favours luxurious simplicity over culinary innovation: a generous plate of lobster spaghetti, say, or a truffle-laced smoked duck salad. The quality of ingredients shone through a succession of bite-sized cicchetti, from plump Umbrian sausages to dainty crostini, topped with creamy goat's cheese and baked aubergine, salty anchovies and rich chicken liver pâté. Lamb cutlets with caponata were faultlessly cooked, if a little underseasoned, but the best dish was the simplest: a tangle of fresh, own-made basil tagliatelle, studded with prawns, peas, garlic, basil and chilli. Unobtrusive but attentive service and a surprisingly wallet-friendly wine list add to Cecconi's easy going appeal; we may not have spotted an A-lister, but we left feeling very content.
Babies and children welcome: high chairs. Booking advisable. Disabled: toilet. Dress: smart casual. Tables outdoors (10, terrace). **Map 9 J7.**

Murano
20-22 Queen Street, W1J 5PR (7495 1127, www.schoolofhartnett.co.uk). Green Park tube. **Lunch served** noon-2.30pm, **dinner served** 6.30-10.15pm Mon-Sat. **Set lunch** £30 3 courses. **Set meal** £65 3 courses, £75 4 courses, £85 tasting menu. **Credit** AmEx, MC, V.

Angela Hartnett's flagship restaurant is a lovely, calm space, in tones of sage and cream, with both retro and modernist touches defying the venue's formality. An initial hush swiftly grows into a soft buzz as the evening progresses; well-versed staff glide along efficiently. These are sound enough reasons to dine here. Another would be the good-value set lunch, which doesn't stint on the adjuncts of simple, delectable nibbles, including outstanding salumi, high-quality breads and oil, a delightful painter's palette of post-main sorbets, fruit, and truffles even if you don't order coffee. Wine by the glass comes in a small measure, but ours all delivered full flavours. Occasional identity crises persist, however, even in the relatively straightforward set menu. At times the 'panache' (to borrow Murano's own term) works fine, as in head chef Diego Cardoso's masterly sea bream ceviche, perfectly in balance. And the following

ITALIAN

fratelli la bufala

45a South End Rd, NW3 2
www.fratellilabufala.c
Telephone: 020 7435 78

If you have visited any Fratelli La Bufala's across Italy, you may think you know what to expect in t Hampstead branch. However, you would be mistaken. The owner Mimmo Rimoli, has lovingly crea his own multi award winning brand that is unique, superior and certainly sets itself apart.

The brand showcases the gastronomic heritage of Naples, with their buffalo meat and mozzar cheese, and the pizzas here are acclaimed far and wide. Unlike many other restaurants that pertair cooking pizzas the Italian way, Mimmo's real wood fired oven ensure authentic pizzas to die for, using finest, freshest toppings just the way you like them.

The emphasis has always been on quality and freshness, and none more so than their fish dishes. Seco to none is their fish casserole, which could easily feed two. A platter of swordfish, lobster, king praw clams and succulent cherry tomatoes, this dish has become a firm favourite and essential to boo advance.

Expect fine dining but a warm and welcoming environment, nothing stuffy! Mimmo and his team always on hand to make your dining experience one that you will be sharing with your friends c crisp-skinned fillet of sea trout was nicely complemented by a sweet-tart tomato vinaigrette. Nevertheless, the accompanying aubergine parmigiana – neatly executed, undeniably delicious – was no foil for the soft-fleshed fish. Risotto and pasta are among the simple delights (but do they really warrant domed service?), and desserts are adroitly prepared and good to eat. In fairness, the overall experience is unlikely to disappoint. *Available for hire. Babies and children welcome: high chairs. Booking essential, dinner Fri and Sat, 1 month ahead. Disabled: toilet. Dress: smart casual. Separate room for parties, seats 12.* **Map 9 H8.**

Ristorante Semplice
9-10 Blenheim Street, W1S 1LJ (7495 1509, www.ristorantesemplice.com). Bond Street tube. **Lunch served** noon-2.30pm Mon-Fri. **Dinner served** 7-10.30pm Mon-Sat. **Main courses** £21-£29. **Set lunch** £23 2 courses incl coffee, £27.50 3 courses incl glass of wine & coffee, £31 4 courses incl glass of wine & coffee. **Credit** AmEx, MC, V.
Every bite of our lunch here was superb, from the exquisite own-made bread rolls down to the petits fours that came with the textbook espresso. Semplice is a tiny room, decorated in rather charmless, hotel-lobby style, but it's comfortable. And in any case, you'd feel privileged to eat this food in an underground car park. In two starters and two mains from the set lunch, not a single element fell short of perfection. Borlotti bean soup, puréed to an unctuous, earthy cream, was enlivened by small chunks of sausage and a fine lace of pungent olive oil. Each ingredient in a salad of french beans, broad beans, leaves and shaved parmesan was improbably flavourful. One main, impeccably timed calf's liver on meltingly soft caramelised onions, was simple and flawless. The other, roasted cod fillet served in a light broth with mussels, samphire and quartered cherry tomatoes, featured top-notch ingredients in a well-judged and completely integrated assembly. This being Mayfair, the wine list hits some heady heights, but there's good choice by the glass, and a few bottles under £30. Dinner prices also climb to Mayfair levels, but the food is breathtaking. Go for lunch and get a bargain.
Available for hire. Babies and children admitted. Booking advisable. Disabled: toilet. Separate room for parties, seats 24. Tables outdoors (4, pavement). **Map 9 H6.** **For branch see index.**

★ Theo Randall at the Intercontinental
1 Hamilton Place, Park Lane, W1J 7QY (7409 3131, www.theorandall.com). Hyde Park Corner tube. **Lunch served** noon-3pm Mon-Fri. **Dinner served** 5.45-11pm Mon-Sat. **Main courses** £27-£35. **Set meal** (lunch, 5.45-7pm, 9-11pm) £27 2 courses, £33 3 courses. **Credit** AmEx, DC, MC, V.
It's a long way from Hammersmith to Park Lane, but it's a transition that Theo Randall (ex-River Café) has made with ease. Yes, the interior is very Mayfair – all hushed tones, soft brown and cream leather, glass screens and pistachio-green gladioli – but the ambience is cheery, warm and intimate, and service unstuffy and unfussy. The food too has made the transition from W6 to W1 with ease. Produce is the star here, whether it's soft, fresh pappardelle with hearty beef ragù, or delicate smoked eel served with

pretty orange beetroot, dandelion and fresh horseradish. Ingredients shine, and will have fans of Italian food in raptures as they discover rustic favourites such as cima di rape, borage leaves, ricotta and sage in a mixed green ravioli, or taste the little pile of creamy aubergines and borlotti beans served with generous hunks of beef sirloin. Staff are charming; our waiter even managed to get a sulky teenager at the next table to smile.
Available for hire. Babies and children welcome: high chairs. Booking advisable. Disabled: lift; toilet. Dress: smart casual. Separate room for parties, seats 25. Vegetarian menu. **Map 9 G8.**

Pimlico

Tinello NEW
87 Pimlico Road, SW1W 8PH (7730 3663, www.tinello.co.uk). Sloane Square tube or Victoria tube/rail. **Lunch served** noon-2.30pm, **dinner served** 6-10.30pm Mon-Sat. **Main courses** £15.50-£22.50. **Credit** AmEx, MC, V.
A welcome addition to Pimlico's rather staid dining scene, Tinello is the brainchild of chef Federico Sali (previously head chef at Locanda Locatelli) and his brother Max (who was Giorgio Locatelli's sommelier). The menu, which includes many antipasti and 'small eats', is both fun and alluring and reflects the cuisine of the brothers' native Tuscany. Witness a traditional Tuscan crostini of toasted bread topped with coarse chicken liver pâté and freshly grated truffle. Another rustic dish taken upmarket was nettle pappardelle served with duck ragu. Also on the pasta list: ingredient of the moment, 'nduja (a spreadable spicy pork sausage from Calabria), melted into a fresh tomato sauce for cloaking tubular mezzi paccheri pasta and topped with burrata cheese. Cornish fish is showcased in the secondi; we chose roast fillet of brill with clams and borlotti beans, but could have had chargrilled mackerel with fennel, pink grapefruit and rocket, or lemon sole with aubergines and salsa verde. Decor is on the sombre side (dangling cords, dark mirrors, steampunk lighting), but staff did a good job of making us feel welcome, aided by a wine list that starts at £2.50 a glass. Nevertheless, the expertly chosen, mainly Italian bottles do quickly reach the £25-plus bracket.
Babies and children welcome: high chairs; nappy-changing facilities. Booking advisable. Separate room for parties, seats 26. Tables outdoors (2, pavement). **Map 15 G11.**

Soho

Bocca di Lupo
12 Archer Street, W1D 7BB (7734 2223, www.boccadilupo.com). Piccadilly Circus tube. **Lunch served** 12.30-3pm Mon-Sat; noon-4pm Sun. **Dinner served** 5.30-11pm Mon-Sat. **Main courses** £7-£25. **Credit** AmEx, MC, V.
Bocca di Lupo was heaving when we came for dinner, and that led to a (minor) grumble about lengthy waits to place orders. But the apologies were heartfelt, and afterwards all proceeded smoothly. There are three keys to the restaurant's success. One: it offers the option of small plates for many dishes, and pricing by the piece for items such as crostini and deep-fried veg, making it easy to eat lightly and to mix and match. Two: it emphasises authentic regionality, thus introducing dishes and ingredients that may be unfamiliar. Three: it chooses ingredients carefully and cooks them beautifully. Octopus and celery salad

featured tender octopus and a lovely dressing of capers and own-made vinegar. Fritto misto had been fried with split-second precision. Luganega, a spicy sausage from the Veneto, was served straight from the grill and was sensationally flavourful. Orecchiette with 'nduja (another spicy sausage, this time from Calabria), featured a fresh tomato sauce of rare excellence. Own-made ice-creams make a perfect finish. The all-Italian wine list offers a generous selection of glasses and carafes, which serves all needs well. It's hard to see how anything can be improved. And there seem to be many people who endorse that view.
Babies and children welcome: booster seats. Booking advisable. Disabled: toilet. Separate room for parties, seats 35. **Map 17 B4.**

Polpo
41 Beak Street, W1F 9SB (7734 4479, www.polpo.co.uk). Piccadilly Circus tube. **Lunch served** noon-3pm Mon-Fri; noon-4pm Sat; noon-5pm Sun. **Dinner served** 5.30-11pm Mon-Sat. **Dishes** £4.50-£8. **Credit** AmEx, MC, V.
Owned by Russell Norman and Richard Beatty, with the kitchen headed by Tom Oldroyd, Polpo and its newer siblings Polpetto and Da Polpo fuse the Venetian bacaro (wine-bar-cum-café) with hip New York West Village eateries. The decor, with peeling paint and battered wooden panelling, looks like something from the 'before' clips on *Homes Under the Hammer*. Brown paper menus and chunky tumblers for wine glasses underline the sense of squatter chic, as does sharing small plates of unfussy food. These stretch from simple olives and a crostino topped with chickpea and anchovy mash (rendered dull by a lack of anchovy flavour), to sirloin steak and calf's liver with onions. A shallow plate of soupy beans – more like bean soup – highlighted that the vogue for sharing dishes is often impractical; neither would we want to spoon linguine vongole across the table. Best dishes were the cuttlefish in squid ink and the spinach and egg pizzette. Service was hard-working and friendly enough. Sitting elbow-to-elbow with the Nathan Barleys who frequent this place could be reassuring or irritating, depending on your point of view; one thing for sure is that this little chain is a hit.
Babies and children welcome: high chairs. Booking advisable lunch. Bookings not accepted dinner. **Map 17 A4.**
For branches (Da Polpo, Polpetto) see index.

South Kensington

Daphne's
112 Draycott Avenue, SW3 3AE (7589 4257, www.daphnes-restaurant.co.uk). South Kensington tube. **Lunch served** noon-3pm, **dinner served** 5.30-11.30pm Mon-Fri. **Meals served** noon-11.30pm Sat; noon-10.30pm Sun. **Main courses** £14-£27.75. **Set meal** (5.30-7pm Mon-Fri; noon-7pm Sat, Sun) £17.50 2 courses, £19.50 3 courses. **Credit** AmEx, DC, MC, V.
The midday shoppers at Brompton's ultra-chic boutiques must have worked up quite an appetite, because by the time we sat down for Daphne's pre-theatre slot, the set menu was looking rather bare. There was no fish, beetroot salad was gone, and the pork was now chicken. Still, there were enough dishes remaining to put together a reasonably interesting three courses. Salad of roast aubergine and mozzarella was prettily presented, the cheese nicely milky. The chicken was a plump, juicy breast

atop flavourful caponata, while vegetarian tagliatelle came with generous blobs of ricotta. Blueberry ice-cream with nutty biscuits made a refreshing end to a good-value meal. The carte, of course, offers a much wider range, but still plays it pretty classic. Staff hovered just a little too close during our meal, though they backed off once the two rooms filled up. The main area, with exposed brick walls, provides people-watching opportunities through the glass front, while at the back there's a large, light conservatory. The wine list is predominantly Italian and in the £20 to £30 per bottle bracket, with a smattering of Bordeauxs and champagnes for the à la carte crowd.

Babies and children welcome: high chairs. Booking advisable. Separate room for parties, seats 40. **Map 14 E10**.

Westminster

Massimo NEW

2011 WINNER BEST NEW DESIGN
Corinthia Hotel, 10 Northumberland Avenue, WC2N 5AE (7998 0555, www.corinthia. com/en/london). Embankment tube.
Oyster Bar **Meals served** noon-11pm Mon-Sat. **Main courses** £8-£40.

Restaurant **Lunch served** noon-3pm, **dinner served** 6-10.30pm Mon-Sat. **Main courses** £16-£38. **Set meal** (noon-2.30pm, 6-7pm) £23 2 courses, £28 3 courses.
Both **Credit** AmEx, MC, V.

David Collins has long been the go-to guy for ambitious restaurateurs wanting glitz and glamour as a backdrop for their high-end menus, and this place shows why. Attached to the five-star Corinthia Hotel, just off Trafalgar Square, where rooms cost in excess of £400 a night, Massimo is a spectacular restaurant and oyster bar headed by Italian chef Massimo Riccioli, also chef-patron of Rome fish specialist La Rosetta. Collins' interior is as much 'wow' as 'mmmmm': huge orbs hang from the vaulted ceiling, great swirls of golden mosaic fill one wall, the showpiece bar another. The dining room is a forest of striped grey and white pillars with low screens creating a sense of intimacy. In keeping with its hotel setting, the food tends to be simple and highly priced. Gnocchi, at £15, may have been stained with beetroot but were essentially potato dumplings in tomato sauce. Consider then the set lunch and pre-theatre menu, which offers a generous choice of four or five dishes per course, such as oxtail meatballs with jerusalem artichoke purée and muscat sauce, and monkfish

gratin with asparagus, capers, olives and almonds. From the dessert list, sweet and salty ginger crème brûlée calls out like *Nessun dorma*.

Babies and children welcome: high chairs; nappy-changing facilities. Booking advisable. Disabled: toilet. Dress: smart casual. Separate room for parties, seats 20. **Map 10 L8**.

Osteria dell'Angolo

47 Marsham Street, SW1P 3DR (3268 1077, www.osteriadellangolo.co.uk). St James's Park tube or bus 88.
Bar **Open/snacks served** noon-11pm Mon-Fri; 6-11pm Sat.
Restaurant **Lunch served** noon-2.30pm Mon-Fri. **Dinner served** 6.30-10.30pm Mon-Sat. **Main courses** £18-£23. **Set lunch** £15.50 2 courses, £20 3 courses.
Both **Credit** AmEx, MC, V.

Pulze group veteran chef Massimiliano Vezzi has settled into this Westminster 'corner' of high-end Italian restaurants. Calm reigns in the highly visible kitchen, and is reflected in the food. There's a clear and enjoyable focus on melding Italian – largely southern – tradition with prime British ingredients. Where Italian produce features, it does so purposefully, as in the darkly grilled strips of cinta

Massimo

senese (rare-breed 'belted' Tuscan pig) pancetta providing crisp contrast to a bright, creamy pea soup. A generous board of cured meats was top-notch, as was an unctuous buffalo mozzarella. On the British side, a 28-day-aged Galloway 'beltie' T-bone steak would have matched any Tuscan Chianina. Accompaniments were strikingly simple and apt, though some sweet-sour zucchini was rather too sweet. The wine list is extensively Italian, with a nod to classical France; a fair selection by the glass features a tantalising and affordable set of Italian sweeties. Service is brisk but warm, quick to correct mistakes, and child-friendly. On a warm summer evening with the sun brightening the terracotta-wash walls and a welcome breeze streaming through an airy expanse of open windows, a cross-section of affluent Londoners created a buzz of contentment.
Babies and children welcome: high chairs. Booking advisable. Disabled: toilet. Separate room for parties, seats 19. **Map 16 K10**.

Quirinale
North Court, 1 Great Peter Street, SW1P 3LL (7222 7080, www.quirinale.co.uk). St James's Park or Westminster tube. **Lunch served** noon-2.30pm Mon-Fri. **Dinner served** 6-10.30pm Mon-Sat. **Main courses** £16-£28. **Set meal** (lunch, 6-7.30pm) £19 2 courses, £23 3 courses. **Credit** AmEx, DC, MC, V.
Although clearly designed with parliamentarians in mind, this surprisingly bright basement space plays host to tourists and Italian food aficionados in the evening; pre-theatre, it attracts bargain hunters for the great-value set meal. Chef Stefano Savio has established a much appreciated pattern of sound sourcing, simple and precise cooking, and trencherman appetite-pleasing. You could dine lightly on grilled fish and sorbets, avoiding the pasta course, but that would miss the point. A recent set menu featured butternut squash passatelli with gloriously rich taleggio sauce – 'best macaroni cheese I've had' was one not-quite-accurate comment. Veal meatballs were executed with a deft hand and the accompanying fresh tomato sauce and spinach were zesty enough to excuse a rich pasta indulgence. Salumi and cheeses are carefully selected, and wine by the glass (each course on the set menu features a recommendation), from a seriously Italian list, is both apt and surprisingly affordable. Reserve a corner for the delicious chocolate pudding: a molten lava of dark chocolate tempered by vanilla ice and fresh fruit. Service was swift, accurate and friendly; an enquiry after the source of a salame resulted in the label being carefully stripped and pasted on paper for us to take home.
Available for hire. Babies and children admitted. Booking advisable lunch. **Map 16 L10**.

West
Bayswater

★ Assaggi
1st floor, 39 Chepstow Place, W2 4TS (7792 5501). Bayswater, Notting Hill Gate or Queensway tube. **Lunch served** 12.30-2.30pm Mon-Fri; 1-2.30pm Sat. **Dinner served** 7.30-11pm Mon-Sat. **Main courses** £18-£24. **Credit** MC, V.
A neighbourhood place serving food that can stand up to any Italian restaurant in London, Assaggi is

a small, simply decorated dining room above a pub. Front-of-house staff usually deliver warm, funny, genuinely friendly service, while the food displays technical skill that is sometimes astonishing, but always focuses on making each ingredient shine. That skill is especially apparent in deep-frying: of big, juicy prawns and a risotto cake in one starter, of stuffed courgette flowers and tiny courgettes in another. The stuffing for the flowers was a runny egg yolk that flowed enticingly when the flower was cut. Another starter comprised creamy burrata cheese wrapped in a strip of grilled aubergine and served on a bed of improbably flavourful salad leaves. Own-made pappardelle had a generous sauce of deeply seasoned crabmeat, including a whole claw. The menu is short, but offers something for everyone. The wine list, also mercifully brief, begins under £25 and delivers high quality at every level. Assaggi's neighbourhood is affluent Bayswater/Notting Hill, so prices are not exactly low, but you can have two courses and a bottle of wine for under £100, which is eminently reasonable for the area. A place to cherish.
Available for hire. Babies and children welcome: high chair. Booking essential. **Map 7 B6**.

Hammersmith

River Café `HOT 50`
Thames Wharf, Rainville Road, W6 9HA (7386 4200, www.rivercafe.co.uk). Hammersmith tube. **Lunch served** 12.30-5pm daily. **Dinner served** 7-11pm Mon-Sat. **Main courses** £30-£37. **Credit** AmEx, DC, MC, V.
The disparity between the River Café's tone – diners and staff are casually dressed; tables are (too) closely packed together – and its prices (most main courses cost over £30) won't sit well with everyone who comes here for a special occasion, but this renowned restaurant works perfectly as a canteen for the well-heeled. Since refurbishment a few years ago, the place looks better than ever. A lovely terrace is dotted with plants, while the big white dining room contains a huge wood-burning oven and an open kitchen. The menu changes twice daily and always makes mouth-watering reading; chargrilled squid with fresh red chilli and rocket is a favourite. In summer, it might be followed by chargrilled, marinated leg of lamb with swiss chard, roast beetroot and fresh horseradish; in winter, by Middle White pork shoulder slow-cooked in milk, lemon peel and sage, accompanied by braised cima di rapa and soft polenta. There are soups, pastas and risottos too, plus a notable regional Italian wine list. Finally, the menu lists regional Italian cheeses, and puddings such as chocolate nemesis or affogato. Satisfaction is pretty much guaranteed, though some of the simpler assemblies just haven't undergone enough kitchen alchemy to justify the prices.
Babies and children welcome: high chairs; nappy-changing facilities. Booking essential. Disabled: toilet. Separate room for parties, seats 18. Tables outdoors (15, terrace). **Map 20 C5**.

South West
Barnes

Riva
169 Church Road, SW13 9HR (8748 0434). Barnes or Barnes Bridge rail or bus 33, 209, 283. **Lunch served** 12.15-2.15pm Mon-Fri,

Sun. **Dinner served** 7-10.30pm Mon-Sat; 7-9pm Sun. **Main courses** £13-£24. **Credit** AmEx, MC, V.
Catering to south-west London suburbanites for over 20 years, Riva is mostly staffed by long-timers. This shows in the efficient, thoughtful service: our waitress reeled off the day's specials with total confidence; tap water was kept topped up; and newspapers were offered to lone diners. There's an old-money vibe to the restaurant, as to the area. Hence Riva doesn't feel the need to be flashy; the walls of its modest-sized dining room are dotted with drawings of Roman architecture. The food isn't overly showy either, with the menu containing rustic dishes such as porchetta with warm beans (admittedly fancied up with a drizzle of balsamic) and shareable starter platters. Main courses of sea bass with fennel, and very rare lamb with peperonata, pleased without wowing, leaving us wondering whether we'd have been better off with a bowl of own-made pasta or gnocchi. The finale, cinnamon ice-cream with crushed amaretti, honey and syrupy balsamic vinegar, was sweet, spicy and sour, and easily enough for two: as well it might be, at £7. The all-Italian wine list deserves attention. With loyal customers welcomed like old friends, a meal here can feel like sitting in on a club you don't belong to – though you might be tempted to join.
Babies and children welcome: high chairs. Booking essential dinner. Tables outdoors (3, pavement).

Chelsea

La Famiglia
7 Langton Street, SW10 0JL (7351 0761, www.lafamiglia.co.uk). Sloane Square tube then bus 11, 22, or bus 19. **Lunch served** noon-2.30pm, **dinner served** 7-11.30pm daily. **Main courses** £14-£30. **Cover** £1.85. **Credit** AmEx, MC, V.
Despite its location on a side street off the less bustling end of the King's Road, La Famiglia cannot be described as quiet. On a weekday lunchtime, conversation was bouncing off the white-tiled walls, from customers who ranged from Chelsea ladies-who-lunch to business folk striking deals. There's a relaxed, jovial feel to the place, helped by black and white family photos lining the walls, and a steadfast bunch of regulars. Perhaps the long-standing customers would be up in arms if their favourite dishes left the menu, but the lengthy collection of risottos, pasta, meat and fish, plus a 15-strong seasonal list, make choosing difficult. Fortunately, the kitchen is strong in all areas; a substantial Tuscan antipasto plate included a selection of cured meats, bruschetta and a crisp polenta slice topped with wonderfully rich ragù. Rigatoni with gorgonzola was creamy and piquant, without overpowering. The waiters are true professionals, wheeling in a dessert trolley loaded with tarts, tortes and tiramisu. We don't resent the cover charge for fantastic bread and focaccia with green olive tapenade, but the same can't be said of the £4.75 price tag for a bowl of over-dressed salad leaves.
Babies and children welcome: high chairs. Booking advisable dinner and Sun. Disabled: toilet. Tables outdoors (30, garden). **Map 13 C13**.

Osteria dell'Arancio
383 King's Road, SW10 0LP (7349 8111, www.osteriadellarancio.co.uk). Fulham Broadway or Sloane Square tube. **Lunch**

served noon-3pm Fri-Sun. **Dinner served** 6.30-11pm Mon-Sat. **Main courses** £15-£17. **Credit** AmEx, DC, MC, V.

The fun, bohemian character of Osteria dell'Arancio has recently become distinctly haute boho, attracting affluent Chelsea folk. A charming, knowledgeable new manager/maître d' runs the front of house, and the kitchen specialises in the food of Le Marche, Tuscany and Piedmont. Head chef Pierluigi Sandonnini trained in Italy under Gualtiero Marchesi (considered the founder of modern Italian cuisine) and brings a new finesse to the food. There's also a fresh focus on wine, with several fine vintages available by the glass from oxygen-free dispensers, and regular wine tastings in the airy upper room. Sadly, we found the new regime somewhat ragged round the edges. The bread, when it eventually came, seemed stale and when more was requested it was much the same. A starter of grilled squid with orange and fennel salad was rather light on both fennel and orange, although the squid was beautifully cooked. Sea bass with courgette ribbons (a main course) was under-seasoned. To cap it all, a cheeseboard that took ages to arrive consisted of a lacklustre assortment of little cubes of hard cheeses, with no blue, creamy or goat's cheese. As with all the maître d's wine recommendations, however, the accompanying sweet Recioto was a perfect match.
Babies and children welcome: high chairs; nappy-changing facilities. Booking advisable dinner. Disabled: toilet. Separate room for parties, seats 35. Tables outdoors (12, terrace). **Map 14 D12.**

Putney

★ Enoteca Turi
28 Putney High Street, SW15 1SQ (8785 4449, www.enotecaturi.com). Putney Bridge tube or Putney rail or bus 14, 74, 270. **Lunch served** noon-2.30pm, **dinner served** 7-11pm Mon-Sat. **Main courses** £11.50-£24.50. **Set lunch** (Mon-Sat) £16.50 2 courses, £19.50 3 courses. **Set dinner** (Mon-Thur) £26.50 2 courses, £30.50 3 courses. **Credit** AmEx, MC, V.

A remarkable restaurant located just by Putney Bridge. Proprietor Giuseppe Turi (previously both sommelier and maître d' at the Athenaeum and the Connaught) has created a unique establishment showcasing both the best Italian regional dishes and the country's finest wines. Enoteca means a 'wine library', where customers can sample a variety of vintages. The enticing menu suggests the best wine, available by the glass, to accompany each dish – something only an establishment with this cellar and expertise could dare to do. A stunning ragù di seppia con ceci e tria (cuttlefish in white wine with chickpeas, scialatelli pasta and deep-fried tagliatelle) was perfectly paired with a citrusy Roncaglia Colli Pesaresi from Le Marche; grilled sardines stuffed with pecorino and mint were set off by a peachy Rami Falanghina. Main courses of monkfish with lobster raviolo, mussels and pea purée; and fedelini with crab, cherry tomato, chilli and rocket were similarly graced with stunning selections. It was hard to resist having wines with the glorious panna cotta and torta al cioccolato, and the dignified but friendly service and soothing earth-toned decor made it difficult to leave. Enoteca Turi isn't cheap, but prices are nowhere near what you would pay for the West End equivalent.
Babies and children welcome: high chairs. Booking advisable. Disabled: toilet. Dress: smart casual. Separate rooms for parties, seating 18 and 30.

South East
Bermondsey

Zucca
184 Bermondsey Street, SE1 3TQ (7378 6809, www.zuccalondon.com). Bermondsey tube or London Bridge tube/rail. **Lunch served** 12.30-3pm Tue-Sun. **Dinner served** 6.30-10pm Tue-Sat. **Main courses** £14.50-£14.95. **Credit** MC, V.

Cool, precise, urbane – the ever-popular Zucca holds on to its position with ease in this hip stretch of Bermondsey. Happily, the slick white plastic surfaces are as accommodating of non-chic gear as the menu is of a not-so-loaded credit card (although being in possession of a forgiving wallet would help one to explore the inspiring wine list). The food is, generally speaking, terrific: generous, prettily but unfussily presented, and always perfectly pitched. Take, for instance the monochrome contrasts of velvety-black ox cheek on gently grainy white polenta; or a tangle of deep gold tagliatelle, ochre girolles and sparkling green flecks of parsley; or glorious medleys of frisky greenery. An excellent array of breads with fine dipping oil features outstanding focaccia. Desserts are homely but beautifully textured, and the coffee as good as you would expect. Niggles, therefore, come as a surprise, whether in the form of a not-so-generous starter of slightly bland salumi; over-zealous water pouring and plate clearing; the absence of a printed dessert list, and the lack of pricing information even in the verbal roll-call. And the initially cheering chatter and clatter from closely packed tables, augmented by an open-plan galley kitchen, grows a touch tiring. But the sheer zest of Zucca will have most punters craving to return.
Babies and children welcome: high chairs; nappy-changing facilities. Booking essential dinner. Disabled: toilet. Separate room for parties, seats 10.

Tower Bridge

Tentazioni
2 Mill Street, SE1 2BD (7237 1100, www.tentazioni.co.uk). Bermondsey tube or London Bridge tube/rail. **Lunch served** noon-2.45pm Mon-Fri. **Dinner served** 6.30-10.45pm Mon-Sat. **Main courses** £13.50-£45. **Set lunch** £11.95 2 courses incl drink, £15 3 courses incl drink & coffee. **Set dinner** £47.50 tasting menu (£68.50 incl wine). **Credit** AmEx, MC, V.

There's plenty to tempt you into splashing out at this smart, romantically lit restaurant, tucked away amid the converted warehouses of Butler's Wharf. A midweek crowd of City boys was doing just that, lured by the seven-course tasting menu.

Polpo. See p161.

Sticking to the carte doesn't prove much more economical; starters are particularly steep at around £10. Ingredients are undoubtedly top-notch (visit Tentazioni's impressive deli around the corner on Queen Elizabeth Street for the take-home-and-enjoy-later proof), but on our latest visit, flavour combinations often fell flat. Raw sliced artichokes made an odd accompaniment to bresaola, while enormous gnocchi (which were too cumbersome to hold on a fork) had been coated in a sickly pear and grappa sauce. Delicate sole fillets were overpowered by mustard, and came with a thickly battered courgette flower, still gooey in the middle. A dessert of 'chocolate ecstasy' didn't quite live up to its name either. Charming (if sometimes forgetful) service, a largely affordable wine list that was grouped by Italian region, and a buzzy atmosphere make this a pleasant spot to spend an evening, but for a better deal, visit at lunchtime.

Available for hire. Babies and children welcome: high chair. Booking advisable dinner Fri, Sat. Separate room for parties, seats 24. **Map 12 S9**.

East
Shoreditch

Fifteen
15 Westland Place, N1 7LP (3375 1515, www.fifteen.net). Old Street tube/rail.
Trattoria **Breakfast served** 7.30-11am Mon-Sat; 8-11am Sun. **Lunch served** noon-3pm, **dinner served** 6-10pm daily. **Main courses** £14-£21.
Restaurant **Lunch served** noon-3pm, **dinner served** 6-10pm daily. **Main courses** £17.50-£23. **Set lunch** £26 2 courses, £30 3 courses, £36 4 courses.
Both **Credit** AmEx, MC, V.
Jamie Oliver's original Fifteen is still going strong. On a recent visit we ate in the ground-floor trattoria: a lively, modern space, with a bar as you enter. The focus is on well-sourced, authentic ingredients, simply prepared and allowed to shine. Starters include a large range of antipasti, along with seafood and vegetable boards featuring some original matchings such as roasted beetroot with orange and oregano, and Sicilian octopus stew on bruschetta. To start, mozzarella di bufala Campana with aubergine, pepper, ricotta salata and bruschetta was a perfect melding of luscious mozzarella, creamy ricotta and lightly roasted veg. A main of poussin with panzanella (a Tuscan bread salad of tomatoes, capers and Volpaia vinegar) came as beautifully tender, moist chicken, the tartness of the capers and vinegar in the salad bringing the dish to life. Fish of the day was an enormous whole bream, perfectly baked. A light, perfect panna cotta completed our dinner. Staff were friendly and professional throughout. The more formal (and pricier) basement restaurant – serving the likes of seared sea trout fillet with fregola sarda, peas, courgettes and taggiasca black olive sauce – is quieter, discreetly retro and elegant, with an open kitchen; we wish it didn't do two-hour sittings, though.
Babies and children welcome: high chairs; nappy-changing facilities. Booking essential restaurant. Disabled: toilet (trattoria). Dress: smart casual. Separate room for parties, seats 65. **Map 6 Q3**.

North
Archway

500 Restaurant
782 Holloway Road, N19 3JH (7272 3406, www.500restaurant.co.uk). Archway tube or Upper Holloway rail. **Lunch served** noon-3pm Fri, Sat. **Dinner served** 5.30-10pm Mon-Sat. **Meals served** noon-9.30pm Sun. **Main courses** £14.30-£16.80. **Credit** MC, V.
Locals are loyal to 500 Restaurant, as shown by the crowd on a quiet Wednesday evening. The small tables filled up quickly between 7.30pm and 8.30pm, by which time it was hard to get a seat. In fact, the clientele creates the atmosphere here, as decor is plain and fairly generic. 500 is one of those rare restaurants that does classic food exceptionally well. You won't find verbose menus or obscure ingredients, just straightforward, trustworthy food. You could confidently take an Italian food connoisseur there – it might even help if they spoke some Italian, as our waiter had limited English (but boundless charm). A menu of old favourites contrasts with regularly changing specials. To start, dense smoked swordfish was delightfully lifted by strawberries and pea shoots. Tagliatelle in a comforting burrata cheese and aubergine sauce, and slow-cooked rabbit were outstanding Italian mamma-style dishes, using rich sauces and robust ingredients. To finish, tiramisu was simple but effective, with caffeine-packed savoiardi biscuits covered in a thick dollop of mascarpone mousse. Portions are generous and prices very reasonable.
Babies and children admitted. Booking essential dinner. **Map 26 C1**.

Camden Town & Chalk Farm

Caponata
3-7 Delancey Street, NW1 7NL (7387 5959, www.caponatacamden.co.uk). Camden Town tube.
Bar **Open** noon-11pm Mon-Sat; noon-10.30pm Sun.

Trullo. See p168.

Restaurant **Brunch served** 10am-3pm Sat, Sun. **Lunch served** noon-3pm Mon-Fri. **Dinner served** 6-10pm daily. **Main courses** £12-£18. **Set meal** £10 2 courses. *Both* **Credit** AmEx, MC, V.
Camden isn't exactly short of places to eat, but Caponata is pretty special. The place attracts local office workers who go for good Italian food (with an emphasis on Sicily), served at very reasonable prices by laid-back, friendly staff. The building is modern and fairly nondescript, with a first-floor dining room and a more informal osteria downstairs – where we enjoyed a pleasurable summer lunch. A rear garden is open in good weather. The quality delivered by the £10 set lunch was unimpeachable: a tart of cherry tomato, oregano and scamorza cheese, followed by linguine with rocket pesto, pachino tomatoes and pecorino shavings. The tart was light and flavour-packed, and the generous portion of pasta showed how fine ingredients can make even simple dishes memorable. The eponymous caponata – mixed vegetables with capers and olives – is rendered here as a thick disc, the flavours well blended, but with all vegetables retaining their integrity. Another starter, of arancina – a deep-fried ball of risotto rice enclosing a nugget of ragù, served with mildly spicy arrabiata sauce – was cooked with precision. Mains from the carte include pastas and a small selection of meat, fish and poultry dishes. Desserts are enticing, and the wine list (plenty of choice by the glass) won't break anyone's bank unless they wish to see it broken.
Babies and children welcome: high chairs; nappy-changing facilities. Booking advisable. Disabled: lift; toilet. Tables outdoors (5, pavement). **Map 3 J1**.

La Collina
17 Princess Road, NW1 8JR (7483 0192). Camden Town or Chalk Farm tube. **Lunch served** noon-3pm, **dinner served** 6-11pm Mon-Fri. **Meals served** noon-11pm Sat, Sun. **Main courses** £12-£20. **Credit** AmEx, MC, V.
La Collina has had a change of ownership, but outwardly continues as it was: a well-established

Osteria dell'Angolo. See p162.

local with its particular strengths to be found in pasta, fish and the warm welcome. Quality has always been sound, with a commitment to traditional Italian cooking, and prices are reasonable. Our starters of vitello tonnato (cold veal loin with tuna mayonnaise) and grilled calamares were done properly, and salt cod cooked in milk and garlic was ample and tasty. Mains were uniformly outstanding: simply and perfectly roasted sea bream, served with sublime sauté potatoes; spaghetti all'astice (with half a lobster and loads of flavourful tomato sauce); and a mixed grill of precisely cooked fish and shellfish that came with just a salad (which was all it needed). The wine list starts with high-quality Sicilians under £20. Our one dessert suggested that puddings aren't a strong point, but cheese is an alternative. The cooking sometimes lacks fine-tuning, in seasoning and dressing, but nothing to get upset about. If there's a problem here, it's in the physical space: ground floor and back garden wonderful, basement room a little cramped. All the more reason to book well in advance and bag a table in a prime position.

Babies and children welcome: high chairs. Booking advisable. Separate rooms for parties, seating 15 and 25. Tables outdoors (15, garden). **Map 27 B2.**

Highbury

Trullo

300-302 St Paul's Road, N1 2LH (7226 2733, www.trullorestaurant.com). Highbury & Islington tube/rail.
Bar **Open/meals served** 7-10.30pm Thur-Sat. **Tapas** £3-£8.50.
Restaurant **Lunch served** 12.30-2.30pm Sat; 12.30-3pm Sun. **Dinner served** 6.30-10.30pm Mon-Sat. **Main courses** £14-£20.
Both **Credit** MC, V.
Blessing or curse? Trullo's connection with Jamie Oliver's Fifteen (head chef Tim Siadatan was an early graduate) meant that it was never going to be allowed to evolve at its own pace. It went from opening (in June 2010) to booked solid within weeks, attracting patrons from far and wide. This has stopped the crowd and mood feeling local, but not

the restaurant's approach. Enthusiastic, solicitous staff behave as if they really care about having you back (on our visit, at least; though not always if reports are to be believed) and prices are fair, at good gastropub level. The short, daily-changing menu marries rustic Italian cooking with British ingredients, big colours and a little kitchen invention. In a July cold snap, we were offered grilled ox heart with borlotti beans and salsa rossa (distinct flavours that fused beautifully), alongside bruschetta with English peas, mint and coppa di parma. Pasta – tagliatelle with Scottish girolles, and pappardelle with beef-shin ragu – was glossy, with bite, and mackerel nicely charcoal-grilled. Caramel panna cotta is halfway to becoming a classic, its creamy taste and texture cut by dense, sharp caramel. A panzanella, though, was poor, the ingredients indistinctly mushed into a tart dressing; we also had problems with a carafe of quite indifferent Morellino di Scansano. The ground-floor dining room makes a decent stab at inhabiting a difficult space; decor is unpretentious, with large windows to the street, exposed pipes and factory-style light fittings. Downstairs is in a similar style with a stand-up bar and more tables; it tends to be easier to get a walk-in spot here than in the heavily booked main room, but the menu is limited so snacks and small dishes.
Babies and children welcome: high chairs; nappy-changing facilities. Booking advisable. Dress: smart casual. Separate room for parties, seats 35.

Outer London
Twickenham, Middlesex

A Cena
418 Richmond Road, Twickenham, Middx, TW1 2EB (8288 0108, www.acena.co.uk). Richmond tube/rail or St Margarets rail.
Lunch served noon-2.30pm Tue-Sun. **Dinner served** 7-10.30pm Mon-Sat. **Main courses** £14-£22. **Set lunch** (Sun) £21 2 courses, £25 3 courses. **Credit** AmEx, MC, V.
Just over Richmond Bridge into Twickenham, behind a deceptively small and understated frontage, lies one of those restaurants locals would love to keep to themselves. A Cena was set up in 2001 by husband-and-wife team Camilla and Tim Healey, and their colleague Nicola Parsons – who all worked together at the former Giorgio Armani restaurant in Knightsbridge. The decor is loosely based on Camilla's grandfather's place in Italy. Bright white, copiously mirrored walls contrast with handsome wooden furniture, in turn accessorised by gleaming white tablecloths and fine silverware, the whole producing a beautifully cool atmosphere. The welcome and service is bright as the ambience is mellow. Food is consistently top-notch. An excellent three-course Sunday lunch menu featured starters of luscious zucchini fritti with basil lemon mayonnaise, and refreshing zuppa d'estiva (a summer soup of mussels, courgettes, lemon, cream and mint). Main courses were equally delightful: barbecued marinated Gressingham duck breast with apricot dressing, watercress and pan-roast potatoes with rosemary; and a grilled sea bass fillet with fennel seeds, white wine and fennel salad. Crema di limone with raspberries made a generous finish to a truly satisfying meal.
Available for hire. Babies and children welcome: booster seats. Booking advisable. Takeaway service.

Budget bites

Fazenda UK

Fazenda UK

13 Leyden Street, E1 7LE (7375 0577, www.fazendauk.com). Aldgate East tube or Liverpool Street tube/rail. **Open** 8.30am-6pm Mon-Sat. **Lunch served** noon-3.30pm Mon-Sat. **Main courses** £6. **No credit cards.**
Owner Antonio Battisti has turned this tiny space just off Petticoat Lane into a charming, homely café. The decor is basic: sacks of wood-roasted coffee beans, bare floorboards and rickety, pastel-coloured tables and chairs. There are also a few tables outside the front windows, and a basement space with a sofa. It's a family affair: Antonio's wife pre-cooks the dishes at home (until they get a full restaurant licence), and her father's farm in Italy supplies the olive oil. We enjoyed a flavourful pumpkin soup as bright and intense as the Mediterranean sun, and beef, dusted in flour then fried, served with mozzarella salad and either top-quality

bread or rotelle (wheel-shaped pasta). Leave room for afters: sponge cake layered with chocolate custard and soaked in vodka tasted sensational.
Babies and children admitted. Bookings not accepted. Tables outdoors (2, pavement). Takeaway service. **Map 12 R6.**

Machiavelli

69 Long Acre, WC2E 9JS (7240 2125, www.machiavellifood.co.uk). Covent Garden tube. **Breakfast served** 8am-11am Mon-Fri; 9am-noon Sat. **Lunch served** 12.20-3pm, **dinner served** 5.30-10.30pm Mon-Sat. **Meals served** 9am-5pm Sun. **Main courses** £8-£15. **Credit** MC, V.
A new venture from the Italian food importer behind the Manicomio restaurants in Chelsea and the City, this classy café-cum-deli mixes tradition (wicker baskets full of fresh lemons) with urban sophistication (black lacquered bistro tables and linen

napkins). Hot dishes such as pasta, steak and sausage-studded lasagne feature on the short menu, alongside some light summery salads; we enjoyed cold orecchiette with intense black olives, pine nuts and sweet cherry tomatoes, all lightly tossed in basil pesto. Sweet cravings can be satisfied with flourless chocolate cake or salted caramel tart. The only downer on our visit was the service, which veered from haughty to hapless.
Available for hire. Babies and children welcome: high chairs; nappy-changing facilities. Booking advisable. Disabled: toilet. Separate room for parties, seats 50. Takeaway service. Vegetarian menu. **Map 18 E3.**

Sardo Cucina

112 Whitfield Street, W1T 5EE (7383 3555, www.sardocucina.com). Warren Street tube. **Open** 8am-9pm Mon-Fri; 9am-4pm Sat. **Meals served** noon-9pm Mon-Fri; noon-4pm Sat. **Main courses** £4.95-£8.95. **Credit** (over £10) MC, V.
An offshoot of the acclaimed Sardo restaurant next door, this place is ideal for a quick dose of Sardinian food and hospitality. The short list of daily changing specials might offer chunky minestrone soup (unusually, containing sweetcorn and croutons), malloreddus (a robust Sardinian pasta) or burger topped with mozzarella and spinach; order at the counter, then take your tray to one of the bare rustic tables. Dishes are reheated for service in a microwave – not always ideal. Breads (all own-made), krafen (doughnuts filled with custard or chocolate) and apple cake topped with pine nuts are among the baked goodies. Drinks include Miscela D'oro coffees, Novus teas and freshly squeezed orange juice.
Available for hire. Babies and children welcome: high chairs. Tables outdoors (8, pavement). Takeaway service. **Map 3 J4.**

ITALIAN

Sardo Cucina

Japanese

Once the exclusive preserve of business dining, Japanese food in London has filtered from rarefied and prohibitively expensive restaurants right down to supermarket chiller cabinets, and bubbled back up again with specialist eateries offering high-quality renditions of even the most basic dishes. Now the capital's diners can be discerning about noodles (udon specialist **Koya** reigns supreme), kushiyaki (try **Zuma** for a dose of glamour, **Bincho** or **Tosa** for informal meals) and even Japanese pancakes (okonomiyaki specialist **Abeno Too** remains a firm favourite). So the days when people thought Japanese cuisine was all rice and raw fish are long gone – and sushi bars, where rice and raw fish abound, are demonstrating a new level of sophistication too, with luxuries such as wagyu beef, truffles and foie gras among the toppings at the most modish establishments. The master chefs at newcomer **Yashin** – winner of Best Sushi Bar in our Eating & Drinking Awards 2011 – carefully creates and seasons each delicious morsel so that even that staple accompaniment, soy sauce, is no longer required.

Central
Chancery Lane

★ Crane & Tortoise
39-41 Gray's Inn Road, WC1X 8PR (7242 9094, www.sohojapan.co.uk). Chancery Lane tube or bus 38, 55. **Dinner served** 5-10.30pm Mon-Fri; 6-10.30pm Sat. **Set meal** £7.70. **Credit** MC, V.
At first glance, the Crane & Tortoise has much the feel of a chain bar with its modern leather chairs, high tables and personality-free white walls. The menu tells a different story, though – teriyaki, katsu curry, Japanese burgers and sushi are all available. Prices are pretty cheap too. Though simple, our chazuke (green tea and rice soup) tasted just right, with plump rice, salty pickled plum and a cleansing broth. A dish of cured squid, bamboo shoots, shredded ginger and chilli packed a punch, with sweet, spicy and sour notes. Bite-sized beef cubes fried in garlic butter were perfectly cooked and tender, though a little bland. Unlike the Yorkshire Grey pub a couple of doors away, the restaurant was far from busy on a Thursday evening – there was a handful of diners in the back room and a few Japanese men at the bar, making the most of the drinks list (Japanese beers and whiskey, Asian-inspired cocktails, saké, shochu and plum wine). A shame: for its reasonable food, value for money and attentive service, the place definitely deserves more customers.
Available for hire. Babies and children admitted. Separate room for parties, seats 30. Tables outdoors (3, pavement). Takeaway service. **Map 4 M4**.

City

★ Moshi Moshi Sushi
24 Upper Level, Liverpool Street Station, EC2M 7QH (7247 3227, www.moshimoshi.co.uk). Liverpool Street tube/rail. **Meals served** 11.30am-10pm Mon-Fri. **Dishes** £1.40-£4. **Main courses** £10-£12. **Credit** MC, V.
Situated, as it is, next to a tanning shop in a far corner of Liverpool Street station, Moshi Moshi Sushi isn't blessed with the most inviting of locations. This doesn't seem to put off local office workers, however, so the place can get busy at peak times. There's a choice of menu and seating options: sushi and salads while perched at the conveyor-belt counter, or à la carte (sushi and other classic Japanese dishes) seated at one of the cosy tables. Sustainability is taken seriously here, so much of the fish used comes from the UK and you'll never see bluefin tuna or eel on the menu. The sushi chef was happy to talk us through the fish offered that day. Our squid and yellowfin tuna nigiri were pleasant enough. The 'sea-fayre' tempura was enjoyable too, containing juicy pollack slices in a light, crisp batter, but the sauce could have had more oomph. Monkfish liver terrine was also let down by a sauce that needed more citrus. Yet in general, Moshi Moshi offers a reliable list of staples at reasonable prices, making it a safe bet for repeat visits.
Babies and children admitted. Disabled: toilet. Takeaway service; delivery service (within 4-mile radius). **Map 12 R5**.

Covent Garden

Abeno Too
17-18 Great Newport Street, WC2H 7JE (7379 1160, www.abeno.co.uk). Leicester Square tube. **Meals served** noon-11pm Mon-Sat; noon-10pm Sun. **Main courses** £9-£24. **Set lunch** (Mon-Fri) £9.80-£19.80. **Credit** MC, V.
Nicknamed 'Osaka soul food' because of its popularity in the Kansai region of Honshu, Japan's main island, you can think of okonomiyaki as akin to Spanish tortilla, but with shredded cabbage dominating the eggy base instead of potato. At Abeno, pioneer of this specialism in Europe, you can order typical Japanese side dishes too; the standout is asparagus and tiger prawn gyoza. There are also not-so-typical combinations of egg and noodles (om-soba) or rice and noodles (soba-rice) – Atkins dieters, beware. But the main event is to select fillings as simple as pork or as outlandish as mushroom, lotus root and cheese, then watch the mixture cooked ('yaki') as you like it ('okonomi') on a hotplate at your table. Service comes with a smile, plus advice on sauces, fish flakes and seaweed sprinkles. The result is comfort food that each diner can help themselves to with their own knife-edged spatula. You may want to decline generous spirals of mayonnaise and okonomiyaki sauce to let the fresh, flavoursome ingredients speak for themselves. The simple menu is matched by no-frills surroundings: cream walls, brushed steel panels, and hollow bench seating in which customers can stow valuables. It's a relatively good-value option

too – if you don't succumb to the temptation of fillet steak teppanyaki or the Kansai special mix. *Babies and children welcome: high chairs. Bookings not accepted. Takeaway service.* **Map 18 C6**. **For branch see index**.

Euston

Sushi of Shiori

2011 RUNNER-UP BEST SUSHI BAR
144 Drummond Street, NW1 2PA (7388 9962, www.sushiofshiori.co.uk). Euston tube/rail. **Lunch served** 11.30am-2.30pm, **dinner served** 5.30-10pm Tue-Sat. **Dishes** £3-£12. **Set lunch** £8.50-£15.50. **Set meal** £12-£50. **Credit** MC, V.

First-time visitors may be surprised by the diminutive size of this sushi restaurant; there are seats for around eight diners, making walk-ins nigh on impossible. But there's a bright side: such a limit means the full attention of the lone chef is channelled into creating extremely intricate plates of food, beautiful from the main event down to the tiny garnishes (radish butterflies, anyone?). As you'd expect, sushi is the focus, and you'd do well to order the temari variations in advance; these small, ball-shaped rice balls are topped with stunningly arranged ingredients, such as scallop with a mound of truffle salsa, and curled botan shrimp with a smidgen of sea urchin. Thoughtfully, pastry brushes are provided to apply soy sauce to the delicate creations. A small but considered saké menu and own-made desserts (cherry blossom ice-cream, red bean cake) round out each meal. Shiori is an outstanding husband-and-wife operation with sweet, smiling service, which somehow makes their table-turning policy a bit easier to stomach. *Available for hire. Babies and children admitted. Booking advisable. Takeaway service. Vegetarian menu.* **Map 3 J3**.

Fitzrovia

Nizuni NEW

22 Charlotte Street, W1T 2NB (7580 7447, www.nizuni.com). Goodge Street or Tottenham Court Road tube. **Lunch served** noon-3pm Mon-Sat. **Dinner served** 6-10.45pm daily. **Main courses** £8-£15. **Set lunch** £8-£13. **Credit** AmEx, MC, V.

Nizuni is not a strictly traditional Japanese restaurant. It has the same owners as nearby Korean eaterie Koba, and ingredients such as gochujang (hot chilli paste) and doenjang (Korean miso) are subtly and successfully integrated into some dishes. There are flashes of Mediterranean influences too, with the use of balsamic syrup to cut through a beautifully creamy butterfish tataki, and garnishes such as gherkins and capers in meat dishes and salads. But the list of appetisers is what's most captivating, with traditional izakaya-style items mixing with more creative dishes. Lightly seared octopus slices in a tart and savoury tosazu sauce (a mix of vinegar, soy sauce and dried bonito fish shavings) was intricately arranged, and had a delicate, yet lingering, flavour. Sushi is equally well-made; a benchmark example of uni (sea urchin) spoke reassuringly of decent sourcing, the creamy roe tasting clean and sweet. Desserts, including a zingy yuzu and cranberry tart, were excellent, but come, disappointingly, from an outside supplier. The building has been tastefully refurbished to create a simple, wood-lined space,

punctuated by paper lanterns and images of swimming carp and cranes in flight. *Available for hire. Babies and children welcome: high chairs. Booking advisable Thur-Sat. Disabled: toilet. Separate room for parties, seats 20. Tables outdoors (4, pavement). Takeaway service.* **Map 17 B1**.

Roka HOT 50

37 Charlotte Street, W1T 1RR (7580 6464, www.rokarestaurant.com). Goodge Street or Tottenham Court Road tube. **Lunch served** noon-3.30pm Mon-Fri; 12.30-4pm Sat, Sun. **Dinner served** 5.30-11.30pm Mon-Sat; 5.30-10.30pm Sun. **Main courses** £4.50-£68. **Set meal** £50-£75 tasting menu. **Credit** AmEx, DC, MC, V.

Roka still impresses with its mastery of the robata grill, which dominates the capacious dining room. It's a swish spot (thanks to acclaimed Tokyo design team Super Potato), with plenty of exotic hardwoods on display and floor-to-ceiling glass windows that open on to the street in good weather (the outdoor tables are much sought after). It's a noisy place when full, however, which is often.

Highlights of the menu, which is split into types of dishes rather than courses, are the grilled items. Order the inch-thick scallops, peppery and sweet from the mix of shiso cress, a slick of soy and a dollop of wasabi cream, or satisfyingly crisp and umami-packed chicken wings with sea salt and lime. It can be difficult to categorise the rest of the menu, which meanders from tokusen ('specially chosen'), featuring the likes of yellowtail sashimi with truffle yuzu dressing, to 'Roka dishes' of creamy, risotto-like rice hotpots and black cod dumplings. A butterfish dish from 'salada and tataki', elegantly presented on a long, heavy plate, featured wonderfully tender pieces of fish wrapped around white asparagus stalks and doused with a sharp yuzu dressing. Desserts, which fuse Japanese and French traditions and ingredients courtesy of pastry chef Juliene Phillipe, are some of the best in town, and worth saving room for. Service has improved since our last visit, with cheerful staff working the packed room with ease. *Babies and children welcome: high chairs. Booking advisable. Disabled: toilet. Tables outdoors (9, terrace).* **Map 17 B1**. **For branch see index**.

Sushi of Shiori

JAPANESE

Abeno Too. See p170.

Soho Japan

*52 Wells Street, W1T 3PR (7323 4661,
www.sohojapan.co.uk). Oxford Circus tube.*
Lunch served noon-2.30pm Mon-Fri. **Dinner
served** 6-10.30pm Mon-Sat. **Main courses**
£6.50-£14 lunch; £10-£22 dinner. **Set lunch**
£10-£20. **Credit** MC, V.
Reminiscent of a wine bar, with its bottle-lined
walls and wood panelling, Soho Japan serves the
local office community well with classic Japanese
cooking (sushi, tempura, sumiyaki grilled dishes
and so on), as well as a reasonable list of wines,
sakés and beers. At lunch there are also set meals
and bento boxes. Teriyaki chicken was moist in the
middle with satisfyingly crunchy skin, while salt-
grilled mackerel and salmon was equally good –
despite the salmon's over-charred skin. A crab and
avocado salad packed with sweet crabmeat and a
sprinkling of flying fish roe was also a success.
Interestingly, when it came to dessert, our waiter
warned us off that day's special (green tea
cheesecake) as he said it wasn't up to par. He
suggested one of their own-made ices instead.
Options included black or white sesame ice-cream,
as well as yuzu sorbet, which we plumped for: it
tasted more of tropical fruit than the Japanese
citrus fruit we'd been expecting, but was
nonetheless enjoyable. Thanks to its quality food,
attentive service and location near Oxford Circus,
Soho Japan is a flexible choice – good for a working
lunch, post-shopping treat or leisurely dinner.
*Babies and children admitted. Booking advisable.
Tables outdoors (3, pavement). Takeaway
service.* **Map 17 A2.**

Knightsbridge

★ Zuma

*5 Raphael Street, SW7 1DL (7584 1010,
www.zumarestaurant.com). Knightsbridge tube.*
Bar **Open** noon-11pm Mon-Fri; 12.30-11pm
Sat, Sun.
Restaurant **Lunch served** noon-2.45pm Mon-
Fri; 12.30-3.15pm Sat, Sun. **Dinner served**
6-10.45pm Mon-Sat; 6-10.15pm Sun. **Main
courses** £14.80-£70.
Both **Credit** AmEx, DC, MC, V.

Japanese food is undeniably fashionable and there
are few sexier places to enjoy this ancient cuisine
than at Zuma. The restaurant bustles day and
night, and a smattering of famous faces among the
good-looking diners guarantees some excitement.
The dining room is decked out in cedar and stone,
but don't expect Zen-like peace and quiet; noise
levels can reach a climax when it's packed. Yet
despite the obvious pressures, service is friendly
and thoughtful. The menu hasn't changed much
over the years, but there's no need to adjust a
winning formula. You don't have to be an oligarch
to enjoy dining here (unlike at many of Zuma's
illustrious rivals), as some of the best food is among
the least expensive. Robata-grilled dishes – such as
chicken wings, and skewers of belly pork with yuzu
and miso – are utterly delicious. To start, try the
ambrosial scallop sashimi and unagi (eel) sushi.
And we can't resist the crispy fried squid with
green chilli and salt – arguably the best in town.
Desserts don't let the side down either, and an
inspired chawan mushi (egg custard) with mango
and pineapple secured a dreamy end to our meal.
*Babies and children welcome: high chairs.
Booking essential. Disabled: toilet. Separate
rooms for parties, seating 12 and 14.*
Map 8 F9.

Marylebone

★ Dinings

2011 RUNNER-UP BEST SUSHI BAR
*22 Harcourt Street, W1H 4HH (7723 0666,
www.dinings.co.uk). Marylebone tube/rail.* **Lunch
served** noon-2.30pm Mon-Fri. **Dinner served**
6-10.30pm Mon-Sat. **Main courses** £6-£28.
Set lunch £12-£25. **Credit** AmEx, MC, V.
Dinings' kitchen takes the best parts of Japanese
minimalism and Latin American flavour profiles,
and melds them into something more than the sum
of their parts. Bookings are essential, as the
restaurant consists of just a ground-floor sushi bar
and a tiny basement room. It makes for intimate
dining, but service is efficient, with staff moving
quickly and unobtrusively through the room.
Luxury meats and seafood – wagyu beef, fatty
tuna, lobster and more – provide the base for the

addition of punchy salsas, hits of citrus and salty-
tangy sauces, as evident in a winning dish of duck
tataki with shiso salsa and ponzu. Prices have risen
considerably since our last visit, but we'd still pinch
together the pennies to order the seared wagyu beef
nigiri topped with truffle salsa and wobbly cubes
of sharp ponzu jelly – one of many creative
variations on sushi that characterises the Dinings
ethos. An overly salty miso soup with tiny shreds
of lobster meat was the only dud note; you're better
off sticking with the more proletarian tofu and
seaweed combinaton. But do save room for the
decadent desserts, including fresh truffle ice-cream
and yuzu champagne sorbet.
*Available for hire. Babies and children admitted.
Booking advisable. Takeaway service. Vegetarian
menu.* **Map 8 F5.**

Tomoe

*62 Marylebone Lane, W1U 2PB (7486 2004,
www.tomoe-london.co.uk). Bond Street tube.*
Lunch served noon-2.15pm Tue-Sat. **Dinner
served** 6-10pm Mon-Sat. **Dishes** £1.80-£15.
Set lunch £9.90-£14.90. **Minimum** (dinner)
£15. **Credit** AmEx, MC, V.
Tomoe is certainly one of the shabbier residents of
Marylebone Lane. Its black and white interior and
menus that look home-printed could do with an
overhaul. Despite this, savvy Londoners keep
returning for the well-presented, high-quality food.
Grilled razor clams and own-made tofu are among
the more unusual options. Unfortunately, the fresh
tofu wasn't available on our visit, so we plumped
for agedashi tofu (deep-fried tofu in fish stock with
dried bonito flakes); surprisingly, it came with
chunks of avocado and green pepper tempura as
well as the expected tofu. The attractive chirashi
sushi (available in two sizes) was served in a
lacquered bowl with a decent variety of firm-
fleshed fish. A hint of yuzu added interest to a
seaweed and cucumber salad. Draught Asahi and
Kirin are popular with the Japanese businessmen
who frequent Tomoe, but you'll also discover a fine
range of saké and shochu. In the evening, there's a
£15 per person minimum charge – take note, if
you're not planning to order much. Service was well
intentioned, but a little patchy.
*Babies and children welcome: high chairs.
Booking advisable dinner. Takeaway service.*
Map 9 H6.

Mayfair

Chisou

*4 Princes Street, W1B 2LE (7629 3931,
www.chisou.co.uk). Oxford Circus tube.*
Lunch served noon-2.30pm, **dinner served**
6-10.15pm Mon-Sat. **Main courses** £12-£23.50.
Set lunch £14.50-£20.50. **Credit** AmEx, MC, V.
Just five minutes from the hustle and bustle of
Oxford Street, Chisou is a welcoming oasis of calm
with its cream and pale wood interior. The menu is
packed with much of the usual repertoire – sushi,
noodles, tempura and grilled dishes. Saké is taken
seriously, with a regularly changing specials menu.
Prices are higher than average, so the bill can mount
up if you aren't careful. On the plus side, the dishes
are often quite generously proportioned. A large
plate of beef tataki featured velvety slices of meat
in a nicely balanced ponzu sauce. Crispy soft-shell
crab was equally ample, and the complimentary
hijiki seaweed salad appetiser was a nice touch.
From the drinks menu, we sampled some fragrant
and refreshing shochu and shiso sours. Surprisingly,

Nizuni. See p171.

however, the sushi assortment on our most recent visit was a little lacklustre: the rice slightly too soft (which prevented the fish from shining), and the filling of a badly rolled tuna maki spilling out. We also found the service to be inconsistent, becoming less attentive as the night went on. We'd expected better from Chisou.

Babies and children welcome: high chairs. Booking essential. Separate rooms for parties, seating 12-20. Tables outdoors (2, terrace). Takeaway service. **Map 9 J6.**

Nobu

1st floor, The Metropolitan, 19 Old Park Lane, W1K 1LB (7447 4747, www.noburestaurants. com). Hyde Park Corner tube. **Lunch served** noon-2.15pm Mon-Fri; 12.30-2.30pm Sat, Sun. **Dinner served** 6-10.15pm Mon-Thur; 6-11pm Fri, Sat; 6-10pm Sun. **Dishes** £4-£35.75. **Set lunch** £33 bento box; £60, £70. **Set dinner** £80, £95. **Credit** AmEx, MC, V.
As we went to press, Nobu was closing for a week of refurbishment. It needed it. We couldn't help but notice the scuffed chair legs, nor the slightly half-hearted 'irrashaimase' welcomes of the staff on our recent visit. Coupled with the fact that you can now get a Friday night table with less than a week's notice (last year, receptionists advised calling one calendar month in advance), this had us a little worried. However, the eccentric menu, mixing Japanese traditions with Peruvian flair, a combination made famous by the eponymous Nobu Matsuhisa, can still be a hot draw. Latin American influences by way of anticucho skewers, salsas and tacos elevate the pure beauty of ingredients such as wagyu beef, raw fish and simple vegetables, but there is also no-nonsense sushi. This is no place for budget eating; the drinks list is pricey, and the set lunch menus are not an accurate reflection of the main menu, though it does offer peeks. Rock shrimp tempura with ponzu, black cod with miso, and sashimi salad with a peppery vinaigrette were all brief glimpses of the kitchen's skill, but the greasy butter-fried vegetables with rice were sub-standard, and the miso soup pedestrian.

Babies and children welcome: high chairs. Booking essential. Disabled: lift; toilet. Separate rooms for parties, seating 14-60. **Map 9 H8. For branches see index.**

Umu

14-16 Bruton Place, W1J 6LX (7499 8881, www.umurestaurant.com). Bond Street or Green Park tube. **Lunch served** noon-2.30pm Mon-Fri. **Dinner served** 6-11pm Mon-Sat. **Main courses** £13-£57. **Set lunch** £25-£50. **Set dinner** £65-£135. **Credit** AmEx, DC, MC, V.
In mid 2009, the executive chef at Umu changed and the menu did too. There are now more fusion dishes and, due to the earthquake of March 2011, fewer Japanese ingredients. The interior and ambience, however, remain constant: dramatic dark wood features, low lighting and well-to-do diners. Although the tasting menu has shot up in price, it still makes a wise choice if you're after the full Umu experience. Highlights included a skilfully constructed starter of cured arctic char with slivers of fried artichoke, trout roe and delicate shiso flowers, and an innovative dessert of light, tangy tomato mousse with own-made shichimi chilli powder. Less successful was the ochazuke, which saw hot green-tea stock combined with cold sea bass sashimi, resulting in an odd temperature and texture. Our à la carte choices were a mixed bag:

foie gras mousse with crab and dashi jelly was a triumph, while the 'modern sushi' seemed confused. From the ample drinks menu, we enjoyed two unusual options: sparkling saké and sesame shochu. Service can be a little clinical, but on our last visit the waiter was charming and informative. The dining experience here is worth trying, just be prepared for a hefty bill.

Babies and children welcome: high chairs. Booking advisable dinner. Dress: smart casual. Separate room for parties, seats 10-12. **Map 9 H7.**

Piccadilly

Yoshino

3 Piccadilly Place, W1J 0DB (7287 6622, www.yoshino.net). Piccadilly Circus tube. **Meals served** noon-9.30pm Mon-Sat. **Dishes** £1.80-£11.80. **Set meal** £11.80-£39.80 bento box. **Credit** AmEx, MC, V.
If you weren't paying attention, you could easily miss Yoshino's neon sign, tucked away on a side alley just off Piccadilly. Downstairs, there's a sushi counter and a few small tables, but for a bit more refinement, head upstairs to the minimalist dining room. Like the decor, the menu here is also pared down. There are à la carte options (tempura, sushi, grilled dishes and more), but set meals and platters are the main attraction. For sashimi lovers, the chirashi sushi makes a good choice; the rice is served in a lacquer box topped with fine shreds of seaweed, omelette and mangetout, but not fish, which is on the side. Sushi assortments come scattered with seaweed flakes in both traditional and more Californian flavours. Unlike many Japanese venues, Yoshino has some interesting desserts too, including green tea tiramisu (a little dry, in our opinion) and a tasty black sesame panna cotta. For a change from saké, try the shochu, or choose from the small selection of wines and Japanese beer. High-quality fish and efficient service make this a great destination for a quick lunch (there's an express menu) or a leisurely dinner.

Babies and children admitted. Booking advisable. Takeaway service. **Map 17 A5.**

St James's

Matsuri

15 Bury Street, SW1Y 6AL (7839 1101, www.matsuri-restaurant.com). Green Park tube. **Lunch served** noon-2.30pm Mon-Sat; noon-3pm Sun. **Dinner served** 6-10.30pm Mon-Sat; 6-10pm Sun. **Dishes** £2.50-£10.50. **Main courses** £6.50-£55. **Set lunch** £15-£17.50 1 course, £18-£22 2 courses, £10-£30 bento box. **Set meal** £48-£160 5 courses. **Credit** AmEx, MC, V.
The theme of this long-standing restaurant is matsuri ('festival' in Japanese), evidenced in subtle ways. A theatrical nebuta mask welcomes diners with its fierce expression, while the jovial chefs who work the teppan (flat steel grill) put on a good show. The den-like space comes alive to the sound of the clanging and scraping of metal-on-metal as everything from premium steaks to asparagus spears and mounds of garlicky fried rice are prepared directly in front of a captivated audience of diners. You can, of course, head to the separate sushi bar for well-crafted nigiri and sashimi if the mood for grilled food doesn't strike. A meal here isn't cheap, but there are set menus that don't skimp on quality or quantity; lunch is a good opportunity

to sample Matsuri's menu for less. We enjoyed the light touch of appetisers such as a cold vinegared crab salad, served in the shell, and a delicate dobin mushi: hot broth served in a teapot, featuring goodies such as prawns, bamboo shoot and fish cake. Soft-spoken Japanese waitresses float in and out of the shadows with impressive efficiency. The clientele consists mainly of Mayfair businessmen, interspersed with the odd family, whose children never fail to be delighted by the theatrics of the 'fireball' ice-cream course.

Available for hire. Babies and children welcome: high chairs. Booking advisable. Disabled: toilet. Takeaway service. **Map 9 J8.**

Saké No Hana

23 St James's Street, SW1A 1HA (7925 8988, www.sakenohana.com). Green Park tube. **Lunch served** noon-3pm Mon-Fri. **Dinner served** 6-11.30pm Mon-Sat. **Main courses** £4-£40. **Set meal** £45-£65. **Credit** AmEx, MC, V.
Alan Yau's high-end Japanese enterprise lost some of its sandy-hued warmth when swathes of tatami were removed in a 2010 refurbishment. But the finely slatted cedar blinds still hang over the enormous windows of the main restaurant, lessening glare yet enhancing the light in the room and shimmering at sunset. Unless you're eating in the ground-floor sushi bar, you need to navigate the peculiar entrance, which involves taking a static escalator or a dimly lit tilt to reach the wide open first-floor space (now with a sushi bar too). Staff assist at the reception desk and at most of the twists and turns; first-time diners will need directions for the toilets. Of the impeccable sushi, the salmon and avocado roll is especially refreshing, with bonus cucumber inside and canny flourishes of cress held in place by translucent sheets of daikon. The tempura has always stood out, for quality of batter and diversity of ingredients – in summer, look out for courgette flowers and luscious halved figs. Other hot highlights range from the simplest, tapas-sized quartet of salt-sprinkled shishito (mini green peppers) to higher-priced, if still small, delicacies such as charcoal-grilled hamachi collar and stocky leg sections of ponzu-tinged king crab. In conclusion: great food, modest portions, substantial prices, bizarre layout and service that blows warm and cool.

Available for hire. Babies and children admitted. Booking advisable. Disabled: lift; toilet. **Map 9 J8.**

Soho

★ Bincho

16 Old Compton Street, W1D 4TL (7287 9111, www.bincho.co.uk). Leicester Square or Tottenham Court Road tube. **Lunch served** noon-3pm Tue-Sat; 1-3.30pm Sun. **Dinner served** 5-11pm Mon-Sat; 5-10.30pm Sun. **Main courses** £1.50-£2.50. **Set lunch** £6.50-£8.50. **Set dinner** £10-£25. **Credit** AmEx, MC, V.
We liked the original Bincho, with great Thames views and space for a theatrically long open grill, but this surviving branch has a better vibe. It's darker, Soho-boisterous, more cramped and closer in feel to the Japanese booze-with-food izakaya model than its spacious but over-refined progenitor. The key feature remains the charcoal grill, here located near the entrance, on to which chefs throw little skewers of meat, fish and vegetables. This is the more enjoyable section of the restaurant, since you can watch the flames and

Budget bites

Centrepoint Sushi

20-21 St Giles High Street, WC2H 8LN (7240 6147, www.cpfs.co.uk). Tottenham Court Road tube. **Lunch served** noon-3pm, **dinner served** 6-11pm Mon-Sat. **Main courses** £8-£17. **Set lunch** £8-£9.50. **Credit** MC, V.
'Hidden gem' is a much-abused term, but in the case of Hana, it's completely appropriate. Accessed via a Korean-Japanese supermarket in the shadow of Centre Point, this old-school sushi bar deals in traditional dishes for salarymen, from made-to-order sushi to the selection of tempura or teriyaki. The set-price bento boxes are particularly popular with local office workers, who appreciate the tranquil atmosphere. Groups tend to head for the leather booths by the window, while solo diners and couples perch at the bar, watching the chefs at work.
Babies and children admitted. Booking advisable. Takeaway service. Vegetarian menu. **Map 17 C2.**

Kulu Kulu

76 Brewer Street, W1F 9TX (7734 7316). Piccadilly Circus tube. **Lunch served** noon-2.30pm Mon-Fri; noon-3.45pm Sat. **Dinner served** 5-10pm Mon-Sat. **Dishes** £1.50-£3.60. **Set meal** £5.20-£12.90. **Credit** MC, V.
The original branch of Kulu Kulu may be looking a tad tired, but it's as popular as ever, with queues often spilling on to Brewer Street. Keen pricing and a superb location are the main draws, as is the lively ambience. The conveyor-belt sushi can be hit and miss, with cheap farmed (though perfectly fresh) fish and sometimes stingy portions. Instead, order off-belt: Kulu Kulu was one of the first places to serve prawn tempura hand rolls, and these continue to be excellent. Staff are often stretched, and at busy times will shamelessly boot you out the instant you've stopped eating.
Bookings not accepted. Takeaway service. **Map 17 A5.**
For branches see index.

Necco

52-54 Exmouth Market, EC1R 4QE (7713 8575, www.necco.co.uk). Farringdon tube/rail or bus 19, 38, 55. **Meals served** noon-9.30pm Mon-Sat. **Main courses** £7.50-£12.50. **Set lunch** (noon-3pm) £5 bento box. **Credit** (over £10) MC, V.
If you share the Japanese penchant for all things *kawaii* (cute), then Necco is the place to go. Even the grout between the white tiles has had the *kawaii* treatment – it's pink. For a small café, the menu is ample: rice dishes, noodles, curries and green tea-laced desserts, as well as Japanese beers, teas and sakés. We weren't convinced by our sun-dried tomato, olive and cream cheese roll, but the plump tako yaki (octopus balls)

hit the spot. Necco has good lunch offers and plenty for vegetarians too. Service can be a little haphazard.
Available for hire. Babies and children admitted. Tables outdoors (3, pavement). Takeaway service. **Map 5 N4.**

Taro

10 Old Compton Street, W1D 4TF (7439 2275, www.tarorestaurants.co.uk). Leicester Square or Tottenham Court Road tube. **Lunch served** noon-2.50pm Mon-Fri; 12.30-3.15pm Sat, Sun. **Dinner served** 5.30-10.30pm Mon-Sat; 5.30-9.30pm Sun. **Main courses** £5.90-£8.90. **Set meal** £8.90-£13. **Credit** MC, V.
You might think that the limited natural light in this basement canteen would put people off: far from it. Taro's reputation for diminutive price tags and generous portions has made it popular with a wide spectrum of bargain-hunters. Clustering around chunky pine communal tables, diners order from a roll-call of traditional Japanese favourites, from sushi to noodles, plus teriyaki, katsu and tempura. It's surprisingly roomy, meaning that at all but the busiest times, staff are happy to leave you to it, appearing only occasionally to offer more drinks, such as cold bottles of Kirin or Asahi.
Babies and children welcome: high chairs. Booking advisable Fri, Sat. Takeaway service. **Map 17 C3.**
For branch see index.

Toku at Japan Centre

14-16 Regent Street, SW1Y 4PH (3405 1222, www.toku-restaurant.co.uk). Piccadilly Circus tube. **Meals served** noon-9.45pm Mon-Thur; noon-10pm Fri, Sat; noon-8.45pm Sun. **Main courses** £3-£26. **Set meal** (3-6pm Mon-Fri) £10 bento box. **Credit** MC, V.
Talk about playing to a tough crowd. Toku is the official restaurant of the Japan Centre, a business that has been a

Necco

magnet for homesick Nipponese for more than 35 years. It's popular with local office workers too. While next door focuses on imported products and produce, Toku majors in fairly priced Japanese cooking of the highest order, from spankingly fresh sushi to traditional hot dishes of gyoza, teriyaki, noodles and donburi (one-bowl rice meals). Don't miss the delicately battered signature tempura.
Babies and children welcome: high chairs; nappy-changing facilities. Bookings not accepted Sat, Sun. Disabled: toilet. Tables outdoors (4, pavement). Takeaway service. **Map 17 B5.**

Tokyo Diner

2 Newport Place, WC2H 7JJ (7287 8777, www.tokyodiner.com). Leicester Square tube. **Meals served** noon-midnight daily. **Main courses** £6.60-£19.90. **Set lunch** (noon-6pm Mon-Fri) £8-£11.90. **Credit** MC, V.
A Japanese jewel in the heart of Chinatown, Tokyo Diner has a long-standing reputation for its affordable menu and friendly service. All the usual suspects are here, from soup noodles to sushi, as well as set lunch boxes and donburi, though you won't find any tuna – TD has taken an active sustainability stance on this. More café than canteen, the airy corner site has plenty of smaller tables if you're not a fan of sharing with strangers, though, be warned: there's sometimes a live webcam running.
Babies and children welcome: high chairs. Bookings not accepted Fri, Sat. Takeaway service. **Map 17 C4.**

Tsuru

4 Canvey Street, SE1 9AN (7928 2228, www.tsuru-sushi.co.uk). Southwark tube or London Bridge tube/rail. **Meals served** 11am-9pm Mon-Fri. **Tapas served** 5.30-9pm Mon-Fri; 11.30am-7pm Sat. **Main courses** £8.20-£14.25. **Set meal** (11.30am-5.30pm) £6.40 bento box; (5.30-9.30pm) £8.20 bento box. **Credit** AmEx, MC, V.
Tucked away behind Tate Modern, the original branch of Tsuru proved such a success with the office crowd that it's spawned City offshoots near Liverpool Street and Bank. The signature dish is katsu curry, cooked for eight hours and served with pieces of golden breadcrumbed pork (Japanese schnitzel, if you like). It's worth exploring the rest of the menu, though, which ranges from hot dishes of gyoza and potato korokke (a type of croquette) ordered at the bar, to cold boxes of sushi or Japanese potato salad, available from the chill cabinet.
Available for hire. Babies and children welcome: high chairs. Disabled: toilet. Tables outdoors (5, pavement). Takeaway service. **Map 11 O8.**
For branches see index.

JAPANESE

smell the smoke, but there are also couply tables in a second room to the rear that are often less hectic. Setting a minimum order of two skewers from the yakitori and kushiyaki lists seems a little mean, but share them around and you'll soon have assembled a tasty meal at not unreasonable cost - perhaps vary favourites like pork belly, eel or asparabacon (asparagus with smoky bacon) with more outlandish options such as sunazuri (chicken gizzard). Among the larger dishes, we enjoy the iwashi shio-yaki (salt-grilled sardine, threaded on a skewer as if still swimming). Do try the premium sakes, served to be drunk from an unwieldy but flavour-enhancing cedar box, the masu.

Available for hire. Babies and children welcome: high chairs. Booking advisable. Disabled: toilet. Separate room for parties, seats 18. Takeaway service. **Map 17 C3**.

★ Koya
49 Frith Street, W1D 4SG (7434 4463, www.koya.co.uk). Tottenham Court Road tube.
Lunch served noon-3pm, **dinner served** 5.30-10.30pm Mon-Sat. **Main courses** £6.70-£14.70. **Credit** MC, V.
Once you step through the navy noren (doorway curtain) of this very plain-looking specialist, it's noodles with everything. Though, without wishing to sound like an M&S advertisement, this is not just noodle. This is thick, white udon, made with wheat flour imported from Japan, then kneaded by foot (in a good, hygienic way) for extra chewiness. Customers can vary how they have their noodles: according to temperature (hot udon with hot broth, cold with hot broth, or cold with cold dipping sauce); and topping (from various meats to mushrooms with walnut miso). Staff seem happy to advise. For a richer udon-slurping experience, crack an onsen ('hot spring' or slow-poached) egg into the mix. Rice lovers aren't entirely neglected; half a dozen donburi choices include tempura and curry. There's even 'fish & chips' – in this case, cod tempura and lotus root chips. Among the usual alcoholic and soft drinks, Echigo rice beer and own-made hot ginger tea make for a list less ordinary. Koya's location in the heart of Soho and its cheap prices are further draws – in fact, the restaurant was an immediate hit when it launched in spring 2010. Time your arrival carefully, or you may have to wait a while for a table.
Bookings not accepted. Vegan dishes.
Map 17 C3.

So Japanese
3-4 Warwick Street, W1B 5LS (7292 0760, www.sorestaurant.com). Piccadilly Circus tube.
Lunch served noon-3pm Mon-Fri. **Dinner served** 5.30-10.30pm Mon-Thur; 5.30-11pm Fri. **Meals served** noon-11pm Sat. **Main courses** £14-£28. **Set lunch** £6.95-£16. **Credit** AmEx, MC, V.
There's no shortage of Japanese restaurants in Soho, but So Japanese stands out for its fusion of European and Japanese ingredients, all presented on attractive ceramics and lacquerware. In the airy ground-floor dining room, you can sit shoulder to shoulder with other diners at the long wooden sushi counter, or at tables. There's seating downstairs too, where you can watch the chefs at work, though it's a little dark. For traditionalists, the sushi is excellent: perfectly cooked rice and achingly fresh fish. Tempura – light, crisp batter encasing sweet prawns, seafood or perfectly cooked veg – is another good option. If you fancy something more

Dinings. See p172.

Koya. See p177.

Hammersmith

★ Tosa

*332 King Street, W6 0RR (8748 0002).
Ravenscourt Park or Stamford Brook tube.*
Lunch served 12.30-2.30pm, **dinner served**
6-11pm daily. **Main courses** £7-£15. **Set
lunch** £11. **Set meal** £30 4 courses. **Credit**
AmEx, MC, V.

It doesn't take long to spot the star attraction at
Tosa – there's a robata grill by the entrance. If you
want to watch the chef at work and don't mind the
smoke, sit at the counter or at one of the small
tables next to the window. Alternatively, head into
the dining room, whose white walls are lined with
decorative kimono belts and Japanese prints. Sticky
glazed yakitori, crispy-skinned tebasaki (chicken
wings) and bacon-rolled asparagus have proved to
be popular skewers, but there are more adventurous
options too, favoured by the Japanese diners (ox
tongue, chicken skin and quail's eggs, for example).
Grilled black bream head was bursting with
flavour, and yellowtail nigiri was well prepared.
However, Tosa salad (a pretty average mixed salad
with radish dressing) seemed overpriced at £5.20.
For dessert, look to the specials tacked up on the
wall. To drink, saké is served in traditional wooden
cups; there's beer and shochu too. We found service
attentive at the beginning of our meal, but it waned
towards the end.
*Babies and children admitted. Booking advisable.
Takeaway service.* **Map 20 A4.**
For branch see index.

Kensington

★ Yashin NEW HOT 50

2011 WINNER BEST SUSHI BAR
*1A Argyll Road, W8 7DB (7938 1536,
www.yashinsushi.com). High Street Kensington
tube.* **Lunch served** noon-2.30pm, **dinner
served** 6-11pm daily. **Set meals** £12.50-£60.
Credit AmEx, MC, V.

Yashin's motto – 'without soy sauce… but if you
want to' – has been lauded and ridiculed in equal
measure. We welcome the absence of soy sauce,
which here is made redundant by the extraordinary
ways in which itamae (sushi chefs) Shinya Ikeda and
Yasuhiro Mineno design their creations. Individual
seasonings and garnishes are paired with each piece
to bring out the flavours of the seafood or meat;
some pieces are lightly blowtorched, resulting in
contrasting textures and a smoky flavour. Each
meticulously crafted morsel had its own merits,
whether it was yellowtail with black pepper, or
torched fatty tuna with a dollop of fresh wasabi. But
well-seasoned fish is only half of the equation: the
consistently well-formed, supple rice completes the
formula for perfect nigiri. The appetisers – intensely
flavoured miso soups, fresh oysters, own-made tofu
and various carpaccio dishes (fish, beef) – make
excellent supplements to the sushi. High-quality
Japanese teas are a relative steal at £1-£1.40 a cup,
but saké buffs will also appreciate the option of
'tasters', featuring three premium sakés served
(weirdly) in test tubes. The design of dark green
tiles, hanging lights and parquet floor is reminiscent
of a kitsch pie and mash shop; the coveted seats are
at the wooden counter, in front of the chefs, though
there's also a small basement room. A meal at
Yashin is incredibly expensive – the sushi set meals
range from £30 for nine pieces to £60 for 15 – but
it's worth saving up for an unbeatable experience.

innovative, try the indulgent, pan-fried foie gras
nigiri – popular, though the pan juices made our
rice crumble slightly. Barbary duck, smoked in-
house with Jack Daniel's wood chips, was silky
textured, but too smoky. The drinks menu shows
some imagination, with saké and shochu cocktails
complementing the wine and saké list. The
somewhat nonchalant service was the only minor
let-down in a quality meal.
*Available for hire. Babies and children admitted.
Separate room for parties, seats 4. Takeaway
service.* **Map 17 A5.**

West
Ealing

★ Atari-ya

2011 RUNNER-UP BEST SUSHI BAR
*1 Station Parade, Uxbridge Road, W5 3LD
(8896 3175, www.atariya.co.uk). Ealing Common
tube.* **Lunch served** 11am-1.30pm, **dinner
served** 4.30-9pm Tue-Sun. **Dishes** 60p-£3.20.
Set meal £8-£18. **Credit** AmEx, MC, V.

What used to be known as Sushi Hiro is now part
of the Atari-ya group (one of London's most prolific
seafood suppliers to Japanese restaurants). But
aside from the front windows, which have been
swapped from uninviting panels of frosted glass to
welcoming floor-to-ceiling panes, it remains pretty
much business as usual at this Ealing staple. The
menu has remained the same, as is the staff. But
somehow the restaurant isn't quite as good as it
used to be. The quality of fish is reassuringly high,
but on our most recent visit, the execution of the
sushi needed more care and attention. Several
pieces of fish were messily cut, with some varying
in thickness and length, which we put down to the
head itamae (sushi chef) not being present. A
generously topped chirashi-don (rice bowl with
mixed sashimi on top) proved to be the better
choice. Aside from a small number of slight flaws
such as these, service is sweet, and despite the odd
opening hours (lunch ends at 1.30pm), there are few
better places to enjoy good sushi at such reasonable
prices in the neighbourhood.
*Babies and children welcome: high chairs.
Booking advisable Fri, Sat. Takeaway service.*
For branches see index.

Available for hire. Babies and children welcome: high chair. Booking advisable weekends.
Map 7 B9.

South West
Putney

Chosan
292 Upper Richmond Road, SW15 6TH (8788 9626). East Putney tube or Putney rail. **Lunch served** noon-2.30pm Tue-Sun. **Dinner served** 6.30-10.30pm Tue-Sat; 6.30-10pm Sun. **Main courses** £3.30-£25. **Set lunch** £7.90-£13.90. **Set dinner** £18.90-£20.90; £20.90-£26.90 bento box. **Credit** MC, V.
Cosy Chosan, with its tatty cushions, Japanese knick-knacks and kind-faced husband-and-wife team, teeters on the verge of cliché, albeit a lovely one. A small reception housing the till and an array of Japanese papers and pamphlets leads to a reasonably sized dining room, with a sushi bar in one corner and tables along the walls. The menu is impressive in its breadth. There is, of course, sushi and sashimi, but also lesser-known kushiage (deep-fried morsels of food on skewers) and a smattering of delicious small dishes that would not be out of place in an izakaya, such as grilled chicken wings with salt, crab croquettes, and grilled squid with ginger. Comforting rice dishes are a popular option at lunch, and our katsu-jyu (deep-fried breaded pork on rice) was a satisfying number. The agedashidofu was expertly fried too, with a thin, crisp exterior giving way to silky bean curd. The sushi wasn't quite as delicate, but the fish was fresh and portions generous; our natto maki was slightly dry, though, without the fermented soybean's distinctive (and desired) sliminess. We'd advise booking at the weekend, as this couple's hospitality and cooking is a hit with Putney locals.
Babies and children admitted. Takeaway service.

South
Clapham

Tsunami
5-7 Voltaire Road, SW4 6DQ (7978 1610, www.tsunamirestaurant.co.uk). Clapham North tube. **Lunch served** 12.30-4pm Sat, Sun. **Dinner served** 6-10.30pm Mon-Thur; 6-11pm Fri; 5.30-11pm Sat; 6-9.30pm Sun. **Main courses** £7.70-£19.50. **Set lunch** (Sat, Sun) £10.50 2 courses. **Credit** MC, V.
Bringing a dash of West End glamour to Clapham North, Tsunami has become a south London mini-destination. From Battersea to Balham, the inhabitants of SW postcodes flock here for upmarket modern Japanese, delivered in dark, swanky surroundings. Smartly dressed staff bustle around the low-lit, open-plan room, serving WAG favourites (yellowtail sashimi with jalapeño, miso black cod) alongside more everyday options (warm udon noodles, chicken with a wasabi sauce). Curls of tender salt-and-pepper squid came delicately battered and suspended in an attractive paper cone; six soft-shell crab maki, the limbs hoiked in the air, also combined flavour, texture and visual appeal. Only the salmon teriyaki, with its stingy proportions and insipid marinade, proved a let-down. On weekend evenings, the tempo goes up several notches, with the small,

amber-topped cocktail bar becoming a magnet for dating couples and groups of young professionals, all eager to indulge in a lychee martini or two. A word of warning, though: at these times, the overspill of noise into the dining room can become well-nigh unbearable. Come summer, the dozen or so alfresco tables, looking on to the railway arches, make a peaceful alternative.
Babies and children welcome: high chairs. Booking advisable; essential weekends. Takeaway service; delivery service (over £15 within 2-mile radius). **Map 22 B1**.

North
Camden Town & Chalk Farm

Asakusa
265 Eversholt Street, NW1 1BA (7388 8533). Camden Town or Mornington Crescent tube. **Dinner served** 6-11.30pm Mon-Fri; 6-11pm Sat. **Main courses** £5.50-£13. **Credit** AmEx, MC, V.
With its down-at-heel exterior and ramshackle dining room, Asakusa is far from being a glamorous spot, but its prices and food are reasonable, so getting a table can prove tricky (best to book). The two dining rooms are often crammed full of trendy Camdenites of all ages. Opt for the upstairs one if you can, as the basement is a little dingy. The menu covers a broad scope of Japanese classics, including noodles, sushi, and simmered and grilled dishes. Teriyaki chicken was just right, with crisp skin and moist meat. Saké ochazuke (green tea and fish stock poured over cooked salmon and rice) had plenty of earthy flavour. However, a mixed prawn and vegetable tempura dish seemed inconsistent – the batter was appropriately thin and crisp, the vegetables nicely cooked, but the prawns had next to no flavour. To drink, the three-glass saké tasting set is good value at just under £8, though there are plenty of other

options. Despite being busy, the staff were polite and fairly proficient, bringing free genmai tea and chocolates with the bill.
Babies and children admitted. Booking advisable Thur-Sat. Takeaway service. Vegetarian menu. **Map 27 D3**.

Crouch End

Wow Simply Japanese
18 Crouch End Hill, N8 8AA (8340 4539, http://wowsimplyjapanese.co.uk). Finsbury Park tube/rail then bus W3, W7, or Crouch Hill rail. **Lunch served** noon-2.30pm Wed-Sat. **Dinner served** 6-10.30pm Mon-Sat; 6-10pm Sun. **Main courses** £7.80-£35. **Set lunch** £5.90-£8.90. **Credit** MC, V.
Smartly informal yet relaxingly untrendy, Wow has seen local competitors come and go over the past few years and remains a popular choice for Crouch Enders. Consistency in the cooking has been a weak point, but our recent visit saw the kitchen in fine form, the only disappointment being some flabby gyoza. The signature sushi, the Wow roll, sees spicy tuna, avocado, tobiko and rice wrapped in nori and deep-fried for an indulgent combination of soft, crisp and chewy – wow indeed. Also outstanding was a generous bowl of prawn and vegetable tempura donburi: the seafood was sweet, the batter crisp, the veg tender. Perhaps the rice could have been a little less gluggy, but that's a minor quibble. Springy yaki soba (fried noodles) with chicken and vegetables tasted wholesome and comforting; so too simple cucumber maki and tomago nigiri. There's an appealing choice of bento boxes, plus main dishes such as grilled black cod with miso, and chicken katsu. Friendly staff went out of their way to be helpful despite the lunchtime rush – even with a generous tip we felt we dined heartily at very persuasive prices.
Babies and children welcome: high chairs. Booking advisable. Takeaway service; delivery service (over £20 within 2-mile radius).

Tosa

JAPANESE

North West
Golders Green

Café Japan
*626 Finchley Road, NW11 7RR (8455 6854).
Golders Green tube or bus 13, 82.* **Lunch
served** noon-2pm Tue-Sun. **Dinner served**
6-10pm Tue-Sat; 6-9.30pm Sun. **Main courses**
£9-£23. **Set lunch** £8-£13.50. **Set dinner** £17.
Credit MC, V.

Its short-lived offshoot around the corner (Sushi
Cafelicious) ceased trading in July 2011, but Café
Japan's been going strong, through changes of
ownership, for nigh on two decades – to wit a plaque
dating back to 1996 when it took Best Japanese in
Time Out's Eating & Drinking Awards, followed by
sundry other nods of approval over the years. Which
explains why you generally need to book, often on
the promise of vacating your table by a certain time.
However, rapid turnover is aided by attentive staff
– and plenty of them. They even fashion cheat-
chopsticks for novices out of waribashi, elastic
bands and wadded napkins. While the odd-coloured
interior and tired-looking furniture wouldn't win any
awards, the sushi is consistently very good. Evening
à la carte prices tend to hike the bill, but you can offset
investment in a 14-piece omakase (£23) that includes
high-end toppings such as chutoro and hotate
(scallop) by, for example, ordering lower-cost
hosomaki sushi. Hot dishes are more of a gamble:
we've been delighted by melt-in-the-mouth butterfish
teriyaki, but disappointed by bland agedofu. Take a
perch at the front sushi counter and grill if you want
to watch the chefs plying their skilful trade.
*Babies and children admitted. Booking advisable.
Takeaway service.*

Hampstead

Jin Kichi
*73 Heath Street, NW3 6UG (7794 6158,
www.jinkichi.com). Hampstead tube.* **Lunch
served** 12.30-2pm Tue-Sun. **Dinner served**
6-10.45pm Tue-Sat; 6-10pm Sun. **Main courses**
£14-£16. **Set lunch** £9-£17. **Credit** AmEx,
MC, V.

Even on Tuesday lunchtime it's wise to book here,
for Jin Kichi is popular with local mums, workers
and Hampstead's fraternity of resting actors. It
only takes someone walking in to make a
reservation for the snug dimensions to feel
cramped. Decor is traditional, with framed Japanese
prints, myriad paper lanterns, and humble
furniture set around a Formica-topped bar, though
the staff (perhaps also resting actors) are
fashionable chaps in lean black T-shirts and long
aprons. The kitchen is known for its kushiyaki
grilled skewers, but the menu spans the gamut of
Japanese cuisine, from sushi and noodles to
simmered dishes and red bean cakes. The chef
expertly works the central grill, using his bare
hands to feel and shift the ingredients (ox tongue,
quails' eggs and chicken gizzards among them),
testing to see if they're done. Choose a skewer set
to narrow the options; ours arrived (we wish a little
quicker) with a majestic king prawn the luxurious
centrepiece, but it was the chicken meatballs, pork
and shiso rolls, and tangy, bacon-wrapped
asparagus that wowed the taste buds. Yaki nasu
was another winner, the pristine aubergine flesh
devoid of bitterness, the generous topping of bonito
flakes waving ethereally. A good place to know.
*Babies and children welcome: high chairs. Booking
advisable. Takeaway service.* **Map 28 B2.**

Willesden

Sushi-Say
*33B Walm Lane, NW2 5SH (8459 2971).
Willesden Green tube.* **Lunch served** noon-
3.30pm Sat, Sun. **Dinner served** 6.30-10pm
Wed-Fri; 6.30-10.30pm Sat; 6-9.30pm Sun.
Main courses £7.20-£24.60. **Set dinner**
£23.50-£39.50. **Credit** MC, V.

The residents of Willesden come back time and
again to enjoy Sushi-Say's quality Japanese food.
However, the casual visitor should beware: this
means the place is usually full, so booking is
recommended. The narrow restaurant has three
areas divided by black slatted screens: a glass sushi
counter at the front, cream dining room in the
middle and a traditional tatami room for larger
groups at the back. The jolly sushi chef turns out
perfectly fresh and generously proportioned
sashimi and nigiri toppings; our yellowtail and
scallop nigiri didn't disappoint. From the kitchen,
a kinpira gobo (sautéed shredded burdock and
carrot) had just the right balance of sweet and
savoury, while the tempura udon saw crisp tempura
prawns and vegetables atop chewy noodles and a
warming broth. If you have room for dessert,
choose from the interesting own-made ice-creams
with flavours that include green tea, sesame,
chestnut and wasabi – we weren't entirely sold on
the last one. Regular patrons can buy whole bottles
of saké and keep them behind the bar, but the drink
is also offered in small flasks. Service on our Sunday
night visit was well meaning, though not as efficient
as on previous occasions.
*Babies and children welcome: high chairs.
Booking advisable. Separate room for parties,
seats 8. Takeaway service. Vegetarian menu.*

Yashin. See p178.

Menu

Agedashidofu: tofu (qv) coated with katakuriko (potato starch), deep-fried, sprinkled with dried fish and served in a broth based on shoyu (qv), with grated ginger and daikon (qv).
Amaebi: sweet shrimps.
Anago: saltwater conger eel.
Bento: a meal served in a compartmentalised box.
Chawan mushi: savoury egg custard served in a tea tumbler (chawan).
Chutoro: medium fatty tuna from the upper belly.
Daikon: a long, white radish (aka mooli), often grated or cut into fine strips.
Dashi: the basic stock for Japanese soups and simmered dishes. It's often made from flakes of dried bonito (a type of tuna) and konbu (kelp).
Dobin mushi: a variety of morsels (prawn, fish, chicken, shiitake, ginkgo nuts) in a gently flavoured dashi-based soup, steamed (mushi) and served in a clay teapot (dobin).
Donburi: a bowl of boiled rice with various toppings, such as beef, chicken or egg.
Dorayaki: mini pancakes sandwiched around azuki bean paste.
Edamame: fresh soy beans boiled in their pods and sprinkled with salt.
Gari: pickled ginger, usually pink and thinly sliced; served with sushi to cleanse the palate between courses.
Gyoza: soft rice pastry cases stuffed with minced pork and herbs; northern Chinese in origin, cooked by a combination of frying and steaming.
Hamachi: young yellowtail or Japanese amberjack fish, commonly used for sashimi (qv) and also very good grilled.
Hashi: chopsticks.
Hiyashi chuka: Chinese-style ramen (qv, noodles) served cold (hiyashi) in tsuyu (qv) with a mixed topping that usually includes shredded ham, chicken, cucumber, egg and sweetcorn.
Ikura: salmon roe.
Izakaya: 'a place where there is saké'; an after-work drinking den frequented by Japanese businessmen, usually serving a wide range of reasonably priced food.
Kaiseki ryori: a multi-course meal of Japanese haute cuisine.
Kaiten-zushi: conveyor-belt sushi.
Karaage: deep-fried
Katsu: breaded and deep-fried meat, hence tonkatsu (pork katsu) and katsu curry (tonkatsu or chicken katsu with mild vegetable curry).
Kushiage: skewered morsels battered then deep-fried.
Maki: the word means 'roll' and this is a style of sushi (qv) where the rice and filling are rolled inside a sheet of nori (qv).
Mirin: a sweetened rice spirit used in many Japanese sauces and dressings.
Miso: a thick paste of fermented soy beans, used in miso soup and some dressings. Miso comes in a wide variety of styles: earthy, crunchy or smooth.

Miso shiru: classic miso soup, most often containing tofu and wakame (qv).
Nabemono: a class of dishes cooked at the table and served directly from the earthenware pot or metal pan.
Natto: fermented soy beans of stringy, mucous consistency.
Nimono: food simmered in a stock, often presented 'dry'.
Noodles: second only to rice as Japan's favourite staple. Served hot or cold, dry or in soup, and sometimes fried. There are many types, but the most common are **ramen** (Chinese-style egg noodles), **udon** (thick white wheat-flour noodles), **soba** (buckwheat noodles), and **somen** (thin white wheat-flour noodles, usually served cold as a summer dish – **hiyashi somen** – with a chilled dipping broth).
Nori: sheets of dried seaweed.
Okonomiyaki: the Japanese equivalent of filled pancakes or a Spanish omelette, whereby various ingredients are added to a batter mix and cooked on a hotplate, usually in front of diners.
Ponzu: usually short for ponzu joyu, a mixture of the juice of a Japanese citrus fruit (ponzu) and soy sauce. Used as a dip, especially with seafood and chicken or fish nabemono (qv).
Robatayaki: a kind of grilled food, generally cooked in front of customers, who make their selection from a large counter display.
Saké: rice wine, around 15% alcohol. Usually served hot, but may be chilled.
Sashimi: raw sliced fish.
Shabu shabu: a pan of stock is heated at the table and plates of thinly sliced raw beef and vegetables are cooked in it piece by piece ('shabu-shabu' is onomatopoeic for the sound of washing a cloth in water). The broth is then portioned out and drunk.
Shiso: perilla or beefsteak plant. A nettle-like leaf of the mint family that is often served with sashimi (qv).
Shochu: Japan's colourless answer to vodka is distilled from raw materials such as wheat, rice and potatoes.
Shoyu: Japanese soy sauce.
Sukiyaki: pieces of thinly sliced beef and vegetables are simmered in a sweet shoyu-based sauce at the table on a portable stove. Then they are taken out and dipped in raw egg (which semi-cooks on the hot food) to cool them for eating.
Sunomono: seafood or vegetables marinated (but not pickled) in rice vinegar.
Sushi: a combination of raw fish, shellfish or vegetables with rice – usually with a touch of wasabi (qv). Vinegar mixed with sugar and salt is added to the rice, which is then cooled before use. There are different sushi formats: **nigiri** (lozenge-shaped), **hosomaki** (thin-rolled), **futomaki** (thick-rolled), **temaki** (hand-rolled), **gunkan maki** (nigiri with a nori wrap), **chirashi** (scattered on top of a bowl of rice), and **uramaki** or **ISO maki** (more recently coined terms for inside-out rolls).

Tare: a general term for shoyu-based cooking marinades.
Tataki: meat or fish quickly seared, then marinated in vinegar, sliced thinly, and seasoned with ginger.
Tatami: a heavy straw mat – traditional Japanese flooring. A tatami room is usually a private room where you remove your shoes and sit on the floor to eat.
Tea: black tea is fermented, while green tea (**ocha**) is heat-treated by steam to prevent the leaves fermenting. **Matcha** is powdered green tea, and has a high caffeine content. **Bancha** is the coarsest grade of green tea, which has been roasted; it contains the stems or twigs of the plant as well as the leaves, and is usually served free of charge with a meal. **Hojicha** is lightly roasted bancha. **Mugicha** is roast barley tea, served iced in summer.
Tempura: fish, shellfish or vegetables dipped in a light batter and deep-fried. Served with tsuyu (qv) to which you add finely grated daikon (qv) and fresh ginger.
Teppanyaki: grilled on an iron plate. In modern Japanese restaurants, a chef standing at a hotplate (teppan) is surrounded by several diners. Slivers of beef, fish and vegetables are cooked and deposited on your plate.
Teriyaki: cooking method by which meat or fish – often marinated in shoyu (qv) and rice wine – is grilled and served in a tare (qv) made of a thick reduction of shoyu (qv), saké (qv), sugar and spice.
Tofu: soy beancurd used fresh in simmered or grilled dishes, or deep-fried (**agedashidofu**, qv), or eaten cold (**hiyayakko**, qv).
Tokkuri: saké flask – usually ceramic, but sometimes made of bamboo.
Tonkatsu: see above katsu.
Tsuyu: a general term for shoyu/mirin-based dips, served both warm and cold with various dishes ranging from tempura (qv) to cold noodles.
Umami: the nearest word in English is tastiness. After sweet, sour, salty and bitter, umami is considered the fifth primary taste in Japan, but not all food scientists in the West accept its existence.
Unagi: freshwater eel.
Uni: sea urchin roe.
Wakame: a type of young seaweed most commonly used in miso (qv) soup and kaiso (seaweed) salad.
Wasabi: a fiery green paste made from the root of an aquatic plant that belongs to the same family as horseradish. It is eaten in minute quantities (tucked inside sushi, qv), or diluted into shoyu (qv) for dipping sashimi (qv).
Yakimono: literally 'grilled things'.
Yakitori: grilled chicken (breast, wings, liver, gizzard, heart) served on skewers.
Zarusoba: soba noodles served cold, usually on a bamboo draining mat, with a dipping broth.
Zensai: appetisers.

Jewish

North-west London is bursting with new kosher establishments. When one restaurant closes, another quickly takes its place. There are well over 20 such venues in NW11 (Golders Green) and NW4 (Hendon) alone. In Edgware – teeming with kosher life – there's new **Papalina** and, in Golders Green, a recently opened branch of **Isola Bella**, competing with **Novellino** (103 Golders Green Road, NW11 8EN, 8458 7273) in providing fish and dairy food. The frustrating lack of kosher eateries in central London continues, however. **Bevis Marks** in the City still leads the field in terms of inventive and elegant cuisine, yet **Reubens** draws the crowds because it's the only kosher dining venue in the West End.

All the restaurants below are kosher (that is, they follow the strict rules of kashrut), but half offer cuisines other than 'Jewish'. Hence, if you're after Chinese cooking, head for **Kaifeng**; visit **Papalina** for Brazilian grills, **La Fiesta** for Argentinian steaks, and **Isola Bella** for food ranging from Italian to Thai. Dishes from the two main branches of specifically Jewish cooking – Sephardi (originating in Mediterranean countries) and Ashkenazi (from eastern Europe) – are getting more difficult to find. **New Yorker Deli** or **Reubens** are the best bets for Ashkenazi classics such as chopped liver or salt beef, while **Solly's** and **Dizengoff** (118 Golders Green Road, NW11 8HB, 8458 7003) are the pick of the Israeli-style restaurants, where you'll find Sephardi dishes such as falafel and shwarma. **Bevis Marks** offers a creative update of both cuisines. But ask any Londoner in the know, and you'll be told that to sample authentic Sephardi and Ashkenazi food in this city, you'll need to find a Jewish mamma.

Central

City

★ Bevis Marks Restaurant

4 Heneage Lane, EC3A 5DQ (7283 2220, www.bevismarkstherestaurant.com). Aldgate tube or Liverpool Street tube/rail. **Lunch served** noon-2.15pm Mon-Fri. **Dinner served** 5.30-8.30pm Mon-Thur. **Main courses** £15.25-£24.95. **Credit** AmEx, MC, V.

The most stylish of London's kosher venues, Bevis Marks has the added advantage of overlooking the adjacent 18th-century synagogue with its impressive brass chandeliers. Expect elegant service and high-end cooking with a nod to traditional Ashkenazi fare. Salt beef is 'Thai style' and chopped liver comes with added pear compote. A starter of satay salad (moist slices of chicken breast and just enough chilli) is a welcome addition to a menu that doesn't change often enough. Meat main courses can be outstanding; try the ribeye steak or herb-crusted rack of lamb, though perhaps staff should mention that the latter comes very pink. The accompaniments (red wine jus with the steaks, latkes, chips) were all well executed. Confit of duck was a little dry. For Sephardi flavours, try the Moroccan spiced salmon, or sea bream with tomato and olive salsa. Desserts here always appeal, as the kitchen concentrates on those not requiring fresh cream. Pear and almond tart with a raspberry coulis vies with the chocolate brownie for top points, but in season why can't the chef add more summer fruits to the list of wintry puds such as crumbles and sticky toffee pudding?
Available for hire. Babies and children admitted. Booking advisable lunch. Disabled: toilet. Kosher supervised (Shephardi). Tables outdoors (2, courtyard). Takeaway service; delivery service (over £10 within 4-mile radius). **Map 12 R6**.

Marylebone

Reubens

79 Baker Street, W1U 6RG (7486 0035, www.reubensrestaurant.co.uk). Baker Street tube. **Lunch served** 11.30am-4pm Mon-Thur; 11.30am-3pm Fri. **Dinner served** 5.30-10pm Mon-Thur. **Meals served** 11.30am-10pm Sun. **Main courses** £9-£29. **Minimum** (restaurant) £10. **Credit** MC, V.

Reubens is the only kosher eaterie in the West End, so has a captive audience of tourists and locals wanting *haimishe* (home-style) food. The ground-floor cafeteria-deli is stark, with cold blue walls and granite tables. This is where to find a quick salt beef sandwich or unexceptional chicken soup. Queue up at the counter, choose from a wide range of Ashkenazi dishes listed on a board, pay, and the plates will be brought to your table. Grilled lamb chops and steak are both good bets, but if you want waiter service and tablecloths, head for the pricier basement restaurant. Here you can order the likes of chicken with mango, beef in ambitious-sounding sauces, or old-fashioned favourites such as chicken kiev. Modern European it ain't, but Reubens draws crowds for its reliable grilled sole or tuna, and the filling, flavourful meats that Orthodox diners enjoy. Sadly, the no-fat salt beef didn't seem as good as it used to be, while chips, latkes and knaidlach were merely competently prepared. After a large portion of grilled chicken wings or stuffed cabbage, you might not manage dessert, but trenchermen could tackle the lockshen pudding or chocolate pud. Ices are made with parev cream.
Available for hire. Babies and children welcome: children's menu; high chairs; nappy-changing facilities. Booking advisable. Kosher supervised (Shephardi). Tables outdoors (3, pavement). Takeaway service. **Map 3 G5**.

North West

Golders Green

La Fiesta

235 Golders Green Road, NW11 9ES (8458 0444). Brent Cross tube. **Dinner served** 6-11pm Mon-Thur. **Meals served** noon-11pm Sun. **Main courses** £16-£50. **Credit** MC, V.
This kosher Argentinian steakhouse has had a makeover, with the dining area enlarged and brightened, though you can still see the white-hot coals of the barbecue and the cuts of meat ready to be grilled. The menu is resolutely meaty, with the best beef and lamb in kosher London – there are few fish choices and little for vegetarians. Starters include roasted pepper soup and empanadas, although with complimentary bread, olives and chimichurri sauce provided, as well as a salad, you might prefer to pass them up. The waitress brings large plates and then a brazier sizzling with thick juicy cuts: asado ribs (less tender and marbled with fat), grilled chicken and chunky kebabs. The best bets are the entrecote steak and the lamb chops. The beef was thick, tender and rare, charred on the outside and full of flavour. Four generous lamb chops were equally succulent. As accompaniments, chunky chips are a better option than the vegetable brochette, which was pretty yet lacking flavour (the onions hadn't been caramelised, and we find green peppers less appealing than the riper red ones). Desserts include Argentinian crêpes with parev ice-creams, but remember this is a steakhouse, so don't expect high-end pâtisserie.
Babies and children welcome: children's menu; high chairs. Booking advisable. Kosher supervised (Beth Din). Takeaway service.

Isola Bella

111A-113 Golders Green Road, NW11 8HR (8455 2228, www.isolabella.co.uk). Golders Green tube. **Meals served** 8am-1am Mon-Thur, Sun; 8am-4pm Fri. **Main courses** £4.50-£18. **Set lunch** £12-£15 2 courses, £20 3 courses. **Credit** AmEx, MC, V.
Transplanted from Hendon in 2011, this large dairy restaurant covers various cuisines. The owners have trimmed the original menu of 300 dishes to a more manageable choice. Sit at a dark, shiny table and start with breakfast (Mexican, Tunisian) or maybe all-day sandwiches or salads. There are pastas and pizzas too, plus 'soup casseroles', fish and a large vegetarian section. Portions are large. A plate of Thai vegetables (here called 'sida loui fay') was enough for three, coming with cashews for crunch. Fish is a forte: teriyaki salmon delivered moist flakes of fish in a rich marinade, with creamy mash. Less successful was the tuna burger – enough enjoyable chips for two, but uninspiring content inside the bun. If you choose salad niçoise, you may have room for dessert: fried banana and pineapple, or the exotic football (deep-fried battered ice-cream with chocolate cream and maple syrup). Or perhaps you'd prefer cheesecake, or one of 17 combinations of whipped cream layered with meringue and sweet glossy mousses? The pinnacle of these must be the Himalaya: coconut, white chocolate and caramel mousse, tiramisu, meringue, praline and milk chocolate ganache. There's a new branch at the Westfield mall in Shepherd's Bush.
Available for hire. Babies and children admitted: high chairs; nappy-changing facilities. Booking advisable. Disabled: toilet. Kosher supervised (Beth Din). Tables outdoors (4, pavement). Takeaway service; delivery service (over £15 within 2-mile radius).
For branch see index.

Bevis Marks Restaurant

Menu

Baklava: filo pastry layered with almonds or pistachios and soaked in scented syrup.
Borekas: triangles of filo pastry with savoury fillings like cheese or spinach.
Borscht: a classic beetroot soup served either hot or cold, often with sour cream.
Challah or **cholla:** egg-rich, slightly sweet plaited bread for the Sabbath.
Chicken soup: a clear, golden broth made from chicken and vegetables.
Cholent: a hearty, long-simmered bean, vegetable and (sometimes) meat stew, traditionally served for the sabbath.
Chopped liver: chicken or calf's liver fried with onions, finely chopped and mixed with hard-boiled egg and chicken fat. Served cold, often with extra egg and onions.
Chrane or **chrain:** a pungent sauce made from grated horseradish and beetroot, served with cold fish.
Cigars: rolls of filo pastry with a sweet or savoury filling.
Falafel: spicy, deep-fried balls of ground chickpeas, served with houmous and tahina (sesame paste).
Gefilte fish: white fish minced with onions, made into balls and poached or fried; served cold. The sweetened version is Polish.
Kataifi or **konafa:** shredded filo pastry wrapped around a nut or cheese filling, soaked in syrup.
Kibbe, kuba, kooba, kubbeh or **kobeiba:** oval patties, handmade from a shell of crushed wheat (bulgar) filled with minced meat, pine nuts and spices. Shaping and filling the shells before frying is the skill.
Knaidlach or **kneidlach:** dumplings made from matzo (qv) meal and eggs, poached until they float 'like clouds' in chicken soup.
Kreplach: pockets of noodle dough filled with meat and served in soup, or with sweet fillings and eaten with sour cream.
Laffa: large puffy pitta bread used to enclose falafel or shwarma (qv).
Latkes: grated potato mixed with egg and fried into crisp pancakes.
Lockshen: egg noodles boiled and served in soup. When cold, they can be mixed with egg, sugar and cinnamon and baked into a pudding.
Matzo or **matzah:** flat squares of unleavened bread. When ground into meal, it is used to make a crisp coating for fish or schnitzel.
Parev or **parve:** a term describing food that is neither meat nor dairy.
Rugelach: crescent-shaped biscuits made from a rich, cream cheese pastry, filled with nuts, jam or chocolate. Popular in Israel and the US.
Shwarma: layers of lamb or turkey, cooked on a spit, served with pitta.
Worsht: beef salami, sliced thinly to eat raw, but usually cut in thick pieces and fried when served with eggs or chips.

New Yorker Deli NEW

122 Golders Green Road, NW11 8HB (8209 0232). Golders Green tube. **Meals served** *Summer* noon-11pm Mon-Thur, Sun. *Winter* noon-11pm Mon-Thur, Sun; 2hrs after sabbath-2am Sat. **Main courses** £16-£17. **Credit** AmEx, MC, V.

Under the same ownership as Dizengoff next door, this feels like the late lamented Bloom's on a quiet day – not a bustling New York deli. The display of dishes at the counter is less inspiring than the list written on the old-style menu, though there's plenty for both takeaway and eat-in customers. You'll find hot and cold deli sandwiches and hefty portions of the type of Ashkenazi food (chopped liver, chicken soup) that sustained our grandparents. Salt beef and tongue are moist and flavourful, the 'gourmet' burger perfect for teenagers. Apart from the great-value food, the table mats feature games and quizzes for children. The Deli also caters for non-meat eaters, with an Israeli-style breakfast and fish options that include traditional fried haddock. Service is hesitant but pleasant; what's lacking is enthusiasm – in a real New York deli, the staff talk up the food, telling you to go for the braised beef or schnitzel, suggesting a side order of latkes or lockshen pudding. While neighbouring Dizengoff offers classier Israeli meze and grills, the kids will prefer to eat here – and if you choose the soup and sandwich combo, it's a bargain.
Available for hire. Babies and children welcome: children's menu; high chairs. Kosher supervised (Beth Din). Tables outdoors (2, pavement).

Solly's

146-150 Golders Green Road, NW11 8HE (8455 2121). Golders Green tube. **Lunch served** 11.30am-1hr before sunset Fri. **Meals served** 11.30am-11pm Mon-Thur, Sun. *Winter* 1hr after sabbath-1am Sat. **Main courses** £10-£16. **Set dinner** £32 3 courses. **No credit cards**.

The regulars at Solly's keep returning for reliable, Israeli-style food, crowding on to closely packed tables. Takeaway options are appetising, with crisp falafel and spicy shwarma, but once you sit down, prices shoot up (and it's cash-only). You're spoilt for choice with starters; there are kibbe and vine leaves and several varieties of houmous, plus an array of deliciously oily aubergine dishes. But the best pick is crunchy, lamb-filled Moroccan cigars, accompanied by a spicy tomato dipping sauce. Traditional dishes include chicken, bean or goulash soups – all served with puffy laffa bread baked in the oven at the back. Main courses are mostly grills: lamb (on skewers or as chops), steaks and burgers. Chicken comes with the breast fried in crumbs or as boneless thighs marinated and chargrilled to tender succulence. All main courses are served with chips (ours were unexceptional) or basmati rice (generous portions cooked in the Iraqi way with vermicelli). A slightly incongruous mixture of vinegary cabbage and lettuce fills the rest of the plate. We found service surly, and staff didn't think to offer us dessert (baklava, perhaps) or coffee.
Babies and children welcome: high chairs. Disabled: toilet. Kosher supervised (Beth Din). Takeaway service.

Hendon

Kaifeng

51 Church Road, NW4 4DU (8203 7888, www.kaifeng.co.uk). Hendon Central tube. **Lunch served** 12.30-2.30pm Mon-Thur, Sun.

Dinner served 5.30-10.30pm Mon-Thur, Sun; 1hr after sabbath-11pm Sat. **Main courses** £6.95-£24. **Set lunch** £20-£23 per person (minimum 2), £27-£42 per person (minimum 4). **Set dinner** £26-£32 per person (minimum 2), £38-£60 per person (minimum 4). **Credit** AmEx, DC, MC, V.

Kaifeng is named after the Chinese city in Hunan province, where Jews lived as long ago as the tenth century. It has traded here – away from the main Hendon restaurant scene – for 25 years. The dining room is a long, dark space with white linen on the tables. The menu lists expensive Chinese kosher food of the old-fashioned kind: generally tasty and slightly oily, though with an encouragingly large choice for vegetarians. Seaweed or spring rolls are reliable starters, as did our five-spices bean curd came in bland cubes. A clear spicy fish soup lacked kick too, as did cold bang bang chicken: the strips of breast were tender enough, but were covered in a cloying sauce with no hint of chilli, ginger or sesame oil. Things looked up with the crispy aromatic duck; a generous portion of pulled duck meat with crispy skin arrived with the requisite pancakes, hoi sin sauce and strips of cucumber and spring onion. We also enjoyed a comforting bowl of phat thai noodles with slivers of beef and lamb. Portions are generous, but presentation could have more finesse. Service (charged at 15%) was competent, yet sometimes lacked attention to detail.
Available for hire. Babies and children welcome: high chairs. Booking advisable. Kosher supervised (Beth Din). Takeaway service.

Outer London
Edgware, Middlesex

Papalina NEW

313 Hale Lane, Edgware, Middx, HA8 7AX (8958 7999, www.papalina.co.uk). Edgware tube. **Lunch served** noon-3pm Sun. **Dinner served** 5.30-11pm Mon-Thur, Sat, Sun. **Main courses** £15-£25. **Set buffet** £25. **Credit** AmEx, MC, V.

Set in the bustling kosher area of Edgware, this new Brazilian-style venture offers a buffet meal for £25, along with à la carte grills and salads. It's a bright, pleasant space, with purple art on the walls and purple napkins. The food is brought to you straight from the rotisserie; choose the churrascaria option and it will keep coming, the flow regulated by diners who indicate with a table-top red/green sign if they are ready for more. 'More' is the operative word: starting with salad, bread and dips, the waiter brings chicken wings, followed almost immediately by sausage (chicken or beef chorizo) and beef kofta. Next come lamb chops, chicken breasts, pieces of duck and even prime rib of beef. As accompaniments, there's a small choice of side dishes: chips, segments of corn on the cob and refreshing grilled pineapple. Understandably, staff don't allow some people to order à la carte while others at the same table choose the all-you-can-eat deal. Quality? Our lamb chops were sliced curiously thinly across the bone, and the kofta was dry, but the duck and slices of rare beef proved worth the wait. Just don't fill up early on too many sausages.
Available for hire. Babies and children welcome: high chairs; nappy-changing facilities. Booking advisable Sat, Sun. Kosher supervised (Federation). Takeaway service; delivery service (over £25 within 2-mile radius).

Korean

We've been predicting this cuisine as the Next Big Thing for a few years now. Korean cooking has much in common with in-vogue Japanese, but packs a chilli-laden punch that appeals to lovers of spicy food. It's big on barbecue too, so what's not to love? There's no shortage of new Korean restaurants opening in London, but the tipping point is still to arrive, we suspect in part because of the mediocrity of so many places – only a couple from the past two years are of a standard we think worthy of this guide (welcome **Ceena** and **Bi Bim Bap**). And not since the closure of Fulham's enigmatic Wizzy restaurant has anyone attempted creative contemporary Korean food – unless you count the cult kimchi burger at Hawksmoor (*see p249*). So our favourite places are well established: **Cah Chi** of Raynes Park and Earlsfield, New Malden's **Jee Cee Neh** and Fitzrovia's **Koba**. Visit them and you too may decide that Korean food is a big trend waiting to happen.

Central
City

Ceena NEW
13 St Bride Street, EC4A 4AS (7936 4941, www.ceena.co). City Thameslink rail, Farringdon tube/rail or bus 17, 45, 46, 63. **Meals served** 11.30am-10.30pm Mon-Fri. **Main courses** £9-£16. **Set meal** £15.30 3 courses. **Credit** AmEx, MC, V.

Ceena hopes to take Korean cooking from this off-Fleet Street launch pad to a global audience by emphasising the cuisine's healthy ingredients and cooking techniques, and selling the sizzle. Grills – galbi, bulgogi and ccochi (barbecued skewers, marinated in soy or red pepper sauce) – are both a menu and dining room focal point, cooked as they are on a grill at the end of the U-shaped bar counter. That other Korean classic, bibimbap, is offered in seven varieties, including squid, fresh salmon and pork belly. We were highly impressed by the chicken and gochujang version, served the traditional way with an egg yolk in a scorching-hot stone bowl that emanates a mouth-watering crackling sound and gives a delightfully toasty crust to the rice. Other dishes include japchae (sweet potato starch noodles with vegetables), jeon (savoury mung bean pancakes) and guk (sizzling-hot soup), though two off-message Italian-style salads suggest a slight nervousness about its market. We liked the fact that Ceena hasn't dumbed down the authenticity of its recipes for the City crowd: witness desserts of caramelised sweet potato in corn malt syrup, and sujung gwa (fruit punch made from dried persimmons and spices). The takeaway service, although rather pricey (£1.95 for barley tea!), is proving popular too. *Babies and children admitted. Booking advisable. Tables outdoors (2, pavement). Takeaway service; delivery service (over £14 within 2-mile radius).* **Map 11 N6**.

Covent Garden

Naru
230 Shaftesbury Avenue, WC2H 8EG (7379 7962, www.narurestaurant.com). Tottenham Court Road tube. **Lunch served** noon-3pm, **dinner served** 6-11pm Mon-Sat. **Main courses** £8-£13. **Credit** MC, V.

Punctuated with clusters of contemporary rice paper lanterns and traditional brush paintings, Naru's interior has an elegance to it, which is only slightly let down by the squeaky banquettes at the back. There's a noticeable absence of cooking equipment on the small tables, as everything is prepared behind the scenes here. This is not necessarily a bad thing: our bulgogi was cooked to melt-in-the-mouth perfection – not always the case with table-top barbecuing. The haemul jeongol (seafood stew) – rich and spicy, with a good mixture of seafood and vegetables – came in a traditional jeongol teul (cooking pot). Many of the other dishes are presented in a less conventional way, so expect rectangular plates with drizzled dressings, smears of sauce, and chapch'ae moulded in a chef's ring. Service was a little too relaxed on our visit and it proved very difficult to catch the waiter's eye, but this didn't detract from an enjoyable evening of accomplished cooking. Naru works equally well for a post-shopping pitstop, casual dinner or special occasion, and is definitely worth a repeat visit. *Babies and children admitted. Booking advisable Thur, Fri. Takeaway service.* **Map 18 D2**.

Fitzrovia

★ Koba
11 Rathbone Street, W1T 1NA (7580 8825). Goodge Street or Tottenham Court Road tube. **Lunch served** noon-2.15pm Mon-Sat. **Dinner served** 6-10.15pm daily. **Main courses** £7.80-£10. **Set lunch** £6.50-£11.50. **Set meal** £25-£35. **Credit** AmEx, MC, V.

This remarkable Korean restaurant is curiously low-key, tucked away in the curve of Rathbone Street. Nevertheless, it stays busy even on quiet weekend evenings. On our visit, most of the bar seats had been booked up. The dining room is understated and comfortable, with sophisticated wooden furniture and beautiful crockery. Service is exemplary and exceedingly polite; one waiter, unable to translate a particular ingredient into English, helpfully looked it up on his smartphone. The food is marvellous: authentic, refined and balanced in flavours and textures. An order of assorted p'ajeon produced a riff on the traditional Korean mung bean pancake, with small medallions of greaseless kimchi and chive variations, along with rounds of silky tofu, crisp courgette and earthy shiitake mushrooms. The chigaes here rival New Malden's best. The wobbly, eggy soondooboo chigae is rich and packed with seafood, while the beef and vegetable version came with tangles of bouncy glass noodles and gosari (bracken stalks), plus the sour sting of kimchi. Prices are fair for the

Menu

Chilli appears at every opportunity on Korean menus. Other common ingredients include soy sauce (different to both the Chinese and Japanese varieties), sesame oil, sugar, sesame seeds, garlic, ginger and various fermented soy bean pastes. Until the late 1970s eating meat was a luxury in Korea, so the quality of vegetarian dishes is high.

Given the spicy nature and overall flavour of Korean food, drinks such as chilled lager and vodka-like **soju/shoju** are the best matches. A wonderful non-alcoholic alternative that's always available, although not always listed on the menu, is barley tea (**porich'a/borich'a**). Often served free of charge, it has a light dry taste that works perfectly with the food. Korean restaurants don't usually offer desserts, though some serve orange or watermelon with the bill.

Spellings on menus vary hugely; we have given the most common.

Bibimbap or **pibimbap**: rice, vegetables and meat with a raw/fried egg dropped on top, often served in a hot stone bowl.
Bindaedok, **bindaedoek** or **pindaetteok**: a mung bean pancake.
Bokum: a stir-fried dish, usually including chilli.
Bulgogi or **pulgogi**: thin slices of beef marinated in pear sap (or a similar sweet dressing) and barbecued at the table; often eaten rolled in a lettuce leaf with shredded spring onion and fermented bean paste.
Chang, **jang** or **denjang**: various fermented soy bean pastes.
Chapch'ae or **chap chee**: mixed vegetables and beef cooked with transparent vermicelli or noodles.
Cheon, **jeon** or **jon**: meaning 'something flat'; this can range from a pancake containing vegetables, meat or seafood, to thinly sliced vegetables, beancurd or other ingredients, in a light batter.
Cheyuk: pork.
Chigae or **jigae**: a hot stew that contains fermented bean paste and chillies.
Gim or **kim**: dried seaweed, toasted and seasoned with salt and sesame oil.
Gu shul pan: a traditional lacquered tray that has nine compartments containing individual appetisers.
Hobak chun or **hobak jun**: sliced marrow in a light egg batter.
Japch'ae, **japchae** or **jap chee**: alternative spellings for chapch'ae (qv).
Jjim: fish or meat stewed for a long time in soy sauce, sugar and garlic.

Ceena. See p185.

quality of food and presentation, and lunch deals offer a good introduction to the various stews, barbecues, and rice and noodle dishes available.
Babies and children welcome: high chairs. Booking advisable. Disabled: toilet. Takeaway service. **Map 17 B1**.

Holborn

Asadal
227 High Holborn, WC1V 7DA (7430 9006, www.asadal.co.uk). Holborn tube. **Lunch served** noon-3pm Mon-Sat. **Dinner served** 6-11pm Mon-Sat; 6-10.30pm Sun. **Main courses** £6-£20. **Set lunch** £8.50-£15.80. **Set dinner** £20-£35. **Credit** AmEx, MC, V.
It may be London's largest Korean restaurant, but Asadal is easy to miss: a discreet doorway beside Holborn tube station leads down to a dimly lit, graceful cavern with spot-lit stone walkways, exposed brickwork, wooden columns and gleaming tabletop barbecues. The main dining room is warmly convivial, and often humming with business people at lunchtime. At the rear are a couple of elegant private dining rooms – handy for groups, though we have felt remote and forgotten when eating there. For a not-too-heavy, not-too-light lunch, the bento boxes are a good choice (albeit with City pricing); the appealing options range from galbi and bulgogi to battered seafood and stir-fried vegetables. Alternatively, there are plenty of diverse

big bowl dishes among the 'lunch sets': five types of bibimbap, three neng myun (cold buckwheat noodles with spicy sauce or chilled soup), slow-cooked mackerel in soy and spicy sauce over rice, and more. Start with the mandu – dumplings made on-site – or pa jeon (spring onion and seafood pancake). Drinks include herbal infusions, soju and Korean beers, plus a serviceable wine list.
Babies and children welcome: high chairs. Booking advisable. Disabled: toilet. Separate rooms for parties, seating 6 and 12. Takeaway service. **Map 18 E2**.

Leicester Square

Jindalle
6 Panton Street, SW1Y 4DL (7930 8881). Piccadilly Circus tube. **Meals served** noon-11pm daily. **Main courses** £6.90-£10.90. **Set lunch** £3.90-£8.90. **Set dinner** (5-9pm) £18.90-£24.90. **Credit** AmEx, MC, V.
Jindalle's location on a shabby street just south of Leicester Square isn't promising, but don't let appearances put you off: the food is good, and the staff lovely. The space too is pleasant, a café-style wood-panelled area out front, balanced by a more formal but relaxed dining room behind. The barbecue section is the best option from the menu, as it includes a huge array of meat – marinated beefsteak, spicy belly pork, short ribs, ox tongue and more. We chose a couple of these with

KOREAN

traditional sides such as kimchi pancake, as well as soba noodles and a hearty beef rib and cabbage stew. Hite beers and soju provided the accompaniment. Presentation and service were above par and the food tasty rather than outstanding. Around us predominantly Asian customers were tucking in with gusto to giant hotpots, sizzling bibimbaps and steaming bowls of noodle soups. The staff do the barbecuing for you, but provide as little distraction as possible, adding to the friendly, familiar atmosphere. It's hard to imagine having a bad night out here.
Babies and children welcome: high chairs. Booking advisable. **Map 17 C5.**

Mayfair

Kaya
42 Albemarle Street, W1S 4JH (7499 0622, www.kayarestaurant.co.uk). Green Park tube. **Lunch served** noon-3pm, **dinner served** 6-11pm Mon-Sat. **Main courses** £9-£20. **Set lunch** £10-£15. **Set dinner** £19-£22.50 per person (minimum 2). **Credit** AmEx, MC, V.
From its smart Mayfair location and brasserie-style façade, you might expect prices to be high at Kaya. In fact, it isn't that much more expensive than many other West End Korean restaurants (unless you opt for one of the set dinner menus). The tranquil dining room is designed to echo elements of a Korean palace; classical music tinkles away in the background as *hanbok*-clad waitresses effortlessly attend to customers. Kaya is more serene than austere, however, so you can kick back. All the dishes we tried were just as polished as the service, and a cup of complimentary porich'a (barley tea) was a nice touch too. Kalbi came in succulent chunks (including bone), with a well-balanced, spicy, soy bean paste. Bindaedok, speckled with finely cut vegetables, was crisp and delicious, while haemul tang (spicy seafood stew) had a decent chilli heat to it, although the fish was a tad overcooked. If you venture downstairs to the toilets, you'll come across a whole different side to Kaya: a sultry karaoke bar, no doubt popular with some of the Korean businessmen who dine here.
Babies and children admitted. Booking advisable. Disabled: toilet. Separate rooms for parties, seating 8 and 12. **Map 9 J7.**

Soho

★ Bi Bim Bap `NEW`
11 Greek Street, W1D 4DJ (7287 3434, www.bibimbapsoho.com). Tottenham Court Road tube. **Lunch served** noon-3pm, **dinner served** 6-11pm Mon-Fri. **Meals served** noon-11pm Sat. **Main courses** £6.45-£9.95. **Credit** DC, MC, V.
With its colourful IKEA-style interior and photos of diners on the wall, Bi Bim Bap is a popular stop-off for hip, young Londoners out and about in town. Other than the speedy service and reasonable prices, the main attraction is the restaurant's namesake rice dish. Bibimbap is taken seriously, with ten varieties to choose from, including classic beef or vegetable and more unusual spicy pork, chilli chicken, or ginseng, ginko, date and chestnut – all served in sizzlingly hot stone bowls. You also have the option of brown or white rice. According to the menu, the key to a good bibimbap is how much you stir it, and staff trust you to do this yourself, adding as much koch'ujang and denjang as you like. Our fillet beef version, packed with plenty of meat and vegetables, filled the mouth with flavour. Another of the signature dishes, chapch'ae, was also tasty, but too heavy on the sesame oil. Sadly, deep-fried chilli squid wasn't particularly crisp or spicy. We'll definitely be back for the bibimbap and Korean drinks (including plum and ginseng wine), but probably not for the side dishes.
Babies and children admitted. Booking advisable dinner Fri, Sat. Takeaway service. **Map 17 C3.**

Myung Ga
1 Kingly Street, W1B 5PA (7734 8220, www.myungga.co.uk). Oxford Circus or Piccadilly Circus tube. **Lunch served** noon-3pm Mon-Thur. **Dinner served** 5.30-11pm Mon-Thur, Sun. **Meals served** noon-11pm Fri, Sat. **Main courses** £7.50-£8.90. **Set lunch** £11-£13.50. **Set dinner** £25-£45. **Credit** AmEx, MC, V.
The cosy booths in this long-established restaurant just off Carnaby Street are filled with a vibrant mix of families, Koreans and the usual West End crowd. Try not to end up in the brightly lit private dining room at the back, as you'll miss out on much of the bustling atmosphere. Hot hand towels are brought to the table as soon as you sit down – a nice touch.

Jeongol or **chungol**: casserole.
Kalbi, **galbi** or **kalbee**: beef spare ribs, marinated and barbecued.
Kimchi, **kim chee** or **kimch'i**: fermented pickled vegetables, usually chinese cabbage, white radishes, cucumber or greens, served in a small bowl with a spicy chilli sauce.
Kkaktugi or **kkakttugi**: pickled radish.
Koch'ujang: a hot, red bean paste.
Kook, **gook**, **kuk** or **guk**: soup. Koreans have an enormous variety of soups, from consommé-like liquid to meaty broths of noodles, dumplings, meat or fish.
Ko sari na mool or **gosari namul**: cooked bracken stalks with sesame seeds.
Mandu kuk or **man doo kook**: clear soup with steamed meat dumplings.
Naengmyun or **neng myun**: cold noodle dishes, usually featuring thin, elastic buckwheat noodles.
Namul or **na mool**: vegetable side dishes.
Ojingeo: squid.
P'ajeon, **pa jeon** or **pa jun**: flour pancake with spring onions and (usually) seafood.
Panch'an: side dishes; they usually include pickled vegetables, but possibly also tofu, fish, seaweed or beans.
Pap, **bap**, **bab** or **pahb**: cooked rice.
Pokkeum or **pokkm**: stir-fry; common types include cheyuk pokkeum (pork), ojingeo pokkeum (squid).
Shinseollo, **shinsonro**, **shinsulro** or **sin sollo**: 'royal casserole'; a meat soup with seaweed, seafood, eggs and vegetables, all of which is cooked at the table.
Teoppap or **toppap**: 'on top of rice'; for example, ojingeo teoppap is squid served on rice.
Toenjang: seasoned (usually with chilli) soy bean paste.
Tolsot (or **dolsot**) **bibimbap**: tolsot is a sizzling hot stone bowl that makes the bibimbap (qv) a little crunchy on the sides.
Tteokpokki: bars of compressed rice (tteok is a rice cake) fried on a hotplate with veg and sausages, in a chilli sauce.
Twaeji gogi: pork.
T'wigim, **twigim** or **tuigim**: fish, prawns or vegetables dipped in batter and deep-fried until golden brown.
Yach'ae: vegetables.
Yuk hwe, **yukhoe** or **yukhwoe**: shredded raw beef, strips of pear and egg yolk, served chilled.
Yukkaejang: spicy beef soup.

Bi Bim Bap

The menu covers the usual Korean repertoire (soups, barbecue, stir-fries and noodles) executed to a reasonable standard. Tolsot bibimbap is available in an assortment of flavours, including beef, pork, chicken, prawn or tofu; egg doesn't come as standard, though, so ask if you want it (for a £1 supplement). Our beef version was tasty enough, but too oily. From the barbecue menu, sweet marinated pork contrasted well with its salt and sesame oil dip. A selection of namul included satisfyingly crunchy blanched bean sprouts and palate-cleansing, sweet, spicy radish. Buzzers brought staff – who were polite if not over-friendly – to the tables quickly. Although barley tea is missing from the drinks list, there are plenty of other Korean options including ginseng tea and soju cocktails.
Babies and children welcome: high chairs. Booking advisable. Separate room for parties, seats 12. **Map 17 A4.**

★ Nara

9 D'Arblay Street, W1F 8DR (7287 2224). Oxford Circus or Tottenham Court Road tube. **Lunch served** noon-3.30pm, **dinner served** 5.30-11pm daily. **Main courses** £6.90-£13. **Set lunch** £6.90. **Set dinner** £8.50. **Credit** AmEx, MC, V.
Business-people of limited height will love the manly, no-nonsense interior of this long-standing Korean/Japanese restaurant: the black and dark wood furnishings are broken by one lone silk painting that does its best to lighten the austere decor. Taller folk will curse the tabletop grill base against which their knees will keep cracking. The mixed clientele, including several Korean diners,

happily tucked into well-presented, generous portions of staples such as hotpots and kimchi, samgyeopsal (pork belly) and bulgogi – or making use of those cursed barbecue grills. Stir-fried squid in a sweet chilli sauce was succulent and not too sugary, its flavours dense and complex. However, tolsot bibimbap came with partially cooked beef and a fried egg, when we'd been expecting both key ingredients to be raw in a dish that's really not so hard to get right. The great-value lunch menu, which also includes miso soup, came with a mixed bag of side dishes: enjoyably fresh pickles and less enjoyable seaweed jelly. On the whole, though, Nara is an ideal place to come if you want something fairly upmarket, without the accompanying price tag. Just don't forget your kneepads.
Babies and children admitted. Takeaway service. **Map 17 B3.**

Ran

58-59 Great Marlborough Street, W1F 7JY (7434 1650, www.ranrestaurant.com). Oxford Circus tube. **Lunch served** noon-3pm Mon-Sat. **Dinner served** 6-11pm daily. **Main courses** £5.90-£12. **Set lunch** £7-£18. **Set dinner** £25. **Credit** AmEx, MC, V.
Korean businessmen and groups of young professionals seem to like Ran, and it's easy to see why: impressive chrome extractor fans suggest barbecue is taken seriously here; the interior is handsomely attired; and service is professional yet convivial. The lengthy menu highlights the house speciality of ssam, a traditional Korean way of eating that involves wrapping morsels of meat in leafy vegetables. We sampled two varieties: a classic bo ssam with tender steamed pork belly and half a

head of salted napa cabbage for wrapping; and a version comprising crisp lettuce, seasoned julienned spring onions, fiery raw garlic and spicy ssamjang paste. Less successful were dry beef rolls wrapped around slivers of pear and spring onions, as the accompanying 'mustard' sauce lacked the promised bite. Bibim naengmyun (chilled spicy cold noodles) was pleasant enough, with the requisite spicy-sour kick, but felt starchier than more accomplished renditions. A plate of kimchi (radish, cabbage, cucumber) was generous in size, as it should be for £9.50; we found ourselves adding the delicious crunchy morsels to our lettuce wraps. To conclude: it's worth sticking to Ran's extensive barbecue and ssam menu, plus a few bottles of icy cold Hite beer.
Babies and children admitted. Booking advisable. Separate rooms for parties, seating 10. Takeaway service. **Map 17 A3.**

South West

Raynes Park

★ Cah Chi [HOT 50]

34 Durham Road, SW20 0TW (8947 1081, www.cahchi.com). Raynes Park rail or bus 57, 131. **Lunch served** noon-3pm, **dinner served** 5-11pm Tue-Fri. **Meals served** noon-10.30pm Sat, Sun. **Main courses** £6-£14. **Set dinner** £20 3 courses. **Corkage** (wine only) £2. **Credit** MC, V.
Cah Chi is the jewel in the crown of south-west London's Korean restaurant scene, despite not being in the Korean heartland of New Malden. From the kids' drawings tacked to the walls of the

light, breezy dining room, to the smiling staff, the place exudes charm. The homely feel is carried through to the clientele, which includes plenty of local Korean families. We were pleased to see more variety than usual on the menu (as well as some amusing typos). For less conventional options, including offal and mountain vegetables, ask the staff to talk you through the specials menu, which is displayed in Korean at the back of the restaurant. They pride themselves on making their own tofu, dumplings, kimchi and soy bean paste. Not to be missed is the own-made tofu and seafood stew ('soon-du-bu jji-gae' on the menu): a rich, creamy, chilli-spiked sauce encased chewy slivers of seafood that contrasted perfectly with pieces of silky tofu. Black pudding stuffed with cellophane noodles, served with a dip of salt and chilli flakes, is also a popular choice. The sweet marinated soy beans were a welcome addition to the free panch'an. Cah Chi offers exceptional food, good value for money and a BYO wine policy too. Korean wine and beer, soju and saké are also available.
Babies and children welcome: high chairs. Booking essential. Separate room for parties, seats 18. Takeaway service.
For branch see index.

North
Finsbury Park

Dotori
3 Stroud Green Road, N4 2DQ (7263 3562). Finsbury Park tube/rail. **Lunch served** noon-3pm, **dinner served** 5-10.30pm Tue-Sun. **Main courses** £6.50-£32. **Set lunch** £6.50-£7 2 courses. **Set meal** £12-£25. **Credit** MC, V.
Dotori's interior is perfectly serviceable, with tables clustered closely together in a small but fairly attractive space. However, it's the food that takes centre stage, the Korean/Japanese hybrid menu happily mixing sashimi and sushi with kimchi and bibambap. Shrimp tempura donburi was one of the best examples we've eaten of this battered shellfish on rice dish, while yukhoe tolsot bibimbap (thin slices of raw beef topped with a raw egg on rice, served in a fiercely hot stone bibambap dish) was delicious, the mixed ingredients continuing to cook while we ate, to produce a scrumptious layer of crispy, sesame oil-flavoured rice on the bottom of the bowl. A shared dish of japch'ae – dangmyeon noodles with fried beef and vegetables – was top-notch, the sweetness perfectly balanced against a panoply of more complex flavours. With two sides of kimchi and soft drinks, the bill for two came to little more than £25, making this one of the dining bargains of the year. Service can get rather haphazard when the restaurant is full, and if you show up without booking you may be in for a long wait, but the food is worth it.
Babies and children admitted. Booking advisable dinner. Takeaway service. Vegetarian menu.

North West
Golders Green

Kimchee
887 Finchley Road, NW11 8RR (8455 1035). Golders Green tube. **Lunch served** noon-2.30pm, **dinner served** 6-11pm Tue-Sun.

Jee Cee Neh

Main courses £5.90-£8.50. **Set meal** £16.50-£21.90 per person (minimum 2). **Credit** MC, V.
Kimchee has been serving classic Korean food from its site on the busy Finchley Road for many years. While the window display of plastic food may have seen better days, the interior is light and airy, with traditional Korean touches. On our visit, the dining room was buzzing with a mix of trendy young Koreans, and Korean and western families. We opted for the good-value Kimchee set dinner, which included seaweed soup, kimchi, chapch'ae, p'ajeon, bulgogi, bibimbap, fruit and barley tea. Both the soup (made with an earthy stock) and the chapch'ae were flavourful. As the barbecue on our table wasn't working, they brought us a portable one. This left the bulgogi a little wetter than we would have liked, but it was pleasant nonetheless. We felt a little short-changed on the tolsot bibimbap, however: there was too much rice, not enough vegetables and egg. Kimchee is a fun place to go for a lively evening, a glass of Korean beer or soju and reasonably priced food. Thanks to buzzers on the tables, the service is pretty efficient too.
Babies and children welcome: high chairs. Booking essential Fri-Sun. Takeaway service.

Outer London
New Malden, Surrey

Hankook
Falcon House, 257 Burlington Road, New Malden, Surrey KT3 4NE (8942 1188). Motspur Park rail. **Lunch served** noon-3pm Mon, Tue, Fri. **Dinner served** 6-11pm Mon-Fri. **Meals served** noon-11pm Sat, Sun. **Main courses** £6.50-£50. **Set meal** £10 per person (minimum 2). **Credit** MC, V.
Situated on a bleak, industrial stretch of Burlington Road, beneath an accountancy firm, Hankook isn't much to look at from the outside. The interior is more appealing – especially the traditional private dining rooms with low seating and sliding paper-screen doors. On a Saturday night, the clientele was a mix of Korean families and businessmen, the latter letting off steam with plenty of soju and singing. Free porich'a (barley tea) and panch'an – including a peppery pasta salad, kimchi and blanched bean sprouts – were delivered as soon as we sat down. The set meal offers good value and variety, but there's plenty more to choose from, including sashimi. A satisfying dish of barbecued pork and squid in a thick, chilli-flecked sauce came sizzling to the table. It made a refreshing change to be allowed to mix the haemul tolsot bibimbap ourselves, although it contained a rather uninspiring selection of seafood. Staff had just the right balance of efficiency and friendliness, and a knack of popping up exactly when needed.
Babies and children welcome: high chairs. Booking essential dinner Fri, Sat.

★ ★ Jee Cee Neh
74 Burlington Road, New Malden, Surrey KT3 4NU (8942 0682). New Malden rail. **Lunch served** noon-3pm, **dinner served** 6-11pm Mon, Tue, Thur, Fri. **Meals served** 11.30am-10.30pm Sat, Sun. **Main courses** £7-£13. **Credit** (over £20) MC, V.
Sitting at the end of a row of local shops, in what could have been a British caff at one point, Jee Cee Neh (or 'Jee's Korean Restaurant', as the sign says) has a charmingly ramshackle feel. The mix-and-match decor includes dark wood tables, candy-striped walls and a clumsily partitioned area at the back of the restaurant. The place was populated mostly by Korean families on our visit. For such an understated venue, the cooking is of a very high standard. Naengmyun was ideal on a hot evening: the ice-chilled broth, filled with lip-smackingly chewy noodles and tender beef slices, had the perfect balance of refreshing sweet, sour and savoury flavours. Yuk hwe was another hit, although, unusually, it was made with apple rather than pear. Even the sweet spicy sauce in a dish of tteokpokki seemed to have a richer, more complex flavour than normal. A bottle of soju and some complimentary panch'an rounded off the meal well. Service, delivered in slightly faltering English, was warm and accommodating. We'll definitely be back.
Available for hire. Babies and children welcome: high chairs. Separate room for parties, seats 20. Takeaway service.

KOREAN

Malaysian, Indonesian & Singaporean

We may think of London as the premier crucible in which cooking styles are forged to create new cuisines – and so it is, but it was certainly not the first. Malaysia has long been a centre of trade, a place where cultures have mixed. The Malay people had their own brand of rich aromatic curries, typified by such dishes as nasi lemak, before the British brought Indians to the peninsula during the colonial era; the delicious fried bread and curry breakfast dish, roti canai, bears witness to the southern Indian influence. Chinese travelled there in the 17th century, and as well as bringing their own Cantonese stir-fries, they intermarried with the Malays. The resulting gastronomic progeny is called Nonya or Peranakan cuisine; otak otak (a coconutty fish cake often served in a banana leaf) is among the more famous dishes of this cooking style. Throw in the extraordinary melting pot that is Singapore (a great place for laksa), and the myriad islands that form Indonesia (where satay and beef rendang were born) and you have some idea of the wealth of influences on this cuisine. In London, there are still relatively few venues that specialise in this food, but they cover the spectrum of dining options pretty well. You want posh? Try the long-established **Singapore Garden** or the newer, trendier **Awana**. Is street food your bag? Head for Chinatown's **Rasa Sayang** or **New Fook Lam Moon**.

Central

Barbican

★ Sedap
102 Old Street, EC1V 9AY (7490 0200, www.sedap.co.uk). Old Street tube/rail. **Lunch served** 11.30am-2.30pm Mon-Fri. **Dinner served** 6-10.30pm daily. **Main courses** £6.80-£8. **Set lunch** £6.95-£7.95 2 courses. **Credit** MC, V.
Sedap's modest frontage conceals a smoothly run, darkly handsome little restaurant, with gold dragon decorations on the walls, exotic tea sets in cabinets, and goldfish in an aquarium on the black counter. The place seemed overstaffed early on a Sunday evening, but the two smart waiters were soon at full stretch, with a packed room and takeaway orders coming in. If you love the nutty flavour of satay sauce, try the achar, a zingy Nonya dish of pickled carrots, cauliflower and cucumber with peanuts and sesame, offered as a starter. Many of the main courses glisten with colour. By comparison, beef rendang looked undistinguished, despite its careful mound of rice, yet it proved to be a delicious version of the 'dry' curry – spiced to prickle the brow and sucking at the tongue. Penang char kway teow (a stir-fry of prawns, chinese sausage, slivers of fish cake, spring onions, egg, beansprouts and soy) suffered only from the slightly soggy noodles. With LSO St Luke's opposite and the Barbican a short walk south, Sedap draws a curious but enthusiastic clientele: a mix of stripy-blazered City boys and their female companions, self-appointed Shoreditch culturati and Asian women.
Available for hire. Babies and children admitted. Booking advisable dinner. Separate room for parties, seats 14. Takeaway service; delivery service (over £10 within 1-mile radius). **Map 5 P4**.

Chinatown

New Fook Lam Moon
10 Gerrard Street, W1D 5PW (7734 7615). Leicester Square or Piccadilly Circus tube. **Meals served** noon-11.30pm Mon-Sat; noon-10.30pm Sun. **Main courses** £11.50-£27. **Credit** MC, V.
Given the display of roast meats hanging out front, you may assume this is just another Hong Kong-style Chinatown café. The simply decorated interior, with its ground-floor and basement dining rooms, does little to dispel that notion. But examine the menu closely, and you will discover some choice Malaysian dishes dotted amid the standard Cantonese fare. Descriptions can mask the true

identity of dishes; 'pork ribs soup with herbs' turned out to be bak kut teh (a soup with reputed medicinal properties that is popular at breakfast), while 'wok-fried flat wide noodles' was actually the hawker-stall favourite, char kway teow. The flavour-dial was turned to high with our dish of okra packed with blachan. The okra was perfectly crunchy and its gooey sap kept well in check. We also wolfed down a juicy Nonya chicken curry (a red curry with chicken on the bone and potatoes), which was good enough to grace the tables of the best home cooks. A little coconut milk was used to add richness and texture, and kaffir lime leaves provided an exotic hint. This crackingly good food is served in generous portions by friendly staff, making New Fook Lam Moon one of our favourite Malaysian restaurants in London.

Babies and children welcome: high chairs. Booking advisable. Takeaway service. **Map 17 C4.**

★ Rasa Sayang

5 Macclesfield Street, W1D 6AY (7734 1382, www.rasasayangfood.com). Leicester Square or Piccadilly Circus tube. **Meals served** noon-11pm Mon-Thur, Sun; noon-midnight Fri, Sat. **Main courses** £6.90-£17.80. **Credit** AmEx, MC, V.
Opened in 2008, Rasa Sayang is now established as one of the better Malaysian restaurants in Soho. There are two dining areas; we prefer the smaller ground-floor space with its pale wood furniture to the darker basement. The room can seem austere and cramped, but prices are still low and service is cheerful. The menu is like a tour of Singapore's hawker stalls, featuring satay, hainanese chicken rice and nasi lemak – real comfort cooking for expatriates – although the execution can be a little slapdash and inconsistent. We started with kon loh mee (flat rice noodles), which arrived with pork won ton, then moved on to the national dish of Singapore: chilli crab topped with egg white, for a velvety touch from the 'heat zone'. Extracting the soft flesh from the crab shell can be a messy affair, but we were rewarded by tasty and spicy flavours. For an authentic finish, try the bubur cha cha – a medley of yam, sweet potato and sago served with warm coconut milk – and a comforting cup of teh tarik.
Babies and children admitted. Booking advisable. Separate room for parties, seats 30. Takeaway service. **Map 17 C4.**

South Kensington

Awana

85 Sloane Avenue, SW3 3DX (7584 8880, www.awana.co.uk). South Kensington tube. **Lunch served** noon-3pm daily. **Dinner served** 6-11pm Mon-Fri, Sun; 6-11.30pm Sat. **Main courses** £10.50-£25. **Set lunch** £12.50 2 courses, £15 3 courses. **Set dinner** £40-£45 tasting menu. **Credit** AmEx, DC, MC, V.
One of London's swankiest Malaysian restaurants, Awana cossets its diners with lush swathes of teak and burgundy leather. For a more casual bite, perch at the satay bar, where the little skewers are top of their class, holding the likes of tender organic chicken or scallops, served with a peanut sauce that's lifted by a hint of lemongrass. Lunchtimes tend to be quiet affairs, but the room was busy at dinner. The menu is long and somewhat confusing, and the kitchen has added a few twists to the standard Malaysian repertoire. Lobster tail, for instance, lends a touch of luxury to the otherwise simple hawker's plate of char kway teow (stir-fried flat rice noodles). We lapped up a tasty beef

rendang, but a curry of fish and prawns, simmered with tomato and okra, lacked spice. Awana's flavours have a tendency to be muted, and prices are high. The upside is that ingredients are of a noticeably high quality – unlike much of the competition. We ended our meal with bakar kirim durian, an innovative take on crème brûlée that featured stinky durian fruit infused with vanilla.
Available for hire. Babies and children welcome: high chairs. Booking advisable Thur; essential Fri, Sat. Takeaway service. Vegetarian menu. **Map 14 E10.**

West
Bayswater

C&R Restaurant

52 Westbourne Grove, W2 5SH (7221 7979). Bayswater tube. **Meals served** noon-11pm Mon, Wed-Fri; noon-11.30pm Sat; noon-10.30pm Sun. **Main courses** £7.50-£24. **Set meal**

£16 vegetarian, £19 meat per person (minimum 2). **Credit** AmEx, MC, V.
C&R is the grown-up sister of Soho's C&R Café. The dining room features grey banquettes, pale wooden chairs and magnolia walls jazzed up with abstract artwork including one of a nude. A stained tablecloth got our meal off to an inauspicious start, and the prawn crackers, complimentary on our last visit, now cost £3. We took time browsing the extensive menu, which doesn't restrict itself to Malaysia, drawing influences from China, Thailand and Vietnam. Singapore laksa is a popular choice here, but this time we decided to sample one of the chef's specials: fish fillet in batter. Sadly, the batter was clumpy and the dish was only just saved by the piquant chilli sauce. Sambal goreng telor – whole hard-boiled egg, quickly fried then mixed with a spicy sambal sauce – was equally ho-hum. Chendol (pandan pearls with coconut milk and gula melaka) brought our meal to a slapdash, excessively sweet and milky end. We've enjoyed meals here in the past, but it seems both the food and service can be unreliable.

Bubble tea shops

Originating in Taiwan but now popular in China and across South-east Asia, bubble teas are flavoured teas served with delectably chewy tapioca balls and shaken to produce a foamy top. They can be milk- or fruit-based, and are fairly similar to iced teas, juices and smoothies. Consumption is great fun, involving chewing and slurping at the same time – the tapioca 'pearls' or 'boba' are sucked up through a very wide straw. Expect to pay about £3.50 per tumbler. In addition to the shops listed below, you'll also find good bubble teas (and more generous seating) at **Café de Hong Kong** and **HK Diner** (for both, *see p70*).

Boba Jam

102 Shaftesbury Avenue, W1D 5EJ (no phone). Leicester Square tube. **Open** noon-11.30pm daily. **Dishes** £4.45-£6.95. **Credit** MC, V.
This simple white-walled venue, a spin-off of Candy Café, is more takeaway than café, with only a few seats at the window. A huge choice of fruit- and milk-based bubble teas is available, featuring a generous number of boba per cup. There's also the option to add other ingredients to your drink, such as jellied nata de coco (fermented coconut water).
Babies and children admitted. Takeaway service. **Map 17 C4.**

Bubbleology

49 Rupert Street, W1D 7PF (7494 4231, www.bubbleology.co.uk). Piccadilly Circus tube. **Open** 11am-11.30pm daily. **Credit** MC, V.
There's a scientific theme at play here, with staff in lab coats, chemistry sets on display, and a high-tech machine for

shaking the drinks. Bubbleology's big, chewy bubbles are a paragon of the art, though we weren't enamoured with the taste of our drinks. Flavours range from simple assam and jasmine teas to taro, almond and kumquat.
Babies and children admitted. Tables outdoors (4, pavement). Takeaway service. **Map 17 B4.**

Candy Café

1st floor, 3 Macclesfield Street, W1D 6AU (7434 4581, www. candycafe.co.uk). Leicester Square tube. **Open** noon-11.30pm daily. **Dishes** £2-£3.95. **Credit** MC, V.
The steps leading to this internet café specialising in Asian drinks and desserts lie next to Leong's Legends restaurant. Head up them and you'll find more than just bubble teas; blueberry coffee, snow pudding drinks and red bean ice drinks are among the 'yet to go mainsteam' options.
Babies and children admitted. Takeaway service. **Map 17 C4.**

Chaboba

8 East Yard, Camden Lock, NW1 8AL (7267 4719, www.chaboba.co.uk). Camden Town tube. **Open** 11am-6.30pm daily. **No credit cards.**
Quirky Chaboba is a great place to sample your first bubble tea. The various types of tea (milk- or fruit-based, or an icy version that's called 'crush' here), and the ratios used for making each drink, are clearly explained in colourful diagrams. Pimp your choice with toppings such as mixed fruit jelly, seasonal fruit, and yoghurt popping boba.
Babies and children admitted. Tables outdoors (2, market). **Map 27 C2.**

Menu

Blachan, **belacan** or **blacan**: dried fermented shrimp paste.

Char kway teow or **char kwai teow**: a stir-fry of rice noodles with meat and/or seafood with dark soy sauce and beansprouts. A Hakka Chinese-derived speciality of Singapore.

Gado gado: a salad of blanched vegetables with a peanut-based sauce.

Gula melaka: palm sugar, an important ingredient with a distinctive caramel flavour added to a sago and coconut-milk pudding of the same name.

Hainanese chicken rice: poached chicken served with rice cooked in chicken stock, light chicken broth and a chilli-ginger dipping sauce.

Ikan bilis or **ikan teri**: tiny fish, often fried and made into a dry sambal (qv) with peanuts.

Laksa: a noodle dish with either coconut milk or tamarind as the stock base.

Mee: noodles.

Mee goreng: fried egg noodles with meat, prawns and vegetables.

Nasi ayam: rice cooked in chicken broth, served with roast or steamed chicken and a light soup.

Nasi goreng: fried rice with shrimp paste, garlic, onions, chillies and soy sauce.

Nasi lemak: coconut rice on a plate with a selection of curries and fish dishes topped with ikan bilis (qv).

Nonya or **Nyonya**: the name referring to both the women and the dishes of the Straits Chinese community.

Otak otak: a Nonya (qv) speciality made from eggs, fish and coconut milk.

Pandan leaves: a variety of the screwpine plant; used to add colour and fragrance to both savoury and sweet dishes.

Peranakan: refers to the descendants of Chinese settlers who first came to Malacca (now Melaka), a seaport on the Malaysian west coast, in the 17th century. It is generally applied to those born of Sino-Malay extraction who adopted Malay customs, costume and cuisine, the community being known as 'Straits Chinese'. The cuisine is also known as Nonya.

Rendang: meat cooked in coconut milk.

Roti canai: a South Indian/Malaysian breakfast dish of fried unleavened bread served with a dip of either chicken curry or dal.

Sambal: there are several types of sambal, often made of fiery chilli sauce, onions and coconut oil; it can be served as a side dish or used as a relish.

Satay: there are two types – **terkan** (minced and moulded to the skewer) and **chochok** ('shish', more common in London). Beef or chicken are the traditional choices, though prawn is now often available too. Satay is served with a rich spicy sauce made from onions, lemongrass, galangal, and chillies in tamarind sauce; it is sweetened and thickened with ground peanuts.

Babies and children welcome: high chairs. Takeaway service; delivery service (within 2-mile radius). **Map 7 B6**.
For branch (C&R Café) see index.

Paddington

Satay House
13 Sale Place, W2 1PX (7723 6763, www.satay-house.co.uk). Edgware Road tube or Paddington tube/rail. **Lunch served** noon-3pm, **dinner served** 6-11pm daily. **Main courses** £5-£18.50. **Set meal** £16.90-£27.90 per person (minimum 2). **Credit** AmEx, MC, V.
From this quiet corner of the Edgware Road, Satay House has been serving Malaysian food to homesick expats for almost 40 years. Today, the area, like the restaurant, has been spruced up. The interior has an easy-on-the eye modern design with hibiscus flower motifs, red leather or beige walls and oak flooring. The menu is loaded with favourites from hawker stalls, so you'll find numerous noodle dishes including laksa. The meat in the chicken and lamb satays seemed more tender than on our last visit, but the peanut sauce lacked oomph. For the adventurous, this is a place to try petai (twisted cluster beans), commonly known as 'stink beans' due to their unusual strong smell. A dish of king prawns stir-fried in fresh ground shrimps was jam-packed with onions, but could have done with more chilli. Blachan (hot shrimp paste) helped to ignite a dish of stir-fried kangkong (water convolvulus, aka morning glory). On our visit, the only Malaysians present were those dining, which could explain why the dishes lacked spiciness. Service was laid-back and cheery. We finished with sago gula melaka (steamed sago pudding with palm sugar) drowning in coconut milk, followed by sweet, milky teh tarik ('stretched tea').
Babies and children welcome: high chairs. Booking advisable. Separate room for parties, seats 35. Takeaway service. Vegetarian menu. **Map 8 E5**.

North West
Swiss Cottage

★ Singapore Garden
83A Fairfax Road, NW6 4DY (7624 8233, www.singaporegarden.co.uk). Swiss Cottage tube. **Lunch served** noon-3pm Mon-Sat; noon-5pm Sun. **Dinner served** 6-11pm Mon-Thur, Sun; 6-11.30pm Fri, Sat. **Main courses** £10-£30. **Set meal** £30-£40 per person (minimum 2). **Minimum charge** (dinner) £15 per person. **Credit** AmEx, MC, V.
This classy restaurant, now part-owned by a shareholder of Awana, has been a beacon of Singaporean cooking for decades. Prices have crept steadily upwards recently, but higher bills haven't diminished Singapore Garden's popularity judging by the packed room on our arrival. You get to sit in a suave room with modern furnishings, and are looked after by friendly, well-drilled staff. The long menu is neatly divided into Chinese and Singaporean dishes, which makes ordering straightforward. Pork satay, accompanied by a tasty peanut sauce, was enjoyable. This was followed by a wok-fried crispy oyster omelette, which transported us back to the humidity of South-east Asia. We couldn't resist asking for more

pork scratchings to bolster a Hokkien hay mee soup (a prawn-based broth served with egg noodles, rice vermicelli, prawns and pork) – a favourite hawker's dish. For the final act, pulot hitam (black glutinous rice) paired with coconut milk was a reminder that this is one of the best Singaporean restaurants in town.
Babies and children admitted. Booking essential. Disabled: toilet. Takeaway service; delivery service (within 1.5-mile radius). **Map 28 A4**.

Satay House

Middle Eastern

It is often the simplest dishes that show the calibre of a Middle Eastern restaurant. Take the ubiquitous kebab. An unadorned grilled skewer with rice and salad might sound boring, but if the meat (or fish) is the perfect combination of seared exterior and interior succulence, if the rice is moist and free-flowing, and if the salad epitomises herby freshness, no further accompaniments are needed – and you know you're on to a winner. The area around Edgware Road, W2, remains a prime hunting ground for top Lebanese restaurants, which also offer a range of enticing meze dishes, but the popularity of newer, on-trend cafés such as Holborn's **Hiba**, Tooting's **Meza**, and **Yalla Yalla** (which has expanded from a tiny spot in Soho to a capacious venue in Fitzrovia) shows that the cuisine is gaining fans from outside the Middle Eastern community. Persian or Iranian food offers an extra, fascinating take on the cooking style, characterised by rich, sweet-sour stews employing the likes of ground walnuts and pomegranate molasses. Newest arrival on the Iranian scene is Maida Vale's **Kateh**, where you'll find sophisticated surroundings matched by ample culinary skill.

Central
Edgware Road

★ Maroush I
*21 Edgware Road, W2 2JE (7723 0773,
www.maroush.com). Marble Arch tube.* **Meals
served** noon-2am daily. **Main courses** £12.95-
£18. **Credit** AmEx, DC, MC, V. Lebanese
One of London's longest-running Lebanese restaurants, Maroush has been going strong for more than three decades, and the company now runs 14 venues including Ranoush Juice and Beirut Express. The enticements at this original location are the musicians and belly dancing, which make evenings in the cavernous basement a riotous affair. For a less over-the-top experience of the excellent food, visit the upstairs lunch counter, where you can watch the chefs at work. The extensive menu lists nearly 60 meze: from favourites like smoky baba ganoush and expertly prepared falafel, to intriguing options such as lamb's tongues, kidneys and lamb tartare. The lunch special of superb starters (zingy tabouleh, fresh flatbread, greaseless sambousek pastries filled with creamy feta), plus shawarma or mixed grill, was too much to finish. Service was quite formal and attentive; we were charmed with complimentary baklava and mint tea at the end of the meal. The Maroush empire has proved a hit across the board, attracting Arab diners, tourists and the inevitable high-spirited groups. Given the

top-notch food and the classy surroundings of gleaming marble and heavy white linens, it's easy to understand its longevity.
*Babies and children welcome: high chairs.
Booking advisable. Entertainment: belly dancers
and musicians 9.30pm daily. Separate room for
parties, seats 25. Takeaway service; delivery
service (over £20 within 2-mile radius).*
Map 8 F6.
**For branches (Beirut Express, Maroush,
Maroush Gardens, Randa) see index.**

Fitzrovia

Yalla Yalla
*12 Winsley Street, W1W 8HQ (7637 4748,
www.yalla-yalla.co.uk). Tottenham Court Road
tube.* **Meals served** 10am-11.30pm Mon-Fri;
11am-11.30pm Sat. **Main courses** £4-£13.75.
Set lunch £6.50 2 courses. **Credit** AmEx,
MC, V. Lebanese
With its jarring mix of neon-yellow, black, white and wood, Yalla Yalla is hardly a place to linger. Tall stools around a communal high table, and an off-Oxford Street location, also suggest pit stop. Yet on our Sunday visit, service was so lethargic and distracted we had no choice but to try and enjoy a leisurely lunch. The food was diverting, sumptuous enough to grace a formal restaurant, and prices are kinder than those often paid for lesser cooking. Sawda djej (chicken livers with garlic and pomegranate molasses) is typical of the style: big-flavoured ingredients harmoniously combined to

thrill the taste buds. Chicken shawarma is nothing short of a feast; even the rice (here with vermicelli) seems ethereally tasty. The menu is dominated by Lebanese meze and main course classics, so the surprises are all on the palate. We loved chargrilled sea bass with citrus rice and tomato and coriander sauce. Specials might include pumpkin kibbeh parcels, filled with spinach and chickpeas, or grilled halloumi and watermelon salad. To drink, there's an appealing range of juice combos and intriguing wines from the Lebanon. Takeaway is available for those who really are in a hurry.
*Babies and children admitted: high chairs.
Disabled: toilet. Tables outdoors (7, pavement).
Takeaway service.* **Map 17 A2.**
For branch see index.

Holborn

Hiba
*113 High Holborn, WC1V 6JQ (7831 5171,
www.hibarestaurant.co.uk). Holborn tube.* **Meals
served** noon-11.30pm daily. **Main courses**
£8.95-£14. **Set meal** £10.95 1 course; £55
3 courses. **Credit** AmEx, MC, V. Lebanese
Despite the local competition, Holborn's stylish new lunch spot is already so popular for takeaway wraps and chips that diners have to break through the queue snaking from the door to the counter. Once settled in a comfortable booth under a large colour photograph of historic Lebanese sites, you can ignore the saps who can't spare time to sit down and eat. Instead, make your own wrap with a

generous pile of toasty, tasty shredded chicken shawarma and excellent flatbread. The lunch plate is a great deal, comprising either said shawarma or a kebab, plus a selection of meze: wonderfully smoky, tahini-rich moutabal, less memorable houmous, refreshingly parsleyed tabouleh and crunchy kibbeh. Topped with a zesty fattoush, slightly stodgy lamb sambousek and fuul medames (broad beans cooked to an earthy, comforting mush), this was a bargain feast for two. Without the time or space for the graciousness that often distinguishes service at Middle Eastern restaurants, staff cope efficiently with the pressure. From the olives that arrive to stave off initial hunger to the final fresh mint tea or authentically dark, bitter coffee, standards at this sleek, fast-ish food place match those of much pricier Lebanese joints.
Available for hire. Babies and children welcome: high chairs. Takeaway service; delivery service (over £15 within 5-mile radius). Vegetarian menu. **Map 18 F2**.

Marylebone

Levant
Jason Court, 76 Wigmore Street, W1U 2SJ (7224 1111, www.levant.co.uk). Bond Street tube.
Bar **Open** 5pm-midnight Mon-Thur; noon-1am Fri, Sat; noon-midnight Sun.
Restaurant **Meals served** 5-11pm Mon-Thur; 6pm-1am Fri; noon-midnight Sat; noon-11pm Sun. **Main courses** £13-£26. **Set lunch** (noon-5.30pm Sat, Sun) £12.50 2 courses. **Set meal** £28-£50 3 courses; £50 kharuf feast.
Both **Credit** AmEx, MC, V. Lebanese
First impressions are good as you open Levant's heavy studded door on to a rosily lit interior with seductive beaded lamps and wafts of incense. But the dim lighting hides slightly shabby tapestry banquettes by the dark wooden tables. The 'ALC Feast' menu entitles diners to five meze per table, plus one main course, mint tea, fruit and pastries per person – a reasonable deal, but it's an intimidating amount of food, even for hearty eaters. All the regulars were in evidence, but seemed to lack the cooked-to-order freshness this type of menu demands. Koussa (a smoky, smooth courgette dip) hit the spot, but kibbeh lacked the essential crisp shell to counteract the stodgy interior, as did the sambousek with lamb. Some greasy fried squid and tired fattoush added to our disappointment, so the arrival of buxom belly dancers provided a welcome distraction. To follow, mixed grill on a huge mound of rice was passable, but the couscous darna was a horror: an unappealingly dark-brown mass of meat and couscous in an far too salty broth, overpoweringly flavoured with allspice. Groups out for a fun Arabian Nights experience and some decent cocktails may go home happy, but we reckon the kitchen needs a shake-up.
Booking advisable. Entertainment: belly dancer 8.30pm Mon-Thur; 8.45pm, 11pm Fri; 8.30pm, 11pm Sat, Sun. Separate room for parties, seats 10-12. Takeaway service. **Map 9 G6**.

Mayfair

Al Sultan
51-52 Hertford Street, W1J 7ST (7408 1155, www.alsultan.co.uk). Green Park or Hyde Park Corner tube. **Meals served** noon-11pm daily. **Main courses** £13.50-£20. **Cover** £2. **Minimum** £20. **Credit** AmEx, DC, MC, V. Lebanese

Kateh. See p197.

There's no informality or Arabian Nights fantasy influencing proceedings at this venerable old-school Lebanese establishment. Al Sultan's corporate hotel-style starchiness clearly finds favour with a cosmopolitan group of diners, from large Gulf family groups to Mayfair business types and well-heeled tourists. Service, although a mite stiff, is never unfriendly. The huge meze menu delivers freshly cooked and prepared Lebanese delicacies – no surprises, but no compromises on quality either. Wines are pricey, though the robust, fruity Lebanese house red, Wardy, stands up well to the richer dishes. A modest cover charge brings olives, a mound of salad vegetables and puffy flatbread (baked in-house). Silky smoky moutabal, crunchy muhamara, crispy kibbeh stuffed with tasty minced lamb, and a spikily fresh green tabouleh were all top-notch. Stick to meze or maybe share a main; the köfte khashkhash (minced lamb kebabs with a rich tomato sauce) were tender and chargrilled to perfection. Afterwards, linger over fragrant mint tea and complimentary sticky pastries to the evocative soundtrack of traditional Arabic divas. *Available for hire. Babies and children welcome: high chairs. Booking advisable dinner. Tables outdoors (4, pavement). Takeaway service; delivery service (over £35 within 4-mile radius). Vegetarian menu.* **Map 9 H8**.

St James's

Noura

122 Jermyn Street, SW1Y 4UJ (7839 2020, www.noura.co.uk). Green Park or Piccadilly Circus tube. **Meals served** noon-midnight daily.

Main courses £14-£22. **Set lunch** £22.50 2 courses. **Set dinner** (5-7pm) £16.50 2 courses. **Credit** AmEx, DC, MC, V. Lebanese

An oasis of Middle Eastern delights among the Piccadilly Circus steakhouses, this branch of the small, Paris-based Noura chain provides consistently top-notch Lebanese food and gracious service. The restaurant has two aspects. Lunch (shame the set menus isn't cheaper) takes place on the white-walled, high-ceilinged side. In the evening, the action shifts to an area of gauzy old-gold curtains and cushions under the blood-red glass droplets of a massive chandelier. The lengthy menu lists masses of meze, grills galore and several oven-baked dishes, plus diverse desserts. Silky smooth as a eunuch's chin, Noura's houmous is peerless. Moutabal (chargrilled aubergine purée) comes peppered with pomegranate seeds to offset its richness. It benefited from a very free hand with lemon juice, which was also the dominant flavour in the fattoush salad and tangy chicken livers. Of other hot meze, crisp falafels were better than doughy kibbeh and fatayer. Extra pitta, warm and puffy, arrived unbidden. Pastries, especially a semolina flour and date morsel accompanying fortifying coffee, are exquisite. Yet although the food is beautifully presented, the serving bowls are plastic, not earthenware, and one white dish was chipped. The banquette looked worse for wear too. We hope these aren't signs that Noura is coasting. *Available for hire. Babies and children welcome: high chairs. Disabled: toilet.* **Map 17 B5**. **For branches see index**.

West

Bayswater

Al Waha

75 Westbourne Grove, W2 4UL (7229 0806, www.alwaharestaurant.com). Bayswater or Queensway tube. **Meals served** noon-11.30pm daily. **Main courses** £10.50-£13.50. **Set lunch** £12.50. **Set dinner** £21 per person (minimum 2) 2 courses, £25 per person (minimum 2) 3 courses. **Cover** £1.50. **Minimum** (dinner) £13.50. **Credit** MC, V. Lebanese

In an area rich in Middle Eastern restaurants, Al Waha's classical Lebanese food competes with the best, both here in Bayswater and the nearby Edgware Road. An understated corner restaurant with white tablecloths, brick walls and an abundance of plastic potted plants, it pulls in an international crowd of enthusiastic diners. On our visit, a friendly welcome was not matched by attentive service, but this place is all about the food. With almost 50 meze choices, you can't go wrong; we suggest ordering a groaning tableful. The classics are good – houmous, topped with curls of grilled lamb and pine nuts, is very smooth; aubergine moutabal has a smoky sourness – but there are plenty more unusual dishes to try, such as fatayer (puffed bread-like pastries stuffed with spinach, onion, pomegranate and walnuts) or basturma (bresaola-thin slices of beef cured with a complex mix of spices). If you can't choose, a set menu at £25 a head will bring a selection of favourites as well as superb meats from the charcoal grill. The shish taouk, succulent boneless chicken smothered in lemon and garlic sauce, takes some beating. End with the complimentary baklava. *Babies and children welcome until 7pm. Booking advisable; essential dinner. Tables outdoors (4, patio). Takeaway service; delivery service (over £20 within 3-mile radius).* **Map 7 B6**.

Olympia

Mohsen

152 Warwick Road, W14 8PS (7602 9888). Earl's Court tube or Kensington (Olympia) tube/rail. **Meals served** noon-midnight daily. **Main courses** £12-£15. **Unlicensed**. **Corkage** no charge. **No credit cards**. Iranian

It is testament to Mohsen's enduring popularity that the place was packed with late lunchers, mostly Iranians, on our recent 4pm visit. The secret? While neighbouring Persian restaurants have bowed to progress – installing fancy lighting and flamboyant outdoor heaters – Mohsen appears not to have altered in the past decade. Still the walls are decorated with the same gaudy dioramas and dog-eared posters of Iranian tourist attractions; still Mrs Mohsen swoops between tables handing out plastic laminated menus and bantering with regulars; and still the food is superb. We started with hot taftoon bread from the clay oven, dipped in zingy masto musir, and a plate of butter-soft ox tongue in a tomato and garlic broth. Mains were brought out before we'd finished our starters – a common occurrence here – but were too good to send back. Baghali polo (lamb shank with dill and lima bean-infused rice) was note perfect, the meat melting in the mouth and the juices adding a rich undertone to the fragrant rice, while both joojeh (marinated chicken) and koobideh (minced lamb) kebabs were as good as we've come to expect.

Yalla Yalla. See p194.

Atmosphere, however, isn't a strong point: Mohsen is bright and noisy, and service can be brisk.
Babies and children admitted. Takeaway service.
Map 13 A10.

Maida Vale

Kateh NEW

5 Warwick Place, W9 2PX (7289 3393, www.katehrestaurant.co.uk). Warwick Avenue tube. **Lunch served** noon-4pm Fri, Sat. **Dinner served** 6-11pm Mon-Sat. **Meals served** noon-9.30pm Sun. **Main courses** £8.50-£17. **Credit** AmEx, MC, V. Iranian
That Kateh's small room of pretty candlelit tables was fully booked on a Wednesday evening shows it's doing something right. You come here for rich Persian stews, served with unabashed directness. A plate bearing a huge pile of rice is brought, beside which, in a metal pot, is set the stew – perhaps khoresht-e fesenjan (dark and tender duck thigh with walnut and pomegranate) or the less successful ghelieh mahi (cod fillet atop a combination of tamarind, tomato and herbs). Dezfouli salad was a terrific concoction of cucumber, pomegranate, lemon juice, mint and 'angelica powder', while the meatballs were solid comfort food, in a slightly spicy tomato sauce – perfect for scooping up with the sensational taftoon, (seeded brown and white flatbreads, a generous portion for £1.50). The combination of rosewater sorbet and lime juice in the fallodeeh made a zingy finish, even if some may find the traditional inclusion of noodles rather disconcerting. Our only criticisms are the eccentricities of the warm and friendly staff: slow delivery of menus can be excused in a bustling restaurant, stern refusal to stave off our hunger by bringing the taftoon ahead of other starters might be a charming eccentricity, but pouring water into a glass half full of wine is startlingly inattentive.
Available for hire. Babies and children welcome: high chairs. Booking advisable. Separate room for parties, seats 10. Tables outdoors (5, terrace). Takeaway service. **Map 1 C4.**

Shepherd's Bush

Abu Zaad

29 Uxbridge Road, W12 8LH (8749 5107, www.abuzaad.co.uk). Shepherd's Bush Market tube. **Meals served** 11am-11pm daily. **Main courses** £5-£14. **Unlicensed** no alcohol allowed. **Credit** MC, V. Syrian
Step off teeming Uxbridge Road into Abu Zaad and you're transported to Damascus – this is the sort of workaday Formica-tabled eaterie that proliferates across the Middle East. Big screens showing BBC Arabic news to a soundtrack of Arabic divas add to the vibe, as do long tables at the back packed with multiple generations of family members tucking into hearty, tasty food. There's no alcohol, so indulge in one of the fab freshly squeezed juices, which include the Damascene favourite, spritzy lemon with mint. Turnover is fast – with lots of takeaway orders as well as all tables full – so the dishes are generally strikingly fresh. From our perfect crunchy shell of kibbeh shamieh (minced lamb) and properly chewy cheese fatayer, to the lemony fattoush with crisp squares of flatbread and the silky houmous, we were treated to honest comfort food. Mains include

the usual chargrilled skewered meats, as well as Syrian specialities such as chicken kabseh: tender roast poultry with spicy tomato rice, served with plump golden sultanas and cooling cucumber yoghurt. Finish with dense Syrian ice-cream packed with pistachios – its characteristic chewiness comes from the addition of mastic (a plant resin) – and wonder at the small size of the bill.
Babies and children welcome: high chairs. Booking advisable weekends. Separate room for parties, seats 36. Takeaway service.
Map 20 B2.
For branch see index.

Sufi

70 Askew Road, W12 9BJ (8834 4888, www.sufirestaurant.com). Hammersmith tube then 266 bus. **Meals served** noon-11pm daily. **Main courses** £6.50-£13.50. **Corkage** £4. **Credit** MC, V. Iranian
Sufi hasn't missed a beat in all the years we've been visiting. It's a restaurant that combines authenticity with familiarity and respects the sense of ceremony in dining out – something that elevates it above more functional contemporaries. The walls are decorated with sitars and framed paintings of old clerics, the shelves lined with shishas and the floors covered with Persian rugs. As evening sets in, the lights are dimmed and staff distribute candles, creating a romantic atmosphere and making this one of few Iranian restaurants in London suitable for a date. The food is first-rate, and takes in many regional dishes seldom seen in the capital. We started with a bowl of zeytoon parvardeh (olives in a crushed walnut and pomegranate sauce), native to the northern Caspian towns, and a plate of buttery tah dig (rice cake from the bottom of the pot) indulgently soaked in sauce from a split-pea stew. Mains were also excellent, from bitter-sweet fesenjoon (a rich chicken, walnut and pomegranate stew) to a daily special of zereshk polo (saffron and barberry-studded rice baked with shredded chicken). Service is friendly and efficient, and there's a good wine list as well as the option of BYO.
Babies and children welcome: children's menu; high chairs. Separate room for parties, seats 40. Takeaway service. **Map 20 A2.**

South West
East Sheen

★ Faanoos

481 Upper Richmond Road West, SW14 7PU (8878 5738, www.faanoosrestaurant.com). Mortlake rail or 33, 337, 493 bus. **Meals served** noon-11pm daily. **Main courses** £4.95-£8.95. **Credit** MC, V. Iranian
Faanoos is a great local restaurant – cheerful, cheap and bustling even midweek. It's also an oasis of colour on an insipid stretch of the Upper Richmond Road: sit facing the windows and you'll look out on stagnant traffic and furniture showrooms; face inwards and your eye alights on straw-matted walls hung with Persian rugs and unframed paintings of bearded merchants, a ceiling strung with coloured lanterns (faanoos) and a turquoise clay oven. All seats were taken on our last visit, but none of our fellow diners was Iranian – a geographical issue (few expats stray south of the river), but one that has allowed standards to slip slightly over the years. A starter of stuffed vine leaves lacked texture and had the limp outer warmth of a dish hastily

reheated, while a plate heaped with sabzi khordan (mixed fresh herbs) was bereft of the all-important coriander. Mains were better: joojeh (chicken kebab) was suitably aromatic from the lemon and saffron marinade, the accompanying grilled tomato nicely blackened, and ghorm-e sabzi (lamb and herb stew) was generous in size, but lacking citrus kick due to insufficient dried limes. Still, at these prices – and with decent house wine at £10.95 per bottle – complaints are rare.
Babies and children admitted. Booking advisable. Tables outdoors (2, pavement). Takeaway service.
For branch see index.

South
Tooting

★ Meza NEW

34 Trinity Road, SW17 7RE (07722 111299 mobile). Tooting Bec tube. **Meals served** noon-11pm Tue-Sat; 1-10pm Sun. **Main courses** £7.50-£9.50. **Set meze** £17. **No credit cards.** Lebanese
What this teensy Lebanese restaurant lacks in flashiness, it more than makes up for in charm. The frontage is brown and unprepossessing, the dining room can seat only 15, and while the gently lit, plain interior is broken up by a smattering of decorative touches (velvet-trimmed mirrors and black and red scatter cushions), it's visually dominated by the tiling and ingredient-stacked shelves of the open kitchen. The super-friendly proprietor stands guard behind the counter, and the soundtrack to your meal is the sizzle of soujouk sausages being tossed in a pan. On our visit, a customer smoking outside was brought an ashtray unbidden, diners unfamiliar with the menu were helpfully discouraged from over-ordering, and the patron's warm, tactile conversation gave the impression that you're a valued guest rather than just another bum on a seat. The menu is divided between a range of punchy, smoky grilled dishes and a meze selection, including the crisp filo tubes of melty, tart cheese that is reaat bil jeben, and a rich, delectably creamy houmous. Those with a sweet tooth, be warned: there's no dessert menu.
Available for hire. Babies and children welcome: high chairs. Booking advisable dinner. Takeaway service.

East
Spitalfields

Zengi

44 Commercial Street, E1 6LT (7426 0700, www.zengirestaurant.co.uk). Aldgate East tube. **Meals served** noon-11pm daily. **Main courses** £2.50-£14. **Credit** MC, V. Iraqi
There's something innately likeable about Zengi, a Middle Eastern fusion restaurant set on a strip otherwise dominated by faceless caffs and fried chicken parlours. Functionality reigns on the ground floor, where a gleaming open kitchen dominates a room otherwise decorated with Arabic prints, the occasional shisha pipe and a handful of engraved metal tables. But there's also a more intimate basement featuring cushioned couches and hanging lanterns in a number of cosy alcoves. Staff

مامونيا لاونج

Finest Lebanese & Moroccan Cuisine

نخبـــة المــــذاق اللبنـــاني والمغـــربـي

Mamounia's name originating from Majorelle, the great gardens of Marrakech, provides a venture into a sanctuary of luxury in an idyllic setting.

Mamounia Lounge is a stylish bar and contemporary Arabic restaurant. The location of each venue is in one of London's finest areas. The new Mamounia Lounge Knightsbridge is just metres away from premier department store Harrods.

With the original branch in the heart of Mayfair, one of London's most fashionable districts, also the previous winner of London's Best Bar and Restaurant Awards.

Experience exquisite Lebanese and Moroccan dishes using the finest ingredients and authentic recipes. There are a variety of dishes to tease your palette with Moroccan and Lebanese mezzes and fusion starters, such as grilled halloumi or homemade falafel and hommus. Followed by an exquisite selection of tagines and couscous in the true essence of North African culture, along with a varied wine list including a selection of Lebanese wines.

We offer glamorous Mamounia signature and premium cocktails from our vibrant and funky bar areas. In addition you can relax and lounge in comfort with a variety of unique Shisha flavours to suit everyone, including one created using a water melon as the water jar giving a wonderful fruity aroma.

All of this topped off by soothing music and regular entertainment. Be swept away with traditional Arabic charm, a luxurious experience and magnificent cuisine.

Private Events / Corporate Dining / Canapé Receptions

Mamounia Offers Lunch and Dinner Set Menus, and local home delivery or takeaway services.

Mamounia Lounge Mayfair,
37a Curzon Street, London, W1J 7TX.

T: 0207 629 2211
info@mamounialounge.com
www.mamounialounge.com

Mamounia Lounge Knightsbridge,
136 Brompton Road, London, SW3

T: 0207 581 7777
info@mamounialounge.com
www.mamounialounge.com

were happy to explain dishes on a menu that mixes Turkish, Lebanese, Syrian and Iraqi influences, but meze orders were hit and miss on our recent visit. Of the hits, böregi combined a rich cheese and spinach filling with crisp filo pastry, while velvety lamb's liver came in an indulgent tomato and parsley sauce; of the misses, we bemoaned the limpness of too-chewy köfte kibbeh and an overdressed fattoush salad. Turkish pizza is better, generously topped with lightly spiced mince, while the patented Zengi burger featured a juicy lamb patty adorned with grilled halloumi and onions. Finish with mint tea and – if you can stomach the roar of the traffic – an apple shisha at one of the pavement tables.
Available for hire. Babies and children admitted. Booking advisable. Tables outdoors (4, pavement). Takeaway service. **Map 12 S5**.

North
Archway
Gilak
663 Holloway Road, N19 5SE (7272 1692). Archway tube or Upper Holloway rail. **Meals served** 11am-midnight Mon-Fri; noon-midnight Sat, Sun. **Main courses** £6.99-£14.50. **Set meal** £42 (minimum 4). **Credit** MC, V. Iranian
Seaside photographs and a red, white and blue fishing net hung from the ceiling are your first clues that Gilak specialises in cooking from Iran's coastal Gilan region. This is not, however, at the expense of better-known Persian dishes such as spinach borani, sabzi-o-panir and khoresht-e fesenjan. Walnuts abound – in starters mixed with aubergine and yoghurt, in marinades for lamb, and in a heavenly, cinnamon-scented rice flour pancake for dessert. Most unusually, however, the creamy nuts appear alongside a dish of rehydrated dried broad beans and a plate of ruddy smoked mackerel; this Gilak triumvirate is a traditional regional adjunct to kebabs, and is also wrapped in the papery, floury flatbread as a starter nibble, but might not be to everyone's taste. A brothy stew of chicken with wild garlic and eggs saw the bird cooked into submission so that even the bones were soft; a huge pile of buttery saffron-capped rice was just right for absorbing the fragrant juices. Bastani, a dessert of saffron and pistachio ice-creams flecked with bright green crisp nuts, made a delicious chewy conclusion. Wines are inexpensive and you'll do fine with the house sangiovese. Service wasn't pushed, but we found it friendly and informative.
Available for hire. Babies and children welcome: high chairs. Booking advisable. Takeaway service. **Map 26 C1**.

Camden Town & Chalk Farm
★ Tandis
73 Haverstock Hill, NW3 4SL (7586 8079). Chalk Farm tube. **Meals served** noon-11.30pm Mon-Thur, Sun; noon-midnight Fri, Sat. **Main courses** £8.90-£14.90. **Credit** AmEx, MC, V. Iranian
We were delighted to see Tandis busier than on our previous visits, for it's one of London's most pleasurable spots to explore Persian cooking. The recently spruced-up terrace area is well worth

considering for a sunny weekend lunch. Inside, the three modestly proportioned dining rooms have something of a nightclub feel, though a skylight adds welcome cheer to the comfortable back room. There we sampled the menu's 'siniyeh mazzeh' deal, offering four starters of our choice for £11.90. Each was excellent, especially the salad olivieh, creamy tasting yet delightfully coarse in texture. Tandis's fruit-fragrant stews of meats and pulses are like a passport to winter sun, but the grills are just the ticket in warm weather. The quality minced lamb kebabs are full flavoured enough not to need heavy use of herbs and spices, and contrast well with cubes of baby chicken infused with saffron. Feather-light rice and piles of springy salad are just so. To drink, you need look no further than the house wines from Sicily (£12.95), including a blend of inzolia and chardonnay that's just right for a lingering lunch. Staff are friendly and unpushy – so much so that a little more momentum could be welcome.
Babies and children welcome: high chairs. Booking advisable Fri, Sat. Separate rooms for parties, seating 14-30. Tables outdoors (7, terrace). Takeaway service; delivery service (over £15 within 3-mile radius).

Budget bites

Comptoir Libanais
65 Wigmore Street, W1U 1PZ (7935 1110, www.lecomptoir.co.uk). Bond Street tube. **Meals served** 8am-10pm Mon-Sat; 8am-9pm Sun. **Main courses** £5.95-£7.45. **Credit** MC, V. Lebanese
Bright, fun and full of local workers taking lunch, Comptoir Libanais is part-canteen, part-delicatessen. One wall is lined with shelves containing preserves and other imported goods. The rest of the space is taken up with colourful tables and chairs. Dishes are clearly displayed behind the counter, and there are plenty to choose from: salads, tagines, wraps, and mountains of glistening pastries and baklava. Service is personable even during the lunchtime rush, but while the decor is appealing, the standard of cooking is no better than the Middle Eastern caffs of the Edgware Road; we think it has slipped a bit. Fruit juices come in a variety of interesting and vitamin-packed flavours, with apple, mint and cucumber a highlight.
Available for hire. Babies and children welcome: high chairs. Bookings not accepted. Tables outdoors (5, pavement). Takeaway service. **Map 8 G6**.
For branch see index.

Fresco
25 Westbourne Grove, W2 4UA (7221 2355, www.frescojuices.co.uk). Bayswater or Royal Oak tube. **Meals served** 8am-11pm daily. **Main courses** £5.95-£9. **Set meze** £11.95. **Credit** MC, V. Lebanese
Light and airy Fresco is furnished with bright yellow walls and rustic wooden furniture. The kitchen rustles up salads and sandwiches for customers swinging past for a quick takeaway, plus cooked meals for those sticking around and taking a seat. Huge portions of meatballs arrived with potatoes, rice and salad (£8), and mixed meze plates came packed with falafel, tabouleh, moutabal garnished with pomegranate seeds, houmous, stuffed vine leaves and aubergine in yoghurt (£9). The juice machine whirs almost constantly as the efficient, friendly staff make fresh juices and refreshing fruit milkshakes. A perfect place to refuel.
Takeaway service. Vegetarian menu. **Map 7 B6**.
For branches see index.

Pilpel
38 Brushfield Street, E1 6EU (7247 0146, www.pilpel.co.uk). Liverpool Street tube/rail. **Meals served** 10am-8pm Mon-Fri, Sun. **Main courses** £4.25-£5.85. **Unlicensed. No credit cards**. Middle Eastern
It may look like an American chain, but Uri Dinay's bijou falafel and houmous bar has become a firm favourite among connoisseurs of the Middle East's fried chickpea dumplings. There are a few tables and chairs for diners who want to eat in (and watch the goings-on at Old Spitalfields Market), but this is mostly back-to-the-office fare, which suits Liverpool Street denizens nicely. You can eat very well for a fiver, or pay a little more and get extra toppings (egg, guacamole, feta, aubergine), and have your dish served in a container with pitta on the side instead of shaped into a wrap. For a change from falafel, try the sabich (houmous, aubergine, egg, tabouleh and salad in pitta). Drinks (no alcohol) include own-made lemonade. Vegetarians can't go wrong, and there's a 10% discount when ordering by phone before 11am.
Babies and children admitted. Takeaway service. **Map 12 R5**.

Ranoush Juice
43 Edgware Road, W2 2JE (7723 5929, www.maroush.com). Marble Arch tube. **Meals served** 8am-3am daily. **Main courses** £3-£10.50. **No credit cards**. Lebanese
Ranoush is all about getting in and out. A few stools, metallic tables and chairs line one side, while the other is filled with juicing machines, huge turning kebab grills and piles of sticky baklava behind the counter. Pay at the till, then watch as flatbreads are filled with shawarma skewers of lamb or chicken, gherkins and tomatoes (£11.50) and served with serious speed. Hot and cold meze is available to those opting to sit in, and there are a couple of tables at the front for watching busy Edgware Road over a fresh fruit juice until the early hours.
Bookings not accepted. Takeaway service. **Map 8 F6**.
For branches (Maroush Ranoush, Ranoush Juice) see index.

Menu

See also the menus in **North African** and **Turkish**.

MEZE

Baba ganoush: Egyptian name for moutabal (qv).

Basturma: smoked beef.

Batinjan or **bazenjan el-rahib**: aubergine mashed with olive oil, garlic and tomato.

Batata hara: potatoes fried with peppers and chilli.

Falafel: a mixture of spicy chickpeas or broad beans ground, rolled into balls and deep fried.

Fatayer: a soft pastry, filled with cheese, onions, spinach and pine kernels.

Fattoush: fresh vegetable salad containing shards of toasted pitta bread and sumac (qv).

Fuul or **fuul medames**: brown broad beans that are mashed and seasoned with olive oil, lemon juice and garlic.

Kalaj: halloumi chees on pastry.

Kibbeh: highly seasoned mix of minced lamb, cracked wheat and onion, deep-fried in balls. For meze it is often served raw (**kibbeh nayeh**) like steak tartare.

Labneh: cream cheese made from yoghurt.

Moujadara: lentils, rice and caramelised onions mixed together.

Moutabal: a purée of chargrilled aubergines mixed with sesame sauce, garlic and lemon juice.

Muhamara: dip of crushed mixed nuts with red peppers, spices and pomegranate molasses.

Sambousek: small pastries filled with mince, onion and pine kernels.

Sujuk: spicy Lebanese sausages.

Sumac: an astringent and fruity-tasting spice made from dried sumac seeds.

Tabouleh: a salad of chopped parsley, tomatoes, crushed wheat, onions, olive oil and lemon juice.

Torshi: pickled vegetables.

Warak einab: rice-stuffed vine leaves.

MAINS

Shawarma: meat (usually lamb) marinated then grilled on a spit and sliced kebab-style.

Shish kebab: cubes of marinated lamb grilled on a skewer, often with tomatoes, onions and sweet peppers.

Shish taouk: like shish kebab, but with chicken rather than lamb.

North West
Cricklewood

Zeytoon
94-96 Cricklewood Broadway, NW2 3EL (8830 7434, www.zeytoon.co.uk). Cricklewood rail. **Meals served** 12.30-11pm daily. **Main courses** £5.95-£11.95. **Set meze** £13.50. **Credit** AmEx, MC, V. Afghan/Iranian

Given the culinary cross-pollination between the two countries, it's strange that it has taken until now for a restaurant to offer an Iranian and Afghan fusion menu. Zeytoon's walls feature tapestries, turquoise mosaics and brick arches decorated with paintings of ethereal Persian women; a wooden shisha terrace is set with heat lamps and plastic trees decked in coloured lights. Service on our visit was erratic; the waiter insisted on taking away starters of boorani (spinach and yoghurt dip) and a superb kashk-e bademjan (mashed aubergine and garlic, topped with crisp fried onions) to make way for mains, despite the fact we were still eating. The mains were excellent: an Iranian ghorm-e sabzi stew was full of meat and greens, with a welcome citrus kick thanks to plentiful dried limes; and the signature Afghan dish of qabli polow (lamb shank with brown rice flavoured with carrot, raisins and almonds) was delicious and hearty enough for two. With more consideration from staff, Zeytoon could be more than just a great local.
Available for hire. Babies and children welcome: high chairs. Booking advisable. Disabled: toilet. Separate room for parties, seats 100. Tables outdoors (6, pavement). Takeaway service.

Kensal Green

★ Behesht
1082-1084 Harrow Road, NW10 5NL (8964 4477). Kensal Green tube/rail. **Meals served** noon-11.30pm daily. **Main courses** £5.95-£9.95. **Unlicensed** no alcohol allowed. **Credit** MC, V. Iranian

Behesht means 'heaven', and to pining Iranian expats that's exactly what this first-rate restaurant is. To others, its gaudy oriental interior is more Disney than Darius. The four main rooms are bedecked with so many cultural trinkets that it's like dining in Tehran's central bazaar. Shelves groan with daf drums, carpet-weaving machines and hand-painted pots stuffed with peacock feathers; the ceiling is covered with Persian rugs; and the sculpted wooden walls converge on a stone fountain knotted with plastic plants, its constant babble blending with the mournful violin music on the stereo and the caw of the restaurant's pet parrot. Service forsakes pleasantries for unsmiling efficiency, but the food is as authentic as any in London. A starter of ash-e reshteh (noodle and bean soup) arrived packed with ingredients and was lent a pleasing pungency by a generous dollop of whey, while both minced lamb koobideh and marinated chicken joojeh kebabs were flavourful and flawlessly cooked, served with saffron-tinted rice and a nicely blackened tomato. Save room for traditional bastani ice-cream, flavoured with rose water, studded with pistachios and presented in a dramatic metal bowl.
Babies and children admitted: high chairs; nappy-changing facilities. Booking advisable. Disabled: toilet. Separate rooms for parties, seating 30-120. Takeaway service. Vegetarian menu.
Map 1 C4.

West Hampstead

★ Mahdi
2 Chantfield Gardens, NW6 3BS (7625 4344). Finchley Road tube. **Meals served** noon-11pm daily. **Main courses** £2.20-£5.90. **Set meal** £6.90-£7.90. **Credit** MC, V. Iranian

Authenticity is something the original Mahdi in Hammersmith has in spades, and this brighter, less cavernous Finchley Road branch is a worthy offspring. The brick arches that line the walls are set with traditional tapestries and topped with calligraphic inscriptions; the glamorous Persian tablecloths are covered with plastic sheets; and a head-high samovar looms in one corner. There's less of the haughtiness among staff here that made visiting the original an occasionally daunting task, yet there's no indication that the menu is taking itself less seriously, with a large range of dishes seldom seen in London's Iranian restaurants. We started with a bowl of sesame seed-scattered sangak bread from a traditional wall oven (sangak is something of a rarity in the capital, where sheets of the simpler taftoon are standard), using it to mop up thick, creamy mirza ghasemi, a dip of baked aubergines mashed with eggs, onions and garlic. Mains were also excellent, and included a hearty bowl of abgoosht – a working man's lamb and potato stew with beans and dried limes. Portions, as in Hammersmith, are overwhelming: expect to live off the leftovers for a while.
Available for hire. Babies and children welcome: high chairs. Takeaway service. **Map 28 A3**.
For branch see index.

Outer London
Wembley, Middlesex

Mesopotamia
115 Wembley Park Drive, Wembley, Middlesex, HA9 8HG (8453 5555, www.mesopotamia.ltd.uk). Wembley Park tube. **Dinner served** 5.30pm-midnight Mon-Sat. **Main courses** £8-£15.50. **Set meal** £19.95-£24.95. **Credit** AmEx, MC, V. Iraqi

Strikingly different from its takeaway neighbours, this beacon of homespun Iraqi cooking reflects well on the talented husband-and-wife team who run it. Bedouin-style cloth draped over the ceiling, animal friezes along stone walls and themed artefacts lend a theatrical flourish. Stars of our marvellous meze platter included silky houmous seasoned with cumin, fattoush (mixed salad tossed in a dressing of pomegranate molasses), and baba ganoush (roasted aubergine blended with tahini, garlic and yoghurt). The acclaimed fesenjoon is a highlight among the main courses: a dressed-up chicken casserole cooked in pomegranate molasses and walnuts. We enjoyed the succulence of herby minced lamb rolled into sausages, each wrapped in an aubergine slice and baked in tomato and toasted cumin sauce. Even simple grills are given the light touch with lemony tahini marinades, served with garlicky yoghurt and red chilli and tahini sauce. The wine list too is notable; look for the surprisingly affordable quality Lebanese bottles. Food portions are generous, but if there's space, conclude with cardamom-laced coffee and sweet, indulgent baklava.
Available for hire. Babies and children welcome: children's menu. Booking advisable. Takeaway service. Vegetarian menu.

Meza. See p197.

DESERTS

Balkava: filo pastry interleaved with pistachio nuts, almonds or walnuts, and covered in syrup.

Konafa or **kadayif**: cake made from shredded pastry dough, filled with syrup and nuts, or cream.

Ma'amoul: pastries filled with nuts or dates.

Muhallabia or **mohalabia**: a milky ground-rice pudding with almonds or pistachios, flavoured with rosewater or orange blossom.

Om ali: bread pudding, often made with filo pastry and including nuts and raisins.

IRANIAN DISHES

Ash-e reshteh: soup with noodles, spinach, pulses and dried herbs.

Ghorm-e sabzi: lamb with greens, kidney beans and dried limes.

Halim bademjan: mashed chargrilled aubergine with onions and walnuts.

Joojeh or **jujeh**: chicken marinated in saffron, lemon and onion.

Kashk, **qurut** or **quroot**: a salty whey.

Kashk-e bademjan: baked aubergines mixed with herbs and whey.

Khoresht-e fesenjan or **fesenjoon**: chicken cooked in ground walnut and pomegranate sauce.

Kuku-ye sabzi: finely chopped fresh herbs with eggs, baked in the oven.

Masto khiar: yoghurt mixed with finely chopped cucumber and mint.

Masto musir: shallot-flavoured yoghurt.

Mirza ghasemi: crushed baked aubergines, tomatoes, garlic and herbs mixed with egg.

Sabzi: a plate of fresh herb leaves (usually mint and dill) often served with a cube of feta.

Salad olivieh: like a russian salad, includes chopped potatoes, chicken, eggs, peas, gherkins, olive oil and mayonnaise.

Modern European

As the largest chapter in this guide, Modern European restaurants are arguably Londoners' favourite places to dine. Why? Perhaps because, while the cooking and surrounds tend to be smart, the menus have something for everybody. Classic French, Italian and British recipes, with an increasing showing from Spain, sit comfortably alongside the occasional dish inspired by Middle Eastern, American, Japanese or South-east Asian cuisines. If one diner wants steak and chips and another pasta, or more creative contemporary cooking, the argument can be settled by choosing a restaurant from this section. Nor would you have to travel far, for Modern European establishments can be found throughout the capital, from **Petersham Nurseries Café** in Richmond to **Wapping Food** in the east – even Finsbury Park, where **Season Kitchen** is a welcome addition. Our current favourites show similar breadth: compare Nuno Mendes' cutting-edge cuisine at **Corner Room** in Bethnal Green, to the classic sophistication of the **Glasshouse** in Kew; south London fares (and dines) particularly well, thanks to the presence of **Tom Ilic**, **Magdalen** and **Lamberts**. Among the clutch of newcomers, we welcome **Medlar**, which made the shortlist for our 2011 Best New Fine Dining award; **Chiswell Street Dining Rooms** from gastropub maestros Tom and Ed Martin; and **Brawn**, an offshoot of popular wine bar **Terriers** (*see p327*).

Central
Barbican

Chiswell Street Dining Rooms NEW
56 Chiswell Street, EC1Y 4SA (7614 0177, www.chiswellstreetdining.com). Barbican or Moorgate tube/rail. **Breakfast served** 7-11.30am, **lunch served** 11.30am-3.30pm, **tea served** 3.30-6pm, **dinner served** 6-10.30pm daily. **Main courses** £12.50-£27. **Credit** AmEx, MC, V.
From the same restaurant group as the Botanist, and the Gun gastropub, Chiswell Street puts on a splendid variety show. Full-on breakfast fry-ups, classy lunchtime pub meals, afternoon tea and even dinners for elastic expense accounts are all available. Throw in a doorstopper of a wine list, snazzy cocktails and speciality British beers, and it feels like the complete package. On our visit, white onion and sage soup, enriched with robust chicken stock, scored top marks for infusing herby mildness into a subtly sweet and creamy onion base. The delicacy of Lincolnshire smoked eel morsels also won us over, their texture contrasting with the crunch of shredded celeriac dressed in lemony mayonnaise. Main courses were equally splendid, from lightly fried Cornish lemon sole, sauced with

citrus dill butter, to a trio of plump, succulent lamb chops, well matched to a summery spin on cassoulet (broad beans, tender peas and butter beans flecked with diced tomatoes). Yet it wasn't all smooth sailing. A summer pudding was overshadowed by too much bread in proportion to squishy berries. The large site – a former brewery – has been tastefully decorated, and also houses a decent, if noisy, bar. Staff were professional, attentive and friendly.
Available for hire. Babies and children welcome: high chairs. Booking advisable. Disabled: toilet. Separate rooms for parties, seating 10, 30, 40, 45, 60. **Map 5 P5.**

Belgravia

Botanist
7 Sloane Square, SW1W 8EE (7730 0077, www.thebotanistonsloanesquare.com). Sloane Square tube. **Breakfast served** 8-11.30am Mon-Fri; 9-11.30am Sat, Sun. **Lunch served** noon-3.30pm Mon-Fri; noon-4pm Sat, Sun. **Tea served** 3.30-5.30pm, **dinner served** 6-10.30pm daily. **Main courses** £14.50-£27. **Set dinner** (5.30-7.30pm) £21 2 courses, £26 3 courses. **Credit** AmEx, MC, V.
A sizeable and lively bar, with pavement tables bending around a corner of Sloane Square, gives way to a smartly elegant restaurant (biscuit leather,

1920s-style chandeliers) with colourful yet restrained botanical wall art. You can come for breakfast (a neat envelope of crêpe complete with golden yolks poking through the top, say, or crusty thick pancakes with blueberries and maple syrup) or afternoon tea (finger sandwiches, sultana scones with Suffolk jams and Devonshire clotted cream, Jing teas). A pre-theatre menu cherry-picks from the carte, offering a choice of three or four dishes for each course. Recipes range from simple (leek vinaigrette with soft-boiled quail egg and anchovy toast) to complex (confit duck ravioli with braised lentils and duck anise consommé), though some of the combinations are interesting rather than heavenly. We weren't entirely convinced by the red wine-braised chicory accompanying delicate royal bream, especially once an Asian-style crab croquette and earthy monk's beard were added. Nor the peanut and whisky ice-cream that accompanied a cake-like sticky toffee pudding. However, service and the extensive drinks list (which includes a good choice of classic and signature cocktails, are hard to fault. Clearly, the Botanist formula has worked for gastropub supremos Tom and Ed Martin, as they've re-employed it at their latest opening, the Chiswell Street Dining Rooms.
Babies and children welcome: high chairs. Booking advisable. Disabled: toilet. Dress: smart casual. Tables outdoors (4, pavement). **Map 15 G10.**

Bloomsbury

Giaconda Dining Room

9 Denmark Street, WC2H 8LS (7240 3334, www.giacondadining.com). Tottenham Court Road tube. **Lunch served** noon-2.15pm Tue-Fri. **Dinner served** 6-9.15pm Tue-Sat. **Main courses** £12-£14. **Cover** £1.50. **Credit** AmEx, MC, V.

The menu changes little at this pocket-sized room: 30 covers in an inauspicious location off Charing Cross Road. And it shouldn't, because everything is just right. The understated decor reminds you of someone's cosy dining room; people at the next table may be only a foot away. No one minds. The food is enjoyable and reasonably priced. It's old-fashioned stuff, largely French in orientation, and substantial. Meat, including offal and extremities, is the most prominent feature (this is no place for vegetarians). A disc of boned pig's trotter, braised, then fried to crispness, conveys the essence of Giaconda cooking. Ditto for a deeply satisfying 'crumble' of creamed shallots and mushrooms, meltingly soft and rich underneath its crisp brown crumble. Ditto again ham hock hash: a hockey puck of meat topped with a fried egg and served with a well-dressed salad. There's also a changing roster of blanquettes, those creamy stews beloved of French grand-mères, and fish and grills of the day. To finish, eton mess and crème brûlée were perfectly executed. The all-European wine list, chosen with love, starts at under £20. Two people can eat three courses of accomplished cooking with wine for under £100: rare indeed in central London. *Available for hire. Babies and children admitted. Booking advisable.* **Map 17 C3**.

Paramount

101-103 New Oxford Street, WC1A 1DD (7420 2900, www.paramount.uk.net). Tottenham Court Road tube. **Breakfast served** 8-10.30am Mon-Fri. **Lunch served** noon-3pm Mon-Fri, Sun; 11.30am-3pm Sat. **Dinner served** 6-11pm Mon-Sat. **Main courses** £14.50-£25.50. **Set lunch** (Mon-Fri) £18.50 2 courses, £23.50 3 courses. **Credit** AmEx, MC, V.

It's a surprise that Centre Point – for so long closed to the public – is now so easily penetrated. There are none of Vertigo 42's airport-style security checks, just a charming lady behind the brass desk in the lobby to confirm your reservation and buzz you into the lift for the 32nd floor. We're told Paramount gets very busy on weekend evenings, but it was almost empty for Saturday brunch. The short menu was predictable, but delivered a superb vegetarian risotto, rich with mascarpone and served with vividly intense confit tomatoes, and an accomplished, frothy-topped asparagus and truffle soup. Attention to detail faltered with bland cod goujons, barely lifted by their tartare sauce, but revived for a nicely presented, deconstructed tiramisu with two scoops of blood orange sorbet, one of them a quenelle of froth. The inventive cocktails are expensive (£11 and upwards), but fun – a Breakfast Martini made with marmalade infusion comes with toast on a swizzle stick; the Cherry & Bubblegum Sour has a glass edged with sherbet. The setting is rather chic, especially the more colourful and more relaxed bar areas, and the waitstaff are straightforward and personable. Are the views worth the prices? Assuredly, yes – especially from the 360° Viewing Gallery upstairs, where there's another tiny bar (with decent bar snacks) and several window seats.

Chiswell Street Dining Rooms

MODERN EUROPEAN

Dock Kitchen. See p213.

Booking advisable. Disabled: lift; toilet. Dress: smart. Separate rooms for parties, seating 16-30, 150. **Map 17 C2.**

City

Prism
147 Leadenhall Street, EC3V 4QT (7256 3888, www.harveynichols.com/ restaurants/prism-london). Bank tube/DLR.
Bar **Open** 11am-11pm, **lunch served** 11.30am-3pm Mon-Fri. **Main courses** £10-£14.
Restaurant **Lunch served** noon-3pm, **dinner served** 6-10pm Mon-Fri. **Main courses** £18-£25. **Set meal** £24.50 2 courses, £29.50 3 courses.
Both **Credit** AmEx, DC, MC, V.
A certain grandeur is guaranteed at Harvey Nichols' City venture, set in a former banking hall/. The space is all white, with the original Ionic columns soaring up to a wonderfully lofty ceiling, and spectacular towers of flowers on the bar and piano. Red leather sofas in the bar area, on one side, and brasserie tables on the other, still leave plenty of airy spaciousness. In contrast, dining prices can be surprisingly un-lofty for the area, and the set menu counts as a City bargain (look out for limited-time frame special deals too). At its best, the food has an enjoyable flair. From the set menu, macaroni with wilted spinach in a subtly creamy mushroom sauce made a lovely, light starter, though parma ham salad was more ordinary. Sauces are a strong point: a fragrantly herby, mushroomy sauce with the baked parmesan polenta and asparagus; or a beautifully deep-flavoured gravy with slow-cooked lamb. Best was a dessert: cinnamon-sugared churros to dunk in sumptuous hot chocolate sauce. House wines are far above average, but there's also an ample fine-wine and cocktail list. Outstanding service, friendly and individual, adds a warm feeling to what could be a brittle space.
Babies and children welcome: high chairs. Booking advisable. Disabled: toilet. Separate rooms for parties, seating 23 and 45. Vegetarian menu. **Map 12 Q6.**

Clerkenwell & Farringdon

Smiths of Smithfield
67-77 Charterhouse Street, EC1M 6HJ (7251 7950, www.smithsofsmithfield.co.uk). Barbican tube or Farringdon tube/rail.
Café-bar **Open** 7am-11pm Mon-Fri; 10am-11.30pm Sat; 9.30am-10.30pm Sun. **Meals served** 7am-4.45pm Mon-Fri; 10am-4.45pm Sat; 9.30am-4.45pm Sun. **Main courses** £5.50-£8.50.
Wine Rooms **Dinner served** 6-10.45pm Tue-Sat; 5-9.30pm Sun. **Main courses** £5.50-£20.
Dining Room **Lunch served** noon-2.45pm Mon-Fri. **Dinner served** 6-10.45pm Mon-Sat. **Main courses** £12-£28.
Top Floor restaurant **Lunch served** noon-2.45pm Mon-Fri; 12.30-3.45pm Sun. **Dinner served** 6-10.45pm Mon-Sat. **Main courses** £16-£30.
All **Credit** AmEx, DC, MC, V.
John Torode may be most familiar nowadays for raising satirical eyebrows on *MasterChef*, but he also has a good line in user-friendly restaurants. Smiths is split into four sections: a slouchily post-industrial ground-floor bar, the first-floor Wine Rooms, the third-floor Dining Room and, for expense accounts, the posh Top Floor. We opted for the Wine Rooms, a relaxed and intimate venue after

the cavernous space downstairs, where you can choose from a friendly range of somewhat modish sharing plates. Three dishes each is plenty (and spares you a bill-time shock), and the options are appealingly straightforward. Ingredients shone in olive and rosemary focaccia with aïoli; salty samphire nicely balanced by beurre blanc; an uncomplicated tomato salad; gorgonzola in a slick of gorgonzola; and a chunky roast cod fillet with soft-boiled egg and strongly flavoured but unnecessary rouille. Only the trendiest dish disappointed: sliders tend to provide proportionally too much bun for the meat patty, but the promised chilli hardly poked its head out from beneath the sweet chutney. All was delivered briskly, if with little affection, by a hilariously lugubrious waiter. Choose from nearly two dozen wines by the glass, or try a cocktail: the Bramble was competently executed.
Babies and children welcome (restaurant): high chairs. Disabled: toilet. Entertainment (ground floor): DJs 7pm Thur-Sat. Separate rooms for parties, seating 12 and 24. Tables outdoors (4, pavement; 6, terrace). **Map 11 O5.**

Covent Garden

L'Atelier de Joël Robuchon
13-15 West Street, WC2H 9NE (7010 8600, www.joel-robuchon.com). Leicester Square tube.
Bar **Open** noon-1.30am Mon-Sat; noon-10.30pm Sun.
Ground floor **Lunch served** noon-2.30pm, **dinner served** 5.30-10.30pm daily. **Main courses** £15-£55. **Set meal** (noon-2.30pm, 5.30-6.30pm) £25 2 courses, £29 3 courses.
1st floor **Lunch served** noon-2.30pm, **dinner served** 6.30-11.30pm Mon-Sat. **Main courses** £15-£55.
All **Credit** AmEx, MC, V.
One of several Ateliers around the world, this is a slick operation, all black lacquer and red highlights, staffed by a team of professionals in smart black uniforms. There's a bar, a first-floor restaurant (La Cuisine) and the ground-floor L'Atelier, where seating is at high tables or around a bar. Various menus are offered, from full-on feasts to a selection of small tasting dishes (confit duck in aubergine caviar, with crunchy vegetables and sesame crust, perhaps, or langoustine ravioli with savoy cabbage and foie gras sauce). The set menu is excellent value; not only are the two or three courses accompanied by a choice of breads, a side vegetable and an amuse-bouche, but the quality is striking. Even simple spaghetti of the day – on this occasion, tomato, black olive, parmesan and basil – was an intensely flavoured, beautifully presented pleasure. To start, jewel-like melon and fromage frais tart with coriander and bayonne ham looked almost too good to eat. Next, an elegantly presented plate of fresh mackerel with preserved lemon and saffron on a spice crumble also found favour. A lovely selection of traditional tarts – miniature wedges of chocolate, coffee, pistachio, cinnamon and lemon – made a great finale, though £4.50 for an espresso took off some of the shine.
Available for hire. Babies and children welcome: high chairs; nappy-changing facilities. Booking advisable. Disabled: toilet. Dress: smart casual. **Map 17 C3.**

Axis
One Aldwych, 1 Aldwych, WC2B 4BZ (7300 0300, www.onealdwych.com). Covent Garden or Embankment tube or Charing Cross tube/rail.

Lunch served noon-2.30pm Tue-Fri. **Dinner served** 5.30-10.30pm Tue-Fri; 5-10.30pm Sat. **Main courses** £19-£24. **Set meal** (noon-2.30pm Mon-Fri; 5.30-7pm, 10-10.45pm Mon-Sat) £18.75 2 courses, £21.75 3 courses. **Credit** AmEx, DC, MC, V.
The unusual cylindrical shape of this basement restaurant gives it a height and grace that compensate for the lack of windows, and, with its serene decor, make for a calming bolthole from the Theatreland crowds. Axis is comfortable, quiet and chic, if not especially memorable, with most of its character coming from personable, experienced staff good at intuiting whether you want to banter or be left alone for a business lunch. So many of the latter are served that they guarantee providing a two-course lunch menu in 40 minutes (or you'll get a free night at the hotel). This was begging to be tested. No sooner had we set our watches than the starters were delivered: a delicate mackerel fillet expertly grilled to a genteel crispness, served prettily with cauliflower polonaise; and a pre-mixed (slightly bland) steak tartare. Mains were gutsier: generous roast loin of pork with an over-intense risotto; and halibut with pea purée and a highly concentrated red wine jus. The former came with victoria plum jam, the latter with succulent girolles – bearing out claims of seasonality. The carte dishes are also mainly based on a few good ingredients prepared to order, with some nice touches but no unnecessary culinary vanities. Catering for its hotel clientele, Axis also serves salads and light main courses (fillet of bream en papillote, for example) plus some crowd-pleasing desserts that are slightly out of keeping with its cultured mood (knickerbocker glory with popping candy, anyone?).
Available for hire. Babies and children welcome: high chairs. Booking advisable. Disabled: toilet. Separate room for parties, seats 18. Vegan dishes. Vegetarian menu. **Map 18 F4.**

The Ivy
1 West Street, WC2H 9NQ (7836 4751, www.the-ivy.co.uk). Leicester Square tube.
Meals served noon-11pm Mon-Sat, noon-10pm Sun. **Main courses** £6.75-£34.50. **Set meal** (4-6pm, 10-11pm Mon-Wed; noon-6pm Sun) £21.75 2 courses, £26.25 3 courses. **Cover** £2. **Credit** AmEx, DC, MC, V.
Any A-listers seem to have shipped upstairs to the Ivy's members' club, covertly entered via the florist next door. The restaurant itself might boast old-world allure – bottle-green carpets abut oak-panelled walls, and there's a pretty perimeter of stained-glass windows – but the crowd these days seems to consists largely of wayfarers and gawkers, attracted by the exclusive reputation, but given slightly short shrift with squeezed-in tables and narrow time slots. A top-hatted doorman ensures a majestic entrance and – a nice touch – a copy of *The Times* is proffered to anyone waiting alone for others in their party. Yet there's something of the assembly line about the operation: Gary Lee's menu of stalwarts, such as Bannockburn rib steak, barnsley lamb chop and corn-fed chicken breast, is duplicated with reliable efficiency and plays safe almost every step of the way. Shepherd's pie and sticky toffee pudding hint at boarding school days of yesteryear. Dishes are almost impossible to dislike, but equally tricky to love. The Ivy thrives on meeting expectations, not challenging them. Tables are as hotly sought after as ever, though – you may find most success around 5.30pm or 10pm.

sketch

A MOSAIC OF EXPERIENCE

From the Michelin Star **LECTURE ROOM & LIBRARY** to the **GALLERY** our gastro-brasserie or tea for two in the **PARLOUR**

Openings 8am to 2am

"Pierre Gagnaire's astonishing food isn't the only talking point at this stylish celebration of art and luxury" - Time Out's Hot 50

9 CONDUIT STREET, LONDON - 0207 659 45 00 - WWW.SKETCH.UK.COM

Babies and children welcome: high chairs. Booking essential, 4-6 wks in advance. Separate room for parties, seats 60. Vegan dishes. Vegetarian menu. **Map 18 D4**.

Knightsbridge

Fifth Floor

Harvey Nichols, Knightsbridge, SW1X 7RJ (7235 5250, www.harveynichols.com). Knightsbridge tube.
Café **Breakfast served** 8am-noon, **lunch served** noon-3.30pm, **dinner served** 6-10.30pm Mon-Sat. **Brunch served** 11am-5pm Sun. **Tea served** 3-6pm daily. **Main courses** £9.50-£15.
Restaurant **Lunch served** noon-2.45pm Mon-Thur; noon-3.45pm Fri, Sat. **Brunch served** noon-4pm Sun. **Tea served** 2.30-5.30pm Mon-Sat; 3-5pm Sun. **Dinner served** 6-10.45pm Mon-Sat. **Main courses** £19.50-£35. **Set lunch** £19.50 2 courses, £24.50 3 courses. **Set dinner** £29.50 tasting menu.
Both **Credit** AmEx, DC, MC, V.
It may be located by the 'Foodmarket', but the Fifth Floor is a luxury restaurant with views across Knightsbridge, and prices to suit prosperous Harvey Nichols customers. Its latest incarnation has more traditional leanings than in the past (the walls a satin taupe, displaying large contemporary mirrors), but the adjacent bar area retains its pearly white brilliance. Service was a touch fawning – 'Two courses? Oh, but we want the pleasure of mademoiselle's company a little longer'. However, if there's a time and a place for dispensing such attention, this is probably it: the fuss reflecting the customer experience elsewhere in the store. The carte is divided into 'From my favourites', and 'From…' the sea, the farm, and the field. This gives a decent balance, although the favourites section (poached eggs, Lyme Bay scallops, crispy Gressingham duck and more) seemed to equate neither to starters nor light meals. Mains were dainty; even roast loin and braised shoulder of lamb left ample room for further edible manoeuvres, while roasted zander lent intrigue, served with a gentle red lentil vinaigrette and a spirited parsley coulis. The market menu presents 'high street' value for those not on designer budgets.
Babies and children welcome: children's menu; high chairs; nappy-changing facilities. Disabled: lift; toilet. Tables outdoors (15, café terrace). **Map 8 F9**.

Marylebone

L'Autre Pied

5-7 Blandford Street, W1U 3DB (7486 9696, www.lautrepied.co.uk). Baker Street tube.
Lunch served noon-2.30pm Mon-Sat; noon-3.30pm Sun. **Dinner served** 6-10pm Sun. **Main courses** £21.50-£27.95. **Set meal** (noon-2.30pm Mon-Sat, 6-7pm daily) £18.95 2 courses, £22.50 3 courses. **Set lunch** (Sun) £29.50 3 courses. **Credit** AmEx, MC, V.
Sibling to fine-dining restaurant Pied à Terre, L'Autre Pied keeps it convivial, melding friendly, upbeat service with an accessible menu devoid of florid description. Hand-painted walls depicting flowers and fruit add an air of fantasia to the otherwise formal room of burgundy leather and slick dark furniture. An affordable lunch and pre-theatre menu doesn't compromise on ingredients nor creativity, and even comes with reasonably

priced by-the-glass wine pairings. Dishes such as 'confit cod, lemon purée, black olive, sweet onion, tomato vinaigrette, coriander oil' left our waitresses a bit breathless – and us too. Despite the terse ticking-off of ingredients, the dish came together as a flawless, refreshing starter. A simple raviolo of guinea fowl with a ragout of chickpeas, parsley crisps and red pepper oil was equally refined, if overly rich for a summer's evening. For an accomplished aubergine dish, a dry, melon- and honeysuckle-scented muscat-furmint blend from Slovakia was an inspired match. The carte is far more enthusiastically priced (ditto the wine list, despite a good first page of options by the glass), but it's worth upgrading if budget allows.
Babies and children welcome: high chairs. Booking advisable. Separate room for parties, seats 16. Tables outdoors (3, pavement). **Map 9 G5**.

Orrery

55 Marylebone High Street, W1U 5RB (7616 8000, www.orrery-restaurant.co.uk). Baker Street or Regent's Park tube. **Lunch served** noon-2.15pm, **dinner served** 6.30-10.15pm daily. **Set lunch** £21.50-£33 3 courses, £24.50-£37 3 courses incl wine. **Set dinner** £48 3 courses, £55 6 courses, £59 tasting menu (£104 incl wine). **Credit** AmEx, MC, V.
Orrery is a safe haven of excellent taste. It offers the top-end tropes, such as appetisers, pre-desserts and petits fours, even to those on promotional set menus and, while there's not much flexibility in the price of dinner, lunch is a good deal. Vegetarians get their own menu – goat's cheese bavarois, beet salad, parsley granité, for example. Dishes are elegant and artful, but don't always live up to expectations. To start: a wonderfully piquant, appetite-sharpening glass of gazpacho under parsley foam; and chicken and mushroom terrine studded with soft baby onions and a ribbon of cabbage, that wasn't as enjoyable as it should have been, despite the obvious effort expended. Scallop mousse on glorious shellfish bisque was less contrived, and more successful. Precision cooking delivered excellent mains of sea trout à la provençale with black olive crust; and pink slices of rump of beef with peas, girolles and parmesan-rich polenta. Presentation is generally delightful, but a plaster-hard strawberry pavlova shaped like a swan was surprisingly naff. Staff seem to share diners' pleasure, and the fine wine list is made accessible thanks to approachable sommeliers. Windows and skylights flood the long, pleasing room with light, making this an uplifting place to dine. The rooftop bar is an excellent outdoor eyrie.
Babies and children welcome: high chairs. Booking essential. Disabled: toilet. Tables outdoors (5, roof terrace). Vegetarian menu. **Map 3 G4**.

Mayfair

Patterson's

4 Mill Street, W1S 2AX (7499 1308, www.pattersonsrestaurant.co.uk). Bond Street or Oxford Circus tube. **Lunch served** noon-3pm Mon-Fri. **Dinner served** 6-11pm Mon-Fri; 5-11pm Sat. **Main courses** £21x. **Set lunch** £25-£29 3 courses. **Credit** AmEx, MC, V.
Set just off fashionable Conduit Street, Patterson's attracts a mature yet fun-loving business crowd. The mood is understated rather than restrained, elegant but not stuffy, with comfortable high-

backed chairs, dark glass vases of greenery, some impressive abstract seascapes, and two fish tanks. They don't make a show of it, but the one near the kitchen isn't decorative: it holds lobsters for lunch. Scottish produce, particularly seafood, features heavily on chef-owner Raymond Patterson's menus, but as forays are made to France, the Mediterranean and Japan, there is no sense of flag-waving from the Scot. Originality seems to be a driver. Miso-cured foie gras, for instance, made no attempt to taste Japanese, despite the strip of nori and smattering of sesame seeds; the sweet duck dumplings that partnered it were more reminiscent of Chinese cuisine, and the consommé of micro-chopped vegetables was classic French. At our request, staff had no hesitation in matching it with a dark honeyed sauternes. Hake with crisp burnished skin came with soft-centred crab gnocchi, tiny sweet vongole and green sauce – a fine dish refreshingly free of trendy styling, again conveying the sense of a kitchen charting its own course. Summer pudding with plum sorbet and clotted cream appealed for dessert, but we chose a compilation of chocolate; highlight was a dark chocolate sorbet as fine and glossy as satin.
Available for hire. Babies and children welcome: high chair. Booking advisable. Separate room for parties, seats 20. **Map 9 H/J6**.

Sotheby's Café

Sotheby's, 34-35 New Bond Street, W1S 2RT (7293 5077, www.sothebys.com/cafe). Bond Street or Oxford Circus tube. **Breakfast served** 9.30-11.30am, **lunch served** noon-2.45pm, **tea served** 3-4.45pm Mon-Fri. **Main courses** £15-£18. **Set tea** £8.25-£13.25. **Credit** AmEx, DC, MC, V.
Eating in what is essentially the entrance corridor of Sotheby's auction house is more fun than it sounds. A cosy but stylish space has been carved out, and the place is always full for lunch (it's a prime people-watching spot). The menu changes regularly, but the lobster club sandwich is a fixture. It's not for the price-conscious, but then neither is the auction house. Typical dishes on the short menu are a soup, such as cauliflower with curry oil, or a starter, such as merguez with braised puy lentils, watercress and salsa rossa. Mains might feature roast partridge with wild rice and mushroom cabbage parcel with paprika sauce, or a vegetarian option – perhaps roast red onion, butternut, courgette and chickpea chilli, with cornbread, avocado salsa and chive crème fraîche. We enjoyed flavour-packed roast cod with cockles, and an almost textbook steak frites with watercress and béarnaise sauce, slightly marred by saltiness. Desserts are dominated by a choice of fabulous ice-creams. Three scoops (marmalade; peanut, chocolate and salted caramel; redcurrant sorbet) were all amazing, but somehow bettered by a rich, creamy rice pudding with damson compote – possibly the best we've ever tasted. Further pluses are top-notch coffee, a short but winning wine list (more places should do grüner veltliner by the glass), and charming, on-the-ball waiting staff.
Babies and children admitted. Booking advisable (lunch). Disabled: toilet. **Map 9 H6**.

★ Wild Honey

12 St George Street, W1S 2FB (7758 9160, www.wildhoneyrestaurant.co.uk). Bond Street or Oxford Circus tube. **Lunch served** noon-2.30pm Mon-Sat; noon-3pm Sun. **Dinner served** 6-11pm Mon-Wed; 6-11.30pm Fri, Sat;

6-10.30pm Sun. **Main courses** £17.50-£19.50. **Set lunch** £18.95 3 courses. **Set dinner** (6-7pm, 10pm-close) £22.95 3 courses. **Credit** AmEx, MC, V.

On our latest visit, Wild Honey exceeded even our high expectations. The kitchen delivered the menu's promises in spades: dishes drew gasps of delight for their sensational flavours and technical brilliance. We were afraid the pre-theatre set menu would be comparatively dull, but a chicken and eel terrine was a terrific earthy, briny, herby dish, offset with sweet chutney and perky salad. Gurnard (currently the most fashionable sustainable fish), spiked with dill, baby capers, raw fennel and an oily, rich tomato dressing, and served with soft gnocchi, was exceptional. From the carte, raw mackerel, accompanied by beetroot, more tiny capers, pine kernels, baby coriander and wafer-thin slices of red and black radish, was stop-in-your-tracks good. Although there's a marked seasonality to the menu, some dishes common to Wild Honey and sister restaurant Arbutus will be familiar to regulars – no bad thing when it comes to the 'floating island' that's a fixture of the set-price menu. The cheeseboard is a sight to behold too. The attractive old oak panelling is brightened by large pretty abstracts; the closely packed tables probably explain why prices aren't higher. As at Arbutus, all wines from the well-chosen list are available in 250ml carafes. Our only complaint is that service was over-eager.
Babies and children admitted. Booking essential. **Map 9 H6**.

Piccadilly

Criterion
224 Piccadilly, W1J 9HP (7930 0488, www.criterionrestaurant.com). Piccadilly Circus tube. **Lunch served** noon-2.30pm, **dinner served** 5.30-11.30pm Mon-Sat. **Main courses** £12.50-£28.50. **Set meal** (lunch, 5.30-7pm, 10-11.30pm) £18 2 courses, £22 3 courses. **Credit** AmEx, MC, V.

With its prime Piccadilly Circus location, Criterion is the restaurant of choice for tourists, theatre-goers, hen parties and those who just fancy a bit of escapist glamour. Step inside, and the garish fluorescent lights and rowdy teens congregating around *Eros* are quickly forgotten, replaced by plush curtains, cushioned banquettes and above all, a glittering, golden mosaic ceiling. When booking the pre-theatre menu, we were delighted by the considerate receptionist, who took notes to ensure we would have enough time to eat before curtain call; staff on the floor, however, left much to be desired. Service skated between condescending and cheerful, depending on whose attention we managed to catch; dishes came out quickly but, once finished, lingered far too long on the table. Enthusiastic salting marred both beef carpaccio (otherwise decent), and chunky ham hock terrine, but things improved with a main of light, satisfying Cornish mackerel, served with crisp rocket and fennel and juicy, peeled cherry tomatoes. Desserts are a highlight, with cherry and frangipane making an impression; they could lose the chewing gum-flavoured mint and yoghurt sorbet, however. The kitchen has potential – some of the main menu offerings were real beauties – but service has some catching up to do.
Babies and children admitted. Booking advisable. Dress: smart casual. Separate room for parties, seats 70. **Map 17 B5**.

Pimlico

Rex Whistler Restaurant at Tate Britain
Tate Britain, Millbank, SW1P 4RG (7887 8825, www.tate.org.uk). Pimlico tube or bus 87. **Breakfast served** 10-11.30am Sat, Sun. **Lunch served** 11.30am-3pm, **tea served** 3.15-5pm daily. **Main courses** £13.25-£18.50. **Set lunch** £16.50 2 courses, £20.50 3 courses. **Credit** AmEx, DC, MC, V.

From the moment we arrived at the Rex Whistler, the service was exemplary: our bags whisked into the cloakroom, a table found outside in the sunshine, a choice of five breads proffered. The menu is all about big flavours – and largely about meat. From the carte, an appetiser of pork crackling would barely yield to the bite, and beef carpaccio lacked flavour (or a notable contribution from the advertised truffle oil), although it came with a feisty celeriac remoulade. However, smoked eel with crispy bacon and two slashes of sweet beetroot sauce (intensified by soy and balsamic vinegar) was both pretty and tasty; and fish of the day – a whole fresh cod, on the bone – was well cooked and beautifully fresh, even if the trimmings of fine diced onion, capers and lemon added little. Set lunch options didn't immediately grab us, but are nicely priced, with a neat by-the-glass system (one £3.75, two £7.25, three £10.50) that encourages you to match wine from the excellent list to each course. The smart, single-room interior gives you a chance to digest Mr Whistler's intriguing 1926-27 mural that encircles the walls.
Babies and children welcome: high chairs. Booking advisable. Disabled: lift; toilet. Tables outdoors (8, terrace). **Map 16 L11**.

St James's

The Avenue
7-9 St James's Street, SW1A 1EE (7321 2111, www.theavenue-restaurant.co.uk). Green Park tube.
Bar **Open** noon-11pm Mon-Fri; 5.45-11pm Sat.
Restaurant **Lunch served** noon-3pm Mon-Fri. **Dinner served** 5.45-11pm Mon-Sat. **Main courses** £13.50-£20.50. **Set lunch** £19.50 2 courses, £22.50 3 courses. **Set dinner** (5.45-7pm, 9.30-11pm) £17.50 2 courses, £21.50 3 courses.
Both **Credit** AmEx, DC, MC, V.

Surrounded by purveyors of fine wines, cigars and yachts to the world's wealthy, Avenue has a glamorous if somewhat clinical sense of occasion. The long narrow bar gleams with bottles of everything you could imagine, but quite possibly can't afford. With tables on two levels, a long skylight and artful lighting attempting to diffuse the overall coolness, it's a handsome place that would impress clients or suit a slightly formal date. Finnish chef Mikko Kataja's hand is clear in the kitchen. Thick slices of Severn & Wye smoked salmon with a silky-smooth broad bean purée and exquisitely nutty warm rye bread, and lacily thin slices of beef carpaccio with celeriac and puréed parsley, were beauties to behold. Mains of chargrilled lamb with spring onion fondue and mint jus, and a perfectly grilled fillet of sea bass with carrots, a rich red pepper purée and buttery crushed new potatoes, demonstrated finesse and top-quality ingredients. Puddings include the trendy sea-buckthorn (served here as a set cream

with yoghurt sorbet), and a rich chocolate delice accompanied by poached cherries and a sour-sweet cherry sorbet: taste bud tinglingly good. To keep down the bill, look out for set menu bargains.
Available for hire. Babies and children welcome: high chairs. Booking advisable. Disabled: toilet. Separate room for parties, seats 20. **Map 9 J8**.

Le Caprice
Arlington House, Arlington Street, SW1A 1RJ (7629 2239, www.caprice-holdings.co.uk). Green Park tube. **Lunch served** noon-3pm Mon-Thur; noon-4pm Fri, Sat. **Dinner served** 5.30pm-midnight Mon-Sat. **Meals served** 11.30am-11pm Sun. **Main courses** £15.75-£32. **Set dinner** (5.30-6.45pm, after 10.15pm) £19.75 2 courses, £24.25 3 courses. **Cover** £2. **Credit** AmEx, DC, MC, V.

As befits a Mayfair glamour-puss with a 30-year-long career, Le Caprice has just splashed out on a facelift. Stark black and white art deco chic is still the order of the day, but gleaming metal and glass shelving and an illuminated, marble-effect cream backdrop now join the long black marble bar and the white panelled walls adorned with David Bailey's monochrome photos of British celebs from the Swinging Sixties. The cocktail menu has been adapted to include a short 'heritage list' of classics (bellinis, bloody marys, manhattans), but the food remains focused on unfussy Modern European fare. Partridge salad came sprinkled with tangy elderberries and little curled wafers topped with blobs of pâté. There was no need for the rich, salty gravy that accompanied a slow-roast duck leg, whose crisp skin was underlaid by such a satisfyingly thick layer of fat that the plate it came on was already swimming in grease. But as the occasional customer posing for photos outside the door proves, this is more a destination restaurant than a place food is the main draw.
Babies and children welcome: high chairs. Booking essential, 2 wks in advance. Entertainment: pianist 6.30pm-midnight Mon-Sat, 7-11pm Sun. Tables outdoors (6, terrace). Vegetarian menu. **Map 9 J8**.

Soho

Andrew Edmunds
46 Lexington Street, W1F 0LW (7437 5708). Leicester Square, Oxford Circus or Piccadilly Circus tube. **Lunch served** 12.30-3pm Mon-Fri; 1-3pm Sat; 1-3.30pm Sun. **Dinner served** 6-10.45pm Mon-Sat; 6-10.30pm Sun. **Main courses** £10-£19. **Credit** MC, V.

Very much a venue that trades on its ambience, this buzzy, pan-European Soho eaterie goes all out for romantic intimacy. The dark wooden interior of the gently lit front room leads to a narrow staircase; downstairs is a low-ceilinged dining area, where small tables are decorated with bunches of flowers, and wax-spattered, candle-filled wine bottles provide most of the lighting. Diners are closely packed, meaning the soundtrack to a meal is the loud buzz of conversation from a couples-heavy crowd. Cooking is highly variable. A portion of pleasing, spice-marinated octopus was garnished with dry chorizo that had been cooked down to the size of 5p pieces. Veal-stuffed chicken leg, already salty, was marred by an even saltier gravy. Best was precision-poached turbot, served with a punchy, tarragon-heavy tartare sauce, and coarsely processed mushy peas. Service is friendly and attentive, although not very well informed about

A NEW WESTFIELD IN EAST LONDON

WHERE EAST MEETS WESTFIELD

ESTFIELD.COM/STRATFORDCITY2011

Westfield

STRATFORD CITY

— E20 —

Medlar. See p215.

the menu. Our questions had to be relayed to the chef, with the waiter's (charmingly delivered) explanation being, 'I don't cook'.
Babies and children admitted. Booking essential. Tables outdoors (2, pavement). **Map 17 A4**.

Arbutus

63-64 Frith Street, W1D 3JW (7734 4545, www.arbutusrestaurant.co.uk). Tottenham Court Road tube. **Lunch served** noon-2.30pm Mon-Sat; noon-3pm Sun. **Dinner served** 5-11pm Mon-Thur; 5-11.30pm Fri, Sat; 5.30-10.30pm Sun. **Main courses** £14-£19.95. **Set lunch** £16.95 3 courses. **Set dinner** (5-6.30pm) £18.95 3 courses. **Credit** AmEx, MC, V.
The trio of restaurants run by Anthony Demetre and Will Smith – the others are Wild Honey (Modern European) and Les Deux Salons (French) – are emblematic of a certain buzzy, modern, metropolitan style of dining and creative cooking. This original Soho base attracts crowds of media lunchers and passers-by. Restrained minimalist decor seems to amplify the chatter; service can be uncoordinated, but is bright and friendly. On our visit the food lacked the expected pzazz. The menu suggests full-on flavours, with gutsy offerings such as pigs' trotters and tripe, but ingredients were inconsistent. Poached egg with wild mushrooms, peas and parma ham was a dainty little pot, yet lacked flavour. And in a salad of green beans, white peach and almond, only the fruit was at all memorable. A main of slow-cooked lamb with cannellini beans, apricot and almonds was also unbalanced, as the sweet fruit and fragrantly nutty beans weren't matched by the bland (but tender) meat. Cod with chickpeas, chorizo and grilled fennel was also a mix of fine (chorizo, chickpeas) and a bit dull (fish, fennel). A big plus, however, is the wine list, with all wines available in 250ml carafes, to encourage tasting.
Babies and children admitted: high chairs. Booking advisable. **Map 17 B3**.

South Kensington

★ Bibendum

Michelin House, 81 Fulham Road, SW3 6RD (7581 5817, www.bibendum.co.uk). South Kensington tube. **Lunch served** noon-2.30pm Mon-Fri; 12.30-3pm Sat, Sun. **Dinner served** 7-11pm Mon-Sat; 7-10.30pm Sun. **Main courses** £18-£32. **Set lunch** £26.50 2 courses, £30 3 courses. **Credit** AmEx, MC, V.
Bibendum resides on the first floor of one of the capital's foremost art nouveau structures. The Grade II-listed former UK headquarters of the Michelin Tyre Company – replete with ornate ironwork and stained-glass panels – makes a failsafe good impression. The capacious dining room is drenched in light during the day, while around the clock an inebriated Michelin man presides, beseeching you that 'nunc est bibendum' ('now is the time to drink'). The blimpish mascot is emblazoned on the monumental arched window, and echoed in the bulbous curves of the glass tumblers. The dining experience is exemplary, from the expertise of the front-of-house staff – a masterclass in professionalism – to the consistently accomplished food. Head chef Matthew Harris flits from British seaside (deep-fried haddock and chips) to Anatolia (spiced lamb koftas with fragrant rice) and beyond (sichuan beef salad). A starter of fritto misto di mare muddled scallops, baby squid and prawns in a melt-in-the-mouth batter. To follow,

mullet fillet was served with a delicate cockle, chive and crème fraîche risotto. Set menu lunches are exceptional value for this class of cooking. The ground-floor oyster bar is a popular stop-off in its own right, though we've had disappointing meals there in the past.

Available for hire. Babies and children welcome: high chairs. Booking advisable. Disabled: lift, toilet. Dress: smart casual. **Map 14 E10.**
For branch (Bibendum Oyster Bar) see index.

West

Bayswater

Le Café Anglais `HOT 50`
8 Porchester Gardens, W2 4DB (7221 1415, www.lecafeanglais.co.uk). Bayswater tube.
Lunch served noon-3.30pm Mon-Fri, Sun.
Brunch served noon-3.30pm Sat. **Dinner served** 6.30-10.30pm Mon-Thur; 6.30-11pm Fri, Sat; 6.30-10pm Sun. **Main courses** £14.50-£22. **Set meal** (Mon-Fri) £20 2 courses, £25 3 courses. **Set lunch** (Sun) £25 2 courses, £30 3 courses. **Cover** £1.85. **Credit** AmEx, MC, V.
A contemporary take on the golden age of travel, Le Café Anglais' huge dining room has the feel of a chic ocean liner, with curved white banquettes, tall windows with heavy red curtains, large mirrors, huge vases of flowers and crisp linen tablecloths. Staff are smartly dressed in traditional brasserie style, and happy to chat when time allows. Chef-proprietor Rowley Leigh was dining there himself on our Sunday lunch visit, when the set menu is an excellent choice. There's a seasonal roast offered – lamb, maybe, or french partridge – but while Le Café Anglais aims to be a neighbourhood favourite, these aren't the pile-'em-high dinners expected at a gastropub. Fiery, flavour-packed bloody marys start things nicely, as do the fresh radishes that come with olives and bread and butter while waiting for starters (there's a £1.85 cover charge per person). Pappardelle with girolles and parmesan was both simple and luxurious. We chose desserts from the extensive carte, but the fun of splashing out was diminished by a burnt tinge to a bitter chocolate soufflé served with hazelnut ice-cream. Black forest 'revisited' tasted OK, but lacked finesse for a pudding priced over £8. Stick to the savouries and you are likely to leave happy.
Available for hire. Babies and children welcome: high chairs. Booking advisable dinner. Disabled: toilet. Separate room for parties, seats 26.
Map 7 C6.

Kensington

Clarke's
124 Kensington Church Street, W8 4BH (7221 9225, www.sallyclarke.com). Notting Hill Gate tube. **Lunch served** 12.30-2pm Mon-Fri; noon-2pm Sat, Sun. **Dinner served** 6.30-10pm Mon-Sat. **Main courses** £18.50-£24. **Set dinner** £40.50 3 courses. **Credit** AmEx, DC, MC, V.
Clarke's can appear rather starchy to outsiders: partly because locals in this chichi district of Kensington naturally don a jacket for dinner, and partly because the maître d' sometimes has a demanding demeanour that dissuades you from feeling entirely relaxed. It's perhaps not what chef-proprietor Sally Clarke would hope for, as she seemed entirely at ease popping out of the kitchen

Corner Room. See p219.

Brawn. See p220.

to fetch items from the bar, or sitting and chatting with familiar faces. The dining room is small, the tables enrobed with heavy linen tablecloths. The menu changes daily and is short and contained, with just four main courses – though this represents a progression from the original 'no choice' dinner menu of the 1980s. Dishes display a modern British leaning with a European flourish; the Jersey royals are served with aïoli, for instance. Own-made breads are a highlight. Pomegranate, chilli and mint glaze gave Aylesbury duck a delightful crispness, but the spice was unannounced. Another main, grilled veal chop, was ample, lean and tender. Dessert of 'dark chocolate soufflé cake' turned out to be a brownie in all but name: delicious nonetheless. Yet although the cooking roused the senses on our visit, it didn't lighten the atmosphere. *Available for hire. Babies and children welcome: high chairs. Booking advisable. Dress: smart casual. Separate room for parties, seats 50.* **Map 7 B7**.

Kensington Place

201-209 Kensington Church Street, W8 7LX (7727 3184, www.kensingtonplace-restaurant. co.uk). Notting Hill Gate tube. **Lunch served** noon-3pm Mon-Sat; noon-3.45pm Sun. **Dinner served** 6.30-10.30pm Mon-Thur; 6.30-10.45pm Fri, Sat. **Main courses** £11-£23. **Set meal** (lunch, dinner Mon; lunch, 6.30-7.30pm Tue-Sat; lunch Sun). **Credit** AmEx, MC, V.
Set at the base of a concrete block, with large metal-framed windows, a vibrant mural at one end and statement designer chairs, Kensington Place feels more like the trendy canteen of an arts centre than an upmarket Notting Hill destination. The absence of soft furnishings means it gets very noisy – or buzzing, depending on your point of view – when packed with office groups and young professionals. This is not the place for an intimate tête-à-tête, but the set menus make it an affordable option for an informal but special meal; just watch out for the wines, liable to bump up the bill considerably. The menu is big on fish, sourced from the adjoining fishmonger; meat dishes tend to be hearty, whatever the time of year. Mackerel escabèche was marinated carefully, without overpowering the fish, and pea soup was light and lemony. Fish pie didn't contain any shellfish (contrary to the waiter's description), but there were good chunks of salmon and smoked haddock, sweet leeks and creamy mash. Vegetarians don't get a lot of choice; the set menu option on our visit was the ubiquitous mushroom risotto.
Babies and children welcome: high chairs. Booking advisable; essential weekends. Disabled: toilet. Separate room for parties; seats 45. **Map 7 B7**.

Kitchen W8

11-13 Abingdon Road, W8 6AH (7937 0120, www.kitchenw8.com). High Street Kensington tube. **Lunch served** noon-2.30pm Mon-Sat; 12.30-3pm Sun. **Dinner served** 6-10.30pm Mon-Sat; 6.30-10pm Sun. **Main courses** £18.95-£31.50. **Set lunch** (Mon-Sat) £17.50 2 courses, £19.50 3 courses. **Set dinner** (Mon-Fri) £21.50 2 courses, £24.50 3 courses. **Credit** AmEx, MC, V.
Sitting pretty on a quiet street in an affluent neighbourhood, Kitchen is a joint venture between chef Philip Howard (The Square) and restaurateur Rebecca Mascarenhas (Sonny's). Dining takes place in a spacious, dimly lit room with a low ceiling,

coffee coloured walls and olive green furnishings. Service is low-key, efficient and polite. The playful dishes initially introduced on the menu have been replaced by mainstream interpretations of modern French-Mediterranean cuisine. We started with a tasty prelude of salt cod beignet, followed by a gazpacho full of the flavours of summer tomatoes and garlic, which came with crab toast so hard it threatened to break teeth. Tender roast rack of lamb arrived with piperade and creamy polenta imbued with rosemary, but again there was a slip: chargrilled lamb's tongue that was slightly burnt. Though the cooking so far failed to knock our socks off, impressive culinary skill was demonstrated by a carpaccio of watermelon; a dash of lemon oil enlivened the paper-thin slices of juicy fruit, and the addition of crushed strawberries soothed by lime ice-cream made it the perfect summer dessert. Look out for the fairly priced fixed-priced menus at lunch and early dinner.
Babies and children welcome: children's menu (lunch Sun); high chairs. Booking advisable. Disabled: toilet. **Map 7 A9**.

Ladbroke Grove

Dock Kitchen

Portobello Docks, 342-344 Ladbroke Grove, W10 5BU (8962 1610, www.dockkitchen.co.uk). Ladbroke Grove tube then bus 52, 70, or bus 452. **Lunch served** noon-2.30pm Mon-Sat; noon-3.30pm Sun. **Dinner served** 7-9.30pm Mon-Sat. **Main courses** £14-£30. **Set dinner** £40 4 courses. **Credit** AmEx, MC, V.
Dock Kitchen is not the positive advertisement for Tom Dixon's furniture that one might expect. Set in the designer's Ladbroke Grove HQ, the restaurant has been open less than two years, yet the Slab chairs, in particular, were looking the worse for wear – and the way the arms butt up against the table drove us crazy, as we kept hitting our elbows. No sale. With drinks company Innocent's head office also just a hop across the canal, this otherwise remote but surprisingly pretty place has the air of an upstart River Café about it – and perhaps not surprisingly, given that chef Stevie Parle used to work there, as well as at Petersham Nurseries Café and Moro. His spin on relaxed, big-flavoured cooking incorporates diverse recipes gleaned from his travels, so a typical menu leaps from Yorkshire to Spain to the Lebanon, then to Kerala and Mexico. Fans of rosé, be warned, there's only one option and it's £32 a bottle (strange, given the spacious alfresco dining terrace), but the £18 vermentino from the Languedoc will do on a hot day. Staff are relaxed, keen to help and friendly – indeed, although it's easy to dislike an overhyped spot such as this, we were utterly charmed, despite those damn chairs. *Available for hire. Babies and children welcome: high chairs; nappy-changing facilities. Booking advisable. Disabled: toilet. Separate room for parties, seats 25. Tables outdoors (6, terrace).*

Notting Hill

Notting Hill Brasserie

92 Kensington Park Road, W11 2PN (7229 4481, www.nottinghillbrasserie.com). Notting Hill Gate tube. **Dinner served** 6.30-11pm Mon-Sat; 6.30-10.30pm Sun. **Main courses** £19.50-£25.50. **Set lunch** (Wed-Sat) £17.50 2 courses, £22.50 3 courses; (Sun) £25 2 courses, £30 3 courses. **Credit** AmEx, MC, V.

Brasserie is an odd choice of name for this spot: the menu suggests something fancier, and the prices certainly do. It's an altogether more serious affair, drawing in Notting Hill's smarter diners for service complete with jazz tinkling through the speakers and from a grand piano at the bar. Original features of the Edwardian townhouses (the restaurant takes up the ground floor of three houses, making the most of the interlocking rooms) are decked with modern fittings, wooden floors and African artefacts on the walls, all in shades of taupe. Heavy white tablecloths and armchairs complete the sumptuous set-up. On a recent visit, food was a little disappointing. Foie gras parfait with rhubarb compote was light and smooth, but tasted cheesy, as if it contained parmesan – surely not? A main of duck came with nicely cooked spring vegetables and sour cherries, but the gravy was insipid. A heavy, coffee-scented crème brûlée didn't lift our spirits either. Perhaps we visited on an off-day, but for these prices we'd hope for something more exciting. Still, service is faultless, the wine list notable and the set lunches are excellent value.
Babies and children welcome: high chairs; supervised crèche (Sun lunch). Booking advisable. Entertainment: jazz/blues musicians 7pm daily, lunch Sun. Separate rooms for parties, seating 12 and 32. **Map 7 A6**.

South West

Barnes

Sonny's

94 Church Road, SW13 0DQ (8748 0393, www.sonnys.co.uk). Barnes or Barnes Bridge rail, or bus 33, 209, 283.
Bar **Lunch served** noon-4pm daily. **Brunch served** 10am-4pm Sat; 10am-noon Sun.
Restaurant **Lunch served** noon-3pm daily. **Dinner served** 7-10.30pm Mon-Thur; 7-11pm Fri, Sat. **Set dinner** (Mon-Thur) £16.50 2 courses, £19.50 3 courses.
Both **Main courses** £16.50-£19.50. **Set lunch** (Mon-Sat) £14.50 2 courses, £16.50 3 courses; (Sun) £18.50 2 courses, £22.50 3 courses. **Credit** AmEx, MC, V.
Rebecca Mascarenhas's Barnes eaterie has notched up a quarter-century of service. The smart rear dining area is still a calm, pale-hued sanctuary (although noisy when busy, thanks to the low ceiling), while the front café-bar has more comfortable seating, including a couple of banquettes, and a charming semi-private room to one side. Artworks dot the walls throughout. The classy service and impressive wine list remain, but the seasonal menu seems to have dulled of late – more prosaic ingredients, simpler dishes – and prices have risen. Cooking can still be good: chilled courgette soup with parmesan chantilly made a velvety, flavoursome starter; and a main of tender braised spring lamb had satisfying Middle Eastern overtones, thanks to a cumin-flavoured jus and imam bayildi. The good-value set menu yielded an excellent fish cake (the right ratio of fish to potato, and a crisp coating) in a lovely chive velouté, but the starter salad of violet artichoke, olives, purple potato crisps and pickled lemons was an incoherent grouping of tastes and textures. Desserts made the most of summer fruits; strawberries, cherries and gooseberries all appeared, the latter in a lovely light, creamy fool. Next door, Sonny's food shop sells enticing if expensive treats.

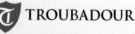

Available for hire. Babies and children welcome: children's menu; high chairs. Booking advisable (restaurant). Separate room for parties, seats 18.

Chelsea

Bluebird

350 King's Road, SW3 5UU (7559 1000, www.bluebirdchelsea.com). Sloane Square tube then bus 11, 19, 22, 49, 319. **Lunch served** noon-2.30pm Mon-Fri. **Brunch served** noon-3.30pm Sat, Sun. **Dinner served** 6-10.30pm Mon-Sat; 6-9.30pm Sun. **Main courses** £13.50-£25. **Set meal** (lunch, dinner Mon-Thur, Sun; lunch, brunch, 6-7pm, 9.30-10.30pm Fri, Sat) £20 2 courses, £25 3 courses. **Credit** AmEx, DC, MC, V.

Now entering its 15th year, this vast former Conran venue wants to be all things to all people. The ground floor is home to food, wine and even clothing stores (though it's the alfresco café on the roadside forecourt that attracts the poseurs); upstairs, a cocktail bar gives way to a large, hard-to-fill restaurant with a split personality. Despite a refurb a few years ago, the claret upholstery, starched linen and oversized flower arrangements are more corporate than cutting-edge, so a soundtrack of 'hip' dance music (cranked up at weekends) is an odd choice. Similarly, the menu plays it safe with a roll-call of upmarket bistro favourites, but can't resist including a few fashionable pan-Asian dishes. Cooking is variable. A hand-chopped steak tartare came not only with all the correct accoutrements, but was mixed at the table with great élan, while a creamy monkfish curry with just the right bite also impressed. A Cumbrian beef burger, however, was overcooked, and overwhelmed by its too-sweet relish. Service is polished, prices stiff and diners varied – from near-naked Saturday night arrivistes being ogled by old boys in blazers, to yummy mummies at weekends. A community centre for Chelsea, if you like.
Available for hire. Babies and children welcome: high chairs; nappy-changing facilities. Disabled: lift; toilet. Dress: smart casual. Separate rooms for parties, seating 10-110. Tables outdoors (25, courtyard). **Map 14 D12.**

Henry Root NEW

9 Park Walk, SW10 0AJ (7352 7040, www.thehenryroot.co.uk). Fulham Broadway tube then bus 211, 414. **Open** 11am-midnight daily. **Meals served** noon-11pm Mon-Sat; noon-9pm Sun. **Main courses** £10.50-£22. **Credit** AmEx, MC, V.

Although it's self-consciously designed, and so clean-living you wonder if anything as mucky as eating would ever be permitted here, the Henry Root is a small, friendly neighbourhood joint. Sit outside and you'll be gawping at footballers, models, Maseratis and other poseurs' marques, but redirect your attention to the food and all is cosy and kind. Upscale starters – juicy oysters, potted Dorset crab, charcuterie – are excellent. Piccalilli and black pudding add a British tinge to proceedings. For mains, the large house VIP burger, served in a small, crisply toasted brioche, with fat, triple-cooked chips and slim slices of gherkin, was at the top of the range for that litmus-test dish. Lemon chicken breast with peas, and ballotine of lamb were also excellent. There are also daily specials and salads. The concise dessert list comprises neat, smallish versions of homely classics (gooseberry fool, lemon meringue pie), plus the odd comedy item (a parfait

made from a Snickers bar). All had the appearance, texture and combination of flavours to indicate loving preparation. The wine list is long, but offers few cheap options (our tempranillo, at £20 a bottle, was only satisfactory). Staff were super-friendly and helpful.
Babies and children welcome: high chairs. Disabled: toilet. Tables outdoors (4, pavement). **Map 14 D12.**

Medlar NEW

2011 RUNNER-UP BEST NEW FINE DINING
438 King's Road, SW10 0LJ (7349 1900, www.medlarrestaurant.co.uk). Fulham Broadway tube or bus 11, 22. **Lunch served** noon-3pm Tue-Sun. **Dinner served** 6.30-10.30pm Tue-Sat. **Set lunch** (Tue-Sat) £25 3 courses; (Sun) £30 3 courses. **Set dinner** £38 3 courses. **Credit** AmEx, MC, V.

We expect Medlar will follow the trajectory of south London's legendary Chez Bruce, where chef-patron Joe Mercer Nairne and business partner David O'Connor, a front-of-house expert, have both done time. A slightly out-of-the-way neighbourhood restaurant of surprising calibre, it has the same feeling of classy informality, with a soothingly chic interior and correct but unfussy service. Full-length windows fold back to lend the front dining room the alfresco vibe of the terrace tables. Grey fabric walls suggest sumptuousness, but contrast with stark, bright green illustrations of medlars, and mood lights with exposed squirrel-cage bulbs. A glossy yet understated Chelsea crowd quickly warmed to the place, so securing a table can be difficult. On our latest visit, desserts were the weak point; in fact, they so lacked the sophistication of the savoury dishes that we suddenly felt as if we were in another restaurant. A bowl of vibrant pink plum ice-cream with ginger brandy snap had great flavour and texture, but couldn't stand up to, say, ham and foie gras terrine, which featured huge chunks of meat, perfectly groomed green beans, milky fresh walnuts and a perfectly balanced dressing of shallots and sweet vinegar. Pretty red mullet with perfectly cooked squid on a flavourful ratatouille was the best of the mains. There's a focused list of wines by the glass, starting at £4.50 for 125ml; 500ml carafes are also available.
Available for hire. Babies and children welcome. Booking essential. Dress: smart casual. Separate room for parties, seats 14. Tables outdoors (3, pavement). **Map 14 D12.**

South

Balham

★ Lamberts

2 Station Parade, Balham High Road, SW12 9AZ (8675 2233, www.lambertsrestaurant.com). Balham tube/rail. **Lunch served** noon-3pm Sat. **Dinner served** 7-10.30pm Mon-Sat. **Meals served** noon-5pm Sun. **Main courses** £14-£18. **Set meal** (Tue-Thur) £17 2 courses, £20 3 courses. **Credit** MC, V.

For many years, Lamberts has been the best restaurant in Balham, but our most recent visit suggests it is rivalling – or surpassing – Chez Bruce as the smartest choice in south-west London. Service is solicitous and attentive as ever, purring along with the easy confidence of a restaurant at the top of its game. But prices barely rise above the level of 'smart neighbourhood place': about £7 for

starters, £17 for mains, £6 for dessert. For this, you get very sophisticated cooking. The sous-vide wood pigeon breast wasn't the pallid meat this slow-cooking technique sometimes imparts; instead, the rich flesh was tender and moist, nicely cut with the sharpness of accompanying apple chunks and hazelnuts. In contrast, line-caught Dorset char was pleasingly blackened on the skin, with the firm flesh resting on crushed Jersey royals with a slick of sauce vierge. We've always found the meat and fish dishes imaginative, but this time it was the desserts that stood out, such as the tiny mattress-like wafers of own-made lemon marshmallow, sandwiching a scoop of strawberry sorbet, the plate peppered with fresh strawberry chunks. The drinks list is well chosen and reasonably priced, offering great wines by the glass or carafe.
Available for hire. Babies and children welcome: children's menu (weekends); high chairs. Booking advisable; essential weekends.

Battersea

Ransome's Dock

35-37 Parkgate Road, SW11 4NP (7223 1611, www.ransomesdock.co.uk/restaurant). Battersea Park rail or bus 19, 49, 319, 345. **Brunch served** noon-5pm Sat; noon-3.30pm Sun. **Meals served** noon-11pm Mon-Fri. **Dinner served** 6-11pm Sat. **Main courses** £11.50-£24. **Set brunch** (Sun) £22.50 3 courses. **Set meal** (noon-7.30pm Mon-Fri) £15.50 2 courses. **Credit** AmEx, DC, MC, V.

A neighbourhood restaurant with an immediate advantage: namely, it belongs to a very desirable neighbourhood. Ransome's has a narrow terrace alongside the dock, and – if you crane your neck – views across the Thames to Chelsea. Despite the riverside allure, it's an unassuming, rather old-fashioned venue, the conservatory giving way to purple-haze walls and nondescript tables and chairs, some of the latter upholstered in a kind of terracotta corduroy. The pared-back Modern European menu is simple, perhaps to a fault. Best call is the fish, which is fresh daily and tastes heavenly. Eel fillet on a buckwheat pancake with horseradish made a good, if costly, starter. The following cod in a gentle pesto sauce was so full-flavoured, it seemed like a different species from the frozen specimens usually encountered. Chicken breast was decent too, but both mains were served with similar vegetables (a sign, at least, of seasonality). Service was fine, though junior staff were a little timid. On the plus side, the wine list is a revelation, with all the hallmarks of an enthusiastic expert (borne out by several accolades and a wine club – details online).
Available for hire. Babies and children welcome: high chairs. Booking advisable. Disabled: toilet. Tables outdoors (10, terrace). **Map 21 C1.**

★ Tom Ilic

123 Queenstown Road, SW8 3RH (7622 0555, www.tomilic.com). Battersea Park or Queenstown Road rail. **Lunch served** noon-2.30pm Wed-Sat; noon-3.30pm Sun. **Dinner served** 6-10.30pm Tue-Sat. **Main courses** £11.50-£15.50. **Set lunch** £14.50 2 courses, £16.95 3 courses; (Sun) £16.95 2 courses, £21.50 3 courses. **Set dinner** £16.95 2 courses, £21.50 3 courses. **Credit** AmEx, MC, V.

Peeping out from the 'O' in Tom Ilic's logo is a cartoon pig. The theme continues inside, in the shape of a few ornamental brass oinkers adding a

grunt of insouciance to what is otherwise a fairly formal deep red and cream dining room. A couple of giant mirrors are judiciously positioned to lend a convincing illusion of space. Typical customers are a fraction older than the norm, perhaps attracted by what is a classic, meat-laden menu. There's plenty of pork, of course, plus oxtail, sweetbreads, rabbit saddle and more – this is not a million miles removed from Fergus Henderson's British brand of nose-to-tail eating. House special is the degustation of pork, which (vegetarians, beware) was a tantalisingly arranged platter of pig's cheek and trotter with medallions of black pudding, sourced from the British Isles. Presentation is something that Tom Ilic does well, and the lamb was equally enticing; a succulent braised shoulder and roast rump were good textural contrasts, set off by the sweet tang of garlic runner beans and gratin potato. In just a few years, Ilic's restaurant has garnered quite a following, and justly so. Given the quality, this is great-value food.
Available for hire. Babies and children welcome: high chairs. Booking advisable weekends.

Brixton

Upstairs
89B Acre Lane, entrance on Branksome Road, SW2 5TN (7733 8855, www.upstairslondon. com). Clapham Common tube or Brixton tube/ rail. **Dinner served** 6.30-10pm Tue-Sat.
Set dinner £26 2 courses, £32 3 courses, £37 4 courses, £39 tasting menu. **Credit** AmEx, MC, V.
Dining at Upstairs is an experience imbued with the personality of its owners, Phillipe Castaing and Stephanie Mercier. Their fingerprints are on every flourish – from the unmarked doorbell access on a side street off Acre Lane, to the jazzy first-floor bar, an assortment of leather couches and spot-lit paintings in a converted living room above their sandwich shop, Opus. But the main event is yet another floor up, in an intimate, largely undecorated dining room, the candle-lit tables too close together to be traditionally romantic, but with superb views to Victoria and beyond. We began with a delicate disc of rabbit lasagne in a fragrant pea and girolle mushroom broth, and a lip-smackingly fresh helping of tuna tartare served with salted crispbread. A main of artichoke ravioli – like all the dishes, lovingly explained by staff – came flavoured with parsley and mint, and served with griddled artichoke hearts, broad beans and balls of spinach, but seemed to sacrifice flavour for flair. Better was pan-fried salmon fillet on a bed of samphire and chipped potatoes, an exercise in taste and texture combinations that – like most things here – is at a level of fine dining seldom associated with Brixton.
Available for hire. Babies and children admitted. Booking advisable Mon-Fri; essential Sat, Sun. **Map 22 C2.**

Waterloo

Oxo Tower Restaurant, Bar & Brasserie
8th floor, Oxo Tower Wharf, Barge House Street, SE1 9PH (7803 3888, www.harveynichols.com). Southwark tube or Waterloo tube/rail.
Bar **Open** 11am-11pm Mon-Wed; 11am-11.30pm Thur-Sat; noon-10.30pm Sun. **Meals served** noon-11pm Mon-Sat; noon-10pm Sun.
Main courses £6-£12.
Brasserie **Lunch served** noon-3pm Mon-Sat;

noon-3.30pm Sun. **Dinner served** 5.30-11pm Mon-Sat; 6-10pm Sun. **Main courses** £13-£33. **Set meal** (lunch, 5.30-6.15pm Mon-Fri) £22.50 2 courses; £26.50 3 courses.
Restaurant **Lunch served** noon-2.30pm Mon-Sat; noon-3pm Sun. **Dinner served** 6-11pm Mon-Sat; 6.30-10pm Sun. **Main courses** £22-£35. **Set lunch** £35 3 courses.
All **Credit** AmEx, DC, MC, V.
Harvey Nichols runs these dining options in the Oxo Tower, and is making a fine job of it. Service is bright and welcoming, and food is inventive and refined, with subtle flavour combinations beautifully executed. The seasonal menus in the buzzy brasserie (at one end of the top floor) have a global outlook, so might include Moroccan merguez sausages with red-pepper muhammara sauce, as well as Loch Duart salmon with gnocchi, pea mousse and goat's cheese, and a full vegetarian menu. The quieter and more spacious restaurant at the other end stays closer to a Mod Euro style, so could feature pork cheeks with fennel choucroute, or truly memorable scallops with an oxtail spring roll and pea vinaigrette. Between the brasserie and restaurant is a very sleek bar. Prices at both dining venues are lofty, especially for wines, but the set menus (lunch in the restaurant, lunch and early dinner in the brasserie) represent good value for this quality of cooking. Oh, and a highlight of a meal at both venues is the fabulous Thames view.
Available for hire. Babies and children welcome: children's menu; high chairs. Booking advisable. Disabled: lift; toilet. Entertainment (jazz lunch Sat, Sun; 7.30pm daily brasserie). Tables outdoors (50, brasserie terrace; 40, restaurant terrace). Vegan dishes. Vegetarian menu. **Map 11 N7.**

Skylon
Royal Festival Hall, Belvedere Road, SE1 8XX (7654 7800, www.skylon-restaurant.co.uk). Waterloo tube/rail.
Bar **Open/snacks served** noon-1am daily.
Brasserie **Meals served** noon-10.45pm daily.
Main courses £12.50-£25. **Set dinner** (5.30-6.30pm, after 10pm) £19.50 2 courses, £23 3 courses.
Restaurant **Lunch served** noon-2.30pm Mon-Sat; noon-3.30pm Sun. **Dinner served** 5.30-10.30pm daily. **Set dinner** £40 2 courses, £45 3 courses; (5.30-6.30pm, after 10pm) £26.75 2 courses, £30.50 3 courses.
All **Credit** AmEx, MC, V.
A large, open-plan space in the Royal Festival Hall complex, glitzy Skylon commands jaw-dropping views across the Thames from its massive windows. It's a great place for sundowners, and the cocktails and wine lists in both the brasserie and restaurant sections are impressive too. In recent visits, the food hasn't quite lived up to the surroundings, but we've noted a recent return to form. A pre-theatre menu in the brasserie (better value than the rather pricey à la carte) had decent choice, with dishes that showed no lack of imagination. A starter of puy lentils, enlivened by a sweet-wine reduction and salty feta and olives, was simple but effective. To follow, roast cod with chickpeas, tomato and chorizo arrived generously proportioned and well cooked (although a crisper skin on the fish would have been welcome). A meaty treat – grilled onglet steak – was well aged and served properly rare. Pudding of vanilla crème brûlée, served in a little Le Creuset pot, was smooth-textured and not too sweet. With chirpy,

professional service rounding things off, Skylon is somewhere that, if you catch it right, has the makings of a special night out.
Babies and children welcome: children's menu; high chairs. Booking advisable. Disabled: lift; toilet. **Map 10 M8.**

South East

Crystal Palace

★ Exhibition Rooms
69-71 Westow Hill, SE19 1TX (8761 1175, www.theexhibitionrooms.com). Crystal Palace rail. **Lunch served** noon-4pm, **dinner served** 6-10.30pm Mon-Sat. **Meals served** noon-9pm Sun. **Main courses** £10.50-£18.50. **Set meal** (noon-4pm, 6-7pm daily) £12 2 courses, £15 3 courses. **Credit** AmEx, MC, V.
The Exhibition Rooms opened in 2009, and in the same year won Time Out's Best Local Restaurant gong. There's nothing especially novel about the menu of beer-battered haddock, steak tartare, Maldon rock oysters, spring vegetable risotto, Loch Duart salmon, or strawberries with shortbread, but it's all top-notch produce superbly cooked and allowed to speak for itself. Pan-fried Cornish mackerel was succulent and salty, with a pleasingly crisp skin; roast beef came rare and lean, served with an enormous puff of yorkshire; and sticky toffee pudding was as wicked as you could hope. There's genuine enthusiasm for all things national and seasonal, and showcasing English aperitifs – cocktails mixing Chapel Down sparkling wine and fruit-based spirits – is a particularly nice touch. Service was welcoming, and staff able to make informed recommendations. Alongside the main menu, the restaurant offers Sunday roasts, weekend brunches, and two-for-one cocktails plus half-price wines on a Wednesday. Downstairs from the light, airy restaurant, there's a cosy bar that opens on to a decked courtyard with squishy leather sofas: the perfect place for a digestif.
Babies and children welcome: children's menu; high chairs. Booking advisable; essential weekends. Disabled: toilet. Tables outdoors (9, courtyard).

Greenwich

Inside
19 Greenwich South Street, SE10 8NW (8265 5060, www.insiderestaurant.co.uk). Greenwich rail/DLR. **Lunch served** noon-2.30pm Tue-Fri; noon-3pm Sun. **Dinner served** 6.30-11pm Tue-Sat. **Main courses** £12.95-£18.95. **Set lunch** (Mon-Fri) £12.95 2 courses, £17.95 3 courses; (Sun) £17.95 2 courses, £22.95 3 courses. **Set dinner** (dinner Tue-Thur; 6.30-8.30pm Fri, Sat) £18.95 2 courses, £23.95 3 courses. **Credit** AmEx, MC, V.
Inside has made it through the past near-dozen years by maintaining high standards, and remains a linchpin of the Greenwich dining scene. The decor is plain and modern, inside and out, sticking to a chic palette of dark brown and cream. Front-of-house operations run like clockwork, and service is so unintrusive as to be considered characterless by some – the atmosphere comes from the warm lighting and the convivial hum of fellow diners. All the passion is evident in a succinct menu of imaginative dishes dreamt up by chef-patron Guy Awford – Modern European in the main, but with

influences from the Middle East and Asia. Almond, honey and rosewater cake was crumbly and delicate, accompanied by a perfect, subtle pistachio ice-cream. The more conventional dishes we tried were just as accomplished; juicy, roast corn-fed chicken breast, perched on top of kernels of pop-in-the-mouth creamed corn, was bettered only by meltingly soft confit duck leg. A comparatively dull cheeseboard (chèvre, stilton, cheddar) felt overpriced at £6.95, but dining here is generally excellent value – the set menus are a steal.
Available for hire. Babies and children admitted. Booking advisable. Other.

London Bridge & Borough

Delfina

50 Bermondsey Street, SE1 3UD (7357 0244, www.thedelfina.co.uk). London Bridge tube/rail. **Breakfast served** 8-11am, **lunch served** noon-3pm Mon-Fri. **Dinner served** 7-10pm Fri. **Meals served** 11am-5pm Sun. **Main courses** £9-£18.95. **Set lunch** £15 2 courses, £18.50 3 courses. **Credit** AmEx, DC, MC, V.
This large, white gallery space-cum-restaurant is perfectly suited to lunchtime dining (it's open for dinner on Fridays only), when the natural light coming through the windows shows it to best advantage. There's a nice atmosphere too, with pleasant staff and low-key background chatter. The kitchen is mostly reliable, with only a dry beef burger disappointing on this visit. Own-made, and served with chorizo, cheese and gherkin, it tasted fine, but failed to meld into a delicious whole. A well-dressed leaf salad helped, as did slightly oily chunky chips. A further annoyance was that it was served on a narrow wooden board, so bits kept falling off. However, everything else passed muster: an excellent and beautifully presented starter of smoked salmon with crab wrapped in pickled carrot, followed by well-flavoured roast cod with sticky rice and pak choi. Veg of the day, runner beans and peas, were fresh and buttery. Gin and tonic sorbet made a bracing dessert, but couldn't compete with a glorious chocolate fondant with macerated cherries and salted caramel ice-cream. An unthreatening wine list has options by the glass, carafe and bottle. Note that on Thursdays, the menu is supplemented with a choice of steaks.

Available for hire. Babies and children admitted: high chairs. Booking advisable. Disabled: toilet. Separate room for parties, seats 250. Tables outdoors (8, pavement). **Map 12 Q9.**

★ Magdalen

152 Tooley Street, SE1 2TU (7403 1342, www.magdalenrestaurant.co.uk). London Bridge tube/rail. **Lunch served** noon-2.30pm Mon-Fri. **Dinner served** 6.30-10pm Mon-Sat. **Main courses** £13.50-£20. **Set lunch** £15.50 2 courses, £18.50 3 courses. **Credit** AmEx, MC, V.
The atmosphere at Magdalen is low-key and quite romantic, with tea lights flickering on white-clothed tables and classical music playing quietly. The small bar area and simple dining room epitomise discreet sophistication; it's as though the big guns have been saved for the menu. What this short, frequently changing carte lacks in length, it makes up for in creativity. Ingredients are chosen with evident care and treated with respect, neither too fussily nor too plainly. The kitchen certainly knows how to pair flavours. A simple fried duck egg was offset beautifully by smoked anchovies. Silky-smooth chilled fennel soup spiked with Pernod sang with Provençal flavours, and a generous portion of wild salmon served on Alsace-style choucroute was cooked to pink translucence. For afters, there's a selection of cheeses from Neal's Yard and from an affineur in France; or, for sweet-lovers, classics such as pear and almond tart or caramelised rice pudding. The wine list focuses on France, with some good bottles from the wider Continent and the New World, and there's a decent by-the-glass selection. Service is friendly and suitably unfussy. Magdalen is excellent value at dinner and the set lunch is more of a bargain.
Babies and children admitted. Booking advisable. Disabled: toilet. Separate rooms for parties, seating 8-35. **Map 12 Q8.**

Tower Bridge

Blueprint Café

Design Museum, 28 Shad Thames, SE1 2YD (7378 7031, www.blueprintcafe.co.uk). Tower Hill tube or Tower Gateway DLR or London Bridge tube/rail or bus 47, 78. **Lunch served** noon-2.45pm daily. **Dinner served** 6-10.45pm Mon-Sat. **Main courses**

£12.50-£21. **Set lunch** £15 2 courses, £20 3 courses. **Set dinner** £17 2 courses, £22 3 courses. **Credit** AmEx, DC, MC, V.
The Blueprint Café feels like a treat: the airy, white-walled dining room has floor-to-ceiling glass windows looking on to one of the finest river views in London (so the opera glasses on the linen-covered tables must be to peer at your fellow diners). Service is friendly and helpful, and the food from head chef Jeremy Lee's kitchen can be really very good indeed. The set dinner is a bargain. A starter of fresh sardines and egg on toast was scrumptious, just pipping the other starter, beetroot salad. Both mains were excellent: perfectly seared onglet (justly known as the 'butcher's choice') and superb preserved duck confit, although the former didn't benefit much from its accompanying pickled walnut. Vegetables were pod-fresh and well flavoured (the addition of fresh mint was a nice touch). For afters, there's the likes of lemon posset, almond cake with caramelised apples or British cheeses. If you don't drink too much – perhaps an aperitif of a kir or mir (the blackberry version) – you'll be surprised at how little you've spent. Then again, as this is a perfect spot for a celebration, perhaps not.
Available for hire. Babies and children welcome: high chair. Booking advisable dinner. Disabled: lift; toilet (in museum). Tables outdoors (4, terrace). **Map 12 S9.**

Le Pont de la Tour

Butlers Wharf Building, 36D Shad Thames, SE1 2YE (7403 8403, www.lepontdelatour. co.uk). Tower Hill tube or Tower Gateway DLR or London Bridge tube/rail.
Bar & grill **Lunch served** noon-3pm Mon-Fri; noon-4pm Sat, Sun. **Dinner served** 6-10.30pm Mon-Sat; 6-10pm Sun. **Main courses** £11.50-£22. **Set lunch** £15 2 courses, £18 3 courses.
Restaurant **Lunch served** noon-3pm Mon-Fri; noon-4pm Sat, Sun. **Dinner served** 6-11pm Mon-Sat; 6-10pm Sun. **Main courses** £16.50-£35. **Set lunch** £27.50 2 courses, £31.50 3 courses.
Both **Credit** AmEx, DC, MC, V.
The impressive spectacle of Tower Bridge provides the backdrop, as well as the name of this riverside restaurant and brasserie. Le Pont is at its best in summer, when outdoor tables (unbookable, alas) are hot property. On the downside, the inverse equation theory (which states that the better the view, the less interesting the food) is at play; this is not the place to come for culinary fireworks. The bar and brasserie menu plays safe, with a selection of seafood, charcuterie, grills and light dishes, though there are some nice wines to be had. Chips with an ultra-crisp exterior were a high point, as was gazpacho finished with a swirl of good olive oil. Grilled asparagus spears were well cooked too, but the accompanying hollandaise was underseasoned and lacked sharpness. Ditto the 'citrus aïoli' that accompanied salt and pepper squid, which was in serious need of an allium or lemon kick. For afters, desserts such as bitter chocolate tart and vanilla crème brûlée hum a well-worn tune. Service was fine, but the kitchen needs to pay more attention to detail and aim a bit higher if the food is ever to live up to the view.
Babies and children welcome: high chairs. Booking advisable. Entertainment: pianist 6pm Tue-Sun, bar & grill). Separate room for parties, seats 20. Tables outdoors (22, terrace). **Map 25 S8.**

Botanist. See p202.

East
Bethnal Green

★ Corner Room `NEW`
*Town Hall Hotel, Patriot Square, E2 9NF
(no phone, www.viajante.co.uk). Bethnal
Green tube or Cambridge Heath rail.*
Breakfast served 7-10am Mon-Fri; 7.30-
10.30am Sat, Sun. **Meals served** noon-
10.30pm daily. **Main courses** £10-£15.
Set lunch (noon-3pm Mon-Fri) £15 2 courses.
Credit AmEx, MC, V.
Eating food by Nuno Mendes (whose first
restaurant, Viajante, is also in this boutique Bethnal
Green hotel) is an adventure. As any hobbit will tell
you, adventures aren't for everyone – but we find it
fascinating. After a terrific amuse-bouche of fat
olives stuffed with anchovy, orange and parsley, we
enjoyed visually arresting mackerel with
gooseberry granita, pistachio and tiny, roe-like balls
of melon. The biggest hit had the simplest twist:
'clam and cod chowder' wasn't soup, just a perfectly
cooked, chunky cod fillet, a scatter of clams,
sweetcorn, diced potato and a little sauce, delivering
an explosive whack of flavour authentic enough to
demand a return ticket from Boston. To finish:
blueberry pudding with chunks of dry brioche and
caramel-streaked goat's cheese, under a grassy-
tasting shiso granita. No bookings are taken, so
you'll probably wait for a table, and there's a 90-
minute maximum stay – not enforced for our early
week visit, even though the quietly arty, first-floor
corner space was full by 9pm. Later diners began
to experience delays, doubtless because of the
amount of hands-on preparation required. Also,
some dishes over-extend themselves: the meat in a
delicious dish of Ibérico pork with Portuguese
bread pudding was seared like sushi tuna: the
texture was superb, but the temperature
disconcertingly lukewarm. But for the price, these
are exciting, surprising eats.
*Babies and children admitted. Bookings not
accepted. Disabled: toilet.*

Palmers
*238 Roman Road, E2 0RY (8980 5590,
www.palmersrestaurant.net). Bethnal Green
tube/rail or 8 bus.* **Dinner served** 6-10.30pm
Mon-Sat. **Meals served** noon-9pm Sun. **Main
courses** £9.50-£16.50. **Credit** AmEx, MC, V.
Palmers is by far the most welcoming spot on an
unlovely stretch of Roman Road, with cooking that
exceeds the norm for London restaurants, never
mind this part of town. Run by a Czech family, with
a talented son in the kitchen, the white-painted,
modern-looking restaurant is minimally decorated
but comfortable. Prices are very reasonable,
particularly as portions are sizeable: a beautifully
seared rump steak, with giant chips, roast tomato,
leaf salad and fresh-tasting chimichurri sauce cost
just £13.50. Other mains were similarly appealing:
spiced lamb with tabouleh and pomegranate salad
was done just-so, with three big pieces of tender
meat, while equally tender, tasty duck came with
gloriously punchy merguez sausage, rosemary
potatoes and spinach. Every plate was wiped clean
– and this after starters of a meat plate (three
meats, toasted sourdough, caperberries and
cornichons), and a refreshing salad of smoked
mackerel with beetroot, soft-boiled egg and little

Season Kitchen. See p223.

MODERN EUROPEAN

gem lettuce. Best of all was a huge bowl of spicy bouillabaisse. The only misstep was a rubbery buttermilk panna cotta; other desserts of sorbet, and affogato (with both chocolate and vanilla ice-cream) went down a treat. The wine list lags behind the menu in scope and quality, but overall this is a lovely local that's also worth a trip.

Available for hire. Babies and children admitted. Booking advisable weekends. Disabled: toilet. Takeaway service.

Docklands

Plateau

Canada Place, Canada Square, E14 5ER (7715 7100, www.plateau-restaurant.co.uk). Canary Wharf tube/DLR.
Bar & grill Meals served noon-10pm Mon-Sat. **Main courses** £12-£22. **Set meal** £15 2 courses, £18 3 courses.
Restaurant **Lunch served** noon-3pm Mon-Fri. **Dinner served** 6-11pm Mon-Sat. **Main courses** £14-£29.50. **Set meal** £23 2 courses, £27.50 3 courses.
Both **Credit** AmEx, DC, MC, V.
Stepping out of the lift at Plateau's fourth-floor location, it was immediately apparent that many of the well-dressed diners hailed from local Canary Wharf offices (though couples out for an intimate meal also eat here). The expansive restaurant sits just beyond an informal bar area, where music plays and the menu is less exalted (fish and chips, say). Both areas are glass-clad, reflecting the Wharf's skyscrapers back at you. The high-design interior is all gleaming steel lamps, white chairs and grey marble-topped tables. Our meal began with a simple but perfectly balanced buffalo mozzarella, pickled beetroot and rocket salad. To follow, slow-cooked pork belly with crisp crackling was accompanied by an inspired baby squid salad. Dessert, a buttery bourbon vanilla cream with strawberries, came with a sprinkling of unadvertised pistachio nuts (allergy sufferers, beware). Ingredients are clearly of a high quality, but provenance isn't mentioned on the menu. When questioned about our Portuguese wine (from an extensive list), the sommelier could only tell us that it was part of a promotion. Service is otherwise unfalteringly pleasant and efficient, but come here for the food rather than the atmosphere.
Babies and children welcome: high chairs; nappy-changing facilities. Booking advisable. Disabled: lift; toilet. Dress: smart casual. Separate rooms for parties, seating 16 and 25. Tables outdoors (17, terrace). Vegetarian menu. **Map 24 B2.**

Shoreditch

Brawn NEW
49 Columbia Road, E2 7RG (7729 5692, www.terroirswinebar.com). Hoxton rail or bus 48, 55. **Lunch served** noon-3pm Mon-Sat; noon-4pm Sun. **Dinner served** 6-11pm Mon-Sat. **Main courses** £16-£27.50. **Set lunch** (Sun) £25 3 courses, £30 incl cheese board. **Credit** MC, V.
As the name suggests, the menu here is a robust affair. Although there's the occasional nod towards salad and vegetables (golden beetroot with watercress and pickled walnuts; English pea and mousseron mushroom risotto) the focus lies elsewhere, with a whole section of the list simply labelled 'pig' (brawn, prosciutto di parma, terrine, rillettes and so on). Many small plates feature (some surprisingly small for the money), such as scallops with gremolata and salted capers. Dishes can be hit and miss – a much-anticipated pigs' trotters with sauce gribiche disappointed, but top-notch smoked sprats with horseradish, and a luscious globe artichoke with vinaigrette, cooked just-so, delighted. Brawn is an offshoot of the very popular wine bar Terroirs, and though the vibe here is altogether cooler (east London hipsters perched on old school chairs in a bare, whitewashed room), it exhibits the same passion for organic or biodynamic 'natural' wines. Beware: such was the waiter's evangelism for these that we ended up with a glass we didn't really like – as well as a delightful 2010 Côtes de Provence rosé cuvée elégance. Bread is scrumptious ('Hackney wild sourdough', by London Fields' bakery E5) and typical of the careful sourcing at work here.
Available for hire. Babies and children welcome: high chairs; nappy-changing facilities. Booking advisable. Disabled: toilet. Separate room for parties, seats 30. **Map 6 S3.**

Spitalfields

The Luxe
109 Commercial Street, E1 6BG (7101 1751, www.theluxe.co.uk). Liverpool Street tube/rail or Shoreditch High Street rail.
Café-bar **Open** 8am-midnight Mon-Thur, Sun; 8am-1am Fri, Sat. **Meals served**

8.30am-4.30pm Mon-Sat; 9.30am-4.45pm Sun.
Main courses £7.50-£11.50.
Restaurant **Lunch served** noon-3pm Mon-Fri;
noon-4pm Sun. **Dinner served** 6-10.45pm
Mon-Sat. **Main courses** £13-£15.
Both **Credit** AmEx, MC, V.
The Luxe is a slightly trendier version of John
Torode's other restaurant-bar complex, Smiths of
Smithfield. There's private dining (top-floor
mezzanine), a restaurant (first floor), a noisy
brasserie (ground floor) and a bar, music and DJ
space (basement). Anyone who wants to talk to their
fellow diners should book a table in the restaurant,
a prettily decorated, light-filled room that runs
around a central kitchen space. The menu is more
interesting than the Mod Euro norm: City boys can
still have a plate of meat (various steaks and a chop
of the day), but other dishes show more originality.
To start, crab and glass noodle salad with thai herbs
and chilli dressing was a generous portion, though
under-flavoured – surprising given the ingredients.
Moreish salt and pepper squid with garlic, chilli and
coriander packed a greater punch. Roast beetroot
salad, with wasabi, edamame houmous, crispy
shallots and watercress was the only starter that
didn't gel, though the individual ingredients were
tasty. Thai jungle curry with guinea fowl was
excellent, the spicing enhancing, rather than
overpowering, the bird. Star of the ice-cream
selection was cherry; even better was the house-
baked cheesecake. Service was attentive, and the
atmosphere relaxing. It's quite a shock to leave via
the jumping joint that is the ground floor – save this
for leisurely weekend brunches, unless you want to
join the party.
*Available for hire. Babies and children welcome:
high chairs; nappy-changing facilities. Booking
advisable restaurant. Bookings not accepted café.
Disabled: lift; toilet. Separate rooms for parties,
seating 30-100. Tables outdoors (3, pavement).
Takeaway service.* **Map 12 R5**.

Victoria Park

Empress

*130 Lauriston Road, E9 7LH (8533 5123,
www.empresse9.co.uk). Mile End tube then bus
277 or 425.* **Brunch served** 10am-noon Sat,
Sun. **Meals served** noon-10.15pm Mon-Sat;
noon-9.30pm Sun. **Main courses** £12-£17.
Credit MC, V.
The Empress has dropped its 'of India' suffix and
British bent in favour of an Italian- and Spanish-
leaning menu that emphasises sharing dishes (its
chefs were previously at Salt Yard and Fino). The
handsome venue now has modern pendant lights
in place of the previous chandeliers and no longer
sports the Empire-era mural, giving it a cleaner
look. The wraparound windows, with enviable
views of Victoria Park, continue to attract passers-
by for drinks and bar snacks (croquetas, tortillas,
charcuterie) in the front section, and flood the airy
space with a beautiful light ideal for weekend
lunches. At dinner, the grazing dishes are appealing:
razor clams with chorizo were a chewy, chilli-
flecked delight, while delicate gnocchi were given
punch with the strong flavours of olive and chard.
A handful of mains included anchovy-stuffed
shoulder of lamb – good quality meat that was
handled well, but stopped short of dazzling. Lemon
polenta cake and panna cotta with strawberries
featured among the simple, seductive desserts.
Portions are smallish, but prettily presented. The
beer selection runs to more than a dozen and

includes Duvel, Chimay and Anchor Steam. Upbeat,
knowledgeable staff play their part in creating a
local gem with plenty of charisma.
*Babies and children welcome: children's menu;
high chairs; nappy-changing facilities. Booking
advisable Fri-Sun. Disabled: toilet. Tables
outdoors (8, pavement). Vegan dishes.*

Wapping

Wapping Food   HOT 50

*Wapping Hydraulic Power Station, Wapping
Wall, E1W 3SG (7680 2080, www.thewapping
project.com). Wapping tube or Shadwell DLR.*
Lunch served noon-3.30pm Mon-Fri; 1-4pm
Sat, Sun. **Brunch served** 10.30am-noon Sat,
Sun. **Dinner served** 6.30-10.30pm Mon-Fri;
7-10.30pm Sat. **Main courses** £15-£22.
Credit AmEx, MC, V.
The Wapping Project has been underway for many
years now. It occupies a barely converted late-
Victorian hydraulic power station that hosts
compelling art and film installations (often in
the stunningly gloomy induction chamber through
a door to the rear), contemporary classical music
concerts and dance shows. The setting is wonderful.
At Wapping Food, you dine under a towering
ceiling, with a backdrop of red-brick walls, hauling
chains and big industrial machines, with rust
showing through their pistachio paint. At weekend
lunchtimes, grown-up families join lushly
bohemian brunchers for simple but largely
successful dishes, such as full-flavoured braised
rabbit and fennel stew; fillet of sea bream served
with cauliflower and lemon butter; or smoked
sprats with pickled cabbage. Only the dessert
disappointed on a recent visit; the gin and tonic
sorbet (a menu regular) seemed to have melted and
been refrozen, as it contained solid blocks of ice.
Our black-clad waitress was detached, though not
inefficient; other staff members were all smiles.
The interesting, all-Australian wine list, which
includes dessert wines and plenty by the glass, has
been joined by some fine cocktails; we enjoyed a
soured elderflower collins in the garden by the
greenhouse bookshop.
*Babies and children welcome: high chairs.
Booking essential Wed-Sun. Disabled: toilet.
Entertainment: performances and exhibitions;
phone for details. Tables outdoors (20, garden).*

Whitechapel

Whitechapel Gallery
Dining Room

*Whitechapel Gallery, 77-82 Whitechapel High
Street, E1 7QX (7522 7888, www.whitechapel
gallery.org/dining-room). Aldgate East tube.*
Lunch served noon-3pm Tue-Sat; noon-
3.45pm Sun. **Dinner served** 6-9.30pm
Wed-Sat. **Main courses** £10.50-£14.95.
Credit AmEx, MC, V.
Recent years have seen the Whitechapel Gallery
cement its reputation as a modern art space, but the
attached dining room hasn't been so consistent,
with two head chefs in as many years. Now, Angela
Hartnett (ex-Gordon Ramsay protégé, and chef-
owner of Murano) is consultant here, along with a
whole new catering firm. Nothing has changed in
the room itself – it's still smart, wood-lined and
warm. The menu is largely British, with only hints
of the Italian influence Hartnett favours elsewhere.
Dishes, though decent, were not hugely exciting,
and not especially good value. Pressed ham terrine

came with nicely tangy piccalilli, but no toast: that
costs extra. Lamb cutlets with salsa verde were just
that – a trio of chops dressed with a smear of rather
polite sauce. Slip sole with brown butter and
shrimps was the highlight, but, again, veg cost
extra. The wine list is better value, with a small
selection peaking at around £30. Water,
commendably, is of the filtered tap variety; £1 per
person gets you unlimited refills, although our
bottle was never replaced. Our tip: if you're visiting
an exhibition at the gallery, remember that the café
is in a different room from the restaurant, well
priced and well worth a visit.
*Babies and children welcome: high chairs;
nappy-changing facilities. Booking advisable.
Disabled: toilet. Separate room for parties,
seats 14.* **Map 12 S6**.

North
Camden Town
& Chalk Farm

Odette's

*130 Regent's Park Road, NW1 8XL (7586 8569,
www.odettesprimrosehill.com). Chalk Farm tube
or bus 31, 168, 274.* **Lunch served** noon-
2.30pm Tue-Fri; noon-3pm Sat, Sun. **Dinner
served** 6.30-10.30pm daily. **Main courses**
£11.50-£25. **Set meal** (lunch Mon-Fri; 6-7pm
daily) £16 2 courses. £20 3 courses; (lunch Sat,
Sun) £20 2 courses, £25 3 courses. **Credit**
AmEx, MC, V.
The grand dame of Primrose Hill sits comfortably
on her laurels, having long been considered one of
the capital's most romantic restaurants. More
recently, it was the showcase for TV chef Bryn
Williams, whose *Great British Menu*-winning dish
of turbot and oxtail has become a menu staple. A
recent refurbishment puts us in mind of a Welsh
stately home, with the intimate series of rooms
decked in moody blue-greens, black and grey – the
colours of Snowdonia in the rain. Service and food
have a formality that is more Mayfair than
Primrose Hill, but the cooking doesn't quite live up
to the prices, and the fiddly presentation seems
pretentious rather than elegant. Wood pigeon with
foie gras, cherries and chocolate sounded good, but
failed to achieve harmony on the plate: the best
element was the little pastry parcel of shredded
pigeon. Do less, achieve more, might be our advice –
yet the straightforward special, of chicken and
mushroom ravioli with chicken broth, wasn't on
the money either, lacking flavour. A tiny scoop of
cheesecake was overwhelmed by fresh
strawberries, jelly cubes, basil, meringues and
honeycomb – about three ingredients too many.
Carefully cooked apricot soufflé with dark chocolate
sorbet made some amends, but, overall, there are
better ways to spend £120.
*Babies and children welcome: high chairs.
Booking essential. Separate room for parties,
seats 20. Tables outdoors (5, garden).*
Map 27 A2.

York & Albany

*127-129 Parkway, NW1 7PS (7388 3344,
www.gordonramsay.com/yorkandalbany).
Camden Town tube.* **Breakfast served**
7-10.30am Mon-Fri; 7-11.30am Sat, Sun.
Lunch served noon-3pm Mon-Fri;

Petersham Nurseries Café

12.15-3pm. **Dinner served** 6-11pm Mon-Sat.
Meals served noon-8.30pm Sun. **Main courses** £15-£22. **Credit** AmEx, MC, V.
Gordon Ramsay's outpost, perched on the edge of Regent's Park, houses a hotel, bar, restaurant and takeaway pizzeria under one lofty Georgian roof. The dining room is faultlessly elegant, with airy vintage decor and serenely formal service to match. It welcomes a well-groomed mix of customers for both business and pleasure, with a menu encompassing pizzas and pasta as well as more typical Modern European dishes. Our meal was topped and tailed by some gorgeous offerings. Plump, crisply coated arancini with harissa made a generous starter for £6; tagliatelle with crab, chilli and lemongrass was fragrant and filling; and a dessert of pistachio cake with melon sorbet and chocolate crumb covered all pudding bases in one exciting plateful. But in the middle, the mains fell short. Lamb rump with coco beans was over-salted and the accompanying caramelised kidney failed to bring much to the dish. Chips were nicely done,but also drowned in salt. Sea bass with crayfish tails, samphire, cauliflower and chorizo sounded lovely, but its fighting textures just didn't work as well on the plate as on the menu. The Y&A provides a pleasant evening's eating, but one that doesn't quite live up to its owner's name.
Babies and children welcome: high chairs; nappy-changing facilities. Booking essential. Disabled: toilet. Separate rooms for parties, seating 24 and 70. Tables outdoors (6, pavement). **Map 3 H1**.

Finsbury Park

Season Kitchen NEW
53 Stroud Green Road, N4 3EF (7263 5500, http://seasonkitchen.co.uk). Finsbury Park tube/rail. **Dinner served** 5.30-10.30pm Tue-Sun. **Main courses** £10.95-£18.50. **Credit** MC, V.
The walk to Season Kitchen, past the wig shops and halal butchers of litter-strewn Stroud Green Road, is part of the dining experience. Once you hit the chalk-drawn menu outside the restaurant – written on the pavement – you know you've arrived. As the name suggests, this neighbourhood joint is big on seasonality. On our visit, the British-leaning menu was playing with comforting winter ingredients, such as cauliflower, jerusalem artichoke and bone marrow. A starter of smoked salmon (prepared in Stoke Newington's Hansen & Lydersen smokehouse) came with sweet and crumbly own-made soda bread, while warm beetroot salad with sorrel and oozing duck egg was delightful in its simplicity. Next: a pleasing vegetarian option of polenta with wild mushroom ragù and smoked mozzarella, even if the tomato sauce slightly overpowered the subtle taste of the funghi. Whole roast wood pigeon was agreeably gamey, though it required plenty of dissection work – and a fingerbowl. We finished with a decadent chocolate and rosemary pot and a warming cup of specially blended Guatemalan filter coffee. The restaurant's stylish grey interior creates a cosy backdrop for dining, whatever the weather.
Available for hire. Babies and children welcome: high chair. Booking advisable. Tables outdoors (4, garden).

Islington

Frederick's
Camden Passage, N1 8EG (7359 2888, www.fredericks.co.uk). Angel tube. **Lunch**
served noon-2.30pm, **dinner served** 5.45-10.30pm Mon-Sat. **Main courses** £12.50-£26. **Set meal** (lunch; dinner Mon, Tue; 5.45-7pm Wed-Sat) £15.50 2 courses, £19 3 courses. **Credit** AmEx, MC, V.
We've had some cause to criticise Frederick's food over the past few years, so were delighted to find some very pleasing dishes on our most recent visit to this spacious restaurant. We still have reservations about some flavour combinations, and prices are on the high side, but the ingredients and culinary skills are of a good standard. After a light waldorf salad – from a selection of ten starters that included squid with chilli sauce, and crab with gazpacho and guacamole – we opted for mains of côte de boeuf, and wild salmon served with broad bean and samphire risotto. The former was perfectly cooked to order, while the latter underlined how different wild salmon can be from farmed; the fish had dense flesh and a complex, almost-earthy flavour. One complaint: vegetarians are barely considered – a note under the fish and meat main courses suggests that diners ask about the vegetarian option. Still, we were pleased by the sophisticated wine list, and an exquisite chocolate tart, served with heavenly coconut ice-cream, was a delicious end to the meal. If dining on a summer evening, ask to be seated near the conservatory's fabulous tree.
Babies and children welcome: children's menu; high chairs. Booking advisable weekends. Separate rooms for parties, seating 16 and 30. Tables outdoors (12, garden). **Map 5 O2**.

North West

West Hampstead

Walnut
280 West End Lane, NW6 1LJ (7794 7772, www.walnutwalnut.com). West Hampstead tube/rail. **Dinner served** 6.30-11pm Tue-Sun. **Lunch served** by arrangement. **Main courses** £13.50-£17.25. **Credit** AmEx, DC, MC, V.
Walnut makes the most of its small space with a kitchen eyrie, the chef calling down to the waitresses when dishes are ready. We had initial qualms about a slightly stained menu and smeary glasses, but these were quickly dispelled by the restaurant's friendly lack of pretension, and the big, honest flavours of the food. Cornish crab cakes were the perfect combination of coarse flavoursome meatiness and crispy crumb crust, while plump seared Scottish scallops were bursting with juicy sweetness. Chef-owner Aidan Doyle is keen on sustainability; all the produce is sourced from good-practice British farmers and fishmongers, and it certainly shows. The quality of meat was exceptional: from the pork belly, falling apart under our forks, to the chargrilled Oxfordshire ribeye with perfect chips. Sides of fresh greens and green beans were just that – unadulterated and delicious. Puddings continue the theme: top-notch ice-creams from a Suffolk creamery, and a warm Fairtrade chocolate tart in the crumbliest of pastries. Walnut attracts a steady stream of loyal (and lucky) locals, so it's worth booking ahead at weekends.
Available for hire. Babies and children welcome: high chairs; nappy-changing facilities. Booking advisable weekends. Tables outdoors (4, pavement). **Map 28 A2**.

Outer London
Kew, Surrey

★ Glasshouse
14 Station Parade, Kew, Surrey, TW9 3PZ (8940 6777, www.glasshouserestaurant.co.uk). Kew Gardens tube/rail. **Lunch served** noon-2.15pm Mon-Sat; 12.30-2.45pm Sun. **Dinner served** 7-10.30pm Mon-Sat; 7-10pm Sun. **Set lunch** (Mon-Fri) £26 3 courses; (Sat) £27.50 3 courses; (Sun) £32.50 3 courses. **Set dinner** £39.50 3 courses. **Credit** AmEx, MC, V.
The Glasshouse (from the same stable as Chez Bruce and La Trompette) continues to fill tables for its beautifully executed food in unpretentious yet elegant surroundings. Unchanged for years, it nonetheless feels timeless. The understated beige interior acts as a blank canvas for rotating pieces of modern art. Likewise, the menu changes daily with seasonal produce, yet familiar favourites are always recurring, keeping regulars happy. Classical flavour combinations are deconstructed, so that each taste sings on its own, as well as combining in perfect balance. Rabbit ballotine had springy chunks of meat offset by salty pancetta shards, sweet prune purée and a quenelle of peppery mustard cream. Succulent saddle of lamb in rich gravy was cut by aniseedy braised fennel, spring onions and roast garlic purée. There are more modern dishes too, such as sea bass sashimi with guacamole and shrimp beignet – a careful balance of textures and bright flavours. Service was slow, so dinner dragged on, but all was forgiven when the Valhrona chocolate pudding arrived with a shattering peanut and praline terrine and silken chocolate sorbet.
Babies and children welcome: high chairs. Booking advisable. Dress: smart casual.

Richmond, Surrey

Petersham Nurseries Café HOT 50
Church Lane, Richmond, Surrey, TW10 7AG (8605 3627, www.petershamnurseries.com). Richmond tube/rail then 30mins walk or bus 65. **Lunch served** 12.30-3pm Wed-Sun. **Main courses** £19.50-£29.50. **Credit** AmEx, MC, V.
A garden-centre café like no other. Bourgeois meets bohemian in the dining area: a large old greenhouse with an earth floor, mismatched furniture and hessian-draped walls hung with art. Head chef Skye Gyngell has been here from the start, in 2004, and it's her use of simple, seasonal ingredients, often from the nursery garden, that has brought the place acclaim. Forget sauces and foams; these ingredients are here to be tasted, and if the flavours don't sing, they won't make it to your plate. From the short menu, a starter of meze with beetroot, red peppers, chickpeas and castelluccio lentils set pulses racing, while a main of Thai-marinated sea bass was delicious if small. As word has spread, prices have crept up, although, notably, not on the wine list: a concise selection of mid-range French and Italian labels. Many diners choose own-made lemonade or fragrant elderflower cordial. The Café is open only for lunch, and booking is essential. If you're not prepared to press redial repeatedly the morning of the month before you want to go, try the non-bookable teahouse next door.
Babies and children welcome: high chairs; nappy-changing facilities. Booking essential, 1 mth in advance. Disabled: toilet. Tables outdoors (25, garden).

North African

Parts of the Maghreb may gave gone through revolutionary tumult in recent times, but London's compact North African dining scene has settled into stability. **Momo** gave the cuisine a burst in the limelight when it opened in the 1990s, attracting A-listers aplenty with its sexy take on Moroccan food and interior design, and though the venue is now more than 15 years old, some of the stardust still lingers. You'll also find sumptuous surroundings, and cocktails, at **Pasha**. However, if you simply want to sample the tagines and couscous dishes that are the bedrock of the cuisine, and prefer low-key, family-run restaurants, make a beeline for **Adam's Café**, where you'll also be able to savour some Tunisian specialities.

Central
Edgware Road

Sidi Maarouf
56-58 Edgware Road, W2 2JE (7724 0525, www.maroush.com). Marble Arch tube.
Meals served noon-12.30pm Mon-Sat; noon-midnight Sun. **Main courses** £14-£18. **Set meal** £30-£35 4 courses. **Credit** AmEx, DC, MC, V.
With shisha smokers stationed two deep under the awning, diners must pass through a haze of smoke before reaching the more sparsely occupied restaurant. Under a silk-canopied ceiling, the interior, dominated by dark wood and leather club chairs, seems comparatively gloomy. All the tempting North African staples are here at the Maroush chain's Moroccan outpost. Of these, the best bets are the briouats. For our vegetarian's sake, we asked the waiter to identify which of the mixed selection of crisp filo triangles and cylinders were meat-free. 'This one or this one is chicken or cheese,' he said cryptically, pointing at two indistinguishable parcels. Along with a lemony-fresh fattoush salad, these subtly seasoned pastries were the highlights. Starter plates including a so-so houmous were whipped away before we'd finished. Vegetable couscous and vegetable tagine were both dishwater dreary, the soggy veg not enhanced by any distinctive spicing. Poor value too. Maybe you pay for the 'live entertainment' – a man behind a synthesiser pumping out insistent music, and at weekends there are belly dancers to make more of an event of it. The couscous certainly wasn't the attraction; some pastries and a pipe on the street might be preferable.

Available for hire. Babies and children admitted. Booking advisable. Entertainment: belly dancer 9.30pm, 10.30pm Thur-Sun. Tables outdoors (6, pavement). **Map 8 F6**.

Gloucester Road

★ Pasha
1 Gloucester Road, SW7 4PP (7589 7969, www.pasha-restaurant.co.uk). Gloucester Road tube. **Meals served** noon-11pm Mon-Wed, Sun; noon-midnight Thur-Sat. **Main courses** £13-£26. **Set meal** £30-£40 per person (minimum 2). **Credit** AmEx, DC, MC, V.
A night out at Pasha is a sumptuous experience. Rich fabrics, flickering candles, beaded lamps, carved doorways and North African music combine to evoke an exotic atmosphere. From the moment you enter, service is quick and attentive, with much effort placed on making you feel welcome. Food lives up to the surroundings, and whether you choose the 'feast' set menu option or pick your own array of dishes, feasting is certainly encouraged. Starters consist of meze-style small plates, among them lamb, ras el hanout (a commonly used spice blend) and prunes enveloped in crisp ouarka pastry; spiced aubergine dip; and prawns wrapped in kataifyi pastry. As a main, s'csou darna deserves special mention: tender morsels of braised lamb, chicken and merguez sausage come with a host of delicious extras, each plated on its own dish (steamed couscous, vegetable broth, plump golden sultanas, spiced chickpeas and a potent harissa). The wine list includes Moroccan and Lebanese entries, and the cocktail menu contains some cheekily adapted favourites such as Bloody Harissa and a Date Old Fashioned. Pasha isn't cheap, but the food and service make it worth the price.

Available for hire. Babies and children welcome: high chairs. Booking advisable. Separate room for parties, seats 20. Tables outdoors (2, pavement). Takeaway service. **Map 13 C9**.

Marylebone

Original Tagines
7A Dorset Street, W1U 6QN (7935 1545, www.original-tagines.com). Baker Street tube.
Meals served 11am-11pm Mon-Fri; 2-11pm Sat. **Dinner served** 6-11pm Sun. **Main courses** £12.95-£15.95. **Set lunch** £8.50 2 courses. **Credit** MC, V.
This small, unpretentious place near Baker Street has a family-run feel. Our amiable waitress also helped out in the kitchen, which has a window on the dining area. The paintwork and mosaic tabletops seem rather shabby, but otherwise the surroundings are simple and inoffensive, featuring brass lamps and colourful ceramic plates. Mixed meze is a fine way to start a meal, the platter crammed with paprika-scented red peppers, aubergines in tomato and cumin sauce, and silky houmous. Mains cover couscous, tagines and grilled meats. Several of the tagines marry lamb with fruit – pear, apricot or prunes, the latter of which we chose. The sweet and salty combination in this soupy dish (which also contained hard-boiled eggs and potatoes) made the flavourful lamb immensely appetising, although the accompanying side of bulky bulgur wheat proved more than we could eat. The couscous in a mixed vegetable main course was far more appealing, the saffron-scented grain beautifully light and moreish, despite the overcooked veg. The extra stock we were given was a homely touch. Our fellow diners on a Thursday night were limited to

two families, though groups also dine here; staff accommodated a walk-in request for a party of 12. *Available for hire. Babies and children welcome: high chairs. Booking advisable. Tables outdoors (5, pavement). Takeaway service.* **Map 3 G5**.

Mayfair

★ Momo   `HOT 50`

25 Heddon Street, W1B 4BH (7434 4040, www.momoresto.com). Piccadilly Circus tube. **Lunch served** noon-3pm Mon-Sat. **Dinner served** 6.30pm-midnight daily. **Main courses** £17-£28. **Set lunch** £15 2 courses, £19 3 courses. **Credit** AmEx, DC, MC, V.

With an outside terrace on Heddon Street – hedonism itself on a summer's evening – and an interior of mesmerising beats, intricate carved wood, filigree metalwork, sumptuous fabrics, and subtle lights playing on crystal glasses, the atmosphere at Momo is intoxicating and seductive. A cosmopolitan clientele ranged from a baby in a buggy through dressed-up couples to smooth businessmen sporting expensive watches. Prominence is nonetheless given to the food, evidenced by the pyrotechnics behind the counter. And there's a finesse to dishes such as the grilled sardine starter, the fish fillets resting on soft roast peppers and a crisp pastry galette. Moroccan salad is Momo's name for a fine fattoush; puffy bread performs juice-mopping duty. Come the main courses, the copper tabletop is laden with fragrant dishes of fruit and meat tagines: orange-zest flavoured chicken, or lamb, prunes and almonds on a bed of sweet, slow-cooked onions, with fluffy couscous. An accompanying dish of chickpeas and sultanas was heady with the scent of orange flower water. All that was missing from the table was the bottle of Moroccan rosé irritatingly kept out of reach in a bucket. A glamorous and enjoyable, if not bargain-priced, evening that ended sweetly with syrupy mint tea in pretty glasses.
Available for hire. Babies and children admitted. Booking advisable weekends. Disabled: toilet. Tables outdoors (14, terrace). **Map 17 A4**. **For branch (Mô Café) see index.**

West

Shepherd's Bush

★ ★ Adam's Café

77 Askew Road, W12 9AH (8743 0572, www.adamscafe.co.uk). Hammersmith tube then 266 bus. **Breakfast served** 7.30am-2pm Mon-Fri; 8.30am-2pm Sat. **Dinner served** 7-11pm Mon-Sat. **Set dinner** £11.50 1 course incl mint tea or coffee, £14.50 2 courses, £16.95 3 courses. **Licensed**. **Corkage** (wine) £3. **Credit** AmEx, MC, V.

With a name like Adam's Café and a daytime menu of full english and other greasy spoon favourites, you might not expect the nightly transformation into a cosy North African bistro. Head here after 7pm, though, and mottled lampshades scatter pretty patterns of light across a candlelit room that's decorated in muted blues and greens, with ornate ceramic tiling. In-the-know locals often fill the place. The menu is helpfully split into prices for one, two or three courses; you can mix and match as you like and it's great value. Briks, doigts de fatma and cigares – all crisp little pastries, surprisingly light and delicately spiced, with meat, seafood or vegetarian fillings – are highlights among the starters. Main courses include tagines and couscous, as well as a variety of grilled meats and fish. The chefs hail from Morocco and Tunisia,

Menu

North African food has similarities with other cuisines; see the menu boxes in **Middle Eastern** and **Turkish**.

Brik: minced lamb or tuna and a raw egg bound in paper-thin pastry, then fried.
Briouats, **briouettes** or **briwat**: little envelopes of deep-fried, paper-thin ouarka (qv) pastry; can contain ground meat, rice or cheese, or be served as a sweet, flavoured with almond paste, nuts or honey.
Chermoula: a dry marinade of fragrant herbs and spices.
Couscous: granules of processed durum wheat. The name is also given to a dish where the slow-cooked grains are topped with a meat or vegetable stew; couscous royale usually involves lamb, chicken and merguez (qv).
Harira: lamb, lentil and chickpea soup.
Harissa: very hot chilli pepper paste flavoured with garlic and spices.
Maakouda: spicy potato fried in breadcrumbs.
Merguez: spicy, paprika-rich lamb sausages.
Ouarka: filo-like pastry.
Pastilla, **bastilla** or **b'stilla**: an ouarka (qv) envelope with a traditional filling of pigeon, almonds, spices and egg, baked then dusted with cinnamon and powdered sugar. Chicken is often substituted for pigeon.
Tagine or **tajine**: a shallow earthenware dish with a conical lid; it gives its name to a slow-simmered stew of meat (usually lamb or chicken) and vegetables, often cooked with olives, preserved lemon or prunes.

Sidi Maarouf

NORTH AFRICAN

and the subtlety of the aromatic dishes shows their homelands' cuisines in their best light. Complimentary appetisers, a leisurely atmosphere and optional BYO add to diners' sense of well-being. *Available for hire. Babies and children admitted. Booking advisable weekends. Separate room for parties, seats 24. Vegetarian menu.* **Map 20 A1**.

North

Islington

Maghreb

189 Upper Street, N1 1RQ (7226 2305, www.maghreb-restaurant.com). Highbury & Islington tube/rail. **Meals served** 6-11.30pm Mon-Thur; 5-11.30pm Fri-Sun. **Main courses** £9.50-£14.50. **Set dinner** £14.95 2 courses, £18.95 3 courses. **Credit** AmEx, MC, V.

The orange glow from Maghreb makes a cheery sight on Upper Street; the welcome is equally warm, with owner Mohamed Faraji often on hand to greet diners. Past experience tells us his kitchen is at its best when cooking the Moroccan classics that comprise most of the menu. A good way to sample a range of these is to order the mixed meze starter. This brought to our table little plates of houmous, marinated olives and artichoke, zaaluk (steamed aubergine with tomato, coriander and preserved lemon), stewed lentils, and carrot and orange with cumin. Unfortunately, the accompanying bread was burnt. Mains (grills, seafood, tajines) are generously proportioned, and while some could be more robustly flavoured, everything is solidly done. Moroccan kebab with couscous had chunks of

Budget bites

Couscous Café

7 Porchester Gardens, W2 4DB (7727 6597). Bayswater tube. **Meals served** noon-11.30pm daily. **Main courses** £9.95-£15.95. **Licensed**. **Corkage** no charge. **Credit** MC, V.

The solitary table outside this small Moroccan restaurant does little to belie the exotic haven that awaits inside. It feels like entering an authentic Moroccan bazaar: a romantic clutter of trinkets (instruments, oil paintings and bellows) dim illumination from ornate lanterns, and the sweet, slow waft of incense in the air. Tagines, skewered meat dishes and stews are served with exceptionally fluffy couscous, rice or flatbread by staff who are more than willing to help you through the menu. Milk and fruit combos feature alongside an unremarkable selection of alcoholic beverages. *Babies and children admitted. Tables outdoors (1, patio). Takeaway service.* **Map 7 C6**.

Le Rif

172 Seven Sisters Road, N7 7PX (no phone). Finsbury Park tube/rail. **Meals served** 8am-10pm Mon-Fri; noon-10pm Sat, Sun. **Main courses** £4-£6. **Unlicensed** no alcohol allowed. **No credit cards**.

While the decoration at Le Rif is far from inventive – several gaudy Arabic weavings tacked to the walls and a slight decked terrace are all that distinguish it from any typical N7 caff – the food remains excellent. We recommend you opt for the tagines: tender lamb sweetened with prunes and cinnamon, or spiced chicken with apricots and almonds served on a light layer of couscous – a steal at less than £6 each. There's no alcohol at this amiable Moroccan, but fruit smoothies and mint tea make for satisfying accompaniments. *Babies and children admitted. Tables outdoors (5, patio). Takeaway service.*

tender, marinated lamb, gently spiced; the large selection of tagines includes lentil and pumpkin, and a more unusual venison with redcurrant and caramelised quince. Throw in drinks (pleasingly, there are several classy Moroccan wines to sample) and things can seem pricey, but the £14.95 two-

course deal balances things out. Not Islington's most exciting restaurant, but a dependable and welcoming stalwart. *Available for hire. Babies and children welcome: high chairs. Booking advisable. Takeaway service.* **Map 5 O1**.

Pan-Asian & Fusion

London has become the world's gastronomic laboratory. This most multicultural of cities is in a unique position to forge new approaches to cooking, using ingredients sourced from across the globe. How come? Talented chefs discover they aren't hidebound by convention here; they can find inspiration, and ample culinary skill, at London's abundance of restaurants from five continents. They can easily purchase exotic herbs, spices and condiments in this major centre of international trade; and they have a ready supply of adventurous diners eager to experiment.

Sometimes, the cooking styles of Asia – from Japan to Malaysia and beyond – are synthesised, as at the excellent **Champor-Champor** or at Will Ricker's chain of sexy, eternally fashionable restaurants, **Great Eastern Dining Room** included. That this hybrid pan-Asian cuisine is popular is further evidenced by the opening of glamorous **Spice Market** (a clone of the New York original). Occasionally, an east-west fusion is produced (try the Franco-Ital-Japanese **L'Etranger** or the French-Calif-Asian flavours of **Rosemary Lane**); and in a few instances ingredients from across the entire world are placed in the culinary crucible (renowned experts the **Modern Pantry** and the **Providores & Tapa Room** have recently been joined by Yotam Ottolenghi's new **NOPI**). The results of such innovation can be abominable, but they can also be exciting. These are the restaurants to convert any doubters.

Central
Clerkenwell & Farringdon

The Modern Pantry
47-48 St John's Square, EC1V 4JJ (7250 0833, www.themodernpantry.co.uk). Farringdon tube/ rail.
Café **Breakfast served** 8-11am Mon-Fri.
Brunch served 9am-4pm Sat; 10am-4pm Sun.
Meals served noon-10pm Mon; noon-11pm Tue-Fri; 6-11pm Sat; 6-10pm Sun.
Restaurant **Lunch served** noon-3pm Tue-Fri; 10am-4pm Sun. **Dinner served** 6-11pm Tue-Sat.
Both **Main courses** £15-£22.50. **Set lunch** (Mon-Fri) £19 2 courses; (Sun) £18.50 2 courses, £23.50 3 courses. **Credit** AmEx, MC, V.
Light and bright, the Modern Pantry is decorated in shades of white and grey. There are formal dining rooms on the first floor, a more relaxed space on the ground floor, and outdoor seating on St John's Square (plus a small 'pantry' selling sandwiches, pies, cakes and so on, to one side). The wonderfully eclectic all-day menu is the same throughout. Dishes run from small plates such as sweetcorn, date and feta fritters with rose yoghurt, or chorizo scotched quail eggs with tomato relish, to main courses such as grilled tamarind miso-marinated onglet steak with cassava chips, smoky apricot relish and salad leaves; or panko and parmesan-crusted veal escalope with asparagus, mustard sauce and salsa verde. Breakfast might feature grilled chorizo with caramelised plantain fritters and slow-roasted vine-ripened tomatoes, while there are green tea scones with gooseberry compote and clotted cream for afternoon tea. The woman responsible for these exhilarating ingredients and combinations is owner/chef Anna Hansen; she grew up in New Zealand (and worked with Peter Gordon for years, running Providores with him until 2005). To see her in action, book a cooking demonstration (£100 a head), which features canapés and prosecco, a 90-minute demo, and a four-course dinner.
Available for hire. Babies and children welcome: high chairs. Booking essential weekends.
Disabled: toilet. Separate room for parties, seats 40. Tables outdoors (13, square). **Map 5 O4**.

Fitzrovia

Bam-Bou
1 Percy Street, W1T 1DB (7323 9130, www.bam-bou.co.uk). Goodge Street or Tottenham Court Road tube.
Bar **Open** 5.30pm-1am Mon-Sat.
Restaurant **Lunch served** noon-3pm Mon-Fri. **Dinner served** 5.30-11pm Mon-Sat. **Main courses** £9.50-£14.50. **Set meal** (noon-3pm Mon-Fri; 5.30-7pm Mon-Sat) £15.25 2 courses, £18.75 3 courses.
Both **Credit** AmEx, MC, V.
Large Buddha carvings and mahogany-framed traditional Chinese paintings – washed over with Sino-Balearic chill-out muzak – are standard issue these days for contemporary pan-Asian restaurants. In this respect, Bam-Bou offers no surprises, and attracts a buzzy crowd of West End shoppers and polished Charlotte Street denizens. What might distinguish it is the high-quality service from attentive, polite and professional staff. The menu, including a good-value set meal, encompasses influences from China to Vietnam, and adds distinctively modern accents; the deep-fried soft-shell crabs with chilli mayonnaise are a digit-sucking case in point. Slow-roasted duck thigh was crispy and fragrant, enhanced by a deliciously salty and tangy plum dipping sauce; yellow curry with sweet squash and meltingly soft aubergine was gently spiced if slightly cloying. Like the decor, however, the exotic fruit platter – with pineapple, mango and melon – wasn't as exotic as it pretended to be, and the crumbly, unremarkable petits fours weren't the meal's strongest point. Yet in a city where broadly oriental food is commonplace, Bam-Bou (which belongs to the group that runs Scott's and the Ivy) succeeds in offering something a little more elevated in terms of flavour and service.

NOPI

Babies and children admitted. Booking advisable. Separate rooms for parties, seating 8-20. Tables outdoors (4, terrace). **Map 17 B1**.

Crazy Bear

26-28 Whitfield Street, W1T 2RG (7631 0088, www.crazybeargroup.co.uk). Goodge Street or Tottenham Court Road tube.
Bar **Open** noon-midnight Mon-Thur; noon-1am Fri; 6pm-1am Sat. **Dim sum served** noon-10.45pm Mon-Fri; 6-10.45pm Sat.
Restaurant **Meals/dim sum served** noon-10.45pm Mon-Fri; 6-10.45pm Sat. **Dim sum** £4-£9. **Main courses** £12-£32. **Set meal** £39-£47 tasting menu.
Both **Credit** AmEx, MC, V.
Crazy Bear is perfectly positioned to appeal to the flashier, cash-rich segment of Fitzrovia's media crowd. Smartly black-clad staff whisk you to restaurant tables, or downstairs to the dimly lit bar, with an appropriate hint of froideur. Decor, like the menu, is all about surface sheen – dig deeper and you'll find those romantic tables for two are, in fact, highly uncomfortable, and the cooking, while pleasant enough, doesn't justify its high prices. Chefs are drawn from Thailand, Japan and China to produce a menu that ranges from familiar maki rolls and shrimp crackers to inventive chargrilled lamb cutlets with French beans, XO sauce, mango and mint. Impressively, the Crazy Bear Group's own farm in Oxfordshire provides Gloucestershire Old Spot pork and Welsh Badger Face lamb. The basement has pretty much everything you want from a cocktail bar, including dim sum and sushi from the restaurant kitchen. Its booze list is well thought out, and the cocktails are elegantly constructed and served with care. They range from traditional – try the sazerac (rye, Peychaud's and Angostura, proper absinthe rinse for the tumbler) – to the likes of 'after dinner' passionfruit brûlée (cognac, honey vodka, passionfruit). On the whole, for a night out we prefer it to the restaurant.
Babies and children admitted. Booking advisable. Vegan dishes. Vegetarian menu. **Map 17 B1**.

Gloucester Road

★ L'Etranger

36 Gloucester Road, SW7 4QT (7584 1118, www.etranger.co.uk). Gloucester Road tube.
Lunch served noon-3pm Mon-Fri. **Brunch served** noon-3pm Sun. **Dinner served** 5.30-11pm Mon-Thur; 5.30-11.30pm Fri, Sat; 5.30-10pm Sun. **Main courses** £16.50-£32.50. **Set meal** (lunch, 5.30-6.45pm Mon-Fri) £21 2 courses, £24 3 courses, £36 4 courses; (6-11pm Mon-Sat, 6-10pm Sun) £59-£109 tasting menu. **Credit** AmEx, MC, V.
Within a large, modishly grey building, with its own wine shop next door, L'Etranger's monochrome dining room features black leather seating and black tables. Considerate staff made us feel relaxed from the start. The Euro-Asian menu is divertingly eclectic; few lists feature dover sole with asparagus and tomato concasse next to grade-nine wagyu beef nigiri with honey-flavoured soy. Raw meat and fish are kitchen favourites. Four different tartare (a twist on steak tartare) are offered, including one of Charolais beef plated with truffled polenta chips. A five-tomato salad was like summer unfolding, an absolute belter of colours and textures: creamy burrata infused with truffle and topped with balsamic caviar played beautifully next to a basil and tomato sorbet, and assorted cuts and

shades of tomatoes. We were equally impressed with a 'surf and turf' main course of pan-fried monkfish in a herb crust, paired with wagyu beef binding together black rice and fennel carpaccio, completed by a hint of shichimi pepper. Desserts are more familiar, and we finished on a high note with a giant pistachio and kalamansi (South-east Asian citrus fruit) macaroon sandwich filled with wild strawberries. To match the extraordinary food, there's an equally diverse blockbuster wine list, including saké. You'll need a fat wallet to dine here, but the quality justifies the prices.
Available for hire. Babies and children welcome: high chairs. Booking advisable. Separate room for parties, seats 20. Vegetarian menu. **Map 13 C9**.

Marylebone

★ The Providores & Tapa Room `HOT 50`

109 Marylebone High Street, W1U 4RX (7935 6175, www.theprovidores.co.uk). Baker Street or Bond Street tube.
The Providores **Lunch served** noon-2.45pm Mon-Fri. **Brunch served** noon-2.45pm Sat, Sun. **Dinner served** 6-10.30pm Mon-Sat; 6-10.15pm Sun. **Main courses** (lunch) £17-£25. **Set dinner** £32 2 courses, £46 3 courses, £56 4 courses, £62 5 courses. **Cover** (brunch) £1.50.
Tapa Room **Breakfast/brunch served** 9-11.30am Mon-Fri; 10am-3pm Sat, Sun. **Meals served** noon-10.30pm Mon-Fri; 4-10.30pm Sat; 4-10pm Sun. **Tapas** £2-£14.40.
Both **Credit** AmEx, MC, V.
This beacon of fusion cuisine in Britain has also done much to inspire the wave of gastro coffee bars and café-brasseries opening across the capital. The ground floor Tapa Room serves food and fabulous coffee (an exclusive blend supplied by Monmouth) almost all day – worth noting, for we've found the kitchen's 11.30am to midday break can be mighty inconvenient. The breakfast/brunch menu, which contains everything you might fancy, from date scones through boiled eggs and fry-ups to grilled chorizo with sweet potato and miso hash, is rightly revered, and attracts killer queues on market days. Vegetarians have a stupendous choice, as do other health fiends (spirulina smoothie, anyone?). Upstairs is the Providores, a tightly packed dining room that's formal but friendly. Here, chef-patron Peter Gordon's talent for combining seemingly disparate flavours and textures really soars: witness the pan-Asian combination of tandoori halibut with brown shrimp and dashi chawanmushi (Japanese savoury custard), vegetable achard (a Malaysian pickle) and chickpea water. Even a bowl of own-made ices is turned into a sensation of new tastes with the addition of caramelised gooseberry cardamom compote. An Officer of the New Zealand Order of Merit, Gordon wears his antipodean heritage with understated pride; note the exclusively New Zealand, very high-end wine list.
Babies and children welcome: high chairs. Booking advisable Providores; bookings not accepted Tapa Room. Disabled: toilet. Tables outdoors (2, pavement). **Map 9 G5**.

Mayfair

Sketch: The Gallery

9 Conduit Street, W1S 2XG (7659 4500, www.sketch.uk.com). Oxford Circus tube. **Dinner served** 7-10.30pm Mon-Wed; 7-11pm Thur-Sat. **Main courses** £12-£32. **Credit** AmEx, MC, V.

The Gallery occupies the middle ground in the gloriously ostentatious (some may say pretentious) surroundings of Sketch, pitched as it is between a bistro and a haute cuisine destination. As with everything in Sketch, it's hugely expensive: not that poverty troubles the high-fashion clientele drawn here by the hip staff and quirky design touches that pepper the vast, chatter-filled room. (Early bookings might find it rather quiet, however.) Animated projections provide most of the light, leaving diners to peer through the gloom at the menu. From its classical French roots, the list takes a footloose and unfettered trip around the world. Foie gras terrine might be accompanied by pickled girolles, tamarillo paste and pine nuts; beef fillet by sarawak black pepper; udon noodles by tofu, pear and lemongrass. It's high-ambition stuff, although sometimes not as mind-blowing in outcome as the esoteric ingredients and setting might suggest. Unlike the upstairs Lecture Room & Library, there are no amuse-bouche or freebies here – bread costs extra, a side order of steamed veg is £5.50. As with the other Sketch venues, the Gallery is a 'scene' as much as a restaurant, and one you'll need to suspend economy to become part of.
Available for hire. Booking essential. Disabled: toilet. Entertainment: DJs 11pm-2am Thur-Sat. Separate rooms for parties, seats 150. **Map 9 J6**.

Soho

NOPI `NEW`

2011 RUNNER-UP BEST NEW DESIGN
21 Warwick Street, W1B 5NE (7494 9584, www.nopi-restaurant.com). Piccadilly Circus tube. **Breakfast/lunch served** 8am-2.45pm, **dinner served** 5.30-11.30pm Mon-Fri. **Meals served** 9am-11.30pm Sat; 10am-4pm Sun. **Main courses** £8-£13. **Credit** AmEx, MC, V.
NOPI, from the Ottolenghi stable, is a sparkling, fresh-faced addition to Soho's dining scene. Interior designer Alex Meitlis has taken elements of the traditional brasserie aesthetic and rehoused them in a light white space. Brass features not in rails but neat square tabletops, champagne buckets and bazaar-style lighting; marble (veined with glowing golden streaks) is used for the floor, and mirrors line the fabulously disorientating toilets. Serene though the ground-floor dining room is, it's hard not to love the basement communal tables next to the open kitchen. It feels as if you're eating in a private home; the space doubles as the supplies store, with chunky shelves heavy with catering packs of oregano and at least six different vinegars. We've had mixed experiences with the food. For breakfast, shakshuka (Tunisian braised eggs) was spot-on with its spicing. Thai black sticky rice porridge was also authentic, but dinky presentation only highlighted the ordinariness of the recipe. Yet creative dishes didn't fare better: courgette and manouri fritters had too much uncooked batter in the centre. Tea came in bags – not classy. On the plus side, we loved dinnertime cured halibut with lemony oil, shiso and samphire, and rich burrata cleverly accompanied by toasted coriander and blood orange.
Available for hire. Babies and children welcome: high chairs. Booking advisable dinner. **Map 17 A4**.

Spice Market `NEW`

W London, 10 Wardour Street, W1D 6QF (7758 1088, www.spicemarketlondon.co.uk). Leicester Square tube. **Breakfast served**

Best oriental chains

For good looks and a quick fix of flavours from across the Far East, try one of these popular chain restaurants.

Banana Tree Canteen

412-416 St John Street, EC1V 4NJ (7278 7565, www.bananatreecanteen. com). Angel tube. **Meals served** noon-11pm Mon-Sat; noon-10.30pm Sun. **Main courses** £5.75-£9.85. **Set meal** (noon-6pm Mon-Fri; noon-5pm Sat, Sun) £5.95-£7.45. **Credit** AmEx, MC, V.

Mini-chain Banana Tree Canteen sells itself on the cooking of Indo-China. In truth, there's little to showcase the traditional dishes of Cambodia, Myanmar or Laos: instead, the menu follows a well-trodden, backpacker-friendly route, majoring on hawker staples such as Vietnamese spring rolls or Malaysian satay chicken ahead of pad thai or the Singaporean version of mee goreng. A few lesser-seen dishes include a fabulous spicy aubergine and tamarind curry. Mains all cost less than a tenner.

Babies and children welcome: children's menu; high chairs; nappy-changing facilities. Disabled: toilet. Takeaway service. **Map 5 N3.**
For branches (Banana Leaf Canteen, Street Hawker) see index.

dim t

56-62 Wilton Road, SW1V 1DE (7834 0507, www.dimt.co.uk). Victoria tube/rail. **Meals served** noon-11pm Mon-Sat; noon-10.30pm Sun. **Dim sum** £3.60-£3.85. **Main courses** £7.65-£8.55. **Credit** AmEx, MC, V.

With its dark, slick interiors, dim t has the oriental swagger of an A-list establishment, but with a much more affordable price-tag. Unfortunately, the cooking doesn't always live up to expectations, particularly in the selection of dim sum that leads the charge: on recent visits, pastry has been thick and doughy, while fillings were bland. Elsewhere, the menu is a pick 'n' mix of popular pan-Asian fare, from crispy duck with pancakes to thai green curry or stir-fried yaki soba. After dark, the compact choice of exotic cocktails is a draw, while weekends cater more to families.

Babies and children welcome: children's menu; high chairs; nappy-changing facilities. Booking advisable. Disabled: toilet. Takeaway service. **Map 15 J10.**
For branches see index.

Feng Sushi

1 Adelaide Road, NW3 3QE (7483 2929, www.fengsushi.co.uk). Chalk Farm tube. **Meals served** 11.30am-10pm Mon, Sun; 11.30am-10.30pm Tue, Wed; 11.30am-11pm Thur-Sat. **Main courses** £7-£18. **Set meal** £12 bento box. **Credit** MC, V.

While its competitors shout loudly, Feng Sushi quietly goes about its business, consistently delivering on quality. Taking its cues from both traditional and modern

Banana Tree Canteen

Japanese kitchens, the menu includes stalwarts such as nigiri, maki and tempura, as well as more fashionable options, such as tuna tartare on pickled cucumber with a yuzu and miso dressing, or seasonal specials such as crispy battered pollock served with a Japanese salsa verde. It's not cheap, but with MSC certification as well as numerous organic or brown rice variations, you're sure to come away feeling wholesome and virtuous.

Babies and children admitted. Disabled: toilet. Takeaway service; delivery service (over £12 within 3-mile radius). **Map 27 B1.**
For branches see index.

Itsu

118 Draycott Avenue, SW3 3AE (7590 2400, www.itsu.com). South Kensington tube. **Meals served** noon-11pm Mon-Sat; noon-10pm Sun. **Main courses** £3-£8. **Set meal** £4.50-£9.99 bento box. **Credit** AmEx, MC, V.

Long a haven for the see-and-be-seen crowd of SW3, this branch of Itsu has much in its favour. The ground floor is home to a traditional kaiten (conveyor belt), albeit with less-than-traditional plates: Vietnamese-inspired rice-paper rolls packed with fresh herbs and chilli crab; seaweed salad with seared tuna; or sashimi 'new style' with strips of ginger and a sesame dressing. The upstairs bar – a more peaceful daytime option – comes with waiter service: order from the conveyor menu or a made-to-order list (crispy baby squid, teriyaki-marinated grilled eel). Be warned: the bill can mount steeply.

Babies and children welcome: booster seats. Bookings not accepted. Takeaway service; delivery service (over £20 within 3-mile radius). **Map 14 E10.**
For branches see index.

Ping Pong

45 Great Marlborough Street, W1F 7JL (7851 6969, www.pingpongdimsum.com). Oxford Circus tube. **Dim sum served** noon-midnight Mon-Sat; noon-10.30pm Sun.

Dim sum 99p-£6.69. **Set meal** £9.99-£36. **Credit** AmEx, MC, V.

Credited with bringing dim sum to the masses, this, the original branch of Ping Pong, opened back in 2005. Since then, it has spawned almost a dozen offshoots across town, all with the same attractive formula of smart, sexy surroundings, decent cocktails and a large selection of the popular steamed parcels – available all day. Standards can be wobbly, with dumplings all too often coming with thick, claggy pastry – it's best to head for dishes that don't require as much finesse, such as Vietnamese prawn paper-rolls, or the signature honey-glazed ribs.

Babies and children welcome: high chairs; nappy-changing facilities. Bookings not accepted for fewer than 8 people. Disabled: toilet. Takeaway service. **Map 17 A3.**
For branches see index.

Wagamama

1 Ropemaker Street, EC2Y 9AW (7588 2688, www.wagamama.com). Moorgate tube/rail. **Meals served** 11.30am-10pm Mon-Fri. **Main courses** £6.75-£13. **Credit** AmEx, MC, V.

Everyone has their favourite Wagamama dish, and this branch of the nation's favourite noodle bar can cater for the lot. Whether it's a slurpy, soupy bowl of chicken (a generous portion of wheat noodles in broth, topped with thick slabs of breast meat), a huge mound of colourful stir-fried udon studded with chicken, prawns and veg, or one of the increasingly popular rice bowls, you're unlikely to leave hungry. Even so, many diners also indulge in side plates (which, as opposed to starters, arrive as soon as they're ready) of gyoza, breaded prawns or chicken yakitori.

Babies and children welcome: children's menu; high chairs. Disabled: toilet. Takeaway service. Vegan dishes. **Map 12 Q5.**
For branches see index.

Yo! Sushi

52 Poland Street, W1F 7NQ (7287 0443, www.yosushi.com). Oxford Circus tube. **Meals served** noon-11pm Mon-Sat; noon-10.30pm Sun. **Dishes** £1.70-£5. **Credit** AmEx, DC, MC, V.

Yo! Sushi's Poland Street branch is where many Londoners got their first taste of conveyor-belt dining. With its loud music and call buttons for service, Yo! Is quirky and fun, but not for sushi aficionados. Special offers and free refills of soft drinks and soup make it popular with wallet-watchers, while the menu constantly reinvents itself, with innovative specials (scallop katsu, salmon and tobiko tartare) supplementing a wide range of sushi, tempura and teriyaki.

Babies and children welcome: high chairs. Disabled: toilet. Takeaway service. Vegetarian menu. **Map 17 A3.**
For branches see index.

7-11am Mon-Fri; 8-11.30am Sat, Sun. **Meals served** noon-11pm Mon-Wed, Sun; noon-11.30pm Thur-Sat. **Main courses** £16-£32. **Set lunch** (noon-4pm) £16 2 courses, £18 3 courses. **Set dinner** (5.30-6.30pm, 10-11pm) £18 2 courses, £20 3 courses; £48 tasting menu. **Credit** AmEx, MC, V.

Chef Jean-Georges Vongerichten now has a 29-restaurant empire across the globe, and his London venture replicates a venue he opened in New York's Meatpacking District. It's a capacious, moodily lit space in the swanky W London hotel. The glitzy, Manhattan-meets-Orient interior features a large open kitchen, black or orange seating at ground-floor and mezzanine level, and parquet flooring. The menu provides a selective jaunt across Asia. It's Thai with the edges taken off, pseudo-Indian, cod Vietnamese, vaguely Malaysian, Japanese redux. Prices are vertiginously high. Yet though dishes are often a hybrid of many cuisines, the food shouldn't be dismissed. Thought has gone into such starters as shaved tuna, chilli tapioca, asian pear and lime, or a main of chargrilled chicken with kumquat and lemongrass dressing. Menus change regularly, but the best choice at our latest meal was turbot cha ca la vong: a prettified version of the Hanoi classic, the fish topped with crushed peanuts and fresh herbs, all resting on a bed of noodles above a thin broth of coconut and turmeric. Service is formal, but in the US way: faultless, yet executed to a rigorous formula that doesn't leave much room for improvisation.
Available for hire. Babies and children welcome: high chairs; nappy-changing facilities. Booking advisable. Disabled: toilet. Separate room for parties, seats 40. **Map 17 C5**.

South
Vauxhall

Chino Latino
Park Plaza Riverbank, 18 Albert Embankment, SE1 7TJ (7769 2500, www.chinolatino.co.uk). Vauxhall tube/rail. **Lunch served** noon-2.30pm Mon-Fri. **Dinner served** 6-10.30pm Mon-Sat; 6-10pm Sun. **Main courses** £14.50-£29. **Set meal** £40-£50 tasting menu. **Credit** AmEx, MC, V.

Despite its name, the Latin influences on Chino Latino are hard to detect – perhaps they've all been poured into the super-strength mojitos. A meal begins with a few showy flourishes: a tablet turns into a hot towel with a splash of water ('ooh!'), and cocktails are garnished with chillies ('ahh!'). Customers are an arbitrary mix of tourists, work colleagues, families and romancing couples, which makes for good people-watching but doesn't bring much atmosphere. However, the pan-Asian sharing menu is consistently delicious. The likes of soft-shell crab tempura, perfectly light and crisp, are presented imaginatively too. Dumplings were another highlight, stuffed with tender crayfish and Chilean sea bass. Grilled scallops arrived dressed with yuzu aïoli and a dusting of wasabi pea, and popcorn crackling made a great addition to the pork belly. Desserts (passionfruit cheesecake with blow-torched marshmallow, say) were equally good. Sadly, though, the setting doesn't do the food justice. The clubby decor, with its slick black leather and backlit screen, would have been stylish a decade ago, and it's hard to escape the starchy hotel surroundings. Service on our visit was brisk and formal, at times verging on rude, which made us reluctant to linger over the lovely food.
Available for hire. Babies and children welcome: high chairs. Booking advisable. Disabled: toilet. **Map 16 L11**.

South East
Herne Hill

★ Lombok
17 Half Moon Lane, SE24 9JU (7733 7131). Herne Hill rail or 37 bus. **Dinner served** 6-10.30pm Tue-Sun. **Main courses** £6-£8. **Credit** MC, V.

Loved by locals, this corner of South-east Asia in south-east London is a consistently safe bet for spice fans, and does well to accommodate cosy dinners and noisy parties alike. Lombok is a family affair behind the counter too – we interrupted a homework session when we arrived early evening. The furnishings strike a happy balance between authentic and elegant, with wood-panelled walls, linen napkins and a few arty trinkets. Service is attentive, if not quite cheerful, and the small space makes for an intimate time with fellow diners. Thai, Malay, Vietnamese and Burmese dishes are all well represented on the menu, which is impressively inexpensive and varied. A plateful of vegetable tempura was tasty, though the carrots, pumpkin and green beans inside were slightly underdone. Thai red curry was fragrant and wonderfully spiced, but let down by gristly chicken pieces. A surer hit is the singapore chilli crab, which comes

The Modern Pantry. See p227.

whole in a lake of sweet, fiery sauce with crispy noodles. Cracking our way through it was messy, but well worth the effort.

Babies and children admitted. Booking essential weekends. Takeaway service. **Map 23 A5**.

London Bridge & Borough

Champor-Champor

62-64 Weston Street, SE1 3QJ (7403 4600, www.champor-champor.com). London Bridge tube/rail. **Lunch served** by appointment. **Dinner served** 6-10pm Mon-Sat. **Set meal** £29.50 2 courses, £33.50 3 courses. **Credit** AmEx, MC, V.

The design of Champor-Champor's dining room, along with the faint scent of incense, will whisk you away to a fantasy land. Where else could you find a kaleidoscope of Asian fabrics alongside tribal bric-a-brac and a miniature teak house on stilts? The exotic vibe is clearly infectious, as the place was busy. The menu is inspired by a pot-pourri of Asian cultures, underpinned by Malaysian customs. We kicked off with Japanese-style barbecued unagi (eel), cooked to sweetness and near opalescence, and perched atop spinach noodles in a piquant penang laksa. This could have been a bonkers combination if the kitchen had failed to pull it off. The cross-cultural theme continued with a pan-fried fillet of black bream juxtaposed with sweet miso, which sat on an omelette lifted by a dash of coconut, and paired with a sassy tomato purée infused with sambal. To end, caramelised palm sugar and cinnamon mousse was teamed with yam pengat, a sauce based on coconut milk. New owners arrived in September 2011 (after our visit), and changes to the menu, including more Thai dishes, are planned.

Available for hire. Babies and children welcome: high chairs. Booking essential. Separate room for parties, seats 8. **Map 12 Q9**.

East

Shoreditch

Great Eastern Dining Room

54-56 Great Eastern Street, EC2A 3QR (7613 4545, www.rickerrestaurants.com). Old Street tube/rail or bus 55.
GG's Bar Open/meals served 8pm-12.30am Wed-Sat. **Main courses** £4.25-£8.
Ground-floor bar **Open/dim sum served** noon-midnight Mon-Fri; 6pm-midnight Sat. **Dim sum** £5-£6.50. **Set meal** £8.50-£9.75 bento box.
Restaurant **Lunch served** noon-3pm Mon-Fri. **Dinner served** 6-10.45pm Mon-Sat. **Main courses** £9-£17.50. **Set meal** (noon-3pm, 6-10.45pm) £13.50-£18.50 bento box.
All **Credit** AmEx, DC, MC, V.

When a place calls itself 'one of London's trendiest restaurants' on its website, it sets itself up for a fall before you've even sat down. This Will Ricker outpost occupies a prime corner of Shoreditch, it's true, but on a busy Thursday evening the clientele was more City workers and tourists than East End hipsters. It does have appeal, though. The bar area is airy and stylishly outfitted; staff are chatty, inventive cocktails flow and the mood is decadedly bohemian. It's a slicker story in the adjacent dining room, with the dark wood, chandeliers and pared-down presentation of so many pan-Asian spots.

Food is a well-considered mix of dim sum, sushi, tempura, curries and grills, all served with efficient charm. We ploughed through cod siu mai and black bean dumplings; a generous portion of vegetable tempura; a perfect example of sweet, nutty pad thai; and a chicken, coconut and peanut sambal that really needed a starchy accompaniment. All were thoroughly tasty and satisfying, but few dishes really excited on the same level as the cocktail menu next door. It's a similar story at E&O and XO, Ricker venues in Notting Hill and Belsize Village, respectively. At their best, they're fun, smart and useful – with friendlier service than you might expect in such fashion-conscious places.

Available for hire. Babies and children admitted. Booking advisable; essential Fri, Sat. Entertainment: DJs 8.30pm Fri, Sat. Takeaway service. **Map 6 R4**.

For branches (Cicada, E&O, Eight Over Eight, XO) see index.

Whitechapel

Rosemary Lane

61 Royal Mint Street, E1 8LG (7481 2602, www.rosemarylane.btinternet.co.uk). Tower Hill tube or Tower Gateway DLR. **Lunch served** noon-2.30pm Mon-Fri. **Dinner served** 5.30-10pm Mon-Fri; 6-10pm Sat. **Meals served** by appointment Sun. **Main courses** £13-£18. **Set meal** £15 2 courses, £18 3 courses. **Set dinner** (Sat) £32 tasting menu. **Credit** AmEx, MC, V.

A London eccentric, Rosemary Lane has survived for some years despite an unlikely location beside a DLR viaduct in the part-redeveloped streets east of Tower Hill. Inside, the converted old pub is cosy and snug, lined with dark wood and colourful paintings, and staff are quietly charming. The restaurant has won its under-the-radar reputation, and a core of regulars, for the refinement and individuality of its part-French, part global-influenced cuisine (ginger, lime and sesame are favourite flavours), and for the painstaking sourcing of fine, mainly organic ingredients. A smoked Bresse chicken and waldorf salad was a lovely, refreshing blend, enhanced with pumpkin seeds and citrus mayonnaise dressing; chicken liver pâté with red onion marmalade and grain mustard also hit the right notes, and complimentary scoops of lemon sorbet between courses were another nice touch. The menu included two vegetarian mains: delicious gnocchi with red chard and mushrooms, in a beurre blanc sauce that was both subtle and richly buttery, and a delicately herby risotto with mixed greens. Meat- and fish-eaters are also well supplied, with excellent roast pork belly and sea bass among menu regulars. Wines include an unusual number of quality Californian labels. It's busier for lunch than dinner.

Available for hire. Babies and children admitted. Booking advisable lunch. Dress: smart casual. **Map 12 S7**.

North

Camden Town & Chalk Farm

Gilgamesh

Stables Market, Chalk Farm Road, NW1 8AH (7482 5757, www.gilgameshbar.com). Chalk Farm tube.
Bar **Open/snacks served** 6pm-2.30am Mon-Thur; noon-2.30am Fri, Sat; noon-midnight Sun.
Restaurant **Meals served** noon-midnight daily. **Dim sum** from £5. **Main courses** £12-£30. **Set lunch** £12 3 courses. **Set meal** £37.50-£57.50 3 courses.
Both **Credit** AmEx, MC, V.

From the moment you take the escalator up to its gilded entrance, Gilgamesh is in danger of putting style before substance. The carved wooden interior and extravagant lighting offer a glamorous escape from Camden Market below for fawning couples and those out to impress. But the spell is quickly broken. Windows overlook rattling freight trains. Staff in headsets, and a toilet attendant, seem to belong in a West End nightclub. Service ranged from overly attentive to stand-offish and slow. The pan-Asian food is equally inconsistent, veering from beautifully crisp son-in-law eggs spiked with chilli and tamarind sauce, to a watery mouthful of pomelo banh trang roll. We ordered one set menu, which was great value for its quantity, but not its quality; the tired-looking house salad and lamb with sweet potato mash were shown up by the tastier à la carte offerings. There's a good selection of Thai and Malaysian curries, dim sum and delicate sushi, as well as predictably modish dishes such as miso black cod and wagyu beef, but the food simply can't compete with the overdone surroundings.

Babies and children welcome: high chairs. Booking advisable. Disabled: lift; toilet. Dress: smart casual. Vegetarian menu. **Map 27 C1**.

Outer London
Barnet, Hertfordshire

★ Emchai

78 High Street, Barnet, Herts EN5 5SN (8364 9993, www.emchai.co.uk). High Barnet tube. **Lunch served** noon-2.30pm daily. **Dinner served** 6-11pm Mon-Thur; 6pm-midnight Fri, Sat; 5-10pm Sun. **Main courses** £4.20-£7.90. **Set meal** £15-£18.50 per person (minimum 2). **Credit** AmEx, MC, V.

Reliable cooking, punchy flavours and warm, smiling service keep outer and north Londoners returning to this soothingly modern restaurant and takeaway. Decorated with vivid jade walls, fairy lights, and orange gerberas smiling from triangular vases, Emchai is a family-friendly spot yet smart enough for a date; spacious proportions and thoughtful staff keep the separate interests at a suitable distance. A South African chenin blanc, one of the cheapest bottles on the list, proved a great complement to the diverse Chinese and Singaporean flavours we chose from the pan-Asian menu. Plump prawns with asparagus and crunchy lily buds was delicate and succulent, while french beans in sambal was an addictive double whammy of chilli heat and fishy umami. From the specials list, chicken and spring onion potstickers featured moist fillings in pleasingly chewy golden wrappers. Aromatic crispy duck, served with flair, is understandably popular, and we have fond memories of the venison fillet in black pepper sauce. The whirr of the juicer punctuates conversation, telling its own story of freshly squeezed fruit concoctions. Finish perhaps with coconut roll served with palm sugar and ice-cream, or banana fritters.

Available for hire. Babies and children welcome: high chairs. Booking advisable weekends. Disabled: toilet. Takeaway service.

Spanish & Portuguese

London's love affair with Spanish cuisine generally, and tapas specifically, shows no sign of abating; we seem to be enjoying some sort of smoked paprika high. This edition has seen no fewer than five noteworthy new openings. Interestingly, the people behind them all have form. **Morito** is the tapas-only, next-door offshoot of Exmouth Market's acclaimed Moro. **Opera Tavern** is the latest outing from husband-and-wife team Simon Mullins and Sanja Morris-Mullins of Salt Yard and Dehesa. Even newer, **José**, which is located in up-and-coming Bermondsey, is the brainchild of José Pizarro, who was the ex-head chef of **Tapas Brindisa** and its siblings. Meanwhile, **Capote y Toros** completes an Old Brompton Road hat-trick for the folk behind highly regarded Cambio de Tercio and Tendido Cero.

While Spanish cuisine is thriving, the capital's Portuguese restaurants seem to be at an impasse. Farringdon's **Portal** strives to promote a contemporary cooking style (and, notably, Portuguese wines), but most of the venues we include here (and it seems to be fewer each year) are traditional. One bright spot – literally – is the fillip that Tom and Ed Martin annually give fondly remembered Algarve holiday dishes at Al Grelha, the appealing al fresco terrace at the **Gun** (*see p111*), their Docklands gastropub.

SPANISH

Central
Bloomsbury

Cigala
*54 Lamb's Conduit Street, WC1N 3LW
(7405 1717, www.cigala.co.uk). Holborn
or Russell Square tube.*
Bar **Open/tapas served** 5.30-10.45pm
Mon-Sat. **Tapas** £3-£25.
Restaurant **Meals served** noon-10.45pm
Mon-Fri; 12.30-10.45pm Sat; 12.30-9.45pm Sun.
Main courses £12.50-£19. **Set lunch** (noon-
3pm Mon-Fri) £16 2 courses, £18 3 courses.
Both **Credit** AmEx, DC, MC, V.
Having got over the brittle trendiness of its early
years, Cigala seems to have settled into position
at the superior, sophisticated end of the London
tapas-restaurant scene. Decor of white walls and
pale wood is unfussy and mellow. Vinophiles can

enjoy an exceptional, adventurous list of modern
Spanish wines – and they're not all at hefty prices
either – that's notably strong in sherries, rosés and
high-quality Catalan regions such as Priorat and
Montsant. Food flavours are delicate and subtle,
evidence of refined cooking skills at work. Blue
cheese croquettes were beautifully smooth and
rich, squid grilled 'a la plancha' ideally tender. Salt
cod fritters with aïoli had a delicious balance of
crunch and saltiness, and Catalan escalivada
(roasted peppers, aubergines and onions) was
enhanced by an unusual, fragrant smokiness.
Even an absolute standard, patatas bravas, had
much more depth of herby flavour than is
normally the case. Tapas are the mainstay, but
Cigala also offers main courses and a set lunch
menu. Minuses: some portions are quite small (a
definite case of quality not quantity); and while
service is charming, the ordering process, given
the size of the menu, could be more organised
(some of our choices had to be asked for twice).
*Available for hire (bar). Babies and children
welcome: high chairs. Booking advisable.
Tables outdoors (11, pavement).*
Map 4 M4.

Clerkenwell & Farringdon

★ Morito NEW
2011 RUNNER-UP BEST NEW RESTAURANT
*32 Exmouth Market, EC1R 4QE (7278 7007).
Angel tube or Farringdon tube/rail.* **Tapas
served** noon-11pm Mon-Sat. **Tapas** £1-£6.50.
Credit MC, V.
Morito is the little sibling of Sam and Samantha
Clark's veteran Moro. As with big bro, the cooking
blurs the lines between Spanish and Middle
Eastern, picking the best of both worlds and
mixing them delectably on the plate. Eating here is
like being transported straight to a tapas bar in
Spain. There's little to the design beyond wipe-clean
orange surfaces and a central bar behind which the
chefs work, plus a smattering of small tables and
stools around the sides. The focus is firmly on the
food – and what food. Andalusian-style ajo blanco,
made with fine-ground almonds and spiked with
sherry vinegar, was silky smooth, served Malaga-
style with a few sweet muscat grapes. The richness
of chicharrones (made from slow-cooked pork belly
that is then cooked until crisp on the plancha grill),

was cut with cumin and lemon. Slices of crisp-fried aubergine, topped with Spanish molasses, skillfully blended savoury and sweet, as did salt cod salad with pine nuts, dill and sweet orange. The cooking is superb and the well-chosen all-Spanish wines are worthy of investigation – don't miss the sherries.
Available for hire. Babies and children welcome: high chairs. Bookings not accepted dinner. Disabled: toilet. Tables outdoors (3, pavement). Map 5 N4.

Moro `HOT 50`

34-36 Exmouth Market, EC1R 4QE (7833 8336, www.moro.co.uk). Angel tube or Farringdon tube/rail.
Bar Open/tapas served 12.30-10.30pm Mon-Sat. **Tapas** £3.50-£14.50.
Restaurant Lunch served 12.30-2.30pm, **dinner served** 7-10.30pm Mon-Sat.
Main courses £15.50-£19.50.
Both Credit AmEx, DC, MC, V.
Although new restaurants pop up regularly in Exmouth Market, well-established Moro still has the edge, serving quality Spanish/North African food that is cooked simply and presented with a twist. Staff are as relaxed as the setting. You can sit inside, perched on a stool at the bar or at a table, or outside, and order from the tapas menu or the grill, or both. The plain interior can be noisy when full. All our dishes pleased, from garlicky boquerones with crusty bread, to tender chargrilled squid coated in harissa; the latter came with fresh broad beans, rocket and pea shoots in a delightfully tangy preserved lemon and coriander dressing. Simple-sounding mains of wood-roasted chicken, pork or fish, and charcoal-grilled wild salmon or lamb chops, are raised to dizzy heights, if our choice was typical. Perfectly grilled mullet fillet, with a sensational creamy dressing of yoghurt, dill, black sesame seeds and chilli, arrived on a bed of lentils with wonderfully light, tempura-battered cucumber. The Spanish-oriented wine list is helpfully divided by style (crisp and dry, fruity, and so on), and includes plenty of sherries, dessert wines and ports, even Jerez brandies. But on a hot summer lunchtime, most diners were opting for glasses of cooling lemonade.
Available for hire. Babies and children welcome: high chairs. Booking essential. Disabled: toilet. Tables outdoors (7, pavement). Map 5 N4.

Covent Garden

Opera Tavern `NEW`

23 Catherine Street, WC2B 5JS (7836 3680, www.operatavern.co.uk). Covent Garden tube.
Tapas served noon-3pm, 5-11.30pm Mon-Sat; noon-3pm Sun. **Tapas** £4.25-£7.95. **Credit** AmEx, MC, V.
From the same stable as hugely popular Italian-Iberican small plates specialists Salt Yard and Dehesa, this one-time Theatreland boozer has been lovingly transformed into a handsome restaurant. Spread over two floors, the exposed bricks, bold artwork and flattering low light make for a darkly sexy ambience, providing the perfect backdrop for good-looking, grown-up plates of modern tapas. Even the bar snacks are special – we enjoyed the winning combination of thyme-spiked pork and soft-boiled yolk in a warm 'Italian-style' scotch egg – while the succulent mini Ibérico pork and foie gras burger from the grill is another must-have. Elsewhere, there are top-notch cuts of meats and full-flavoured cheeses, plus perfectly executed

tapas: a plate of lightly battered sea purslane and squid, or rich and comforting truffle croquettes with just a hint of the forest. Only the chargrilled salt marsh lamb, teamed with an ill-judged mix of hulled wheat, broad beans and overpowering feta cheese, fell wide of the mark. The by-the-glass selection of Italian and Spanish wines, supplemented by a compact, well-compiled list of dry sherries, make this a destination bar in its own right. The genial staff are a delight too.
Babies and children welcome (dining room): high chairs. Booking essential. Dress: smart casual. Separate room for parties, seats 45. Tables outdoors (3, pavement). Map 18 E4.

Fitzrovia

Barrica

62 Goodge Street, W1T 4NE (7436 9448, www.barrica.co.uk). Goodge Street or Tottenham Court Road tube. **Tapas served** noon-11pm Mon-Fri; 1-11pm Sat. **Tapas** £1.95-£10.
Credit AmEx, MC, V.
Noisy, busy, a bit cramped and sometimes chaotic, Barrica provides an authentic Spanish tapas bar

experience. Arrive late for lunch or on impulse in the evening, and you may be crushed into a tiny space near the bar or asked to share a table with other diners perched on stools. Staff do their best to add warmth to the welcome, and the food comes fast, most of the time. Bread and oil are delivered as you sit down – always a good sign. The short fixed tapas menu, featuring standards such as padrón peppers (small, sharply salty and doused in high-grade olive oil) and classy bellota ham (tender and slightly nutty), is enhanced by daily specials. Moist baked hake with peas was a refreshing combination of clean flavours; grilled squid was buttery in texture and full of flavour; and a small lamb chop was sweet and nicely browned. Two different Spanish waiters looked after us, both of them friendly and informed. The carefully compiled all-Spanish wine and sherry list has some decent by-the-glass options. If you want to both wake up and wind down before you leave, try a carajillo: a super-strong espresso with a generous shot of Spanish brandy.
Available for hire. Babies and children admitted. Booking advisable Tue-Sat. Tables outdoors (2, pavement). Map 17 A1.

Morito

Fino

*33 Charlotte Street, entrance on Rathbone Street,
W1T 1RR (7813 8010, www.finorestaurant.com).
Goodge Street tube.* **Tapas served** noon-
2.30pm, 6-10.30pm Mon-Fri; 6-10.30pm Sat.
Tapas £2-£25. **Credit** AmEx, MC, V.
After almost a decade in business, Fino is showing
no signs of losing its touch. True, the basement
setting, done out in pale woods and modern art, is
rather dull, but this has never been a place of style
over substance: cooking is king. Premium versions of
everyday tapas – with price tags to suit – and
downsized portions of regional specialities come
together to form a small plates menu designed for
sampling and sharing. We kicked off with two
flawless classics: creamy croquetas studded with
generous chunks of top-notch jamón; and a plump,
golden pillow of tortilla oozing runny egg from its
middle. Equally memorable were dishes from the
plancha (grill), such as meaty razor clams simply
cooked in their own juices, or a marinated queen
scallop in its shell. Black-as-night arroz negro (rice
cooked in squid ink), beautifully presented in a little
copper pan, provided warmth and comfort. Only a
trio of dry and doughy cinnamon-sugared doughnuts
disappointed; churros (deep-fried batter fingers)
would have been better. Clued-up staff are happy to
suggest matches from the excellent selection of
Spanish wine. There's good people-watching here too,
with a jovial 'meedja' crowd in residence most days.
*Available for hire. Babies and children welcome:
high chairs. Booking advisable. Disabled: lift;
toilet.* **Map 17 B1.**

Ibérica Food & Culture

*195 Great Portland Street, W1W 5PS (7636
8650, www.ibericalondon.com). Great Portland
Street tube.* **Tapas served** 11.30am-11pm

Opera Tavern. See p235.

Mon-Sat; noon-4pm Sun. **Set tapas** (11.30am-
6.30pm Mon-Fri) £16.50. **Tapas** £3.50-£12.50.
Credit AmEx, MC, V.
If your idea of Spanish restaurants begins and
ends with bullfighting posters and ceiling hams,
then Ibérica may seem a tad unsympathetic. All
glass and cool colours, and set on a business-
minded corner of Great Portland Street, it looks
officious rather than Iberian. The food, though, is
good reason to linger. The lunch deal offers two
tapas for £16.50 – good value, but three tapas is
usually enough for two diners, so it may be wiser
to order individual dishes unless you're very
hungry. The starter of cold cuts is generous, with
moist, peppery salami, succulent cured ham, and
plain Spanish cheeses, decorated with a sweet
chutney. For a sweatier, more pungent sensation,
opt for the pricier bellota ham. Two salads –
spinach and goat's cheese, and prawn and alioli –
were crisp, light and full of flavour. Octopus came
fondue-style, with melted cheese: it looked ugly and
heavy, but the combination of fishy and creamy
worked surprisingly well. Desserts are not wildly
ambitious, but caramelised rice pudding was a
treat with a glass of pedro ximénez. Many wines
are available by the glass, starting at a very
reasonable £4.50 – and quality was above average.
More suited to a lunchtime bite than a romantic
sojourn, Ibérica is a solid, reliable choice. The
house paellas are ideal for groups: abundant,
authentic and heavily laced with saffron.
*Available for hire. Babies and children welcome:
high chairs; nappy-changing facilities. Booking
advisable. Separate room for parties, seats 30.
Takeaway service.* **Map 3 H4.**

Salt Yard

*54 Goodge Street, W1T 4NA (7637 0657,
www.saltyard.co.uk). Goodge Street tube.*
Open noon-11pm Mon-Fri; 5-11pm Sat.
Tapas served noon-3pm, 5.30-11pm Mon-Fri;
5-11pm Sat. **Tapas** £4.75-£9. **Credit** AmEx,
DC, MC, V.
Hidden behind a discreet, slate-grey frontage, this
polished tapas joint is an unexpected apparition to
find on brash Goodge Street. Late afternoon, it's a
low-key spot to perch at the bar for sherry and
charcuterie; from 6pm, the pace quickens as the
after-work set descends. Salt Yard buzzes at
lunchtime and at night – though on our midweek
visit, blaring disco tunes threatened to drown out
the sociable hum, and didn't make for a restful
supper. The food, like the decor, tends towards
sophistication, offering an artful, Spanish-Italian
take on tapas. Although the menu frequently
changes, confit of Old Spot pork is a constant,
pairing beautifully tender, crackling-topped meat
with a layer of rosemary-infused, near-dissolving
cannellini beans. Jamón-studded manchego
croquetas were also wonderful: miraculously light,
but indulgently rich. Other dishes, though,
disappointed: rather bland slow-roasted lamb,
rescued only by a punchy mojo verde; and a
curiously cloying escabeche of mackerel, fennel
and baby broad beans, its flavours lost in a surfeit
of lemon and bay. With attention perhaps diverted
to newer sister restaurant, the Opera Tavern, Salt
Yard seems to have lost its way a little. We'll return
to give the place another chance – though at a safe
remove from those speakers.
*Available for hire. Babies and children admitted.
Booking essential. Tables outdoors (3, pavement).*
Map 17 A1.
For branch (Dehesa) see index.

King's Cross

Camino

*3 Varnishers Yard, Regents Quarter, N1 9FD
(7841 7331, www.camino.uk.com). King's Cross
tube/rail.*
Bar **Open** noon-midnight Mon-Wed; noon-1am
Thur-Sat; noon-11pm Sun. **Tapas served**
noon-4pm, 4.30-11pm daily.
Restaurant **Tapas served** 8-11.30am, noon-
3pm, 6.30-11pm Mon-Fri; 8-11.30am, noon-4pm,
6-11pm Sat; 8-11.30am, noon-4pm Sun.
Both **Tapas** £2.75-£39.50. **Credit** AmEx, MC, V.
You have to admire the sheer boldness of Richard
Bigg's Camino. The huge site comprises bar, lounge,
casual and formal dining areas, outdoor tables, plus
the Time Out award-winning sherry specialist Bar
Pepito across the courtyard, all tucked away inside
an office development opposite King's Cross station.
The ornate, metal-topped, multi-room bar counter
alone must have cost a stylish penny; indeed, it's all
smartly appointed, if built to withstand a cavalier
post-work crowd. The set-up has thrived, with a
branch opening recently in the arguably easier
Docklands location of Westferry Circus. Camino
might not fit your ideal of a romantic little tapas
bar in Seville, but Spanish staff underline the
authenticity of the food and drink on offer, and the
cooking is rather good. From a list of brunch
specials, we enjoyed Cornish sardines with garlic,
chilli and tomato sofrito, plus a punchy salad of
tomatoes, pickled fennel, red onions and an anchovy
and orange dressing. But it was the parrillada mixta
to share, featuring perfectly cooked ribeye, Ibérico
pork shoulder, chorizo, chicken romesco and
morcilla, that really wowed. Ice-creams with pedro
ximénez, and tarta de santiago (Galician almond
tart) outclassed an overcooked chocolate pudding
when it came to dessert. The wine list is great fun
to explore, our bottle of Quinta el Refugio a
delightful way to spend £23.50.
*Available for hire. Babies and children welcome
(before 6pm Thur-Sat): high chairs; nappy-
changing facilities. Booking advisable. Disabled:
toilet. Tables outdoors (10, garden; 4, pavement).*
Map 4 L3.
For branch see index.

Mayfair

El Pirata

*5-6 Down Street, W1J 7AQ (7491 3810,
www.elpirata.co.uk). Green Park or Hyde Park
Corner tube.* **Meals served** noon-11.30pm
Mon-Fri. **Dinner served** 6-11.30pm Sat.
Main courses £13.95-£17.95. **Tapas** £1.90-
£10.50. **Set lunch** (noon-3pm) £10.25 2 dishes
incl glass of wine. **Set meal** £16.35 6 dishes.
Credit AmEx, MC, V.
The Piccadilly side of Mayfair is not the most
convivial part of London, which makes a trip to El
Pirata all the more pleasurable. Warm and
welcoming, with a menu that is stridently traditional
and (mostly) fairly priced, it's like a little piece of pre-
gastro London. The interior is noisy but pleasantly
low-lit, while a pavement table gets you a view on to
a street with a ghost tube station entrance (Down
Street, closed since 1932) and a church. Six or seven
tapas will satisfy even a ravenous duo. Crisply grilled
sardines, moist ham and pungent morcilla were
generous, tasty dishes, but the lentil stew deserves
special mention. Rich, smoky and chocolatey, it was
a late-in-the-order tapa we wished we'd chosen earlier

– and twice. Padrón peppers also tempted, but cost
more than a fiver, which would buy you a bag's
worth in Spain. Bread (which we had to request) was
decent, though the pan con tomate lacked zing. Our
waiter's wine recommendation – a bottle of 2008 Hito
from the ever-popular Duero region – didn't quite
deliver the body or bouquet we expected for £30.
Finish with crema catalana, rice pudding or chocolate
pancake – not the lightest desserts, but good to share.
*Babies and children admitted. Booking advisable
dinner. Separate room for parties, seats 65.
Tables outdoors (4, pavement). Takeaway
service.* **Map 9 H8.**

Soho

Aqua Nueva

*5th floor, 240 Regent Street, entrance on Argyll
Street, W1B 3BR (7478 0540, www.aqua-
london.com). Oxford Circus tube.* **Lunch served**
noon-3pm Mon-Sat. **Dinner served** 6-10.45pm
Mon-Wed; 6-11.15pm Thur-Sat. **Brunch served**
noon-3pm Sun. **Main courses** £12-£29. **Tapas**
£4-£22. **Credit** AmEx, MC, V.

José. See p241.

On leaving tourist-thronged Argyll Street to check
into the Aqua 'concept', you're greeted by a dark,
sinful-looking lobby. Take the lift to the fifth floor,
where, after bypassing Japanese restaurant Aqua
Kyoto, you arrive at the large, glitzy dining room and
terrace of the Spanish part of the operation. The
location, hybrid offering and high prices (expect to
blow £80 on a tapas lunch for two, including a couple
of glasses of house wine) may make diners wonder
who all this is for – but the stylish presentation and
panoramic views temper such misgivings. Pan con
tomate was big, rustic and bold, with the required
garlicky kick. Sardines with sun-dried tomato and
creamed cheese terrines were also moist and
moreish. Braised cabbage wrapped in pancetta and
served with morcilla sounded amazing, but didn't
quite live up to expectations. Apart from a £22 ham
platter, no cold dishes were on offer during our visit –
on a hot August lunchtime. Wines range from a
decent £9 glass of albariño white to high-end Riojas;
the dessert menu is well stocked with small, creamy
classics. Service needs some work: staff stood around
with quickly-cooling dishes, looking lost, until a
maitre d' came to sort things out.

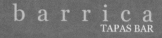

Available for hire. Babies and children admitted. Booking advisable Wed-Sat. Disabled: lift; toilet. Dress: smart casual. Separate room for parties, seats 16. **Map 9 J6**.

Barrafina `HOT 50`

54 Frith Street, W1D 4SL (7440 1463, www.barrafina.co.uk). Leicester Square or Tottenham Court Road tube. **Tapas served** noon-3pm, 5-11pm Mon-Sat; 1-3.30pm, 5.30-10.30pm Sun. **Tapas** £2-£18.50. **Credit** AmEx, MC, V.

The younger, sexier sibling of Fino, Barrafina is a glossy take on the classic Spanish tapas bar. Thanks to its no-bookings policy, the queue for seats often snakes out along a side counter to the street, but there's an excellent selection of nibbles to keep the wolf from the door as you shuffle along the line. On our visit, giant caper berries, salted almonds and moreish ham croquetas made the perfect foil for a cold glass of Manzanilla Pasada sherry. When you're finally perched at the bar, the real fun starts. Amiable chefs chat with the assembled diners, recommending dishes while you watch them at work. Ingredients are impeccably sourced from key regional providers, and simply prepared to allow the flavours to sing. Highlights included folds of butter-soft, piquant chorizo ibérico, ahead of a soft-centred jamón and spinach tortilla. Sweet, meaty giant prawns, grilled in their shells and served with own-made aïoli, also got the thumbs-up. Of the salads, the crunchy, bitter centres of a row of halved baby gems were beautifully offset by fresh shallot vinaigrette, soft anchovies and crisp strips of smoked pancetta. Prices are on the stiff side, but Barrafina's legions of fans remain undeterred.

Babies and children admitted. Bookings not accepted. Tables outdoors (4, pavement). **Map 17 C3**.

South Kensington

Cambio de Tercio

163 Old Brompton Road, SW5 0LJ (7244 8970, www.cambiodetercio.co.uk). Gloucester Road or South Kensington tube. **Lunch served** noon-3pm daily. **Dinner served** 7-11.30pm Mon-Sat; 7-11pm Sun. **Main courses** £13.90-£32. **Credit** AmEx, DC, MC, V.

The menu at this beautiful, highbrow tapas bar is the stuff of foodie novels. It all sounds better in Spanish, of course, but who doesn't feel a little bit magic-realist – and hungry – when they read of Basque-style crab ravioli with leek emulsion, sea asparagus and Galician seaweed. Such dishes are not only gorgeously presented, but tap deeply into Spain's many regional cuisines and serve as a showcase for the best food that the peninsula offers. Portions are on the small side, so take it slowly and enjoy the art-filled, brightly painted room, tranquil atmosphere and the whisperings of the posh clientele – rich Spanish residents, embassy types and holidaying Argentines. The classics – patatas bravas, padrón peppers, pata negra ham (£22.50 for a few small slices!) – are all a cut above the usual you'll find, and the house tortilla ('deconstructed chorizo omelette') is an audacious, flavour-filled borrowing from El Bulli. The oxtail is not the hefty slab of black meat you'd probably get in a Madrid eaterie, but a carefully caramelised allusion to the real thing. Even the desserts are experimental and ethereal: Bombay Sapphire gelée and tonic water sorbet with lime

foam was bold, but oh so brief. That's what Cambio de Tercio is all about: suggestive, seductive, stylised food. One for a very special occasion, when you've £100 to spare.

Available for hire. Babies and children admitted. Booking advisable dinner. Separate room for parties, seats 20. Tables outdoors (3, pavement). **Map 13 C11**.

Capote y Toros `NEW`

157 Old Brompton Road, SW5 0LJ (7373 0567, www.cambiodetercio.co.uk). Gloucester Road or South Kensington tube. **Tapas served** 6-11pm Tue-Sat. **Tapas** £4.50-£22. **Credit** AmEx, MC, V.

Another sherry-and-tapas joint from the crew behind Cambio de Tercio and Tendido Cero, Capote y Toros is built along the same winning lines. The regularly changing menu is a mini gastro-tour of Spain's great and good, so there's cured cecina (beef ham) from Leon, spicy Andalusian chorizo cooked with fino sherry, and juicy meatballs in a mellow tomato sauce (a regional speciality of Jerez). Long, luscious folds of premium cured meats (jamon Ibérico Sánchez Romero Carvajal), or cuts of creamy cheeses served with plump grapes, are also worth a look. Much like its sister restaurants, Capote y Toros is done out in vibrant colours: the deep pink and ultra-orange echo the bullfighters' capes in the framed pictures that line the walls, while the same sense of bravado carries over to the bill of fare. The wine list explores the great names (Rioja, Ribera del Duero) and lesser-known regions of Spain. The main liquid attraction here, though, is not the wines, but the sherries. Taste them in all their multifaceted glory: 48 varieties are available by the glass, ranging from bone-dry, pale straw-coloured finos and manzanillas to unctuously rich, raisiny sweet pedro ximénez.

Babies and children admitted. Bookings not accepted. Tables outdoors (1, pavement). **Map 13 C11**.

Tendido Cero

174 Old Brompton Road, SW5 0BA (7370 3685, www.cambiodetercio.co.uk). Gloucester Road or South Kensington tube. **Tapas served** noon-3pm, 6.30-11pm daily. **Tapas** £4-£14. **Credit** AmEx, MC, V.

Most tapas bars are noisy, but Tendido Cero makes a virtue of what could be a fault. The waiters and cooks communicate freely between the small main room and the tiny semi-open kitchen, and service is dashingly fast. The food, however, is quirky rather than brash: tiny cuts of oxtail were wrapped in sweet, succulent peppers; a delicate bream came cut into three neat triangles, swimming in ratatouille. And the names of dishes parody the titles of Spanish noblemen; witness the carrillera de cerdo ibérico guisada con pedro ximénez y parmentier de patata (pork cheeks in dessert wine). Even that most elementary of appetisers, cured ham on tomato bread, is presented artfully – and without an excess of olive oil that might drip on to the immaculate clothes of the generally well-heeled customers. The design is also striking: walls are daubed in bright ochre and pink, and hung with huge, rather camp photographs of matadors. It's certainly a lively, fun place (those looking for a more formal experience should head across the road to sober sister restaurant Cambio de Tercio), but, in this instance, cheerful certainly doesn't equate to cheap. To curb the bill, you could try sharing a dessert – the crema catalana is a decently

Barrica. See p235.

Capote y Toros. See p239.

sized variation on crème brûlée, lovely with a glass of moscatel – and have beer rather than the underwhelming and expensive house wines. *Available for hire. Babies and children admitted. Booking advisable dinner Wed-Sat. Tables outdoors (5, pavement).* **Map 13 C11**. **For branch (Tendido Cuatro) see index**.

West

Bayswater

El Pirata Detapas
115 Westbourne Grove, W2 4UP (7727 5000, www.elpiratadetapas.co.uk). Bayswater or Royal Oak tube. **Tapas served** noon-3pm, 6-11pm Mon-Fri; noon-11pm Sat, Sun. **Tapas** £3-£7. **Set tapas** £20 7 dishes, £25 8 dishes. **Credit** AmEx, MC, V.
The tapas-serving sibling to Mayfair's esteemed El Pirata restaurant, this modish spot is packed to the gunnels all week. Black leather banquettes, a

wall made up of wine racks (the impressive wine and sherry list offers bottles from across Spain) and dark wooden tables give the restaurant a smart business feel. But in among the suits, you'll also find families and affluent west Londoners enjoying the quality cooking. The young head chef, an El Bulli protégé, produces standard tapas (croquettes, Iberian cured meats and so on), as well as more daring dishes. Meaty recipes, such as heady wood pigeon with fig purée or delicious pork cheeks with carrot purée, show a careful respect for balancing sweet and savoury flavours. However, we were disappointed that our tortilla was far too soft-set and crumbly, taking the idea of deconstructed food to the sort of level we'd prefer not to reach. The clementine 'caviar' that came with our otherwise faultless octopus carpaccio also lacked a certain pop. Don't miss dessert, though – we loved the combination of chocolate truffle and mousse with a slick of saffron toffee.
Available for hire. Babies and children welcome: high chairs. Booking advisable. Separate room for parties, seats 30. Takeaway service. **Map 7 B6**.

South

Battersea

Lola Rojo [HOT 50]
78 Northcote Road, SW11 6QL (7350 2262, www.lolarojo.net). Clapham Junction rail. **Tapas served** noon-3pm, 6-10.30pm Mon-Thur; noon-10.30pm Fri-Sun. **Tapas** £4-£15.50. **Credit** MC, V.
The original Lola Rojo – there is a second branch in Fulham – remains a destination for good, fun Spanish food. The stylishly modern dining room is lively, the tables close-packed and the service a bit erratic, though most regulars don't seem to mind. Possibly because interesting *nueva cocina* (new-wave Spanish cooking) dishes leap from the menu like caged bulls into a ring. There's piquillo peppers, laid flat like a matador's cloak, then topped with garlicky prawns plus a few leaves of spinach for the shock of colour; or tiny clam shells in a tomato and bean broth that evokes the coast and tastes of summer. Such tapas-sized dishes are very tempting,

but they are also small, so the bill adds up fast. Larger helpings include paellas, such as black rice with squid and saffron alioli. The wine list takes almost as much pride of place as the dishes, with well-chosen wines from good emerging Spanish regions and producers, though the choice of crisp sherries by the glass is curiously limited. On warm market days, the tiny terrace becomes the place to sit on a bar stool and observe the *paseo* down Northcote Road.
Babies and children welcome: booster seats. Tables outdoors (16, terrace). Takeaway service. **Map 21 C5.**
For branch see index.

Vauxhall

Rebato's
169 South Lambeth Road, SW8 1XW (7735 6388, www.rebatos.com). Stockwell tube. ***Bar*** **Open/tapas served** 5.30-10.45pm Mon-Fri; 7-11pm Sat. **Tapas** £3-£10. ***Restaurant*** **Lunch served** noon-2.30pm Mon-Fri. **Dinner served** 7-10.45pm Mon-Sat. **Main courses** £12-£19. **Set meal** £19.99 3 courses.
Both **Credit** AmEx, MC, V.
Despite its location on a parade of Portuguese restaurants and shops, there's no doubt Rebato's is Spanish. As you step in from busy South Lambeth Road, you're immersed in a typical taverna: from long bar with tapas on display, via bullfighting posters, to leg of serrano in pride of place. Go no further if you're looking for a traditional tapas experience. All the old favourites are here – albóndigas, patatas bravas, ensalada rusa, gambas al ajillo – and they're prepared with precision. Spanish beer, wine and sherry are on hand as accompaniments. Even during the day, this cosy, dimly lit oasis conjures up an atmosphere far removed from its location. If you're after old-school formality, however, step through to the main restaurant, with its white tablecloths, whitewashed walls, tiled flooring, well-spaced tables and lush foliage. There's even a dessert trolley. Although you can enjoy mains in the bar, the restaurant is where to sit down and savour such dishes as seafood casserole, grilled sea bass with garlic and olive oil, or the signature roast suckling pig. A little piece of Spain in Vauxhall.
Available for hire. Babies and children admitted. Booking advisable. **Map 16 L13.**

Waterloo

Mar i Terra
14 Gambia Street, SE1 0XH (7928 7628, www.mariterra.co.uk). Southwark tube. **Tapas served** noon-3pm, 6-11pm Mon-Fri; 5-11pm Sat. **Tapas** £2.70-£9. **Credit** MC, V.
The former pub that now houses Mar i Terra on a narrow street near a railway viaduct has a slightly Dickensian look, contrasting with the area's new glass-and-steel towers. Inside, there's traditional polished wood tapas bar decor in both the main bar and the first-floor dining room. A neat walled garden at the back adds to the feel of a snug, relaxing hideaway. The place is deservedly popular, but thanks to the three distinct spaces you'll rarely have difficulty getting a table, despite the 'no evening bookings for fewer than ten' rule. The wine range includes less common Spanish labels at accessible prices, and the tapas menu also features unusual offerings such as habas tiernas

de lodosa (small broad beans sautéed with ham and mint) and a richly tasty rabbit casserole with wine, mushrooms and potatoes. All the classics are here too: Catalan spinach with raisins and pine nuts, and cumin-flavoured albóndigas were also enjoyable; only piquillo peppers stuffed with rather dull crab disappointed. Young, friendly Spanish staff keep things going nicely. The restaurant is generally good value too, although charging £1.50 per head for bread and oil and £2.70 for a bowl of olives seems cheeky.
Available for hire. Babies and children welcome: high chairs. Bookings not accepted for fewer than 10 people dinner. Separate room for parties, seats 50. Tables outdoors (15, garden). **Map 11 O8.**
For branch see index.

South East
Bermondsey

José NEW
104 Bermondsey Street, SE1 3UB (7403 4902, http://joserestaurant.co.uk). London Bridge tube/rail. **Tapas served** noon-10.30pm daily. **Tapas** £3.50-£5. **Credit** AmEx, DC, MC, V.
José is its own worst enemy. This tiny, mostly standing-room-only tapas bar is the first independent project from acclaimed chef José Pizarro (previously of the hugely successful Brindisa group), but is so popular it's annoying. The no-bookings policy means you have to take your chances on finding a space to stand (let alone sit), especially if you visit during peak hours, and securing the attention of staff can be equally fraught. Visit off-peak, and José's appeal is more obvious. The chef and his crew are doing a great job at turning out top-quality Spanish food from a kitchen the size of a caravan's galley. From the day's specials board, razor clams were served piping hot from the grill; 'caramelised' chicory was also grilled to order, served with shards of walnut and a sharp picos de europa blue cheese. The

flavour combinations worked well, particularly with glasses of sapid manzanilla and fino sherries. Lamb meatballs in tomato sauce were also a cut above the norm, and head-on sardines were as fresh as if they'd just come off the boat.
Babies and children admitted. Bookings not accepted. Disabled: toilet. **Map 12 Q9.**

Camberwell

★ Angels & Gypsies
29-33 Camberwell Church Street, SE5 8TR (7703 5984, www.angelsandgypsies.com). Denmark Hill rail or bus 36, 436, 185. **Lunch served** noon-3pm Mon-Thur; noon-3.30pm Fri, Sat; noon-4pm Sun. **Dinner served** 6-10.30pm Mon-Thur, Sun; 6-11pm Fri, Sat. **Tapas** £3.50-£12. **Credit** AmEx, MC, V.
An unexpected gem on Camberwell Church Street. The decor is appealing, the focal point being a horseshoe-shaped bar, with simple wooden tables surrounding it. Chairs look like they were sourced from the local Sunday school, with a cross motif on the back and a pocket for hymn books. The religious theme doesn't end there, with stunning stained glass at the windows and the only piece of art on the exposed-brick walls being a backlit stained-glass scene depicting the restaurant's name. The food, served by proficient staff, includes plenty of treats for the discerning palate: apricot-stuffed meatballs with manchego, organic slow-roast pork belly with clementines and plum jam, farina cake with orange syrup and bergamot. Don't expect too many old classics; emphasis is put on fresh and exciting flavour combinations using high-quality, seasonal ingredients. Dishes are small, so you'll want three per person. It's worth booking if you plan to head here of an evening, as A&G certainly draws a crowd. The assembled trendies and foodies sit comfortably together enjoying the indisputably good food.
Available for hire. Babies and children welcome: high chairs. Booking advisable. Separate room for parties, seats 25. Takeaway service. **Map 23 B2.**

Angels & Gypsies

Herne Hill

Number 22

*22 Half Moon Lane, SE24 9HU (7095 9922,
www.number-22.com). Herne Hill rail or bus
3, 37, 68.* **Tapas served** 5-11pm Mon-Fri;
noon-3pm, 5-10.30pm Sat; noon-9.30pm Sun.
Tapas £3-£10. **Credit** MC, V.
Ever reliable for good Spanish nosh, Number 22 has
a modest menu of beautifully crafted tapas. There's
a combination of traditional favourites (chorizo in
cider, seared tuna with fennel and olives) and more
exotic dishes such as roasted quail with sweet potato
mash, or pumpkin roasted with sesame. A section
devoted to pintxos gives the opportunity to try
smaller-sized appetisers: great for those who love to
pick. Paellas are made fresh to order, so you have to
wait a little, but this is time well spent if you prefer
a more substantial main course. There are various
set deals depending on when you visit, so it's worth
checking these beforehand. The wine list is
extensive, but not exclusively Spanish, and desserts
come with a recommendation for sweet wine or
sherry. The backdrop isn't particularly Spanish in
style; the dining room is sleek and contemporary,
with dark flooring and furnishings. Number 22 is a
cosy little local that's as good for couples as it is for
an intimate evening with friends.
*Available for hire. Babies and children welcome:
high chairs. Booking advisable. Tables outdoors
(6, patio).* **Map 23 A5**.

London Bridge & Borough

★ Tapas Brindisa

*18-20 Southwark Street, SE1 1TJ (7357 8880,
www.brindisa.com). London Bridge tube/rail.*
Tapas served 11am-3pm, 5.30-11pm Mon-
Thur; 9-11am, noon-4pm, 5.30-11pm Fri, Sat;
noon-10pm Sun. **Tapas** £4-£12.90. **Credit**
AmEx, MC, V.
The upsurge in Spanish food quality in London
since the 1990s can in part be dated from the arrival
in Borough Market of food importers Brindisa,
bringing first-rate Iberian hams, cheeses and other
essentials to the city almost for the first time. The
firm's showcase tapas restaurants are equally a
benchmark. In early 2011, star chef José Pizarro left
to start José, but we haven't noticed any drop in
standards, so you'll still find an ideal blend of
superb ingredients and refined cooking (the latter
normally confined to larger dishes). At the original
Brindisa in Borough Market, 'black rice' (cooked
with squid in its ink, with unusually fragrant aïoli)
had a superbly smooth flavour, without any acridity;
ham croquettes gained extra depth from the quality
of the meat. Padrón peppers (Galician peppers
simply fried and salted) exemplified wonderful
produce being allowed to shine. The style is easy
going, prices very reasonable – though inescapably
higher for delicacies such as the finest Ibérico meats.
Wines are sophisticated and priced accordingly. The
only drawback is that it's often impossible to get a
seat at the Borough and Soho branches, as there's
no booking; fortunately, South Ken's Casa Brindisa
does now take reservations.
*Babies and children admitted. Bookings not
accepted. Disabled: toilet. Tables outdoors (8,
pavement).* **Map 11 P8**.
**For branches (Casa Brindisa,
Tapas Brindisa Soho) see index.**

East
Shoreditch

★ Laxeiro

*93 Columbia Road, E2 7RG (7729 1147,
www.laxeiro.co.uk). Hoxton rail.* **Tapas served**
noon-3pm, 7-11pm Tue-Sat; 9am-4pm Sun.
Tapas £4.50-£7.95. **Credit** AmEx, MC, V.
A Columbia Road old-timer, Laxeiro is at its convivial
best on Sunday afternoons. When the flower market
is in full swing outside, its small, airy dining room
provides welcome respite; space may be tight, but it's
nothing to the crush outside. Although the
paintwork has moved with the times (it's now a
modish grey, rather than cheery yellow), the menu
holds less truck with passing fads. Classic tapas,
barbecued meat and seafood, and heaped, two-
person portions of paella are the order of the day.
Should the latter prove too much, you'll be dispatched
home with a box of leftovers. The approach is more
rustic than refined, but the flavours sing. Teaming
sautéed fennel with slow-roasted hunks of garlic
worked wonderfully well, while rough-chopped
chillies added fire to a plate of baby squid and
chorizo. The best dish was the simplest of all:
succulent strips of Ibérico pork shoulder, cooked on
the barbecue, scattered with rock salt and served
with a handful of peppery rocket leaves. We finished
with a plate of rich, slightly salty manchego and
translucent slices of own-made membrillo, before
being politely but firmly presented with the bill; if
you like to linger over coffee, avoid the Sunday rush.
*Babies and children welcome: high chairs. Booking
advisable; not accepted Sun. Tables outdoors
(3, pavement). Takeaway service.* **Map 6 S3**.

North East
Walthamstow

Orford Saloon

*32 Orford Road, E17 9NJ (8503 6542).
Walthamstow Central tube/rail.* **Tapas served**
6-10.30pm Tue-Fri; noon-3pm, 6-10.30pm Sat;
noon-3pm, 6-9.30pm Sun. **Tapas** £4.15-£7.25.
Credit MC, V.
Clearly a popular spot in E17's gentrified enclave –
aka Walthamstow Village – this tapas bar has full
tables and a chatty buzz most nights. Decor is a mix
of Moroccan-style tiled tables, plain colours and
modern art; the menu is a little book with laminated
covers. Only the music, a soundtrack of Spanish pop,
began to grate after a while – and a while it was, for
service seemed disorganised. We waited 40 minutes
between ordering and the arrival of the first tapas,
which then all came separately over another long
stretch. Still, crunchy patatas aïoli featuring
excellent, punchy fresh garlic helped cheer us, as did
one of the day's specials, deep-fried cuttlefish in
crisp, delicate batter. Lamb chuletas (cutlets) were
also tender, juicy and well flavoured (even if they had
taken an inexplicable hour to cook). However, green
beans with garlic and ham shavings were crunchy
but bland, and a mixed salad was bog-standard. The
wine range is short yet to the point, beginning around
£14.50. Local regulars are obviously willing to
overlook the glitches that seem to have crept in – and
we've had very good experiences here in the past.
*Babies and children welcome: high chairs.
Booking advisable. Disabled: toilet. Tables
outdoors (2, pavement).*

North
Camden Town & Chalk Farm

El Parador

*245 Eversholt Street, NW1 1BA (7387 2789,
www.elparadorlondon.com). Mornington
Crescent tube.* **Tapas served** noon-3pm,
6-11pm Mon-Thur; noon-3pm, 6-11.30pm Fri;
6-11.30pm Sat; 6.30-9.30pm Sun. **Tapas** £4.60-
£7.80. **Credit** MC, V.
Open since the 1980s, Camden standby El Parador
has clearly never felt the urge for a makeover, still
sporting the same white walls and slightly wacky
blue-mosaic bar. Stairs lead down to a darker
basement, and a neat garden where tables are in big
demand in summer. There have been innovations,
though, in the tapas menu, with an unusually large
vegetarian range and ingredients that rarely feature
in routine tapas, such as capers, samphire, harissa,
and various herbs and spices. Results are rather hit
and miss. In merluza con hinojo (hake with roast
fennel, dill and Madeira), the fennel has been
overcooked to the point of losing nearly all flavour,
and we couldn't detect the dill; grilled squid
marinated in mint and garlic was also bland. On the
other hand, belly pork braised in cider came with
unannounced strong chilli. Much more enjoyable
were green beans 'del Parador' (with roast
artichokes and red onions) and samphire with
Japanese mushrooms. The wine and beers list is
good value. Amiable service and a laid-back vibe
keep regulars coming. Lone diners and pairs note,
though: bookings are only taken for three and up.
*Babies and children admitted. Booking
advisable for 3 or more. Separate room for
parties, seats 30. Tables outdoors (12, garden).*
Map 27 D3.

Tufnell Park

Del Parc

*167 Junction Road, N19 5PZ (7281 5684,
www.delparc.co.uk). Archway or Tufnell Park
tube.* **Dinner served** 7.30-10.30pm Wed-Sat.
Tapas £6-£10. **Credit** MC, V.
Dining at this small tapas restaurant is a very
intimate experience. Soft lighting and a soundtrack
of chill-out classics create a romantic vibe that
attracts plenty of couples. A dozen tables are
spread around the open-plan kitchen, where you can
observe chef Steve at work (staying consistently
calm and gracefully arranging plates), while waiter
Alan chirpily works the room. The menu mixes
Spanish and North African influences. Serrano ham
rolls came wrapped around honeyed goat's cheese
with hints of fennel. Del Parc's version of migas, a
Spanish dish made with breadcrumbs, combined
crunchy olive oil croutons with buttery broad
beans, seaweed and dukka (a Middle Eastern herb
and nut mix); paprika added a deep smokiness. We
loved the Moroccan meatballs. Snuggled in a
tomato sauce and contrasted with mint labneh, they
were bursting with Moorish favours of cumin and
paprika. Not everything hit the spot, though. Two
salt cod fritters contained too much floury potato
mash, with only a hint of fish, and the
accompanying pea and mint purée seemed a tad too
British to feature in a tapa dish.
*Booking advisable; essential weekends. Tables
outdoors (5, pavement).* **Map 26 B2**.

PORTUGUESE

Central
Clerkenwell & Farringdon

Portal
88 St John Street, EC1M 4EH (7253 6950, www.portalrestaurant.com). Barbican tube or Farringdon tube/rail. **Lunch served** noon-3pm Mon-Fri. **Dinner served** 6-10.15pm Mon-Sat. **Main courses** £12-£29. **Credit** AmEx, MC, V.
Classic Portuguese ingredients are given a Modern European makeover at Portal. Here, bacalhau (salt cod) comes as a tartare with a coriander sauce, or is served confit-style next to a risotto. The results are far removed from the homely style of cooking of most of London's Portuguese restaurants. This forward-thinking approach extends to the decor, which is all exposed brickwork, modernistic chairs and statement-piece lighting. We loved the braised Bisaro (rare-breed pork from northern Portugal), which was slow-cooked to perfection and served alongside pea mash and roasted baby peppers. A stew of favas à portuguesa was one concession to the cuisine's more rustic roots. Brought to the table in a cast-iron pot, it was a heady mix of pork belly, broad beans and chouriço. Only a starter of prawn tagliatelle missed the mark, owing to an ill-advised garnish of raspberry on a balsamic glaze. Informal dining comes in the form of tapas in the front bar, which also serves as a showcase for Portuguese wines and ports. Those celebrating should head to the shimmering glass-encased garden at the back.
Available for hire. Babies and children welcome: high chairs; nappy-changing facilities. Booking advisable. Disabled: toilet. Separate room for parties, seats 14. Tables outdoors (5, patio). **Map 5 O4**.

Knightsbridge

O Fado
50 Beauchamp Place, SW3 1NY (7589 3002, http://ofado.co.uk). Knightsbridge or South Kensington tube. **Lunch served** noon-3pm, **dinner served** 6.30-11pm Mon-Sat. **Main courses** £15.99-£20.95. **Credit** AmEx, MC, V.
With its basement location, starched white cloths and faux leather-bound menus, there's a definite air of the old school about O Fado. We were hoping for an evening of Portuguese folk music, from which the restaurant takes its name, but instead our meal was accompanied by an organist crooning Neil Diamond and Carpenters classics. Sadly, the disappointment didn't stop there. With 365 ways to serve bacalhau in Portugal, we had the misfortune to choose the very one that presents the country's national dish so badly: an unseasoned hunk of salt cod with new potatoes, served with a smattering of raw olives. The mixed grill was no better: a solitary lamb cutlet accompanied by half a chouriço, a tiny spare rib and a piece of minute steak. When Harrods is the local corner shop, it's no wonder main courses hit the £20 mark, but this didn't seem to deter the tables of tourists and couples. It's a shame our meal lacked lustre, as on our last visit we'd experienced a much better standard of cooking. O Fado would do well to take seriously its status as London's oldest Portuguese restaurant and work to make improvements.

Pastelaria

Those coffee shop stalwarts, pastéis de nata or custard tarts, are perhaps the most recognisable dish in Portuguese cuisine. These places sell them, along with a range of other traditional pastries and bica (Portuguese espresso).

Café Oporto
62A Golborne Road, W10 5PS (8968 8839). Ladbroke Grove or Westbourne Park tube or bus 23, 52. **Open** 7.30am-7pm Mon-Sat; 8am-5pm Sun. **Snacks** £1-£3.50. **No credit cards.**
This corner site is larger than Lisboa Pâtisserie, its rival on the opposite side of the road, and has a more relaxing vibe that's great for people-watching and grazing en famille. The counter is well stocked with sandwiches, but we prefer the savoury pastries (salt cod, chicken, cheese) or a toasted cheese and ham croissant.
Babies and children admitted. Tables outdoors (3, pavement). Takeaway service. **Map 19 B1**.

Funchal Bakery
141-143 Stockwell Road, SW9 9TN (7733 3134). Stockwell tube. **Open** 7am-7pm daily. **Snacks** £1-£5. **Credit** MC, V.
Available for hire. Babies and children admitted. Booking advisable; essential dinner weekends. **Map 14 F9**.

South
Brixton

Lisboa Grill
256A Brixton Hill, SW2 1HF (8671 8311). Brixton tube/rail or bus 45, 109, 118, 250. **Meals served** 7-10.30pm Mon-Fri; noon-10.30pm Sat, Sun. **Main courses** £7.50-£15. **Credit** MC, V.
In the past, those in search of a spicy chicken hit had to press a Prohibition-style buzzer at the back of Lisboa Grill's unassuming takeaway in order to gain entry to its main dining room. With a recent expansion, the cloak-and-dagger tactics are no longer necessary; a new café area next door now leads to the wood-panelled restaurant, which is decorated with frescos of Lisbon landmarks. Lisboa Grill is still one of the best places in town to enjoy franchise-free peri-peri chicken. Delicious platters of charcoal-grilled chicken were the common denominator on all tables, with the dishes distinguished by the medium, hot or extra hot level of spice offered. The rest of the menu consists of seafood dishes of varying quality. A starter of breaded prawns was meagre, and a main of bacalhau à brás (salt cod and fried potatoes) was almost inedibly oily. Stick to the main attraction and you won't be disappointed, proving that peri-peri chicken still rules the roost at Lisboa Grill.
Available for hire. Babies and children welcome: high chairs. Booking advisable weekends. Disabled: toilet. Tables outdoors (5, garden). Takeaway service. **Map 22 D3**.

Reflecting the Stockwell area's Madeiran immigrants (Funchal is a city on the island of Madeira), this friendly, functional spot offers keenly priced groceries and deli items plus cut-above cakes. We're very fond of the bolo con arroz. Expats gather to watch football on the TV in the café. *Babies and children admitted. Takeaway service.* **Map 22 D1**.

Lisboa Pâtisserie
57 Golborne Road, W10 5NR (8968 5242). Ladbroke Grove or Westbourne Park tube or bus 23, 52. **Open** 7.30am-7.30pm daily. **Snacks** 75p-£2.65. **Credit** MC, V.
A friendly spot – with delicious baking that attracts customers from some distance away, and inevitable queues – though the humble environs may surprise first-timers. For a change from custard tarts, try the scrumptious orange and coconut cake or a custard doughnut. Savouries include salt cod croquettes and ham and chorizo pastries; the breadcrumbed pork and chicken escalopes also win plaudits.
Babies and children admitted. Tables outdoors (3, pavement). Takeaway service. **Map 19 B1**.
For branches see index.

Vauxhall

Casa Madeira
46A-46C Albert Embankment, SE11 5AW (7820 1117, www.madeiralondon.co.uk). Vauxhall tube/rail. **Meals served** Coffee shop 6am-9pm daily. Restaurant noon-11pm Mon-Fri, Sun; noon-midnight Sat. **Main courses** £6.95-£15.95. **Tapas** £3-£5.95. **Credit** (over £5) AmEx, MC, V.
The ever-expanding Madeira empire now boasts nine delis, cafés and restaurants, from Paddington to Stockwell. This is the biggest and smartest of the group, situated in an imposing railway arch off the Albert Embankment. The menu encompasses tapas, grills, seafood and pizzas, helping the restaurant attract a varied post-work crowd on weekdays. On Sundays, it becomes a hub for the local Portuguese community, when the massive dining area is filled to capacity. We enjoyed the tapas-sized portions of sardines and lamb cutlets, both benefiting from a smoky blast from the charcoal grill. Octopus in paprika had a pleasant hit of chilli, but the flaming chouriço, set alight at our table, was a little too fatty. A main course of bacalhau con natas was Portuguese comfort cooking at its best: a heavenly combination of salt cod, cream and cheese, topped with toasted mashed potato. The soundtrack of satellite TV is replaced by music at the weekend, when Portuguese DJs and bands rock up and Casa Madeira becomes the ideal place to linger over a Super Bock beer or two.
Babies and children admitted. Booking advisable weekends. Entertainment: musicians 7pm Fri, Sat. Tables outdoors (40, pavement). Takeaway service. **Map 16 L11**.
For branches (Bar Madeira, Café 89, Pico Bar & Grill, Madeira Café) see index.

Steakhouses

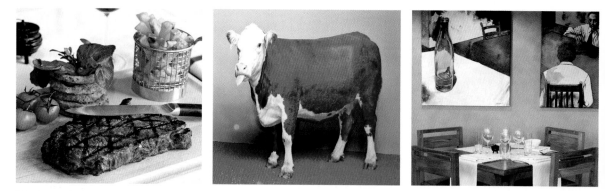

Britain has long been renowned for the quality of its beef, so London should be able to produce some top-flight steakhouses, yet it's a genre that often sees restaurateurs mimicking New York establishments. The team at **Hawksmoor**, however, has tried to forge a new style of British steakhouse at its huge Seven Dials premises – and the results are stunning: it won Best New Restaurant in the 2011 Time Out Eating & Drinking Awards. Other strong performers include **Maze Grill** and **High Timber**, both fairly costly and aiming for a well-heeled clientele. High prices don't always guarantee a great experience, however, and there are times when the functionality of a limited-choice spot such as **Le Relais de Venise l'entrecôte** or **Popeseye** appeal. Carnivores, take note: Argentinian parrilla restaurants are also great places to enjoy steak (Argentinian, of course) and we feature several in our Latin American section (*see p30*). Also recommended is the luxurious setting of **Top Floor at Smiths** (*see p205* Smiths of Smithfield), which specialises in dry-aged beef from British rare-breed cattle.

Central

Belgravia

Palm

1 Pont Street, SW1X 9EJ (7201 0710, www. thepalm.com/london). Knightsbridge or Sloane Square tube. **Dinner served** 6-11pm Mon-Fri. **Meals served** noon-11pm Sat; noon-10pm Sun. **Main courses** £11.50-£49. **Credit** AmEx, MC, V.

Palm originated in New York in the 1920s; it now has outposts across the States, from Boston to Los Angeles, but this is its only location in Europe. It fits right into its Belgravia milieu of embassies and designer handbag shops, but stands out in the London dining scene as an American import that doesn't quite translate. Low lighting, white napery and large, solid booths create a perfectly comfortable setting, and the welcome basket of assorted breads was lovely. However, having a monotone waitress deliver a rehearsed spiel about different cuts of meat, while presenting them on a tray plastered with cling film, smacked a little of David Lynch and didn't do much for the appetite. A wedge salad starter (based on iceberg lettuce) was fine, but topped with onions that were chewy, not crispy. On a previous trip here, the steaks were overcooked; this time, they were bloodier than they should have been ('rare' came just on the right side of cooked, but 'medium-well' was still oozing plenty of juice). The meat was certainly delicious – in the US, there's nothing better than these grain-fed cattle

– but grass-fed British beef is just as good. Perhaps the import duty is also responsible for the elevated prices, with steaks topping £40. On our visit, most diners were Americans reluctant to step out of their comfort zone.

Babies and children welcome: booster seats; high chairs. Booking advisable. Disabled: toilet. Separate room for parties, seats 40. **Map 15 G10**.

City

Butcher at Leadenhall

6-7 Leadenhall Market, EC3V 1LR (7283 1662, www.butcheratleadenhall.com). Bank tube/DLR. **Meals served** 7.30am-3pm Mon-Fri. **Main courses** £10.50-£23.50. **Credit** MC, V.

It may lack the sheer heft of the nearby Gherkin or Lloyd's building, but Leadenhall Market is a City presence as uncompromising as any of those young upstarts. Businesses that set up shop here must play by the market's rules – from Orange to Reiss, they share the same red and gold colour scheme – while several feature hooked metal frames that once served as display apparatus when Leadenhall dealt exclusively in meat. This is the only butcher here nowadays, with a grill area that sends tempting, smoky smells over to the lunchtime drinkers outside the Lamb and New Moon pubs. Sit out on the cobbles at one of the lightweight metal tables and choose from chops of pork, steaks of grass-fed beef and cutlets of Bretby lamb. The market interior – from the meat hooks to ceiling details – is a pleasing contrast between the dainty and the

bulky, and the platefuls here follow suit, pairing the no-nonsense goodness of grilled meat with a few adornments, such as sautéed spinach and roasted tomatoes. Non-grill dishes, such as a roast beef open sandwich, and duck breast with tuscan salad, are a little lighter, but only just. Overall, Butcher at Leadenhall does the old market's heritage proud. *Available for hire. Babies and children admitted. Booking advisable. Tables outdoors. Takeaway service.* **Map 12 Q7**.

Goodman City

11 Old Jewry, EC2R 8DU (7600 8220, www.goodmanrestaurants.com). Bank tube/ DLR. **Meals served** noon-10.30pm Mon-Fri. **Main courses** £30-£70. **No credit cards**.

Goodman opened its first London restaurant, in Mayfair, in 2009. It dry-ages its beef on site in a temperature-controlled environment, but the new City branch turns this into a visual feature with a glass-walled dry-ageing room. Cuts of the day are chalked on a blackboard. Nebraska is a favoured source for the USDA prime corn-fed beef, though the company also buys from this side of the Atlantic, so you may find Black Label Angus from south Devon, Buccleuch estate beef from Scotland, or rare-breed Belted Galloway from the Lake District. The menu is reassuringly straightforward, but speckled with luxury ingredients such as lobster, truffle and foie gras. A sweet herring starter salutes the Russian owners (there are several branches in Moscow), while wedge salad, caesar salad and creamed spinach defer to their New York inspirations. If you're not here for the steak,

Hawksmoor Seven Dials. See p249.

consider opting for grilled lobster, fish of the day or roast chicken breast with chorizo and spinach risotto. We clocked a pleasing choice of wines by the glass, with the reds offering the most diversity (including Californian zinfandel, Sicilian nero d'avola and Marlborough pinot noir). Prices are City-ruthless, though, with bottles starting at £28. The main dining area near the open kitchen feels slightly like a theme park canteen; we prefer the look of the bar with its old herringbone-patterned wooden floor, polished leather chairs and inviting booths. Another branch, in Canary Wharf, is scheduled to open at the end of 2011.
Map 11 P6.
For branch see index.

High Timber

8 High Timber Street, EC4V 3PA (7248 1777, www.hightimber.com). Mansion House tube.
Lunch served noon-3pm, **dinner served** 6.30-10pm Mon-Fri. **Main courses** £13.25-£32. **Set lunch** £16.50 2 courses, £20 3 courses.
Credit AmEx, MC, V.
High Timber has a neat location on the unfavoured north bank of the Thames, with a good view west to the Millennium Bridge and Tate Modern. It's a smart place, with minimalist decor perked up by some boisterous sculpture and paintings, and a tight focus on serving a mostly City crowd with high-spec meat and robust wine from the South African owners' Jordan Wine Estate. The 28-day-aged steaks are terrific, and not badly priced for the quality, but beware the cost of the extras. Given the tastiness of the bare steak, small pots of wonderfully intense bordelaise sauce (with redundant marrow plopped in, £5.30), or whipped foie gras butter (£4.30), are mere show-off additions aimed beadily at the banker's bonus. A shame, since our ox-cheek bourguignon showed real attentiveness, with 'smoked mashed potato' well judged in its subtle support of the stew. Although the menu is mostly gents' club favourites (bacon with black pudding, foie gras and chicken liver parfait, potted crab), there are also delicate touches: Kentish strawberries with rosé wine jelly and strawberry and Sichuan pepper gel. Service is appropriately crisp and obliging, if veering towards over-attentiveness.
Available for hire. Babies and children admitted. Booking advisable. Disabled: toilet. Separate room for parties, seats 18. Tables outdoors (4, riverside). **Map 11 O7.**

Covent Garden

★ Hawksmoor
Seven Dials [HOT 50]

2011 WINNER BEST NEW RESTAURANT
11 Langley Street, WC2H 9JJ (7856 2154, www.thehawksmoor.co.uk). Covent Garden tube.
Lunch served noon-3pm, **dinner served** 5- 10.30pm Mon-Sat. **Meals served** noon-5pm Sun. **Main courses** £15-£30. **Set meal** (5-6.30pm, 10-10.30pm Mon-Fri) £20 2 courses, £22.50 3 courses. **Credit** AmEx, MC, V.
Hawksmoor is a carnivore's paradise, a homage to top-quality British beef. Yet it's more than a steakhouse. The Covent Garden outpost is quite a different animal from the Spitalfields original, and makes the most of its basement location with a gorgeous bar that feels like an old school chemistry lab, from which palate-dazzling alco-concoctions emerge. Starters focus on British fish (Dorset oysters and blue lobster, Poole clams); our crab on

Burger joints

London is well provided with burger bars, both chains and one-offs – these are our favourites.

Byron

222 Kensington High Street, W8 7RG (7361 1717, www.byronhamburgers. com). High Street Kensington tube.
Meals served noon-11pm Mon-Thur; noon-11.30pm Fri; 11am-11.30pm Sat; 11am-10.30pm Sun. **Main courses** £6.50-£10.50. **Credit** AmEx, MC, V.
The Kensington branch of this popular burger chain is an airy, minimalist space with yellow walls, dark brick flooring and an open grill in the middle. A similar simplicity rules the menu. There are no elaborate reinventions of the burger here, just five easy options – classic, cheese, bacon cheese, chicken or veggie – with the traditional accompaniments, leaving you free to enjoy what is superior comfort food. Assorted salads cater to the calorie-conscious, and a strong list of craft beers will please enthusiasts. With such an informal atmosphere, cordial staff and high-quality, unpretentious fare, it's not surprising that Byron continues to expand at such a rate – the business, established in 2007, opened its 17th restaurant in 2011.
Babies and children welcome: children's menu; high chairs; nappy-changing facilities. Bookings not accepted lunch Sat & Sun. Disabled: toilet. Tables outdoors (4, pavement). Takeaway service. **Map 7 A9.**
For branches see index.

Gourmet Burger Kitchen

Upper Southern Terrace, Westfield Shopping Centre, W12 7GB (8749 1246, www.gbk.co.uk). Wood Lane tube. **Meals served** noon-11pm Mon-Fri; 11am-11pm Sat; 11am-10pm Sun. **Main courses** £5.96-£9.95. **Credit** AmEx, MC, V.
With around 30 branches in London alone, this ever-expanding New Zealand-inspired chain continues to serve huge, tasty burgers in its canteen-style restaurants. The Westfield branch is clean and bright, opening out on to the boardwalk, complete with water feature and the noisy hum of shoppers. The menu makes for a slightly bewildering read, with burgers coming in an array of options ranging from a basic cheeseburger to the more adventurous wellington, with mushroom, rocket, mayo and horseradish sauce. If the thought of tackling one of the high-stacked burgers seems too much, fear not: smaller sizes are available. There are also chicken, lamb, chorizo and vegetarian versions (including one with puy lentils, potato and green curry) and salads. The drinks list is standard stuff: milkshakes, bottled beers and a few wines.
Babies and children welcome: high chairs; nappy-changing facilities. Bookings not

accepted. Disabled: toilet. Tables outdoors (45, terrace). Takeaway service. Vegetarian menu. **Map 20 C1.**
For branches see index.

Haché

24 Inverness Street, NW1 7HJ (7485 9100, www.hacheburgers.com). Camden Town tube. **Meals served** noon-10.30pm Mon-Wed; 10.30am-11pm Thur-Sat; noon-10pm Sun. **Main courses** £6.95-£12.95. **Credit** AmEx, MC, V.
Patties might rule the menu here, but the experience of dining at Haché is closer to that of an urbane modern restaurant than a burger bar. The interior is chic and intimate; the glow of hanging candelabra and mirrored wall panels soften the dark wooden furniture and beams to create a surprisingly romantic mood. The attention of the young staff varied, but this was soon forgotten when a glass of tart real lemonade and a creamy vanilla milkshake arrived. Prime Scotch beef is used in the burgers, and the range of combinations is lengthy and innovative – roasted red pepper and goat's cheese, say, or portobello mushroom and basil pesto. Cooked to tender perfection, they're served on floury ciabatta or brioche, with generous sides of skin-on chips or sweet potato frites. Alternatives include burgers made with fish, chicken, lamb and even crispy duck, as well as several vegetarian falafel burgers, and salads. Pricing is very reasonable considering the premium ingredients and restaurant-standard cooking.
Available for hire. Babies and children welcome: high chairs. Booking advisable weekends. Tables outdoors (2, terrace). Takeaway service. Vegan dishes. Vegetarian menu. **Map 27 C2.**
For branches see index.

Honest Burgers

Unit 12, Brixton Village, Coldharbour Lane, SW9 8PR (07739 182955 mobile, www.honestburgers.co.uk). Brixton tube/ rail. **Lunch served** noon-4pm Tue-Sun. **Dinner served** 6-10pm Thur-Sat. **Main courses** £6.50-£8. **No credit cards**.
One of a score of new cafés in 'Brixton Village', this burger joint occupies a former shop unit and retains a shack-like feel and appearance. Seating is either in the tiny kitchen-diner or outside, in the covered market formerly called Granville Arcade. The brief menu is chalked on a blackboard. Aged beef from Ginger Pig is used for the patties, which are cooked medium-rare unless you request otherwise. The buns are firm with good bite, but we found our hand-cut, triple-cooked chips to be excessively salted. Service was on the slow side, but genial.
Available for hire. Babies and children admitted. Bookings not accepted. Takeaway service. **Map 22 E2.**

toast, a huge mound of brown and white meat served on good crusty bread, was straightforward and delectable. This is a place that chooses its ingredients carefully, then serves them simply. The steaks are a case in point. All the meat comes from excellent, Yorkshire-based butcher Ginger Pig. The beef is from Longhorn cattle, the meat dry-aged for at least 35 days. Steaks are cooked on a Josper grill, emerging with a crusty black exterior and luxe red interior. We're fans of the deep-flavoured rump, and were blown away by the ribeye, served medium-rare to melt the fat in the well-marbled meat. Side dishes of bone marrow and two kinds of chips (beef dripping or triple-cooked) complete the feast. Clued-up staff are keen to advise on the various meat cuts and the lengthy, well-chosen wine list. Make sure you arrive hungry.

Available for hire. Babies and children welcome: high chairs; nappy-changing facilities. Booking advisable. Disabled: toilet. Separate room for parties, seats 16. **Map 18 D4.**
For branch see index.

Holborn

Bountiful Cow
51 Eagle Street, WC1 4AP (7404 0200, www. thebountifulcow.co.uk). Holborn tube. **Lunch served** noon-3pm, **dinner served** 5-10.30pm Mon-Sat. **Main courses** £9-£22.50. **Set lunch** £7 1 course. **Set meal** (5-7pm) £12.50 2 courses, £14.50 3 courses. **Credit** AmEx, MC, V.
Describing itself as a 'a public house devoted to beef', this converted 1960s corner boozer nowadays looks more like a cocktail bar. A short row of smart stools face the counter; the rest of the seating is diner-style booths. Jocular film posters (cowboy movies, zombie flick *Raw Meat*) set the tone and get the carnivorous juices running. The steak is good. We were delighted that our 11oz sirloin arrived on the bloody side of rare, with neat charred lines and accompanied by a little pot of béarnaise and chips. Unsurprisingly, few concessions are made to vegetarians on the very meat-heavy menu, but the £8.50 tomato bruschetta with capers and anchovies balanced by sweet piquillo peppers proved to be keenly priced – it arrived overlapping the plate. Puddings provide few surprises, but there's good drinking to be had: draught Dark Star Hophead, perhaps or a feisty pays d'oc merlot, available by the 500ml carafe. The B-Cow was quiet on our Saturday night visit, but hooks in weekday business custom with a reliable set lunch (pork chop, macaroni cheese, corned beef hash) and early-dinner deal. Not a destination venue, then, but a solid performer.
Available for hire. Babies and children admitted. Disabled: toilet. Tables outdoors (3, pavement). Takeaway service. **Map 18 F1.**

Marylebone

Le Relais de Venise l'entrecôte
120 Marylebone Lane, W1U 2QG (7486 0878, www.relaisdevenise.com). Bond Street tube. **Lunch served** noon-2.30pm Mon-Thur; noon-2.45pm Fri; 12.30-3.30pm Sat, Sun. **Dinner served** 6-10.45pm Mon-Thur; 6-11pm Fri; 6.30-11pm Sat; 6.30-10.30pm Sun. **Set meal** £21 2 courses. **Credit** AmEx, MC, V.
This self-consciously Gallic steak restaurant aims to fit diners into a stereotypically Parisian postcard scene. Waitresses in black and white uniforms flit

between tables covered in primary-coloured cloths and a dark wooden service counter lined with bottles of vin rouge – even the blades of the knives announce the place's Parisian heritage. On a Saturday afternoon, it was rammed with casually dressed young couples with cut-glass accents. The limited-choice menu means that all diners are served a walnut-sprinkled green salad with a dijon mustard vinaigrette to start, followed by steak frites, the meat cooked to order and drenched in a mustardy 'secret sauce'. A pleasingly rare steak came cut into chunky slices, with the waitress keeping half of it back on a silver platter to offer second portions. Those who'd like to exercise some culinary choice should partake of the small dessert menu of tartelettes, sorbets and gateaux. A boozy Grand Marnier semifreddo featured a generous studding of vanilla seeds and chantilly cream scattered with precision-toasted almonds, although the difficulty of fitting a dessert spoon into the narrow wine glass it was served in is evidence that the Frenchiness occasionally goes too far.
Babies and children welcome: high chairs. Bookings not accepted. Disabled: toilet. **Map 9 G5.**
For branch see index.

Mayfair

Maze Grill
10-13 Grosvenor Square, W1K 6JP (7495 2211, www.gordonramsay.com/mazegrill). Bond Street tube. **Breakfast served** 6.45am-10.30am, **meals served** noon-11pm daily. **Main courses** £13.50-£28. **Set lunch** (noon-6.30pm Mon-Thur, Sun; noon-4pm Fri, Sat) £21 2 courses, £24 3 courses. **Credit** AmEx, MC, V.
Very much a venue that aims equally for style and substance, this Gordon Ramsay-owned restaurant is all minimalist, contemporary chic. The space is light and bright, with pale wood furniture and flooring and a muted colour scheme. At the far end, a separate, white-tiled chef's table (known as the Butcher's Block) is walled off by etched glass. It overlooks the kitchen, where the steaks are cooked over coals, and a top-of-the-range salamander grill finishes the meat at 650°C. As diners are seated, they're greeted by a waiter bearing a tray laden with hunks of raw beef swaddled in white linen, and a lengthy explanation of the five cuts, which range from 21-day-aged grain-fed Casterbridge to a '9th grade' wagyu ribeye for £85. A smoky rump, cooked rare, was impressive: piping hot yet bloody enough to ooze all over the stylish wooden board on which it was presented. Sichuan pork ribs had a salty crust and delicate lemongrass scenting, but a starter of gazpacho bordered on bland. Those who don't fancy shelling out for dessert (treacle tart with yoghurt sorbet, perhaps) are well catered for too, as everyone gets a substantial, complimentary oat and chocolate chip cookie.
Babies and children welcome: children's menu; high chairs. Booking essential. Disabled: toilet. Separate room for parties, seats 12. **Map 9 G6.**

West
Olympia

Popeseye Steak House
108 Blythe Road, W14 0HB (7610 4578, www.popeseye.com). Kensington (Olympia) tube/rail. **Dinner served** 7-10.30pm Mon-Sat. **Main courses** £9.95-£55.95. **No credit cards.**

Stuck on a lonely block between the Olympia exhibition centre and Shepherd's Bush Road is this pared-down restaurant that offers just three types of mains, doesn't do starters, doesn't take cards and doesn't – at least on our Monday visit – have many customers. It has a cosy junk-shop sort of interior, with wooden floors and ample natural light. The idea is that by serving only high-grade, grass-fed, grilled Aberdeen Angus beef steaks (fillet, sirloin and a slender rump known in Scotland as a popeseye, ranging in size from 6oz to 30oz), quality can be assured. With a single gratis side dish of chips (nicely golden, but rather homogeneous in appearance) and a single paid-for extra of salad (in a pleasingly tart french dressing), you can't go wrong. Only, you can: our steak was too charred to show off the flavour of the beef. A great pity, as the meat inside was pinkly medium-rare, as requested. Factor in the waitress's admission that the house wines were 'so-so', compelling us to part with £20 for a satisfactory Chilean cab sav, and the absence of any seasonal desserts (we couldn't face sticky toffee pudding or rhubarb crumble on a balmy summer's night), and the result was disappointing.
Available for hire. Babies and children admitted. Booking advisable. **Map 20 G3.**
For branch see index.

South
Battersea

Butcher & Grill
39-41 Parkgate Road, SW11 4NP (7924 3999, www.thebutcherandgrill.com). Clapham Junction rail or bus 19, 49, 170, 319, 345. **Breakfast served** 9am-noon daily. **Lunch served** noon-3.30pm Mon-Sat; noon-4pm Sun. **Dinner served** 5.30-11pm Mon-Sat. **Main courses** £7.50-£25. **Credit** AmEx, MC, V.
Really, that should be 'Butcher, Grill & Deli', as the delicatessen part of this operation gets as much custom as does the glass counter of meat. At the weekend, expect to see middle-class couples browsing the artisan jars of pâté, kitschy American confectionery, organic white carrots and gigantic, own-made scotch eggs. Adjacent to the deli, in an attempt to add a café-like ambience, are a couple of long communal tables. The airy main dining area is raised above the shop floor, providing a view of a post-industrial decor that takes in bare bricks, white-painted metal girders and ventilation pipes. Huge black and white framed photos of cows and sheep remind you that meat is this place's speciality – and the steaks certainly impress. A medium-rare ribeye offered hunks of crisped-up fat, dotted with chunks of black peppercorn and topped with a garlicky half-tomato. But the chips were disappointingly supermarket-like, and a portion of grilled ox heart on toast was drowned in a gloopy, brown, oniony jam that wasn't mentioned on the menu. Service was slightly impersonal, but swift – partly because there were few other diners during our Sunday afternoon visit. There's also a branch in chi-chi Wimbledon Village.
Available for hire. Babies and children welcome: children's menu; high chairs; nappy-changing facilities. Booking advisable weekends. Disabled: toilet. Tables outdoors (5, pavement; 6, terrace). Takeaway service. **Map 21 C1.**
For branch see index.

Thai

There's really no excuse. If venues such as Brixton's new café, **KaoSarn**, or South Norwood's long-esteemed **Mantanah** can produce authentic Thai cooking at low prices, then why can't it be more readily available across our city? We don't employ the 'A' word lightly; authenticity, that over-used culinary buzzword, is especially important to Thai cuisine in Britain. All too often, ingredients that are crucial to the distinctiveness of Thai food – bitter pea aubergines, the aniseed tang of holy basil, outrageously hot bird's-eye chillies, pungent dried shrimps, and many more – are substituted by cheaper foodstuffs. A Thai chef in the Scottish highlands might have no option in doing this, but many London restaurateurs, who have a wealth of fresh produce close at hand, sold at one of several good Thai supermarkets around the city, are simply cutting corners. That's not to say the food shouldn't evolve. David Thompson, an acknowledged master of Thai cuisine, produces some innovative, thrilling cooking at the luxurious **Nahm**, but his flavours are grounded in the herbs and spices of Thailand. At a less exalted level, recent developments have seen the growth of the decent **Busaba Eathai** chain, and the arrival of **Suda**, a stylish venture from the folk behind Patara.

Central
Belgravia

★ Nahm HOT 50
The Halkin, Halkin Street, SW1X 7DJ (7333 1234, www.nahm.como.bz). Hyde Park Corner tube. **Lunch served** noon-2.30pm Mon-Fri. **Dinner served** 7-10.45pm Mon-Sat; 7-9.45pm Sun. **Main courses** £17.50-£26.50. **Set lunch** £20 2 courses, £25 3 courses. **Set dinner** £60 3 courses. **Credit** AmEx, MC, V.
Located within the discreetly luxurious Halkin hotel, off Belgrave Square, Nahm is plush yet minimalist. Its windows face a delightful garden, and the warm wood panelling and gilded columns gives a regal feel to match the royal Thai food. Service is unobtrusively helpful and the menu – devised by David Thompson, celebrated Australian chef and author – is full of intriguing delights, making choice difficult, if pleasant. Opting for the Nahm arharn ('traditional Thai meal') at £60 per person allows diners to select a dish from each of the menu's six sections. As it gives no indication of degree of heat, so the waitress advised us not to order nam prik bpuu (crab relish with pea aubergines) or the geng gati (yellow seafood curry) as they were 'both very hot'. In fact, the curry was fairly mild, while the geng gari gradtai (rabbit curry with butternut squash) was palate-numbingly fierce, but elicited no such warning. Nevertheless, every ingredient was perfectly cooked and flavoured, although the textures of one or two dishes (including the 'crispy' noodles) were just a little disappointing. Don't miss the superb geng jeut fak (clear soup of green melon, chanterelles, egg and crab).
Available for hire. Babies and children welcome: high chairs; nappy-changing facilities (hotel). Booking advisable. Disabled: toilet. Dress: smart casual. Separate room for parties, seats 30.
Map 9 G9.

Covent Garden

Suda NEW
23 Slingsby Place, WC2E 9AB (7240 8010, www.suda-thai.co.uk). Covent Garden or Leicester Square tube. **Meals served** 11am-10.30pm Mon-Wed; 11am-11pm Thur-Sat; noon-10.30pm Sun. **Main courses** £7.50-£10. **Credit** AmEx, MC, V.
Darkly stylish, 2010 newcomer Suda is the latest addition to pristine St Martin's Courtyard, the recently developed enclave between Long Acre and St Martin's Lane. It comes from the same crew as the successful Patara chain and, on the whole, lives up to expectations. Spread over two floors, the large, industrially sized space is stark and monochrome (black walls and exposed girders, gleaming white tiles), with muzak beats adding to the nighttime vibe. The menu is equally contemporary, delivering clean – if occasionally sanitised – interpretations of Thai classics, from salads and noodles to curries. Our seafood and meat dishes were perfectly cooked, showing a deft hand in the kitchen, and there are plenty of fresh, fragrant ingredients. Highlights of our visit included a soft, steamed skinned aubergine (European substituted for the more bitter Thai version), served with sweet, plump scallops and a zesty dressing; a full-flavoured (though not 'hot', as advertised) red duck curry accompanied by a choice of rice; and a generous bowl of delicately sweet pad thai studded with peanut crumbs and tiny pieces of marinated tofu. Service is professional and accommodating, making Suda a safe bet for a meal with clients or dates.
Available for hire. Babies and children welcome: high chairs; nappy-changing facilities. Booking advisable weekends. Disabled: lift; toilet. Tables outdoors (4, pavement). Takeaway service.
Map 18 D4.

Thai Square
166-170 Shaftesbury Avenue, WC2H 8JB (7836 7600, www.thaisquare.net). Covent Garden or Tottenham Court Road tube. **Lunch served** noon-3pm daily. **Dinner served** 5.30-11.30pm Mon-Sat; 5.30-10.30pm Sun. **Main courses** £6.50-£22. **Set lunch** £8.95 3 courses. **Set meal** £17.95-£23.95 4 courses. **Credit** AmEx, MC, V.
The Covent Garden branch of this London-wide chain is something of a mixed bag. Our visit started well, with Thai staff warmly greeting us with a traditional 'sawadee ka'; the sweet-natured service continued throughout. On a quiet midweek evening, we weren't seated in the smart rear area, with its vaulted ceiling and adjoining courtyard garden, but in the middle section: a no-man's-land in need of a facelift, where cheap wood-effect floor tiles and

sickly lighting do little for the ambience. Likewise, the cooking showed promise, but never quite hit the mark. A beautifully presented som tam, complete with artfully carved garnishes, combined all the essential ingredients, from shredded green papaya to snake beans, dried shrimp and roasted peanuts, but its dressing lacked balance: the heat and saltiness of red chilli and fish sauce overpowering any sweet or sour flavours. Similarly, monkfish green curry correctly used bitter pea aubergines and holy basil, but was bulked up with tinned bamboo shoots; and pad thai was well seasoned but a touch overcooked. Come here if you need an urgent – and tasty – Thai fix, but Thai Square is a far cry from the stalls of Thong Lor.

Babies and children welcome: high chairs. Booking advisable Fri, Sat. Disabled: toilet. Takeaway service. **Map 18 D3**.
For branches see index.

Leicester Square

Busaba Eathai   `HOT 50`
35 Panton Street, SW1Y 4EA (7930 0088, www.busaba.com). Leicester Square or Piccadilly Circus tube. **Meals served** noon-11pm Mon-Thur; noon-11.30pm Fri, Sat; noon-10pm Sun. **Main courses** £6.20-£10.90. **Credit** AmEx, MC, V.

This chain of budget Thai eateries is experiencing a growth spurt. After years of just three branches, several more are cropping up around London. The Panton Street outlet is ideal for Leicester Square, and spacious enough to accommodate the inevitable tourist rush. Staff continue to seat patrons tightly around the large communal tables, despite plenty of empty seats nearby. Otherwise, service is generally upbeat and efficient. The menu – both food and drink – has also been growing, but is still compact and offers a decent variety of salads, soups, stir-fries, curries and noodle dishes. We enjoyed the new refreshing 'muddled' drinks of coconut water (mixed with either raspberry or lychee juice), and iced earl grey and raspberry tea. Stir-fried pepper ostrich sounded interesting, but wasn't: the meat coated in a heavy cornflour sauce that obliterated any natural flavours of the bird. Chinese broccoli with shiitake mushrooms came in quite a mean portion, with only a few slivers of flavoursome fungi. We would also avoid the new 'Thai roti', which was dry and grainy. But the old favourites are still worth returning for, such as a soothing, galangal-rich tom kha noodle soup with chargrilled chicken and slippery glass noodles, or aromatic pandan chicken.

Babies and children admitted: high chairs. Bookings not accepted. Disabled: toilet. Takeaway service. **Map 17 C5**.
For branches see index.

Marylebone

Chaopraya Eat-Thai
22 St Christopher's Place, W1U 1NP (7486 0777, www.eatthai.net). Bond Street tube. **Meals served** noon-11pm daily. **Main courses** £10.50-£23.95. **Set lunch** £8.95-£15.95 bento box. **Set dinner** £30-£40 per person (minimum 2-6). **Credit** AmEx, MC, V.

It may look rather unassuming, but Chaopraya has gastronomic aspirations. Outside, an oversized easel enthusiastically advertises lunchtime deals, which offer a more affordable way of sampling the menu of Thai delights. Massaman curry – a rich

KaoSarn. See p257.

THAI

concoction of coconut-tinged sauce cloaking tender lamb, al dente sweet potatoes and crunchy cashew nuts – came beautifully presented in a shallow bowl set on a rectangular plate. Even better, from the à la carte, was the roasted duck red curry, all smoky and sweet thanks to the chargrilled meat (though we'd have preferred the duck a touch pinker) and the medley of Thai fruits: mangosteens, lychee, longan and pineapple. Decorated with sprigs of deep violet basil and a splayed chilli made to look like a flower, the dish was as wonderfully presented as it was balanced in flavour. Less successful but by no means unpalatable, was a sweet basil and chicken soup; the broth was clear and deeply flavoured, but lacked aromatic basil. The ground-floor dining room is small and slightly narrow, skirting the line between romantic and intrusive; the basement is less appealing. Staff are all smiles. During the day, Chaopraya is a popular destination for West End shoppers and business lunchers. *Babies and children welcome: high chairs. Takeaway service. Vegetarian menu.* **Map 9 G6.**

Mayfair

Patara
3&7 Maddox Street, W1S 2QB (7499 6008, www.pataralondon.com). Oxford Circus tube. **Lunch served** noon-2.30pm, **dinner served** 5.30-10.30pm daily. **Main courses** £6.75-£19.95. **Set lunch** £12.50-£15.50 2 courses. **Credit** AmEx, DC, MC, V.
Concentrate on the food and you won't be disappointed by the Patara chain. The menu has a wide choice of dishes, with good use of UK produce weaved into classic and modern, upmarket Thai cuisine. The satay is better than most, with mouth-wateringly tender morsels of chicken, beef and prawn, and a sauce that begs to be mopped up to the last drop. Corn-fed chicken with pineapple and ginger in a garlic sauce was equally delicious, and all dishes displayed competent cooking and a clear respect for quality ingredients. There's a fantastic cocktail menu too, making this a great venue for a night on the town. Unfortunately, on our visit there was a large party dining, and a 9pm table didn't materialise until 9.30pm. We were left waiting with no drinks and no apology. Decor is stylish, with wood panelling, cosy low lighting and minimalist furnishings. Ask for a table in the main section, or downstairs if you prefer a cosier vibe, but avoid the small corridor of tables by the bar. Overall, this is a pleasing restaurant, but its popularity can lead to shortcomings in service. *Available for hire, up to 45. Babies and children admitted. Booking advisable Fri, Sat. Takeaway service. Vegetarian menu.* **Map 9 J6. For branches see index.**

West

Bayswater

★ Nipa
Lancaster London Hotel, Lancaster Terrace, W2 2TY (7262 6737, www.niparestaurant.co.uk). Lancaster Gate tube. **Bar Open** 10am-10pm daily. *Restaurant* **Lunch served** noon-2pm Mon-Fri. **Dinner served** 6.30-10.30pm Mon-Sat. **Main courses** £9.50-£15.50. **Set meal** £29-£34 4 courses. *Both* **Credit** AmEx, DC, MC, V.

Everything about the Lancaster London Hotel's smart Thai restaurant is impeccably presented – from the intricate carved vegetables artfully arranged on traditional pottery plates, to the super-nice staff with their air-hostess smiles and neat outfits. Bar a 1970s-style orange carpet, the decor is easy on the eye, combining wooden panelling with carved details, golden Thai artefacts and a view to be proud of over Hyde Park. The place was buzzing on a Monday evening, with a Thai family tucking in among the crowd of tourists, families and business folk. Feast-like set menus are priced between £29 and £34 per person; given the length of the menu, these are good ways to sample the gamut of options. We ordered kao lao nuea, a deliciously sweet, garlicky beef consommé. Soft-shell crab and green mango salad was a chef's recommendation, and we could see why: eat it quickly to retain the crunch. Aubergine and prawn dumpling curry came with a flavourful sweet basil sauce, yet was somewhat let down by its gloopiness. Desserts include the likes of coconut rice pudding, passionfruit tart and fried bananas – a step above most Thai restaurants, as indeed is Nipa itself. *Babies and children welcome: high chairs; nappy-changing facilities (hotel). Booking essential Fri, Sat. Disabled: toilet (hotel). Dress: smart casual. Vegetarian menu.* **Map 8 D6.**

Shepherd's Bush

Esarn Kheaw
314 Uxbridge Road, W12 7LJ (8743 8930, www.esarnkheaw.com). Shepherd's Bush Market tube or 207, 260, 283 bus. **Lunch served** noon-3pm Mon-Fri. **Dinner served** 6-11pm daily. **Main courses** £7.95-£10.95. **Credit** MC, V.
In its first decade after opening in 1992, this small establishment was nominated for various awards. Now, it seems tired. The decor of green walls, with faux timbers, pictures of Thai royalty and a plastic clock, looks almost like contemporary pastiche, but the weariness is evident in other ways. The kitchen is renowned for its authentic north-eastern (Isarn) Thai cuisine, yet this time the cooking felt slightly apathetic. A tasty tom yum talay was fiery without numbing the palate; it was jammed with prawns, squid and mussels, but spoilt by rubbery white mushroom quarters scattered on top. The som tam was tasty and crunchy, yet seemed to lack something, perhaps the salted crab mentioned by habitués but not now listed on the menu. Despite this, the salad made a nice textural foil for a highly enjoyable pad thai koong (with king prawns), where the noodles had a lovely unguent texture. Service was perfectly nice, if abrupt, but our meal (including a glass of Thai wine) cost more than £30 a head; it seems as if Esarn Kheaw is not only resting on its laurels, but possibly being cynical with its pricing. *Babies and children welcome: high chairs. Booking advisable. Takeaway service.* **Map 20 B1.**

South West

Earlsfield

Amaranth
346-348 Garratt Lane, SW18 4ES (8874 9036). Earlsfield rail or bus 44, 77, 270. **Dinner served** 6.30-10.30pm Mon-Sat. **Main courses** £8-£10. **Set dinner** £16.50-£22 3 courses. **Unlicensed. Corkage** (wine) £2.75. **Credit** MC, V.
Amaranth has built a loyal following over the past decade for its bold flavours and low prices (helped by a BYO policy). In fact, it's so popular that booking is required every night, and table-turning after 90 minutes is the norm. Dining takes place on two floors (ground level with kitchen, and a slightly more spacious basement), both caff-like in demeanour, sporting vividly patterned wallpaper. Service is brisk, though polite, from young Thai staff. But on this visit we couldn't help feeling that culinary standards had slackened. Pad thai comprised flaccid, broken noodles, with bean sprouts the dominant taste; the flavours provided by salty fish sauce, sour tamarind juice and hot pepper were notably subdued. A crisp som tam was better, as it used proper green papaya and not substitutes, but again it lacked kick. A steamboat dish of prawns was fine, the aroma of lemongrass filling the air as the lid was lifted, though the stock was a little one-dimensional. Let's hope this meal was a glitch, and there's a return to the consistent form of recent years. *Booking essential. Takeaway service.*

Fulham

Blue Elephant
4-6 Fulham Broadway, SW6 1AA (7385 6595, www.blueelephant.com). Fulham Broadway tube. **Lunch served** noon-2.30pm Mon-Sat; noon, 2.30pm Sun. **Dinner served** 6.30-11pm Mon-Thur; 6-11.30pm Fri, Sat; 7-10.30pm Sun. **Main courses** £11.90-£30. **Set buffet** (lunch Sun) £30. **Credit** AmEx, DC, MC, V.
Dining out is as much about the experience as the food, and few deliver the former as well as Blue Elephant. The re-creation of a Thai palace garden is beguiling: cleverly divided-off areas amid lofty plants, ponds, fountains and bridges. What's truly transporting, though, is the easy but dignified warmth of the welcome, service and even the farewell. Some critics claim this is at the expense of the food's authenticity, which they deem muted to suit westerners. The restaurant is, however, part of an international chain with establishments across the world, all receiving many ingredients flown in daily from Bangkok. Each branch promotes refined royal Thai cuisine, derived from the ancient palace cookery of the Ayutthaya kingdom in central Thailand. Here, the basic royal Thai banquet menu provides a memorable and satisfying tour of royal Thai flavours. Joys as diverse as chicken satay with peanut sauce, luscious dim sim (parcels of minced pork, shrimp and crab meat), a little mound of perfect som tam (green papaya salad), imperial fish (crisp-fried tilapia with sweet and sour sauce) and patani (lamb with cloud-ear mushrooms in oyster sauce) all combine with the surroundings to waft diners from Fulham to Phuket. *Babies and children welcome: crayons; high chairs; nappy-changing facilities. Booking advisable Sun lunch. Disabled: toilet. Entertainment: face painting Sun lunch. Takeaway service.* **Map 13 B13.**

Parsons Green

Sukho
855 Fulham Road, SW6 5HJ (7371 7600, www.sukhogroups.com). Parsons Green tube. **Lunch served** noon-3pm, **dinner served**

THAI

Menu

Spellings are subject to considerable variation. Word divisions vary too: thus, kwaitiew, kwai teo and guey teow are all acceptable spellings for noodles.

Thailand abandoned chopsticks in the 19th century in favour of chunky steel spoons and forks. Using your fingers is usually fine, and essential if you order satay sticks or spare ribs.

STARTERS

Khanom jeep or **ka nom geeb**: dim sum. Little dumplings of minced pork, bamboo shoots and water chestnuts, wrapped in an egg and rice pastry, then steamed.
Khanom pang na koong: prawn sesame toast.
Kratong thong: tiny crispy batter cups ('top hats') filled with mixed vegetables and/or minced meat.
Miang: savoury appetisers with a variety of constituents (mince, ginger, peanuts, roasted coconut, for instance), wrapped in betel leaves.
Popia or **porpia**: spring rolls.
Tod mun pla or **tauk manpla**: small fried fish cakes (should be lightly rubbery in consistency) with virtually no 'fishy' smell or taste.

SOUPS

Poh tak or **tom yam potag**: hot and sour mixed seafood soup.
Tom kha gai or **gai tom kar**: hot and sour chicken soup with coconut milk.
Tom yam or **tom yum**: a hot and sour soup, smelling of lemongrass. **Tom yam koong** is with prawns; **tom yam gai** with chicken; **tom yam hed** with mushrooms.

RICE

Khao, **kow** or **khow**: rice.
Khao nao: sticky rice.
Khao pat: fried rice.
Khao suay: steamed rice.
Pat khai: egg-fried rice.

SALADS

Laab or **larb**: minced and cooked meat incorporating lime juice and other ingredients like ground rice and herbs.
Som tam: a popular cold salad of grated green papaya.
Yam or **yum**: refers to any tossed salad, hot or cold, but it is often hot and sour, flavoured with lemon and chilli.
Yam nua: hot and sour beef salad.
Yam talay: hot and sour seafood salad (served cold).

NOODLES

Generally speaking, noodles are eaten in greater quantities in the north of Thailand. There are many types of **kwaitiew** or **guey teow** noodles. Common ones include **sen mee**: rice vermicelli; **sen yai** (river rice noodles): a broad, flat, rice noodle; **sen lek**: a medium flat noodle, used to make pad thai; **ba mee**: egg noodles; and **woon sen** (cellophane noodle): transparent vermicelli made from soy beans or other pulses. These are often prepared as stir-fries.

Common noodle dishes are:
Khao soi: chicken curry soup with egg noodles; a Burmese/Thai dish, referred to as the national dish of Burma.
Mee krob or **mee grob**: sweet crispy fried vermicelli.
Pad si-ewe or **cee eaw**: noodles fried with mixed meat in soy sauce.
Pad thai: stir-fried noodles with shrimps (or chicken and pork), beansprouts and salted turnips, garnished with ground peanuts.

CURRIES

Gaeng, **kaeng** or **gang**: the generic name for curry. Yellow curry is the mildest; green curry (**gaeng keaw wan** or **kiew warn**) is medium hot and uses green chillies; red curry (**gaeng pet**) is similar, but uses red chillies.
Jungle curry: often the hottest of the curries, made with red curry paste, bamboo shoots and just about anything else to hand, but no coconut cream.
Massaman or **mussaman**: also known as Muslim curry, because it originates from the area along the border with Malaysia where many Thais are Muslims. For this reason, pork is never used. It's a rich but mild concoction, with coconut, potato and some peanuts.
Penang, **panaeng** or **panang**: a dry, aromatic curry made with 'Penang' curry paste, coconut cream and holy basil.

FISH & SEAFOOD

Hoi: shellfish.
Hor mok talay or **haw mog talay**: steamed egg mousse with seafood.
Koong, **goong** or **kung**: prawns.
Maw: dried fish belly.

6.30-11pm daily. **Main courses** £11.25-£18.95. **Set lunch** £9 1 course, £12.15 2 courses. **Credit** AmEx, MC, V.
Located towards the Putney end of the Fulham Road, Sukho is a tranquil, airy place where the simple decor (dark wood tables dotted with potted green plants) is enlivened by a huge carved wooden panel on one wall. Service is reassuringly attentive. The extensive menu offers classic dishes as well as some intriguing surprises, with an emphasis on seafood. A starter of 'seared' scallops with young lemongrass and lime juice was exquisite, although the (albeit perfectly cooked) scallops were in no way seared; the curly parsley garnish, however, was slightly jarring. A main course of delicious crisp-fried confit of duck leg with lemongrass and tamarind arrived amid a splendid array of leaves and carved vegetables on a decorative platter, together with a large empty white plate. We then had to transfer the food to the plate, resulting in ungainly scraping to get all the lovely sauce. Top marks for the perfectly cooked fragrant rice. A Chilean viognier from the lengthy wine list suited the food nicely, but a pot of fresh mint tea was rather flavourless.
Babies and children admitted. Booking advisable. Takeaway service.
For branches (Suk Saran, Suksan) see index.

South

Brixton

★ KaoSarn NEW

2011 RUNNER-UP BEST NEW CHEAP EATS
Brixton Village Shopping Arcade, Coldharbour Lane, SW9 8PR (7095 8922). Brixton tube/rail.
Lunch served 12.30-3.30pm Tue-Sat; noon-3.30pm Sun. **Dinner served** 5.30-10pm Tue-Sat; 5.30-9pm Sun. **Main courses** £6.90-£11.50. **Unlicensed. Corkage** no charge.
No credit cards.
This tiny café sprawls by the entrance to the rebranded 'Brixton Village' (formerly Granville Arcade), one of Brixton's covered markets. KaoSarn's tables spill out into the arcade corridor and also the market's outdoor forecourt, thus providing one of the area's few alfresco dining spots. Book well ahead, because it's hugely popular – if you just turn up, as we did (on a Wednesday evening), you'll probably be turned away. Food is just like you get in Thailand, complete with slivers of fiercely hot bird's-eye chilli in some dishes. The som tam is a must-try, the sharp citrus crunch of green papaya given sour notes by the addition of ground dried shrimps. Chicken satay was also excellent, and a beef massaman curry correctly rich and sweet. Gai yang – half a chicken, marinated then grilled – was a bit dry, and accompanied by sticky rice (curiously, served in a microwave-ready plastic bag): it transported us back to Bangkok's backpacker ghetto, the Khao San Road. Although vegetarian dishes aren't prominent, tofu and vegetable versions can be prepared to order; our katoi waitress handled this with charm and efficiency. KaoSarn's rough-edged allure may not be for everyone – the toilet facilities are shared with the market – but the traffic noise, BYO policy and occasional whiff of ganja (from passers-by) give it some edge for hipster diners.
Booking advisable. Takeaway service.
Map 22 E2.

South East
South Norwood

★ Mantanah

*2 Orton Building, Portland Road, SE25 4UD
(8771 1148, www.mantanah.com). Norwood
Junction rail.* **Lunch served** noon-3pm Sun.
Dinner served 6-11pm Tue-Sun. **Main
courses** £6.95-£13.95. **Set dinner** £17 per
person (minimum 2) 3 courses, £25 per person
(minimum 2) 4 courses. **Set buffet** (lunch Sun)
£7.95. **Credit** AmEx, MC, V.

Decor is simple and inexpensive in this unassuming
little restaurant – all sparkly decorations, wood-
effect panelling and, of course, the prerequisite
photographs of the Thai royal family. Thus far, it's
a typical local Thai eaterie; what isn't typical is the
food. The menu is big on choice, with additional
sections devoted to vegetarian food, signature
dishes, regional delicacies and set meals. Don't be
overwhelmed: you'll almost invariably find your
selection doesn't disappoint (though ask for advice
if you're unused to fiery food). We selected three
very spicy dishes with a potent heat familiar to
those who have enjoyed native Thai cooking. Our
meal was impeccable, with fresh and exhilarating
flavours. Staff are extremely obliging and clearly
take pride in their food. They happily explained
various dishes and made recommendations when
asked. The gelatinous green and white Thai
pudding – made with, and served in pandan leaves
– might otherwise have been overlooked, but was
as delicious as it was unusual. An essential stop-
off for a reasonably priced and authentic Thai meal.

*Available for hire. Babies and children admitted:
high chairs. Takeaway service. Vegetarian menu.*

East
Spitalfields

★ Rosa's

*12 Hanbury Street, E1 6QR (7247 1093,
www.rosaslondon.com). Liverpool Street tube/rail
or Shoreditch High Street rail.* **Lunch served**
11am-3pm Mon-Fri, Sun. **Dinner served**
5-10.30pm Mon-Thur, Sun; 6-11pm Fri. **Meals
served** 11am-11pm Sat. **Main courses** £5.50-
£15.25. **Credit** AmEx, MC, V.

Rosa's is located in the heart of trendy Spitalfields,
and so often packed. The cool basement has proper
seats, not the red stools of the rather dark ground
floor. Service was fast and friendly, and the menu
enticing. Deep-fried crispy squid with plum sauce
was just right, and poo nim ('deep-fried soft-shell
crab topped with Thai herbs') suitably tasty. But the
'Thai herb' was a strange scattering of chopped
salad completely shrouding the crab, and containing
hidden chunks of fierce dried chilli. The signature
grills – pla yang (sea bass) and gaeh yang (rack of
lamb) – were both perfectly cooked and came with
chilli sauce and 'cooled steamed vegetables'. Given
such spicy dishes, it was a joy to find among the
latter chunks of perfectly cooked cauliflower.

*Available for hire. Babies and children welcome:
high chairs. Bookings not accepted for fewer than
6 people; advisable Fri, Sat. Takeaway service.
Vegetarian menu.* **Map 12 S5**.
For branch see index.

North
Tufnell Park

★ Charuwan

*110 Junction Road, N19 5LB (7263 1410,
http://charuwan.co.uk). Archway or Tufnell Park
tube.* **Dinner served** 6-11pm daily. **Main
courses** £4.95-£8.95. **Set dinner** £18-£20 per
person (minimum 2) 3 courses. **Credit** MC, V.

An intimate shopfront room with just 12 tables and
a tiny bar, Charuwan offers a friendly welcome that
increases to genuine warmth for regulars. Decor is
soothingly traditional, with a Thai pavilion roof
embedded in the ceiling, framed landscape photos
and a painting of the Buddha. Squarish white
plates and etched-glass tea lights are among the
token nods to modernity. The tone continues in the
menu: starters are as expected (satay, spring rolls,
fish cakes), but there are treats to explore among
the larger dishes. From the list of house specials,
squid tubes stuffed with a spicy paste of prawns
and chicken then deep-fried and served with chilli
sauce, looked as cheerful as sunflowers. We loved
the fresh fragrance of kung obb mor din (king
prawns with glass noodles, spring onion and herbs),
and the kick of hot and sour black mushroom salad.
A simple stir-fry of beef, garlic, spinach and pepper
scored for its tender meat and rich yet clean-tasting
sauce. Speaking of cleanliness: few places score the
maximum five stars for hygiene from the Food
Standards Agency; this is one of them.

*Babies and children welcome: high chairs.
Booking advisable. Takeaway service; delivery
service. Vegetarian menu.* **Map 26 B2**.

Turkish

Only last year we were bemoaning the lack of upmarket Ottoman restaurants in London – now we're welcoming a smart neighbourhood spot specialising in the dishes of Antep, and a ritzy hotel dining room introducing inventive eastern Mediterranean cooking to its celebrity guests. Set in Mayfair, **Quince**, fronted by TV cook Silvena Rowe, is about as far removed from the kebab joints of Green Lanes, the heartland of London's Turkish community, as it's possible to be. **Antepliler**, meanwhile, has grown organically from humble beginnings as a Harringey pâtisserie and is currently proving a strong competitor among the mid-priced restaurants on Islington's Upper Street. Among our top-rated places this year are two perennial favourites specialising in grills: **19 Numara Bos Cirrik** and **Mangal Ocakbaşi**. So, whether you're looking for a special occasion treat or a late-night takeaway, the capital has a first-rate Turkish restaurant to suit.

Central

Fitzrovia

Özer
5 Langham Place, W1B 3DG (7323 0505, www.sofra.co.uk). Oxford Circus tube.
Bar **Open** noon-11pm daily.
Restaurant **Breakfast served** 8am-noon, **meals served** noon-midnight daily. **Main courses** £8.95-£23.95. **Set meal** (noon-6pm) £12.95; (6pm-midnight) £14.95-£22.
Both **Credit** AmEx, MC, V.
Though it's a branch of the plush Sofra chain, Özer sits slightly uncomfortably in the Turkish section. In appearance it resembles a fine-dining operation: there's a long cocktail bar, a relaxed area with low seating and cushions, and a more starched section at the back with linen tablecloths and burnished walls. Perfect service is overseen by a besuited maître d'. The menu is too wide-ranging to be pigeon-holed: along with a range of Mediterranean dishes such as meatballs, moussaka and meze, incongruous items such as prawns with sweet chilli, or roast beef and yorkshire pud pop up. (Plastered across the menu is owner Huseyin Özer's peculiar promise/threat: 'If it is not to your taste, I'll eat it myself.') There are also several dishes that seem to be aimed at Regent Street shoppers – see the grilled salmon salad and good-value lunch platter offering 12 meze (£12.95). Nothing wrong with all this, of course, but treat Özer like a better sort of Turkish restaurant and you'll be best rewarded. Meze are made with care and high-quality ingredients, and many of the mains (lamb stew with smoked aubergine caviar; lahmacun, here called lahmazza) take care to steer away from the well-trodden kebab route.
Available for hire. Babies and children welcome: high chairs. Booking advisable. Disabled: toilet. Tables outdoors (5, pavement). Takeaway service. **Map 9 H5.**
For branches (Sofra) see index.

Marylebone

★ Ishtar
10-12 Crawford Street, W1U 6AZ (7224 2446, www.ishtarrestaurant.com). Baker Street tube.
Meals served noon-11pm Mon-Thur, Sun; noon-11.30pm Fri, Sat. **Main courses** £9.95-£15.95. **Set lunch** (noon-6pm) £8.95. **Set meal** £25-£27.50. **Set meze** £6.50. **Credit** MC, V.
You can feel the buzz at Ishtar the minute you arrive. The smart location, mainly business clientele and stylish basement with its arches, large tables and ample space between tables appeal from the word go. The waiters welcome you in the manner of discreet hotel concierges and are keen to explain the menu, which includes grand dishes such as meyveli kuzu (falls-off-the-fork stewed lamb with apricots and pears) and cupra bugulama (sea bream stew with wild mushrooms, new potatoes and asparagus), as well as a range of the more familiar grilled and minced lamb platters. There's a good-value lunch and early evening menu too, as well as a £27.50 set menu that features lots of vegetarian dishes (such as cali fasulye: green beans cooked in olive oil and tomato sauce). A variety of fattening but moreish creamy puddings and fine pastries means you don't have to plump for baklava when you finish. The wine list contains some decent Cappadocian bottles – though, again, the waiters will be honest if you're after a great vintage for a special occasion. Come the evening, this is definitely a restaurant suited for a romantic soirée or a birthday treat.
Babies and children welcome: high chairs. Booking advisable Thur-Sat. Entertainment: musicians Wed-Sat; belly dancer Fri, Sat. Separate room for parties, seats 120. Tables outdoors (6, pavement). Takeaway service. Vegetarian menu. **Map 2 F5.**

Mayfair

Quince NEW
The May Fair Hotel, Stratton Street, W1J 8LT (7915 3892, www.quincelondon.com). Green Park tube. **Breakfast served** 7-10.30am Mon-Fri; 7.30-11am Sat, Sun. **Lunch served** 12.30-3pm Mon-Fri; 1-4pm Sat, Sun. **Afternoon tea served** 3-5.30pm Mon-Fri; 2.30-5.30pm Sat, Sun. **Dinner served** 6-10.30pm daily. **Main courses** £14.50-£29. **Credit** AmEx, DC, MC, V.
The May Fair Hotel is a favourite with the partying *OK! Magazine* type of celebrity crowd thanks to its popular spa and cocktail bar, but until now has lacked a flagship restaurant. While the decision to make it an eastern Mediterranean spot may raise a few eyebrows, the owners have cleverly chosen a chef-patron with the sort of television profile that will both reassure regular guests and tempt new diners. Silvena Rowe's cooking is fresh, vibrant and deceptively simple. Witness spiced pork belly glazed with blueberry and coriander molasses – it may seem like a straightforward grill, but the pork

is cooked twice, and the molasses is made from scratch, not poured out of a food importer's bottle. Other riffs on familiar Mediterranean ingredients and recipes include tahini-flavoured hollandaise, grapefruit za'atar and tzatziki made with fennel. Or, for afternoon tea, orange and orange blossom filo pastry, and a cake made from figs, almonds and white chocolate. Martin Brudnizki's decor is not to everyone's taste; the designer of such elegant dining rooms as Scott's of Mayfair has here combined plush red banquettes (as seen in Angus steakhouses) and blue and green tiles (as seen in Turkish bathhouses), but, on the plus side, service seems to be finding its feet at last.

Available for hire. Babies and children welcome: high chairs; nappy-changing facilities (hotel). Booking essential. Disabled: toilet. Dress: smart casual. **Map 9 H7.**

Pimlico

★ Kazan
93-94 Wilton Road, SW1V 1DW (7233 7100, www.kazan-restaurant.com). Victoria tube/rail.

Lunch served noon-3pm Mon-Fri; noon-4.30pm Sat, Sun. **Dinner served** 5.30-10.30pm Mon-Sat; 5.30-9.30pm Sun. **Main courses** £11.95-£15.95. **Set meal** £13.95-£14.95 2 courses. **Credit** MC, V.

Smart yet relaxed, Kazan is a fine example of how a restaurant can showcase Turkish cuisine without being either a prosaic ockabaşı or an opulent Ottoman pastiche. Verdigris walls and just-so table settings immediately give the impression of a thoughtful operation; decor is restrained, with only a few screens, well-placed ornaments and hanging lanterns providing any clue of what's on the menu. Efficient, smiling staff bring upmarket renditions of meze and classic Mediterranean and Anatolian dishes: köfte, chops, moussaka, slow-cooked lentil stews and güveç. A few of these aren't often seen and are worth seeking out. Delicately spiced lentil köfte comes with pearls of fresh pomegranate and molasses (and is described as 'ladies' navels'. Not men's, of course – who would want to eat those?). Mualle is an aubergine-based vegetable stew with tomato and pepper that, although filling, perhaps could have been more assertive in taste; it required

the proffered chilli sauce to enliven it. Nevertheless, all freebies – bread, vegetable pilav, olives and pistachio turkish delight brought with the bill – are of a high quality. There's a basement room for larger groups, which means the ground-floor atmosphere remains calm.

Babies and children welcome: high chairs. Booking advisable Fri, Sat. Disabled: toilet. Takeaway service. **Map 15 J11.**

South East
London Bridge & Borough

Tas
72 Borough High Street, SE1 1XF (7403 7200). London Bridge tube/rail. **Meals served** noon-11.30pm daily. **Main courses** £7.95-£12.90. **Credit** AmEx, MC, V.

The Borough branch of Tas neatly embodies the traits that make this Anatolian chain so popular. The pillared white interior is simply decorated – a wall mosaic here, a framed painting of Turkish women there – but with its artful spot-lighting and liberal arrangement of potted plants, it offers a Mediterranean ambience that on our last visit was bolstered by an elderly guitarist plucking away in the background. The menu lists more than 40 starters alongside a huge range of grills, casseroles and fish dishes, but our selections varied from delicious to disappointing. A hot starter of patlıcan-biber kizartma featured generous chunks of aubergine in a fresh-tasting tomato and yoghurt sauce, but was served lukewarm; better was a cold confection of zeytinli ahtapot salatasi (marinated baby octopus in a salad of red onions, olives and coriander). A main of slow-cooked incik lamb shank was tender enough to fall off the bone, and came in a rich tomato sauce, but a vegetarian kabak stew of courgettes with tomatoes, chickpeas and potatoes was watery and under-seasoned. As a window into the breadth of Anatolian cuisine, Tas does a commendable job; as a mainstream chain, it might benefit from a less ambitious menu.

Available for hire. Babies and children welcome: high chairs; nappy-changing facilities. Booking advisable. Disabled: toilet. Takeaway service. **Map 11 P8.** **For branches (EV Restaurant, Bar & Delicatessen, Tas, Tas Café, Tas Pide) see index.**

North East
Dalston

Mangal II
4 Stoke Newington Road, N16 8BH (7254 7888, www.mangal2.com). Dalston Kingsland rail or 76, 149, 243 bus. **Meals served** noon-1am Mon-Sat; noon-midnight Sun. **Main courses** £8.45-£14.45. **Credit** AmEx, MC, V.

In business for more than 20 years, Mangal II is the unflagging granddaddy of ockabaşı – with its very own celebrity diners-in-residence, Gilbert & George, still a nightly fixture. It's lasted well, considering it faces stiff competition in this Turkish heartland, notably from its slightly cheaper (unrelated) rival round the corner, Mangal Ocakbaşı, which is still full to bursting despite a recent expansion. Mangal II also appears to have lost its tablecloths and with them any comfort advantage over the competition.

Quince. See p259.

But it's easy to see why G&G never cook at home. The menu is long enough to offer different choices every night of the week, and at lunchtime there are meaty, beany stews too. Meze, though well presented, aren't the main attraction (halloumi a bit rubbery, calamares with salad-creamy dip, dinky dolmas, iceberg lettuce). The siren call emanates from the ocakbaşı barbecue trough at the back, which is expertly tended by guys crouching over the coals. This is the source of the irresistible grilled meats – including sweetbreads, liver, kidney, quail and the usual şiş, spicy beyti and succulent lamb chops – or veg speared on metal skewers. Plates overflow with colourful, crunchy salad and there's warm absorbent bread for the smoky juices. Pudding choices are minimal, but few make it that far. Service is swift and tables are turned as fast as the hipsters pack in.
Babies and children welcome: high chairs. Booking advisable weekends. Takeaway service. **Map 25 C4.**

★ Mangal Ocakbaşı
10 Arcola Street, E8 2DJ (7275 8981, www.mangal1.com). Dalston Kingsland rail or 67, 76, 149, 243 bus. **Meals served** noon-midnight daily. **Main courses** £9.50-£13.50. **Corkage** no charge. **No credit cards.**
Hidden for more than 20 years down a side street off Stoke Newington Road, this no-frills grill is where London's kebab connoisseurs head for some of the best Turkish food in the city. There's often a scrum as customers cram in to wait for tables or a takeaway, but the meat-packed display by the door proves an incentive to patience, as does the compelling sight of the chef behind his smoky charcoal grill expertly flipping skewers. Despite this theatre, the best seats are at the back, where things are somewhat calmer. Once ensconced, order the mixed meze – it will arrive in minutes with a free basket of superb bread – while you mull over the mains. Remember, pretty much everything that comes off those coals is of outstanding quality. (Vegetarians might not be so impressed.) We especially rate the spicier minced lamb kebabs, such as adana köfte and beyti; also good is cubed chicken with tomato and yoghurt sauce. Although you can buy alcohol, corkage-free BYO and bargain prices make the restaurant a magnet for groups, so it's not the place for a quiet meal. Service is friendly but brisk – don't expect to hang around when you're finished.
Babies and children admitted. Booking advisable. Disabled: toilet. Takeaway service. **Map 25 C4.**

★ ★ 19 Numara Bos Cirrik I
34 Stoke Newington Road, N16 7XJ (7249 0400). Dalston Kingsland rail or 76, 149, 243 bus. **Meals served** noon-midnight daily. **Main courses** £7.50-£10.50. **Corkage** £1-£5. **Credit** MC, V.
It's appropriate that the dominating feature of this single-room ocakbaşı is the embossed copper extractor hood at the right-hand end of the counter: the place is all about that smoking charcoal grill. The setting might be simple (plain paper tablecloths, blue plates on the wall, evil eyes over the grill to ward off curses, wandering Turkish melodies and, bizarrely, some Egyptian friezes), but the welcome from the black-clad staff is warm. You'll be presented with a big bowl of excellent pide and three salads shortly before your food order arrives, and offered free Turkish tea to finish. In between, the main event is the meat: şiş, adana and

Mangal Ocakbaşı

chicken kebabs, spare ribs, beyti and köfte – perfectly charred without being burnt, and all saltily, juicily magnificent. Only the şiş was a little chewy on our most recent visit. The extras are done right too: those free salads look rough-handed, but we really liked the roasted onion variant with a fruity pomegranate sauce, and the accompanying rice is deliciously plump. We won't vouch for the starters, simply because we rarely have enough appetite to try them. Expect a great feed for pleasingly little cash.
Available for hire. Babies and children admitted. Booking advisable. Separate room for parties, seats 40. Takeaway service. **Map 25 C4. For branches see index.**

North
Camden Town & Chalk Farm

Ottoman Palace NEW
14-16 Camden High Street, NW1 0JH (7383 7245, www.ottomanpalace.co.uk). Mornington Crescent tube. **Meals served** noon-midnight daily. **Main courses** £9-£16. **Set lunch** £9.95 2 courses, £11.95 3 courses. **Set meze** £14.95-£24.95 per person (minimum 2). **Credit** AmEx, MC, V.
Think 'Ottoman palace' and Istanbul's Topkapı Sarayı, might spring to mind, not Camden High Street, whose most palatial building is the unappetising Koko club. This so-called palace may lack a harem, but the owners have made a decent, sabre-edged stab at evoking Turkish luxury (albeit via the site's previous incarnation as a Vietnamese restaurant), with intricately cut wooden screens and velvet cushions. The back area is oddly constructed: exposed sloping roofs and skylights imply that an al fresco effect was the aim, yet these are juxtaposed with backlit mirrors and glistening, obsidian-like floors. Starters were served on very 1990s plates, and the non-traditional mixed leaf salad that accompanied them was a disappointment – we missed those masterclasses of chopping that are typical of traditional Turkish salads such as çoban. Nevertheless, lamb's liver was good, and pallid-

looking squid surprisingly savoury, though the famous imam bayıldı left us unmoved. One of our main courses – iskender kebab – was decent, despite the fundamental failing of soggy bread at its base. Another of za'atar chicken with green lentils, baby spinach and chestnut stew was tasty and light (as Turkish mains go), even if the name given on the menu – tavuk göğsü – usually refers to a chicken-based dessert.
Babies and children welcome: high chair; nappy-changing facilities. Booking advisable. Disabled: toilet. Takeaway service. **Map 3 J2.**

Finsbury Park

Petek
94-96 Stroud Green Road, N4 3EN (7619 3933). Finsbury Park tube/rail. **Meals served** noon-11pm daily. **Main courses** £9.45-£15.70. **Set meal** £8.45-£9.95 2 courses. **Set meze** £7.45-£9.45 per person (minimum 2). **Credit** AmEx, MC, V.
Local restaurants often have to do that bit more to hang on to customers, and Petek certainly works hard to please a mixed clientele: witness the list of cocktails, from a decent gin martini to a surprising chilli and pear margarita. The menu offers the expected hot and cold meze and kebabs as well as less common dishes (mongol liver) and more outlandish combinations (salmon and pear). Sticking to the classics, we were delighted by a warmly spiced and big-flavoured adana (spicy mince kebab), which came with tomato sauce and a rich, delicious aubergine paste. The mackerel and prawns wasn't so successful – the dish showed a steady hand at the grill, but it was hard to see what the three skewered prawns added (surf and surf, perhaps?). Both these main courses were generously sized; the large plates on which they were served were barely able to contain the accompanying salad, pitta strips and sun-dried tomatoes. Our friendly waitress was swift in her patrols of the restaurant's parallel rooms, the prettier of which adds a multitude of multicoloured hanging lamps to interior decor of historical photos and navy-blue tiles. In all, a relaxed and accommodating venue.
Babies and children welcome: high chairs. Booking advisable. Tables outdoors (3, pavement). Takeaway service.

Harringay

★ Hala NEW

29 Green Lanes, N4 1LG (8802 4883). Manor House tube, then bus 29. **Meals served** 7am-2am daily. **Main courses** £3.50-£11.50. **No credit cards**.

Linger a little at this Turkish café-restaurant and takeaway and it will appear that Hala – meaning 'Aunt' – is a fitting name. The easy warmth, unhurried atmosphere and free tea at the end of the meal make it feel rather like hanging out in a family kitchen. The rectangular space, hung with 'evil eye' ornaments and kilim, is heavy on the wood, with cool stone floors that recall hotter climes than Harringay. At the takeaway counter area, the overarching brownness is interrupted by metal panelling and a yellow wall menu. Staff may be predominantly male, but (as befits the name) it's the two ladies at their windowside work station who most intrigue as they manipulate dough into gözleme (filled pancakes) and tiny mantı. The latter – springy, beef-filled pasta nuggets – may not represent the high point of Turkish cuisine, but think of them rather as comforting nursery food. Mantı is one of two Hala specialities; the other, içli köfte, is also recommended. The usual range of grilled meat, fish and kebabs are present, and our meze starters were flawless, particularly the lamb's liver, its richness tempered by a sprinkle of chilli and plentiful parsley and onion.
Available for hire. Babies and children welcome: high chairs; nappy-changing facilities. Disabled: toilet. Takeaway service. Vegetarian menu.

Highbury

Iznik

19 Highbury Park, N5 1QJ (7354 5697, www.iznik.co.uk). Highbury & Islington tube/ rail or 4, 19, 236 bus. **Meals served** 10.30am-11pm daily. **Main courses** £10-£14. **Credit** AmEx, MC, V.

Half a borough away from the hubbub of Hackney's rougher-hewn, charcoal-fuelled Turkish scene, Highbury's Iznik emits a pretty glow of lamplight and vibrant paint shades at night. Flavours come not from the grill, but the oven, and slower cooking creates some unusual and subtly complex tastes. In sebzeli sarma, chicken, hand-chopped into a kind of sausage, is flavoured with dill, wrapped in aubergine and courgette to keep it succulent, baked in a tomato sauce, then served on puréed potato with a fresh, contrasting crunch of pomegranate seeds. Karniyarik, melting aubergine baked with herby minced lamb, is another winner. Though painstakingly prepared, meze, especially peynirli börek (cheesy filo parcels), can be salty. That's feta for you. Though there are grills for the meat-minded, Iznik also has vegetarian main courses that are better than the meze. Taratorlu kabak is a skewer of courgette and apple, grilled and served with a nutty, cheesy, herby sauce. Under the turquoise ceiling there's decorative clutter and appreciative clatter from a local clientele. Note that the wooden benches aren't as comfortable as embroidery seat covers make them look. Eat enough of the notable puddings, such as semolina cake with thick cream and fruit, and in time you'll provide your own padding.
Available for hire. Babies and children welcome: high chairs. Booking advisable; essential weekends. Takeaway service.

Islington

Antepliler

139 Upper Stret, N1 1QP (7226 5541, www.anteplilerrestaurant.com). Angel tube or Highbury & Islington tube/rail. **Meals served** noon-11pm daily. **Main courses** £3.90-£14.50. **Credit** MC, V.

Antepliler (meaning someone from the Turkish city of Antep) started life as a pâtisserie in Newington Green nearly 20 years ago; the original site was extended to include a restaurant and now commands four shopfronts. This new, more upmarket branch, which has a holiday nightclub feel to the decor, is broader in its appeal and Londoners have taken to it like gulls to the Mediterranean. Prices are keen, service is excellent and dishes are true to the flavours of south-eastern Anatolia. Antep is famous throughout Turkey for its cuisine, especially kebabs and pistachio baklava. Here, Gaziantep ('Glorious Antep') specialities are

helpfully marked on the menu. Sogan kebabs (ground lamb with chargrilled shallots, topped with pomegranate sauce) had the pleasingly sour-sweet flavours found along the Silk Road. Diced lamb fillet with spiced butter was rich and tender. Among the intriguing meze are occe (parsley and red pepper fritters), bakla (marinated broad beans served on strained yoghurt) and içli köfte (minced lamb with pistachios and spices in a bulgar wheat crust). The brief wine list is international, though the house red and white (£13.50 per bottle) come, appropriately, from Turkey. A welcome addition to Islington's dining scene.
Available for hire. Babies and children welcome: high chairs. Tables outdoors (4, pavement). Takeaway service. **Map 5 O1**. **For branch see index**.

Pasha

301 Upper Street, N1 2TU (7226 1454, www.pasharestaurant.co.uk). Angel tube or Highbury & Islington tube/rail. **Meals**

Pasha

Menu

It's useful to know that in Turkish 'ç' and 'ş' are pronounced 'ch' and 'sh'. So şiş is correct Turkish, shish is English and sis is common on menus. Menu spelling is rarely consistent, so expect wild variations on everything given here. See also the menu boxes in **Middle Eastern** and **North African**.

COOKING EQUIPMENT

Mangal: brazier.
Ocakbaşı: an open grill under an extractor hood. A metal dome is put over the charcoal for making paper-thin bread.

MEZE DISHES & SOUPS

Arnavut ciğeri: 'albanian liver' – cubed or sliced lamb's liver, fried then baked.
Barbunya: spicy kidney bean stew.
Börek or böreği: fried or baked filo pastry parcels with a savoury filling, usually cheese, spinach or meat. Commonest are **muska** or **peynirli** (cheese) and **sigara** ('cigarette', so long and thin).
Cacik: diced cucumber with garlic in yoghurt.
Çoban salatası: 'shepherd's' salad of finely diced tomatoes, cucumbers, onions, perhaps green peppers and parsley.
Dolma: stuffed vegetables (usually with rice and pine kernels).
Enginar: artichokes, usually with vegetables in olive oil.
Haydari: yoghurt, infused with garlic and mixed with finely chopped mint leaves.
Hellim: Cypriot halloumi cheese.
Houmous kavurma: houmous topped with strips of lamb and pine nuts.
Imam bayıldı: literally 'the imam fainted'; aubergine stuffed with onions, tomatoes and garlic in olive oil.
İşkembe: finely chopped tripe soup, an infallible hangover cure.
Kısır: usually a mix of chopped parsley, tomatoes, onions, crushed wheat, olive oil and lemon juice.
Kizartma: lightly fried vegetables.
Lahmacun: 'pizza' of minced lamb on thin pide (qv).
Mercimek çorbar: red lentil soup.
Midye tava: mussels in batter, in a garlic sauce.
Mücver: courgette and feta fritters.
Patlıcan: aubergine, variously served.
Pide: a term encompassing many varieties of Turkish flatbread. It also refers to Turkish pizzas (heavier and more filling than lahmacun, qv).
Pilaki: usually haricot beans in olive oil, but the name refers to the method of cooking not the content.
Piyaz: white bean salad with onions.
Saç: paper-thin, chewy bread prepared on a metal dome (also called saç) over a charcoal grill.
Sucuk: spicy sausage, usually beef.
Tarator: a bread, garlic and walnut mixture; **havuç tarator** adds carrot; **ıspanak tarator** adds spinach.
Yayla: yoghurt and rice soup (usually) with a chicken stock base.
Yaprak dolması: stuffed vine leaves.

MAIN COURSES

Alabalik: trout.
Güveç: stew, which is traditionally cooked in an earthenware pot.
Hünkar beğendi: cubes of lamb, braised with onions and tomatoes, served on an aubergine and cheese purée.
İçli köfte: balls of cracked bulgar wheat filled with spicy mince.
İncik: knuckle of lamb, slow-roasted in its own juices. Also called kléftico.
Karni yarik: aubergine stuffed with minced lamb and vegetables.
Mitite köfte: chilli meatballs.
Sote: meat (usually), sautéed in tomato, onion and pepper (and sometimes wine).

KEBABS

Usually made with grilled lamb (those labelled **tavuk** or **piliç** are chicken), served with bread or rice and salad. Common varieties include:
Beyti: usually spicy mince and garlic, but sometimes best-end fillet.
Böbrek: kidneys.
Çöp şiş: small cubes of lamb.
Döner: slices of marinated lamb (sometimes mince) packed tightly with pieces of fat on a vertical rotisserie.
Halep: usually döner (qv) served over bread with a buttery tomato sauce.
İskender: a combination of döner (qv), tomato sauce, yoghurt and melted butter on bread.
Kaburga: spare ribs.
Kanat: chicken wings.
Köfte: mince mixed with spices, eggs and onions.
Külbastı: char-grilled fillet.
Lokma: 'mouthful' (beware, there's a dessert that has a similar name!) – boned fillet of lamb.
Patlıcan: mince and sliced aubergine.
Pirzola: lamb chops.
Şiş: cubes of marinated lamb.
Uykuluk: sweetbread.
Yoğurtlu: meat over bread and yoghurt.

DESSERTS

Armut tatlısı: baked pears.
Ayva tatlısı: quince in syrup.
Kadayıf: cake made from shredded pastry dough, filled with syrup and nuts or cream.
Kazandibi: milk pudding, traditionally with very finely chopped chicken breast.
Kemel pasha: small round cakes soaked in honey.
Keşkül: milk pudding with almonds and coconut, topped with pistachios.
Lokum: turkish delight.
Sütlaç: rice pudding.

served noon-11.30pm Mon-Sat; noon-11pm Sun. **Main courses** £7.95-£14.95. **Set meze** lunch £9.95, dinner £12.95 (minimum 2). **Set meal** £20.95 3 courses. **Credit** AmEx, MC, V.
On first impression, Pasha almost seems to resemble a late-night club, with its feature lights, low seating, UV toilets and well-stocked bar. It's a smart place, with a few Ottoman design flourishes providing the only clues to its direction. Rather than straight-up Turkish, think of the menu as a stylish but safe trip around the Med, stopping mainly in Turkey but also North Africa, Albania and the Middle East. Pasha never actually wows with any of the countries it represents, but everything is well executed, thoughtfully plated and tasty. Along with a warm wholemeal pitta, our waistcoated waiter brought a starter of fine renditions of mücver: deep-fried, bhajia-style fritters of courgette and cheese. A meze offer includes these, as well as skewers and the usual houmous and tabouleh, but it's only available for groups of two or more. Steer clear of the grilled mains (you can get them elsewhere) and try some of the more interesting dishes: lamb kléftico, say (slow-cooked shoulder with potatoes and oregano). Pasha's trad Sunday roasts seem to signify a slight lack of confidence, but there's no need: the Turkish offerings are still among the best on Upper Street.
Available for hire. Babies and children welcome: high chairs. Booking advisable. Tables outdoors (2, pavement). Takeaway service. **Map 5 O1**.

North West
Belsize Park

Zara
11 South End Road, NW3 2PT (7794 5498). Belsize Park tube or Hampstead Heath rail. **Meals served** noon-11.30pm daily. **Main courses** £9-£15. **Credit** AmEx, MC, V.
When this homely neighbourhood café-restaurant gets things right, a lovely time is guaranteed. Little has changed over the years and that's how locals seem to like it. Simple traditional furniture sits in a terracotta-tiled, white-walled room. Occasionally we've been disappointed by the cooking and service, but our most recent visit saw staff and kitchen in fine fettle. We're still salivating over the tavuk iskender, one of 12 dishes available from the grill (16 if you include the fish options). Delectable pockets of smoky chicken, rich tomato sauce and creamy seasoned yoghurt interspersed with nuggets of chewy pitta bread made each mouthful a textural, flavour-packed delight. Also terrific was the lamb shish featuring lamb and chicken shish, köfte and lamb chop, chargrilled to perfection and served with loose-grained rice and crisp salad. Traditional Anatolian dishes are available too: meatballs baked with vegetables, for example, or chicken tava, sautéed with mushrooms and vegetables and served in a herby cream sauce. Share one of the mixed meze plates if you can't decide where to start. The Turkish wines aren't numerous but worth choosing – this time, çankaya, made with indigenous Turkish grapes emir and narince, flowed very nicely indeed.
Available for hire. Babies and children welcome: high chairs. Booking essential weekends. Tables outdoors (4, pavement). Takeaway service. Vegetarian menu. **Map 28 C3**.

Vegetarian

2011 may not have seen the launch of any hot new vegetarian restaurants, but the old guard is still going strong. From the relaxed, welcoming ambience of the **Gate** in Hammersmith or **Mildred's** in Soho, to a more polished approach at Primrose Hill's **Manna**, or **Vanilla Black** in the City, there's something to suit every occasion. Eating on the run? We also have some great suggestions for a veggie pit-stop. For special occasions, don't forget to think outside the box: the capital boasts a number of fine dining restaurants that cater exceptionally well for non-meat eaters. We're especially fond of the **Greenhouse** (*see p132*), **Morgan M** (*see p99*), **Murano** (*see p159*) and **Roussillon** (*see p84*), all of which offer classy vegetarian menus. For something more casual, consider favourites such as the **Modern Pantry**, **NOPI** and the **Providores & Tapa Room** from our Pan-Asian & Fusion chapter (*see p227*), where bold ingredients add va-va-voom to veggie fare. Alternatively, there's the tried-and-trusted veg-friendly cuisines of South India (*see p137*) and the Middle East (*see p194*).

Central
Chancery Lane

★ Vanilla Black
17-18 Tooks Court, off Cursitor Street, EC4A 1LB (7242 2622, www.vanillablack.co.uk). Chancery Lane tube. **Lunch served** noon-2.30pm Mon-Fri. **Dinner served** 6-10pm Mon-Sat. **Set lunch** £18.50 2 courses, £23.50 3 courses. **Set meal** £24.50 2 courses, £32.50 3 courses. **Credit** AmEx, MC, V.
Contemporary, innovative and refined, Vanilla Black occupies a top spot in the pecking order of London's vegetarian restaurants. Attention to detail is the defining quality, from its imaginative culinary creations to its beautiful plating. Obscure ingredients such as sea aster (a coastal plant) and cheffy embellishments – gels, infusions, smoked ingredients – pepper the elaborate menu. To start, a duck egg poached for two hours to retain a loose wobble and served cold was too adventurous for our tastes, but potato cakes with a surprising smoked olive oil mayonnaise were delicate and delectable. Mains included a tomato tarte tatin that paired vibrant cherry tomatoes with light, flaky pastry. Peanut butter cheesecake was a far cry from the doorstop dessert you might expect, instead exemplifying the restaurant's intelligent way with contrasting textures. It involved slender cream cheese cigars balanced on perfectly sweetened toffee sauce swirls, sprinkled with shards of bitter cocoa beans to resemble a deconstructed, high-class Snickers bar. That VB manages to pull off such culinary sophistication while sidestepping overt formality is largely thanks to its expert yet friendly staff. Decoration is limited to expensive flowers and streamlined mirrors on walls painted soft grey. The venue livens up as it fills with diners from the nearby legal quarter and folks out for a celebration. *Babies and children admitted. Booking advisable. Disabled: toilet.* **Map 11 N6**.

King's Cross

Itadaki Zen
139 King's Cross Road, WC1X 9BJ (7278 3573, www.itadakizen.com). King's Cross tube/rail. **Lunch served** noon-3pm Mon, Tue, Thur, Fri. **Dinner served** 6-10.30pm Mon-Sat. **Main courses** £6.50-£12. **Set menu** £15 3 courses, £21 4 courses. **Credit** MC, V.
With neutral colours, pale wooden tables, scattered plants and a sculptural branch hanging near the entrance, Itadaki Zen has the air of tranquillity you might hope for in a place aiming to serve foods with 'healing properties'. The menu holds vegan versions of many classic Japanese dishes, as well as giving a few nods to other Asian cuisines. Expect plenty of whole grains, tofu, seasonal vegetables and seaweed varieties, along with some intriguing restorative teas. Mixed grain maki rolls had a satisfying nutty flavour and a good variety of fillings. On the other hand, the white rice nigiri were chalky, with toppings that, although inventive, were too wet for the rice to hold its shape. Crispy kakiage tempura was attractively threaded with tiny fronds of seaweed, but the dipping sauce was a little too salty and lacked depth of flavour – a recurring theme with much of the food we tried. On our midweek visit, the service was friendly yet unhurried, with the drinks and dishes taking some time to arrive. We suspect a laid-back attitude comes with the territory here.
Available for hire. Babies and children welcome: high chair. Separate room for parties, seats 14. Tables outdoors (2, pavement). Takeaway service. Vegan dishes. **Map 4 M3**.

Mayfair

★ Tibits
12-14 Heddon Street, W1B 4DA (7758 4110, www.tibits.co.uk/e). Oxford Circus or Piccadilly Circus tube. **Meals served** 9am-midnight Mon-Sat; 11.30am-10.30pm Sun. **Buffet** lunch £2/100g, dinner £2.20/100g. **Credit** MC, V.
Thanks to ample seating on Tibits's peaceful courtyard terrace, we didn't have to wait for a table, even at the lunchtime peak when shoppers and tourists throng the place. It's a bit like a canteen inside, despite the decor of black ceilings, richly coloured patterned fabrics and the odd ornate candle holder. Friendly staff explained the help-yourself buffet system. Around 30 hot and cold dishes are displayed in an oval 'food boat', priced per 100g (4oz); prices are raised slightly for dinner. The usual pasta salads, gratins and antipasti dishes make an appearance, but seemed dull and bland, and not worth their weight. A mangetout and red onion stir-fry was too oily. Red rice salad with courgette, peppers and a peperoncini oil dressing offered more complex, satisfying flavours. We also tried a mini calzone; the filling of lightly spiced

Mildred's

mushrooms and peppers was promising, but cardboard-like pastry let it down. Thankfully, desserts (such as the light chocolate coconut mousse, and the berry tiramisu), and the fresh juice combinations, didn't disappoint. A wholesome, healthy food experience? Perhaps not, but Tibits makes for a tranquil lunch break in between the Regent Street shops.

Babies and children welcome: crayons; high chairs; nappy-changing facilities. Disabled: toilet. Separate room for parties, seats 50. Tables outdoors (18, piazza). Takeaway service. Vegan dishes. **Map 17 A4.**

Soho

Mildred's

45 Lexington Street, W1F 9AN (7494 1634, www.mildreds.co.uk). Oxford Circus or Piccadilly Circus tube. **Meals served** noon-11pm Mon-Sat. **Main courses** £8-£10.50. **Credit** MC, V.

Reservations aren't taken at this Soho old-timer, so arrive promptly for lunch or dinner to secure one of the nicer tables under the skylight at the back, and to avoid peak-time clatter. Mildred's has lost none of the qualities that made it successful at its original Greek Street premises. Clean white walls, Formica tables and muddy orange banquettes create a simple aesthetic, and friendly staff are helpful and answer questions knowledgeably. As we dithered over the fresh juice selection, the waitress (unbidden) brought over a beetroot, apple and ginger concoction to sample. The menu features regulars like burger and chips, sausage and mash and vegetable stir-fry on brown rice, but also reveals an enticing range of global influences. We shared some perfectly judged gyoza dumplings, followed by a surprisingly mild (but deeply flavoured) Sri Lankan curry, and a hefty burrito. Afterwards, the likes of fruit crumble, and banana and coconut tofu cheesecake had to be ignored in favour of pavlova. This lacked a soft centre, but strawberries, cream and sugar work in any manifestation. We weren't the only happy

customers; the young women next to us were so keen they asked if the manager was hiring. *Babies and children welcome: high chairs. Bookings not accepted. Separate room for parties, seats 24. Tables outdoors (2, pavement). Takeaway service. Vegan dishes.* **Map 17 A4.**

West
Hammersmith

The Gate

51 Queen Caroline Street, W6 9QL (8748 6932, www.thegate.tv). Hammersmith tube. **Lunch served** noon-2.30pm Mon-Fri. **Dinner served** 6-10.30pm Mon-Sat. **Main courses** £10.50-£13.75. **Credit** AmEx, MC, V.

This long-established destination is an oasis of calm in noisy Hammersmith. Leased from a church, the Gate has a prime location in an expansive artist's loft overlooking a picturesque courtyard. It's a smart set-up, with the bright, sunny interior making for a relaxed atmosphere, helped by friendly, well-versed staff. Food lovers of all backgrounds come here for seasonal creative dishes inspired by Middle Eastern, Mediterranean and Asian flavours. A lightly fried Indo-Iraqi potato cake made a tasty first course: crushed potatoes spiced with popped mustard seeds and filled with lightly curried peas and carrots – a more-ish contrast to fresh-tasting apple and coriander chutney. Equally impressive, fried courgette flowers filled with sweet potatoes and tart goat's cheese made a marvellous marriage with lemon-dressed lentils. Our mains weren't quite as memorable; a sizeable crumbed and fried aubergine slice was too greasy to do justice to its crunchy okra garnish and accompaniment of guacamole and chipotle chilli salsa. Thankfully, rotola, a herby ricotta and sliced potato roll, wrapped around crisp-cooked courgettes, asparagus and roasted red pepper, brought things

back on track. Even carnivores won't miss the meat at this doyenne of vegetarian restaurants. *Available for hire. Babies and children welcome: high chairs. Booking advisable. Tables outdoors (15, courtyard). Vegan dishes.* **Map 20 B4.**

Shepherd's Bush

Blah Blah Blah

78 Goldhawk Road, W12 8HA (8746 1337, www.blahvegetarian.com). Goldhawk Road tube or 94 bus. **Lunch served** 12.30-3.30pm, **dinner served** 6.30-10.30pm Mon-Sat. **Main courses** £9.95. **Unlicensed. Corkage** £1.45 per person. **Credit** MC, V.

With the likes of Yotam Ottolenghi showing that vegetarian food need have no limits (apart from the obvious one of meat, of course), we can't help but find the canteen-style nosh in this long-established veggie restaurant just a little, well, blah. The venue is nicely presented, with playful touches including a theatrical crimson shopfront looking on to Goldhawk Road, massive TV-like spotlights and pots of crayons provided for doodling on the paper tablecloths. The menu reaches around the globe: greek salad beside caribbean curry, mushroom wellington, vietnamese spring rolls and halloumi tikka skewers (the latter of which were well spiced). The Middle Eastern filo pie is one of those hearty traditional vegetarian dishes: a dense mound of lentil-stuffed pastry with a generous selection of dips. Both the pie and the parmesan-crusted aubergine schnitzels skimped a little on seasoning. Plum crumble was actually a crumble tart swimming in what tasted – not altogether unpleasantly – like Bird's custard. Blah Blah Blah could be cheaper, even though the BYOB policy helps reduce bills, and despite the odd high note, the cooking lacks the verve of the best contemporary vegetarian cuisine. *Available for hire. Babies and children admitted: high chairs. Booking advisable. Separate room for parties, seats 35. Takeaway service. Vegan dishes.* **Map 20 B2.**

West Kensington

222 Veggie Vegan

222 North End Road, W14 9NU (7381 2322, www.222veggievegan.com). West Kensington tube or West Brompton tube/rail or bus 28, 391. **Lunch served** noon-3.30pm, **dinner served** 5.30-10.30pm daily. **Main courses** £7.50-£10.50. **Set lunch** £7.50 buffet. **Credit** MC, V.

On an uninspiring stretch of the North End Road, this modest restaurant attempts an impressive feat by creating an exclusively vegan menu. Its nondescript decor – cream walls, blonde wood, bright lighting – provides a blank canvas for the food. The formula is clearly popular as, on a recent weeknight visit, the tightly packed tables were full with a young, multinational crowd. The varied menu not only takes on the challenge of vegan cooking, but also avoids high fat, salt and refined carbohydrates. Raw food features heavily. The approach may be admirable, but it results in dishes that can be stodgy and, dare we say, a little bland. A tart of carrots mixed with soya mayonnaise, with a pastry base, came with a steamed vegetable medley and boiled potatoes; pumpkin risotto finished with cashew-nut cream was more school rice pudding than Italian gastronomy. We were also disappointed by the reliance on soya protein rather than letting pulses and vegetables shine. But although dishes may lack a little zip for non-vegans, the bargain-priced all-you-can-eat lunchtime buffet and daily specials keep 222 vibrant and its regulars happy.

Available for hire. Babies and children welcome: high chairs. Booking advisable. Takeaway service. Vegan dishes. **Map 13 A12.**

East

Shoreditch

★ Saf

152-154 Curtain Road, EC2A 3AT (7613 0007, www.safrestaurant.co.uk). Old Street tube/rail or 55, 243 bus. **Lunch served** noon-3.30pm daily. **Dinner served** 6.30-11pm Mon-Sat; 6.30-10.30pm Sun. **Main courses** £13.50-£14.25. **Credit** AmEx, MC, V.

With a fusion of modern Mediterranean and Asian flavours, and a commitment to serving food as raw as possible, Saf ('Simple Authentic Food') continues to provide stylish and stimulating dining. It's a great place to spend a sunny afternoon in the herb garden or a late evening in the dusky neon bar. The main eating area is airy and contemporary, featuring blonde wood, sleek light fixtures and abstract digital art prints. As an alternative to pasta, try the zucchini marinara where slivers of raw courgette are drizzled in tomato and spotted with briny capers and olives. Farinata, one of several cooked dishes on the menu, was a light but under-seasoned chickpea pancake enlivened by aïoli. Saf's enduring strength, however, is its raw food. There are also carefully calibrated juice blends and an outstanding cocktail menu, with drinks boosted by leaves and berries from the garden's greenhouse. Staff are chirpy and the customers laid-back. The innovative menu is filled with bright, appealing dishes that are the polar opposite of the leaden vegan fare of popular imagination. What's more, Saf pulls off this feat with panache.

Available for hire. Babies and children welcome: high chairs; nappy-changing facilities. Booking advisable weekends. Disabled: toilet. Tables outdoors (10, courtyard). Vegan dishes. **Map 6 R4.** **For branch see index**.

North

Camden Town & Chalk Farm

Manna

4 Erskine Road, NW3 3AJ (7722 8028, www.mannav.com). Chalk Farm tube or bus 31, 168. **Lunch served** noon-3pm Sat, Sun. **Dinner served** 6.30-10.30pm Tue-Sun. **Main courses** £10-£14. **Credit** AmEx, MC, V.

A well-dressed gentleman approaches with clipboard: 'Do you have a reservation?' We didn't. No problem, but it underlines that Manna is a restaurant rather than a café. Still, there are plenty of people who come during the day for one-dish meals – a rich plate of tomatoey pasta, say, or vegetable tart made with cashew cheese. The decor suits dressing up or down. Etched glass by the door echoes the silhouetted trees and birds of the wallpaper inside; a small, shimmering rear dining room continues the leafy theme. Jerk tofu kebabs with chewy grilled plantain and succulent sweet potato were not as fiery or aromatic as expected, but pleasing nevertheless, with gingery ribbons of raw courgette and carrot adding vitality. A special of white bean falafel worked well with olive, sun-dried tomato and caper dressing, although the latter was far too oily. The wine list is vegan and organic, but even so seems overpriced at £19-plus a bottle, as do the £4 smoothie-style mocktails, though the tie-dye swirls of our mango and coconut number were undeniably pretty. The friendly yet formal service seemed a little pressed on our visit, but the restaurant wasn't full.

Babies and children welcome: high chairs. Booking essential weekends. Tables outdoors (2, conservatory). Takeaway service. Vegan dishes. **Map 27 A1.**

Budget bites

Beatroot

92 Berwick Street, W1F 0QD (7437 8591, www.beatroot.org.uk). Oxford Circus, Piccadilly Circus or Tottenham Court Road tube. **Meals served** 9.15am-9pm Mon-Fri; 11am-9pm Sat. **Main courses** £4.30-£6.50. **Credit** MC, V.

This popular Soho spot is the place to go to for honest, wholefoods-based grub. The colourful interior may not be terribly sophisticated, with its lime green walls, red food counter and orange tables, but it's a pleasant, clean space in which to chow down on a box full of goodness – tofu stir-fry, say, or lentil-based shepherd's pie with quick-blanched broccoli and lots of salad. Boxes come in three sizes: small for £4.30, medium for £5.50, or large for £6.50. The expected fresh juices and smoothies are available, as well as vegan cakes and organic coffee. Seating is in the form of comfortable curved leather benches, with outside tables arranged next to the friendly chaos of Berwick Street Market.

Babies and children admitted. Tables outdoors (5, pavement). Takeaway service. Vegan dishes. **Map 17 B3.**

Food for Thought

31 Neal Street, WC2H 9PR (7836 0239, http://foodforthought-london.co.uk). Covent Garden tube. **Meals served** noon-8.30pm Mon-Sat. **Lunch served** noon-5pm Sun. **Main courses** £4.90-£8. **Minimum** (noon-3pm, 6-7.30pm Mon-Sat) £3.50. **No credit cards.**

The queues may no longer run down Neal Street, but Food for Thought, open since 1974, still attracts a loyal crowd that comes here as much for the eccentric, sociable vibe as for the wholesome food. The Covent Garden institution is less health-obsessed than some of the more puritanical veggie spots, with the emphasis on proper, unprocessed food in all its forms – from Moroccan chickpea tagine or stir-fried vegetables and rice, to indulgent desserts such as the infamous 'scrunch' (chunks of oat biscuit base mixed with fresh fruit and lashings of whipped cream). Takeaway food is ordered from the small upstairs space; head to the basement if you want to eat in.

Babies and children admitted. Bookings not accepted. Takeaway service. Vegan dishes. Vegetarian menu. **Map 18 D3.**

Vitao

74 Wardour Street, W1F 0TE (7734 8986, www.vitaorganic.co.uk). Leicester Square, Piccadilly Circus or Tottenham Court Road tube. **Meals served** noon-11pm Mon-Sat; noon-10pm Sun. **Set meal** (noon-5.30pm Mon-Fri) £5.60-£6.50 1 course; (5.30-11.30pm Mon-Fri; noon-11pm Sat; noon-10pm Sun) £8.90 buffet. **No credit cards.**

While the basic concept remains the same, a recent spruce-up has left Vitao looking healthier than ever. The good-value buffet is arranged around one wall and the front counter. Choose the size of plate you want – small (£5.50), large (£6.50) or a plate that can be refilled within the space of an hour (£8.90) – pay, and then help yourself to the array of vegetarian, vegan, macrobiotic, gluten-free and/or raw food dishes that span the globe, from sprouted chickpea curry to vegetable paella via greek salad. Dishes can be on the watery side, and veg a little undercooked, but the health-factor is taken seriously, and staff are helpful and friendly. What's more, the juice/smoothie/espresso bar is extensive.

Available for hire. Babies and children welcome: high chairs. Takeaway service. Vegan dishes. Vegetarian menu. **Map 17 B4.**

Vietnamese

Hooray – at last, Vietnamese cuisine has spread from its London heartland, the Kingsland Road in Shoreditch (where long-running **Song Que** still rules the roost), to other parts of the capital. The estimable **Cây Tre** is the latest of the established players to branch away from east London, opening a chic little restaurant in Soho's Dean Street. **Mien Tay** continues to work the Kingsland Road as well as Battersea's Lavender Hill. Newcomer **Vy Nam Café** is helping **Khoai Café** acquaint Finchley residents with the delights of this fresh, vibrant and generally inexpensive cuisine. Add **Saigon Saigon** in the west and all compass points are covered. If you're looking for a fast bite, you have even more options as London goes bonkers for bánh mì; the Franco-Viet baguette has become a street food sensation and can be found on sale from Islington and Bloomsbury to Camberwell and Deptford.

West
Hammersmith

Saigon Saigon
313-317 King Street, W6 9NH (0870 220 1398, www.saigon-saigon.co.uk). Ravenscourt Park or Stamford Brook tube. **Lunch served** noon-2.30pm Mon-Fri; 12.30-3pm Sat, Sun. **Dinner served** 6-10pm Mon, Sun; 6-11pm Tue-Thur; 6-11.30pm Fri, Sat. **Main courses** £6.95-£15. **Credit** MC, V.
At the quiet end of King Street, this largish restaurant with a basement bar is deservedly popular with locals, as well as many from further afield – it serves probably the best Vietnamese food in west London. Dark wood tables, carved wooden artwork and low lighting comprise the simple decor; bamboo screens help break up the space to create more intimate seating. In summer, tables occupy an uncommonly wide and set-back stretch of pavement. The welcome is warm, and service both pleasant and informative. Saigon Saigon's once lengthy menu has shrunk, but retains all the favourites. Starters include chargrilled quail marinated with honey, minced garlic and five spice, and crispy soft-shell crab with garlic, chilli and sea salt. Main courses of 'beef on fire' (baked sliced beef fillet in coconut juice and wine vinegar) and stewed king prawns in spicy caramel sauce, served in a clay pot, are among the most popular. The beef and chicken pho are unmissably flavourful. Seafood is also worth trying, as are the 'special' steamboats (also with meat) of raw ingredients that diners cook themselves in a bowl of simmering stock.

Available for hire (bar). Babies and children welcome: high chairs. Booking advisable. Tables outdoors (4, pavement). **Map 20 A4**.

South East
Surrey Quays

★ Café East
Surrey Quays Leisure Park, 100 Redriff Row, SE16 7LH (7252 1212, www.cafeeast.co.uk). Canada Water tube/rail or Surrey Quays rail. **Lunch served** 11am-3pm, **dinner served** 5.30-10.30pm Mon, Wed-Fri. **Meals served** 11am-10.30pm Sat; noon-10pm Sun. **Main courses** £6-£7.50. **Unlicensed** no alcohol allowed. **No credit cards.**
'Cash only.' 'We don't serve tap water.' 'Closed Tuesdays.' Café East doesn't offer the warmest of welcomes, and the decor – stark walls, closely packed canteen furniture, and net curtains shutting out the daylight – may not convince visitors they've come to the right place. And all this in one of the least appetising locations you'll (struggle to) find: the arse end of a leisure complex car park in Surrey Quays, past a Frankie & Benny's and a tenpin bowling alley. But there's a reason the seats are full (largely with young South-east Asians) most evenings, and that's the food: a relatively concise menu of interesting and consistently high-quality Vietnamese dishes. A choice of six mainly rolled starters includes bi cuon (soft rice papers filled with crisp lettuce, roasted rice and shredded pork skin); another option is cha hue (deep-fried sausage with fish sauce). Mains move through pho, dry dishes

(try the bun cha, with pleasingly fatty pork instead of minced patties) and rice dishes. There's no alcohol, either: a good reason to sample the che ba mau (three-colour drink made from kidney beans). Café East is one of our favourites: always an uncompromisingly authentic experience.
Babies and children welcome: high chairs. Bookings not accepted. Disabled: toilet. Takeaway service.

East
Shoreditch

★ Cây Tre
301 Old Street, EC1V 9LA (7729 8662, www.vietnamesekitchen.co.uk). Old Street tube/rail or bus 55, 243. **Lunch served** noon-3pm Mon-Sat. **Dinner served** 5.30-11pm Mon-Thur; 5.30-11.30pm Fri, Sat. **Meals served** noon-10.30pm Sun. **Main courses** £5-£9. **Set dinner** £20 per person (minimum 2) 2 courses. **Credit** MC, V.
The distance Cây Tre keeps from Kingsland Road's concentration of Vietnamese restaurants seems to give the place a forward-thinking attitude its near-neighbours lack. Although a few years old, the decor – printed wallpaper, coloured lamps, shiny white furniture – attracts a hipster crowd whose conversations you'll inevitably overhear as you squeeze into the closely packed seating. The slightly cringe-producing menu descriptions sound like Jamie Oliver wrote them, with their 'piggy grilled aubergine', 'wicked frogs' and 'wokked french beans'. But there's substance behind the

style, and in both presentation and execution the food demonstrates that the kitchen has skill. The repertoire is as lengthy as you'll find anywhere, with the usual selection of soups, salads, rolls, noodles and rice, but there are also plenty of inventive touches – summer rolls are stuffed with duck instead of prawn; there's pomelo salad with dried shrimp; and crab and lobster come as a spicy 'ceviche' salad. It's the 'meat' section that contains the most unusual items; try the simmered brisket with lemongrass and anise as proof Vietnam can do slow cooking well too. The wine and beer list is intelligent, and for a Vietnamese restaurant, the service can veer dangerously close to friendly.
Babies and children admitted. Booking advisable. Takeaway service. **Map 6 R4**.
For branches (Viet Grill) see index.

★ ★ Mien Tay
122 Kingsland Road, E2 8DP (7729 3074, www.mientay.co.uk). Hoxton rail. **Lunch served** noon-3pm, **dinner served** 5-11pm Mon-Sat. **Meals served** 11am-10pm Sun. **Main courses** £4-£7. **Unlicensed. Corkage** no charge. **Credit** MC, V.
Nothing much about the appearance of Mien Tay would suggest it's worth a visit. This is one of the more 'unreconstructed' Vietnamese restaurants on Kingsland Road, with a look that's not so much tired as exhausted, including garlands of plastic plants, oriental fans and little else. The annoying doorbell, which sounds every time there's food to be sent out, doesn't do much for the ambience either, and service, although well meaning, can occasionally slacken off alarmingly. So why are we recommending it? One reason: the food, which seems to appear through the poky kitchen hatch from another dimension. The menu is extensive, travelling the length and breadth of Vietnam and taking in everything from pho to spicy salads, but a few dishes really stand out. Whole fishes are a highlight, fried in a wok until crisp; sea bass with chilli and lemongrass was a near-perfect dish. Try too the 'Mien Tay' fried spring rolls, which hide a mixture of pork, chicken, prawn and vegetables in a lattice of thread noodles. And don't miss the chargrilled quail, marinated in honey, garlic and chilli, and served with aromatic salt for dipping – one of the best versions we've tried in London.
Babies and children welcome: high chair. Takeaway service. **Map 6 R3**.
For branch see index.

★ Song Que `HOT 50`
134 Kingsland Road, E2 8DY (7613 3222, http://songque.co.uk). Hoxton rail. **Lunch served** noon-3pm, **dinner served** 5.30-11pm Mon-Sat. **Meals served** 12.30-11pm Sun. **Main courses** £4.80-£14.80. **Credit** MC, V.
There are several great places for Vietnamese food in this part of London, but the undisputed pho king of Hackney is Song Que. The sparse, sterile space, unchanged in years, offers little in the way of sophistication (although the loos were tarted up in 2010). Atmosphere is instead provided by the sometimes raucous crowd of in-the-know diners and the bustling staff (who, if truth be told, could smile a bit more: don't expect much of a welcome). The cooking has consistently scored top marks in our guides, so choose with confidence from the sprawling menu. We find it hard to look past la lot, a starter of juicy ground beef wrapped in wild betel leaves; the smoky barbecued quail with its almost effervescent ginger and citrus dipping sauce; the

prawn-stuffed summer rolls; and the spicy soft-shell crab. Pho, though, is the star of the show, based on a broth so deep you could swim in it; the soup is almost a meal in itself, but the added Vietnamese herbs and water vegetables are always vibrant and plentiful, and the version with rare beef isn't stingy with the meat. It's advisable to book most evenings, as queues are common.
Babies and children welcome: high chairs. Disabled: toilet. Vegetarian menu. **Map 6 R3**.

North East
Hackney

★ Green Papaya
191 Mare Street, E8 3QE (8985 5486, www. green-papaya.com). London Fields rail or bus 26, 48, 55, 277, D6. **Dinner served** 5-11pm Tue-Sun. **Main courses** £5-£8. **Credit** MC, V.

Song Que

VIETNAMESE

It's sad to see a restaurant we once rated highly slip, but Green Papaya doesn't seem to be quite the place it was. There are things to recommend – this is still one of the better Vietnamese establishments on Mare Street, and the casual atmosphere created by the stream of locals wandering in makes for a relaxing meal. Yet the specials board above the bar (still a rarity in restaurants like this) is, sadly, blank more often than not, and the 'new dishes' on the A4 sheet accompanying the menu (wing-bean salad, tofu with asparagus, and barbecue pork belly) have been doing the rounds unchanged for some time. On our most recent visit, almost everything we ordered – green papaya salad, bo nam bo (stir-fried beef with peanuts and shallots) and stir-fried turmeric pork with aubergine, chilli, lemongrass, purple basil and la lot – seemed restrained, with flavours indistinct. It's as if everything needs shaking back to life. There aren't many better places locally for a reviving bowl of pho, which Green Papaya still does well, but for a more exciting Vietnamese meal, we fear Kingsland Road is a better bet.
Babies and children welcome: high chairs. Booking advisable. Takeaway service.

Tre Viet

247 Mare Street, E8 3NS (8986 8885, www.treviet.co.uk). London Fields rail or bus 26, 48, 55, 277, D6. **Meals served** noon-11pm Mon-Thur, Sun; noon-11.30pm Fri, Sat. **Main courses** £4.70-£13. **Credit** MC, V.
A short distance from the Vietnamese restaurant corridor that runs north from Shoreditch, Tre Viet on more mundane Mare Street lacks the manic explosion of drunken youth attracted to its hipper cousins – and benefits from it enormously. Staff are patient and friendly, fellow diners a broad mix of locals, all tucking into an equally broad menu that ranges across the expected Vietnamese dishes (pho, summer rolls), but also includes goat and galangal, along with old oriental stalwarts that seem to be present because people insist on ordering them. If you find peking duck served with less pomp than here, let us know – the duck arrived pre-shredded and the pancakes still sealed in their plastic microwave wrapping. But there are some cracking dishes to be had; the aubergine hotpot with tofu and/or minced pork is a thing of rich, silky beauty, and laudable too are the noodle soups and the soft-shell crab. So while Tre Viet may not offer the most authentic Vietnamese cuisine to be found in London, it handles the influences that have shaped it well. Hence you're unlikely to have a dull or tasteless meal here.
Booking advisable weekends. Disabled: toilet. Takeaway service.
For branch (Lang Nuong) see index.

North
Finchley

Khoai Café

362 Ballards Lane, N12 0EE (8445 2039, www.khoai.co.uk). Woodside Park tube or bus 82, 134. **Lunch served** noon-3.30pm, **dinner served** 5.30-11.30pm daily. **Main courses** £5-£11.25. **Set lunch** £5.95 1 course, £8.45 2 courses. **Credit** AmEx, MC, V.
This simply designed contemporary canteen, sister to a long-established restaurant of the same name

Bánh mì cafés

Kêu

Bánh mì are an increasingly common sight on the capital's streets. A legacy of French colonialism, these Vietnamese baguettes are made from wheat and rice flour, with fillings inspired by both nations: cold meats and pâté; pickled carrots, coriander and chilli. Try them for yourself at these specialists.

Bánh Mì Bay

4-6 Theobald's Road, WC1X 8PN (7831 4079). Chancery Lane tube. **Meals served** 10am-9.45pm Mon-Fri; noon-9.45pm Sat, Sun. **Main courses** £6-£7.50. **Credit** MC, V.
From the same crew as Camberwell's Café Bay, who were crafting bánh mì long before they became trendy. This Holborn hotspot boasts an impressive selection, most of which cost less than £5. Service is friendly.
Available for hire. Babies and children welcome: high chairs. Takeaway service. **Map 4 M5.**

Cà Phé

47 Clerkenwell Road, EC1M 5RS (07780 784696 mobile, www.caphevn.co.uk). Farringdon tube/rail. **Meals served** 11am-6pm Mon-Fri. **Main courses** £3.50. **Credit** MC, V.
Hot on the heels of their successful ventures in Hackney and Islington, husband-and-wife team Rob Athill and Tuyen Hong have opened this Clerkenwell café. As well as bánh mì, daily specials include Vietnamese salads, summer rolls or bánh cuon (steamed rice flour pancakes, stuffed with pork and mushrooms).
Available for hire. Babies and children welcome: high chairs. Bookings not accepted. Tables outdoors (2, pavement). Takeaway service. **Map 5 O4.**
For branch see index.

Café Bay

75 Denmark Hill, SE5 8RS (7703 2531). Denmark Hill rail or bus 36, 185, 436. **Meals served** 8am-5pm Mon-Fri. **Main courses** £2.60-£4. **No credit cards.**
Against the odds, this utilitarian sandwich bar in Camberwell makes excellent bánh mì as well as the more prosaic takeaway

fare. We can't get enough of the caramel pork, layered with crisp pickles, cucumber, coriander and chilli.
Booking advisable. Takeaway service; delivery service (over £25 within 1-mile radius). **Map 23 A2.**

City Càphê

17 Ironmonger Lane, EC2V 8EY (no phone, www.citycaphe.com). Bank tube/DLR. **Meals served** 7.30am-4pm Mon-Fri. **Main courses** £3.65-£6.50. **Credit** MC, V.
City Càphê, which opened in 2010, remains one of the best places to buy bánh mì in the capital. The small but vibrant space also serves summer rolls packed with fresh herbs, warming pho, colourful salads and full-strength Vietnamese coffee.
Available for hire. Bookings not accepted. Takeaway service. **Map 11 P6.**

Kêu

332 Old Street, EC1V 9DR (7739 1164, www.keudeli.co.uk). Old Street tube/rail or bus 55, 243. **Meals served** 8am-8pm Mon-Sat. **Main courses** £4-£5.50. **Credit** AmEx, MC, V.
From the team behind Cây Tre and Viet Grill, this Vietnamese baguette deli looks the part, with bare lightbulbs and shelves stacked with produce. The bánh mì can be a little hit and miss, but other dishes, such as well-executed curries or salads, are more consistent.
Babies and children admitted. Bookings not accepted. Takeaway service. **Map 6 R4.**

Panda Panda

8 Deptford Broadway, SE8 4PA (8616 6922, www.panda-panda.co.uk). Deptford Bridge DLR or Deptford rail or bus 177, 453. **Meals served** 11am-5pm Mon-Fri; 10am-11pm Sat. **Main courses** £1.99-£4.95. **No credit cards.**
Bringing sunshine to Deptford Broadway, Panda Panda serves properly made bánh mì filled with traditional ingredients: slices of rolled pork and Vietnamese ham layered with tart pickled veg, crushed peanuts and fresh coriander. Look out for Hong Kong-style street snacks too.
Babies and children welcome: high chairs. Takeaway service.

Menu

Banh cuon: pancake-like steamed rolls of translucent fresh rice pasta, sometimes stuffed with minced pork or shrimp (reminiscent in style of Chinese cheung fun, a dim sum speciality).

Banh pho: flat rice noodles used in soups and stir-fries, usually with beef.

Banh xeo: a large pancake made from a batter of rice flour and coconut milk, coloured bright yellow with turmeric and traditionally filled with prawns, pork, beansprouts and onion. To eat it, tear the pancake apart with your chopsticks, roll the pieces with sprigs of herbs in a lettuce leaf, and dip in nuoc cham (qv).

Bo la lot: grilled minced beef in betel leaves.

Bun: rice vermicelli, served in soups and stir-fries. They are also eaten cold, with raw salad vegetables and herbs, with a nuoc cham (qv) sauce poured over, and a topping such as grilled beef or pork – all of which are tossed together at the table.

Cha ca: North Vietnamese dish of fish served sizzling in an iron pan with lashings of dill.

Cha gio: deep-fried spring rolls. Unlike their Chinese counterparts, the wrappers are made from rice paper rather than sheets of wheat pastry, and pucker up deliciously after cooking.

Chao tom: grilled minced prawn on a baton of sugar cane.

Goi: salad. There are many types in Vietnam, but they often contain raw, crunchy vegetables and herbs, perhaps accompanied by chicken or prawns, with a sharp, perky dressing.

Goi cuon (literally 'rolled salad', often translated as 'fresh rolls' or 'salad rolls'): cool, soft, rice-paper rolls usually containing prawns, pork, fresh herbs and rice vermicelli, served with a thick sauce similar to satay sauce but made from hoi sin mixed with peanut butter, scattered with roasted peanuts.

Nem: north Vietnamese name for cha gio (qv).

Nom: north Vietnamese name for goi (qv).

Nuoc cham: the generic name for a wide range of dipping sauces, based on a paste of fresh chillies, sugar and garlic that is diluted with water, lime juice and the ubiquitous fish sauce, nuoc mam.

Nuoc mam: a brown or pale liquid derived from fish that have been salted and left to ferment. It's the essential Vietnamese seasoning, used in dips and as a cooking ingredient.

Pho: the most famous and best-loved of all Vietnamese dishes, a soup of rice noodles and beef or chicken in a rich, clear broth flavoured with aromatics. It's served with a dish of fresh beansprouts, red chilli and herbs, and a squeeze of lime; these are added to the soup at the table.

Rau thom: aromatic herbs, which might include Asian basil (**rau que**), mint (**rau hung**), red or purple perilla (**rau tia to**), lemony Vietnamese balm (**rau kinh gioi**) or saw-leaf herb (**ngo gai**).

in Crouch End, would be an ideal destination in any area for those nights when you can't be bothered to cook – but in dreary North Finchley it stands out as a superior dining choice. Service is caring and friendly. La lot leaves aside, our dishes lacked the speciality herbs that make Vietnamese cooking distinctive; maybe if we hadn't visited on a Monday we would have enjoyed more than coriander and mint. The cooking was certainly good. Aubergine fritters made a crisp yet succulent topping for finely grated goi salad punctuated with crispy shallots and peanuts. Chao tom, prawn paste on fat slabs of sugar cane (deliciously juicy to gnaw on once the meat has gone), were cooked to a burnished hue and served with rice vermicelli, salad and nuoc cham dipping sauce. Admittedly, the menu features a few Chinese takeaway favourites, but there's also a dedicated list of regional Vietnamese dishes (tom cang rim nuoc dua, cha ca la vong), plus classics such as pho and summer rolls. For a satisfying alternative to the Vietnamese beers, try the Portuguese house red.

Available for hire. Babies and children welcome: high chairs. Takeaway service.
For branch see index.

★ Vy Nam Café

371 Regents Park Road, N3 1DE (8371 4222, www.vynamcafe.com). Finchley Central tube. **Lunch served** noon-3pm, **dinner served** 5-11pm daily. **Main courses** £6.80-£13. **Credit** MC, V.

Anyone familiar with the kitschy surroundings and brusque service found in many of Hackney's Vietnamese joints will find this Finchley newcomer a refreshing change. Interiors are bright, clean and homely, with displays of dried and fresh flowers, while staff are welcomingly courteous and friendly. Happily, the menu, which takes in all the classics of both the north and south of the country (including more unusual dishes made with frogs' legs or goat), is just as on-song. On our visit, beef with la lot (wild betel leaves) came with meat thinly sliced rather than more conventionally minced, but nonetheless impressed. A dish of soft-shell crab produced a generous pile of deep-fried spindly limbs and tender body. We also enjoyed a zesty papaya salad with sliced prawns, beautifully presented and sharply dressed with a fish sauce and chilli dressing. Perhaps most impressively, Vy Nam's pho (a real test of any Vietnamese kitchen's skill) was pitch-perfect, featuring a richly layered beef broth and plenty of rare beef – and it was excellent value at £7.20. A great addition for the area's locals, and a reason to travel to Zone 4 for the rest of us.

Available for hire. Babies and children welcome: high chair. Booking advisable weekends. Takeaway service; delivery service (over £15 within 15-mile radius).

Vy Nam Café

Cheap Eats

Budget

London may be one of the most expensive cities in the world, and you can certainly spend a fortune eating out here, but there are alternatives. Some remarkably good-value cafés and restaurants manage to turn out flavourful, imaginative food without stinting on ingredient quality or cooking skill, in pleasant surroundings, at cheap-as-chips prices. Certain types of eaterie seem to lend themselves to budget dining, such as candlelit French brasseries (**Pierre Victoire**, **Passage Cafe**, **Le Mercury**) and updated pie and mash shops (**Mother Mash**, **Square Pie**). Chains also have their place – Portuguese chicken specialist **Nando's** has been a family favourite for years, while the steady growth of **Leon** shows that nutrition and sustainability aren't at odds with the concept of fast food – but most of the venues listed here are one-offs. Top performers this time are chickpea specialist **Hummus Bros**, catering college showcase **Vincent Rooms** and the capital's very own Bavarian-style beer garden, **Stein's**.

Central

City

Grazing

19-21 Great Tower Street, EC3R 5AR (7283 2932, www.grazingfood.com). Monument or Tower Hill tube. **Meals served** 7am-4pm Mon-Fri. **Main courses** £1-£6.95. **Credit** MC, V.
Hungry City workers with a taste for meat are well catered for at this cleverly conceived breakfast and lunch spot. The spick-and-span white-tiled room, with a large window at one end, is light, modern and airy. A counter steams with huge joints ready to be carved. A bacon and cheese burger was mountainous and juicy; chips (which cost an extra £2) were tasty and well cooked, but perhaps unnecessary considering the burger's size. The varied menu also features pies, wraps and rolls, as well as breakfast options, such as sausage and bacon, or egg and black pudding butties for those needing an early fix of flesh – or fruit and yoghurt pots for those who don't. Service was welcoming, attentive and eager. Office and event catering services are offered, and there's free delivery on big orders when you just can't leave your desk. *Babies and children admitted. Tables outdoors (2, pavement). Takeaway service.* **Map 12 R7.**

Passage Café

12 Jerusalem Passage, EC1V 4JP (3217 0090, www.thepassagecafe.com). Farringdon tube/rail. **Lunch served** noon-4pm Tue-Fri. **Dinner served** 6pm-midnight Tue-Fri; 5-11pm Sat. **Main courses** £12.95. **Credit** AmEx, MC, V.

This tiny yet ambitious venue offers a French neighbourhood feel in central London. Intimate dining is guaranteed in the small, candlelit interior decorated with art deco posters. The French owners have decided to drop their savoury crêpes and now focus solely on a bistro-style menu – with all mains costing £12.95, starters £6.50 and puds £5. An expertly presented starter of beetroot-cured salmon came with a quenelle of horseradish cream and miniature pieces of pickled vegetables. Pan-fried gnocchi were crisp on the outside, giving way to a creamy interior flavoured with herbes de provence, aptly complementing the Mediterranean vegetables that came with them. Our portion was on the small side, though. Calf's liver arrived a tad too pink for our taste, and an intense flavour of sage overpowered the onion and sultana raviolo. Nevertheless, the innovative French cooking convinced overall, and puddings continue the theme: baked chocolate soup with black pepper ice-cream, for instance.
Available for hire. Babies and children admitted. Tables outdoors (2, pavement). Takeaway service. **Map 5 O4.**

Clerkenwell & Farringdon

Little Bay

171 Farringdon Road, EC1R 3AL (7278 1234, www.little-bay.co.uk). Farringdon tube/rail. **Meals served** noon-midnight Mon-Sat; noon-11pm Sun. **Main courses** £7.95-£11.95. **Credit** MC, V.
The folk at Little Bay are pretty clever. Last year, this budget chain caused some furore by letting diners pay as much (or as little) as they wanted. On our most recent visit, all dishes were slashed to half their usual price. A starter of crab choux burst with a spicy seafood filling; however, the puffs were so hard, they seemed like rocks covered in hollandaise sauce. Our burger tasted nicely chargrilled, and so did the lamb steak, but the goose-fat chips were limp and puny. So, the cooking is not at all perfect, but at such cut-throat prices it's easy to forgive the odd shortfall. Decor at this Farringdon branch is flamboyant; red walls decorated with baroque frescoes and golden mirrors make for a kitsch boudoir atmosphere.
Babies and children welcome: high chairs. Booking advisable. Disabled: toilet. Separate room for parties, seats 120. **Map 5 N4.** **For branches see index.**

Covent Garden

Battersea Pie

Lower ground floor, 28 The Market, WC2E 8RA (7240 9566, www.batterseapiestation. co.uk). Covent Garden tube. **Meals served** 11am-9pm Mon-Sat; 11am-8pm Sun. **Main courses** £7.50-£8.50. **Credit** AmEx, MC, V.
With bargain prices and proper British food, this pie and mash house – signed simply 'The Pie Shop' – is something of an anomaly among the tourist traps of Covent Garden Market. It's housed in one of the refurbished arches, keeping the traditional exterior and flagstone floor, but the fixtures and fittings are stylish and modern: bright white tiles, polished marble tables and a shiny aluminium counter. On a busy summer day, a firm pie crust seasoned with rosemary enclosed a hearty chicken and mushroom filling, accompanied by well-

whipped, buttery mash. Rich red-wine gravy arrived separately in a miniature jug. Unfortunately, a counter-side fan did little to alleviate the sweltering heat in the small room, and a soundtrack of brash dance music only increased our desire for a swift exit. A few tables outside provide an escape, if only to view the market's stream of ambling tourists.
Babies and children admitted. Tables outdoors (4, market). **Map 12 E4.**

Canela
33 Earlham Street, WC2H 9LS (7240 6926, www.canelacafe.com). Covent Garden tube. **Meals served** 10.30am-10pm Mon-Sat; 10.30am-7pm Sun. **Main courses** £5.90-£9.50. **Credit** MC, V.
Canela – meaning cinnamon stick in Portuguese – has done a decent job of providing the peasant food of Portugal and Brazil some sex appeal. This branch has a dramatic black and red interior, which, coupled with an energetic musical soundtrack, serves to give the place the feel more of a nightclub than a café. By contrast, service is laid-back and amenable, with staff happy to talk first-timers through the options. We appreciated the depth of flavour in a classic feijoada: a rich stew of black beans dotted with smoky, fatty meats and served, Brazilian-style, with rice, farofa (coarse roasted cassava flour) and sliced orange – though for workers' fare, it cost a decidedly bourgeois £10.60. The deli counter is packed with bold, appetising salads and quiches, as well as Brazilian streets eats: chewy cheese bread (pão de queijo), a starchy drumstick-shaped snack of breaded chicken and potato (coxinha), and a thick-set lemon curd tart with a coconutty base (quindim). Coffee comes with a cinnamon stick for stirring: just as in Lisbon.
Babies and children admitted. Tables outdoors (4, pavement). Takeaway service. **Map 18 D3.** **For branch see index**.

Soho

★ Hummus Bros
88 Wardour Street, W1F 0TJ (7734 1311, www.hbros.co.uk). Oxford Circus or Tottenham Court Road tube. **Meals served** noon-10pm Mon-Wed, Sun; noon-11pm Thur-Sat. **Main courses** £6.65-£8.45. **Credit** AmEx, MC, V.
When Hummus Bros first opened, onlookers genuinely wondered how it could possibly survive: after all, chickpea dip doesn't usually set pulses racing. But survive (and thrive) it has, with the two entrepreneurial 'bros' – actually, two university chums – having since launched branches near Holborn and St Paul's. The concept is simple and done well. Queue at the counter for one of the chickpea-based snacks; at its most basic, this is an ample bowl of creamy houmous with a slick of tahini (sesame paste), drizzle of olive oil and sprinkling of paprika, served with warm wholemeal pitta. Other Middle Eastern-inspired riches include a 'pimped-up' version of houmous topped with tender chunks of beef; or fresh, fragrant side salads made with bulgar wheat and chopped parsley (tabouleh), or pulpy smoked aubergine (baba ganoush). Tiny plastic pots of fresh garlic or lemon juice are available for extra zing. A youthful sense of fun adds to the experience: the hip staff are hospitable, the communal tables vibrant, the music festively loud and the Wi-Fi free of charge.

Passage Café

Babies and children welcome: high chairs. Bookings not accepted. Disabled: toilet. Takeaway service. Vegan dishes. **Map 17 B3.**
For branches see index.

Leon

36-38 Old Compton Street, W1D 4TT (7434 1200, www.leonrestaurants.co.uk). Tottenham Court Road tube. **Meals served** 11am-11pm Mon-Thur, Sun; 11am-1am Fri, Sat. **Main courses** £3.95-£6.75. **Set dinner** (6pm-close Mon-Sat) £27.50 2 courses (2 people). **No credit cards.**
Fast-food chain Leon currently has ten branchs in London, including this one slap-bang in the heart of Soho. Grab a meal and watch Old Compton Street's flamboyant fauna parade in front of the big windows. If you prefer some quieter entertainment, hide downstairs in the basement, where hundreds of cookery books wait to be devoured. Leon prides itself on using sustainably sourced ingredients in its (mostly) healthy dishes. Grilled chicken salad was happily satisfying, the moist, chargrilled meat resting on a bed of crunchy salad leaves. Moroccan meatballs were flavourful, but refused to reveal the slightest hint of Moorish spices. And our hearts sunk when presented with the fish finger wrap; the barely discernible thin, mushy fish strip was sadly snuggled against a few lonely salad leaves – all wrapped in layers of dry tortilla. Compensation arrived, however, with pudding: a superb chewy orange chocolate brownie.
Babies and children welcome: children's menu; high chairs; nappy-changing facilities. Disabled: toilet. Separate room for parties, seats 50. Tables outdoors (4, pavement). Takeaway service. **Map 17 C4.**
For branches see index.

Mother Mash

26 Ganton Street, W1F 7QZ (7494 9644, www.mothermash.co.uk). Oxford Circus tube. **Meals served** 8.30am-10pm Mon-Fri; noon-10pm Sat; noon-5pm Sun. **Main courses** £6.95-£7.50. **Credit** AmEx, MC, V.
At first sight, this narrow, white-tiled room seems cramped with its booths, stools and marble countertops, but Mother Mash is a lively place for tucking into some prime comfort food. The three-step ordering process adds to the fun – choose your mash, choose your main, choose your gravy – although a variety of enticing options at each stage ensure this isn't as simple as it sounds. On our visit, a daily special of toulouse sausages was served with a creamy helping of mustard mash and farmer's gravy (likeably flavoured with red wine, mushroom and onion). Opposite, a steak and ale pie arrived well puffed (deceptively so, as it would have benefited from a more generous helping of the rich filling) and set at a jaunty angle atop its bed of mash. Lateish opening hours, a decent wine and beer list and animated staff make Mother Mash an excellent beginning or end to a night on the town.
Babies and children admitted. Tables outdoors (2, pavement). Takeaway service. **Map 17 A4.**

Pierre Victoire

5 Dean Street, W1D 3RQ (7287 4582, www.pierrevictoire.com). Tottenham Court Road tube. **Meals served** noon-11pm Mon-Wed, Sun; noon-11.30pm Thur-Sat. **Main courses** £9.90-£14.90. **Set lunch** (noon-4pm) £8.90 2 courses. **Set dinner** (4-7pm) £10.90 2 courses. **Credit** AmEx, MC, V.
In the 1990s, there was a chain of these inexpensive French bistros across London; now there's just this one, plus the newer Prix Fixe down the road. Mercifully, Pierre Victoire shows no corporate symptoms. It's a well-run, convivial little place occupying ground floor and basement, with mismatched furniture, scrubbed floorboards and white walls displaying colourful paintings. At night, dripping candles emerge. Service is proficient and kind-hearted. The carte prices are at the top end of budget dining, but the lunch and pre-theatre set menus are a bargain, offering ample choice of tasty (if not especially accomplished) cooking. Yes, the 'escargot-style' mussels starter could have had more Pernod and parsley punch, but the bivalves (de-shelled and resting, like snails, in melted butter) were tender. And a handsome portion of roast pork may have had a mushy accompaniment (orange braised savoy cabbage, sage jus, apple, sichuan pepper), but the flavours gelled. Tarte tatin was passable – if more puréed apple tart than tatin – and wines are fairly priced.
Babies and children welcome: high chairs. Booking advisable. Separate room for parties, seats 25. Tables outdoors (2, pavement). **Map 17 B3.**

Stockpot

18 Old Compton Street, W1D 4TN (7287 1066). Leicester Square or Tottenham Court Road tube. **Meals served** 9am-11.30pm Mon, Tue; 9am-midnight Wed-Sat; noon-11.30pm Sun. **Main courses** £3.95-£9.10. **Set meal** £7.10 2 courses. **No credit cards.**
No frills abound at this long-running Soho institution. Walls are covered with anaglypta wallpaper and wooden slatting; scored tables look like they've been varnished time and again; and the decorations vary between unframed posters for West End productions of *Jersey Boys* and cartoon depictions of period military figures. The menu's heart is in the 1960s, with an emphasis on solid cooking that takes in portions of thinly sliced fried liver and onions, duck à l'orange, and roast potatoes sprinkled with dried rosemary. For dessert, the selection of rice pudding, golden sponge, and jelly with ice-cream could come straight from a school canteen, but there's no arguing about the value: most main courses cost around £6, with starters and desserts rarely straying over £3. Such reliability and lack of pretension draw customers from across the social divide. Groups of Japanese tourists ask staff to take their photos, student couples tuck into retro desserts, pensioners sip tea, and business-suited female diners push grilled salmon around their plate. Something for everyone, then.
Babies and children admitted. Tables outdoors (2, pavement). Takeaway service. **Map 17 C3.**
For branches see index.

Westminster

★ Vincent Rooms

Westminster Kingsway College, Vincent Square, SW1P 2PD (7802 8391, www.westking.ac.uk). St James's Park tube or Victoria tube/rail. **Lunch served** noon-1pm Mon-Fri. **Dinner**

Hummus Bros. See p275.

served 6-7pm Wed, Thur. Closed June-Aug. **Main courses** £4-£12. **Set meal** Escoffier Room £25 3 courses incl coffee. **Credit** MC, V.

There's often a nervous note in the air at the Vincent Rooms around the beginning of term. Adjoined to Westminster Kingsway College's school of hospitality and culinary arts, the restaurant's waiters and kitchen staff are almost all students, learning their trade on the job. While the atmosphere mellows (and the skills improve) as the year goes on, there's a perennial interest in a quality menu, as well as a genuine attempt at professional service. This well-meaning approach makes a meal in the brasserie – or a tasting menu in the classier Escoffier Room – a wonderfully novel experience. A honey-grilled goat's cheese starter was gently sweet and devastatingly creamy, while a more technically challenging main of roast cod and squid tempura with saffron potatoes was full of flavour and culinary style. Pearl barley and caerphilly risotto was less successful, more milky than creamy. But the cheap-as-chips prices, and a real sense of effort, make it easy to forgive faults.
Babies and children welcome: high chairs.
Booking advisable. Disabled: toilet.
Separate room for parties, seats 30.
Map 15 J10.

South

Battersea

Fish in a Tie

105 Falcon Road, SW11 2PF (7924 1913, http://fishinatie.co.uk). Clapham Junction rail.
Meals served noon-midnight Mon-Sat; noon-11pm Sun. **Main courses** £6-£11.25. **Set lunch** (noon-5pm Mon-Sat) £5 2 courses. **Set dinner** (5pm-close) £10 2 courses. **Credit** MC, V.

The name is odd, as is much about this Battersea haunt. Mismatched chandeliers, and candles wedged-in bottles, vie with a 'Mediterranean' menu random enough to keep even regulars on their toes. But weirdest of all are the prices, kept down by the every-day set menus. Fresh-off-the-boat salmon gravadlax (definitely not Mediterranean) followed by spinach and ricotta-packed filo pastry pie for only £10 was lunacy (and the lunch deal is even cheaper). Especially when generous portions, delicate presentation and smiley service are included. So what's the catch? Aside from a few bits of fatty meat in the sweet 'n' spicy gypsy lamb, a soggy base to our banoffi pie, and needing to be quick to beat the locals to the seats – we can't find one.
Babies and children welcome: high chairs.
Booking advisable. Separate rooms for parties,
seating 25 and 40. **Map 21 C3**.

Galapagos Bistro-Café

169 Battersea High Street, SW11 3JS (8488 4989). Clapham Junction rail. **Meals served** 9.30am-9.30pm Tue-Sat. **Main courses** £7.50-£9.95. **Set lunch** (noon-4pm) £10.95 2 courses, £13.95 3 courses. **Set dinner** (6.30-9.30pm) £12.95 2 courses, £15.95 3 courses. **Credit** MC, V.

Galapagos is the kind of place where neighbours drop by for a cuppa, couples come for a casual supper and lone diners feel at ease. The Ecuadorian owner makes everyone feel comfortable with his cheery chatter about current affairs and cultural differences. The menu is a gallop across the globe, from the sunny tortilla of the Med, to a North

Stockpot

African tagine with lots of cinnamon, to Indonesian nasi goreng (spicy rice with eggs and peanuts). We found the Asian dishes particularly successful, thanks to the long-standing chef from Burma; try the Burmese sweet and sour salad of tomatoes, onions, peanuts and roasted chickpea flour. Puds too are a draw: all super-fresh, own-made and firmly European, from warm hazelnut cake to lush bread and butter pudding. And then there are the prices – £15.95 for a three-course dinner, plus decent wines with honest mark-ups. Fabulous.
Available for hire. Babies and children admitted. Booking advisable. Tables outdoors (2, pavement). Takeaway service.

East
Bethnal Green

E Pellicci
332 Bethnal Green Road, E2 0AG (7739 4873). Bethnal Green tube/rail or bus 8. **Meals served** 7am-4pm Mon-Sat. **Main courses** £6.40-£8.20. **Unlicensed. Corkage** no charge. **No credit cards.**
Established in 1900, Pellicci's is an East End institution with its Formica tables, gorgeous original marquetry and old-fashioned cash register. But it's the warm, friendly atmosphere that owner Nev Pellicci and his family create that draws a busy crowd of market traders and locals. On our visit, Nev was ribbing a couple of lads that they only came to the caff to meet girls; they could get chatting to them once he'd had broken the ice. Regulars on another table then suggested Nev start a speed-dating service. As well as a chat and a laugh, everyone is here for the traditional greasy-spoon grub cooked in the kitchen by Maria, Nev's mum. Rumour has it that a 'healthy option' breakfast exists, but most opt for the big breakfasts listed on the menu or pick and mix from bubble, bacon, bangers, blood pudding, eggs, mush, toms and beans, accompanied by a mug of strong tea or coffee. Lunch includes favourites such as chicken pie, spag bol and lasagne, all served with two veg or Maria's awesome chips. Follow that, if you can, with a bowl of bread and butter pudding with custard. A gem.
Available for hire. Babies and children admitted. Bookings not accepted. Tables outdoors (4, pavement). Takeaway service.

Spitalfields

S&M Café
48 Brushfield Street, E1 6AG (7247 2252, www.sandmcafe.co.uk). Liverpool Street tube/ rail or Shoreditch High Street rail. **Meals served** 7.30am-10pm Mon-Fri; 8.30am-10pm Sat, Sun. **Main courses** £4.95-£9.95. **Credit** AmEx, MC, V.
The cheekily named S&M café pays tribute to the great greasy spoons of yesteryear, and appeals to both local hipsters and the more among curious tourists. A determinedly un-gourmet selection of stodgy British favourites forms the menu: sausage and mash being the mainstay, with a good choice of meat (including steak and horseradish) and vegetarian (caerphilly and leek, mushroom and tarragon) versions. Two bangers, mash and gravy costs £7.95, add a quid for a third sausage. Generously proportioned pies, fish and chips, sponge puddings and a few token salads fill up the list.

Service is cheery, the food consistently hearty, and everything is accompanied by a healthy dose of nostalgia. Sadly, trouble is afoot somewhere: where S&M had a half-dozen branches a couple of years ago, it's now down to just this one, in Spitalfields.
Babies and children welcome: high chairs. Bookings not accepted weekends. Tables outdoors (3, pavement). **Map 12 R5.**

Square Pie
Old Spitalfields Market, 105C Commercial Street, E1 6BG (7375 0327, www.squarepie. com). Liverpool Street tube/rail or Shoreditch High Street rail. **Meals served** 10.30am-4.30pm Mon-Fri; 10.30am-5.30pm Sat, Sun. **Main courses** £3.50-£6.90. **Credit** MC, V.
As Spitalfields Market continues to bustle and change around it, Square Pie remains a bastion of all things pie and mash. The sleek, red-tiled counter provides tasty pies, mash and mushy peas to shoppers and local workers, who sit and devour their cardboard boxes of hearty goodness at either the bar stools inside or the tables outside in the market itself. The menu ranges from trad options (steak and Guinness, chicken and mushroom) to the more adventurous (jerk chicken), all coming

Stein's

with mounds of soft mash. Smaller pies, Devon-made pasties and veggie options are available, as well as non-pie dishes, such as beef stew, jacket potatoes, macaroni cheese and sausages. If you can fit in anything afterwards, there are lamingtons, carrot cake, victoria sponge and apple pie, and coffees from Monmouth. All in all, great filling grub at a persuasive price.
Available for hire. Babies and children welcome: high chairs. Bookings not accepted. Tables outdoors (25, marketplace). Takeaway service. **Map 12 R5.**
For branches see index.

North East
Dalston

LMNT
316 Queensbridge Road, E8 3NH (7249 6727, www.lmnt.co.uk). Dalston Junction rail or bus 236. **Meals served** noon-11pm Mon-Sat; noon-10.30pm Sun. **Main courses** £8.95-£10.95. **Credit** MC, V.
LMNT wouldn't be out of place among Covent Garden's theatre-themed restaurants, thanks to its quirky decor rife with Egyptian and Roman imagery, tucked-away tables and soundtrack of operatic music. It certainly stands out in Dalston, though, and draws all sorts of curious diners. The menu is more standard than the surroundings might suggest: Mediterranean-skewed dishes such as calamari or grilled halloumi with houmous. A dish of mussels in a cream and wine sauce was tasty enough and a chocolate tart with passionfruit sauce did the trick, though a pork steak with chorizo was overcooked. But you definitely get a lot for your money at LMNT – and a fun experience too. Do pay a visit to the toilets: their erotic imagery, in both the men's and women's, gives the murals in Pompeii a run for their money.
Babies and children admitted. Booking advisable. Tables outdoors (3, garden). **Map 25 C5.**

Stoke Newington

Blue Legume
101 Stoke Newington Church Street, N16 0UD (7923 1303, www.thebluelegume.co.uk). Stoke Newington rail or bus 73, 393, 476. **Meals served** 9.30am-11pm Mon-Sat; 9.30am-6.30pm Sun. **Main courses** £7.95-£11.95. **Credit** (Mon-Fri) MC, V.
Church Street certainly has no shortage of cafés, and somehow they always seem to be heaving with yummy mummies and other Stokey residents. The Blue Legume – bustling café by day, more bistro-like in the evening, with bare-boards flooring and colourful wall and ceiling decorations – is no exception. There is plenty in on offer here, including a large breakfast menu and anything from bangers and mash to pasta, salads or braised lamb shank among the lunch and dinner options. Of note on our visit was a special of fresh cinnamon- and sugar-coated churros with thick hot chocolate. Freshly pressed celery, beetroot and carrot juice was also good, in contrast to an unremarkable halloumi and spicy sausage salad. The food is unlikely to rock your world, but it does arrive in generous portions. Make sure to bring cash with you (credit cards are accepted only during the week) and don't be put off by the sometimes-chaotic service.

Babies and children welcome: high chairs. Booking advisable (dinner). Tables outdoors (5, pavement). Takeaway service. **Map 25 B1.**
For branch see index.

North
Camden Town & Chalk Farm

Marine Ices
8 Haverstock Hill, NW3 2BL (7482 9003, www.marineices.co.uk). Chalk Farm tube. **Lunch served** noon-3pm, **dinner served** 6-11pm Tue-Fri. **Meals served** noon-11pm Sat; noon-10pm Sun. **Main courses** £4.40-£13.75. **Credit** MC, V.
The green raffia chairs, hard tiled floor and wall decorations couldn't look more dated, but write off this family-run Chalk Farm favourite at your cost. As the celebrity endorsements on the wall suggest (from Ted Danson and Samantha Morton to Bob Hoskins), this restaurant and ice-cream parlour is an absolute gem. Prices are reasonable, portions generous and the service warm. The pasta, pizza and meat dishes are classics, produced with real verve; there's no pretension here. Flavour is king. A spaghetti carbonara tasted so much better than our home version; we speculated about secret ingredients. Anything featuring the own-made neapolitan sausage with fennel seeds is worth ordering. We skipped starters to save room for the ice-cream, and most other diners (a mix of couples, families, locals and tourists) were doing the same. Sundaes, coppe and a knickerbocker glory are all on the menu, but the ice-cream (from honey and ginger to maple and walnut) is good enough to need no adornments.
Babies and children welcome: high chairs; nappy-changing facilities. Booking advisable weekends. Takeaway service. **Map 27 B1.**

Islington

Le Mercury
140A Upper Street, N1 1QY (7354 4088, www.lemercury.co.uk). Angel tube or Highbury & Islington tube/rail. **Meals served** noon-1am Mon-Sat; noon-11.30pm Sun. **Main courses** £8.45. **Credit** AmEx, MC, V.
It's one of countless restaurants on Upper Street, but Le Mercury has an evangelistic following. Three candlelit floors are crammed with animated diners, and the sweetly eclectic decor makes the place feel like a stumbled-upon holiday café. Aside from atmosphere, the appeal is clear from a glance at the menu – the food is fantastically cheap. A reassuring selection of French bistro-style dishes is listed, with starters (all £3.95) ranging from grilled goat's cheese to a more adventurous crayfish and lobster ravioli. Even foie gras makes an appearance, and it isn't half bad. Roast barbary duck made a delicious main, while sea bass with minted potatoes tasted almost too good for its price tag. Desserts (crème brûlée, poached pear, chocolate tart) were less impressive and service was a little patchy, but with change from £20 per person, no one's complaining.
Available for hire. Babies and children welcome: high chairs. Booking advisable weekends. Separate room for parties, seats 50. **Map 5 O1.**

Kentish Town

Nando's
227-229 Kentish Town Road, NW5 2JU (7424 9363, www.nandos.co.uk). Kentish Town tube/rail or Kentish Town West rail. **Meals served** 11.30am-11pm Mon-Thur, Sun; 11.30am-11pm Fri, Sat. **Main courses** £6-£12. **Credit** AmEx, MC, V.
Offering swift rather than fast food, Portuguese-inspired Nando's distinguishes itself from other chain restaurants with a mix of counter and table service, relatively comfortable surrounds, a short wine list and a menu focused on chicken flame-grilled to order. You'll either appreciate the lack of ceremony and meal deals, or not. People of all persuasions do, and Nando's is a shoo-in for families, who are no doubt reassured by the generally wholesome tone of the menu. Workaday chips don't seem quite as appealing when side dishes include grilled corn on the cob, spiced rice, 'macho' peas given oomph with mint and chilli, and hot, chunky ratatouille. Peri-peri chicken is available in various shapes, sizes and levels of spicy heat. On a chaotic Saturday night at the popular Kentish Town branch, the classic grilled half-chicken fared better than the new, premium-priced butterfly chicken breasts, which were disappointingly dry. Perhaps the grill chef wasn't yet familiar with them – the guy who took our order certainly wasn't: we had to point them out on the menu when we ordered.
Babies and children welcome: children's menu; high chairs; nappy-changing facilities. Bookings not accepted. Disabled: toilet. Vegetarian menu. **For branches see index.**

Outer London
Richmond, Surrey

★ Stein's
55 Richmond Towpath, Richmond, Surrey, TW10 6UX (8948 8189, www.stein-s.com). Richmond tube/rail then 20mins walk or bus 65. **Meals served** *Summer* noon-10pm Mon-Fri; 10am-10pm Sat, Sun. *Winter* noon-10pm Sat, Sun. Times vary depending on weather, call to check. **Main courses** £2.90-£9.90. **Credit** MC, V.
You're in Richmond, just south of the bridge. You're hungry. Make your choice: spend £150 on premium steak and red wine for two at Argentinian restaurant Gaucho, or less than a third of that on sausages, spuds and lager. But Stein's, an alfresco-only riverside joint that's been serving Bavarian fare since 2004, is not to be sniffed at. When you're in the mood, the fantastically unfashionable dishes (goulash, wursts, dumplings, white cabbage, potato salad) put the comfort back into cuisine. A sausage platter and side will serve two handsomely, and cost about £30. Desserts are superfluous, but if you're in a group, do sample a single apple strudel or sachertorte – they're scrumptious. First-rate beers include Erdinger Weissbier and cool, refreshing Paulaner Helles. The form: pick a numbered table, queue, collect your beers at the hatch, sit down – imagine you're in a leafy, riverine suburb of Munich – and pay at the end. Weather and daylight determine opening hours, so check Stein's iPhone app for opening times.
Babies and children welcome: crayons; high chairs; nappy-changing facilities; play area. Disabled: toilet. Tables outdoors (29, towpath). Takeaway service.

Cafés

With good cafés spreading across London like icing on a lemon drizzle cake, you don't have to go far to find a cup of cheer. Morning or afternoon, pit-stop or hangout, there's a café here to suit every mood, from quirky **Towpath** or the **Deptford Project**, to traditional **Orange Pekoe** (which has long been our star pick for afternoon tea) and sleek, style-conscious establishments such as **Cocomaya**, **Teasmith** and the **Grocer on King's**. Look around and you may find your new breakfast or lunchtime choice hiding within, say, the headquarters of the English Folk Dance & Song Society (**Nice Green Café**), Camberwell's South London Gallery (**No 67**), Greenwich's National Maritime Museum (**Museum Café**) or east London's Stour Space (**Counter Café**). Among our favourites this edition are **Nordic Bakery** (now an old favourite, despite it's perennially hip interior), **Lantana** (winner of our Best New Café award in 2009), the revamped **Jack's** – Dulwich's new foodie hub – **Tina, We Salute You** in Hackney, and the glamorous **Lido Café** at Brockwell Lido, worthy, family-friendly winner of our hotly contested 2011 Best Park Café award.

CAFÉS, PÂTISSERIES & TEAROOMS

Central

City

Bea's of Bloomsbury

One New Change, 83 Watling Street, EC4M 9BX (7242 8330, www.beasofbloomsbury.com). St Paul's tube. **Open** 8am-7pm Mon-Fri; noon-7pm Sat, Sun. **Main courses** £5-£10. **Credit** (over £5) AmEx, MC, V.

Toto, we're no longer in Bloomsbury. This quirky purveyor of fine cakes and sweet treats has shown its ambitious hand with this second branch in the City, and, as we went to press, a third was about to open on the King's Road. Bea's has also moved on from the aesthetics of its original diminutive premises; One New Change is a split-level beauty. Architects have worked small wonders with the oddly-shaped space, a long and narrow squeeze with plenty of natural light through floor-to-ceiling windows. Punters are greeted with a lavish display of cupcakes. There is no proper kitchen to speak of, so savouries are largely limited to doorstop sandwiches and tureens of hot soup; our 'small' bowl of fragrant wild mushroom soup with a wedge of excellent sourdough could have fed two. Afternoon tea is the main deal here, and Bea's repertoire of brownies, meringues, cakes and scones is a natural match for the excellent Jing teas and Square Mile coffees. Depending on your outlook, the odd mezzanine level can feel reassuringly private or sadly detached, and it can be difficult to get the attention of staff.

Available for hire. Bookings not accepted Mon-Fri. Takeaway service. **Map 11 P6**.
For branch see index.

Clerkenwell & Farringdon

Clerkenwell Kitchen

27-31 Clerkenwell Close, EC1R 0AT (7101 9959, www.theclerkenwellkitchen.co.uk). Angel tube or Farringdon tube/rail. **Open** 8am-5pm Mon-Fri. **Main courses** £4.80-£14. **Credit** MC, V.

While ordering at the bar can add unwelcome faff to dining out, the system works well enough here, ensuring service moves swiftly for the glut of local workers that fill the sleek white and pine space from midday. The opening hours – weekdays only, until 5pm – means the place is geared toward this lunchtime clientele, and a daily changing menu features quick-to-serve, seasonal dishes that use mainly organic ingredients. Hot mains range from the supremely simple (fettuccine with Scottish girolles) via familiar comfort classics (steak and kidney pie) to brasserie-style dishes, such a perfectly flaky fillet of pollack on a too-small bed of swiss chard and a filling sea of lentils. A brief selection of doorstop sandwiches and own-made cakes are well executed, and the coffee is excellent. Food is reliable and the atmosphere calm and friendly, making Clerkenwell Kitchen a prime spot for informal business meetings or a smart lunchtime treat.

Babies and children welcome: high chairs. Disabled: toilet. Tables outdoors (8, courtyard). Takeaway service. **Map 5 N4**.

J&A Café

4 Sutton Lane, EC1M 5PU (7490 2992, http://jandacafe.com). Barbican tube or Farringdon tube/rail. **Breakfast served** 8-11am Mon-Fri. **Brunch served** 9am-1pm Sat. **Lunch served** noon-3.30pm Mon-Sat. **Tea served** 3.30-5.45pm Mon-Fri; 3-5pm Sat. **Main courses** £3.50-£10.50. **Credit** MC, V.

At lunchtimes, a crowd of creative types descend down the small alley leading to J&A – named after sister owners Johann and Aoise Ledwidge – and sit at communal tables in the buzzing main room or the backyard of this former diamond-cutting factory. The upstairs room is much calmer and has the same lovely look of bare brick walls and cast-iron windows. The menu tempts with dishes made on site from scratch: slow-roast tomato, rocket and courgette tart, full of flavour and laden with sparkling fresh vegetables, or baked potatoes with premium toppings such as the steak, rocket, tomato, capers and horseradish sauce combo. Be quick to order as it's not unusual for mains to sell out by 1.30pm. When a neighbouring table complained about a delay in food arriving, apologetic staff offered free cakes. If those disgruntled customers had opted for the victoria sponge – delicious flavour and perfect texture – the delay would no doubt have been forgiven instantly.

Available for hire. Babies and children admitted. Disabled: toilet. Tables outdoors (13, pavement). Takeaway service. **Map 5 O4**.

St Ali NEW

27 Clerkenwell Road, EC1M 5RN (7253 5754, www.stali.co.uk). Farringdon tube/rail. **Meals served** 7am-6pm daily. **Main courses** £4.50-£13.75. **Credit** MC, V.

St Ali is the English sibling of a well-regarded café established in Melbourne around 12 years ago – if you didn't know that already, you'd probably guess. The bush-meets-warehouse decor is spot-on, as is the friendly service and relaxed, fusion-style menu – think soy- and mirin-spiced pulled pork ciabatta with Asian-style courgette 'slaw, cos lettuce and chilli jam. Being Australian, St Ali turns breakfast into something of an art, serving Antipodean staples (banana bread and corn fritters), as well as complex combos such as house-brasied beans with salted ricotta, lemon, mint and a poached egg, to which you can, if you wish, add a kipper. Espresso, filter and decaf coffees are roasted on site in the huge roaster at the back of the room, and the baristas are undeniably expert. You can have the usual espresso drinks from the handmade American machine, or opt for a cup of black coffee, such as Buf Café from Rwanda, made using an Aeropress. The handful of teas is pretty serious too. A concise, simple wine list cherry-picks from Old and New Worlds, as does the beer selection, with excellent bottles from Southwark's Kernel Brewery, and Cooper's Pale Ale representing the Aussies.

Available for hire. Bookings not accepted. Disabled: toilet. Separate room for parties, seats 60. Tables outdoors (2, pavement). Takeaway service. **Map 5 O4**.

Edgware Road

Cocomaya NEW

3 Porchester Place, W2 2BS (7706 2770, http://cocomaya.co.uk). Marble Arch tube. **Open** 10am-7pm Mon-Sat; 10am-5pm Sun. **Main courses** from £1.50. **Credit** AmEx, MC, V.

It's no surprise that Cocomaya attracts a chic clientele. Masterminded by three of fashion's big names – Agent Provocateur co-founder Serena Rees, accessories designer Walid al Damirji and former Liberty man Joel Bernstein – this chocolatier and bakery are stamped with style. The bakery, all pale wood and marble, offers an expansive array of uniformly good breads, cakes and pastries, including mousse-soft flourless chocolate cake, and juicy quince and almond tart. The more vibrant decor of the adjacent chocolate parlour suits its inventive, exquisite artisan chocolates. Pretty plates are topped with novelty chocs (skulls, blood red hearts) and interesting flavours (lavender, sour cherry), as well consummate classic creations. Drinks, ice-creams and cakes made with chocolate are also available.

Available for hire. Tables outdoors (2, pavement). Takeaway service. **Map 8 F6**.
For branches see index.

Euston

Peyton & Byrne

Wellcome Collection, 183 Euston Road, NW1 2BE (7611 2138, www.peytonandbyrne.com).

St Ali

Organic Butternut Lemongrass curd & crisp serano £4.50.

Pain Au Chocc £1.40

Nice Green Café. See p290.

See p290.

CAFÉS

Euston Square tube or Euston tube/rail. **Open** 10am-6pm Mon-Wed, Fri, Sat; 10am-10pm Thur; 11am-6pm Sun. **Main courses** £3.50-£9.50. **Credit** MC, V.

These days it seems as if you can't visit a museum or gallery without finding that Messrs Peyton and Byrne have got there first, installing a Brit-themed eaterie. Happily, though, this café's food – displayed in a long deli counter – isn't the stuff of mass production. We were impressed by a warm, doughy shortcrust pie packed with succulent slow-cooked beef, teamed with two simple but effective salads from a colourful Med-leaning selection (roasted butternut squash; puy lentils with diced peppers and red onions), all for £7.90. Sweet treats are a forte, with pastries, flapjacks and own-made cakes offered. Walnut-studded carrot cake was moist and fluffy, though a pretty fairy cake had been suffocated by an excess of sickly butter-cream. Service can be perfunctory, but the dining area is bright and futuristic, with high ceilings, candy-coloured seating and a shimmering light installation overhead. Thanks to the café's hidden location inside the Wellcome Collection (with bags checked at the door), you'll rarely have to fight for seats; it's a fairly well-kept secret.
Babies and children welcome: high chairs; nappy-changing facilities. Disabled: lift; toilet. Takeaway service. **Map 4 K4.**
For branches see index.

Fitzrovia

★ Lantana
13 Charlotte Place, W1T 1SN (7637 3347, www.lantanacafe.co.uk). Goodge Street tube. **Meals served** 8am-6pm Mon, Tue; 8am-10.30pm Wed-Fri; 9am-5pm Sat, Sun. **Main courses** £5-£12.50. **Credit** MC, V.
Owner Shelagh Ryan's determination to bring Australian café culture to a London that was, back then, bereft of Antipodean cuisine has worked to turn Lantana into a cult destination. The small café has now expanded next door to include a takeaway outpost (the former marked as 'In', the latter 'Out'). Menus change and evolve, with snacks such as sweetcorn fritter stacks with crispy bacon, Spanish-style baked eggs with chorizo, and the BRAT (bacon,

rocket, avocado, tomato) among the list of hot hits. A new dish – spicy pork burger served with fresh mango salsa and asian coleslaw – was as good as it gets, served daringly pink and juicy; ditto meatballs with a melted taleggio cheese centre. Customers mostly come from Fitzrovia's media crew, who drop by for breakfast, lunch or afternoon cakes and coffees. They're also treated to a hip soundtrack and plenty of old-fashioned Aussie bonhomie.
Babies and children admitted. Tables outdoors (2, pavement). Takeaway service.
Map 17 B1.

Holborn

Fleet River Bakery
71 Lincoln's Inn Fields, WC2A 3JF (7691 1457, www.fleetriverbakery.com). Holborn tube. **Open** 7am-6pm Mon-Fri; 10am-4pm Sat. **Main courses** £6.50-£8. **Credit** AmEx, MC, V.
Enter this bakery's small front room and order at a bar displaying salads, sandwiches and cakes. If you wish to eat-in, balance your tray up and down the steps leading to the rustic backrooms, filled with a random mix of tables, mismatched chairs, an old radiator, an art deco clock and even a church hymn board. We can see what the owners are trying to achieve, but the decor slightly misses the mark. Unsurprisingly, the best things to choose here are the baked goods. All breads and cakes are freshly made on site and taste wonderful. The varied daily lunch menu is available from noon. On our visit, a precisely balanced gazpacho came with fruity olive bread. 'Forbidden fruit cake' was simply an apple slice, but it had a juicy filling and was baked to perfection. Wholemeal bread for breakfast is also delightful, and best warmed in the toaster provided – enjoy it with a cup of Monmouth coffee.
Babies and children admitted. Tables outdoors (4, pavement). Takeaway service.
Map 18 F2.

Marylebone

La Fromagerie `HOT 50`
2-6 Moxon Street, W1U 4EW (7935 0341, www.lafromagerie.co.uk). Baker Street or Bond Street tube. **Open** 8am-7.30pm Mon-Fri;

9am-7pm Sat; 10am-6pm Sun. **Main courses** £6-£15. **Minimum** (12.30-2.30pm) £10. **Credit** AmEx, MC, V.
There's no doubt about the quality offered at La Fromagerie – in the shop, the provenance of everything from cheese to cherries is clearly shown – though the prices can make you wince. The café tables are in two areas of the attractively arranged shop premises; this time around we sat at the long communal table (and tried not to eavesdrop on Benedict Cumberbatch). Dishes are mostly assemblies, but what excellent ones they are: cheese plates, charcuterie plates, a salmon tasting plate (which includes Hansen & Lydersen salmon smoked in Stoke Newington); and a superior ploughman's with pork pie or ham, Keen's cheddar, smooth piccalilli and balsamic vinegar pickled onions. There are also several hot dishes, savoury tarts, salads, sandwiches and a soup of the day (a hearty gazpacho on this visit). The bread is moreish, and a plate of rare roast beef with beetroot and leaves was good enough to justify the £12 charged. A short wine list is as thoughtfully put together as the menu. Service is leisurely (and slightly po-faced), but no one seems to mind, underlining the impression that the regulars tend not to have jobs to rush back to.
Available for hire (evenings). Babies and children admitted. Takeaway service. **Map 3 G3.**
For branch see index.

Scandinavian Kitchen
61 Great Titchfield Street, W1W 7PP (7580 7161, www.scandikitchen.co.uk). Oxford Circus tube. **Meals served** 8am-7pm Mon-Fri; 10am-6pm Sat; 10am-3pm Sun. **Main courses** £4.95-£7.50. **Set lunch** £4.95-£7.95. **Credit** AmEx, MC, V.
The combination of café and specialist grocery shop, with a tasty smörgåsbord of food, makes Scandinavian Kitchen a favourite with expat Nordic folk and local office workers. Friendly and good-looking Swedish staff chat away to regulars from behind cabinets displaying a flavoursome array of open sandwiches featuring all things pickled, cured and smoked, plus salads and wraps. You can choose a plate of three or five items; smoked salmon and fish roe on rye, and pickled herring with onion are favourites. Beetroot and apple salad with crème

fraîche was also delicious. Relax on sofas by the window and listen to the sounds of Abba, or sit at tables towards the back where a vast array of Scandinavian goods fills the shelves. Useful 'what is this?' signs explain some of the bestsellers. If you're just popping in for a cup of coffee and a slice of freshly baked cake, don't miss the gooey chocolate kladdkaka.

Babies and children welcome: high chairs. Tables outdoors (4, pavement). Takeaway service; delivery service (over £35). Map 9 J5.

Mayfair

Bond & Brook

2nd floor, Fenwick Bond Street, 63 New Bond Street, W1S 1RQ (7629 0273, www.fenwick. co.uk). Bond Street tube. **Breakfast served** 10am-noon Mon-Sat. **Lunch served** noon-6.30pm Mon-Wed, Fri, Sat; noon-8pm Thur. **Tea served** 3-6.30pm Mon-Wed, Fri, Sat; 3-8pm Thur. **Main courses** £10.50-£18.50. **Set tea** £17.50. **Credit** AmEx, MC, V.

Ideally located on the second floor of department store Fenwick, Bond & Brook has ladies-who-lunch firmly in its sights. The elegant mid-century furniture, white palette, flashy pewter bar and framed fashion photography make the venue a stylish stop for shoppers, while its all-day menu has feminine appeal. Breakfast and brunch run the gamut from yoghurt on granola to smoked salmon with scrambled egg and brioche; lunch features light tapas options alongside more substantial main meals. From the tapas menu, artichokes alla giudia were charred rather than crunchy, but the slivers of duck breast with orange salad were sublime. We liked the main dish of black ink linguine with crab meat, chilli and parsley, despite the fact the pasta had been boiled well past al dente. Next time, though, we might stick to the frou-frou afternoon tea. Dainty sandwiches, fondant fancies and a cheeky champagne cocktail make for a suitably wicked break from frocks and shoes.

Available for hire. Babies and children welcome: high chairs; nappy-changing facilities. Disabled: toilet. **Map 9 H7.**

Mount Street Deli

100 Mount Street, W1K 2TG (7499 6843, www.themountstreetdeli.co.uk). Bond Street tube. **Open** 8am-8pm Mon-Fri; 9am-6pm Sat. **Main courses** £3-£9.95. **Credit** AmEx, MC, V.

Situated in the heart of Mayfair, Mount Street Deli has a suitably exclusive air. Its well-heeled clientele are unlikely to blanch at the prices, though a stray tourist may well gasp on being charged more than £10 for an ordinary houmous and roast pepper sandwich with side salad. Still, this is what you'd expect from Caprice Holdings, the restaurant group with J Sheekey, Scott's and the Ivy under its umbrella. Keeping things firmly in the family, much of the food is ferried over from the adjacent Scott's; daily specials tend to outclass some of the duller sandwich and bakery options. The salmon en croute special, for example, had a substantial fish centre encrusted with thick, crisp pastry. The standard spinach and ricotta roll, on the other hand, was limp and bland. A breakfast menu includes own-made granola as well as boiled eggs with soldiers, and the tempting selection of sweets comprises oversized brownies, meringues and fruit tarts. On the deli's traditional shelving you'll find an abundance of international, upmarket goods, from Alain Milliat juices to Amedei chocolate.

Available for hire. Babies and children admitted. Tables outdoors (2, pavement). Takeaway service. **Map 9 G7.**

Pimlico

William Curley

198 Ebury Street, SW1W 8UN (7730 5522, www.williamcurley.co.uk). Sloane Square tube. **Open** 9am-7pm Mon-Thur; 9am-8pm Fri, Sat; 10am-6pm Sun. **Main courses** £4-£6. **Credit** AmEx, MC, V.

This beautifully appointed pâtisserie-chocolatier and café showcases an array of delectable specialities, including truffles sharpened with Japanese vinegar, shiny-glazed mousses, tea-infused sponges, ices and artisan chocolates. There's a bespoke dessert bar at weekends, where you might sink a spoon into lavender panna cotta or classic savarin. The pâtisserie and chocolates are hard to fault for their creativity, but dishes from the café's brunch menu weren't as memorable (despite being priced at the sharp end). Scotch pancakes were dense and cloying, saved only by lashings of creamy chocolate sauce. Equally disappointing, french toast, rendered soggy by too much sugar syrup, didn't do itself any favours. Curley's speciality work is to- class, but the café menu needs more attention.

Babies and children admitted. Tables outdoors (2, pavement). Takeaway service. **Map 15 G11.** **For branch see index.**

Soho

Maison Bertaux

28 Greek Street, W1D 5DQ (7437 6007, www.maisonbertaux.com). Leicester Square, Piccadilly Circus or Tottenham Court Road tube. **Open** 9am-10pm Mon-Sat; 9-8pm Sun. **Main courses** £3.60-£4.75. **No credit cards.**

A long-time Soho favourite, Maison Bertaux doesn't beguile every visitor, but if you can see the charm in its hard-worn furniture, chaotic decor and unruly service, you'll be rewarded with an enlivening café experience. The pâtisserie was opened in 1871 by French Communards and continues to stick to what it knows best: viennoiseries and classic, cream-loaded confections baked here daily. The mont blancs, éclairs and millefeuilles all glisten temptingly enough from the large window, but their execution varies. If you're not up to the risk, choose the reliably delicious frangipanes or go for a savoury snack. The selection is brief – the choice is essentially quiche (again, uniformly good) or the popular dijon slice (a pastry involving mustard and melted cheese) – but it comes with a good fresh salad. There's usually space to sit downstairs and watch the world go by, or else you can head up to the shabby first floor where there's a madcap gallery starring the art world's more eccentric talents.

Babies and children admitted. Tables outdoors (7, pavement). Takeaway service. **Map 17 C4.**

★ Nordic Bakery

14A Golden Square, W1F 9JG (3230 1077, www.nordicbakery.com). Piccadilly Circus tube. **Meals served** 8am-8pm Mon-Fri; 9am-7pm Sat; 11am-6pm Sun. **Main courses** £3.25-£4. **Credit** MC, V.

We love this Finnish-owned spot, and its new Marylebone offshoot. The counter set-up looks like any modern sandwich bar, but a quick glance at the food on offer immediately sets it apart as authentic, gourmet and health-minded. Exquisite rye breads of unusually light texture surround fillings such as salmon tartare, or egg and herring (there's usually smoked salmon, ham and cheese, and cheese and pickle for the less adventurous). Karelian pies filled with rice or mashed potato and topped with egg-butter spread are not to be missed – and are filling, despite their modest size and £1.60 price tag. We also adore the tender rye and blueberry muffins, oatmeal cookies and hefty, sticky cinnamon buns with their addictive sugar-and-spice filling. Even when busy, the café exudes serenity – perhaps because of the relaxed yet achingly stylish decor of pine panelling and petrol blue paint. You'll probably sit there, as we tend to, sipping coffee from the designer cups and glasses, wondering if you can get them to redecorate your place.

Kipferl. See p290.

South Kensington

Hummingbird Bakery
47 Old Brompton Road, SW7 3JP (7851 1795, www.hummingbirdbakery.com). South Kensington tube. **Open** 9am-7pm Mon-Thur, Sun; 9am-8pm Fri, Sat. **Main courses** £2-£3. **Credit** AmEx, MC, V.
Popular with all ages, especially young mums, this branch of Hummingbird Bakery celebrates Stateside sweetness with some classic all-American flavours. There's a tiny café area attached to the shop, along with a couple of coveted outdoor tables. The eye candy is provided by a veritable parade of indulgence – sparkly frosted cupcakes decorated in rainbow colours, lemon meringue pies, devil's food cake and whoopee pies. We loved our darkly seductive chocolate cupcake and whipped icing, but found the red velvet cake disappointingly dry. Brownies come in various guises; our favourite is the deliciously soggy walnut version, topped with rich chocolate and cream cheese frosting. Supplies can run low by the evening; for the best choice, visit earlier in the day. Service, although friendly, is sometimes slow and chaotic during busy times.
Babies and children admitted. Tables outdoors (4, pavement). Takeaway service. **Map 14 D10.** **For branches see index.**

West
Ladbroke Grove

Books for Cooks
4 Blenheim Crescent, W11 1NN (7221 1992, www.booksforcooks.com). Ladbroke Grove tube. **Open** 10am-6pm Mon-Sat. **Lunch served** noon-2pm Tue-Fri; 11.30am-2pm Sat. **Set lunch** £5 2 courses, £7 3 courses. **Credit** MC, V.
A food-lover's delight, this specialist cookbook shop has a small kitchen and handful of tables at the back, where co-owner Eric Treuille puts recipes from the cookbook of the day to the test. The results are offered as a set lunch from noon – arrive promptly or you'll miss out. On our visit, a roasted pepper stew with sausages (all meat is organic) came from Antonio Carluccio and Gennaro Contaldo's Italian cookbook, and passed the test with flying colours. Complementing this was a puy lentil salad starter with own-made focaccia, and, for afters, a choice of cakes. We opted for a delightful chocolate caramel soufflé cake with pecans. Enjoy it all with a glass of red from the owner's own vineyard. If you want to recreate the dishes yourself, pick up the cookbook on your way out – or sign up for the cooking classes offered.
Bookings not accepted. Disabled: toilet. **Map 19 B3.**

St Helen's Foodstore NEW
55 St Helen's Gardens, W10 6LN (8960 2225). Ladbroke Grove tube. **Open** 7.30am-6.30pm Mon-Fri; 9am-5pm Sat, Sun. **Main courses** £5-£12. **Credit** AmEx, MC, V.
On a largely residential street, tucked away from throbbingly busy Ladbroke Grove and Portobello Road, St Helen's appears to cater solely to in-the-know locals. Regulars are greeted warmly, and the café's mix of Italian and British dishes, as well as

its packed shelves of dry and fresh deli items, keeps them coming back. On our visit, a couple of hot bakes and savoury pastries, as well as four or five interesting salads, were available for lunch. We opted for a portion of parmigiana accompanied by rocket, dolcelatte and walnut salad, as well as that Sicilian favourite, arancini balls. While there wasn't enough meat, sauce or flavour in the latter, the parmigiana's tangy tomato and firm aubergine compensated. The cake choice is plentiful, ranging from a slightly wet brownie to voluptuous bread and butter bake. The small interior is lacklustre, but the pleasant outdoor seating makes this a sunny-day destination.
Available for hire. Babies and children welcome: high chairs. Tables outdoors (20, pavement). Takeaway service.

Westbourne Grove

Tom's Deli
226 Westbourne Grove, W11 2RH (7221 8818, www.tomsdelilondon.co.uk). Notting Hill Gate tube. **Open** 8am-6.30pm Mon-Sat; 9am-6.30pm Sun. **Main courses** £10-£12. **Credit** (over £5) MC, V.
Tom's Deli is a happy place. You enter through a sweet shop displaying sugary treats in jars and retro packaging; bright wall art, kaleidoscopic paper lanterns and finds from Portobello market add more colour. Downstairs is the deli. Friendly staff led us up to the diner-like café, past yummy mummies and young couples, to the back garden. Small tables, plus the odd gnome, fill a tiny bohemian terrace under a fig tree. The menu isn't especially innovative, but if you're after breakfast egg dishes, sandwiches or salad, it comes up trumps. We opted for some daily specials: spinach, pine nut and goat's cheese quiche for a light lunch; and a more substantial dish of tender beef goulash packed with paprika and caraway flavours on buttered pappardelle. The beautifully arranged cakes – including raspberry chequerboard, and pistachio rosewater – are hard to resist, though the latter was a bit dry. The waitress waved us goodbye with a 'come again'. We certainly will.
Babies and children welcome: high chairs. Tables outdoors (6, garden; 2, terrace). Takeaway service. **Map 7 A6.**

South West
Barnes

★ Orange Pekoe
3 White Hart Lane, SW13 0PX (8876 6070, www.orangepekoetea.com). Barnes Bridge rail or bus 209. **Meals served** 7.30am-5.30pm Mon-Fri; 9am-5.30pm Sat, Sun. **Main courses** £4.70-£8. **Credit** AmEx, MC, V.
It's wise to book whatever time you visit Orange Pekoe, so popular is this charming little tearoom near the river on the Barnes/Mortlake border. The front room sets the tone: black and gold tea canisters line one wall, while the wooden counter is laden with chunky sandwiches and classy-looking cakes. Further in, flamboyant wallpaper and pretty vintage crockery provide a decorative feminine touch. On a sunny afternoon, the wobbly metal tables outside are packed, despite being close to a busy roundabout. Affable staff explain the deal for afternoon tea: a pot of tea of your choice, finger sandwiches (including cucumber and mint, smoked

salmon, and egg mayo), a fat scone with Cornish clotted cream and strawberry jam, and your choice of cake. The baking (orange and almond cake, lemon chiffon cake) is tip-top. Elegant white bone china or glass teapots and a three-tier cake stand add to the sense of occasion. Breakfast, light lunches (soup of the day, ploughman's and pâté platters) and a decent array of coffee drinks are also available.
Babies and children welcome: crayons; high chairs; nappy-changing facilities. Tables outdoors (6, pavement). Takeaway service.

Chelsea

Grocer on King's
184A King's Road, SW3 5XP (7351 5544, www.thegroceron.com). Sloane Square tube. **Open** 8.30am-7pm Mon-Fri; 10am-6pm Sat, Sun. **Main courses** £6-£7. **Credit** MC, V.
Temptingly packaged prepared foods, choice grocery items and gorgeous bakes line the walls of this deli-cum-café. Design is sleek and functional and the 'menu' is limited to what can be toasted or plated – salads, sandwiches, pizzas and cakes, which you select from the shop. A tuna niçoise salad, presented on a pretty flower plate, featured high-quality ingredients and showed a refreshing lightness of touch for something that, only minutes before, had been sitting on a shelf in a plastic container. This is not the location for a leisurely lunch, but the Grocer does provide a welcome haven in the middle of a shopping trip. And whatever standard of cook you may be, it's hard to leave the shop without a little package to take home.
Available for hire. Takeaway service. **Map 14 E11.**

South
Balham

Trinity Stores
5-6 Balham Station Road, SW12 9SG (8673 3773, www.trinitystores.co.uk). Balham tube/rail. **Open** 8am-6pm Mon-Fri; 9am-5.30pm Sat; 9.30am-5pm Sun. **Main courses** £2.15-£9.55. **Credit** AmEx, MC, V.
It's all change at Trinity Stores. This time last year, every nook of the bijoux site was crammed with attractive deli goods, but the tiny 'café' section felt like an afterthought. Nevertheless, the dry-goods sales went into decline while demand for the handful of tables regularly exceeded supply. So, out went the store cupboard section, in came more seating: a please-all mix of counter, communal and bistro. The boho-chic surroundings (scuffed wooden floorboards, farmhouse furniture) are nicely matched by high-quality organic picnic foods. We enjoyed the crumbly pastry and wholesome flavours of a sweet potato, spinach and feta quiche, teamed with a colourful salad of chickpeas, roasted parsnips, parsley and carrots. For the sweet-toothed, the moist walnut-studded carrot cake, with its light butter-cream icing, is a must, though a gratifyingly sticky treacle tart was spoiled by the inclusion of lemon. The chiller cabinet survived the cull, and continues to offer for sale all the ingredients for a top-notch organic brekkie, from juice and yoghurts to sausages and vine-ripened tomatoes. Trinity's rosy-cheeked staff are hugely welcoming, and passionate about the produce.
Available for hire. Babies and children welcome: high chairs. Takeaway service.

Counter Café. See p290.

CAFÉS

Battersea

Crumpet

66 Northcote Road, SW11 6QL (7924 1117).
Clapham Junction rail. **Open** 8.30am-6pm
Mon-Sat; 9.30am-6pm Sun. **Main courses**
£4.20-£7.50. **Credit** AmEx, MC, V.
Situated on a bustling stretch of Northcote Road,
sandwiched in by pretty boutiques, Crumpet is an
ideal stop for mums-that-lunch. A substantial
children's menu is at the heart of the café, full of
tot-pleasing fare from Marmite on toast to fairy
cakes and ice-cream. For the grown-ups, there are
deep-filled sarnies on granary bread, beefy jacket
potatoes and an outstanding welsh rarebit
smothered with quality mature cheddar and just a
smattering of worcestershire sauce. To drink, the
Union coffee is overshadowed by loose-leaf tea that
arrives in a pot large enough for two. There are
more than ten blends from which to choose, and
staff are happy to recommend something to suit
your taste. Crumpet isn't always the most serene
spot to enjoy a cuppa – after all, the spacious café
comes complete with a kids' play den and a family
bathroom with a mini-toilet – but it's an
accommodating and cheerful neighbourhood joint.
Babies and children welcome: children's menu;
high chairs; nappy-changing facilities; play area.
Disabled: toilet. Tables outdoors (2, pavement).
Takeaway service. **Map 21 C5**.

Clapham

Breads Etcetera

127 Clapham High Street, SW4 7SS (07717
642812 mobile, http://breadsetceterabakery.com).
Clapham Common or Clapham North tube.
Open 10am-10pm Tue-Sat; 10am-4pm Sun.
Main courses £5.50-£12. **No credit cards**.
Breads Etcetera is a hug in café form. The ambience
is cosy, with low ceilings and every inch of wall
covered in pictures, mirrors and blackboards – the
exposed brick is hardly exposed at all. Staff are
friendly and the dressed-down diners huddle
together, sharing tables. A toaster sits on each table
and for most of the week, and all day on Sundays,
meals are based around rustic breads (baked on the
premises) accompanied by comfort food: various
iterations of full english, smoked salmon and cream
cheese, buttery wild mushrooms with chicken liver
pâté, baked beans and smoked bacon, or
sandwiches. From around 5pm, pasta, sourdough
pizzas, stews and soups take over. Come here for
the relaxed atmosphere and the homely fare.
Babies and children admitted. Tables outdoors
(2, pavement). Takeaway service. **Map 22 B2**.
For branch see index.

Macaron

22 The Pavement, SW4 0HY (7498 2636).
Clapham Common tube. **Open** 7.30am-7pm
daily. **Main courses** £2.85-£12. **Credit**
MC, V.
Step into this quirky French pâtisserie and you
immediately leave the hustle and bustle of Clapham
for a place that would seem more at home in a small
French town. As the name suggests, macaroons are
available to eat in or to take away, and they are
excellent. Deep-filled sandwiches, croque monsieur,
glazed fruit tarts, pastries and brownies are
similarly tempting. Decor is eclectic, with stained-
glass windows depicting various baked goods, a
faux-sky ceiling complete with cherubs, a collection

of ornate lights and china crockery that looks like it came from your nan's. Stop by for lunch or a cup of tea – rose, blackberry, hibiscus and jasmine are just part of the selection – or take away French supermarket goodies such as Teisseire cordials, Banania chocolate drink, and bakery favourites. *Babies and children admitted. Tables outdoors (3, pavement). Takeaway service.* **Map 22 A2**.

South East
Camberwell

No 67 NEW
South London Gallery, 67 Peckham Road, SE5 8UH (7252 7649, www.southlondon gallery.org). Bus 12, 36 or 171. **Breakfast served** 9am-11.30pm, **lunch served** noon-3.30pm Tue-Fri. **Brunch served** 10am-3.30pm Sat, Sun. **Dinner served** 6.30-10pm Wed-Sat. **Main courses** £9.80-£13.80. **Credit** AmEx, MC, V.

These days, any art gallery worth its salt must have an ace café attached – and the South London Gallery is no exception. The elegantly converted ground floor of an adjacent Victorian house provides the setting for quality Union coffee, freshly made smoothies, and delicious and reasonably priced food. A shady bar at the front displays luscious home-baked cakes and a menu of daily-changing, inventive dishes (succulent köfte kebabs with grilled vegetables and couscous; ox heart stew; mackerel, beetroot and new potato salad), while a light-filled atrium gallery opens on to a walled garden and terrace for diners à deux. No 67 serves easily the best breakfast for miles around, ranging from a massive bowl of thick, creamy porridge to the 'full Spanglish' – grilled mushrooms, fried eggs, grilled chorizo slices, dense, black morcilla and own-made spicy baked beans. *Available for hire. Babies and children welcome: high chairs; nappy-changing facilities. Disabled: toilet. Tables outdoors (6, terrace; 5, garden). Takeaway service.* **Map 23 B2**.

Deptford

Deptford Project
121-123 Deptford High Street, SE8 4NS (07545 593279 mobile, www.thedeptford project.com). Deptford rail or Deptford Bridge DLR. **Open** 9am-6pm Mon-Sat; 11am-4pm Sun. **Main courses** £3.50-£4.75. **No credit cards.**
A collaborative creative enterprise sited in a former railway yard a few minutes' train ride from London Bridge, the Deptford Project is a make-do world away from the Shard or tourist hotspot Borough. While the 'up-cycling' artists and open-air cinema make good use of the arches and railway yard, a community café has been created in and around a recovered train carriage. Both the artfully designed interior and outdoor decked area are bright and inviting. Filling, good-value family fare such as baked potatoes and local sausages in a bun is enhanced by inventive and neatly presented relishes and chutneys. There's a good range of health-conscious salads too, and juices as befits a child-friendly place, but the generous, moist wedges of own-made cakes alongside great coffee are the highlights. *Babies and children welcome: high chairs; nappy-changing facilities. Disabled: toilet. Tables outdoors (11, terrace). Takeaway service.*

East Dulwich

Blue Mountain Café
18 North Cross Road, SE22 9EU (8299 6953, www.bluemo.co.uk). East Dulwich rail. **Open** 9am-6pm Mon-Sat; 10am-6pm Sun. **Main courses** £4.50-£8. **Credit** AmEx, MC, V.
Before the area was filled with free-range butchers and Bugaboo pushchairs, Blue Mountain was already serving its famous 'full monty' fry-up and squishy cakes to an appreciative clientele. This may not be the cheapest full english you'll ever eat, but it's substantial, with meaty cumberland sausages, quality bacon, and all the trimmings, served with hunks of toast. More interesting dishes are to be found among the lunchtime specials: for example, fiery jerk chicken (which could have done with some salad or plantain as accompaniment), or vegetable fricassee. If the weather's good, pick a table on the forecourt – a great spot for people-watching on one of East Dulwich's liveliest roads. *Babies and children welcome: children's menu; high chairs; nappy-changing facilites. Disabled: toilets. Separate room for parties, seats 10. Tables outdoors (5, garden; 5, terrace).* **Map 23 C4.**
For branch see index.

★ Jack's Tea & Coffee House
85 Pellatt Road, SE22 9JD (7183 9135, http://chocolateconcreteandpinkcustard.blog spot.com). East Dulwich rail. **Meals served** 10.30am-5pm Mon; 8.30am-5pm Tue-Fri; times vary, call for details Sat, Sun. **Main courses** £3.95-£7.95. **Credit** MC, V.
If there's a neighbourhood with a friendlier local café serving such high-quality food, we're moving there. Di Brindley, who earned her cheffing stripes at Michelin-starred London restaurants, only took over this tiny café a year ago, but has already turned it into a local foodie hub. The lunch menu changes according to available produce and whatever's inspiring Di that day, but you can rely on there being a cooked breakfast made with top ingredients, healthy granolas with fresh berries, own-made seasonal soup, doorstop-sized BLTs, sensational brownies, and the best coffee in the area. Jack's also occasionally hosts intimate Saturday night dinners, monthly Sunday roasts, pudding contests and Saturday brunch. The flipside to having a small team with big ideas is unpredictability – phone ahead if you're coming far. *Available for hire. Babies and children welcome: children's menu; high chairs. Booking essential Sat, Sun. Tables outdoors (4, pavement; 4, garden). Takeaway service.* **Map 23 C4.**

Luca's
145 Lordship Lane, SE22 8HX (8613 6161, www.lucasbakery.com). East Dulwich rail. **Open** 8.30am-5pm Mon-Sat; 9am-4.30pm Sun. **Main courses** £3.50-£7.50. **Credit** (over £10) AmEx, MC, V.
Spacious and light, Luca's is a popular meeting place for parents after the school drop-off, ladies who lunch, and East Dulwich's large home-working population. You'll find light savoury snacks – soup, salads, eggs benedict/florentine/royale/scrambled, a passable croque monsieur – and the counter heaped with buns and pastries is difficult to ignore. Austrian influences predominate, with glistening fruit tarts, a hearty baked cheesecake, a spicy carrot cake, fat cinnamon buns, and, of course, black forest gateau. There's also a wide selection of freshly baked breads, from crusty bloomers and sourdough loaves to heavy dark rye, making for some super sarnies. We found the coffee a little flavourless, but enjoyed the range of very English juices and cordials. *Babies and children admitted. Tables outdoors (12, garden). Takeaway service.* **Map 23 C4.**

Greenwich

Museum Café NEW
National Maritime Museum, Romney Road, SE10 9NF (8858 4422, www.nmm.ac.uk).

Boulangerie Bon Matin. See p290.

Greenwich rail/DLR. **Open** 8am-6pm daily.
Main courses £3.25-£8.50. **Credit** (over £5)
AmEx, MC, V.
Located at the base of the National Maritime
Museum's new Sammy Ofer Wing, the sun terrace
of the recently opened Museum Café is a pleasant
place to relax, but the views of the park are just as
good from the seats inside. The kitchen is shared
with another newcomer (the 16" West Brasserie
upstairs), so take note of the strict 11.30am deadline
for the short breakfast and brunch menu, which
includes the likes of porridge and eggs benedict.
Aside from the sandwiches and baguettes, food is
on the expensive side, with brunch items rising to
as much as a stonking £8.25 (for a full english); a
meagre portion of poached salmon was £3.75. The
cakes that we sampled were dry and uninspiring,
but drinks – including Union hand-roasted coffee
and an excellent coconut, banana and pineapple
juice – were a cut above.
Available for hire (evenings). Babies and children
welcome: children's menu; high chairs; nappy-
changing facilities. Bookings not accepted.
Disabled: toilet. Tables outdoors (12, terrace).
Takeaway service.

Peckham

Petitou
63 Choumert Road, SE15 4AR (7639 2613,
www.petitou.co.uk). Peckham Rye rail. **Open**
9am-5pm Mon-Wed, Sun; 9am-8pm Thur-Sat.
Main courses £6.60-£7. **Credit** MC, V.
In Peckham-by-Hampstead, Petitou lies on a tree-
lined street just off the bustling main drag. A
lovely wrought-iron plant holder forms a pretty
border around the tiled seating area outside, where
a group of older ladies and gents take tea and cake.
Inside, the wooden tables and chairs fill up with
young families looking for a late breakfast (free-
range scrambled eggs with various extras,
including sustainable salmon, are served until
1pm). Lunch might be mackerel pâté with pitta,
falafel with flatbread or a range of sandwiches on
thick granary bread. Own-made warm chickpea
and potato samosas with raita arrived with a big
pile of salad, as did halloumi and sun-dried
tomatoes. There's a range of teas served in a two-
cup or four-cup pot, plus great coffee and a choice
of delicious cakes. Peruse one of the daily papers,
order a glass of wine or beer, and you could easily
lose an entire day here.
Babies and children welcome: high chairs.
Tables outdoors (5, pavement). Takeaway
service. **Map 23 C3**.

East
Docklands

Mudchute Kitchen
Mudchute Park & Farm, Pier Street, E14
3HP (3069 9290, www.mudchutekitchen.org).
Mudchute DLR. **Open** 9.30am-4.50pm
Tue-Sun. **Main courses** £2.50-£9. **Credit**
MC, V.
After a period of closure, the popular café serving
crowds of visitors to this 32-acre Isle of Dogs park
and city farm has reopened. It is now under the
management of Frizzante, which successfully runs
a number of London city farm eateries in the
manner of an agriturismo. Lunch features own-
grown organic greenery; brunch offers golden-

yolked free-range eggs. British favourites such as
plump grilled sausages rub shoulders with
Italianate dishes, including thyme-scented steak
and roast new potatoes, and tender gnocchi in a
herby own-made tomato sauce. Doorstep
sandwiches with fresh fillings, appealing cakes,
Italian ices and a wide range of soft drinks keep all
family members happily fed. A word of caution: hot
days can bring hordes of flies that somehow evade
the zappers…
Babies and children welcome: children's menu;
high chairs; nappy-changing facilities. Disabled:
toilet (farm). Tables outdoors (20, courtyard).
Takeaway service. **Map 24 C4**.

Shoreditch

Frizzante@Hackney City Farm
Hackney City Farm, 1A Goldsmith's Row,
E2 8QA (7739 2266, www.frizzanteltd.co.uk).
Hoxton rail. **Lunch served** 10am-4pm Tue-Sun.
Dinner served 7-10pm Thur. **Main courses**
£5-£17. **Credit** MC, V.
It's the clamour of families ruddy-cheeked from a
visit to Hackney City Farm that saves the large
main space of the farm's high-ceilinged café from
feeling a little cold. The outdoor area, buffered from
Hackney Road by a container garden, is a more
atmospheric spot. Yes, Frizzante has a functionality-
over-style vibe, but it also has a confident-sounding
menu. Sadly, the cooking was found wanting on our
most recent visit. An octopus and cuttlefish salad
was clean-tasting, though the grilled polenta
underneath was soggy, while a frittata was almost
as chewy as the woodchip underfoot. Potato, leek
and stilton soup may have been a mite autumnal
for an August menu, but it hit an appropriately
rustic note. Breakfasts – meat or vegetarian options
– looked to be better value than our choices. That
sausage might repeat on you when you visit the
pigsty, though.
Available for hire (autumn and winter only).
Babies and children welcome: children's menu;
high chairs; nappy-changing facilities. Booking
advisable dinner. Disabled: toilet. Tables outdoors
(10, park). **Map 6 S3**.

Jones Dairy Café
23 Ezra Street, E2 7RH (7739 5372,
www.jonesdairy.co.uk). Liverpool Street tube/
rail then bus 26, 48 or Old Street tube/rail
then bus 55. **Meals served** 9am-3pm Fri;
9am-4.30pm Sat; 8am-3pm Sun. **Main courses**
£3-£8. **No credit cards.**
If a Sunday morning trip to Columbia Road's flower
market can feel like holidaying in your own city –
it's a bit out of the way, and boasts plentiful natural
beauty – then this is where you'd sit and write your
postcard. The interior at Jones Dairy Café is all
higgledy-piggledy retro chic (an infestation of
vintage teapots, a huge 'Thomas' stove sitting
totem pole-like in the corner), and may make some
think 'knitting club', but the food is worth writing
home about. The quality of ingredients in dishes
such as Norfolk-caught kipper with a poached egg,
and Sladbury's smoked salmon with egg, avocado
and other verdant goodies left us satisfied long into
the day. Fine Colchester oysters are available, raw
or grilled with pecorino, and the milk leaves old-
fashioned globules on the surface of your coffee.
Babies and children welcome: high chairs. Tables
outdoors (4, pavement). Takeaway service.
Map 6 S3.

Spitalfields

Tea Smith
6 Lamb Street, E1 6EA (7247 1333,
www.teasmith.co.uk). Liverpool Street tube/rail.
Open 11am-6pm daily. **Afternoon tea** £20.
No credit cards.
Betray even a passing interest in loose-leaf tea and
the wonderful staff at this Spitalfields teahouse will
happily share their seemingly endless knowledge.
Sit up at the long, wooded bar by the hot water taps
and you can watch them ceremonially brewing your
choice using the traditional Chinese method of
gongfu. By adhering to exact water temperatures
and steeping a small amount of leaves in a gaiwan
(a small lidded bowl), staff can make several
infusions, giving you a chance to linger over a few
rounds of tea together with some William Curley
confections. The pâtissier's exquisite sweets come
with an innovative Asian twist here; the sesame-
coated walnut and miso biscuit is a stand-out hit.
You can also try chocolate chunks with a matcha
honey dip – tooth-achingly sweet, even with the
powdered green tea – as well as chocolate sables and
shortbread. Perfect treats to accompany an
expansive tea menu.
Babies and children admitted. Takeaway service.
Map 12 R5.

North East
Clapton

Venetia
55 Chatsworth Road, E5 0LH (8986 1642).
Homerton rail or bus 242, 308. **Open** 8am-5pm
daily. **Main courses** £4-£4.85. **Credit** MC, V.
Chatsworth Road may not rival Broadway Market
just yet, but thanks to the likes of Venetia, it's well
on the way. If you're after a fry-up, you're best off
going over the road to Chatsworth Kitchen as you
won't find one here. The kitchen did rustle up a
mean bacon and egg sandwich on our visit, though,
with sweet smoky bacon, still-warm egg mayo and
fresh bread from Flour Station. Various other
sandwiches are also offered, as well as cakes (the
raspberry, pear and sour cream cake was light,
moist and delicious) and pastries. There's also a
daily salad, perhaps herby lentil, panzanella or fig,
mozzarella and basil. The menu may be short, but
the quality is high, and there are kids' options too.
Babies and children welcome: high chairs;
nappy-changing facilities; toys. Tables outdoors
(6, garden). Takeaway service.

Dalston

★ Tina, We Salute You
47 King Henry's Walk, N1 4NH (3119 0047,
www.tinawesaluteyou.com). Dalston Kingsland
rail or bus 38. **Open** 8am-7pm Tue-Fri; 9am-7pm
Sat; 10am-7pm Sun. **Main courses** £3.60-£6.
No credit cards.
And we really do… salute Tina, that is. The stylish
interior of this corner café – white walls decorated
with Ben Murphy's wonderful electrical tape
'drawings' of trees, snogging couples and cryptic
phrases – belies the genuinely friendly service. Top
breakfasts and sarnies are the order of the day,
accompanied by really good coffee, which is
probably why all the pavement tables were taken.
The sofa had been commandeered by a young

CAFÉS

No 67. See p287.

couple eager to talk coffee machines with the owners (they're opening a café nearby), and the window ledge hosted a couple of laptop junkies. We only just managed to squeeze on to the big table inside, where Marmite, jams and marmalade are on hand to slather over toast or crumpets. Breakfast pide was a delicious toasted ham, egg, spinach and ketchup combo, and breakfast trifle consisted of healthier but equally lush layers of stewed fruit, granola and yoghurt. Sandwiches are huge, with high-quality fillings (serrano ham, sun-dried tomatoes and the like).

Babies and children admitted. Bookings not accepted. Disabled: toilet. Tables outdoors (3, pavement). Takeaway service.

Hackney

Wilton's NEW

63 Wilton Way, E8 1BG (7249 0444). Hackney Central rail or bus D6, 48, 106, 254. **Open** 8am-5pm Mon-Fri; 8am-6pm Sat; 9am-6pm Sun. **Main courses** £2.50-£5.50. **No credit cards**.

Nestled between a hip new hairdresser's and a cool clothing/design store, Wilton's has made locals very happy indeed. The pared-back design of corrugated iron and stripped-wood floors, stools and tables means the interior is not exactly cosy, but the steady stream of regulars don't seem to mind a jot. They come to pick up pastries and scrumptious-sounding delights involving cheese, meats and bread from the likes of Neal's Yard, Ginger Pig, Brindisa and Seven Seeded. Coffee (beans provided by Broadway Market's Climpson & Sons) is reliably excellent too. A bacon bap with avocado was delicious: well-cooked bacon piled on freshly sliced avocado laced with just the right amount of lemony tang (though the bap could have been fresher). Sourdough with goat's cheese and honey was equally moreish, but not toasted as advertised. Further inducements include free internet access, art on the walls (beautiful delicate

tangerine wrappers on our visit), and, if you time it right, London Fields Radio, which broadcasts from here.

Babies and children admitted. Entertainment: live radio station. Tables outdoors (4, pavement). Takeaway service.

Hackney Wick

Container Cafe

The View Tube, The Greenway, Marshgate Lane, E15 2PJ (07 702 125081, www.theview tube.co.uk). Pudding Mill Lane DLR. **Open** 9am-4.30pm daily. **Main courses** £4-£7. **Credit** AmEx, MC, V.

At the end of the Greenway, past the View Tube Gallery, lies this fine new café housed within stacked-up acid-green shipping containers. It's not especially cosy: apart from a button-back sofa, seating is on stools, benches and fold-up chairs. However, there's a decked viewing terrace and a

little sculpture garden for sunny days, and the constant influx of tourists, cyclists, joggers and the curious can't get enough of the place. Perhaps it's the fact that, like its sibling the Counter Café, the Container boasts terrific views of the Olympic Stadium – Anish Kapoor's ArcelorMittal Orbit sculpture is directly opposite. A great draw too is the excellent coffee, moreish pastries and decent breakfasts, such as bacon baguettes or own-made baked beans on a bed of spinach with halloumi and toast. Portions are smaller than at the Counter, but chirpy staff, an even chirpier soundtrack and cheaper prices make up for it. Community cycling centre Bikeworks is just outside if you feel like working off your breakfast.
Available for hire. Babies and children admitted. Disabled: toilet. Tables outdoors (15, park). Takeaway service.

★ Counter Café NEW

Stour Space, 7 Roach Road, E3 2PA (07 834 275920, www.thecountercafe.co.uk). Hackney Wick tube/rail or bus 488. **Open** 7.30am-5pm Mon-Wed, Fri; 7.30am-11pm Thur-Sun. **Main courses** £3.50-£8. **Credit** AmEx, MC, V.
Head down Dace Road and take a left on Bream Street to Fish Island's Roach Road and you'll discover the wonderful Counter Café. The enormous two-floored establishment is attached to the Stour Space and perched on the banks of the Regent's Canal, with views to the Olympic Stadium. Young and middle-aged couples, dads and kids, groups of friends, as well as singletons with laptops, take up every chair, sofa and theatre-seat. There's free Wi-Fi, newspapers, a decent soundtrack and huge windows and skylights offering great weather- and people-watching opportunities until the dishes arrive. The food – breakfasts, brunches, cakes and own-made pies – is excellent. In spite of the café's popularity, service remains efficient. A perfect flat white coffee and an enormous vegetarian breakfast (own-made potato cake and 'baked' butter beans, wilted spinach, two eggs, fried tomatoes, mushrooms, and two slices of Bürgen toast) made it up to the second floor with no perceptible loss of temperature. By lunchtime, there was a queue. Come the evening, from Thursday to Sunday, the café turns into a bar and serves tapas. A winner.
Available for hire. Babies and children admitted. Bookings not accepted. Disabled: toilet. Tables outdoors (4, pavement). Takeaway service.

Haggerston

Towpath HOT 50

Regent's Canal towpath, between Whitmore Bridge and Kingsland Road Bridge, N1 5SB (no phone). Haggerston rail. **Open** Mar-Nov 8am-dusk Tue-Fri; 9am-dusk Sat, Sun. **Main courses** £3-£8. **No credit cards.**
Situated beside the Regent's Canal, Towpath is an idyllic place to stop and take in the passing water, ducks and people. Since opening in 2010, it has been committed to serving simple, tasty food and coffee. Wooden tables and chairs in a mix of primary colours sit alongside mirrored tables that reflect the sunlight bouncing off the water; seating also extends a little further west on a raised deck complete with cycle parking. On our early morning visit, the chalked-up breakfast menu ran from toast with a selection of preserves to grilled cheese sandwiches, muesli and porridge. The din of building work blocking off the towpath did little to

deter customers, and the seats rapidly filled as the café's devoted followers ambled in for their morning fix. Later on, food is seasonal and mostly Italian – think pork rillettes with piccalilli or roast lamb with anchovy and chard. Order at the counter and grab a seat: there's no takeaway service.
Available for hire. Babies and children admitted. Bookings not accepted. Tables outdoors (3-10, towpath). **Map 6 R1.**

North
Camden Town & Chalk Farm

Lanka

71 Regent's Park Road, NW1 8UY (7483 2544, www.lanka-uk.com). Chalk Farm tube. **Open** 9am-6.30pm Tue-Sat; 9am-5pm Sun. **Main courses** £5-£12. **Credit** AmEx, MC, V.
Lanka always looks busy, but that's because it's a veritable pencil of a room. The kitchen out back is so tiny that the mostly Japanese staff decorate their fusion cakes and pastries at a workstation behind the limited bar-style seating. Chef-patron Masayuki Hara (who often appears to talk to customers) produces an extensive range of not-too-sweet treats, many containing green tea (tarts, cakes, gateaux of cream and strawberries, panna cotta). Typical is the crumbly white chocolate and aduki bean gateau: not unpleasant, but perhaps more interesting than delicious. You're on safer ground with the heady rum baba, a generous portion that, if eaten in situ, is presented like a restaurant dessert, with mango purée (an intelligent addition) and brandy snap on a rectangular white plate. There's a short list of savouries – usually a soup, salad, ham and cheese croissant, or omelette – with breakfast scrambled eggs served all day. The coffee is good enough, though not expertly made. Party catering is a growing facet of the business; Lanka offers private cookery lessons too.
Babies and children admitted. Tables outdoors (2, pavement). Takeaway service.
Map 27 A2.

Nice Green Café NEW

Cecil Sharp House, 2 Regent's Park Road, NW1 7AY (7485 2206, www.efdss.org). Camden Town tube. **Open** 10am-7.30pm daily. **Main courses** £3.50-£6. **No credit cards.**
Looking for an alternative to Camden's hyper-trendy/touristy alternative scene? Believe it or not, you'll find it inside the imposing 1930s hall of the English Folk Dance & Song Society, just across the tracks in Primrose Hill. Below the main performance halls lies a suitably retro-styled interior, where pastel-coloured tablecloths with polka dots provide a stage for vintage cake stands (the cakes are freshly baked throughout the day). While dance students burn off calories in the adjacent rehearsal rooms, you can munch on daily-changing delights, the kind of fresh, healthy and tasty food Jamie Oliver was trying to get his school dinner ladies to cook. A hearty tomato and bean soup was heaving with chunky vegetables, and a zesty tabouleh came with a refreshing yoghurt and cucumber relish. For more substantial grub, try the organic pork sausages or lamb pie.
Available for hire. Babies and children welcome: children's menu. Tables outdoors (4, terrace). Takeaway service. **Map 27 B2.**

Finsbury Park

Boulangerie Bon Matin NEW

178 Tollington Park, N4 3AJ (7263 8633). Finsbury Park tube/rail. **Open** 7am-6.30pm daily. **Main courses** 80p-£5.90. **Credit** MC, V.
North London stalwart Sablé D'Or cleverly realised that not every discerning cake eater wants to climb the hill to visit its branches in Muswell Hill and Crouch End, hence this recent venture in pâtisserie-starved Finsbury Park. With its display of mouth-watering French pastries and pretty cakes, Boulangerie Bon Matin has been attracting lustful gazes from passers-by. A frangipane apple tart was a fantastic rendition of the French classic – the buttery pastry crust filled with a moist almond mix, topped with apple slices and sweet 'gelée'. Savoury options include quiches, open sandwiches and galettes – savoury buckwheat pancakes filled with various cheesy stuffings. The café's rustic, brick-walled interior is flooded with light from the large atrium above, making it a lovely space in which to linger. As the name suggests, it also serves breakfasts, including crêpes and cinnamon french toast, with last orders at 3.30pm.
Available for hire. Babies and children welcome: high chairs. Bookings not accepted. Takeaway service.

Hornsey

Haberdashery NEW

22 Middle Lane, N8 8PL (8342 8098, www.the-haberdashery.com). Turnpike Lane tube or Crouch Hill or Hornsey rail. **Open** 8am-6pm Mon-Fri; 9am-6pm Sat, Sun. **Main courses** £5.95-£9.50. **Credit** AmEx, MC, V.
This Crouch End newcomer is well named: it's got cutesy village charm aplenty. There's vintage crockery, bunting and a dinky back garden, as well as a community programme that includes craft-oriented evening bazaars, charity gig nights and a produce box scheme with an out-of-town farm. The menu isn't half bad, either. Hearty sandwiches, soups and a brief selection of hot dishes (meatballs with mashed swede and beetroot coleslaw, for example), join a good range of baked goods, from billowy muffins served in terracotta pots to child-friendly rainbow cake. At the weekends, local parents are replaced with sustenance-searching brunch-eaters who pack out the place, and artisan breads fly off the shelves.
Available for hire. Babies and children welcome: children's menu; high chairs; nappy-changing facilities. Tables outdoors (12, garden; 2, pavement). Takeaway service.

Islington

Kipferl

20 Camden Passage, N1 8ED (7704 1555, www.kipferl.co.uk). Angel tube. **Open** 9am-6pm Tue; 9am-10pm Wed-Sat; 10am-6pm Sun. **Main courses** £8.20-£16.80. **Credit** MC, V.
Having relocated from a tiny site in Barbican to a large and bright space in Angel, Kipferl now has plenty of room to accommodate its many admirers. They come for Austrian and Central European classics, and the notably stylish café serves them with aplomb. A zingy, spiced debreziner sausage (you can also get the standard wiener, or a kasekrainer with nuggets of emmental cheese) came with extremely good rye bread, pickle,

CAFÉS

horseradish and salad. The goulash, with its thick chunks of beef, rich sauce and egg pasta, could put hairs on your chest. If fact, everything on the menu, from dumpling soup to mountain cheese omelette, is hearty and homely. If you're after something lighter, stay towards the front of the café, where Viennese patisserie (exemplary sachertorte, apfelstrudel and the like) are served with coffee. Interestingly, a colour palette is provided to help you decide how strong you like your coffee; your drink then arrives, the traditional way, on a little metal tray with a glass of water. Polished, authentic and charming.

Available for hire. Babies and children welcome: high chairs. Disabled: toilet. Tables outdoors (2, pavement). Takeaway service. **Map 5 O2**.
For branches see index.

Muswell Hill

Feast on the Hill

46 Fortis Green Road, N10 3HN (8444 4957). East Finchley or Highgate tube then bus 43, 134. **Open** 8.30am-5pm Mon; 8.30am-10pm Tue-Sat; 8.30am-5.30pm Sun. **Main courses** £6-£12. **Credit** MC, V.

Feast Delicatessen has been a popular Muswell Hill deli for years. Its next-door café, Feast on the Hill, is also a favourite, particularly with thirtyish locals who head here for all-day breakfasts. Perfectly polite but not especially enthusiastic staff took our orders over the clatter of a smoothie maker; the noise echoed around a white-walled room furnished with brown bistro tables and wooden flooring. Portions are generous, so you may only need one course. Own-made granola with yoghurt came with sweet, fresh melon, pineapple and grapes – very pleasing. Pancakes, however, disappointed: they weren't sweet enough, and had been drowned in tangy yoghurt, leaving them cold. Eggs benedict arrived with high-quality salmon and a chive oil dressing, which added a welcome flavour dimension (though we'd have appreciated a more generous drizzle). A longer evening menu, with pasta dishes, burgers and the like, is available from Tuesday to Saturday when Feast is open until 10pm.

Babies and children welcome: children's menu; high chairs. Tables outdoors (6, pavement). Takeaway service.

Newington Green

That Place On the Corner

1-3 Green Lanes, N16 9BS (7704 0079, www.thatplaceonthecorner.co.uk). Canonbury rail or bus 73, 141, 341. **Open** 9.30am-6pm Mon-thur; 9.30am-8pm Fri; opening varies, call for details Sat, Sun. **Main courses** £5.95-£8.50. **Credit** MC, V.

The two mums who run this café-cum-children's activity venue welcome customers like friends. When they have a spare five minutes, the staff even seem to enjoy playing with their small visitors. There's a well-stocked dressing-up cupboard, a new giant doll's house, ride-on toys, many books and a large cushion area. We happily spent four hours here on a rainy day, and there weren't even any activities scheduled (which include music sessions, arts and crafts, story-time and face-painting). In that time, we sampled good strong coffee and various dishes. The egg in the bacon sandwich was slightly overcooked, but everything tasted homemade in all the right ways, and the kids lapped up their spag bol and penne with tomato and herbs. As we settled our very reasonable bill, the staff gave the children some Monopoly money for being good, and explained they could spend it on cakes or ice-creams next time. Next time will be soon.

Available for hire. Babies and children welcome: children's menu; colouring books; crayons; high chairs; nappy-changing facilities; toys. Disabled: toilet. Takeaway service. **Map 25 A4**.

North West
Kensal Green

Gracelands

118 College Road, NW10 5HD (8964 9161, www.gracelandscafe.com). Kensal Green tube. **Open** 8.30am-5pm Mon-Fri; 9am-4.30pm Sat; 9.30am-3.30pm Sun. **Main courses** £7-£12.95. **Credit** AmEx, MC, V.

You don't need a pal in nappies or short trousers to eat at Gracelands, but bring a bambino and you'll sure feel welcome. While many places claim to be child-friendly, this café means it, with its toy-filled play area, a healthy tots-own menu and chefs cooing at high-chair diners from the open-plan kitchen. Don't let all that put you off if you're sans enfants, though – both the main menu and the lofty industrial interior are really for grown-ups. There's a licence too, which means bloody marys with your all-day breakfast. The burger, from 21-day matured beef, has proper foodie pedigree, or you might equally choose one of the well-constructed salads or the enticing-sounding daily specials: slow-braised brisket, say, or devilled mackerel. Our eggs florentine was made with love: two plump, ultra-fresh eggs, perfectly wilted spinach and pleasingly yellow hollandaise. Elvis appears on the odd mug, but despite its name, Gracelands is more about healthy complementary therapies in the suntrap courtyard than deep-fried peanut butter sarnies.

Babies and children welcome: children's menu; high chairs; nappy-changing facilities; play area; toys. Tables outdoors (4, pavement; 8, garden). Takeaway service.

PARK CAFÉS

Central
Knightsbridge

Lido Café

2011 RUNNER-UP BEST PARK CAFÉ
South side of the Serpentine, Hyde Park, W2 2UH (7706 7098, www.companyof cooks.com). Hyde Park Corner or Knightsbridge tube. **Open** 8am-5.30pm daily (times may vary). **Credit** MC, V.

With its stupendous position overlooking the Serpentine in London's most famous park, right next to the Lido and the Diana Memorial Fountain, this café could serve mud and leaves washed down with a cup of mildew, and still attract customers. It's a lovely spot for an early evening cocktail, but the interior can be loud and clattery, so head outside if you can – there's masses of outdoor seating. The breakfasts, lunches and small plates (the food comes courtesy of Company of Cooks) sound enticing, but some of our dishes lacked attention to detail. Pizzettes were low on cheese and herbs, and tiny for £4.75. Grilled chicken was dry – a yoghurt and harissa dressing gave it some oomph, but while the accompanying couscous was studded with lots of interesting things, it tasted too much of spring onion. Best was a moist, flavourful, well-seasoned burger, served with fat chips and relish. Coffee was good too, as was a zesty lemon drizzle cake. Staff were very helpful, taking the initiative to set up a table for us inside as rain drenched the terrace.

Available for hire. Babies and children welcome: children's menu; high chairs; nappy-changing facilities. Bookings not accepted. Tables outdoors (80, park). Takeaway service. **Map 8 E8**.

Serpentine Bar & Kitchen

Serpentine Road, Hyde Park, W2 2UH (7706 8114, www.serpentinebarandkitchen. com). Hyde Park Corner tube. **Open** 8am-8pm daily. **Main courses** £4.90-£18. **Credit** AmEx, MC, V.

The food here is pretty standard, but the setting is outstanding. Weeping willows drape over the waterside terrace, while a varied clientele of tourists, joggers and Londoners enjoy views across the Serpentine. Patrick Gwynne's sweeping architectural roof and angular glass walls contrast playfully with the English country-cottage interiors. Hot and cold food is available all day: takeaway sandwiches, cake or ice-cream for a picnic in the park; or visit the restaurant for wood-fired pizzas, salads, dry-aged steak and seasonal fish. A vintage piano accompanies Sunday brunch. Our fish finger sandwich was in fact upmarket goujons in a granary bun, and pea risotto was crowned with lotus root crisps. Hire a rowing boat after lunch if you've eaten too many cakes for dessert.

Babies and children welcome: children's menu; high chairs; nappy-changing facilities. Bookings not accepted. Disabled: toilet. Tables outdoors (20, pavement; 10, balcony). Takeaway service. **Map 8 E7**.

Marylebone

Garden Café

Inner Circle, Regent's Park, NW1 4NU (7935 5729, www.thegardencafe.co.uk). Baker Street or Regent's Park tube. **Open** 9am-8pm daily. **Breakfast served** 9-11.30am, **lunch served** noon-4pm, **dinner served** (summer) 5-8pm daily. **Main courses** £8.50-£12.50. **Set meal** £14.75 2 courses, £18.95 3 courses. **Credit** MC, V.

This Regent's Park café has two delineated areas for either counter or table service, with each sporting an oasis-like garden surrounded by tall flora. If it's wet, you'll have to plump for the no-frills 1960s aesthetic indoors, though this barely matters if you're opting for a quick-stop sandwich, salad or soup – or a slice of seedy beetroot sponge (one of a strong selection of cakes) – at the self-service station. For a more formal meal in the dining room, you're best insisting on a snug window-side table and directing your gaze outdoors. Company of Cooks manages the menu here, which bears both stars and duds. The chilli con carne, for example, was disappointing and unremarkable, but the perfectly grilled mackerel with samphire was a salty hit. This mix of pub standards (sticky toffee pudding) and interesting seasonal fare (gooseberry and elderflower crumble) is presumably designed to suit all tastes, and proof of success comes in the shape of a packed house during the park's Open Air Theatre season.

Babies and children welcome: children's menu; high chairs. Booking advisable. Disabled: toilet. Tables outdoors (38, garden). Takeaway service. **Map 3 G3**.

West
Kensington

Kensington Palace Orangery
The Orangery, Kensington Palace, Kensington Gardens, W8 4PX (3166 6112, www.hrp.org.uk). High Street Kensington or Queensway tube. **Open** *Mar-Oct* 10am-6pm daily. *Nov-Feb* 10am-5pm daily. **Main courses** £8.75-£13.50. **Set tea** £15.15-£34.45. **Credit** AmEx, MC, V.
Though now largely dominated by tourists, Kensington Palace Orangery retains all the grandeur you'd expect from a former royal, alfresco entertainment space. Imposing colonnades, vaulted ceilings and a spacious terrace make it a lovely place to stop for breakfast, lunch or afternoon tea. The latter is a relatively simple affair, with sandwiches, scones and orange-themed petits fours arriving all together on a tiered stand. It's not the best spread in town (the orange-flavoured scones were particularly unpleasant), but the setting helps things along. Breakfast focuses mainly on pastries, and lunch options are equally brief. Our seasonal mains included a goat's cheese, fig and pomegranate salad (wonderful once we'd asked for additional figs) and a convincing combination of warmed smoked salmon, green beans and new potatoes. The filling, tasty food is elevated unquestionably by the incredible backdrop.
Babies and children welcome: children's menu; high chairs; nappy-changing facilities. Disabled: toilet. Tables outdoors (20, terrace). **Map 7 C8**.

South West
Fulham

Fulham Palace Café
2011 RUNNER-UP BEST PARK CAFÉ
Bishop's Avenue, SW6 6EA (7610 7160, www.fulhampalacecafe.org). Putney Bridge tube. **Open** 9am-5pm daily. **Main courses** £8.50-£9. **Credit** AmEx, MC, V.
The Bishops of London knew how to live. This secluded palace by the river was their official residence from 704 until 1975. These days, locals and clued-up visitors can enjoy the quiet lawns, walled garden, museum and plush café within the palace itself. The large terrace tables are popular on warm days when a barbecue gazebo operates on the lawn, serving burgers and sausages. The café menu is sophisticated, offering a range of sandwiches, fish, meat and vegetarian platters, salads and hot mains. Garden herb burger with mozzarella and tomato chutney was juicy and full of flavour; butternut squash and leek risotto was creamy and lively, with flecks of thyme, and rice that had just the right amount of bite. Mackerel salad and a butternut gratin were also a success, and the children's meals are some of the most imaginative and tasty we've found. Service was slow – perhaps inevitably on a busy bank holiday Monday – and our cakes came a full 15 minutes after our coffees, but they were good. A lovely place for a treat lunch, that's no more expensive than other park cafés serving distinctly inferior fare.

Pavilion Café, Highgate

Babies and children welcome: children's menu; high chairs; nappy-changing facilities. Bookings not accepted Sat, Sun. Disabled: toilet. Tables outdoors (12, terrace).

Wandsworth

Common Ground
Wandsworth Common, off Dorlcote Road, SW18 3RT (8874 9386). Wandsworth Common rail. **Open** 9am-5pm daily. **Main courses** £3.50-£9. **Credit** MC, V.
Surrounded by the greenery of Wandsworth Common, this in-park café should be an idyllic destination. Sadly, on our visit the dreary interior and lacklustre food made it about as appealing as a school dinner. A children's menu featuring chicken goujons and fish fingers joins a standard selection of sandwiches and jacket potatoes; the specials consist of a pie and tart of the day. We can't speak for the tart, but our chicken pie was a depressing affair, its thick, soup-like filling topped with an undersized disc of puff pastry. The side salad of lettuce and seemingly tinned mixed beans

hardly helped matters. If you happen to be stopping by at around teatime, you'll find a varied range of classic bakes, from victoria sandwich to carrot cake, but the orange and poppyseed slice that we tried was hideously stodgy. Best order a failsafe tea, sit outside and put your back to Common Ground. *Available for hire. Babies and children welcome: children's menu; high chairs; nappy-changing facilities; play area. Takeaway service. Vegetarian menu.*

South East
Dulwich

Pavilion Café
Dulwich Park, SE21 7BQ (8299 1383, www.pavilioncafedulwich.co.uk). West Dulwich rail or bus P4. **Open** *Summer* 8.30am-6.30pm daily. *Winter* 9am-4pm daily. **Main courses** £3.50-£7.50. **Credit** MC, V.
Even midweek, this place is packed to its quaint rafters with parents, grandparents and other groups making the most of Dulwich Park's varied amenities (recumbent bikes, the new all-weather ping-pong tables, horse riding). But the café used to be better. The menu above the counter still looks convincing – meat is from Dulwich butcher William Rose, and fish from Moxon's – but on a recent visit, the specials board listed only two dishes, eggs benedict and salad niçoise. An interminable queue tailed around the central ordering station all afternoon, but at least the food came quickly once our order was placed. We tried both specials, plus bacon, egg and chips; while everything was well executed, nothing was memorable. Staff were chaotic and ill-informed. There's a well-stocked play area and plenty of outdoor tables overlooking the park, but nice touches such as selling baby food and sun-cream don't make up for impersonal service and a lack of verve in the kitchen.
Available for hire. Babies and children welcome: children's menu; high chairs; nappy-changing facilities; play area. Tables outdoors (12, terrace). Takeaway service.

Greenwich

Pavilion Tea House
Greenwich Park, Blackheath Gate, SE10 8QY (8858 9695, www.companyofcooks.com). Blackheath rail or Greenwich rail/DLR. **Open** 9am-5.30pm Mon-Fri; 9am-6pm Sat, Sun. **Main courses** £4.95-£6.60. **Credit** MC, V.
Situated a stone's throw from the Royal Observatory, the Pavilion Tea House (run by Company of Cooks) has white picket fences surrounding lush greenery, making its grounds a safe haven for children to play, as well as a prime spot for taking in the magnificent City views from the outdoor tables. In winter, you may prefer to sit on the mezzanine level inside, which is bathed in natural light even on the most dreary of days. Hot food is ordered at the counter, but delivered to your table; pizzas with crisp bases and peppy toppings (chorizo and caper, artichoke and mushroom) are great value at around £5. An unctuous salmon and dill fish cake was on the pricier side at £7.25. Decent sandwiches and baked potatoes are also available, though you may prefer to drop in simply for the Fairtrade tea and coffee, a glass of wine or a hefty slice of cake.

Babies and children welcome: children's menu; high chairs; nappy-changing facilities. Disabled: toilet. Tables outdoors (20, terrace).

Herne Hill

★ Lido Café
2011 WINNER BEST PARK CAFÉ
Brockwell Lido, Dulwich Road, SE24 0PA (7737 8183, www.thelidocafe.co.uk). Herne Hill rail or Brixton tube/rail then bus 37. **Open** *Summer* 7.30am-6pm Mon, Tue, Sun; 7.30am-11pm Wed-Sat. *Winter* 9am-6pm Mon, Tue, Sun; 9am-11pm Wed-Sat. **Main courses** £7.25-£15.95. **Credit** MC, V.
The café inside Brockwell Hall at the top of Brockwell Park's central hill is decent, but foodies should head straight to the Lido Café. Its latest incarnation, inside the light, bright 1930s building overlooking the pool, is fantastic. We arrived one Saturday lunchtime, when the café was full to bursting. Staff took constant care of us until we were able to sit down at a freshly wiped table, with extra chairs already added to suit our number. The mouth-watering menu changes monthly, offering salads, savoury tarts and a selection of imaginative main courses. Burgers of aged beef and chorizo came with supremely good hand-cut chips and well-dressed salad. Courgette, crème fraîche and pecorino tart featured light pastry and an expert, refined filling. Burgers for kids are almost as large as those for adults, and sausage and chips comes with a proper butcher's banger. Superlative breakfasts and cakes are also offered, and on evenings from Wednesday to Saturday the place turns into a fairly priced restaurant-bar. There's even a children's toy box.
Available for hire. Babies and children welcome: children's menu; high chairs; nappy-changing facilities. Disabled: toilet. Tables outdoors (10, terrace). Takeaway service. **Map 22 E1**.

East
Victoria Park

Pavilion Café
Victoria Park, Crown Gate West, E9 7DE (8980 0030, www.the-pavilion-cafe.com). Mile End tube then bus 277, 425. **Meals served** *Summer* 8am-4.30pm Mon-Fri; 8am-5pm Sat, Sun. *Winter* 8am-4pm daily. **Main courses** £4-£9. **Credit** MC, V.
This lovely domed café is the old pavilion for Victoria Park lake. In summer, seating is all outdoors. There's plenty of it – on a terrace, on stools perched breakfast-bar style against lakeside balustrades, and sheltering beneath the café's eaves – but on a sunny day it's all full by noon. Staff can get a little overloaded at peak times, but they're generally efficient and warmly friendly. This is a big breakfast destination, offering all the classic dishes, both plebby (beans on toast) and posh (eggs florentine, benedict and royale) in huge portions. It's all expertly cooked but occasionally bland. Lunch is a matter of fancy sandwiches plus the odd burger and salad. Whatever time you visit, leave room for the satisfying house-made cakes, which are good and moist: the chocolate and marmalade is a classic.
Babies and children welcome: children's menu; high chairs; nappy-changing facilities. Bookings not accepted. Disabled: toilet. Tables outdoors (20, park). Takeaway service.

North
Highgate

Pavilion Café
2011 RUNNER-UP BEST PARK CAFÉ
Highgate Woods, Muswell Hill Road, N10 3JN (8444 4777). Highgate tube. **Open** 9am-1hr before park closing daily. **Main courses** £6-£10. **Credit** AmEx, MC, V.
Set in a grassy clearing in the ancient woodlands between Muswell Hill and Highgate tube, this café has a prime location. There are only six tables inside (popular at breakfast/brunch time), but on chilly days, the covered outdoor tables are warmed with wall heaters. The large hedged-in terrace is packed with families in fine weather, but the last time we visited it was wet and stormy, and the juicy beefburger and chips was off the menu, as were all other main courses. We settled for the only warm things to be had: carrot and ginger soup, and cheese and ham toastie, ordering some feta and red pepper dip, artichokes and pitta to bulk it out. We didn't need the extras, as the soup was a hearty bowl, a little salty, but full of hot root-ginger undertones and rich carrot flavour. We can never decide between the almond, lemon and polenta cake, or the warmed brownies with ice-cream. So we had both. On busy days, you can buy coffee and ice-creams at a serving hatch to take away.
Babies and children welcome: children's menu; crayons; high chairs; nappy-changing facilities. Disabled: toilet. Tables outdoors (30, garden). Takeaway service.

North West
Hampstead

Brew House
Kenwood House, Hampstead Lane, NW3 7JR (8341 5384, www.companyofcooks.com). Archway or Golders Green tube then bus 210. **Open** *Apr-Sept* 9am-6pm daily (7.30pm on concert nights). *Oct-Mar* 9am-dusk daily. **Main courses** £4.75-£9.95. **Credit** MC, V.
Such is the popularity of the cafeteria at Kenwood House that, frankly, we give it a wide berth at weekends, when the place is overrun with extended family groups; weekdays are another matter. You can avoid the unruly toddlers and panting canines at the front by taking your tray of victuals straight from the service area to the bucolic terrace, which shows this place at its best. We've been disappointed by the scones and the occasional piece of dried cake (tip: the adjacent Steward's Room sells many of them wrapped for take-out and in noticeably better nick), but otherwise the food is impressive. Sandwiches (Singleton cheddar with caramelised onion, say, or coronation chicken) may seem pricey, but the ingredient quality is first-rate and portions generous. Thoughtfully conceived and carefully cooked hot meals showcase seasonal British ingredients and artisan sources; we've even seen samphire-topped fish here. Soups (get the meal deal that includes bread, British cheese and fruit), sausages and mash and the cooked breakfasts are exemplary – as, usually, are the courteous staff.
Available for hire. Babies and children welcome: children's menu; high chairs; nappy-changing facilities. Separate room for parties, seats 120. Tables outdoors (400, garden). Takeaway service. Vegetarian menu. **Map 28 C1**.

Coffee Bars

London's coffee scene is thriving, thanks in large part to an influx of enthusiasts from Australia and New Zealand, but also to the emergence of new artisan roasters promoting a wider range of speciality beans. An increasing number of coffee bars do their own roasting, adding to the diversity of flavours to explore – check out **Nude Espresso** (who invite customers into their Brick Lane roastery) and **Allpress Espresso**, as well as **St Ali** (*see p281*) and **Caravan** (*see p37*). Now too there are more ways of making a brew, and with siphons and Aeropress machines adding to the paraphernalia behind the counter, some new coffee bars are starting to look more like chemistry labs than cafés. Any questions? Pop along to a class, such as those offered by **Prufrock Coffee** and **Kaffeine**, to learn how to perfect the coffee you make at home. Time Out's critics (some of whom are trained baristas) have taste-tested coffee all over town – from espressos to cortados – and here you'll find our favourites.

Central
Bloomsbury

★ Espresso Room
31-35 Great Ormond Street, WC1N 3HZ (07932 137380 mobile, www.theespressoroom.com). Russell Square tube. **Open** 7.30am-5pm Mon-Fri; 9.30am-2.30pm Sat. **No credit cards.**
'Room' pretty much says it all. This shoebox of a coffee bar opposite Great Ormond Street Hospital (and its handy cashpoint, because, note, they don't take cards) is barely big enough to swing a teabag let alone a cat, yet when we surveyed the spate of new coffee bars for the 2010 Time Out Eating & Drinking Awards, this spot was the hands-down winner. Since then, London has become even more heavily endowed with potential caffeine fixes and, short of roasting its own beans, we reckon Espresso Room still beats most of them. And who could be more deserving of great coffee than the staff of the hospital opposite? They come in a steady stream for drinks made from Has Bean and Square Mile beans, plus 'builder's', 'posh' or herbal teas. The range of food isn't huge, but it's top-quality, with a daily soup (pea, spinach and coriander, on our visit), sandwiches (lovely smoked chicken and artichoke hearts on sourdough, or cheese and pickle) and well-made cakes (the choc chip and walnut blondie would convert doubters). Pleasant, intelligent staff offer a glass of water with the brews and are happy to grind bags of beans for customers to take home. *Babies and children admitted. Tables outdoors (6, pavement). Takeaway service.* **Map 4 L4**.

Chancery Lane

Department of Coffee & Social Affairs
14-16 Leather Lane, EC1N 7SU (no phone, www.departmentofcoffee.co.uk). Chancery Lane tube. **Open** 7.30am-5pm Mon-Fri; 10am-4pm Sat, Sun. **Credit** (over £5) MC, V.
A small coffee revolution is brewing on Leather Lane, and this smartly named café is at the forefront. Just a few doors down from the esteemed Prufrock Coffee, the Department of Coffee & Social Affairs serves a sophisticated, changing roster of hand-ground beans, presenting a new espresso blend and filter blend from an independent roaster every two weeks. A creamy and rich house coffee from Climpson & Sons is a reliable back-up, but the enthusiasm of the knowledgeable staff is infectious and you'll no doubt find yourself adventurously opting for the feature coffees. Our piccolo (made with a Has Bean blend) was a heavenly, milky short; while a filter coffee from Yirgacheffe in Ethiopia was a smooth roast, the kind you might find in a good continental café. Food comes in the shape of tempting sandwiches and own-made cakes, and the decor is industrial-chic, all exposed brick walls and black furniture. *Babies and children admitted. Separate room for parties, seats 25. Tables outdoors (3, market). Takeaway service.* **Map 11 N5.**

★ Prufrock Coffee **NEW**
23-25 Leather Lane, EC1N 7TE (07853 483479 mobile, www.prufrockcoffee.com). Chancery Lane tube. **Open** 8am-6pm Mon-Fri; 10am-5pm Sat; 10am-4pm Sun. **Credit** AmEx, MC, V.

Not the first coffee company to get its start piggybacking in unusual premises, Prufrock began with (and continues to run) a counter inside menswear boutique Present in Shoreditch. This spacious new outlet couldn't be more different. Customers are mostly besuited high-achievers who need their espresso fix and expect the very best. They don't want to discuss the science of heating milk sugars, but are reassured that someone here does. A blackboard advertises classes in milk texturing and latte art, while downstairs is the London BRAT (Barista Resource and Training). Don't come expecting mochamacchilattecino, let alone hazelnut syrup. You can have espresso with milk (4oz, 6oz or 8oz – their philosophy is 'to approach your coffee like you are a cook'), or coffee brewed using one of the other methods that make the area behind the counter look like a high-school chemistry lab. The choice of food has improved since opening, but still isn't an attraction – zeppelin-shaped pretzels were the best-looking items on our last visit; tomato, sultana and coconut loaf cake just didn't appeal. *Available for hire. Babies and children admitted. Disabled: toilet. Takeaway service.* **Map 11 N5.** **For branch see index.**

Clerkenwell & Farringdon

Dose Espresso
70 Long Lane, EC1A 9EJ (7600 0382, www.dose-espresso.com). Barbican tube. **Open** 7am-5pm Mon-Fri; 9am-4pm Sat. **Credit** MC, V.
Dose Espresso has moved next door, into Kipferl's ex-premises, giving it a bright, clean-lined makeover in its trademark mix of wood, white and red. Although the welcome is friendly, staff are

inclined to lecture on subjects such as grinding beans for home use – the problem is, people are then less inclined to forgive slips such as the lukewarm warm milk in our latte (though it was speedily replaced with a smile). Otherwise, there's much to like about the clear-mindedness of this spot, which attracts a steady stream of City workers. Fairtrade is, as owner James Phillips rightly attests, the very minimum standard to work to as far as responsible sourcing goes. He offers Square Mile blends, plus changing guest coffees, such as Machacamarca single estate from Bolivia, or simply Climpson & Sons espresso. The milk is organic, as are the breads, and the daily soup and sweet bakes are provided by Bea's of Bloomsbury.
Babies and children admitted. Takeaway service. **Map 11 O5**.

Fitzrovia

Kaffeine

66 Great Titchfield Street, W1W 7QJ (7580 6755, www.kaffeine.co.uk). Oxford Circus tube. **Open** 7.30am-6pm Mon-Fri; 9am-6pm Sat; 9.30am-5pm Sun. **Credit** (over £6) MC, V.
They won't exactly chuck a prawn on the barbie, but this affable Australian-New Zealand outfit has a discerning selection of foods to enjoy alongside the coffees expertly made on its Synesso machine. After a couple of years of trading, Kaffeine has attracted a loyal fan-base despite quality local competition and although the peak-time queues are relentless, the atmosphere is as enlivening as the espresso. The tight space is neatly and chicly handled, with high tables and benches near the counter, and regular tables at the back. Trademark Antipodean snacks (banana bread, anzac biscuits, melting moments, friands) feature, but the weekly-changing menu also reflects the rich pickings of the British countryside, with goodies such as damson muffins, and pear and ale bread with mascarpone (from the new brunch selection). Salads and sarnies are mostly Mediterreanan in inspiration, with artisan suppliers the bedrock of the recipes. Office catering is available, as are coffee-making classes.
Available for hire. Babies and children welcome: high chair. Takeaway service. Vegan dishes. **Map 9 J5**.

Tapped & Packed

26 Rathbone Place, W1T 1JD (7580 2163, www.tappedandpacked.co.uk). Tottenham Court Road tube. **Open** 8am-7pm Mon-Fri; 9am-7pm Sat. **Credit** AmEx, MC, V.
Something of a default Time Out staff room, this seductive spot offers rather louche, brown velvety seating cleverly separated by armrest-cum-tables, plus a couple of bench-and-table options at the back. The crew are chatty (as are the customers), promptly offering water while your espresso brews in the La Marzocco machine. Old tins of Lyle's black treacle hold the sugar. A changing roster of featured artists (on our visit, moody black and white photographs), and an ornate white-framed mirror provide wall interest. We've never had cause to complain about the coffee, but, sadly, detected a sour finish to a flat white on our last visit – we suspect an unfortunate blip. In addition to espresso drinks, Tapped & Packed offers a choice of coffees brewed by filter, siphon or Aeropress. Like the espresso blends, these change seasonally: you might find the jasmine and fruit flavours of Duncan Organic Kotowa Farm coffee from Panama, or the sweet almond and peanut notes of Brazil's Capim

Branco. Filled baguettes, salads, fruit tarts, victoria sponge and cupcakes are enticingly displayed by the window, making this a no-brainer for lunch.
Babies and children admitted. Takeaway service. **Map 17 B2**.
For branch see index.

Soho

Fernandez & Wells

73 Beak Street, W1F 9RS (7287 8124, www.fernandezandwells.com). Oxford Circus or Piccadilly Circus tube. **Open** 7.30am-6pm Mon-Fri; 9am-6pm Sat; 9am-5pm Sun. **Credit** (over £5) MC, V.
The three outposts of classy Fernandez & Wells bustle all day with the clatter and chatter of Soho folk on breaks; this plainly decorated yet welcoming café branch (the other two are dubbed 'food and wine bar' and 'espresso bar') is near perfect on every front. Coffee is roasted to F&W's own specifications and produces a consistently smooth, clean-flavoured cup: a black coffee had not a hint of bitterness, even at the last sip. Staff are earnest, polite and eager to please. The food – inventive sandwiches and an irresistible selection of own-made cakes – clearly uses top-end ingredients. The counter seating and stools don't make Fernandez & Wells a place to linger, but it's hard to find a better place in Soho to stop for a coffee.
Babies and children admitted. Takeaway service. **Map 17 A4**.
For branches see index.

Flat White

17 Berwick Street, W1F 0PT (7734 0370, www.flatwhitecafe.com). Leicester Square, Oxford Circus or Tottenham Court Road tube. **Open** 8am-7pm Mon-Fri; 9am-6pm Sat, Sun. **No credit cards.**
The name is Antipodean, as are the cheery, slightly dishevelled staff at this hip little coffee bar by Berwick Street Market. Clued-up Soho folk drop by for their caffeine dose, perhaps also ordering from the all-day breakfast list (croissants, porridge, own-made baked beans with goat's cheese on ciabatta). They cram into the narrow dark interior, sitting at

scarred wooden tables and listening to a soundtrack of indie tunes. Lunches include salads and toasted sandwiches: soba salad was a colourful assembly of well-dressed noodles and crunchy veg; chorizo sandwich had a generous helping of spicy fried sausage and roast pepper wrapped in toasted flatbread. Specials tend to run out by mid-afternoon. The main event, our flat white, was an expertly tuned balance of the bitter and the creamy (the creaminess created by microscopic bubbles in the milk) – but arrived lukewarm. There's also a choice of a dozen other coffee styles, plus juices, shakes and gooey cakes. In all, a decent pit-stop: Australian, yes, but oh so Soho.
Babies and children admitted. Takeaway service. Vegan dishes. **Map 17 B4**.

Milk Bar

3 Bateman Street, W1D 4AG (7287 4796). Leicester Square or Tottenham Court Road tube. **Open** 8am-7pm Mon-Fri; 9am-6pm Sat, Sun. **No credit cards.**
Milk Bar opened in 2008 as an offshoot of Flat White, one of the original Antipodean cafés in London. If we awarded stars for coffee alone, Milk Bar would get top marks: the baristas clearly love their trade, and use a signature blend of Square Mile beans to coax perfect flat whites, piccolos and long blacks from a top-of-the-range La Marzocco machine. But other aspects could do with a refresh. The decor is rather uninspiring, with teenage-bedroom black walls not adding much ambience. Simple salads and sandwiches are own-made, but the cakes we tried on our last visit were too sweet, unremarkable and lacked a home-baked flavour.
Babies and children admitted. Takeaway service. **Map 17 C3**.

Sacred

13 Ganton Street, W1F 9BL (7734 1415, www.sacredcafe.co.uk). Oxford Circus tube. **Open** 7.30am-8pm Mon-Fri; 10am-8pm Sat; 9.30am-7pm Sun. **Credit** (over £2.50) AmEx, MC, V.
Sacred now has six locations, but the original is still thriving in its restaurant-crowded enclave just off Carnaby Street. Nothing much changes here, though we did encounter something we'd never

Espresso Room

Ben's Canteen

This great little neighbourhood venue serves more than just great coffee. Offering simple yet fantastic food and drink in a relaxed environment at affordable prices it is a great spot for a light lunch or cosy supper. Try its ever changing menu of small plates created with the best quality produce from independent artisan suppliers.

140 St John's Hill, SW11 1SL
020 7585 0511
www.benscanteen.com

Foxcroft & Ginger

A contemporary espresso bar and food emporium in the heart of Soho run with passion and flair. The chic, relaxed décor has a cool New York vibe with skilled baristas serving the perfect coffee using their own blend of beans. Homemade sandwiches are grilled, dressed with a herb salad and served on homemade sourdough bread made fresh daily. It offers a large range of delicious tarts and cakes.

3 Berwick Street, W1
Boxpark, Shoreditch, E1
www.foxcroftandginger.com

vida e caffé

It is the journey from bean to cup that makes vida e caffé's coffee one of the best in London. First the finest beans are selected from the plantations of South America before being transferred to the café's very own roastery in the heart of Cape Town. The quality Portuguese-inspired blend is then delivered its buzzy London cafés and served with South African energy and a friendly smile.

Golden Sq, Goodge St and Stratford
www.vidaecaffe.com

COFFEE WITH A TWIST

Russi Espresso Bar

A buzzy Latin corner bar in the heart of Fritzrovia serving the perfect espresso. The owner, Carlos, believes the secret of the perfect coffee lies in the espresso shot. Pop in to experience its quality coffee and delicious homemade sandwiches, pastas and salads. Not only are its freshly made fillings extremely popular, you also get a free homemade soup with every filled bap/ciabatta/foccacia.

23 Rathbone Place, W1T 7H2
020 7436 6123
www.russiespressobar.co.uk

Shoreditch Grind

Shoreditch Grind is not your regular coffee shop – expect a vintage-style neon cinema sign with weekly slogans, and a stripped-back Shoreditch-meets-New York interior. Watch through the wraparound windows while expert baristas serve perfect flat whites, homemade sandwiches and organic cakes. Coming soon: alfresco seating, an extended menu and alcohol at night.

213 Old Street, EC1V 9NR
020 7490 7490
www.shoreditchgrind.com

Bertie and Boo

Once upon a time there was a magical double act called Bertie and Boo. One day they decided it would be really fun to open a coffee shop in Balham. It would be a place that was unique and different, bright and quirky – a delicious treat for all ages. Somewhere which served fine coffee, fresh fruit smoothies, unusual milkshakes, hot toasty melts and amazing handmade cakes... so they did. Go and find them!

162 Balham High Road, SW12 9BW
020 8772 9987
www.bertieandboo.com

seen before: espresso that fell short of perfection. The brew lacked body, and the crema – the tan/brown foam that is an essential component of espresso – was decidedly anaemic. This could have been because the cup had taken too long to reach us; the brew was not properly hot. Apart from that, no problems. Earl Grey tea was good, and the baked goods are terrific: five stars for the chocolate and raspberry brownie. Just another note for the owners: by 5pm, some of the sandwiches in the chill cabinet start looking as if they need embalming – wrapping them in plastic would solve the problem. *Available for hire. Babies and children admitted. Tables outdoors (6, pavement). Takeaway service.* **Map 17 A4.**
For branches see index.

East
Shoreditch

★ Allpress Espresso NEW
58 Redchurch Street, E2 7DP (7749 1780, http://uk.allpressespresso.com). Liverpool Street tube/rail or Shoreditch High Street rail. **Open** 8am-5pm daily. **Credit** (over £5) MC, V.
The giant coffee roaster immediately catches your eye as you enter this neat little Shoreditch coffee shop. A combination of wooden tables and communal bar seating gives an informal charm to the place. The New Zealand baristas take good coffee seriously: come on Mondays or Thursdays to see the roaster in action, purchase a bespoke blend or learn how to make 'The Perfect Cup' in a masterclass. Allpress also uses only Fairtrade coffee bought directly from growers. A full-bodied flat white had good textured foam, and the Costa Rican espresso from the La Marzocco machine was perfection. Salmon toast came with a hearty gherkin, incredible horseradish cream cheese and a lemon wedge. Locals receive a personal welcome, and a few felt so at home they even wheeled in their bikes to pick up a coffee. Breakfast, cake and sandwiches are available – or you could just have another cup of coffee.
Babies and children admitted. Disabled: toilet. Takeaway service. **Map 6 S4.**

Shoreditch Grind NEW
213 Old Street, EC1V 9NR (7490 7490, http://shoreditchgrind.com). Old Street tube/ rail. **Open** 7am-8pm Mon-Fri; 9am-6pm Sat; 10am-6pm Sun. **Credit** AmEx, MC, V.
Occupying a prime spot on Old Street roundabout, Shoreditch Grind aims to supply decent coffee to hipster locals. With a knowing nod to its clientele, the café signage looks like a retro cinema with a changing bill of pretty poor puns ('your perfect cup size' or 'sex coffee and rock 'n' roll'), while the interior decor features on-trend brick tiling and those ubiquitous metal pendant lampshades. The glass-fronted café also has plenty of bar seats by the window: perfect for people-watching, but facing a drab and ugly medley of roads and offices. Coffee comes from an independent roaster in Brighton and tends to vary slightly each week. On this occasion, an americano was quite bitter, perhaps needing a longer roast for that ideal smooth finish, and a cappuccino lacked froth. The food selection is brief but attractive, with handmade, Italian-style sandwiches and assorted own-made cakes.
Babies and children admitted. Takeaway service. **Map 6 Q5.**

Spitalfields

Nude Espresso
26 Hanbury Street, E1 6QR (07804 223590 mobile, www.nudeespresso.com). Liverpool Street tube/rail or Shoreditch High Street rail. **Open** 7.30am-5pm Mon-Fri; 10am-6pm Sat, Sun. **Credit** AmEx, MC, V.
This genial spot near Spitalfields (and with a new branch in Soho) now has its own roastery on Brick Lane – which is where they produce their signature East espresso blend, and also roast small batches of Ethiopian Sidamo or Harrar, and decaf organic Columbia del Obispo. But Nude wears its expertise lightly: the cafés are unpretentious, perfect for meeting friends or for taking a shopping break. The pillar-box-red Hanbury Street branch is roomy (with good loos downstairs); it's not as sleek as some newer arrivals, but possibly more relaxing. Table service was being trialled on our most recent visit, so an element of confusion was to be expected – but our excellent coffees arrived promptly and with a smile. The display of food (all made from scratch on the premises) is tempting: feta and spinach scones, focaccia sarnies filled with cheese and charcuterie, white chocolate and banana muffins, anzac biscuits. You can buy Nude's whole bean coffee to take home, visit the roastery to pick some up, or order online.
Available for hire. Babies and children admitted. Tables outdoors (2, pavement). Takeaway service. Vegan dishes. **Map 12 S5.**

Taylor Street Baristas
1A New Street, EC2M 4TP (7929 2207, www.taylor-st.com). Liverpool Street tube/rail. **Open** 7am-5pm Mon-Fri; 10am-4pm Sun. **Credit** MC, V.
Don't try searching for Taylor Street Baristas in Taylor Street. In fact, there isn't such a street in London: the name comes from a road in Sydney, straight away revealing the Antipodean ethos behind this mini-chain. Although it's an independent company, with highly trained staff and well-sourced beans, it has a slightly corporate air, befitting its City location and the fact there are now several branches in London (and one in Brighton). At busy times, it can resemble a production line, with suits queuing for their morning eye-opener, and it's pretty much takeaway only. But these aren't criticisms: Taylor Street is an example of how consistently brilliant coffee can be served at high volumes without compromise. The almost geeky commitment to all aspects of the barista's art is evident in every cup.
Babies and children admitted. Bookings. Takeaway service. **Map 12 R5.**
For branches see index.

North West
Hampstead

Ginger & White
4A-5A Perrin's Court, NW3 1QS (7431 9098, www.gingerandwhite.com). Hampstead tube. **Open** 7.30am-5.30pm Mon-Fri; 8.30am-5.30pm Sat, Sun. **Credit** MC, V.
On a bright pedestrianised alley in Hampstead Village, with chichi shops adding interest, Ginger & White's location is almost idyllic. Unfortunately, the interior is cramped, with counter, kitchen and

toilet shoehorned into one side; when staff and customers are milling around, things get very awkward. God help you, if you have a pram. Nab one of the smart outdoor tables, though, and staff seem to forget your existence. A couple standing outside on our last visit summed up our usual feelings: 'No, don't go in there,' said the man. 'It'll take ages and I'll just get upset.' Having said that, the coffee is great and the baristas skilled. Ginger loaf with vanilla icing is the pick of the cakes; sandwiches are pricey, but usually worth it thanks to superb Flour Station breads and generous fillings of quality ingredients (free-range chicken, Quickes cheddar, Wicks Manor ham). Fellow customers tend to be the cooler breed of locals; luckily, tourists tend to settle in the chains on the high street.
Babies and children welcome: high chairs. Tables outdoors (4, pavement). Takeaway service. Vegan dishes. **Map 28 B2.**

Shoreditch Grind

Fish & Chips

Maybe it's the need for comfort food in times of recession, maybe it's the desire to eat out inexpensively, but London's chippies seem to be enjoying a renaissance. Bustling newcomers such as **Poppies** in Spitalfields, **Kerbisher & Malt** in Hammersmith and **Oliver's** in Belsize Park make good old fish and chips seem positively fashionable, while the revamped **Sea Shell** is strutting its stuff with a glossy new confidence. One problem, however, is the continuing lack of clarity regarding threatened species and their sources. Charles Clover's online guide www.fish2fork.com highlights a number of London venues claiming to make efforts in this area, which, in reality, score pretty badly compared to other eateries such as Japanese chain **Feng Sushi** (*see p231*), gastropub the **Duke of Cambridge** (*see p114*) and fine-dining restaurant **One-0-One** (*see p130*).

Central

Barbican

Fish Central
149-155 Central Street, EC1V 8AP (7253 4970, www.fishcentral.co.uk). Old Street tube/rail or bus 55. **Lunch served** 11.30am-2.30pm Mon-Sat. **Dinner served** 5-10.30pm Mon-Thur; 5-11pm Fri, Sat. **Main courses** £9.55-£18.95. **Credit** AmEx, MC, V.
Plonked in the middle of a housing estate, Fish Central has been serving fish 'n' chips for decades, but these days it's a rather more upmarket spot: tables are clothed and adorned with fresh flowers; diners are treated to an amuse-bouche of, say, a salmon bite; and, if you haven't booked, you might have to settle for a takeaway. On our visit, a group of taxi drivers (clearly regulars) began with buttered rolls and wallies (pickled cucumbers), but could have opted for jellied eels or something a little more exotic. Our slightly undercooked pan-fried scallops were delicious, sweet and juicy, though the freshly made salsa verde lacked poke. Traditional cod and chips was excellent: an enormous fillet in crispy batter and a great pile of crunchy-outside, fluffy-inside chips. The special of turbot (one of very few sustainable fish on the menu), served in a creamy chive sauce with fried fennel, was another success. Portions are huge, service solicitous and the special menus a bargain.
Babies and children welcome: children's menu; high chairs. Booking advisable. Separate room for parties, seats 70. Tables outdoors (4, pavement). Takeaway service. **Map 5 P3**.

Bloomsbury

North Sea Fish Restaurant
7-8 Leigh Street, WC1H 9EW (7387 5892, www.northseafishrestaurant.co.uk). Russell Square tube or King's Cross tube/rail. **Lunch served** noon-2.30pm, **dinner served** 5.30-10.30pm Mon-Sat. **Main courses** £9.95-£21.05. **Credit** MC, V.
Enter Bloomsbury's North Sea and you instantly feel you've been beamed out of London and transported to a quaint, old-fashioned seaside town. The cosy room is lined with dark wooden tables, and plastic table settings display drawings of various fish found on the menu. A huge seafood platter was plenty for two to share; battered goujons of cod, haddock and plaice were served with deep-fried sardines, calamares and scampi – all with chips, of course. If you prefer a less greasy alternative, order boiled potatoes and remember that all big fish portions can be grilled. Our dessert, a square piece of trifle, was sweetly reminiscent of school dinners, complete with fluorescent cherries and lashings of cream.
Babies and children welcome: children's menu; high chairs. Booking advisable Thur-Sat. Separate room for parties, seats 40. Takeaway service. **Map 4 L4**.

Covent Garden

Rock & Sole Plaice
47 Endell Street, WC2H 9AJ (7836 3785). Covent Garden tube. **Meals served** 11.30am-10.30pm Mon-Sat; noon-9.30pm Sun. **Main courses** £9-£12. **Credit** MC, V.

According to the menu at Rock & Sole Plaice, London's third ever chippy opened on this site in 1871. Today, a jolly fish with Union Jack bib and entertainer's cane presides over a green and white frontage with several benches outside. At lunchtimes, office workers and tourists tussle for custody of the couple of tables on the ground floor, while takeaway customers place their orders at the fryer. Below, the walls of a stuffy basement are decorated with a fading submarine mural of strange smiling dolphins and teeth-gnashing sharks. Any minor lack of comfort is worth enduring, though, as the food is good – especially the fish. Delicate, flaky cod arrived encapsulated in a light, crisp batter and was served with oversized, golden chips; other options (pies and sausages) and sides (mushy peas, pickled onions) are at least equal to the standard fare normally found in chip shops. Prices exceed the norm, however, being pretty steep for food that is simply plated up from the fryer.
Babies and children welcome: high chairs. Separate room for parties, seats 40. Tables outdoors (7, pavement). Takeaway service. **Map 18 D3**.

Holborn

Fryer's Delight
19 Theobald's Road, WC1X 8SL (7405 4114). Holborn tube or bus 19, 38, 55. **Meals served** noon-11pm Mon-Sat. **Main courses** £4.75-£7.65. **Unlicensed**. **Corkage** no charge. **No credit cards**.
Fryer's Delight is a defiantly unreconstructed chippy, which is great if you like tradition: black and white tiled floors, Formica-topped tables, big

portions, small prices, and that simply indefinable satisfaction that comes from tucking into a plate of fish and chips with bread and butter and a cuppa. The 50-year-old bill of fare on the wall offers 'peas (mushy)', as well as the intriguing 'chop' sauce (Hammond's brand brown sauce). If you're looking for reassurances on sustainable fish, own-made tartare sauce or interactive service, then look elsewhere. But the stream of customers (Fryer's has a reputation as a cabbies' favourite) who crowd in throughout the day to share the booths don't care a jot about such niceties. Everything fried here is reliably good, if not astounding. Fish and chips as it should be, some might say.
Babies and children admitted. Takeaway service. **Map 4 M5**.

Marylebone

Golden Hind

73 Marylebone Lane, W1U 2PN (7486 3644). Bond Street tube. **Dinner served** 6-10pm Mon-Fri. **Dinner served** 6-10pm Mon-Sat. **Main courses** £6.30-£10.50. **Minimum** (dinner) £5. **Unlicensed**. **Corkage** £1. **Credit** AmEx, MC, V.
Like the vicars of a long-established parish church, the owners of the Golden Hind are displayed on a roll of honour, dating back to 1914. The current Greek family (at the tiller since 2002) has recently expanded the business into the neighbouring premises, where plate-glass windows and cream floor tiles create a bright if slightly anodyne space. In the original section, black and white photos of old London and a splendid art deco deep-fryer (which is now used to store cutlery) are pleasingly fitting. Customers range from 'twin-set and pearls' pensioners pecking at their weekly skate wing, to construction workers wolfing down rock salmon and chips during their breaks. Own-made fish cakes feature on the short list of starters, but most punters head straight for the battered fish (all

species available are offered steamed too). Golden-clothed plaice arrived brilliant white and almost wobbly in its impeccable freshness. We readily forgave the odd bone. Chips, hot from the fryer, and mushy peas were prosaic in comparison. Finish, if you have room, with a steamed pudding wallowing in a sea of custard.
Babies and children welcome: high chairs. Takeaway service. **Map 9 G5**.

★ Sea Shell

49-51 Lisson Grove, NW1 6UH (7224 9000, www.seashellrestaurant.co.uk). Marylebone tube/rail. **Lunch served** noon-2.30pm, **dinner served** 5-10.30pm Mon-Fri. **Meals served** noon-10.30pm Sat. **Main courses** £12-£30. **Credit** AmEx, DC, MC, V.
Badly damaged by fire in 2009, the Sea Shell has finally risen phoenix-like in a somewhat glossier incarnation, complete with gleaming brass, chequered marble floor and backlit aquarium (a magnet for children). The latter must be proving a challenge, as the brown banquettes around which the fish tank wraps are also the seating of choice for dating couples, but then, that's the Sea Shell – popular with everyone. Service has cranked up a notch since our last visit, our waiter knowledgeably talking about the wines, and the pros and cons of screw-cap bottles. The menu, more extensive and varied than most chippies, remains much the same. Start maybe with prawn cocktail or chargrilled halloumi. There's a large choice of sides including broccoli with chilli and garlic, and jacket potatoes with soured cream, plus steaks for fish-fearers. A decision to opt for Japanese panko crumbs on our deep-fried haddock was well rewarded. The chips, fried in groundnut oil, taste much better than they look, and the tartare sauce is surely London's best.
Babies and children welcome: children's menu; high chairs. Booking advisable Thur-Sat. Disabled: toilet. Tables outdoors (8, pavement). Takeaway service. **Map 2 F4**.

Soho

Golden Union Fish Bar

38 Poland Street, W1F 7LY (7434 1933, www.goldenunion.co.uk). Oxford Circus tube. **Meals served** noon-9pm Mon-Sat; noon-6pm Sun. **Main courses** £4.50-£7.50. **Credit** AmEx, MC, V.
The boundaries of Soho contain culinary representatives of a great many different nations, so it's heartening to see proper fish and chips flying the British flag at Golden Union. The café mixes traditional and modern, with a takeaway at the front for those who consider greasy fingers as important as the salt and vinegar. Through the back there's a bright seating area with lemon-yellow tables and white-tiled walls. Table service comes from breezy and cheerful young ladies who bring generous, fried-to-order portions of cod and haddock, as well as the lesser-spotted pollock or coley. The beer batter was pleasingly crisp, and the chips were proficiently executed if unremarkable. There's a drinks licence too, so you can jazz up a meal with a glass of wine or something from the decent beer list, which features Deuchars and London Pride.
Babies and children welcome: children's menu; high chairs. Bookings not accepted lunch Fri. Disabled: toilet. Takeaway service. **Map 17 A3**.

Victoria

Seafresh Fish Restaurant

80-81 Wilton Road, SW1V 1DL (7828 0747, www.fishandchipsinlondon.com). Victoria tube/rail. **Lunch served** noon-3pm, **dinner served** 5-10.30pm Mon-Fri. **Meals served** noon-10.30pm Sat. **Main courses** £10.75-£25.95. **Set lunch** £12.05 2 courses incl tea or coffee. **Credit** AmEx, MC, V.
Located on the main thoroughfare that links Victoria to Pimlico, this large, airy establishment

Poppies. See p301.

does brisk business among locals. Seafresh is certainly a restaurant rather than a mere chippy – tables are firm and widely spaced, cutlery is reassuringly heavy, and the menu has a strong line in grilled fish for diners who aren't tempted by the battered selection. Indeed, the options of grilled sardines or fisherman's pie could be a slightly better bet than the fish and chips themselves. We found the batter oily and the chips anaemic, while the sardines were superb and the pie tasty and filling. There's also a takeaway area for those on the move. *Available for hire. Babies and children welcome: high chairs. Booking advisable. Takeaway service.* **Map 15 J10.**

West

Bayswater

Mr Fish

9 Porchester Road, W2 5DP (7229 4161, www.mrfish.uk.com). Bayswater or Royal Oak tube. **Meals served** 11am-11pm daily. **Main courses** £6.25-£12.95. **Set lunch** (11am-3pm) £6.95 2 courses, £7.95 3 courses. **Credit** AmEx, MC, V.

This popular neighbourhood chippy always seems to have a queue of locals waiting for its freshly battered fish and thick-cut chips. A partition conceals the takeaway punters from a small dining room, where dated seaside decor meets canteen crockery and a pleasantly nostalgic menu. There's prawn cocktail to start and school dinner-style puddings, such as jam sponge slathered in electric-yellow custard, to finish. For mains, fish and chips is the real deal. Light, crispy batter envelops fresh, flaky cod (you can also have haddock, plaice, lemon sole or halibut), while the chips are refreshingly free of finger-drenching oil. The tartare sauce might be a little thin and overly sharp, and the side salad reliant on uninspiring iceberg, but Mr Fish is a consistently reliable quick-stop venue worth discovering. *Babies and children welcome: children's menu; high chairs. Takeaway service.* **Map 7 C5.**
For branch see index.

Hammersmith

Kerbisher & Malt [NEW]

164 Shepherd's Bush Road, W6 7PB (3556 0228, www.kerbisher.co.uk). Hammersmith tube. **Lunch served** noon-2.30pm, **dinner served** 4.30-10pm Tue-Fri. **Meals served** noon-10pm Sat; noon-9pm Sun. **Main courses** £4-£8.60. **Credit** MC, V.

A modern, maritime-themed café and takeaway, Kerbisher & Malt is furnished with sleek white tiles, monochrome photos and a chunky communal table. While waiting for your order, watch behind-the-scenes kitchen action on the flatscreen TV. The menu offers the usual hearty staples, including fish that tick some ecological boxes (pollock and coley, as recommended by the Marine Stewardship Council). Mushy peas, big fat gherkins, and fennel and dill salad are among the classic extras. Go for whitebait, fish cakes, fried squid or a fishfinger butty, or sample batter-free daily specials such as garlicky, Mediterranean-style langoustines. Coley fillet, encased in light, crunchy golden batter, was beautifully succulent, as was a perfectly grilled chunk of pollack. We weren't bowled over by the chips, however, which, though crisp in texture and fluffy inside, seemed over-fried. Tartare sauce was let down by a raw mustardy flavour and a shortfall of gherkins and herbs, but the onion rings were good. Service is spot-on: attentive and enthused. Judging by the evening queues, K&M is just what W6 has been crying out for. *Babies and children welcome: children's menu; high chairs. Bookings not accepted dinner Fri. Tables outdoors (2, pavement). Takeaway service.* **Map 20 C3.**

South West

Wandsworth

Brady's

513 Old York Road, SW18 1TF (8877 9599, www.bradysfish.co.uk). Wandsworth Town rail. **Lunch served** 12.30-2.30pm Fri, Sat. **Dinner served** 6.30-10pm Tue-Thur, Sat; 6.30-10.30pm Fri. **Main courses** £7.85-£12.95. **Credit** MC, V.

Blackboard menus, a pastel colour scheme and mermaids on the mirror – Brady's fish bar is an unlikely seaside getaway in the heart of south-west London. 'Freshest fish, simply cooked' is the mantra, and a chunky salmon fish cake starter – crisp outside, fluffy inside – was a steal at £2.95. Dark golden, slightly chewy batter gave our cod an upmarket feel, and a grilled-to-perfection haddock fillet was enjoyed alongside dollops of own-made herb sauces, including tangy tomato and basil mayonnaise. Service was friendly, chips were plentiful, but claggy mushy peas needed a squirt of lemon to bring them to life. English puddings

are too heavy to follow fish and chips; our lemon pie was like eating a tub of zesty clotted cream. Finish with a cup of tea instead.
Babies and children welcome: high chairs. Takeaway service. **Map 21 A4.**

South

Battersea

Fish Club
189 St John's Hill, SW11 1TH (7978 7115, www.thefishclub.com). Wandsworth Town rail. **Dinner served** 5-10pm Mon. **Meals served** noon-10pm Tue-Sun. **Main courses** £6.70-£14.95. **Credit** AmEx, MC, V.
More café than restaurant, Fish Club offers sustainable fish and chips and other seafood to take away or to eat in its trendy, rather chilly interior. Watch your food being prepared behind a counter stocked with fresh fish and inviting salads. The friendly, knowledgeable staff recommended a special of sprats: fried whitebait-style, served with aïoli, and very munchable. Battered coley came in an oddly shaped chunk, but it flaked into succulent mouthfuls. 'Catch of the day' was a generous helping of two dabs, though it's worth noting that, as with many of the dishes, the fish came unadorned. Add sauces and side dishes and the overall cost becomes less of a bargain. Drink local ales or Asahi beer with your feast, the latter chosen because of the Japanese nation's love of fish.
Babies and children welcome: children's menu; high chairs. Disabled: toilet. Tables outdoors (3, courtyard; 2, pavement). Takeaway service. **Map 21 B4.**
For branch see index.

Waterloo

Masters Super Fish
191 Waterloo Road, SE1 8UX (7928 6924). Southwark tube or Waterloo tube/rail. **Lunch served** noon-3pm Tue-Sat. **Dinner served** 5.30-10.30pm Mon; 4.30-10.30pm Tue-Thur, Sat; 4.30-11pm Fri. **Main courses** £7.25-£16. **Set lunch** £7 1 course incl soft drink, tea or coffee. **Credit** MC, V.
Bare brickwork, metal deep-fat fryers and a queue of cabbies distinguish the busy takeaway counter at the entrance to this no-frills chippy. The retro feel is continued by the wipe-clean tables and wilted hanging plants of the conservatory-like dining room, with its collection of celebrity photos (Ian McShane, Lenny Henry). The menu lists several more exotic options than the takeaway, including cod in mustard batter and various grilled fish (swordfish, tuna steak). The accompaniments, however, are of the back-to-basics ilk. Three chewy baguette slices and cooked king prawns arrive as complimentary starters. Mains are served along with metal jugs filled with ketchup and tartare sauce; staff offer to heap pickled gherkins and onions on to plates. Portion sizes are vast. A Masters '247g piece of cod' special was unfinishable, and a crisply battered rock salmon was the size of a house brick. Most tables were empty on our Saturday afternoon visit, but just as we finished, tables were hastily crammed together as a coach-load of pensioners descended.
Babies and children welcome: children's menu; high chairs. Bookings not accepted Fri. Takeaway service. **Map 11 N9.**

South East

Dulwich

Sea Cow
37 Lordship Lane, SE22 8EW (8693 3111, www.theseacow.co.uk). East Dulwich rail or bus 176. **Meals served** noon-10pm Mon, Sun; noon-11pm Tue-Sat; noon-8.30pm Sun. **Main courses** £8.50-£10. **Credit** MC, V.
Posh fish and chips brand Sea Cow may now be a frequent presence at festivals and events, but this is where it all began, back in 2003. Sadly, the place no longer feels the sensation it once was – though we find it hard to tell whether this is because the quality has gone down or whether the competition has upped its game. Fish is bought fresh, displayed on ice and seaweed, and only cooked when ordered, so it's not sitting around under heated lamps going flaccid. There's a commendable emphasis on sustainability, with native catches such as mackerel enthusiastically promoted. Although you'll find several alternatives to the straight battered fish supper (crab cakes, tuna with cracked pepper and coriander, spicy prawns), we've discovered that these can be disappointing. Note: children eat free at weekends until 4pm.
Babies and children welcome: children's menu; high chairs. Takeaway service. **Map 23 C4.**

Herne Hill

Olley's
65-69 Norwood Road, SE24 9AA (8671 8259, www.olleys.info). Herne Hill rail or bus 3, 68, 196. **Lunch served** noon-3pm Tue-Sun. **Dinner served** 5-10pm Tue-Sat; 5-9pm Sun. **Main courses** £5.50-£19.50. **Set lunch** £5.50 1 course. **Credit** AmEx, MC, V.
Olley's occupies a prominent spot opposite Brockwell Park. Inside, it resembles a Mediterranean taverna, with a smattering of nautical paraphernalia and extremely friendly service. The menu features a dozen types of fish (battered, steamed or grilled), with a selection of meal options named after local celebrities or famous customers. After more than 20 years' practice, the kitchen has got things down to a fine art: batter is crisp and not too oily; chips and mushy peas are expertly judged too. Food is complemented by a small drinks list, including wine and the excellent Innis & Gunn beer. Olley's may not be the best chippy in London, but it's certainly in the top bracket. The only drawback is the bill, which can sometimes pinch a little if you haven't come for one of the early-bird deals.
Babies and children welcome: children's menu; crayons; high chairs; nappy-changing facilities. Booking advisable weekends. Disabled: toilet. Separate room for parties, seats 40. Takeaway service. **Map 23 A5.**

Lewisham

Something Fishy
117-119 Lewisham High Street, SE13 6AT (8852 7075). Lewisham rail/DLR. **Meals served** 9am-5.30pm Mon-Sat. **Main courses** £4-£7.25. **No credit cards.**
This two-room workers' caff majoring in fish and chips serves its appreciative Lewisham clientele (mainly market workers and shoppers) with pride. The Formica tables and plastic chairs are as clean

and bright as the blue-tiled floor and fishy-themed wall decor. Service is brisk and friendly, and the food consists of spanking fresh fish (the classics, including skate) cooked to order in gloriously crisp batter – or simply steamed for diners with a regard for their waistline. Chips, fluffy and golden, come in three portion sizes; fish, where appropriate, in two. Mash is served in a gargantuan mound to accompany Pukka pies or, more interestingly (if all too rarely ordered), jellied eels. Most punters have little room left for the choice of traditional puds, though a cuppa goes down nicely.
Babies and children welcome: children's menu; high chairs. Tables outdoors (5, pavement). Takeaway service.

East

Spitalfields

★ Poppies NEW HOT 50
6-8 Hanbury Street, E1 6QR (7247 0892, www.poppiesfishandchips.co.uk). Aldgate East tube or Liverpool Street tube/rail. **Meals served** 11am-11pm daily. **Main courses** £9.90-£18.90. **Credit** AmEx, MC, V.
Unlike many restaurants in squeaky-clean 'new' Spitalfields, Poppies isn't a concept dreamed up by a branding exec in Hoxton; it's run by Pat 'Pop' Newland, a time-served fryer who began salting and battering on the Roman Road in 1953. He's come out of retirement to launch this venture, which, with its location, appealing decor and good food, skates a perfect line between pukka and posh. There's nothing to alarm the traditionalist looking for a no-frills fish supper, but the carefully considered 1950s interior will appeal to local trendsetters seeking an authentic backdrop for their haircuts. Fresh fish from Billingsgate (cod, haddock, rock, scampi, halibut – all sustainably caught, we're told) combines with a perfect batter, hand-cut chips, home-made tartare sauce and mushy peas. Table service is provided by sharply dressed, authentically amiable Italian chaps, although on our visit they could have been a bit sharper in performance. Further incentives: there's wine by the glass, Meantime beers and Fentimans bottled soft drinks, if a cuppa doesn't do it for you. Prices are decent given the quality of the food. Poppies is already busy, even midweek, and rightly so: it's a Spitalfields place with heart.
Babies and children welcome: children's menu; high chairs. Booking advisable. Disabled: toilet. Separate room for parties, seats 25. Tables outdoors (4, pavement). Takeaway service. **Map 12 S5.**

Victoria Park

★ Fish House
126-128 Lauriston Road, E9 7LH (8533 3327, www.fishouse.co.uk). Mile End tube then 277 bus. **Meals served** noon-10pm Mon-Fri; 11am-10pm Sat, Sun. **Main courses** £8.95-£12.95. **Credit** AmEx, MC, V.
Situated on the leafy borders of Victoria Park, Fish House serves outstanding fish and chips. Customers queue for takeaways on the left, their anticipation reverberating off retro white-tiled walls. To the right, upmarket fish dishes are served in the quieter, sit-down restaurant: the likes of lobster bisque or Greenland halibut with samphire. Only certified, eco-friendly, seasonal fish approved

by the Marine Conservation Society's 'Good Fish Guide' are cooked here (see the blackboard above the kitchen door to discover in exactly which ocean your fish has been swimming), and even the chips are approved by the British Potato Council. Our battered fish was close to perfection, with a crunchy, light batter coating steamed Atlantic cod. Breaded fish cakes were fragrant with tarragon, and the chips fresh and crisp. Being very picky, we'd say the mushy peas were bland, but overall we've rarely found a better local chippy. The most convincing sign of quality – beyond insulated takeaway bags, authentic gelato and Irish skate on the menu – was that we left without greasy fingers. *Babies and children welcome: children's menu; crayons; high chairs. Booking advisable Fri dinner; Sat, Sun. Tables outdoors (8, pavement). Takeaway service.*

North East

Dalston

Faulkner's
424-426 Kingsland Road, E8 4AA (7254 6152). Haggerston rail or bus 67, 149, 242. **Lunch served** noon-2.30pm Mon-Fri. **Dinner served** 5-10pm Mon-Thur; 4.30-10pm Fri. **Meals served** 11.30am-10pm Sat; noon-9pm Sun. **Main courses** £10-£18.90. **Credit** MC, V.
Faulkner's feels like a relic of the Kingsland Road that's currently being swept away by a wave from the north, leaving in its wake fashionable bars, cafés and boutiques. The takeaway on the left-hand side does a brisk trade; the restaurant features white tablecloths, heavy napkins, branded crockery and net curtains. Above, fake beams stripe the artex ceiling. Tropical fish watch from their tank, as fried or grilled portions of their distant relatives are served to diners; the menu also advertises jellied eels, oysters and mussels. This sort of nostalgic dining experience is brilliant if the food matches up, but we can't say it always does. Battered haddock came crispy and fresh, but scampi seemed to have rested in a freezer on its way to the plate, and the less said about the wimpy, pallid chips the better. The food is by no means terrible, but Faulkner's has that curious combination of formality and disappointment that characterises so many traditional British establishments. *Babies and children welcome: children's menu; high chairs. Booking advisable weekends. Separate room for parties, seats 25. Takeaway service.* **Map 6 R1**.

Stoke Newington

Sutton & Sons
90 Stoke Newington High Street, N16 7NY (7249 6444). Stoke Newington rail or bus 149, 243. **Meals served** noon-10pm Mon-Thur; noon-10.30pm Fri, Sat. **Main courses** £5.90-£8.40. **No credit cards.**
With a new name and a new, stylish interior, the former Fishery Fish Bar has upped the game for Stoke Newington chip joints. Wine comes in chic tumblers, wooden communal tables line the elegant white interior, and the main wall is covered in a drawing of local landmarks. If it weren't for the aromas of frying, you might almost forget you were in a chippy. The menu consists of a selection of deep-fried fish and, if your arteries are up to it, you can order a battered Mars bar for dessert.

Nevertheless, there are also some more healthy and intriguing alternatives; on our visit, the handwritten blackboard menu offered swordfish with vegetable couscous. Grilled British sea bass was moist and came stuffed with lemon and garlic. If only the accompanying chips – pale and limp – had spent longer in the fryer. *Babies and children welcome: children's menu; high chairs. Booking advisable Fri. Disabled: toilet. Takeaway service; delivery service (over £15 within 3-mile radius).* **Map 25 C2**.

North

Finchley

Two Brothers Fish Restaurant
297-303 Regent's Park Road, N3 1DP (8346 0469, www.twobrothers.co.uk). Finchley Central tube. **Lunch served** noon-2.30pm, **dinner served** 5.30-10.15pm Tue-Sun. **Main courses** £12.95-£25.95. **Credit** AmEx, MC, V.
Although it doesn't seem so long ago that this north London stalwart was refurbished, the vaguely New England coastal decor is starting to look, like the fish, quite battered – a result, we'd suggest, of Two Brothers' extreme popularity (Friday night queues are legendary) rather than lack of care. Staff are on the ball, though it can take surprisingly long for orders to arrive at the close-set tables. Fortunately, the multi-generational crowd is friendly. Apart from several bones in our haddock, the fish was superb, with a crisp coating and perfectly steamed fillet within; the cod was exceptionally hunky and flaky. It's worth splashing out the extra 50p for matzo. Portions stretch generously beyond the rims of the long oval plates, and accompaniments of chips, fresh-tasting coleslaw and mushy peas are good. Specials such as asparagus soup, caesar salad with prawns, and grilled kingfish with tomato relish, help mix things up. Among the appealing drink options are reliable party-style house wines, Old Speckled Hen and Asahi beer. *Babies and children welcome: high chairs. Takeaway service.*

Highgate

Fish Fish
179 Archway Road, N6 5BN (8348 3121). Highgate tube. **Dinner served** 5-10pm Mon-Fri. **Meals served** noon-11pm Sat, Sun. **Main courses** £9.95-£17.50. **Credit** MC, V.
This spot, formerly known as the Lighthouse, may have reined back on its ambitious Black Sea-inspired menu, but it's a welcome source of reliable fish and chips and other seafood treats on the dreary Archway Road. Just stepping inside can put you in a holiday mood: there are cheerful hanging nets and lanterns, simple pine furniture, a long, shiny open kitchen and a tempting rear conservatory. Locals coming for takeaway lean on the counter and chat amicably with the friendly staff. Battered haddock and cod with chips hit all the right notes; calamari rings were good too. 'Scallop terminator' (scallops and mussels in white wine and cream) didn't destroy the shellfish at all – they were cooked just-so – but more effort with presentation would be welcome. Chargrilled salmon was overdone, to our bitter disappointment: the huge portion was too smoky and dry – curious given the menu's promotion of this 'healthy living'

cooking technique. More attention to detail is evident in the choice of coffees and teas. Wines, such as our Esperanza merlot, may be readily available in big-name retailers, but Fish Fish's mark-ups are not offputting. *Available for hire. Babies and children welcome: high chairs; nappy-changing facilities. Tables outdoors (7, pavement). Takeaway service.*

Muswell Hill

Toff's
38 Muswell Hill Broadway, N10 3RT (8883 8656, www.toffsfish.co.uk). Highgate tube then bus 43, 134. **Meals served** 11.30am-10.30pm Mon-Sat. **Main courses** £11.95-£24.95. **Set meal** £8.95 1 course. **Credit** AmEx, DC, MC, V.
Despite Muswell Hill's march upmarket, its denizens still enjoy their chips. Toff's is always bustling, and come early evening, there are usually queues at the takeaway counter and for the narrow restaurant behind. Staff are a friendly, efficient team at this family-run establishment. A child's fork landed on the floor during peak serving time; the waiter immediately came over with another one. Everything is fried to order and arrives on the plate glistening with hot, fresh groundnut oil; our cod and haddock (both with chips) were faultless. We'd have preferred garden peas to the salad garnish, but that's a small complaint. The portions are enormous, though staff still asked if we'd like a chip top-up. We declined in favour of puddings: local Marine Ices ice-cream, school-dinner classics such as spotted dick and custard, and a huge tranche of light, creamy tiramisu. Locals appreciate the photos of Muswell Hill in bygone times posted around the walls. *Babies and children welcome: children's menu; crayons; high chairs. Disabled: toilet. Separate rooms for parties, seating 20 and 24. Takeaway service.*

North West

Belsize Park

Oliver's **NEW**
95 Haverstock Hill, NW3 4RL (7586 9945). Chalk Farm tube. **Meals served** noon-10.15pm Tue-Sun. **Main courses** £9.20-£11.45. **Credit** AmEx, MC, V.
You have to love an outfit so discriminating as to specify deep-fried Mars Sensations rather than simply battering a Mars bar, but then this is Steele's Village rather than mere Chalk Farm. The pong of oil is slightly offputting, though the compact interior is spick and span, with closely packed tables to the rear and more 'below decks'. Cheerful green and white tiles and modish furniture make the setting pleasant enough for a casual night out or a family meal. Oliver's claim is that fish comes from sustainable stocks, and the chain is a 'Hugh's Fish Fight' supporter, offering battered mackerel bap and the likes of coley as specials (though the tiny specials board is easily overlooked). We liked the flavour of the fish cake (made from cod, smoked halibut and smoked salmon), and its fruity salsa, but the leafy salad tasted as if it had come out of a packet. Good, crunchy, brown-tinged batter encased the (slightly overcooked) fish. In all, this is an attractive spot that's reassuringly careful about the details of a meal, including freshly ground coffee and terrific ice-cream.

FISH & CHIPS

Babies and children welcome: high chairs.
Booking advisable. Tables outdoors
(2, pavement). Takeaway service. **Map 28 C4.**

West Hampstead

Nautilus

27-29 Fortune Green Road, NW6 1DU
(7435 2532). West Hampstead tube/rail then
bus 328. **Lunch served** 11.30am-2.30pm,
dinner served 4.30-10pm Mon-Sat. **Main**
courses £10.50-£22.50. **Credit** MC, V.
Nautilus has been owned by the same Greek family
for 50 years (witness the pinewood panelling), but
despite this it's no stickler for tradition. Instead of
standard batter, fish is only available grilled or
fried, Jewish-style, in matzo meal. Nevertheless,
this is a blessing given the gargantuan portions.
The thin, crispy matzo coating on our soft, creamy
plaice rendered the dish so light that we were easily
able to manage the accompanying large platter of
piping-hot chips (fried in groundnut oil). Service is
comically helpful, with our matronly server going
into lengthy explanations about the popularity of
cod, greeting customers with exhortations to 'Sit
anywhere. Anywhere!' and even providing hand
gestures to demonstrate 'the way I chop the fish'.
There's a touch of the tacky too, with the Disotto
dessert menu offering orange ice-cream in frozen
half-orange shells, and design touches such as
turquoise-blue glass panelling, plastic flowers and
shiny dolphin statuettes. Customers include in-the-
know fish hunters and many pensioner couples,
whose warmly familiar greetings suggest that they
make Nautilus a regular haunt.
Babies and children welcome: high chairs.
Booking advisable. Takeaway service.
Map 28 A1.

Outer London

Kingston, Surrey

fish! kitchen

58 Coombe Road, Kingston, Surrey, KT2 7AF
(8546 2886, www.fishkitchen.com). Norbiton
rail or bus 57, 85, 213. **Meals served** noon-
10pm Tue-Sat. **Main courses** £11.95-£24.95.
Credit AmEx, MC, V.
With its bare-brick walls, decent wines (available
by the glass or bottle), blackboard of daily specials
and cheery waitresses, Norbiton's best chippy is
somewhere between a snack bar and bistro. The
creative likes of hand-picked Dorset crab with
toast (delicious, and one order was enough to share)
and smoked haddock rarebit make great taste bud
tinglers to start. Fish is no longer a cheap
ingredient, and fish! kitchen makes no bones about
being pricey. Halibut and chips costs £18.95, for
which you get dark-golden beer batter wrapped
around a densely packed fillet of moist halibut –
not tastier than cod, if we're honest, but currently
a more sustainable catch. The chips, peas and
tartare sauce were all average, but the fish really
stood out. At least as good is the fish pie:
scrumptious comfort food packed with white and
smoked fish under a cheesy topping. Desserts are
locally produced ice-creams, crumbles and sticky
toffee pudding. There's also a good fishmonger's
next door if you want to try dishes out at home.
Babies and children welcome: children's menu;
high chairs. Disabled: toilet. Tables outdoors
(20, terrace). Takeaway service.

Kerbisher & Malt. See p300.

FISH & CHIPS

Ice-cream Parlours

Suddenly, London has the taste for ice-cream or, more usually, Italian-syle gelato – yes, despite the weather. We're starting to lose count of the number of new parlours and kiosks to open in the capital, not least because some old favourites such as **Scoop**, **Oddono's** and **Gelato Mio** are expanding. Then there's the fabulous ice-cream being sold to take away from other eateries and shops – first-rate gastropub the **Bull & Last** (*see p114*), chocolatier **William Curley** (*see p283*) and, in season, the Camden Passage branch of **Paul A Young Fine Chocolates** (www.paulayoung.co.uk). And, of course, we can't forget Chalk Farm family favourite **Marine Ices** (*see p279*). Competition keeps standards high, but has also encouraged the rise of more theatrical, attention-grabbing establishments: you can have your ice-cream frozen in front of your eyes in the chemistry-lab setting of nitro-parlour **Chin Chin Laboratorists**, or have a 'vice cream' cocktail blowtorched by the fetish cap-wearing **Icecreamists** in Covent Garden. Chills and thrills, then.

Central
Charing Cross

Gino Gelato
3 Adelaide Street, WC2N 4HZ (7836 9390, www.ginogelato.com). Charing Cross tube/rail.
Open noon-10.30pm Mon-Thur, Sun; noon-11.30pm Fri, Sat. **Credit** MC, V.
Just a stone's throw from Charing Cross station, Gino Gelato pair traditional Italian methods with organic British milk to make their high-quality ice-cream. In pride of place at the back of the vanilla and chocolate coloured gelateria sits an ice-cream churner, used daily to turn out different kinds of gelato from a collection of 200 or so recipes. Of the 26 flavours on offer on our latest visit, vin santo with crushed cantucci was the shining star; a slightly salty pistachio was also extremely good. The tiramisu flavour was rich and creamy with actual cake crumbs, and a fresh and fruity frutti di bosco had nothing artificial about it. We'll definitely be back to sample more, including the chocolate and chianti sorbet, and the olive oil ice-cream that staff were raving about.
Takeaway service. Vegan dishes. **Map 18 D5**.

Covent Garden

Gelatorino
2 Russell Street, WC2B 5JD (7240 0746, www.gelatorino.com). Covent Garden tube.
Open 11am-9pm Mon-Wed; 11am-11pm Thur-Sat; 11am-8pm Sun. **No credit cards**.

This Covent Garden parlour, fittingly decorated in cool stripes of coffee and vanilla, offers one of the most authentic Italian gelateria experiences in London. Old-fashioned machines run behind the counter all day, making the freshest possible gelato, with a light, velvety texture. Recipes draw on ingredients from the owners' native Turin – high-quality dark chocolate, milk and nuts – and steer clear of preservatives and artificial colourings. A real and infectious enthusiasm for ice-cream prevails: when you make your choice, staff are quick to suggest the perfect complement – for example, fior di latte (an extremely light, milk-based ice-cream) with an exceptionally soft strawberry sorbetti – and encourage you to taste other flavours before making your decision. On our visit, one of the owners even brought round tasters of pistachio, hazelnut and the specialty, Breakfast in Turin (coffee ice-cream with Ecuadorian dark chocolate), so that customers could sample even more.
Babies and children welcome: high chairs. Tables outdoors (3, pavement). Takeaway service. Vegan dishes. **Map 18 E4**.

Icecreamists
Market Building, Covent Garden Market, WC2E 8RF (8616 0721, www.theicecreamists.com). Covent Garden tube. **Open** noon-10.30pm daily. **Credit** MC, V.
Although the black and electric-pink decor, thumping music and neon signage is more sex shop than ice-cream parlour, the Icecreamists isn't all garish style over substance. The gimmick-laden gelatos are actually pretty good. Towering extremely high on a cone, our gigantic scoop of 'Sex, Drugs & Choc 'n' Roll' was laced with sea salt, giving the creamy milk chocolate a superb lift. White-chocolate 'Priscilla Queen of Desserts' came with a malty hit of Horlicks and a naughty kick of Baileys. There's even more razzle-dazzle in the sundaes. The 'Molotoffee Cocktail', for example, brings together dulce de leche, apple juice and banana syrup, and the concoction is then blowtorched at your table. The spectacle is perhaps better experienced at the roomy Covent Garden Piazza branch, where tables spill out on to the cobbled courtyard; the original Maiden Lane shop is much smaller and a little less brash.
Babies and children admitted. Tables outdoors (16, market). Takeaway service. Vegan dishes. **Map 18 E4**.
For branch (Queen of the Desserts) see index.

★ Scoop
40 Shorts Gardens, WC2H 9AB (7240 7086, www.scoopgelato.com). Covent Garden tube.
Open noon-10.30pm daily. **Credit** AmEx, MC, V.
The gelato packs a punch at this always busy Covent Garden parlour (there's also a handy new branch in Soho's Brewer Street). Entirely free of artificial flavourings and preservatives, the scoops are not short on taste. Malaga is spiked with a lot more than a dash of Sicilian marsala wine, and the intensely dark, bittersweet chocolate sorbet (extra fondente) could almost suck the liquid from your mouth – opt for the cioccolato fondente ice-cream made with a changing array of grand-cru single-origin varieties if you're not looking for a such a

chocolate hit. A few alternative flavours (green tea, cinnamon) are outnumbered by familiar Italian options, from stracciatella to a beautiful pistachio, as well as some vibrant-looking fruit sorbets. Space is tight for such a popular shop, and after dinner there's a clamour for the few seats at the back, with punters spilling into the street to enjoy their mountain-high ice-cream cones.

Takeaway service. Vegan dishes. **Map 18 D3.**
For branch see index.

Fitzrovia

Polka Gelato
45 Fitzroy Street, W1T 6EB (7387 3841, www.polkagelato.co.uk). Warren Street tube. **Open** 8.30am-8pm Mon-Fri; 1-8pm Sat, Sun. **Credit** (over £5) AmEx, MC, V.
A relative newcomer to the ever increasing ice-cream offering in London, Polka Gelato's interior is far from extravagant: concrete walls, minimal seating and a chilled counter packed with colourful ice-creams and sorbets. Always available are chocolate, pistachio, nocciola and an outstanding salt caramel with just a hint of bitterness. Other flavours change from day to day. Chocolate and chilli had just the right amount of heat and the odd fleck of real chilli running through it. Also of note were the fragrant blueberry ice-cream and a vibrant pink raspberry sorbet crammed with fruit, pips and all. Monmouth Coffee drinks are also sold, and there should be pastries coming soon. Look out for the own-made ice pops in summer.
Takeaway service. Vegan dishes. **Map 3 J4.**

Knightsbridge

Ice-Cream Parlour at Harrods
2nd floor, Harrods, 87-135 Brompton Road, SW1X 7XL (7893 8959, www.harrods.com). Knightsbridge tube. **Open** 10am-7.30pm Mon-Sat; 10am-5.30pm Sun. **Credit** AmEx, MC, V.
At Harrods' art deco-inspired ice-cream parlour, chandeliers of inverted sundae glasses sprinkle coloured light on to an undulating marble counter, while customers swivel on sorbet-coloured bar stools, peering over their towering knickerbocker glories. The epic menu includes the classic sundaes you'd expect, as well as an unusual deconstructed gelato platter and gelato served in spaghetti shapes. For a retro treat, try an ice-cream float with your favourite fizzy drink. Our banana split was good, but the vanilla gelato was too plain. Banana and dulce de leche gelato, although refined, also lacked intensity of flavour. Better was the wild berry gelato – rich and fresh, with swirls of fruit. Service was lax, but very polite once we'd got the staff's attention. Pay a visit after wandering Harrods' sparkling shopping halls, although the venue's sense of occasion and setting is perhaps a better selling point than the gelato itself.
Babies and children welcome: high chairs; nappy-changing facilities. Disabled: lift; toilet. Takeaway service. Vegan dishes. **Map 14 F9.**

Mayfair

Freggo
27-29 Swallow Street, W1B 4QR (7287 9506, www.freggo.co.uk). Piccadilly Circus tube. **Open** 8am-11pm Mon-Thur; 8am-12.30am Fri; 9am-12.30am Sat; 10am-8pm Sun. **Credit** MC, V.
Set just off Regent Street, Freggo, with its striking purple and silver interior and lively music, makes a great post-shopping treat. It may not offer the largest range of flavours, but what it does have tucked away behind the counter is certainly good. Along with the usual vanilla and chocolate, you'll find Irish cream, chocolate-speckled banana split, and a must-try malbec and berry sorbet that testifies to the shop's Argentinian roots. Another nod to Argentina comes in the three different dulce de leche ice-creams: one regular, one with extra dulce de leche sauce (best left to the seriously sweet-toothed) and one with bittersweet dark chocolate chips that balance the sweetness perfectly. The empanadas also warrant attention; their crumbly pastry and chilli-spiked meat make the perfect antidote to an ice-cream-induced sugar rush.
Babies and children welcome: high chairs. Tables outdoors (2, pavement). Vegan dishes. **Map 17 A5.**

Soho

Amorino
41 Old Compton Street, W1D 6HF (7494 3300, www.amorino.com). Leicester Square or Piccadilly Circus tube. **Open** noon-midnight daily. **Credit** (over £7) MC, V.
Already a chain in Paris, Amorino still feels like a one-off in Soho. Styling itself as a traditional gelateria (rather than today's typically bright contemporary parlour), it's a warm and cosy spot in which to partake of an Italian gelato. The quality of flavours is key, and many of the ice-creams boast the provenance of their ingredients: lemons come from Sorrento, alphonso mangoes from India and coconut from Sri Lanka. All scoops are churned without artificial colours or flavourings, and, perhaps as a result, can lack intensity. Madagascan bourbon vanilla, for example, was beautifully creamy, but far too mild; and the amarena lacked the sour smack of a good cherry scoop. Flavours using more naturally vibrant ingredients, such as a powerfully sweet Ecuadorian banana, faired better. But with 28 intriguing hot chocolates, as well as waffles, panettone and biscuits on the menu, you don't even have to be a fan of the cold stuff to enjoy a visit here.
Tables outdoors (2, pavement). Takeaway service. **Map 17 B4.**

★ Gelupo ⬛HOT 50
7 Archer Street, W1D 7AU (7287 5555, www.gelupo.com). Piccadilly Circus tube. **Open** noon-11pm Mon-Wed, Sun; noon-1am Thur-Sat. **Credit** MC, V.
From the people behind the Italian restaurant Bocca di Lupo just across the road, this gelateria and delicatessen is a joyous celebration of authentic Sicilian ices. Gelato, sorbet and granita are all made with a chef's sensibility of ingredient quality, seasonality and flavour, and the results are spectacular. Around 20 flavours are offered each day and, apart from a few classics such as pistachio ice-cream and strawberry sorbet, recipes tend to be sophisticated. Take the summer pudding gelato – not merely a mix of berries, but one that is marbled with vodka- and mulberry-soaked sponge. Among our favourites at Gelupo are the sheep's milk ricotta and black pepper ice-cream marbled with chocolate sauce, and refreshing, jewel-coloured mint granita. Can't decide? Order three in a tub or large cone, or scooped into a sugar-crusted brioche-cum-doughnut, which adds a delicious layer of wickedness to the experience. Sit at one of the bar stools in the front or at the park bench in the rear deli section; with its pale blue painted boards and blue and white tiling, you can almost believe you're in Sicily.
Tables outdoors (2, pavement). Vegan dishes. **Map 17 B4.**

South Kensington

Oddono's
14 Bute Street, SW7 3EX (7052 0732, www.oddonos.co.uk). South Kensington tube. **Open** 11am-11pm Mon-Thur, Sun; 11am-midnight Fri, Sat. **Credit** AmEx, MC, V.
Oddono's ice-cream wins awards for a reason. This little shop on a South Ken side street looks unremarkable, but the ice-cream is outstanding. Fifteen indulgent flavours of gelato and sorbet glisten under a glass counter. Chocoholics are well catered for, as billows of dark chocolate, milk chocolate, and cookies and cream gelato are voluptuously covered in chunks and swirls of chocolate. Fruit lovers can enjoy pomegranate sorbet, mango sorbet or no-added-sugar banana sorbet. Four gelato flavours change weekly; try to get there when salted caramel is on the menu – it's a revelation. The simple decor of bright yellow walls and candy-coloured stools keeps the focus on gelato; you can even watch it being freshly made in the kitchen at the back. Staff chat excitedly in Italian, their T-shirts emblazoned with the motto 'Life's too short for bad ice-cream'. How right they are.
Tables outdoors (2, pavement). Takeaway service. Vegan dishes. **Map 14 D10.**

West
Ladbroke Grove

Dri Dri Gelato
189 Portobello Road, W11 2ED (3490 5027, www.dridrigelato.com). Ladbroke Grove or Notting Hill Gate tube. **Open** noon-10.30pm Mon-Thur, Sun; 11am-11pm Fri, Sat. **Credit** MC, V.
'Dri Dri' is an affectionate diminutive of Adriano, the Italian proprietor, who's usually to be found behind the long marble counter and its 20 silvery pozzetti lids that hide the gelato and sorbet from view. All ices are made in-house, with organic milk (in the gelato) and without the use of artificial additives: the pistachio is a natural creamy-beige colour, for instance, rather than vivid green. A few of the flavours were too sweet for our taste, but the deep ruby-red French cherry sorbet, when paired with the astringent Sorrento lemon sorbet, was just right; and the crema 'dri dri' (the house special) was a decadent, velvet-smooth cream with swirls of sesame caramel. Dri Dri's popularity has led to a second outlet in Chelsea Farmers' Market, and a pop-up summer shop in Covent Garden (check the website for news of a repeat).
Babies and children welcome: high chairs. Takeaway service. **Map 19 B3.**
For branch see index.

South West
Chelsea

Gelateria Valerie
9 Duke of York Square, SW3 4LY (7730 7978, www.patisserie-valerie.co.uk). Sloane Square tube. **Open** 7.30am-7.30pm daily. **Credit** AmEx, MC, V.

Gelato here is good, but it's the location that really sells Pâtisserie Valerie's gelateria. The impressive glass building has a long glass counter with tall swivel stools running along one window. Customers tuck into colourful bowls of gelato while looking out on to Duke of York Square, as shoppers look back enviously at the ice-cream sundaes. If weather allows, the patio is a relaxing place to sip Italian coffee too. Portions are generous; three balls looked more like five, piled into an old-fashioned glass. Mandarin sorbet tasted creamy and had a fresh fruity aftertaste, and double chocolate was, indeed, double delicious with its dark chocolate swirls. Pistachio had a creamy nuttiness and vibrant green colour – ask for a drizzle of dark caramel sauce for a real treat. *Babies and children admitted. Tables outdoors (30, terrace). Takeaway service.* **Map 14 F11**.

North
Camden Town & Chalk Farm

★ Chin Chin Laboratorists
49-50 Camden Lock Place, NW1 8AF (07885 604284 mobile, www.chinchinlabs.com). Camden Town tube. **Open** noon-7pm Tue-Sun. **No credit cards**.
Within months of opening, Chin Chin Labs become a Camden Market legend. Europe's first nitro ice-cream parlour (the mixes are fast-frozen in front of customers' eyes using liquid nitrogen) has staff who wear white lab coats and protective goggles, and takes inspiration from the molecular gastronomy movement for its manufacturing process and flavour combinations. Co-founder Ahrash Akbari-Kalhur initially trained to be a pastry chef and has a gourmet's appreciation of technique and ingredients. Specials, such as blueberry buttermilk pancake ice-cream, served with bacon sugar shards and Valrhona chocolate sauce, or the comparatively simple orange and bayleaf ice-cream, change weekly and cleverly tempt customers back. Visit off-peak and they'll happily talk you through the creation process, pointing out the gas tank by the door. Once your ice-cream is made and scooped, choose from toppings such as salted caramel sauce, raspberry coulis and caramelised pecans. Space is limited; there's just a few items of garden furniture to perch on, plus swings by the door, so head down to Camden Lock to enjoy. *Babies and children admitted. Tables outdoors (3, pavement). Takeaway service. Vegan dishes.* **Map 27 C1**.

North West
Belsize Park

Gelato Mio
204 Haverstock Hill, NW3 2AG (7998 9276, www.gelatomio.co.uk). Belsize Park tube. **Open** 7.30am-10pm Mon-Thur; 7.30am-11pm Fri, 9am-11pm Sat; 9am-10pm Sun. **Credit** AmEx, MC, V.
From its first shop in Holland Park, Gelato Mio is now scattered across north and west London like nuts on a sundae. The spacious Belsize Park branch makes the most of the wide pavement and leafy surrounds with plenty of outdoor tables and a

Icecreamists. See p304.

swing seat that pleases both kids and adults. As the name suggests, Italian-style gelato is the draw; ingredient quality is high and the flavours are true, with options changing weekly. The cioccolato, made with dark Belgian chocolate, and amarena (black cherries mixed with fior di latte) are especially good; children will love the clean-tasting banana flavour, and parents can rest assured there's nothing artificial in the mix. For parties, you can order gelato cakes, customised flavours or even a full-sized ice-cream display, complete with staff to scoop. Take-home tubs are available, though, at £10 for 500ml, they're no bargain. *Babies and children welcome: high chairs. Disabled: toilet. Tables outdoors (8, pavement). Takeaway service.* **Map 28 C3**.
For branches see index.

Hampstead

Slice of Ice
8 Flask Walk, NW3 1HE (7419 9908, www.slice-of-ice.co.uk). Hampstead tube. **Open** *Summer* 11am-7pm Mon-Fri; 11am-10pm Sat, Sun. *Winter* 11am-7pm daily. **Credit** AmEx, MC, V.
Tucked away on a pedestrianised strip of Hampstead Village that's as skinny as the jeans of the local glitterati, this cheerful white and lime green spot fuses an Italian-style gelateria with the health appeal of machine-dispensed frozen yoghurt and the likes of matcha (green tea) fruit smoothies. Gelato isn't made on the premises, but bought in from north London producer Il Gelato di Ariela, whose standards are high. The dark, almost black, chocolate sorbet is a winning choice for evenings, but perhaps a bit heady in the morning. Our hazelnut and pistachio scoops had clear nutty flavours, and we loved the chewy, sour cherry pieces in the yoghurt-based amarena. Slice of Ice's

discerning choice of suppliers extends to L'Artisan du Chocolat, Teapigs and local cake makers (the brownie, and lemon and almond cake are terrific). Union lattes and cappuccinos are well made too. A few trendy white tables (and a toilet) are available for those who want to eat in. *Babies and children welcome: high chairs. Disabled: toilet. Takeaway service. Vegan dishes.* **Map 28 C2**.

Outer London
Richmond, Surrey

Gelateria Danieli
16 Brewers Lane, Richmond, Surrey, TW9 1HH (8439 9807, www.gelateriadanieli.com). Richmond tube/rail. **Open** *Summer* 10am-10pm daily. *Winter* 10am-6pm daily. Times may vary, phone to check. **No credit cards**.
The tiny lanes between Richmond Green and the high street are full of delightful little surprises, though you'll be forewarned about Gelateria Danieli by the queue extending from the door on warm summer days. Two dozen flavours of superior gelato and sorbet are available at one time, drawn from a house list of more than 100 recipes. Standards, such as Sicily-grown pistachio and the not-guilty pleasure of dairy-free chocolate sorbet, are supplemented by seasonal berry sorbets in summer and more fanciful inventions such as Christmas pudding ice-cream. Wooden floorboards and a couple of chairs inside make it cosy in winter and at quieter times, when you can also enjoy a coffee without feeling too cramped; if the weather's good, you'll be happier lazing about on the Green, watching the cricketers, tub in hand. *Takeaway service.*
For branches see index.

Pizza & Pasta

So simple, so cheap, so ubiquitous – and yet so rarely done right. Pizza and pasta joints are ten-a-penny in London, and the relatively low cost of production has meant the corporate big boys have been quick to muscle-in. Nearly every high street has a chain pizza outlet, where concept is all (Ital-American, bizarre toppings, smoochy setting), but food is average. Most also offer a batch of cooking-by-numbers pasta dishes too. Where did they go wrong? In a word: texture. Sample the best Italy has to offer and the pasta sauces and pizza toppings can seem ludicrously simple, but the dishes sing like Caruso because the basic ingredients have been cooked to split-second perfection: succulent, al dente pasta; light, crisp pizza bases with soft interiors. Such exactitude needs a feel for cookery rarely found in the chain gangs. Brixton's **Franco Manca** led the way in boosting the standards of London's pizzerias when it opened in 2008; let's hope their expansion doesn't dilute quality – we've found the Chiswick outlet equally good so far. More recently, Ealing's **Santa Maria**, which sources ingredients direct from Italy, has joined the top of the tree; and the new Portobello Road branch of **Pizza East** is a typically slick outfit from the fashionable Soho House group. As we went to press, our long-time favourite **Story Deli** was on the move again (this time, to 3 Redchurch Street, E2 7DJ, 07918 197352, www.storydeli.com).

Central

Clerkenwell & Farringdon

Santoré
59-61 Exmouth Market, EC1R 4QL (7812 1488). Farringdon tube/rail or bus 19, 38, 341. **Meals served** noon-11pm daily. **Main courses** £7.65-£15.95. **Set lunch** (noon-3pm) £8.95 2 courses. **Set dinner** (3-7pm) £12.95 2 courses. **Credit** AmEx, MC, V.

Santoré seems to divide opinion: some diners can't get enough of its authentic Neapolitan food; others can't forgive the occasionally tetchy service. On our most recent midweek visit, however, we were greeted warmly by the staff who happily recommended their favourite dishes on the menu. The place was packed with diners. As with many a good trattoria, the decor – unspectacular brown furniture with wine bottles and a pizza oven for decoration – means little compared to the food. A generous plate of antipasti included at least ten items (from a moreish warm aubergine salad to own-cured salmon with pink peppercorns) – and was a gift at £8.95. 'I panuozzi' pizza, where the dough is first baked and then filled (in our case, with spring greens, mozzarella and porky fennel sausage), was simply delicious if just slightly burnt. Fresh fusilli pasta with clams and succulent

Sicilian prawns was brilliantly spicy. Only the desserts of own-made tiramisu and sorbets were average. We're inclined to forgive the uneven service for such big-hearted food and prices.
Available for hire. Babies and children welcome: booster seats. Tables outdoors (10, pavement). Takeaway service; delivery service (over £8 within 3-mile radius). **Map 5 N4**.

Covent Garden

Fire & Stone
31-32 Maiden Lane, WC2E 7JS (0844 371 2550, www.fireandstone.com). Covent Garden or Leicester Square tube. **Lunch served** noon-4.30pm daily. **Dinner served** 4.30pm-12.30am Mon-Wed; 4.30pm-1am Thur-Sat; 4.30pm-midnight Sun. **Main courses** £6.95-£10.25. **Set meal** £16.50 3 courses incl drink. **Credit** AmEx, DC, MC, V.

There's no shortage of passably good pizza spots in Covent Garden, but sheer novelty value sets Fire & Stone apart. Its outlandish menu keeps classic Italian toppings to a bare minimum, preferring to make a sometimes-crude stab at reflecting international flavours. So you get cumberland sausage, mushrooms and egg on the London pizza, and a rather frightening combination of yellow coconut curry, sweet potato and mozzarella on the koh samui. The gimmick seems to go down well

with large groups of young diners, as well as families looking to keep the little ones entertained. For the timid, there are also toppings that make a less jarring fit with the doughy, flatbread-like bases. The marrakech, for example, tastes akin to a lahmacun (Turkish-style pizza with minced lamb), and the bombay, with its tandoori chicken and mango chutney, is pleasing enough. The huge restaurant – set over two floors and featuring long banquettes and a modish orange and brown colour scheme – can accommodate 250 diners.
Available for hire. Babies and children welcome: children's menu; high chairs; nappy-changing facilities. Booking advisable weekends. Disabled: toilet. Takeaway service. **Map 18 E5**. **For branches see index**.

Rossopomodoro
50-52 Monmouth Street, WC2H 9EP (7240 9095, www.rossopomodoro.co.uk). Covent Garden tube. **Meals served** noon-11.30pm daily. **Main courses** £7-£14. **Set lunch** (noon-3pm Mon-Fri) £9.99 2 courses. **Credit** AmEx, MC, V.

Part of a global chain of some 80 outlets (but with just three in London), this cheery restaurant clearly retains its modern Neapolitan roots – and its popularity. The paintwork and crockery are as bright as the smiles of the welcoming staff, while the mosaic-tiled pizza unit (complete with wood-fired oven) inspires confidence. This carries through, in part, to the swiftly supplied dishes. Neapolitan flour makes for a nicely chewy pizza dough, charred and smoky, while the tomato sauce is zesty; handmade scialatielli pasta had intrinsic flavour and sound texture; air-freighted buffalo milk cheeses delighted with their freshness. Stray too far from Naples, though, and disappointment might ensue. On our 'affettati' plate, the caponatina from Sicily was barely more than chopped, bland tomato on toast; parma ham was young, crude and ill-flavoured. Among the ices, buffalo milk 'fior di late' was great, others less so. Prices aren't too steep, but don't quite carry the lapses. Nonetheless, the place was buzzing with Italians eager for a taste of home.

Babies and children welcome: high chairs. Booking advisable pre-theatre, weekends. Separate room for parties, seats 60. Tables outdoors (5, pavement). Takeaway service. **Map 18 D4.**
For branches see index.

Euston

Pasta Plus

62 Eversholt Street, NW1 1DA (7383 4943, www.pastaplus.co.uk). Euston tube/rail. **Lunch served** noon-2.30pm Mon-Fri. **Dinner served** 5.30-10.30pm Mon-Sat. **Main courses** £6.50-£16. **Credit** AmEx, DC, MC, V.
Far better than its name and dingy location suggest, this unassuming Italian eaterie is a favourite with nearby office workers and those seeking a more leisurely lunch than Euston station can offer. Inside, it's light and airy, with a glass roof at the back and tasteful art on the walls. The menu covers a well-considered selection of pasta, meat and seafood: mostly conventional, but with a few more exciting dishes. Cannelloni and ravioli were both tastily stuffed; sea bass arrived well presented, with a generous side of veg; and veal milanese was delicious and impressively huge. Prices are low and service is understated yet efficient. If not quite a diamond in the rough, Pasta Plus is still a surprisingly good find.
Available for hire. Babies and children welcome: high chairs. Separate room for parties, seats 26. Tables outdoors (26, conservatory). **Map 4 K3.**

Mayfair

Rocket

4-6 Lancashire Court, off New Bond Street, W1S 1EY (7629 2889, www.rocket restaurants.co.uk). Bond Street or Oxford Circus tube.
Bar **Open** noon-11pm Mon-Sat; noon-10pm Sun. **Meals served** noon-10pm Sun. **Main courses** £8-£17.
Restaurant **Lunch served** noon-3pm, **dinner served** 6-11pm Mon-Fri. **Meals served** noon-11pm Sat. **Main courses** £8-£17.
Both **Credit** AmEx, MC, V.
Secreted in an atmospheric Mayfair mews, Rocket feels like it should have an 'in the know' vibe – but judging by our Saturday evening visit, plenty of people are in the know. The ground-floor bar bustles, and caters for the post-shopping/post-work crowds; upstairs is an uncluttered and bright space dominated by a floor-to-ceiling wine display (there's a good selection by the glass). Food is largely of the pizza/pasta variety, although it is far too molested by international influences to be called Italian. Some of the dishes work well. The thin, crispy pizza bases feature interesting toppings; a starter of serrano

ham, broad beans and manchego with almonds was bright and fresh. We ordered a 'rare beef and chip salad with rocket, deep-fried green beans, radish and crispy garlic with gingered black bean dressing and a ginger mayonnaise' to find out whether such a collection of ingredients could be wrestled into a coherent whole. They couldn't.
Babies and children welcome: high chairs. Booking advisable. Separate rooms for parties, seating 10 and 26. Tables outdoors (7, pavement). **Map 9 H6.**
For branches see index.

West

Ealing

★ Santa Maria

15 St Mary's Road, W5 5RA (8579 1462, www.santamariapizzeria.com). South Ealing tube. **Meals served** noon-10.30pm daily.
Main courses £4.95-£10.50. **Credit** MC, V.

Lucky Ealing to harbour such a perfectly formed little gem as Santa Maria. Within months of its opening in 2010, this Neapolitan pizzeria was nominated for Best Cheap Eats in our annual Eating & Drinking Awards. Everything, from the quality ingredients to the super-swift firing in the authentic wood oven, is Italian-imported, giving Ealing an experience as close as possible to that you'd enjoy at a streetside table in Naples, apart from the hooting cars and the heat. The secret is consistency; the base will be beautifully chewy and the topping charred to loveliness, whether you keep it simple with a santa margherita or dress things up with, say, neapolitan salame and chilli (santa caterina) or olives, anchovies and capers (san gennaro) – all this for £6.50 for a margherita, and around £8 for something more elaborate. It's a miniscule place and bookings aren't accepted, so be prepared to wait for a table – brisk business also means that service is occasionally brusque.
Babies and children welcome: high chairs. Bookings not accepted. Tables outdoors (2, pavement). Takeaway service.

Santa Maria

Ladbroke Grove

Pizza East Portobello

310 Portobello Road, W10 5TA (8969 4500, www.pizzaeastportobello.com). Ladbroke Grove tube. **Meals served** 8am-11.30pm Mon-Thur; 8am-midnight Fri, Sat; 8am-10.30pm Sun. **Main courses** £7-£17. **Credit** AmEx, DC, MC, V.

The former Fat Badger pub has transformed into a swan under the wing of the achingly fashionable Soho House Group, a company that seems to specialise in charging more than its cooking is worth, but compensates diners with fabulous interiors and a feeling of being in with the in-crowd. Refreshingly, this branch of the Pizza East concept doesn't imitate the hit Shoreditch original. Barring a predilection for white porcelain tiles and the option of bar seating, the two are like night and day: the East Ender's converted warehouse decor just right for clubbers; this sunny spot (with bright blue chairs, large windows and blue and white striped awnings) inspiring alfresco brunches with friends and family. We liked the veal meatball pizza, made still more luxurious with cream, and the spicy sausage, mozzarella and broccoli combo – but the desserts left us cold. Apart from around a dozen pizzas, mains include fillet of beef and roast chicken. Breakfast is also served and, as with the original, there's an on-site deli – though the idea that the Portobello area needs any more retailers of polenta and taleggio is just ridiculous.

Babies and children welcome: high chairs; nappy-changing facilities. Bookings not accepted. Disabled: toilet. Tables outdoors (11, pavement; 4, terrace). **Map 19 B1**.

For branch see index.

Maida Vale

Red Pepper

8 Formosa Street, W9 1EE (7266 2708, http://theredpepper.net). Warwick Avenue tube. **Dinner served** 6.30-11pm Mon-Fri. **Meals served** 11am-11pm Sat; 11am-10.30pm Sun. **Main courses** £9-£17. **Credit** MC, V.

An upmarket haunt for Maida Vale locals, this slightly cramped venue is spread over a ground floor and basement, and also does brisk business in takeaway orders. Dine-in customers come here mainly for posh pizzas, pastas and risottos, though they might also choose one of the rustic Italian specialities for added interest. A crisp first course of shredded raw beetroot, almonds, courgette and carrots, tossed in a lemony dressing, worked well as a light tease. To follow, Red Pepper's own-made pasta delivers quality results; ravioli, generously filled with chunky chopped prawns, fresh tuna and chilli, made a lovely match with a simple buttery sauce. Sadly, our pizza wasn't in the same league, let down by a chewy, too doughy base. Well-priced wines keep costs on the right side of good value. *Babies and children admitted. Booking essential. Separate room for parties, seats 25. Tables outdoors (4, pavement). Takeaway service.*

Westbourne Grove

Mulberry Street

84 Westbourne Grove, W2 5RT (7313 6789, www.mulberrystreet.co.uk). Bayswater or Royal Oak tube. **Meals served** noon-midnight Mon-Sat; noon-11pm Sun. **Main courses** £7.55-£14.95. **Credit** AmEx, MC, V.

It's from New York that this Notting Hill pizzeria takes its cues – a wraparound Times Square street scene covers the walls; a 'walk/don't walk' traffic light flashes in the window. Spacious booths accommodate groups and families, and screens show US sports. From the oven come massive, thick-crust, piping-hot pies, loaded with the usual combination of toppings: pepperoni, parma ham, mozzarella, peppers, gorgonzola, mushrooms. You can order them by the slice for variation. The rest of the menu is made up of solid renditions of Italian-American carby classics and salads (chicken milanese, pastas arrabbiata and bolognese, caesar salad). Hot fudge sundae and tiramisu are among the standard desserts – though die-hard fans could try the chocolate pizza. Mulberry Street is a reliable all-rounder and fun, if unremarkable.

Available for hire. Babies and children welcome: high chairs. Booking advisable. Separate room for parties, seats 30. Takeaway service; delivery service (over £20 within 5-mile radius). **Map 7 B6**.

South West

Fulham

Napulé

585 Fulham Road, SW6 5UA (7381 1122, www.madeinitalygroup.co.uk). Fulham Broadway tube. **Lunch served** noon-3.30pm Sat, Sun. **Dinner served** 6-11.30pm Mon-Sat; 6-10.30pm Sun. **Main courses** £6.50-£16. **Credit** MC, V.

Napulé's smudgy exterior may need a lick of paint, but it's the wood-burning pizza oven inside that counts. That's jumping ahead, though: first was antipasto misto, highlighted by oozing, garlicky bruschetta. Shame about the vegetables though: aubergines starved of olive oil lacked nuttiness; and charred potato slices were out of place. Stick to pizza if you appreciate good dough. Our siciliana – own-made ricotta and aubergine with charred chewy crust, eaten to the beat of crazed Italian music – was a triumph, but the rubbery fra rosario (mozzarella, sun-dried tomatoes, roast potatoes, sausage, onion, capers) with its inexplicable lack of rosemary left us cold. The all-Italian waiters

Donna Margherita

recommended little cantucci biscuits dipped in plummy passito wine for pudding: a posh touch, but not as satisfying as the tiramisu.

Available for hire. Babies and children welcome: high chairs. Booking advisable. Separate room for parties, seats 14. Takeaway service. **Map 13 A13**.

For branches (Luna Rossa, Made In Italy, Marechiaro, Regina Margherita, Santa Lucia) see index.

South

Balham

Ciullo's

31 Balham High Road, SW12 9AL (8675 3072). Clapham South tube or Balham tube/rail. **Dinner served** 6-11pm Mon-Thur; 6-11.30pm Fri, Sat. **Meals served** noon-10.30pm Sun. **Main courses** £7-£16.90. **Credit** MC, V.

Concessions to modernity in this traditional Italian restaurant are few: a sudden interjection of sculpted design in the dessert plates; downlighters to boost tea lights set in candelabras. Yet the comforting, generously portioned dishes and warm service, set against a background of Italian repartee, are no more outdated or undesirable than the cheery Beryl Cook prints lining the walls. Toddlers tuck in happily alongside grandparents; groups of young Italians rub shoulders with evening shoppers. Nothing startles on the menu: the seafood and meat dishes, pastas and pizzas are all variants of long-established combos. Our pasta was al dente but no challenge to dentures; the pizza crust was nicely charred and chewy; greenery included deep-fried battered courgettes; sorbet in a hollowed-out lemon was sit-up zesty; and decent coffee made a robust finale. Half-bottles of house wine were gluggable and good value. Leftovers are deftly packed up in microwave plastic or cardboard boxes to polish off at home (Ciullo's has a popular takeaway service). Locals no doubt wish the place many more years of service.

Available for hire. Babies and children welcome: high chairs. Booking advisable. Tables outdoors (3, terrace). Takeaway service.

Battersea

Donna Margherita
*183 Lavender Hill, SW11 5TE (7228 2660,
www.donna-margherita.com). Clapham Junction
rail.* **Dinner served** 5-10.30pm Mon-Thur;
5-11pm Fri. **Meals served** noon-11pm Sat;
12.30-10.30pm Sun. **Main courses** £7-£18.50.
Credit AmEx, DC, MC, V.
Much-praised Donna Margherita might well be the
closest you'll get to an authentic Neapolitan pizzeria
in London, which is to say it's loud and chaotic, the
waiters are a little mad – and maddeningly slow –
but it's good fun, with a constant stream of local
and expat custom. Choose from own-made pastas,
pricier meat and fish dishes, and a good list of both
classic and unusual wood-fired pizzas. Our cone-
shaped pizza wasn't quite as adventurous as we
imagined, the 'cone' being more of a flap filled with
a slightly bland ricotta and ham mix; the base could
have been crisper too. Desserts include soufflé-like
tortino di ricotta. The three Italian bottled beers
offered make the best match with the pizzas.
*Available for hire. Babies and children welcome:
high chairs. Booking advisable. Tables outdoors
(8, terrace). Takeaway service; delivery service
(over £10 within 1-mile radius).* **Map 21 C3**.

Pizza Metro
*64 Battersea Rise, SW11 1EQ (7228 3812,
www.pizzametropizza.com). Clapham Junction
rail.* **Dinner served** 6pm-midnight Mon-Fri.
Meals served noon-midnight Sat, Sun.
Main courses £8.50-£16.50. **Credit** MC, V.
Tables are hard to come by, even midweek, at the
original branch of this jolly pizza joint. Pizza Metro
is popular with groups, including children
celebrating birthdays, when the trademark
shareable 'metre-long' pizzas come into their own.
Consequently, couples can find themselves a bit
squeezed in. The menu is extensive, with a lengthy
list of pasta dishes and more than 20 pizzas, as well
as a few meat and fish dishes (ribeye, swordfish). A
slab of lasagne crammed with extras including
sausage pieces looked too big to manage, but
manage it we very happily did. The pizza toppings
are a little more restrained, the combinations well
chosen; salami and buffalo ricotta had a lovely
balance of creaminess and spice. You won't want
to cut off the crusts – they're as flavoursome as the
centre. Desserts, though, are an afterthought; ice-
cream tartufo was pleasant, but not a patch on the
mains. The all-Italian wine list has some high-end
bottles for special occasions.
*Babies and children welcome: high chairs.
Booking advisable. Takeaway service; delivery
service (Tue-Sun, over £15 within 2-mile radius).*
Map 21 C4.
For branch see index.

Brixton

★ Franco Manca
*4 Market Row, Electric Lane, SW9 8LD
(7738 3021, www.francomanca.co.uk). Brixton
tube/rail.* **Meals served** noon-5pm Mon-Wed;
noon-9pm Thur-Sat; noon-4pm Sun. **Main
courses** £5-£7.50. **Credit** MC, V.
Giuseppe Mascoli's much-lauded pizza joint began
trading in 2008, and investment has since seen
branches opening in Chiswick and Westfield
Stratford, along with talk of expansion into the
West End. But you wouldn't know that from a visit

to the original, still in the same spot split by a
corridor across two sites at the unfashionable end
of Brixton market. The place continues to be full
(fit to bursting, in fact) most afternoons, thanks to
the best – and given that, the most reasonably
priced – pizza in London. The secret is in the bases,
which are prepared the day before and then cooked
for 40 seconds at high temperature. The menu is
simple: six different pizzas, none with fancy names,
but instead with excessively generous toppings that
are impeccably sourced – the ham comes from
Gloucester Old Spot pigs, the ricotta and mozzarella
from Alham Wood Organics in Somerset, the
tomatoes from Salerno. To drink, there's organic
wine, beer and lemonade. Ridiculously satisfying.
*Babies and children admitted. Bookings not
accepted. Disabled: toilet. Tables outdoors
(10, market). Takeaway service. Vegan dishes.*
Map 22 E2.
For branches see index.

Clapham

Eco
*162 Clapham High Street, SW4 7UG (7978
1108, www.ecorestaurants.com). Clapham
Common tube.* **Meals served** 11am-11.30pm
Mon-Fri, Sun; 11am-midnight Sat. **Main
courses** £6.75-£14.90. **Credit** AmEx, MC, V.
Once on the frontline of the new wave of pizza
restaurants, Eco now seems something of an old-
timer. The curvy decor still demonstrates a
commitment to breaking up the lines of a long, thin
room, but the contoured boards on the ceiling and
around the bar are looking a little battered. It's the
same with the pizzas, which were once about the
best you could get in the capital, yet have now been
left trailing by newcomers such as Franca Manca.
Portions are generous and the toppings fresh, but
our sourdough base was a little chewy. In contrast,
the pasta – so often an afterthought in a pizza joint
– was excellent, with a rich but not too creamy
carbonara sauce going down well. Reasonable
prices help paper over any culinary cracks.
*Babies and children welcome: high chairs. Booking
advisable; essential weekends. Tables outdoors
(4, pavement). Takeaway service.* **Map 22 A2**.
For branch see index.

South East

Peckham

Gowlett
*62 Gowlett Road, SE15 4HY (7635 7048,
www.thegowlett.com). East Dulwich or Peckham
Rye rail or bus 12, 37, 63.* **Open** noon-midnight
Mon-Thur; noon-1am Fri, Sat; noon-11.30pm
Sun. **Lunch served** 12.30-2.30pm, **dinner
served** 6.30-10.30pm Mon-Fri. **Meals served**
12.30-10.30pm Sat; 12.30-9pm Sun. **Main
courses** £7.50-£9.50. **Credit** AmEx, DC, MC, V.
Located up a sidestreet almost exactly halfway
between East Dulwich and Peckham – but proudly
labelling itself a Peckham local on its website – the
Gowlett is a large, old-fashioned, open-plan corner
pub, shabby and down-at-heel in a reassuringly
unpretentious way. It's an unexpected place to find
food of any quality, let alone pizzas as impressive
as the beauties that emerge from the kitchen. Huge
discs of thin, crusty bases come saturated in
toppings to form pizzas that would grace just
about any specialist establishment. Our siciliana
was a salty feast of anchovies and capers, while
an american hot was spicy and filling. The menu
isn't extensive and warns that pizzas can take a
while to appear at busy times, but locals seem
happy to wait, content in the knowledge that
they're on to a good thing.
*Babies and children welcome until 9pm: high
chairs; nappy-changing facilities. Disabled: toilet.
Tables outdoors (4, garden; 4, pavement).
Takeaway service.*

East

Bethnal Green

StringRay Globe Café,
Bar & Pizzeria
*109 Columbia Road, E2 7RL (7613 1141,
www.stringraycafe.co.uk). Hoxton rail or bus
26, 48, 55.* **Meals served** 11am-11pm daily.
Main courses £6.95-£11.95. **Credit** AmEx,
MC, V.

Franco Manca

Located towards the east end of Columbia Road, this friendly branch of the StringRay mini-chain is buzzing during and after the Sunday flower market. Dark wooden tables are crammed into a former pub space, now painted in bright red, orange and blue. The inexpensive menu focuses on pizza and pasta, but also has a few meat and fish options, as well as a special children's menu. Enormous calzones are the main attractions; all regular pizzas can be folded into dough pockets, generously filled with the usual toppings, starting at the bargain price of £4.95. Maybe it's not the best idea to transform a capricciosa pizza into a calzone, however – the egg white was still runny and came oozing out of our otherwise delicious pizza. No complaints, though, about a garlicky cannelloni with spinach and rocket.
Babies and children welcome: children's menu; high chairs. Booking essential. Tables outdoors (7, pavement). Takeaway service. **Map 6 S3**.

Shoreditch

Furnace
1 Rufus Street, N1 6PE (7613 0598, www.hoxtonfurnace.com). Old Street tube/ rail or Shoreditch High Street rail. **Dinner served** 6-11pm Sat. **Meals served** noon-11pm Mon-Fri. **Main courses** £6.95-£11.50. **Credit** MC, V.
Furnace's crisp logo recalls the plentiful design agencies round Shoreditch these days. Inside, the old building has an airy industrial feel created by exposed brick and wooden beams – plus a Banksy print and a wall-mounted bicycle. Starters are hearty considering the carb-fest to follow; a poached blade of beef with salsa verde and horseradish was rather blunt in flavour. The 'porketta' pizza (sliced suckling pig, sour cream, fennel and salsa verde) is just one of the many bells-and-whistles examples of toppings here. A few pasta, meat and fish options are chalked up as specials; sea bass with fennel was moist and light. To finish, a zabaglione-filled tartufo nero was the sort of dessert you hankered after as a kid from the saturated-colour picture menus on holidays abroad.
Babies and children admitted. Separate room for parties, seats 50. Takeaway service. **Map 6 R4**.

Wapping

Il Bordello
81 Wapping High Street, E1W 2YN (7481 9950). Wapping rail. **Lunch served** noon-3pm Mon-Fri. **Dinner served** 6-11pm Mon-Sat. **Meals served** 1-10.30pm Sun. **Main courses** £8.45-£26.95. **Credit** AmEx, DC, MC, V.
There can't be many Italian restaurants where a queue forms before the doors have opened, but Il Bordello is one such – though, frankly, we find it hard to see why. Service was friendly and solicitous, and families with young children were particularly in evidence on our visit. Portions were ample, stopping all but the hardiest trenchermen in their tracks. A misto starter of salami, cheese and olives provided a bite for all our party of five, and pizzas were generously topped, but the olives tasted like they came from a jar, and the mozzarella was flavourless. We began to feel we might have been happier at one of the big pizza chains. Spaghetti alla vongole was better, the sauce nicely poked up with chilli. A huge specials board covers everything from swordfish to fillet steak with dolcelatte

(another generous serving, costing £26), but we couldn't help feeling that quality had generally been sacrificed for quantity. Prices are hefty too – up to £13.95 for a pizza and a positively cheeky £2.85 for a glass of generic lemonade.
Babies and children welcome: high chairs. Booking advisable. Disabled: toilet. Takeaway service. Vegetarian menu.

North East
Stoke Newington

Il Bacio
61 Stoke Newington Church Street, N16 0AR (7249 3833). Stoke Newington rail or bus 73, 393, 476. **Dinner served** 6-11.15pm Mon-Fri. **Meals served** noon-11.15pm Sat, Sun. **Main courses** £9-£16. **Credit** MC, V.
There's a lot of exposed flesh in cosy little Il Bacio – mostly on the walls. If you're on a date, you might want to consider your choice of table: set under a painting of a naked man with a leaf between his legs, or maybe the fresco of two embracing lovers. This is the original branch of a small group of Italian restaurants with a focus on Sardinia (look out for the likes of malloreddus pasta with spicy barbaricina sausage, or spaghetti with bottarga – dried mullet roe – and clams). A starter of parma ham and poached pear looked as if it had come straight from a 1950s cookbook; the salty ham went well with the pears, but these tasted more tinned than poached. We continued with an excellent pizza bacione, its crisp base generously topped with creamy mozzarella and courgette, contrasted with bitter slices of radicchio and gorgonzola. Share a big slab of tiramisu for the perfect finish.
Babies and children welcome: high chairs. Booking advisable. Tables outdoors (3, pavement). Takeaway service; delivery service (over £10 within 2-mile radius). **Map 25 B1**.
For branches see index.

North West
Hampstead

★ Fratelli la Bufala
45A South End Road, NW3 2QB (7435 7814, www.fratellilabufala.com). Belsize Park tube or Hampstead Heath rail. **Lunch served** noon-3pm Fri. **Dinner served** 6-11pm Mon-Fri. **Meals served** noon-11pm Sat, Sun. **Main courses** £8-£29. **Set lunch** (Fri) £9.50 2 courses. **Credit** MC, V.
Not the animal it was when it first opened, this (posh) neighbourhood Italian has dropped its colourful buffalo-themed decor. The new creamy-toned interior with comfortable high-backed chairs, coupled with solicitous, uniformed service, makes Fratelli la Bufala more restaurant than pizzeria or trattoria. But the white-tiled, wood-fired oven still takes centre stage, pumping out excellent pizzas to eat in or take away. Our bianco-style nuraghe pizza was a sumptuous affair contrasting creamy buffalo mozzarella with the salty, fishy kick of anchovies. From the specials board, which emphasises fresh fish dishes such as sea bass cooked in cartoccio (a bag), we chose one of the least expensive options, a homely and satisfying mixed seafood lasagne, which arrived as a hearty high-rise slab. City high-flyers and American expats living locally tend to

use this place as a premium alternative to family restaurant chains, but Fratelli la Bufala welcomes a variety of Hampstead Heath visitors – and if you choose carefully, it need not cost a lot.
Available for hire. Babies and children welcome: high chairs. Booking advisable dinner. Separate room for parties, seats 20. Tables outdoors (4, pavement). Takeaway service. **Map 28 C3**.

Kilburn

Betsy Smith
77 Kilburn High Road, NW6 6HY (7624 5793, www.thebetsysmith.co.uk). Kilburn Park tube. **Meals served** 9am-10pm daily. **Main courses** £8.75-£14.95. **Credit** AmEx, MC, V.
Formerly a shabby local called the Bridge, this pub has been spruced up with a resolutely on-trend 'junk shop chic' look – birdcages, charity shop paintings and other vintage stuff. If as much effort went into the food, the owners would be on to a winner. Yet despite the £180 champagne and a massive cocktail list, we reckon the Betsy Smith is all fur coat and no knickers: an apt description for some of the scantily clad punters too. The menu covers all bases (breakfasts, nachos, burgers and bistro dishes like spaghetti with clams), including a long list of pizzas from the wood-fired oven. The pizzas are the best bet, and are reasonably priced; the toppings may be more notable for their quantity than quality, but after a few drinks, they'll do.
Available for hire. Babies and children welcome: high chairs. Booking advisable. Tables outdoors (15, decking). Takeaway service. **Map 1 B1**.

West Hampstead

La Brocca
273 West End Lane, NW6 1QS (7433 1989, www.labrocca.co.uk). West Hampstead tube/ rail or bus 139, C11. **Bar Open** noon-11pm Mon-Thur; noon-1am Fri; 11am-1am Sat; 11am-midnight Sun. **Lunch served** noon-5pm Mon-Fri; 11am-5pm Sat, Sun. **Main courses** £9-£15. *Restaurant* **Dinner served** 6-11pm daily. **Main courses** £9-£15. *Both* **Credit** AmEx, MC, V.
Food is served in La Brocca's ground-floor bar during the day, but at 6pm, the pizza restaurant opens downstairs. The staircase from the street looks a bit unlikely, though there's a friendly welcome at the bottom. The basement has been extended to fill the garden, with the back half a glass conservatory. It looks more cheerful when dark has fallen and the lights outside add some atmosphere. Pizza and pasta account for most of the menu, but the specials board always includes a few meat and fish dishes. Pizzas have a thin base and generous toppings; the egg on a capricciosa was perfectly soft. Alterations to accommodate children's palates were met with a friendly 'of course' by the warm, patient waitress. La Brocca isn't trying to be inventive. It's an old-fashioned spot that plays well to its fortes. Spaghetti bolognese looked like it lacked sauce, but proved very tasty. To finish, we lingered over dishes of Jude's ice-cream and a sunken chocolate cake – a warm molten slice of heaven.
Babies and children welcome: high chairs. Booking advisable weekends. Separate room for parties, seats 40. Tables outdoors (3, pavement). Takeaway service. **Map 28 A2**.

Drinking

Bars

The newcomers shortlisted for the 2011 Best New Bar award exemplify recent trends in the capital's ever-evolving bar scene: the **Experimental Cocktail Club** is a speakeasy-style drinking den; **Zetter Townhouse** takes antiques shop clutter to new heights; the **Booking Office** sits within the High Victorian magnificence of the refurbished St Pancras Hotel; and the **Worship Street Whistling Shop** channels Dickensian London in its setting, staff costumes and historical libations. What unites them all is the flair and creativity of their drinks lists, masterminded with geek-like fervour and attention to detail by enthusiastic staff. As for less recent arrivals and long-established favourites, it's often easiest to choose the type of bar by area of town: head to swankier parts of the West End for classic hotel bars, the City and the South Bank for stunning views, and Shoreditch for hipster-oriented hangouts. You'll find excellent neighbourhood operations futher afield too, in the likes of Balham, Greenwich and Tooting.

Central
Chinatown

Experimental Cocktail Club NEW
2011 RUNNER-UP BEST NEW BAR
13A Gerrard Street, W1D 5PS (7434 3559, www. chinatownecc.com). Leicester Square tube. **Open** 6pm-3am Mon-Sat; 5-11pm Sun. **Credit** MC, V.
'Speakeasies' are a current trend, but as bar owners balance covertness with the economic reality of bringing in punters, some of the thrill is lost. ECC is perhaps the closest London has to a genuine hidden drinking den, and the fact that it's on touristy Gerrard Street makes it even more interesting. Head through the scruffy door to find two floors designed in a tasteful blend of fin-de-siècle opulence and antiques shop chic. A gang of clearly fanatical barmen work in front of a display of top-end spirits that includes vintage 1950s Gordon's (made into a martini for £150). The concise list shows astounding creativity, but never lets 'molecular mixology' get in the way of drinkability: a St-Germain-des-Prés, for example, contained Hendrick's gin with elderflower liqueur, egg white, chilli, lime and cucumber. Cocktails are perfectly balanced and unusual; the fact they're a decent £10 adds to their appeal.
Map 17 C4.

City

★ Vertigo 42
Tower 42, 25 Old Broad Street, EC2N 1HQ (7877 7842, www.vertigo42.co.uk). Bank tube/DLR or Liverpool Street tube/rail. **Open** noon-4.30pm, 5-11pm Mon-Fri; 5-11pm Sat. **Food served** noon-2.30pm, 5-9.30pm Mon-Fri; 5-9.30pm Sat. **Credit** AmEx, DC, MC, V.
You'll need to make a reservation, promise a £10 minimum spend, head through airport-style security gates ('no coins, keys or mobiles?'), take the escalator to your left and then find the lift dedicated to level 42. But the views make it worth the effort. By day, they're amazing, even discombobulating: the sort of clichéd bird's-eye views not even aeroplane windows can deliver. Within a small circle of bar space with a walk-round mirror at its core, you see 360° views of building upon building for mile after mile. As you gawp from a sci-fi retro chair in Teletubby colours (purple predominates), champagne is the way to go, from entry-level Pannier Brut to a magnum of Krug Clos du Mesnil. House wine costs a shade over £9 a glass, but house wine you can have in the real world.
Booking essential. Disabled: lift, toilet. Dress: smart casual. **Map 12 Q6**.

Clerkenwell & Farringdon

Giant Robot
45-47 Clerkenwell Road, EC1M 5RS (7065 6810, www.gntrbt.com). Farringdon tube/rail. **Open** 10am-midnight Mon-Wed; 10am-2am Thur-Sat; 10am-10pm Sun. **Food served** 10am-11pm Mon-Wed; 10am-1am Thur-Sat; 10am-5pm Sun. **Credit** MC, V.
The building that formerly held Match EC1 was revamped in 2010 by Match supremo Jonathan Downey, and in pretty fine style. Lined with brick walls and a handsome tin ceiling, Giant Robot pulls off the neat and unusual trick of feeling both industrial and cosy, and the split-personality nature of the decor extends to the food and drinks. During the day, it's a café-diner offering coffees, snacks and Italo-American food favourites such as spaghetti with meatballs, and salt beef. In the evenings, you can dine or just drink from a fine, American-themed cocktail list (the manhattan stars Rittenhouse rye, a Brooklyn cocktail comes with Woodford Reserve). And the later it gets, the more the drinks come to the fore. A welcome and successful reinvention.
Babies and children admitted until 8pm. Disabled: toilet. Function room (160 capacity). Tables outdoors (7, pavement). Wireless internet. **Map 5 O5**.

Zetter Townhouse NEW
2011 RUNNER-UP BEST NEW BAR
49-50 St John's Square, EC1V 4JJ (7324 4545, www.thezettertownhouse.com). Farringdon tube/rail. **Open** 10am-midnight Mon-Thur, Sun; 10am-1am Fri, Sat. **Food served** noon-5pm, 6-10.30pm daily. **Credit** AmEx, MC, V.
Imagine an eccentric antiques shop where the owner is reluctant to actually sell anything, and instead sees an empty shelf, table or area of wall as an invitation to show off a seemingly discordant but holistically pleasing collection of curios. The lounge here is stuffed with framed portraits, landscapes and photographs, ironmongery and all manner of lamps, urns, vases and statues, elegant Queen Anne-style furniture and a menagerie of taxidermy. Imagine too that the shop served some of the best cocktails in London – and you're somewhere near Zetter Townhouse. Perfectly mannered staff bring drink menus whose simple descriptions belie the invention

and attention inherent in every glass – a dainty coupe is the receptacle for a Koln martini, the standard gin and martini combo brought dazzlingly to life with a pipette of own-made citrus aromatics. Head barman Tony Conigliaro has dug out many forgotten British libationary techniques (and created a few of his own), so you'll see intriguing ingredients such as 'port evaporation', nettle cordial and gunpowder tea tinctures among the premium spirits. *Babies and children admitted. Booking advisable. Disabled: lift; toilet. Function room (20-40 capacity). Wireless internet.* **Map 5 O4**.

King's Cross

★ Bar Pepito

Varnishers Yard, Regents Quarter, N1 9FD (7841 7331, www.camino.uk.com/pepito). King's Cross tube/rail. **Open** 5pm-midnight Mon-Fri; 6pm-midnight Sat. **Food served** 5-11pm Mon-Fri; 6-11pm Sat. **Credit** AmEx, MC, V.
Tucked away in a courtyard accessible via an alley at the foot of Pentonville Road, this rustic, Andalusian-themed bar is dedicated to sherry. With room for only four or five tables, all shaped from sherry casks, it's a tiny place – so small, in fact, that the toilet is across the road at Camino (run by the same folks, *see p237*) – but no less appealing for its lack of size. The 15 sherries span all styles: fino, which is dry, delicate and pale; manzanilla, comparatively brusque and briny; the sweeter, fruitier styles made with the pedro ximénez grape; and so on. You can sample the breadth of flavours by buying a sherry flight for around £8. The tapas-style cold-food menu features cured meats, olives, regional cheeses, pickled anchovies and figs coated in dark chocolate. The candelabra and bare-brick walls make it cosy, if squeezed; thankfully, there's room outside in summer.
Available for hire. Disabled: toilet. Tables outdoors (14, courtyard). **Map 4 L3**.

★ Booking Office NEW

2011 RUNNER-UP BEST NEW BAR
St Pancras Renaissance London Hotel, NW1 2AR (7841 3540, www.bookingofficerestaurant. com). King's Cross or St Pancras tube/rail. **Open** 6.30am-2.45am daily. **Credit** AmEx, DC, MC.

The superlatives come easy when describing the Booking Office: it is epic, soaring, dramatic, downright magnificent. As part of Sir George Gilbert Scott's 1873 Midland Grand Hotel, it was designed to instil in passengers a sense of awe and wonder at the power of the railways. These days, it serves as an awe-inspiring bar, and the refit has made the most of the Victorian splendour while introducing the comforts expected in a modern five-star hotel. Around the sides are deep, comfortable sofas and armchairs, perfect for taking in the original arched windows, the ribbed vaulting, the ornate brickwork – all cleverly lit to impressive effect. The drinks show equal attention to detail: the cocktail list was created by great London mixers Nick Strangeway and Henry Besant, and shows a deep respect for the history of British drinking. Sours, fizzes and cobblers are represented, but perhaps most exciting are the punches, served with dash from handmade copper mugs – the Billy Dawson Punch Rocks was a dark and complex mixture of lemon peel, demerara sugar, rum, cognac, porter and nutmeg.
Available for hire. Babies and children admitted. Disabled: toilet. Tables outdoors (27, terrace). **Map 4 L3**.

Simmons

32 Caledonian Road, N1 9DT (7278 5851). King's Cross tube/rail. **Open/food served** 4pm-midnight Mon-Wed; 4pm-2am Thur; 4pm-3am Fri, Sat. **No credit cards**.
This now evening-only DJ bar still attracts a studenty, music-savvy crowd to what looks like a cross between an old-style corner newsagents and a Shoreditch-like retro bar. Fantastic Four comic albums, board games in tatty boxes and furniture both wobbly and ratty are juxtaposed with a disco ball and a United Nations of beer cans displayed on a shelving unit. As for actual liquid nectar, there's no drinks menu ('Nah mate, we just don't bother'), only taps of Amstel and Tiger atop a tiny bar counter behind which packets of Refreshers and Wizz Fizz provide fizzy trips into childhood memories. A fridge contains bottles of Moretti, Tsingtao and Singha beers; standard cocktails are mixed according to request; and, on Mondays, everything seems to cost £2.50.

Babies and children admitted (until 7pm). Disabled: toilet. Entertainment (DJs 9pm Thur-Sat). Function room (60 capacity). Tables outdoors (2, pavement). Wireless internet. **Map 4 L2**.

VOC NEW

2 Varnishers Yard, Regents Quarter, N1 9AW (7713 8229, www.voc-london.co.uk). King's Cross tube/rail. **Open** 5pm-1am Mon-Thur; 5pm-2am Fri, Sat. **Food served** 5-10pm Mon-Thur; 5-11pm Fri, Sat. **Credit** AmEx, MC, V.
Looking like Phileas Fogg's front room, this 17th-century-inspired punch house (by the chaps behind Worship Street Whistling Shop) has cartography adorning the brick walls, swashbuckling busts, telescopes and cosy candlelight. Back in the days of the British Empire, punches were a bit of a big deal in the colonies, and the punches packed here run a gamut of styles. Some are individually bottled, while others are aged in casks and dangle in mini-barrels from the ceiling; the 'Dog's Nose' brings together Tanqueray Rangpur with fresh horseradish, Meantime porter, fresh citrus, spices and honey. The shelves are stacked with Dutch genevers, arracks, bourbons and rums sourced from the Americas, yet, punches aside, it's the bespoke bottlings that are of most interest. As well as a house-blended spiced rum, there's an array of bottle-matured cocktails decanted into apothecary-style vessels, including the impressive Vieux Carre, made with Hennessy VS cognac, sweet vermouth, Jim Beam rye and Benedictine.
Available for hire. Booking advisable. Disabled: toilet. Tables outdoors (2, pavement; 4, terrace). Wireless internet. **Map 4 L3**.

Knightsbridge

★ Blue Bar

The Berkeley, Wilton Place, SW1X 7RL (7235 6000, www.the-berkeley.co.uk). Hyde Park Corner tube. **Open/food served** 4pm-1am Mon-Sat; 4-11pm Sun. **Credit** AmEx, DC, MC, V.
The name isn't just a caprice: this David Collins-designed bar really is as blue as a Billie Holiday album. The sky-blue armchairs, the deep-blue ornate plasterwork and the navy blue leather-

Zetter Townhouse

bound menus combine with discreet lighting to striking effect. It's a see-and-be-seen place, but staff treat all-comers like royalty, and the cocktails are a masterclass in sophistication. Not everyone can afford to scale the frightening heights of the bar list, worth perusing just to confirm that there is such a thing as a £4,210 bottle of champagne or a £925 shot of whisky (Macallan 55-year-old). Leave those to the A-list, and just enjoy the elegance and luxury of one of the finest hotel bars in the city. *Disabled: toilet (hotel). Dress: smart casual.* **Map 9 G9**.

Marylebone

Artesian
Langham Hotel, 1C Portland Place, W1B 1JA (7636 1000, www.artesian-bar.co.uk). Oxford Circus tube. **Open/food served** noon-midnight daily. **Admission** (non-guests) £5 after 11pm Mon-Tue, Sun; £7 after 11pm Wed-Sat. **Credit** AmEx, DC, MC, V.
David Collins' redesign of this handsome room in the Langham Hotel updated the pillars, marble fittings and high ceilings with a considered yet glamorous touch. The result has an impressive visual impact, blending grand Victorian decadence (a marble bar, soaring inset mirrors, embroidered napkins) with modern details (purple snakeskin-effect leather seats, a carved pagoda-style back bar, faultless service). Cocktail highlights include the heady Artesian Punch (Poire William, pineapple, citrus and three rums); indeed, rum is a speciality of the house, with a list running to 60 varieties, from Gosling's Black Seal (£9) to Havana Club Maximo (£300). A cut above.

Babies and children admitted (until 6pm). Disabled: toilet (hotel). Wireless internet. **Map 9 H5**.

★ Purl
50 Blandford Street, W1U 7HX (7935 0835, www.purl-london.com). Bond Street tube. **Open** 5-11.30pm Mon-Thur; 5pm-midnight Fri, Sat. **Credit** AmEx, MC, V.
A lovable place that aims to recreate the atmosphere of a New York speakeasy, Purl's decor is simple but endearingly eclectic. The bar occupies the basement of a Georgian house and features low vaulted ceilings and plenty of individual seating areas. The list of original cocktail creations is divided between molecular mixology and a confident mastery of classicism. Among the former, an Absinthe Sazerac, served in a silver egg cup, blends cognac, sugar and bitters with absinthe bubbled on top; meanwhile, a Silver Fizz, a variant on the gorgeous Ramos gin fizz using gin, lemon, sugar syrup, egg white and fizzy water, is made with precise two-stage shaking to guarantee the right texture: this is as good a cocktail as you'll find anywhere.
Available for hire. Booking advisable. **Map 9 G5**.

Mayfair

Coburg Bar
The Connaught, Carlos Place, W1K 2AL (7499 7070, www.the-connaught.co.uk). Bond Street or Green Park tube. **Open** 11am-11pm Mon, Sun; 11am-1am Tue-Sat. **Food served** 11am-11pm daily. **Credit** AmEx, MC, V.
There's no velvet rope barring your way to the Connaught's destination bar, and no door-nazi

attitude: refreshingly, you can just walk straight on in. And once you've done so, the service will be faultless. The room oozes sophistication, with modern touches (grey velvet wing-backed chairs, black-glass tables) that enhance its historic character. The drinks list charts the evolution of the cocktail, with each drink – the greatest hits of the last two centuries, more or less – well worth the expense. The wine list is exemplary, if pricey, with an emphasis on fine French marques. Tip-top nibbles are free of charge; better, a tiny skewer of iced fruit on a silver dish appears with each cocktail as a palate-cleanser. Luxurious, elegant and discreet, the Coburg is everything a good hotel bar should be. *Disabled: toilet. Wireless internet.* **Map 9 H7**.

St James's

Dukes Bar
Dukes Hotel, 35 St James's Place, SW1A 1NY (7491 4840, www.dukeshotel.com). Green Park tube. **Open** 2pm-midnight Mon-Thur, Sun; noon-midnight Fri, Sat. **Credit** AmEx, DC, MC, V.
With its engravings and fringed chairs, the tiny, comfortable bar at this exclusive hotel looks like an upper-class Georgian sitting room, but few butlers could manage martinis of this calibre. If the art looks simple, that's because it is: the quiet waiters simply flick dry vermouth into an iced glass, fill it with gin or vodka (various premium options, all priced accordingly) and then drop in a sliver of lemon peel. Whether the secret is the elegant wooden tray, the vermouth flask that resembles a vinegar bottle in a cheap chippie or the staff's mannered method of delivery, sipping a drink amid the murmur of the grown-up clientele while

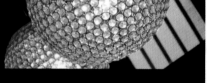

munching nuts and olives is one of the most soothing, elegant drinking experiences in the city. *Dress: smart casual. Tables outdoors (4, garden). Wireless internet.* **Map 9 J8.**

Soho

★ Mark's Bar `HOT 50`

Hix, 66-70 Brewer Street, W1F 9UP (7292 3518, www.marksbar.co.uk). Piccadilly Circus tube. **Open/food served** noon-1am Mon-Sat; 11am-11pm Sun. **Main courses** £14.75-£32.50. **Set meal** (4.30-6.30pm Mon-Fri; noon-6.30pm Sat; noon-10pm Sun) £15.50 2 courses, £19.50 3 courses. **Credit** AmEx, DC, MC, V.
Opened in 2009, together with the Mark Hix-operated restaurant (*see p53*) on the ground floor, this is a destination in its own right. It's a subterranean speakeasy with plenty of style – low zinc bar, tin ceiling panels, comfortable chesterfields, bar billiards table – but with precious little attitude. Former Hawksmoor bartender Nick Strangeway celebrates the seasons on his fascinating, history-minded cocktail list; highlights include the Hanky Panky (Beefeater, Fernet Branca and red vermouth), created in the 1930s for Charles Hawtrey by a Savoy bartender, and the Scoff-Law Cocktail, a rye-whisky-based drink from the same period. There are plenty of appetising alternatives on the 150-strong wine list and the enlightened beer menu, with pale ales, bitters, stouts and Hix's own porter all served in gleaming tankards. The conditions of the licence mean drinkers have to order food, either selections from the restaurant menu or lovely bar snacks (pork crackling, fennel sausage, posh fish fingers). *Babies and children admitted (until 5pm). Disabled: toilet. Wireless internet.* **Map 17 A4.**

Milk & Honey

61 Poland Street, W1F 7NU (7065 6840, www.mlkhny.com). Oxford Circus tube. **Open** *Non-members* 6-11pm Mon-Sat (2hrs max, last admission 9pm). *Members* 6pm-3am Mon-Sat. **Credit** AmEx, DC, MC, V.
You could walk past the door of this Soho speakeasy every day and never know it was there, and that's just how the owners like it. For the busiest times of the week, Milk & Honey is open only to members (£250 a year, plus a £50 joining fee), but mere mortals can book a table until 11pm; it's well worth the effort. The Prohibition ideal is carried through to the vaguely art deco interior (dimly lit, adding to the air of secrecy), the jazz and ragtime soundtrack, and the perfectly executed classic cocktails. Granted, the atmosphere isn't at its most kinetic at, say, 7pm on a Tuesday, but the excellent cocktails more than make up for it. Everywhere you look, the emphasis is on quality, from the daily squeezed juices and twice-frozen ice to the stock of premium spirits. It's almost enough to make you want to join – and membership will also get you in late to nearby sister bar, the Player (8 Broadwick Street, 7065 6841, www.thplyr.com). *Booking essential for non-members. Function rooms (50 capacity). Other.* **Map 17 A3.**

Strand

Beaufort Bar at the Savoy `NEW`

The Savoy, 100 Strand, WC2R 0EW (7836 4343, www.the-savoy.com). Charing Cross tube/rail or Embankment tube. **Open** 5.30pm-1.30am Mon-Sat. **Credit** AmEx, MC, V.

Following its recent multi-million pound revamp, the Savoy's devotion to debonair drinking now stretches beyond the iconic American Bar. The Beaufort might be less famous, but it's definitely the looker of the pair, and combines a wow-factor interior with good service and top-quality (if pricey) drinks. Art deco opulence abounds, £38,000 of gold leaf adorns the alcoves and ornate cornicing, and the black velvet furnishings are suitably plush. The broad range of bubbly leans heavily towards Louis Roederer, starting at around £16 a glass; beers include Meantime Pale Ale and Guinness. While the Beaufort doesn't boast the wealth of cocktails available at the American Bar, the seven-strong list is worth exploring: the Sugar Strut is a terrific twist on a rum old-fashioned that blends Bacardi 8 Year Old with Guinness Foreign Syrup; the Gilded Cage (vodka, fresh passionfruit and chartreuse) comes served in a birdcage. Be warned, though: at both bars, you may need to queue to get in. *Bookings not accepted. Disabled: toilet (hotel). Dress: smart casual. Entertainment (cabaret 8pm daily). Wireless internet.* **Map 18 E5.**

Trafalgar Square

Albannach

66 Trafalgar Square, WC2N 5DS (7930 0066, www.albannach.co.uk). Charing Cross tube/rail. **Open** noon-1am Mon-Sat; noon-7pm Sun. **Food served** noon-11pm Mon-Sat; noon-6.30pm Sun. **Credit** AmEx, DC, MC, V.
Albannach flies the flag of Scotland as deep inside enemy territory as you can get: right on Trafalgar Square. The decor is sleek and modish, but the house speciality is welded to tradition – the drinks list is all about the whiskies. A map on the menu details the origins of the Highland and Island malts, the likes of a 16-year-old, sherry-matured, cask-strength Bowmore, Bruichladdich 15-year-old and Bunnahabhain 1968 Auld Acquaintance (£65). The menu isn't capped at Scots varieties: there are also Irish and Japanese whiskies, along with bourbons. The cocktails aren't solely reliant on the Gaelic grain, but you may as well investigate a Smoky Martini (Tanqueray or Smirnoff Black with a spoonful of Laphroaig ten-year-old) or Albannach Stag (Pampero Special rum, fresh berries, angostura bitters, lime, ginger ale). Salmon and haggis feature prominently among the decent if pricey food offerings. *Disabled: toilet. Dress: smart casual. Function rooms (150 capacity). Tables outdoors (5, terrace). Wireless internet.* **Map 10 K7.**

South

Balham

Balham Bowls Club

7-9 Ramsden Road, SW12 8QX (8673 4700, www.antic-ltd.com). Balham tube/rail. **Open** 4-11pm Mon-Wed; 4pm-midnight Thur, Fri; noon-midnight Sat; noon-11pm Sun. **Food served** 6-9.30pm Tue-Fri; noon-3.30pm, 6-9.30pm Sat; 1-5pm Sun. **Credit** AmEx, MC, V.
Despite its upper-crust appearance, the Balham Bowls Club welcomes all-comers to its clubhouse. The bowls club's history has been sensitively preserved, with a warren of small, wood-panelled rooms decorated with rosettes, chesterfields and an old wooden scoreboard. The bar itself is cosy and crowded, with a crackling fire in winter;

VOC. See p315.

draught Ubu, Peroni and Grolsch are served along with bottled Honey Dew, Fursty Ferret and Abbot. Food is a focus, with sharing platters of cured meats, comfort-food mains and generous Sunday lunches. There's plenty of space in the back rooms to dine in comfort – space enough, in fact, for two snooker tables. A crazy-paved front terrace accommodates the smokers. *Babies and children admitted (until 8pm). Entertainment (quiz 8pm Tue). Function room (50 capacity). Tables outdoors (10, garden; 4, terrace). Wireless internet.*

Battersea

Ink Rooms

14 Lavender Hill, SW11 5RW (7228 5300, www.inkrooms.co.uk). Clapham Common tube or Wandsworth Road rail. **Open** 5pm-midnight Mon-Thur, Sun; 4pm-2am Fri, Sat. **Food served** 5-10pm Mon-Thur, Sun; 4-10pm Fri, Sat. **No credit cards.**
The folk behind Lost Society and Lost Angel have remodelled this place as an American dive bar, albeit one without the drunks, the divey-ness or, for that matter, the Americans. Decked out in black leather banquettes and stools, the main bar is coated in 1950s Sailor Jerry-style tattoo art, with the odd flash of neon and an old-school jukebox. Purple drapes partition a laid-back lounge area; downstairs, the cellar room leads out into a beer garden. The 60-strong, American-accented beer list contains superb craft brews, including Cutthroat Porter from Odell and Doggie Style Pale Ale from Flying Dog, as well as a selection of Trappist beers; the dozen taps pour the likes of Brooklyn Lager and Sierra Nevada, and you might see Truman's among the ales. The back bar offers a well-chosen selection of spirits, including such lesser-known labels as small-batch Old Pogue bourbon. *Babies and children admitted (until 6pm). Entertainment (bands 7.30pm Thur, 6.30pm Sun; DJs 9pm Fri, Sat; quiz 7pm Sun). Tables outdoors (10, garden). Wireless internet.* **Map 21 C3.**

Tooting

Tooting Tram & Social NEW
46-48 Mitcham Road, SW17 9NA (8767 0278, www.antic-ltd.com). Tooting Broadway tube. **Open** 5pm-midnight Tue-Thur; 4pm-2am Fri; noon-2am Sat; noon-midnight Sun. **Credit** MC, V.

Hard to spot but impressive once you find it, this converted tram shed incorporates a cavernous, chandelier-lit main bar and a smaller mezzanine, filled with decorative quirks and televisions for football viewing. Don't expect a laddish crowd, though: the offbeat tone is set by a pair of winkle-pickers displayed under glass as you walk in, while Lionel Ritchie beams a Lionel Ritchie smile from an album cover mounted on the back bar. It's a laid-back bunch that mingles here, either parked on turquoise-topped bar stools or lounging on the banquettes and antique armchairs. There's draught Purity Mad Goose, Doom Bar and Grolsch, with ten wines by the glass among the 20-strong selection. *Disabled: toilet. Entertainment (bands/cabaret/DJs 8pm daily). Tables outdoors (6, pavement). Wireless internet.*

Waterloo

Oxo Tower Bar
8th floor, Oxo Tower Wharf, Barge House Street, SE1 9PH (7803 3888, www.harveynichols.com). Southwark tube or Waterloo tube/rail. **Open** 11am-11pm Mon-Wed; 11am-11.30pm Thur-Sat; noon-10.30pm Sun. **Food served** noon-11pm Mon-Sat; noon-10pm Sun. **Credit** AmEx, DC, MC, V.

Diners at the restaurant and brasserie (*see p217*) have long gazed across to St Paul's Cathedral and Somerset House, but it's only since owners Harvey Nicks reshuffled things that drinkers can also properly enjoy uninterrupted views. Bar designer Shaun Clarkson has updated the interior too, the most notable addition being a slick boomerang-shaped white bar behind which an army of attentive bartenders bustle. It's not the cosiest of places, and it still conjures up something of the feel of a cruise ship, but the refit has also brought in its wake some better booze. The cocktail list covers the classics using some house-made ingredients – lime cordial in the gimlet, an OXO-branded ice cube in the negroni – while the Earl Grey Mar-tea-ni comes in tea cups for two. The extensive French-leaning wine list provides sufficient choice of wines by the glass; bottled beers include Meantime Pale Ale and Schneider Weisse. The bar menu brings sharing plates with charcuterie, manchego and quince, and boutique snacks such as mini truffled honey chorizo. *Available for hire. Babies and children welcome. Booking advisable. Disabled: lift; toilet.* **Map 11 N7.**

Skylon
Royal Festival Hall, Belvedere Road, SE1 8XX (7654 7800, www.skylon-restaurant.co.uk). Waterloo tube/rail. **Open** noon-1am daily. **Food served** *Brasserie* noon-10.45pm daily. *Restaurant* noon-2.30pm, 5.30-10.30pm Mon-Sat; noon-3.30pm, 5.30-10.30pm Sun. **Credit** AmEx, MC, V.

Passing the throngs standing listening to Hindustani drumming in the Royal Festival Hall foyer, take the lift to the third floor, turn left and enter this light space. An attractive blend of contemporary style and retro chic (look out for nods to the 1951 Festival of Britain), it makes terrific use of its cathedral ceilings and vast windows, which provide views of river, skyline and people on the move. In the middle of the room, surrounded by restaurant tables (*see p217*), is a cocktail oasis, consisting of a slate bar counter, swivel bar stools, banquettes and, nearer the window, seats for sipping à deux. It's not cheap: wines start at £5.55, beer is £4.50 a bottle, and the excellent cocktails, both classics (margaritas with Don Agustin) and variations such as the signature Skylon (muddled grapes and ginger with Ciroc vodka, Manzana Verde, lime and apple juice) go for a tenner-plus. But as destination drinking venues go, this one can't easily be topped. *Babies and children admitted. Booking advisable. Disabled: toilet.* **Map 10 M8.**

South East

Greenwich

Old Brewery
Pepys Building, Old Royal Naval College, SE10 9LM (3327 1280, www.oldbrewerygreenwich.com). Cutty Sark DLR. **Open** 11am-11pm daily. **Food served** noon-5pm, 6-10.30pm daily. **Credit** MC, V.

Rather than make cask-conditioned English ales for an already crowded market, Alastair Hook and his team at Meantime specialise in more unusual artisan beers, which they've rolled out in increasing numbers across London over the last few years. In 2010, he opened this ambitious operation, a microbrewery, pub and café-restaurant (*see p57*) in part of the recently refurbished Old Royal Naval College. The modern bar area is small, but has a huge outdoor seating area. Meantime's own beers, chiefly brewed using bottom-fermented, low-temperature continental methods, take pride of place; among them are Helles, a pale lager, and the potent Hospital Porter. But the menu extends beyond Greenwich to cover around 50 beers on draught or in bottles, arranged by style on the menu from 'hoppy ales' to 'Belgian Lambic and crisp beers'. The food, billed on the menu as 'Modern British', takes in such hearty dishes as pork terrine served with strips of pig's ear. *Babies and children admitted (until 6pm). Disabled: toilet. Tables outdoors (20, garden). Wireless internet.*

East

Shoreditch

Book Club
100-106 Leonard Street, EC2A 4RH (7684 8618, www.wearetbc.com). Old Street tube/rail or Shoreditch High Street rail. **Open** 8am-midnight Mon-Wed; 8am-2am Thur, Fri; 10am-2am Sat; 10am-midnight Sun. **Food served** 8am-10pm Mon-Fri; 10am-10pm Sat, Sun. **Admission** *Club* free-£8. **Credit** MC, V.

This commendable bar-club comprises one expansive room – divided by a wall with an oval hole in the middle, giving the illusion that half of Hoxton is here – and a small pool room downstairs. Cocktails are scrawled up in black felt-tip on white tiles by the bar; most cost around £7 and have in-joke names, such as Shoreditch Twat (Jägermeister, tequila and Chartreuse shaken with vanilla and egg) and Don't Go to Dalston (Bombay Sapphire gin, Martini Bianco and falernum). All but one of the dozen beers come by the glass, while the draught beer option is Sagres. Sharing platters include fajitas and English barbecue ribs, while light bites involve whitebait with garlic aïoli and own-made pork scratchings. *Babies and children admitted: until 8pm. Entertainment (bands/DJs 7pm Thur-Sat). Function room (100 capacity). Wireless internet.* **Map 6 R4.**

Happiness Forgets

8-9 Hoxton Square, N1 6NU (7613 0325, www.happinessforgets.com). Old Street tube/rail or Shoreditch High Street rail. **Open** 5-11pm Mon-Sat. **Food served** 6-10.30pm Mon-Sat. **Credit** MC.

Defying recent trends, this cosy cocktail cavern on Hoxton Square is just a bar with down-to-earth decor, extremely well-crafted cocktails, switched-on staff and good music. The maroon brick walls are mellowed by candles and lanterns; the scattering of 1960s furniture is accented by bits of booze-related bric-a-brac, including an old absinthe fountain. The wild 'green fairy' liquid features heavily in the Green Beast (absinthe shaken with cucumber water, sugar and lime), one of 11 cocktails on a fortnightly-changing list devised by Alastair Burgess, formerly of Milk & Honey. The masculine Harry Palmer – made from rye whiskey, vermouth and Suze – was excellent, and so too was the Perfect Storm, bringing together dark rum, brandy, honey, lemon juice and ginger. As well as beers from Meantime and the Aussie Coopers, there's Breton cider and up to a dozen reasonably priced wines. The Thai restaurant upstairs supplies dim sum, prawn rolls and pad thai. *Available for hire. Wireless internet.* **Map 6 R3**.

Mason & Taylor

51-55 Bethnal Green Road, E1 6LA (7749 9670, www.masonandtaylor.co.uk). Liverpool Street tube/rail or Shoreditch High Street rail. **Open** 5pm-midnight Mon-Thur; 5pm-2am Fri; noon-2am Sat; noon-midnight Sun. **Food served** 5-10pm Mon-Thur; 5-10.30pm Sat; noon-9pm Sun. **Credit** MC, V.

The guys behind the Duke of Wellington in Dalston have taken over this two-floor, urban/industrial space to showcase boutique beer. Behind a concrete bar, a dozen draught taps draw both the obscure and the accessible: Brooklyn Lager, Bitburger and De Koninck alongside Thornstar (a collaboration from Thornbridge and Dark Star) and a milk stout from Colorado, as well as some decent ciders. The friendly staff are happy to advise on putting together a taster flight. The 40-strong bottled-beer menu changes regularly: local beers include Kernel IPA and Meantime Raspberry, and there are American craft beers, barrel-aged brews, 'oddities', and the best of Belgium and Germany. Tapas-style small plates with a British bent include whitebait, smoked salmon with horseradish cream, and roast butternut squash with bacon. On Sundays, it's all about the roasts.

Babies and children admitted. Booking advisable. Disabled: toilet. Entertainment (DJs 9pm Fri, Sat). Function room (120 capacity). Wireless internet. **Map 6 S4**.

Nightjar

129 City Road, EC1V 1JB (7253 4101, www.barnightjar.com). Old Street tube/rail. **Open** 6pm-1am Tue, Wed, Sun; 6pm-3am Thur-Sat. **No credit cards**.

With its inconspicuous entrance and subterranean setting, Nightjar is a stylised stab at a Shoreditch speakeasy: a late-opening cocktail bar and music venue that leads with live jazz, swing and cabaret, and debonair drinking. First and foremost, the cocktails here are excellent and original: liquid legacies from cocktail's golden era and pre-Prohibition drinks incorporating own-made infusions, and liqueurs and bitters. Brought to your table by (maybe overly) meticulous staff and accompanied by an array of canapés, they both look and taste the business. The BBC, made with calvados and Becherovka cordial, is served with 'absinthe smoke', while misty 'dry ice' vapours add allure to the Fog Cutter, an alcoholic orgy of rum, sherry, gin and Cognac. With its trio of open-plan areas big on brass, black leather booths and dark wood, it's a dapper, dusky place to drink. *Booking advisable Fri, Sat. Disabled: toilet. Entertainment (live music 9pm Wed, Thur, Sat).* **Map 6 Q4**.

★ Worship Street Whistling Shop NEW

2011 WINNER BEST NEW BAR

63 Worship Street, EC2A 2DU (7247 0015, www.whistlingshop.com). Old Street tube/rail. **Open** noon-1am Mon-Thur; noon-2am Fri, Sat. **Food served** noon-10pm Mon-Sat. **Credit** AmEx, MC, V.

We've noticed a few conspicuous themes appearing in London's bars. A semi-secret location, Victoriana, faithful interpretations of classic British drinks – Worship Street Whistling Shop does them all, and very well. Located at the City end of Shoreditch on a backstreet deserted at night, it's almost without signage. The darkly Dickensian cellar room is full of cosy corners, leather armchairs and select antiquities. At the back is a windowed laboratory (worthy of a Jekyll and Hyde fantasy), crammed with equipment modern and antiquated that is used to create the wondrously described ingredients that constitute the cocktails. Behold 'removed cream', 'high pressure hydrosol', 'WS2 exhaustion tonic', 'clorophyll bitters' – all are used to create original and stimulating drinks that rarely exceed £10. But it's the staff who really turn this from a great bar into a brilliant one. It would be easy to come across po-faced or pretentious with such a studied approach to drink-making, but they were staunchly friendly and helpful throughout. A fun night out can be thought-provoking too, and the Whistling Shop captures this idea perfectly. *Babies and children admitted (until 7pm). Booking advisable Mon-Sat. Function room (10 capacity). Wireless internet.* **Map 6 Q4**.

Spitalfields

Hawksmoor

157 Commercial Street, E1 6BJ (7247 7392, www.thehawksmoor.com). Liverpool Street tube/rail. **Open** noon-midnight Mon-Fri; 11am-midnight Sat; 11am-4pm Sun. **Food served** noon-3pm, 6-10.30pm Mon-Fri; 11am-4pm, 6-10.30pm Sat; 11am-4pm Sun. **Credit** AmEx, MC, V.

How much of Hawksmoor is given over to drinkers depends on how busy the restaurant is. On quieter nights, you may be able to snag a table; otherwise, you'll have to hope there's room at the corner bar. The reason to squeeze in is simple: the cocktails are among the best in town. Bartender Nick Strangeway may have moved to Mark's Bar in Soho, but his influence is still visible on a menu that nods in the direction of pre-FDR America, with a lengthy list of variations on the mint julep, an array of 'expat classics' enjoyed by travelling Yanks during Prohibition, and an assortment of other arcane recipes, some of which date back the better part of 150 years. But while the education provided by the descriptions of each drink on the menu is welcome, the drinks sell themselves without them, especially given the reasonable prices. *See also p249.* *Babies and children admitted. Disabled: toilet. Wireless internet; free.* **Map 6 R5**.

North

Islington

★ 69 Colebrooke Row

69 Colebrooke Row, N1 8AA (07 540 528593, www.69colebrookerow.com). Angel tube. **Open** 5pm-midnight Mon-Wed, Sun; 5pm-1am Thur; 5pm-2am Fri, Sat. **Credit** AmEx, MC, V.

Tucked away off the Islington Green end of Essex Road, 69 Colebrooke Row bears an impressive pedigree. It's the brainchild of Tony Conigliaro, familiar from his work at the likes of Isola, Roka and Shochu Lounge, and Camille Hobby-Limon, who runs the nearby Charles Lamb pub. With just a handful of tables supplemented by a few stools at the bar, it may be smaller than your own front room, but the understated, intimate space proves a fine environment in which to enjoy the pristine cocktails (liquorice whisky sours, raspberry and rosehip bellinis, gimlets with own-made rhubarb cordial, depending on the season), mixed with quiet ceremony by an elegantly bow-tied Conigliaro. Still, for all the excellence of the drinks, it's the little touches (impeccably attired staff, handwritten bills, tall glasses of water poured from a cocktail shaker) that elevate this lovely enterprise from the pack. *Booking advisable. Entertainment (pianist 8pm Thur). Wireless internet.* **Map 5 O2**.

Worship Street Whistling Shop

Eating & Entertainment

Sometimes you want a little extra entertainment to accompany a meal, and the following places should be able to help. Whether it's waiters bursting into operatic arias (**Sarastro**), salsa classes (the aptly named **Salsa!**), Austrian kitsch and beers (the long-established **Tiroler Hut**), big-name jazz musicians (the legend that is **Ronnie Scott's**) or dining in the dark (the unique **Dans Le Noir?**), the capital has more than enough venues where you can shake a leg, sing your heart out or, better still, watch someone else do it for you. Here's our pick of the bunch.

Blues, jazz & soul

Blues Kitchen
111-113 Camden High Street, NW1 7JN (7387 5277, www.theblueskitchen.com). Camden Town tube. **Open** noon-midnight Mon, Tue; noon-1am Wed; noon-2am Thur; noon-3am Fri; 11am-3am Sat; 11am-1am Sun. **Meals served** noon-10.30pm Mon-Fri; 11am-10.30pm Sat, Sun. **Music** *Bands* 9.30pm Mon-Thur; 10pm Fri, Sat; 7pm Sun. *DJs* 1am-3am Fri, Sat. **Main courses** £9-£15. **Admission** Gigs free; £4 after 9pm Fri; £5 after 9pm Sat. **Credit** AmEx, MC, V.
This bar-diner channels the spirit of America's Deep South with dark wood fittings, booths furnished in weathered leather and colourful portraits of legendary bluesmen (Blind Willie McTell, Skip James). A dedicated bourbon bar stocks around 50 varieties, and the food menu takes inspiration from traditional New Orleans diners – gumbo, ribs and jambalaya. Past acts include Pete Doherty, The Drums and Seasick Steve. *Available for hire. Babies and children welcome until 7pm: high chairs.* **Map 27 D3**.

Green Note
106 Parkway, NW1 7AN (7485 9899, www.greennote.co.uk). Camden Town tube. **Dinner served** 7-10pm Wed, Thur, Sun; 7-10.30pm Fri, Sat. **Music** 9-11pm daily. **Tapas** £2.50-£4.95. **Main courses** £7.95-£9.95. **Admission** £4-£15. **Credit** MC, V.
An international line-up of acts at this relaxed Greenwich Village-style hangout has included the Coal Porters (the 'world's first alt-bluegrass band'), Tift Merritt, and folk heros Martin Simpson and Jackie Leven. Paintings of music icons including Joni Mitchell and Bob Dylan line the walls. Food is vegetarian and organic; daily specials, salads and tapas can be eaten in the café/restaurant area out front, or in the music venue at the back. *Babies and children admitted: high chair. Booking advisable. Vegan dishes. Vegetarian menu.* **Map 27 C3**.

Jazz After Dark
9 Greek Street, W1D 4DQ (7734 0545, www.jazzafterdark.co.uk). Leicester Square or Tottenham Court Road tube. **Open** 2pm-2am Tue-Thur; 2pm-3am Fri, Sat. **Meals served** 2pm-midnight Tue-Sat. **Music** 9pm Mon-Thur; 10.30pm Fri, Sat. **Main courses** £8.50-£10.95. **Set meal** £12.95 3 courses. **Admission** £5 Tue-Thur; £10 diners, £15 non-diners Fri, Sat. **Credit** AmEx, DC, MC, V.
An old-school jazz club with few pretensions. It's a popular after-work spot, where a young crowd enjoys a live blend of jazz, plus blues, funk and soul. The menu concentrates on comfort food classics – burgers, pasta dishes, fish and chips, grills – while a tacky cocktail list (fancy a Blow Job or Slippery Nipple?) appeals to hen and stag parties. *Booking essential Fri, Sat. Dress: smart casual. Tables outdoors (2, pavement).* **Map 17 C3**.

Jazz Café
5-7 Parkway, NW1 7PG (7688 8899, http://venues.meanfiddler.com). Camden Town tube. **Open/meals served** varies; phone for details. **Music** daily; phone for details. **Main courses** £16.50. **Set meal** £26.50 2 courses. **Admission** varies; phone for details. **Credit** MC, V.
Not only jazz, but also soul, funk and world musicians perform here. Cheesy Saturday club night 'I love the '80s' caters for students, but the Jazz Café is best known for its excellent live music programme, notably soon-to-be-huge US acts: Mary J Blige and John Legend played their first European dates here. An adventurous menu (lobster and scallop lasagne in fire-roasted red pepper sauce; asparagus, artichoke and mushroom risotto) is served in the balcony restaurant overlooking the stage. Note that it's open only on show nights. *Booking advisable. Disabled: toilet.* **Map 27 D2**.

Pizza Express Jazz Club
10 Dean Street, W1D 3RW (0845 602 7017, www.pizzaexpresslive.com). Tottenham Court Road tube. **Meals served** *Club* 7-11pm daily. *Restaurant* 11.30am-midnight Mon-Sat; 11.30am-11.30pm Sun. **Music** 8.30-10.30pm Mon-Thur; 9-11pm Fri, Sat; 8-10pm Sun. **Main courses** £6.50-£10.95. **Admission** Gigs £15-£25. **Credit** AmEx, DC, MC, V.
There are shows every night at this long-standing Soho club, taking in everything from hotly tipped newcomers to established mainstream acts such as jazz vocalists Jamie Cullum and revered American Gregory Porter. The atmosphere in the basement space is laid-back and friendly, and, it being a Pizza Express, the food is reliable and affordable. *Babies and children welcome (restaurant): high chairs. Booking advisable. Takeaway service.* **Map 17 B3**.

Le Quecum Bar

42-44 Battersea High Street, SW11 3HX
(7787 2227, www.quecumbar.co.uk). Clapham
Junction rail. **Open** 7pm-midnight Mon-Thur;
6pm-1am Fri, Sat; 6pm-midnight Sun. **Meals
served** 7-10pm Mon-Thur; 6-10pm Fri-Sun.
Music varies Mon, Sun; 8pm Tue-Sat. **Main
courses** £9.50-£15. **Admission** varies
Mon, Sun; free Tue; £5 after 8pm Wed-Sat.
Membership £65/yr. **Credit** AmEx, MC, V.
Django Reinhardt-style gypsy jazz performances
provide the nightly entertainment at this wine
bar – Le Quecum Bar claims to be the world's only
venue dedicated to the genre. A French menu lists
the likes of coq au vin and french onion soup.
Kronenburg and Amstel beers are on draught, and
wine is reasonably priced. Sunday and Monday
nights see the bar host ticketed concerts, a recent
highlight being a visit from the French gypsy
musician Aurélien Bouly. Regular events include
the (free) Tuesday Gypsy Swing Jam – bring your
own instrument if you want to join in.
*Booking advisable Fri, Sat. Dress: smart casual.
Tables outdoors (5, garden).* **Map 21 B2**.

Ronnie Scott's

47 Frith Street, W1D 4HT (7439 0747,
www.ronniescotts.co.uk). Leicester Square or
Tottenham Court Road tube. **Open** 6pm-late
Mon-Sat; 6.30pm-late Sun. **Meals served**
6pm-1am Mon-Sat; 6-11pm Sun. **Music**
7.30pm-2am Mon-Thur; 7.15pm-1.30am Fri,
Sat; 8am-10.30pm. **Main courses** £15.40-
£24. **Admission** (non-members) £20-£40.
Membership £175/yr. **Credit** AmEx,
MC, V.
Ronnie Scott's remains one of the oldest and most
renowned jazz venues in the world. Bookings tend
to be high-calibre veterans of the jazz circuit, with
recent shows from Wynton Marsalis, Ramsey
Lewis and Michel Legrand. Although the music is
obviously the main draw here, the food is of a high
standard too: butternut squash risotto and pan-
fried sea bream are on the menu, alongside more
typical burgers and steaks.
*Available for hire. Booking advisable. Disabled:
toilet. Dress: smart casual.* **Map 17 C3**.

606 Club

90 Lots Road, SW10 0QD (7352 5953,
www.606club.co.uk). Earl's Court tube then bus
C3 or Sloane Square tube then bus 22. **Open**
7pm-midnight Mon-Thur, Sun; 8pm-2am Fri, Sat.
Meals served 7-11pm Mon-Thur, Sun; 8pm-
midnight Fri, Sat. **Music** 8.30pm Mon, Thur,
Sun; 7.30pm Tue, Wed; 9.30pm Fri, Sat. **Main
courses** £9.95-£19.45. **Admission** (non-
members) £8-£12. **Membership** £95 1st yr,
£60 subsequent yrs. **Credit** AmEx, MC, V.
A long-established basement club (it opened its
doors in now dim and distant 1976), with low
ceilings and candlelight creating a relaxed,
intimate hangout. There's music every night; the
website is regularly updated with the latest line-
ups, ranging across jazz, latin, R&B and soul. Food-
wise, expect the likes of baked salmon fillet
teriyaki served with cardamom rice and vegetables
or grilled wild boar sausages, herb mash, apple
chutney and gravy. The 606 is now also open for
Sunday lunch. The club's licence means non-
members can only drink alcohol with meals, and
are admitted at weekends only if they're eating.
*Available for hire. Babies and children admitted.
Booking advisable Fri, Sat.* **Map 13 C13**.

Burlesque

Brickhouse

152C Brick Lane, E1 6RU (7247 0005,
www.thebrickhouse.co.uk). Liverpool Street
tube/rail or Shoreditch High Street rail. **Open**
6pm-2am Tue-Thur; 6pm-3am Fri, Sat. **Dinner
served** 6.30-9pm Tue-Sat. **Main courses**
£14-£27.50. **Set dinner** £35 4 courses incl
entertainment cover charge. **Credit** MC, V.
Whitewashed walls, wooden floors and red velvet
curtains present a modern take on traditional
cabaret in this converted warehouse. There's
something of a 1930s speakeasy vibe, with two
mezzanine levels rising above the ground-floor
stage. Here you can catch performances from tassel-
twirling burlesque dancers, cabaret acts, magicians
and DJs. A £5 to £10 cover charge is included in the
dinner price during shows; it goes directly to the
performers. The menu features dishes such as
goat's cheese and piquillo pepper rigatoni with
cream sauce and black olives, or minute steak in
cheese bread with shallot rings and basil pesto.
*Available for hire. Booking advisable. Disabled:
toilet. Entertainment: live acts, DJs 9pm daily.*
Map 6 S5.

Volupté

7-9 Norwich Street, EC4A 1EJ (7831 1622,
www.volupte-lounge.com). Chancery Lane tube.
Open 5pm-1am Tue, Wed; 5pm-3am Thur,
Fri; 1.30-3am Sat; 1-6.30pm Sun. **Dinner
served** 7-10pm Tue, Wed; 6-11pm Thur-Sat.
Tea served 2.30-5pm Sat; 3-5.30pm Sun.
Main courses £16.50-£24. **Admission**
£14-£42. **Credit** AmEx, MC, V.
Ivy hangs from the ceiling and candlelit tables
surround a small stage and piano at this retro
basement supper club. Cabaret shows provide the
entertainment from Wednesday to Saturday, while
'Afternoon Tease' – a traditional champagne
afternoon tea with a burlesque slant – is held on
selected Saturdays and the last Sunday of the
month. Evening highlights might include Ivy
Paige's performances in *Femmes Fatales* and
Moulin Rouge; there's also the Volupté Vintage Ball,
a 1940s and '50s swing night and dinner. Food leans
towards Modern European, with dishes such as
grilled sirloin with cherry tomatoes and swiss
chard. Reasonably priced retro cocktails are
available from the upstairs bar.
*Available for hire. Booking essential. Dress:
smart casual. Entertainment: cabaret 8pm
Wed-Fri; 2.30pm, 7pm, 10pm Sat; 3pm Sun.*
Map 11 N5.

Latin

Nueva Costa Dorada

47-55 Hanway Street, W1T 1UX (7631 5117,
www.costadorarestaurant.co.uk). Tottenham
Court Road tube. **Open/meals served** noon-
3am Mon-Sat. **Main courses** £9.95-£16.45.
Credit MC, V.
Flamenco shows from Thursday to Saturday draw
the crowds to this Spanish stalwart. There's a
relaxed atmosphere, with tables arranged around
the stage. Unsurprisingly, it's popular with office
parties and birthday bashes. A solid à la carte menu
(which includes paella) accompanies a selection of
tapas. There's an exclusively Spanish wine list and
a short cocktail list.

*Available for hire. Babies and children admitted
(until 11pm). Entertainment: flamenco shows
8.30pm Thur, 10pm Fri, Sat; DJ 11pm Fri, Sat.*
Map 17 B2.

Salsa!

96 Charing Cross Road, WC2H 0JG
(7379 3277, www.barsalsa.info). Leicester
Square or Tottenham Court Road tube.
Bar **Open** 5pm-2am daily.
Café **Open** 9am-5pm Mon-Sat. **Snacks
served** noon-5pm Mon-Sat. **Set buffet**
(noon-6pm Mon-Sat) £1.10/100g.
Restaurant **Meals served** 5-11pm daily.
Main courses £4.75-£11.50.
Bar & Restaurant **Admission** £4 after 9pm
Mon-Thur; £2 after 7pm, £4 after 8pm, £8 after
9pm, £10 after 11pm Fri, Sat; £4 after 8pm Sun.
All **Credit** AmEx, MC, V.
Dance classes take place every evening in the bar,
catering for everyone from complete beginners to
salsa pros (from £5, £3 for diners), as well as a free
two-hour introduction to latin dance on Friday
nights, taking in salsa, merengue and lambada.
Latin-themed drinks will help guests overcome their
inhibitions before taking to the floor. Food is a mix
of tapas and larger dishes such as steaks and
quesadillas. There's also a Brazilian-style buffet.
*Booking advisable; essential weekends. Dress:
smart casual. Entertainment: dance classes
6.30pm, DJs 9.30pm daily. Tables outdoors
(14, pavement).* **Map 17 C3**.

Music & dancing

Dover Street

8-10 Dover Street, W1S 4LQ (7629 9813,
www.doverstreet.co.uk). Green Park or Piccadilly
Circus tube. **Open** 5pm-3am Mon-Sat. **Dinner
served** 6pm-2am Mon-Thur; 7pm-2am Fri,
Sat. **Music** Bands 9.30pm Mon; 10pm Tue-Sat.

Green Note

DJs until 3am Mon-Sat. **Main courses** £13.95-£21.95. **Set dinner** £25-£45 3 courses. **Admission** £7 after 10pm Mon; £8 after 10pm Tue; £10 after 10pm Wed; £15 after 10pm Thur, Fri; diners only until 10pm, then £15 Sat. **Credit** AmEx, DC, MC, V.
Enjoy early evening cocktails at one of the three elegant bars, all decked out in black and white fashion prints, at this jazz and dining venue. The Modern European menu is served until late, with last orders for food taken at 2am. After dinner, guests take to the dancefloor to the sounds of regular bands, such as the Jazz Dynamos, Funkification and the Blues Engineers. Check the website for events.
Booking advisable; essential weekends. Dress: smart casual. Separate rooms for parties, seating 20-100. **Map 9 J7**.

Roadhouse
35 The Piazza, WC2E 8BE (7240 6001, www.roadhouse.co.uk). Covent Garden tube. **Open** 5.30pm-3am Mon-Sat; 5.30pm-12.30am Sun. **Meals served** 5.30pm-1.30am Mon-Sat; 5.30pm-midnight Sun. **Main courses** £8.25-£17. **Admission** £5 after 10pm Mon-Wed, Sun; £7 after 10pm Thur; £10 after 9pm Fri; £5 after 7pm, £12 after 9pm Sat. **Credit** AmEx, MC, V.
Roadhouse is more than a popular spot for beer-swigging lads and lasses, who come for the drinks promotions and diner-style food. There's music every night, while Rocky-oke on Sundays offers a new slant on karaoke, giving customers the chance to sing their favourite hits with a real backing band. Roadhouse is also the setting for the World Flair Championships in which bartenders compete to find who's best at looping and spinning bottles while mixing a pina colada; a £10,000 first prize ensures it's a serious affair.
Booking advisable. Dress: smart casual. Entertainment: bands/DJs times vary daily. **Map 18 E4**.

Tiroler Hut
27 Westbourne Grove, W2 4UA (7727 3981, www.tirolerhut.co.uk). Bayswater or Queensway tube. **Open** 6.30pm-1am Tue-Sat; 6.30pm-midnight Sun. **Dinner served** 6.30pm-12.30am Tue-Sat; 6.30-11.30pm Sun. **Main courses** £14.90-£17.50. **Set meal** (Tue-Thur, Sun) £24.50 3 courses; (Fri, Sat) £28.50 3 courses. **Credit** AmEx, MC, V.
'Nothing changes here, except the colour of my hair,' says Joseph, the accordion-wielding owner of this uber-kitsch Austrian restaurant. (It's designed to resemble an Alpine ski chalet.) Each night, Joseph takes charge of festivities with his cowbell performance, encouraging diners to get up and sing along. Less jocular is the menu, filled with authentic fare (schnitzel, sauerkraut, stuffed cabbage and goulash) and the admirable selection of German and Austrian beers (served in steins, of course) and wines. We recommend going in a group for a hearty dose of raucous communal cheer.
Available for hire. Babies and children admitted. Booking essential. Entertainment: cowbell show times vary Tue-Sun. **Map 7 B6**.

One-offs

Dans Le Noir?
30-31 Clerkenwell Green, EC1R 0DU (7253 1100, www.danslenoir.com/london). Farringdon tube/rail. **Lunch served**
by appointment. **Dinner served** (fixed sittings) 7-7.30pm Mon-Wed; 7-7.30pm, 9-9.30pm Thur-Sat. **Set dinner** £40 2 courses, £45 3 courses. **Credit** AmEx, MC, V.
The premise here is that you dine in absolute darkness, allowing you to focus entirely on the taste, texture and smell of the food. It starts in the main bar, where you choose one of four simple, but secret colour-coded menus: blue for fish, green for vegetarian, red for meat, and white for the chef's surprise. Blind staff guide you to your table and serve you in the pitch-black dining room. To answer two frequently asked questions: Are the chefs blind? No, they're not. And are the toilets also in the dark? Again, thankfully, no.
Booking essential. Children admitted. Disabled: toilet. Separate room for parties, seats 60. **Map 5 N4**.

Lucky Voice
52 Poland Street, W1F 7LR (7439 3660, www.luckyvoice.co.uk). Oxford Circus tube. **Open/meals served** 5.30pm-1am Mon-Thur; 3pm-1am Fri, Sat; 3-10.30pm Sun. **Main courses** £7.50. **Credit** AmEx, MC, V.
Food here is limited to pizzas and snacks, but the Japanese-style private karaoke booths will appeal to those usually too shy (or too sober) to take to the microphone and sing. There are nine rooms at this Soho branch, with space for four to 12 people; the larger rooms have hats, wigs and other props to enhance the fun. A long drinks list features saké, cocktails, spirits by the bottle, and plenty of beer and wine – press the 'thirsty' button for waiter service. Go online before your visit to create a playlist from the website's song database of somewhere around a million tracks (yes, they do have Journey's 'Don't Stop Believin').
Booking essential. Entertainment: karaoke pods for hire, £5-£11.50/hr per person. Over-21s only. **Map 17 A3**.
For branch see index.

Rainforest Café
20 Shaftesbury Avenue, W1D 7EU (7434 3111, www.therainforestcafe.co.uk). Leicester Square or Piccadilly Circus tube. **Meals served** noon-10pm Mon-Fri; 11.30am-8pm Sat; 11.30am-10pm Sun.. **Main courses** £12.95-£18.90. **Credit** AmEx, MC, V.
A host of animatronic wildlife models bring this jungle-themed restaurant to life. The emphasis is very much on having fun, making it a hit with children's parties. Bag a table upstairs to sit among the fish, elephants and gorillas, and choose from the global menu of meze, pasta, seafood, ribs, steaks and burgers. Pay an extra £3 for the Adventure meal to keep youngsters entertained with a mask, stationery and sticker book. If they're still looking for mementos, and your wallet can take it, stop at the shop on your way out. No advance bookings are taken, but a priority seating system operates online (where the next available table is yours within a certain time slot).
Babies and children welcome: children's menu; crayons; high chairs; nappy-changing facilities. Entertainment: face painting weekends & school hols. Separate rooms for parties, seating 11-100. **Map 17 B5**.

Troubadour
263-267 Old Brompton Road, SW5 9JA (7370 1434, www.troubadour.co.uk). West Brompton tube/rail. **Open** 9pm-midnight
Mon-Thur, Sun; 9pm-2am Fri, Sat. **Food served** 9-11pm daily. **Main courses** £8.25-£13.50. **Credit** AmEx, MC, V.
A key player in London's 1950s folk scene, the Troubadour has a lot of history. Bob Dylan played his debut London show here; the first issues of *Private Eye* were produced and distributed from the café, and it was here that Ken Russell and Oliver Reed became friends. The ground-floor café, with coffee pots in the windows, steel pans dangling overhead, and stained glass and wood-panelling, retains a bohemian vibe. The bistro-style menu offers burgers, omelettes, salads and pastas. Poetry readings and music gigs take place in the basement club. Next door is a wine bar/shop holding regular wine-tastings, and you can even spend the night in 'The Garret', the top-floor apartment lavishly decorated with antique furniture and an imposing Philippe Starck bed.
Available for hire. Babies and children welcome (café): high chair. Booking advisable. Entertainment: bands 7.30pm Mon-Sat. Separate rooms for parties, seating 15-32. Tables outdoors (8, garden; 6, pavement). **Map 13 B11**.

Opera

Bel Canto
Corus Hotel Hyde Park, 1 Lancaster Gate, W2 3LG (7262 1678, www.lebelcanto.com). Lancaster Gate tube. **Dinner served** 7-11pm Tue-Sat. **Set dinner** £39 2 courses, £46 3 courses. **Credit** AmEx, MC, V.
Having recently moved to Bayswater's Corus Hotel, Bel Canto continues to provide classic French cuisine (there's a sister restaurant in Paris) with a musical twist – the waiting staff are classically trained opera singers and break into song every 15 minutes. Dark wood panelling, velvet curtains and red chairs provide a suitably theatrical look to the establishment. The music centres on mainstream classics such as *The Marriage of Figaro* and *Carmen*. Audience participation is encouraged, with guests invited to join the well-known toast 'Brindisi' from *La Traviata*.
Available for hire. Booking essential. Children admitted. Disabled: lift; toilet. Dress: smart casual. **Map 8 D7**.

Sarastro
126 Drury Lane, WC2B 5QG (7836 0101, www.sarastro-restaurant.com). Covent Garden or Holborn tube. **Meals served** noon-11pm Mon-Thur; noon-11.30pm Fri, Sat; noon-10.30pm Sun. **Main courses** £9-£16.50. **Set lunch** (noon-6.30pm Mon-Sat) £14.50 2 courses. **Set meal** £29.50 3 courses incl coffee. **Credit** AmEx, DC, MC, V.
Named after a character from Mozart's *The Magic Flute*, this restaurant provides an operatic theme with ten individually-styled opera boxes, velvet drapes and theatrical props. Musicians from the ENO and Royal Opera House, along with students and talented newcomers, appear in opera and string quartet performances on Monday and Sunday evenings and on Sunday lunchtimes. Food is Mediterranean-Turkish.
Babies and children welcome: high chairs. Booking advisable. Disabled: toilet. Entertainment: opera, string quartet 8.30pm Mon, 2.30pm, 8.30pm Sun; swing & Motown vocalist 8pm Wed or Thur. **Map 18 F3**.

Wine Bars

London has plenty of places in which you can simply drink wine. Here, we point out the wine bars that proffer accompanying food with equal seriousness. Among our favourites is **Vinoteca** – well established in Farringdon but now with a Portman Village sibling that turns out terrifically gutsy cooking to partner the modern-minded, intelligently egalitarian wine list. Like many of the establishments in this section, it is based on the enoteca model, which allows you to drink on site or buy a bottle to take away. The increased blurring of distinctions between on and off sales is also reflected in the retailing operations of recommended restaurants such as **Gaucho** (*see p30*), **St John** (*see p50*), **RSJ** (*see p95*) and **L'Absinthe** (*see p96*). The other key trend among wine bars in recent years has been the spread of 'natural' wines (those with as little added or taken away from the pure fermented grape juice as possible). Newcomer **Bar Battu** has pinned its French flag to that mast, joining venues such as **Terroirs** (plus its new offshoot **Brawn**, *see p220*) and **Green & Blue** in promoting their virtues. Whatever your views on viticulture and vinification, at least these wines are interesting.

Central
Chancery Lane

★ 28°-50° Wine Workshop & Kitchen
140 Fetter Lane, EC4A 1BT (7242 8877, www.2850.co.uk). Chancery Lane tube.
Bar **Open** 11am-11pm Mon-Fri. **Snacks served** noon-10pm Mon-Fri.
Restaurant **Lunch served** noon-2.30pm, **dinner served** 6-9.30pm Mon-Fri. **Main courses** £12-£15.95. **House wine** £19.50 bottle, £3.60 glass.
Both **Credit** AmEx, MC, V.
This exciting collaboration between sommelier Xavier Rousset and executive chef Agnar Sverrisson (their second, following haute cuisine restaurant Texture) is focused on wine, but has much more attention on food than the average wine bar. You can eat from the bar or restaurant menu in either area; both are informally furnished with rough-hewn wood tables and teal blue walls hung with mirrors and restrained wine-abilia. The bar menu lists a handful of charcuterie and cheese accompaniments; the restaurant menu is French-oriented, with British accents conferred by much of the produce. Starters of tangy whitebait, prawns and capers on toast and beet salad indicated that something special was happening in the kitchen; Devon cod served with foraged seashore herbs and vegetables confirmed it. Wine comes from either of two lists. One is 40-strong

and eminently explorable – seldom repeating a grape variety, and with everything available in sampler glasses. The other is a fine wine list, unusually compiled: 28°-50° effectively acts as an agent for collectors selling stock; there are some celebrated vintages from heavy-hitting winemakers. This system sometimes (though not always) results in good value. A grape or producer of the month is honoured with a special section.
Available for hire. Booking advisable.
Separate rooms for parties, seating 6 and 12.
Map 11 N6.

City

Bar Battu NEW
48 Gresham Street, EC2V 7AY (7036 6100, www.barbattu.com). Bank tube/DLR. **Open** 11.30am-11pm Mon-Fri. **Food served** noon-9pm Mon-Fri. **Main courses** £10.50-£24.50. **Set meal** £17.50 2 courses, £19.50 3 courses. **House wine** from £17.50 bottle, from £4 glass. **Credit** AmEx, MC, V.
A French spot with a stylish New York edge, Bar Battu occupies the former site of Molloy's in the heart of the City, and is a fully signed-up exponent of natural wines. Many of these are available by the glass or carafe; the menu comes with user-friendly symbols that denote cloudiness, body and 'wild' or 'semi-wild' to indicate how unfettered the wines really are. Regardless of anyone's views on growing techniques, the term biodynamic, in particular, usually indicates a high level of

artisanship and care; the resulting wines tend to be striking, sometimes cloudy due to a lack of sulphites, and often featuring uninhibited, expressive characters that can alarm as many tasters as they excite. An enthusiastic sommelier is on hand to guide drinkers (who can sit at the bar if they don't want to eat) through the list, which also includes French ciders and a few sherries. We like the water policy too: it's unlimited, filtered, from the mains, still or sparkling, and comes with a boundless supply of bread for £1.50 per person. Food is equally on-trend: small plates of tapas/cicchetti drawing on French, Italian and Spanish cuisines; everything we tried was superb.
Available for hire. Babies and children admitted.
Booking advisable lunch. Disabled: toilet.
Map 11 P6.

Clerkenwell & Farringdon

Bleeding Heart Tavern
Bleeding Heart Yard, 19 Greville Street, EC1N 8SJ (7404 0333, www.bleedingheart.co.uk). Farringdon tube/rail.
Tavern **Open** 7am-11pm Mon-Fri. **Lunch served** noon-3pm, **snacks served** 3-6pm, **dinner served** 6-10.30pm Mon-Fri. **Main courses** £8.95-£15.45.
Bistro **Lunch served** noon-3pm, **dinner served** 6-10.30pm Mon-Sat. **Main courses** £8.95-£18.90.
Restaurant **Lunch served** noon-2.30pm, **dinner served** 6-10.30pm Mon-Fri.

Main courses £13.45-£28.95.
All House wine £19.25 bottle, £3.95 glass.
Credit AmEx, DC, MC, V.
Upstairs: a buzzy bare-brick space with elaborate carved-wood bar and close-packed tables heaving with shirts-and-ties. Downstairs: a demure, even dowdy, dining room with spacious booths sporadically occupied by a quieter, older crowd. Both: a menu that reads somewhere between nursery food and gastropub, and service that manages to look professional but act erratically. The food is well priced yet hit and miss: potted prawns, venison scotch egg, and pea and ham hock soup all serviceable but unexciting; fish pie well made and generous with the salmon; other mains poor, with flaccid roast (we presume) potatoes accompanying dry spit-roast pork, and a nasty haddock-flavoured roux sauce swamping an omelette. In all, a drab background against which the excellent wines shone brightly. The Bleeding Heart owns a vineyard in Hawkes Bay, New Zealand, and offers several of its cuvées here at good prices. The 2010 sauvignon blanc (£9.75 for a free-poured half bottle) was sophisticated yet vivid, and the 2009 pinot noir smooth and silky; the shiraz has been lauded by Robert Parker. Overall, a slightly odd experience: we suspect the Bleeding Heart trades a little too much on its two-century history while feeling, ironically, dated.
Booking advisable. Dress: smart; no shorts, jeans or trainers (restaurant). Separate rooms for parties, seating 12-125. Tables outdoors (10, terrace). **Map 11 N5**.
For branch (The Don) see index.

Cellar Gascon
59 West Smithfield, EC1A 9DS (7600 7561, www.cellargascon.com). Barbican tube or Farringdon tube/rail. **Open** noon-midnight Mon-Fri. **Food served** noon-11.30pm Mon-Fri. **Main courses** £6-£7. **Set meal** £7.50 1 course. **House wine** from £19 bottle, from £2.70 glass. **Credit** AmEx, MC, V.
Something seems awry at the clubby wine-bar adjunct of the usually reliable Gascon operation. Its banquette cushions are sagging, and the veneer is wearing thin on its tables. The kitchen too has lost some gloss. Now only one dish of the day supplements the tapas-style snacks (an uninspiring salmon and ratatouille, on our visit) and the snacks themselves lack excitement. Most of these French South-western regional dishes are assembled cold, rather than cooked to order, though quality is undoubtedly high: interesting charcuterie, well-kept cheese, prawns with herb butter, foie gras carpaccio. Hot dishes weren't special; Basque-style braised lamb shank was reasonable, but chipolatas in another Basque sauce, sakari, was dreadful. Nevertheless, the Cellar continues to offer an outstanding wine list, exclusively – champagnes excepted – from the south of France. It is well curated and well organised by region (Languedoc-Roussillon, Provence, Corsica), and shows specialist knowledge in its selection of fortified wines, sparkling reds and late-harvest dessert wines. The otherwise distracted staff came passionately alive when asked for a recommendation, offering us samples even though we were only choosing a single glass. But you have to wonder whether this expertise is wasted when the only other customers on a Friday night wanted frozen vodka.
Available for hire. Babies and children admitted. Tables outdoors (3, pavement). **Map 11 O5**.

For branches (Le Cercle, Club Gascon, Le Comptoir Gascon) see index.

Mayfair

★ Vinoteca   `HOT 50`
15 Seymour Place, W1H 5BD (7724 7288, www.vinoteca.co.uk). Marble Arch tube. **Open** noon-10pm Mon-Sat; noon-4pm Sun. **Lunch served** noon-3pm daily. **Dinner served** 6-10pm Mon-Sat. **No credit cards**.
Vinoteca's new outlet is a mere cork's pop from Oxford Street, yet completely removed in spirit. Set

Sip and tucker

You can drink-in or take home at these tremendous wine bars, which also offer platters of carefully selected deli delights to enjoy alongside their first-rate wine lists.

Finborough Wine Cafe
118 Finborough Road, SW10 9ED (7373 0745, www.finboroughwine cafe.co.uk). West Brompton tube/rail. **Open** 8am-11pm Mon-Sat; 10am-10pm Sun. **Meals served** 8am-10pm Mon-Sat; 10am-10pm Sun. **Main courses** £8-£20.60. **House wine** £18.95 bottle, from £3.50 glass. **Credit** MC, V.
An all-day café, wine bar and shop rolled into one – with a fringe theatre. The ground-floor bar has a real fire, leather sofas and welcoming young staff, while downstairs you'll find wine-tasting tables and the cellar. Around 50 wines are stocked at any one time, offering a range of styles, origins and prices. Tempted to explore? For £8 you can taste 12 wines of your choice. Nibble on the cheese and charcuterie platters, or order one of the wood-fired pizzas brought in from Firezza next door.
Available for hire. Babies and children admitted. Booking advisable. Disabled: toilet. Tables outdoors (5, pavement). **Map 13 B12**.

Green & Blue
36-38 Lordship Lane, SE22 8HJ (8693 9250, www.greenandbluewines. com). East Dulwich rail. **Open/meals served** 9am-11pm Mon-Wed; 9am-midnight Thur-Sat; 11am-8pm Sun. **Main courses** £5-£10. **House wine** £14 bottle, £3.50 glass. **Credit** MC, V.
Every high street could do with a place like this (and there are plans for expansion). Green & Blue's wine list isn't huge, but there's much to love. Owner Kate Thal does an excellent job combining big-name superstars with some oddities and new discoveries. Monday nights feature tastings and masterclasses (booking required) – and there's also a 13-week wine course. Food ranges from charcuterie and cheese platters to vegetarian antipasti, Mediterranean dips, and hot jacket potatoes. The bar is surprisingly family-friendly too, with high chairs and a children's menu.

on a villagey parade of upmarket shops, it repeats the successful Farringdon blend of wine bar, restaurant and shop and adds some new ideas. One is a feasting table, where groups of five to nine people can enjoy sharing dishes such as slow-roast shoulder of mutton. But you can also come alone, order a prosecco (from the tap) and enjoy bar nibbles. We opted for a three-course meal with matching wines, a great way to experiment. Denbie's Surrey Gold (yes, that Surrey) worked well with smoked eel, leeks and lovage dressing; more striking was the thick, honeyed vin doux from Samos, Greece, served with rhubarb jelly, palmier

Babies and children welcome: high chairs; nappy-changing facilities. Booking advisable weekends. Disabled: toilet. Map 23 C4.

Negozio Classica
283 Westbourne Grove, W11 2QA (7034 0005, www.negozioclassica.co.uk). Ladbroke Grove or Notting Hill Gate tube. **Open/meals served** 3.30pm-midnight Mon-Thur; 11am-midnight Fri, Sun; 9am-midnight Sat. **Main courses** £8.40-£14.70. **House wine** £7.99 bottle (retail), £3.95 glass. **Corkage** £8.50. **Credit** AmEx, MC, V.
It may look as if a European trade fair stand has been plonked beside Portobello Road, but we can't fault Negozio Classica for the quality of its deli goods (pasta, saffron, olive oil, honey) or wines. Tuscany and Piedmont are the list's mainstays, alongside interesting selections from Sicily and Slovenia. A wine dispenser allows sale of fine wines by the glass, but this is also a place to try relatively inexpensive vintages from iconic names; bargains include dolcetto and barbera from leading Barolo wine-makers. Alternatively, sip on Teo Musso beer, grappa or a cappuccino. *Separate room for parties, seats 13. Tables outdoors (3, pavement).* **Map 7 N6**.

Wonder Bar
Selfridges, 400 Oxford Street, W1A 1AB (7318 2476, www.selfridges.com). Bond Street or Marble Arch tube. **Open/meals served** 11am-10pm Mon-Fri; 11am-9pm Sat, Sun. **Main courses** £9.50-£15. **House wine** £35 bottle, £5.25 glass. **Credit** AmEx, DC, MC, V.
A slim red mezzanine right-angle above Selfridges' wine department, Wonder Bar offers a varied choice of wines with a pleasing mix of favourites and new, challenging flavours. An Enomatic machine dispensing wines by the glass encourages sampling (in so far as the minimum 125ml glass sizes allow), but so too does the beautifully written wine list, which enthuses and educates rather than lectures. To eat, there's a range of meat, cheese and fish boards, plus salads (waldorf, goat's cheese, prosciutto), oysters and a few rich desserts. Handy.
Available for hire. Babies and children admitted. Booking advisable. Disabled: lift; toilet. Map 9 G6.

28°-50° Wine Workshop & Kitchen. See p324.

and vanilla ice-cream. The cooking was mostly terrific, with hot, double-crusted meat pies (pork and prune, say, or mutton and oyster) a highlight. Wines are always brought before the food to allow time to savour, and served with brief comments from staff. If this sounds pretentious, rest assured it's not – Vinoteca is classily relaxed, a place that makes wine buffery fun. The smart-casual crowd of carefully matured groovers who've flocked here since November 2010 confirm it.

Bookings not accepted. **Map 8 F6**.
For branch see index.

Piccadilly

1707

Fortnum & Mason, 181 Piccadilly, W1J 9FA (7734 8040, www.fortnumandmason.com). Piccadilly Circus tube. **Meals served** noon-10pm Mon-Sat. **Main courses** £2.75-£32. **House wine** from £18.50 bottle, from £6.25 glass. **Credit** AmEx, MC, V.

The idea works well in principle: position a wine bar-restaurant in the downstairs deli heartland of Fortnum & Mason, lay on wine-friendly food and allow customers either to choose from a list showcasing house wines, or purchase from the wine department and pay £10 corkage. It works less well in practice. The wood-walled room-within-a-room is stylish, but the food – other than deli goods (cheese, smoked salmon, cured meats) – is nothing special, or, in the case of our first two dishes from the short, snacky menu (grape and almond gazpacho, dressed crab) virtually non-existent. A skewer of merguez sausage and rabbit was the only hot dish, and ours seemed to have been reheated judging by its dry exterior. For £14, with just some green leaves and cardboardy toast triangles, this was poor. The house red burgundy wasn't great either, but it was at the cheerier price of £6.50, for 175ml: the smallest measure available by the glass. Fortunately, the ten flights of three wines grouped by region or type come in 125ml measures – though even these total a half bottle (share!). Customers seemed as likely to order champagne or cocktails at the attractive central bar, and the punctilious staff better briefed to serve them.

Available for hire. Babies and children admitted. Booking advisable. Disabled: lift; toilet (ground floor). **Map 9 J7**.

Strand

★ Terroirs HOT 50

5 William IV Street, WC2N 4DW (7036 0660, www.terroirswinebar.com). Charing Cross tube/rail. **Open** noon-11pm Mon-Sat. **Lunch**

Terroirs

Bar Battu. See p324.

served noon-3pm, **dinner served** 5.30-11pm Mon-Sat. **Main courses** £13-£15. **House wine** £17 bottle, £4.25 glass. **Credit** AmEx, MC, V.

Terroirs was among the first places in London to serve 'natural wines': unfiltered wines with no added acid, sugar or sulphur, made from biodynamically grown organic grapes (here marked by a horse icon). All the wines on the 200-strong list come from artisan growers, mostly from France or Italy, who work sustainably, organically or biodynamically, with minimal interventions at the winery. There's a good choice by the glass and pot, but it's a shame to miss the tasting notes on the main list. A 2008 Domaine Sébastien Riffault Sancerre is described as 'a thunderous gallop through wild forests and murky thickets'. However, what makes everyone so keen on Terroirs is that the food is just as good. Served in the small ground floor, and an attractive, roomy basement, the menu runs from charcuterie and cheese, through small plates (salade paysanne, fish soup, smoked duck with beetroot and hazelnuts) to bigger plats du jour, such as braised rabbit leg with glazed carrots, celeriac purée and tarragon. Service is brisk but friendly; we were in a hurry and the waiter made sure we hit our deadline. Terroirs is often fully booked, but always has unreserved seats at the bar. *Babies and children admitted. Booking advisable. Tables outdoors (3, pavement).* **Map 18 D5**.

West
Notting Hill

Kensington Wine Rooms
127-129 Kensington Church Street, W8 7LP (7727 8142, www.greatwinesbytheglass.com). Notting Hill Gate tube. **Open** noon-midnight daily. **Meals served** noon-11pm daily. **Main courses** £13-£20. **House wine** £18 bottle, £4 glass. **Credit** AmEx, MC, V.

KWR's front-of-house wine bar and shop are textbook examples of how single-glass Enomatic dispensers have changed the game. An evening's drinking can be a self- or staff-guided exploration, taking in both low-priced small producers and landmark clarets. A wide-ranging, well-explained list, with 40 varieties by the glass and some 200 in the bottle, facilitates this admirably, along with a cosy, low-lit bar space and a deli-style tapas menu. In the back room – a comfortable den of dark furniture and open brickwork – the concept has been extended into a restaurant with a wine suggestion given for each dish on the short international menu, but here it stumbles. First, the food is of decidedly mixed rendition, from excellent gazpacho and a creamy-tasting buffalo steak tartare, to indifferent fish and chips and a poor prawn, grapefruit and mangetout salad with neither dressing nor seasoning. Second, the suggested glasses – a Loire Chinon Rouge with the buffalo – weren't always an immediately harmonious match. Had a sommelier explained the taste journey, this needn't have been disappointing, but the staff exuded kooky charm rather than wine expertise. We wonder if the management's attention is distracted by the attractive new Fulham operation. Both venues offer various tasting events. *Babies and children welcome: high chairs. Booking advisable evenings.* **Map 7 B7**. **For branch (Fulham Wine Rooms) see index**.

Maps & Indexes

The following maps highlight London's key restaurant areas: the districts with the highest density of good places to eat and drink. They show precisely where each restaurant is located, as well as major landmarks and tube stations.

Key to Maps

© Copyright Time Out Group 2011

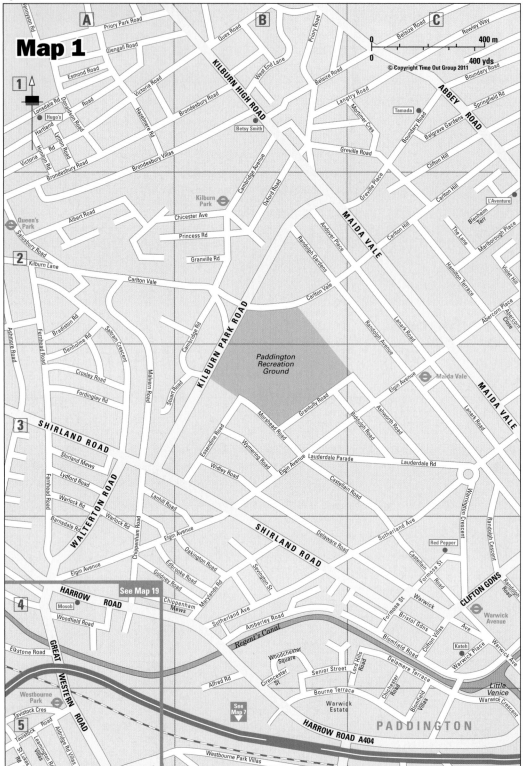

Map 1

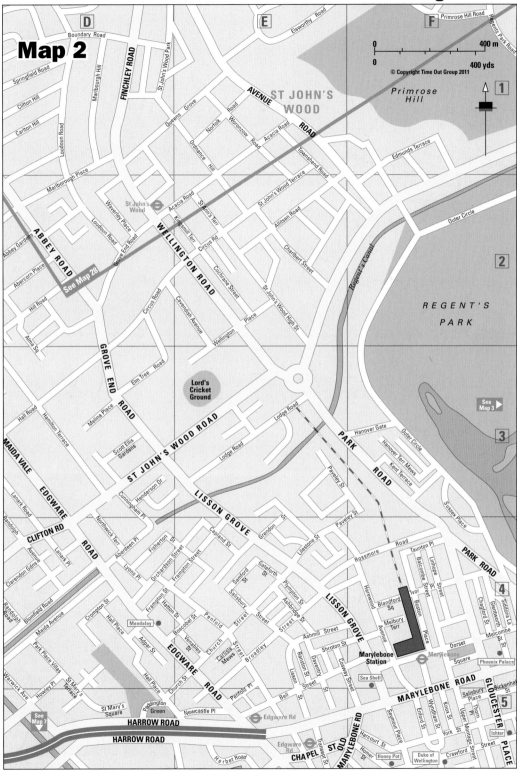

Camden Town & Marylebone

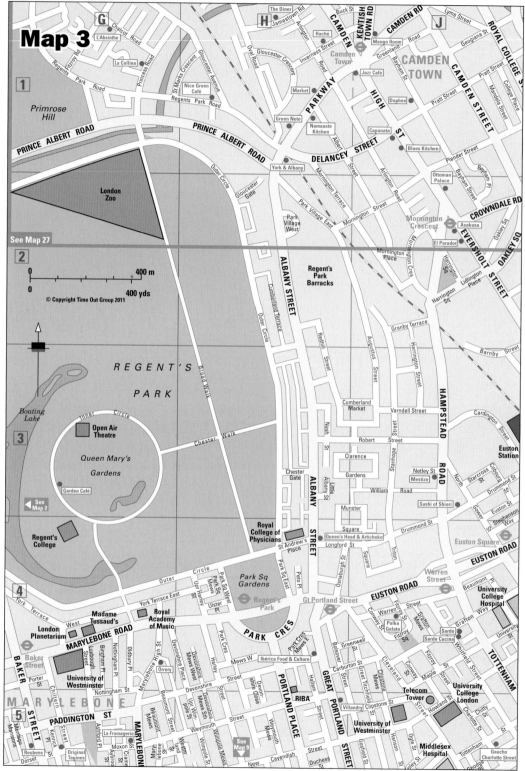

Map 3

1

Primrose Hill

2

See Map 27

0   400 m
0   400 yds
© Copyright Time Out Group 2011

London Zoo

REGENT'S PARK

Boating Lake

3

Open Air Theatre

Queen Mary's Gardens

Inner Circle

Garden Café

See Map 2

Regent's College

4

York Terrace

West

Madame Tussaud's

London Planetarium

Baker Street

Royal Academy of Music

York Terrace East

Ulster Pl

Outer Circle

Park Sq West

Upr Harley St

MARYLEBONE ROAD

University of Westminster

Luxborough Street

Brigham Pl

Nottingham Pl

Oldbury Pl

Orrery

Devonshire Place

Harley Street

Devonshire Mews West

Devonshire Mews Sth

Park Square East

Park Sq Gardens

Peto Pl

Regent's Park

Park Cres

St Andrew's Place

St Andrew's Place

Royal College of Physicians

ALBANY STREET

Chester Gate

Chester Walk

Broad Walk

Outer Circle

Cumberland Terrace

ALBANY STREET

Redhill Street

Nash Street

Robert Street

Clarence Gardens

Stanhope St

Munster Square

Longford St

William Road

Gardens

Varndell Street

Cumberland Market

Augustus Street

Harrington Street

Granby Terrace

HAMPSTEAD ROAD

North

Drummond St

Euston Square

EUSTON ROAD

Euston Station

Cardington St

Netley St

Mestizo

Sushi of Shiori

Queen's Head & Artichoke

Triton St

Drummond St

Starcross St

Cobourg St

Drummond St

Euston St

Gower St

Stephenson Way

PRINCE ALBERT ROAD

PRINCE ALBERT ROAD

Gloucester Gate

Park Village East

Park Village West

Outer Circle

Regent's Park Barracks

Mornington Terrace

Mornington St

Mornington Place

Mornington Cres

Mornington Crescent

Asakusa

El Parador

EVERSHOLT STREET

CROWNDALE RD

Oakley Sq

OAKLEY SQ

Harrington Sq

Lidlington Place

Harrington Sq

Barnby Street

DELANCEY STREET

York & Albany

Namaaste Kitchen

Green Note

Market

PARKWAY

Albert Street

HIGH ST

Jazz Café

Daphne

Caponata

Blues Kitchen

Plender Street

Arlington Road

Bayham Street

Bayham Pl

Ottoman Palace

CAMDEN TOWN

Greenland Road

Pratt Street

Pratt Street

College Place

Georgiana St

CAMDEN STREET

Mandela St

ROYAL COLLEGE ST

Lyme Street

CAMDEN RD

Camden Town

Buck St

Arlington Street

Inverness Street

Gloucester Crescent

Gloucester Avenue

KENTISH TOWN RD

Mango Room

Haché

The Diner

Jamestown Rd

H

J

G

L'Absinthe

Chalcot Road

La Collina

Regents Park Road

Princess Road

St Marks Crescent

Fitzroy Rd

Regent's Park Road

Nice Green Café

Regents Park Road

5

MARYLEBONE

PADDINGTON ST

La Fromagerie

Reubens

Original Tagines

Dorset St

BAKER STREET

Chiltern St

Porter St

Kendrick Pl

Moxon St

Cramer

Aybrook St

Ashford St

MARYLEBONE HIGH ST

Weymouth Mews

Beaumont Mews

Upr Wimpole St

Wimpole Mews

Wimpole St

Devonshire Close

Weymouth Street

New Cavendish Street

Mansfield Mews

Duchess St

See Map 9

PORTLAND PLACE

RIBA

Hallam Street

Great Portland Street

GREAT PORTLAND STREET

Bolsover St

Carburton St

Clipstone Mews

Clipstone Street

Cleveland Street

Maple St

Conway St

Howland St

Charlotte St

Telecom Tower

Villandry

University College London

Middlesex Hospital

Gaucho Charlotte Street

Hanson St

Goodge St

Ogle St

Gosfield St

Riding Ho St

University of Westminster

TOTTENHAM

Chitty St

Tottenham St

EUSTON ROAD

Gt Portland Street

Warren Street

Beaumont Pl

Warren St

Conway St

Grafton Way

Grafton Mews

Fitzroy St

Grafton Way

Maple St

Whitfield St

Tottenham Court

University College Hospital

Beaumont Pl

Polka Gelato

Sardo

Sardo Cucina

Ibérica Food & Culture

Park Cres Mews E

Park Cres Mews W

Greenwell St

Bolsover St

Osnaburgh St

Albany St

Little Albany St

PARK CRES

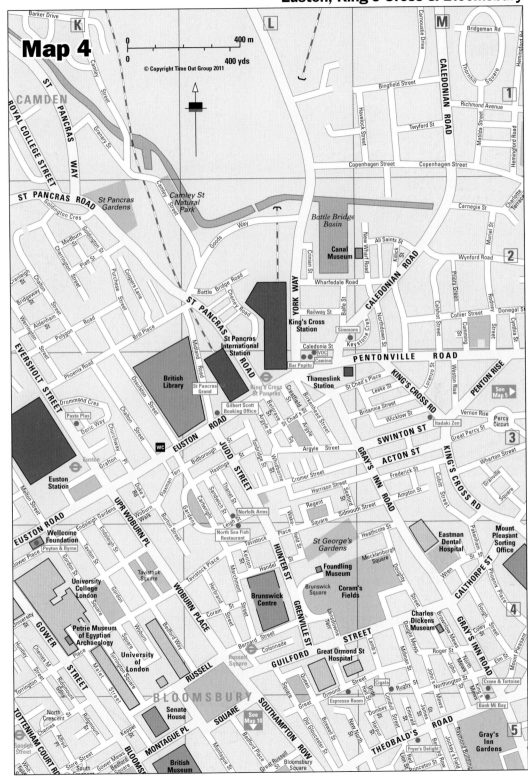

Map 4

0   400 m
0   400 yds
© Copyright Time Out Group 2011

K

CAMDEN

ROYAL COLLEGE STREET
ST PANCRAS WAY
Barker Drive
Camley Street
Granary St

ST PANCRAS ROAD
St Pancras Gardens
Goldington Cres
Medburn St
Goldington St
Charrington Street
Platt St
Polygon Road
Cranleigh St
Chalton St
Bridgeway St
Aldenham St
Warrington St
Phoenix Road
Drummond Cres
Doric Way
Churchway
Chalton Street
Ossulston Street
Midland Road
Cooper's Lane
Purchese St
Brill Place
Battle Bridge Road
Cheney Road

EVERSHOLT STREET

Pasta Plus

British Library

St Pancras Grand
Gilbert Scott Booking Office
St Pancras International Station

King's Cross St Pancras

WC

EUSTON ROAD
JUDD STREET
Grafton Pl
Euston
Euston Station
Melton Street

L

St Pancras Natural Park
Camley St
Goods Way
Battle Bridge Basin
York Way

Canal Museum
New Wharf Road
Crinan St
Wharfedale Road
Balfe St

King's Cross Station
Simmons

ST PANCRAS ROAD
Railway St
Caledonia St
VOC
Camino
Bar Pepito
Keystone Cres

Thameslink Station
St Chad's Place
Belgrove St
St Chad's St
Argyle St
Birkenhead Street
Crestfield St
Britannia Street
Wicklow St
Leeke St

Argyle Street
Tonbridge St
Whidborne St
Cromer Street
Hastings St
Bidborough St
Sandwich St
Thanet St

Harrison Street
Regent Square
Wakefield St
Sidmouth Street

Norfolk Arms
North Sea Fish Restaurant
Tavistock Place
Leigh St
Cartwright Gardens
Burton Street
Marchmont Street
Kenton St
Handel St
Hunter St

M
Bridgeman Rd
Hemingford Rd

CALEDONIAN ROAD
Thornhill Rd
Carnoustie Drive
Bingfield Street
Richmond Avenue
Havelock Street
Twyford St
Matilda Street
Copenhagen Street
Copenhagen Street
Carnegie St
Charlotte Terrace
Muriel St
All Saints St
Wynford Road
Killick St
Priory Green
Calshot Street
Rodney St
Collier Street
Cumming St
Donegal St
Cynthia St
Vernon Rise

PENTONVILLE ROAD
KING'S CROSS RD
SWINTON ST
ACTON ST
Percy Circus
Gt Percy St
Itadaki Zen
KING'S CROSS RD
Wharton Street
Granville Square
Frederick St
Ampton St
GRAY'S INN ROAD
Sidmouth Street
Pakenham St
Cubitt Street
Weston Rise
Penton Rise
See Map 5

See Map 5

1

2

3

MAPS

WELLCOME FOUNDATION
Peyton & Byrne
Gower Place
University College London
Petrie Museum of Egyptian Archaeology
Gordon Square
UPR WOBURN PL
Endsleigh Gardens
Endsleigh St
Taviton St
Tavistock Square
Woburn Walk
Duke's Rd
Flaxman Terr
Gordon St

EUSTON ROAD
GOWER STREET
University St
Chenies M
Ridgmount Gdns
Huntley St
Torrington Place

TOTTENHAM COURT RD
North Crescent
Chenies St
Ridgmount St
Alfred Place
Store Street
Gower Mews
Bedford Ave
South
Whitfield

WOBURN PLACE
RUSSELL SQUARE
Bedford Way
Coram Street
Bernard Street
Woburn Square
Torrington Square
Malet Street
Keppel Street
Montague Place
Montague St

BLOOMSBURY
Senate House
University of London
Russell Square
Colonnade
Tavistock Place

St George's Gardens
Foundling Museum
Brunswick Square
Coram's Fields
Mecklenburgh Square
Doughty Street
Wren
Lansdowne Terr

Brunswick Centre
GRENVILLE ST
HUNTER ST
GUILFORD STREET
Great Ormond St Hospital
Lamb's Conduit St
Millman St
Roger St
John's Mews
Northington St
John St
Doughty Mews
Rugby St
Emerald St
Dombey St
Harpur St
Boswell St
New North St
Old Gloucester St
Great Russell St
Bloomsbury Square

Charles Dickens Museum
Brownlow Mews
CALTHORPE ST
GRAY'S INN ROAD
Mount Pleasant Sorting Office
Eastman Dental Hospital
Phoenix Place
Gough St
Mount Pleasant
Coley St
Elm St
Pakenham St

Espresso Room
Cigala
Ormond
Gt Ormond St
King's Mews
Crane & Tortoise
Bánh Mi Bay

THEOBALD'S ROAD
Jockey's Fields
Gray's Inn Gardens
Fryer's Delight
Raymond Buildings
Jockey's Fields
Princeton St
Red Lion St
Lamb's Conduit St

SOUTHAMPTON ROW
Bloomsbury Place
Bedford Place
Queen Square
Great James St
James St

See Map 10

British Museum

4

5

Islington, Clerkenwell & Farringdon

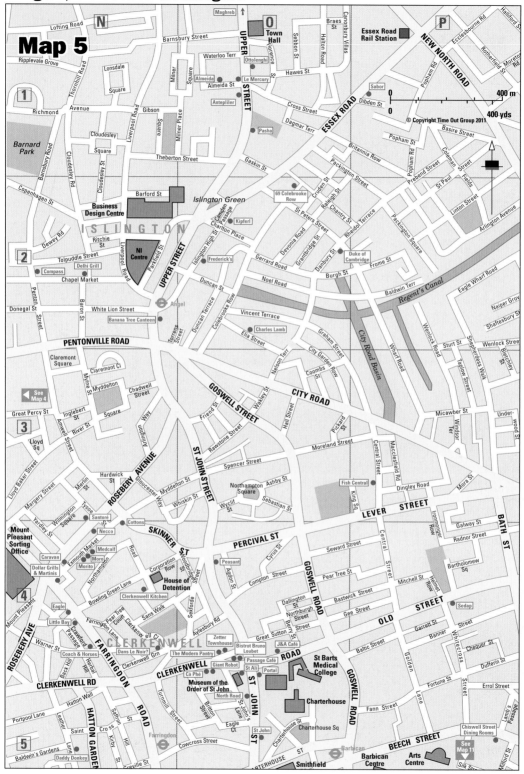

Map 5

Lofting Road
Ripplevale Grove
Lonsdale
Square
Barnsbury Street
Waterloo Terr
Florence
Ottolenghi
Almeida
Le Mercury
Almeida St
Cross Street
Dagmar Terr
Antepliler
Pasha
Richmond
Avenue
Gibson
Milner Place
Theberton Street
Gaskin St
Cloudesley
Square
Barnard
Park
Thornhill Road
Barnsbury Road
Copenhagen St
Dewey Rd
Ritchie
St
Cloudesley Rd
Cloudesley St
Tolpuddle Street
Compass
Delhi Grill
Chapel Market
Penton St
Donegal St
White Lion Street
Banana Tree Canteen
Angel
Business
Design Centre
ISLINGTON
Barford St
Islington Green
NI
Centre
Liverpool Road
Parkfield St
Islington High St
Frederick's
Camden
Passage
Charlton Place
Kipferl
Duncan St
St Peters Street
Devonia Road
Gerrard Road
Noel Road
Burgh St
69 Colebrooke
Row
Cruden St
Raleigh St
Chantry St
Danbury St
Rheidol Terrace
Duke of
Cambridge
Frome St
Baldwin Terr
Maghreb
UPPER STREET
Town
Hall
Sebbon St
Halton Road
Braes
St
Canonbury Villas
ESSEX ROAD
Essex Road
Rail Station
Britannia Row
Packington Street
Prebend St
St Paul
Coleman
Street
Packington Square
Linton Street
Arlington Avenue
NEW NORTH ROAD
Sabor
Dibden St
Popham Rd
Basire Street
Popham Rd
© Copyright Time Out Group 2011
Ecclesbourne Rd
Rotherfield
St
Halliford St
Moreto
Rd
400 m
400 yds
PENTONVILLE ROAD
Claremont
Square
Claremont Cl
Myddelton
Square
Chadwell
Street
Great Percy St
Amwell Street
Inglebert St
River St
Myddelton
St
Myrtle St
Duncan Terrace
Colebrooke Row
Vincent Terrace
Charles Lamb
Elia Street
Nelson Terr
City Garden Row
Coombs St
Graham Street
Wakley St
Regent's Canal
City Road Basin
Wharf Road
Wenlock Road
Eagle Wharf Road
Naper Grov
Shaftesbury Av
Sturt St
Shepherdess Walk
Wenlock Street
Taplow Street
Blanch
Under-
wood St
GOSWELL STREET
CITY ROAD
Friend St
Hall Street
Pickard St
Micawber St
Windsor
Ter
Mora Rd
See
Map 4
Lloyd
Sq
Lloyd Baker Street
Margery Street
Merlin
St
Hardwick
St
ROSEBERY AVENUE
Gloucester Way
Myddelton St
Whiskin St
Wyclif St
ST JOHN STREET
Spencer Street
Rawstone Street
Northampton
Square
Ashby St
Sebastian St
Moreland Street
Central
Street
Macclesfield Rd
Dingley Road
Fish Central
King St
LEVER   STREET
Galway St
Radnor Street
BATH
STREET
Ironmonger
Row
Wilmington
Square
Yardley St
Tysoe
St
Santoré
Necco
Cottons
SKINNER   ST
PERCIVAL ST
Cyrus St
Seward Street
Central
Street
Bartholomew
Sq
Caravan
Dollar Grills
& Martinis
Exmouth Market
Medcalf
Moro
Morito
Northampton
St
Peasant
Agdon St
Compton Street
Pear Tree St
Mitchell St
Helmet
Row
Sedap
Mount
Pleasant
Sorting
Office
Corporation
Row
House of
Detention
Bowling Green Lane
Clerkenwell Kitchen
GOSWELL ROAD
Dallington
Street
Northburgh
Street
Berry St
Gee Street
Bastwick Street
OLD
STREET
Garrett St
Banner
Whitecross
Golden
Chequer St
Dufferin St
Mount Pleasant
ROSEBERY AVE
Eagle
Little Bay
Pear Tree
Court
Warner St
Back Hill
Herbal
Hill
Crawford
Passage
Coach & Horses
FARRINGDON
Clerkenwell
Lane
Sans Walk
Sekforde
Aylesbury Rd
CLERKENWELL
Zetter
Townhouse
Dans Le Noir?
The Modern Pantry
Cà Phê
Clerkenwell Grn
Giant Robot
St Ali
Great Sutton St
Berry St
Bistrot Bruno
Loubet
Passage Café
Portal
J&A Café
ROAD
GOSWELL ROAD
Baltic Street
Banner
Street
Fortune St
Errol Street
Lever Street
CLERKENWELL RD
Portpool Lane
Hatton Wall
HATTON GARDEN
Leather
Lane
Saint
Cross
St
Kirby
Hill
Museum of the
Order of St John
Gt
Sutton
St
North Road
ST
JOHN
ST
Britton
Street
St John's
Lane
Eagle
Ct
St John
TURNMILL
STREET
Baldwin's Gardens
Daddy Donkey
Farringdon
Greville St
Cowcross Street
CHARTERHOUSE
St Barts Medical
College
Charterhouse
Charterhouse St
Charterhouse Sq
Smithfield
Barbican
Barbican
Centre
Fann Street
BEECH STREET
Golden
Lane
Arts
Centre
Chiswell Street
Dining Rooms
See
Map 11
Silk St

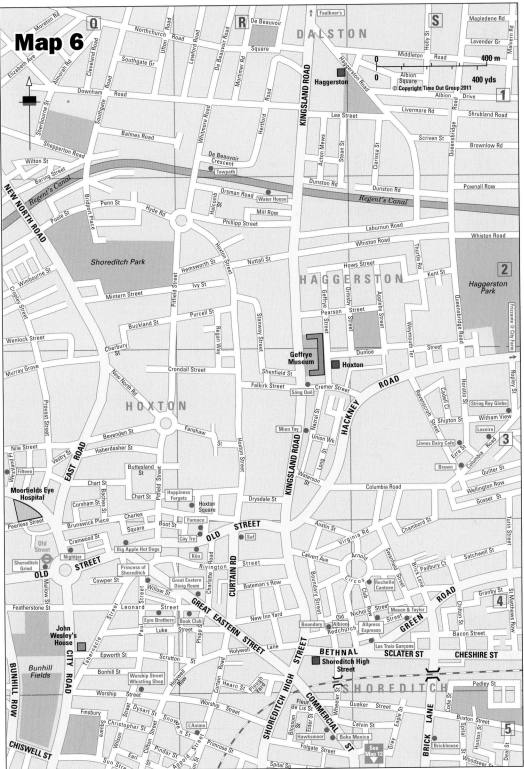

Map 6

DALSTON

HAGGERSTON

HOXTON

SHOREDITCH

BETHNAL

MAPS

Notting Hill, Bayswater & Kensington

Map 7

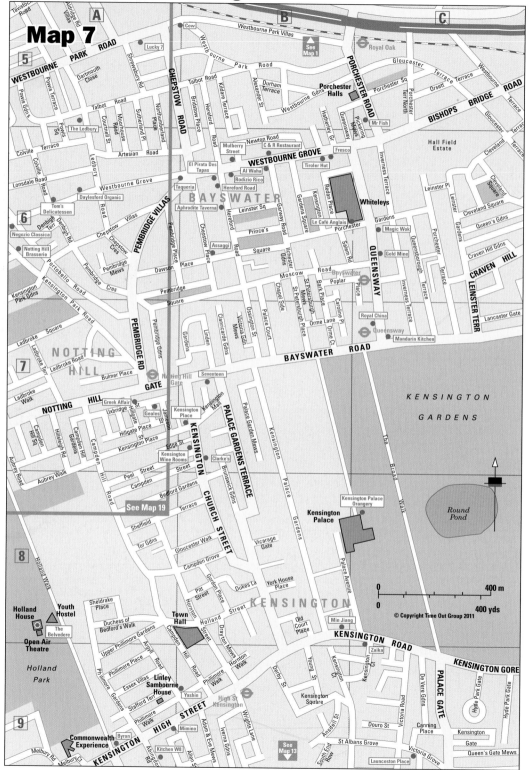

See Map 1
See Map 19
See Map 13

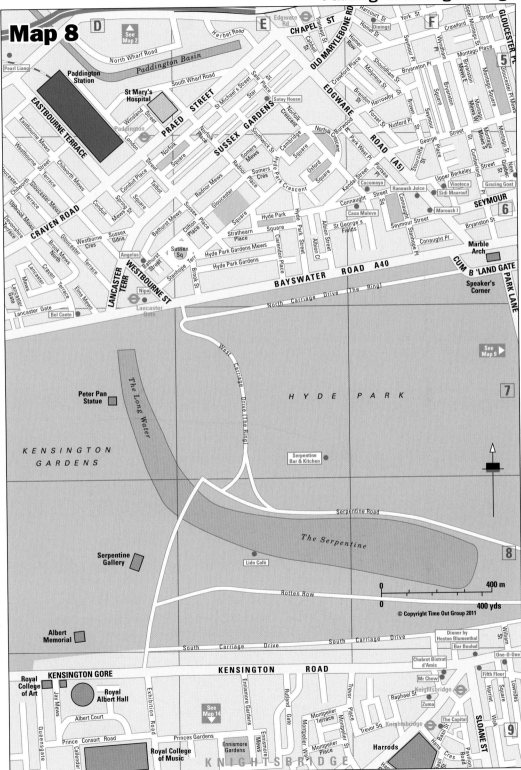

Map 8

Marylebone, Fitzrovia, Mayfair & St James's

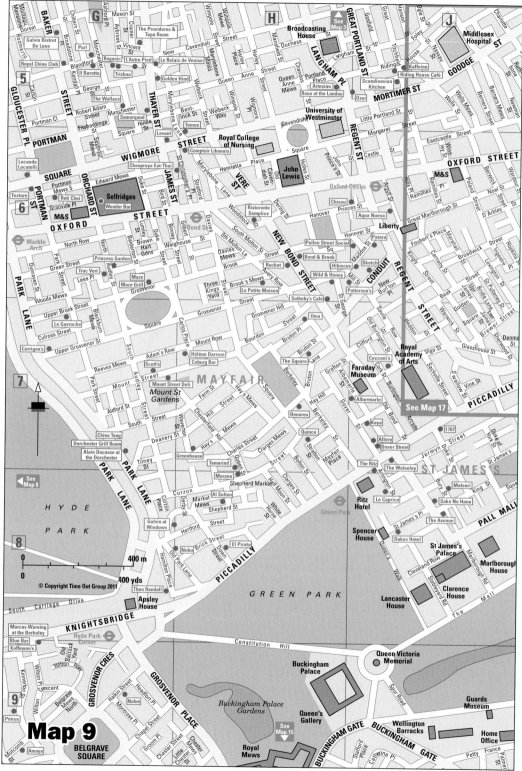

MAPS

Map 9

BELGRAVE SQUARE

© Copyright Time Out Group 2011

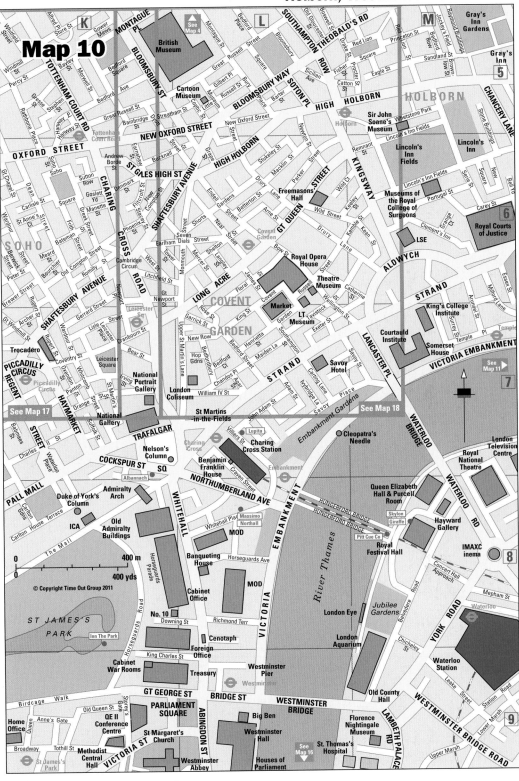

Map 10

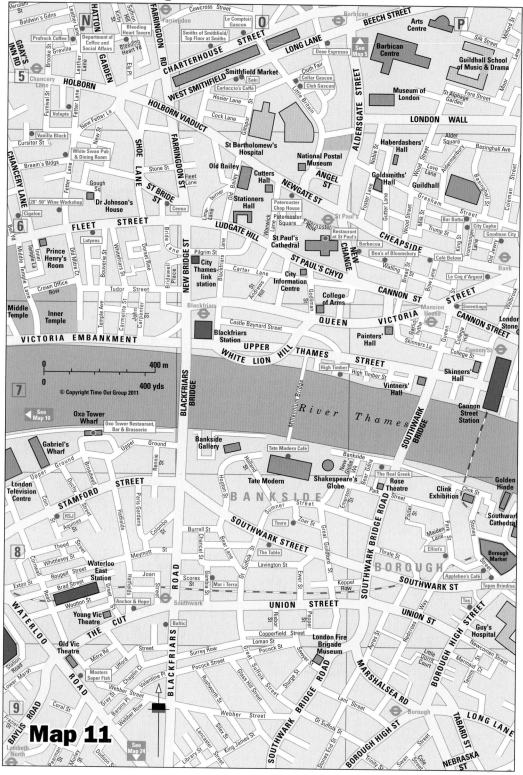

Map 11

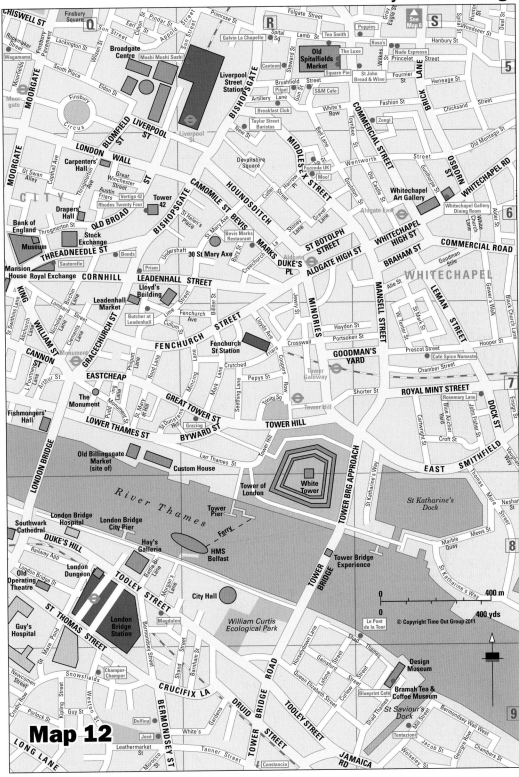

Map 12

MAPS

Earl's Court, Gloucester Road & Fulham

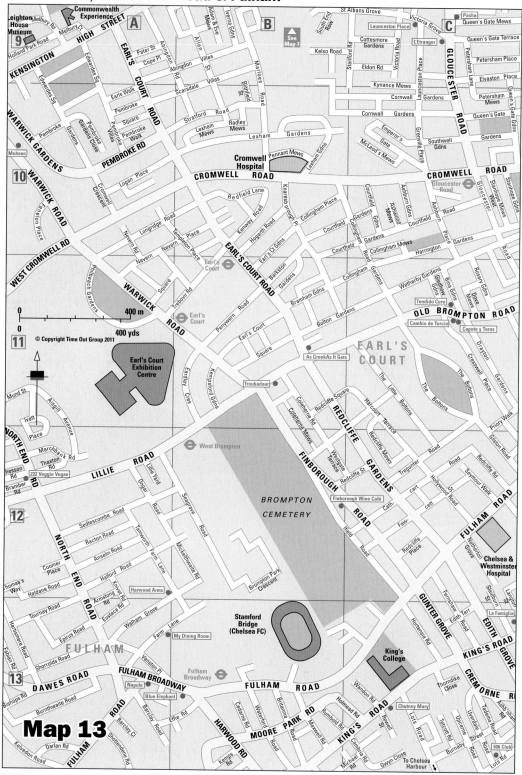

MAPS

Map 13

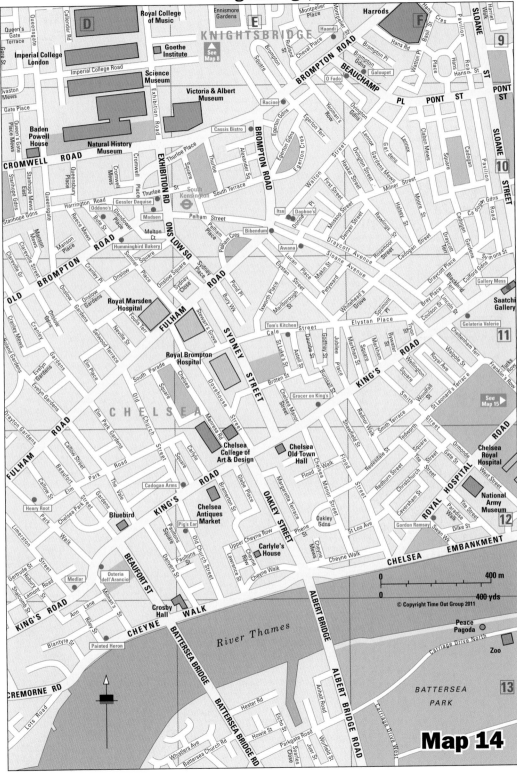

Belgravia, Victoria & Pimlico

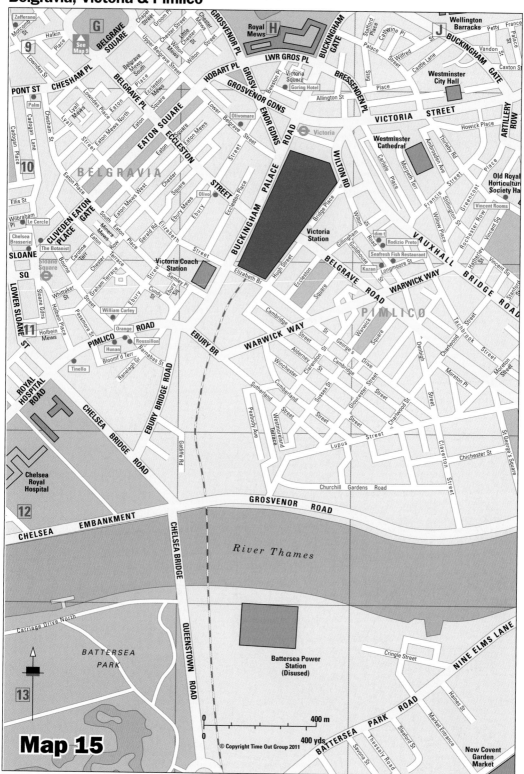

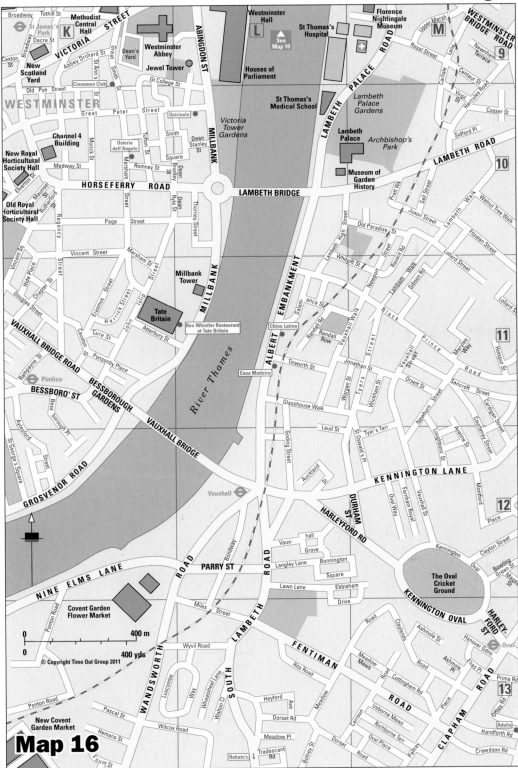

Map 16

Fitzrovia, Soho & Chinatown

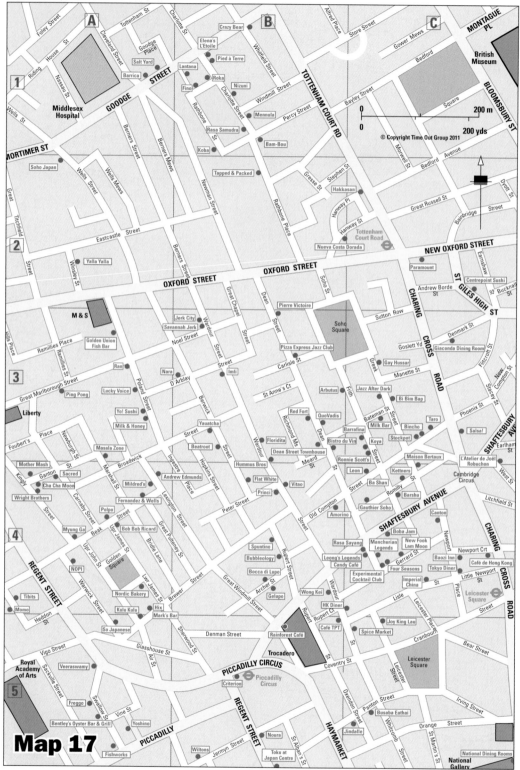

MAPS

Map 17

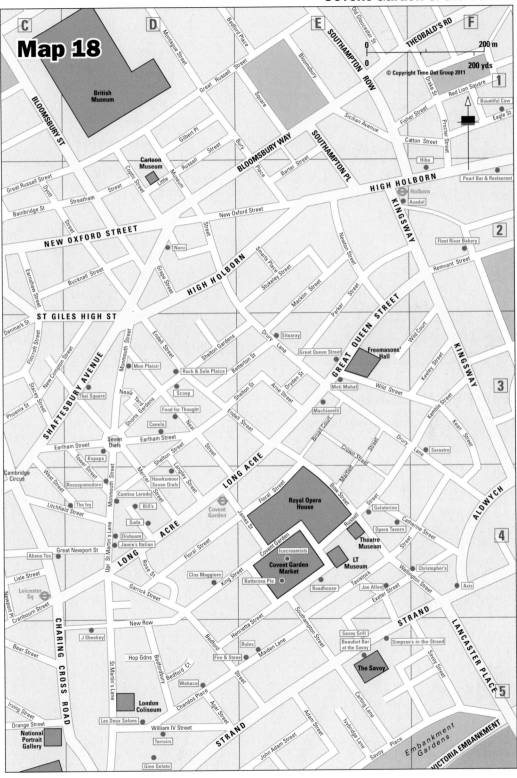

Map 18

C D E F

British Museum

Cartoon Museum

BLOOMSBURY ST

Montague Street

Bedford Place

Great Russell Street

Bloomsbury Square

SOUTHAMPTON ROW

Old Gloucester St

THEOBALD'S RD

Drake St

Red Lion Square

Bountiful Cow

Eagle St

Fisher Street

Proctor Street

Catton Street

0 200 m
0 200 yds

© Copyright Time Out Group 2011

Sicilian Avenue

Gilbert Pl

Russell Street

Coptic Street

Little Russell Street

Museum Street

Bury Place

Barter Street

BLOOMSBURY WAY

SOUTHAMPTON PL

Hiba

HIGH HOLBORN

Holborn
Asadal

KINGSWAY

Pearl Bar & Restaurant

Great Russell Street

Dyott Street

Streatham Street

Bainbridge St

Museum Street

New Oxford Street

Fleet River Bakery

NEW OXFORD STREET

Naru

HIGH HOLBORN

Newton Street

Remnant Street

Earnshaw Street

Bucknall Street

Grape Street

Sheurts Place Street

Stukeley Street

Macklin Street

Parker Street

Wild Court

Denmark St

ST GILES HIGH ST

Sitaaray

Drury Lane

Great Queen Street

GREAT QUEEN STREET

Freemasons' Hall

Wild Street

Keeley Street

KINGSWAY

Filtcroft Street

New Compton Street

Endell Street

Shelton Gardens

Betterton St

Dryden St

Arne Street

Moti Mahal

Kemble Street

Kean Street

Mon Plaisir

SHAFTESBURY AVENUE

Rock & Sole Plaice

Scoop

Shelton St

Endell Street

Machiavelli

Broad Court

Crown Street

Martlett

Drury Lane

Sarastro

Phoenix St

Stacey Street

Neal's Yard Gardens

Thai Square

Food for Thought

Neal Street

ALDWYCH

Earlham Street

Shorts Gardens

Canela

Earlham Street

Seven Dials

Shelton Street

Langley Street

Bow Street

Gelatorino

Catherine Street

Cambridge Circus

Tower Street

Kopapa

Mercer Street

Hawksmoor Seven Dials

LONG ACRE

Floral Street

Russell Street

Opera Tavern

West Street

Rossopomodoro

Cantina Laredo

Royal Opera House

Theatre Museum

Christopher's

Litchfield Street

The Ivy

Bill's

Covent Garden

James St

LT Museum

Wellington Street

Axis

Suda

Dishoom

Jamie's Italian

Icecreamists

Tavistock Street

Joe Allen

Exeter Street

Great Newport St

Abeno Too

LONG ACRE

Rose St

Floral Street

Covent Garden Market

Clos Maggiore

Battersea Pie

Roadhouse

STRAND

Lisle Street

Leicester Sq

Garrick Street

King Street

Southampton Street

LANCASTER PLACE

Newport Pl

Cranbourn Street

New Row

Henrietta Street

Maiden Lane

Savoy Grill

Beaufort Bar at the Savoy

Simpson's-in-the-Strand

Bear Street

CHARING CROSS ROAD

J Sheekey

Hop Gdns

Bedford Street

Rules

Fire & Stone

The Savoy

Savoy Street

Irving Street

St Martin's Lane

Bedfordbury

Wahaca

Chandos Place

Agar Street

Adam Street

Corning Lane

Orange Street

London Coliseum

Les Deux Salons

William IV Street

Ivybridge Lane

Embankment Gardens

National Portrait Gallery

Terroirs

STRAND

John Adam Street

Savoy Place

VICTORIA EMBANKMENT

Gino Gelato

MAPS

Hammersmith & Shepherd's Bush

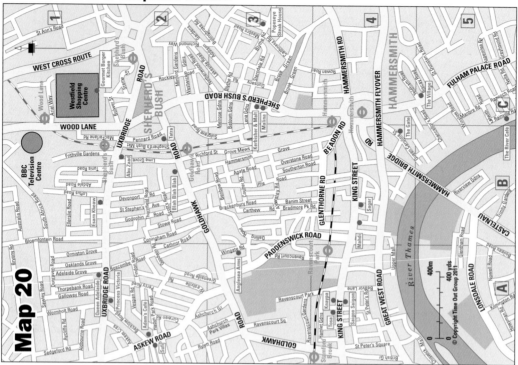

Notting Hill & Ladbroke Grove

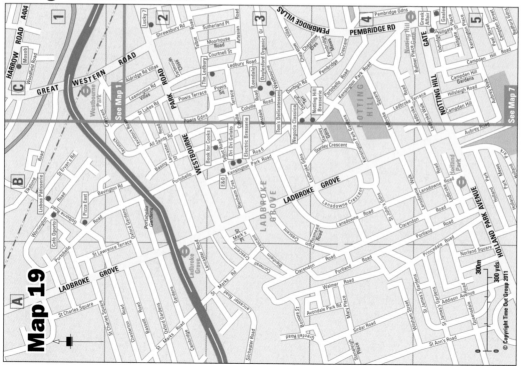

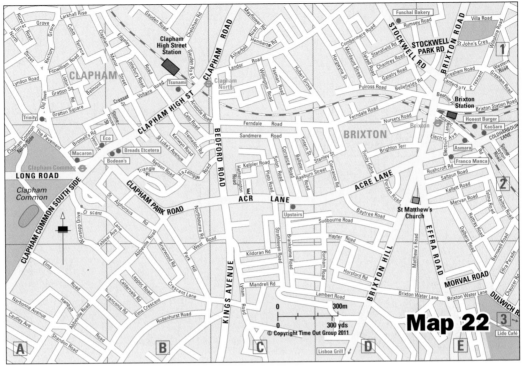

Map 22

MAPS

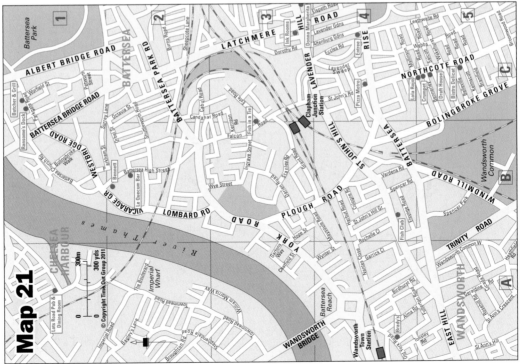

Map 21

Docklands

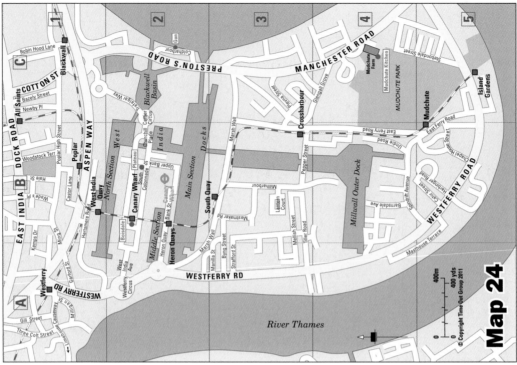

Map 24

Camberwell & Dulwich

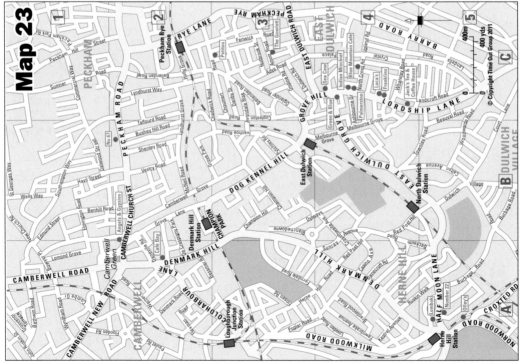

Map 23

MAPS

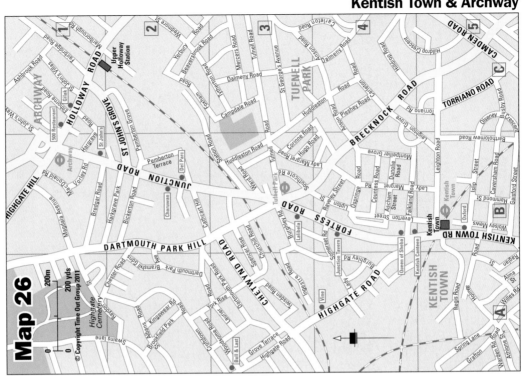

Map 26

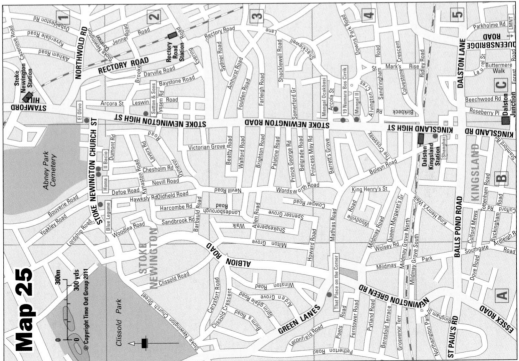

Map 25

Hampstead & St John's Wood

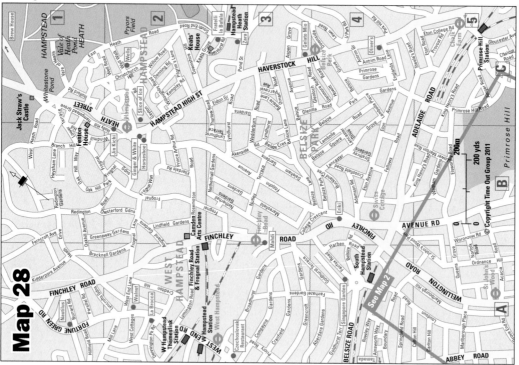

Camden Town & Chalk Farm

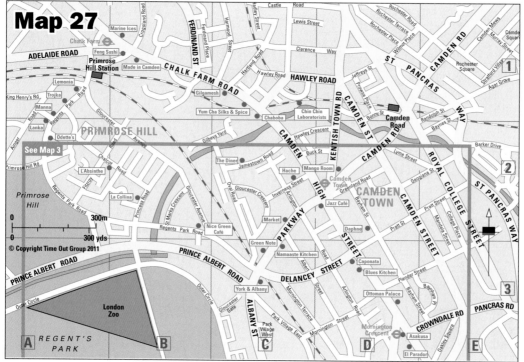

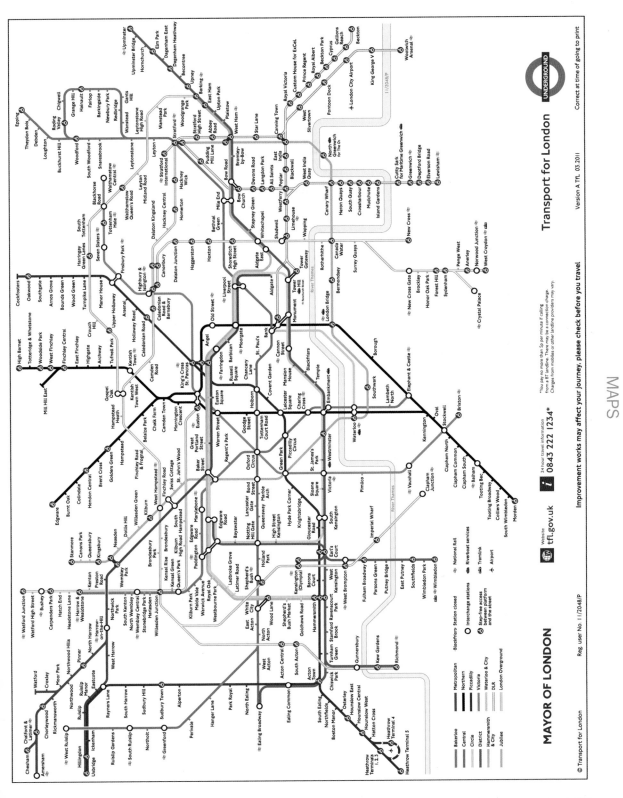

MAPS

Area Index

AREA INDEX

Cafés

Nice Green Café p290
2 Regent's Park Road, NW1 7AY
(7485 2206, www.efdss.org).

Eating & Entertainment

Blues Kitchen p320
111-113 Camden High Street, NW1 7JN
(7387 5277, www.theblueskitchen.com).

Green Note p320
106 Parkway, NW1 7AN (7485 9899,
www.greennote.co.uk).

Jazz Café p320
5-7 Parkway, NW1 7PG (7688 8899,
http://venues.meanfiddler.com).

Greek

Daphne p124
83 Bayham Street, NW1 0AG
(7267 7322).

Ice-cream Parlours

Chin Chin Laboratorists p307
49-50 Camden Lock Place, NW1 8AF
(07885 604284, www.chinchinlabs.com).

Indian

Namaaste Kitchen p153
64 Parkway , NW1 7AH (7485 5977,
www.namaastekitchen.co.uk).

Italian

Caponata p167
3-7 Delancey Street, NW1 7NL (7387
5959, www.caponatacamden.co.uk).

Japanese

Asakusa p179
265 Eversholt Street, NW1 1BA
(7388 8533).

Malaysian, Indonesian & Singaporean

Chaboba p191
8 East Yard, Camden Lock, NW1 8AL
(7267 4719, www.chaboba.co.uk).

Modern European

York & Albany p221
127-129 Parkway, NW1 7PS (7388 3344,
www.gordonramsay.com/yorkandalbany).

Spanish & Portuguese

El Parador p243
245 Eversholt Street, NW1 1BA
(7387 2789, www.elparadorlondon.com).

Steakhouses

Haché p249
24 Inverness Street, NW1 7HJ
(7485 9100, www.hacheburgers.com).

The Americas

The Diner p28
2 Jamestown Road, NW1 7BY
(7485 5223, www.goodlifediner.com).

Turkish

Ottoman Palace p261
14-16 Camden High Street, NW1 0JH
(7383 7245, www.ottomanpalace.co.uk).

Catford

Branches

Nando's
74-76 Rushey Green, SE6 4HW
(8314 0122).

Chalk Farm

Branches

Cottons
55 Chalk Farm Road, NW1 8AN
(7485 8388).

Nando's
57-58 Chalk Farm Road, NW1 8AN
(7424 9040).

Sardo Canale
42 Gloucester Avenue, NW1 8JD
(7722 2800).

Brasseries

Made in Camden p47
Roundhouse, Chalk Farm Road, NW1 8EH
(7424 8495, www.madeincamden.com).

Budget

Marine Ices p279
8 Haverstock Hill, NW3 2BL (7482 9003,
www.marineices.co.uk).

Chinese

Yum Cha Silks & Spice p72
27-28 Chalk Farm Rd, NW1 8AG
(7482 2228, www.yumchasilksand
spice.co.uk).

East European

Trojka p77
101 Regents Park Road, NW1 8UR (7483
3765, www.troykarestaurant.co.uk).

French

L'Absinthe p96
40 Chalcot Road, NW1 8LS
(7483 4848, http://labsinthe.co.uk).

Greek

Lemonia p125
89 Regent's Park Road, NW1 8UY
(7586 7454).

Italian

La Collina p167
17 Princess Road, NW1 8JR
(7483 0192).

Middle Eastern

Tandis p199
73 Haverstock Hill, NW3 4SL
(7586 8079).

Modern European

Odette's p221
130 Regent's Park Road, NW1 8XL (7586
8569, www.odettesprimrosehill.com).

Pan-Asian & Fusion

Feng Sushi p231
1 Adelaide Road, NW3 3QE
(7483 2929, www.fengsushi.co.uk).

Gilgamesh p233
Stables Market, Chalk Farm
Road, NW1 8AH (7482 5757,
www.gilgameshbar.com).

Vegetarian

Manna p267
4 Erskine Road, NW3 3AJ
(7722 8028, www.mannav.com).

Chancery Lane

Branches

Gaucho Chancery
125-126 Chancery Lane, WC2A 1PU
(7242 7727).

Coffee Bars

**Department of Coffee
& Social Affairs** p294
14-16 Leather Lane, EC1N 7SU
(www.departmentofcoffee.co.uk).

Prufrock Coffee p294
23-25 Leather Lane, EC1N 7TE (07853
483479, www.prufrockcoffee.co.uk).

French

Cigalon p88
115 Chancery Lane, WC2A 1PP
(7242 8373, www.cigalon.co.uk).

Japanese

Crane & Tortoise p170
39-41 Gray's Inn Road, WC1X 8PR
(7242 9094, www.sohojapan.co.uk).

Vegetarian

Vanilla Black p265
17-18 Tooks Court, off Cursitor
Street, EC4A 1LB (7242 2622,
www.vanillablack.co.uk).

Wine Bars

**28°-50° Wine Workshop
& Kitchen** p324
140 Fetter Lane, EC4A 1BT (7242 8877,
www.2850.co.uk).

Chelsea

Branches

Bea's of Bloomsbury
370 King's Road, SW3 5UZ.

Byron
300 King's Road, SW3 5UH
(7352 6040).

Dri Dri Gelato
Chelsea Farmers' Market, 125 Sydney
Street, SW3 6NR (8616 5718).

**Eight Over Eight (branch of Great
Eastern Dining Room)**
392 King's Road, SW3 3UZ (7349 9934).

Gaucho Sloane
89 Sloane Avenue, SW3 3DX (7584 9901).

Geales
1 Cale Street, SW3 3QT (7965 0555,
www.geales.com).

Haché
329-331 Fulham Road, SW10 9QL
(7823 3515).

Lisboa Pâtisserie
6 World's End Place, off King's Road,
SW10 0HE (7376 3639).

Made In Italy (branch of Napulé)
249 King's Road, SW3 5EL (7352 1880).

Marechiaro (branch of Napulé)
257 King's Road, SW3 5EL (7351 2417).

Ranoush Juice
338 King's Road, SW3 5UR
(7352 0044).

Santa Lucia (branch of Napulé)
2 Hollywood Road, SW10 9HY
(7352 8484).

Stockpot
273 King's Road, SW3 5EN (7823 3175).

Suksan (branch of Sukho)
7 Park Walk, SW10 0AJ (7351 9881).

Brasseries

Gallery Mess p43
Duke of York's HQ, King's Road,
SW3 4LY (7730 8135, www.saatchi-
gallery.co.uk).

Tom's Kitchen p43
27 Cale Street, SW3 3QP (7349 0202,
www.tomskitchen.co.uk).

Cafés

Grocer on King's p285
184A King's Road, SW3 5XP
(7351 5544, www.thegroceron.com).

Eating & Entertainment

606 Club p321
90 Lots Road, SW10 0QD (7352 5953,
www.606club.co.uk).

Gastropubs

Cadogan Arms p105
298 King's Road, SW3 5UG (7352 6500,
www.thecadoganarmschelsea.com).

Lots Road Pub & Dining Room p107
114 Lots Road, SW10 0RJ (7352 6645,
www.lotsroadpub.com).

Pig's Ear p107
35 Old Church Street, SW3 5BS
(7352 2908, www.thepigsear.info).

Hotels & Haute Cuisine

Gordon Ramsay p136
68 Royal Hospital Road, SW3 4HP
(7352 4441, www.gordonramsay.com).

Ice-cream Parlours

Gelateria Valerie p305
9 Duke of York Square, SW3 4LY
(7730 7978, www.patisserie-
valerie.co.uk).

Indian

Chutney Mary p147
535 King's Road, SW10 0SZ
(7351 3113, www.chutneymary.com).

Painted Heron p149
112 Cheyne Walk, SW10 0DJ
(7351 5232, www.thepaintedheron.com).

Italian

La Famiglia p163
7 Langton Street, SW10 0JL
(7351 0761, www.lafamiglia.co.uk).

Osteria dell'Arancio p163
383 King's Road, SW10 0LP (7349
8111, www.osteriadellarancio.com).

Modern European

Bluebird p215
350 King's Road, SW3 5UU (7559
1000, www.bluebirdchelsea.com).

Henry Root p215
9 Park Walk, SW10 0AJ (7352 7040,
www.thehenryroot.com).

Medlar p215
438 King's Road, SW10 0LJ
(7349 1900, www.medlar
restaurant.co.uk).

Pan-Asian & Fusion

Itsu p231
118 Draycott Avenue, SW3 3AE
(7590 2400, www.itsu.com).

Chinatown

Branches

Leong's Legends II
26-27 Lisle Street, WC2H 7BA
(7734 3380).

St John Hotel
1 Leicester Street, off Leicester
Square, WC2H 7BL (7251 0848,
www.stjohnhotellondon.com).

Bars

Experimental Cocktail Club p314
13A Gerrard Street , W1D 5PS
(7434 3559, www.chinatownecc.com).

Chinese

Baozi Inn p70
25 Newport Court, WC2H 7JS
(7287 6877).

Café de Hong Kong p70
47-49 Charing Cross Road,
WC2H 0AN (7534 9898).

Canton p70
11 Newport Place, WC2H 7JR
(7437 6220).

Four Seasons p70
12 Gerrard Street, W1D 5PR (7494
0870, www.fs-restaurants.co.uk).

Imperial China p60
White Bear Yard, 25A Lisle Street,
WC2H 7BA (7734 3388, www.imperial-
china.co.uk).

Joy King Lau p60
3 Leicester Street, WC2H 7BL
(7437 1132, www.joykinglau.com).

Leong's Legends p71
4 Macclesfield Street, W1D 6AX
(7287 0288).

Manchurian Legends p61
12 Macclesfield Street, W1D 5BP
(7437 8785).

Japanese

Tokyo Diner p176
2 Newport Place, WC2H 7JJ
(7287 8777, www.tokyodiner.com).

Malaysian, Indonesian & Singaporean

Boba Jam p191
102 Shaftesbury Avenue, W1D 5EJ.

Candy Café p191
1st floor, 3 Macclesfield Street, W1D 6AU
(7434 4581, www.candycafe.co.uk).

New Fook Lam Moon p190
10 Gerrard Street, W1D 5PW
(7734 7615).

Rasa Sayang p191
5 Macclesfield Street, W1D 6AY
(7734 1382, www.rasasayangfood.com).

Chiswick

Branches

Carluccio's Caffè
324-344 Chiswick High Road, W4 5TA
(8995 8073).

Côte
50-54 Turnham Green Terrace, W4 1QP
(8747 6788).

Eco
144 Chiswick High Road, W4 1PU
(8747 4822).

Faanoos II
472 Chiswick High Road, W4 5TT
(8994 4217).

Franco Manca
144 Chiswick High Road, W4 1PU
(8747 4822).

**French Kitchen
(branch of Villandry)**
219-221 Chiswick High Road, W4 2DW
(8747 9113).

Gelato Mio
272 Chiswick High Road, W4 1PD
(8616 0891).

Giraffe
270 Chiswick High Road, W4 1PD
(8995 2100).

Gourmet Burger Kitchen
131 Chiswick High Road, W4 2ED
(8995 4548).

Nando's
187-189 Chiswick High Road, W4 2DR
(8995 7533).

Brasseries

High Road Brasserie p40
162-166 Chiswick High Road,
W4 1PR (8742 7474,
www.highroadhouse.co.uk).

Sam's Brasserie & Bar p41
11 Barley Mow Passage, W4 4PH
(8987 0555, www.samsbrasserie.co.uk).

French

La Trompette p91
5-7 Devonshire Road, W4 2EU
(8747 1836, www.latrompette.co.uk).

AREA INDEX

Wagamama
Jubilee Place, 45 Bank Street, E14 5NY
(7516 9009).
Wahaca
Park Pavilion, 40 Canada Square,
E14 5FW (7516 9145).
British
Boisdale Canary Wharf   p58
Cabot Place, E14 4QT (7715 5818,
www.boisdale-cw.co.uk).
Cafés
Mudchute Kitchen   p288
Mudchute Park & Farm, Pier
Street, E14 3HP (3069 9290,
www.mudchutekitchen.org).
Chinese
Yi-Ban   p71
London Regatta Centre, Dockside
Road, E16 2QT (7473 6699,
www.yi-ban.co.uk).
Gastropubs
Gun   p111
27 Coldharbour, E14 9NS (7515 5222,
www.thegundocklands.com).
Modern European
Plateau   p220
Canada Place, Canada Square,
E14 5ER (7715 7100, www.plateau-
restaurant.co.uk).

Dulwich
Cafés
Pavilion Café   p293
Dulwich Park, SE21 7BQ (8299 1383,
www.pavilioncafedulwich.co.uk).
Gastropubs
Rosendale   p109
65 Rosendale Road, SE21 8EZ
(8761 9008, www.therosendale.co.uk).
Wine Bars
Green & Blue   p325
36-38 Lordship Lane, SE22 8HJ
(8693 9250, www.greenandblue
wines.com).

Ealing
Branches
Carluccio's Caffè
5-6 The Green, W5 5DA (8566 4458).
Côte
9-10 The Green, High Street, W5 5DA
(8579 3115).
Gourmet Burger Kitchen
35 Haven Green, W5 2NX (8998 0392).
Nando's
1-2 Station Buildings, Uxbridge Road,
W5 3NU (8992 2290).
Nando's
1-5 Bond Street , W5 5AP
(8567 8093).
Gastropubs
Ealing Park Tavern   p104
222 South Ealing Road, W5 4RL (8758
1879, www.ealingparktavern.com).
Japanese
Atari-ya   p178
1 Station Parade, Uxbridge Road,
W5 3LD (8896 3175, www.atariya.co.uk).
Pizza & Pasta
Santa Maria   p309
15 St Mary's Road, W5 5RA (8579
1462, www.santamariapizzeria.com).

Earl's Court
Branches
Byron
242 Earl's Court Road, SW5 9AA
(7370 9300).
Gourmet Burger Kitchen
163-165 Earl's Court Road, SW5 9RF
(7373 3184).
Masala Zone
147 Earl's Court Road, SW5 9RQ
(7373 0220).
Nando's
204 Earl's Court Road, SW5 9QF
(7259 2544).
Wagamama
180-182 Earl's Court Road, SW5 9QG
(7373 9660).

Eating & Entertainment
Troubadour   p323
263-267 Old Brompton Road, SW5 9JA
(7370 1434, www.troubadour.co.uk).
Greek
As Greek As It Gets   p123
233 Earl's Court Road, SW5 9AH (7244
7777, www.asgreekasitgets.co.uk).
Spanish & Portuguese
Capote y Toros   p239
157 Old Brompton Road, SW5 0LJ
(7373 0567, www.cambiodetercio.co.uk).
Wine Bars
Finborough Wine Cafe   p325
118 Finborough Road, SW10 9ED (7373
0745, www.finboroughwinecafe.co.uk).

Earlsfield
Branches
Cah Chi
394 Garratt Lane, SW18 4HP (8946
8811).
Carluccio's Caffè
537-539 Garratt Lane, SW18 4SR
(8947 4651).
Thai
Amaranth   p255
346-348 Garratt Lane, SW18 4ES
(8874 9036).

East Dulwich
Branches
Gourmet Burger Kitchen
121 Lordship Lane, SE22 8HU
(8693 9307).
British
Franklins   p57
157 Lordship Lane, SE22 8HX (8299
9598, www.franklinsrestaurant.com).
Cafés
Blue Mountain Café   p287
18 North Cross Road, SE22 9EU
(8299 6953, www.bluemo.co.uk).
Jack's Tea & Coffee House   p287
85 Pellatt Road, SE22 9JD (7183
9135, http://chocolateconcreteand
pinkcustard.blogspot.com/).
Luca's   p287
145 Lordship Lane, SE22 8HX
(8613 6161, www.lucasbakery.com).
Fish & Chips
Sea Cow   p301
37 Lordship Lane, SE22 8EW
(8693 3111, www.theseacow.co.uk).
Gastropubs
Herne Tavern   p109
2 Forest Hill Road, SE22 0RR
(8299 9521, www.theherne.net).
Palmerston   p111
91 Lordship Lane, SE22 8EP
(8693 1629, www.thepalmerston.net).
Indian
Indian Mischief   p151
71 Lordship Lane, SE22 8EP
(8693 1627).

East Finchley
Gastropubs
Bald-Faced Stag   p113
69 High Road, N2 8AB (8442 1201,
www.thebaldfacedstagn2.co.uk).

East Sheen
Indian
Mango & Silk   p147
199 Upper Richmond Road West,
SW14 8QT (8876 6220,
www.mangoandsilk.co.uk).
Middle Eastern
Faanoos   p197
481 Upper Richmond Road West,
SW14 7PU (8878 5738,
www.faanoosrestaurant.com).

Edgware Road
Branches
Abu Zaad
128 Edgware Road, W2 2DZ
(8749 5107).

Beirut Express
(branch of Ranoush Juice)
112-114 Edgware Road, W2 2JE
(7724 2700).
Maroush Gardens
1-3 Connaught Street, W2 2DH
(7262 0222).
Maroush III
62 Seymour Street, W1H 5BN (7724 5024).
Maroush IV
68 Edgware Road, W2 2EG (7724 9339).
Global
Mandalay   p118
444 Edgware Road, W2 1EG
(7258 3696, www.mandalayway.com).
Middle Eastern
Maroush I   p194
21 Edgware Road, W2 2JE (7723 0773,
www.maroush.com).
Ranoush Juice   p199
43 Edgware Road, W2 2JE (7723 5929,
www.maroush.com).
North African
Sidi Maarouf   p224
56-58 Edgware Road, W2 2JE
(7724 0525, www.maroush.com).

Edgware, Middx
Branches
Haandi
301-303 Hale Lane, Edgware, Middx,
HA8 7AX (8905 4433).
Nando's
137-139 Station Road, Edgware, Middx,
HA8 7JG (8952 3400).
Jewish
Papalina   p184
313 Hale Lane, Edgware, Middx, HA8 7AX
(8958 7999, www.papalina.co.uk).

Elephant & Castle
Branches
Nando's
Metro Central, 119 Newington Causeway,
SE1 6BA (7378 7810).
Chinese
Dragon Castle   p71
100 Walworth Road, SE17 1JL
(7277 3388, http://dragoncastle.eu).
East European
Mamuska!   p77
1st floor, Elephant & Castle Shopping
Centre, SE1 6TE (07986 352810,
www.mamuska.net).

Enfield, Middx
Branches
Nando's
2 The Town, Enfield, Middx, EN2 6LE
(8366 2904).

Euston
Branches
Nando's
The Piazza, Euston Station, NW1 2RT
(7387 5126).
Peyton & Byrne
British Library, 96 Euston Road,
NW1 2DB (7412 5520).
Rasa Express
327 Euston Road, NW1 3AD (7387 8974).
Cafés
Peyton & Byrne   p281
Wellcome Collection, 183 Euston
Road, NW1 2BE (7611 2138,
www.peytonandbyrne.com).
Japanese
Sushi of Shiori   p171
144 Drummond Street, NW1 2PA
(7388 9962, www.sushiofshiori.co.uk).
Pizza & Pasta
Pasta Plus   p309
62 Eversholt Street, NW1 1DA (7383
4943, www.pastaplus.co.uk).

Farringdon
Branches
Gaucho Smithfield
93A Charterhouse Street, EC1M 6HL
(7490 1676).

Hix Oyster & Chop House
36-37 Greenhill Rents, off Cowcross
Street, EC1M 6BN (7017 1930,
www.hixoysterandchophouse.co.uk).
Tas
37 Farringdon Road, EC1M 3JB
(7430 9721).
Yo! Sushi
95 Farringdon Road, EC1R 3BT
(7841 0785).
Bars
Zetter Townhouse   p314
49-50 St John's Square, EC1V 4JJ (7324
4545, www.thezettertownhouse.com).
Budget
Little Bay   p274
171 Farringdon Road, EC1R 3AL
(7278 1234, www.little-bay.co.uk).
Cafés
St Ali   p281
27 Clerkenwell Road, EC1M 5RN
(7253 5754, www.stali.co.uk).
Coffee Bars
Dose Espresso   p294
70 Long Lane, EC1A 9EJ (7600 0382,
www.dose-espresso.com).
French
Club Gascon   p87
57 West Smithfield, EC1A 9DS
(7796 0600, www.clubgascon.com).
Le Comptoir Gascon   p87
61-63 Charterhouse Street, EC1M 6HJ
(7608 0851, www.comptoirgascon.com).
Global
North Road   p118
69-73 St John Street, EC1M 4AN (3217
0033, www.northroadrestaurant.co.uk).
Italian
Carluccio's Caffè   p156
12 West Smithfield, EC1A 9JR
(7329 5904, www.carluccios.com).
Modern European
Smiths of Smithfield   p205
67-77 Charterhouse Street, EC1M 6HJ
(7251 7950, www.smithsofsmithfield.com).
Pizza & Pasta
Santoré   p308
59-61 Exmouth Market, EC1R 4QL
(7812 1488).
Spanish & Portuguese
Morito   p234
32 Exmouth Market, EC1R 4QE
(7278 7007).
Vietnamese
Cà Phê   p271
47 Clerkenwell Road, EC1M 5RS
(07780 784696, www.caphevn.co.uk).
Wine Bars
Cellar Gascon   p325
59 West Smithfield, EC1A 9DS
(7600 7561, www.cellargascon.com).

Finchley
Branches
Nando's
Great North Leisure Park, Chaplin
Square, N12 0GL (8492 8465).
Tosa
152 High Road, N2 9ED (8883 8850).
Yo! Sushi
O2 Centre, 255 Finchley Road, NW3 6LU
(7431 1488).
Fish & Chips
Two Brothers Fish Restaurant   p302
297-303 Regent's Park Road, N3 1DP
(8346 0469, www.twobrothers.co.uk).
Vietnamese
Khoai Café   p271
362 Ballards Lane, N12 0EE
(8445 2039, www.khoai.co.uk).
Vy Nam Café   p272
371 Regents Park Road, N3 1DE
(8371 4222, www.vynamcafe.com).

Finsbury Park
Branches
Il Bacio Highbury
178-184 Blackstock Road, N5 1HA
(7226 3339).

AREA INDEX

Chinese
Seventeen p71
17 Notting Hill Gate, W11 3JQ
(7985 0006, www.seventeen-
london.com).

Fish
Geales p81
2 Farmer Street, W8 7SN (7727 7528,
www.geales.com).

Greek
Greek Affair p123
1 Hillgate Street, W8 7SP (7792 5226,
www.greekaffair.co.uk).

Ice-cream Parlours
Dri Dri Gelato p305
189 Portobello Road, W11 2ED
(3490 5027, www.dridrigelato.com).

Modern European
Notting Hill Brasserie p213
92 Kensington Park Road,
W11 2PN (7229 4481,
www.nottinghillbrasserie.com).

Wine Bars
Kensington Wine Rooms p328
127-129 Kensington Church
Street, W8 7LP (7727 8142,
www.greatwinesbytheglass.com).

Olympia

Middle Eastern
Mohsen p196
152 Warwick Road, W14 8PS
(7602 9888).

Steakhouses
Popeseye Steak House p251
108 Blythe Road, W14 0HB
(7610 4578, www.popeseye.com).

Oxford Street

Branches
Carluccio's Caffè
8 Market Place, W1W 8AG (7636 2228).
Fresco
34 Margaret Street, W1G 0JE
(7493 3838).
Hix Restaurant & Champagne Bar
Selfridges, 400 Oxford Street, W1U 1AT
(7499 5400, www.hixatselfridges.co.uk).
Yo! Sushi
Selfridges, 400 Oxford Street, W1S 2RT
(7318 3944).

Paddington

Branches
Cocomaya
12 Connaught Street, W2 2AF
(7706 2883, http://cocomaya.co.uk).
Fresco
93 Praed Street, W2 1NT (7402 0006).
Madeira Café
127 Praed Street, W2 1RL (7262 3384).
Yo! Sushi
The Lawn, Paddington Station, W2 1HB
(7706 4619).

Cafés
Cocomaya p281
3 Porchester Place, W2 2BS
(7706 2770, http://cocomaya.co.uk).

Chinese
Pearl Liang p67
8 Sheldon Square, W2 6EZ
(7289 7000, www.pearlliang.co.uk).

Malaysian, Indonesian & Singaporean
Satay House p193
13 Sale Place, W2 1PX (7723 6763,
www.satay-house.co.uk).

Parsons Green

Branches
Côte
45-47 Parsons Green Lane, SW6 4HH
(7736 8444).
Tendido Cuatro
108-110 New King's Road, SW6 4LY
(7371 5147).

British
Manson p56
676 Fulham Road, SW6 5SA (7384
9559, www.mansonrestaurant.co.uk).

Thai
Sukho p255
855 Fulham Road, SW6 5HJ (7371 7600,
www.sukhogroups.com).

Peckham

African & Caribbean
805 Bar Restaurant p21
805 Old Kent Road, SE15 1NX
(7639 0808, www.805restaurant.com).

Cafés
No 67 p287
South London Gallery, 67 Peckham
Road, SE5 8UH (7252 7649,
www.southlondongallery.org).
Petitou p288
63 Choumert Road, SE15 4AR
(7639 2613, www.petitou.co.uk).

Pizza & Pasta
Gowlett p311
62 Gowlett Road, SE15 4HY
(7635 7048, www.thegowlett.com).

Piccadilly

Branches
Gaucho Piccadilly
25 Swallow Street, W1B 4QR
(7734 4040).
Yo! Sushi
Trocadero, 19 Rupert Street,
W1D 7DH (7434 2724).

Brasseries
The Wolseley p40
160 Piccadilly, W1J 9EB (7499 6996,
www.thewolseley.com).

Fish
Bentley's Oyster Bar & Grill p80
11-15 Swallow Street, W1B 4DG
(7734 4756, www.bentleysoyster
barandgrill.co.uk).
FishWorks p81
79 Swallow Street, W1B 4DE
(7734 5813, www.fishworks.co.uk).

Hotels & Haute Cuisine
The Ritz p135
150 Piccadilly, W1J 9BR (7493 8181,
www.theritzhotel.com).

Ice-cream Parlours
Freggo p305
27-29 Swallow Street, W1B 4QR
(7287 9506, www.freggo.co.uk).

Japanese
Yoshino p175
3 Piccadilly Place, W1J 0DB (7287 6622,
www.yoshino.net).

Modern European
Criterion p208
224 Piccadilly, W1J 9HP (7930 0488,
www.criterionrestaurant.com).

Wine Bars
1707 p327
181 Piccadilly, W1J 9FA (7734 8040,
www.fortnumandmason.com).

Pimlico

Branches
Daylesford Organic
44B Pimlico Road, SW1W 8LP
(7881 8060).
Nando's
107-108 Wilton Road, SW1V 1DZ
(7976 5719).

Gastropubs
Orange Public House & Hotel p102
37 Pimlico Road, SW1W 8NE
(7881 9844, www.theorange.co.uk).

Italian
Tinello p161
87 Pimlico Road, SW1W 8PH
(7730 3663, www.tinello.co.uk).

Modern European
Rex Whistler Restaurant p208
at Tate Britain
Tate Britain, Millbank, SW1P 4RG
(7887 8825, www.tate.org.uk).

Pan-Asian & Fusion
dim t p231
56-62 Wilton Road, SW1V 1DE
(7834 0507, www.dimt.co.uk).

The Americas
Rodizio Preto p33
72 Wilton Road, SW1V 1DE (7233 8668,
www.rodiziopreto.co.uk).

Turkish
Kazan p260
93-94 Wilton Road, SW1V 1DW (7233
7100, www.kazan-restaurant.com).

Primrose Hill

Cafés
Lanka p290
71 Regent's Park Road, NW1 8UY
(7483 2544, www.lanka-uk.com).

Putney

Branches
Byron
22 Putney High Street, SW15 1SL
(8246 4170).
Carluccio's Caffè
Brewhouse Street, Putney Wharf,
SW15 2JQ (8789 0591).
Fish & Grill
200-204 Putney Bridge Road,
SW15 2NA (8246 4140,
www.fishandgrillputney.co.uk).
Gourmet Burger Kitchen
333 Putney Bridge Road, SW15 2PG
(8789 1199).
Nando's
148 Upper Richmond Road, SW15 2SW
(8780 3651).
Popeseye Steak House
277 Upper Richmond Road, SW15 6SP
(8788 7733).
Prince of Wales (branch of Bull & Last)
138 Upper Richmond Road, SW15 2SP
(8788 1552,
www.princeofwalesputney.co.uk).
Thai Square
2-4 Lower Richmond Road, SW15 1LB
(8780 1811, www.thaisquare.net).
Wagamama
50-54 Putney High Street, SW15 1SQ
(8785 3636).

Gastropubs
Spencer p107
237 Lower Richmond Road, SW15 1HJ
(8788 0640, www.thespencerpub.com).

Italian
Enoteca Turi p165
28 Putney High Street, SW15 1SQ
(8785 4449, www.enotecaturi.com).

Japanese
Chosan p179
292 Upper Richmond Road, SW15 6TH
(8788 9626).

Queen's Park

Branches
Mr Fish
51 Salusbury Road, NW6 6NJ
(7624 3555).

Brasseries
Hugo's p47
21-25 Lonsdale Road, NW6 6RA
(7372 1232).

French
Penk's p99
79 Salusbury Road, NW6 6NH
(7604 4484, www.penks.com).

Raynes Park

Korean
Cah Chi p188
34 Durham Road, SW20 0TW
(8947 1081, www.cahchi.com).

Richmond, Surrey

Branches
Carluccio's Caffè
31-35 Kew Road, Richmond, Surrey,
TW9 2NQ (8940 5037).
Côte
24 Hill Street, Richmond, Surrey,
TW9 1TW (8948 5971).
FishWorks
13-19 The Square, Richmond, Surrey,
TW9 1EA (8948 5965).

Gaucho Richmond
The Towpath, Richmond, Surrey,
TW10 6UJ (8948 4030).
Giraffe
30 Hill Street, Richmond, Surrey,
TW9 1TW (8332 2646).
Gourmet Burger Kitchen
15-17 Hill Rise, Richmond, Surrey,
TW10 6UD (8940 5440).
Nando's
2&4 Hill Rise, Richmond, Surrey,
TW10 6UA (8940 8810).
Taylor Street Baristas
27D The Quadrant, Richmond,
Surrey, TW9 1DN (07969 798650,
www.taylor-st.com).
Thai Square
29 Kew Road, Richmond, Surrey,
TW9 2NQ (8940 5253).
Wagamama
3 Hill Street, Richmond, Surrey,
TW9 1SX (8948 2224).
William Curley
10 Paved Court, Richmond, Surrey,
TW9 1LZ (8332 3002,
www.williamcurley.co.uk).

Budget
Stein's p279
55 Richmond Towpath, Richmond,
Surrey, TW10 6UX (8948 8189,
www.stein-s.com).

French
Chez Lindsay p99
11 Hill Rise, Richmond, Surrey,
TW10 6UQ (8948 7473,
www.chezlindsay.co.uk).

Hotels & Haute Cuisine
The Bingham p136
61-63 Petersham Road, Richmond,
Surrey, TW10 6UT (8940 0902,
www.thebingham.co.uk).

Ice-cream Parlours
Gelateria Danieli p307
16 Brewers Lane, Richmond, Surrey,
TW9 1HH (8439 9807,
www.gelateriadanieli.com).

Modern European
Petersham Nurseries Café p223
Church Lane, off Petersham
Road, Richmond, Surrey,
TW10 7AG (8605 3627,
www.petershamnurseries.com).

St James's

Bars
Dukes Bar p316
35 St James's Place, SW1A 1NY
(7491 4840, www.dukeshotel.com).

British
Inn The Park p52
St James's Park, SW1A 2BJ
(7451 9999, www.innthepark.com).
Wiltons p53
55 Jermyn Street, SW1Y 6LX
(7629 9955, www.wiltons.co.uk).

Japanese
Matsuri p175
15 Bury Street, SW1Y 6AL
(7839 1101, www.matsuri-
restaurant.com).
Saké No Hana p175
23 St James's Street,
SW1A 1HA (7925 8988,
www.sakenohana.com).
Toku at Japan Centre p176
14-16 Regent Street, SW1Y 4PH
(3405 1222, www.toku-
restaurant.co.uk).

Middle Eastern
Noura p196
122 Jermyn Street, SW1Y 4UJ
(7839 2020, www.noura.co.uk).

Modern European
The Avenue p208
7-9 St James's Street, SW1A 1EE
(7321 2111, www.theavenue-
restaurant.co.uk).
Le Caprice p208
Arlington House, Arlington Street,
SW1A 1RJ (7629 2239, www.caprice-
holdings.co.uk).

St John's Wood

Branches
Carluccio's Caffè
60 St John's Wood High Street,
NW8 7SH (7449 0404).
Gelato Mio
138 St John's Wood High Street,
NW8 7SE (0011 3889).
Sofra (branch of Özer)
11 Circus Road, NW8 6NX (7586 9889).
East European
Tamada   p78
122 Boundary Road, NW8 0RH
(7372 2882, www.tamada.co.uk).
French
L'Aventure   p99
3 Blenheim Terrace, NW8 0EH
(7624 6232, www.laventure.co.uk).

Shepherd's Bush

Branches
Busaba Eathai
Westfield Shopping Centre,
W12 7GA (3249 1919).
Byron
The Loft, Westfield Shopping Centre,
W12 7GF (8743 7755).
Comptoir Libanais
The Balcony, Westfield Shopping Centre,
W12 7GE (8811 2222).
Fire & Stone
Southern Terrace, Westfield Shopping
Centre, W12 7GB (0844 371 2550).
Isola Bella
Westfield Shopping Centre, W12 7SL
(8740 6611).
Jamie's Italian Westfield
Westfield Shopping Centre, Ariel Way,
W12 7GB (8090 9070).
Nando's
284-286 Uxbridge Road, W12 7JA
(8746 1112).
Nando's
The Loft, Westfield Shopping Centre,
W12 7GF (8834 4658).
The Real Greek
Southern Terrace, Westfield Shopping
Centre, W12 7GB (8743 9168).
Sacred
The Atrium, Westfield Shopping Centre,
W12 7GQ (07727 454350).
Square Pie
The Balcony, Westfield Shopping Centre,
W12 7GF (8222 6697).
Wagamama
Southern Terrace, Westfield Shopping
Centre, W12 7GF (8749 9073).
Wahaca
1074 Westfield Shopping Centre,
Ariel Way, W12 7GB (8749 4517).
Yo! Sushi
The Balcony, Westfield Shopping Centre,
Ariel Way, W12 7GE (3130 1430).
East European
Tatra   p75
24 Goldhawk Road, W12 8DH (8749
8193, www.tatrarestaurant.co.uk).
Gastropubs
Anglesea Arms   p104
35 Wingate Road, W6 0UR
(8749 1291).
Princess Victoria   p105
217 Uxbridge Road, W12 9DH
(8749 5886, www.princess
victoria.co.uk).
Queen Adelaide   p105
412 Uxbridge Road, W12 0NR
(8746 2573, www.thequeen
adelaidew12.co.uk).
Middle Eastern
Abu Zaad   p197
29 Uxbridge Road, W12 8LH
(8749 5107, www.abuzaad.co.uk).
Sufi   p197
70 Askew Road, W12 9BJ (8834 4888,
www.sufirestaurant.com).
North African
Adam's Café   p225
77 Askew Road, W12 9AH
(8743 0572, www.adams
cafe.co.uk).

Steakhouses
Gourmet Burger Kitchen   p249
Upper Southern Terrace, Westfield
Shopping Centre, W12 7GB (8749 1246,
www.gbk.co.uk).
Thai
Esarn Kheaw   p255
314 Uxbridge Road, W12 7LJ
(8743 8930, www.esarnkheaw.com).
Vegetarian
Blah Blah Blah   p266
78 Goldhawk Road, W12 8HA
(8746 1337, www.blahvegetarian.com).

Shoreditch

Branches
Breakfast Club
2-4 Rufus Street, N1 6PE
(7729 5252).
Busaba Eathai
313-319 Old Street, EC1V 9LE
(7729 0808).
Byron
46 Hoxton Square, N1 6PB (3487 1230).
The Diner
128-130 Curtain Road, EC2A 3AQ
(7729 4452).
Pizza East Shoreditch
56 Shoreditch High Street, E1 6JJ
(7729 1888, www.pizzaeast.com).
Prufrock Coffee
140 Shoreditch High Street, E1 6JE
(7033 0500, http://prufrockcoffee.com).
The Real Greek
14-15 Hoxton Market, N1 6HG
(7739 8212).
Rivington Grill
28-30 Rivington Street, EC2A 3DZ
(7729 7053, www.rivingtongrill.co.uk).
Taylor Street Baristas
110 Clifton Street, EC2A 4HT.
Viet Grill (branch of Cây Tre)
58 Kingsland Road, E2 8DP
(7739 6686).
Bars
Book Club   p318
100-106 Leonard Street, EC2A 4RH
(7684 8618, www.wearetbc.com).
Happiness Forgets   p319
8-9 Hoxton Square, N1 6NU (7613 0325,
www.happinessforgets.com).
Mason & Taylor   p319
51-55 Bethnal Green Road, E1 6LA
(7749 9670, www.masonandtaylor.co.uk).
Nightjar   p319
129 City Road, EC1V 1JB (7253 4101,
www.barnightjar.com).
Worship Street Whistling Shop   p319
63 Worship Street, EC2A 2DU
(7247 0015, www.whistlingshop.com).
Brasseries
Water House   p45
10 Orsman Road, N1 5QJ (7033 0123,
www.waterhouserestaurant.co.uk).
British
Albion   p59
2-4 Boundary Street, E2 7DD
(7729 1051, www.albioncaff.co.uk).
Rochelle Canteen   p59
Rochelle School, Arnold Circus,
E2 7ES (7729 5677, www.arnold
andhenderson.com).
Cafés
Frizzante@Hackney City Farm   p288
1A Goldsmith's Row, E2 8QA
(7739 2266, www.frizzanteltd.co.uk).
Jones Dairy Café   p288
23 Ezra Street, E2 7RH (7739 5372,
www.jonesdairy.co.uk).
Coffee Bars
Allpress Espresso   p297
58 Redchurch Street, E2 7DP (7749
1780, http://uk.allpressespresso.com).
Shoreditch Grind   p297
213 Old Street, EC1V 9NR (7490 7490,
http://shoreditchgrind.com).
French
Boundary   p95
2-4 Boundary Street, entrance at
9 Redchurch Street, E2 7DD
(7729 1051, www.theboundary.co.uk).

Les Trois Garçons   p96
1 Club Row, E1 6JX (7613 1924,
www.lestroisgarcons.com).
Gastropubs
Princess of Shoreditch   p112
76-78 Paul Street, EC2A 4NE
(7729 9270, www.theprincessof
shoreditch.com).
Global
Eyre Brothers   p121
70 Leonard Street, EC2A 4QX
(7613 5346, www.eyrebrothers.co.uk).
Italian
Fifteen   p167
15 Westland Place, N1 7LP
(3375 1515, www.fifteen.net).
Pan-Asian & Fusion
Great Eastern Dining Room   p233
54-56 Great Eastern Street,
EC2A 3QR (7613 4545,
www.rickerrestaurants.com).
Pizza & Pasta
Furnace   p312
1 Rufus Street, N1 6PE (7613 0598,
www.hoxtonfurnace.com).
Spanish & Portuguese
Laxeiro   p243
93 Columbia Road, E2 7RG
(7729 1147, www.laxeiro.co.uk).
The Americas
Big Apple Hot Dogs   p27
Outside 239 Old Street,
EC1V 9EY (07989 387441,
www.bigapplehotdogs.com).
Vegetarian
Saf   p267
152-154 Curtain Road, EC2A 3AT
(7613 0007, www.safrestaurant.co.uk).
Vietnamese
Cây Tre   p268
301 Old Street, EC1V 9LA (7729 8662,
www.vietnamesekitchen.co.uk).
Kêu   p271
332 Old Street, EC1V 9DR (7739 1164,
www.keudeli.co.uk).
Mien Tay   p269
122 Kingsland Road, E2 8DP (7729
3074, www.mientay.co.uk).
Song Que   p269
134 Kingsland Road, E2 8DY (7613
3222, http://songque.co.uk).

Soho

Branches
Banana Tree Canteen
103 Wardour Street, W1F 0UQ
(www.bananatree.co.uk).
Bodean's
10 Poland Street, W1F 8PZ (7287 7575,
www.bodeansbbq.com).
Breakfast Club
33 D'Arblay Street, W1F 8EU
(7434 2571, www.thebreakfast
clubsoho.com).
Busaba Eathai
106-110 Wardour Street, W1F 0TR
(7255 8686).
Byron
97-99 Wardour Street, W1F 0UF
(7297 9390).
C&R Café
4-5 Rupert Court, W1D 6DY
(7434 1128).
Canela
1 Newburgh Street, W1F 7RB
(7494 9980).
Cây Tre
42 Dean Street, W1D 4PZ (7317 9118,
www.caytresoho.co.uk).
Côte
124-126 Wardour Street, W1F 0TY
(7287 9280).
Dehesa (branch of Salt Yard)
25 Ganton Street, W1F 9BP (7494 4170,
www.dehesa.co.uk).
The Diner
16-18 Ganton Street, W1F 7BU
(7287 8962).
Fernandez & Wells
43 Lexington Street, W1F 9AL
(7734 1546).

Fernandez & Wells
16A St Anne's Court, W1F 0BG
(7494 4242).
Four Seasons
23 Wardour Street, W1D 6PW
(7287 9995).
Giraffe
11-13 Frith Street, W1D 4RB
(7494 3491).
Gourmet Burger Kitchen
15 Frith Street, W1D 4RF
(7494 9533).
Hummingbird Bakery
155A Wardour Street, W1F 8WG
(7851 1795).
Leon
35-36 Great Marlborough Street,
W1F 7JB (7437 5280).
Mar i Terra
17 Air Street, W1B 5AF (7734 1992).
Nando's
10 Frith Street, W1D 3JF (7494 0932).
Nando's
46 Glasshouse Street, W1B 5DR
(7287 8442).
Patara
15 Greek Street, W1D 4DP
(7437 1071).
Polpetto (branch of Polpo)
2nd floor, French House, 49 Dean
Street, W1D 5BG (7734 1969,
www.polpetto.co.uk).
Rosa's
48 Dean Street, W1D 8BF (7494 1638).
Sacred
Kingly Court, off Carnaby Street, W1B
5PW (07598 939876).
Scoop
53 Brewer Street, W1F 9UJ
(7494 3082).
Tapas Brindisa Soho
46 Broadwick Street, W1F 7AF
(7534 1690).
Taro
61 Brewer Street, W1F 9UW
(7734 5826).
Thai Square
27-28 St Annes Court, W1F 0BN
(7287 2000, www.thaisquare.net).
Wagamama
10A Lexington Street, W1F 0LD
(7292 0990).
Wahaca
80 Wardour Street, W1F 0TF
(7734 0195).
Yalla Yalla
1 Green's Court, W1F 0HA
(7287 7663, www.yalla-yalla.co.uk).
African & Caribbean
Jerk City   p23
189 Wardour Street, W1F 8ZD
(7287 2878).
Savannah Jerk   p23
187 Wardour Street, W1F 8ZB
(7437 7770, www.savannahjerk.com).
Bars
Mark's Bar   p317
Hix, 66-70 Brewer Street, W1F 9UP
(7292 3518, www.marksbar.co.uk).
Milk & Honey   p317
61 Poland Street, W1F 7NU (7065 6840,
www.mlkhny.com).
Brasseries
Bob Bob Ricard   p40
1 Upper James Street, W1F 9DF
(3145 1000, www.bobbobricard.com).
Kettner's   p40
29 Romilly Street, W1D 5HP
(7734 6112, www.kettners.com).
Princi   p40
135 Wardour Street, W1F 0UT
(7478 8888, www.princi.co.uk).
British
Dean Street Townhouse   p53
69-71 Dean Street, W1D 4QJ (7434
1775, www.deanstreettownhouse.com).
Hix   p53
66-70 Brewer Street, W1F 9UP
(7292 3518, www.hixsoho.co.uk).
Quo Vadis   p53
26-29 Dean Street, W1D 3LL
(7437 9585, www.quovadissoho.co.uk).

Wagamama
Roof garden level, Cardinal Place, off
Victoria Street, SW1E 5JE (7828 0561).
Yo! Sushi
Main concourse, Victoria Station, SW1V
1JT (3262 0050).
British
Goring Hotel p55
Beeston Place, Grosvenor Gardens,
SW1W 0JW (7396 9000,
www.goringhotel.co.uk).
Fish & Chips
Seafresh Fish Restaurant p299
80-81 Wilton Road, SW1V 1DL (7828
0747, www.fishandchipsinlondon.com).

Victoria Park
Cafés
Pavilion Café p293
Victoria Park, Crown Gate West,
E9 7DE (8980 0030, www.the-
pavilion-cafe.com).
Fish & Chips
Fish House p301
126-128 Lauriston Road, E9 7LH
(8533 3327, www.fishouse.co.uk).
Modern European
Empress p221
130 Lauriston Road, E9 7LH (8533
5123, www.empresse9.co.uk).

Walthamstow
Spanish & Portuguese
Orford Saloon p243
32 Orford Road, E17 9NJ (8503 6542).

Wandsworth
Branches
Nando's
Southside Shopping Centre, SW18 4TF
(8874 1363).
British
Steam p56
55-57 East Hill, SW18 2QE (8704 4680,
www.steamwinebar.com).
Cafés
Common Ground p292
Wandsworth Common, off Dorlcote
Road, SW18 3RT (8874 9386).
Fish & Chips
Brady's p300
513 Old York Road, SW18 1TF
(8877 9599, www.bradysfish.co.uk).
French
Chez Bruce p93
2 Bellevue Road, SW17 7EG
(8672 0114, www.chezbruce.co.uk).

Wapping
Modern European
Wapping Food p221
Wapping Hydraulic Power Station,
Wapping Wall, E1W 3SG (7680 2080,
www.thewappingproject.com).
Pizza & Pasta
Il Bordello p312
81 Wapping High Street, E1W 2YN
(7481 9950).

Waterloo
Branches
Canteen
Royal Festival Hall, Belvedere Road,
SE1 8XX (0845 686 1122).
Feng Sushi
Festival Terrace, Royal Festival Hall,
Belvedere Road, SE1 8XX (7261 0001).
Madeira Café
1 Wootton Street, SE1 8TG (3268 2127).
Ping Pong
Festival Terrace, Royal Festival Hall,
Belvedere Road, SE1 8XX (7960 4160).
Tas
33 The Cut, SE1 8LF (7928 2111).
Wagamama
Riverside Level 1, Royal Festival Hall,
Belvedere Road, SE1 8XX (7021 0877).
Yo! Sushi
County Hall, Belvedere Road, SE1 7GP
(7928 8871).

Yo! Sushi
Unit 3, Royal Festival Hall, Belvedere
Road, SE1 8XX (3130 1997).
Bars
Oxo Tower Bar p318
8th floor, Oxo Tower Wharf, Barge
House Street, SE1 9PH (7803 3888,
www.harveynichols.com).
Skylon p318
Royal Festival Hall, Belvedere Road,
SE1 8XX (7654 7800, www.skylon-
restaurant.co.uk).
Brasseries
Giraffe p44
Riverside Level 1, Royal Festival Hall,
Belvedere Road, SE1 8XX (7928 2004,
www.giraffe.net).
East European
Baltic p77
74 Blackfriars Road, SE1 8HA (7928
1111, www.balticrestaurant.co.uk).
Fish & Chips
Masters Super Fish p301
191 Waterloo Road, SE1 8UX
(7928 6924).
French
RSJ p95
33 Coin Street, SE1 9NR (7928 4554,
www.rsj.uk.com).
Gastropubs
Anchor & Hope p109
36 The Cut, SE1 8LP (7928 9898).
Modern European
Oxo Tower Restaurant,
Bar & Brasserie p217
8th floor, Oxo Tower Wharf, Barge
House Street, SE1 9PH (7803 3888,
www.harveynichols.com).
Skylon p217
Belvedere Road, SE1 8XX (7654 7800,
www.skylon-restaurant.co.uk).
Spanish & Portuguese
Mar i Terra p241
14 Gambia Street, SE1 0XH
(7928 7628, www.mariterra.co.uk).

Wembley, Middx
Branches
Nando's
420-422 High Road, Wembley, Middx,
HA9 6AH (8795 3564).
Indian
Sakonis p155
129 Ealing Road, Wembley, Middx, HA0
4BP (8903 9601, www.sakonis.co.uk).
Middle Eastern
Mesopotamia p200
115 Wembley Park Drive, Wembley,
Middx, HA9 8HG (8453 5555,
www.mesopotamia.ltd.uk).

West Hampstead
Branches
Banana Tree Canteen
237-239 West End Lane, NW6 1XN
(7431 7808).
Gourmet Burger Kitchen
331 West End Lane, NW6 1RS
(7794 5455).
Nando's
252-254 West End Lane, NW6 1LU
(7794 1331).
East European
Czechoslovak Restaurant p78
74 West End Lane, NW6 2LX
(7372 1193, www.czechoslovak-
restaurant.co.uk).
Fish & Chips
Nautilus p303
27-29 Fortune Green Road, NW6 1DU
(7435 2532).
Middle Eastern
Mahdi p200
2 Chantfield Gardens, NW6 3BS
(7625 4344).
Modern European
Walnut p223
280 West End Lane, NW6 1LJ
(7794 7772, www.walnutwalnut.com).

West Kensington
Vegetarian
222 Veggie Vegan p267
222 North End Road, W14 9NU
(7381 2322, www.222veggievegan.com).

Westbourne Grove
Branches
Carluccio's Caffè
108 Westbourne Grove, W2 5RU
(7243 8164).
Brasseries
Daylesford Organic p42
208-212 Westbourne Grove,
W11 2RH (7313 8050,
www.daylesfordorganic.com).
Cafés
Tom's Deli p285
226 Westbourne Grove, W11 2RH
(7221 8818, www.tomsdelilondon.com).
Hotels & Haute Cuisine
The Ledbury p136
127 Ledbury Road, W11 2AQ
(7792 9090, www.theledbury.com).
Malaysian, Indonesian & Singaporean
C&R Restaurant p191
52 Westbourne Grove, W2 5SH
(7221 7979).
Pizza & Pasta
Mulberry Street p310
84 Westbourne Grove, W2 5RT (7313
6789, www.mulberrystreet.co.uk).
Wine Bars
Negozio Classica p325
283 Westbourne Grove, W11 2QA
(7034 0005, www.negozioclassica.co.uk).

Westbourne Park
African & Caribbean
Mosob p20
339 Harrow Road, W9 3RB
(7266 2012, www.mosob.co.uk).
Gastropubs
Cow p105
89 Westbourne Park Road, W2 5QH
(7221 0021, www.thecowlondon.com).
The Americas
Lucky 7 p27
127 Westbourne Park Road, W2 5QL
(7727 6771, www.lucky7london.com).

Westminster
British
Northall p55
10 Northumberland Avenue, WC2N 5AE
(7930 8181, www.thenorthall.co.uk).
Budget
Vincent Rooms p276
Westminster Kingsway College, Vincent
Square, SW1P 2PD (7802 8391,
www.westking.ac.uk).
Indian
Cinnamon Club p145
Old Westminster Library, 30-32 Great
Smith Street, SW1P 3BU (7222 2555,
www.cinnamonclub.com).
Italian
Osteria dell'Angolo p162
47 Marsham Street, SW1P 3DR (3268
1077, www.osteriadellangolo.com).
Quirinale p163
North Court, 1 Great Peter Street, SW1P
3LL (7222 7080, www.quirinale.co.uk).

Whitechapel
Indian
Café Spice Namaste p151
16 Prescot Street, E1 8AZ (7488 9242,
www.cafespice.co.uk).
Lahore Kebab House p151
2 Umberston Street, E1 1PY (7488 2551,
www.lahore-kebabhouse.com).
Needoo Grill p151
87 New Road, E1 1HH (7247 0648,
www.needoogrill.co.uk).
Tayyabs p153
83 Fieldgate Street, E1 1JU
(7247 9543, www.tayyabs.co.uk).

Middle Eastern
Zengi p197
44 Commercial Street, E1 6LT
(7426 0700, www.zengirestaurant.co.uk).
Modern European
Whitechapel Gallery Dining
Room p221
77-82 Whitechapel High Street,
E1 7QX (7522 7888,
www.whitechapelgallery.org/dining-room).
Pan-Asian & Fusion
Rosemary Lane p233
61 Royal Mint Street, E1 8LG
(7481 2602, www.rosemarylane.
btinternet.com).
The Americas
Moo! p36
4 Cobb Street, E1 7LB (7377 9276,
www.moogrill.co.uk).

Willesden
Japanese
Sushi-Say p180
33B Walm Lane, NW2 5SH
(8459 2971).
The Americas
Amber Grill Rodizio p33
47 Station Road, NW10 4UP
(8963 1588, www.ambergrill.co.uk).

Wimbledon
Branches
Butcher & Grill
33 High Street, SW19 5BY
(8944 8269).
Carluccio's Caffè
25 High Street, SW19 5XD
(8946 1202).
Côte
8 High Street, SW19 5DX
(8947 7100).
Giraffe
21 High Street, SW19 5DX
(8946 0544).
Gourmet Burger Kitchen
88 The Broadway, SW19 1RH
(8540 3300).
Nando's
1 Russell Road, SW19 1QN
(8545 0909).
Suk Saran (branch of Sukho)
29 Wimbledon Hill Road, SW19 7NE
(8947 9199).
Wagamama
46-48 Wimbledon Hill Road, SW19 7PA
(8879 7280).
Gastropubs
Earl Spencer p107
260-262 Merton Road, SW18 5JL
(8870 9244, www.theearlspencer.co.uk).
Fox & Grapes p107
9 Camp Road, SW19 4UN
(8619 1300, www.foxandgrapes
wimbledon.co.uk).
Global
Chakalaka p119
Horse & Groom, 145 Haydons
Road, SW19 1AN (8544 2693,
www.chakalakarestaurant.com).

Wood Green
Branches
Lahore Kebab House
159 High Road, N22 6YQ (8881 4037,
www.lahore-kebabhouse.com).
Nando's
Hollywood Green, Redvers Road, off
Lordship Lane, N22 6EJ (8889 2936).
Greek
Vrisaki p126
73 Myddleton Road, N22 8LZ
(8889 8760).

Advertisers' Index

Please refer to relevant sections for addresses/telephone numbers

A-Z Index

A

A Cena p168
418 Richmond Road, Twickenham, Middx, TW1 2EB (8288 0108, www.acena.co.uk). Italian

Abeno p170
47 Museum Street, WC1A 1LY (7405 3211). Branch

Abeno Too p170
17-18 Great Newport Street, WC2H 7JE (7379 1160, www.abeno.co.uk). Japanese

L'Absinthe p96
40 Chalcot Road, NW1 8LS (7483 4848, http://labsinthe.co.uk). French

Abu Zaad p197
29 Uxbridge Road, W12 8LH (8749 5107, www.abuzaad.co.uk). Middle Eastern

Abu Zaad
128 Edgware Road, W2 2DZ (8749 5107). Branch

Adam & Eve p117
The Ridgeway, NW7 1RL (8959 1553, www.adamandevemillhill.com). Gastropubs

Adam's Café p225
77 Askew Road, W12 9AH (8743 0572, www.adamscafe.co.uk). North African

Adulis p21
44-46 Brixton Road, SW9 6BT (7587 0055, www.adulis.co.uk). African & Caribbean

Al Sultan p195
51-52 Hertford Street, W1J 7ST (7408 1155, www.alsultan.co.uk). Middle Eastern

Al Waha p196
75 Westbourne Grove, W2 4UL (7229 0806, www.alwaha restaurant.com). Middle Eastern

Alain Ducasse at the Dorchester p132
The Dorchester, 53 Park Lane, W1K 1QA (7629 8866, www.alainducasse-dorchester.com). Hotels & Haute Cuisine

Albannach p317
66 Trafalgar Square, WC2N 5DS (7930 0066, www.albannach.co.uk). Bars

Albion p59
2-4 Boundary Street, E2 7DD (7729 1051, www.albioncaff.co.uk). British

Alloro p159
19-20 Dover Street, W1S 4LU (7495 4768, www.alloro-restaurant.co.uk). Italian

Allpress Espresso p297
58 Redchurch Street, E2 7DP (7749 1780, http://uk.allpress espresso.com). Coffee Bars

Almeida p97
30 Almeida Street, N1 1AD (7354 4777, www.almeida-restaurant.co.uk). French

Amaranth p255
346-348 Garratt Lane, SW18 4ES (8874 9036). Thai

Amaya p139
Halkin Arcade, Motcomb Street, SW1X 8JT (7823 1166, www.amaya.biz). Indian

Amber Grill Rodizio p33
47 Station Road, NW10 4UP (8963 1588, www.ambergrill.co.uk). The Americas

Amorino p305
41 Old Compton Street, W1D 6HF (7494 3300, www.amorino.com). Ice-cream Parlours

Anchor & Hope p109
36 The Cut, SE1 8LP (7928 9898). Gastropubs

Andrew Edmunds p208
46 Lexington Street, W1F 0LW (7437 5708). Modern European

Angels & Gypsies p241
29-33 Camberwell Church Street, SE5 8TR (7703 5984, www.angelsand gypsies.com). Spanish & Portuguese

Angelus p91
4 Bathhurst Street, W2 2SD (7402 0083, www.angelusrestaurant.co.uk). French

Anglesea Arms p104
35 Wingate Road, W6 0UR (8749 1291). Gastropubs

L'Anima p156
1 Snowden Street, EC2A 2DQ (7422 7000, www.lanima.co.uk). Italian

Antelope p109
76 Mitcham Road, SW17 9NG (8672 3888, www.theantelopepub.com). Gastropubs

Antepliler p263
139 Upper Stret, N1 1QP (7226 5541, www.anteplilerrestaurant.co.uk). Turkish

Antepliler
46 Grand Parade, Green Lanes, N4 1AG (8802 5588). Branch

Aphrodite Taverna p123
15 Hereford Road, W2 4AB (7229 2206, www.aphrodite restaurant.co.uk). Greek

Apollo Banana Leaf p149
190 Tooting High Street, SW17 0SF (8696 1423, www.apollobanana leaf.co.uk). Indian

Applebee's Café p81
5 Stoney Street, SE1 9AA (7407 5777, www.applebeesfish.com). Fish

Aqua Nueva p237
5th floor, 240 Regent Street, entrance on Argyll Street, W1B 3BR (7478 0540, www.aqua-london.com). Spanish & Portuguese

Arbutus p210
63-64 Frith Street, W1D 3JW (7734 4545, www.arbutus restaurant.co.uk). Modern European

Ariana II p122
241 Kilburn High Road, NW6 7JN (3490 6709). Global

Ark Fish Restaurant p83
142 Hermon Hill, E18 1QH (8989 5345, www.arkfishrestaurant.com). Fish

Artesian p316
1C Portland Place, W1B 1JA (7636 1000, www.artesian-bar.co.uk). Bars

As Greek As It Gets p123
233 Earl's Court Road, SW5 9AH (7244 7777, www.asgreekasitgets.co.uk). Greek

Asadal p186
227 High Holborn, WC1V 7DA (7430 9006, www.asadal.co.uk). Korean

Asakusa p179
265 Eversholt Street, NW1 1BA (7388 8533). Japanese

Asmara p20
386 Coldharbour Lane, SW9 8LF (7737 4144). African & Caribbean

Assaggi p163
1st floor, 39 Chepstow Place, W2 4TS (7792 5501). Italian

Atari-Ya p178
1 Station Parade, Uxbridge Road, W5 3LD (8896 3175, www.atariya.co.uk). Japanese

Atari-Ya
31 Vivian Avenue, NW4 3UX (8202 2789). Branch

Atari-Ya
75 Fairfax Road, NW6 4EE (7328 5338). Branch

Atari-Ya
20 James Street, W1U 1EH (7491 1178). Branch

L'Atelier de Joël Robuchon p205
13-15 West Street, WC2H 9NE (7010 8600, www.joel-robuchon.com). Modern European

L'Autre Pied p207
5-7 Blandford Street, W1U 3DB (7486 9696, www.lautrepied.co.uk). Modern European

Avalon p108
16 Balham Hill, SW12 9EB (8675 8613, www.theavalon london.com). Gastropubs

L'Aventure p99
3 Blenheim Terrace, NW8 0EH (7624 6232, www.laventure.co.uk). French

The Avenue p208
7-9 St James's Street, SW1A 1EE (7321 2111, www.theavenue-restaurant.co.uk). Modern European

Awana p191
85 Sloane Avenue, SW3 3DX (7584 8880, www.awana.co.uk). Malaysian, Indonesian & Singaporean

Axis p205
One Aldwych, 1 Aldwych, WC2B 4BZ (7300 0300, www.onealdwych.com). Modern European

B

Ba Shan p67
24 Romilly Street, W1D 5AH (7287 3266). Chinese

Il Bacio p312
61 Stoke Newington Church Street, N16 0AR (7249 3833). Pizza & Pasta

Il Bacio Express
90 Stoke Newington Church Street, N16 0AD (7249 2344). Branch

Il Bacio Highbury
178-184 Blackstock Road, N5 1HA (7226 3339). Branch

Bald-Faced Stag p113
69 High Road, N2 8AB (8442 1201, www.thebaldfacedstagn2.co.uk). Gastropubs

Balham Bowls Club p317
7-9 Ramsden Road, SW12 8QX (8673 4700, www.antic-ltd.com). Bars

Baltic p77
74 Blackfriars Road, SE1 8HA (7928 1111, www.balticrestaurant.co.uk). East European

Bam-Bou p227
1 Percy Street, W1T 1DB (7323 9130, www.bam-bou.co.uk). Pan-Asian & Fusion

Banana Leaf Canteen
75-79 Battersea Rise, SW11 1HN (7228 2828). Branch

Banana Tree Canteen p231
412-416 St John Street, EC1V 4NJ (7278 7565, www.bananatree canteen.com). Pan-Asian & Fusion

Banana Tree Canteen
237-239 West End Lane, NW6 1XN (7431 7808). Branch

Banana Tree Canteen
103 Wardour Street, W1F 0UQ (www.bananatree.co.uk). Branch

Banana Tree Canteen
21-23 Westbourne Grove, W2 4UA (7221 4085). Branch

Bánh mì Bay p271
4-6 Theobald's Road, WC1X 8PN (7831 4079). Vietnamese

Baozi Inn p70
25 Newport Court, WC2H 7JS (7287 6877). Chinese

Bar Battu p324
48 Gresham Street, EC2V 7AY (7036 6100, www.barbattu.com). Wine Bars

Bar Boulud p88
66 Knightsbridge, SW1X 7LA (7201 3899, http://danielnyc.com/barboulud_hub.html). French

Bar Madeira (branch of Casa Madeira)
130 Stockwell Road, SW9 0HR (7737 4785). Branch

Bar Pepito p315
Varnishers Yard, Regents Quarter, N1 9FD (7841 7331, www.camino.uk.com/pepito). Bars

Bar Trattoria Semplice
22 Woodstock Street, W1C 2AP (7491 8638, www.bartrattoria semplice.com). Branch

Barbecoa p25
20 New Change Passage, EC4M 9AG (3005 8555, www.barbecoa.com). The Americas

Il Baretto p159
43 Blandford Street, W1U 7HF (7486 7340, www.ilbaretto.co.uk). Italian

Barrafina p239
54 Frith Street, W1D 4SL (7440 1463, www.barrafina.co.uk). Spanish & Portuguese

Barrica p235
62 Goodge Street, W1T 4NE (7436 9448, www.barrica.co.uk). Spanish & Portuguese

Barshu p67
28 Frith Street, W1D 5LF (7287 6688, www.bar-shu.co.uk). Chinese

Battersea Pie p274
Lower ground floor, 28 The Market, WC2E 8RA (7240 9566, www.battersea piestation.co.uk). Budget

Bea's of Bloomsbury p280
83 Watling Street, EC4M 9BX (7242 8330, www.beasof bloomsbury.com). Cafés

Bea's of Bloomsbury
370 King's Road, SW3 5UZ. Branch

Bea's of Bloomsbury
44 Theobalds Road, WC1X 8NW (7242 8330). Branch

Beatroot p267
92 Berwick Street, W1F 0QD (7437 8591, www.beatroot.org.uk). Vegetarian

Beaufort Bar at The Savoy p317
The Savoy, 100 Strand, WC2R 0EW (7836 4343, www.the-savoy.com). Bars

Behesht p200
1082-1084 Harrow Road, NW10 5NL (8964 4477). Middle Eastern

Beirut Express (branch of Ranoush Juice)
65 Old Brompton Road, SW7 3JS (7591 0123). Branch

Beirut Express (branch of Ranoush Juice)
112-114 Edgware Road, W2 2JE (7724 2700). Branch

Bel Canto p323
Lancaster Gate, W2 3LG (7262 1678, www.lebelcanto.com). Eating & Entertainment

Belvedere p93
Holland House, off Abbotsbury Road, in Holland Park, W8 6LU (7602 1238, www.belvedererestaurant.co.uk). French

Benares p142
12A Berkeley Square House, Berkeley Square, W1J 6BS (7629 8886, www.benaresrestaurant.com). Indian

Bennett Oyster Bar & Brasserie p81
7-9 Battersea Square, SW11 3RA (7223 5545, www.bennetts brasserie.com). Fish

Bentley's Oyster Bar & Grill p80
11-15 Swallow Street, W1B 4DG (7734 4756, www.bentleysoyster barandgrill.co.uk). Fish

Betsy Smith p312
77 Kilburn High Road, NW6 6HY (7624 5793, www.thebetsysmith.co.uk). Pizza & Pasta

Bevis Marks Restaurant p182
4 Heneage Lane, EC3A 5DQ (7283 2220, www.bevismarks therestaurant.com). Jewish

A-Z INDEX

Mount Street Deli p283
100 Mount Street, W1K 2TG
(7499 6843, www.themountstreet
deli.co.uk). Cafés

Mr Chow p63
151 Knightsbridge, SW1X 7PA (7589
7347, www.mrchow.com). Chinese

Mr Fish p300
9 Porchester Road, W2 5DP (7229 4161,
www.mrfish.uk.com). Fish & Chips

Mr Fish
51 Salusbury Road, NW6 6NJ
(7624 3555). Branch

Mudchute Kitchen p288
Mudchute Park & Farm, Pier Street,
E14 3HP (3069 9290, www.mudchute
kitchen.org). Cafés

Mulberry Street p310
84 Westbourne Grove, W2 5RT
(7313 6789, www.mulberrystreet.co.uk).
Pizza & Pasta

Murano p159
20-22 Queen Street, W1J 5PR (7495
1127, www.schoolofhartnett.co.uk).
Italian

Museum Café p287
Romney Road, SE10 9NF (8858 4422,
www.nmm.ac.uk). Cafés

My Dining Room p93
18 Farm Lane, SW6 1PP (7381 3331,
www.mydiningroom.net). French

Myung Ga p187
1 Kingly Street, W1B 5PA (7734 8220,
www.myungga.co.uk). Korean

N

Nahm p252
Halkin Street, SW1X 7DJ (7333 1234,
www.nahm.como.bz). Thai

Namaaste Kitchen p153
64 Parkway , NW1 7AH (7485 5977,
www.namaastekitchen.co.uk). Indian

Nando's p279
227-229 Kentish Town Road, NW5 2JU
(7424 9363, www.nandos.co.uk). Budget

Nando's
9 Widmore Road, Bromley, Kent,
BR1 1RL (8290 5010). Branch

Nando's
199-203 High Street, Beckenham, Kent,
BR3 1AH (8658 8084). Branch

Nando's
26 High Street, Croydon, Surrey,
CR0 1GT (8681 3505). Branch

Nando's
Croydon Valley Leisure Park, Hesterman
Way, Croydon, Surrey, CR0 4YA
(8688 9545). Branch

Nando's
9-25 Mile End Road, E1 4TW
(7791 2720). Branch

Nando's
114-118 Commercial Street, E1 6NF
(7650 7775). Branch

Nando's
120 Middlesex Street, E1 7HY
(7392 9572). Branch

Nando's
Cabot Place East, E14 4QT (3200 2096).
Branch

Nando's
Jubilee Place, off Bank Street, E14 5NY
(7513 2864). Branch

Nando's
1A Romford Road, E15 4LJ (8221 2148).
Branch

Nando's
366 Bethnal Green Road, E2 0AH
(7729 5783). Branch

Nando's
Westfield Stratford, 2 Stratford Place,
Montifichet Place, E20 1EJ (8519 4459).
Branch

Nando's
552 Mile End Road, E3 4PL (8981 9867).
Branch

Nando's
148 Kingsland High Street, E8 2NS
(7923 3555). Branch

Nando's
Level 1 South, One New Change,
Cheapside Passage, EC4M 9AF
(7248 0651). Branch

Nando's
2 The Town, Enfield, Middx, EN2 6LE
(8366 2904). Branch

Nando's
300-302 Station Road, Harrow, Middx,
HA1 2DX (8427 5581). Branch

Nando's
309-311 Northolt Road, Harrow, Middx,
HA2 8JA (8423 1516). Branch

Nando's
137-139 Station Road, Edgware, Middx,
HA8 7JG (8952 3400). Branch

Nando's
420-422 High Road, Wembley, Middx,
HA9 6AH (8795 3564). Branch

Nando's
I-Scene, Clements Road, Ilford, Essex,
IG1 1BP (8514 6012). Branch

Nando's
Odeon, Longbridge Road, Barking, Essex,
IG11 8RU (8507 0795). Branch

Nando's
37-38 High Street, Kingston, Surrey,
KT1 1LQ (8296 9540). Branch

Nando's
324 Upper Street, N1 2XQ (7288 0254).
Branch

Nando's
12-16 York Way, N1 9AA (7833 2809).
Branch

Nando's
Great North Leisure Park, Chaplin
Square, N12 0GL (8492 8465).
Branch

Nando's
139-141 Stoke Newington Church Street,
N16 0UH (7923 1019). Branch

Nando's
Hollywood Green, Redvers Road, off
Lordship Lane, N22 6EJ (8889 2936).
Branch

Nando's
106 Stroud Green Road, N4 3HB
(7263 7447). Branch

Nando's
The Piazza, Euston Station, NW1 2RT
(7387 5126). Branch

Nando's
57-58 Chalk Farm Road, NW1 8AN
(7424 9040). Branch

Nando's
Tesco Extra, Great Central Way, NW10
0TL (8459 6908). Branch

Nando's
O2 Centre, 255 Finchley Road, NW3 6LU
(7435 4644). Branch

Nando's
Brent Cross Shopping Centre, Prince
Charles Drive, NW4 3FP (8203 9131).
Branch

Nando's
252-254 West End Lane, NW6 1LU
(7794 1331). Branch

Nando's
308 Kilburn High Road, NW6 2DG
(7372 1507). Branch

Nando's
658-660 Kingsbury Road, NW9 9HN
(8204 7905). Branch

Nando's
111-113A High Street, Hornchurch,
Essex, RM11 1TX (01708 449537).
Branch

Nando's
Metro Central, 119 Newington Causeway,
SE1 6BA (7378 7810). Branch

Nando's
225-227 Clink Street, SE1 9DG
(7357 8662). Branch

Nando's
The O2, Millennium Way, SE10 0AX
(8269 2401). Branch

Nando's
UCI Cinema Complex, Bugsby's Way,
SE10 0QJ (8293 3025). Branch

Nando's
Bugsby's Way, SE10 0QJ (8293 3025).
Branch

Nando's
16 Lee High Road, SE13 5LQ
(8463 0119). Branch

Nando's
88 Denmark Hill, SE5 8RX (7738 3808).
Branch

Nando's
74-76 Rushey Green, SE6 4HW
(8314 0122). Branch

Nando's
9-11 High Street, Sutton, Surrey,
SM1 1DF (8770 0180). Branch

Nando's
1A Northcote Road, SW11 1NG
(7228 6221). Branch

Nando's
116-118 Balham High Road, SW12 9AA
(8675 6415). Branch

Nando's
148 Upper Richmond Road, SW15 2SW
(8780 3651). Branch

Nando's
6-7 High Parade, Streatham High Road,
SW16 1ES (8769 0951). Branch

Nando's
224-226 Upper Tooting Road, SW17 7EW
(8682 2478). Branch

Nando's
Southside Shopping Centre, SW18 4TF
(8874 1363). Branch

Nando's
1 Russell Road, SW19 1QN (8545 0909).
Branch

Nando's
Tandem Centre, Tandem Way, SW19 2TY
(8646 8562). Branch

Nando's
17 Cardinal Walk, Cardinal Place,
SW1E 5JE (7828 0158). Branch

Nando's
107-108 Wilton Road, SW1V 1DZ
(7976 5719). Branch

Nando's
59-63 Clapham High Street, SW4 7TG
(7622 1475). Branch

Nando's
204 Earl's Court Road, SW5 9QF
(7259 2544). Branch

Nando's
Fulham Broadway Retail Centre, Fulham
Road, SW6 1BY (7386 8035). Branch

Nando's
117 Gloucester Road, SW7 4ST
(7373 4446). Branch

Nando's
234-244 Stockwell Road, SW9 9SP
(7737 6400). Branch

Nando's
2&4 Hill Rise, Richmond, Surrey,
TW10 6UA (8940 8810). Branch

Nando's
1-1A High Street, Hounslow, Middx,
TW3 1RH (8570 5881). Branch

Nando's
The Chimes Centre, High Street,
Uxbridge, Middx, UB8 1GE (01895
274277). Branch

Nando's
58-60 Notting Hill Gate, W11 3HT
(7243 1647). Branch

Nando's
The Loft, Westfield Shopping Centre,
W12 7GF (8834 4658). Branch

Nando's
284-286 Uxbridge Road, W12 7JA
(8746 1112). Branch

Nando's
46 Glasshouse Street, W1B 5DR
(7287 8442). Branch

Nando's
10 Frith Street, W1D 3JF (7494 0932).
Branch

Nando's
57-59 Goodge Street, W1T 1TH
(7637 0708). Branch

Nando's
2 Berners Street, W1T 3LA (7323 9791).
Branch

Nando's
113 Baker Street, W1U 6RS
(3075 1044). Branch

Nando's
63 Westbourne Grove, W2 4UA
(7313 9506). Branch

Nando's
Royal Leisure Park, Kendal Avenue,
W3 0PA (8896 1469). Branch

Nando's
187-189 Chiswick High Road, W4 2DR
(8995 7533). Branch

Nando's
1-2 Station Buildings, Uxbridge Road,
W5 3NU (8992 2290). Branch

Nando's
1-5 Bond Street, W5 5AP (8567 8093).
Branch

Nando's
9-10 Southampton Place, WC1A 2EA
(7831 5565). Branch

Nando's
The Brunswick Centre, Marchmont Street,
WC1N 1AE (7713 0351). Branch

Nando's
66-68 Chandos Place, WC2N 4HG
(7836 4719). Branch

Napulé p310
585 Fulham Road, SW6 5UA
(7381 1122, www.madeinitaly
group.co.uk). Pizza & Pasta

Nara p188
9 D'Arblay Street, W1F 8DR
(7287 2224). Korean

Narrow p111
44 Narrow Street, E14 8DP
(7592 7950, www.gordonramsay.com/
thenarrow). Gastropubs

Naru p185
230 Shaftesbury Avenue,
WC2H 8EG (7379 7962,
www.narurestaurant.com). Korean

National Café
East Wing, National Gallery, Trafalgar
Square, WC2N 5DN (7747 2525,
www.thenationalcafe.com). Branch

National Dining Rooms p55
Sainsbury Wing, National Gallery,
WC2N 5DN (7747 2525, www.the
nationaldiningrooms.co.uk). British

Nautilus p303
27-29 Fortune Green Road, NW6 1DU
(7435 2532). Fish & Chips

Necco p176
52-54 Exmouth Market, EC1R 4QE
(7713 8575, www.necco.co.uk).
Japanese

Needoo Grill p151
87 New Road, E1 1HH (7247 0648,
www.needoogrill.co.uk). Indian

Negozio Classica p325
283 Westbourne Grove, W11 2QA
(7034 0005, www.negozioclassica.
co.uk). Wine Bars

**New Asian Tandoori
Centre (Roxy)** p155
114-118 The Green, Southall, Middx,
UB2 4BQ (8574 2597). Indian

New Cross House p111
316 New Cross Road, SE14 6AF
(8691 8875, www.thenewcross
house.com). Gastropubs

New Fook Lam Moon p190
10 Gerrard Street, W1D 5PW
(7734 7615). Malaysian, Indonesian
& Singaporean

New Yorker Deli p184
122 Golders Green Road, NW11 8HB
(8209 0232). Jewish

Nice Green Café p290
2 Regent's Park Road, NW1 7AY
(7485 2206, www.efdss.org).
Cafés

Nightjar p319
129 City Road, EC1V 1JB (7253 4101,
www.barnightjar.com). Bars

19 Numara Bos Cirrik I p261
34 Stoke Newington Road, N16 7XJ
(7249 0400). Turkish

19 Numara Bos Cirrik II
194 Stoke Newington High Street,
N16 7JD (7249 9111). Branch

19 Numara Bos Cirrik III
1-3 Amhurst Road, E8 1LL (8985 2879).
Branch

19 Numara Bos Cirrik IV
665 High Road, N17 8AD (8801 5566).
Branch

Nipa p255
Lancaster London Hotel, Lancaster
Terrace, W2 2TY (7262 6737,
www.niparestaurant.co.uk). Thai

Nizuni p171
22 Charlotte Street, W1T 2NB
(7580 7447, www.nizuni.com).
Japanese

A-Z INDEX